Contents

KU-327-179

OPPOSITE TAKING THE PLUNGE, THE RED SEA **PREVIOUS PAGE** THE PYRAMIDS OF GIZA

Introduction to
Egypt

Egypt is the oldest tourist destination on earth. Ancient Greeks and Romans started the trend, coming to goggle at the cyclopean scale of the Pyramids and the Colossi of Thebes. During colonial times, Napoleon and the British looted Egypt's treasures to fill their national museums, sparking off a trickle of Grand Tourists that eventually became a flood of travellers, taken on Nile cruises and Egyptological lectures by the enterprising Thomas Cook. Today, the attractions of the country are not only the monuments of the Nile Valley and the souks, mosques and madrassas of Islamic Cairo, but also fantastic coral reefs and tropical fish, dunes, ancient fortresses, monasteries and prehistoric rock art.

The land itself is a freak of nature, its lifeblood the River Nile. From the Sudanese border to the shores of the Mediterranean, the Nile Valley and its Delta are flanked by arid wastes, the latter as empty as the former are teeming with people. This stark duality between fertility and desolation is fundamental to Egypt's character and has shaped its development since prehistoric times, imparting continuity to diverse cultures and peoples over seven millennia. It is a sense of permanence and timelessness that is buttressed by **religion**, which pervades every aspect of life. Although the pagan cults of ancient Egypt are as moribund as its legacy of mummies and temples, their ancient fertility rites and processions of boats still hold their place in the celebrations of Islam and Christianity.

The result is a multi-layered **culture**, which seems to accord equal respect to ancient and modern. The peasants of the Nile and the Bedouin tribes of the desert live much as their ancestors did a thousand years ago. Other communities include the Nubians of the far south, and the Coptic Christians, who trace their ancestry back to pharaonic times. What unites them is a love of their homeland, extended family ties, dignity, warmth and hospitality towards strangers. Though most visitors are drawn to Egypt by its monuments, the enduring memory is likely to be of its people and their way of life.

ABOVE MOUNTAIN ABOVE THE VALLEY OF THE KINGS **OPPOSITE** FELUCCAS AT DUSK

Where to go

Egypt's capital, **Cairo**, is a seething megalopolis whose chief sightseeing appeal lies in its **bazaars** and medieval **mosques**, though there is scarcely less fascination in its juxtapositions of medieval and modern life, the city's fortified gates, villas and skyscrapers interwoven by flyovers whose traffic may be halted by donkey carts. The immensity and diversity of this "Mother of Cities" is as staggering as anything you'll encounter in Egypt. Just outside Cairo are the first of the pyramids that range across the desert to the edge of the Fayoum, among them the unsurpassable trio at **Giza**, the vast necropolis of **Saqqara** and the pyramids at **Dahshur**. Besides all this, there are superb **museums** devoted to Ancient, Coptic and Islamic Egypt, and enough **entertainment** to occupy weeks of your time.

However, the principal tourist lure remains, as ever, the **Nile Valley**, with its ancient monuments and timeless river vistas – Nile cruises on a luxury vessel or a felucca sailboat being a great way to combine the two. The town of **Luxor** is synonymous with the magnificent temples of **Karnak** and the **Theban Necropolis**, which includes the **Valley of the Kings** where Tutankhamun and other pharaohs were buried. **Aswan**, Egypt's southernmost city, has the loveliest setting on the Nile and a languorous ambience. From here, you can visit the island **Philae temple of Isis** and the rock-hewn colossi at **Abu Simbel**, or embark on a cruise to other temples around **Lake Nasser**. Other sites not to be missed are **Edfu** and **Kom Ombo**, between Luxor and Aswan, and **Abydos** and **Dendara**, north of Luxor.

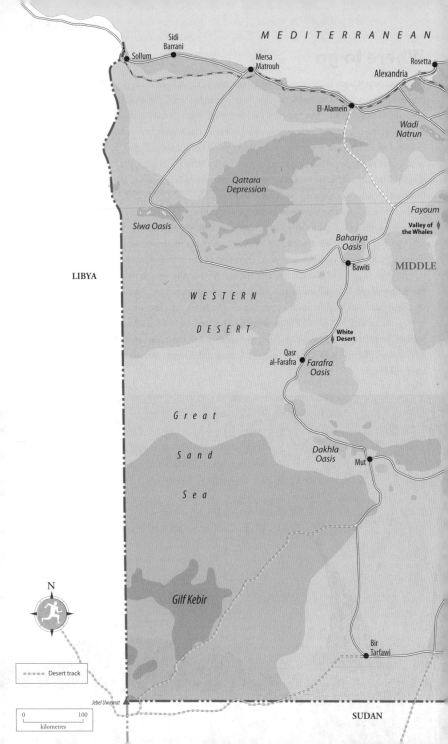

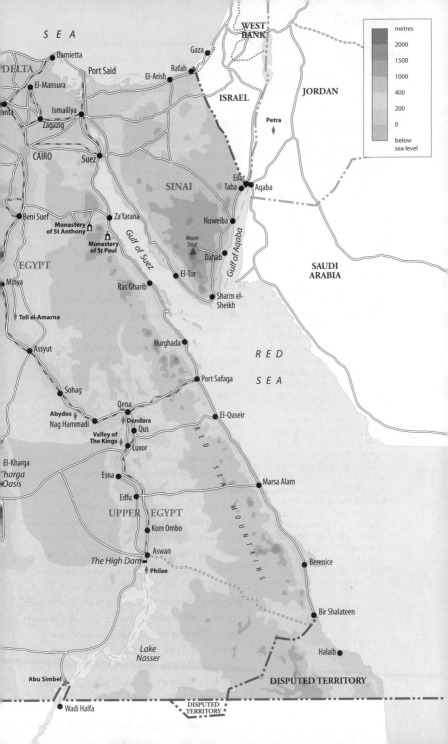

FACT FILE

• The Arab Republic of Egypt covers 1,001,450 square kilometres, but 96.4 percent of that is **desert**. Only the Nile Valley, its Delta and some oases are fertile.

• Egypt's **population** of 83.7 million is over twice that of the next most populous Arab country (Algeria) and a quarter of the population of the Arab world. 71 percent of Egyptians are literate. Average life expectancy is 73 years.

• **Islam** is the biggest religion, and some ninety percent of Egyptians are Muslim; most of the rest are **Coptic Christians**, with a small number of other Christians, and a tiny but ancient **Jewish** community.

• All Egyptians speak **Arabic**, but there are other Egyptian languages too: **Nubian**, related to the Nilotic languages of East Africa, is spoken around Aswan and Lake Nasser; **Siwi**, a Berber language like those of Morocco and Algeria, is spoken in Siwa Oasis; and **Coptic**, which is derived from ancient Egyptian, is used in church services, but not otherwise.

• Since the monarchy was ousted in 1952, Egypt has been a **republic**, ruled by a succession of military strongmen up until the 2011 revolution that overthrew Hosni Mubarak. Elections in 2012 resulted in an Islamist government under **President Mohammed Morsi**. The Muslim Brotherhood's Freedom and Justice Party is the largest in parliament, followed by the Salafist Al-Nour party, the liberal Wafd party and Egyptian Bloc.

• **Tourism** has long been Egypt's biggest money-earner, followed by tolls on the Suez Canal, and exports of oil, petroleum products, natural gas, cotton and textiles. Over forty percent of the population lives below the poverty line, and the **economy** would collapse without $2 billion a year in financial and food-aid from the US.

Besides monuments, Egypt abounds in natural wonders. Edged by coral reefs teeming with tropical fish, the **Sinai Peninsula** offers superb diving and snorkelling, and palm-fringed beaches where women can swim unmolested. Resorts along the Gulf of Aqaba are varied enough to suit everyone, whether you're into the upmarket hotels of **Sharm el-Sheikh**, nearby **Na'ama Bay** or **Taba** further north, or cheap, simple living at **Dahab** and **Nuweiba**. From there it's easy to visit **St Catherine's Monastery** and **Mount Sinai** (where Moses received the Ten Commandments) in the mountainous interior. With more time, cash and stamina, you can also embark on **jeep safaris** or **camel treks** to remote oases and spectacular wadis.

Egypt's **Red Sea Coast** has more reefs further offshore, with snorkelling and diving traditionally centred around **Hurghada**, while barely touched island reefs from **Port Safaga** down to **Marsa Alam** beckon serious diving enthusiasts. Inland, the mountainous **Eastern Desert** harbours the Coptic monasteries of St Paul and St Anthony, Roman quarries, and a host of pharaonic and prehistoric rock art, seen by few apart from the nomadic Bedouin.

While the Eastern Desert is still barely touched by tourism, the **Western Desert Oases** have been on the tourist trail for forty years and nowadays host safaris into the wilderness. **Siwa**, out towards the Libyan border, has a unique culture and history, limpid pools and bags of charm. Travellers can also follow the "Great Desert Circuit" (starting from Cairo, Luxor or Assyut) through the four "inner" oases – though **Bahariya** and **Farafra** hold the most appeal, with the lovely **White Desert** between them, the larger oases of **Dakhla** and **Kharga** also have their rewards once you escape their modernized "capitals". And for those into serious desert expeditions, there's the challenge of exploring the **Great Sand Sea** or the remote wadis of the

...est diving destinations in the world. The **Red Sea** and the **Gulf of Aqaba**
...d home to a wonderful array of dive sites, with plenty of options for both
...s alike: remarkably preserved World War II wrecks, coral reefs filled with
...coloured anemone gardens, and shallow bays visited by turtles are just a
...u can explore. The Sinai (p.534) and Red Sea Coast (p.581) chapters have
...ion on dive sites and recommended dive companies, as well as tips on safety
(p.5... ...onmental issues (p.586).

REEFS

The Red Sea's stable climate, shallow tides and exceptionally high salinity provide perfect conditions for unusually brilliant **corals and sponges** – a revelation if you have previously dived in such places as Hawaii or the Caribbean, whose reefs will forever after seem dull by comparison. Created by generations of miniscule polyps depositing their limestone exoskeletons on the remains of their ancestors, coral reefs can grow by 4–5cm a year. Beside **hard corals** such as brain and fire coral, which have a rigid outer skeleton, the Red Sea hosts an abundance of **soft corals**, including whip coral and sea fans. Because most types of coral need a moderate amount of warm sunlight to flourish, the most spectacular formations are found within 30m of the surface.

Most Red Sea reefs are of the fringing type, with a shallow lagoon just offshore, whose warm water and rubble-strewn bottom attracts starfish and sea slugs. Clams and sea urchins hide in crevices, and schools of damselfish and butterflyfish flit about. Its seaward boundary is the reef flat, whose crest is usually a barren, rough-surfaced shelf, while deeper areas are rich in flora and fauna. Beyond is a coral-encrusted slope, leading to a drop-off like the edge of a cliff. Flatter areas may be dotted with coral pillars or knolls. Lower down, the coral is sparser, and you may find sandy terraces overgrown with seagrass, sustaining sea horses and pipefish. Beyond the drop-off lies open water.

SEA LIFE

Some of the Red Sea's most colourful and endearing species are easy to spot in the **shallows**, where the sunlight is brightest. Among the commonest are beak-mouthed parrotfish and exotic-looking pennantfish, whose long dorsal fins end in filaments.

Wherever stinging anemones cling to the reef, you'll see clownfish (or anemone fish). Angelfish are usually found close to the coral, while clouds of gold and vermillion anthias gather around coral heads and fans. Slopes and fore reefs are the habitat of snappers, goatfish and wrasses (the largest of these, the Napoleon Wrasse, can dwarf a person).

In **deeper waters** you may see sharks, including whitetip reef sharks, grey reef sharks and (occasionally) scalloped hammerheads. Spotted reef stingrays are often seen on the sandy bottom of the sea. Turtles are among the most thrilling species to encounter underwater; the Red Sea has several species, including green turtles and hawksbill turtles. Dolphin encounters are possible too, and those lucky enough to come across a pod of bottlenose or spinner dolphins on a dive are likely to count it among the highlights of their trip.

Gilf Kebir, whose prehistoric rock art featured in the film *The English Patient*. In contrast to these deep-desert locations are the quasi-oases of the **Fayoum** and **Wadi Natrun**, featuring the fossil-strewn Valley of the Whales, diverse ancient ruins and Coptic monasteries.

On the Mediterranean, Egypt's second city, **Alexandria**, boasts a string of beaches to which Cairenes flock in summer, and excellent seafood restaurants. Despite being founded by Alexander the Great and lost to the Romans by Cleopatra, the city today betrays little of its ancient glory; however, its magnificent new **library**, featuring statues raised from the sunken remains of Cleopatra's Palace, and the Lighthouse of Pharos (which divers can explore) are restoring an air of majesty. Famous, too, for its

DUNES AT SUNRISE, BAHARIYA

Author picks

Our authors have spent hours on jeeps crossing vast tracts of desert, floated down the Nile in motley feluccas, and spent nights carousing in dens that most outsiders wouldn't imagine existed. Here are their favourite things to see and do in Egypt.

Be alone in a pyramid field The pyramid site at Dahshur (see p.168) is a world away from the tourist circus at Giza, its pyramids arguably even more impressive.

See the real Egypt Most Egyptians don't live in places like Luxor or Dahab, but in the teeming towns of the Delta. Aside from Rosetta (see p.500) there aren't many "sights" here, but scooting around it by service taxi, you get a feel for the Egypt that beach resorts and pharaonic temples won't give you.

Enjoy the Nile The river is best appreciated from a felucca or a *dahabiya* (see p.241), from which

you can trail your hand in the cool water, watch birds fishing and farmers bathing in the river.

Try something new Learn camel-handling at the *Tala Ranch* in Siwa Oasis (see p.449) or have a go at deciphering the texts in tombs in the Valley of the Kings (see p.297) with a copy of *How to Read Egyptian Hieroglyphs: A Step-By-Step Guide* (see p.625).

Indulge your senses Try aroma-massage or a sand-sauna in Aswan (see p.352), wallow in a hot pool amid the Great Sand Sea (see p.454) or relish the tastes and smells of civilization after a safari to the remote Gilf Kebir (see p.431).

See Egypt from the air The dramatic contrast between the lush Nile Valley and the surrounding desert wastes is best appreciated on an EgyptAir flight from Cairo, Luxor or Aswan to Abu Simbel (see p.366), or a hot-air balloon ride over the Theban Necropolis (see p.264).

Our author recommendations don't end here. We've flagged up our favourite places – a perfectly sited hotel, an atmospheric café, a special restaurant – throughout the guide, highlighted with the ★ symbol.

HUSSEIN OR HOUSSEIN?

There's no standard system of transliterating Arabic script into Roman, so you're sure to find that the **Arabic words** in this book don't always match the versions you'll see elsewhere. Maps and street signs are the biggest sources of confusion, so we've generally gone for the transliteration that's the most common on the spot. However, you'll often need to do a bit of lateral thinking, and it's not unusual to find one spelling posted at one end of a road, with another at the opposite end. See p.629 for an introduction to Egyptian Arabic.

decadence during colonial times, Alexandria still allows romantics to indulge in a nostalgic exploration of the city immortalized in Durrell's *Alexandria Quartet*, while further along the Mediterranean coast is the World War II battlefield of **El-Alamein**. For divers, the waters off Alexandria offer an array of sunken cities and wartime wrecks to explore.

The Nile **Delta**, east of Alexandria, musters few archeological monuments given its major role in ancient Egyptian history, and is largely overlooked by tourists. However, for those interested in Egyptian culture, the Delta hosts colourful religious **festivals** at Tanta, Zagazig and other towns. Further east lies the **Canal Zone**, dominated by the Suez Canal and its three cities: **Suez** is grim, but a vital transport nexus between Cairo, Sinai and the Red Sea Coast; **Port Said** and **Ismailiya** are pleasant, albeit sleepy places, where you can get a feel of "real Egypt" without tripping over other tourists.

When to go

Egypt's traditional tourist season runs from **late November to late February**, though in recent years Luxor and Aswan have only really been busy with tourists during the peak months of December and January. The Nile Valley is balmy throughout this winter season, although Cairo can be overcast and chilly. Winter is also the busiest period for the Sinai resorts, while Hurghada is active year round. Aside from the Easter vacation, when there is a spike in tourism, **March or April** are also good times to visit, with a pleasant climate.

In **May** the heat is still tolerable but, after that, Egyptians rich enough to do so migrate to Alex and the coastal resorts. From **June to September** the south and desert are ferociously hot and the pollution in Cairo is at its worst, with only the coast offering a respite from the heat. During this time, sightseeing is best limited to early morning or evening. **October into early November** is perhaps the best time of all, with easily manageable climate and crowds. For more on the Egyptian climate, see p.47.

Weather and tourism apart, the **Islamic calendar** and its related festivals can have an effect on your travel. The most important factor is **Ramadan** (see p.39), the month of daytime fasting, which can be problematic for eating and transport, though the festive evenings do much to compensate.

FROM TOP LITTLE EGRETS ON THE BANKS OF THE NILE; TEMPLE OF QUEEN NEFERTARI, ABU SIMBEL

28

things not to miss

It's not possible to see everything that Egypt has to offer in one trip – and we don't suggest you try. What follows, in no particular order, is a selective taste of the country's highlights: outstanding temples and tombs, spectacular landscapes and opportunities for Nile cruises. All highlights have a page reference to take you into the Guide, where you can find out more. Coloured numbers refer to chapters in the Guide.

1

 1 MOUNT SINAI
Page 563

This awesome peak is revered as the site where Moses received the Ten Commandments from God.

 2 ISLAMIC CAIRO
Page 90

City of a thousand minarets, teeming with life and chock-full of architectural masterpieces and historic monuments. Head for Khan el-Khalili bazaar, or the Citadel.

 3 DIVING AND SNORKELLING
See p.41

Amazing coral reefs, tropical fish and wrecks make the Red Sea a paradise for scuba divers and snorkellers, while Egypt's Mediterranean coast has ancient underwater ruins and warships to explore.

 4 VALLEY OF THE KINGS
Page 292

The descent into the Underworld, the Judgement of Osiris and the rebirth of the pharaoh are vividly depicted on the walls and ceilings of the royal tombs.

CATACOMBS OF KOM ES-SHOQAFA
Page 476
Beneath the Karmous quarter of Alexandria are the spookiest tombs in Egypt, with a bizarre fusion of pharaonic, Greek and Roman funerary motifs reflecting the city's ancient diversity.

 MEZZE
Page 36
Dining in a restaurant, try mezze, consisting of many delicious, small dishes (particularly good for vegetarians).

 FELUCCAS
Page 242
These lateen-sailed boats can be hired for an afternoon lazing on the Nile, or a two- or three-day journey from Aswan, visiting the temples at Kom Ombo and Edfu.

 ALEXANDRIA
Page 462
With its fabulous seafood and vintage coffee houses, its dazzling new library and the chance to dive the ruins of Cleopatra's Palace, there's plenty to discover in this Mediterranean port city.

 WHITE DESERT
Page 409
A tract of weird wind-eroded rock formations in Farafra Oasis, often visited on overnight safaris from the neighbouring oasis of Bahariya.

 THE PYRAMIDS OF DAHSHUR
Page 168
Less famous than the Giza trio but no less fascinating – and far less crowded. The Bent Pyramid, resting place of Snofru, has a distinctive angled top.

8

9

10

11 BALLOON RIDES
Enjoy a magnificent view of the Theban Necropolis on Luxor's west bank.

12 ASWAN
Aswan has been Egypt's gateway to Nubia since ancient times, and its islands, bazaars and riverside restaurants can keep you happy in between excursions to sites such as Abu Simbel.

13 KARKADAY
This infusion of hibiscus flowers makes a delicious hot or cold drink and tonic.

14 ABU SIMBEL
The monumental sun temple of Ramses II is the most spectacular of the Nubian antiquities that were relocated to higher ground on the shores of Lake Nasser.

15 JEWELLERY
There's an endless choice of pharaonic, classical, Islamic and contemporary designs in the bazaars of Cairo, Luxor and Aswan, and oases such as Siwa.

16 THE EGYPTIAN MUSEUM
Home to Tutankhamun's treasures, monumental statues from the Old Kingdom and the Amarna era, a dozen royal mummies and countless other artefacts, some engagingly humble.

17 DAHAB
Sinai chill-out zone, renowned for its diving, beach cafés, and camel and jeep safaris into the rugged interior.

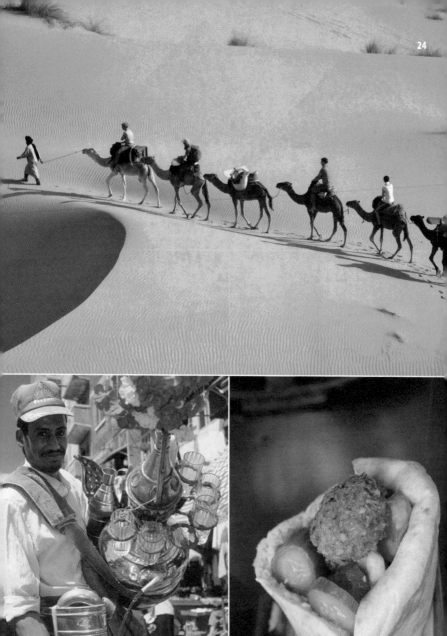

24 JEEP OR CAMEL SAFARIS
Pages 42 & 376

Make tracks into the dunes of the Western Desert or the canyons of Sinai – overnight trips or major expeditions are easily arranged.

25 FRESH JUICE
Page 37

Most towns have a sprinkling of juice bars or carts, where you can quench your thirst with whatever's in season, from freshly pressed oranges and mangoes to strawberries and sugar cane.

26 STREET FOOD
Page 35

Sold from pushcarts or in sit-down diners, *taamiya*, *kushari*, *fuul* and *shawarma* are tasty, cheap and nourishing.

27 RAS MOHAMMED
Page 538

Egypt's oldest marine nature park boasts spectacular shark reefs and the wreck of the *Dunraven*.

28 SIWA OASIS
Page 441

With its unique culture, hilltop citadel and spring-fed pools, Siwa is rated by many as the best of Egypt's oases.

Itineraries

The following itineraries range right across Egypt, taking in both classic attractions and little-visited sights, from temples to turtles. Don't worry if you can't complete the list – even a handful of places will give you a feel for the themes.

TEMPLES AND TOMBS

Egypt's world-famous ancient tombs and temples range the length of the Nile Valley, from the Pyramids of Giza outside Cairo to Abu Simbel. It takes about ten days to explore them, using intercity trains, local taxis and minibuses.

❶ Pyramids of Giza These gargantuan Old Kingdom monuments were constructed as tombs for three IV Dynasty rulers, Egyptologists believe – but there are many alternative theories as to why (and how) they were built. **See p.149**

❷ Abydos One of the foremost healing centres of Ancient Egypt, dedicated to the god Osiris enshrined in the exquisitely carved mortuary-temple of Seti I. **See p.245**

❸ Luxor The ancient New Kingdom capital has more tombs and temples than anywhere else in Egypt, from the awesome complex at Karnak to the Theban Necropolis across the river, with its fabulous Valley of the Kings. **See p.255**

❹ Edfu Sacred to the falcon-headed sky-god Horus, Egypt's best-preserved cult-temple dates from the Greco-Roman era, but respects all the Ancient Egyptian traditions of temple architecture. **See p.325**

❺ Philae An exquisite island shrine to the goddess Isis, which was semi-submerged by the Nile before its reconstruction between the two Aswan Dams. **See p.355**

❻ Abu Simbel This great sun temple, with its colossi of Ramses II hewn from a hillside, was also saved from submersion by Lake Nasser. **See p.366**

WILDLIFE

Egypt is one of the world's major flyover zones for birdlife, and the Red Sea abounds in corals and other aquatic life. You could visit all of these sites in about two weeks using a combination of buses and liveaboard boats.

❶ Lake Manzala This Mediterranean wetland is a wintering ground for egrets, avocets, cormorants, plovers, lapwings, redshanks, terns and other bird species. **See p.507**

❷ Ras Mohammed A marine national park at the southern tip of Sinai, which sustains a thousand-odd species of fish, from the child-friendly Crevice Pools to offshore dive-sites. **See p.538**

❸ Careless Reef Two coral-encrusted pinnacles just below the sea's surface, whose depths harbour semi-tame moray eels (normally known for their ferocity). **See p.581**

❹ The Brothers These two isolated reef-pillars are magnets for pelagic fishes and the hunting grounds of hammerhead, tiger, reef and whale sharks. **See p.581**

❺ Marsa Alam The Red Sea's southernmost resort serves as a springboard to wildlife sites in

ABOVE ROCK FORMATIONS, THE WHITE DESERT

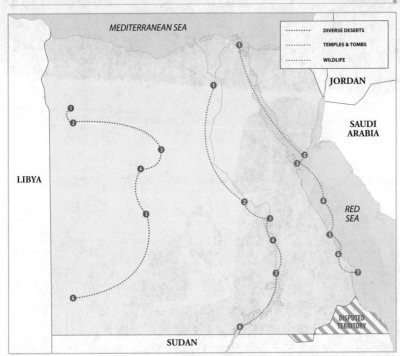

the far south, from Wadi Gimal to Ras Banata. **See p.591**

❻**Wadi Gimal** This national park is especially rewarding during the spring and autumn migrations, to observe ospreys, falcons and flamingos. **See p.592**

❼ **Ras Banata** One of the few undisturbed breeding colonies for sea turtles, accessible by dive-boat from eco-lodges 80km south of Wadi Gimal. **See p.592**

DIVERSE DESERTS

Over 96 percent of Egypt's landmass is desert, from the arid peaks of Sinai and the Eastern Desert to the dunes and escarpments of the Western Desert, where most of Egypt's oases are located. A jeep-safari to all these sites lasts 11 to 18 days, but you could do most of the highlights in a week, using buses in conjunction with local safari outfits.

❶ **Siwa Oasis** Way out near Libya, Siwa has a unique character, romantic ruins, natural springs and other beauty spots. **See p.441**

❷ **Great Sand Sea** A 72,000-square-kilometre wilderness of dunes up to 100m high, stretching from Siwa to the Gilf Kebir. The Sand Sea can be entered from Siwa, or traversed on deep-desert safaris from Bahariya or Farafra Oasis. **See p.440**

❸ **El-Qaf** A 500,000-year-old stalactite cave, accessible by jeep from Bahariya or Farafra. **See p.411**

❹ **White Desert** This surreal landscape of chalk rock-formations within Farafra Oasis is actually best reached from Bahariya, visiting the Black Desert en route. **See p.409**

❺ **Al-Qasr** A labyrinthine medieval Islamic settlement in Dakhla Oasis, reached by off-road safari from Bahariya, or by bus along the road between these oases. **See p.418**

❻ **Gilf Kebir** This super-arid plateau at the remotest corner of Egypt is the site of extraordinary prehistoric rock art at the Cave of the Swimmers (featured in *The English Patient*) and other sites, accessible by long-range safari from Bahariya, Farafra and Dakhla. **See p.431**

THROUGH THE DESERT BY DONKEY

Basics

Getting there

It is possible to get to Egypt by land, but most visitors fly in. Cairo has direct scheduled flights from London and New York, with indirect routes from pretty much everywhere, and there are low-cost flights from Britain to Luxor and the beach resorts.

The best airfares are available in low season, November through March, excluding Christmas and New Year, which counts as high season along with June, July and August. Flights on weekends can cost more than on weekdays; prices quoted below are for the cheapest round trip midweek including tax. Many have restrictions such as fixed dates, and may require advance booking.

Flights from the UK and Ireland

EgyptAir (W egyptair.com.eg), British Airways, (W ba .com) have scheduled flights to **Cairo** from London Heathrow (5hr). EgyptAir also has weekly direct flights to Luxor and twice weekly to Sharm el-Sheikh. EasyJet (W easyjet.com) flies from Manchester, Luton and Gatwick to Sharm el-Sheikh, and from Gatwick to Hurghada and Luxor. Flying indirectly, most airlines serve Cairo only, but Royal Jordanian (W rj.com) and Saudi Arabian Airlines (W saudiairlines.com) also fly from Heathrow to Alexandria and Sharm el-Sheikh, and Austrian Airlines (W austrian.com) fly from Heathrow via Vienna to Sharm el-Sheikh and Hurghada, while BA, KLM (W klm.com), Air France (W airfrance.com) and Lufthansa (W lufthansa.com) all offer indirect flights to Cairo from a number of British and Irish airports. Flights can cost as little as £275 return in low season, depending on the airline.

From the UK, there are also flights with low-cost charter airlines such as Thomsonfly (W flights .thomson.co.uk), First Choice Airways (W flights .firstchoice.co.uk) and Thomas Cook (W book .flythomascook.com), who fly from the UK to Luxor and the main resorts – Sharm el-Sheikh, Hurghada and sometimes Marsa Alam and Taba. These may operate only once or twice a week, and prices are generally similar to those on scheduled services, though you may occasionally turn up a bargain out of season. Most flights depart from London Gatwick or Manchester, but a few – particularly to Sharm el-Sheikh – use other UK airports too. Dive companies such as Planet (W planetdiveholidays .com), Regal (W regal-diving.co.uk) and Crusader (W crusadertravel.com) occasionally have cheap flight-only deals to the Red Sea resorts, but these are not usually advertised, so you'd need to approach the company direct. You may even find it cheaper to take a package tour than just a flight; there are some amazing bargains to be had among the basic Luxor-plus-Cairo or Luxor-only packages, and many smaller independent operators feature felucca trips on the Nile, diving holidays on the Red Sea or camel trekking in Sinai.

From **Ireland**, you can either make your own way to London and fly from there, or take an indirect flight, changing planes in Britain or Europe. Fares to Cairo start at around €300, with many (but not all) airlines hiking their prices by around €100 in high season.

Flights from the US and Canada

From **the US**, EgyptAir (W egyptair.com.eg) fly direct to Cairo from New York (10hr), and several European and Middle Eastern airlines offer indirect flights from a range of departure points, though New York still offers the biggest choice. West Coast flights are routed via the airlines' hub cities, so check that you won't have to wait overnight for your onward connection. You should be able to pick up a round-trip ticket for as little as $805 out of New York in low season, $1000 in high season. Flying from the West Coast, expect to pay $975 in low season, $1330 in high.

From **Canada**, Air Canada (W aircanada.com) offer through tickets from most Canadian airports in combination with Lufthansa (W lufthansa.com) or EgyptAir. Otherwise BA (W ba.com) and Air France

A BETTER KIND OF TRAVEL

At Rough Guides we are passionately committed to travel. We believe it helps us understand the world we live in and the people we share it with – and of course tourism is vital to many developing economies. But the scale of modern tourism has also damaged some places irreparably, and climate change is accelerated by most forms of transport, especially flying. All Rough Guides' flights are carbon-offset, and every year we donate money to a variety of environmental charities.

(Ⓦairfrance.com) fly via London or Paris from Toronto, Montreal or Vancouver, or you could fly to New York to pick up EgyptAir's daily flight from there. Low/high-season fares start at around Can$1300/1800 from Montreal or Toronto, Can$1450/1950 from Vancouver.

Flights from Australia, New Zealand and South Africa

A number of European, Middle Eastern and Asian carriers offer indirect flights to Egypt from **Australia and New Zealand**, changing planes at their hub airports. Cairo fares start at around Aus$2050 in low season, or Aus$2180 in high season from Australia, around NZ$3100 year-round from New Zealand. Emirates (Ⓦemirates .com) and Etihad (Ⓦetihadairways.com) are usually the cheapest and most convenient airlines; if flying into Dubai with Emirates, you might want to investigate low-cost flights on Air Arabia (Ⓦairarabia.com) from nearby Sharjah to Alexandria, Assyut or Luxor.

From **South Africa**, there are direct Cairo flights from Johannesburg (8hr) with EgyptAir (Ⓦegyptair .com.eg); SAA (Ⓦflysaa.com) codeshare this flight, offering through tickets from most South African airports. Otherwise, you can take an indirect flight with an East African airline such as Kenya Airways (Ⓦkenya-airways.com) or Ethiopian Airlines (Ⓦethiopianairlines.com), or a Middle Eastern Airline such as Emirates (Ⓦemirates.com) or Etihad (Ⓦetihadairways.com). Most serve only Johannesburg, but Emirates flies from Cape Town as well. Fares start at around R5,800 in low season (winter), R6,900 in high season (summer).

From Israel and Cyprus by land and sea

At the time of writing, the Rafah border crossing between Gaza and Egypt was closed, and all traffic between Israel and Egypt was using the crossing at **Taba** near Eilat (open 24/7 except Eid al-Adha and Yom Kippur). Entering Egypt via Taba, you're subject to an Israeli departure tax of NIS96 ($25.50), plus a NIS5 handling fee ($1.30) and an Egyptian entry tax of £E75 ($12.50).

Mazada Tours (141 Rehov Ibn Gvirol, Tel Aviv ☎03 544 4454; 6 Yanai St, West Jerusalem ☎02 623 5777; Ⓦmazada.co.il) used to run buses from Tel Aviv and Jerusalem to Cairo, but this service has been suspended since the revolution, though it may be reinstated in the future. Their office in Tel Aviv is just around the corner from the Egyptian embassy.

Taba makes a fine jumping-off point for the Sinai coast resorts, St Catherine's Monastery or Cairo. From Eilat, a taxi or a #15 bus (which doesn't run on Shabbat) will get you to the Israeli checkpoint at Taba for an exit stamp; you then walk over to the Egyptian side, where Sinai-only visas can be obtained on the spot. It usually takes a good hour to cross the border, longer at holiday times. A few banks in Sharm el-Sheikh and one or two banks and foreign exchange bureaux in Cairo are the only places in Egypt where you can legally exchange Israeli shekels. You are not allowed to drive rented cars across the Israeli–Egyptian border. The Israel Airports Authority keep some current information about the Taba border crossing on their website at Ⓦiaa.gov.il/Rashat/en-US/Borders/Taba.

The passenger ferry service from **Limassol** (Cyprus) to Port Said, with some services calling at Haifa (Israel), is often suspended, but usually runs approximately weekly from May to October. For current information contact Varianos Travel, 8C Pantelides Ave, PO Box 22107, 1517 Nicosia, Cyprus ☎357 22 680500, Ⓦvarianostravel.com/Cruises/ferry_service.htm. The ferry does not carry vehicles.

From Jordan by land and sea

Direct buses do the 23-hour journey from **Amman** to Cairo, but they are neither pleasant nor economical. Unless time is of the essence, it's better to do the journey in stages taking a ferry from Aqaba to Sinai.

JETT, on King Hussein Street in Amman (☎06 566 4146, Ⓦjett.com.jo), 900m north of Abdali station, has two weekly departures (Tues & Sat) direct to Cairo for JD28 (approximately $40) one-way, plus $75 for the ferry and JD8 ($11.50) exit tax. Afana, next door to JETT and at Abdali station (☎06 568 1560), run buses (currently daily at 2pm) for JD75 (approximately $106) including the boat. Most of these services will drop you in Cairo at Almaza terminal (see p.175), but some arrive at the more convenient Sinai bus terminal (see p.174). These direct buses usually take the Aqaba–Nuweiba ferry (see p.29), but some may travel overland through Eilat (Israel), a route whose drawbacks are discussed below, so you may want to check which route the bus will take before buying your ticket.

From **Aqaba**, the quickest route to Egypt is by land via Eilat in Israel, using local transport. Disincentives are the telltale Arava and Taba border stamps (see box, p.50), and the hefty exit and entry taxes (totalling around $46.50) payable at Eilat and Taba.

Alternatively, there are **ferries** from Aqaba to Sinai. Arab Bridge Maritime Co. (**W** abmaritime.com.jo) run a fast ferry (daily; 1hr; $75) and a slow ferry (daily; 3hr 30min; $65); both take vehicles but are subject to unpredictable delays, and the slow ferry is notoriously unpunctual. You can buy tickets from the company's offices in Amman (beside the Royal Jordanian building just off 7th Circle; **T** 06 585 9554) or Aqaba (Sharia al-Batra, by Humam Supermarket; **T** 03 209 2000), from agents in Aqaba, or up to an hour before departure at the passenger terminal itself, 6km south of Aqaba (**T** 03 201 3236). The terminal is served by local buses from Aqaba's fort (heading towards the Saudi border at Durra), or costs around JD5 by taxi.

An alternative is provided by Meenagate (next to the JETT bus park opposite the *Kempinski* hotel; **T** 03 201 3100, **W** meenagate.com), who run a **catamaran** service from the Royal Yacht Club, next to McDonald's in central Aqaba (daily 7.30pm, arrive an hour before departure; $85), sometimes supplemented by a ferry service from the main terminal. This service does not take vehicles, but bicycles are carried free so long as you arrange this when booking. You need to book by email, 24 hours ahead, attaching a scan of your passport (or alternatively fax it on **T** 03 201 9461).

You pay a JD8 exit tax when boarding the ferry (and don't expect any change back if you don't have the exact money). Egyptian visas are available on arrival in Nuweiba (one-month full visa $15, two-week Sinai-only visa free).

AGENTS AND OPERATORS

Ancient World Tours UK **T** 020 7917 9494, **W** ancient.co.uk. In-depth archeological and historical tours led by experts to over 120 sites in Egypt, including special access to many sites otherwise off-limits to tourists.

Discover Egypt UK **T** 0844 880 0462, **W** discoveregypt.co.uk. Packages and tailor-made itineraries including Nile cruises and multi-centre holidays.

Egypt Tours US **T** 1 800 TO EGYPT, **W** egyptours.com. Packages ranging from a six-night highlights tour to a nineteen-night "In Depth" trip, as well as combined tours with Jordan and Israel.

North South Travel UK **T** 01245 608 291, **W** northsouthtravel .co.uk. Friendly, competitive travel agency, offering discounted fares worldwide. Profits are used to support projects in the developing world, especially the promotion of sustainable tourism.

Soliman Travel UK **T** 020 7244 6855, **W** solimantravel.com/eg. One of the longest-established UK-based Egypt tour operators, with charter flights and a large range of packages and tailor-made holidays, mainly in five-star accommodation.

STA Travel UK **T** 0871 230 0040, **W** statravel.co.uk; US **T** 1 800 781 4040, **W** statravel.com; Australia **T** 134 782, **W** statravel.com.au; New Zealand **T** 0800 474400, **W** statravel .co.nz; South Africa **T** 0861 781 781, **W** statravel.co.za. Independent travel specialists, offering good discounts for students and under-26s.

Trailfinders UK **T** 020 7408 9000, Ireland **T** 01 677 7888; **W** trailfinders.com. One of the best-informed and most efficient agents for independent travellers.

Travel Cuts Canada **T** 1 800 667 2887, US **T** 1 800 592 2887, **W** travelcuts.com. Canadian youth and student travel firm.

USIT Republic of Ireland **T** 01 602 1906, Northern Ireland **T** 028 9032 7111; **W** usit.ie. Ireland's main youth and student travel specialists.

Ya'lla Tours US **T** 800 644 1595, **W** yallatours.com. Middle East specialists offering a variety of Egypt tours and packages.

Getting around

Egyptian public transport is, on the whole, pretty good. There is an efficient rail network linking the Nile Valley, Delta and Canal Zone, and elsewhere you can travel easily enough by bus or shared (service) taxi. On the Nile you can indulge in feluccas or cruise boats, while in the desert there's the chance to test your camel-riding prowess. For those in a hurry, EgyptAir provides a network of domestic flights.

While you can travel without restriction through most areas of Egypt, **travel permits** are required for desert travel between Bahariya and Siwa oases (permits available in Siwa), to Ain Della and the Gilf Kebir/Jebel Uwaynat in the western desert (see p.376), for the desert east of Marsa Alam (see p.590), and if you want to camp around Berenice and the Red Sea coast south of Marsa Alam (see p.591). In principle, permits to visit restricted areas in the eastern and western deserts are obtainable from Military Intelligence (Mukharabat), whose office is next-door to the Nasser Mosque at Abbassiya in Cairo (you'll need two photos and photocopies of the identifying pages of your passport and your Egyptian entry visa, plus a detailed intinerary), but in

---

TOP 5 EGYPTIAN JOURNEYS

Nile cruise Aswan to Luxor (p.239)
Sleeper train Cairo to Aswan (p.346)
Plane Aswan to Abu Simbel (p.366)
Jeep Siwa to Bahariya (p.457)
Camel safari Sinai (p.556)

practice, you are very unlikely to get a permit by approaching them directly, and it's much easier to go through an authorized travel agency or, failing that, **Misr Travel**, 1 Sharia Talaat Harb, Cairo ☎02 2393 0010, ✉misrtrav@link.com.eg. You don't currently need a permit to travel directly from Mersa Matrouh to the Libyan border, for example if taking a bus or service taxi to Benghazi or Tripoli, but the rules sometimes change, so it's wise to check first.

By rail

Covering a limited network of routes (Cairo to Alexandria, the Delta and the Canal Zone, along the coast to Mersa Matrouh and up the Nile Valley to Luxor and Aswan), Egypt's trains are best used for long hauls, when air-conditioned services offer a comfier alternative to buses and taxis. For shorter journeys, trains are slower and less reliable.

Timetables are posted up in major stations, but in Arabic only. Schedules and fares for services between major stations are posted on the Egyptian Railways website (🌐enr.gov.eg), where you can also buy tickets online. Schedules for sleeper services are available on the website of the company which operates them, Watania (🌐wataniasleepingtrains.com).

From Cairo to Alexandria or Aswan, there are fast a/c trains, including sleepers (also called wagons-lits) and snail-like non-a/c local services. However, on the Cairo–Luxor/Aswan route, foreigners are only allowed to use four "**tourist trains**" (two of which are sleepers), whose compartments are guarded by gun-toting plainclothes cops.

Buying tickets can get complicated at the largest stations, where separate queues exist for different ticket classes.

Air-conditioned trains

Air-conditioned trains nearly always have two classes (although occasionally a/c trains will be first or second class only). The most comfortable option is **first class** (*daraga awla*), with waiter service, reclining armchairs and no standing. They also screen videos until midnight. **Second class superior** (*daraga tania mukayyifa*) is less plush and more crowded – but two-thirds the price of first class. Both classes are comfortable enough to allow you to sleep on an overnight journey, at a fraction of the cost of a sleeper (see below).

Seats are **reservable** up to seven days in advance. There is occasional double booking but a little baksheesh to the conductor usually sorts out any problem. One common difficulty is that return tickets can't necessarily be booked at the point of origin. The peak seasons for travel are summer for Alexandria and winter for Upper Egypt.

In terms of **fares**, a ticket from Cairo to Luxor costs around ££165 in first class (the only class allowed for tourists), while Cairo to Alexandria costs ££50 in first class, ££35 in second. **Students** with ISIC cards (see p.47) get at least a third off on all fares except on sleepers. Many travel agencies sell first-class tickets for a small commission, saving you from having to queue.

Wagons-lits (sleepers)

Many tourists cough up for a bed in a sleeper car (wagons-lits), which may comprise an entire train, or be limited to a couple of carriages tacked on to a regular service. Fares are relatively hefty (though still cheaper than flying) at $60 one way from Cairo to Luxor or Aswan. Passengers get a comfortable two-bed cabin (a single traveller can book one exclusively for $120, or pay the normal fare and share with someone of the same sex) with a sink, plus breakfast and dinner, and access to a dining car and a bar. In summer (mid-June to mid-Sept) there's also a sleeper service from Cairo to Mersa Matrouh.

Bookings for wagons-lits can be done at Ramses station (see p.173), through the operator, Watania (☎02 3748 9388, 🌐wataniasleepingtrains.com), or through American Express; payment must be made in US dollars or euros.

Non-air-conditioned trains

Non-a/c trains comprise **ordinary second class** (*daraga tania aadia*) carriages, with padded bench seating, or **third class** (*daraga talata*), with wooden benches. Both are invariably crowded, the rolling stock ancient and often filthy, and schedules fanciful. Few foreigners use them, but on a few routes they are the only services available, and over short distances you might enjoy the disorder.

There is no advance booking for seats on these services and you needn't even queue for a ticket at the station – these can be bought on-board from the conductor, with just a small penalty fee of ££1–2 added to the fare.

By bus

Egypt's three main **bus companies**, all based in Cairo, are: Upper Egypt Bus Company (Nile Valley, Fayoum, inner oases and the Red Sea Coast down to El-Quseir); East Delta Bus Company (Sinai and the Canal Zone); and West and Middle Delta Bus Company (Alexandria, Mersa Matrouh, Siwa and the

Nile Delta). An independent firm, El Gouna, runs buses from Cairo to Hurghada and Sharm el-Sheikh. Key routes (Cairo to Alexandria, Sharm el-Sheikh and Hurghada) are also covered by Superjet (red, black and gold livery, known as "Golden Arrows" or "Golden Rockets"), a subsidiary of the Arab Union Transport Company which operates international services to Libya, Jordan, Syria and Saudi Arabia.

Major routes are plied by a/c buses, usually new(ish) and fast. Local routes usually have cheaper non-a/c buses, generally old rattletraps. Superjet buses have a/c, toilets, videos and expensive snacks.

Terminals and bookings

Though most towns have a single bus depot for all destinations, cities such as Cairo and Alexandria have several. English- or French-speaking staff are fairly common at the larger ones, but rare in the provinces. **Schedules** – usually posted in Arabic only – change frequently. Bus information can be obtained from hotels in Sinai and the oases, and tourist offices in Luxor, Aswan and the oases.

At city terminals, **tickets** are normally sold from kiosks, up to 24 hours in advance for air-conditioned or long-haul services. In the provinces, tickets may only be available an hour or so before departure, or on the bus itself in the case of through services, which are often standing-room only when they arrive. Passengers on a/c services are usually assigned a seat (the number is written in Arabic on your ticket), but seats on "local" buses are taken on a first-come, first-served basis. Fares are very reasonable: Cairo to Alexandria costs £E17 by ordinary bus, or £E30 on the deluxe Superjet service, while Cairo to Luxor is £E100 by Superjet.

By service taxi

Collective **service taxis** (known as *servees*) are one of the best features of Egyptian transport. They operate on a wide variety of routes, are generally quicker than buses and trains, and fares are very reasonable. On the downside, maniacal driving on congested roads calls for strong nerves; accidents are not uncommon.

The taxis are usually big **Peugeot saloons** carrying seven passengers, or **microbuses** (*meecros*) seating a dozen. Most business is along specific routes, with more or less nonstop departures throughout the day on the main ones, while cross-desert traffic is restricted to early morning and late afternoon. Show up at the terminal (locations are detailed in the guide) and ask for a *servees* to your destination, or listen for drivers

shouting it out. As soon as the requisite number of people (or less, if you're willing to pay extra) are assembled, the taxi sets off. Fewer people travel after dark in winter or on Friday, when you might have to wait a while for a ride to a distant town; travelling in stages can be quicker.

Service taxis have **fixed fares**, which you can ascertain by asking at your hotel (or the tourist office), or seeing what Egyptians pay. You can also **charter a taxi** – useful for day excursions or on odd routes, but you'll have to bargain hard to get the right price.

By car

Driving in Egypt is not for the faint-hearted or inexperienced motorist. Cities, highways, backroads and *pistes* each pose a challenge to drivers' skills and nerve. Pedestrians and carts seem blithely indifferent to heavy traffic. Though accidents are less frequent than you'd think, the crumpled wrecks alongside highways are a constant reminder of the hazards of motoring.

The **minimum age** for driving in Egypt is 25 years, the **maximum** is 70. Foreigners require an International Driving Licence (obtainable from motoring organizations at home).

The highest **speed limit** outside towns is 90km/h (56mph), despite old signs on some highways which still say 100km/h. In built-up areas, the highest speed limit is 60km/h (37mph), and on some stretches of road, the limit can be as low as 30km/h (18mph). Road signs are similar to those in Europe, but speed limits are usually posted in Arabic numerals (see p.631). Vehicles drive on the right, although traffic in cities is relentless and anarchic, with vehicles weaving to and fro between lanes, signalling by horn. Two beeps means "I'm alongside and about to overtake." A single long blast warns "I can't (won't) stop and I'm coming through!" Extending your hand, fingers raised and tips together, is the signal for "Watch out, don't pass now"; spreading your fingers and flipping them forwards indicates "Go ahead." Although the car in front usually has right of way, buses and trams always take precedence. On **country roads** – including the two-lane east- and west-bank "highways" along the Nile Valley – trucks and cars routinely overtake in the face of incoming traffic. The passing car usually flashes its lights as a warning, but not always.

Most roads are bumpy, with potholes and all manner of traffic, including donkey carts and camels. Beware, especially, of children darting into the road. If you injure someone, relatives may take revenge on the spot. Avoid driving **after dark**, when Egyptians drive without lights, only flashing them on to high beam when they see another car approaching. Wandering pedestrians and animals, obstructions and sand drifts present extra hazards. In spring, flash floods can wash away roads in Sinai. On **pistes** (rough, unpaved tracks in the desert or mountains) there are special problems. You need a good deal of driving and mechanical confidence – and shouldn't attempt such routes if you don't feel your car's up to scratch.

Police or military road checks – signposted in English as "Traffic Stations" – occur on the approach roads to towns and oases and along major trunk routes. Foreign motorists are usually waved through, but you might be asked to show your passport or driving licence.

Car rental

Renting a car pays obvious dividends if you are pushed for time or plan to visit remote sites, but whether you'd want to drive yourself is another matter – it's not much more expensive to hire a car and driver. Branches of Misr Travel (see p.30), and numerous local tour agencies, can fix you up with one, or you can charter a taxi (see p.31). If you bring your own vehicle, you are required to re-export it when you leave – even if it gets wrecked.

A self-drive car can be rented through one of the international franchise chains, or a local firm (addresses are given in the guide). It's worth shopping around as rates and terms vary considerably. At the cheaper end, you can get a car with unlimited mileage for around £50/$75 a day. Most companies require a hefty deposit, and not all accept credit cards. You cannot bring a rented car across the border into Egypt.

Before making a reservation, be sure to find out if you can pick up the car in one city and return it in another. Generally, this is only possible with cars from Hertz, Avis or Budget. Before setting out, make sure the car has a spare tyre, tool kit and full documentation – including insurance cover, which is compulsory with all rentals.

Fuel and breakdowns

Petrol (*benzene*) and diesel stations are plentiful in larger towns but few and far between in rural and desert areas. Replace oil/air filters regularly, lest impurities in the fuel, and Egypt's ubiquitous dust, clog up the engine.

Egyptian **mechanics** are usually excellent at coping with breakdowns, and all medium-sized towns have garages (most with a range of spare parts for French, German and Japanese cars). If you break down miles from anywhere, however, you can pay a lot to get towed back.

Vehicle insurance

All car rentals must by law be sold with third-party insurance. Accident and damage insurance should be included, but make sure. In the case of an **accident**, get a written report from the police and from the doctor who first treats any injuries, without which your insurance may not cover the costs. Reports are written in Arabic.

Driving your own vehicle, you will need to take out **Egyptian insurance**. Policies are sold by Misr Insurance (☎02 3335 5350 or ☎19114, ☎misrins .com.eg); offices are found in most towns and at border crossings. Premiums vary according to the size, horsepower and value of the vehicle.

Motorbikes and bicycles

Motorcycling could be a good way to travel around Egypt, but the red tape involved in bringing your own bike is diabolical (ask your national motoring organization and the Egyptian consulate for details). It's difficult to rent a machine except in Luxor or Hurghada. Bikers should be especially wary of potholes, sand and rocks, and other road-users (see p.31).

Bicycles, useful for getting around small towns and reaching local sights or beaches, can be rented in Luxor, Aswan, Hurghada, Siwa Oasis and other places for a modest sum. Cycling in big cities or over long distances is not advisable. Traffic is murderous, the heat brutal and foreign cyclists are sometimes stoned by children (particularly in the Delta). If you're determined to cycle the **Nile Valley**, the east bank expressway that runs down as far as Aswan is the safest route.

Most towns have **repair shops**, well used to servicing local bikes and mopeds. They're unlikely to have the right spare parts but can usually sort out some kind of temporary solution.

Hitchhiking

Hitchhiking is largely confined to areas with minimal public transport, or trunk routes if passing service taxis or scheduled buses are full. You usually pay anyway, and foreigners who hitch where proper transport is available may inspire contempt rather than sympathy. Women should never hitch without a male companion.

By air

In general, it's only worth flying if your time is very limited, or for the view – the Nile Valley and Sinai look amazing from the air – although the trip from Aswan to Abu Simbel (see p.366) is easiest by plane. EgyptAir (W egyptair.com) flies between Cairo and Alexandria, Mersa Matrouh, Port Said, Sharm el-Sheikh, Hurghada, Marsa Alam, Assyut, Sohag, Luxor, Aswan and Abu Simbel, as well as between Aswan and Luxor and between Aswan and Abu Simbel. Details of flights and addresses of local offices appear in the text.

Fares rise as seats on the plane get booked up, so it's best to book early if possible. In winter season, it's wise to book at least a week ahead for flights between Cairo and Luxor, Aswan, Abu Simbel or Sharm. Always reconfirm 72 hours prior to the journey, as overbooking is commonplace.

By boat

The colonial tradition of **Nile cruises** has spawned an industry with over two hundred steamers. Most sail from Luxor to Aswan (or the other way), a three- to five-day trip, stopping at Esna, Edfu and Kom Ombo.

The most reliable cruises are sold with package holidays, and week-long cruises plus air fare are available for as little as £560 from the UK or $2700 from North America. In Egypt you can arrange a trip on the spot from around $50–60 per day (all per person in a twin cabin). Prices escalate dramatically for a luxury cruise.

Looking for a Nile cruise in Egypt, shop around and don't necessarily go for the cheapest deal – some leave a lot to be desired in terms of hygiene and living conditions. If possible, check the vessel first. Deluxe boats with swimming pools can be wonderful, but not all offer value for money. The best deals are available from local agents in Luxor and Aswan (or directly from the boats). Beware in particular of the overpriced trips sold by touts and some hotels in Cairo (see box, p.173).

Feluccas, the lateen-sailed boats used on the Nile since antiquity, still serve as transport along many stretches. Favoured by tourists for sunset cruises, they allow you to experience the changing moods of the Nile while lolling in blissful indolence. Many visitors opt for a felucca cruise between Aswan and Luxor. It's easy to arrange a cruise yourself (see pp.242–245), and several tour operators offer packages.

Local **ferries**, generally battered, crowded and cheap, cross the Nile and Suez Canal at various points. There are fast and slow ferries from Nuweiba

in Sinai to Aqaba in Jordan (see p.29); the catamaran service between Hurghada and Sharm el-Sheikh was suspended at the time of writing, though it may possibly be reinstated in the future. There is also a sporadic and not very reliable boat service from Aswan to Wadi Halfa in Sudan.

City transport

Most Egyptian towns are small enough to cover on foot, especially if your hotel is in the centre. In larger cities, however, local transport is useful. Learn to recognize Arabic numerals (see p.631) to take full advantage of the cheap **buses**, **minibuses** and **trams** that cover most of Alexandria and Cairo (which also has river taxis and an excellent metro).

Four-seater **taxis** often operate on a **shared** basis, making stops to pick up passengers heading in the same direction. To hail a cab, pick a major thoroughfare with traffic heading in the right direction, stand on the kerb, and wave and holler out your destination as one approaches. If the driver's interested he'll stop, whereupon you can state your destination again, in more detail. If the driver starts talking money, say "*maalesh*" (forget it) and look for another cab.

Don't expect drivers to speak English or to know every street; you may need to name a major landmark or thoroughfare in the vicinity instead. If your destination is obscure or hard to pronounce, get it written down in Arabic. Near the end of the journey, direct the driver to stop where you want (bearing in mind one-way systems and other obstacles) with "*hina/hinak kwayes*" (here/there's okay). You need to know the right fare in advance; hand it over with confidence when you arrive, together with any tip you consider appropriate. If you've underpaid, the driver will let you know. Don't take taxis waiting outside expensive hotels or tourist sites, nor those that hustle you in the street, as they are sure to overcharge you.

ADDRESSES

Words for street (*sharia*), avenue (*tariq*) and square (*midan*) precede the name. Narrower thoroughfares may be termed *darb*, *haret*, *sikket* or *zuqaq*. The word *bab* signifies a medieval gate, after which certain quarters are named (for example, Bab al-Khalq in Cairo); *kubri* a bridge; and *souk* a market. Whole blocks often share a single street number, which may be in Arabic numerals (see also p.631), but are commonly not shown at all.

Calèches (or *hantour*) – horse-drawn buggies – are mainly for tourists, who are often accosted by drivers in Luxor and Aswan, Alexandria and at other places. Fares are higher than taxis and, regardless of official tariffs, are negotiable. In a few small towns, mostly in Middle Egypt, the *hantour* remains part of local city transport. Ask locals about fares before climbing on board, or simply pay what you see fit at the end. Some of the horses and buggies are in pristine condition; others painful to behold. Tourists can help by admonishing drivers who abuse their animals or gallop their horses, and by not travelling more than four to a carriage.

Accommodation

The main tourist centres offer a broad spectrum of accommodation, with everything from luxury palaces to homely pensions and flea-ridden dives. Even in high season, in Cairo, Sinai or the Nile Valley, you should be able to find something in your preferred range. Elsewhere, the choice is generally more limited, with only basic lodgings available in some towns and cities. Cairo is generally more expensive for accommodation of all types.

Hotels

Egyptian hotels are loosely categorized into star ratings, from one-star to five-star deluxe. Below this there are unclassified hotels and *pensions*, some tailored to foreign backpackers, others mostly used by Egyptians.

Deluxe hotels are almost exclusively modern and chain-owned (Sofitel, Mövenpick, Hilton, etc), with swimming pools, bars, restaurants, air conditioning and all the usual facilities. **Four-star** hotels can be more characterful, including some famous names like the *Old Cataract* in Aswan and the *Winter Palace* in Luxor. There is also the odd gem among **three-star** hotels, though most are slightly shabby 1970s-style towers, where facilities like plumbing and a/c can be less than reliable. Upmarket hotels, especially at the top of the range, are invariably much cheaper if booked from home through a travel agent or online than if you simply turn up and pay the rack rate.

At **two- and one-star** level, you rarely get air conditioning, though better places will supply fans, and old-style buildings with balconies, high ceilings

TOP 5 EGYPTIAN HOTELS
Le Riad Cairo (p.183)
Old Cataract Aswan (p.349)
Al-Moudira Haggar Daba'iyya (p.272)
Winter Palace Luxor (p.268)
Al-Tarfa Desert Sanctuary Dakhla (p.415)

and louvred windows are well designed to cope with the heat, but can be chilly in winter, as they rarely have heating.

Some cheaper hotels are classified as **pensions**, which makes little difference in facilities, but may signify family ownership and a friendlier ambience.

Hotel room **prices** are quoted in the listings throughout the book. Unless otherwise stated, quoted rates are for the **cheapest double room in high season**, not including breakfast.

Hotel touts

"Fishing" for guests (as Egyptians call it) is common in tourist centres, where new arrivals are approached by touts at train and bus stations, airports and docks. Some work in the hotel they're touting, but most are hustling for commissions and will use trickery to deliver clients to "their" establishment – swearing that other places are full, or closed, or whatever. Usually it's grotty and overpriced places that depend on touts. In any case, their commission will be added to your bill – another reason to avoid using them. In Cairo especially, many touts work for hotels that exist purely to hold foreigners and sell them overpriced excursions or souvenirs.

Hostels

Egypt's twelve official youth hostels are cheap but have daytime lock-outs, night-time curfews and segregation of men from women and (usually) foreigners from Egyptians (which you might appreciate when noisy groups are in residence). The most salubrious hostels are in Cairo, Sharm el-Sheikh and Ismailiya – but all are far from where the action is.

It seems to be up to individual hostels whether you need a Hostelling International (HI) card, and their rules change constantly. Non-HI members, if admitted, are sometimes charged slightly extra. For more information, contact the Egyptian Youth Hostel Association in Cairo (1 Sharia al-Ibrahimy, Garden City, Cairo ☎02 2796 1448, ⓦegyptyha .com). There are also a few YMCA hostels, which admit anyone.

Camping

Most campsites are for holidaying Egyptian families on the coast, often shadeless, with few facilities, and not recommended. Rather better are the occasional campsites attached to hotels, which may offer ready-pitched tents with camp beds, plus the use of hotel showers and toilet facilities. As for camping rough, you should always check with the authorities about any coastal site – some beaches are mined, others patrolled by the military. In the oases it's less of a problem, though any land near water will belong to someone, so again, ask permission.

Food and drink

Egyptian food combines elements of Lebanese, Turkish, Syrian, Greek and French cuisines, modified to suit local conditions and tastes, with more Mediterranean influences, for example, in Alexandria, and spicy Nubian cooking in the south.

Cafés, diners and street stalls offer simpler dishes than more formal restaurants catering to middle-class Egyptians and tourists, with proper menus and a broader range of dishes. Restaurant **prices** do not usually include service and taxes, which generally add around seventeen percent to the bill. **Tips** are a couple of pounds per person in cheap places, ten to fifteen percent in pricier establishments if service is not included (or even if it is). In the text we've given the price of a sample dish per restaurant, but note that this does not include tax or service.

Cafés and street food

Egypt's staples are bread ('aish, which also means "life"), fuul and taamiya. **Bread**, eaten with all meals and snacks, comes either as pitta-type 'aish shamsi (sun-raised bread made from white flour) or 'aish baladi (made from coarse wholewheat flour).

Fuul (pronounced "fool"; fava beans) is extremely cheap and can be prepared in several ways. Boiled and mashed with tomatoes, onions and spices, it becomes fuul madammes, often served with a chopped boiled egg for breakfast. A similar mixture stuffed into 'aish baladi constitutes the fuul sandwiches sold on the street.

Taamiya (falafel) is deep-fried patties of spiced green beans, usually served in pitta bread with salad, pickles and **tahina** (a sauce made from

TOP 5 EGYPTIAN MEALS
Kushari Abou Tarek, Cairo (p.185)
Roast goat Rifai, Cairo (p.187)
Fish supper Fish Market, Alexandria (p.486)
Mezze Sofra, Luxor (p.274)
Chicken molukhiyya Abou el Sid, Cairo (p.187)

sesame paste), for which you can expect to pay the grand sum of ££1–1.50.

Another cheap café perennial is **makarona** – macaroni baked into a cake with minced lamb and tomato sauce. It's rather bland but very filling. Similarly common is **kushari**, a mixture of noodles, rice, macaroni, lentils and onions, in a spicy tomato sauce (another sauce, made of garlic, is optional). It's served in small, medium and large portions (££5–7) in tiled stand-up diners, also called kushari.

Fiteer, a cross between pizza and pancake, consists of flaky filo pastry stuffed with white cheese, peppers, mince, egg, onion and olives, or with raisins, jams, curds or a dusting of icing sugar, costs ££5–25 (depending on size and ingredients) at café-like establishments known as fatatri.

Most **sandwiches** are small rolls with a minute portion of basturma (pastrami) or cheese. Other favourite fillings include grilled liver (kibda) with spicy green peppers and onions; tiny shrimps; and mokh (crumbed sheep's brains).

A common appetizer is **torshi**, a mixture of pickled radishes, turnips, gherkins and carrots; luridly coloured, it is something of an acquired taste, as are pickled lemons, another favourite.

Lastly, there's **shawarma** – slices of marinated lamb, stuffed into pitta bread or a roll and garnished with salad and tahina – somewhat superior to the similar-looking doner kebabs sold abroad. A shawarma sandwich from a street stall can cost as little as ££7, while a plate of shawarma in a cheap diner will set you back around ££10.

On the **hygiene** front, while cafés and tiled eateries with running water are generally safe, street grub is highly suspect unless it's peelable or hot.

Restaurant meals

The classic Egyptian restaurant meal is a lamb **kebab** or **kofta** (spiced mince patties), accompanied or preceded by a couple of mezze (salads and dips) – usually **hummus** (made from chickpeas), tahina and **babaghanoug** (tahina with aubergine). Many restaurants sell kofta and kebab by weight: a

VEGETARIAN EATING

Most Egyptians eat vegetables most of the time – meat and fish are luxuries – yet the concept of **vegetarianism** is incomprehensible. Even if you say that you're vegetarian (in Arabic, *ana nabati* if you're male, *ana nabatiya* if you're female) people may offer you chicken or fish as a substitute. Still, vegetarians and vegans will have no trouble feeding themselves in *kushari* and falafel joints, and *fatatris* offer reasonable pickings too, even for vegans (who can try ordering a veg or mushroom *fiteer* without cheese). Restaurants and hotels that cater particularly to tourists often feature a few vegetarian dishes on the menu, such as omelettes, vegetable *tageens*, pasta and salads.

For **vegans** the magic word is *siami*, which means "for fasting". Coptic Christians have a huge number of fast days in which they eat no meat, fish, eggs or dairy products, and *siami* versions of many dishes are available for their benefit. Thus a *siami* pizza, for example, is one without cheese.

quarter of a kilo is one portion, while a full kilo is usually enough for three to four people. **Chicken** (*firakh*) is a standard, both in cafés and as takeaway food from spit-roast stands. **Pigeon** (*hamam*) is common too, often served with *freek* (spicy wheat) stuffing. There's not much meat on a pigeon, so it's best to order a couple each. In slightly fancier places, you may also encounter pigeon in a **tageen** or *ta'gell*, stewed with onions, tomatoes and rice in an earthenware pot. A meal in an inexpensive restaurant should set you back around £E35–50 per person.

Posher restaurants offer a larger selection of **mezze**, often including olives and stuffed vine leaves, as well as soups, and dishes such as **molukhiyya** (Jew's mallow stewed in stock – a lot tastier than its disconcertingly slimy appearance suggests), **mahshi** (stuffed vegetables), and **torly** (mixed vegetable casserole with lamb or occasionally beef).

Fish (*samak*) – including sea bream, snapper, Nile perch, squid and prawns – is particularly good in Alexandria, Aswan, the Red Sea Coast and Sinai. You often pick your own from an ice box, priced by weight, then grilled or fried, and served with salad and chips.

Confusingly, **pasta**, **rice**, **chips** (French fries) and even **crisps** (potato chips) are often considered interchangeable – so you may order rice and get chips instead. Also note that the shaker with one hole is for pepper, the one with several holes for salt.

Snacks, sweets and fruit

There are two main types of **cheese**: *gibna beyda* (white), which tastes like Greek feta, and *gibna rumi* ("Roman"), a hard yellow cheese tasting a bit like Edam. For breakfast you will often be given imported processed cheeses such as La Vache Qui Rit ("The Laughing Cow" – a popular nickname for ex-president Mubarak).

Nut shops (*ma'la*) are a street perennial, offering all kinds of peanuts (*fuul sudani*) and edible seeds. *Lib abyad* and *lib asmar* are varieties of pumpkin seeds, *lib battikh* come from watermelon, and chickpeas (hummus) are roasted and sugar-coated or dried and salted; all of these are sold by weight. Most nut shops also stock candies and mineral water.

Cakes are available at patisseries (some attached to quite flash cafés) or street stalls. The classics include baklava (filo pastry soaked in honey and nuts – called *basbousa* in Upper Egypt, though elsewhere the term usually applies to syrup-drenched semolina cake); *katif* (similar but with shredded wheat); and a variety of milk- or cornflour-based puddings, such as *mahalabiyya* (blancmange) and *Umm Ali* (made with pastry, milk, sugar, coconut and cinnamon, usually served hot).

Fruits are wonderful in Egypt, all readily available at street stalls, or pressed into juice at juice bars (see p.37). In winter there are oranges, bananas and pomegranates, followed by strawberries in March. In summer you get mangoes, melons, peaches, plums and grapes, plus a brief season (Aug & Sept) of prickly pears (cactus fruit). Fresh dates are harvested in late autumn. Only apples are imported, and thus expensive.

Drinks

As a predominantly Muslim country, Egypt gives **alcohol** a low profile. Public drunkenness is unacceptable, and sale of alcohol is prohibited on the Prophet Mohammed's birthday and – except for a few places serving tourists – during the month of Ramadan.

Tea, coffee and karkaday

Egypt's national beverage is **tea** (*shai*). Invitations to drink tea (*shurub shai?*) are as much a part of life in Egypt as in Britain, although it is served quite differently, generally prepared by boiling the leaves, and served black and sugared to taste (though an increasing number of cafés use tea bags and may supply milk). Tea with milk is *shai bi-laban*, tea-bag tea is *shai libton* – to avoid it ask for loose-leaf tea (*shai kushari*). Tea with a sprig of mint (*shai bi-na'ana*) is refreshing when the weather is hot.

Coffee (*'ahwa*) is traditionally **Turkish** coffee, served in tiny cups pre-sugared to customers' specifications: *saada* (unsugared), *'ariha* (slightly sweetened), *mazboota* (medium sweet) or *ziyaada* (syrupy). In some places you can get it with cardamom (*'ahwa mahawega*). Most middle-class or tourist establishments also serve **instant coffee**, with the option of having it with milk (*'ahwa bi-laban*). Upmarket places increasingly have espresso machines.

Traditional **coffee houses** (*'ahwa*) are usually shabby hole-in-the-wall places with chairs overlooking the street. Until very recently, it was unusual for women to frequent *'ahwas*, and unheard of to see them puffing away on a *sheesha*, but times change, and in more upmarket establishments younger, less inhibited women can now be seen with a waterpipe to their lips. Foreign women won't be turned away from *'ahwas* but may feel uneasy, especially if unaccompanied by a man. For a more relaxed tea or coffee, try one of the middle-class *'ahwas* found in larger towns and often attached to patisseries.

Karkaday (or *karkadé*) is a deep-red infusion of hibiscus flowers. Most popular in Luxor and Aswan, it is equally refreshing drunk hot or cold. Elsewhere, they may use dehydrated extract instead of real hibiscus, so it doesn't taste as good. Other **infusions** sold in *'ahwas* include *helba* (fenugreek), *yansoon* (aniseed) or *'irfa* (cinnamon).

On cold winter evenings you might enjoy **sahleb**, a thick, creamy drink made from milk thickened with ground orchid root, with cinnamon and nuts sprinkled on top. In hot weather Egyptians imbibe **rayeb** (soured milk), which is something of an acquired taste.

Juice

Every main street has a couple of tiled, stand-up **juice bars**, recognizable by their displays of fruit. Normally, you order and pay at the cash desk, where you're given a plastic token or receipt to exchange at the counter for your drink.

Juices made from seasonal fruit include *burtu'an* (orange), *mohz* (banana; with milk *mohz bi-laban*), *manga* (mango), *farawla* (strawberry), *gazar* (carrot), *rummaan* (pomegranate), *subia* (coconut) and *'asab* (the sickly sweet, creamy, light-green juice of crushed sugar cane). You can also order blends; *nus w nus* (literally "half and half") usually refers to carrot and orange juice, but other combinations can be specified.

Street vendors also ladle out iced *'asiir limoon* (strong, sweet lemonade), bitter-sweet *er'a sous* (liquorice-water), and deliciously refreshing *tamar hindi* (tamarind cordial).

Soft drinks and mineral water

Despite this profusion of cheap fresh juices, the usual **soda** pops – Coca-Cola, Fanta, Sprite and 7-Up (referred to as "Seven") – are widely available in bottles and cans. Local brand Fayrouz offers unusual flavours such as mango or pineapple. Bottled sodas are normally drunk on the spot; you have to pay a deposit on the bottle to take one away.

Bottled **water** (*mayya ma'adaniyya*) is widely available, particularly Baraka; Siwa and Hyat (from Siwa Oasis) are less widely distributed. It's wise to check that the seal is intact, or you may be palmed off with tap water (*mayya baladi*), which is safe to drink in major towns and cities, but highly chlorinated; people with sensitive stomachs should stick to bottled water.

Alcohol

Alcohol can be obtained in most places, but outlets are limited. In the Western Desert oases or Middle Egypt, sale is prohibited or severely restricted. If

---

THE SHEESHA

The **sheesha**, or waterpipe, is inseparable from Egyptian café society. It takes *ma'azil*, rough tobacco with molasses, whose distinctive aroma is guaranteed to take you right back to Egypt if you smell it again elsewhere. Posh coffee houses may also stock other flavours of tobacco (apple, strawberry, mint and so forth) and provide disposable plastic mouthpieces. A *sheesha* is normally shared among friends, but you can decline to partake without causing offence. Don't call it a hubbly-bubbly, as in Egypt the term refers to smoking hashish.

there are no bars, then hotels or restaurants are the places to try; if you can't see anyone drinking it, there's none to be had. Keep in mind that the hot, dry climate makes for dehydration, and agonizing hangovers can easily result from overindulgence.

Beer, whose consumption goes back to pharaonic times, is the most widely available form of alcohol. Native Stella beer is a light lager (4 percent ABV) which is OK if it hasn't sat in the sun for too long. To check that bottled beer hasn't gone flat, invert the bottle before opening and look for a fizzy head. Stella retails in liquor stores for £E6.50, and in most bars for £E8–12, though discos may charge as much as £E30, and cruise boats even more. Sakkara is a similarly light lager (4 percent) that most foreigners seem to prefer. Premium or "export" versions of Stella and Sakkara have a slightly fuller flavour. Also worth trying is Luxor lager, availaible in "classic" (5 percent) or "gold" (4.7 percent) varieties. There's also a locally brewed Heineken, plus kamikaze (7–10 percent) versions of Sakkara and Meister, which are worth avoiding. Marzen, a dark bock beer, appears briefly in the spring; Aswali is a dark beer produced in Aswan. There is also Birrel, a non-alcoholic beer.

A half-dozen or so **Egyptian wines**, produced near Alexandria, include Omar Khayyam (a very dry red), Cru des Ptolémées (a dry white) and Rubis d'Egypte (a rosé). None are especially good, though Obélisque Red Cabernet Sauvignon and Chateau des Rêves are slightly better than most. These retail for about £E80 a bottle in most restaurants, but more like £E120 on a cruise boat.

Spirits are usually mixed with sodas or fruit juice. The favourite is **brandy**, known as *jaz* ("bottle"), and sold under three labels: Ahmar (the cheapest), Maa'tak (the best) and Vin (the most common). **Zibiba** is similar to Greek ouzo. Avoid vile Egyptian-made **gin** and **whisky** whose labels imitate famous Western brands – they may contain wood alcohol and other poisons. A vodka-based **alcopop** called ID is available in various flavours at liquor stores and some bars and duty-free shops.

Foreigners could formerly buy up to three litres of imported spirits (or two bottles of spirits plus a two-dozen-can carton of beer) at **duty-free** prices within 24 hours of arrival in Egypt, in addition to the two litres allowed in from abroad, These rules have fluctuated since the revolution, however, and the Islamist majority in parliament may well restrict this allowance in the future. There is a black market for duty-free booze (Johnny Walker Black Label is the most sought-after), and Egyptians in the street may ask you to buy them duty-free booze "for my sister's wedding", but never allow them to be involved in the transaction inside the store: the paperwork for any duty-free purchase is in Arabic, and some travellers have discovered on leaving Egypt that a TV or video has been bought duty-free with their passport. Unable to produce the item for customs officials, they've had to pay duty on it, just as if they'd purchased and then sold it.

The media

Newspapers

The press is now a lot freer than it was before the revolution. The **English-language** *Egyptian Gazette* (on Sat, the *Egyptian Mail*) carries agency reports, articles on Middle Eastern affairs and tourist features, but it's pretty lightweight – you can read it in a few minutes. The same applies to the *Egypt Daily News* (W thedailynewsegypt.com), though it's more independent and has more foreign news. The English weekly edition of *Al-Ahram* (see below) has interesting opinion pieces on politics and international affairs, but tends to reflect official thinking.

Among the **Arabic** papers, *Al-Ahram* ("The Pyramids", founded in 1875 and thus Egypt's oldest newspaper), reflects official thinking, as do *Al-Akhbar* and *Al-Gomhouriya*. Other dailies with a party affiliation include the conservative *Al-Wafd* ("The Delegation"), the liberal *Al-Destour* ("The Constitution") and *Al-Da'wa* ("The Call"), the journal of the Muslim Brotherhood. The left-leaning (and pro-revolution) *Almasry Alyoum* has an online English version at W egyptindependent.com and covers many issues not discussed in the rest of the English-language (or indeed Arabic) press.

Various British, US, French and German newspapers are available in Cairo, Alexandria, Luxor and Aswan, as are *Newsweek* and *Time* magazines. Elsewhere, however, you'll be lucky to find even the *Egyptian Gazette*.

Radio

With a short-wave radio you can pick up the BBC World Service (W bbc.co.uk/worldservice), Voice of America (W voanews.gov) and other broadcasters. You can also pick up the BBC World Service on 1323kHz MW on the Mediterranean coast, in Cairo and, when conditions are right, as far south as Luxor or even Aswan, as well as on a number of shortwave frequencies.

A number of FM **music stations** have sprung up in Cairo in recent years, most notably the privately run Nogoum Radio (100.6FM), which plays mainly Arabic pop music. The other privately owned station, Nile FM (104.2FM), plays Western pop and has talk shows in English. State-run stations include the Music Programme (98.8FM), broadcasting folk and classical music, and Radio Nagham (105.3FM), which plays Arabic pop songs old and new.

TV

Arab music channels with sexy dancing, or news from Al-Jazeera or Al-Arabiya, are staple viewing in coffeehouses. Foreigners may be shocked by their gory reportage, and bored by Egyptian channels, whose programming is heavy on local football matches, Koranic recitations and chat shows. Nile TV often has English subtitles, most notably with classic old Egyptian movies, and has news in English and French. Channel 2 often screens American films (generally after 10pm, or between midnight and 4.30am during Ramadan). It's not worth paying extra for a TV set in your hotel room unless it gets cable or satellite and, even then, many channels will be Middle Eastern, though you might get the BBC, CNN, Star Plus or sports channels. Daily TV schedules appear in the *Egyptian Gazette*, whose Monday edition lists all the movies for the forthcoming week.

Festivals

Most Islamic holidays and festivals follow the lunar Islamic calendar, with twelve months of 29 or 30 days each. The Islamic year is ten or eleven days shorter than a solar year, so dates move back each year in relation to the Western calendar. You can convert dates at websites such as ⓦoriold.uzh.ch/static/hegira.html. A day in the Islamic calendar begins at sundown, so Islamic festivals start on the evening before you'd expect.

Ramadan

During the month of **Ramadan**, most Muslims (ninety percent of Egyptians) fast, with no food, drink, smoking or sex from dawn to sunset. This can pose problems for travellers, but the celebratory evenings are good times to hear music and share hospitality.

The ninth month of the Islamic calendar, Ramadan parallels the Christian Lent, commemorating the first revelation of the Koran to Mohammed. Opening times and transport schedules are affected (almost everything pauses at sunset so people can break the fast), and most local cafés and restaurants close during the day or stop selling food. Ramadan is in many respects a bad time to travel. It is certainly no time to try camel trekking in the Sinai – no guide would undertake the work – and it is probably safer to travel by bus during the mornings only, as drivers will be fasting, too (although airline pilots are forbidden from observing the fast).

But there is a compensation in witnessing and becoming absorbed in the pattern of the fast. At **sunset**, signalled by the sounding of a siren and the lighting of lamps on the minarets, an amazing calm and sense of well-being fall on the streets, as everyone eats *fuul* and *taamiya* and, in the cities at least, gets down to a night of celebration and entertainment. Throughout the evening, urban cafés – and main squares – provide venues for live music and singing, while in small towns and poorer quarters of big cities, you will often come across ritualized *zikrs* – trance-like chanting and swaying.

Non-Muslims are not expected to observe Ramadan, but should be sensitive about not breaking the fast (particularly smoking) in public. The best way to experience Ramadan, however, is to enter into it. You may not be able to last without an occasional glass of water, and you'll probably breakfast later than sunrise, but it is worth an attempt – and you'll win local people's respect.

Islamic holidays

At the end of Ramadan, the feast of **Eid al-Fitr** marks the climax of the month's festivities in Cairo, though observed more privately in the villages. Equally important is **Eid al-Adha** (aka Eid al-Kabir or Korban Bairam – the Great Feast), celebrating Abraham's willingness to obey God by sacrificing his son. God didn't make him go through with it, and he ended up sacrificing a sheep instead. In commemoration of this, every household that can afford to slaughters a sheep, often on the street. For weeks beforehand, you will see sheep tethered everywhere, even on rooftops.

Eid al-Adha is followed, about three weeks later, by **Ras al-Sana al-Hegira**, the Muslim new year, on the first day of the month of Muharram. The fourth main religious holiday is the **Moulid al-Nabi**, the Prophet Mohammed's birthday. This is widely observed, with processions in many towns and

RAMADAN AND ISLAMIC HOLIDAYS

Exact dates are impossible to predict, being set by the Islamic authorities on sighting of the new moon, but approximate dates for the next few years are:

	2013	2014	2015	2016	2017	2018
Moulid al-Nabi	24 Jan	13 Jan	3 Jan & 23 Dec	12 Dec	1 Dec	20 Nov
1st Ramadan	9 July	28 June	18 June	6 June	27 May	16 May
Eid al-Fitr	8 Aug	28 July	17 July	5 July	25 June	15 June
Eid al-Adha	15 Oct	4 Oct	23 Sept	11 Sept	1 Sept	22 Aug
Ras al-Sana	5 Nov	25 Oct	14 Oct	2 Oct	21 Sept	11 Sept

cities. For the approximate dates of these four festivals according to the Western calendar, see the box on Islamic holidays (above).

Moulids

Moulids are the equivalent of medieval European saints' fairs, popular events combining piety, fun and commerce. Their ostensible aim is to obtain blessing (*baraka*) from a local saint, but they are also an opportunity for people to escape the monotony of working life in several days of festivities, and for friends and families from different villages to meet. Farming problems are discussed, as well as family matters – and marriage – as people sing, dance, eat and pray together. Upper-class Egyptians and religious conservatives, however, look down on moulids as vulgar and unorthodox; in 2009 they used the threat of swine flu as an excuse to ban them, and though the ban has now been lifted, Sufi religious gatherings at moulids are much reduced, with Salafists, in particular, claiming that they are un-Islamic.

Apart from Moulid al-Nabi, most moulids are local affairs, centred around the tomb (*qubba*) of a holy man or woman. Most follow the Islamic calendar, but some start (or finish) on a particular day (eg a Tues in a given month), rather than on a specific date, and a few occur at the same time every year, generally following the local harvest. It's wise to verify the (approximate) dates given in this guide by asking locally or at a tourist office.

If you are lucky enough to attend a big one, you'll see Egyptian popular culture at its richest. Some moulids draw crowds of over a million, with companies of *mawladiya* (literally, "moulid people") running stalls and rides, and music blaring into the small hours. Smaller, rural moulids tend to be heavier on the practical devotion, with people bringing their children or livestock for blessing, or the sick to be cured.

The largest moulids are in Cairo, Tanta and Luxor. **Cairo** hosts three lengthy festivals in honour of Al-Hussein, Saiyida Zeinab and the Imam al-Shafi'i (held during the months of Rabi al-Tani, Ragab and Sha'ban, respectively), plus numerous smaller festivals (see pp.196–198). Following the cotton harvest in October, the Moulid of al-Bedawi in **Tanta** starts a cycle of lesser **Nile Delta festivals** that runs well into November (see p.499). Equally spectacular is the Moulid of Abu al-Haggag in **Luxor**, held during the month of Sha'ban, and featuring a parade of boats (see p.276). Elsewhere, the procession may be led by camels or floats. Accompanying all this are **traditional entertainments**: mock stick fights, conjurers, acrobats and snake charmers; horses trained to dance to music; and, sometimes, belly dancers. All the longer moulids climax in a *leyla kebira* (literally "big night") on the last evening or the eve of the last day – the most spectacular and crowded phase; some moulids also have a corresponding "big day".

Music and singing are a feature of every moulid and people even make cassettes to play back for the rest of the year. At the heart of every moulid is at least one **zikr** – a gathering of worshippers who chant and sway for hours to attain a trance-like state of oneness with God. *Zikr* participants often belong to a **Sufi brotherhood**, identified by coloured banners, sashes or turbans, and named after their founding sheikh. The current incumbent of this office may lead them in a **zaffa** (parade) through town, and in olden times would ride a horse over his followers – a custom known as "the Treading".

Coptic festivals

Egypt's Christian Copts often attend Islamic moulids – and vice versa. **Coptic moulids** share many of the functions of their Islamic counterparts and usually celebrate a saint's name-day. Major **Christian festivals**, as in Eastern Orthodox churches, follow the old Julian calendar, so Christmas is on January 7, Epiphany (Twelfth

Night) on January 19, and the Annunciation on March 21, although Easter and related feast days are reckoned according to the solar Coptic calendar, so they differ from Orthodox and Western dates by up to a month (**⑩**copticchurch .net/easter.html, has the dates, which include May 5, 2013, April 20, 2014, April 12, 2015, May 1, 2016, April 16, 2017 and April 8, 2018).

Major Coptic **saints' days** include the Feast of the Apostles Peter and Paul (July 12), and various moulids of the Virgin and St George during August. Many of these are celebrated at monasteries in Middle Egypt and the Red Sea Hills.

Lastly, a Coptic festival (of pharaonic origin) celebrated by all Egyptians on Coptic Easter Monday is **Sham al-Nessim**, a coming-of-spring festival whose name literally means "Sniffing the Breeze". It provides the excuse for mass picnics in parks and on riverbanks throughout the country.

Sports and outdoor activities

Many tourists visit Egypt simply to dive or snorkel in the Red Sea, whose coral reefs put the Caribbean and the South Pacific in the shade. Besides all kinds of other watersports and some swanky golf courses, Egypt offers horse- and camel-riding, trekking, jeep safaris and hot-air ballooning, but for Egyptians the only sport that counts is football (soccer) – a national obsession.

Diving and watersports

The fantastic coral reefs and tropical fish of the Red Sea are the bedrock of tourism from Sinai to Marsa Alam, while the Mediterranean coastline has sunken wrecks and ancient ruins to explore. All this makes Egypt an excellent place to go **diving**, on a package holiday or through local dive centres. Many people learn to dive here, gaining a PADI, BSAC or CMAS certificate. The initial step is a five-day PADI Open Water course, costing around €200–350/$250–425 including equipment, plus about €35/$45 for the certificate if it isn't included. You progress from classroom theory to dives in the hotel swimming pool or from the shore, finishing with a few boat dives. Most centres offer a supervised introductory dive (around €35–70/$42–85) for those uncertain about shelling out for a full course.

Kids aged 8–10 can try the PADI "Bubble Maker" course (€50/$65), which includes a short dive close to the shore. Qualified divers can progress through advanced open-water, dive master and instructor certification, and take specialized courses in night or wreck diving. Note that if you're certified but haven't logged a dive in the past three months, you might have to take a "check dive" before you can go on a sea trip.

Boat trips to dive sites usually include tanks and weights; lunch on the boat may cost about £E50 extra. Dive packages can be a good deal, costing around €260/$340 for a five-day package (ten dives), with discounts sometimes available for advance or online bookings. **Liveaboards** (safari boats) allow you to spend days or weeks at sea, cruising dive sites and shipwrecks. This can work out cheaper than a hotel and dive package, averaging around €100/$130 per person per day, including full board; where equipment rental isn't covered, expect to pay an extra €25/$33 per day. Most are pre-booked by groups, who may not welcome people joining them at the last moment, so it's better (and cheaper) to buy a package deal at home, though during quiet periods vacant berths might be found by asking around boats in marinas.

If you're aiming to arrange things yourself, be careful when choosing a **dive centre**. Ones attached to big hotels or with longstanding links with organizations like PADI are safer bets than backstreet outfits, but smart premises are less important than how they treat their equipment. If left lying about, chances are it'll also be poorly maintained. Also note the location of the compressor used to fill the tanks; if it's near a road or other source of pollution, you'll be breathing it in underwater. Misunderstandings can be dangerous underwater, so you need an instructor who speaks your language well.

Anybody who can swim can **snorkel**. Due to its coastal reefs, Sinai (especially Na'ama Bay) offers better snorkelling than further down the Red Sea, where most coral is on islands. Masks and flippers may be rented at any resort, and many also offer windsurfing and kiteboarding (notably Ras Sudr and Dahab), yachting (Hurghada), **waterskiing** and **parasailing** (also at Almaza Bay on the Mediterranean coast).

While a few resorts offer shark-fishing, Egypt is chiefly renowned for **angling** on Lake Nasser, the vast reservoir behind the Aswan High Dam, which teems with massive Nile perch, carp and tilapia. Fishing trips can be arranged in Aswan or abroad (see p.357 for details).

Riding, trekking and jeep safaris

Around the Pyramids and the major Nile sites, donkeys, horses and camels are all available for hire. **Horses** are fun if you want to ride across stretches of sand between the Pyramids or in the Sinai desert. **Donkeys** are best used for visiting the Theban Necropolis, where they traverse mountains that you'd never cross on foot, and enliven the trip no end. Elsewhere they have less appeal, but you might rent a *caretta* (donkey-drawn taxi cart) to explore the pools and ruins in Siwa Oasis.

Camels (the dromedary, or one-humped Arabian camel) make for rigorous but exhilarating riding, and you'll probably want to try them at least once. They are good for short rides around Aswan, but really come into their own in Sinai or the Western Desert oases, where you can go trekking up wadis or across dunes that horses could never cope with. Trips – lasting anything from a half-day to a week – are easily arranged with local operators, or as part of "adventure holiday" packages from home.

If you've never ridden a camel before, try a half-day excursion before committing to a longer trip. Even a few hours in the saddle can leave you with aches in muscles that you never knew existed, so it's advisable to alternate between walking and riding. The mounting is done for you but be sure to hold on to the pommel of the saddle as the camel raises itself in a triple-jerk manoeuvre. Once on, you have a choice of riding it like a horse or cocking a leg around the pommel, as the Bedouin do, in which case you should use a lot of padding around the pommel to avoid soreness. It's easy to get the hang of steering: pull firmly and gradually on the nose rope to change direction; a camel should stop if you turn its head to face sideways.

Trekking on foot requires more stamina, especially in the High Mountain Region of Sinai (see p.565). The ideal number of trekkers is three to five people; larger groups travel more slowly. You'll need comfortable hiking boots, warm clothes, a sleeping bag, sunglasses, sunscreen, lip salve, bug repellent and toilet paper. In the Western Desert, your baggage may be transported by camel or jeep (in which case blankets are provided).

Jeep safaris are the best way to experience the oases, from an overnight stay in the White Desert or the Great Sand Sea to a deep-desert expedition to the Gilf Kebir. See Chapter 3 for details of sites and safari outfits in the Western Desert.

Golf and hot-air ballooning

There are **golf** courses around Cairo (one within sight of the Pyramids), as well as at Sharm el-Sheikh, Soma Bay, El Gouna and Luxor. For details, visit Ⓦ touregypt.net/golfcourses.htm.

From October to May, visitors to Luxor can enjoy the thrill of drifting above the temples and tombs of the Theban Necropolis in a **hot-air balloon**. Trips start at around $50 (see p.264).

Football

The only sport screened on Egyptian television, **football** (soccer; *kurat 'adem* in Arabic) transfixes the nation during international and premier matches. The national team won the African Nations' Cup in 1986, 1998, 2006, 2008 and 2010, and the two rival Cairo clubs, **Ahly** and **Zamalek**, have long dominated the domestic league, and regularly win African club competitions. Clashes between them can be intense – and have occasionally led to rioting – but games are in general relaxed: Cairo Stadium (see p.144) is the main venue. As well as the big two, other teams include **Ismaily** (from Ismailiya), **Masry** (Port Said) and **Al Ittihad** (Alexandria), while in recent years a new wave of corporate-sponsored teams such as Petrojet and ENPPI have also muscled their way into the premier league.

Should their team win, thousands of supporters drive around Cairo honking horns and waving flags attached to lances – beware of being run over or impaled.

Culture and etiquette

To get the most from a trip to Egypt, it is vital not to assume that anyone who approaches you is on the make. Too many tourists do, and end up making little contact with an extraordinarily friendly people. Even in response to insistent offers or demands, try to avoid being rude or aggressive in refusing.

Intimate behaviour in public (kissing and cuddling) is a no-no, and even holding hands is disapproved of. Be aware, too, of the importance of **dress**: shorts are socially acceptable only at beach resorts (and for women only in private resorts or along the Gulf of Aqaba coast), while shirts (for both sexes) should cover your shoulders. Many tourists ignore these conventions, unaware of how it demeans them in the eyes of the Egyptians. Women wearing halter-necks, skimpy T-shirts, miniskirts and the like will attract gropers, and the disapproval of both sexes. If you're visiting a mosque, you're expected to be "modestly" dressed (men should be covered from below the shoulder to below the knee, women from wrist to ankle). It's also obligatory to remove shoes (or don overshoes).

When **invited to a home**, it's normal to take your shoes off before entering the reception rooms. It is customary to take a gift: sweet pastries (or tea and sugar in rural areas) are always acceptable.

One important thing to be aware of in Egypt is the different functions of the two hands. Whether you are right- or left-handed, the **left hand** is used for "unclean" functions, such as wiping your bottom or putting on shoes, so it is considered unhygienic to eat with it. You can hold bread in your left hand in order to tear a piece off, but you should never put food into your mouth with your left hand, nor put it into the bowl when eating communally.

Egyptians are likely to feel very strongly about certain subjects – Palestine, Israel and Islam, for instance, and these should be treated diplomatically if they come up in conversation. Some Egyptians are keen to discuss them, others not, but carelessly expressed opinions, and particularly open contempt for religion, can cause serious offence.

Tipping and baksheesh

As a presumed-rich *khawaga* (foreigner), you are expected to be liberal with **baksheesh**, which can be divided into three main varieties. The most common is tipping: a small reward for a small service – anything from waiter service to unlocking a tomb or museum room. Try to strike a balance between defending your own wallet and acquiescing gracefully when appropriate. There's little point getting upset or offending people over what are trifling sums for a Western tourist but an important part of people's livelihood in a country where many people live on less than £50/$75 a month.

Typical **tips** might be £E1–2 for looking after your shoes while you visit a mosque (though congregants don't usually tip for this), or £E5–10 to a custodian for opening up a door to let you enter a building or climb a minaret. In restaurants, you do not usually leave a percentage of the bill: typical tips (regardless of whether the bill claims to include "service") are as little as £E3 in an ultra-cheap place such as a *kushari* joint, £E3–5 in a typical cheap restaurant, or £E10–25 in a smarter establishment. Customers also usually give tips of £E1–2 in a café, and sometimes 50pt–£E1 in a juice bar.

A more expensive and common type of baksheesh is for rewarding the **bending of rules** – many of which seem to have been designed for just that purpose. Examples might include letting you into an archeological site after hours (or into a vaguely restricted area), finding you a sleeper on a train when the carriages are "full", and so on. This should not be confused with bribery, which is a more serious business with its own etiquette and risks – best not entered into.

The last kind of baksheesh is simply **alms-giving**. For Egyptians, giving money and goods to the needy is a natural act – and a requirement of Islam. The disabled are traditional recipients of such gifts, and it seems right to join locals in giving out small change. Children, however, are a different case, pressing their demands only on tourists. If someone offers genuine help and asks for an *alum* (pen), it seems fair enough, but to yield to every request encourages a cycle of dependency that Egypt could do without.

Since most Egyptian money is paper, often in the form of well-used banknotes that can be fiddly to separate out, it can make life easier to keep small bills in a separate "baksheesh pocket" specifically for the purpose. If giving baksheesh in foreign currency, give notes rather than coins (which can't be exchanged for Egyptian currency).

Hustlers

Hustling is a necessity for millions of Egyptians – cadging money for errands or knowing a "cousin" who can sort things out. The full-time *khirtiyya* who focus on tourists are versatile, touting for hotels (see p.173), pushing excursions (often vastly marked up), steering tourists into shops or travel agencies (where their commission will be quietly added to your bill), and even being gigolos (see "Women travellers", below). They'll latch on to you as soon as you arrive (at the airport in Cairo or Luxor), hail you on the street like an old friend ("Hey! Remember me?"), or say anything to grab your attention ("You've dropped your wallet"). If they don't already know, they'll try to discover where you're staying, what your plans are, and pester you regularly.

It's easy to get fed up with being hassled and react with fury to any approach from strangers – even a sincere "Welcome to Egypt". Try to keep your cool and respond politely; intoning *la shukran* (no thanks) with your hand on your heart, while briskly moving on, will dissuade most street peddlers. Or you could try a humorous riposte to classic come-ons like "I know what you need" – *Fil mish mish* ("In your dreams!") works well. If necessary, escalate to a gruff *khalas* ("Enough!") and if that doesn't suffice, bawling *shorta* ("Police!") is sure to send any hustler packing.

Women travellers

Sexual harassment is rife in Egypt: 98 percent of foreign women visitors and 83 percent of Egyptian women have experienced it, according to one survey. The perception that women tourists are "easy" is reinforced by their doing things that no respectable Egyptian woman would: dressing "immodestly", showing shoulders and cleavage, sharing rooms with men to whom they are not married, drinking alcohol in bars or restaurants, smoking in public, even travelling alone on public transport without a relative as an escort. While well-educated Egyptians familiar with Western culture can take these in their stride, less sophisticated ones are liable to assume the worst. Tales of affairs with tourists, especially of Hurghada's Russian visitors, who are regarded as being quite scandalous, are common currency among Egyptian males. In Sinai, however, unaccompanied women experience few hassles, except from construction workers from "mainland" Egypt.

Without compromising your freedom too greatly, there are a few steps you can take to improve your image. Most important and obvious is **dress**: loose opaque clothes that cover all "immodest" areas (thighs, upper arms, chest) and hide your contours are a big help, and essential if travelling alone or in rural areas (where covering long hair is also advisable). On public transport (buses, trains, service taxis), try to sit with other women – who may invite you to do so. On the Cairo metro and trams in Alexandria there are carriages reserved for women. If travelling with a man, wearing a wedding ring confers respectability, and asserting that you're married is better than admitting to being "just friends".

Looking confident and knowing where you're going always helps, and it's worth avoiding eye contact with Egyptian men (some women wear sunglasses for the purpose), and best to err on the side of standoffishness, as even a friendly smile may be taken as a come-on. Problems – most commonly hissing or groping – tend to come in downtown Cairo and in the public beach resorts (except Sinai's Aqaba coast, or Red Sea holiday villages – probably the only places you'll feel happy sunbathing). In the oases, where attractions include open-air springs and hot pools, it's okay to bathe – but do so in at least a T-shirt and leggings: oasis people are among the most conservative in the country.

Some women find that verbal hassle is best ignored, while others may prefer to use an Egyptian brush-off like *khalas* (enough!) or *uskut* (be quiet!). If you get groped, the best response is to yell *aram!* (evil!) or *sibnee le wadi* (don't touch me), which will shame any assailant in public, and may attract help, or scare them away by shouting *shorta!* (police!).

FEMALE GENITAL MUTILATION

Most Egyptian women – as many as 97 percent according to one survey – have been subjected to a horrific operation known euphemistically as "female circumcision", and more correctly as female genital mutilation (FGM). In this procedure, typically carried out on girls aged between 7 and 10, the clitoris and sometimes all or part of the inner vaginal lips are cut off to prevent the victim from enjoying sex.

Egypt has the world's highest prevalence of FGM, which is an African rather than an Islamic practice, performed by Copts as much as by Muslims. Nonetheless, spurious religious reasons are sometimes given to justify it, including two disputed hadiths (supposed quotations from Mohammed). In 1951, the Egyptian Fatwa Committee decreed that FGM was desirable because it curbs women's sex drive, and in 1981 the Sheikh of Al-Azhar Mosque and University said that it was the duty of parents to have their daughters genitally mutilated.

The good news is that things have changed since then. FGM is now illegal – the government banned it in 1996 and again in 2007. Former first lady Suzanne Mubarak has spoken out against it, and the Islamic religious authorities issued a fatwa declaring it *haram* (forbidden). FGM is now in decline, but it remains at high levels, and the law is hard to enforce, especially in rural communities. Worse, the rise of religious fundamentalist parties since the revolution means there is now less political pressure to enforce the ban on FGM, and one Salafist MP has already called for it to be re-legalized.

Spending time with **Egyptian women** can be a delight. The difficulty is that fewer women than men speak English, and that you won't run into women in traditional cafés. Public transport can be a good meeting ground, as can shops. Asking directions in the street, it's always better to ask a woman than a man.

Gigolos are part of the tourist scene in Luxor, Aswan, Hurghada, Sinai and Cairo. The exchange of sex for cash usually occurs under the guise of true love, with misled women spending money on their boyfriends or "husbands" until their savings run out and the relationship hits the rocks. Enough foreigners blithely rent toyboys and settle into the scene for locals to make the point that neither side is innocent, but be aware that HIV is a big danger on the gigolo scene – always use protection.

Many enter into so-called Orfi (or "Dahab") **marriages**, usually arranged by a lawyer, to circumvent the law that prohibits unmarried couples from sleeping under the same roof. These allow couples to rent a flat without hassle from the Vice Squad and can be annulled without a divorce. However, an Orfi marriage does not confer the same legal rights as a full marriage in a special registry office (Sha'ar al-Aqari) in Cairo, which is the only kind that allows women to bring their spouse to their own country or gives them any rights in child-custody disputes. Women can bolster their position by insisting on a marriage contract (pre-nuptial agreement).

Shopping

Visitors to Egypt are spoilt for choice when it comes to souvenirs: traditional crafts such as jewellery, textiles, glassware, leatherwork, brass and copperware all offer good value for money if you're prepared to haggle and be choosy. One thing not to buy is any kind of supposed antiquity. The export of antiquities is strictly prohibited, and you could end up in prison if caught trying to smuggle them out. Another thing to avoid is ivory products: their sale is legal, but almost all Western countries prohibit their importation. Inlaid or carved bone makes an acceptable substitute.

Many Westerners are intimidated by **haggling**, but it needn't be an ordeal. Decide before you start what price you want to pay, offer something much lower, and let the shopkeeper argue you up, but not above your maximum price. If you don't reach an agreement, even after a lengthy session, nothing is lost. But if you state a price and the seller agrees, you are obliged to pay – so it is important not to start bidding for something you don't really want, nor to let a price pass your lips if you are not prepared to pay it. Haggling should be goodnatured, not acrimonious, even if you know the seller is trying to overcharge you outrageously.

Don't be put off by theatrics on the part of the seller, which are all part of the game. Buyers' tactics include stressing any flaws that might reduce the object's value; talking of lower quotes received elsewhere; feigning indifference or having a friend urge you to leave. Avoid being tricked into raising your bid twice in a row, or admitting your estimation of the object's worth (just reply that you've made an offer).

Cairo's **bazaars** offer an infinite choice of jewellery, textiles, leatherwork, glassware, brass and copperware and perfumes, plus the world's best selection of bellydancing costumes (see p.199). Alabaster figurines and vases are cheaper on Luxor's west bank (p.308), while Aswan's bazaar (see p.337) is best for spices, incense and basketwork. Siwa Oasis has its own crafts tradition (p.451), as do the thoroughly un-touristy bazaars in Assyut (p.232) and Medinet Fayoum (p.385).

Jewellery, brass and copperware

Jewellery comes in all kinds of styles; gold and silver are sold by the gram, with a percentage added on for workmanship. The current ounce price of gold is printed in the daily *Egyptian Gazette*; one troy ounce equals about 31 grams. Barring antiques, all gold work is stamped with Arabic numerals indicating purity: usually 21 carat for Bedouin, Nubian or *fellaheen* jewellery; 18 carat for Middle Eastern and European-style charms and chains. Sterling silver (80 or 92.5 percent) is likewise stamped, while a gold camel in the shop window indicates that the items are gold-plated brass.

The most popular souvenirs are gold or silver **cartouches** with names in hieroglyphics. Prices depend on the size, the number of characters and whether they're engraved or glued on, but expect to pay around £E500–1000.

Among **brass and copperware** items favoured as souvenirs are candlesticks, waterpipes, gongs, coffee sets, embossed plates and inlaid or repoussé trays (the larger ones are often mounted on stands to serve as tables). Be sure that anything you intend to drink out of is lined with tin or silver, since brass and copper react with certain substances to form toxic compounds. Remember also to test water-pipes for leaky joints.

Perfume and spices

Egypt produces many of the **essences** used by French perfumiers, sold by the ounce to be diluted 1:9 in alcohol for perfume, 1:20 for eau de toilette and 1:30 for eau de cologne. Local shops will duplicate famous perfumes for you, or you can buy fakes (sometimes unwittingly – always scrutinize labels). Salesmen boasting that their "pure" essence is undiluted by alcohol will omit to mention that oil has been used instead, which is why they rub it into your wrist to remove the sheen.

Spices such as **cinnamon** (*'irfa*) and **sesame** (*simsim*) are piled high in bazaars, but what is sold as **saffron** (*za'faraan*) is actually safflower, which is why it seems ridiculously cheap compared with what you'd pay for the real thing (consisting of fine red strands only, hence the ruse of dying safflower red). You'll also see **dried hibiscus** (*karkaday*); the top grade should consist of whole, healthy-looking flowers.

Textiles, leatherwork and basketwork

Most Egyptian **kilims** (woven rugs) and knotted carpets have half as many knots (sixteen per centimetre) as their Turkish counterparts, so should be cheaper – especially ones made from native wool rather than the high-grade imported stuff used in finer kilims. More affordable are **tapestries** and **rugs** woven from coarse wool and/or camel hair, which come in two basic styles. Bedouin rugs have geometric patterns in shades of brown and beige and are usually loosely woven, while the other style, deriving from the Wissa Wassef School (see p.160), features images of birds, trees and village life. Beware of stitched-together seams and gaps in the weave (hold pieces up against the light) and unfast colours – if any colour wipes off on a damp cloth, the dyes will run when the rug is washed. Another high-quality brand that's (less widely) imitated is Akhmim silk (see p.236), woven into tapestries or hand-printed scarves and robes, sold by selected shops in major tourist centres. Decorative **appliqué** work (cushion covers, bedspreads and wall-hangings) and riotously patterned printed tent fabric are best bought in Cairo's Tentmakers Bazaar (p.200).

Although few tourists can wear them outdoors without looking silly, many take home a **kaftan** or **galabiyya** for lounging attire. Women's kaftans are made of cotton, silk or wool, generally A-line, with long, wide sleeves and a round or mandarin collar (often braided). Men's *galabiyyas* come in three basic styles: *Ifrangi* (a floor-length tailored shirt with collar and cuffs), *Saudi* (with a high-buttoned neck and no collar) and *baladi* (very wide sleeves and a low, rounded neckline).

Egyptian **leatherwork** is nice and colourful, if not up to the standards of Turkey. Jackets, sandals, handbags, pouffes (tuffets) and decorative camel saddles are all made in Cairo's workshops for sale throughout Egypt. Cairo also offers a range of palm-frond basketwork, mostly from the Fayoum and Upper Egypt. Fayoumi baskets (for storage, shopping or laundry) are more practical, but it's hard to resist the woven platters from Luxor and Aswan, as vibrantly colourful as parrots. You may also find baskets from Siwa Oasis, trimmed with tassels.

Glassware

Hand-blown Muski glass, made since medieval times (nowadays from recycled bottles), is recognizable by its air bubbles and comes in navy blue, turquoise, aquamarine, green and purple, fashioned into glasses, plates, vases, candle holders and ashtrays. Elegant handmade perfume bottles are another popular souvenir. The cheaper ones are made of glass and are as delicate as they look. Pyrex versions cost roughly twice as much and are a little sturdier (they should also be noticeably heavier).

Travelling with children

Children evoke a warm response in Egypt and are welcome more or less everywhere. It's not unusual to see Egyptian children out with their parents in cafés or shops past midnight. The only child-free zones tend to be bars and clubs frequented by foreigners. Most hotels can supply an extra bed and breakfast. Pharmacies sell formula milk, baby food and disposable nappies, and the last two may also be stocked by corner stores in larger towns. Things worth bringing are a mosquito net for a buggy or crib, and a parasol for sun protection.

Potential hazards to guard against include traffic (obviously dangerous), stray animals (possible disease carriers), fenced-off beaches (probably mined – see p.48), elevators with no inner doors (keep small hands away) and poisonous fish and coral in the Red Sea (see box, p.579). Children (especially young ones) are more susceptible than adults to **heatstroke** and **dehydration**, and should always wear a sunhat, and have high-factor sunscreen applied to exposed skin. If swimming, they should do so in a T-shirt, at least for the first few days. Children can also be very susceptible to an **upset tummy**, and antidiarrhoeal drugs should generally not be given to young children; read the literature provided with the medication or consult a doctor for guidance on child dosages.

If children balk at unfamiliar **food**, outlets of all major American fast-food chains are always close at hand. Ice cream is cheap and ubiquitous, as is *ruz bi-laban* (rice pudding) and *mahalabiyya* (a blancmange-like pudding made with powdered rice).

Children should enjoy camel, horse and donkey rides, but choose carefully – AA Stables in Cairo (see p.153), for example, has a good reputation. Activities such as felucca rides, snorkelling and visiting a few of the great monuments can also be enjoyable. Activities in Cairo that will especially appeal to younger travellers are listed in that chapter (pp.195–196). For more travel tips, see *The Rough Guide to Travel with Babies & Young Children*.

Travel essentials

Costs

Egypt is inexpensive and good value. Providing you avoid luxury hotels and tourist-only services, costs for food, accommodation and transport are very low, though Sinai and Hurghada are pricier than other parts.

Most prices in this book are in Egyptian pounds. The main exceptions – airfares, prices for top-flight accommodation and dive or safari packages – are given in US dollars or euros, depending on what establishments quote. Despite this, you can almost always pay in Egyptian pounds, according to the prevailing exchange rate.

If you're trying to keep expenses down, it is possible to get by on £25/$40 a day by staying in the cheapest hotels and eating street food, but you won't have much left over for sightseeing or activities. On £65/$100 a day, you can eat well and stay in a reasonable two-star hotel. If you want to stay in tip-top accommodation, you could be paying upwards of £200/$300 a night, but even if you travel everywhere by taxi and eat in the very best restaurants, you'll be hard put to add more than £50/$75 a day to that figure.

Although Egypt is cheap, there are hidden costs that can bump up your daily budget. Most restaurant and hotel bills are liable to a **service charge** plus **local taxes** (Cairo, Luxor and Hurghada have the highest), which increase the final cost by 17–25 percent (unless already included in the price). You'll also need to add in the cost of **tickets** for archeological sites such as the Pyramids and the monuments of the Nile Valley (typically £E20–60 a throw), and don't forget the tips you'll need for custodians of tombs and temples and the medieval mosques of Islamic Cairo.

Inflation peaked at over twenty percent in early 2008, before falling back to just over eight and a half percent in mid-2012. Costs of luxury goods, services and most things in the private sector rise faster than for public transport, petrol and basic foodstuffs, whose prices are held down by subsidies that the government dare not abolish.

Student and other discount cards

ISIC **student cards** entitle holders to a discount of fifty percent or slightly less on most museums and sites, thirty-percent discount on rail fares and around fifteen percent on ferries. It's best to get the card at home (see ⓦisic.org for outlets) or – with proof that you are a full-time student – for £E100 at Egyptian Student Travel Services (ESTS), 23 Sharia al-Manial, on Roda Island in Cairo (daily 9am–4pm ⓣ02 2363 7251, ⓦestsegypt.com); you can get there on foot from the El-Malek el-Saleh metro. The **International Youth Travel Card** (available to anyone under 26), and **International Teacher Identity Card** (for teachers), at the same price from the same places, give similar discounts. Note however that, due to the number of forged cards in circulation in Egypt, some archeological sites have stopped accepting them.

Climate

Spring (March–May) and **autumn** (Oct & Nov) are the best times to visit, when it's hot but not debilitatingly so. In **summer** (June–Sept) the south and desert are ferociously hot and the pollution in Cairo is at its worst, with only the coast offering a respite from the heat. During this time, sightseeing is best limited to early morning or evening. In **winter** (Dec–Feb), most places are reasonably warm during the day, but chilly at night, while the desert can get very cold indeed. The Mediterranean Coast can be windy and wet in winter.

The **temperatures** given in the chart (see below) show the average for each month – although of

AVERAGE TEMPERATURES IN DEGREES CENTIGRADE:											
	Jan	Feb	Mar	Apr	May	June	July	Aug	Sept	Oct	Nov	Dec
Cairo	13	15	17	20	24	27	28	28	27	23	19	15
Sharm	17	18	21	25	28	31	32	33	30	27	22	19
Aswan	16	17	21	27	32	33	34	34	32	27	21	16

course the temperature is not always average. Summer peaks in Aswan, Hurghada or Sinai, for example, can hit 50°C (120°F) in hot years. The dryness of the air and absence of cloud cover makes for drastic fluctuations, though they do also make the heat tolerably unsticky outside Cairo and the Delta.

Crime and personal safety

Egypt has always had a low crime rate, and tourist-related crime has traditionally consisted either of sly forms of **theft** such as pickpocketing or stealing unguarded baggage, or else **scams** and cons of one sort or another. Robbery as such was extremely unusual. Since the revolution the crime rate has increased, and although it is still low by Western standards, certain areas have become unsafe to drive in at night due to the rise in carjackings, while street muggings and burglaries, though nothing like as common as in other countries, are nonetheless on the rise.

Minefields (the Arabic for "mines" is *algham*, with the stress on the second syllable) still exist: from World War II along the Mediterranean coast, and from Israeli conflicts in the interior of Sinai and along the Red Sea coast (detailed in chapters 3, 4, 6 and 7). Don't take any risks in venturing into fenced-off territory unless locals go there often.

Terrorism and direct action

In the 1990s and 2000s, Egypt's image as a safe country to visit was shattered by sporadic waves of **terrorism**, with bomb attacks in Cairo and Sinai. Then in 2011, the **Arab Spring** arrived, accompanied at times by violent confrontations and shootings. The former terrorists are now represented in parliament by the Salafists, who are increasingly part of the political establishment, which has to a certain extent neutralized Islamism as a direct threat to tourists.

Since the revolution there has been an increase in lawlessness, banditry and political direct action. The **Sinai** in particular has seen a string of incidents, with regular attacks on a pipeline delivering Egyptian gas to Israel, an attack on an under-construction nuclear power station, and a siege in January 2012 of a tourist resort near Taba, though no tourists were actually in it at the time. Bedouins in Sinai also **kidnapped** 25 Chinese workers in Sinai and (a week later) two American tourists, though all were released unharmed, and the two Americans praised their captors' hospitality in what seems to have been a very Egyptian kidnapping. Sinai Bedouins feel they have been neglected and discriminated against since Mubarak's time, and the revolution has emboldened them to take action, which can directly affect tourists. It is particularly inadvisable to travel in remote regions of Sinai away from major roads.

Meanwhile, there are still armed police and often metal-detecting arches at tourist sites, stations and upmarket hotels, and plainclothes agents in bars and bazaars. Along the Nile Valley, foreigners travelling by rail are only supposed to use services designated for tourists, which have plainclothes guards riding shotgun. Tourist buses from Aswan to Abu Simbel must travel in a **convoy** (*kol*) with a police escort. There is no ban as such on visiting once "risky" areas of Middle Egypt such as Assyut, Sohag or Qena, but the local police will keep a close eye on you if you do.

Revolutionary violence

In 2011, **revolution** broke out across Egypt, and particularly in Cairo. Violent clashes left hundreds dead. Since then, revolutionaries opposing military rule have clashed several times with police and troops in Cairo, Suez and other cities. Foreign tourists are not directly involved, and are advised to steer well clear, but the military invariably blame the violence on foreign spies and agents provocateurs, and while most people do not take this very seriously, there is an undertone of **xenophobia** and hostility to non-Muslims within the population which it plays to. Even among the protestors, use by troops of American-made tear gas has led to claims that "This is a conspiracy between the United States and Israel to slaughter us," and there have been a series of attacks on and arrests of foreigners in Egypt. Mostly these have affected only journalists, but the Slovenian ambassador was beaten up in December 2011 by a mob who took him for a spy because he was photographing the neighbouhood. Especially in times of trouble therefore, it is wise to keep a low profile, and not to go around taking snaps of things that Egyptians might not expect a tourist to be interested in.

Crime

While relatively few in number, **pickpockets** are skilled and concentrate on tourists. Most operate in Cairo, notably in queues. To play safe, keep your valuables in a money belt or a pouch under your shirt (leather or cotton materials are preferable to nylon, which can irritate in the heat). Overall, though, **casual theft** is more of a problem. Campgrounds and cheap hotels often have poor security, though at most places you can deposit valuables at reception (always get a receipt for cash). If you are driving, it goes without saying that you shouldn't leave anything you cannot afford to lose visible or accessible in your car.

Since the revolution, the police (in disgrace for supporting the old regime) have massively reduced their presence, which has led to a rise in certain types of crime, notably burglaries and **carjackings**. Some roads are now unsafe to travel, especially at night, with SUVs being particular targets. The Sinai is the biggest hotspot (see p.531) and it is inadvisable, for example, to drive from Sharm el-Sheikh or even Suez to Cairo overnight. Middle Egypt is also tricky, and even the road from Cairo to Saqqara and the Fayoum Desert Road are considered unsafe to drive on at night. There has also been an increase in **sexual assaults**. Women should avoid being alone with an Egyptian man (for example with a microbus driver if you are the last passenger left), and always sit in the back of taxis.

As a result of this increase in insecurity, a lot of people are now **armed**, mostly with things like cattle-prods or pepper spray, although some people carry guns – in January 2012, for example, a motorist shot dead a microbus driver in a Cairo road rage incident. Other crimes, especially high-publicity ones, may be related to the political situation – a spate of incidents in early 2012, for example, was attributed by many Egyptians to the ruling junta (SCAF) deliberately causing instability to justify retention of military rule.

While most of this is unlikely to affect tourists, you should obviously keep your ear to the ground, and keep your eyes open when wandering around at night, as you would in any Western city. Central Cairo remains pretty safe, but in some suburban areas it is wise to avoid deserted streets at night.

Insofar as any danger can be predicted, it is wise before leaving home to check government travel advisory websites such as the UK's Ⓦ fco.gov.uk/travel, the US State Department's Ⓦ travel.state.gov, the Canadian government's Ⓦ voyage.gc.ca, or the Australian government's Ⓦ smartraveller.gov.au.

To reduce the risk of petty squabbles or misunderstandings developing, always **respect local customs** (see p.42).

The police

If you've got a problem or need to report a crime, always go to the **Tourist and Antiquities Police** (❶ 126). Found at tourist sites, museums, airports, stations and ports, they are supposedly trained to help tourists in distress, and should speak a foreign language (usually English). Ordinary ranks wear a regular police uniform with a "Tourist Police" armband; officers wear black uniforms in winter and white in summer. The more senior the officer, the better the chance they'll speak English.

The **Municipal Police** (❶ 122) handle all crimes and have a monopoly on law and order in smaller towns. Their uniform (khaki in winter, tan or white in summer) resembles that of the **Traffic Police**, who wear striped cuffs. Both get involved in accidents and can render assistance in emergencies, though few speak anything but Arabic.

The largely conscript **Central Security** force (dressed all in black and armed with Kalashnikovs) guard embassies, banks and highways. Though normally genial enough, they shift rapidly from tear gas to live rounds when ordered to crush demonstrations, strikes or civil unrest.

Egyptian **Military Intelligence** (Mukhabarat) is only relevant to travellers wanting to travel to remote parts of the Western Desert or south beyond Berenice on the Red Sea coast, for which you need travel permits (see p.29). The **State Security Investigations Service** (Amn al-Dawla) may take an interest in foreigners in border areas or Middle Egypt.

All of these forces deploy **plainclothes agents** who hang around near government buildings and crowded places, dressed as vendors or peasants – hence their nickname, the "Galabiyya Police".

Drugs

Egypt has its own *bango* (marijuana) industry, based in Sinai and in the far south, and supplemented by hashish from Morocco and Lebanon. Despite a tradition of use stretching back to the thirteenth century, Egypt was one of the first countries in modern times to ban **cannabis**: possession merits a severe prison sentence and a heavy fine (plus legal costs); trafficking is punishable by up to 25 years' hard labour, or even execution. Nonetheless, many Egyptians still smoke, and though Islam clearly forbids alcohol, the position of hashish is less clear. A few hotels in Luxor and Sinai even facilitate dealing to tourists.

As a foreigner, the least you can expect if caught is immediate deportation and a ban from visiting Egypt. You may be able to buy your way out of trouble, but this should be negotiated discreetly and as soon as possible, while the minimum number of cops are involved: once you're at the police station, it will be a lot more difficult. Needless to say, your embassy will be unsympathetic. The best advice is to steer clear of all illegal drugs while in the country.

Electricity

The current in Egypt is 220V, 50Hz. North American travellers with appliances designed for 110V should bring a converter. Most sockets are for two-pin round-pronged plugs (as in Continental Europe), so you may need an adapter.

Entry requirements

Visitors to Egypt must hold **passports** valid for at least six months beyond their date of entry. Citizens of most countries also need visas.

Most nationalities, including British, Irish, Americans, Canadians, Australians, New Zealanders and EU citizens, can obtain **visas** on arrival at officially designated international airports and sea ports, but not at land borders. The process is generally painless and cheaper than getting a visa through an embassy or consulate, although visas issued on arrival are valid for one month only, whereas embassies issue single-visit and multiple-entry visas entitling

you to stay in Egypt for three months (the latter allow you to go in and out of the country three times within this period). Visas are not available at overland border crossings or sea ports, apart from Sinai-only visas (see below).

Visa **applications** can be made in person or by post. If applying in person, turn up early in the day. Postal applications take between seven working days and six weeks to process. Don't be misled by statements on the application form indicating "valid for six months"; this simply means that the visa must be used within six months of the date of issue. When returning the form, you need to include a registered or recorded SAE, your passport, one photo and a postal or money order (not a personal cheque).

Getting a standard visa on arrival costs $15, irrespective of your nationality. The cost of getting a visa in advance of your trip varies according to your nationality, and from place to place. Some consulates may demand that you pay in US dollars instead of local currency, or ask you to supply extra photos. It's wise to allow for all these eventualities.

Free **Sinai-only visas** (available to EU, North American and Australasian nationals) are issued at Taba on the Israel–Egypt border, at Sharm el-Sheikh and St Catherine's airports, and at the sea ports at Sharm el-Sheikh and Nuweiba. They are valid for fourteen days only and restrict you to the Gulf of Aqaba coast down to Sharm el-Sheikh and the vicinity of St Catherine's; they are not valid for Ras Mohammed, the mountains around St Catherine's (except for Mount Sinai), or any other part of Egypt. They can't be extended, and there's no period of grace for overstaying.

In Egypt, carry your passport with you: you'll need it to register at hotels, change money at banks, and possibly to show at police checkpoints. If travelling for any length of time, it may be worth registering with your embassy in Cairo, which will help speed things up if you lose your

---

ISRAELI PASSPORT STAMPS

At the time of writing, many Arab countries other than Egypt and Jordan – and in particular Syria, Lebanon, Libya and Sudan – will deny entry to anyone whose passport shows evidence of a visit to Israel. Although Israeli immigration officials will usually agree not to stamp your passport if you ask them clearly, an Egyptian entry stamp at Taba or Rafah in the Sinai will give you away – and the Egyptians will insist on stamping your passport. If you are travelling around the Middle East, either visit Israel *after* you have been to Syria, Lebanon, or wherever, or else travel from Jordan to the West Bank and back via the Allenby (King Hussein) Bridge to avoid getting any stamps at that border, and visit Israel from the West Bank. This will not of course allow you to travel directly between Israel and Egypt.

passport. At the least, it's wise to photocopy the pages recording your particulars and keep them separately (or carry them in the street instead of your passport itself). If travelling to areas of the country that require permits (see p.29), spare sets of photocopies are useful for producing with your application.

EGYPTIAN EMBASSIES AND CONSULATES

Links to the web pages of Egyptian embassies and consulates worldwide can be found at Ⓦ mfa.gov .eg (choose English and then "Diplomatic Missions").

Australia 1 Darwin Ave, Yarralumla, ACT 2600 ☎ 02 6273 4437, Ⓔ embassy.canberra@mfa.gov.eg; Level 3, 241 Commonwealth St, Surry Hills, NSW 2010 ☎ 02 9281 4844, Ⓔ info@egypt.org.au; Level 6, 50 Market St, Melbourne, Vic 3000 ☎ 03 9614 1888 Ⓔ consul@egyptianconsulate.org.au.

Canada 454 Laurier Ave E, Ottawa, ON K1N 6R3 ☎ 613 234 4931, Ⓔ egyptemb@sympatico.ca; 1000 Rue de la Gauchetière Ouest, Suite 3320, Montreal PQ H3B 4W5 ☎ 514 866 8455, Ⓦ egyptianconsulatemontreal.org.

Cyprus 14 Ayios Prokopios, 2406 Nicosia ☎ 2244 9050, Ⓔ info@egyptianembassy.org.cy.

Ireland 12 Clyde Rd, Ballsbridge, Dublin 4 ☎ 01 660 6566, Ⓔ info@embegyptireland.ie.

Israel 54 Rehov Basel, Tel Aviv 62744 ☎ 03 546 4151; 68 Rehov Afrouni, Eilat ☎ 08 637 6882.

Jordan 14 Riyad Mefleh St, Amman (between 4th and 5th circles, next to the *Dove Hotel*) ☎ 06 560 5175, Ⓔ egypt@embegyptjordan.com; Zahra (3rd Residential District, in the northern outskirts), Aqaba ☎ 03 201 6171, Ⓔ egypicon@wanadoo.jo.

Libya Sharia Omar al-Mokhtar, Tripoli ☎ 021 444 8909, Ⓔ eg.emb_tripoli@mfa.gov.eg; Sharia Marg Bani Amer, District 19, Western Fuwaihat, Benghazi ☎ 061 223 2522, Ⓔ egyptian_Consulate_Ben@yahoo.com.

New Zealand Level 10, 5–7 Willeston St, Wellington 6011, ☎ 04 472 4900, Ⓔ eg.emb_newzealand@mfa.gov.eg.

South Africa 270 Bourke St, Muckleneuk, Pretoria ☎ 012 343 1590, Ⓔ egyptemb@global.co.za.

Sudan Sharia al-Gomhuria (University St), Khartoum ☎ 0183 777646, Ⓔ sphinx-egysud@yahoo.com; Sharia Yehia, Port Sudan ☎ 0311 823666, Ⓔ egyptian_consulate_portsudan@yahoo.com.

UK 2 Lowndes St, London SW1X 9ET ☎ 020 7235 9777, Ⓔ info@egyptianconsulate.co.uk.

USA 3521 International Court NW, Washington DC 20008 ☎ 202 895 5400; 1110 2nd Ave, Suite 201, New York, NY 10022 ☎ 212 759 7120, Ⓦ egyptnyc.net; 276 Mallorca Way, San Francisco, CA 94123 ☎ 415 346 9700, Ⓔ egypt@egy2000.com; 500 N Michigan Ave, Suite 1900, Chicago, IL 60611 ☎ 312 828 9162, Ⓔ consulateofegypt@hotmail.com; 5718 Westheimer Rd, Suite 1350, Houston, TX 77057 ☎ 713 961 4915, Ⓔ eg.com_houston @mfa.gov.eg.

Visa extensions

Tourists who **overstay** their visa are allowed a fifteen-day period of grace in which to renew it or leave the country. After this, they're fined £E150 unless they can present a letter of apology from their embassy (which may well cost more).

Visa **extensions** cost around £E11, and are obtainable from Al-Mugamma in Cairo or from passport offices in governorate capitals such as Alexandria, Luxor, Aswan, Suez, El-Tor, Mersa Matrouh and Ismailiya (addresses are detailed in the guide). Depending on how long you wish to extend by, and on the whim of the official, you may have to produce exchange or ATM receipts proving that you've cashed sufficient hard currency during your stay, and you'll need to supply one or two photos. Procedures vary slightly from office to office, but shouldn't take longer than an hour outside Cairo. **Re-entry visas** (to leave the country and then come back if you don't already have a multiple entry visa) can be obtained at the same places as visa extensions.

Gay and lesbian travellers

As a result of sexual segregation, homosexuality is relatively common in Egypt, but attitudes towards it are schizophrenic. Few Egyptian men will declare themselves gay – which has connotations of femininity and weakness – and the dominant partner in gay sex may well not consider himself to be indulging in a homosexual act. Rather, homosexuality is tacitly accepted as an outlet for urges that can't otherwise be satisfied. Despite this, people are mindful that homosexuality is condemned in the Koran and the Bible, and reject the idea of Egypt as a "gay destination" (although male prostitution is an open secret in Luxor and Aswan). The common term for gay men in Egyptian Arabic, *khawal*, has derogatory connotations.

Homosexuality is not illegal in Egypt, but that doesn't stop the authorities from persecuting gay men, and places that are well known as gay locales have become dangerous for Egyptians. Foreigners seem to be safe from arrest, but if you have a gay relationship with an Egyptian man, be aware that discretion is vital. Lesbians do not face this kind of state harassment, but they have never been visible in Egyptian society. As a Western woman, your chances of making contact are virtually zilch.

ONLINE RESOURCES

Gay Egypt Ⓦ gayegypt.com. News, practical advice and contacts, but don't log on to it within Egypt, as the Security Police monitor the site and may take an interest in computers which access it.

Globalgayz ⓦ globalgayz.com/country/Egypt/EGY. Their Egypt page has articles about the current situation facing gays in Egypt.
International Gay and Lesbian Human Rights Commission ⓦ iglhrc.org. Posts information about civil rights for gay people in Egypt.

Health

Changes of diet and climate accounts for most visitors' health problems, usually nothing worse than a bout or two of diarrhoea. Some people adapt quickly, others take longer, especially children and older people. If you're only here for a week or two, it makes sense to be cautious, while for longer-staying visitors it is worth trying to acclimatize.

Unless you're coming from an area where yellow fever is endemic (mainly sub-Saharan Africa), there are no compulsory **inoculations** for Egypt, though you should always be up to date with polio and tetanus, if not typhoid (which occasionally flares up in parts of Egypt). For vaccination clinics see ⓦ masta.org (in Britain), ⓦ cdc.gov/travel (US), ⓦ csih.org (Canada) or ⓦ tmvc.com.au (Australia, New Zealand and South Africa).

Health hazards

Tap water in Egyptian towns and cities is heavily chlorinated and mostly safe to drink, but is unpalatable and rough on tender stomachs. In rural areas, Sinai campsites and desert rest-houses there's a fair risk of contaminated water. Consequently, most tourists stick to bottled mineral water, which is widely available and tastes better. However, excessive fear of tap water is unjustified and hard to sustain in practice if you're here for long. Once your stomach has adjusted, it's usually okay to drink it without going to the hassle of purifying it (which you can do with Halazone tablets or iodine, or by boiling it).

What you should avoid is any contact with stagnant water that might harbour **bilharzia** (schistosomiasis) flukes. These minute worms, which breed in the blood vessels of the abdomen and liver (the main symptom is blood in the urine), infest irrigation canals and the slower stretches of the Nile. Don't drink or swim there, nor walk barefoot in the mud, or even on grass that's wet with Nile water. The saline pools of desert oases are fine to bathe in.

Heat and dust

Many visitors experience problems with Egypt's intense **heat**, particularly in the south, in summer and in the middle of the day (going out in the early morning and late afternoon is better). Wear a hat and loose-fitting clothes (preferably not synthetic fabrics), and a high-factor sunscreen to protect from sunburn, especially in summer. Wear a T-shirt when snorkelling, for the same reason. Sprinkling water on the ground cools the surrounding area by evaporation, and also levels the dust.

Because sweat evaporates immediately in the dry atmosphere, you can easily become dehydrated without realizing it. Dehydration is exacerbated by both alcohol and caffeine. Drink plenty of other fluids (at least three litres per day; more if you're exerting yourself) and take a bit of extra salt with your food.

Heat exhaustion – signified by headaches, dizziness and nausea – is treated by resting in a cool place and drinking plenty of water or juice with a pinch of salt. An intense headache, heightened body temperature, flushed skin and the cessation of sweating are symptoms of **heatstroke**, which can be fatal if not treated immediately. The whole body must be cooled by immersion in tepid water, or the application of wet towels, and medical assistance should be sought. If walking long distances in the sun, it is vital to carry drinking water. A sunhat can be drenched with water, wrung to stop it dripping, and worn wet so that the evaporation cools your head – you'll be amazed how quickly it dries out. Less seriously, visitors may suffer from **prickly heat**, an itchy rash caused by excessive perspiration trapped beneath the skin. Loose clothing and frequent bathing can reduce it.

Desert **dust** – or grit and smog in Cairo – can irritate your eyes. Contact-lens users may find switching to glasses helps. If ordinary eye drops don't help, try antihistamine decongestant eye drops such as Vernacel, Vascon-A or Optihist. Persistent irritation may indicate trachoma, a contagious infection which is easily cured by antibiotics at an early stage, but eventually causes blindness if left untreated. Dust can also inflame sinuses. Covering your nose and mouth with a scarf helps prevent this; olbas oil or a nasal decongestant spray can relieve symptoms.

Digestive complaints

Almost every visitor to Egypt gets **diarrhoea** at some stage. Rare meat and raw shellfish top the danger list, which descends via creamy sauces down to salads, juices, raw fruit and vegetables. Visitors who insist on washing everything (and cleaning their teeth) in mineral water are overreacting. Just use common sense, and accustom your stomach gradually to Egyptian cooking. Asking for dishes to be served very hot (*sukhna awi*) will reduce the risk of catching anything.

If you have **diarrhoea**, the best initial treatment is to simply adapt your diet, eating plain boiled rice and vegetables, while avoiding greasy or spicy food, caffeine, alcohol and most fruit and dairy products (although some say that bananas and prickly pears can help, while yogurt provides a form of protein that your body can easily absorb). Most importantly, keep your bodily fluids topped up by drinking plenty of bottled water. Especially if children are affected, you may also want to add rehydration salts (brands include Rehydran) to the water, or failing that, half a teaspoon of salt and eight of sugar in a litre of water will help the body to absorb the fluid more efficiently.

Drugs like Imodium or Lomotil can plug you up if you have to travel, but undermine your body's efforts to rid itself of infection. Avoid Enterovioform, which is still available in Egypt despite being suspected of damaging the optic nerve. Antinal (nifuroxazide) is widely prescribed against diarrhoea in Egypt and available over the counter in pharmacies. Note that having diarrhoea may make orally administered drugs (such as contraceptive pills) less effective, as they can pass straight through you without being absorbed.

If symptoms persist longer than a few days, or if you develop a fever or pass blood in your faeces, get medical help immediately, since acute diarrhoea can also be a symptom of dysentery, cholera or **typhoid.**

Rabies and malaria

Rabies is endemic in Egypt, where many wild animals (including bats, sometimes found in temples, tombs and caves) carry the disease. Avoid touching any strange animal, wild or domestic. Treatment must be given between exposure to the disease and the onset of symptoms; once these appear, rabies is invariably fatal. If you think you've been exposed, seek help immediately.

Malaria, spread by the anopheles mosquito, exists in the Fayoum in summer, but you won't need malaria pills unless you're staying in that area for a while. You should nevertheless take extra steps to avoid mosquito bites in the Fayoum – use repellent and cover bare skin, especially feet and ankles, after dusk (see below).

Mosquitoes and other bugs

Even without malaria, **mosquitoes** are a nuisance, ubiquitous in summer and never entirely absent. Fans, mosquito coils, repellent and plug-in vaporizers (sold at pharmacies) all help. A lot of Egyptians use citronella oil, obtainable from many pharmacies, as a repellent, but tests have shown it to be less effective (and to require more frequent applications) than repellents containing DEET (diethyltoluamide), which are the ones recommended by medical authorities. Don't forget to put repellent on your feet and ankles if they are uncovered when you go out in the evening. The best guarantee of a bite-less night's sleep is to bring a mosquito net.

Flies transmit various diseases, and only insecticide spray or air conditioning offer protection. Some cheap hotels harbour fleas, scabies, mites, cockroaches and other bugs. Consult a pharmacist if you find yourself with a persistent skin irritation.

Scorpions and snakes

The danger from scorpions and snakes is minimal, as most are nocturnal and avoid people, but don't go barefoot, turn over rocks or stick your hands into dark crevices anywhere off the beaten track. Whereas the sting of larger, darker **scorpions** is no worse than a bad wasp sting, the venom of the pale, slender-clawed fat-tailed scorpion (*Androctonus australis* and a few related species) is highly toxic. If stung, cold-pack the affected area and seek medical help immediately. Photographs of the most danegrous species, plus sound information and advice can be found on the Scorpion Venom website at Ⓦweb.singnet.com.sg/~chuaeecc/venom/venom.htm.

Egypt has two main types of poisonous **snake**: vipers and cobras. Vipers vary in colour from sandy to reddish (or sometimes grey) and leave two-fang punctures. The horned viper, Egypt's deadliest snake, is recognizable by its horns. Cobras have a distinctive hood and bite mark (a single row of teeth plus fang holes). The smaller Egyptian cobra (coloured sandy olive) is found throughout the country, the longer black-necked cobra (which can spit its venom up to three metres) only in the south.

All snakebites should be washed immediately. Try not to move the affected body part, get immediate medical help, and stay calm, as panicking sends the venom through your bloodstream more quickly.

HIV and AIDS

Levels of HIV infection are low in Egypt but so is AIDS awareness – even among those involved in sex tourism, an industry catering to Western women or gays (in Luxor, Aswan and Hurghada) and male Gulf Arabs (in Cairo). Pharmacies in these cities, plus a few outlets in Sinai, are the only places in Egypt sure to sell condoms (*kabout*) – Egyptian brands such as Sportex are cheaper but less reliable than imported Durex. It's best to bring your own supply.

Women's health

Travelling in the heat and taking antibiotics for an upset stomach make women much more susceptible to vaginal infections. The best precautions are to wash regularly with mild soap, and wear cotton underwear and loose clothing. **Yeast infections** can be treated with Nystatin pessaries (available at pharmacies), "one-shot" Canesten pessaries (bring some from home if you're prone to thrush), or douches of a weak solution of vinegar or lemon juice. Sea bathing can also help. Trichomonas is usually treated with Flagyl, which should only be taken under medical supervision.

Bring your own **contraceptives**, since the only forms widely available in Egypt are old-fashioned, high-dosage pills, the coil, and not too trusty condoms (see p.53). Cap-users should pack a spare, and enough spermicide and pessaries. Note that persistent diarrhoea can render the pill ineffective. **Sanitary protection** is available from pharmacies in cities and tourist resorts, but seldom anywhere else, so it's wise to bring a supply for your trip.

Medical services in Egypt

Egyptian **pharmacists** are well trained, usually speak English and can dispense a wide range of drugs, including many normally on prescription. If necessary, they can usually recommend a doctor – sometimes on the premises.

Private **doctors** are just as common as pharmacies, and most speak English or French. They charge for consultations: expect to pay about £E100–200 a session, which doesn't include drugs, but should cover a follow-up visit. There is a call-out charge for private and public ambulances (❶123).

If you get seriously ill, **hospitals** (*mustashfa*) that are privately run are generally preferable to public-sector ones. Those attached to universities are usually well-equipped and competent, but small-town hospitals are often abysmal. Private hospitals usually require a cash deposit of at least £E150 (it can go as high as £E1500) to cover the cost of treatment, and often require payment on the spot; you will then have to claim it back from your insurance provider. Despite several good hospitals in Cairo and Alexandria, Egypt is not a country to fall seriously ill in. In particular, if you need surgery, it's best to get back home for it if you can.

Hiring guides

Professional guides can be engaged through branches of Misr Travel (see p.30) or American Express, local tourist offices and large hotels, and on the spot at sights such as the Egyptian Antiquities Museum in Cairo and the Pyramids of Giza. They normally charge a fixed hourly rate, and a tip is also expected.

Guides can be useful at major sites, like the Valley of the Kings, where they will be able to ease your way through queues at the tombs. If you feel intimidated by the culture, too, you might welcome an intermediary for the first couple of days' sightseeing. In general, however, and armed with this book, you shouldn't need a guide.

At ancient sites, there are always plenty of hangers-on posing as "guides", who will offer to show you "secret tombs" or "special reliefs" or just present themselves in tombs or temples, with palms outstretched. They don't have a lot to offer you, and encouraging them makes life more difficult for everyone else.

On the other hand, especially in small towns or villages, you may meet local people, often teenagers, who genuinely want to help out foreigners, and maybe practise their English at the same time. They may offer to lead you from one taxi depot to another, or show you the way to the souks or to a local site. Most people you meet this way don't expect money and you could risk offence by offering – if they want money, they won't be shy about asking.

Insurance

It's frankly reckless to travel without insurance cover. Home insurance policies occasionally cover your possessions when overseas, and some private medical schemes include cover when abroad. Bank and credit cards often have certain levels of medical or other insurance included and you may automatically get travel insurance if you use a major credit card to pay for your trip. Otherwise, you should contact a specialist travel insurance company, or consider the travel insurance deal we offer (see p.55). When choosing a policy, you may want to ask whether you're covered to take part in "dangerous sports" or other activities – in Egypt, this could mean, for example, camel trekking or scuba diving.

If you need to **make a claim**, you should keep receipts for medicines and medical treatment, while in the event you have anything stolen you must obtain an official theft report from the police (called a *mahdar*). You may also be required to provide proof that you owned the items that were stolen, in the form of shop receipts or a credit-card statement recording the purchase.

ROUGH GUIDES TRAVEL INSURANCE

Rough Guides has teamed up with WorldNomads.com to offer great travel insurance deals. Policies are available to residents of over 150 countries, with cover for a wide range of adventure sports, 24hr emergency assistance, high levels of medical and evacuation cover and a stream of travel safety information. Roughguides.com users can take advantage of their policies online 24/7, from anywhere in the world. And since plans often change when you're on the road, you can extend your policy and even claim online. Roughguides.com users who buy travel insurance with WorldNomads.com can also leave a positive footprint and donate to a community development project. For more information, go to ⓦ roughguides.com/shop.

Laundry

Wherever you are staying, there will either be an in-house laundry (*mahwagi*), or one close by to call on, charging piece rates. Some budget hotels in Luxor, Aswan and Hurghada allow guests to use their washing machine for a small charge, or gratis. You can buy washing powder at most pharmacies. Dry cleaners are confined to Cairo, Aswan and Hurghada.

Living in Egypt

Some foreigners make a living in Egypt, teaching English or diving, writing for the English-language media, or even bellydancing. Getting a work permit involves getting a job offer, then taking evidence of this to Al-Mugamma in Cairo (see p.205) to apply. So long as the offer is for a job where foreigners rather than Egyptians are needed, it is then simply a question of jumping through the necessary bureaucratic hoops.

Private **language schools** are often on the lookout for English teachers, and the British Council (192 Corniche el-Nil, Aguza ⓣ 19789, ⓔ inform ation@britishcouncil.org.eg) may be able to supply a list of schools to approach; the more reputable firms will want an EFL qualification. You may also be able to find work with the local English-language **media**: *Egypt Today* sometimes accepts articles and photos, and the *Egyptian Gazette* may need sub-editors from time to time.

Most jobs in **tourism** are restricted to Egyptians, and locally based companies usually insist on a work permit, but you can sometimes fix up a season's work with a foreign tour operator as a rep or tour guide. In Sinai, Hurghada and Luxor there may be a demand for people with foreign languages (English, German, French, Italian, Japanese, or – on the Red Sea and Sinai coasts – Russian) to sell dive courses or work on hotel reception desks. Ask around dive centres or upmarket hotels.

Divers with Divemaster or Instructor certificates can often find work with diving centres in Hurghada or Sinai, which may also take on less qualified staff and let them learn on the job, at reduced rates of pay or in return for free tuition. Dive centres commonly turn a blind eye to the lack of a work permit, or might procure one for a valued worker.

Foreign **bellydancers** are much in demand in nightclubs in Cairo, Alexandria, Luxor and Hurghada. The work can be well paid, but you have to be careful: financial and sexual exploitation are real hazards. Aside from work, many foreign dancers come to Egypt to improve their art or buy costumes (see p.193 & p.199).

Studying

The **American University in Cairo's Arabic Language Institute** (ⓣ 02 2794 2964, ⓦ aucegypt .edu/huss/ali) offers year-abroad and non-degree programmes, a summer school and intensive Arabic courses. A full year's tuition (two semesters and summer school) costs roughly $30,000. US citizens may apply to the Stafford Loan Program, at Office of Admissions, 420 5th Ave, 3rd Floor, New York, NY 10018-2729 (ⓣ 212 730 8800).

Foreign students may also attend one- or two-term programmes at **universities** such as Cairo (ⓦ cuportal.cu.edu.eg), Ain Shams (ⓦ shams .edu.eg) and Al-Azhar (ⓦ azhar.edu.eg). Like the AUC's courses, these are valid for transferable credits at most American and some British universities. In the US, you can get information on exchange programmes from the Egyptian Cultural and Educational Bureau, 1303 New Hampshire Ave NW, Washington DC 20036 (ⓣ 202 296 3888, ⓦ eecous.net) or AmidEast, 1730 M St NW, Suite 1100, Washington DC 20036–4505 (ⓣ 202 776 9600, ⓦ amideast.org).

A number of schools in Cairo offer courses in **Arabic language**, both in colloquial Egyptian Arabic and Modern Standard Arabic (see p.204).

Mail

Airmail letters from Egypt generally take a week to ten days to reach Western Europe, two to three weeks to North America or Australasia. It speeds up the delivery if you get someone to write the name of the country in Arabic. As a rule, around fifteen percent of correspondence (in either direction) never arrives; letters containing photos or other items are especially prone to go astray. It's best to send letters from a major city or hotel; blue mailboxes are for overseas airmail, red ones for domestic post.

Airmail (*bareed gawwi*) **stamps** can be purchased at post offices, hotel shops and postcard stands, which may charge a few extra piastres on top of the stamp's official price (£E2.50 for a postcard/letter to anywhere in the world). Registered mail (£E10 extra) can be sent from any post office. Selected post offices in the main cities offer an Express Mail Service.

To **send a parcel**, take it unsealed to a major post office (in Cairo, you'll need to use the one at Ramses Square) for customs inspection, weighing and wrapping. Private **courier firms** such as DHL and UPS are limited to a few cities, and are a lot more expensive.

Post office **hours** are generally daily except Fridays from 8am to 6pm (Ramadan 9am–3pm), though in big cities post offices may stay open until 8pm.

If **receiving mail**, note that any package or letter containing goods is likely to be held, and you will have to collect it and pay customs duty; you should be informed that it has arrived and where you need to pick it up. Poste restante (general delivery) services exist, but are unreliable and best avoided if possible (you could have people write to you at a hotel). If you do use the service, have mail addressed clearly, with the surname in capital letters, and bear in mind that even then, it may well be misfiled.

Internet

Most towns in Egypt have **internet cafés**, and an increasing number of hotels, as well as a few modern cafés, now offer **wi-fi**. Unless you're well off the beaten track, therefore, you should have no trouble checking your email or the websites of newspapers from home, as well as those of Egyptian papers (see p.38) or, for regional news, the English-language website of Qatari broadcaster Al Jazeera (Ⓦ aljazeera.com).

Maps

If you can find a copy, the best **general map** of Egypt is our own Rough Guide map (now out of print but still available in some places) at a scale of 1:1,125,000, on tear-proof paper, with roads, railways and contours clearly marked; Freytag & Berndt's (1:800,000) is a good second-best, as is Nelles (1:2,500,000, with insets at 1:750,000), and Gizi (1:1,300,000, with place names in Arabic as well as English). Kümmerly & Frey (1:950,000; published in Egypt by Lehnert & Landrock) makes a reasonable alternative.

City maps cover Cairo (see p.179), but few other places. **Diving maps** of the Red Sea are available in Egypt, but some do not cover sites in the Sinai, the main diving area for most tourists.

Full-blown **desert expeditions** require detailed maps that can be obtained in Cairo from the Survey Office (*heyat al-misaha*) on Sharia Abdel Salam Arif at the corner of Sharia Giza, open daily except Friday 9am–1pm (see map, p.139), who may demand an official letter explaining why you need the maps.

Money

Egypt's basic unit of currency is the **Egyptian pound** (called a *ginay* in Arabic, and written £E or LE), divided into 100 piastres (*'urush*, singular *'irsh*, abbreviated as "pt"). At the time of writing, exchange rates were around £E9.25 to the pound sterling, £E6 to the US dollar and £E7.35 to the euro.

Egyptian **banknotes** bear Arabic numerals on one side, Western numerals on the other, and come in denominations of 25pt, 50pt, £E1, £E5, £E10, £E20, £E50, £E100 and £E200. There are **coins** for 5pt, 10pt, 20pt, 25pt, 50pt and £E1. Some banknotes are so ragged that merchants refuse them. Trying to palm off (and avoid receiving) decrepit notes can add spice to minor transactions, or be a real nuisance. Conversely, some vendors won't accept high-denomination notes (£E20 upwards) due to a shortage of change. Some offer sweets in lieu of coins, others round prices up. Try to hoard coins and small-value notes for tips, fares and small purchases.

Carrying your money

The easiest way to access your money in Egypt is with plastic, though it's a good idea to also have some back-up in the form of cash or travellers' cheques. Using a Visa, MasterCard, Plus or Cirrus card, you can draw cash using **ATMs** at branches of the main banks in cities, major towns and tourist resorts. Machines are usually outside banks or inside airports and shopping centres. By using ATMs you get trade exchange rates, which are somewhat better than those charged by banks for changing cash, though your card issuer may well add a foreign transaction fee, sometimes as much as five percent. Note also that there is a daily limit on ATM cash withdrawals, usually £E3000–4000. If you use a credit card rather than a debit card, note also that all cash advances and ATM withdrawals obtained are treated as loans, with interest accruing daily from the date of withdrawal.

It's wise to make sure your card is in good condition and, before you leave home, make sure that the card and PIN will work overseas. Where there is no ATM, **cash advances** on Visa and MasterCard can be obtained at most branches of the Banque Misr on the same basis.

Credit cards are accepted for payment at major hotels, top-flight restaurants, some shops and airline offices, but virtually nowhere else. American Express, MasterCard and Visa are the likeliest to be accepted.

To have **money wired**, Western Union's main agents are branches of the Arab African International Bank and a firm called International Business Associates (check ⓦwesternunion.com for specific locations); Moneygram's main agents (ⓦmoneygram.com) are branches of United Bank or Bank du Caire.

Banks and exchange

Arriving by land or sea, you should have no trouble changing money at the border, and airport banks are open around the clock. It is illegal to import or export more than £E5000 in local currency. **Banking hours** are generally from Sunday to Thursday 8.30am to 2pm (9.30am–1.30pm during Ramadan). Branches in five-star hotels may open longer hours, sometimes even 24/7. For arriving visitors, the banks at Cairo airport and the border crossings from Israel are open 24 hours daily, and those at ports whenever a ship docks.

The best exchange rates for cash can be found at **foreign exchange bureaux** – private money-changers found in large towns and tourist resorts (although they seldom take travellers' cheques and will offer poor rates if they do). They are also open longer hours and perform transactions more quickly than Egyptian banks, where forms are passed among a bevy of clerks. You'll also generally get faster service at foreign banks in Cairo and Alexandria, branches in hotels, or offices of American Express (in Cairo, Hurghada, Luxor, Aswan and Port Said) or Thomas Cook (in Cairo, Alexandria, Luxor, Aswan, Port Said, Hurghada and Sharm el-Sheikh; ⓦthomascookegypt.com). **Commission** is not generally charged on currency exchange.

US dollars, euros and English sterling notes are easy to exchange, although due to forgeries some banks may not accept worn or pre-1992 $100 bills. Hard currency (usually US dollars) may be required for visas, border taxes and suchlike. Don't bring New Zealand dollars, or Scottish or Northern Irish sterling banknotes, which are not accepted; Israeli shekels can only be changed at the Taba border crossing, and at one or two banks (in five-star hotels) and some Cairo foreign exchange bureaux. Sudanese pounds and Libyan dinars are similarly hard to change.

There's sometimes a currency **black market**, but it's best to avoid illegal street money changers, who are usually rip-off artists.

Opening hours and public holidays

Offices tend to open Sunday to Thursday from 8.30am to 5pm. **Shops** are usually open from around 10am to around 8pm, sometimes later, with small places often closing briefly for prayers, especially Friday lunchtime between noon and 3pm.

During **Ramadan**, all these hours go haywire. Since everybody who keeps the fast will want to eat immediately after it ends at sunset, most places close early to allow this, and may open early to compensate. Offices may open 7am–4pm, shops may simply close to break the fast, reopening afterwards, while banks open 9.30am–1.30pm. Ramadan opening times are given, where available, throughout the text.

Public holidays include Eid el-Adha, Ras el-Sana el-Hegira, the Moulid el-Nabi and Eid el-Fitr, all following the Islamic calendar (see p.39). Others, following the Gregorian calendar, are: Coptic Christmas (Jan 7), Sinai Liberation Day (April 25), Labour Day (May 1), Evacuation Day (June 18), Revolution Day (July 23), Flooding of the Nile (Aug 15), Armed Forces Day (Oct 6), Suez Liberation Day (Oct 23) and Victory Day (Dec 23). Sham al-Nassim (Coptic Easter Monday) falls according to the Coptic calendar (see p.41). Banks

USEFUL TELEPHONE NUMBERS

EMERGENCIES AND INFORMATION

Ambulance	☎123
Police	☎122
Tourist police	☎126
Fire brigade	☎180
Directory enquiries	☎140 or ☎141
International operator	☎120

INTERNATIONAL CALLS

Omit the initial zero from the area code when dialling Egypt, the UK, Ireland, Australia, New Zealand or South Africa from abroad.

	From Egypt	To Egypt
UK	☎00 44	☎00 20
Ireland	☎00 353	☎00 20
US and Canada	☎001	☎011 20
Australia	☎00 61	☎0011 20
New Zealand	☎00 64	☎00 20
South Africa	☎00 27	☎09 20

and offices close on public holidays; most shops and transport operate as usual.

Phones

All towns and cities have at least one 24-hour telephone and telegraph office (*maktab al-telephonat*, or *centraal*) for calling long-distance and abroad, or you can buy a card at grocers or kiosks to use in public phones on the street. Rates are around twenty percent cheaper at night (8pm–8am).

Cards such as Egypt Telecom's Marhaba card, with a scratch-off panel covering a PIN, can be used from private landline phones (but not public phones or mobiles) by dialling a toll-free number, then the PIN on the card (sometimes in two separate parts, the second part being your "password"), and finally the number you wish to call. They are available from Egypt Telecom offices, and sometimes from grocers or kiosks.

Mobile phones

If you want to take your mobile phone with you, you'll need to check with your phone provider whether it will work in Egypt and what the charges are. You may pay extra for international roaming, and to receive calls in Egypt. A US cellphone must be GSM/triband to work in Egypt.

If planning to use your phone a lot in Egypt, especially for local calls, it's worth getting a SIM card from one of the Egyptian providers, Mobinil, **Etisalat or** Vodafone. You may need to pay a small fee to

have your phone unlocked (assuming it's possible to unlock it). You can get a SIM card (*khatt*) for £E5–10, and top-up cards in denominations from £E10 to £E200. Mobinil tends to have better coverage than Vodafone, especially in the Western Desert and on the Mediterranean coast; for optimum coverage in remote areas, you might even consider buying two SIM cards and swapping between them.

Photography

Proceed with care. Before taking a picture of someone, ask their permission – especially in rural areas, where you can cause genuine offence. Also be aware that during the revolution, foreigners

MOBILE NUMBER CHANGES

Since the beginning of 2012, all Egyptian mobile numbers have been eleven-digit. If you have an old, ten-digit number, here's how to update it:

☎010 becomes ☎0100
☎011 becomes ☎0111
☎012 becomes ☎0122
☎014 becomes ☎0114
☎016 becomes ☎0106
☎017 becomes ☎0127
☎018 becomes ☎0128
☎019 becomes ☎0109
☎015 becomes ☎0120 if Mobinil,
☎0101 if Vodaphone and ☎0112 if Etisalat.

taking photographs have been set upon as suspected spies, so assess the situation before snapping away, and be particularly wary of photographing anything militarily sensitive (even bridges, train stations, dams, etc). People may also stop you from taking photos that show Egypt in a "poor" or "backward" light.

Religious buildings

Most of the **mosques** and **madrassas** (Islamic colleges) that you'll want to visit are in Cairo and, apart from Al-Hussein and Saiyida Zeinab mosques, are classed as historic monuments, so they're open to non-Muslim sightseers (though you should avoid prayer times, especially at noon on Friday). Elsewhere in Egypt, mosques are not used to seeing tourists and people may object to non-Muslims entering. If you are not Muslim, tread with care and if possible ask someone to take you in.

At all mosques, dress is important. Shorts, short skirts and exposed shoulders are out, and women may be asked to cover their hair (a scarf may be provided). Above all, remember to remove your shoes upon entering the precinct. They will either be held by a shoe custodian (small baksheesh expected) or you can leave them outside the door, or carry them in by hand (if you do this, place the soles together, as they are considered unclean).

Egyptian **monasteries** (which are Coptic, save for Greek Orthodox St Catherine's in Sinai) admit visitors at all times except during the Lenten or other fasts (local fasts are detailed in the guide where appropriate). Similar rules of dress etiquette to those for mosques apply, though unless you go into the church itself you don't need to remove your shoes.

Smoking

Most Egyptian men smoke, and offering cigarettes around is common practice. The most popular brand is Cleopatra. Matches are *kibreet*; a lighter is a *wallah*. Traditionally, respectable women aren't supposed to smoke in public, but women are increasingly seen nowadays smoking *sheeshas* in Cairo's coffee shops. Don't expect restaurants or public transport to be non-smoking, though Cairo's Metro is.

Time

Egypt is on GMT+2, which means that in principle it is two hours ahead of the UK, seven hours ahead of

the US East Coast (EST), eleven hours ahead of the US West Coast (PST), six hours behind Western Australia, eight hours behind eastern Australia and ten hours behind New Zealand. Daylight Saving Time at home or in Egypt may affect these differences. Egypt's clocks move forward for daylight saving on the last Friday in April and back again on the last Friday in September.

Tourist information

The **Egyptian Tourist Authority** (sometimes abbreviated as EGAPT; Ⓦegypt.travel) has offices in several countries. Their website gives a good overview of Egypt's tourist attractions. Better still, Ⓦtouregypt.net has quite a lot of useful information, including details of main tourist attractions and listings of hotels, nightclubs and internet cafés.

In Egypt itself, you'll get a variable response from local tourist offices (addresses given throughout the guide), where the level of knowledge and assistance may depend on who exactly you speak to.

Egyptian historical and archeological sites are the responsibility of the **Supreme Council of Antiquities** (SCA; Ⓦsca-egypt.org), whose website carries information about most sites open to the public, and certainly all the important ones. For more detailed archeological information on ancient Egyptian sites, including the more obscure ones, see Ⓦegyptsites.wordpress.com.

EGYPTIAN TOURIST OFFICES ABROAD

Canada 2020 University St, Suite 2260, Montreal, PQ H3A 2A5 ☏ 1 514 861 8071, Ⓔ info.ca@egypt.travel.
UK 170 Piccadilly, London W1J 9EJ ☏ 020 7493 5283, Ⓔ info.uk@egypt.travel.
USA 630 5th Ave, Suite 2305, New York, NY 10111 ☏ 1 212 332 2570, Ⓔ info.us@egypt.travel.

Travel agencies and hotels

Private travel agencies can advise on (and book) transport, accommodation and excursions, though their advice may not be unbiased. The state-run **Misr Travel** (Ⓦmisrtraveleg.net; offices in major cities, listed in the guide) operates hotels, buses and limos, and can make bookings for most things. They also have an office in New York (1270 Ave of The Americas, Suite 604, New York, NY 10020 ☏ 212 332 2600). American Express and Thomas Cook also offer various travel services. In Luxor, Aswan, Hurghada, Sinai and the Western Desert oases, many hotels and campgrounds double as information exchanges and fixers.

Tourist publications

The monthly magazine *Egypt Today* has features on Egyptian culture and travel, and some useful listings of restaurants, cinemas, theatres, galleries and language schools in Cairo and Alexandria, which are the cities where it's sold. Selected events are listed in the daily *Egyptian Gazette*, and the weekly English-language edition of *Al-Ahram*, which are more widely available (see also p.38).

Toilets

Public toilets are almost always filthy, and there's never any toilet paper (though someone may sell it outside). They're usually known as *toileta*, and marked with WC and Men and Women signs. Expect squat toilets in bus stations, resthouses and fleapit hotels. Sit-down toilets have a nozzle that squirts water into your bottom – make sure you're positioned right before you turn it on. Though it's wise to carry toilet paper (£E2.50/double roll in grocers and pharmacies), paper tissues, sold on the streets (50pt–£E1), will serve at a pinch.

Travellers with disabilities

Disability is common in Egypt. Many conditions that would be treatable in the West, such as cataracts, cause permanent disabilities here because people can't afford the treatment. People with disabilities are unlikely to get jobs (though there is a tradition of blind singers and preachers), so the choice is usually between staying at home being looked after by your family, and going out on the streets to beg for alms.

For a blind or wheelchair-using tourist, the **streets** are full of obstacles which, if you walk with difficulty, you will find hard going. Queuing, steep stairs, unreliable elevators and the heat, will take it out of you if you have a condition that makes you tire quickly. A light, folding camp-stool is invaluable if you have limited walking or standing power. In that case, it's a good idea to avoid arriving in the summer months.

For **wheelchair users**, the country's monuments are a mix of accessible and impossible. Most major temples are on relatively level sites, with a few steps here and there – manoeuvrable in a wheelchair or with sticks if you have an able-bodied helper. Your frustrations are likely to be with the tombs, which are almost always a struggle to reach – often sited halfway up cliffs, or down steep flights of steps. The Pyramids of Giza (p.149) are fine to view but not enter, though the sound-and-light show is wheelchair accessible; Saqqara (p.158) is difficult, being so sandy. If you opt for a Nile cruise, bear in mind that you'll be among a large throng and will need to be carried on and off the boat if you depend on a wheelchair (often by people who don't understand English), an experience you may well not relish.

Cairo is generally bad news, especially Islamic Cairo, with its narrow, uneven alleys and heavy traffic, but with a car and helper, you could still see the Citadel and other major monuments. There's a lift in the Egyptian Museum, and newer metro stations have elevator access from street level to the platforms, though none of the older ones do, which unfortunately includes all those in the city

---

USEFUL THINGS TO BRING

- **Earplugs** Help muffle the noise of videos on long-distance buses and trains, if you're trying to sleep.
- **Film/memory cards** For a digital camera, it doesn't hurt to bring more memory card capacity than you think you'll need. If using film, Kodak and Fuji film is available in most towns and major resorts, but may be old stock, so bring adequate supplies.
- **Mosquito net** The best guarantee of a mozzie-free night's sleep in the oases and the Nile Valley. Alternatively, buy a plug-in device (such as Ezalo) at any Egyptian pharmacy.
- **Sleeping bag** A decent bag is required if you're planning to sleep out in the desert in spring or autumn, or in any low-budget hotel over winter. In the summer, a sheet sleeping bag or silk sleeping bag liner is handy if you're staying at cheap hotels, where just one (not necessarily clean) sheet is provided.
- **Suitable clothes** Dress should be appropriate given Egypt's conservative sensibilities (see p.42). Northern Egypt can be cold and damp in the winter, while the desert gets freezing at night, even in spring and autumn, so a warm sweater is invaluable.
- **Torch/flashlight** For exploring dark tombs, and for use during power cuts.

centre. Most five-star hotels in Cairo are wheelchair-accessible and have adapted rooms.

Taxis are affordable and quite adaptable; if you charter one for the day, the driver is certain to help you in and out, and perhaps even around the sites you visit. If you employ a guide, they may well also be prepared to help you with steps and other obstacles. Some **diving** centres in Sinai and Hurghada accept disabled students on their courses, and the hotels in these resorts tend to be wheelchair-friendly.

There are **organized tours** and holidays specifically for people with disabilities, and some companies, such as Discover Egypt in the UK (see p.29), offer packages tailor-made to your specific needs. Egypt for All (58 Sharia al-Gabal al-Shamali, Hadaba District, Hurghada ☎0122 396 1991, ⓦegyptforall.com) run a range of tours, offer tailor-made holidays to your specifications, and may be able to arrange transport or equipment rental.

It's a good idea to carry spares of any clothing or equipment that might be hard to find; if there's an association at home for people with your particular disability, contact them early for more specific advice. And always make sure that travel agencies, package firms and insurance companies, even travelling companions, are aware of, and can cover, your particular needs.

Cairo and the Pyramids

READING IN A MOSQUE, CAIRO

1

Cairo and the Pyramids

Whoso hath not seen Cairo hath not seen the world. Her dust is golden and her Nile a miracle holden; and her women are as Houris fair; puppets, beautiful pictures; her houses are palaces rare; her water is sweet and light and her mud a commodity and a medicine beyond compare.

The Arabian Nights

Cairo has been the Islamic world's greatest city since the Mongols sacked Baghdad in 1258. Egyptians have two names for the city: Masr, meaning both the capital and the land of Egypt (for Egyptians abroad, "Masr" means Egypt, but within the country it means the capital), is a timeless name rooted in pharaonic civilization; the city's other name, Al-Qahira (The Triumphant), is linked specifically to the Fatimid conquest which made it the capital of an Islamic empire embracing modern-day Libya, Tunisia, Palestine and Syria, but the name is rarely used in everyday speech.

In monumental terms the two names are symbolized by two dramatic **landmarks**: the **Pyramids of Giza** at the edge of the Western Desert, and the great **Mosque of Mohammed Ali** – the modernizer of Islamic Egypt – which broods atop the Citadel. Between these two monuments sprawls a vast city, the colour of sand and ashes, of diverse worlds and epochs and gross inequities. All is subsumed into an organism that somehow thrives in the terminal ward: medieval slums and Art Deco suburbs, garbage-pickers and marbled malls, donkey carts and limos, piousness and what

Highlights

❶ The Egyptian Museum One of the world's truly great museums, containing a massive collection of ancient statues, sarcophagi, frescoes, reliefs, and incredible treasures from the tomb of Tutankhamun. **See p.73**

❷ Islamic Cairo The medieval city of Saladin (Salah al-Din) is Cairo's true heart, teeming with life and chock-a-block with stunning architecture. **See p.90**

❸ The Citadel Dominating Cairo's skyline, the great fort commissioned by Saladin boasts a plethora of quirky museums, the Mohammed

Ali mosque and commanding views of the city. **See p.111**

❹ Old Cairo This compact quarter contains the city's most ancient Coptic churches and its oldest synagogue. **See p.122**

❺ The Pyramids of Giza The sole surviving wonder of the ancient world, and still stunning to this day. **See p.149**

❻ The Pyramids of Dahshur Still largely unknown to tour groups, these are some of the most fascinating and significant of all Egypt's pyramids. **See p.168**

HIGHLIGHTS ARE MARKED ON THE MAP ON P.66

1

Desmond Stewart calls "the oaths of men exaggerating in the name of God". Cairo lives by its own contradictions. Its **population** is today estimated at around twenty million and is swollen by a further million commuters from the Delta and a thousand new migrants every day. An estimated half a million people reside in squatted cemeteries – the famous **Cities of the Dead**. The amount of green space per citizen has been calculated at thirteen square centimetres, not enough to cover a child's palm. Whereas earlier travellers noted that Cairo's air smelt "like hot bricks", visitors now find throat-rasping **air pollution**, chiefly caused by traffic.

Cairo's genius is to humanize these inescapable realities with **social rituals**. The rarity of public violence owes less to the armed police on every corner than to the *dowshah*: when conflicts arise, crowds gather, restraining both parties, encouraging them to rant, sympathizing with their grievances and then finally urging "*Maalesh, maalesh*" ("Never mind"). Everyday life is sweetened by flowery gestures and salutations; misfortunes evoke thanks for Allah's dispensation (after all, things could be worse). Even the poorest can be respected for piety; in the mosque, millionaire and beggar kneel side by side.

Brief history

Ancient **Memphis**, the first capital of pharaonic Egypt, was founded around 3100 BC across the river and to the south, but it was 2500 years before a sister city of priests and

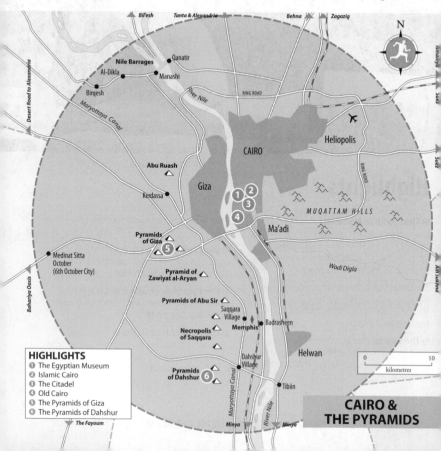

HIGHLIGHTS
1. The Egyptian Museum
2. Islamic Cairo
3. The Citadel
4. Old Cairo
5. The Pyramids of Giza
6. The Pyramids of Dahshur

CAIRO & THE PYRAMIDS

solar cults, known to posterity as **ancient Heliopolis** (see p.145), flourished on the east bank. It took centuries of Persian, Greek and Roman rule to efface both cities, by which time a new fortified town had developed on the east side. **Babylon-in-Egypt** was the beginning of the tale of cities that culminates in modern Cairo, the first chapter of which is described under "Old Cairo" (see p.122).

Babylon's citizens, oppressed by foreign overlords, almost welcomed the army of Islam that conquered Egypt in 641. For strategic and spiritual reasons, their general, Amr, chose to found a new settlement beyond the walls of Babylon – **Fustat**, the "City of the Tent" (see p.134), which evolved into a sophisticated metropolis.

Fatimid and Ayyubid Cairo

Under successive dynasties of caliphs who ruled the Islamic Empire from Iraq, three more cities were founded, each to the northeast of the previous one, which was either spurned or devastated. When the Shi'ite Fatimids took control in 969, they created an entirely new walled city – **Al-Qahira** – beyond this teeming, half-derelict conurbation. **Fatimid Cairo** formed the nucleus of the later, vastly expanded and consolidated capital that Saladin left to the Ayyubid dynasty in 1193. But the Ayyubids' reliance on imported slave-warriors – the Mamlukes – brought about their downfall: eventually, the Mamlukes simply seized power for themselves, ushering in a new era.

Mamluke and Ottoman Cairo

Mamluke Cairo encompassed all the previous cities, Saladin's Citadel (where the sultans dwelt), the northern port of Bulaq and vast cemeteries and rubbish tips beyond the city walls. Mamluke sultans like Baybars, Qalaoun, Barquq and Qaitbey erected mosques, mausoleums and caravanserais that still ennoble what is now known in English as "Islamic Cairo". The Islamic Cairo history section (p.90) relates their stories, the Turkish takeover, the decline of **Ottoman Cairo** and the rise of Mohammed Ali, who began the modernization of the city.

Modern Cairo

Under Ismail, the most profligate of Mohammed Ali's successors, a new, increasingly **European Cairo** arose beside the Nile – see the "Central Cairo" section (p.68). By 1920, the city's area was six times greater than that of medieval Cairo, and since then its residential suburbs have expanded relentlessly.

When **revolution** hit Egypt during the Arab Spring of 2011, Cairo was of course its epicentre, with events in Tahrir Square in particular an inspiration for the entire Arab world. Most of the events of that revolt played out in the square, on 6th October Bridge, and in the streets of Qasr al-Aini, in particular around the Interior Ministry, whose control was vital to the military in their bid to rein in the revolution and cling onto power.

Downtown Cairo

Most people prefer to get accustomed to **Downtown Cairo** before tackling the older Islamic quarters, for even in this westernized area, known in Arabic as *wust al-balad* (literally, "the town centre"), the culture shock can be profound. The area is essentially a lopsided triangle, bounded by Ramses Station, Midan Ataba and Garden City, and for the most part it's compact enough to explore on foot. Only the Ramses quarter and the further reaches of Garden City are sufficiently distant to justify using transport. At the heart of the Downtown area is the broad, bustling expanse of **Tahrir Square**, its most famous landmark the domed **Egyptian Museum**, which houses the finest collection of its kind in the world.

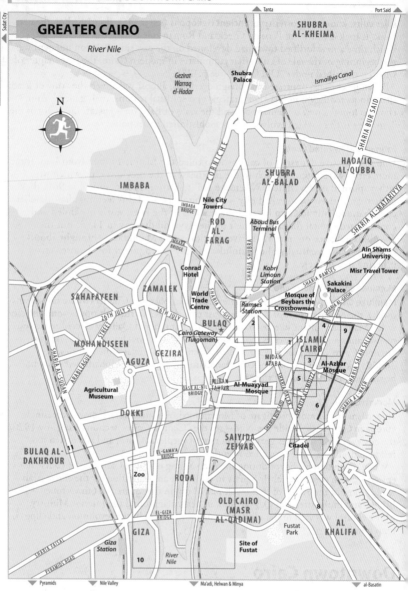

GREATER CAIRO

River Nile

N

The **layout** of the downtown area goes back to the 1860s, when Khedive Ismail had it rebuilt in the style of Haussmann's new Paris boulevards to impress dignitaries attending the inauguration of the Suez Canal, and had it named the **Ismailiya quarter**. Cutting an X-shaped swathe through the area are the main thoroughfares of **Talaat Harb** and **Qasr al-Nil** (each about a kilometre long). Though the area was founded in the nineteenth century, most of the buildings you see today date from the early twentieth century and, behind the inevitable layers of dust and grime, reflect the elegance of that period's architecture.

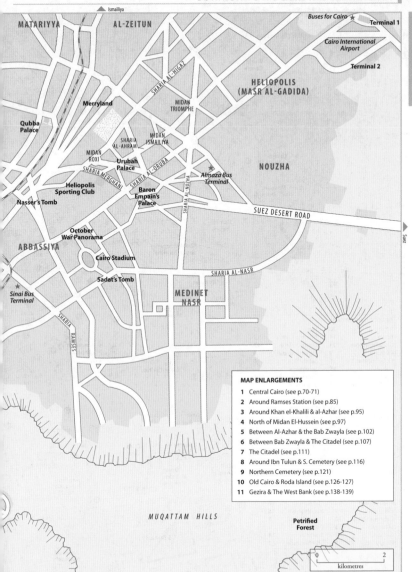

MAP ENLARGEMENTS

1 Central Cairo (see p.70-71)
2 Around Ramses Station (see p.85)
3 Around Khan el-Khalili & al-Azhar (see p.95)
4 North of Midan El-Hussein (see p.97)
5 Between Al-Azhar & the Bab Zwayla (see p.102)
6 Between Bab Zwayla & The Citadel (see p.107)
7 The Citadel (see p.111)
8 Around Ibn Tulun & S. Cemetery (see p.116)
9 Northern Cemetery (see p.121)
10 Old Cairo & Roda Island (see p.126-127)
11 Gezira & The West Bank (see p.138-139)

Tahrir Square (Midan Tahrir)

At the very heart of Cairo is the broad expanse of **Tahrir Square** (Midan Tahrir in Arabic), which gained worldwide fame as the centre of events during Egypt's **2011 revolution**. Originally called Ismailiya Square, it was nicknamed Midan Tahrir (Liberation Square) during an uprising against British rule in 1919 and was officially renamed as such after the revolution of 1952. It was only in 2011, however, that it really lived up to its new name (see box, p.72).

ACCOMMODATION

Amin	20	Luna	13
Berlin	14	Nile Ritz-Carlton	19
Cairo Downtown	21	Odeon Palace	12
Carlton	3	Pension Roma	9
Cosmopolitan	16	Select	10
Dahab	15	Semiramis	
Four Seasons	27	Intercontinental	24
Garden City House	23	Shepheard	25
Grand	5	Sultan	4
Happyton	1	Talisman	7
Isis	11	Travelers House	6
Ismailia House	22	Tulip	17
Kempinski Nile	26	Venice	
King Tut Hostel	8	Hosokawaya	4
Lotus	18	Windsor	2

BARS, NIGHTCLUBS & MUSIC VENUES

After Eight	8	Le Bistro	12
Barrel Lounge	3	Le Grillon	6
Bodega Orabi	1	MakAn	16
Café Riche	9	Napoleon Bar	15
Cafeteria Stella	10	Odeon Palace	5
El Horryia	13	Palmyra	4
Gamayka	7	Scarabee	14
Happy City	11	Scheharazade	2

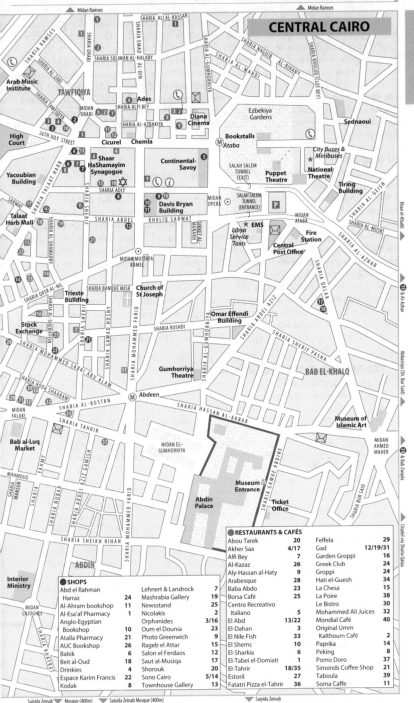

CENTRAL CAIRO

1

RESTAURANTS & CAFÉS

Abou Tarek	20	Felfela	29
Akher Saa	4/17	Gad	12/19/31
Alfi Bey	7	Garden Groppi	16
Al-Kazaz	26	Greek Club	24
Aly-Hassan al-Haty	9	Groppi	24
Arabesque	28	Hati el-Guesh	34
Baba Abdo	23	La Chesa	15
Borsa Café	25	La Poire	38
Centro Recreativo		Le Bistro	30
Italiano	5	Mohammed Ali Juices	32
El Abd	13/22	Mondial Café	40
El-Dahan	3	Original Umm	
El Nile Fish	33	Kalthoum Café	2
El Shems	10	Paprika	14
El-Sharkia	6	Peking	8
El-Tabei el-Domiati	1	Pomo Doro	37
El-Tahrir	18/35	Simonds Coffee Shop	21
Estoril	27	Taboula	39
Fatatri Pizza el-Tahrir	36	Soma Caffe	11

SHOPS

Abd el Rahman		Lehnert & Landrock	7
Harraz	24	Mashrabia Gallery	19
Al-Ahram bookshop	11	Newsstand	25
Al-Esa'af Pharmacy	1	Nicolakis	2
Anglo-Egyptian		Orphanides	3/16
Bookshop	10	Oum el Dounia	23
Atalla Pharmacy	21	Photo Greenwich	9
AUC Bookshop	26	Rageb el Attar	15
Babik	6	Salon el Ferdaos	12
Beit al-Oud	18	Saut al-Musiqa	17
Drinkies	4	Shorouk	20
Espace Karim Francis	22	Sono Cairo	5/14
Kodak	8	Townhouse Gallery	13

Saiyida Zeinab Mosque (400m) · Saiyida Zeinab Mosque (400m) · Saiyida Zeinab

1

The entrances to **Sadat metro station** serve as pedestrian underpasses linking the various buildings around Tahrir Square and the main roads leading off it. Despite clear signage in English, some of the exits are sometimes closed, and it's always easy to go astray in the maze of subways and surface at the wrong location; most Cairenes prefer to take the chances crossing by road, though that can be a nerve-wracking experience for newcomers.

To watch the square over tea, try one of the **cafés** to the west of Sharia Talaat Harb, the main street leading north through the downtown area. The café nearest to Sharia Talaat Harb, the *Wadi al-Nil*, was the target of a 1993 bomb attack by Islamic radicals, apparently because they didn't like the Sudanese cannabis dealers who used to hang out in it.

Al-Mugamma

Dominating the southern side of Tahrir Square is a concave office block that inspires shuddering memories: **Al-Mugamma**. A "fraternal gift" from the Soviet Union in the 1960s, this Kafkaesque warren of gloomy corridors, dejected queues and idle bureaucrats houses the public departments of the Interior, Health and Education ministries, and the Cairo Governorate, and is the place to go for visa renewals and extensions (see p.205). How many of the fifty thousand people visiting Al-Mugamma each day suffer nervous breakdowns from sheer frustration at the bureaucratic nightmare is anyone's guess – according to legend more than one person has thrown themselves to their death from its windows in despair.

The street heading past the east side of Al-Mugamma, **Sharia Qasr al-Aini**, leads on to the **National Assembly**, and, further east, the main building of the **Interior Ministry** (see p.87). The result is that, at the time of writing, the first two blocks of Sharia Qasr al-Aini (down to Sharia Rustam) and the streets to its east are sealed off with barbed wire and blockades, necessitating long detours to get around them.

TAHRIR AND THE REVOLUTION

On **25 January 2011**, inspired by the revolution in Tunisia which kicked off the Arab Spring, Cairenes held a **"Day of Rage"** protest, which steadily grew and eventually became irresistable as more and more people joined in. By 1 February, the crowd had swelled to well over a quarter of a million people (some reports even claimed a million), noisily demanding the resignation of dictator Hosni Mubarak, The next two days saw violent attacks on the protestors by regime supporters – including horse and camel hustlers from the Giza pyramids, mounted on their beasts, thus giving the events their popular name, **Battle of the Camel**. Among those defending the square were fighting football supporters ("ultras") of the Cairo clubs Zamalek and, in particular, Ahly. During the battle, rooftop snipers fired on the protestors, and the **death toll** mounted to some three hundred, but the people stood firm. Eventually, on 11 February, finally bowing to the inevitable, **Mubarak resigned**. As celebrating Egyptians streamed into Tahrir across the 6th October Bridge, news reports worldwide made Tahrir (Liberation) Square an international symbol of people power, inspiring protestors in Syria, Libya, Yemen and even Spain, the United States and Britain.

Since then, the square has had a semi-permanent encampment of protestors demanding full democracy and the retirement of the army from political life. **Violence** has sometimes flared up anew, as on 20 November 2011, when police tried unsuccessfully to clear the square, and on the first anniversary of the Battle of the Camel, after the killing of **74 Ahly supporters** at a football match in what was seen as revenge for the Ahly ultras' defence of the revolutionaries the previous year. Foreign reporters have also on occasion been targeted. On the other hand, there sometimes seems to be an almost carnival atmosphere around the protestors' encampment, with street food on offer and the inevitable revolution T-shirts on sale (on the corner of Sharia Talaat Harb in particular). Nonetheless, it's wise to **exercise caution** when visiting the square, take advice from local people such as your hotelier, don't wave your camera about too ostentatiously, and stay away when there is trouble in the air. Tensions rise on **Fridays** in particular, especially after midday prayers.

West of Tahrir Square to the Nile

On the west side of the Mugamma the **Omar Makram Mosque** is where funeral receptions for deceased VIPs are held in brightly coloured marquees. Behind it is Egypt's **Ministry of Foreign Affairs**, still army-controlled. Across Sharia Tahrir from here, the secretariat of the **Arab League**, a tan-coloured edifice built during the 1960s, is a vestige of the time when Egypt was acknowledged leader of the "progressive" Arab cause. After Sadat's treaty with Israel, the Arab League moved its headquarters to Tunis, but in 1992 the League returned to Cairo and, with it, posses of limos and gun-toting guards.

West from here, **Sharia Tahrir** leads past two guardian lions and across **Tahrir Bridge** to Gezira Island (see p.137) and on to Dokki (see p.142). Just south of the bridge down the Corniche (the road that runs along the bank of the Nile), roughly opposite the **Shepheard Hotel**, was the site of the Thomas Cook landing stage, where generations of tourists embarked on Nile cruises, and where British General Gordon's ill-fated expedition set off for Khartoum in 1883 in a vain attempt to wrest Sudan from the Mahdi's nationalist forces.

The Egyptian Museum

Downtown Cairo's star attraction is the **Egyptian Museum**, or to give it its full title, the Museum of Egyptian Antiquities. Founded in 1858 by Auguste Mariette, who excavated the Serapeum at Saqqara and several major temples in Upper Egypt (and who was later buried in the museum grounds), it has long since outgrown its present building and can now scarcely warehouse all its pharaonic artefacts, with 136,000 exhibits, and forty thousand more items still crated in the basement. A new Grand Egyptian Museum (see p.157), which will house some or all the exhibits in the present one, is already under construction by the pyramids of Giza, and is due to open in around 2013. Meanwhile, for all the chaos, poor lighting and captioning of the old museum, the richness of the collection makes this one of the world's few truly great museums.

A single visit of three to four hours suffices to cover the Tutankhamun exhibition and a few other **highlights**. Everyone has their favourites, but a reasonable shortlist might include, on the ground floor, the Amarna galleries (**rooms 3 and 8**), and the cream of statuary from the Old, Middle and New kingdoms (**rooms 42, 32, 22 and 12**), and, on the upper floor, the Fayoum Portraits (**Room 14**), and of course the Royal Mummies (**Rooms 52 and 56**) – though these cost extra. **Information** on the exhibits themselves is extremely sparse. Due to different systems of numbering being added at different times, some exhibits in the museum now have three different numbers, but very often no other labelling at all. When identifying exhibits by number in the account which follows, we have given the number which is the most prominent.

The **water lilies** growing in the pond in front of the main entrance are the now-rare blue lotus, a mildly psychoactive plant used by the ancient Egyptians – frescoes and reliefs from ancient Egypt show these lotuses being dipped into wine to enhance their effects.

INFORMATION

EGYPTIAN MUSEUM

Address Northern end of Tahrir Square

Opening hours Sat–Thurs 9am–7pm, Fri 9am–5pm (Ramadan daily 9am–4pm); last ticket sold one hour before closing.

Admission £E60

Photography No cameras are allowed inside (they can be deposited at the entrance)

Guides You'll probably be offered a guided tour outside the museum, by the camera deposit; these generally last

two hours (at around £E80/hour, depending on your bargaining skills), though the museum deserves more like six. The guides are extremely knowledgeable and do help you to make sense of it all. Alternatively, audioguides can be rented (£E20) from just inside the museum entrance.

Guidebooks The museum's bookshop (by the exit, and still under construction at the time of writing) should stock guidebooks, such as the full-colour *The Egyptian Museum in Cairo – An Illustrated Guide* (Farid Atiyah Press;

£E250) and the smaller *Pocket Book of the Egyptian Museum in Cairo* (Abydos Publications; £E150), both of which locate the featured exhibits by room (though not in order). Another excellent book, sold at the American University bookshop (see p.201) is the AUC's *Illustrated Guide to the Egyptian Museum* (£E150), which has a room-by-room picture index at the back to help you find what you are looking at in the text.

Ground floor

Exhibits are arranged more or less chronologically, so that by starting at the entrance and walking in a clockwise direction round the outer galleries you'll pass through the Old, Middle and New kingdoms, before ending up with the Late and Greco-Roman periods in the east wing. A snappier alternative is to proceed instead through the Atrium – which samples the whole era of pharaonic civilization – to the superb Amarna gallery in the northern wing, then backtrack to cover sections that sound interesting, or instead head upstairs to Tutankhamun. Whichever approach you decide on, it's worth starting with the Atrium foyer (**Room 43**), where the dynastic saga begins.

The Rotunda

The **Rotunda**, inside the museum entrance, kicks off with **monumental sculptures** from various eras, notably (in the four corners) three colossi of the XIX Dynasty pharaoh

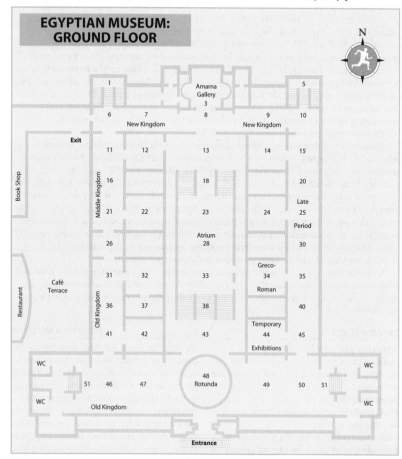

Ramses II and a statue of Amenhotep, son of the XVIII Dynasty royal architect Hapu (near right-hand corner). In a glass case to the left as you enter is the limestone **statue of King Zoser** (#16), installed within its *serdab* beside his step pyramid at Saqqara (see p.161) in the 27th century BC and removed by archeologists 4600 years later.

The forging of dynastic rule is commemorated by a famous exhibit in **Room 43**. A decorative version of the slate palettes used to grind kohl eye make-up, the **Palette of Narmer** (#111) records the unification of the Two Lands (c.3100 BC) by a ruler called Narmer or Menes. One side of the palette depicts him wearing the White Crown of Upper Egypt, smiting an enemy with a mace, while a falcon (Horus) ensnares another prisoner and tramples the heraldic papyrus of Lower Egypt. The reverse face shows him wearing their Red Crown to inspect the slain, and ravaging a fortress as a bull. Dividing these tableaux are mythical beasts with entwined necks, restrained from conflict by bearded men, an arcane symbol of his political achievement.

Ahead and to the left, just before the steps down into the Atrium, are fragments of two **Libyan palettes**, the first of which (missing its top half) is beautifully carved with trains of bulls, donkeys and goats, and a grove of olive trees. A century or so older than Narmer's palette, it seems to have been made to commemorate the payment of a tribute to the Upper Egyptian ruler by the Tjemehu tribe of Libya.

The Atrium

Descending into **Room 33**, the Atrium proper, you'll find two black, polished **pyramidions** (pyramid capstones) from Dahshur, and several sarcophagi from the New Kingdom. Outshining those of Tuthmosis I and Queen Hatshepsut (before she became pharaoh) is the **sarcophagus of Merneptah** (#213), surmounted by a figure of the XIX Dynasty king as Osiris, protectively embraced from within by a bas-relief of the sky goddess Nut. When discovered at Tanis in 1939, Merneptah's sarcophagus actually held the coffin of Psusennes, a XXI Dynasty ruler whose gold-sheathed mummy now lies upstairs in Room 2 (see p.81).

At the centre of the Atrium is a **painted floor** from Akhenaten's palace at Tell el-Amarna in Middle Egypt showing a river brimming with ducks and fish and framed by reeds where waterfowl and cows amble – a fine example of the lyrical naturalism of the Amarna period. For more of this revolutionary epoch in pharaonic history, head upstairs past the **colossal statues** of Akhenaten's parents, Amenophis III and Queen Tiy, with their three daughters, to rooms 3 and 8 in the North Wing (see p.77).

At the top of the stairs into **Room 13**, off to the right of two reconstructed gateways, you'll find Merneptah's Victory Stele from the temple of Karnak, otherwise known as the **Israel Stele** (#134). Its name derives from the boast "Israel is crushed; its seed is no more", among a list of Merneptah's conquests – the sole known reference to Israel in all the records of Ancient Egypt. Partly on the strength of this, some scholars believe that Merneptah, the son of Ramses II, was the pharaoh of the biblical Exodus.

Room 47

The southwest corner of the ground floor is devoted to the **Old Kingdom** (c.2700–2181 BC), when the III–VI dynasties ruled Egypt from Memphis and built the Pyramids. On the north side of **Room 47**, six wooden panels from the tomb of Hesy-Re (#21) portray this senior scribe of the III Dynasty, who was also the earliest known dentist. Three slate triads, or triple statues, represent the III Dynasty ruler Menkaure, flanked by the goddess Hathor and a lesser provincial deity. The two alabaster lion tables were probably used for sacrifices or libations during the II Dynasty. The room's most striking exhibit is a case (#54 and 65, just before Room 46) containing statuettes of Khnumhotep, Overseer of the Wardrobe, a man evidently afflicted by Pott's disease (tuberculosis of the spine), which left him with a hunchback, a deformed head and reduced stature.

1

Room 42

Around the corner, **Room 42** boasts a superb **statue of Chephren**, the pharaoh of Giza's second pyramid (see p. 155), his head embraced by the hawk-headed god Horus (#31). Carved from black diorite, whose white marbling emphasizes the sinews of his knee and clenched fist, the statue comes from Chephren's valley temple at Giza. Even more arresting, on the left, is the wooden **statue of Ka-aper** (#40), an amazingly lifelike figure with an introspective gaze, which members of the digging team at Saqqara called "Sheikh al-Balad" because it so resembled their own village headman. One of the two restored wooden statues just beyond him may well be the same man. To the left of the doorway as you exit, the **statue of a scribe** (#43) shows him poised for notation, with an open scroll across his knees.

Rooms 31, 32 and 37

Usually, the highlight of **Room 31** is a beautiful life-size **copper statue** of VI Dynasty pharaoh Pepi I (#129) from Hierakonpolis in Upper Egypt (see p.324), and another of his son Merenre. Both have been taken away for restoration, but should be back in place by the time you read this.

Next door, **Room 32** is dominated by life-size seated **statues of Prince Rahotep and Princess Nefert** (IV Dynasty) from their mastaba at Maidum (#27). His skin is painted brick-red, hers a creamy yellow – a distinction common in Egyptian art. Nefert wears a wig and diadem and swathes herself in a diaphanous wrap; the prince is simply clad in a waist cloth. Look out for the **tableau of the dwarf Seneb and his family** on the left (#39). Embraced by his wife, this Overseer of the Wardrobe seems contented; his naked children hold their fingers to their lips. In the second niche on the north (left-hand) wall, don't miss the perfectly observed, vividly stylized mural, known as the **Maidum Geese** (III/IV Dynasty), depicting three different types of goose in superbly realistic detail, nor the painted relief of boatmen fighting (#60, to the right of the door as you exit).

In the adjoining **Room 37**, the **furniture of Queen Hetepheres** (III Dynasty) has been expertly reconstructed from heaps of gold and rotten wood. As the wife of Snofru and mother of Cheops, she was buried near her son's pyramid at Giza with a sedan chair, gold vessels and a canopied bed. Also in the room, in a cabinet of its own, is a tiny **statuette of Cheops** (#143), the only known likeness of the Great Pyramid pharaoh.

Rooms 26, 22 and 16

With **Room 26** you enter the **Middle Kingdom**, when centralized authority was restored and pyramid building resumed under the XII Dynasty (c.1991–1786 BC), but the enthroned **statue of Mentuhotpe Nebhepetre** (on the right) is a relic of the previous era of civil wars, termed the First Intermediate Period (in fact, it was Mentuhotpe Nebhepetre, founder of the XI Dynasty, who finally ended the wars and reunited the country). Glum-faced, and endowed with hulking feet and black skin to symbolize his royal power, plus crossed arms and a curly beard to link him to Osiris, the statue was buried near his funerary shrine at Deir el-Bahri, and was discovered by Howard Carter when his horse fell through the roof.

The statuettes at the back of **Room 22** (#92) are striking for the uncharacteristic expressiveness of their faces, in contrast to the manic staring eyes of the wooden statue of Nakhti on the south (right-hand) side of the room, but the room's main exhibit is the **burial chamber of Harhotpe** from Deir el-Bahri, covered inside with pictorial objects, charms and texts. Surrounding the chamber are ten limestone **statues of Senusret** from his pyramid complex at Lisht, stiffly formal in contrast to his cedarwood figure in the case to the right as you enter the room (#88). The sides of these statues' thrones bear variations of the *sema-tawy* symbol of unification: Hapy the Nile god, or Horus and Seth, entwining the heraldic plants of the Two Lands.

At the northern end of **Room 16**, on the east side, an unusual **wooden ka-statue** of the XIII Dynasty ruler Hor (#75) is mounted on a sliding base, probably to signify his posthumous wanderings. The pair of hands sprouting from his head are the hieroglyphic symbol for the *ka*, or life-force which the ancient Egyptians believed would live on after their death, though it had to be sustained by offerings of food (either genuine, or depicted in their tomb).

Rooms 11 and 12

With **Room 11** you pass into the **New Kingdom**, an era of renewed pharaonic power and imperial expansion under the XVIII and XIX dynasties (c.1567–1200 or 1150–1186 BC). Egypt's African and Asian empires were forged by Tuthmosis III, who had long been frustrated while his unwarlike stepmother, Hatshepsut, ruled as pharaoh. The commanding stone head of Hatshepsut comes from one of the pillars of her great temple at Deir el-Bahri, in the Theban Necropolis across the river from Luxor.

In **Room 12** you'll find a grey schist statue of Tuthmosis III (#62, on the south side of the room) and other masterpieces of XVIII Dynasty art, but the main exhibit is the **Hathor Shrine** from Tuthmosis III's ruined temple at Deir el-Bahri. Inside it, a statue of the goddess in her bovine form emerges reborn from a papyrus swamp. Tuthmosis stands beneath her cow's head, and is suckled as an infant in the fresco behind Hathor's statue.

To the right of the shrine is a block statue (#418) of Hatshepsut's vizier, **Senenmut**, with the queen's daughter Neferure – the relationship between the queen, her daughter and her vizier has inspired much speculation. A smaller statue of the same duo is also usually on display here, but was absent on our last visit.

From the same period comes a section of the Deir el-Bahri "**Punt relief**" (#130, in the second niche on the room's north wall), showing the Queen of Punt, whose oddly shaped body suggests that she may have suffered from elephantiasis, although it could also indicate that she belonged to a Khoisan people like the San Bushmen of modern-day Namibia.

To the right of the Punt relief stands a grey granite **statue of the god Khonsu** with a sidelock denoting youth and a face thought to be that of the boy pharaoh Tutankhamun, which was taken from the temple of the moon-god at Karnak. Flanking this statue and the Punt relief, two statues of a man named **Amenhotep** portray him as a young scribe of humble birth (#6014, on the left) and as an octogenarian priest (#98, on the right), honoured for his direction of massive works like the Colossi of Memnon (see p.291).

Rooms 6 and 7

Before turning the corner into the northern wing, you encounter in **Room 6** two **lion-headed statues of Sekhmet**, found at Karnak. Right in the corner is a statue supposedly of the last XVIII Dynasty pharaoh, Horemheb, but the face looks a lot more like that of Tutankhamun, and the suspicion is that Horemheb simply took one of the boy king's statues and had his own cartouche inscribed on it.

A **sphinx** with the head of Hatshepsut welcomes you to **Room 7**, where among the first set of reliefs on the southern wall is one from the Tomb of Maya at Saqqara. The tomb was uncovered in the nineteenth century but subsequently lost, and only rediscovered in 1986.

The Amarna Gallery

Room 3 and much of the adjoining **Room 8** focus on the **Amarna period**, a break with centuries of tradition which barely outlasted the reign of Pharaoh Akhenaten (c.1352–1336 BC) and Queen Nefertiti (see box, pp.226–227). Rejecting Amun and the other deities of Thebes, they decreed the supremacy of a single god, the Aten, built a new capital at Amarna in Middle Egypt to escape the old bureaucracy, and left enigmatic works of art that still provoke a reaction. Some have suggested that the religion of the ancient Israelites – and hence Judaism, Christianity and Islam – was derived from the monotheistic cult instituted by Akhenaten.

In the centre of Room 3 is Akhenaten's carnelian-, gold- and glass-inlaid **coffin**, the upper half displayed alongside the gilding from the bottom part of the coffin. This gilding disappeared from the museum at some time between 1915 and 1931 but resurfaced in Switzerland in the 1980s. It has now been restored and mounted on a Plexiglas cast in the presumed shape of the original coffin.

Staring down from the walls of **Room 3** are four **colossi of Akhenaten**, whose attenuated skull and face, flaring lips and nostrils, rounded thighs and belly are suggestive of a hermaphrodite or a primeval earth goddess. Because these characteristics are carried over to the figures of his wife and daughters on certain **stelae** (such as those in the stele case in Room 8), **statuettes** (such as those in case #169 in Room 8) and tomb reliefs, it has been argued that the Amarna style pandered to some physical abnormality in Akhenaten (or the royal family). Others retort that the famous head of Nefertiti in Berlin proves that it was just a stylistic device.

Another feature of Amarna art was its note of **intimacy**: a statuette in Room 8 (case #162) portrays Akhenaten kissing their eldest daughter, Meritaten, and steles show Nefertiti cradling her sisters. For the first time in Egyptian art, breakfast was depicted. The Amarna focus on this world rather than the afterlife infused traditional subjects with new vitality – witness the freer brush strokes on the fragments of a **marsh scene**, displayed around the walls of Room 3 A case on the south side of Room 8 contains some of the **Amarna Letters** (others are in London and Berlin), recording pleas for troops to aid the pharaoh's vassals in Palestine. The letters were originally baked into earthen "envelopes" for delivery.

The Northeastern Galleries

The eastern section of Room 8 also contains a monumental **dyad of Amun and Mut**, smashed to pieces by medieval limestone quarriers and lovingly pieced together from fragments long lost in the vaults of the museum and at Karnak, where it originally stood. Those pieces that could not be fitted into the jigsaw are displayed in a case just behind it.

To the left of the stairs in **Room 10**, note the painted **relief** on a block from Ramses II's temple at Memphis, which shows him subjugating Egypt's foes. In a motif repeated on dozens of temple pylons, the king grabs the hair of a Libyan, Nubian and Syrian, and wields an axe. The room is dominated by a **statue of Ramses II and Haroun**, embodying an elaborate pun. Haroun was a Levantine sun-god whom the Ancient Egyptians regarded as an avatar of their own solar deity Re (or Ra); shown here protecting the child (mes) king, who holds in his left hand the heraldic sedge plant (su) – thereby combining the syllables Ra-mes-su, to form the pharaoh's name.

The East Wing

As an inducement to follow the New Kingdom into the East Wing, **Room 15** starts with, directly facing the statue of Ramses II as a child, a sexy statue of his daughter and consort Merytamun. The centrepiece of **Room 14** is a restored pink granite triple statue of Ramses III being crowned by Horus and Seth, representing order and chaos respectively. Of the diverse statues of deities in **Room 24**, the most striking by far is that of **Taweret** (or Tweri), the pregnant hippopotamus goddess of childbirth, on the left (#248). Very sleek, in smooth black slate, the statue was found in a sealed shrine at Karnak, which is why it is so well preserved.

Rooms 34 and **35** cover the **Greco-Roman Period** (332 BC onwards), when Classical art engaged with Ancient Egyptian symbolism. Facing you as you enter Room 34 is a coiled serpent, ready to strike, and to the left of it, in case D, an alabaster head of a very young-looking Alexander the Great. The meld of Egyptian and Greco-Roman styles is typified by the bizarre statues and sarcophagi down the corridor in **Room 49**, especially the **statue of a Ptolemaic king** (possibly Alexander II) at the threshold of the room. Room 44, on your way, sometimes hosts temporary exhibitions.

Upper floor

The museum's upper floor is dominated by the **Tutankhamun galleries**, which occupy the best part of two wings, comprising 1700 items in a dozen rooms, laid out roughly as they were packed into the boy-king's tomb. Given the brevity of his reign (c.1336-1327 BC) and the almost unassuming nature of his tomb itself when compared with others in the Valley of the Kings, the mind boggles at the treasure that must have been stashed with great pharaohs like Ramses or Seti.

The floor's other highlights are the Jewellery Rooms, the Mummy Room and the Fayoum Portraits, but Tutankhamun's treasures are best taken in together before going on to the rest of the upper floor.

Rooms 45 to 25

When Howard Carter's team penetrated the sealed corridor of the tomb in 1922 (see p.298), they found an antechamber, stuffed with caskets and detritus, that had been

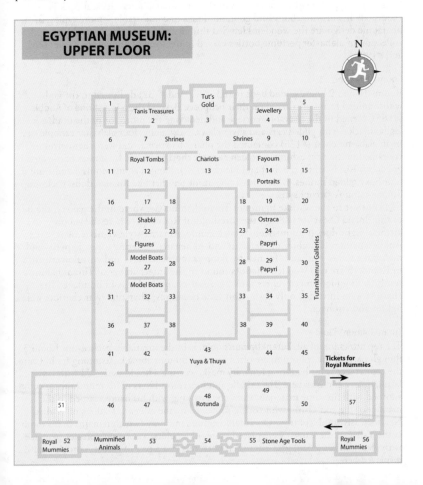

1

ransacked by robbers, and two life-size **ka statues of Tutankhamun** (flanking the doorway to **Room 45**), whose black skin symbolized his rebirth. Just beyond are golden **statues of Tutankhamun**, mostly depicting him hunting with a harpoon.

Room 35 is dominated by a **gilded throne** with winged-serpent arms and clawed feet (#179). Its seat back shows the royal couple relaxing in the rays of the Aten, their names given in the Amarna form – dating it to the time when Tutankhamun still observed the Amarna heresy. Tutankhamun's clothes were stored in the magnificent "**Painted Chest**", whose lid depicts him hunting ostriches and devastating ranks of Syrians in his war chariot; the end panels show him trampling other foes in the guise of the sphinx. Among the other worldly goods that the boy pharaoh carried with him into the next world are an ebony and ivory **gaming set** for playing *senet*, a game similar to draughts or checkers, seen in the next case on (#189), and a host of small **shabti figures** to fulfil any tasks the gods might set him.

Room 30 has a case of "**Prisoners' Canes**" (#187, by the doorway to Room 29), whose ebony- and ivory-inlaid figures symbolize the unity of north and south. A bust of the boy king emerging from a lotus (#118) shows the continued influence of the Amarna artistic style during Tutankhamun's reign. The "**ecclesiastical throne**" (#181) in **Room 25** is a prototype for episcopal thrones of the Christian Church. Its seat back is exquisitely inlaid with ebony and gold, but looks uncomfortable – more typical of pharaonic design are the wooden Heb-Sed throne and footstools. Beyond is a collection of **alabaster perfume bottles** carved in the form of animals or deities (#61 and #190).

Rooms 10–7 and 13

Rooms 10 and 9 house **gilded beds** (#183, #221 and #732) dedicated to the gods whose animal forms are carved on their bedposts. Beyond these is a **shrine of Anubis** (#185), carried in the pharaoh's cortege and depicting the protector of the dead as a vigilant jackal with gilded ears and silver claws. Next along, four alabaster **canopic jars** in an alabaster chest (#176) contained the pharaoh's viscera, and were themselves contained in the next exhibit, a golden **canopic chest** protected by statues of the goddesses Isis, Nephthys, Selket and Neith (#177). Ranged along rooms 8 and 7 are four boxy **gilded shrines**, which fitted one inside another like Russian dolls, enclosing Tutankhamun's sarcophagus.

In contrast to the warlike figures of Tutankhamun elsewhere in the gallery, the lid of the "**Inlaid Chest**" (#188) on the threshold of Room 13 (where the yellow artificial light does it no justice) shows a gentle, Amarna-style vignette of Ankhesenamun (daughter of Nefertiti and Akhenaten) offering lotus, papyrus and mandrake to her husband, framed by poppies, pomegranates and cornflowers. Also in Room 13 are two wooden **chariots** found in the antechamber of Tutankhamun's tomb, with gilded stucco reliefs showing Asiatics and Nubians in bondage. The chariots were intended only for use on state occasions; pharaonic war chariots were lighter and stronger.

Tutankhamun's Gold

The top attraction of all, **Tutankhamun's gold**, is in the invariably packed-out Room 3, though parts of the collection are often sent out on tour abroad. Assuming it's in Cairo, the centrepiece is his haunting **funerary mask**, wearing a headdress inlaid with lapis lazuli, quartz and obsidian. The middle and innermost layers of his mummiform **coffin**, adorned with the same materials, show the boy king with his hands clasped in the manner of the god Osiris, while being protected by the *cloisonné* feathers of Wadjet, Nekhbet, Isis and Nephthys. On Tutankhamun's mummy (which remains in his tomb at the Valley of the Kings) were placed scores of **amulets**, a *cloisonné* **corselet** spangled with glass and carnelian, gem-encrusted **pectorals** and a pair of golden **sandals** – all displayed here.

The Jewellery Rooms

Flanking Tutankhamun's gold in Room 3, the two **Jewellery Rooms** (Rooms 4 and 2) are almost as breathtaking. The star attraction and centrepiece of **Room 4** is the VI Dynasty golden **head of a falcon** (once attached to a copper body) from Hierakonpolis (see p.324). On the right-hand side of the room (anticlockwise from the door), is the **Treasure of Queen Hetephres** (IV Dynasty) apparently discovered by accident in 1925 when a phtographer's tripod fell through a hole in the ground at Giza. Treasures from the XII Dynasty **Princess Mereret** and **Queen Weret** include necklaces, bracelets and anklets of gold, carnelian, lapis lazuli and turquoise, a classic Egyptian combination, as well as necklaces of amethyst.

On the left-hand side of the room (anticlockwise from the back), the ceremonial **axe of Ahmosis** (founder of the XVIII Dynasty), commemorating his expulsion of the Hyksos from Egypt, was buried in the tomb of his mother, Queen Ahhotep. From the same cache (discovered by the museum's founder, French Egyptologist Auguste Mariette, in 1859) came some stunning **gold collars** and the bizarre **golden flies** of the Order of Valour – bug-eyed decorations for bravery. The last exhibits, by the door, include some very chunky **gold necklaces** of Apis bulls (see p.165) in their shrines, hung on fine gold wire.

Displayed in **Room 2**, the **Treasure of Tanis** comes from the XXI–XXII Dynasty, when northern Egypt was ruled from the Delta. Of the three royal caches unearthed by French Egyptologist Pierre Montet in 1939, the richest was that of Psusennes I, whose coffin, made of silver and electrum (an alloy of silver and gold), was found inside the sarcophagus of Merneptah (which is downstairs). His gold necklace is made from rows of discs, in the New Kingdom style.

The Mummy Room

££100 • Sat–Thurs 9am–6pm, Fri 9am–5pm (Ramadan daily 9am–4pm)

The famous **Mummy Room** (previously Room 52) was closed by President Sadat in 1981 because the exhibition of human remains offended many religious people, but this gave the museum and the Getty Institute an opportunity to restore the badly decomposed royal mummies. The results of their work are now displayed in Room 56, where you have to buy another ticket to see them. In deference to the deceased, no guiding is allowed, and the low hum of *sotto voce* chatter is only broken by the attendant periodically calling for "Silence, please!"

The eleven mummies on display were found in a spare chamber in the tomb of Amenophis II in the Valley of the Kings, and in a cache at nearby Deir el-Bahri, where they had been reburied during the XXI Dynasty to protect them from grave robbers. They include those of some of the most famous pharaohs, including the great conquerors of the XIX Dynasty, **Seti I** and his son **Ramses II**, the latter looking rather slighter in the flesh than the massive statues of him at Memphis and elsewhere. Most of them seem remarkably peaceful – **Tuthmosis II** and **Tuthmosis IV** could almost be sleeping – and many still have hair.

Mummification techniques evolved over millennia, reaching their zenith by the New Kingdom, when embalmers offered three levels of mummification. The deluxe version entailed removing the brain (which was discarded) and the viscera (which were preserved in canopic jars), dehydrating the cadaver in natron salts for about forty days, and packing it to reproduce lifelike contours. For a graphic demonstration of the hollowness of a mummy, take a look up Ramses V's right nostril – from this angle you'll be able to see straight out through the hole in his skull.

Even if you decide not to view the royal mummies, the **mummified animals** in Room 53 can be seen at no extra cost. Drawn from necropolises across Egypt, they evince the diversity of animal cults in ancient times, when devotees embalmed everything from crocodiles to birds and fish. Here too you'll find a series of **panels** from the Sun Temple of Userkaf at Saqqara, the first known example of natural scenes being used as

1

decoration within a royal edifice – a pied kingfisher, purple gallinule and sacred ibis are clearly recognizable.

The West Wing

Starting down the **west wing** of the upper floor from Tutankhamun's galleries, **Room 12**'s hoard of objects from **XVIII Dynasty royal tombs** includes priestly wigs and wig boxes (in Case L), a libation table flanked by two leopards from the funerary cache of Amenophis II (#3842), and part of the chariot of Tuthmosis IV (#4113). **Room 17** holds the **contents of private tombs**, notably that of Sennedjem, from the Workmen's Village near the Valley of the Kings. With skills honed on royal tombs, Sennedjem carved himself a stylish vault; its door (#215) depicts him playing *senet* (see p.80). The beautiful gold-painted sarcophagus of his son Khonsu carries a design showing the lions of Today and Yesterday supporting the rising sun, while Anubis embalms his mummy under the protection of Isis and Nephthys.

The South Wing

By the southeast stairway in Room 50 is the cubic **leather funerary tent** (#3848) of an XXI Dynasty queen, decorated in red-and-green checkered squares. **Room 43** houses objects from the **tomb of Yuya and Thuya**, who, as parents of Queen Tiy (wife of Amenophis III), were buried in the Valley of the Kings; their tomb was found intact in the late nineteenth century. The finest objects from it are the two mummiform coffins, Thuya's gilded funeral mask and statuettes of the couple. Hidden away by the entrance to Room 42 is a panel of blue faïence tiles from Zoser's burial hall at Saqqara (#17).

In Room 48, on the west side, is a display case (#155) containing a stone head of Akhenaten's mum, and Yuya and Thuya's daughter, **Queen Tiy**, that prefigures the Amarna style. The same case also contains statues of "**dancing dwarves**", believed to be modelled on equatorial Forest People ("Pygmies"), who were far more widespread throughout Africa in those days. The same case also holds a beautiful, very lifelike wooden statuette of a Nubian woman, possibly Queen Tiy, with her hair in braids, looking surprisingly modern. Next to it, another case (#82) contains a striking bright blue faïence hippopotamus.

The East Wing

If approached from the north, the **eastern wing** begins with **Room 14**, containing a couple of mummies and the superbly lifelike but sadly ill-lit "**Fayoum Portraits**" found by British egyptologist Flinders Petrie at Hawara. Painted in encaustic (pigments mixed into molten wax) while their sitters were alive, the portraits were glued onto Greco-Roman mummies (100–250 AD). The staggering diversity of Egypt's pantheon by the late pagan era is suggested by the **statues of deities** in **Room 19**. The tiny statuettes are worth a closer look, especially those of the pregnant hippo goddess Sekhmet (in Case C), Harpocrates (Horus as a child), Ibis-headed Thoth and the dwarf god Ptah-soker (all in Case E), a couple of whose figurines (third shelf down, on the left), look almost Mexican, as do some of the statuettes of Bes in Case P. In the centre of the room, look out for the gold and silver image of Horus in Case V, apparently the case for a mummified hawk.

Room 24 next door, and Room 29 beyond that, are devoted to **ostraca and papyri**. Ostraca were limestone flakes or potsherds on which were scratched sketches or ephemeral writing; papyrus was used for finished artwork and lasting **manuscripts**. Besides the *Book of the Dead* (**rooms 1 and 24**) and the *Book of Amduat* (depicting the Weighing of the Heart ceremony; on the south side of **Room 29** above Cabinet 51), note the *Satirical Papyrus* (#232 in Cabinet 9 on the north side), showing mice being served by cats. Painted during the Hyksos period (see p. 598), the cats represent the Egyptians, the mice their rulers, who came from countries that were part of Egypt's former empire, implying that rule of Egyptians by foreigners is not the natural order.

Talaat Harb and around

The main road through the former Ismailiya quarter, Suleyman Pasha Street was once an elegant boulevard lined with trees and sidewalk cafés. Since being renamed **Sharia Talaat Harb** (many Cairenes still use its old name) the street has seen its once elegant facades effaced by grime and neglect, tacky billboards and glitzy facings. Yet its vitality and diversity have never been greater, as thousands of Cairenes come here to window-shop, pop into juice bars and surge into cinemas. Number 17, decorated with old postcards of the city, is the **Café Riche** (see p.190), where the Free Officers supposedly plotted their overthrow of Egypt's monarchy; another version maintains that they communicated over the telephone in **Groppi** (see p.188), a famous coffee house on **Midan Talaat Harb**, at the intersection with Qasr al-Nil. Here too stands a statue of Talaat Harb himself (1876–1941), nationalist lawyer and founder of the National Bank. Further north, Number 34, next door to the Miami Theatre, is the **Yacoubian Building**, immortalized in Alaa Al Aswany's bestselling 2002 novel of the same name (see p.627), though the real building differs somewhat from the fictional version.

Shaar HaShamayim Synagogue

Sharia Adly • Daily 10am–6pm • Donation expected • Bring your passport to get in

A couple of blocks east of Sharia Talaat Harb, on the north side of Sharia Adly, you'll see a buff, temple-like edifice like something out of a Cecil B. de Mille movie. This is the **Shaar HaShamayim Synagogue**, the main house of prayer for Cairo's now much reduced Jewish community. Because of the threat of attack by Islamic fundamentalists, the synagogue is surrounded by armed police, who don't take kindly to tourists pointing cameras at it – which is a pity, because it's actually one of downtown Cairo's most photogenic buildings. Though it looks like a piece of Art Deco, the synagogue was actually built well before that era, in 1905. The palm trees on the facade are a symbol peculiar to Egyptian Jewry; the interior is also impressive, with its high dome, stained-glass windows and opulent marble fittings. Nowadays services are held only at the Jewish New Year (around Sept), and Yom Kippur (the Day of Atonement, ten days after the New Year).

26th July Street

The busiest, widest thoroughfare of downtown Cairo is **Sharia Setta w'Ashreen Yulyu** – more easily rendered as **26th July Street** – which runs west across the Nile to Zamalek and Mohandiseen, and east to Midan Opera. It was once called Sharia al-Malik Fouad (a name still quite commonly used), after King Fouad, who reigned 1917–36; the current name commemorates the date on which his son King Farouk abdicated in 1952, following a bloodless coup by the Free Officers three days earlier. The **Cicurel building**, on the corner of Sharia Emad al-Din, and the **Ades building**, with its stylish corner tower, a couple of blocks north, were both originally Jewish-owned department stores, expropriated after the Suez Crisis in 1957.

Midan Opera

At the eastern end of 26th July Street is **Midan Opera**, named after an opera house constructed here in the 1860s, when Cairo's centre was rebuilt; symbolically, the building faced west, overlooking the Ismailiya quarter rather than Islamic Cairo. The square's centrepiece, an equestrian statue of **Ibrahim Pasha**, by Cordier, honours Ismail's father. The Opera House burned down in 1971 (a multistorey car park now occupies the site) while other colonial buildings were torched on "**Black Saturday**" (January 26, 1952), when protestors reacted to the killing of Egyptian police by British troops in Ismailiya (see p.512) by burning down numerous of colonial institutions.

1

THE CONTINENTAL-SAVOY HOTEL

On the west side of Midan Opera, the **Continental-Savoy Hotel** was once the city's top hotel, rivalling *Shepheard*'s just up the street and boasting the finest restaurant in colonial Cairo. It opened in 1869, and was soon a favourite among visiting VIPs. Guests included Lawrence of Arabia, who stayed here at the beginning of World War One, and at the end of the war, Australian soldiers celebrated with a massive pillow fight on the hotel's grand staircase. Lord Carnarvon, who financed the excavation of Tutankhamun's tomb, died in his room here in 1923, supposedly a victim of the pharaoh's curse, and other guests included American journalist Henry Morton Stanley, of "Dr Livingstone, I presume" fame. In 1941, Orde Wingate, the eccentric military genius who later led the British commandos known as Chindits against the Japanese in Burma, attempted suicide in his room here by stabbing himself in the neck with a Bowie knife. Luckily for Britain's southeast Asian war effort, he failed.

The hotel closed in the 1980s, and is now largely disused, its grand halls empty and neglected, inaccessible to the public and largely derelict. Much of the building is in danger of collapse. Its future remains uncertain, but it would need a huge amount of rebuilding to ever open again as a hotel.

Midan Ataba and around

Behind Midan Opera car park, a minibus depot and split-level thoroughfares render **Midan Ataba** just as Yusuf Idris described it in *The Dregs of the City*: "a madhouse of pedestrians and automobiles, screeching wheels, howling klaxons, the whistles of bus conductors and roaring motors".

Nearby are three wonderful **belle époque department stores**, though all are now but shadows of their former selves. Only **Sednaoui**, just off Sharia Khulud (aka Clot Bey), still functions as a single grand store, and it's worth popping in to check out the atrium with its huge chandeliers and spectacular glass ceiling. **Omar Effendi** on Sharia Abdel Aziz, and **Tiring**, just off Midan Ataba itself, have long been divided up into offices and smaller shops, but their early twentieth-century exteriors are still impressive. Tiring, topped by a globe upheld by four Atlas figures, is known to Egyptians as the Al-Tofaha Building after a 1997 film of that name, in which the star, Leila Elwi admires the globe from her rooftop hovel.

Ezbekiya Gardens

The **Ezbekiya Gardens**, to the north of Midan Ataba, were laid out in the 1870s by the former chief gardener of Paris, forming a twenty-acre park. Subsequent extensions to 26th July Street reduced them to trampled islands amid a sea of commerce and traffic, and construction of metro line 3 has reduced the gardens even further, leaving only the southwestern corner (now enclosed to preserve its magnificent banyan tree). The **secondhand book market** on the gardens' eastern side is increasingly hemmed in by all the building work going on around it, but it's still a draw for English- and Arabic-speaking bibliophiles.

EZBEKIYA BACK IN THE DAY

In medieval times a lake fed by the Nasiri Canal and surrounded by orchards existed on the site of present Ezbekiya Gardens, but in 1470 the Mamluke emir (general) **Ezbek** built a palace, inspiring other beys and wealthy merchants to follow suit. During the French occupation Napoleon commandeered the sumptuous palace of **Alfi Bey**, and his successor Kléber promoted Western innovations such as windmills, printing presses and a balloon launch – which embarrassingly failed. Later in the nineteenth century, two of Egyptian tourism's founding institutions overlooked Ezbekiya from a site bounded by Alfi Bey and Sharia Al-Gumhorriya. Here, **Shepheard's Hotel** (founded in 1841) once flourished alongside the **Thomas Cook Agency**, which pioneered tourist "expeditions" in the 1870s. Rebuilt more grandly in 1891, Shepheard's famous terrace, Moorish Hall and *Long Bar* were destroyed in 1952 by Black Saturday rioters (see p.83).

Sharia Clot Bey

When Mohammed Ali created a military high road to link the Citadel with Cairo's new railway station, he named it after the French physician Antoine Clot – whom he ennobled for introducing Western ideas of public health to Egypt. Mohammed Ali little dreamed that **Sharia Clot Bey** (spelt Klot Bek on some street signs, but now officially Sharia Khulud) and the then-fashionable area north of Ezbekiya would

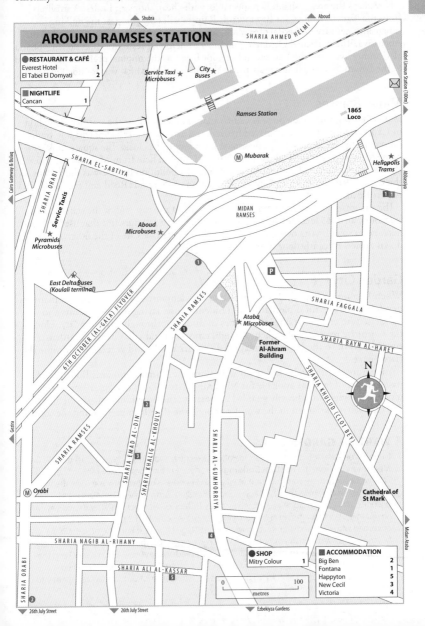

AROUND RAMSES STATION

● **RESTAURANT & CAFÉ**
Everest Hotel 1
El Tabei El Domyati 2

■ **NIGHTLIFE**
Cancan 1

● **SHOP**
Mitry Colour 1

■ **ACCOMMODATION**
Big Ben 2
Fontana 1
Happyton 5
New Cecil 3
Victoria 4

Shubra
Aboud
SHARIA AHMED HELMI
Kobri Limoun Station (100m)
Service Taxi Microbuses
City Buses
Ramses Station
1865 Loco
Mubarak
Heliopolis Trams
Abbassiya
Cairo Gateway & Bulaq
SHARIA EL-SABTIYA
SHARIA ORABI
Service Taxis
Pyramids Microbuses
Aboud Microbuses
MIDAN RAMSES
East Delta Buses (Koulali terminal)
6TH OCTOBER (AL-GALA) FLYOVER
SHARIA RAMSES
SHARIA FAGGALA
Ataba Microbuses
SHARIA BAYN AL-HARET
Former Al-Ahram Building
Gezira
SHARIA RAMSES
SHARIA EMAD AL-DIN
SHARIA KHALIG AL-KHOULY
SHARIA AL-GUMHORRIYA
SHARIA KHULUD (CLOT BEY)
N
Orabi
Cathedral of St Mark
Midan Ataba
SHARIA NAGIB AL-RIHANY
SHARIA ORABI
SHARIA ALI AL-KASSAR
0   100
metres
26th July Street
26th July Street
Ezbekiyza Gardens

1

degenerate into a red-light district, the **Wasa'a**, known to generations of foreign soldiers. During World War II, activities centred on Wagh al-Birket, known as "**the Berka**": a long street with curtained alleys leading off beneath balconies where the (mainly Italian) prostitutes would sit fanning themselves. The area's bars, brothels and hashish dens all paid protection to the "king of the Wasa'a", Ibrahim al-Gharby, an obese Nubian gangster known for dressing in feminine silk gowns.

Nowadays the area is shabbily respectable, with cheap shops and cafés. A stroll up from the gardens along Clot Bey towards Ramses will take you past the hulking nineteenth-century **Cathedral of St Mark**, now superseded by the Coptic cathedral in Abbassiya. The porticoed Ottoman pile (now undergoing restoration) at no. 117 Sharia al-Gumhorriya, near the Ramses end of Clot Bey, was the **original premises of Al-Ahram** ("The Pyramids"), the first newspaper in the Arab world, which was founded in 1875.

Midan Ramses

Midan Ramses, the square outside Cairo's main rail terminal, is the northern ganglion of Cairo's transport system. Splayed flyovers and arterial roads, haemorrhaging traffic onto darting pedestrians, keep the square busy round the clock. The square took its name from a red granite Colossus of Ramses II, moved here from Memphis in 1955. By 2006 poor Ramses had become so corroded by pollution that he was shifted out to the Giza Pyramids, now standing at the junction of Pyramids Road and the Alexandria Desert Road.

The square's main focus is **Ramses Station** itself. At the east end of the station forecourt, an **1865 locomotive** is the only remnant of a rail museum that used to stand here. For a superb vista over the square, head to the terrace café of the otherwise rather down-at-heel fifteenth-floor *Everest Hotel* (see p.185).

Garden City

When Ibrahim Pasha's al-Dubbarah Palace was demolished in 1906, British planners developed the site for diplomatic and residential use, laying down crescents and cul-de-sacs to create the illusion of lanes meandering through a **Garden City**. Until the Corniche road was ploughed through, embassies and villas boasted gardens running down to the Nile; nowadays, fishermen's shacks and vegetable plots line the river's edge.

Aside from the traffic, it's a pleasant walk along the Corniche towards Roda Island, past a cluster of **feluccas** available for Nile cruises (see p.178). Further inland, Art Deco residences mingle with heavily guarded **embassies**. The American embassy on Sharia Tawfik Diab is the largest in the world, although the British embassy round the corner

---

WARTIME GARDEN CITY

During World War II, Britain's Special Operations Executive plotted sabotage across the Mediterranean from the **Rustum Buildings** on Sharia Rustum (now Sharia Mohammed Fahmy). Security there was so tight that when SEO people asked taxi drivers to take them there, they would smile and say, "Oh yes, Secret Building." Army General Headquarters (GHQ) occupied a rusticated stone pile known as "**Grey Pillars**" or "Number Ten" after its address on Sharia Tolombat (now Ittihad al-Muhamiyin al-Arab). SAS officers held wild parties in a flat crammed with captured ammunition at 13 Sharia Naguib Pasha, where the novelist Olivia Manning also lived. British sang-froid only cracked once, when the Afrika Korps seemed poised to seize Alexandria and advance on Cairo. On "**Ash Wednesday**" (July 1, 1942) GHQ and the Embassy burned their files, blanketing Garden City with smoke. Half-charred classified documents were wafted aloft to fall on the streets, where peanut vendors twisted them into cones to sell their wares in.

on Sharia Amerika Latina enjoys grander buildings with more spacious grounds, a legacy of their pre-eminence in the colonial days of Lord Cromer and Sir Miles Lampson.

Qasr al-Aini Hospital

Just south of Garden City, on the east bank of the Nile by Manial Bridge, the **Qasr al-Aini Hospital**, erected in the 1960s, is Cairo's largest public hospital. It stands on the site of an early nineteenth-century medical school, which itself replaced a palace (*qasr*) erected for a Mamluke emir, Shihabeddin al-Aini, in 1466. The palace gave its name to the hospital, and also to the adjoining Qasr al-Aini neighbourhood. Antoine Clot (see p.85) was the hospital's first director, and Egypt's most famous short-story writer, Yusuf Idris, practised as a doctor here before dedicating himself to writing.

Qasr al-Aini

The neighbourhood of **Qasr al-Aini**, named after an old Mamluke palace (see above), lies immediately east of Garden City, separated from it by Sharia Qasr al-Aini. It hosts not only Egypt's **National Asembly**, on Sharia Maglis al-Shaab, but also a number of other important government buildings, including the **Interior Ministry**, on Sharia Sheikh Rihan. This is one of three ministries (the others being foreign affairs and defence) which the military insisted on retaining control of after the 2011 revolution, and because it is responsible for the police and security services, it is key to continuing military control of the state in general – whoever may be elected to the assembly or the presidency. For this reason, it is guarded like a fortress, with armoured vehicles, barbed wire and barricades. Some of the streets around it (notably Sharia Qasr al-Aini itself, and also Sharia Mohammed Mahmoud and Sharia Sheikh Rihan) are completely blocked in parts; others are open, but ready to be closed off at a moment's notice. Deadly clashes broke out in the surrounding streets in November 2011 and February 2012. Always be aware of the situation before venturing into this area, and give it a wide berth in times of trouble.

Mausoleum of Sa'ad Zaghloul

Opposite the end of Sharia Darih Sa'ad, and to the south of the National Assembly and Interior Ministry, a colossal pharaonic-style **mausoleum** marks the resting place of **Sa'ad Zaghloul**, an early twentieth-century revolutionary who dreamed of a democratic Egypt free from British colonial control. A revolt by his supporters in 1919 forced the British to give Egypt a parliamentary constitution. Zaghloul's Wafd Party went on to win the subsequent polls, as a result of which he became, in 1924, the country's first elected prime minister. The mausoleum is closed to the public, but is an impressive local landmark.

Abdin quarter

East of Qasr al-Aini, the ex-royal, then presidential **Abdin Palace** lends its name to the **Abdin quarter**. With hindsight, several rulers must have regretted the move by Khedive Ismail of the seat of state from the more easily defensible Citadel. The European-style palace, flanked to the north by the Cairo Governorate building, subsequently became the state headquarters of Egypt's president. In Mubarak's time, the palace held a **Palace Museum** containing a large collection of eccentric historical weaponry among other royal and presidential curios. The museum closed following the revolution, though may well reopen in the future.

The rest of the neighbourhood is still chiefly residential and working-class, divided from the Saiyida Zeinab quarter to its southeast by **Sharia Bur Said**, which marks the course of the Khalig al-Masri canal, filled in after the Aswan Dam reduced Cairo's dependency on Nile floodwater. Another effect of the dam's construction was the displacement of much of the Nubian population who had lived the area to its south.

1

Many of them ended up as servants in the palace, and to this day, many of Abdin's residents are of Nubian origin.

The Museum of Islamic Art

Junction of Sharia Ahmed Maher, Sharia Bur Said and Sharia Qalaa (entrance on Sharia Qalaa) • Daily 9am–5pm except during Fri prayers • £E50 • ☎ 02 2390 1520 • The museum is wheelchair-accessible, but you will have to call ahead, or get someone to go up the steps to the main entrance to arrange for the wheelchair entrance to be opened

Refurbished and reopened after eight years' work, the **Museum of Islamic Art** contains one of the best collections of Islamic art in the world, with exhibits including glassware, jewellery, ceramics and architectural ornaments from Egypt and across the Muslim world spanning all the major periods of Islamic history – well worth at least an hour of your time.

The museum's **history** goes back to 1880, when the ruinous state of Cairo's mosques and mansions impelled Khedive Tewfiq to ask two foreign historians, Hungarian Max Herz and Londoner K.A.C. Creswell, to establish an Islamic collection. Originally housed in Al-Hakim's Mosque (see p.100), the collection had grown to over seven thousand pieces by the time the museum opened here in 1903.

The lobby and central room

Entering from Sharia Qalaa, you are immediately faced in the lobby with a **seventh-century Koran** – a reminder of what stands at the core and base of everything Islamic – and two fearsome **stone panthers**, symbol of the greatest of all Mamluke sultans, Baybars the Crossbowman (ruled 1260–77). Straight ahead, a display of glass lamps marks what is effectively the museum's central anchor room, and the place to start your tour. Displays on the walls tell you about the main **dynasties** whose rule defined the periods of the art in the museum: the Umayyads, who ruled the Islamic empire from Damascus (661–750 AD); the Abbasids, who booted them out and ruled from Baghdad (750–1258); the Fatimids, who ruled Egypt 969–1171; the Ayyubids who succeeded them (1171–1250); the Mamlukes, who took over next (1250–1517); and the Ottoman Empire, which supplanted the Caliphates and ruled Egypt from 1517 until its khedives (viceroys) established their de facto independence in 1805.

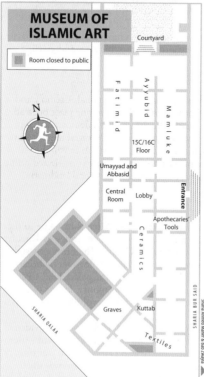

MUSEUM OF ISLAMIC ART

Courtyard

Room closed to public

N

Fatimid

Ayyubid

Mamluke

15C/16C Floor

Umayyad and Abbasid

Central Room

Lobby

Entrance

Apothecaries' Tools

Ceramics

Graves

Kuttab

Textiles

SHARIA QALAA

Sharia Ahmed Maher & Bab Zwayla

SHARIA BUR SAID

Umayyad and Abbasid art

If you take a right from the central room, you pass through a small room displaying art from the **Umayyad and Abbasid periods**. The top exhibit here is a bronze ewer with a spout in the form of a crowing cockerel, which probably belonged to the last Umayyad caliph,

Marwan II, notable for burning down Fustat (see p.134). This may come as a surprise: images of people and animals are usually absent from Islamic art, as making a graven image is considered to smack of idolatry, but the taboo was evidently not yet established at this early stage, as this and other exhibits in the same room clearly show.

Fatimid art

The next three rooms are devoted to art from the **Fatimid period** (969–1171). That the taboo on images had still not taken hold is clear from the eleventh-century **frescoes of people** exhibited in the first of these rooms, originally from the niches in a bathhouse. There are also carved wooden beams depicting people hunting and playing music. In the same room are two **wooden doors** from one of the Fatimid palaces which once flanked Bayn al-Qasrayn (see p.96).

Ceramics in the next room depict **mythical beasts**, but the third Fatimid room is rather more pious, with a pair of **original doors** from Al-Azhar Mosque, and a selection of **mihrabs**, including portable wooden ones from the shrines of Saiyida Nafisa (see p.118) and Saiyida Ruqqaya, as well as one in stucco from Ibn Tulun's mosque.

The Ayyubid rooms and neighbouring exhibits

The next room and the adjoining one are dedicated to **Ayyubid art**. The exhibits include two bronze-clad wooden doors which originally adorned the shrine of Saiyida Nafisa, but nothing else really compelling. Beyond the second Ayyubid room, a spectacular fifteenth- or sixteenth-century (late Mamluke or early Ottoman) **inlaid marble floor** has been laid out, centred around a fountain. From the first Ayyubid room, don't forget to pop out and check the **courtyard**, where columns from various periods are displayed.

Mamluke art

Islamic Egypt's golden age, so far as art is concerned, was that of the **Mamlukes** (1250–1517). The rooms dedicated to them begin in the museum's northeast corner, next to the first Ayyubid room. Exhibits in the first Mamluke room include some beautiful **tables** made of wooden inlay and of different-coloured metals. On the wall, a **stone medallion** featuring a crescent moon, a Picasso-like bull's head and a double-headed eagle.

The curved **swords** in the next room once belonged to the last two Mamluke sultans, Al-Ghuri (ruled 1501–16) and Tumanbey (ruled 1516–17). The third Mamluke room displays a superb **calligraphic frieze** made of inlaid ceramic pieces, and the room beyond that has a Mamluke **wooden minbar** (mosque pulpit).

Ceramics

The other half of the museum is divided by craft rather than by historical period. The room immediately to the south of the entrance lobby (on the left when entering) kicks off with some ceramic sixteenth-century **Ottoman tiles in** vivid blue. The **ceramics** continue in the long gallery beyond, where they are mostly from Iran. Top items include a magnificent twelfth-century turquoise **bull's head ewer** and a cobalt blue **camel** and **leopard** from the days of the Ilkhanids (1256–1335), when Iran was under Mongol rule.

At the far end of this gallery, a small room on the left houses a section of a **kuttab** (koranic school) from Rosetta incorporating a niche for the teacher to sit beneath its *muqarna* (stalactite) ceiling.

The south wing

The room beyond the long gallery contains three Ottoman **graves** and a Mamluke one, illustrating clearly the difference in style. You'll see a lot more of these, of course, if you visit the Northern and Southern Cemeteries (see pp.117–122). On the wall are three Persian **ceramic tombstones**, and facing them, a wonderful ceramic **tile panel** depicting the Kaaba in Mecca, and three smaller, single-tile versions of the same thing. The display cases next to them contain some magnificent hand-copied **Korans** dating from the fourteenth to the twentieth century.

Two rooms on from this, in a small, triangular room at the museum's southern end, two **basalt tombstones** from the twelfth century have inscriptions carved straight onto their naturally curved faces, making them look as if they are made of warped metal.

Textiles, windows and apothecaries' tools

Turning the corner to head back towards the entrance, a sumptuous seventeenth-century red and blue Persian rug on the floor of the next room kicks off the **textile and carpet** section, with a red and green Mamluke rug and a red and gold **Ottoman saddle cloth** on the wall. The textiles in the next room are mostly older, and include fragments of cloth from Umayyad and Tulunid times embroidered with **hunting scenes**, and a richly coloured sixteenth-century Persian carpet in wool and silk.

Numerous **stained-glass windows** of various periods can also be found scattered around the various rooms, usually placed to allow you to see both sides, demonstrating their construction and allowing you to appreciate their colours.

The last room before you get back to the centre of the museum contains **tools and implements** used by apothecaries, herbalists and perfumiers. Aside from the vials, scales and surgical instruments, there are a couple of medieval **medical books**, and two Abbasid-era **prescriptions** written out on papyrus.

Islamic Cairo

Few foreigners enter Islamic Cairo without equal measures of excitement and trepidation. Streets are narrow and congested, overhung with latticed balconies. Mosques, bazaars and medieval lanes abound; the smell of *sheeshas* and frying offal wafts through alleys where muezzins wail "Allahu akbar!" (God is most great) and beggars entreat "Ya mohannin, ya rabb" (O awakener of pity, O master) – as integral to street life as the artisans and hawkers. The sights, sounds, smells and surprises draw you back time after time, and getting lost or dispensing a little baksheesh is a small price to pay for the experience. You can have a fascinating time exploring this quarter of the city without knowing anything about its history or architecture, but a little knowledge of both will bring it more to life; our potted history section below should help, and architectural expressions used in the text are explained in the glossary on pp.635–637. In 1992 an **earthquake** caused a lot of damage in Islamic Cairo, which ironically led to many mosques and monuments being repaired and restored to their original glory after years of neglect (some of them already having been given a knocking by an earlier earthquake in 1884). Most are now open once again, but one or two are still undergoing restoration and thus closed to the public.

Brief history

New cities in Cairo have invariably been constructed to the north of the old, an east–west spread being prevented by the Muqattam Hills and the Nile, while the prevailing northerly wind blew the smoke and smell of earlier settlements away from newer areas. Thus when Amr's Muslim troops took Egypt for Islam in 641 AD, they sited their city, **Fustat**, north of Coptic Babylon (see "Old Cairo", p.134). Similarly, when the last Umayyad caliph, Marwan II, burned down Fustat while retreating from the **Abbasids** in 750, they ordered the city rebuilt further north. In 870, the Abbasids' viceroy, Ahmed **Ibn Tulun**, asserting his independence, founded a new city further north again. Inspired by the imperial capital of Samarra, it consisted of a gigantic congregational mosque, palace and hippodrome, surrounded by military quarters. In 905, however, the Abbasids invaded Egypt and razed it, sparing only the great Mosque

1

of Ibn Tulun. After this, people lived wherever they could amid the remains of these earlier cities, together known as **Masr**.

Foundation of Al-Qahira

The **Fatimids**, who took Egypt in 969, distanced themselves from Masr by building a new city further north again, which they called **Al-Qahira** (The Triumphant), and key features of their city still remain. It was at the Al-Azhar Mosque that Al-Muizz, Egypt's first Fatimid ruler, delivered a sermon before vanishing into his palaces (which survive only in name); the Mosque of Al-Hakim commemorates the caliph who ordered Masr's destruction after residents objected to proclamations of his divinity. The great Northern Walls and the Bab Zwayla gate date from 1092, when the Armenian-born army commander Al-Gyushi, having reconquered Al-Qahira for the Fatimids following its 1068 fall to the Seljuk Turks, expanded the city's defences northwards and southwards.

The Ayyubids and Mamlukes

The disparate areas of Masr and Al-Qahira only assumed a kind of unity after **Saladin** (Salah al-Din al-Ayyubi), having booted out the Fatimids in 1171, built the **Citadel** on a rocky spur between Al-Qahira and Masr, and walls which linked up with the aqueduct between the Nile and the Citadel, so as to surround the whole. His successors, the **Ayyubids**, erected pepperpot-shaped minarets and the magnificent tombs of the Abbasid caliphs and Imam al-Shafi'i in the Southern Cemetery, but when the sultan died heirless and his widow needed help to stay in power, the Mamlukes who ran the army took control.

The Mamluke era is divided into periods named after the garrisons of troops from which the sultans intrigued their way to power: the Qipchak or Tartar **Bahri Mamlukes** (1250–1382), originally stationed by the river (*bahr* in Arabic); and their Circassian successors, the **Burgi Mamlukes** (1382–1517), quartered in a tower (*burg*) of the Citadel. Despite their brutal politics of assassinations and poisonings, the Mamlukes were also aesthetes, commissioning mosques, mansions and *sabil-kuttabs* (koranic schools with fountains) that are still the glory of today's Islamic Cairo. Although urban life was interrupted by their bloody conflicts, the city nevertheless maintained public hospitals, libraries and schools. Caravanserais overflowed with the spices of the East, and with Baghdad laid waste by the Mongols, Cairo had no peer in the Islamic world, its wonders inspiring many of the tales in the *Thousand and One Nights*.

The Ottoman period

In 1517 the **Ottoman Turks** reduced Egypt from an independent state to a vassal province in their empire, and the Mamlukes from masters to mere overseers. When the French and British extended the Napoleonic War to Egypt they found a city living on bygone glories, introspective and archaic, its population dwindling as civil disorder increased.

The city's renaissance – and the ultimate shift from Islamic to modern Cairo – is owed to **Mohammed Ali** (1805–48) and his descendants. An Ottoman servant who turned against his masters, Mohammed Ali effortlessly decapitated the vestiges of Mamluke power and raised a huge mosque and palaces upon the Citadel. Foreigners were hired to advise on urban development, and Khedive Ismail's Minister of Public Works ordered Boulevard Mohammed Ali (now Sharia Qalaa) to be ploughed through the old city (asking rhetorically: "Do we need so many monuments? Isn't it enough to preserve a sample?"). As Bulaq, Ezbekiya and other hitherto swampy tracts were developed into a modern, quasi-Western city, Islamic Cairo ceased to be the cockpit of power and the magnet for aspirations. But as visitors soon discover, its contrasts, monuments and vitality remain as compelling as ever.

ISLAMIC CAIRO: MAIN ARCHITECTURAL PERIODS

1

Tulunid 870–905
Fatimid 909–1171
Ayyubid 1171–1250

Mamluke 1250–1517
Ottoman 1517–1882

EXPLORING ISLAMIC CAIRO

The best way to explore Islamic Cairo is by **walking**. Decide on a starting point that's readily accessible, and follow one of our maps on foot from there. The most **obvious starting points** are Khan al-Khalili, Bab Zwayla and the Citadel; see the beginning of each of these sections for details on getting there (and the bus/minibus routes on pp.176–178).

APPROACHES FROM DOWNTOWN

There are four main ways to approach Islamic Cairo on foot from Midan Ataba in downtown Cairo:

Sharia al-Azhar Overshadowed by a flyover and buzzing with traffic and cottage industries, this is the fastest and most direct route to Khan al-Khalili and the al-Azhar Mosque, at the heart of Islamic Cairo, a ten-to-fifteen-minute walk from Midan Ataba.

Sharia al-Muski This narrow bazaar (see p.95) is the classic approach to Khan al-Khalili, though it takes a lot longer than Sharia al-Azhar due to its permanent state of congestion. To reach it, take the first right off Sharia al-Geish heading north from Sharia al-Azhar, identifiable by the crowds squeezing into it.

Sharia Qalaa Across from Ataba fire station, this runs directly to the Citadel (2km) via the Museum of Islamic Art.

Sharia al-Geish Topped by a flyover, "Army Street" runs out towards Abbassiya and Heliopolis. The main reason for venturing up it is to visit the Mosque of Baybars the Crossbowman (see p.143), and the Sakakini Palace (see p.143).

ORIENTATION

The main north-south axis within Islamic Cairo itself is Sharia al-Muizz, which runs from the Northern Gates (see p.101), along the western side of the Khan al-Khalili bazaar area, past the Ghuriya (see p.104), through Bab Zwayla (see p.105), crossing Sharia Qalaa near the Citadel, and Sharia Saliba near the Mosque of Ibn Tulun (see p.115). A large number of the sights you'll want to see are on Sharia al-Muizz, and you'll probably spend much of your time wandering along it in one direction or another.

GUIDES

The streets of Islamic Cairo are labyrinthine and, while getting lost among them can result in the richest experiences, some visitors prefer to be shown round by a guide. The tourist office can put you in touch with authorized guides, and unofficial guides may accost you on the street, but frankly, armed with this book and a map, you really don't need one to visit Islamic Cairo. If you do decide to hire a guide, whether official or not, make it clear before you

start how much you are prepared to pay, where you want to go, and how long you want the tour to last. Above all, make it abundantly clear that you do not want to visit any shops, since taking a guide into any shop with you will oblige the shopkeeper to pay them a hefty commission, which will be added to your bill (indeed, most unofficial guides are really only intent on steering you into commission-paying shops rather than showing you around the old city).

GUIDEBOOKS AND MAPS

Most of Islamic Cairo's monuments are described in detail in *Islamic Monuments in Cairo: A Practical Guide*, published by the AUC. Although the area maps printed in this book should suffice, the AUC book and four fold-out maps published by SPARE (the Society for the Preservation of the Architectural Resources of Egypt) show even more detail. The al-Shorouk, AUC and Lehnert & Landrock bookshops (see p.201) are the best places to look for the SPARE maps, which are not always easy to come by.

ENTRANCE CHARGES

Historic buildings may charge admission, but mosques generally don't, though unscrupulous custodians and other opportunists may try to charge visitors for entry. If this happens, demand an official ticket – if they have none, the charge is spurious and you should refuse to pay it, though of course custodians may expect (and deserve) baksheesh, especially for looking after shoes (£E1–2) or showing you round and opening things up (£E5–20).

OPENING HOURS

Opening hours for mosques, madrassas and other religious and historical buildings are usually roughly 9am to 5pm daily (where they're significantly different, details are given in the text), though places may well open up later, depending on when the guardian turns up, and they may close an hour or two earlier in winter. During Ramadan, you will not be able to visit after about 4pm. Unless you are Muslim and want to pray, you will also not be welcome during prayer times, including the Friday noon assembly, which lasts over an hour but should be finished by 2pm. A couple of mosques (indicated in the text) are closed to non-Muslims.

1

Khan al-Khalili to the Northern Gates

The bazaar quarter of **Khan al-Khalili** is the commercial heart of Islamic Cairo, and the best starting point from which to explore it. Located right by **Midan al-Hussein**, the city's main religious focus, the Khan is slap-bang in the middle of the old walled city of Al-Qahira, just above its main east–west axis, **Sharia al-Azhar**, and right next to its main north–south axis, **Sharia al-Muizz**, which leads from here to the northern city gates of Bab al-Futuh and Bab al-Nasr. Along the way are some of the most important – and most beautiful – of Cairo's famous thousand **minarets**, including the amazing triple complex of the Mamluke sultans Qalaoun, Al-Nasir and Barquq. Also here are the great **Fatimid mosques** of Al-Aqmar and Al-Hakim, and Darb al-Asfur, a beautifully restored medieval city street. Of all the neighbourhoods in Islamic Cairo, this is the most atmospheric, the most evocative and, in terms of sights, the densest.

GETTING TO KHAN AL-KHALILI

By bus Bus #66 serves Al-Azhar from Abdel Mouneem Riyad bus station.
By taxi A taxi from downtown Cairo to Midan al-hussein – the main square adjoining Khan al-Khalili that's best given as your destination – shouldn't cost more than £E5, although drivers often try to overcharge tourists.

Sharia al-Muski

Running eastwards from Sharia al-Guesh by Midan Ataba is the narrow, incredibly congested street of Sharia al-Muski. Worming your way through the crowds, past windows full of wedding gear, and vendors peddling everything from salted fish to socks, beware of mopeds and other traffic thrusting up behind. Barrow-men still yell traditional warnings – "Riglak!" (your foot!), "Dahrik!" (your back!), "Shemalak!" (your left side!). Itinerant drinks-vendors are much in evidence: although water-sellers have been made redundant by modern plumbing, *susi* dispensing liquorice-water and *sherbutli* with their silver-spouted lemonade bottles remain an essential part of street life. Halfway along the Muski you'll cross Sharia Bur Said, which you cannot cross directly (you'll have to head 50m south and dodge under the flyover, or use the footbridge 50m to the north).

Midan al-Hussein

Midan al-Hussein is a central point of reference in Islamic Cairo. To the north stands the tan-coloured **Mosque of Saiyidna Hussein**, where the Egyptian president and other dignitaries pray on special occasions, and off-limits to non-Muslims. Its cool marble, green and silver interior guards the **head of Al-Hussein**. The grandson of the Prophet Mohammed, Hussein was killed in Iraq in 680 by the Umayyads, who had earlier been recognized as Mohammed's successors against the claims of his son-in-law, Ali, Hussein's father. This generational power struggle over the caliphate caused an enduring schism within Islam. The Muslim world's Sunni ("followers of the way") majority not only recognized the Umayyad caliphate but forbade the office to anyone of Ali's line. Conversely, the Shia ("partisans of Ali") minority refused to accept any leader but a descendant of Ali, and revered Hussein as a martyr. In Egypt, whose Muslim population is almost completely Sunni, Hussein is nevertheless regarded as a popular saint, ranked beside his sister, Saiyida Zeinab (see p.117).

AL-HUSSEIN FESTIVITIES

Al-Hussein's annual **moulid** is one of Cairo's greatest festivals – a fortnight of religious devotion and popular revelry climaxing on the *leyla kebira* or "big night", the last Wednesday in the Muslim month of Rabi al-Tani. Here the Sufi brotherhoods parade with their banners and drums, and music blares all night, with vast crowds of Cairenes and *fellaheen* from the Delta (each of whose villages has its own café and dosshouse in the neighbourhood). Midan al-Hussein is also a focal point during the festivals of Moulid al-Nabi, Eid al-Adha, Ramadan and Eid al-Fitr.

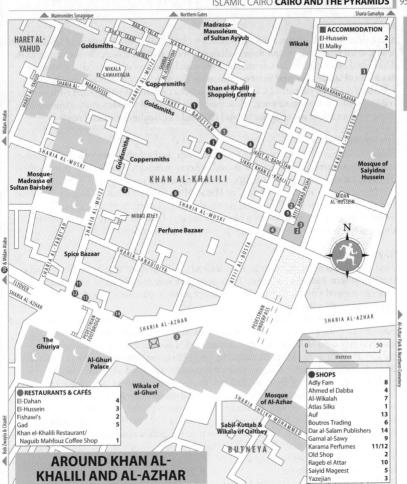

AROUND KHAN AL-
KHALILI AND AL-AZHAR

Khan al-Khalili

In 1382, the Fatimid tombs beside the Al-Hussein Mosque were demolished and the bodies within unceremoniously dumped in the dung heaps beyond the city walls. In their place, Sultan Barquq's Master of the Horse, an emir (military commander) by the name of Gaharkas al-Khalili, funded the establishment of a caravanserai which became the core of a network of bazaars now known as **Khan al-Khalili**. Most of the shopfronts conceal workshops or warehouses, and the system of selling certain goods in particular areas still applies, if not as rigidly as in the past.

Goldsmiths, jewellers and souvenir shops congregate along the lanes, which retain a few arches and walls from Mamluke times. The majority of shops open from 10am till 9pm or later, except on Sundays, when most are shut. The *khan* proper is quite compact, bounded by the Al-Hussein Mosque, Sharia al-Muizz and Sharia al-Muski, with two medieval lanes (Sikket al-Badestan and Sikket Khan al-Khalili) penetrating its maze-like interior – but the name is also applied to other bazaars in the vicinity.

1

The Spice Bazaars

South off the Muski, along Sharia al-Muizz, you'll find the Souk al-Attarin or **Spice Bazaar**, selling dried crushed fruit and flowers alongside more familiar spices. On the corner of the Muski and Sharia al-Muizz, screened by T-shirt and *galabiyya* stalls, stands the **Mosque-Madrassa of Sultan al-Ashraf Barsbey** who made the spice trade a state monopoly, thus financing his 1426 capture of Cyprus. The *madrassa*'s exterior is resplendent with red-and-white striped stonework, while the interior is full of wooden *mashrabiya*-work, along with an inlaid wooden *minbar* and the tombs of Barsbey's wife and son.

The Perfume Bazaar

Sharia Sanadiqiya (off Sharia al-Muizz) leads into the **Perfume Bazaar**, a dark, aromatic warren sometimes called the Souk es-Sudan because much of the incense is from there. The first passage on your left off Sharia Sanadiqiya leads up a flight of steps to a tiny cul-de-sac. This is Zuqaq al-Midaq, or **Midaq Alley**, immortalized by Naguib Mahfouz (see p.627) in his novel of the same name, the film adaptation of which was shot here. There is no street sign apparent; it's kept in the tiny (and easy to miss) café, where they'll ask if you want to photograph it – for baksheesh, of course.

Bayn al-Qasrayn

North of Sharia al-Muski, **Sharia al-Muizz** leads past jewellers' shops overflowing from the **Goldsmiths Bazaar** to its west. These soon give way to vendors of pots, basins and crescent-topped finials, after whom this bit of street is popularly called Al-Nahaseen, the **Coppersmiths Bazaar**.

In Fatimid times this bazaar was a broad avenue culminating in a great parade ground between caliphal palaces – hence the name **Bayn al-Qasrayn** (Between the Two Palaces), which is still used today to describe this section of Sharia al-Muizz, although the palaces are long gone. More recently, the street has given its name to the first novel of Naguib Mahfouz's *Cairo Trilogy*, where it is usually translated as "Palace Walk".

Along the west side of Bayn al-Qasrayn, the medieval complex of buildings endowed by the sultans Qalaoun, Al-Nasir and Barquq forms an unbroken and quite breathtaking 185-metre-long facade, especially after nightfall, when they are bathed in coloured lighting. All were severely damaged in the 1992 earthquake, but have now been beautifully restored, and most are open to the public once again.

The Mausoleum of al-Salih

Bayn al-Qasrayn • Daily 9am–3pm • Free

At the southern end of Bayn al-Qasrayn, set slightly back on the east side, the **Mausoleum of al-Salih** set a trend by being the first sultan's tomb to be built with an

---

HARET AL-YAHUD

Behind the palace that once stood on the western side of Bayn al-Qasrayn, there was a garden called Bustan al-Kafuri, which was known in Ayyubid times for the fine hashish that was grown there. After the garden was destroyed (which the historian al-Maqrizi reckoned a fitting punishment for such sinfulness), the area became Cairo's Jewish quarter, and still bears the name **Haret al-Yahud**. Most of Cairo's Jews left after the triple blows of Israeli independence, the Suez Crisis and the Six-Day War made their position increasingly difficult, and though a few still live in the downtown area, none now live in the Haret al-Yahud. Two synagogues still survive among the quarter's labyrinthine lanes, but are not open to the public. From Sharia al-Muizz, you can enter the quarter at its southern end along Sharia al-Makassisse (second left heading north from al-Muski; see map, p.95), or at its northern end along Sharia al-Khurunfush, by the Sabil-Kuttab of Abd al-Rahman Katkhuda (see map, p.97). You'll probably get lost in the maze of alleys and covered passageways, crammed with workshops and dwellings, but local residents are generally very helpful, and will often go out of their way to guide you through the labyrinth.

attached *madrassa*. The mausoleum was commissioned for the Ayyubid sultan Najm al-Din al-Salih (ruled 1240–49) by his widow, Shagar al-Durr (see p.118) and is noticeably simpler in style than the Mamluke buildings which succeeded it. Its *mihrab* was the first in Egypt to be decorated with marble ablaq (variegated stonework). Al-Salih himself reposes in a wooden tomb in the centre of the mausoleum's main chamber.

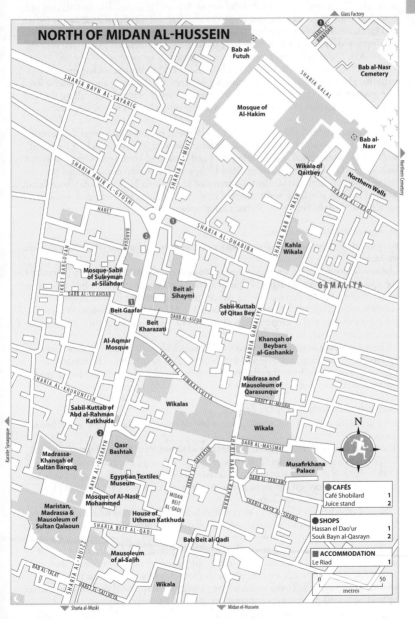

NORTH OF MIDAN AL-HUSSEIN

Glass Factory

HARET BARADOAR

Bab al-Futuh

SHARIA GALAL

Bab al-Nasr Cemetery

SHARIA BAYN AL-SAYARIG

Mosque of Al-Hakim

SHARIA AL-MUIZZ

Bab al-Nasr

Northern Cemetery

SHARIA AMIR EL-GYUSHI

Wikala of Qaitbey

SHARIA BAB AL-NASR

Northern Walls

SHARIA AL-IRAQI

HARET

SIKKET BARGUAN

BARQUAN

SHARIA AL-DHABIBA

Kahla Wikala

Mosque-Sabil of Suleyman al-Silahdar

GAMALIYA

DARB AL-SILAHDAR

Beit al-Sihaymi

Sabil-Kuttab of Qitas Bey

Beit Gaafar

Beit Kharazati

DARB AL-ASFUR

SHARIA GAMALIYA

Al-Aqmar Mosque

Khanqah of Beybars al-Gashankir

SHARIA EL-TUMBAKSHEYA

SHARIA AL-KHURUNFISH

Madrasa and Mausoleum of Qarasunqur

HARET AL-MEDAH

Sabil-Kuttab of Abd al-Rahman Katkhuda

Wikalas

Wikala

Karaite Synagogue

DARB AL-MASSMAT

Qasr Bashtak

SHARIA HABS EL-RAHBA

N

Madrassa-Khanqah of Sultan Barquq

BAYN AL-QASRAYN

Musafirkhana Palace

DARB AL-TABLAWI

Egyptian Textiles Museum

HARET QIRMIZ

MIDAN BEIT AL-QADI

SHARIA QASR AL-SHAWQ

Maristan, Madrassa & Mausoleum of Sultan Qalaoun

Mosque of Al-Nasir Mohammed

House of Uthman Katkhuda

SHARIA BEIT AL-QADI

Bab Beit al-Qadi

SHARIA AL-MUIZZ

BAB AL-TALAT

Mausoleum of al-Salih

HARET EL-SAILIYEYA

Wikala

● CAFÉS
Café Shobilard   1
Juice stand   2

● SHOPS
Hassan el Dao'ur   1
Souk Bayn al-Qasrayn   2

■ ACCOMMODATION
Le Riad   1

0   50
metres

Sharia al-Muski

Midan el-Hussein

1

The Qalaoun complex

Bayn al-Qasrayn • Daily 9am–3pm • Entrance currently free, though a ticket (£E30) may be introduced, possibly also covering the Madrassa and Khanqah of Sultan Barquq (see below)

Opposite Al-Salih's mausoleum, the **Maristan, Madrassa and Mausoleum of Sultan Qalaoun** is a jewel of Mamluke architecture not to be missed. Qalaoun, who ruled 1279–90, was the seventh Mamluke sultan, and a tireless foe of the Crusaders – he died aged 79 en route to booting them out of Acre in Palestine. The architecture of his complex, with its grand scale and lavish ornamentation, was influenced by the Syrian and Crusader architecture he had encountered while fighting abroad. If modern visitors are impressed by the fact that the whole structure was completed in thirteen months (1284–85), Qalaoun's contemporaries were amazed.

The main entrance to the complex, a huge door clad in bronze with geometric patterns, gives access to a corridor running between the *madrassa* and the mausoleum. The **madrassa** (entered to the left off this corridor) has a prayer hall recalling the three-aisled churches of northern Syria, with Syrian-style glass mosaics around its prayer niche.

But the real highlight of the ensemble is Qalaoun's **mausoleum**, across the corridor. First comes an atrium court with a *mashrabiya* doorway, surmounted by a beautiful stucco arch worked with interlocking stars and floral and koranic motifs, as intricate as lace. Beyond is the tomb chamber, 30m high, with its soaring dome pierced by stained-glass windows in viridian, ultramarine and golden hues. Elaborately coffered, painted ceilings overhang walls panelled in marble, with mother-of-pearl mosaics spelling out "Mohammed" in abstract calligraphy.

Mosque of Al-Nasir Mohammed

Bayn al-Qasrayn • Not generally open, although the caretaker of the Qalaoun complex next door may be persuaded to open it up for a little baksheesh.

Qalaoun's second son, responsible for the **Mosque of Al-Nasir Mohammed** (next door to the Qalaoun complex on Bayn al-Qasrayn), had a rough succession. Only 9 years old when elected, he was deposed by his regent, then restored but kept in miserable conditions for a decade by Baybars al-Gashankir. He finally had Baybars executed and subsequently enjoyed a lengthy reign (1293–1340, with interregnums), which marked the zenith of Mamluke civilization.

The **mausoleum** here was intended for Al-Nasir, although he actually lies next door in Qalaoun's mausoleum, his wife and son being buried in this one. The **minaret** is particularly noteworthy, a superb ensemble of stuccoed Kufic and Naskhi inscriptions, ornate medallions and stalactites, probably made by Moroccan craftsmen.

Madrassa and Khanqah of Sultan Barquq

Bayn al-Qasrayn • Daily 9am–3pm • Free, although an entrance ticket may be introduced, also covering the Qalaoun complex (see above)

The broad facade of the adjacent **Madrassa and Khanqah of Sultan Barquq**, divided into shallow recesses, echoes Qalaoun's *madrassa*, although Barquq's complex (1384–86) has the taller dome. It also boasts a minaret, which you may be able to ascend (second door on the right in the entrance passage and over the roof) for excellent views of Islamic Cairo.

Barquq was the first Circassian sultan (1382–98), a Burgi Mamluke who seized power by means of intrigue and assassination. His name, meaning "plum" in Arabic, appears on the raised boss in the centre of the bronze-plated doors, behind which a vaulted passageway leads to an open court. The *madrassa*'s prayer hall (on the right as you enter) has a beautiful blue-and-gold ceiling supported by porphyry columns of pharaonic origin; upstairs are the cells of the Sufi monks who once inhabited the **khanqah** (monastery). To the north of the prayer hall, a splendid domed mausoleum upheld by gilded pendentives contains the tomb of Barquq's daughter.

PARTS OF A MOSQUE

All mosques are aligned towards Mecca, which from Cairo means towards the southeast. Larger mosques will have a **courtyard** (*sahn*) in the centre of which there may be a **fountain** for pre-prayer ablutions, with the covered **prayer hall** at the Mecca-facing end. In mosques with a courtyard, the prayer hall is also sometimes called the **liwan**, which more generally means a covered area off an open yard.

Inside the prayer hall, the **qibla** (Mecca-facing) wall is marked by a niche called the **mihrab**, usually beautifully decorated. The mihrab is not religiously significant in itself: it merely marks the direction of prayer. Usually placed next to it is a wooden pulpit called the **minbar**, from which the **imam** (not a priest, but the person who leads the service and looks after the mosque, like a Protestant pastor) reads the Friday sermon.

The most striking feature of most mosques is the **minaret**, from which the call to prayer is issued. Nowadays, loudspeakers are used, but at one time the **muezzin** (the man who makes the call, sometimes the mosque's imam) would have climbed the minaret five times a day and bellowed it out without any artificial aid.

The Egyptian Textiles Museum

Bayn al-Qasrayn • Daily 10am–5pm • £E20

A recent addition to Islamic Cairo, the **Egyptian Textiles Museum** stands opposite the Barquq complex on Bayn al-Qasrayn. Attractively laid out and signed in English throughout, it reveals all you might wish to know about the country's textiles from pharaonic times up until the modern era. Egypt was an exporter of textiles since ancient times – linen, chiffon, mohair and fustian (the medieval equivalent of denim, named after Fustat) were all of local origin – although Egypt gradually became dependent on imports from Iran, India and, eventually, Europe, a situation only remedied in the late nineteenth century.

The museum's collection includes one of the 145 linen loincloths found in Tutankhamun's tomb in the Valley of the Kings, mummy shrouds, Greco-Roman and Coptic tunics, cloaks and tapestries. Don't miss the magnificent silver-embroidered qiswa covering for the sacred Kaaba shrine in Mecca, which was replaced annually with a new one brought by pilgrims from Egypt performing the Hajj.

The Sabil-Kuttab of Abd al-Rahman Katkhuda

Bayn al-Qasrayn • Daily 9am–5pm in theory, although in practice whenever the caretaker happens to be around • Free, although charges (£E10) may be introduced

At a fork in the road on Bayn al-Qasrayn just north of the Qalaoun and Barquq complexes, the **Sabil-Kuttab of Abd al-Rahman Katkhuda** rises in tiers of airy wooden fretwork above solid masonry and grilles at street level. The *sabil* (public fountain) and *kuttab* (boys' primary school) are common charitable institutions throughout the Islamic world, but uniquely in Cairo they were usually combined. At one time there were some three hundred such *sabil-kuttabs* in the city, of which around seventy survive. This one, founded by an eighteenth-century emir who wanted to make amends for his roistering youth, betrays a strong Ottoman influence, notable in the floral carvings between the arches. As usual, the *sabil* is on the ground floor (where the Kaaba at Mecca is depicted in Syrian tilework); exhibitions of ceramics from the Fustat Traditional Crafts Centre are often held here. Upstairs, the *kuttab* affords a bird's eye view over Bayn al-Qasrayn.

Al-Aqmar Mosque

Bayn al-Qasrayn • Daily, approximately 9am–5pm • Free

Towards the northern end of Bayn al-Qasrayn (70m north of the Sabil-Kuttab of Abd al-Rahman Katkhuda) rises the **Al-Aqmar Mosque**, originally located at the northwest corner of one of the great Fatimid palaces. Its most notable feature is the facade, whose

1

ribbed shell hood, keel arches and stalactite panels were the first instance of a decorated mosque facade in Cairo. Built between 1121 and 1125 by the caliph's grand vizier, the mosque gets its name – "the moonlit" – from the glitter of its masonry under lunar light. The intricate medallion above the door bears the names of both Mohammed and his son-in-law Ali, from whom the Fatimids claimed descent and legitimacy as the Prophet's successors. The mosque's entrance is at what was the street level when it was built. At the northern end of the facade, notice how the corner of the mosque has been cut away to allow heavily laden camels to turn more easily into the narrow lane along its north side.

Darb al-Asfur

Between Sharia al-Muizz and Sharia Gamaliya • Combined entry to Beit al-Sihaymi, Beit Kharazati and Beit Gaafar £E30 (daily 9am–5pm)

Heading off the east side of Sharia al-Muizz a block north of the Al-Aqmar Mosque, **Darb al-Asfur** ("The Yellow Street") was probably named for the pale honey-hued facades of its buildings, most of which were private homes, dating from different periods. The first three houses on the left are all open to the public, offering a unique chance to see what lies behind the walls of these old-city streets, and view the interior of a traditional wealthy Cairene's home, although the family life that once filled it is missing.

Entrance to the houses is through the broad wooden door of no.19, the seventeenth-century **Beit al-Sihaymi**, which is the finest of the three. Its rooms surround a lovely courtyard filled with birds and shrubbery, overlooked by a *maq'ad*, or loggia, where men enjoyed the cool northerly breezes; the ground-floor reception hall with its marble fountain was used during winter or for formal occasions. The *haramlik* section, reserved for women, is equally luxurious, adorned with faïence, stained glass, painted ceilings and delicate latticework. From here, you pass through the similarly restored early eighteenth-century **Beit Kharazati**, to emerge via the smaller, nineteenth-century **Beit Gaafar** on the corner at no.25.

Mosque-Sabil of Suleyman al-Silahdar

Sharia al-Muizz • Daily 9am–5pm • £E30

On the west side of Sharia al-Muizz, some 20m north of the junction with Darb al-Asfur, the **Mosque-Sabil of Suleyman al-Silahdar** is recognizable by its "pencil" minaret, a typically Ottoman feature. Built in 1839, the mosque reflects the Baroque and Rococo influences that reached Cairo via Istanbul during Mohammed Ali's reign – notably the fronds and garlands that also characterize *sabil-kuttabs* from the period. Its most remarkable feature is the huge underground cistern discovered in 2001 (accessible by a blue door just beyond the *sabil* beneath the *kuttab*), an austere hall whose only adornment is a painted ceiling frieze and ultramarine-coloured horn-shaped lamps.

Mosque of Al-Hakim

Sharia al-Muizz • Daily, approximately 9am–5pm • Free

The **Mosque of Al-Hakim**, abutting the Northern Walls, commemorates one of Egypt's most notorious rulers, the Fatimid caliph **Al-Hakim**, known as "Egypt's Caligula" (see box, p.101). After his death, the mosque was shunned or used for profane purposes until 1980, when it was restored by a group of Bohara Isma'ili Shi'ites from India who have dedicated themselves to looking after Cairo's Fatimid mosques. Their addition of brass lamps, glass chandeliers and a new *mihrab* outraged purists, but the original wooden tie-beams and stucco frieze beneath the ceilings remain. From the roof, you can gaze over Bab al-Nasr Cemetery and admire the mosque's minarets, which resemble bastions and are another of the mosque's original surviving features. One advantage of modernization is that the courtyard has some degree of wheelchair access (via the side door, to the left of the main one; you'll need to get someone to open it for you).

EGYPT'S CALIGULA

Al-Hakim bi-Amr Allah ("Ruler by God's Command") was only 11 years old when he became the sixth Fatimid caliph in 996, and was 15 when he had his tutor murdered. His 25-year reign was characterized by the persecution of merchants, Jews and Christians (he had Jerusalem's Church of the Holy Sepulchre burned down), and by rabid misogyny: he forbade women to leave their homes and once had a group of noisy females boiled alive in a public bath. Merchants found guilty of cheating during Al-Hakim's inspections were summarily sodomized by his Nubian slave, Masoud, while the caliph stood upon their heads – comparatively restrained behaviour from a man who once dissected a butcher with his own cleaver.

In 1020, followers proclaimed Al-Hakim's divinity in the Mosque of Amr, provoking riots which he answered by ordering **Fustat's destruction**. Legend ascribes the conflagration to Al-Hakim's revenge on the quarter where his beloved sister, **Sitt al-Mulk** ("Lady of Power"), allegedly took her lovers; only after half of Fustat-Masr was in ruins was she examined by midwives and pronounced a virgin. Allegedly, it was Al-Hakim's desire for an incestuous marriage that impelled Sitt al-Mulk to arrange his "disappearance" during one of his nocturnal jaunts in the Muqattam Hills in 1021, though his body was never found.

Though Al-Hakim's declaration of divinity was considered blasphemous by Muslims, his follower Hamza Ibn Ali and Ibn Ali's disciple, Mohammed al-Durzi, persuaded some foreign Muslims that Al-Hakim was a manifestation of God similar to the Christian Messiah, thus giving rise to the **Druze** faith, whose tightly knit communities still exist in Syria, Lebanon and Israel. In Coptic legend, Al-Hakim experienced a vision of Jesus, repented, and became a monk.

The Northern Gates

Entrance from the gate just west of Bab al-Futuh • Daily 8am–3pm • Free

Erected under the Fatimid vizier Al-Gamali in 1087 to replace the original mud-brick ramparts of Al-Qahira, the city's **walls** were intended to rebuff the Seljuk Turks, but never put to the test, although they later provided barracks for Napoleonic, and then British, grenadiers. The French also attempted to rename the bastions of Bab al-Futuh and Bab al-Nasr (Victory Gate), where the inscriptions "Tour Julien" and "Tour Pascal" can still be seen. The walls have now been restored following damage sustained in the 1992 earthquake, and you can usually now climb up on to the top of them by the gates.

In times past, the annual pilgrim caravan returning from Mecca would enter Cairo via the **Bab al-Futuh** (Open Gate), drawing vast crowds to witness the arrival of the Mahmal, a decorative camel litter symbolizing the sultan's participation in the hajj. In Mamluke times during festivities marking the end of Ramadan, acrobats walked along a tightrope stretched between the top of the Bab al-Nasr and the ground. Islamic pageantry is still manifest during the **Moulid of Sidi Ali al-Bayoumi**, in early October, when the Rifai brotherhood parades behind its mounted sheikh with scarlet banners flying. The procession starts from Midan al-Hussein, passes through the Bab al-Futuh and north along Sharia Husseiniya (where locals bombard the sheikh and his red-turbanned followers with sweets) through Bab al-Nasr, re-entering the old city via the Bab al-Futuh.

Inside the Walls

If you are able to gain access to the **interior** of the Northern Walls (entrance from the gate just to the west of Bab al-Futuh; a little baksheesh to the gurardian may help you gain entry), you can see the archers' slits and bombardiers' apertures, shafts for pouring boiling oil onto enemies entering through Bab al-Futuh, and bits of pharaonic masonry (featuring Ramses II's cartouche and a hippo) filched from Memphis. The ceiling of the two-hundred-metre tunnel is vaulted, which allowed mounted guards passage through. At its end lies a cavernous judgement room where the condemned, if found guilty, were hanged immediately, their corpses dumped through a hole in the floor, into the moat.

1

Al-Azhar to Bab Zwayla

Egypt's most important mosque, **Al-Azhar**, sits on the south side of Sharia al-Azhar, the main road named after it, which neatly bisects the old walled Fatimid city. To avoid having to brave the traffic when you cross Sharia al-Azhar, it's best to take the **pedestrian underpass** from Midan al-Hussein. Alternatively, you can use the **footbridge** 100m to the west, which connects the northern and southern parts of Sharia al-Muizz. In either case, beware the predatory tourist hustlers who seem to haunt the southern side of both crossings.

Heading south from the Muski across Sharia al-Azhar (over the pedestrian bridge), Sharia al-Muizz continues south to the medieval gate known as **Bab Zwayla**. Named after the conquering Fatimid caliph who founded Al-Qahira, **al-Muizz** was the main thoroughfare of medieval Cairo. Traditionally, each stretch of it had its own name, usually derived from the merchandise sold there. The section from Sharia al-Azhar to

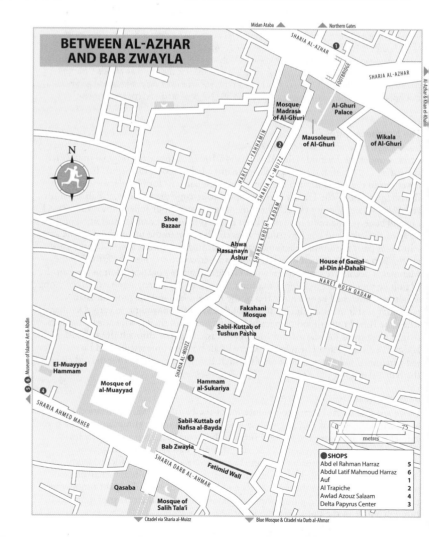

BETWEEN AL-AZHAR AND BAB ZWAYLA

Midan Ataba ◢   ◣ Northern Gates

SHARIA AL-AZHAR

FOOTBRIDGE

SHARIA AL-AZHAR

Al-Azhar & Khan el-Khalili

Mosque-Madrasa of Al-Ghuri

Al-Ghuri Palace

Mausoleum of Al-Ghuri

Wikala of Al-Ghuri

HARET AL-FAHHAMIN

SHARIA AL-MUIZZ

SHARIA KHOSH KADAM

Shoe Bazaar

Ahwa Hassanayn Ashur

House of Gamal al-Din al-Dahabi

HARET HOSH QADAM

Fakahani Mosque

Sabil-Kuttab of Tushun Pasha

SHARIA AL-MUIZZ

El-Muayyad Hammam

Museum of Islamic Art & Abdin

Mosque of al-Muayyad

Hammam al-Sukariya

SHARIA AHMED MAHER

Sabil-Kuttab of Nafisa al-Bayda

Bab Zwayla

Fatimid Wall

Qasaba

SHARIA DARB AL-AHMAR

Mosque of Salih Tala'i

0 ———— 75
metres

● **SHOPS**
Abd el Rahman Harraz	5
Abdul Latif Mahmoud Harraz	6
Auf	1
Al Trapiche	2
Awlad Azouz Salaam	4
Delta Papyrus Center	3

▽ Citadel via Sharia al-Muizz   ▽ Blue Mosque & Citadel via Darb al-Ahmar

Bab Zwayla is a short walk of just 300m. Shops along this part sell mostly household goods, making fewer concessions to tourism than Khan al-Khalili.

Al-Azhar Mosque

Sharia al-Azhar • Daily 9am–5pm, except during prayers (including Fri 11am–1pm) • Free

The **Al-Azhar Mosque**, whose name can be translated as "the radiant", "blooming" or "resplendent", was founded in 970, and claims to be the world's oldest university (a title disputed by the Kairaouine Mosque in Fez, Morocco). As the ultimate theological authority for Egyptian Muslims, the mosque has always been politically significant. Saladin changed it from the hotbed of Shi'ite heresy it had been under the Fatimids into a bastion of Sunni orthodoxy, while Napoleon's troops desecrated it to punish Cairenes for revolting against French occupation in 1798. A nationalist stronghold in colonial times, Al-Azhar was the venue for Nasser's speech of defiance during the Suez invasion of 1956.

The **mosque** is an accretion of centuries and styles, harmonious if confusing. You come in through the fifteenth-century **Barber's Gate**, where students traditionally had their heads shaved, onto a great **sahn** (courtyard) that's five hundred years older, overlooked by three minarets. The *sahn* facade, with its rosettes and keel-arched panels, is mostly Fatimid, but the latticework-screened *riwaqs* (residential quarters) of the *madrassas* on your right-hand side date from the Mamluke period. While these are rarely opened for visitors, you can walk into the carpeted, alabaster-pillared **prayer hall**, where the *mihrab*, or niche facing Mecca, is located. The **roof** and **minarets** (closed to visitors at time of writing, but it's worth asking if you can go up) offer great views of Islamic Cairo's vista of crumbling, dust-coloured buildings, the skyline bristling with dozens of minarets.

Butneya

The neighbourhood of **Butneya**, a warren of lanes and tenements to the south and west of Al-Azhar, was traditionally Cairo's "Thieves' Quarter", where the main business was **hashish**, openly sold outdoors in slabs on trestle tables by local drugs barons who enjoyed high-level protection – President Sadat's brother was said to take a commission on every kilo. Within days of Sadat's assassination in 1981, police armoured cars entered Butneya, ending the drug lords' impunity. It's now a fairly respectable quarter, and the heroin addiction rife in Cairo's poorest neighbourhoods makes Butneya's once outrageous hashish trade seem rather quaint by comparison.

Midan al-Aini

Mansions: daily 9am–5pm • £E15 each (tickets from the caretaker, who can usually be found in the House of Zeinab Khatun, or hanging out in the square)

Along the south side of Al-Azhar Mosque, Sharia Sheikh Mohammed leads past a *sabil-kuttab* (school with drinking fountain) and *wikala* (merchants' hostel) facing the mosque's south wall, commissioned in 1477 by Sultan Qaitbey, who also provided a drinking trough on the next corner. Immediately east of the *sabil-kuttab* and *wikala*, a turning south off Sharia Sheikh Mohammed leads into **Midan al-Aini**, a lovely little plaza with a small café (see p.189) surrounded by a trio of interesting Mamluke and Ottoman mansions. The **House of Zeinab Khatun**, on the north side of Midan al-Aini was built around 1468 and restored in 1713. You can wander around the upper and lower floors, checking out the *mashrabiya* screens and *ablaq* floors and recesses. Opposite across the square, the 1731 **House of Abd al-Rahman al-Harawi** is now a school for lute players, so a visit here is as much a musical experience as an architectural one.

By far the most interesting house on the square, however, is the next-door **House of Sitt Wasilia**, named after a nineteenth-century resident (*sitt* is like "Mrs"), but actually built in 1664. Exploring it, you'll find an in-house hammam hidden away in one of the

1

back rooms, but the house's most impressive feature is the fresco of Istanbul in the first-floor portico overlooking the main patio, as well as one of Mecca and Medina.

The Ghuriya

The array of buildings to the west of al-Azhar, known collectively as **the Ghuriya**, were erected by the penultimate Mamluke sultan, Qansuh al-Ghuri. Sixty years old when he took power in 1500, Al-Ghuri loved perfume, flowers, playing polo, writing poetry and discoursing with Sufis – none of which equipped him to deal with the warlike Ottoman Turks, who signalled their intent by stripping his ambassador naked and forcing him to carry a bucket of manure on his head. In 1516 Al-Ghuri perished in battle in Syria, his intended tomb being occupied by his luckless successor Tumanbay, who was swiftly defeated by the Ottoman ruler Selim the Grim – bringing three centuries of Mamluke rule over Egypt to an inglorious end. Al-Ghuri's legacy was a monumental ensemble instantly recognisable by its striped facades – a decorative motif termed *ablaq*, which is one of the hallmarks of latter-day Mamluke architecture.

The Wikala of al-Ghuri

On a side street off Sharia al-Azhar: turn left when leaving Al-Azhar Mosque, then follow the alley round past a market • Daily 10am–5pm • £E15

The nearest part of the Ghuriya to Al-Azhar is the **Wikala of al-Ghuri**, the finest example of the merchants' hostels which once characterized Cairo's bazaars. It was built in 1505, just as the Europeans' new sea route round the Cape to the East Indies was diminishing Cairo's role as a spice entrepôt. With its stables and lock-ups beneath tiers of spartan rooms, the *wikala* is uncompromisingly functional, yet the rhythm of *ablaq* arches muted by the sharp verticals of shutters, and the severe masonry lightened by *mashrabiyas* and a graceful fountain, achieves elegance. On Wednesday and Saturday evenings, the *wikala* hosts a free performance of spectacular Sufi **dervish dancing** (see p.194), which you shouldn't miss if you are in town.

Just west of here, the **Palace of Al-Ghuri** now hosts occasional concerts (details from the *wikala*)

Al-Ghuri's Mausoleum

Sharia al-Muizz • Daily 9am–5pm • Free, although a charge (£E15) may be introduced in the future

Immediately to the west of Al-Ghuri's Palace, **Al-Ghuri's Mausoleum** forms one half of a set-piece pair of buildings flanking Sharia al-Muizz where it meets Sharia al-Azhar. Vistors can usually (for a little baksheesh) descend into a dank medieval cistern, and climb to the roof to admire the view. From here, you can see the lofty wooden roof that shades the narrow section of Al-Muizz between Al-Ghuri's mausoleum and his mosque-*madrassa*. This was formerly the **Silk Bazaar**, where fine carpets were sold, and is the subject of a famous drawing by the nineteenth-century Scottish artist **David Roberts** (of which prints and postcards are often sold in souvenir shops).

The Mosque-Madrassa of al-Ghuri

West side of Sharia al-Muizz • Daily, approximately 9am–5pm • Free

Boldly striped in buff and white, the **Mosque-Madrassa of al-Ghuri** has a lofty stalactite portal, leading to the tomb of his successor Tumanbay, who was executed by the Ottomans not far away. Its rooftop offers glimpses of the Spice Bazaar and a grand view of the neighbourhood – the door to the rooftop is diagonally opposite the entrance to the main part of the mosque, but you may have to ask a custodian for access.

The House of Gamal al-Din al-Dahabi

6 Haret Hosh Qadam • Daily 9am–5pm • £E15

Some 200m south of the Ghuriya, a turning east off Sharia al-Muizz leads along the north side of the Fakahani Mosque and then (after a left turn and then a right) to the

House of Gamal al-Din al-Dahabi. Now open to the public (though it seems to close sporadically), this magnificent Ottoman mansion was the home of seventeenth-century Cairo's foremost gold merchant, and visitors are free to explore its dusty rooms and rooftops. The most impressive features are the large upstairs portico, overlooking the inner patio, so typical of mansions of this period – you'll see it in the House of Sitt Wasilia, for example, (see p.103) – and the wonderful *ablaq* inlays of the adjoining *haramlik* (women's quarters), where the ladies of the house could look down upon any male visitors in the courtyard while remaining unseen behind *mashrabiya* screens. The roof affords a fine view over the adjoining neighbourhood, revealing a shocking amount of dereliction.

Opposite the western end of Haret Hosh Qadam, an old-school spit-and-sawdust café called 'Ahwa Hassanayn Ashur offers a surprisingly good 'ahwa mahawega (Turkish coffee with cardamom).

The Sabil-Kuttab of Tusun Pasha
Sharia al-Muizz • Daily 10am–5pm • ££10

Around 300m south of the Ghuriya, Sharia al-Muizz curves around the flowery Baroque facade of the 1820 Ottoman-built **Sabil-Kuttab of Tusun Pasha**, adorned with wrought-iron sunbursts, garlands and fronds. It's well worth the entry fee to see the beautiful painted interior of the dome and well-labelled exhibits. You can also descend into the 455,000-litre cistern beneath, whose sweet water fed the *sabil* (drinking fountain), and then ascend to the *kuttab* (primary school) upstairs to see a classroom, and a display on the life of the nineteenth-century pasha and later khedive Mohammed Ali (see p.92), who brought in the Baroque style from Turkey.

Mosque of al-Muayyad
Sharia al-Muizz • Daily, approximately 9am–5pm • Free

On Sharia al-Muizz, 100m south of the Sabil-Kuttab of Tusun Pasha, the **Mosque of al-Muayyad** is commonly known as the "**Red Mosque**" for the colour of its exterior – its minarets are actually built atop the turrets of Bab Zwayla, the adjoining city gate. The mosque occupies the site of a prison where its founder, who was sultan from 1412 to 1421, was himself previously incarcerated for plotting against Sultan Barquq. Plagued by lice and fleas, he vowed to transform it into a "saintly place for the education of scholars" once he came to power.

Entrance is via a nine-tiered stalactite portal with a red-and-turquoise geometric frame around its bronze door. From here a vestibule leads to a mausoleum, where Al-Muayyad is buried, together with his son. In the *liwan* (prayer hall, on the southeast side of the courtyard), a carpeted sanctuary precedes the *qibla* (Mecca-facing) wall, where the *mihrab* is patterned with polychrome marble and blue ceramic tiles.

Bab Zwayla
Entrance next to Al-Muayyad Mosque • Daily 8.30am–5pm • ££15

In Fatimid times, the mighty **Bab Zwayla** was the city's main southern gate. It was constructed during the 1090s, when the Fatimid city's defences (including sixty gates) were being reinforced using Anatolian and Mesopotamian Christian architects and Egyptian labour. In the Mamluke city, which had outgrown the Fatimid walls and extended southward, Bab Zwayla became a central point rather than the southern extremity, but the practice of barring the gates each night continued well into the nineteenth century, maintaining a city within a city. The minarets of Al-Muayyad's Mosque, added to its turrets some four hundred years after they were built, make it look far more imposing than the Northern Gates; its full awesomeness is best taken in from the south side. The barbells high up on the western gatetower are apparently a relic of medieval keep-fit enthusiasts.

> ### ONWARD ROUTES FROM BAB ZWAYLA
>
> Bab Zwayla is an important crossroads in the Islamic city, and a good starting point for exploring the area. The **route north** (see pp.104–105) leads along Sharia al-Muizz to the Ghuriya and Khan al-Khalili. **Southward**, Sharia al-Muizz continues through the tentmakers' souk towards Sharia Qalaa and the Citadel. The more scenic route to the Citadel is east along Sharia Darb al-Ahmar (see pp.108–110). **Westward**, Ahmed Maher takes you towards the Museum of Islamic Art (see p.88) and on to Abdin (see p.87) through the neighbourhood known as Bab al-Khalq after a long-since-vanished medieval gate. On the way, you'll pass stalls selling waterpipes and braziers, a nineteenth-century *sabil-kuttab* and a fifteenth-century mosque.

Bab Zwayla was named after Fatimid mercenaries of the **Berber al-Zwayla** tribe, quartered nearby, whom the Mamlukes displaced. For centuries the gate was the point of departure for caravans to Mecca and the source of drum rolls greeting the arrival of Mamluke generals. Besides dancers and snake charmers, punishments were another spectacle: dishonest merchants were hung from hooks; common criminals were garrotted, beheaded or impaled; and losers in the Mamluke power struggles were nailed to the doors. It was here that Tumanbay, the last Mamluke sultan, was hanged by the Ottomans in 1517. The gate's reputation was subsequently redeemed by its association with Mitwalli al-Qutb, a miracle-working local saint who is still said to manifest himself to the faithful as a gleam of light within the gatehouse.

The **western gatetower**, the **turret** and the **minarets** house displays finds from the site, as well as votive offerings left by local residents for Mitwalli al-Qutb. You can also climb to the top of the two minarets for great views over Islamic Cairo and a bird's-eye perspective over the Al-Muayyad and Salih Tala'i mosques below.

Sabil-Kuttub of Nafisa al-Bayda

Opposite Bab Zwayla • Daily 8.30am–5pm • £E8 (if no one is selling tickets, ask at Bab Zwayla)

Across the street from the entrance to Bab Zwayla the restored, eighteenth-century **Sabil-Kuttub of Nafisa al-Bayda** has accounts of the building and some of the artefacts found there, but nothing hugely compelling. It stands at the beginning of a strikingly medieval passage, at the end of which is a section of the old **Fatimid city wall**.

Between Bab Zwayla and the Citadel

There are two routes from Bab Zwayla to the Citadel: via the Qasaba, **Sharia al-Muizz** and Sharia Qalaa; or following the old **Darb al-Ahmar** (after which this quarter of Islamic Cairo is named). It's possible to get the best of both worlds by combining the Darb al-Ahmar with a detour into the **Qasaba** and **Saddlemakers Bazaar**, located on the other route, a total distance of about 1.5km. If you're starting from Bab Zwayla, it's logical to visit the Qasaba before embarking on the Darb al-Ahmar, but the reverse is true if you're coming from the Citadel, in which case you'll want to start with the "Blue Mosque" of Aqsunqur on Sharia Bab al-Wazir and backtrack through the text from there.

The Zawiya of Farag ibn Barquq

Across the street from Bab Zwayla, where Sharia al-Muizz continues southward, there's a cluster of Islamic monuments. On the west side of Al-Muizz stands a Sufi establishment, the 1408 Mamluke **Zawiya of Farag ibn Barquq** (not normally open to the public) whose inlaid marble lintels and *ablaq* panels have now been restored to their original splendour. The *zawia* (also called a *khanqah*) was a hostel and meeting place for dervishes following a particular Sufi sheikh's tariqa (path). Such Sufi brotherhoods were a conspicuous feature of Cairo until the 1940s when the British curtailed them for fear of public disorder, but they flourish to this day.

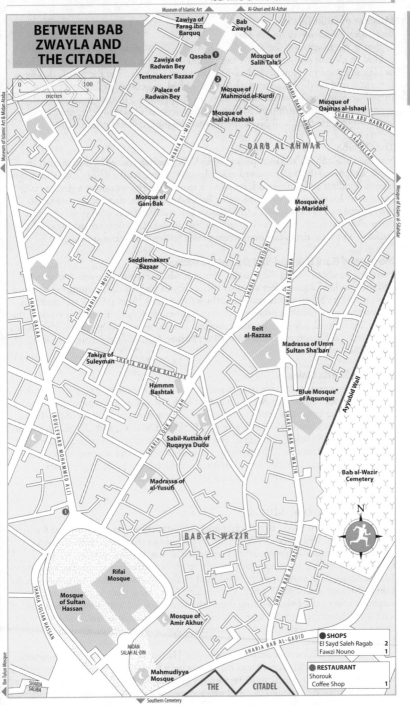

BETWEEN BAB ZWAYLA AND THE CITADEL

Museum of Islamic Art

Al-Ghuri and Al-Azhar

Zawiya of Farag ibn Barquq

Bab Zwayla

Qasaba ❶

Zawiya of Radwan Bey

Mosque of Salih Tala'i

Tentmakers' Bazaar

❷

Palace of Radwan Bey

Mosque of Mahmoud al-Kurdi

Mosque of Qajmas al-Ishaqi

SHARIA ABU HARBEYA

Mosque of Inal al-Atabaki

HARET SAADALLAH

DARB AL AHMAR

Museum of Islamic Art & Midan Ataba

0   100

metres

Mosque of Gani Bak

Mosque of al-Maridani

Mosque of Aslam al-Silahdar

Saddlemakers' Bazaar

Takiya of Suleyman

SHARIA HAMMAM BASHTAK

Beit al-Razzaz

Madrassa of Umm Sultan Sha'ban

Hammm Bashtak

"Blue Mosque" of Aqsunqur

Ayyubid Wall

Sabil-Kuttab of Ruqayya Dudu

Madrassa of al-Yusufi

Bab al-Wazir Cemetery

N

BAB AL-WAZIR

(BOULEVARD MOHAMMED ALI)

❶

Rifai Mosque

Mosque of Sultan Hassan

Mosque of Amir Akhur

Ibn Tulun Mosque

SHARIA SULTAN HASSAN

MIDAN SALAH AL-DIN

SHARIA BAB AL-GADID

SHARIA SALIBA

Mahmudiyya Mosque

THE   CITADEL

Southern Cemetery

● SHOPS	
El Sayd Saleh Ragab	2
Fawzi Nouno	1

● RESTAURANT	
Shorouk Coffee Shop	1

1

Mosque of Salih Tala'i
Sharia al-Muizz • Daily, approximately 9am–5pm • Free

Opposite the *zawiya*, on the east side of al-Muizz, the **Mosque of Salih Tala'i** withdraws behind an elegant portico with five keel arches – a unique architectural feature. The last of Cairo's Fatimid mosques, the building shows an assured use of the motifs that were first employed on the Mosque of Al-Aqmar: ribbed and cusped arches and panels, carved tie beams and rosettes. Rents from the shops around its base (now restored, but as yet unoccupied) contributed to the mosque's upkeep. Originally they were at street level, but this has risen well over a metre since the mosque was built in 1160.

The Qasaba
Straight ahead, Sharia al-Muizz passes through the **Qasaba**, erected by Ridwan Bey in 1650, and one of the best-preserved examples of a covered market left in Cairo. Colourful fabrics, appliqué and leatherwork are piled in dens ranked either side of a gloomy, lofty passageway known as the Khiyamiyya, or **Tentmakers Bazaar**, after the printed fabrics used to make tents for moulids and weddings (see p.200). If you want to see the tents themselves and don't happen to coincide with a moulid, small ones are usually to be found in a yard off the bazaar on the eastern side (entered near its southern end).

Mosque of Gani Bak and Saddlemakers Bazaar
From the southern end of the Qasaba, Sharia al-Muizz extends between two mosques and the facade of Ridwan Bey's former palace, beyond which the monuments thin out as vegetable stalls and butchers congest the narrow street. About 150m on you'll pass the **Mosque of Gani Bak**, a protégé of Sultan Barsbey, who was poisoned by rivals at the age of 25. Beyond, a few stalls selling donkey- and camel-wear constitute what remains of the Souk es-Surugiyyah, or **Saddlemakers Bazaar**, formerly the centre of Cairo's leather industry.

South to Sharia Qalaa
Assuming you don't turn back here to pursue the Darb al-Ahmar, it's a fairly mundane 350-metre walk to Sharia al-Muizz's junction with **Sharia Qalaa**. From this junction, Sharia al-Muizz continues south to cross Sharia Saliba near the Mosque of Ibn Tulun, where it becomes Sharia al-Khalifa (see p.115). Down Sharia Qalaa, the Sultan Hassan and Rifai mosques below the Citadel (see p.114) are plainly visible at the boulevard's southern end, 300m away. Alternatively, use bus services in the opposite direction to reach the Museum of Islamic Art, 1km up Sharia Qalaa (see p.88). Some buses continue on to Midan Ataba, others to Abdin or Al-Azhar.

Along the Darb al-Ahmar
The scenic route between Bab Zwayla and the Citadel follows the medieval **Darb al-Ahmar** ("The Red Street"). Originally a cemetery beyond the Fatimid city walls, this became a fashionable residential area after Sultan al-Nasir developed the Citadel, and during the fourteenth and fifteenth centuries it was the true heart of Islamic Cairo. The street is even mentioned in the Arabian Nights. Its name became grimly appropriate in 1805 when Mohammed Ali tricked the Mamlukes into staging a coup before slaughtering them; the street ran red with their blood. Stuffed with straw, their heads were sent to Constantinople as a sign of his power; six years later the surviving Mamlukes fell for another ruse, and were massacred in the Citadel (see p.111).

Nowadays the local neighbourhood (also called Darb al-Ahmar) is very down-at-heel, with much poverty and unemployment, but has been the object of a regeneration project financed by the Aga Khan Trust along with the building of Al-Azhar Park (see p.122) and the excavation of the Ayyubid city wall which runs along the eastern edge of the quarter.

Mosque of Qajmas al-Ishaqi

200m east of Bab Zwayla along Darb al-Ahmar, on the corner where the Darb turns south • Daily, approximately 9am–5pm • Free

East of Bab Zwayla, the **Mosque of Qajmas al-Ishaqi** looms over workshops sunk beneath street level. A marble panel with a rosette of swirling leaf forms in red, black and white surmounts the entrance to a vestibule with a gilded ceiling; left off this is the mosque itself. Notice the *mihrab*'s sinuous decorations (incised grooves filled with red paste or bitumen) and the fine panelling on the floor near the qibla wall (ask the custodian to lift a mat). Best of all are the stained-glass windows in the tomb chamber occupied by one Abu Hurayba. A raised passage connects the mosque with a *sabil-kuttab* across the street; both were built in the 1480s.

Mosque of Aslam al-Silahdar

Off Darb al-Ahmar; walk under the raised passage on the north side of Qajmas al-Ishaqi's Mosque, past a shrine and then bear right where the street forks: Al-Silahdar's Mosque lies 250m ahead • Daily, approximately 9am–5pm • Free

East off Darb al-Ahmar, the **Mosque of Aslam al-Silahdar** was named after its founder, a Qipchak Mamluke who lost his position at court after Sultan al-Nasir believed rumours spread by his enemies, and imprisoned him, only to reinstate him as *silahdar* (swordbearer) six years later. The marble panel outside is typical of exterior decoration during the Bahri Mamluke period; inside, the layout is that of a cruciform *madrassa*. Students used to live in rooms above the north and south *liwans*, behind an ornate facade of stucco mouldings and screened windows.

To return to the Darb al-Ahmar, either retrace your steps or take the street running southwest off the square, which joins the Darb further south, beyond Al-Maridani's Mosque. It is also possible to access Al-Azhar Park (see p.122) from here – follow the street along the east side of the mosque (signposted) and take the first right to enter the park through a gap in the old Ayyubid city wall (Bab al-Mahrouk).

Mosque of al-Maridani

Darb al-Ahmar • Daily, approximately 9am–5pm • Free

South from the Qajmas Mosque stands the **Mosque of al-Maridani**, built in 1340 and still a peaceful retreat from the streets. The mosque is usually entered via its northern portal, offset by a stalactite frieze with complex patterns of joggled voussoirs and *ablaq* panels. Inside, a splendid *mashrabiya* screen separates the open courtyard from the prayer hall with its stained-glass windows and variegated columns (Mamluke, pre-Islamic and pharaonic). Architecturally, the minaret marks the replacement of the Ayyubid "pepperpot" finial by a small dome on pillars, which became the hallmark of Mamluke minarets.

Madrassa of Umm Sultan Sha'ban

Sharia Tabbana • Daily, approximately 9am–5pm • Free

Some 200m south of Al-Maridani's Mosque, the hulking **Madrassa of Umm Sultan Sha'ban** is named after a daughter-in-law of the Mamluke sultan Al-Nasir, and mother of Sultan Sha'ban. It was Sha'ban who had the *madrassa* erected (1368–69) as a gesture of gratitude after he became sultan at the age of 10. This pious act failed to guarantee his good fortune, however. Murdered in 1377, he preceded his mother to the grave and ended up interred here himself, since his own *madrassa* was still unfinished. A wealth of *muqarnas* and *ablaq* rims the entrance, which is flanked by a *sabil* and a drinking trough for animals.

Adjoining the *madrassa* (entered through the doorway just to the left of the mosque entrance) is the rambling **Beit al-Razzaz** palace (daily except Fri 9am–5pm). The caretaker will probably offer to show you around the restored upper rooms, with their *mashrabiya* screens, painted ceilings and stained-glass windows (tip expected).

1

The Blue Mosque

Sharia Bab al-Wazir • Daily, approximately 9am–5pm • Free

A hundred metres south of Umm Sultan Sha'ban's *madrassa*, the **"Blue Mosque"** or **Mosque of Aqsunqur** was restored after the 1992 earthquake but closed again for further restoration at the time of writing. When originally built in 1347, the mosque was plainer, its *ablaq* arches framing a *sahn*, now battered and dusty, with a palm tree and chirping birds. The Iznik-style tiles (imported from Turkey or Syria) were added in the 1650s by Ibrahim Agha, who usurped and redecorated the fourteenth-century mosque. The indigo and turquoise tiles on the *qibla* wall – with cypresses, tulips and other floral motifs either side of the magnificently inlaid *mihrab* – were added at the same time. Along with similar tiles around the tomb of Ibrahim Agha in the mosque's southwest corner, they were probably made in Damascus, and explain the mosque's name and its popularity with tourists. The circular minaret affords a superb **view** of the Citadel (on a clear day you can even make out the Pyramids).

The mosque's founder, **Shams al-Din Aqsunqur**, intrigued against the successors of Sultan al-Nasir, his father-in-law – pitting eight sons in turn against their siblings, of whom one, Al-Ashraf Kuchuk, was enthroned at the age of 6, "reigned" five months, and was strangled by his brother three years later (his tomb is just inside the mosque's entrance). Eventually, a brother-in-law became sultan, and promptly had the scheming Aqsunqur garrotted.

The Hammam Bashtak and Sharia Souk al-Silah

Some 200m west of the Blue Mosque, on a small open square where Sharia Hammam Bashtak meets Sharia Souk al-Silah, the **Hammam Bashtak** was once a bathhouse serving the Darb al-Ahmar quarter, many of whose tenements lack washing facilities, but like most such old hammams (baths) is now closed. Its elaborate portal is worth a second glance, however, the ribbed keel arch bearing the napkin motif of a jamdar or Master of Robes. This surrounding area is one of the most traditional quarters of Islamic Cairo, and it's worth pausing for a tea at the café on the square just to enjoy the passage of daily life here.

From the hammam, **Sharia Souk al-Silah** leads 300m south to the Citadel past the now derelict Ottoman **Sabil-Kuttab of Ruqayya Dudu** at no. 41 and the 1373 **Madrassa of al-Yusufi**, whose founder was a Cupbearer, as shown by the goblet motif in the inscription above the door.

The Citadel and around

Alongside Khan al-Khalili, the **Citadel** is the natural focus of a visit to Islamic Cairo. Just below it, **Midan Salah al-Din** features two of the city's greatest monuments: the **Sultan Hassan** and **Rifai mosques**. A visit to all of these will probably take you a good half a day.

Heading **onward** from the Citadel, you could continue north from the entrance along Sharia Salah Salem to Al-Azhar Park and the Northern Cemetery (see pp.120–122), or from Midan Salah al-Din you could head north up Sharia al-Muizz or Sharia Darb al-Ahmar (see p.108), or west along Sharia Saliba past the Mosque of Ibn Tulun (see p. 115).

GETTING TO THE CITADEL

If you ask for the Citadel (Al-Qalaa – usually pronounced "al-'alaa"), most Cairenes will assume you want to go to Midan Salah al-Din, the large square immediately beneath it. The actual entrance to the Citadel is at **Bab al-Gabal**, however, on the Citadel's east side on Sharia Salah Salem, nearly 1km by road from Midan Salah al-Din.

By bus/microbus The Bab al-Gabal entrance is served by bus #951 from Abdel Mouneem Riyad terminal behind the Egyptian Museum, and by service taxi microbuses from Ramses and Ataba along Sharia Salah Salem. Midan Salah al-Din is served by bus #72 and minibus #124 from Abdel Mouneem Riyad.

By taxi A taxi from downtown will cost around £E10–15.

The Citadel

Entrance at Bab al-Gabal • Daily 8am–5pm (mosques closed Fri during midday prayers; last entry to museums 30min before closing) • £E50

The Citadel presents the most dramatic feature of Cairo's skyline: a centuries-old bastion crowned by the needle-like minarets of the great Mosque of Mohammed Ali. The complex was begun by Saladin, the founder of the Ayyubid dynasty, the Crusaders' chivalrous foe. Saladin's reign (1171–93) saw much fortification of the city, though it was his nephew, Al-Kamil (ruled 1218–38), who developed the Citadel as a royal residence.

The main features of the Citadel as it is today, however, are associated with **Mohammed Ali**, a worthy successor to the Mamlukes and Turks. In 1811 he feasted with 470 leading Mamlukes in the Citadel palace, bade them farewell with honours, then had them ambushed in the sloping lane behind the **Bab al-Azab**, the locked gate (now closed to the public) opposite the Akhur Mosque. An oil painting in the Manial Palace on Roda Island depicts the apocryphal tale of a Mamluke who escaped by leaping the walls on his horse; in reality he survived by not attending the feast.

The Citadel remained the residence of Egypt's rulers for nearly seven hundred years. Mohammed Ali prophesied that his descendants would rule supreme as long as they resided here, and his grandson Ismail's move to the Abdin Palace did indeed foreshadow an inexorable decline in their power.

On entering the Citadel, keep the wall to your right and follow it round into the southern courtyard of the **southern enclosure**, whose buildings include the former **Mint** (currently closed). A passage from the courtyard's north side leads through to the central courtyard; to the left of this passage, stairs lead up to the back of the Citadel's most dominant structure, the Mohammed Ali Mosque.

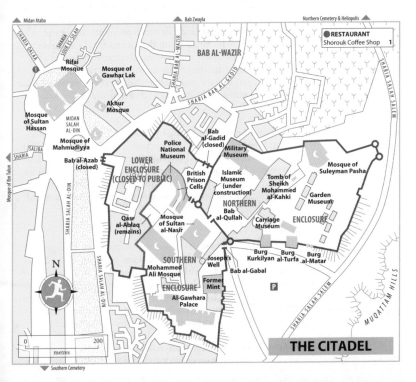

Mohammed Ali Mosque

The Turkish-style **Mohammed Ali Mosque**, which so ennobles Cairo's skyline, disappoints at close quarters: its domes are sheathed in tin, its alabaster surfaces grubby. Nonetheless, it exudes *folie de grandeur*, starting with the ornate clock given by the French king Louis Philippe (in exchange for the obelisk in the Place de la Concorde, Paris), which has never worked; and the Turkish Baroque ablutions fountain, resembling a giant Easter egg. Inside the mosque, whose lofty dome and semi-domes are decorated like a Fabergé egg, the use of space is classically Ottoman, reminiscent of the great mosques of Istanbul. A constellation of chandeliers and globe lamps illuminates Thuluth inscriptions, a gold-scalloped *mihrab* and two *minbars*, one faced in alabaster, the other strangely Art Nouveau. Mohammed Ali is buried beneath a white marble cenotaph, behind a bronze grille on the right of the entrance. The mosque itself was erected between 1824 and 1848, but the domes had to be demolished and rebuilt in the 1930s.

Due south of Mohammed Ali's Mosque is the entrance to what remains of his **Al-Gawhara Palace**, also known as the Bijou ("Jewelled") Palace, where he waited while the Mamlukes were butchered. Its French-style salons contain a dusty display of nineteenth-century dress, royal furniture and tableware.

Mosque of Sultan al-Nasir

For an idea of the Citadel's appearance before Mohammed Ali's grandiose reconstruction programme, descend from the front entrance of the Mohammed Ali Mosque into the Citadel's central courtyard. On your right, at the end of the passage from the southern courtyard, is the **Mosque of Sultan al-Nasir** (also called the Mosque of Ibn Qalaoun, after Al-Nasir's father).

The Mamlukes and the Mongols of Persia enjoyed good relations when the mosque was constructed (1318–35), and a Tabriz master mason probably designed the corkscrew minarets with their bulbous finials and faïence decorations, if not the dome, which also smacks of Central Asia. Since Selim the Grim carted its marble panelling back to Turkey, the mosque's courtyard has looked ruggedly austere, with rough-hewn pillars supporting *ablaq* arches linked by Fatimid-style tie-beams – although the *mihrab* itself is a feast of gold and marble. Notice the stepped merlons around the parapet, and the blue, white and silver decorations in the prayer hall.

Joseph's Well

Just south of Al-Nasir's Mosque is **Joseph's Well**, dug by prisoners between 1176 and 1182, although now filled in. Dubbed "The Well of the Snail", it spiralled down 97m to the level of the Nile, whence water percolated through fissures in the bedrock. Its steps were strewn with soil to provide a footing for the donkeys that carried up water jars. To reach the well, turn right when exiting the mosque and walk clockwise around it, past one of Mohammed Ali's cannons, and up a ramp to one of the Barbicans and along the adjoining rampart.

The Police National Museum

On the northwestern side of the Citadel's central courtyard, a gate leads through to another courtyard, at whose northern end is the **Police National Museum**. As you pass through the gateway, the door to your right (with a plaque that reads "Citadel's Prison Museum") leads to **cells** that were used when the Citadel was a prison. Famous detainees included Anwar Sadat, arrested by the British for wartime espionage (see box, p.142), as well as Osama Bin Laden's mentor, Ayman al-Zawahiri. Although the cells are officially closed to the public, police at the entrance may offer to let you in for a look if you show an interest.

Taken clockwise, the **exhibition rooms** off the main hall begin with Ancient Egypt (antique weapons and an exposition of the conspiracy to kill Ramses III), moving on to the Islamic period (Ottoman swords, a cartoon of prisoners from Fatimid times and a scale model of the 1952 Battle of Ismailiya that galvanized public opinion against the British occupation). A "Political Assassination" room illustrates three famous cases – including the 1944 murder of the British minister Lord Moyne by the Zionist Stern Gang in Zamalek – but oddly omits President Sadat's 1981 assassination. The next room contains a killer's death mask and a forger's press, leading to the "Forgery and Counterfeiting" room, whose ancient coins and seals are all clever fakes.

There is a superb **view** of the entire city from the terrace outside the Police Museum, where you'll also find toilets and a **café**. At the southern end, in a pit, are the excavated remains of Sultan al-Nasir's **Qasr al-Ablaq**, or Striped Palace, which amounted to a luxury prison, and finally an execution cell, for many of the hapless boy-sultans chosen by the Mamlukes.

The Northern Enclosure

Passing through Bab al-Qullah, you'll enter the Citadel's northern enclosure, which is the oldest section of the Citadel, and the only part that dates back to Saladin's time. Straight ahead from the gate, beyond a parade of tanks from four Arab–Israeli Wars, is Mohammed Ali's old Harim Palace, now a **Military Museum** full of ceremonial accoutrements, with spectacular *trompe-l'oeil* in the main salon. By turning right at the barracks near the enclosure entrance and following the lane around, you'll emerge into the **Garden Museum**, a formal garden decorated with assorted columns, gateways and the top of a minaret from the mosque of Qaitbey al-Jatkasi.

To its south is a **Carriage Museum**, boasting six royal carriages and two picnic buggies (one an infant prince's); the largest state carriage was a gift to Khedive Ismail by Napoleon and his wife, Empress Eugénie.

Behind the Carriage Museum, the bastions along the Citadel's ramparts carry evocative names. Although the derivation of **Burg Kirkilyan** (Tower of the Forty Serpents) is unknown, the **Burg al-Matar** (Tower of the Flight Platform, nowadays used to mean an airport flight tower) probably housed the royal carrier pigeons. Neither is open to the public.

It's worth visiting a neglected treasure at the other end of the compound, where a cluster of verdigris domes and a pencil-sharp minaret identify the **Mosque of Suleyman Pasha** as an early sixteenth-century Ottoman creation. This is confirmed by the lavish arabesques and rosettes adorning the interior of the cupola and semi-domes. Inside, cross the courtyard to find a mausoleum where stones over the tombs of emirs and their families indicate their rank, with turbans or hats for the men, floral-patterned columns for the women. Adjacent to the courtyard is a **madrassa** where students took examinations beneath a *riwaq* supported by painted beams.

Midan Salah al-Din

Humdrum traffic islands and monumental grandeur meet beneath the Citadel on **Midan Salah al-Din**, where makeshift swings and colourful tents are pitched for local moulids. The tents have a long pedigree: in 1517, when they took Cairo, the victorious Ottomans set up three large marquees in the square to supply their troops with, respectively, beer, hashish and boys. A bevy of small mosques around the square set the scene for a vocal confrontation of its two behemoths, the **Rifai** and **Sultan Hassan mosques**, five times daily when their powerfully voiced muezzins call the faithful to prayer, their cacophanous duet echoing off the surrounding tenements. This amazing aural experience is best enjoyed from one of the seats on the sidewalk outside the **Shorouk coffee shop**, on the corner of Sharia Sultan Hassan and Sharia Qalaa; check prayer times in the newspapers or by asking around. From this vantage point you can survey both mosques, built so close as to create a knife-sharp, almost perpetually shadowed canyon between them. A few centuries ago, all this area would have been swarming with mounted Mamlukes, escorting the sultan to polo matches or prayers.

1

The Mosque of Sultan Hassan

Midan Salah al-Din • Sat–Thurs 8am–4pm, Fri 8–10.30am & 3–4pm • £E25 (tickets from the booth between the Sultan Hassan and Rifai mosques)

Commissioned by a Mamluke who was placed on the throne by manipulative emirs at the age of 13, and then had them arrested and jailed when he was 16, the **Mosque of Sultan Hassan** was unprecedentedly huge in scale when it was begun in 1356 – covering an area of 7906 square metres, 150m in length, with walls rising to 36m and its tallest minaret to 68m. Design flaws soon became apparent, however. The plan to have a minaret at each corner was abandoned after the one directly above the entrance collapsed, killing three hundred people. Hassan himself was assassinated in 1391, two years before the mosque's completion. After another minaret toppled in 1659, the weakened dome collapsed; and if this wasn't enough, the roof was also used as an artillery platform during coups against sultans Barquq (1391) and Tumanbey (1517).

The interior

The mosque is best seen when the morning sun illuminates its deep courtyard and cavernous mausoleum, revealing subtle colours and textures disguised by shadows later in the day. Entering beneath a towering stalactite hood, you're drawn by instinct through a gloomy domed vestibule with *liwans*, out into the central **courtyard** – a stupendous balancing of mass and void. Vaulted **liwans** soar on four sides, their height emphasized by hanging lamp chains, their maws by red-and-black rims, all set off by a bulbous-domed ablutions fountain (probably an Ottoman addition). Each was assigned to one of Sunni Islam's four schools of legal thought, providing theological justification for the cruciform plan. Four *madrassas* have been skilfully fitted into an irregular area behind the *liwans* to maintain the internal cruciform.

Soft-hued marble inlay and a band of monumental Kufic script distinguish the prayer hall *liwan* from its roughly plastered neighbours. To the right of the *mihrab* is a bronze door, exquisitely worked with radiating stars and satellites in gold and silver; on the other side is Hassan's **mausoleum**, cleverly sited to receive homage and *baraka* from prayers to Mecca while overlooking his old stamping grounds. The mausoleum is sombre beneath its restored dome, upheld by stalactite pendentives. Around the chamber runs a carved and painted inscription, from the Throne verse of the Koran.

The Rifai Mosque

Midan Salah al-Din • Sat–Thurs 8am–4pm, Fri 8–10.30am & 3–4pm • £E25 (tickets from the booth between the Sultan Hassan and Rifai mosques)

Adjoining Sultan Hassan, the **Rifai Mosque** is pseudo-Mamluke, built between 1869 and 1912 for Princess Khushyar, the mother of Khedive Ismail. With the royal entrance now closed, you enter on the side facing Sultan Hassan. Straight ahead in a sandalwood enclosure lies the **tomb of Sheikh Ali al-Rifai**, founder of the Rifai *tariqa* of dervishes, whose moulid occurs during Gumad al-Tani (see p.198). Off to your left are the *mashrabiya*-screened **tombs of King Fouad** (reigned 1917–36) and his mother, the last **Shah of Iran** and **King Farouk** of Egypt (who both died in exile).

Amir Akhur Mosque

Facing the Rifai Mosque, you can't miss the **Mosque of Amir Akhur** (on the left), with its bold red-and-white *ablaq*, breast-like dome and double minaret finial, incorporating a *sabil-kuttab* at the lower end of its sloping site. The same red-and-white *ablaq* is repeated on the neighbournig **Mahmudiyya Mosque**, facing the Citadel.

West of the Citadel

From Midan Salah al-Din, **Sharia Saliba** leads west to the **Mosque of Ibn Tulun** and the **Saiyida Zeinab quarter**. At its eastern end, next to a prison, the lofty1479 **Sabil-Kuttab**

of Qaitbey is now beautifully restored. Its bold red, white and black facade is distinguished by its use of oxblood-red sandstone offset by small pieces of blue glass in the inlay.

Further west, beyond the Khanqah of Shaykhu and Shaykhu's Mosque, opposite, with a sundial on its wall, **Sharia al-Khalifa** (actually a southward continuation of Sharia al-Muizz) turns off towards the Southern Cemetery (see p.118). West of this junction, past the nineteenth-century **Sabil of Umm Abbas**, with its blue-and-red panels and gilt calligraphy, you'll see the huge walls of Ibn Tulun's Mosque come into view on the south side of Saliba.

GETTING TO SAIYIDA ZEINAB

By metro Saiyida Zeinab metro station is on the western edge of the quarter, ten minutes' walk from Midan Saiyida Zeinab.

By bus Buses #72 and #160 serve Saiyida Zeinab from Midan Lazoghli and Sharia Khayrat.

Sharia al-Galaa by Abdel Mouneem Riyad.

By foot A 15min walk along Sharia Saliba from Midan Salah al-Din, or a twenty-minute walk from downtown via Midan Lazoghli and Sharia Khayrat.

The Mosque of Ibn Tulun

Entrance from Sharia Ibn Tulun, on the east side of the mosque • Daily 8am–4.30pm • Free

Ibn Tulun's Mosque is a rare survivor of the classical Islamic period of the ninth and tenth centuries, when the Abbasid caliphs ruled the Muslim world from Iraq. Their purpose-built capital, Samarra, centred upon a congregational mosque where the entire population assembled for Friday prayer, and this most likely provided the inspiration for the Ibn Tulun.

You enter the mosque via a **ziyada**, or enclosure, designed to distance the mosque from its surroundings. It's only within the inner walls that the vastness of the mosque becomes apparent: the courtyard is 92m square, while the complex measures 140m by 122m – sufficient to accommodate the entire population of Al-Qitai, which was effectively the city of Cairo in Tulunid times. Besides its sheer size, the mosque impresses by its simplicity. Ibn Tulun's architects understood the power of repetition – see how the merlons echo the rhythm of the arcades – and also restraint: small floral capitals and stucco rosettes seem at first glance to be the only decorative motifs. Beneath the arcades you'll find a sycamore-wood frieze over 2km long, relating roughly one-fifth of the Koran in Kufic script. The severely geometric ablutions fountain, an inspired focal point, was added in the thirteenth century, when the *mihrab* was also jazzed up with marble and glass mosaics – the only unsuccessful note in the complex.

The **minaret** (entered from the ziyada) is unique for its exterior spiral staircase, which gives the structure a helical shape. Supposedly, Ibn Tulun twisted a scrap of paper into a spiral, and then justified his absent-minded deed by presenting it as the design for a minaret, although the great minaret at Samarra (itself influenced by ancient Babylonian ziggurats) seems a likelier source of inspiration. Expect to pay baksheesh to climb the minaret (£E10–20), and for looking after your shoes or providing shoe covers (£E1–2), but resist excessive demands, especially if you are told (falsely) that they are official charges.

The Gayer-Anderson House

Entrance from Sharia Ibn Tulun or from the ziyada of Ibn Tulun Mosque • Daily 9am–4pm • £E35, video camera £E20

Abutting the southeast corner of Ibn Tulun Mosque is the **Gayer-Anderson House**, otherwise known as the Beit al-Kritiliya ("House of the Cretan Woman"). Gayer-Anderson was a retired British major who, during the 1930s and 1940s, refurbished two mansions dating from the sixteenth and eighteenth centuries, filling them with Oriental bric-a-brac. **Tours** of the house (the buildings are linked by a passage on the third floor) feature Persian, Chinese and Queen Anne rooms, and an amazing guest bedroom named after Damascus, whence its opulent panelling originated. It's possible to sneak through a camouflaged *dulab* (wall cupboard) into the screened gallery

1

Sharia Bur Said & Abdin

Sharia Qadry

Sharia Abdel Meguid

Saiyida Zeinab Mosque (500m)

Mosque of
Sultan Hassan

Mosque of
Shaykhu

Sabil of
Umm Abas

Madrasa of
Sarghatmish

Sharia Saliba

Sabil-Kuttab
of Qaitbey

Prison

Citadel

Khanqah of
Shaykhu

Madrasa
of Qaitbey

Mosque of
Ibn Tulun

Gayer-Anderson
House

Sharia Ibn Tulun

Sharia Ibn Tulun

Sharia Salah al-Din

Sharia Salah al-Din

Mosque of
Saiyida Sukayna

Sharia al-Khalifa

Tomb of
Shagar al-Durr

Mashhad of
Saiyida Ruqayya

Mosque
of Saiyida
Aisha

Sharia Badr al-Din al-Zanati

Sharia Salah Salem

Bird
Market

Citadel entrance

Mosque of
Saiyida Nafisa

Tombs of
Abbasid
Khalifs

Sharia Salah Salem

Ayyubid Wall

Sharia al-Khalifa

Souk al-Gom'a

Funm al-Khalig

Sharia al-Khalifa

Aqueduct

Sharia Magra al-Ayoun

Sharia Salah Salem

Aqueduct

AL-KHALIFA

Sharia Imam al-Shafi'i

**Southern
Cemetery**

N

Sharia Salah Salem

Sharia Ain al-Sira

Hosh
al-Basha

Mausoleum of
Imam al-Shafi'i

Fustat
Park

Cairo
Land

0 — 250
metres

**AROUND IBN TULUN AND
THE SOUTHERN CEMETERY**

Al-Basatin

overlooking the *salamlik*, as women did in the olden days. With its polychrome fountain, decorated ceiling and kilim-covered pillows, this is the finest reception hall left in Islamic Cairo, and served as the set for a tryst and murder in the James Bond film *The Spy Who Loved Me*.

South of the Gayer-Anderson House, you can continue down into the southern cemetery (see p.118). Alternatively, return to Sharia Saliba and continue on into Saiyida Zeinab.

The Madrassa of Sarghatmish

Sharia Saliba • Daily, approximately 9am–5pm • Free

Directly north of Ibn Tulun's Mosque is the **Madrassa of Sarghatmish**. The courtyard, resplendent in white marble inlaid with red, black and green porphyry, is quite stunning, with a cool, light feel that makes a pleasant change from the rather heavy architecture of Cairo's classic mosques. It centres around a fountain surmounted with an *oba* (canopy), and surrounded by the cell-like quarters formerly used by students. The Sarghatmish who had the *madrassa* built, a Mamluke commander assassinated on the orders of Sultan Hassan in 1358, is interred in a chamber adjoining the courtyard.

Saiyida Zeinab quarter

The **Saiyida Zeinab quarter** is named after Egypt's beloved saint, who was the Prophet's granddaughter and sister of Al-Hussein. Its heart is the **Saiyida Zeinab Mosque** where she is buried. The mosque is closed to non-Muslims, but everyone can join in her **moulid** (see p.198).

Bayt al-Sinnari and Sabil-Kuttab of Sultan Mustafa III

Two interesting Ottoman buildings in Saiyida Zeinab have also now been restored and opened to the public. The lovingly restored **Bayt al-Sinnari** mansion (Sun–Thurs 11am–7pm; free), built in 1794, features a first-floor portico, and a wind trap on the roof to catch the cooling breezes and direct them into the house. To reach the mansion, go up the alley (signed "Mongi District") on the left just past the Rifai roast-goat-and-kofta house (see p.187), then go round to the right and turn left into the first alley.

Staff from Bayt al-Sinnari will then take you to the 1759 **Sabil-Kuttab of Sultan Mustafa III** on Sharia Bur Said, which you'll have passed when coming to Bayt al-Sinnari. The *sabil-kuttab* is of particular interest, as it's decorated inside with Dutch blue Delft tiles showing scenes of eighteenth-century daily life in the Netherlands – not something you expect to find in an Ottoman *sabil-kuttab* in Cairo. Sultan Mustafa evidently had the tiles brought over from Turkey rather than directly from the Netherlands.

Cities of the Dead

It's thought that at least five hundred thousand Cairenes live amid the **Cities of the Dead**, two vast cemeteries that stretch away from the Citadel to merge with newer shantytowns below the Muqattam. The **Southern Cemetery**, sprawling to the southeast of Ibn Tulun's Mosque, is only visible from the Muqattam, or at close quarters. The **Northern Cemetery**, by contrast, is an unforgettably eerie sight, with dozens of mausoleums rising from a sea of dwellings along the road from Cairo Airport.

Although tourists generally – and understandably – feel uneasy about viewing the cemeteries' splendid **funerary architecture** with squatters living all around or in the tombs, few natives regard the Cities of the Dead as forbidding places. Egyptians have a long tradition of building "houses" near their ancestral graves and picnicking or even staying there overnight; other families have simply occupied them. By Cairene standards these are poor but decent neighbourhoods, with shops, schools and electricity, maybe even piped water and sewers. The saints buried here provide a moral touchstone and *baraka* for their communities, who honour them with moulids.

Though these are generally not dangerous quarters, it's best to exercise some caution when **visiting**. Don't flaunt money or costly possessions, and be sure to dress modestly; women should have a male escort, and will seem more respectable if wearing a headscarf. You'll be marginally less conspicuous on Fridays, when many Cairenes visit their family plots; but remember that mosques can't be entered during midday prayers. At all events, leave the cemeteries before dark, if only to avoid getting lost in their labyrinthine alleys – and don't stray to the east into the inchoate (and far riskier) slums around the foothills of the Muqattam.

The Southern Cemetery

The older and larger **Southern Cemetery** – known to Egyptians as "the Great Cemetery" (Al-Qarafah al-Kubra) – is broadly synonymous with the residential quarter of **Al-Khalifa**, named after the Abbasid caliphs buried amid its mud-brick tenements. The area is respectable enough by day, but is known for drug dealing and is unsafe after dark. Although the Abbasid tombs aren't half as imposing as those of the Mamlukes in the Northern Cemetery, one of the approach routes passes several shrines famous for their moulids.

Mosque of Saiyida Sukayna

Sharia al-Khalifa, 250m south of the junction with Sharia Saliba and just around the corner from the Gayer-Anderson House •Daily, approximately 9am–5pm • Free

The yellow-and-white **Mosque of Saiyida Sukayna** is the burial place of Al-Hussein's daughter, the great-granddaughter of the Prophet Mohammed, whose **moulid** (see p.198) is attended by several thousand people and features traditional entertainments such as stick-twisters and dancing horses, not to mention more modern ones such as DJ sound systems.

The Tomb of Shagar al-Durr

Sharia al-Khalifa, 100m south of Saiyida Sukayna's mosque

The **Tomb of Shagar al-Durr** is a derelict edifice sunk below street level. Shagar al-Durr (Tree of Pearls) was the widow of Sultan Ayyub, who ruled as sultana of Egypt for eighty days (1249–50) until the Abbasid caliph demanded that she abdicate, quoting the Prophet's dictum "Woe unto nations ruled by a woman". She therefore married Aybak, the first Mamluke sultan, and governed "from behind the *mashrabiya*". In 1257 she ordered Aybak's murder after learning that he wanted another wife, but then tried to save him. The assassins objected, "If we stop halfway through, he will kill both you and us!" Rejecting her offer to marry their new leader, the Mamlukes handed Shagar al-Durr over to Aybak's former wife, whose servants beat her to death with bath clogs and threw her body to the jackals.

The Mosque of Saiyida Nafisa

Sharia al-Khalifa • Daily, approximately 9am–10pm • Free

Egypt's third-holiest shrine is the **Mosque of Saiyida Nafisa**, 100m south of the Tomb of Shagar al-Durr, by a roundabout planted with grass and flowers. It holds the tomb of a great-granddaughter of the Prophet (she was the granddaughter of al-Hussein's brother al-Hassan) and is closed to non-Muslims, though all visitors can appreciate the good-natured crowd that hangs around after Friday noon prayers, or during Nafisa's **moulid** (see p.198). Honoured during her lifetime as a descendant of the Prophet and a *hafizat al-Qur'an* (one who knows the Koran by heart), Nafisa was famed for working miracles and conferring saintly blessings (*baraka*) on visitors to her shrine. Indeed, the Southern Cemetery possibly began with devotees wanting to be buried near her grave. She lived in a house on this site until her death in 824 AD, but the mosque you see today was constructed in 1897, after the original building burned down.

The Abbasid Tombs

Daily 9am–5pm (assuming the caretaker's around; tip expected)

The alley on the north side of Saiyida Nafisa's Mosque leads through a passage, beyond which a green-painted gate to the right (just before the street turns) leads into a compound enclosing the **Tombs of the Abbasid Caliphs**. Having been driven from Baghdad by the Mongols in 1258, the caliphs gratefully accepted Baybars' offer to re-establish them in Egypt, only to discover that they were mere puppets. Baybars appropriated the domed mausoleum (usually kept locked) for his own sons; the caliphs were buried outdoors in less than grandiose tombs. Notice the beautiful foliate Kufic inscription on the cenotaph of Khadiga, under the wooden shed. The last Abbasid caliph was formally divested of his office in 1517.

The Mosque of Saiyida Aisha and around

Sharia Salah al-Din • Daily, approximately 9am–5pm • Free • Microbus service taxis run between the mosque and Midan Ataba

At the southern end of Sharia Salah al-Din, the eighteenth-century Ottoman **Mosque of Saiyida Aisha** is the scene of a colourful **moulid** held during the Muslim month of Sha'ban. Immediately to the south, alongside Sharia Salah Salem, is a section of Saladin's medieval **aqueduct**, which once carried water from the Nile to the Citadel (see p.134). If you can't coincide with the moulid, the best time to be here is on a Friday morning, when a bird and pet animal market stretches south from the Salah Salem overpass.

The Mausoleum of Imam al-Shafi'i

Sharia Imam al-Shafi'i, around 1km south of the Mosque of Saiyida Aisha • Daily, approximately 9am–10pm • Free • You can reach the mausoleum by taxi from Midan Salah al-Din (£E12–15) or by minibus #154 from Abdel Mouneem Riyad (behind the Egyptian Museum), which turn off Sharia Imam al-Shafi'i 100m short of the mausoleum itself.

At the far end of the street that bears his name, the **Mausoleum of Imam al-Shafi'i** is Egypt's largest Islamic mortuary complex, instantly recognizable by its graceful ribbed dome, crowned by a metal boat like a weather vane. The mausoleum marks the final resting place of Mohammed Ibn Idris al-Shafi'i, founder of one of the four Sunni schools of Islamic jurisprudence and theology. Born in Gaza in 767 AD, Imam al-Shafi'i grew up in Mecca and practiced law in Baghdad under Caliph Haroun al-Rashid (of *Arabian Nights* fame) before moving to Cairo, where he died in 820. His legal rulings (*fatwas*) form the basis of the Shafi'ite school of Islamic jurisprudence, whose rulings are followed by most Egyptian Muslims. Al-Shafi'i's moulid (see p.198) attracts many sick and infirm people seeking his *baraka*.

The mausoleum was constructed in 1211 on the orders of the Ayyubid sultan Al-Kamil (Saladin's nephew), who was a great propagator of Sunni orthodoxy, like the imam himself. It was the first Sunni monument to be officially commissioned in the city following the demise of the Shi'ite Fatimids fifty years earlier. Inside, Al-Shafi'i's teak cenotaph – into which the faithful slip petitions – lies beneath a magnificent dome perched on stalactite squinches and painted red and blue, with gilt designs. The walls are clad in variegated marble, dating from Qaitbey's restoration of the building in the 1480s.

Hosh al-Basha

Sharia Salah al-Din • Daily, approximately 9am–5pm • Free

Directly behind the Mausoleum of Imam al-Shafi'i stands the **Hosh al-Basha**, a five-domed complex where Mohammed Ali's sons, their wives, children and retainers are buried. Inside the courtyard are clumps of cenotaphs decorated with garlands and fronds, topped by a turban, fez or other headdress to indicate the deceased's rank. The conspicuously plain cenotaph belongs to a princess with radical sympathies, who abhorred ostentation. In a separate room, forty statues commemorate the 470 Mamlukes butchered by Mohammed Ali in the Citadel (see p.111).

1

The Northern Cemetery

The finest of Cairo's funerary monuments – erected by the Burgi Mamlukes from the fourteenth to sixteenth centuries – are spread around the **Northern Cemetery**. The majority of tourists who venture in from Sharia Salah Salem are content to see three main sites, plus whatever crops up in between. This takes an hour or two, plus any time you care to spend hanging out in cafés or just wandering around the old cemetery, checking out the less well-known tombs and absorbing the area's unique atmosphere.

GETTING TO THE NORTHERN CEMETERY

By minibus Take minibus #102 from Tahrir Square or minibus #10 from Ramses and Ataba to Dirasa bus terminal, from where it's a short walk to Qaitbey's Mausoleum, whose ornate dome and minaret are clearly visible. Dirasa can also be reached by service-taxi microbus from Midan Ramses.

By taxi Ask for *al-qarafat ash-sharqiyyah* – the Eastern Cemetery

By foot Around 15min from Al-Azhar, following the dual carriageway Bab al-Ghuriyab past university buildings and uphill to its roundabout junction with Salah Salem.

Opening hours Opening hours of the monuments in the cemetery seem to change very frequently. Most are generally open from at least 10am and 5pm, while some are open until as late as 10pm, but it often seems to depend on when the caretaker happens to be around. Non-Muslims are not allowed in during prayers.

Sultan Qaitbey's Mausoleum

Northern Cemetery • Daily 10am–5pm • Free

Sultan Qaitbey was the last strong Mamluke ruler and a prolific builder of monuments from Mecca to Syria; his funerary complex is among the grandest in the Northern Cemetery. His name means "the restored" or "returned", indicating that he nearly died at birth; as a scrawny lad, he fetched only fifty dinars in the slave market. The rapid turnover in rulers after 1437 accelerated his ascent, and in 1468 he was acclaimed sultan by the bodyguard of the previous incumbent. His 28-year reign was only exceeded by Al-Nasir's, and Qaitbey remained "tall, handsome and upright as a reed" well into his eighties.

An irregularly shaped complex built in 1474, the **Mausoleum of Sultan Qaitbey** is dynamically unified by the bold stripes along its facade, which is best viewed from the north. The trilobed portal carries one's eye to the graceful **minaret**, soaring through fluted niches, stalactite brackets and balconies to a teardrop finial. Inside, the *madrassa's* floors, walls and *liwans* are a feast of marble and geometric patterns, topped by elaborately carved and gilded ceilings, with a lovely octagonal roof lantern. Qaitbey's **tomb chamber** off the prayer hall is similarly decorated, its lofty dome upheld by squinches. One of Mohammed's footprints, brought over from Mecca, is also preserved in the tomb chamber. Ask to climb the minaret for a close view of the marvellous stone carving on the dome's exterior: a raised star-pattern is superimposed over an incised floral one, the two designs shifting as the shadows change. From this minaret vantage point you can also plot a course to Barsbey's complex, further up the narrow, winding street.

Mausoleum of Sultan al-Ashraf Barsbey

Northern Cemetery • Daily 10am–10pm • Free

North of Qaitbey's Mausoleum, the street jinks past (on the left) his **rab**, a residential building endowed by Qaitbey so that the rent from its apartments would provide income for the mausoleum's upkeep and employment for his poorer relations. Such bequests could not be confiscated, unlike merchants' and Mamlukes' personal wealth, which partly financed the **Mausoleum of Sultan al-Ashraf Barsbey**, 200m beyond the building. Barsbey was the sultan who acquired young Qaitbey at a knockdown rate. He himself had been purchased in Damascus for eight hundred dinars, but was "returned to the broker for a filmy defect in one of his blue eyes". Unlike other sultans, who milked the economy, Barsbey troubled to pay his Mamlukes regularly and the reign (1422–38) of this well-spoken teetotaller was characterized by "extreme security and low prices".

Based on a now-ruined *khanqah*, the complex was expanded to include a mausoleum and mosque-*madrassa* (1432) after Barsbey's funerary pile near Khan al-Khalili was found lacking. If there's a curator around, ask him to lift the mat hiding the marble mosaic floor inside the long mosque, which also features a superb *minbar*. At the northern end, a great dome caps Barsbey's tomb, its marble cenotaph and mother-of-pearl-inlaid *mihrab* softly lit by stained-glass windows, added at a later date. The stone carving on the dome's exterior marks a transition between the early chevron patterns and the fluid designs on Qaitbey's Mausoleum.

Fifty metres north, another finely carved dome surmounts the **Tomb of Gani Bak**, a favourite of Barsbey's, whose mosque stands near the Saddlemakers Bazaar (see p.108). To the west of here, you could seek out nearby **smaller tombs** such as those of Barsbey al-Bagasi and Amir Suleyman.

Mausoleum of Sultan Barquq

Northern Cemetery • Daily 9am–10pm • Free

The third – and oldest – of the Northern Cemetery's great funerary complexes can be found 100m north of Barsbey's mausoleum, on the far side of a square with a direct through road onto Sharia Salah Salem. Recognizable by its twin domes and minarets, the 1411 **Mausoleum of Sultan Barquq** was the first royal tomb in a cemetery that was previously noted for the graves of Sufi sheikhs. Its courtyard is plain, with stunted tamarisks, but the proud chevron-patterned domes above the prayer hall uplift the whole ensemble. Barquq and his son Farag are buried in the northern tomb chamber, his daughters Shiriz and Shakra in the southern one, with their faithful nurse in the corner. Both are soaring structures preceded by *mashrabiyas* with designs similar to the window screens in Barquq's *madrassa* on Sharia al-Muizz (see p.98). The sinuously carved *minbar* was donated by Qaitbey to what was then a Sufi *khanqah* (dervish hostel); stairs in the northwest corner of the courtyard lead to a warren of dervish cells on the upper floors, long since deserted.

The complex was actually commissioned by Farag, who had his father's body transferred here from the *madrassa*. Farag was crowned at the age

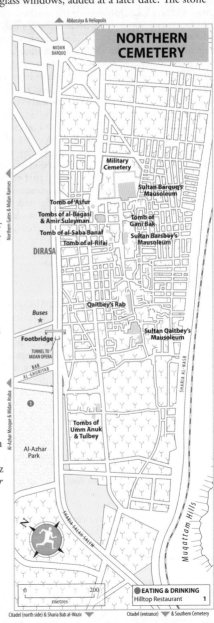

NORTHERN CEMETERY

Abbassiya & Heliopolis

MIDAN BARQUQ

Military Cemetery

Sultan Barquq's Mausoleum

Tomb of 'Asfur

Tombs of al-Bagasi & Amir Suleyman

Tomb of Gani Bak

Tomb of al-Saba Banaf

Sultan Barsbey's Mausoleum

Tomb of al-Rifai

DIRASA

Northern Gates & Midan Ramses

Qaitbey's Rab

Buses

Sultan Qaitbey's Mausoleum

Footbridge

TUNNEL TO MIDAN OPERA

BAB AL-GHURIYAB

Al-Azhar Mosque & Midan Ataba

SHARIA AL-NASR

Tombs of Umm Anuk & Tulbey

Al-Azhar Park

SHARIA SALAH SALEM

N

Muqattam Hills

0   200
metres

● **EATING & DRINKING**
Hilltop Restaurant   1

Citadel (north side) & Sharia Bab al-Wazir

Citadel (entrance) & Southern Cemetery

1

of 10 and deposed and killed in Syria thirteen years later after a reign marked by rebellion and civil strife; all in all, it's quite amazing that the mausoleum was ever completed.

Al-Azhar Park

Daily 9am–10pm • Mon–Wed £E5, Thurs–Sun and public holidays £E7 • ⓦ alazharpark.com/index.html

Across Sharia Salah Salem from the northern cemetery, its entrance about 200m south of Dirasa, and 500m north of the Citadel's Bab Gadid, is the new and very welcome **Al-Azhar Park**. Funded by a $45m grant from the Aga Khan Trust, the park is part of a regeneration project for the Darb al-Ahmar area and was built on the site of a filthy and rather dangerous stretch of waste ground, used as a rubbish dump and the haunt of junkies. Now all that has changed: in its place is a scrupulously kept recreational area that has provided local employment and given one of Cairo's most deprived areas a new lease of life. Scattered around the park's lawns and fountains are trees, plants and shrubs from around the world, all labelled. The park also contains a lakeside café and a classy **restaurant** (see p.187), while its highest point offers a panoramic view over Islamic Cairo, especially impressive at night when many monuments are illuminated.

The park's western boundary is marked by a 1300-metre stretch of **Ayyubid city wall**, most of it uncovered during construction of the park. Work is still continuing on the very northern section of the wall, and part of the ramparts should be open to the public when that is complete. In the meantime you can walk alongside the wall, and climb one of the bastions adjoining the park's back gate, Bab al-Mahrouk, which leads into Darb al-Ahmar (see p.108). When work on the northern section of the wall is finished, there will also be an entrance (Bab al-Barkiyya) directly accessible from Sharia al-Azhar.

Old Cairo

In a city with two names – Masr and Al-Qahira (see p.64) – Cairenes distinguish between *al-Qahira al-Qadima* (Old al-Qahira, known in English as Islamic Cairo) and *Masr al-Qadima*, Old Masr, or as it's known in English, **Old Cairo**. Depending on whether it's broadly or narrowly defined, this covers everything south of Garden City and Saiyida Zeinab, or a relatively small area near the Mar Girgis metro station, known to foreigners as "**Coptic Cairo**", which remains the heart of Cairo's Coptic community. Featuring several medieval churches, the superb Coptic Museum and an atmospheric synagogue, it totally eclipses the neighbouring site of **Fustat** – Egypt's first Islamic settlement, of which little now remains.

GETTING TO OLD CAIRO

By metro The Coptic quarter is most easily accessible via Mar Girgis metro station (four stops from Tahrir Square in the Helwan direction).

By bus Buses from Abdel Mouneem Riyad (#235) and Ramses (#134, minibus #94) serve Al-Amr Mosque.

By taxi A taxi from downtown Cairo to Old Cairo should cost around £E8.

Brief history

Perhaps as early as the sixth century BC, a town grew up in this area around a fortress intended to guard the canal linking the Nile and the Red Sea. Some ascribe the name of this settlement – **Babylon-in-Egypt** – to Chaldean workmen pining after their home town beside the Euphrates; another possible derivation is Bab il-On, the "Gate of Heliopolis". Either way, it was Egyptian or Jewish in spirit long before Emperor Trajan raised the existing fortress in 130 AD. Many of Babylon's inhabitants, resentful of Greek domination and Hellenistic Alexandria, later

1

embraced Christianity, despite bitter persecution by the pagan Romans. Even after the Empire adopted Christianity, the Copts were oppressed by Byzantines for their adoption of the Monophysite "heresy" (see box below). Thus when the Muslim army besieged Babylon in 641, promising to respect Copts and Jews as "People of the Book", only its garrison resisted.

The Coptic Museum

Sharia Mari Girgis • Daily 9am–4pm (closes at 3pm during Ramadan) • £E50 • ⓦ coptic-cairo.com

Founded in 1908 under the patronage of Khedive Kamil and the Coptic Patriarch Cyril V, the **Coptic Museum** is one of the highlights of Old Cairo. The museum was intended to save Christian antiques from the ravages of neglect and foreign collectors, but soon widened its mandate to embrace secular material. With artefacts from Old Cairo, Upper Egypt and the desert monasteries, the museum traces the evolution of Coptic art from Greco-Roman times into the Islamic era (300–1000 AD). The collection can be seen in detail in a couple of hours, or covered at a trot in half that time.

The Roman Gates

Flanking the museum entrance, almost opposite the Mar Girgis (St George) metro station are the circular towers of Babylon's **western gate**. In Trajan's day, the Nile lapped the base of this gate and was spanned by a pontoon bridge leading to the southern tip of Roda Island. Today, Babylon's foundations are buried under ten metres of accumulated silt and rubble, so the churches within the compound and the streets outside are nearly at the level of the fortress's ramparts.

COPTIC CHRISTIANITY

While Egypt's **Copts** share a common national culture with their Muslim compatriots, they remain acutely conscious of their separate identity. Intercommunal marriages are extremely rare and bring problems from both sides. **The Coptic church** belongs (along with the Armenian Orthodox and Ethiopian churches) to the Monophysite branch of Christianity, which split from Eastern and Roman Catholic orthodoxy very early on, and the Copts even have their own pope, chosen from the monks of Wadi Natrun. The Coptic Bible (first translated from Greek c.300 AD) predates the Latin version by a century. While Coptic services are conducted in Arabic, portions of the liturgy are sung in the old Coptic language descended from ancient Egyptian, audibly prefiguring the Gregorian chants of Eastern Orthodoxy.

CHRISTIANITY IN EGYPT

Tradition holds that **St Mark** made his first Egyptian convert (a Jewish shoemaker from Alexandria) in 45 AD. From Jews and Greeks the religion spread to the Egyptians of the Delta – which teemed with Christian communities by the third century – and thence southwards up the Nile. The Christian faith appealed to Egyptians on many levels. Its message of resurrection offered ordinary folk the eternal life that was previously available only to those who could afford elaborate funerary rituals, and much of the new religion's **symbolism** fitted old myths and images. God created man from clay, as did Khnum on his potter's wheel, and weighed the penitent's heart, like Anubis; Confession echoed the Declaration of Innocence; the conflict of two brothers and the struggle against Satan echoed the myth of Osiris, Seth and Horus. Scholars have traced the **cult of the Virgin** back to that of the Great Mother, Isis, who suckled Horus, and the resemblance between early **Coptic crosses** and pharaonic ankhs has also led some to argue that Christianity's principal symbol owes more to Egypt than Golgotha.

Emperor Constantine's 313 AD legalization of Christianity eased matters until 451, when the Copts rejected the decision of the Council of Chalcedon that Christ's human and divine natures were unmixed, insisting that his divinity was paramount. For this **"Monophysite" heresy** (monophysite meaning "single nature") they were expelled from the fold, and persecuted by the Byzantines. Most Egyptians remained Christian long after the Arab conquest (640–41) and were treated well by the early Islamic dynasties. Mass **conversions to Islam**

1

The towers are encased in alternating courses of dressed stone (much of it taken from pharaonic temples) and brick, a Roman technique known as *opus mixtum* or "mixed work". The **south tower** is ruined, exposing a central shaft buttressed by masonry rings and radial ribs, which enabled it to withstand catapults and battering rams. Atop the **north tower** stands the **Church of St George** (daily 8am–4pm; free). It's been there since the tenth century but was rebuilt in 1904 after the original was destroyed by fire. Notwithstanding the church's Greek Orthodox allegiance, its **Moulid of Mari Girgis** (on St George's Day, April 23) is one of the largest Coptic festivals in Cairo.

Steps from the museum forecourt lead down into the old **Water Gate** beneath the Hanging Church, but these are usually closed to the public. It was through this gate (then lapped by the river) that the last Byzantine viceroy, Melkite bishop Cyrus, escaped by boat under cover of darkness before Babylon surrendered to the Muslims.

Rooms 2–4

From the museum entrance, the **New Wing**, built in 1937, is straight ahead. The **ground floor** is arranged in chronological order in an anticlockwise direction, starting with **Room 2**, which kicks off with a fourth- or fifth-century tapestry of (on one side) a piper, possibly African, and (on the other side) people dancing and frolicking. There's also a fresco of saints from the Monastery of St Jeremiah at Saqqara. Amid the shell-shaped cornices in **Room 3**, one relief shows the goddess Aphrodite emerging from a seashell, just as she does in Botticelli's famous painting. Another image of Aphrodite, in the centre of the room, looks almost Indian. Behind her, second-century gravestones still feature the Egyptian gods Anubis and Horus, but pagan gods disappeared and

followed harsher taxation, abortive revolts, punitive massacres and indignities engendered by the Crusades, until the Muslims attained a nationwide majority (probably during the thirteenth century, earlier in Cairo). Thereafter Copts still participated in Egyptian life at every level, but the community retreated inwards and its monasteries and clergy stagnated until the nineteenth century.

THE COPTS TODAY

In recent decades the Coptic monasteries have been revitalized by a new generation of well-educated monks, and community work and church attendances are flourishing, but Coptic solidarity reflects alarm at rising **Islamic fundamentalism** and sectarianism. In Egypt religion is recorded on official ID cards (Egyptians may only be Muslim, Christian or Jewish), and it is illegal for a Muslim to convert to Christianity. There have been several cases of Christian children being abducted and "converted" to Islam, making it extremely difficult for them to return to their original faith. To build or even repair a church requires permission from the local governor, usually denied, and even when given, it often results in sectarian attacks from local Muslims. The Mubarak regime happily pandered to sectarian sentiment, using the 2009 swine flu epidemic, for example, as an excuse to slaughter all of the country's pigs and close down all butchers selling pork, despite the fact that swine flu cannot be caught from pigs, and that pigs played a vital role in Egypt's rubbish recycling.

Meanwhile, Egypt's liberal intelligentsia became more vocal in their opposition to sectarianism, satirizing it, for example, in a 2008 movie, *Hassan and Morqos*, starring Omar Sharif and Adel Imam. **During the revolution** (which came shortly after a bomb attack on an Alexandria church that killed 21 people), intercommunal solidarity was a theme commonly voiced by those in Tahrir Square, symbolized by a ubiquitous crescent-and-cross symbol. Salafists and regime supporters had different ideas, however, with attacks by Salafists on Christian communities in Upper Egypt leading to a demonstration in Cairo in October 2011 which was in turn attacked by regime supporters and soldiers, leaving 24 dead. In the face of this, the high vote obtained by the Salafists in the elections has heightened the fear now felt by Egypt's Christian community. The most forthright reporting on this comes from the Coptic diaspora, especially in the US, with regular updates at ⊛copts.com and ⊛freecopts.net.

1

OLD CAIRO & RODA ISLAND

N

Saiyida Zeinab Mosque   Saiyida Zeinab Mosque

Al-Abdin Mosque

Slaughterhouse

SHARIA BAHRAM EL TONSI

SHARIA BUR SAID

SHARIA BUR SAID

AL-BARRANI

SHARIA MAGRI AL-AYUN

Institut Français

Saiyida Zeinab (M)

SHARIA MANSUR

Monastery of St Menas

Ayyubid Aqueduct

QASR AL-AINI

Bird Market

ABU RISH

SHARIA AL-SADD

GARDEN CITY

Qasr al-Aini Hospital

MANIAL BRIDGE

SHARIA MANSUR

Burg al-Saqiyya

QASR AL-AINI BRIDGE

CORNICHE AL-NIL

FUMM AL-KHALIG

Manial Palace

SHARIA SAYALA

Cairo University Medical Faculty

SHARIA AL-MANIAL

RODA ISLAND

Umm Kalthoum Garden

SHARIA AL-MANIAL

River Taxi

GAMA'A BRIDGE

River Nile

Gold's Gym

SHARIA EL-NIL (CORNICHE)

Mahmoud Khalil Museum

SHARIA EL-GIZA

DOKKI

Nasr Building

Former Israeli Embassy

SHARIA MARUUN

Survey Office

Saudi-Arabian Embassy

Zoological Garden

SHARIA AL-MISHA

Nahdet Misr Statue

El-Urman Garden

SHARIAAL-DOKKI

SHARIA ABDEL SALAM ARIF

0   250
metres

▲ Tahrir Square   ▲ Maspero Dock   ▲ Aguza

▼ Cairo University

■ ACCOMMODATION
Grand Nile Tower   1
Youth Hostel   2

● RESTAURANTS
Abou Shakra   3
Foontana   2
Revolving Restaurant   1

■ NIGHTSPOT
Pharaohs Floating
Festaurants   1

● SHOPS
APE   1
AUEED   1
Icon Art Gallery   1
Nefertari   1

1

El-Khalifa & Citadel

Tanneries

SHARIA SALAH SALEM

SHARIA MANSUR

CORNICHE AL-NIL

El-Malek
El-Saleh

AL-SALIH BRIDGE

SHARIA AL-MALIK AL-SALEH

SHARIA EL-MANIAL

Student
cards

GIZA BRIDGE

SHARIA SIDI HASSAN AL-ANWAR

Mosque
of Amr

Buses

Church of
St Shenute

Church of
St Mercurius

Church of
the Holy Virgin

OLD CAIRO

CORNICHE AL-NIL

FOOTBRIDGE

Bus to Tahrir

Umm
Kalthoum
Museum

Manasterly Palace

Nilometer

Jacob
Island

SITE
OF
FUSTAT

Ticket
Office

SHARIA AL-IMAM

Souk al-
Fustat

SHARIA MARI GIRGIS

SHARIA AL-QABWA

SEE INSET FOR DETAIL

Mari
Girgis

Ma'adi & Helwan

SHARIA AL-GIZA

SHARIA MURAD

GIZA

MIDAN
GIZA

SHARIA FAYSAL

PYRAMIDS ROAD

SHARIA GAMI'AT AL-QAMIRA

Giza Station & Pyramids

COPTIC CAIRO

Footbridge

Underpass

Mari
Girgis

SHARIA MARI GIRGIS

Monastery
of St George

Convent of
St George

Church of
the Virgin

Church of
St George

Nuptial
Hall

Church of
St George

Church of
St Sergius

Church of
St Barbara

Ben Ezra
Synagogue

Roman
South
Tower

Coptic
Museum

Hanging
Church

Water Gate

Roman Walls

N

0   20

metres

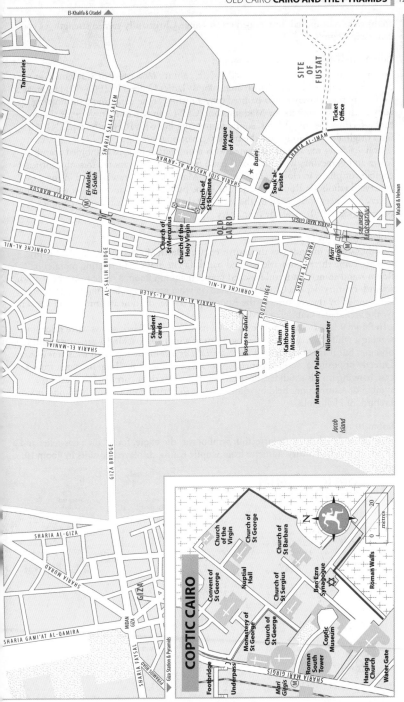

ankhs were transmuted into looped crosses once Christianity gained strength, as you can see in **Room 4**.

Objects from the Monastery of St Jeremiah

Rooms 5 and 6 display objects from the sixth-century **Monastery of St Jeremiah** at Saqqara, unearthed by the British archeologist James Quibell in 1906–10. His greatest finds were seven lovely fresco-painted **prayer niches**, some depicting Jesus holding up a copy of the Bible, others the Madonna and Child – in two of them Mary is shown breast-feeding the infant Jesus, subtly identifying her with Isis (see box, p.124). All were originally used to inspire the monks' devotional prayers.

Stone-carving was a craft associated with monasteries; masons combined acanthus leaves and grapevines with pharaonic palm fronds and lotus motifs to sculpt intricate capitals for pillars in cloisters and churches. Many of these are displayed in the courtyard adjoining Room 6, where the stone **pulpit** – the oldest one known anywhere – may have been influenced by the Heb-Sed thrones of Zoser's funerary complex at Saqqara (see p.160), near the monastery.

Objects from Bawit

Another source of finds was the fourth-century **Bawit Monastery** in Middle Egypt, whence came three geometric painted panels (a cheap way of imitating mosaic) in **Room 7** and some wonderful frescoed prayer niches in **Room 8**. One from the sixth or seventh century depicts Christ enthroned on what appears to be a flaming chariot, surrounded by the creatures of the Apocalypse (eagle, ox, lion and man), and flanked by the archangels Gabriel and Michael.

In **Room 9**, a cartoon from the wall of a monk's cell at Bawit shows three mice (one waving a white flag, another offering a cup of wine) approaching a cat – its meaning is obscure, but it is reminiscent of the *Satirical Papyrus* in the Egyptian Museum (p.82). Directly opposite, a wooden panel depicts a haloed monk reaching for a pen from a case hanging on his shoulder; the peacock in the top right corner of the panel is a symbol of resurrection, held by some scholars to derive from the mythical phoenix, or firebird, of Heliopolis.

Room 10

Another early Christian resurrection symbol was the **eagle**, found on a bas-relief and a third- or fourth-century statuette from Coptic Cairo, displayed upstairs in **Room 10**.

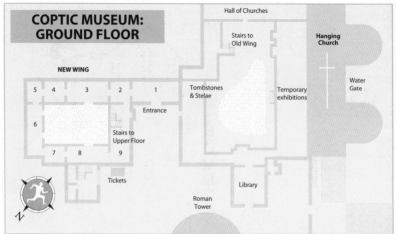

COPTIC MUSEUM: GROUND FLOOR

Hall of Churches

Stairs to Old Wing

Hanging Church

NEW WING

5 4 3 2 1

Tombstones & Stelae

Temporary exhibitions

Water Gate

Entrance

6

Stairs to Upper Floor

7 8 9

Tickets

Library

Roman Tower

This harks back to Greek mythology (whose supreme deity Zeus often took an eagle's form), as do an embroidered piece of cloth and a carving depicting centaurs (one ridden by a faun playing pan pipes). Behind is a trove of gold coins from the White Monastery near Sohag in Middle Egypt. Another case displays fourth- to sixth-century linen, woollen tunics and leather shoes, while beyond are handwritten copies of the **gospels** in Coptic and Arabic.

Room 11

Minutely detailed carving in ivory was as much a devotional task as copying the gospels. In **Room 11**, a comb depicts the raising of Lazarus, while a panel (probably from a box) shows the resurrected Jesus appearing to the apostles Peter, James and John, and beneath, chatting to Moses and Elijah. A sixth- or seventh-century fresco from St Jeremiah's Monastery portrays Abraham preparing to sacrifice his son on God's orders (Genesis 22:1–14; Koran 37:102–105); sadly, the top half is missing.

Rooms 12 to 14

The liturgical vestments in **Room 12** jump forward to the nineteenth century before **Room 13** returns to the fourth and fifth centuries, with **tapestries** and **embroideries** including a tiny one of Hercules feeding a lion. A strip of cloth from the same period depicts Aphrodite partying, but the goddess is notably absent from the neighbouring seventh- or eighth-century black-and-white depiction of similar scenes. In **Room 14**, the textiles get more colourful and elaborate, including a particularly good one featuring dancing animals.

The Nag Hammadi Gospels

Room 15 is devoted to the **Gospels of Nag Hammadi**, whose 1200 pages shed light on the development of early Christianity and its mystic tradition. These non-canonical gospels – omitted from the Bible – were mostly translated into Coptic from Greek for local members of the heretical Gnostic church. Probably buried during anti-Gnostic purges in the fourth and fifth centuries, they were found in a sealed jar by farmers near the Upper Egyptian town of Nag Hammadi in 1945. Sadly only two pages are on show here, along with the covers in which the gospels were found. The two pages contain the end of a book called the Apocryphon of John, and the beginning of the Gospel of Thomas, which may actually be earlier than the official, canonical gospels. Translations of these and other Nag Hammadi gospels can be found at ⓦgnosis.org/naghamm/nhl.html.

Rooms 16 and 17

The rest of the museum is rather less interesting, though bibliophiles may enjoy the books in **Room 16**, which include paper ones from a time before paper was known in Christian Europe. You can also see inkpots, a scribe's pen case (similar to the one shown on the panel in Room 9), and letters, doodles and orders for grain, mostly inscribed on potsherds but with two on pieces of animal bone. **Room 17** has only one exhibit: a fourth- or fifth-century book of psalms with an ankh-shaped bookmark.

Rooms 18 to 19

Passing through a corridor into the **Old Wing**, **Room 18** contains wooden panels carved with Nile scenes including two from the fifth or sixth century featuring crocodiles, still endemic in Egypt at that time. The exquisite **painted ceiling** with stained-glass windows in **Room 19**, dating from the museum's inauguration in 1910, was lovingly restored in 2006 and rather outshines the other exhibits, including some wooden pull-along toys with wheels, dating from Byzantine times, and a Fayoum-style funerary portrait (see p.82).

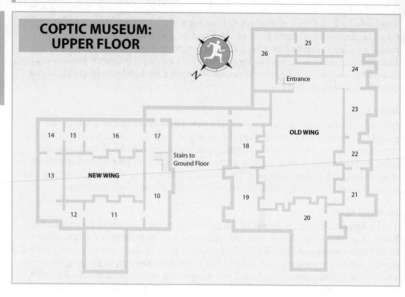

COPTIC MUSEUM: UPPER FLOOR

N

26 | 25 | 24 | 23

Entrance

OLD WING

14 | 15 | 16 | 17 | 18 | 22

Stairs to Ground Floor

13 | **NEW WING**

10 | 19 | 21

12 | 11 | 20

Icons and other artefacts

Room 20 is dedicated to **icons**, including a thirteenth-century triptych of Jesus on the cross surrounded by pictures of events (on the left) preceding and (on the right) following his crucifixion. An eighteenth-century image of two saints with the heads of dogs harks back to ancient times, and sits oddly on a Christian icon. Gruesome icons in **Room 21** include one of St Zacharias being throttled to death, and one of John the Baptist holding his own decapitated head on a dish. Also in Room 21, an eighteenth-century icon on a cloth was a typical souvenir sold to pilgrims in Palestine, which they could roll up and take home. The icons continue in **Room 22**, where one, of St Thomas touching Jesus's stigmata, shows Jesus and the disciples as they probably were – rather swarthier than as usually depicted in European churches. **Rooms 23–25** are dedicated to metalware, glassware and ceramics, and **Room 26** has an Ottoman litter in which rich female pilgrims were carried to Jerusalem.

You then descend to the courtyard, to pop into the **Hall of Churches of Old Cairo**, whose prime exhibit is a fifth-century wooden altar from the Church of St Sergius (see p.132) topped by a wooden dome from the Hanging Church (see below), dating from Fatimid times (tenth to twelfth centuries).

The Hanging Church

Sharia Mari Girgis • Daily 9am–5pm; Coptic Mass Wed 8–10am, Fri & Sun 9–11am (no public entry until after mass) • Free

Built directly above the water gate, the **Hanging Church** (in Arabic, *al-Mu'allaqah*, "The Suspended") can be reached via an ornate portal on Sharia Mari Girgis south of the Western Gate and the Coptic Museum. Ascending a steep stairway, you enter a nineteenth-century vestibule displaying cassettes and videos of Coptic liturgies and papal sermons. Above this are the monks' quarters; beneath it lies a secret repository for valuables, only discovered last century. Through the door and to the right, a glass panel in the floor of the church allows you to see that the church is indeed "suspended" bridge-like, above the water gate.

The main **nave** – whose ceiling is ribbed like an upturned boat or ark – is separated from the side aisles by sixteen pillars, formerly painted with images of saints. Behind the marble pulpit, beautifully carved altar screens hide three separate

1

haikals (altar sanctuaries) from the congregation. Their star patterns, accentuated by inlaid bone and ivory, are similar to those found in mosques. Both the pulpit and the altar screens date from the thirteenth century, but the church was founded at least six hundred years earlier and may even have originated in the fourth century as a chapel for the soldiers of the bastion. Among its relics, the church once claimed to own an olive stone chewed by the Virgin Mary, to whom Al-Mu'allaqah is dedicated.

If you want to attend a Coptic **mass**, the Hanging Church is the best place to do so, for both its choir and atmosphere.

The Old Quarter
Entrance from Sharia Mari Girgis • Daily 8am–4pm • Free

A hundred metres north of the Coptic Museum, just north of St George's Monastery, steps lead down via a **subterranean gateway** into the oldest part of Old Cairo, whose cobbled lanes flanked by high-walled houses wend between medieval churches and cemeteries. Described as a "constricted slum" by British satirist Evelyn Waugh in 1929, the quarter has been gradually sanitized and tarted up for tourists since the 1970s, and now seems quite spruce compared to Islamic Cairo.

The Convent of St George
Coptic Cairo, Old Quarter • Daily 10am–4pm (if door is closed, ring bell for entry) • Free

The most interesting of the Old Quarter's churches is reached through the first gate on the left after you pass through the subterranean gateway. This is the Coptic **Convent of St George**, whose main building, still a nunnery, is closed to visitors. Underneath however, and usually open to visitors (despite still being under restoration during our last visit) is a lofty hall that once belonged to a Fatimid mansion. The chapel beyond, with tall, narrow wooden doors, boasts a cedarwood casket containing relics of St George.

To the left of this building is the **Chaplet of St George**, a small chapel holding the very chain with which St George was restrained while being tortured by the Romans. Visitors may touch the chain for *baraka*, and the nuns may even offer to wrap it around you for a souvenir photo.

Church of the Virgin
Coptic Cairo, Old Quarter • Daily 8am–4pm • Free

The **Church of the Virgin** is also known as **Qasriyyat al-Rihan** ("Pot of Basil") after the favourite herb of the Orthodox Church. Because the mother of the Fatimid Caliph al-Hakim was a Greek Orthodox Christian, the church was given to the Greek community for the duration of his reign, but later returned to the Copts. Largely rebuilt in the eighteenth century, with a new roof added quite recently, it's chiefly notable for several icons painted in 1778 by John the Armenian, a well-known icon painter of the time.

FEATURES OF A COPTIC CHURCH

As in Anglican and Catholic churches, the congregation of a Coptic church sit in the **nave**, the main body of the building, and pray towards an **altar** – a consecrated table covered with a cloth, on which the wine and wafer used for mass are placed. As in Greek and Russian Orthodox churches, however, the altar is hidden behind an **altar screen** (iconostasis), usually decorated with **icons** (paintings of saints), and only priests may enter the **haikal** (sanctuary area) behind the screen.

In front of the screen, the **pulpit** is typically made of marble. The thirteen **pillars** holding it up represent Jesus and the twelve disciples. Usually, one of the pillars is black, for Judas, and another, perhaps rather unfairly, is grey, for "doubting" Thomas.

1

Church of St Sergius

Coptic Cairo, Old Quarter • Daily 8am–4pm • Free

The **Church of St Sergius** (Abu Serga) is the oldest church in Egypt, its great age attested by its site below modern-day street level. Probably founded in the fifth century, though most of the current building dates from the eleventh, Abu Serga retains the basilical form typical of early Coptic churches. Antique columns topped with Corinthian capitals support the women's gallery, where you can inspect the thirteenth-century altar screen, and bits of frescoes and mosaics in the central apse. Steps to the right of the altar descend into a **crypt** where the Holy Family are believed to have stayed, a sojourn commemorated by a Coptic **festival** (June 1). Unfortunately, the crypt itself is open only for services (Sat 6–7pm). A recently discovered thirteenth-century painting in the apse of the church's south chapel could not be seen at the time of writing due to restoration work in progress.

Church of St Barbara

Coptic Cairo, Old Quarter • Daily 8am–4pm • Free

The eleventh-century **Church of St Barbara** replaced an earlier Church of Saints Cyrus and John, which was razed during Al-Hakim's assault on Fustat (see p.134). Unlike others in the quarter, its wooden-vaulted roof is lofty, with skylights and windows illuminating a nave flanked by Arabic arches with Fatimid tie-beams. Its *minbar*-esque pulpit and inlaid altar screen would not look amiss in a mosque. The western sanctuary (remove shoes to enter) contains the cloth-wrapped relics of Saint Barbara. Tradition holds that she was the daughter of a pagan merchant who was murdered for preaching Christianity in the third century.

The Ben Ezra Synagogue

Coptic Cairo, Old Quarter • Daily 8am–4pm • Free (but donation requested)

The **Ben Ezra Synagogue** is a unique relic of Cairo's ancient Jewish community which persisted long after most Jews had moved to Fustat or the Haret al-Yahud (see box p.96), leaving only twelve impoverished families by 1864, and not one a century later. The synagogue would have crumbled away were it not for the efforts of one "Rabbi" Cohen, who shamelessly overcharged for souvenir postcards to fund repairs for twenty years, until the American Jewish Congress and the Egyptian government stepped in to restore it in the 1990s.

In form, the synagogue resembles a basilical church of the kind that existed here between the fourth and ninth centuries. Sold to the Jews so that the Copts could pay taxes to finance Ibn Tulun's Mosque, this church was either demolished or incorporated within the synagogue, which Abraham Ben Ezra, the Rabbi of Jerusalem, restored in 1041. The inlaid marble and gilded stalactite niche date from around then, but most of the arabesque mouldings and floral swirls are the result of repairs following the discovery of a vast cache of medieval manuscripts: the **geniza** (see box opposite) after 1864. **Photography** isn't allowed inside, to the frustration of visitors dying to snap the opulent decor.

Jewish and Coptic traditions invest the site of the synagogue with ancient significance. Here, it is said, the pharaoh's daughter found Moses in the bulrushes (Exodus 2:1–6), the biblical prophet Jeremiah gathered survivors after Nebuchadnezzar destroyed Jerusalem, and the temple named after him provided a haven for the Holy Family, who lived among the Jews of Babylon for three months of their sojourn in Egypt (Matthew 2:13–15). Moreover, the Copts believe that saints Peter and Mark pursued their apostolic mission in Egypt, and that from here Peter issued the First Epistle General (the New Testament's First Epistle of Peter). The rest of Christendom disagrees, however, arguing that the Biblical reference to Babylon (I Peter 5:13) is only a metaphor for Rome.

Fustat

Entrance from Sharia al-Imam • Daily (not set hours, but the the family who live on site will let you in at any reasonable hour) • 24hr • £E10

To the northeast of Coptic Cairo is the vast site of the once-great city of **Fustat**, Cairo's

THE BEN EZRA GENIZA

In the Jewish religion, any document in Hebrew, or one which might bear God's name, must be preserved. Since Ben Ezra's restoration in 1041, therefore, nearly all the papers of Cairo's Jewish community were consigned to a special storeroom in the synagogue, known in Hebrew as a **geniza**. In 1864, a Lithuanian Talmudist, Jacob Sapir, was the first outsider to explore this geniza, but although he realized that some of the ancient documents might be of historical interest, he was a religious scholar rather than a historian, and did not alert anybody in the academic community. Scrolls and texts subsequently began to leak onto the black market, and in 1896, two Scottish sisters, **Agnes Lewis** and **Margaret Gibson**, who were familiar with a number of Semitic languages, including Hebrew, bought some mansucript fragments in Cairo which had come from the geniza. The two sisters realized that these might be important and, when they got back to Britain, they took them to **Solomon Schechter**, a rabbi who was a professor of Talmudic studies at Cambridge University. Schechter identified one of the fragments as a unique copy of a lost Hebrew text from the Apocrypha, and immediately rushed to Egypt to acquire everything that was left in the geniza. The 280,000 letters, contracts and legal rulings amounted to the most complete record of any medieval society ever discovered. Thanks to Schechter, most of them are now in Cambridge's university library.

first Islamic incarnation. Leading southeastward from the northern end of Coptic Cairo, Sharia al-Imam runs alongside it. About 300m down this road on the left you can access what's left of the **ruins of Fustat**, comprising some remains of mud-brick houses and fallen pillars, still being organized by archeologists. A caretaker will show you round the site, which is a necessary precaution given that there are a lot of unfenced wells, which you wouldn't want to fall down. Smoke from neighbouring potteries can be seen rising around the perimeter of the site, and the combination of smoke and ruins gives the feel of a city that had the misfortune to be burned down no less than three times (see box p.134).

On the corner of Sharia Hassan al-Anwar with Sharia al-Imam, the relatively new **Souk al-Fustat** (daily 10am–6pm), contains shops showcasing handicrafts by local artisans (see p.199). A small park has also been created behind the souk, accessed from the bus station just to the north.

The far side of the Fustat site, accessible from Sharia Dalah Saleh (see map, p.116) has been grassed over and landscaped to create **Fustat Park** (daily 9am–9pm; £E2), funded, like Al-Azhar Park (see p.122), by the Aga Khan Trust.

Mosque of Amr

Sharia Sidi Hassan al-Anwar • Daily, approximately 9am–8pm • Free • Buses serve the mosque from Abdel Mouneem Riyad (#235) and Ramses (#134, minibus #94); Mar Girgis and El-Malek el-Saleh metro stations are within walking distance

North of Coptic Cairo, the **Mosque of Amr** was founded by Egypt's Arab conqueror, **Amr Ibn al-As**. Though altered several times and doubled in size in 827, it boasts direct descent from Egypt's first-ever mosque, built in 641. A simple mud-brick, thatch-roofed enclosure without a *mihrab*, courtyard or minaret, it was large enough to contain the Muslim army at prayer.

The existing building follows the classic congregational pattern, arched *liwans* surrounding a pebbled courtyard centred on an ablutions well. Believers pray or snooze on fine carpets in the prayer hall *liwan*. When Amr introduced a pulpit, he was rebuked by Caliph Omar for raising himself above his Muslim brethren. The *mashrabiya*'d **mausoleum** of his son, Abdullah, marks the site of Amr's house in Fustat. A nearby column bears a gash caused by people licking it until their tongues bled to obtain miraculous cures. The pair of columns on the left as you come in are said to part to allow the truly righteous to squeeze through, and another was whipped from Mecca by Omar. From the mosque's **well**, it is said, a pilgrim retrieved a goblet dropped into the Well of Zemzem in the Holy City.

1

THE THRICE-BURNED CITY

Fustat was founded in 642 AD by the victorious Arab general **Amr Ibn al-As**, near the fortress of Babylon which had just fallen to his troops. According to tradition, its location was chosen by a dove, which laid an egg in Amr's tent before he was to march on Alexandria. Amr declared this as a sign from God, and the tent was left untouched as they went off to battle. When they returned victorious, Amr told his troops to pitch their tents around his, giving his new capital its name, **Masr al-Fustat**, "City of the Tents". From an array of tribal encampments around a mosque, it grew into a wealthy city populated by Copts and Jews and settlers from Yemen and Arabia, communicating in Arabic and Coptic, and trading as far away as India.

In 750 AD, the final Umayyad caliph, **Marwan II**, made his last stand here, and then had Fustat **burned behind him** as he fled the victorious Abbasids, who proceeded to usurp the caliphate from him. The Abbasids ordered a new city to be built further north, but Fustat was never depopulated, and never stopped growing: in the early eleventh century, the Persian poet and traveller **Nasir Khusraw** saw fourteen-storey buildings with roof gardens here, irrigated by ox-powered waterwheels, which drew from a **piped water system** unmatched anywhere else until the eighteenth century.

This huge conurbation peaked demographically long after the **Fatimids** had founded Al-Qahira (see p.92), when its population topped two hundred thousand. Even the **sacking and burning** of Fustat ordered by the "mad caliph" **Al-Hakim** in 1020 (see p.101) left such vast remains that in 1168 the Fatimid vizier Shawar decided to **evacuate and burn** it yet again, rather than let the invading Crusaders occupy the defenceless old city and use it as a base outside Al-Qahira's walls. Set ablaze with ten thousand torches and twenty thousand barrels of naphtha, "flames and smoke engulfed the city and rose to the sky in a terrifying scene", wrote the historian **Al-Maqrizi**. Fustat burned for 54 days, and was not occupied again. Under the **Mamlukes**, its ruins became a rubbish dump, entirely ignored except for the Mosque of Amr – the sole surviving monument to its bygone glory.

Deir Abu'l-Sayfayn

Sharia Ali Salem • Daily 9am–5pm • Free • Metro to Mari Girgis or El-Malek el-Saleh

If the Coptic quarter hasn't satisfied your curiosity about medieval churches, pay a visit to **Deir Abu'l-Sayfayn**, a walled enclosure northwest of Amr's Mosque, entered via a door at its southwest corner. Inside, the first church to the right is the early seventh-century **Church of St Shenute** (Anba Shenouda), featuring a beautiful cedarwood and ebony altar screen. Beyond it, the **Church of St Mercurius**, first mentioned in the tenth century (when it served as a sugar-cane warehouse), was totally rebuilt after the burning of Fustat, and was closed for renovation on our last visit. Beneath its northern aisle you can descend into a tiny crypt where St Barsum the Naked lived with a snake until his death in 317; a special Mass is held here on his name day (Sept 10).

Across the way, the diminutive, icon-packed **Church of the Holy Virgin** (Al-Damshira), originally dating from the seventh century, was destroyed in 785, rebuilt in 809 and restored in the eighteenth century, looking very modern on the outside, and beautifully restored within. It also has a very fine inlaid altar screen, while a cabinet at the back of the anteroom holds some archeological finds, unfortunately unlabelled.

Adjacent to Deir Abu'l-Sayfayn are extensive Protestant and Maronite **cemeteries**, including a military cemetery for Commonwealth servicemen killed in World War II.

Burg al-Saqiyya

Sharia Magri al-Ayun at Corniche al-Nil • Daily 9am–8pm • Free

Near the Corniche stands a massive hexagonal water-wheel tower, the **Burg al-Saqiyya**, formerly used to raise river water to feed the great **aqueduct** that carried water from the river to the Citadel, and which can be seen alongside Sharia Magri al-Ayoun and Sharia

Salah Salem – by the Saiyida Aisha Mosque, for example (see p.119). Originally a mere conduit supported by wooden pillars, the aqueduct was rebuilt in stone under Sultan al-Nasir in 1311 and extended under Al-Ghuri in 1505 to accommodate the Nile's westward shift, to a total length of 3405m.

On the Burg al-Saqiyya's western wall you can still see Al-Ghuri's heraldic emblem and slots for engaging the six oxen-powered water wheels, which remained in use until 1872. Stairs to the top of the tower allow visitors to see one of the oxen tread-wheels and enjoy a fantastic **view** west over Roda Island or eastwards to the Muqattam Hills. The locality is called **Fumm al-Khalig** (Mouth of the Canal) after the Khalig Masri (Egyptian Canal) that once ran inland from here and along what is now Sharia Bur Said. In an annual ceremony to mark the Nile flood, the dike that separated the canal from the river was breached, sending fresh water coursing through the city to fill boating lakes near Bab al-Luq and Ezbekiya.

Roda Island

The narrow channel between **Roda Island** and the mainland is bridged in such a way that the island engages more with Garden City than with Old Cairo – a reversal of historic ties. As the much-rebuilt **Nilometer** suggests, it was the southern end of Roda that was visited by ferries en route between Memphis and Heliopolis, and Roman ships bound for Babylon-in-Egypt. However, Roda reverted to agricultural use as Cairo's focus shifted northeastwards, and nothing remains of the Byzantine fortress that defied the Muslim invasion, nor the vast Ayyubid *qasr* where the Bahri Mamlukes were garrisoned. Its sights are very spread out, and you wouldn't normally visit them together. **Manial Palace**, at the island's northern end, is most conveniently reached from Garden City, while the Nilometer and **Umm Kalthoum Museum** at its southern end are easiest to get to from Old Cairo.

The Nilometer

Southern end of Roda Island, off Sharia al-Malik al-Saleh • Daily 8am–4pm • £E15 (tickets are sold just inside the compound containing the Nilometer and Umm Kalthoum Museum)

Roda's **Nilometer** is the best-preserved example of a device invented by the ancient Egyptians (see box below) that was adopted by later civilizations and remained in use for millennia. This particular one dates from Abbasid times (861 AD), though others existed here earlier. A stone-lined shaft descending below the level of the Nile, it was connected to the river by three tunnels (now sealed) at different heights – only the uppermost is still accessible. Around the shaft's interior are koranic verses extolling rain as God's blessing. The central column is graduated into 16 *ells* of roughly 54cm each and enclosed by a 1947 replica of a kiosk that covered it in Ottoman times.

NILOMETERS

From ancient times to the present century, Egyptian agriculture depended on the annual **flooding of the Nile**. Crop yields were predicted and taxes were set according to the river's level in August, as measured by a series of **Nilometers** from Aswan down the valley to Roda and the Delta. Readings were sent to Egypt's ruler and provincial governors; the basin-system of irrigation dictated that dikes must be breached at certain levels, making the Nile's rise essential to the whole nation. A reading of 16 *ells* (8.6m) foretold the valley's complete irrigation; significantly more or less meant widespread flooding or drought. Public rejoicing followed the announcement of the Wafa al-Nil ("Abundance of the Nile"), while any other verdict caused gloom and foreboding.

THE STAR OF THE EAST

Umm Kalthoum, known as Kawkab al-Sharq (Star of the East), was born in a Delta village some time between 1898 and 1904, when girls' births weren't registered. Her father was an imam who taught her to recite the Koran (she reportedly memorized the entire book) and, when she was 12, disguised her as a boy and entered her in a performing troupe where she was later noticed by an established singer who taught her the classical repertoire. Moving to Cairo in 1923 she was taught to play the lute, and mentored in Arabic literature by the poet Ahmed Rami (who wrote 137 songs for her), but never became part of the bohemian set, proudly espousing her humble origins and conservative values. Her powerful and wide-ranging voice had an immediate emotional impact which very quickly brought her to public attention – King Farouk became a big fan, as did Nasser. Her funeral drew 2.5 million mourners, so many that their combined weight almost brought down the Qasr al-Nil Bridge. A **café** at 21 Sharia Orabi dedicated itself to playing her music all day long and was soon followed by imitators such as the *Soma Caffe* (see p.189).

Umm Kalthoum Museum

Southern end of Roda Island, off Sharia al-Malik al-Saleh • Daily 9am–4pm • £E2 (tickets are sold at the gate to the compound containing the museum and Nilometer)

In the same compound as the Nilometer is a **museum** dedicated to the life and work of Egypt's most popular singer, **Umm Kalthoum**, who lived in Zamalek until her death in 1975. It does a fair job of recreating the life and work of this giant of Arab music through audiovisual clips, photos, press cuttings and a film show. The exhibits include 78rpm wax records, letters from Arab heads of state including Nasser, Sadat and King Farouk, and, most poignantly, her trademark pink scarf and dark glasses.

Manial Palace

Sharia Sayala • Bus #95 or minibus #58 from Abdel Mouneem Riyad terminal, or minibus #56 from Ramses; alight on Sharia Sayala, near the palace gates.

Previously Roda's chief attraction, the **Manial Palace** across from Qasr al-Aini Hospital (see p.87) is **closed** for restoration until at least 2013 (would-be visitors can enquire at the tourist office downtown or ask the policemen at the palace gates, as scheduled opening dates mean little in Egypt). Once it reopens the palace will certainly be worth a visit. Built in 1903, its fabulously eclectic decor reflects the taste of King Farouk's uncle, Prince Mohammed Ali, author of *The Breeding of Arabian Horses*. Each of the main buildings manifests a different style – Persian, Syrian, Moorish, Ottoman and Rococo – or mixes them together with gay abandon.

In the **Reception Palace** just inside the gateway, a magnificent *salamlik* (guest-greeting room) adorned with stained glass, polychrome tiles and ornate woodcarving prepares visitors for the opulent guest rooms upstairs. The finest is the Syrian Room, literally transplanted from Damascus. Leaving this building and turning right, a pseudo-Moroccan tower harbours the prince's **mosque**, whose lavish decor is reminiscent of the great mosque of his namesake in the Citadel, and a grotesque **Hunting Museum** featuring scores of mounted ibex heads, a hermaphrodite goat, a table made from elephants' ears and a vulture's-claw candlestick.

Deeper into the banyan-shaded garden, the **Prince's Residence** is richly decorated in a mixture of Turkish and Occidental styles. The drab-looking building out the back contains an elongated **Throne Hall**, whose red carpet passes life-size royal portraits hung beneath a sunburst ceiling. If accessible, visitors can admire the Obsidian Salon and the private apartments of the prince's mother upstairs, enriched by a silver four-poster bed from the Abdin Palace. Lastly there's the **Private Museum**, a family hoard of manuscripts, carpets, glassware and silver plate, including some huge banqueting trays.

Gezira and Zamalek

The island of **Gezira** dominates the waterfront from Garden City to Bulaq, nearly 4km long and connected to either bank of the Nile by three sets of bridges. The southern half is Gezira proper (literally "island"), and includes the **Gezira Sporting Club** (see p.204), laid out by the British Army on land given by Khedive Tewfiq and occupying almost a third of the island. The northern half, **Zamalek**, is full of apartments, villas, offices and embassies, with a Westernized ambience and nightlife. Both seem so integral to Cairo that it's hard to envisage their absence, yet the island itself only coalesced out of mudbanks in the river in the early 1800s, and remained unstable until the first Aswan Dam regulated the Nile's flood in the 1900s. For more on the history and architecture of Gezira and Zamalek, check out Samir Raafat's website at ⓦ egy.com/zamalek.

GETTING TO GEZIRA AND ZAMALEK

Despite the traffic, it's enjoyable to walk across the Qasr al-Nil Bridge (200m west of Tahrir Square), catching the breeze and watching barges and feluccas on the river. Further north, the 6th October Bridge, high above the Sporting Club, is more of a direct link between Aguza and central Cairo than a convenient approach to Zamalek, although you can access Gezira from it via stairs down to both the eastern and western sides of the island.

By metro The only metro station in Gezira at present is Opera station by the Opera House. Line 3 will eventually have a station in Zamalek.

By bus Buses from Tahrir Square to Zamalek will drop you on Sharia Gabalaya on the western side of the district; buses from Tahrir to Dokki will drop you on Sharia Tahrir near the Opera House.

By service taxi Service taxi microbuses can be picked up at Al-Esa'af Pharmacy, at the junction of 26th July St and Sharia Ramses, and will drop you at Sharia Abul Feda on the west side of the island.

By taxi A taxi from downtown to Gezira or Zamalek should cost around £E5–8.

By calèche *Calèches*, horse-drawn carriages seating up to five people, are available from Sharia al-Gezira between Qasr al-Nil and 6th October bridges, and from Sharia Tahrir by Gala'a Bridge for tours of Gezira. A short trip around the Cairo Tower will cost about £E40, while a 30min circuit all the way round the Gezira Sporting Club is about £E60.

The Cairo Tower

Sharia al-Borg • Daily 8am–midnight • £E70 • ⓦ cairotower.net

Rising 187m above Gezira, the **Borg al-Qahira** or **Cairo Tower** offers a stupendous view of the city's seething immensity. Entering the tower from Sharia al-Borg, visitors take a lift to the mediocre **restaurant** on the fourteenth floor (minimum charge £E150) that – when working – slowly revolves for a 360° view. Above, on the fifteenth floor, a

NASSER'S COLUMN

The **Cairo Tower** is the world's tallest all-concrete structure, built with Soviet help between 1956 and 1961. Combining pharaonic and socialist-realist motifs, it takes the form of a cylindrical lattice of poured concrete, flared at the top to symbolize a lotus flower. The tower was funded with money passed to Nasser by CIA bagman **Kermit Roosevelt** as a bribe to stay on America's side during the Cold War. Nasser spent it on the tower to be, as historian Samir Rafaat called it, "a giant middle finger [that] even the Americans would see". Egyptian officials nicknamed it waqf Roosevelt, which can be taken to mean "Roosevelt's endowment" or "Roosevelt's erection". The Americans retaliated by calling it "**Nasser's prick**", and this was apparently taken literally by an Islamist group in the 1990s, who issued a fatwa declaring the tower "against religion and sharia law. It must be destroyed," they said, "as its shape and construction amid greenery could excite Egyptian women". In fact the tower is a popular locale for discreet lovers' trysts, and remains so to this day, much to the ire of the religious lobby.

1

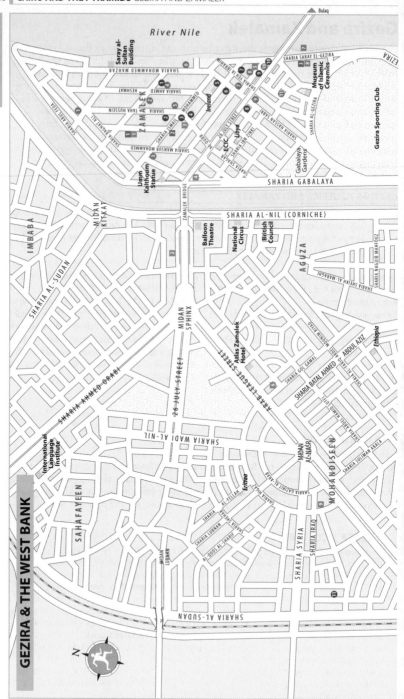

GEZIRA & THE WEST BANK

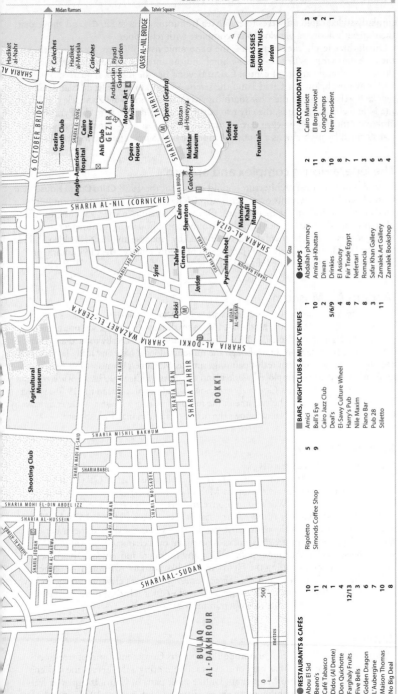

RESTAURANTS & CAFÉS

Abou El Sid	10
Beano's	11
Café Tabasco	2
Didos (Al Dente)	1
Don Quichotte	4
Farghaly Fruits	12/13
Five Bells	3
Golden Dragon	6
L'Aubergine	7
Maison Thomas	10
No Big Deal	8
Rigoletto	10
Simonds Coffee Shop	11

BARS, NIGHTCLUBS & MUSIC VENUES

Amici	1
Bull's Eye	10
Cairo Jazz Club	2
Deal's	5/6/9
El-Sawy Culture Wheel	4
Harry's Pub	8
Nile Maxim	7
Piano Bar	8
Pub 28	3
Stiletto	11

SHOPS

Abdallah pharmacy	5
Amira al-Khattan	9
Diwan	2
Drinkies	11
El Assiouty	9
Fair Trade Egypt	8
Nefertari	7
Romancia	1
Safar Khan Gallery	3
Zamalek Art Gallery	6
Zamalek Bookshop	5

ACCOMMODATION

Cairo Marriott	3
El Borg Novotel	4
Longchamps	2
New President	1

EMBASSIES SHOWN THUS:

Jordan

1

similarly styled **cafeteria** serves tolerable tea (minimum charge £E30), and above that, the sixteenth floor is a **viewing room** complete with telescopes.

On all three levels, the attraction is the **panoramic vista** of Cairo. East across the river, the blue-and-white *Nile Ritz-Carlton* hotel and the antenna-festooned Television Building delineate an arc of central Cairo. Beyond lies the medieval quarter, bristling with minarets below the Citadel and the serene Muqattam Hills. Roda Island and deluxe hotels dominate the view south (upriver); to the north are Zamalek, Shubra and the Nile Delta. Westwards, the city extends to meet the desert, with the Pyramids visible on the horizon on clear days. Come a while before sunset to witness Cairo transformed by nightfall, as a thousand muezzins call across the vast metropolis.

The Opera House complex and around

Fans of postmodernist architecture should check out the 1988 **Cairo Opera House** near Qasr al-Nil Bridge, with its own metro stop (signed "Opera" on the platform but marked as "Gezira" on the metro map). Outwardly Islamic in style, the interior melds pharaonic motifs with elements of the Baroque opera houses of the nineteenth century: an audacious blend of Oriental and Occidental by Japanese architect Koichiro Shikida. It was a US$30 million gift from Japan, and belatedly replaces the old building on Midan Opera, which burned down in 1971.

Modern Art Museum

Opera House Complex, off Sharia Tahrir, Gezira • Daily except Mon & Fri 10am–2.30pm & 5–9pm • £E10

East of the Opera House, the **Modern Art Museum** displays paintings, sculptures and graphics by Egyptian artists since 1908. The collection is periodically rotated and there is always something new on show, though the museum doesn't have any really famous works. Highlights include modern realist paintings such as Mohamed Owais's 1989 *Fellah*, depicting a weeping unemployed worker, and the grimly industrial *Factory Workers*. On a jollier note, Ragheb Ayad's *Café in Aswan* shows a traditional *'ahwa* in the 1930s, with a band playing and a rather hefty dame in the middle smoking a *sheesha*, while *Hammam* by Coptic artist Marguerite Nakhla shows the inside of a traditional Turkish bath.

Mukhtar Museum

Daily except Mon 10am–1.30pm & 5–9pm • £E5

Across Sharia Tahrir from the Opera House Complex, just east of Gala'a Bridge, the **Mukhtar Museum** honours the sculptor Mahmoud Mukhtar (1891–1934), who is buried in the basement. Working in bronze and marble, he created several patriotic sculptures, most famously *Nahdet Misr*, "Egypt's Renaissance" (see p.142). Mukhtar was a keen supporter of the nationalist Wafd Party, and is considered the father of modern Egyptian sculpture. His works are typified by a characteristic rounded smoothness, but are somehow staid, lacking any feeling of movement. The museum houses 85 of them, including the Henry Moore-like abstract *Khamsin* (the name refers to hot, dusty, spring wind) and *The Water Drawer*, Mukhtar's elegant homage to Egypt's hardworking village women. The museum was closed for refurbishment on our last visit, but was supposedly due to reopen in mid-2012.

Zamalek

Originally a very British neighbourhood, despite its Continental grid of tree-lined boulevards, **Zamalek** still has bags of social cachet: renting a flat here is the Cairene equivalent of moving into Manhattan. Unlike most parts of Cairo, the quarter feels very private; residents withdraw into air-conditioned high-rises or 1930s apartment

> **MURDER MOST FOUL**
>
> Although Zamalek is young by Egyptian standards, it isn't without its **history**, some of it quite grisly. Number 4 Sharia Hassan Sabry, for example, occupies the site of a villa where the UK's senior representative in wartime Egypt, **Lord Moyne**, was shot dead in 1944, along with his driver, by members of a maverick Zionist paramilitary group known as the Stern Gang.
>
> A more recent Zamalek murder, which shocked the Middle East no less, was that of Tunisian singer **Zikra** in November 2003, at her swanky apartment in the Saray al-Sultan building at 123 Sharia Mohammed Mazhar (next to what is now the *Hilton Hotel*). Zikra was killed by her husband, apparently in a fit of jealousy, after refusing his demand that she give up her career. Having produced two pistols and a machine gun, he pumped her with 25 rounds, then shot two of their friends, and finally himself. Thousands attended the singer's funeral. Perhaps predictably, the apartment is now said to be haunted.

buildings, and with so many foreign companies and **embassies** in the area, most of the streets are lifeless after dark.

The portions of Sharia Shagar al-Durr and Sharia Mansur Mohammed south of 26th July Street, were once home to **Edwardian villas** constructed by the British government in 1906–7 to house important official employees. Of the nine still standing, the grandest is at 20 Sharia Ibn Zinki (on the corner of Mansur Mohammed) with its imposing triple-arched portico.

Southeast of here, on the riverfront, the modern annexes of the **Cairo Marriott Hotel** (see p.184) screen what was originally a "madly sumptuous palace" built for Napoleon III's wife Empress Eugénie, later sold to wealthy Copts in lieu of Ismail's debts and turned into a hotel.

The singer **Umm Kalthoum** (see p.136) lived at 5 Sharia Abul Feda, just north of Zamalek Bridge, until her death in 1975, when her home was immediately taken over by property developers. They promptly demolished it and erected a hotel in its place, which is named after her. A **statue** of the great diva stands outside.

Museum of Islamic Ceramics

Sharia al-Gezira • Daily except Fri 10am–1.30pm & 5–9pm • £E25

Housed in a white-domed villa close to the *Cairo Marriott Hotel*, the **Museum of Islamic Ceramics** is one of Cairo's most agreeable museums. Built by Prince Amru Ibrahim in the late nineteenth century, the structure itself is worth a look for its elaborate marble inlays and floors. The collection contains pieces from Egypt, Persia, Syria, Turkey, Morocco, Iraq and Andalusia, ranging from the seventh century to the present. Downstairs there's an art gallery (same hours; free) exhibiting original paintings and sculptures as well as prints by modern Egyptian artists such as Asraf and Alzamzami. The museum was closed for refurbishment on our last visit, but was supposedly due to reopen in mid-2012.

The west bank

The districts on the **west bank** of the Nile are administered by the **Giza** governorate, which is separate from that of Cairo, though transport and utilities are effectively integrated. If you cross over to the west bank of the Nile from Zamalek, you arrive at **Mohandiseen**, laid out during the 1960s to house Egypt's new technocrats. Medinat Mohandiseen ("Engineers' City"), as the suburb was initially called, responded to an influx of business and media folk during the Sadat era by shortening its name and trying to be more American in style. Its main axis, **Arab League Street** (Sharia Gameat al-Dowal al-Arabiya) is bisected by palms and shrubbery for its three-kilometre length, and on a clear day (admittedly a rare occurrence in Cairo), you can look down it and see the Giza Pyramids, to which it is aligned.

1

The Mahmoud Khalil Museum

Sharia al-Giza • Daily except Mon 10am–6pm • £E25 • Wheelchair accessible

South of Aguza and Mohandiseen, **Dokki** (usually pronounced "Do'i", with a glottal stop in the middle) is notable for the **Mahmoud Khalil Museum**, housed in the refurbished mansion on Sharia al-Giza, where Khalil, a prewar politician and agriculture minister, lived with his French-born wife. Together they built up this magnificent collection of art and sculpture, mostly French Impressionist and post-Impressionist works. Highlights include Gauguin's *Life and Death*, in which both conditions are portrayed as nude women, and Gustave Moreau's *Salome in the Garden*, a depiction of the biblical *femme fatale* in Pre-Raphaelite style. There's also one of Monet's waterlily canvases, and paintings by Renoir and Pissaro, not to mention sculptures by Rodin. Van Gogh's *Poppy Flowers* was heisted from the museum in 2010 (for the second time), and was still missing at the time of writing.

Giza

South of Dokki is **Giza** proper, which in pharaonic times lay en route between Heliopolis and Memphis, and probably also housed the skilled corps of pyramid-builders. Coming over the Gama'a Bridge from Garden City, you pass (on the north side of the road) the former **Israeli Embassy**, now closed. Never popular with the Egyptian public, the embassy was stormed by protestors in September 2011 after Israeli troops had shot dead six Egyptian police officers in a border incident. Six staff members, forced to hide in a reinforced safe room, were only evacuated by commandos after a personal intervention by US president Barrack Obama.

Regaining terra firma after crossing the bridge, motorists are greeted at the next road junction by Mahmoud Mukhtar's most famous statue, **Nahdet Misr** –"Egypt's Renaissance" or "Egypt Awakes" (see p.140). For all its pharaonic stolidity, this 1928 sculpture, of a woman lifting her veil while a sphinx stirs at her feet, was supposed to represent a cultural renewal heralded by early twentieth-century Egyptian nationalism.

The Pyramids of Giza are nowhere near central Giza at all, but at the far end of **Pyramids Road** (Sharia al-Ahram), 8km of tourist bazaars and nightclubs, many of the latter trashed during the 2011 revolution. A couple of kilometres before the pyramids, it crosses two canals in quick succession, which lead south to Saqqara and Dahshur.

Giza Zoo

Sharia Nahdet Misr (entrance in northwest corner, opposite Nahdet Misr statue) • Daily 9am–5pm • £E20, video camera £E30

Besides creating the Ezbekiya Gardens (see p.84), the French landscaper **Jean-Pierre Barillet-Deschamps** (responsible for the Bois de Boulogne and the Champs de Mars in

---

MESSING ABOUT ON THE NILE

Boats have been synonymous with **misbehaviour** in Cairo since they were used in the Middle Ages on the seasonal lakes that filled when the Nile rose (see p.135). In the mid-twentieth century, the neighbourhood of Aguza, wedged between Mohandiseen and the Nile, was a popular mooring place for houseboats. One of them was occupied during World War II by a famous bellydancer, **Hekmet Fathy**, who used to entice Allied staff officers aboard to inveigle secrets from them on behalf of the Nazis. Also involved was a young Egyptian officer, **Anwar Sadat**, who attempted to convey messages to Rommel and was subsequently jailed by the British for treason. Even today, the Aguza and the surrounding area is known for naughtiness: many Gulf Arabs spend the summer here, and "**Saudi flats**" has become a euphemism for prostitution in this part of town. What the Saudi-linked Salafists now prominent in Egyptian politics, will do about this remains to be seen.

Paris) also laid out vast grounds for Khedive Ismail's palace in Giza. Ismail had hoped for a botanical garden in time for the opening of the Suez Canal but this wasn't realized until 1891, under his son Tewfik, a venture that soon grew into a **Zoological Garden** with a suspension bridge by **Gustav Eiffel**, man-made waterfalls and grottos, and flora and fauna from Africa and Asia, covering nearly 80 acres. For further information see the "Kids' attractions" section (p.195).

Across Sharia Najdet Misr, the smaller **Al-Urman Garden** (daily 8.30am–4pm; free) is a rather formal garden that was also originally part of Ismail's palace grounds.

The northern suburbs

During the last century, Cairo's **northern suburbs** swallowed up villages and farmland and expanded far into the desert to form a great arc of residential neighbourhoods stretching from the Nile to the Muqattam. **Heliopolis**, with its handsome boulevards and Art Deco villas, is still favoured above the satellite suburbs that have mushroomed in recent decades, and retains a sizeable foreign community.

Abbassiya

The sprawling **Abbassiya** district gets its name from a palace built by Mohammed Ali's grandson, Pasha Abbas I, who dreaded assassination during his brief reign (1848–54) and kept camels saddled here for rapid flight into the desert. The ornate Rococo **Sakakini Palace**, on Sharia Sakakini near Ghamra metro station, was built in 1898 for an Italian nobleman. It's currently used as offices by the Ministry of Health and is closed to the public, though there has long been talk of turning it into a museum of medicine. If you're in the area, it's worth a detour for its outrageously kitsch facade.

Mosque of Baybars

Midan al-Zahir (at southern end of Sharia Sakakini) • Daily, approximately 9am–5pm • Free

The 1268 **Mosque of Baybars** was the first Cairo mosque to be located outside the city's walls. After it ceased to be a place of worship in the sixteenth century, it was subsequently used as a military storehouse by the Ottomans, a barracks by Napoleon and a slaughterhouse by the British. Restoration started in the early 1990s but soon petered out, and part of the southwest side is now again in use as a mosque; the rest of it remains a building site, but work is in progress for its eventual restoration.

Medinet Nasr

During the 1960s and 1970s, **Medinet Nasr** ("Victory City") was created as a new satellite suburb on the site of the Abbassiya Rifle Ranges, and many government departments were relocated here. Today it is best known for its shopping malls, of which the newest and biggest is **City Stars** on Sharia Omar Ibn al-Khattab (⊕citystars.com.eg), chock-full of glitzy shops, most of which are foreign.

Victory Memorial and Sadat's Tomb

Sharia al-Nasr • Daily 7am–7pm • Free, but bring your passport

Alongside the Sharia al-Nasr boulevard is a landscaped parade ground centred on a pyramid-shaped **Victory Memorial** to the 1973 October (Yom Kippur) War, beneath which lies **Sadat's Tomb**. In 1981, Islamic radicals infiltrated the October 6 anniversary parade and blasted the reviewing stand with machine guns and grenades, fatally wounding President Sadat (his successor, Hosni Mubarak, who was standing beside him, was unharmed).

BAYBARS THE GREAT

The most illustrious of all the Mamluke sultans, **Baybars I** was originally a Kipchak slave from Crimea. Known as Baybars al-Bunduqari ("the Crossbowman", actually the surname of one of his former owners), or just as Baybars the Great, it was he who brought legitimacy to the idea of a Mamluke sultanate after its brutal start with the rise and fall of Aybak and Shagar al-Durr (see p.118), which had not gone down well with public opinion.

As a general, Baybars made his name in Palestine, where he inflicted the first ever defeat on the **Mongol Empire** at the 1260 Battle of Ain Jalut. On his triumphal entry into Cairo after the battle, he simply seized power from the previous sultan. Baybars cemented his legitimacy by putting a puppet Abbasid caliph in Cairo (see p.119) to sanction him as sultan, and by courting the religious establishment. He gave equal rights to the four Sunni schools of Islamic law, and appointed a chief justice from each of them. In Palestine, he all but drove out the **Crusaders**, leaving them just a few coastal footholds. He also clamped down on corruption, and made sure that food was distributed equitably during times of famine, and took steps to ban prostitution, beer and hashish, although he himself was partial to an alcoholic brew called *qumiz*, made from fermented mare's milk. In the end, this little tipple proved his downfall: in 1277, after drinking a cup of dodgy *qumiz*, he died. It may simply be that the drink was just off, but according to one story, Baybars poisoned a cup meant for one of his rivals, and then accidentally drank it himself.

As a hero of Islam against corruption, vice and, of course, the Crusader foe, Baybars was long remembered. A romanticized popular epic of his life, the Sirat Baybars, was a favourite among café storytellers for centuries after his death, and even today Baybars is revered as the greatest of all Mamluke sultans, and among the country's Islamic rulers, second only to Saladin.

October War Panorama

Sharia al-Oruba • Shows daily except Tues at 9.30am, 11am and 12.30pm, also during winter at 5pm and 6.30pm, and summer at 6pm and 7.30pm • £E20, camera £E2

East of Abbassiya on Sharia al-Oruba, the huge **October War Panorama** was built on a suggestion made to Hosni Mubarak by his fellow dictator Kim Il Sung of North Korea. Construction was supervised by North Korean technicians, and the building looks like a pavilion in some 1950s Communist theme park, decorated with Maoist-style reliefs, but instead of East Asian peasants and workers striding purposefully forward, it's Egyptian soldiers in front of the pyramids. Visits here start with a look at two rather silly dioramas illustrating the opening round of the 1973 October (Yom Kippur) War. You are then taken to a platform surrounded by an impressive three-dimensional theatrical panorama of the war in Sinai, where you hear a commentary on the events of the war in Sinai while being rotated through 360° to take in the scenes around you. The commentary (in Arabic, with an English version via headphones) explains the action with such phrases as "the glorious minutes passed rapidly" and the whole thing is so over-the-top in its triumphalism that you might almost think the Egyptians had actually won the October War.

Behind the Panorama is **Cairo Stadium**, where Cairo football clubs Ahly and Zamalek usually play their home matches, and where international ties and cup finals are also held.

Heliopolis (Masr al-Gadida)

By the beginning of the twentieth century, the doubling of Cairo's population and the exponential growth of its foreign community had created a huge demand for new accommodation, which fired the imagination of a Belgian entrepreneur, **Baron Édouard Empain**, itching for new projects after his successful construction of the Paris Metro. Baron Empain proposed creating a garden city in the desert, linked to the downtown

1

ANCIENT HELIOPOLIS, THE ENNEAD AND THE CULT OF RE

Although Anthony Trollope scoffed "Humbug!" when he saw what little remained of it in 1858, the site of **ancient Heliopolis**, near modern day Matariyya, originally covered some five square kilometres. The City of the Sun (called On by its founders, but better known by its Greek appellation) evolved in tandem with Memphis, the first capital of Dynastic Egypt. As Memphis embodied the political unification of Upper and Lower Egypt, Heliopolis syncretized diverse local cults into a hierarchical cosmogony that surpassed other creation myths of the Old Kingdom. In the **Heliopolitan cosmogony**, the world began as watery chaos (Nun) from which Atum the sun god emerged onto a primal mound, spitting forth the twin deities Shu (air) and Tefnut (moisture). They engendered Geb (earth) and Nut (sky), whose own union produced Isis, Osiris, Seth and Nephthys. Later texts often regarded this divine **Ennead** (Nine) as a single entity, while the universe was represented by the figures of Shu, Nut and Geb. Meanwhile, the primal deity Atum was subsumed by **Re** (or Ra), a yet mightier aspect of the sun god, who manifested himself as hawk-headed Re-herakhte (Horus of the Horizon), the beetle Khepri (the rising sun), the disc Aten (the midday sun), or as Atum (the setting sun). From the V Dynasty onwards, pharaohs claimed descent from Re by identifying themselves with Horus and Osiris, and the rituals in Re's sanctuary (exclusively accessible to pharaohs and priests) were adopted by other cults and fused with Osiris-worship (see p. 246 & p.279).

area by tram: a venture attractive to investors since Empain's company would collect both rents and fares from commuting residents of the new suburb, which was named **Heliopolis** after the ancient City of the Sun nearby in Matariyya. The suburb's wide avenues were lined with apartment blocks ennobled by pale yellow Moorish facades and bisected by shrubbery. Wealthy Egyptians settled here from the beginning; merely prosperous ones moved in as foreigners left in droves during the 1950s. Heliopolis is known in Arabic as **Masr al-Gadida** ("New Cairo").

GETTING TO HELIOPOLIS

BY TRAM

The fastest way to Heliopolis, especially during the rush hour, is on the suburb's original tram system, known as the "Heliopolis metro", which begins at Midan Ramses. From there, its three tram lines follow the same track through Abbassiya, diverging shortly before Midan Roxi. Each has its own colour-coded direction boards.

Abd al-Aziz Fahmi line This line (destination written in blue) runs past Midan Roxi and along Sharia al-Ma'had al-Ishtiraki and Sharia al-Higaz, past Merryland and Heliopolis Hospital, to Midan Heliopolis, where it turns off up Abd al-Aziz Fahmi towards Ain Shams.

Nouzha line The more central Nouzha line (destination

written in red) veers off Sharia Merghani near the Heliopolis Sporting Club, and follows Al-Ahram and Osman Ibn Affan to Midan Triomphe, then heads up Sharia Nouzha to Midan al-Higaz.

Merghani line Initially running alongside the Nouzha line, the Merghani line (destination usually written in yellow) follows the street of that name to Midan Triomphe, and out towards the Armed Forces Hospital.

BY BUS

Heliopolis is a 15–30min bus ride from downtown. Buses #400, #400/ and #500, and minibus #27 run to Heliopolis from Tahrir and Ramses squares.

Sharia al-Ahram

Nouzha-line trams run through the heart of Heliopolis, up **Sharia al-Ahram**, its handsome villas rich with flowery Art Nouveau and Neoclassical details. Here you'll find classy cafés like *Amphytryon* and a branch of the downtown coffee shop *Groppi* (see p.188), where the bourgeoisie of the district's 1920s heyday would relax with a cake and a coffee, as indeed you can today (unlike its downtown namesake, the Heliopolis branch of *Groppi's* still retains some of its original elegance). At the top of Al-Ahram, the tram sidles to the right to pass around the suburb's centrepiece, the Byzantine-style "jelly-mould" **Basilica**, which is also Baron Empain's last resting place.

Sharia Laqqani, Midan Roxi and Sharia Ibrahimi

Some of Heliopolis's finest neo-Moorish facades can be seen along the streets leading off from Al-Ahram, most notably **Sharia Laqqani**, which leads north to **Midan Roxi**, and **Sharia Ibrahimi**, which crosses Al-Ahram a couple of blocks before the Basilica; both streets are lined by arcades topped with Andalucían-style balconies and pantiles. At the start of Al-Ahram, where it branches off from Sharia Merghani, the wonderful neo-Moorish pile, known as the **Urubah Palace**, was used as a palace by former dictator Mubarak and is out of bounds to the public.

Baron Empain's Palace
Sharia al-Oruba

Heliopolis's most impressive landmark is **Baron Empain's Palace** (known to locals as Qasr al-Baron). Modelled on Hindu temples from Cambodia and Orissa, the palace originally boasted a revolving tower that enabled its owner to follow the sun throughout the day. Although the building, completed in 1910, is generally closed to the public, it has been spruced up and is illuminated at night. As Sharia al-Oruba is the main road to the airport, you may see it on your way to or from taking a plane.

The Pyramids

All things dread Time, but Time dreads the Pyramids.

Anonymous proverb

For millions of people the three great **Pyramids of Giza** epitomize Ancient Egypt: no other monuments are so instantly recognized around the world. Yet comparatively few foreigners realize that there are at least 115 further pyramids spread across 70km of desert, from the outskirts of Cairo to the edge of the Fayoum. The mass of theories, claims and counterclaims about how and why the Pyramids were built contributes to the sense of mystery that surrounds them. You can read up on some of the wackier ones – including some involving Martians – at ⓦparanormal.about.com/cs/ancientegypt. Most visitors are content to see the Giza Pyramids and part of the sprawling necropolis of **Saqqara**, both easily accessible from Cairo (tours to Saqqara often include a visit to the ruins of the ancient city of **Memphis**). Only a minority get as far as the **Dahshur** pyramid field, while there are also a host of even more obscure pyramids to explore (see box, p.149).

Brief history

The derivation of the word "pyramid" is obscure. *Per-em-us*, an Ancient Egyptian term meaning "straight up", seems likelier than the Greek *pyramis* – "wheaten cake", a facetious descriptive term for these novel monuments. Then again, "obelisk" comes from *obeliskos*, the ancient Greek for "skewer" or "little spit".

Whatever, the Pyramids' sheer **antiquity** is staggering. When the Greek chronicler Herodotus visited them in 450 BC, as many centuries separated his lifetime from their creation as divide our own time from that of Herodotus, who regarded them as ancient even then. For the Pyramid Age was only an episode in three millennia of pharaonic civilization, reaching its zenith within two hundred years and followed by an inexorable decline, so that later dynasties regarded the works of their ancestors with awe.

The Pyramid Age began at Saqqara in the twenty-seventh century BC, when the III Dynasty royal architect Imhotep enlarged a mastaba tomb to create the first **step pyramid**. As techniques evolved, an attempt was made to convert another step pyramid at Maidum into a true pyramid by encasing its sides in a smooth shell, but it seems that the design was faulty and the pyramid collapsed at some time under its

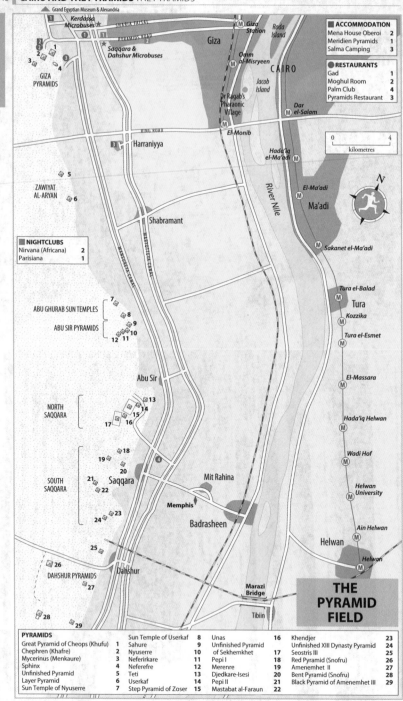

Kerdassa
Microbuses ☆

SHARIA FAISAL

PYRAMIDS ROAD

Saqqara &
Dahshur Microbuses

Giza
Station

Giza

Roda
Island

GIZA
PYRAMIDS

Omm
al-Misryeen

CAIRO

Jacob
Island

Dr Ragab's
Pharaonic
Village

Dar
el-Salam

El-Monib

Harraniyya

RING ROAD

Hada'iq
el-Ma'adi

ZAWIYAT
AL-ARYAN

Shabramant

El-Ma'adi

Ma'adi

River Nile

Sakanet el-Ma'adi

ABU GHURAB SUN TEMPLES

ABU SIR PYRAMIDS

Tura el-Balad

Tura

Kozzika

Tura el-Esmet

Abu Sir

El-Massara

NORTH
SAQQARA

Hada'iq Helwan

Wadi Hof

SOUTH
SAQQARA

Saqqara

Mit Rahina

Helwan
University

Memphis

Badrasheen

Ain Helwan

Helwan

DAHSHUR PYRAMIDS

Dahshur

Helwan

Marazi
Bridge

**THE
PYRAMID
FIELD**

Tibiin

■ ACCOMMODATION	
Mena House Oberoi	2
Meridien Pyramids	1
Salma Camping	3

● RESTAURANTS	
Gad	1
Moghul Room	2
Palm Club	4
Pyramids Restaurant	3

■ NIGHTCLUBS	
Nirvana (Africana)	2
Parisiana	1

0 _____ 4
kilometres

N

PYRAMIDS							
Great Pyramid of Cheops (Khufu)	1	Sun Temple of Userkaf	8	Unas	16	Khendjer	23
Chephren (Khafre)	2	Sahure	9	Unfinished Pyramid		Unfinished XIII Dynasty Pyramid	24
Mycerinus (Menkaure)	3	Nyuserre	10	of Sekhemkhet	17	Seostris III	25
Sphinx	4	Neferirkare	11	Pepi I	18	Red Pyramid (Snofru)	26
Unfinished Pyramid	5	Neferefre	12	Merenre	19	Amenemhet II	27
Layer Pyramid	6	Teti	13	Djedkare-Isesi	20	Bent Pyramid (Snofru)	28
Sun Temple of Nyuserre	7	Userkaf	14	Pepi II	21	Black Pyramid of Amenemhet III	29
		Step Pyramid of Zoser	15	Mastabat al-Faraun	22		

LESSER-KNOWN PYRAMID SITES

Even if you've been to the famous Pyramids of Giza, all the pyramids at Saqqara (of which the Step Pyramid is the best-known) and those at Dahshur, you still won't have come anywhere near to having exhausted Egypt's pyramid sites. Between Giza and Saqqara, for example, lies the group of V Dynasty pyramids at **Abu Sir** (about £E3 by tuk-tuk from Abu Sir village). Nearby at **Abu Ghurab** are two temples dedicated to the sun god Re, while on the way down from Giza, you pass two fragmentary pyramids at **Zawiyat al Aryan** dating from the III and IV dynasties. All of these are currently closed to the public, but you may be able to make private arrangements with the guards.

Much further south, the dramatic "Collapsed Pyramid" of **Maidum** (see p.391) and the lesser Middle Kingdom pyramids of **Hawara** and **Lahun** (see p.392) are easier to reach from the Fayoum, and are covered in Chapter 3. West of Cairo, a kilometre north of the Ring Road's junction with the Cairo–Alex Desert Road, **Abu Ruash** (see Ⓦ talkingpyramids.com/abu-roash) is a very ruined IV Dynasty pyramid which belonged to Cheops' son, Djedefre. Again, it's currently closed to the public, but if you have a particular interest you may be able to come to an arrangement with the guards.

own weight. According to one theory, this happened during construction of what became the Bent Pyramid at Dahshur, necessitating a hasty alteration to the angle of its sides. The first sheer-sided **true pyramid**, apparently the next to be constructed, was the Red Pyramid at Dahshur, followed by the Great Pyramid of Cheops at Giza, which marked the zenith of pyramid architecture. After two more perfect pyramids at Giza, fewer resources and less care were devoted to later pyramids (such as those at Abu Sir, South Saqqara and Lisht), and no subsequent pyramid ever matched the standards of the Giza trio.

The Pyramids of Giza

Of the Seven Wonders of the ancient world, only the **Pyramids of Giza** have withstood the ravages of time. "From the summit of these monuments, forty centuries look upon you", cried Napoleon. Resembling small triangles from afar and corrugated mountains as you approach, their gigantic mass can seem oddly two-dimensional when viewed from below. Far from being isolated in the desert as carefully angled photos suggest, they rise just beyond the outskirts of Giza City. During daytime, the tourist hordes dispel the mystique (though the site is big enough to escape them), but at sunset, dawn and late at night their brooding majesty returns.

The Pyramids' **orientation** is no accident. Their entrances are aligned with the Pole Star (or rather, its position 4500 years ago); the internal tomb chambers face west, the direction of the Land of the Dead; and the external funerary temples point eastwards towards the rising sun. Less well preserved are the causeways leading to the so-called valley temples, and various subsidiary pyramids and mastaba tombs.

GETTING TO THE PYRAMIDS OF GIZA

The site is directly accessible from Cairo via the 8km-long Sharia al-Ahram (Pyramids Rd) commissioned by Khedive Ismail for Napoleon III's consort, the Empress Eugénie. Though heavy traffic can prolong the journey, getting there is straightforward. A minimum-effort way to visit the Giza Pyramids, and also Saqqara, is to go on a guided tour (see box, p.150).

By bus Take a/c bus #355 or #357 (£E2), or ordinary bus #900 (£E1) from Abdel Mouneem Riyad terminal (behind the Egyptian Museum) to the main entrance, or #997 to the Sphinx entrance.
By service taxi (£E1.25) from Ramses (by Sharia Orabi) or Abdel Mouneem Riyad – drivers heading for the Pyramids shout, "Ahram, Ahram", but check they're going all the way.
By taxi Taxi drivers may quote upwards of £E30, but a white cab should cost around £E25 on the meter.

1

THE PURPOSE OF THE PYRAMIDS

The Pyramids' **enigma** has puzzled people ever since they were built. Whereas the Ancient Greeks vaguely understood their function, the Romans were less certain; medieval Arabs believed them to be **treasure houses** with magical guardians; and early European observers reckoned them the biblical **granaries of Joseph**. Most archeologists now agree that the Pyramids' function was to preserve the pharaoh's **ka**, or double: a vital force which emanated from the sun god to his son, the king, who distributed it amongst his subjects and the land of Egypt itself. Mummification, funerary rituals, false doors for his ba (soul) to escape, model servants (*shabti* figures) and anniversary offerings – all were designed to ensure that his *ka* enjoyed an **afterlife** similar to its earthly existence. Thus was the social order perpetuated throughout eternity and the forces of primeval chaos held at bay, a theme emphasized in tomb reliefs at Saqqara. On another level of symbolism, the pyramid form evoked the **primal mound** (*benben*) at the dawn of creation, a recurrent theme in ancient Egyptian cosmogony. This was represented first by megalithic *benben* stones, then obelisks, whose pyramidal tips were sheathed in glittering electrum (an alloy of silver and gold), and finally pyramids, topped by electrum-covered pyramidion capstones, as seen in the Egyptian Museum (see p.75).

INFORMATION

Opening hours Summer 8am–6pm; winter 8am–4pm, Ramadan 8am–3pm

Entrance charge £E60. Extra tickets (sold at the attractions themselves) are required for entry to the Solar Boat Museum, and to go inside the Great Pyramid of Cheops, Chephren's Pyramid and the Pyramid of Mycerinus.

Entrance The main entrance is just uphill from the *Mena House Oberoi* hotel. Ignore touts and other dubious characters en route trying to persuade you that the ticket office is closed, or has moved to the nearby horse stables (which are worth avoiding; see p.153 for better ones). There is another entrance and ticket office near the Sphinx.

Information There's a tourist office (daily 9am–4pm; ☎02 3383 8823) across the street from the *Mena House Oberoi* hotel.

Timing your visit Plan on spending at least half a day at the Giza Pyramids. Early morning is best, ahead of the heat and crowds (tour buses start arriving around 10.30am). You may also want to adjust your timings so as to get tickets for the pyramid interiors as soon as they go on sale.

Going inside the pyramids Usually the interiors of only two pyramids are open at any one time, while the third is closed for conservation reasons, meaning it's pot-luck as to which interiors you'll be able to see when you visit. The pyramid which is closed changes every year or two. Going inside is quite safe, but anyone with claustrophobia or asthma should forget it, and clambering through all three shafts in the Great Pyramid can make your leg muscles ache the following day. To keep down humidity inside the Great Pyramid, the number of visitors for the pyramid interiors is limited to 150 in the morning and 150 in the afternoon for each pyramid (250 for the Great Pyramid in winter). If you want to buy tickets, you'll need to look sharp. In the morning, tour groups tend to snap up all of them before anyone else can get a look in; it is generally less difficult to get afternoon tickets, especially if you can be at the ticket office as soon as they go on sale at 1pm, but be prepared to jostle for position (or, if you go in the morning, to sprint to the ticket office as soon as the main gate opens).

THE PYRAMIDS IN A DAY?

With three main sites to see, leisurely tourists will want to spend a day visiting Giza, a second day at Saqqara and a third day at Dahshur. If you're very energetic and really determined, however, it's possible to visit all three, plus Memphis, in a single day, assuming you line up a taxi driver the day before and don't mind making an early start (say 7.30am from town). Make sure the driver understands exactly what you want, and negotiate hard. In principle, you should be able to visit all four sites for around £E200, but £E250–350 is a reasonable rate, especially if there's a group of you. Some hotels such as the *Berlin* (see p.180) have their own drivers who are used to taking tourists on such excursions. Alternatively, you could opt for a guided tour like the ones run by Samo Tours (see p.166), which takes in both Giza and Saqqara in one day.

The Great Pyramid of Cheops (Khufu)

£E100

The oldest and largest of the Giza Pyramids is that of the IV Dynasty pharaoh **Khufu** – better known as **Cheops** – who probably reigned 2589–2566 BC. It originally stood 140m high and measured 230m along its base, but the removal of its casing stones has reduced these dimensions by three metres. The pyramid is estimated to weigh six million tons and contain over 2,300,000 blocks whose average weight is 2.5 tons (though some weigh almost 15 tons). This gigantic mass actually ensures its stability, since most of the stress is transmitted inwards towards its central core, or downwards into the underlying bedrock. It is thought to contain three main chambers: one in the bedrock and two in the superstructure. By the time archeologists got here, their contents had long since been looted, and the only object left *in situ* was Khufu's sarcophagus. In 1993, a German team using a robot probe accidentally discovered a door with handles supposedly enclosing a fourth chamber, apparently never plundered

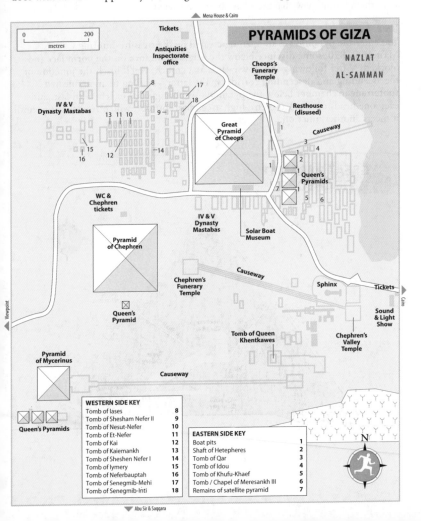

PYRAMIDS OF GIZA

▲ Mena House & Cairo

Tickets

Antiquities
Inspectorate
office

Cheops's
Funerary
Temple

NAZLAT

AL-SAMMAN

Resthouse
(disused)

Causeway

8

17

18

IV & V
Dynasty Mastabas

13 11 10

9

Great
Pyramid
of Cheops

1

3

4

2

Queen's
Pyramids

15

16

12

14

1

7

5

6

WC &
Chephren
tickets

IV & V
Dynasty
Mastabas

Solar Boat
Museum

Pyramid
of Chephren

Causeway

Sphinx

Tickets

Chephren's
Funerary
Temple

Sound
& Light
Show

Queen's
Pyramid

Chephren's
Valley
Temple

Tomb of Queen
Khentkawes

Pyramid
of Mycerinus

Causeway

Queen's Pyramids

0 ——— 200
metres

Viewpoint

N

▼ Abu Sir & Saqqara

WESTERN SIDE KEY

Tomb of Iases	8
Tomb of Shesham Nefer II	9
Tomb of Nesut-Nefer	10
Tomb of Et-Nefer	11
Tomb of Kai	12
Tomb of Kaiemankh	13
Tomb of Sheshen Nefer I	14
Tomb of Iymery	15
Tomb of Neferbauptah	16
Tomb of Senegmib-Mehi	17
Tomb of Senegmib-Inti	18

EASTERN SIDE KEY

Boat pits	1
Shaft of Hetepheres	2
Tomb of Qar	3
Tomb of Idou	4
Tomb of Khufu-Khaef	5
Tomb / Chapel of Meresankh III	6
Remains of satellite pyramid	7

THE SOUND AND LIGHT SHOW

After dark there is a **Sound and Light Show** (three 1hr performances nightly) accompanied by a rather crass, melodramatic commentary in various languages. For schedules, call ☎ 02 3385 2880 or ☎ 02 3384 7823, or check Egypt Today or ⊛ soundandlight.com.eg. Seats cost £E75, plus £E35 for a video camera; the Arabic version costs £E11, though non-Arab nationals are not allowed to buy tickets for it. Seats are on the grandstand (wheelchair-accessible) facing the Sphinx, and the ticket office is by the Sphinx entrance to the site. Bring a sweater, as nights can be cold, even in summer.

by thieves, which might contain the mummy and treasures of Cheops himself. Another robot, sent down in 2002, pushed a camera through a hole drilled in the door to reveal another, similar door behind it. Further probes have been sent down since then, but no new chambers have been discovered.

The entrance

You enter the pyramid via an opening created by the treasure-hunting Caliph Ma'mun in 820, some distance below the original entrance on the north face (now blocked). After following this downwards at a crouch, you'll reach the junction of the ascending and descending corridors. The latter – leading to an **unfinished subterranean chamber** below the pyramid – is best ignored or left until last, and everyone heads up the 1.6-metre-high **ascending corridor**, which runs for 36m until it meets another junction.

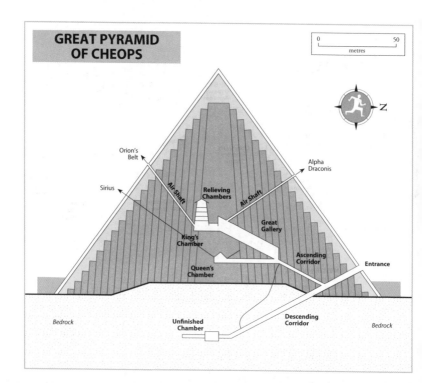

GREAT PYRAMID OF CHEOPS

The Queen's Chamber

To the right of the junction at the end of the ascending corridor is a **shaft** that ancient writers believed to be a well connected to the Nile. It's now recognized as leading into the unfinished subterranean chamber and thought to have been an escape passage for the workmen.

Straight ahead is a horizontal passage 35m long and 1.75m high, leading to a semi-finished limestone chamber with a pointed roof which Arabs dubbed the "**Queen's Chamber**", though there's no evidence that a queen was ever buried here. In the northern and southern walls are two holes made in 1872 for the purpose of discovering the chamber's ventilation shafts; it was through one of these that the 1993 robot probe found a 65-metre shaft, twenty centimetres high and the same distance wide, aligned with the Dog Star (Sirius), which was believed to be an embodiment of the goddess Isis.

The Great Gallery

Opening out from the same junction where the horizontal passage to the Queen's Chamber began, the **Great Gallery**, dark, sepulchral and almost church-like, is the best part of the pyramid's insides. Built of Muqattam limestone, so perfectly cut that a knife blade can't be inserted between its joints, the 47-metre-long shaft narrows to a corbelled roof 8.5m high. The incisions in its walls probably held beams that were used to raise the sarcophagus or granite plug blocks up the steep incline (nowadays overlaid with wooden steps). Though no longer infested by giant bats, as nineteenth-century travellers reported, the Great Gallery is sufficiently hot and airless to be something of an ordeal, and you'll be glad to reach the horizontal antechamber at the top, which is slotted for the insertion of plug blocks designed to thwart entry to the putative burial chamber.

King's Chamber

At the far end of the Great Gallery, the so-called **King's Chamber** lies 95m beneath the apex of the pyramid and half that distance from its outer walls. Built of red granite blocks, the rectangular chamber is large enough to accommodate a double-decker bus. Various people have claimed that its dimensions (5.2m by 10.8m by 5.8m) have a special significance, and speculation surrounding this claim has inspired many an abstruse calculation and wacky prophecy. The size and shape of the chamber, for example, are supposed by some to generate infrasonic vibrations which, according to some New Age pundits, bathe the body in "sonic energy". Adolf Hitler ordered a replica built beneath the Nuremberg Stadium, where he communed with himself before Nazi rallies. To one side of the chamber lies a huge, lidless **sarcophagus** of Aswan granite, bearing the marks of diamond-tipped saws and drills. Being too large to fit through the Great Gallery, it must have been placed here while

---

RENTING HORSES AND CAMELS

Horse and camel **touts** were formerly excluded from the Giza pyramid site by a fence, which made visiting a lot more pleasant, but since the revolution, the ban on their entry has not been enforced and they have become a major **nuisance** again. Ironically, many of them were among the crooks and thugs used by the regime to attack the revolutionaries during the "Battle of the Camel" (see p.72). Aside from their continual pestering and the bad conditions under which they keep their animals, they are also prone to little tricks like quoting a low price, riding you far out into the desert, and then saying that the cheap rate was only for the outward journey, and that the return journey will cost you many times more. If you do want to ride a horse or camel, ignore the touts and choose a **reputable operator** such as KG (☎02 3385 1065) or AA (☎0122 153 4142). A four-hour ride down to the next set of pyramids (at Abu Sir) and back should cost around £E250–300.

the pyramid was being built. On the northern and southern walls, at knee height, you'll notice two air shafts leading to the outer world, aligned with the stars of Orion's Belt and Alpha Draconis (representing Osiris and the hippo goddess Reret respectively).

Unseen above the ceiling, five **relieving chambers** (usually closed to the public) distribute the weight of the pyramid away from the burial chamber; each consists of 43 granite monoliths weighing 40 to 70 tons apiece. These chambers can only be reached by a ladder from the Great Gallery, and then a passage where Khufu's name is inscribed in red (the only inscription within the Giza Pyramids).

On your way back down, consider investigating the 100-metre-long **descending corridor**, which leads to a crudely hewn **unfinished chamber** beneath the pyramid. There's nothing to see, but the nerve-wracking descent is worthy of Indiana Jones.

Satellite pyramids

East of the Great Pyramid, it's just possible to discern the foundations of Khufu's **funerary temple** and a few blocks of the causeway that once connected it to his valley temple (now buried beneath the village of Nazlat al-Samman). Nearby stand three ruined **Queens' Pyramids**, each with a small chapel attached. The northern and southern pyramids belonged to Merites and Hensutsen, Khufu's principal wife (and sister), and the putative mother of Chephren, respectively; the middle one may have belonged to the mother of Djedefre, the third ruler of the dynasty. Between that and the Great Pyramid, the remains of a fourth satellite pyramid were discovered in 1993, its capstone the oldest yet found, its purpose so far unknown.

Subsidiary tombs

Just northeast of Queen Merites' pyramid is a **shaft** where the sarcophagus of IV Dynasty pharaoh Snofru's wife **Queen Hetepheres** was found, having been stashed here following lootings at its original home in Dahshur. To the east of it are the **tombs of Qar** and his son **Idou**, which contain life-size statues of the deceased and various reliefs. To the east of Queen Hensutsen's pyramid are the tombs of Cheops' son **Khufu-Khaef**, and Chephren's wife (also Hetepheres' daughter) **Meresankh III**, the best preserved of all the tombs on the Giza plateau, complete with statues in the niches and reliefs showing scenes of daily life, with much of the paintwork intact. To get into these tombs, ask at the custodian's hut beside Hetepheres' shaft; naturally, he'll expect a tip for opening up.

To the west of the Great Pyramid lie dozens of **IV and V Dynasty mastabas**, where archeologists have uncovered a 4600-year-old mummified princess, whose body had been hollowed out and encased in a thin layer of plaster – a hitherto unknown method of mummification. The **tombs** are less interesting than those on the eastern side, though Neferbauptah's has a dinosaur fossil preserved in the fifth block from the right of the second row up on its north side. Should you want to enter any of these tombs, ask at the Antiquities Inspectorate office to the north. Note that there are a number of deep shafts among these tombs, with no fences round them, so watch your step when exploring the area.

The Solar Boat Museum

Daily: May–Sept 9am–6pm; Oct–April 9am–4pm • £E40

Perched to the south of the Great Pyramid, across the road from another cluster of mastabas, is a humidity-controlled pavilion containing a 43-metre-long "solar boat". The boat's purpose is unknown but it seems to be a version of the solar barques which were believed to carry the pharaoh through the underworld (as shown in XVII–IX Dynasty tombs in the Valley of the Kings), and which accompanied the sun god on his daily journey across the heavens, as in the Heliopolitan cosmology (see p.145). This one was probably used in Cheops' funeral ceremony, after which it was dismantled and buried in a pit sunk into the ground next to the pyramid, one of five such pits around the monument. The boat was made of fragrant cedar, and when the pit's limestone roofing blocks were removed in 1954, a faint odour of cedarwood could still be smelt. A tiny camera inserted into another of the pits has revealed that it too contains the remains of a boat, but this has not been excavated.

After the solar boat was excavated, restorer Ahmed Yussef spent fourteen years re-assembling 1200 pieces of wood that fitted together like a three-dimensional jigsaw puzzle, originally held together by halfa-grass ropes, threaded from the inside, which tightened when wet – thus ensuring a watertight fit. In Ancient Egyptian art, ropes were associated with royalty and divinity: they enclose cartouches, and symbolically bind together the Two Lands of Upper and Lower Egypt.

The Pyramid of Chephren (Khafre)

Sited on higher ground, with an intact summit and steeper sides, the middle or second pyramid appears taller and is actually more imposing than Cheops'. Built for his son **Khafre** (known to posterity as **Chephren**), its base originally covered 214.8 square metres and its weight is estimated at 4,883,000 tons. As with Cheops' Pyramid, the original rock-hewn burial chamber was never finished and an upper chamber was subsequently constructed.

The Roman writer Pliny said that the pyramid had no **entrance**. In 1818, however, when Venetian explorer Giovanni Belzoni located and blasted open the sealed portal on its north face, he found that Arab tomb robbers had already gained access nearly a thousand years earlier – apparently undeterred by legends that the pyramid was protected by an idol "with fierce and sparkling eyes" bent on slaying intruders.

The pyramid's exterior retains a large number of **casing stones** at its summit (best viewed with binoculars). Also notice the huge **paving blocks** to the east of the pyramid, fitted precisely together in an irregular mosaic fashion. These led nineteenth-century pyramidologist Moses Cotsworth to suggest that the entire plateau was a gigantic sundial, with the Great Pyramid casting shadows on a flat pavement (now largely destroyed), calibrated to show equinoxes and other astral events.

HOW THE PYRAMIDS WERE BUILT

Although the limestone scarp at the edge of the Western Desert provided an inexhaustible source of building material, finer stone for casing the pyramids was quarried at Tura across the river, or came from Aswan in Upper Egypt. Blocks were quarried using wooden wedges (which swelled when soaked, enlarging fissures) and copper chisels, then transported on rafts to the pyramid site, where the final shaping and polishing occurred. Shipments coincided with the inundation of the Nile (July–Nov), when its waters lapped the feet of the plateau and Egypt's workforce was released from agricultural tasks.

Herodotus relates that a hundred thousand slaves took a decade to build the causeway and earthen ramps, and a further twenty years to raise the Great Pyramid of Cheops. Archeologists now believe that, far from being slaves, most of the workforce were peasants paid in food for their three-month stint (papyri enumerate the quantities of lentils, onions and leeks), while a few thousand skilled craftsmen were employed full time. One theory holds that a single ramp wound around the pyramid core, and was raised as it grew; when the capstone was in place, the casing was added from the top down and the ramp was reduced. Other ramps (recently found) led from the base of the pyramid to the quarry.

Whether or not the Ancient Egyptians deemed this work a religious obligation, the massive levies certainly demanded an effective bureaucracy. Pyramid-building therefore helped consolidate the state. Its decline paralleled the Old Kingdom's, its cessation and resumption two anarchic eras (the First and Second Intermediate Periods) and the short-lived Middle Kingdom (XII Dynasty). By the time of the New Kingdom, other monumental symbols seemed appropriate. Remembering the plundered pyramids, the rulers of the New Kingdom opted for hidden tombs in the Valley of the Kings.

Chephren's Funerary Complex

The **funerary complex** of Chephren's Pyramid is the best-preserved example of this typically Old Kingdom arrangement. When a pharaoh died, his body was ferried across the Nile to a riverside valley temple where it was embalmed by priests. Then mourners gathered there to purify themselves before escorting his mummy up the causeway to a funerary (or mortuary) temple, where further rites preceded its interment within the pyramid. Thereafter, the priests ensured his *ka*'s afterlife by making offerings of food and incense in the funerary temple on specific anniversaries.

The funerary and valley temples

Chephren's **funerary temple** consists of a pillared hall, central court, niched storerooms and a sanctuary, but most of the outer granite casing has been plundered over centuries and the interior is not usually accessible. Among the remaining blocks is a 13.4-metre-long monster weighing 163,000kg. Flanking the temple are what appear to be boat pits, although excavations have yielded nothing but pottery fragments. From here you can trace the foundations of a **causeway** that runs 400m downhill to his valley temple, near the Sphinx.

The **valley temple** lay buried under sand until its discovery by French Egyptologist Auguste Mariette in 1852, which accounts for its reasonable state of preservation. Built of limestone and faced with polished Aswan granite, the temple faces east and used to open onto a quay. Beyond a narrow antechamber you'll find a T-shaped hall whose gigantic architraves are supported by square pillars, in front of which stood diorite statues of Chephren.

The Sphinx

Everyone has seen pictures of the **Sphinx** but this legendary monument is far more impressive in real life, especially from the front, where it gazes down at you from twenty metres up, with Chepren's pyramid for a backdrop. The Sphinx is carved from an outcrop of soft limestone supposedly left standing after the harder surrounding stone was quarried for the Great Pyramid; however, since most of the outcrop was too friable to work on directly it was clad in harder stone before finishing. Egyptologists credit Chephren with the idea of shaping it into a figure with a lion's body and a human head, which is often identified as his own (complete with royal beard and *uraeus*), though it may represent a guardian deity. Some thousand years later, the future Tuthmosis IV is said to have dreamt that if he cleared the sand that engulfed the Sphinx it would make him ruler: a prophecy fulfilled, as recorded on a stele that he placed between its paws.

The **name** "Sphinx" was actually bestowed by the Ancient Greeks, after the legendary creature of Thebes (the Greek city, not the Egyptian one now known as Luxor) that put riddles to passers-by and slew those who answered wrongly. The Arabs

---

THE AGE OF THE SPHINX

In 1991, maverick Egyptologist **John West** – who had long claimed that Ancient Egyptian civilization was the inheritor of the lost culture of Atlantis – got together a team of American scientists led by geologist Robert Schoch to investigate apparent signs of water erosion on the sides of the Sphinx's enclosure. Schoch's team duly announced that the erosion could only have been caused by water, meaning the Sphinx was older than Egypt's last known flood era back in **10,000–15,000 BC** – several millennia before the date assigned to its creation by conventional Egyptology. Despite this evidence, most Egyptologists continue to believe that the Sphinx was built to honour **Chephren**; apart from anything else, a New Kingdom inscription on a stele in front of it bore Chepren's name, and statues of the pharaoh have been uncovered in the neighbouring valley temple. The water erosion, they argue, can be explained by flooding from the Nile and severe storms in relatively recent times..

called it **Abu al-Hol** (the awesome or terrible one); medieval chronicles relate how its nose and ears were mutilated by a Sufi sheikh in 1378, whereupon the Sphinx blew sand over the village at its feet and enraged residents lynched the sheikh. While there's no evidence to support the oft-repeated story that the Sphinx was used for target practice by Mamluke and Napoleonic troops, much of its beard ended up in the British Museum in London – although the British were respectful enough to sandbag the monument for protection during World War II.

Three **tunnels** exist inside the Sphinx, one behind its head, one in its tail and one in its north side. Their function is unknown, but none goes anywhere. Other tunnels have been unearthed in the vicinity of the Sphinx; again, who built them or what they were for is unknown, but one suggestion is that they were created by later Ancient Egyptians looking for buried treasure.

The Pyramid of Mycerinus (Menkaure)

£E30

Sited on a gradual slope into undulating desert, the smallest of the three main Giza Pyramids, dinkier and less imposing, speaks of waning power and commitment. Though started by Chephren's successor, **Menkaure** (called **Mycerinus** by the Greeks), it was finished with unseemly haste by his son Shepseskaf, who seemingly enjoyed less power than his predecessors and depended on the priesthood. Herodotus records the legend that an oracle gave Mycerinus only six years to live, so to cheat fate he made merry round the clock, doubling his annual quantum of experience and using myriad lamps to turn nights into days, thus doubling his allotted number of the latter. Another story (related by the Greek geographer Strabo) has it that the pyramid was actually built by Rhodophis, a Thracian courtesan who charged each client the price of a building block.

Because its lower half was sheathed in Aswan granite, this is sometimes called the **Red Pyramid** (a name more usually applied to one of Snofru's pyramids at Dahshur). Its relative lack of casing stones is due to Saladin's son Abdel Aziz, whose courtiers persuaded him to attempt the pyramid's demolition in 1196 – a project abandoned after eight months.

The interior

The **interior** of Mycerinus's pyramid is unlike that of any others, having an unfinished chamber in the superstructure and the final burial chamber underground – though no one knows why. It's also a mystery why the lower passageway (now used to enter the pyramid) and the burial chamber should be lined with granite when they are hewn from the bedrock, and why the Ancient Egyptians carved a false barrel-vaulted ceiling in the burial chamber. There, nineteenth-century amateur archeologist Richard Howard Vyse discovered a basalt sarcophagus, later lost at sea en route to Britain, plus human remains (now in the British Museum) that he assumed were Menkaure's, but which are now reckoned to be a XXVI Dynasty replacement.

Satellite pyramids

The complex also features three small pyramids for the pharaoh's wives, a relatively intact funerary temple, and a causeway to the now-buried valley temple. Northwest of the latter lies the sarcophagus-shaped tomb of **Queen Khentkawes**, an intriguing figure who appears to have bridged the transition between the IV and V dynasties. Apparently married to Shepseskaf, the last IV Dynasty ruler, Khentkawes may have wed a priest of the sun god after Shepseskaf's demise and gone on to give birth to several future kings who were buried at Saqqara or Abu Sir (where she also had a pyramid built).

The Grand Egyptian Museum

A swanky new **Grand Egyptian Museum** is currently under construction 2km north of the Giza Pyramids site, at the junction of the Alexandria Desert Road and the Cairo

VIEWS OF THE PYRAMIDS

The best **viewpoints** over the Giza pyramids are south of Mycerinus's pyramid. Most tourists gather along the tarmac road some 400m west of the pyramid, which is particularly popular in the late afternoon when the sun is in the right direction. In the morning, however, **photos** are better taken from the southeast, though it can often be hazy early on. For the best view of the Pyramids close together, the ridge to the south of Mycerinus's pyramid is the place to head for.

Ring Road. Scheduled to open in 2015, it is meant to alleviate the strain on Cairo's venerable Egyptian Museum (see p.73), enabling items from its basement depository to be displayed, and the downtown museum to be modernized. One exhibit, a colossal statue of Ramses II, which formerly stood outside Ramses Station (see p.86), has already been moved here, and will stand at the museum's entrance when it is opened. The museum will be part of a grandiose development with an IMAX cinema, conference and seminar halls, and educational facilities, while the top floor will have commanding views over the Pyramids.

North Saqqara

While Memphis (see p.166) was the capital of the Old Kingdom, Egypt's royalty and nobility were buried at **Saqqara**, the limestone scarp that flanks the Nile Valley to the west – the traditional direction of the Land of the Dead. Although superseded by the Theban necropolis during the New Kingdom, Saqqara remained in use for burying sacred animals and birds, especially in Ptolemaic times, when these cults enjoyed a revival. Over three thousand years it grew to cover 7km of desert – not including the associated necropolises of Abu Sir and Dahshur, or the Giza Pyramids. As such, it is today the largest archeological site in Egypt. Its name – usually pronounced "sa'-'ah-rah" by Cairenes, with the q's as glottal stops – probably derives from Sokar, the Memphite god of the dead, though Egyptians may tell you that it comes from *saq*, the Arabic word for a hawk or falcon, the sacred bird of Horus. The easiest part of the Saqqara necropolis to visit is the **northern area**, which also contains the most interesting sights, including the main attraction, Zoser's Step Pyramid, and its surrounding funerary complex. **South Saqqara** is more remote and gets far fewer visitors.

The Imhotep Museum
Daily 8am–4pm, Ramadan 8am–3pm • Entrance with site ticket

Just beyond the ticket kiosk, to the right of the road leading onto the site, is the small but very interesting and well laid-out **Imhotep Museum**, containing many fine items found at the site. It is named after Imhotep, the architect who started the whole pyramid craze by designing the step pyramid for Pharaoh Zoser back in 2650 BC or thereabouts. Revered throughout pharaonic history, he was worshipped at Saqqara in later pharaonic times as a god of healing. The Ptolemies even identified Imhotep with Asclepius, the Greek god of medicine. Imhotep's tomb is thought to lie among a cluster of III Dynasty tombs to the east of the Mastaba of Ti (see p.164).

To the right of the entrance hall, a door marked "Saqqara Missions" leads to a prettily **painted mummy** from the XXX Dynasty, Imhotep's wooden coffin (his body has yet to be found) and some copper **surgical instruments** from the tomb of a palace physician called Qar. The main hall, dominated by a reconstruction of the facade from Zoser's tomb, contains the original green faïence panels found at the site, a **cobra frieze** similar to the one in situ (see p.160) and a bronze statuette of Imhotep made nearly a millennium after his death.

Next to the museum is a "Visual Setting Hall", which features a large-scale model of Zoser's funerary complex. A nine-minute **film** about Imhotep and Saqqara (narrated

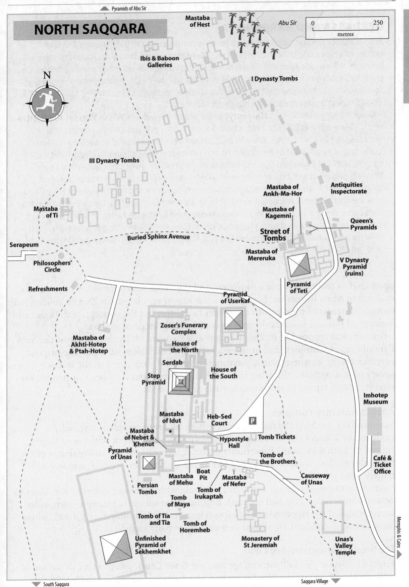

NORTH SAQQARA

by Omar Sharif) is sometimes shown in this hall, and is worth seeing if you aren't pressed for time.

The Step Pyramid

Zoser's **Step Pyramid** heralded the start of the Pyramid Age. When **Imhotep**, the king's chief architect, raised it in the 27th century BC, it was the largest structure ever built in stone – the "beginning of architecture", according to one historian. Imhotep's achievement was to break from the tradition of earthbound mastabas, raising level

1

KERDASSA AND HARRANIYYA

The villages of Kerdassa and Harraniyya have no connection with the Pyramids, but tour groups often pay one or both of them a visit. **Kerdassa** (accessible by microbus from the junction of Pyramids Road with Sharia Mansureya) is where most of the scarves, *galabiyyas* and shirts in Cairo are made, plus carpets, which are sold by the metre. Although no longer a place for bargains, it's still frequented by collectors of ethnic textiles, particularly Bedouin robes and veils (the best-quality ones sell for hundreds of dollars).

Guided tours often take in **Harraniyya**, the site of the famous **Wissa Wassef Art Centre** (daily 10am–5pm; ☏ 02 3381 5746, ⓦ wissa-wassef-arts.com and ⓦ wissawassef.com). Founded in 1952 by Ramses Wissa Wassef, an architect who wanted to preserve village crafts and alleviate rural unemployment, the centre teaches children to design and weave carpets, and has branched out into batik work and pottery. The pupils, supervised by Wassef's widow, daughters and the original generation of students, produce beautiful tapestries which now sell for thousands of dollars and are imitated throughout Egypt. You can see them at work (except at lunchtime, Thurs afternoons and Fri) and admire a superb collection, laid out in a mud-brick museum designed by Hassan Fathy. To reach the Art Centre under your own steam, take a taxi or minibus 4km south along the Saqqara road (Maryotteya Canal, west bank) from Pyramids Road, or bus #335 (hourly) from Midan Giza and get off at Harraniyya.

upon level of stones to create a four-step, and then a six-step pyramid, which was clad in dazzling white limestone. None of the blocks was very large, for Zoser's builders still thought in terms of mud-brick rather than megaliths, but the concept, techniques and logistics all pointed towards the true pyramid, finally attained at Giza.

Before it was stripped of its casing stones and rounded off by the elements, the Step Pyramid stood 62m high and measured 140m by 118m along its base. The original entrance on the northern side is permanently blocked, and access to the interior via a gallery on the opposite side (dug in the XXVI Dynasty) has long been suspended for vital structural repairs to its subsidence-ruptured innards.

Zoser's funerary complex

Surrounding the Step Pyramid is an extensive **funerary complex**, originally enclosed by a finely cut limestone wall, 544m long and 277m wide, now largely ruined or buried by sand. False doors occur at intervals for the convenience of the pharaoh's *ka*, but visitors can only enter at the southeastern corner, which has largely been rebuilt.

Entrance to the complex is through a vestibule with simulated double doors (detailed down to their hinge pins and sockets). Beyond the vestibule is a narrow colonnaded corridor, called the **Hypostyle Hall** (hypostyle meaning "columned" in Greek), whose forty "bundle" columns are ribbed in imitation of palm stems.

The Great Court and Heb-Sed Court

From the Hypostyle Hall you emerge into the **Great Court**, where a rebuilt section of wall (marked * on our site plan) is topped by a frieze of cobras, like the one in the Imhotep Museum (see p.158). Worshipped in the Delta as a fire-spitting goddess of destruction called Wadjet or Edjo, the cobra was adopted as the emblem of royalty and always appeared on pharaonic headdresses – a figure known as the *uraeus*.

Nearby, a deep shaft plummets into Zoser's **Southern Tomb**, decorated with blue faïence tiles and a relief of the king running the **Heb-Sed race**. During the jubilee festival marking the thirtieth year of a pharaoh's reign, he had to sprint between two altars representing Upper and Lower Egypt and re-enact his coronation, seated first on one throne, then upon another, symbolically reuniting the Two Lands. Although the festival was held at Memphis, pairs of altars, thrones and shrines were incorporated in

Zoser's funerary complex to perpetuate its efficacy on a cosmic timescale. The B-shaped structures near the centre of the Great Court are the bases of these altars; the twin thrones probably stood on the platform at the southern end of the adjacent **Heb-Sed Court**. Both shrines were essentially facades, since the actual buildings were filled with rubble. This phoney quality is apparent if you view them from the east: the curvaceous roof line and delicate false columns wouldn't look amiss on a yuppie waterfront development A shelter near the northern end of the court covers four **stone feet** which once belonged to ancient statues.

Houses of the South and North

North of the Heb-Sed Court, near the Step Pyramid's northeastern corner, is the partially ruined **House of the South**, whose chapel is fronted by proto-Doric columns with lotus capitals, and a spearhead motif above the lintel. Inside you'll find several examples of XVIII–IXX Dynasty tourist graffiti, expressing admiration for Zoser or the equivalent of "Ramses was here". Continuing northwards, you'll pass a relatively intact row of casing stones along the eastern side of Zoser's Pyramid. The **House of the North** has fluted columns with papyrus capitals; the lotus and the papyrus were the heraldic emblems of Upper and Lower Egypt.

Statue of Zoser

On the northern side of the pyramid, a tilted masonry box or *serdab* contains a life-size **statue of Zoser** gazing blindly towards the north and circumpolar stars, which the ancients associated with immortality; seated thus, his *ka* was assured of eternal life. The statue is a replica, however; the original is in the Egyptian Museum (see p.75).

South of Zoser's funerary complex

South of Zoser's funerary complex are several tombs and ruins dating from various dynasties including a handful of the table-like tombs known as mastabas, as well as a couple of minor pyramids. Some of the tombs contain well-preserved painted reliefs, which are well worth a look, even if it means locating the caretaker and haggling over baksheeh to get in.

Mastabas of Idut, Nebet and Khenut

During the Old Kingdom, nobles were buried in subterranean tombs covered by large mud-brick superstructures; the name **mastaba** (Arabic for "bench") was bestowed upon them by native workmen during excavations in the nineteenth century. A trio – the mastabas of Idut, Khenut and Nebet – stand outside the southern wall of Zoser's complex; they're often closed for no apparent reason, but it's usually just a question of locating and tipping the caretaker to get them opened up.

The **Mastaba of Idut** is the most worthwhile of the three, with interesting reliefs in five of its ten rooms. Among the fishing and farming scenes, notice the crocodile eyeing a newborn hippo, and a calf being dragged through the water so that cows will ford a river. The chapel contains a false door painted in imitation of granite, scenes of bulls and buffaloes being sacrificed, and Idut herself. Idut was the daughter of Pharaoh Unas, whose two wives, **Nebet and Khenut**, share a double mastaba. Inside it, Nebet gets the best of the reliefs, including a beautiful one of her sniffing a sacred blue lotus.

Pyramid of Unas

The **Pyramid of Unas**, at the end of the causeway, looks like a mound of rubble from the front, but retains many casing stones around the back, some carved with hieroglyphs. Inside (though it is usually closed), the walls are covered with Pyramid Texts, on which the Egyptian *Book of the Dead* is based. They speak of the pharaoh becoming a star and travelling to Sirius, and are the earliest-known example of decorative writing within a pharaonic tomb chamber.

1

Tombs of the Brothers, Nefer and Irukaptah

Tickets (£E30) from a kiosk by the Step Pyramid car park are supposed to cover all three tombs, but the caretaker may claim not all are open (although even without an official ticket you should be able to negotiate entry to all of them for baksheesh, which should not exceed the price of the ticket)

Three more tombs stand next to the causeway of Unas. The most worthwhile is the **Tomb of the Two Brothers**, belonging to Niankh-khnum and Khnum-hotep, two V Dynasty officials depicted kissing each other and performing various activities together. They were probably brothers, and possibly twins, rather than a gay couple, as their families are also pictured in the tomb. The nearby **Tomb of Nefer** is smaller and less interesting; the **Tomb of Irukaptah**, if the caretaker can be persuaded to open it up, has no lights inside, so you'd need a torch.

Persian Tombs

South of Unas's Pyramid, a stone hut gives access to a spiral staircase that descends 25m underground to where three low corridors lead into the vaulted **Persian Tombs**. Chief physician Psamtik, Admiral Djenhebu and Psamtik's son Pediese were all officials of the XXVII Dynasty of Persian kings founded in 525 BC, yet the hieroglyphs in their tombs invoke the same spells as those written two thousand years earlier. The dizzying descent and claustrophobic atmosphere make this an exciting tomb to explore. Though often locked, it's not "forbidden" as guards sometimes pretend, hoping to wangle excessive baksheesh.

Tombs of Horemheb, Tia and Maya

Southeast of the Persian Tombs lies the **Tomb of Horemheb**. Built when he was Tutankhamun's army chief, the tomb became redundant after Horemheb seized power from Tutankhamun's successor Ay, and ordered a new tomb to be dug in the Valley of the Kings, the royal necropolis of the New Kingdom, as befitted his new statius as pharaoh. Many of the finely carved blocks from his original tomb are now in museums around the world.

Another set of paving stones and truncated columns marks the nearby **Tomb of Tia and Tia**, the sister of Ramses II and her husband, who both had the same name. The tomb was discovered in 1982, but the courtyard in front of it was only excavated in 2005. Just to its north, the **Tomb of Maya**, Tutankhamun's treasurer, was unearthed nearby in 1986. Unfortunately, all three of these tombs were closed at the time of writing.

Unfinished Pyramid of Sekhemkhet

It's indicative of how much might still be hidden beneath the sands at Saqqara that the **unfinished Pyramid of Sekhemkhet** was only discovered in 1950. Beyond his monuments, nothing is known of Sekhemkhet, whose step pyramid and funerary complex were presumably intended to mimic those of his predecessor, Zoser, and may also have been built by Imhotep. The alabaster sarcophagus inside the pyramid (which is unsafe to enter) was apparently never used, but the body of a child was found inside an auxiliary tomb.

From Sekhemkhet's pyramid it's roughly 700m to the nearest part of South Saqqara (see p.167).

Pyramids of Userkaf and Teti, and street of tombs

From Zoser's funerary complex, it's only a short walk northeast to the pulverized **Pyramid of Userkaf**, the founder of the V Dynasty, whose successors were buried at Abu Sir (see p.149). From here, a track runs northwards to the **Pyramid of Teti**, which overlooks the valley from the edge of the plateau and belongs to the first pharaoh of the VI Dynasty. Excavated by French Egyptologist Auguste Mariette in the 1850s, it has since been engulfed by sand, but can still be entered. In one of the funeral chambers (accessible by a sloping shaft and low passageway), the star-patterned blocks of its vaulted roof have slipped inwards due to an earthquake some time in the last 4500 years. East of here you'll find the scant remains of a **V Dynasty pyramid**, while a couple of satellite **queens' pyramids** lie to the northeast.

Although most of the VI Dynasty kings who followed Teti chose to be buried at South Saqqara, several of their courtiers were interred in a **"street of tombs"** beside his pyramid, which was linked to the Serapeum by an Avenue of Sphinxes (now sanded over). To do justice to their superbly detailed reliefs takes well over an hour, but it's rare to find all of them open.

Mastaba of Mereruka

The largest tomb in the street belongs to **Mereruka**, Teti's vizier and son-in-law, whose 32-room complex includes separate funerary suites for his wife Watet-khet-hor, priestess of Hathor, and their son Meri-Teti. In the entry passage, Mereruka is shown playing a board game and painting at an easel; the chamber beyond depicts him hunting in the marshes with Watet-khet-hor (the frogs, birds, hippos and grasshoppers are beautifully rendered), along with the usual farming scenes. Goldsmiths, jewellers and other artisans are inspected by the couple in a room beyond the rear door, which leads into another chamber showing taxation and the punishment of defaulters. A pillared hall to the right portrays them watching sinuous dancers; a room to the left depicts offerings, sacrifices and birds being fed, with a *serdab* at the far end.

Beyond the transverse hall, with its tomb shaft, false door and reliefs of grape-treading and harvesting, lies the main **offerings hall**, dominated by a statue of Mereruka emerging from a false door. The opposite wall shows his funeral procession; around the corner are boats under full sail, with monkeys playing in their rigging. To the left of the statue, Mereruka is supported by his sons and litter-bearers, accompanied by dwarfs and dogs; on the other side, children frolic while dancers sway above the doorway into Meri-Teti's undecorated funerary suite.

To reach **Watet-khet-hor's suite**, return to the first room in the mastaba and take the other door. After similar scenes to those in her husband's tomb, Watet-khet-hor is carried to her false door in a lion chair.

Mastabas of Kagemni and Ankh-ma-hor

East of Mereruka's tomb and left around the corner, the smaller **Mastaba of Kagemni** features delicate reliefs in worse shape. The pillared hall beyond the entrance corridor shows dancers and acrobats, the judgement of prisoners, a hippo hunt and agricultural work, all rich in naturalistic detail. Notice the boys feeding a puppy and trussed cows being milked. The door in this wall leads to another chamber where Kagemni inspects his fowl pens while servants trap marsh birds with clap-nets; on the pylon beyond this he relaxes on a palanquin as they tend to his pet dogs and monkeys. As usual in the offerings hall, scenes of butchery appear opposite the false door. On the roof of the mastaba (reached by stairs from the entrance corridor) are two boat pits. As vizier, Kagemni was responsible for overseeing prophets and the estate of Teti's pyramid complex.

The **Mastaba of Ankh-ma-hor** is also known as the "Doctor's Tomb" after its reliefs showing circumcision, toe surgery and suchlike, as practised during the VI Dynasty. If the tomb is open, it's definitely worth a look, unlike the sand-choked **I Dynasty tombs** that straggle along the edge of the scarp beyond the **Antiquities Inspectorate**.

Double Mastaba of Akhti-Hotep and Ptah-Hotep

West of Zoser's Funerary Complex lies the **Double Mastaba of Akhti-Hotep and Ptah-Hotep**. This mastaba belonged to **Ptah-Hotep**, a priest of Maat during the reign of Unas's predecessor, Djedkare, and his son **Akhti-Hotep**, who served as vizier, judge and overseer of the granaries and treasury. Though it's smaller than Ti's mastaba, its reliefs are interesting for being at various stages of completion, showing how a finished

1

product was achieved. After the preliminary drawings had been corrected in red by a master artist, the background was chiselled away to leave a silhouette, before details were marked in and cut. The agricultural scenes in the entrance corridor show this process clearly, although with the exception of Ptah-Hotep's chapel, none of these reliefs was ever painted.

Off the pillared hall of Akhti-Hotep is a T-shaped chapel whose inside wall shows workers making papyrus boats and jousting with poles. More impressive is the chapel of his father, covered with exquisitely detailed reliefs. Between the two door-shaped stele representing the entrance to the tomb, Ptah-Hotep enjoys a banquet of offerings, garbed in the panther-skin of a high priest. Similar scenes occur on the facing wall, whose upper registers show animals being slaughtered and women bringing offerings from his estates. The left-hand wall swarms with activity, as boys wrestle and play *khaki la wizza* (a leapfrog game still popular in Nubia) and wild animals mate or flee from hunting dogs, while others are caged. A faded mural above the entrance shows the priest being manicured and pedicured.

Mastaba of Ti

Discovered by Auguste Mariette in 1865, the V Dynasty **Mastaba of Ti** has been a rich source of information about life in the Old Kingdom. A royal hairdresser who made an advantageous marriage, **Ti** acquired stewardship over several mortuary temples and pyramids, and his children bore the title "royal descendant".

Ti makes his first appearances on either side of the doorway, receiving offerings and asking visitors to respect his tomb [a] – letters refer to the Mastaba of Ti site plan. The reliefs in the courtyard have been damaged by exposure, but it's possible to discern men butchering an ox [b], Ti on his palanquin accompanied by dogs and dwarves [c], servants feeding cranes and geese [d], and Ti examining accounts and cargo [e]. His unadorned tomb (reached by a shaft from the courtyard) contrasts with the richly decorated interior of the mastaba.

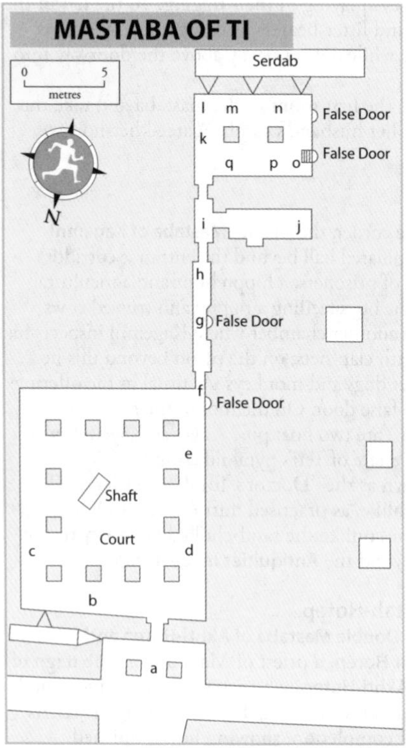

MASTABA OF TI

Near his son's false door, variously garbed figures of Ti [f] appear above the portal of a corridor where bearers bring food and animals for the sustenance of his *ka* [g]. Beyond a doorway [h] over which Ti enjoys the marshes with his wife, funerary statues are dragged on sledges above scenes of butchery, and his Delta fleets are arrayed [i]. Potters, bakers, brewers and scribes occupy the rear wall of a storage room [j], while dancers shimmy above the doorway to Ti's chapel.

In the harvesting scene, notice the man twisting a donkey's ear to make it behave [k]. Further along, Ti inspects shipwrights shaping tree trunks, and sawing and hammering boards [l]. Goldsmiths, sculptors, carpenters, tanners and market life are minutely detailed [m], like the musicians who entertain Ti at his offerings table [n]. Peer through one of the apertures and you'll see a cast of his statue inside its *serdab*. The original is in the Egyptian Museum.

Reliefs on the northern wall depict fishing and trapping in the Delta [o]; Ti sailing through the marshes while his servants spear hippopotami [p]; harvesting papyrus for boat-building; and ploughing and seeding fields [q]. The scene of hunting in the marshes is also allegorical, pitting Ti against the forces of chaos (represented by fish and birds) and evil (hippos were hated and feared). If you aren't claustrophobic and like cold, dark spaces, it is possible to squeeze down the steps of the shaft into the burial chamber below.

The Serapeum

Saqqara's weirdest monument (closed for restoration at the time of writing) lies underground near a derelict building downhill from the refreshments tent. Discovered by Mariette in 1851, the rock-cut galleries of the **Serapeum** held the mummified corpses of the Apis bulls, which the Memphites regarded as manifestations of Ptah's "blessed soul" and identified with Osiris after death. The **cult of the Apis bulls** was assailed by Egypt's Persian conqueror, Cambyses, who stabbed one to disprove its divinity, whilst Artaxerxes I avenged his nickname "the donkey" by having a namesake beast buried here with full honours. But the Ptolemies encouraged native cults and even synthesized their own. "Serapeum" derives from the fusion of the Egyptian Osarapis (Osiris in his Apis form) and the Greeks' Dionysus into the cult of **Serapis**, whose temple stood in Alexandria.

The galleries

Although robbers had plundered the galleries centuries before, Auguste Mariette, excavating in 1850, found a single tomb miraculously undisturbed for four thousand years. The oldest of the galleries dates from that era, and is now inaccessible; the second is from the Saite period, and the main one from Ptolemaic times. Enormous granite or basalt **sarcophagi** weighing up to seventy tons are ranged either side of the Ptolemaic gallery, at the end of which is a narrow shaft whereby robbers penetrated the Serapeum. The finest sarcophagus squats on the right, while another one lies abandoned near the entrance to the Ramessid gallery. Sadly, none of the mummified bulls remains *in situ*.

Philosopher's Circle

En route to the Serapeum you'll notice a concrete slab sheltering broken statues of Plato, Heraclitus, Thales, Protagoras, Homer, Hesiod, Demetrius of Phalerum and Pindar – the **Philosopher's Circle**, now rather rubbish-strewn and neglected. The statues formerly stood near a temple that overlaid the Serapeum, proof that the Ptolemies juxtaposed Hellenistic philosophy and Ancient Egyptian religion with no sense of incongruity.

GETTING TO NORTH SAQQARA

North Saqqara lies 21km south of the Giza Pyramids as the camel strides, or 32km from Cairo by road. There are a number of ways to get here by public transport, but all leave you in Saqqara village, over a kilometre from the site entrance. If **driving your own vehicle**, note that the Cairo–Saqqara road is currently considered unsafe after dark due to the possibility of carjackings, although this situation may change in future.

Via Pyramids Road The most direct way to Saqqara by public transport (about 1hr–1hr 30min) is to take a bus or service taxi to Pyramids Road, and get off at Maryotteya Canal (about 1km before the Pyramids), where you'll find service taxi microbuses to Saqqara village (20min; £E1).

Via Midan Giza Bus #335 runs hourly from Midan Giza to Saqqara village.

Via Helwan A slightly more adventurous route, which avoids the Cairo traffic, is to take the metro to Helwan (30min; £E1), then a service taxi minibus to Tibiin, near the Marazi Bridge (15min; £E1), another

1

service taxi (often a Peugeot rather than a microbus) across to Badrasheen on the west bank (15min; 75pt); and finally one to Saqqara (15min; 75pt), by way of Memphis.

Via Ramses–Badrasheen Bus #987 runs from Midan Ramses to Badrasheen, where you can get a microbus to Saqqara village as described above.

Getting back to Cairo Don't leave too late or you may not find transport in Saqqara village, and have either to pay well over the odds for a taxi, or walk another 5km to Badrasheen (or at least to the Maryotteya Canal) to get a bus back to Cairo, or a microbus to Midan Giza.

INFORMATION

Tickets £E60; sold at the Imhotep Museum.

Opening hours Daily 8am–4pm, Ramadan 8am–3pm.

Visiting the tombs It's a good idea when buying your ticket to check which tombs are open – especially those further afield – as they often close due to restoration work. When you do visit, some guards will encourage unauthorized photography in the tombs in the expectation of baksheesh, but aside from this you're not obliged to give anything unless they help with lighting or provide a guided tour (and if you don't want a running commentary, make this clear at the outset). Note that guards also start locking up the tombs at least half an hour before closing time.

Tours Tours, such as the ones run by Samo Tours (☎0122 313 8446 or ☎02 2299 1155, ✉samo@link net), include Memphis, North Saqqara, the Wissa Wassef tapestry school at Harraniyya and the Pyramids of Giza. All are accompanied by an English-speaking Egyptologist, with transport in an a/c minibus; tours leave around 8am (9am in winter), returning to Cairo at

4–5pm. Be sure to ask to see the Mastaba of Ti during your trip. The price of the tour (US$23.50) doesn't include admission tickets, but *Rough Guide* readers who book direct get a £E5 discount, with a free airport transfer to your hotel on arrival also thrown in. Misr Travel (see p.30) and American Express (see p.202) also run half-day tours to Saqqara for around £E200/person. Another option is to rent a private taxi for the day (around £E200–250 for Giza and Saqqara, £E250–300 if you add on Dahshur). Be sure to specify which sites are included and how long you expect to stay when you negotiate with the driver.

Camel rides Camels can be hired outside the refreshments hut near the Serapeum (around £E60/hr).

Swimming pool At the *Palm Club* (see below).

Weather conditions Over winter, the site can be swept by chill winds and clouds of grit; during the hottest months walking around is exhausting.

Dangers Beware of deep pits, which aren't always fenced off.

EATING AND DRINKING

Bring at least one litre of water per person, as vendors at Memphis and the refreshments hut at North Saqqara are grossly overpriced, as is every restaurant along the Saqqara road. A packed lunch is also a good idea.

Palm Club ☎02 3819 1555 or ☎02 3819 1999. Just over the Mansureya Canal from the site entrance, this place has a swimming pool set amid pleasant gardens and charges £E175 (April–Oct), or £E95 (Nov–March, when

the pool is out of use) for a day's access including lunch – definitely an option worth considering if you have kids in tow. Daily 9am–6pm

Memphis

Daily 8am–4pm • £E35

Most tour excursions to Saqqara include a flying visit to the scant remains of **Memphis** in the village of Mit Rahina. Something of its glory is still evident in the great necropolises ranged across the desert and the countless objects in Cairo's Egyptian Museum, but alas for posterity, most of this garden city was built of mud-brick, which returned to the Nile silt whence it came, and everyone from the Romans onwards plundered its stone temples for fine masonry.

Brief history

The foundation of Memphis is attributed to **Menes**, the quasi-mythical ruler (known also as Narmer – and possibly a conflation of several rulers) who was said to have unified Upper and Lower Egypt and launched the I Dynasty around 3100 BC. At that time, Memphis was sited at the apex of the Delta and thus controlled overland and

THE CULTS OF PTAH AND SOKAR

In pre-Dynastic times, **Ptah** was the Great Craftsman or Divine Artificer who invented metallurgy and engineering. However, the people of Memphis esteemed him as the Great Creator who, with a word, brought the universe into being – a concept that never really appealed to other Egyptians. Like most creator gods, he was subsequently linked with death cults and is shown dressed in the shroud of a mummy. The Greeks equated him with Hephaestus, their god of fire and the arts.

Another deity closely associated with Memphis is **Sokar**, originally the god of darkness but subsequently of death, with special responsibility for necropolises. He is often shown, with a falcon's head, seated in the company of Isis and Osiris. Although his major festival occurred at Memphis towards the end of the inundation season, Sokar also rated a shrine at Abydos, where all the Egyptian death gods were represented.

river communications. It was surrounded by levees and battlements, giving it its original name, the White Wall.

Egypt's **capital** throughout the Old Kingdom (III–IV Dynasty, c.2650–2134 BC), Memphis regained its role through the Middle Kingdom (XI–XIV Dynasty, c.2040–1640 BC), and was still Egypt's second most important city during the New Kingdom (the classic period of ancient Egypt, XVII–XX Dynasty, c.1550–1040 BC), when Thebes was the capital. Memphis remained the nation's second city until well into the Ptolemaic era, when Alexandria gradually took over, while the creation of Babylon-in-Egypt (Old Cairo) by the Persians sowed the seed of the city that would supplant it – Cairo. By Roman times Memphis was in terminal decline, though it wasn't completely abandoned until early Muslim times, after four thousand years of continuous occupation.

At peak times, the city's **population** may have exceeded one hundred thousand, making it the most populous city in the ancient world until the rise of Mesopotamian Babylon in the seventh century BC. Core-sampling has shown that, in Roman times, Memphis was the shape and size of Manhattan, stretching for over 19km along the west bank of the Nile, to the outskirts of modern-day Giza.

The site

Nowadays, the site of ancient Memphis is occupied by leftover statues and stelae sharing a garden with souvenir kiosks. The star attraction, found in 1820, is a limestone **Colossus of Ramses II**, similar to the one that used to stand in Midan Ramses, but laid supine within a concrete shelter. A giant **alabaster sphinx** weighing 80 tons is also mightily impressive. Both these figures probably stood outside the vast Temple of Ptah, the city's patron deity.

If you leave the garden and walk west along the road, you'll notice (on the right) several alabaster **embalming slabs**, where the holy Apis bulls were mummified before burial in the Serapeum at Saqqara. In a pit across the road are excavated chambers from Ptah's temple complex; climb the ridge beyond them and you can gaze across the cultivated valley floor to the Step Pyramid of Saqqara.

South Saqqara

A number of pharaohs, particularly during the VI Dynasty (c.2345–2181 BC) used a necropolis – nowadays called **South Saqqara** – which starts 700m beyond Sekhemkhet's unfinished pyramid (see p.162) and extends for over 3km. Unfortunately, the most interesting monuments are those furthest away across the site; renting a donkey, horse or camel (£E30–50 for the round trip) will minimize slogging over soft sand. It's also possible to walk from Saqqara village: just keep heading west until you emerge from the palm trees. If you stop to ask directions,

1

bear in mind that, whatever you say (even if you say it in Arabic), villagers will almost certainly assume you are looking for the Step Pyramid, and direct you accordingly; to remedy this, the key word you need to get across is "Pepi", the name of South Saqqara's main pyramid.

The site is quite large, with the **northern part** (around Pepi I's pyramid) pretty much due west of Saqqara village, while the **southern area** (around the Mastabat al-Faraun) lies to the village's southwest. There is no official entrance fee to the site, and you probably won't see another tourist. Apart from the tranquillity, what you get here – with North Saqqara's pyramids clearly visible to the north, and Dahshur's to the south – is the feeling of being in the midst of a massive pyramid field, somewhere vast and very ancient.

The northern area

South Saqqara's northern area centres on a low mound of rubble identified as the **Pyramid of Pepi I**. The name "Memphis", which Classical authors bestowed upon Egypt's ancient capital and its environs, was actually derived from one of this pyramid's titles, Men-nefer-Pepi (The Beauty of Pepi Endures). To the southwest, another insignificant heap indicates the **Pyramid of Merenre**, who succeeded Pepi. French archeologists are excavating the latter's pyramid, but neither site is really worth a detour.

Directly east of Pepi's pyramid, sand drifts over the outlying temples of the **Pyramid of Djedkare-Isesi**. Known in Arabic as the "Pyramid of the Sentinel", it stands 25m high and can be entered via a tunnel on the north side. Although a shattered basalt sarcophagus and mummified remains were found here during the 1800s, it wasn't until 1946 that Abdel Hussein identified them as those of Djedkare, the penultimate king of the V Dynasty.

The southern area

The **mortuary complex of Shepseskaf** (son of Mycerinus of Giza's third pyramid) is the most important monument in South Saqqara, and lies well to the south of Pepi's, Merenre's and Djedkare-Isesi's pyramids, Built of limestone blocks, the complex resembles a gigantic sarcophagus with a rounded lid. Locally, it's known as **Mastabat al-Faraun** – the Pharaoh's Bench. If you can find a guard, it's possible to venture through descending and horizontal corridors to reach the burial chamber and various storerooms. The monument was almost certainly commissioned by Shepseskaf, who evidently felt the need to distance himself from his father's pyramid at Giza. However, the early twentieth-century Swiss Egyptologist Gustave Jequier doubted that the complex was ever used for any actual burial and Shepseskaf's final resting place remains uncertain.

Just northwest of Shepseskaf's complex lie the mortuary temple and pyramid of **Pepi II**. These form the most complete example of a VI Dynasty mortuary complex still in existence, even though they are missing casing stones and other masonry that was plundered in medieval times. The **mortuary temple**, whose vestibule and sanctuary retain fragments of their original reliefs, stands at the end of a causeway which starts 600m to the northeast, where Pepi's valley temple once stood. Immediately to the west of the mortuary temple rises the **Pyramid of Pepi II**, whose reign supposedly lasted 94 years, after which the VI Dynasty expired. A descending passage leads to his rock-cut **burial chamber**, whose ceiling and walls are inscribed with stars and Pyramid Texts (also found within the subsidiary pyramids of Pepi's queens, Apuit and Neith, which imitate his mortuary complex on a smaller scale).

Dahshur

The **Dahshur pyramid field** contains some of the most impressive of all the pyramids, and some of the most significant in the history of pyramid-building. The pyramids are in two groups. To the east are three **Middle Kingdom complexes**, dating from the revival of pyramid-building (c.1991–1790 BC) that culminated near the Fayoum (see p.383). Though the pyramids proved unrewarding to nineteenth-century excavators, their subsidiary tombs yielded some magnificent jewellery (now in the Egyptian Museum).

To the north, the pyramids of XII Dynasty pharaohs Seostris III and Amenenmhat II are little more than piles of rubble, but the southernmost of the three, the **Black Pyramid of Amenemhat III** (Joseph's pharaoh in the Old Testament, according to some), is at least an interesting shape: though its limestone casing has long gone, a black mud-brick core is still standing (its black basalt capstone is in the Egyptian Museum).

More intriguing, however, are the two **Old Kingdom pyramids** further into the desert, which have long tantalized archeologists with a riddle. Both of them are credited to **Snofru** (c.2613–2588 BC), father of Cheops and founder of the IV Dynasty, whose monuments constitute an evolutionary link between the stepped creations of the previous dynasty at North Saqqara and the true pyramids of Giza.

GETTING TO DAHSHUR

Public transport leaves you in Dahshur village, 2km from the site entrance. Taking a taxi from there is a good idea since the site is extremely spread out: it's 1km from the gate to the Red Pyramid, and another 1km from there to the Bent Pyramid. A tuk-tuk (Indian-style auto-rickshaw) should cost £E2–3 from the village to the site entrance, or you may find a place in a shared one for 50pt. Alternatively, it's a pleasant walk to the site.

Via Saqqara Service taxi microbuses run from Saqqara to Dahshur. You may even occasionally find a direct one from the Saqqara servees station on Pyramids Rd.

Via Badrasheen There are regular service taxi microbuses to Dahshur village from Badrasheen, which is accessible by bus #987 or by service taxi from Tibiin (see p.165).

Getting back to Cairo Transport from Dahshur tends to dry up at around 5pm so don't leave too late or you may find yourself stranded, with the nearest public transport 5km away in Saqqara.

INFORMATION

Opening hours Daily 8am–4pm, last ticket sold an hour before closing.

Entrance charge £E30.

The Red Pyramid

Arriving in Dahshur, the first pyramid you come to (if you follow the road from the village past the ticket office) is the northern **Red Pyramid**, named after the pinkish limestone from which it's built. No less impressive than any of the Giza trio (see p.149), it differs from them by standing in perfect isolation. Despite its lower angle (43.5°) and height (101m), Snofru's the Red Pyramid clearly prefigures Cheops' edifice at Giza, which is also the only pyramid that exceeds it in size. It was probably Snofru's final attempt at pyramid building, but he was not laid to rest here, as no sarcophagus was ever found. Indeed, the Red and Bent pyramids are only attributed to Snofru because his cartouche appears on their respective mortuary temples.

The interior

The Red Pyramid's **interior** configuration is unusual: a typical entrance shaft on the north face leads down to just above bedrock level, where you pass through two large chambers with corbelled ceilings (slabs laid overlapping the ones below until they meet in the middle) and ascend a (modern) staircase to reach the burial chamber, situated on a higher level, perpendicular to the other two. You may well be alone to absorb the rather eerie, fetid, atmosphere.

The Bent Pyramid

From the Red Pyramid, a road leads south to the **Bent Pyramid**, which is not only the most intriguing of all the pyramids, but, because of its state of preservation, also the most breathtaking. What makes it different from all the other pyramids is its change of angle towards the top: it rises more steeply (54.3°) than the Red or Giza pyramids for three-quarters of its height, before abruptly tapering at a gentler slope (43.2°) – hence its name. The explanation for its shape, and why Snofru should have had two pyramids built barely a kilometre apart, is a longstanding conundrum of Egyptology (see box below).

Of all the pyramids, the Bent Pyramid is the only one constructed with **two entrance shafts** at right angles to each other – one on the north side (as usual) and the other on its western face. The former leads to two chambers carved from the bedrock, connected to a separate upper chamber within the superstructure, directly accessible by the latter shaft. All three chambers have corbelled ceilings. While they are unlikely to be open to the public in the near future, you can see inside on ⓦguardians.net/egypt.

Externally, the pyramid is remarkable for its largely intact **limestone casing**, whose smooth, once pristine white, surface gives a clear impression of how it once looked. All the Old Kingdom pyramids were originally clad in limestone, their surfaces as smooth as this one, but most have been stripped, their stone burned for lime. The Bent Pyramid escaped that fate because its narrower angle made it harder to remove the facing, though this has disappeared from much of the base. Where the casing blocks have fallen away at the northwest corner (now being repaired), you can see how closely they were slotted together, and also pits and grooves carved into the bedrock, presumably carved before the pyramid was begun, marking out its base on the plateau.

To its south is a subsidiary **Queen's Pyramid**, possibly belonging to Snofru's wife Hetepheres. If it did, she didn't stay there too long: after robbers had entered both of

---

THE RIDDLE OF SNOFRU'S PYRAMIDS

Snofru, the founder of the IV Dynasty, is associated with three different pyramids: the Red and Bent Pyramids at Dahshur and the Collapsed Pyramid at Meidum (see p.391). Given that a pyramid was the pharaoh's tomb, the question arises, why would Snofru want three of them? And why is the Bent Pyramid such a funny shape, changing its angle halfway up?

Some scholars reasoned that the **Bent Pyramid**'s strange form resulted from a change of plan prompted by fears for its stability, and when these persisted, a second, safer pyramid was built to guarantee Snofru's afterlife. But for this theory to hold, it's necessary to dismiss Snofru's claim to have commissioned the pyramid at **Maidum** as a mere usurpation of an earlier structure. Two pyramids can be explained, three cannot.

Then, in 1977, Oxford professor **Kurt Mendelssohn** came up with a better answer. He suggested there was something like a pyramid production line. As one pyramid neared completion, surplus resources were deployed to start another. The reason for this was that building a single pyramid required gigantic efforts over ten to thirty years; inevitably, some pharaohs lacked the time and resources. A stockpile of half-constructed, perhaps even finished, pyramids was thus an insurance policy on the afterlife.

According to Mendelssohn, Snofru did indeed start off by commissioning the pyramid at Maidum. Unfortunately, this was built at too steep an angle and its outer layer collapsed. When this happened, the Bent Pyramid was already under construction, so its angle was hastily altered to make it more stable. The **Red Pyramid**, which followed, was then built at this new, shallower angle.

Not everyone agrees with Mendelssohn: other scholars argue that the Bent Pyramid's shape had nothing to do with the Collapsed Pyramid, but expressed a deliberate symbolic **duality**, echoed in its two burial chambers and the two entrance shafts at right angles to each other. At any rate, Snofru decided against using either Maidum or the Bent Pyramid, and was finally interred in the Red Pyramid.

Even if one discounts the attribution of the Collapsed Pyramid of Maidum to Snofru, it is a staggering fact that, during his twenty-five-year reign, the construction of the Bent and Red pyramids involved the quarrying, transport and shaping of some nine million tons of stone – more than three times the quantity of the Great Pyramid of Giza. Yet Herodotus wrote that Snofru was remembered by the Egyptians as benign, and his successor Cheops as a tyrant.

Snofru's pyramids at Dahshur, her sarcophagus was moved to Giza for safekeeping and hidden down a shaft beside the Great Pyramid of her son Cheops.

Excursions from Cairo

The Nile Valley – most people's target after Cairo – is too distant for a **day excursion** from the city. Elsewhere, however, you can choose between such possibilities as a jaunt to the seaside or remoter pyramids, a river trip or desert monasteries – and still be back in Cairo the same night. See Chapter 3 for details of the "Collapsed Pyramid" of Maidum (p.391) and the Monasteries of Wadi Natrun (p.378); Chapter 4 for Alexandria (p.462); Chapter 6 for the canal city of Ismailiya (p.518); and Chapter 8 for the Red Sea monasteries (p.570) and beaches of Ain Sukhna (p.570).

Those without the time to organize their own excursions might consider taking a set or **tailor-made** tour. There are plenty of disreputable tour operators about, but we list some of the better ones under "Tour Operators" in our Directory (see p.205).

The Nile barrages at Qanatir

Roughly 20km downriver from Cairo, the Nile divides into two great branches which define the Delta, and whose flow is controlled by the **Nile barrages** at **Qanatir**. Decoratively arched and turreted, this splendid piece of Victorian civil engineering is surrounded by shady parks and lush islets – an ideal spot for a picnic, provided you don't come on Friday, when the area is ridiculously crowded.

Originally conceived by Mohammed Ali's French hydro-engineer, Mougel Bey, the barrages were later realized as part of the nationwide hydrological system designed by Scottish military engineer Colin Scott-Moncrieff. At the eastern end of the 438-metre-long Rosetta Barrage lies the Istarahah al-Qanatir or **Presidential Villa**. Egypt's **State Yacht** (originally King Farouk's, on which he sailed into exile) is often moored at the quay.

GETTING TO QANATIR

By bus Bus #210 from the Abdel Mouneem Riyad terminal.
By boat From the Maspero Dock (hourly 8–10am, returning 2–4pm; ££5) in front of the Television Building, or by pleasure boat (daily round trips departing around 9am; ££10) from just north of the Maspero Dock. Travelling by felucca is slow, since the mast has to be lowered at every bridge.

The Muqattam Hills and Wadi Digla

The **Muqattam Hills** plateau, rising beyond Cairo, are seldom visited by tourists but readily accessible on #951 bus from Abdel Mouneem Riyad, or #401 from Midan Ataba. Zigzagging up the hillside past caves and quarries, ruined shrines and guarded outposts, buses terminate at **Medinet Muqattam**, an upmarket suburb whose avenues are flanked by villas and casinos. The Muqattam Corniche, circling the edge of the plateau, offers spectacular views across the Citadel and most of Cairo – an unforgettable vista at sunset.

People planning self-drive desert expeditions might consider a few training runs below the Muqattam. Victorian travellers used to engage a dragoman to lead them to the **Petrified Forests** – two expanses littered with broken, fossilized trunks, thought to date from the Miocene Period. The larger one (see map, p.69) is really only accessible with a guide, but would-be explorers can easily find the "Little Forest" on the Jebel al-Khasab plateau, north of the Digla–Ain Sukhna road, which turns east off the Nile Valley expressway near a *zebaleen* village beyond Ma'adi.

The **Digla–Ain Sukhna road** turns east off the Nile Valley expressway near a *zebaleen* village beyond Ma'adi. Roughly 25km from the turn-off, you'll pass the Jebel al-Khasab

1

on the left; if you keep on, you'll notice various tracks leading off to the right, which eventually converge on a main desert track running east–west. By following it west, back towards Digla, you'll pass through several meandering wadis before the way is blocked by **Wadi Digla**. This miniature canyon is good for **rock-climbing** and **birdwatching**. Bring water, food and shade.

Birqesh Camel Market

Held 35km north of the city at **Birqesh** (pronounced "Bir'esh"), Cairo's **Camel Market** is a twice-weekly feast of drama and cruelty. Beaten into defecating ranks, the hobbled camels are assessed by traders who disregard their emaciation (caused by a month-long trek from northwestern Sudan to Aswan, followed by an overnight truck ride to Cairo), unperturbed by throat-slittings and disembowelments in the vicinity. An adjacent compound hosts a furniture and bric-à-brac market.

The Souk al-Gamal (pronounced "Gah*mell*") lasts from dawn till early afternoon every Friday (and also Mon, when the market is smaller), but is busiest between 6am and 8.30am.

GETTING TO BIRQESH CAMEL MARKET

By bus In principle, you can catch bus #214 from Abdel Mouneem Riyad to Manashi by the Nile barrage at Qanatir (45min) and take a service taxi microbus from there (1hr), but in practice, especially if you arrive late-ish, you may find there are no connecting services once you get to Manashi, so you may then have to take a service taxi to Al-Dikla (45min), and if there's nothing there, take a taxi

(£E5, though they'll try to charge you more). You can also get to Manashi by microbus from Imbaba al-Matba'a (30min), which can in turn be reached by microbus from Al-Esa'af Pharmacy at the junction of 26th July St with Sharia Ramses (15min). If you're already at Qanatir, there are service taxis from there to Manahi too (15min).
By taxi Roughly £E150–200 for the round trip.

ARRIVAL AND DEPARTURE

CAIRO

BY AIR

Cairo International Airport About 15km northeast of the city centre, Cairo airport (⌨ cairo-airport.com) comprises three terminals which are roughly 3km apart. Terminal 1, known as the "old airport", Terminal 2 (currently closed for refurbishment) and the new Terminal 3, used by EgyptAir and other Star Alliance airlines. The terminals will eventually be connected by a monorail; in the meantime a free shuttle bus service provides transport between them. There are 24-hour currency exchange facilities, ATMs and tourist offices in all terminals. Leaving Cairo by air, make sure you know which terminal you're flying from before heading out to the airport.
Flight information ☎ 0900 77777 from a landline or ☎ 2777 from a mobile. For other information, call ☎ 02 2265 5000 for Terminal 1 or ☎ 16707 for Terminal 3.
Airlines Austrian (also Lufthansa and Swiss), 6 Sharia Sheikh al-Marsafi, Zamalek ☎ 02 2269 0971; British Airways, City Star Complex, Sharia al-Forsan, Heliopolis ☎ 02 2480 0380; EgyptAir, 9 Sharia Talaat Harb ☎ 02 2392 7664, and 6 Sharia Adly ☎ 02 2390 0999, airport ☎ 02 2267 7010, call centre ☎ 0900 70000; Emirates, 18 Sharia Batal Ahmed Abdel Aziz, Mohandiseen ☎ 19899; Ethiopian Airlines, 3A Sharia Rafat Saleh Tawfik (off Farid Semeka Hegaz), Heliopolis ☎ 02 2621 4934; Etihad, World Trade Center, 1191 Corniche al-Nil, Bulaq ☎ 02 2578 1303; Kenya

Airways, 11 Sharia Qasr al-Nil ☎ 02 2579 8529; Royal Jordanian, 6 Sharia Qasr al-Nil ☎ 02 2575 0614.

GETTING INTO TOWN

By taxi Taxi drivers will waylay you as you emerge from customs, claiming that they're the only way of getting into town, which isn't so. They will almost certainly refuse to use the meter and will probably demand at least £E60, and then quite likely start giving you nonsense of the "your hotel is no good/closed/burnt down, but I know a better one" variety (see box p.173) – don't pay them until you're sure you've reached the right hotel. Alternatively, your hotel may be able to arrange to send a vehicle for you (around £E75–100, but confirm the price in advance). A white cab (see p.178) from town to the airport should use the meter, and cost around £E40, though they may also ask for a £E5 surcharge, which is what they pay to enter the airport precincts.
By limousine A limousine taxi service in the arrivals halls offers prices which are fixed, but higher than regular taxi rates.
By bus/minibuses Buses and minibuses stop by the Awlad Ragab (Ragab Sons) supermarket, outside the airport precincts (about 200m straight ahead from Terminal 1). The most comfortable service is a/c bus #356

(£E2), which serves Midan Ramses and Abdel Mouneem Riyad terminal in downtown Cairo. This service runs from about 7am to 11pm, as does minibus #27 (£E2), which follows the same route. After hours, you can use bus #400 (£E1; 24hr), which plies the same route round the clock, though it's less comfortable and takes longer – over an hour in rush hour, about forty minutes at night. Bus #948 also runs 24/7, serving Midan Ataba on the eastern edge of downtown.

Domestic flights EgyptAir (☎ 02 2696 6798 or ☎ 0900 70000) domestic flights leave from Terminal 3. In addition, the oil company Salit Khadramaat Betrol, 45 Akfit al-Mahdi, off Sharia al-Azhar (☎ 02 2392 1674) runs flights from hall 2 at Terminal 1 to Kharga (Tues & Sun; 1hr), which will take passengers for £E400 if there's room.

Destinations: Abu Simbel (2–3 daily, mostly very early morning; 2hr 40min); Alexandria (2–4 daily; 45min); Assyut (3 weekly; 1hr); Aswan (8–10 daily; 1hr 25min); Hurghada (9 daily; 1hr 5min); Kharga (Tues & Sun; 1hr); Luxor (11–14 daily; 1hr); Marsa Alam (1–2 daily; 3hr); Port Said (2 weekly; 45min); Sharm el-Sheikh (8–10 daily; 1hr); Sohag (3 weekly; 1hr 10min).

BY TRAIN

Heading to Luxor, Aswan, Alexandria and the Delta and Canal Zone towns, trains are the most comfortable way to travel, though not always the fastest. Timetables for services heading south are posted in the Upper Egypt ticket office by platform 11 of Ramses Station, but are in Arabic only, as are those for services to the Delta posted in Kobra Limoun. Timetables for some first- and second-class services can be found at ⓦ enr.gov.eg.

Ramses Station Most trains terminate at Ramses Station (see map, p.85), which is currently undergoing renovation. Entering Ramses Station from Midan Ramses, Platforms 1–4, serving Alexandria, the Delta and Canal Zone, are to your right. The tourist office (☎ 02 2579 0767), tourist police and sleeper booking offices should be on your left, but have been closed while the station is being renovated and are temporarily by platform 11. The railway information office (☎ 02 2574 8279) is just beyond where they usually are. There was a 24hr left luggage office by platform 1, but this was closed during the renovations and it's not clear whether it will return. To reach platforms 8–11, go straight ahead from the entrance, through the doors on the far side of the hall (with the Delta ticket office to your left) and onto platform 8, where there's an underpass to your left which will take you to platforms 9–11. Buying tickets at Ramses is rarely easy, and you will probably have to try a couple of times before you find the right window. Tickets for Alexandria and the Delta are sold in an office opposite platform 4 (on the left at the far end of the hall if you're coming in through the main entrance, just beyond the information office). Tickets for all points south are sold in an office by platform 11. Sleeper tickets are currently sold there too, but should move back to an office opposite platform 2 (to your left as you come in through the main entrance). One way to avoid the queues and chaos is to get your ticket through a downtown travel agent (such as De Castro at 12 Sharia Talaat Harb), who will add a small commission.

Kobra Limoun Station Third-class trains to Zagazig and Mansura use the small Kobra Limoun Station, 100m east of Ramses Station, just past the post office building.

Giza Station Trains between Cairo and Upper Egypt halt at Giza Station, 15min out of Ramses, and some must be boarded at Giza if heading south.

CAIRO COMMISSION SCAMS

Arriving at Cairo airport you may be approached by "travel agents" wearing ID badges who'll try to dissuade you from going to the hotel you had in mind by saying it's closed, or pretending to call the hotel for a voice to announce "We're full". Similar stories from taxi drivers, and strangers who get talking to you on the bus into town or on the streets, should also be disbelieved; some even lurk outside popular hotels, claiming to be the manager. Their aim is to steer you into hotels which will pay them a commission (added to your bill). Many hotels that work with touts pressure guests to buy souvenirs, horse and camel trips, or excursions to Luxor and Aswan sold at a huge mark-up, and touts on the street aim to steer you into commission-paying perfume or souvenir shops. Checking into a hotel, it's best not to pay for more than one night upfront so you can leave the next day if necessary. Never buy any tour without first shopping around – you'll get a better deal direct from operators such as Samo Tours, Adventure in Egypt or Eastmar (p.205). See "Culture and etiquette" (p.43) for more on hustlers. In Cairo they favour specific areas: Sharia Talaat Harb (especially between Tahrir Square and Midan Talaat Harb); around the Egyptian Museum (which they may try to steer you away from by telling you that it's closed); the Ghuriya and Spice Bazaar in Islamic Cairo; and around the Sultan Hassan and Rifai mosques.

1

GETTING INTO TOWN

From Ramses Station Getting downtown from Ramses Station is very easy. The start of the downtown area is only ten minutes on foot from the station down Sharia Ramses, taking a left at Sharia Emad al-Din or Sharia Orabi, but the other end of downtown (Tahrir Square) is over a kilometre further, so you might want to take a cab (around £E3–6), the metro (Al-Shohadaa Station, beneath Midan Ramses), or a bus along Sharia Ramses.

From Giza Station Around £E15 from downtown by taxi, and also reachable by metro.

DESTINATIONS

To Alexandria Currently 19 daily a/c services, with limited stops (reservations required). Of these, seven are non-stop, and four halt only at Tanta (journey time 2hr 30min). The others stop at five to eight stations en route (2hr 45min–3hr 30min). There are also some forty non-a/c trains, with third- and sometimes second-class carriages only; they cost a fraction of the price of the a/c services, stop everywhere, and can take four hours or more to reach Alex.

To Mersa Matrouh Direct services run only in summer, when there's a thrice-weekly sleeper (Mon, Wed & Sat at 11pm, arriving 6am) and a daily early-morning a/c service – see the "To Luxor and Aswan" section (below) for booking options. Failing this, you would have to change trains at Alexandria, and it's far better to travel to Mersa by bus from Cairo (or Alex) than to endure the interminable journey in ordinary 2nd or 3rd class from Alex to Mersa by train.

To Luxor and Aswan There are two daily sleeper services from Giza Station at 8pm and 8.40pm (theoretically arriving in Luxor at 5.30am and 6.40am, and Aswan at 8.55am and 10.20am respectively; tickets cost US$60 one-way to Luxor or Aswan per person sharing a double cabin including dinner and breakfast. Solo travellers can share with a stranger of the same sex, or reserve the entire cabin for US$120. You can book at the sleeper office in Ramses Station (cash dollars or euros only; daily 9am–8pm; ☎02 2576 1319) until around 5pm on the day of departure, but you're best off reserving a few days in advance if possible. You can also book through American Express (see p.202) or Watania (phone and online bookings only; ☎02 3748 9388, ⊛wataniasleepingtrains.com). Aside from these, there are nine daily services to Luxor, of which two continue to Aswan. In theory tourists are allowed to use only one of these trains, leaving Ramses at 10pm, but enforcement of this rule is haphazard, and in practice it may be possible to travel on other trains. You are strongly advised to reserve in advance, or you may end up standing all the way, especially at weekends.

BY BUS

Inter-city buses are often faster than trains. They depart from three main terminals: Cairo Gateway, aka Turgoman

(for most Egyptian destinations, especially the Canal Zone), Aboud (especially to Alexandria, the Delta, Middle and Upper Egypt) and Sinai Terminal, aka Abbassiya Terminal (for services to the Sinai). Some services (particularly Superjet buses to Alexandria and the Canal Zone, as well as international services to Jordan and Libya) leave from, or call at, Almaza Terminal in Heliopolis (see p.175). A few buses also leave from Sharia al-Galaa near the *Ramses Hilton*, and one or two services from Aboud may be picked up off Sharia Orabi near Ramses Station. Some destinations may be served by buses from more than one departure point, notably Alexandria (Aboud, Turgoman, Almaza and the *Ramses Hilton*), Hurghada (Cairo Gateway, Aboud and *Ramses Hilton*), Sharm el-Sheikh and Dahab (Sinai and Cairo Gateway) and Tanta and Mahalla (Aboud and Cairo Gateway). On buses from Turgoman to Mansura and Damietta, you can buy tickets and board at the old Koulali terminal off Sharia Orabi. Tickets must be purchased at the relevant terminal.

Aboud Terminal 4km north of Ramses Station, up Sharia Ahmed Helmi, most easily reached by service taxi microbus (£E1) from Sharia al-Galaa near Ramses Station (see map, p.85). A taxi will cost around £E6 from Ramses Station, £E12 from downtown. Arriving at Aboud, the easiest way into town is to climb up the steps to the main road where microbus service taxis will take you to Sharia Orabi by Ramses Station (see map p.85).

Destinations The West and Middle Delta Bus Co. runs buses to Alexandria (hourly 7am–6pm; 3hr) via Damanhur (2hr); Tanta (hourly 6.45am–6.45pm; 1hr 30min); and Mahalla (every 30min 7am–7pm; 2hr 30min). The East Delta Bus Co. covers Zagazig (every 30min 7.30am–9pm; 1hr 30min); Mansura (every 30min 7am–7pm; 2hr 30min); and Faqus (1 daily; 2hr). For destinations south, the Upper Egypt Bus Co. has departures to Fayoum (hourly 9.30am–3.30pm; 2hr); Minya (hourly 6.30am–midnight; 4hr); Assyut (12 daily; 6–7hr); Qena (2–3 daily; 9–10hr); Luxor (1 daily; 9hr); and Aswan (1 daily; 12hr). Most Upper Egypt destinations, however, are far more comfortably reached by train.

Sinai Terminal (Mahattat Seena, aka Abbassiya Station), 4km from the centre in Abbassiya, can be reached by bus (#230, #611 and #998) from Abdel Mounem Riyad or Midan Ramses (#14, #69, #178, #710 and #998, and minibus #203), with more buses to Midan Abbassiya, a short walk away. A taxi will cost around £E15 from downtown. Arriving at the terminal, cross the street outside (Sharia Ramses) to get a cab into town, or take a bus or minibus from the stop 100m to the right. Alternatively, if you turn left outside the terminal and walk 300m on past the flyover to the hospital, you have an even wider choice of buses and minibuses to Ramses, Tahrir and Ataba.

Destinations El-Arish (2 daily; 5hr); Dahab (4 daily; 9hr); Sharm el-Sheikh (9 daily; 5hr); Taba (3 daily; 10hr); plus international services to Amman (1 daily; 22hr) and to Tripoli (1 daily; 36hr) via Benghazi (24hr).

Cairo Gateway In Bulaq, 600m southwest of Ramses Station on Sharia Waboor al-Turgoman (see map, p.70), and often referred to by its old name, Turgoman. The terminal isn't really served by local public transport but is an easy walk from Ramses Station or from downtown. A taxi from Tahrir Square should cost around £E5, and certainly not more than £E8. To get to downtown Cairo on arrival, it's easiest to take a cab; on foot, turn right out of the front, then left at the next junction (by a mosque), along Sharia al-Sahafa to the end; cross Sharia al-Galaa (under the flyover), then head right and take the next left (26th July St), and Sharia Talaat Harb is 250m ahead. For Midan Ramses, turn left when you come out of the terminal, to the flyover (Sharia Shanan), then right and right again up Sharia al-Galaa. The brand-new terminal incorporates a cavernous shopping mall and a barely functioning food court at the far end.

Destinations Alexandria (West Delta Bus Co. hourly 5.30am–8.30pm; Superjet hourly 7am–1am; 3hr); Aswan (1 daily; 12hr); Bahariya (6 daily; 5–6 hr); Dahab (4 daily; 9hr); Dakhla (3 daily; 14hr); Farafra (2 daily; 9hr); Hurghada (8 daily; 6hr); Ismailiya (every 30min 6am–7.30pm; 2hr); Kharga (2 daily; 9hr); Luxor (2 daily; 9hr); Mahalla (hourly 7am–9pm; 2hr); Mersa Matrouh (7 daily; 6hr); Nuweiba (3 daily; 9hr); Port Said (hourly 6.30am–9.30pm; 3hr); Sharm el-Sheikh (5 daily; 5hr); Siwa Oasis (7.45pm daily; 9hr); St Catherine's Monastery (1 daily; 9hr); Suez (every 30min 6am–7.30pm; 2hr); Taba (3 daily; 10hr); Tanta (hourly 7am–9pm; 1hr 30min).

Sharia al-Galaa Near the *Ramses Hilton* hotel (see map, p.70), Go Bus (☎ 19567) runs buses to Hurghada (13 daily; 6hr) and Sharm el-Sheikh (10 daily; 6hr 30min). A hundred metres north, Superjet has a booth selling tickets for its buses to Alexandria (hourly 7am–1am; 3hr), which stop here to pick up passengers.

International services For Amman East Delta Bus Co. has a daily service from Sinai Terminal, travelling via the Nuweiba–Aqaba ferry, (US$65 plus £E220; 22hr). Superjet also runs weekly buses to Amman (Thurs 7am) from their terminal at **Almaza** at the far end of Heliopolis. Likewise, there is a daily service to Tripoli (36hr; US$130) from Sinai Terminal, plus a weekly service from Almaza. Arriving at Almaza, a taxi into town will cost £E20–30, while bus #54 and minibus #39 go to Ramses and Tahrir, and minibus #40

to Ramses and Ataba. Alternatively, you can pick up the Heliopolis metro (see p.145) to Ramses; to reach the Heliopolis metro, head 500m northwest, under the flyover at the junction of Sharia Merghani with Sharia Abu Bakr al-Siddiq. Buses to Israel (Tel Aviv or Jerusalem; 14hr) used to leave twice weekly from the *Cairo Sheraton* in Dokki (see map, p.139), but have been suspended sice the revolution. Tickets were sold by Misr Travel at the *Pyramisa Hotel*, 60 Sharia al-Giza ☎ 02 3335-5470 (see map, p.139), who are the best people in Cairo to call for updates; for tour operators in Israel, see p.28.

BY SERVICE TAXI

Service taxis (see p.31) are the fastest way to get to most destinations, though they don't generally go as far afield as trains or buses, and they're also a lot less comfortable. Service taxis are also the least safe form of transport so far as road traffic accidents are concerned.

To Alexandria and the Delta Service taxis to Alexandria (3hr), Damanhur (2hr), Damietta (4hr), Faqus (2hr), Mahalla (1hr 45min), Mansura (2hr 30min), Tanta (1hr 15min) and Zagazig (1hr 15min) all leave from Aboud Terminal (see p.174), with very frequent departures and a direct route out of town. Vehicles to several of these destinations, in particular Alex and Tanta, can sometimes be picked up around Ramses Station too, especially during rush hours, but they may take a roundabout route out of town, and end up taking longer than vehicles from Aboud.

To the Canal Zone Service taxis to Suez (2hr) and Ismailiya (2hr) leave from Sharia Orabi near Ramses Station (see map, p.85). Taxis for Port Said (3hr) depart from a station in Al-Marg, not far from the metro station at the end of line 1.

To Fayoum The most convenient station for Fayoum (2hr) is Sharia Orabi near Ramses Station (see map, p.85), but there's a more frequent service from Midan Giza (see p.178), reached by regular bus and service taxi from Abdel Mouneem Riyad. You probably won't want to depart from it, but coming back to Cairo, you may end up at Al-Mounib, under a flyover 300m north of El-Monib metro station.

To Middle Egypt Taxis for Beni Suef (2hr), Minya (3hr 30min) and Mallawi (4hr) leave from Al-Mounib (see above).

To Libya Service taxis to Benghazi (20hr) and Tripoli (30hr) leave twice weekly (Mon & Thurs) around 8pm from the office of Wikala Suessi on Midan Opera ☎ 02 2395 4480 (see map, p.71). It's wise to book a day or two ahead if possible.

CITY TRANSPORT

Getting around Cairo is relatively straightforward. The **metro** is simple to use and **taxis** are inexpensive. Familiarize yourself with Arabic numerals (see p.631) and you can also use **buses** and **minibuses**, which reach most parts of the city. You might as well resign yourself to the fact that everyone drives like participants in the Paris–Dakar Rally, but accidents are surprisingly rare, all things considered. The streets are busy from 8am to midnight, and, unless you enjoy sweltering in traffic jams, it's best to try and avoid travelling (except by metro) during **rush hours** (Sun–Thurs 7–10am & 4–7pm). Friday mornings, on the other hand, are a joy, with very little traffic on the roads.

1

USEFUL METRO STATIONS

From a tourist's standpoint, there are six crucial stations:

Mubarak (Lines 1 & 2) Beneath Midan Ramses; the metro stop for Ramses Station.

Nasser (Line 1) On 26th July Street near the top of Talaat Harb (take the High Court exit).

Sadat (Lines 1 & 2) The most used (and useful) station, beneath Tahrir Square.

Saiyida Zeinab (Line 1) Midway between the Saiyida Zeinab quarter and the northern end of Roda Island.

Mar Girgis (Line 1) The best stop for Coptic Cairo and Amr's Mosque.

Opera (Gezira) (Line 2) By the Opera complex in south Gezira.

THE METRO

Cairo's metro (for background and updates see ⑩ urbanrail .net/af/cairo/cairo.htm) works like nothing else in the city. Trains run every few minutes from 5.30am to midnight; outside of the rush hours they're no more crowded than in other cities around the world. The front (and sometimes also the middle) carriage of each train is reserved for women, worth keeping in mind if you're a lone female traveller. Stations are signposted with a large "M"; signs and route maps appear in Arabic and English. Tickets are purchased in the station (75pt–£E1); twin sets of booths cater for passengers heading in opposite directions, sometimes with separate queues for either sex. Hang on to your ticket to get through the automatic barriers at the other end. Line 1 connects the northeastern suburb of New el-Marg with the southern industrial district of Helwan (via Mubarak, Sadat, Saad Zaghoul, Saiyida Zeinab, Mar Girgis and Maadi), with Line 2 running from Shubra in the north to El Monib (via Mubarak, Ataba, Sadat, Opera and Giza). The new stations on Line 2 are wheelchair-accessible, but stations on Line 1 are not. Line Three is currently under construction (the first section, from Ataba to Abbassiya, is already open); when completed, hopefully by 2014, the line will run from the airport via the city centre to Zamalek, Mohandiseen and Imbaba. A fourth line is planned (with work planned to start in late 2012) which will run west from El-Malek el-Saleh station (on Line 1) to the Grand Egyptian Museum near the Giza Pyramids (see p.157), and on to 6th October City, a satellite town west of Cairo.

BUSES

Cairo's buses mainly operate from 5.30am to 12.30am daily (6.30am–6.30pm & 7.30pm–2am during

Ramadan). Fares are cheap enough to be affordable for everyone, so buses are usually full and overflow during rush hour, when passengers hang from doorways. Though many foreigners are deterred from using buses by the crush, not to mention the risk of pickpockets and gropers, the network reaches virtually everywhere. Because buses tend to make slow progress against the traffic, however, service taxis are generally a better option, where available, though there are air-conditioned buses on some routes to prosperous suburbs such as Heliopolis and Medinet Nasr, and to tourist sights such as the Pyramids.

Tickets and fares Conductors sell tickets (the flat fare on most routes is £E1, or £E2 on a/c buses) from behind a crush-bar by the rear door. The front of the bus is usually less crowded, so it's worth squeezing your way forwards; start edging towards the exit well before your destination.

Bus stops Not always clearly signposted (look for metal shelters, plaques on lampposts or crowds waiting), and buses often just slow down instead of halting, compelling passengers to board and disembark on the run. Some bus stops (mostly on the west bank of the river) have route information posted, but in Arabic only. Most buses start from (or pass through) at least one of the main city-centre nuclei at Tahrir Square, Abdel Mouneem Riyad terminal (behind the Egyptian Museum), Midan Ramses or Midan. At each of these locations, there are several bus stops, and where exactly you pick up your bus will depend on which direction it is going in and whether it starts there or is simply passing through. If possible, ask the conductor "*Rayih...?*" (Are you going to...?) to make sure. Except at terminals, you are supposed to enter

USEFUL BUS ROUTES

Abdel Mouneem Riyad and Midan Ramses to: Airport #400 (24hr), #356 (a/c), #27; Abbassiya and Heliopolis (Midan Roxi) #400, #400/, #500.
Abdel Mouneem Riyad to: Citadel (Bab Gabal) #951; Midan Salah al-Din #72,

minibus #154; Saiyida Zeinab and Ibn Tulun Mosque #72//, #160/; Immam al-Shafi'i minibus #154; Manashi #214; Muqattam Hills #951; Pyramids #355, #357, #900; Qanatir #210; Sphinx #997.

through the rear door (often removed to facilitate access) and exit from the front.

Route numbers Buses should have route numbers in Arabic numerals on the front, side and back. Those with a slash through the number (represented in this guide as, for example, #13/) may follow different routes from buses with the same number unslashed; some route numbers even have two slashes.

MINIBUSES

Supplementing the bus network, minibuses use the same terminals and stops as full-size buses. They usually make better headway through traffic than full-size buses, actually halt at stops and are also more comfortable than ordinary buses and never crowded, as standing is not permitted. Tickets (£E1–2) are bought from the driver. Numbered minibuses should not be

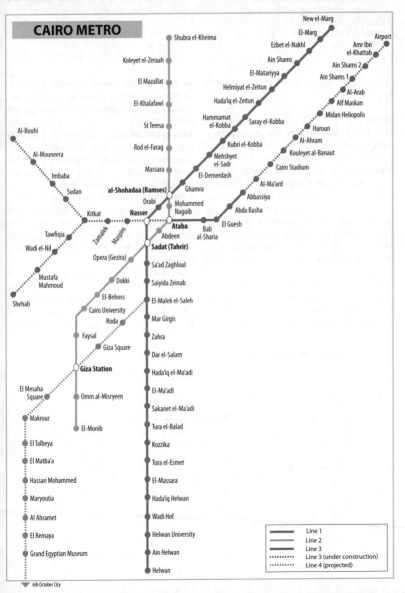

CAIRO METRO

New el-Marg
El-Marg
Shubra el-Kheima
Ezbet el-Nakhl
Airport
Amr Ibn el-Khattab
Koleyet el-Zeraah
Ain Shams
Ain Shams 2
El Mazallat
El-Matariyya
Ain Shams 1
El-Khalafawi
Helmiyat el-Zeitun
Hada'iq el-Zeitun
Al-Arab
St Teresa
Hammamat el-Kobba
Saray el-Kobba
Alf Maskan
Midan Heliopolis
Al-Bouhi
Rod el-Farag
Kubri el-Kobba
Haroun
Al-Mouneera
Massara
Mehshyet el-Sadr
Al-Ahram
Imbaba
El-Demerdash
Kouleyet al-Banaut
Sudan
al-Shohadaa (Ramses)
Ghamra
Cairo Stadium
Kitkat
Orabi
Mohammed Naguib
Al-Ma'ard
Nasser
Abbassiya
Tawfiqia
Zamalek
Maspiro
Ataba
Bab al-Sharia
Abda Basha
Wadi el-Nil
Abdeen
El Guesh
Sadat (Tahrir)
Mustafa Mahmoud
Opera (Gezira)
Sa'ad Zaghloul
Shehab
Dokki
Saiyida Zeinab
El-Behoss
El-Malek el-Saleh
Cairo University
Roda
Mar Girgis
Faysal
Zahra
Giza Square
Dar el-Salam
Giza Station
Hada'iq el-Ma'adi
El Mesaha Square
El-Ma'adi
Omm al-Misryeen
Sakanet el-Ma'adi
Makrour
El-Monib
Tura el-Balad
El Talbeya
Kozzika
El Matba'a
Tura el-Esmet
Hassan Mohammed
El-Massara
Maryoutia
Hada'iq Helwan
Al Ahramet
Wadi Hof
El Remaya
Helwan University
Grand Egyptian Museum
Ain Helwan
Helwan

6th October City

	Line 1
	Line 2
	Line 3
···········	Line 3 (under construction)
···········	Line 4 (projected)

1

USEFUL SERVICE TAXI ROUTES

Abdel Mouneem Riyad (behind the Egyptian Museum) to the Pyramids, Midan Giza, Mohandiseen, Bulaq, Imbaba, Ma'adi, Helwan and Qanatir.

Around Ramses Station From Ahmed Helmi terminal, behind the station, to Abbassiya, Medinet Nasr, Ma'adi and Helwan; from Sharia al-Gala to Aboud terminal; from Sharia Orabi to Midan Giza and the Pyramids; from al-Fath Mosque to Midan Ataba.

Midan Giza (at the eastern end of Pyramids Road, around 1km west of Al-Giza bridge) to Ramses, the Pyramids and Badrasheen (for Saqqara).

Maryotteya Canal/Pyramids Road along Pyramids Road to Ramses, Abdel Mouneem Riyad and sometimes Ataba; from the west bank of canal to Abu Sir and Saqqara, usually changing at the latter for Dahshur, though direct services sometimes run.

confused with service taxis (usually smaller microbuses, see p.179).

TAXIS

Cairo's old-style black-and-white cabs are being phased out in favour of newer white cabs, which are metred and therefore much easier for tourists to use.

White cabs White cabs cost £E2.50 basic flag fare, plus £E1.25/km and £E10/hr waiting time. Because the rate is fixed, they generally work out cheaper than black-and-white cabs, and are certainly a lot more convenient. If you feel like tipping the driver you can do so, but it isn't expected. And if the driver starts giving you any nonsense about the meter not working, just get out and hail another cab. It's true that cabs with meters could increase your fare by taking you round the houses, but it isn't common. Note also that the meter shows distance travelled as well as the fare, and should rise in 25pt increments every 200m; it isn't unknown for drivers to fiddle the meter to rise in 60pt increments, but you'll be able to see it if they do, and getting caught means

very big trouble for them indeed. The only little trick they do usually pull is to claim not to have change, so if you don't want to pay them an involuntary tip, make sure you have plenty before you get in.

Black-and-white cabs In unmetred black-and-white cabs you'll need to know the fare in advance or risk being outrageously overcharged. Find out the fare in advance, get in and ask for your destination, and hand over the fare with confidence at the end – the driver will soon let you know if you've underpaid. Don't give the driver any hint that you aren't sure what the fare is, or he'll almost certainly try to overcharge you. As a general guide, expect to pay a £E5 minimum, £E5–10 for a downtown hop, and £E20–25 if heading further out (to Heliopolis for example). Drivers may expect more late at night.

Limousines Limousines, usually Mercedes or Peugeot 406s, operated by firms such as Limousine Misr (☎02 2342 2581) and Target Limousine (☎02 2588 0095), are stationed at five-star hotels and at the airport. Fares are fixed (£E80 from the airport to downtown, for example),

BOAT TRIPS ON THE NILE

If you're planning to take a **Nile cruise** in Upper Egypt, you may want to book ahead in Cairo, although better deals may well be available from local agents in Luxor or Aswan. **Luxury cruises** offered by five-star hotels in Cairo are extremely expensive (often as much as $500/person/night), although Thomas Cook (☎16119, ⊕thomascookegypt.com) may offer more reasonably priced deluxe cruises. **Budget travellers** might consider less ritzy boats run by agencies such as Eastmar Tours, in the passage of 13 Sharia Qasr al-Nil (☎02 2579 7686, ⊕eastmar-travel.com), which charges – depending on season – US$85–123 a night per person for a four to seven-night cruise. For more on Nile cruises, see chapter 2 (p.239).

Shorter **pleasure trips** are available on the river in Cairo. Most of the **feluccas** moored along the river bank opposite the *Shepheard Hotel* and the northern tip of Roda can seat eight people and charge around £E60 per hour for the boat. Bring a picnic and lots of mosquito repellent. For rather less money you can join one of the boats just south of Maspero Dock, which do round trips to the Nile barrages at Qanatir (see p.171) costing £E10 per person for the six-hour round trip. Shorter jaunts are available on boats from the quay just south of Tahrir Bridge on the Corniche (£E5 per person for a 30min trip). For an even cheaper no-frills ride on the Nile, catch a river-taxi (£E1) from Maspero Dock up to Giza or down to Qanatir (£E5 each way).

and they can also be rented by the day (around £E600 for 12hr and up to 100km).

SERVICE TAXIS

Service taxis travel various set routes – see the box (p.178) for some of the most useful – and can be flagged down anywhere if there is space aboard; they are especially useful for longer-distance journeys such as from downtown to the Pyramids. Within Cairo, service taxis are invariably microbuses (*arrabeya bin nafar*, or just *servees*).

Fares From 75pt to £E1.50, according to the distance travelled.

Terminals The main terminals are at Abdel Mouneem Riyad (behind the Egyptian Museum and in front of the *Ramses Hilton* hotel), and from various streets behind and around Ramses Station. For Saqqara (and occasionally Dahshur), they leave from Maryotteya Canal near its junction with Pyramids Rd, easily reached on a pyramids-bound service taxi from Ramses or Abdel Mouneem Riyad.

TRAMS

Trams As the metro and minibus systems expand, Cairo's original colonial-era tram network has been all but phased out, apart from the Heliopolis tram system (see p.145). Like buses, the trams are cheap and battered, sometimes with standing room only; their Arabic route numbers are posted above the driver's cab.

RIVER-TAXIS

River-taxis (aka waterbuses) leave from the Maspero Dock outside the Television Building, 600m north of the Egyptian Museum. Boats run every hour from 7am to Gama'a Bridge in Giza (see map, p.126). You can buy tickets (£E1) at the dock. On Fri and Sun, they also run up to the Nile barrages (see p.171) at Qanatir (£E5 one-way).

DRIVING

The only thing scarier than driving in Cairo is cycling, which is tantamount to suicide. Dashes, crawls and finely judged evasions are the order of the driver's day. Renting a car with a driver costs around $20 a day more than doing the driving yourself.

Car rental Avis (ⓦavisegypt.com), 16a Sharia Maamal al-Sukar, Garden City ☏02 2794 7400 and Midan Simon Bolivar, Garden City ☏02 2793 2400; Budget (ⓦbudget-egypt.com), Ring Road, Mirage City ☏0122 235 5290 and airport ☏0122 355 3628; Hertz (ⓦhertzegypt .com), 195 26th July St, Aguza ☏02 3347 4172, *Ramses Hilton* hotel ☏02 2575 8914, and airport Terminals 1 and 3 (☏0128 000 0822 and 0823; open 24hr). A number of local agencies can be found on Sharia al-Misaha in Dokki.

Car parks Multistorey car parks, such as the one on Midan Ataba, are ignored as motorists park bumper-to-bumper along every kerb, leaving their handbrakes off so vehicles can be shifted by the local *minaidy* (street parking attendant), whom they tip £E2–5 or so.

Accidents Jaywalkers trust in motorists' swift reactions. Any collision draws a crowd. Minor dents (and you won't see many undented cars about) are settled by on-the-spot payoffs, but should injury occur, it's wise to involve a cop right away.

INFORMATION

Tourist office The downtown tourist office, at 5 Sharia Adly (daily 9am–6pm, Ramadan and public holidays 9am–3pm; ☏02 2391 3454), is rather useless, but may be able to answer simple queries. There are also 24hr tourist offices at all the airport terminals, and an office at the Giza Pyramids (daily 9am–4pm; ☏02 3383 8823). The tourist office in Ramses Station should reopen as soon as renovations are completed (daily 9am–4pm; ☏02 2579 0767), and there's also one at Giza train station (daily 9am–4pm; ☏02 3570 2233).

Maps If you can find a copy, the *New Handy Map of Cairo* is generally the best map of the city; Cairo City Key's *Detailed Map of Greater Cairo* comes second. Alternatives (all available sporadically) include the Cairo Engineering and Manufacturing Company's *Cairo Tourist Map*, which extends out to Heliopolis, and Lehnert & Landrock's map of the same name, which is better for downtown. Geodia's *Cairo City* map, on laminated paper, is a lot less detailed. Of more use for longer stays are the American University in Cairo's (AUC) *Cairo: The Practical Guide Maps* (£E50), and the *Cairo City Key* (£E60). The best place to buy maps is at a bookshop such as Lehnert & Landrock (44 Sharia Sherif) or Shorouk (1 Midan Talaat Harb).

Asking for directions Don't expect Cairenes themselves to relate to maps, or even to street names; they comprehend their city differently. Also be aware when asking directions that people are unlikely to admit they don't know where something is, and will make up directions instead; for that reason it's always best to ask more than one person.

ACCOMMODATION

Cairo's hotels reflect the city's diversity: deluxe chains overlooking the Nile; functional high-rises; colonial piles, homely *pensions* and bug-infested flophouses. **Room rates** are usually the same year-round, though rates at some five-stars change daily depending on demand. Inexpensive hotels tend to be located on the upper floors of downtown office buildings; one or two are locked at midnight, so if you arrive later you'll have to rouse the doorman (*bowab*), who will expect a tip for

1

> ## CAIRO ADDRESSES AND PHONE NUMBERS
>
> All Cairo landline **telephone numbers** are now eight-digit. If you have an old, seven-digit number, add a 2 in front of the number for phones east of the river and in Zamalek (Cairo governorate), or a 3 for phones west of the river (Giza governorate).
>
> **Street names** may be posted in English (or French) as well as Arabic, but spellings vary, and often there is no sign at all. The same goes for house numbers, rendered in Western and Arabic numerals, or just the latter; note that a single number may denote a whole block with several entrances.

his trouble. Many budget hotels offer a choice between cheap rooms, with shared bathrooms, and slightly pricier ones with en suite, though sometimes that is just a shower in the corner of the room. Downtown traffic is noisy – earplugs may help. Many hotels offer **tours**, usually on commission, and not uncommonly at several times over their actual price (see p.173); always shop around before buying a tour, and be especially suspicious of any hotel whose staff try to push tours.

CENTRAL CAIRO

Amin 38 Midan Falaki, opposite Bab al-Luq market ☎ 02 2393 3813; map p.71. Recently redecorated small hotel whose rooms, all with fans, are located on the sixth, seventh and tenth floors. It's worth paying £E15 more for a room with private bathroom and constant hot water as the shared facilities aren't so clean. **£E75**

Berlin 4th floor, 2 Sharia al-Shawarby ☎ 02 2395 7502 (UK ☎ 076 2408 0432), ✉ berlinhotelcairo@hotmail.com; map p.71. Small city-centre hotel with high-ceilinged double and triple rooms, each with its own shower, a/c and comfortable mattresses, and looking nice and fresh now that most of them have been given a facelift. The owner is extremely helpful, and services include laundry, free wi-fi and use of a computer, their own drivers to take you round the pyramid sites or elsewhere at decent rates, and good-value Arabic and bellydancing lessons. B&B **£E130**

Big Ben 33 Sharia Emad al-Din ☎ 02 2590 8881; see map, p.85. Good-value budget hotel north of the main downtown area with clean, fresh rooms, all en suite, not frequented much by foreign tourists, and rather cheaper than its centre-of-downtown equivalents as a result. **£E80**

Cairo Downtown 3rd floor, Sharia Amir Qadada ☎ 02 2792 8932, ⊕ cairodowntownhotel.com; map p.70. In a great old building with a bifurcating staircase and Art Nouveau metalwork, this little budget hotel gained itself a big reputation among shoestring journalists during the revolution (among other things, it offers direct views from some balconies onto Tahrir Square), but it's equally popular with ordinary tourists for its friendly staff, relaxed atmosphere and decent-sized rooms, some en suite. Dorm beds **£E8**, rooms **£E28**

Carlton 21 26th July St ☎ 02 2575 5022, ⊕ carltonhotelcairo.com; map p.71. A pleasantly creaky old hotel, once quite swanky, built in 1935 and still retaining some wood-panelled period charm, albeit rather worn. All rooms are a/c, and the pricier deluxe rooms have satellite TV and minibar. Rooms at the back

are much quieter than those at the front. There's a restaurant on the seventh floor and a very pleasant rooftop garden with a café-bar. You usually have to take half-board, though they may do you a bed-and-breakfast rate. Half-board **£40**

Cosmopolitan 1 Sharia Ben Talaab, off Qasr al-Nil ☎ 02 2392 3956, ✉ 02 2393 3531; map p.71. This rather grand monumental belle époque hotel, located in the trendy Borsa area, has certainly seen better days, but is still quite stately in a modest way. The rooms are carpeted and quite sedate, if not as spic and span as they might be, and there's a European restaurant and English-style bar, but avoid the tours sold at the travel desk. All rooms have a/c and private baths. B&B **£103**

★ **Dahab** Seventh floor, 26 Sharia Bassiouni ☎ 02 2579 9104, ⊕ dahabhostel.com; map p.70. A very laidback hostel that's like a beach camp from the Red Sea backpacker resort of Dahab transported – surprisingly convincingly – to the roof of a building in downtown Cairo, with poky rooms, friendly staff and lots of interesting people staying. Plenty of vegetation and an open area to socialize in make it a pleasant hangout; facilities include a Bedouin-style café, laundry service, free wi-fi and hot water – though the last of those is a bit erratic. **£E55**

Fontana Off Midan Ramses ☎ 02 2592 2321; map, p.85. A bit scuffed in places, but this hotel definitely has a slightly kitsch charm about it, with pink marble in the lobby and a touch of the Louis Farouks in the rooms (that's Louis XIV as interpreted by King Farouk). There's a small rooftop swimming pool (summer only), bar, restaurant, café and a disco (see p.192). Rooms have TV, fridge and a/c; some have views as far as the Citadel, and the staff are extremely friendly. B&B **£60**

Four Seasons 1089 Corniche al-Nil, Garden City ☎ 02 2791 7000, ⊕ fourseasons.com/c+aironp; map p.70. Sleek, sophisticated and luxurious to a fault, this branch of the *Four Seasons* chain is better suited to Western tastes

1

than its gaudier sister establishment opposite the zoo in Giza. The rooms have a classic charm with little extras like DVD player and high-speed internet connection. Spa packages are available, and two rooms are adapted for wheelchair users. $298

Garden City House 3rd floor, 26 Sharia Kamal al-Din Salah ☎02 2794 8400, ✉garden77house@yahoo.com; map p.70. 1930s pension on the edge of the Garden City, behind the *Semiramis* (see p.183) and popular with impecunious Egyptologists. Some rooms have Nile views, some have en-suite bathrooms, and some have a/c, but all are rather well worn, and the entrance is flanked by predatory perfume and papyrus shops. B&B ££143

Grand 17 26th July St (entrance in the alley off Sharia Talaat Harb) ☎02 2575 7801 to 5, ⊛grandhotelcairo .com; map p.71. Art Deco edifice featuring original lifts and furniture, a fountain, coffee shop and old-fashioned, homely rooms with immaculately varnished wooden floors, attached to spacious and immaculate tiled bathrooms, though the plumbing can be temperamental. B&B ££381

Happyton 10 Sharia Ali al-Kassar ☎02 2592 8600; map p.71. Functional but friendly and excellent-value two-star hotel with en-suite a/c rooms of variable sizes, all decent and well-kept, but nothing fancy. There's a café and small restaurant, but no bar, though you can buy beer in the lobby and drink it on the roof terrace. B&B ££125

★ **Isis** Marouf Tower, 16th floor, 33B Sharia Ramses ☎02 2578 1895, ⊛isiscairo.com; map p.70. Worth staying at for the spectacular views alone, over the river on one side, and over downtown to the Citadel on the other. Staff are friendly and rooms are spacious, with large windows, wooden floors and furnishings, some with private bathroom and a/c, and there's free internet. On the downside, the location isn't great (two blocks off Talaat Harb among car spares shops), and the lift only reaches the fifteenth floor, so you have to walk the last one. B&B ££170

Ismailia House 8th floor, 1 Midan Tahrir ☎02 2796 3122, ⊛ismailiahotel.com; map p.70. Advance booking is advisable for this easy-going, cheerful backpackers' haven. Slightly worn around the edges, it offers a variety of singles, doubles, triples and dorm beds, plus 24hr hot water and plenty of communal areas to hang out in. The Tahrir-facing rooms are noisy at night but have great views. B&B: dorm beds $6, rooms $17

Kempinski Nile 12 Sharia Ahmed Ragheb ☎02 2798 0000, ⊛kempinski.com/Cairo; map p.70. This sleek, deluxe boutique hotel, purring with understated plushness, and creamy as its cool decor, gets consistent rave reviews. It's got all the facilities you'd expect from a larger five-star, including a pool, spa and fitness centre. The rooms aren't quite as large as they might be in some places, but this is more than made up for by the efficient and courteous staff. $246

King Tut Hostel 8th floor, 37 Sharia Talaat Harb ☎02 2391 7897, ⊛kingtuthostel.com; map p.71. Kitsch but wonderful pharaonic decor in the entrance and public areas welcomes you to this bright hotel (not really a hostel, despite the name). It's often full, so worth booking ahead (or try the very similar *Ramses II Hotel*, four floors up in the same building, run by the same firm). Don't be pressurized into buying their tours, however. B&B ££150

Lotus 7th floor, 12 Sharia Talaat Harb (entrance in the arcade) ☎02 2575 0966, ⊛lotushotel.com; map p.70. Its claim to have "an authentic Art Deco ambience" is a slight exaggeration, though one or two of the fittings do seem to date from the 1930s, and the rooms are suitably sombre. There's a restaurant and a bar, and the staff are friendly; it's worth paying the extra $5 for an en-suite room with a/c (hot water 6–11am and 6–11pm). Those of a nervous disposition may care to note that the staircase is kept locked, so in case of an emergency, the only way out is by elevator. B&B $25

★ **Luna** 5th floor, 27 Sharia Talaat Harb (entrance in a courtyard off the street) ☎02 2396 1020, ⊛hotellunacairo.com; map p.71. Better looked after and generally cleaner than other hotels in this price range, with large a/c rooms, some en suite. It's worth asking for the Egyptian breakfast (*fuul* and falafel) in preference to the continental. Rooms at the back are quieter and slightly pricier. There's also an a/c annexe, the *Bella Luna*, on the third floor. B&B ££140

New Cecil (or New Cicil) 22 Sharia Emad al-Din ☎02 2591 3859; map, p.85. Situated north of the centre, near Ramses Station, this is a reasonable ultra-low budget option so long as you aren't fussy – the rooms are a bit grimy, but adequate considering the price, with fans and shared bathroom facilities. ££45

Nile Ritz-Carlton 1113 Corniche al-Nil ☎02 2578 0444 or ☎02 2578 0666, ⊛ritzcarlton.com/en/Properties/Cairo; map p.70. Cairo's most central five-star, closed for refurbishment until at least 2013. This 1950s building (formerly the *Nile Hilton*) is on the river right by the Egyptian Museum; it boasts the choicest location in town, and the biggest rooms, which will no doubt be top-of-the-range when renovation is completed.

Odeon Palace 6 Sharia Abdel Hamid Said, just off Sharia Talaat Harb ☎02 2577 6637, ✉odeon@hodeon .com; map p.70. Creaky old place with a certain sombre, old-fashioned charm, but give your room a once-over, and make sure the shower and plug sockets are working, before checking in. The hotel's main attractions are 24hr room service and a 24hr roof bar. $56

★ **Pension Roma** 169 Sharia Mohammed Farid (entrance around the side of Gattegno department store) ☎02 2391 1088, ⊛pensionroma.com.eg; map p.71. The stylish 1940s ambience of this charming little *pension*, immaculately maintained by Madame Cressaty, is highly recommended and it's wise to book in advance. The rooms are cosy, spic and span, some with private bathrooms, though most have shared bathroom facilities. B&B **£E125**

Select 8th floor, 19 Sharia Adly, beside the synagogue ☎ 02 2393 3707, ✉ hostelselect@yahoo.com; map p.71. A bright little place, homely, friendly and recently refurbished, in a 1930s building with one or two period touches. The rooms are en suite, all with balconies and views, though the best are on the east side (worth asking for when booking). B&B **£E120**

Semiramis Intercontinental Corniche al-Nil ☎ 02 2795 7171, ⊛ intercontinental.com; map p.70. Spacious, elegant rooms, plus a gym, a pool, the *Haroun al-Rashid* nightclub (see p.194), and seven restaurants offering cuisine from around the world. Rooms on the upper floors give excellent views – the views over Cairo from the slightly cheaper city-side rooms are better than from the Nile side. **$400**

Shepheard Corniche al-Nil ☎ 02 2792 1000, ⊛ shepheard-hotel.com; map p.70. Nile-side version of the famous nineteenth-century establishment that stood on Midan al-Opera, rebuilt on the present site in 1957, and still retaining a certain 1950s feel. Rooms on the quieter side facing the Muqattam Hills are cheaper than those facing the Nile. Facilities include two restaurants and a 24hr casino, but no swimming pool. B&B **$150**

Sultan First floor, 4 Sharia Tawfiqia ☎ 02 2577 2258, ✉ hotel.sultan@hotmail.com; map p.71. Dorm beds only in this friendly but basic ultra-cheapy located in a colourful market street near Midan Orabi, very handy for inexpensive eating and groceries, and just the right distance from the centre of downtown. Guests get free use of the kitchen and there's satellite TV in the common room. Dorm beds **£E20**

Talisman In the passage by 39 Sharia Talaat Harb ☎ 02 2393 9431, ✉ talisman_hoteldecharme@yahoo .fr; map p.71. Well-situated boutique hotel with some five-star facilities (a/c, satellite TV, minibar, safe) but no pool or fitness centre. Excellent service and attentive staff give it a real personal touch. The whole hotel is decorated with antiques and objets d'art, and rooms are double-glazed to keep out the street noise. **€81.50**

Travelers House 4th floor, 43 Sharia Sherif ☎ 02 2396 4362, ✉ travellershousehotel@yahoo.com; map p.71. Travellers rave about this small budget hotel, which boasts pharaonic motifs in its public areas and shiny polished wooden floors in its rooms (some of which are en suite), not to mention free wi-fi. What most distinguishes this place from others in the same price bracket, however, is the friendliness and attentiveness of its staff. B&B **£E120**

Tulip 1st floor, 3 Midan Talaat Harb ☎ 02 2393 9433, ⊛ tulip-hotel.com; map p.70. Decently refurbished old place facing *Groppi's* across Midan Talaat Harb. It's extremely well-located and the rooms are bright and

cheerful. Free wi-fi, and discounts if staying five nights or more. B&B **£E120**

Venice Hosokawaya 4th floor, 4 Sharia Tawfiqia ☎ 02 2773 5307, ⊛ venicehosokawaya.net; map p.71. In the same building as the *Sultan* (see p.183) but pricier, this is the Japanese backpackers' budget hotel of choice in Cairo, and ninety percent of its clientele are from Japan. It's very clean and well-run, with dorm beds and private rooms, free wi-fi and a laundry service. B&B: dorm beds **£E35**, rooms **£E120**

Victoria 66 Sharia al-Gumhorriya ☎ 02 2589 2290 to 94, ⊛ victoriahotel-egypt.com; map p.85. A three-star 1930s hotel once frequented by George Bernard Shaw. Lots of wood panelling, attractive a/c rooms with shiny wooden floors (some with mahogany furniture) and a comfortably worn, lived-in feel, plus a bar, restaurant and spacious lounge area. Advance reservation advisable. B&B **€58**

Windsor 19 Sharia Alfi Bey (entrance round the back) ☎ 02 2591 5810, ⊛ windsorcairo.com; map p.71. This colonial hotel retains much character and is home to one of the nicest bars in Cairo (the *Barrel Lounge*, see p.190), but it has definitely seen better days, though some of the rooms have been refurbished, and the bathrooms are new. All rooms have a/c and satellite TV; all but the very cheapest are en suite. Fifteen percent discount for *Rough Guide* readers. B&B **$58**

ISLAMIC CAIRO

El-Hussein Muski, entered via a passage to Fishawi's ☎ 02 2591 8089; map, p.95. Rather grimy, and rooms overlooking the square are harangued by Cairo's loudest muezzins, and festivals are celebrated all night long in Midan al-Hussein, just outside. On the other hand, if you don't mind the noise, a balcony overlooking the square gives you a ringside view, and if you want to be in the thick of it, this really is right in the heart of Islamic Cairo. B&B **£E165**

El Malky 4 Sharia al-Hussein ☎ 02 2589 0804, ⊛ server2002.net/malky; map, p.95. Behind the Saiyidna Hussein Mosque, this quiet little hotel, with a mainly Muslim clientele, is good value, and well located. It's less than 100m from Al-Hussein, but out of the noise and bustle. Rooms are carpeted, with a/c and private bathrooms, some with balconies overlooking the bazaars. B&B **£E120**

★ **Le Riad** 114 Sharia al-Muizz ☎ 02 2787 6074, ⊛ leriad-hoteldecharme.com; map p.97. Immaculate boutique hotel in the heart of Gamaliya, containing seventeen individually themed suites (including a pharaoh suite, a Mamluke suite and a King Farouk suite), all with sparkling bathrooms, free wi-fi (plus loan of a laptop if you need it) and plasma TV with DVD player. There's a library of DVDs and books, and a roof terrace with great views over Islamic Cairo. B&B **€240**

1

ELSEWHERE IN THE CITY

Cairo Marriott Sharia Saray al-Gezira, off 26th July St, Zamalek ☎02 2728 3000, ⓦcairomarriotthotel.com; map, p.138. A classy five-star where you can choose between garden rooms or slightly pricier tower rooms with a better view (some of the river and downtown), all built around a lavish palace constructed to house Napoleon III's wife Empress Eugénie. The hotel's extensive facilities include five restaurants, two bars, a casino, nightclub and, of course, a pool. Rooms have fast internet connections and the hotel is wi-fi-enabled throughout. $312

El Borg Novotel 3 Sharia Saraya el Gezira, Gezira ☎02 3735 6725, ⓦnovotel.com; map p.139. Just over Tahrir Bridge in Gezira, this hotel is rather ugly on the outside but cool and stylish inside, with modern cream and beige rooms, plus deluxe accessories such as a/c and plasma TV. €160

Grand Nile Tower Roda Island (north end) ☎02 2365 1234, ⓦgrandniletower.com; map p.126. Superior five-star at the northern tip of Roda Island, best accessed via its own bridge from Garden City. Rooms, all in a sumptuous new wing, are stylish; north-facing ones offer killer views of central Cairo and the Nile. Facilities include everything you'd expect from a top hotel, including a sauna, health club, business centre and two swimming pools. There are also eight restaurants, including a revolving restaurant with panoramic views (see p.185). $248

Le Meridien Pyramids Midan al-Remaya, Alexandria Desert Rd, Giza Pyramids ☎02 3377 7070, ⓦlemeridien.com/pyramids; map p.148. Just over 1km from the pyramids, and a 20min drive from central Cairo, the vast sandy-coloured Le Meridien Pyramids has spacious rooms with subdued decor and balconies, but the real draw are the stunning views of the pyramids that many of the rooms boast. Service is smart and efficient, and there's an appealingly curvy pool and a spa. You'll find several decent restaurants in-house, and breakfasts are bountiful. Promotional offers are usually available, often reducing the price by as much as fifty percent. B&B $360

★ **Longchamps** 5th floor, 21 Sharia Ismail Mohammed, Zamalek ☎02 2735 2311, ⓦhotellongchamps.com; map p.138. Spotless, quiet and well-run three-star hotel with a/c, satellite TV, internet connection and a fridge in all rooms, plus a pleasant terrace and meals available. It's advisable to book at least a couple of weeks ahead; if it's full, the similarly priced *Horus House* downstairs isn't a bad fallback. B&B $84

Mena House Oberoi Near the Giza Pyramids ☎02 3377 3222, ⓦoberoihotels.com; map p.148. Set in lush grounds by the Giza Pyramids, and with views of them from the pricier rooms, this one-time khedival hunting lodge witnessed Roosevelt and Churchill initiate the D-Day plan, and the formal signing of the peace treaty between Israel and Egypt. Its renovated arabesque halls and nineteenth-century "palace" rooms are delightful; the modern Mena Gardens annexe isn't so grand, though the rooms are plush enough. Facilities include the *Moghul* restaurant (the best Indian restaurant in Egypt; see p.188), a pool, golf course (closed until 2013) and tennis courts. €135

New President 20 Sharia Taha Hussein, Zamalek ☎02 2737 2780; map, p.138. An unassuming two-star in a quiet street away from the busier parts of Zamalek, nothing fancy, but calm and peaceful, with warm but sober decor in

---

LONG STAYS AND FLAT-HUNTING

If you're staying in the city for longer than a week or two, renting an apartment is worth considering. Upscale areas popular with foreigners include **Ma'adi** (home to most of Egypt's American community), **Zamalek** (favoured by embassies and European expats) and **Heliopolis**. **Aguza** and **Mohandiseen** are also possible, but few flats are available downtown except in Bulaq, Qasr al-Aini or Abdin.

Places to look for apartment rentals include the small ads in *Egypt Today*, the *Egyptian Gazette* and *Community Times* (ⓦcommunitytimesonline.com) and expat community newssheets such as the *Maadi Messenger* (ⓦmaadimessenger.com). It's also worth checking the noticeboards at English-language institutes and cultural centres (see p.203). Flats are also advertised online, at ⓦe-dar.com and ⓦalgomhoria.com. The AUC's regularly updated *Cairo: the Practical Guide* contains a lot of useful advice on apartment rental and Cairo living in general; it can be found at the AUC's bookshop (see p.201), or ordered online at ⓦaucpress.com.

Foreigners working or studying in Cairo often seek flatmates or want to sublet during temporary absences. Aside from checking the newssheets and noticeboards mentioned above, another way of finding a flat is via a **simsar** (flat agent), who can be found in any neighbourhood by making enquiries at local shops and cafés. Unless you spend a long, fruitless day together, simsars are only paid when you settle on a place; ten percent of your first month's rent is the normal charge. Flat agencies in Ma'adi levy the same commission on both tenant and landlord. You can usually rent a flat in the centre for around £E1500–2500 per person per month, and occasionally even less; prices are lower in winter than in summer.

CAIRO'S BEST VIEWS

The roof of the *Nile Ritz-Carlton* on the Corniche, when it opens, will have top views over Tahrir Square, but the front rooms at the *Ismailia House* hotel (see p.182) can equal them. The best budget hotel for views over the city in general is the *Isis* (see p.182). The Citadel (p.111) overlooks Islamic Cairo, where certain minarets give you a vista as far as the Pyramids on a clear day if they're open (the Qalaoun complex, the Blue Mosque and the al-Muayyad minarets atop Bab Zwayla), but the finest view is from the high point in Al-Azhar Park (p.122). To look down on the mayhem that is Midan Ramses, the terrace café of the *Everest Hotel* (p.188) is the place. The Cairo Tower on Gezira (p.137) is also great for views, while the revolving restaurant at the *Grand Nile Tower* hotel on Roda Island (p.184) offers what must rate as Cairo's best panoramic view, encompassing the Pyramids, the Citadel, the Nile and most of downtown.

brown, cream and gold. Not to be confused with the *President* next door. **££326**

Salma Camping Harraniyya, past Giza ☎ 02 3381 5062 or ☎ 0100 487 1300, ✉ salma.camp@yahoo.com; map p.148. Cairo's only campsite is a bit run-down, but handy for the Pyramids Giza and Saqqara. The camping price (in either a tent or campervan) includes electricity and hot showers; there are also a small number of double rooms. Breakfast isn't included, but there's a kitchen you can use. The campsite is reached by turning off Pyramids Rd towards Saqqara at Maryotteya Canal (1km before the pyramids), then after 4km taking a signposted turn-off at Harraniyya

village; continue for 100m, and the site is about 100m away on your right. Camping **££30**/person; rooms **££100**

Youth Hostel 135 Sharia Abdel Aziz al-Saoud, by Kobri al-Gamaa, Roda Island ☎ 02 2364 0729, ✉ info @egyptyha.com; map p.126. The dorms here (single-sex and mostly three-bed) are clean and en suite but the location is inconvenient, staff are not very friendly and don't usually speak English, and doors are closed from midnight to 7am, so no carousing unless you aim to make a full night of it. The only advantage, aside from the ultra-cheap price, is that you can meet young Egyptians and practice your Arabic. Dorm bed **££35**

EATING

Restaurants run the gamut from posh salons to backstreet kebab houses – those places serving up *kushari* or *fuul* and *taamiya* provide the cheapest nutritious meals going. At the other end of the gastro-cultural spectrum, every hotel rated three stars or above has at least one restaurant and coffee shop that's open to nonresidents. There's a huge variation in standards of cleanliness and presentation, and whether somewhere seems okay or grotty depends partly on your own values. Running water remains a crucial factor – anywhere without it (such as street stalls) is risky. A number of places off Ramses, Orabi, Ataba, Falaki, Lazoghli and Giza squares and midway down Sharia Qalaa function all night. Increasingly, restaurants in Cairo, from fast-food joints through to posh eateries, offer home delivery (or hotel delivery, if your hostelry will allow it). In addition to places listed here, there are restaurants which double as discos, bars or nightclubs (see p.192), as well as **floating restaurants** (see p.194) – boats offering dinner cruises plus entertainment.

DOWNTOWN DINERS AND STREET FOOD

★ **Abou Tarek** 40 Sharia Champollion, corner of Sharia Maarouf ☎ 02 2577 5935, ☻ aboutarek.com; map p.70. You can't miss this a/c diner, spread over two floors and lit up like a Christmas tree. It dishes up the best *kushari* in Cairo (££5–7), with rice pudding for dessert. Daily 7.30am–11.30pm.

Akher Saa 8 Sharia Alfi Bey, next to the Nile Christian Bookshop ☎ 02 2575 3521; map p.71. A very popular 24hr *fuul*, *taamiya* (falafel) and *shawarma* takeaway (*taamiya* in pitta costs just ££1.75) with a sit-down restaurant attached. Not bad for breakfast either – *fuul*, omelette, bread and *tahina* will set you back ££12.50. There's another branch at 14 Sharia Abdel Khaliq Sarwat, just off Talaat Harb (☎ 02 2579 8557). Daily 24hr.

Al-Kazaz 38 Sharia Abo Alaam ☎ 02 2392 3994; map p.71. Clean, inexpensive 24hr diner, just off Midan Talaat

Harb serving up tasty *shawarma* (££3.75–9.25), *taamiya* (££1) and other fried food in a tiny a/c dining room upstairs, or downstairs to take away. Daily 24hr.

Baba Abdo 3 Sharia Borsa al-Gadida ☎ 02 2393 1490; map p.71. Popular *kushari* joint, hidden away in the backstreets between Talaat Harb and Qasr al-Nil. Also serves spaghetti and macaroni with meat sauce or liver on top (££6–8). Daily 7am–midnight.

El-Tabei el-Domiati 31 Sharia Orabi, north of Midan Orabi ☎ 02 2575 4211 or ☎ 16015, ☻ eltabei-eldomyati .com; map p.71. The pick-and-mix mezze (££3–4.50 each) is the best thing in this eat-in or take-out diner, which also does Egyptian puddings (such as Umm Ali; ££5). They also have a small takeaway branch in the food court of the mall on Sharia Talaat Harb (☎ 02 2577 9784). Daily 5am–1am.

El-Tahrir Sharia Tahrir, between Tahrir Square and Midan Falaki ☎ 02 2795 8418; map p.70. A long-established rival to Abou Tarek (see p.185). Its *kushari* (£E5–10) isn't quite as tasty nor its premises as clean, but it's not a bad option. There's another branch at 19 Sharia Abdel Khaliq Sarwat (☎ 02 2396 1740). Daily 8am–1am.

Fatatri Pizza el-Tahrir Sharia Tahrir, one block east of Tahrir Square; map p.70. The marbled facade belies this place's humble interior. Their *fiteers* (£E5 to £E25) with meat and egg (or crustier versions topped with hot sauce, cheese and olives) make a delicious meal, and they also serve pancake *fiteers* filled with apple jam and icing sugar. Daily 24hr.

DOWNTOWN RESTAURANTS

★ **Alfi Bey** 3 Sharia Alfi Bey ☎ 02 2577 1888; map p.71. A classic colonial-era restaurant, with teak panelling, chandeliers and gilt furniture, *Alfi Bey* is best for traditional Egyptian meat dishes, including lamb, poultry and their signature neck of mutton (£E45). Daily 1pm–1am.

Aly Hassan Al-Haty 3 Sharia Halim, off 26th July St, behind the Windsor Hotels ☎ 02 2591 6055; map p.71. Vintage colonial decor in a cavernous dining room, with huge mirrors and ceiling fans. The traditional and good-value fare includes mezze, roast lamb, kofta and kebabs – their tasty chargrilled half-chicken (£E19) is a meal in itself. Daily noon–1am.

Centro Recreativo Italiano Off Sharia al-Galaa, behind the Italian embassy ☎ 02 2575 9590; map p.70. The city's club for Italian expats, but they usually let in other foreigners on payment of a £E15 guest fee (plus £E5 cover charge). As you'd expect, the pizzas (£E30–45) and pasta dishes (£E19–28) are excellent, and there's also wine and Italian aperitifs such as Campari and vermouth. The dining room is a/c, but most people prefer to eat outside on the terrace. Daily 7–11pm.

El-Dahan 52 26th July St, Bulaq ☎ 02 2575 6949; map p.70. A decent imitation of the Muski kebab house (see p.187), but cheaper, and with special meal deals usually on offer. A quarter kilo of kofta and kebab with salad and *tahina* wil set you back around £E34. Daily 10am–1am.

El Nile Fish 25 Sharia al-Bustan, just off Midan Falaki ☎ 02 2794 0042; map p.71. Popular fish restaurant with a choice of various denizens of the deep freshly caught and fried or grilled to order (£E22–100/kilo), served with salad, *tahina* and pickles. Daily noon–1am.

Estoril 12 Sharia Talaat Harb ☎ 02 2574 3102; map p.70. Tucked away in a passage off Talaat Harb, this cosy bistro-style restaurant serves mainly French and Lebanese dishes, and also has a splendid 1930s-style bar. Dishes include Tripoli-style spicy grouper (£E48) and a French-style take on chicken in ginger and soy sauce (£E42). Daily noon–midnight.

Felfela 15 Sharia Hoda Shaarawi ☎ 02 2392 2833; map p.70. A tourist favourite, serving Egyptian dishes in a long hall with Arabesque decor and waiters in traditional livery. Reliably good, with plenty of veg options, though service can be a little snooty if you're scruffily dressed, and prices are above-average (kofta and kebab £E35; stuffed pigeon £E45). Alcohol served. *Felfela*'s takeaway, around the corner on Talaat Harb (daily 7am–midnight), serves *shawarmas* and *taamiya* sandwiches, though again slightly pricier than elsewhere. Daily 8am–midnight.

★ **Gad** 13 26th July St ☎ 02 2577 7962 or ☎ 16098; map p.71. Cairo's shiniest, most popular takeaway is always crowded, with table seating upstairs. Besides high-quality *taamiya*, *fuul*, *shawarma* and burgers, *Gad* serves delicious specialities such as *kibda skanderani* (Alexandria-style liver with chilli; £E24), baked-on-the-premises Syrian-style pitta bread (*'aish shaami*), and some of the best *fiteers* in town (£E6–26). They also deliver, and have branches at 21 Sharia Abdel Khaliq Sarwat (☎ 02 2396 4621) and 11 Midan Falaki (☎ 02 2392 9133). Daily 24hr (branches daily 8am–2am).

Greek Club Midan Talaat Harb, above Groppi's (entrance on Sharia Bassiouni) ☎ 02 2575 0822; map p.70. The cuisine here is mostly Egyptian, or generic east Mediterranean, rather than specifically Greek, but the Greek salad (£E14) is good, and the rest of the food isn't bad either (fried squid and chips £E36; stuffed vine leaves £E10). The terrace is pleasant in summer, and they serve alcohol, including ouzo. Entry for non-members is £E10, plus a £E30 minimum charge. Tues–Sun 7pm–1am.

Hati el-Guesh (aka *Emara*) 32 Midan Falaki, corner of Tahrir and Falaki streets ☎ 02 2794 5438; map p.70. An immaculate little place serving well-prepared Egyptian standards such as kofta and kebab (£E42.80) and stuffed pigeon (£E30.80), with better-than-average mezze and side dishes, and a takeaway and home delivery service. Daily noon–midnight.

La Chesa 21 Sharia Adly ☎ 02 2393 9360; map p.71. Salubrious, Swiss-managed café serving good Western food, including fondues (£E179 for up to four people); hearty Swiss breakfasts (£E34), scrumptious pastries and great coffee. Daily 7am–midnight.

Le Bistro 8 Sharia Hoda Shaarawi ☎ 02 2392 7694; map p.71. A cheerful little bistro with immaculate service and well-presented French food including sea bass in mustard sauce (£E45), tournedos of beef in red wine sauce (£E64), crêpes (£E12–15) and chocolate mousse (£E12). Serves alcohol. Daily noon–midnight.

Paprika 1129 Corniche al-Nil, just south of the TV Building ☎ 02 2578 9447; map p.70. A slightly faded fusion bistro frequented by media folk (including Omar Sharif) and footballers, *Paprika* gets especially busy at weekends. Its menu offers a mix of Hungarian and Egyptian food – mezze and tasty paprika-flavoured dishes like the speciality goulash (£E55). Alcohol served. Daily noon–midnight.

Peking 14 Sharia Saray al-Azbakiya ☎02 2591 2381 or ☎16078, ⓦpeking-restaurants.com; map p.71. Central branch of a citywide chain of Chinese restaurants, with eight more branches around town, plus a floating restaurant. It's not the best or most authentic Chinese food you'll ever taste, but makes a change – try the prawn *kun pao* in a spicy peanut sauce (£E47.50), or old favourites such as duck with ginger and garlic (£E44). Daily 7am–midnight.

★**Pomo Doro** 197 Sharia Tahrir, Abdin ☎02 2795 6848; map p.71. Formerly little more than a hole-in-the-wall, this place has now expanded both its premises and the menu, but the best offering here is still the dish with which it made its name: spaghetti, with a choice of chicken, bolognaise, vegetarian or (especially recommended) seafood sauces, in £E35 (small), £E40 (medium), £E50 (large) or £E60 (greedy pig) sizes. Daily 1pm–midnight.

ISLAMIC CAIRO AND SAIYIDA ZEINAB

★**El-Dahan** Sharia al-Muski, beneath the El-Hussein Hotel ☎02 2593 9325; map p.95. Excellent kebab house, where a quarter kilo of mixed kebab with salad and *tahina* costs £E45. There's also roast lamb and other meat dishes. Daily 11am–2am.

El-Gahsh Saiyida Zeinab, a block along Sharia Abdel Meguid from Midan Saiyida Zeinab, on the way to Ibn Tulun Mosque; map p.116. It may not look like much, but this insalubrious little diner is generally held to do the finest *fuul* in Cairo. Come at night, when they lay out tables in the neighbouring streets, but don't expect super-clean hygiene. A plate of *fuul* with all the trimmings will set you back the princely sum of £E8. Daily 24hr.

El-Hussein On the roof of the El-Hussein Hotel ☎02 2591 8089; map p.95. Only worth a visit for its fantastic view of Khan al-Khalili; the food is poor, but no one minds if you just drink juice or tea, or smoke a *sheesha*. Daily 24hr.

Gad 165 Sharia al-Azhar ☎02 2514 5901; map p.95. Al-Azhar branch of the popular downtown eatery (see p.186). Daily 8am–2am.

★**Hilltop Restaurant** (aka *Citadel View*) Al-Azhar Park, Sharia Salah Salem ☎02 2510 9150; map p.121. Set in a lovely park with stunning views over Islamic Cairo, this restaurant pays homage to Egypt's Mamluke heritage, with Arab classical music playing in the background. The classy ambience is matched by the quality of the grills and kebabs (mixed grill £E85), while on Fri there's an all-you-can-eat buffet (£E150) with soups, salads, half-a dozen main dishes and a gluttonous choice of desserts. Daily noon–11pm.

Khan el-Khalili Restaurant 5 Sikket al-Badestan ☎02 2590 3788; map p.95. Managed by the *Mena House Oberoi* (see p.184), this Mamluke-themed café-restaurant

is a short stroll from Al-Hussein's Mosque. Western and Egyptian snacks (£E16–22) and meals (main dishes from £E65), such as rabbit *molukhiyya*, are served in the a/c dining room. Daily 10am–2am.

★**Rifai** 37 Midan Saiyida Zeinab, opposite Saiyida Zeinab Mosque (hidden up an alley by the sabil-kuttab of Sultan Mustapha, signposted "Mongy Destrict") ☎012 334 4278; map p.116. A renowned night-time kofta joint best known for its roast goat (*nifa*) – people are known to drive from Heliopolis for a takeaway because it's so good. A quarter-kilo each of kofta and *nifa* with *tahina, babaghanoug,* salad and a glass of salad juice with chilli, comes to £E85 and easily serves two, even three. Daily 5pm–5am.

ZAMALEK

As befits an affluent, cosmopolitan neighbourhood, Zamalek boasts several upmarket restaurants devoted to foreign cuisine, with lots of choice for vegetarians at *L'Aubergine*, and popular bars such as *Deals* and *Pub 28* (see p.191), both of which also do good food. All are shown on the "Gezira & The West Bank" map, as is the Zamalek branch of the *Peking* chain of Chinese restaurants (see above) at 23b Sharia Ismail Mohammed (☎02 2736 3894).

★**Abou El Sid** 157 26th July St, Zamalek ☎02 2735 9640, ⓦabouelsid.com; map p.138. The food here is classic Egyptian fare, on the pricey side of moderate (the signature dish is chicken *molukhiyya* at £E48), but it isn't especially outstanding in itself. What you really come here for is the venue and the decor, which have a wonderfully old-fashioned colonial feel, warmly dark and golden, augmented by odd little touches such as the tent-fabric upholstery on the bar stools. Daily 11am–2am.

Didos (Al Dente) 26 Sharia Bahgat Ali ☎02 2735 9117; map p.138. Besides great pasta (£E21–40.50), this little place also has excellent salads, and specialities such as Portuguese-style fish (£E32). Daily noon–2am.

Don Quichotte 9a Sharia Ahmed Heshmat ☎02 2735 6415; map p.138. Small, elegant, lounge-style restaurant serving French and Italian cuisine. Dishes include sole meunière (£E110) and steak in gorgonzola sauce (£E110), with desserts such as chocolate soufflé (£E43). Alcohol served. Reservations advisable. Daily 1pm–2am.

Five Bells Corner of Adil Abu Bakr and Ismail Mohammed ☎02 2735 9980; map p.138. It's worth dressing up for this swish Italianate joint, with a choice of indoor lounge or outside marquee dining. Specialities include meat fondue, grill-it-yourself charbonnade (£E130 for two) and fish with squid and prawns (£E65). Alcohol served. Daily 12.30pm–2am.

Golden Dragon 1 Sharia Mohammed Mahzar ☎02 2738 2972; map p.138. Done out in the bright red decor that's become such a cliché for Chinese restaurants, this new place doesn't offer any surprises, but the food is decent enough, with offerings like crispy duck and seafood sizzler (both £E55). Daily noon–midnight.

L'Aubergine 5 Sharia Sayed al-Bakri ✆ 02 2738 0080; map p.138. *L'Aubergine*'s adventurous menu is regularly refreshed, and features a good variety of vegetarian dishes, such as cheese and spinach crêpes (£E25), or pan-fried halloumi (£E30). The food is usually delicious, though some of the more ambitious dishes may disappoint. There's also a bar upstairs. Daily 7am–2am.

Maison Thomas 157 26th July St, opposite the Marriott Hotel ✆ 02 2735 7057; map p.138. Deli-diner-takeaway serving freshly made baguettes and pizzas as well as light meals (from £E55). They also make their own mozzarella, and serve good breakfasts (7–11am; £E40). Daily 24hr.

GARDEN CITY AND RODA ISLAND

Abou Shakra 69 Sharia Qasr al-Aini, opposite the hospital ✆ 02 2531 6111, ⊛ aboushakra.net; map p.126. Lavishly decorated in marble and alabaster, this famous establishment specializes in kofta and kebab sold by weight (£E115/kg), to eat in or take out, although despite its pretensions, the food isn't as good as in humbler establishments such as El-*Dahan* or *Rifai* in Islamic Cairo. Daily noon–2am.

Revolving Restaurant 40th floor, Grand Nile Tower Hotel, Roda Island ✆ 02 2365 1234; map, p.126. "Semi-formal" dress is required and children under 12 are barred at this tip-top restaurant, which serves the finest French cuisine in Cairo and enjoys a panoramic view of the entire city. The menu changes regularly, but typical starters include scallop carpaccio (£E120) or lobster with smoked salmon and asparagus (£E130), followed by main courses like salmon in basil sauce (£E180), duck breast with cherry and endive (£E210), or vegetarian options such as tomato and asparagus risotto (£E80) followed by rosemary crème brulée (£E60). Alcohol served. Daily 7pm–1am.

★ **Taboula** 1 Sharia Amerika al-Latina, Garden City ✆ 02 2792 5261; map, p.70. One of Cairo's best Lebanese restaurants, whose opulent Arabesque decor and fine ambience complement its huge range of excellent mezze (£E16–27), various preparations of kofta and Lebanese *fattehs* (stews made with toasted pitta pieces; £E35–50). Daily noon–2am.

PYRAMIDS AREA

Felfela Village Maryotteya Canal ✆ 02 3384 1515 or ✆ 02 3384 1616; map, p.148. Unabashedly kitsch and touristic, this place features a similar menu to *Felfela*'s (see p.186) plus a rambling outdoor complex including a zoo and playground. The chief attraction, however, is a lavish show (1–7.30pm; daily in summer, Fri in winter) with acrobats, puppets, bellydancers, camel rides and dancing horses. It's located beside a canal that crosses Pyramids Rd, 1km north of Pyramids Rd on the east bank of the canal.

Daily 10am–midnight.

Gad Sharia al-Ahram (Pyramids Rd) ✆ 02 3741 2222; map p.148. The pyramids branch of the popular downtown eatery (see p.186) is a godsend if you need some reliable budget food while checking out the pyramids. Daily 8am–2am.

The Moghul Room Mena House Oberoi (see p.184) ✆ 02 3377 3222; map p.148. Cairo's top Indian restaurant. As the name suggests, north Indian Mughal dishes are the mainstay here, notably rogan josh (£E130), but they also do veg curries and Goan fish curry (£E120). They usually stint on the chilli, so tell them if you want it spicy. Reservations required. Daily 7pm–midnight & Fri 12.30–2.30pm.

Pyramids Restaurant 9 Sharia Abu al-Hol ✆ 02 3386 5111; map, p.148. A decent kebab house, now tarted up and quite pricey (quarter-kilo kofta and kebab £E65; chicken *shish tawook* £E55; salad and *tahina* extra). Nonetheless, it's still an oasis amid the tourist traps. Daily 24hr.

COFFEE HOUSES, TEAROOMS AND BUFFETS

DOWNTOWN

Borsa Café 5 Sharia al-Sheriffein ✆ 02 2237 7575; map p.71. This was the first coffee-drinking establishment in the little area of streets around the stock exchange (Al-Borsa) which now seemingly becomes one huge outdoor café in the evenings, although in fact various cafés are involved, some supplying free wi-fi. Massively trendy, the area is characterized by such racy modern novelties as groups of women smoking *sheeshas* together with no men involved, and groups of friends of both sexes hanging out together. Whether such outrageous behaviour will survive the rise of the Islamists remains to be seen. Daily 24hr.

El Shems (*Sun Café*) In the passage by 4 Sharia Tawfiqia, off Midan Orabi; map p.71. A grimy, city-centre 'ahwa, distinguished by its incredibly kitsch decor and a general feeling of old-school Cairene authenticity. Daily 7am–2am.

Everest Hotel Midan Ramses ✆ 02 2574 2506; map p.85. On the fifteenth-floor terrace of an otherwise unremarkable cheap hotel. The coffee isn't the best in town, but you can sit on the balcony and enjoy a view over Midan Ramses and as far as the Citadel and the Muqattam Hills. Daily 10am–2am.

Garden Groppi 48 Sharia Abdel Khaliq Sarwat/12 Sharia Adly ✆ 02 2391 1871; map p.71. The more spacious, "garden" branch of the *Groppi* chain (see below), a favourite with British officers during the war, when non-commissioned ranks were barred. You can sit in the salon with your coffee and pastry, or on the outside terrace and enjoy a *sheesha*. Daily 7am–11pm.

Groppi 21 Sharia Bassiouni, on Midan Talaat Harb ✆ 02 2574 3244; map p.70. The once-palatial flagship branch of this classic chain was in its heyday synonymous with Cairo's "café society". Renovations have destroyed much of its charm, and the coffee itself is pretty terrible, but it still has a restful a/c salon, great pastries and offers a taste, albeit a very faded one, of what Cairo's elegant Ismailiya Quarter was like in the days of King Fouad and King Farouk. Minimum charge £E10. Daily 7am–11pm.

Mondial Café 4 Sharia Darih Sa'd; map p.70. This unassuming 'ahwa is the place to come for football fans, and can generally be relied on to show all the most important English, European and international matches live. Daily 24hr.

Simonds Coffee Shop 29 Sharia Sherif ☎02 2393 8519; map p.71. A downtown branch of Zamalek's French-style café (see below) with espresso coffee, Egyptian and European-style pastries and free wi-fi (when it's working). Daily 7am–9pm.

Soma Caffe Sharia al-Azbakiya; map p.71. "Soma" is the nickname of Umm Kalthoum (see p.136), and this is one of several Cairo cafés dedicated to the great lady. It isn't the original Umm Kalthoum Café (that's at 21 Sharia Orabi), but it's the most fun, fronted by two giant busts of the Arab diva and filled with memorabilia of the singer and other stars of her day. Daily 24hr.

ISLAMIC CAIRO

'Ahwa al-Aini Midan al-Aini, Butneya; map p.102. This hole-in-the-wall coffee house used to come alive in the evening, when music played and the whole square became a lovely open-air hangout. The café was temporarily closed at the time of writing, but should hopefully reopen soon, with coffee and music in the square again by the time you read this, insha'allah. Daily 5pm–2am.

Café Shobilard 30 Sharia al-Dhabiba, Gamaliya; map p.97. A cut above your average 'ahwa, with a strange collection of furniture and bric-a-brac – an excellent place to stop for a breather amid the chaos of Islamic Cairo. Daily 24hr.

Fishawi's Behind the El-Hussein Hotel in Khan al-Khalili; map p.95. Cairo's oldest tea house has been managed by the same family since 1773. Soak up the atmosphere – cracked mirrors, battered furniture, haughty staff and wandering vendors – with a pot of mint tea and a *sheesha*. Prices (about double those of most 'ahwas) are posted up in Arabic, but expect to be overcharged if you can't read it. Daily 24hr (except in daylight hours during Ramadan).

Naguib Mahfouz Coffee Shop 5 Sikket al-Badestan, Khan al-Khalili; map p.95. Part of the *Khan el-Khalili Restaurant*, this upmarket a/c tourist café in the heart of the bazaar serves snacks, coffee, mint tea and orange juice. Daily 10am–2am.

ZAMALEK

Beano's 8 Sharia al-Marsafy ☎02 2735 0576, ⓦ beanoscafe.com; map p.138. Hot and cold espresso-based coffee concoctions, plus crêpes, pastries, salads and sandwiches, in a lovely a/c space with free wi-fi. There's a downtown branch on Sharia Mohammed Mahmoud, but it isn't as good. Daily 7am–1am.

Café Tabasco 18b Sharia al-Marashly ☎02 2735 8465, ⓦ deyafa.net; map p.138. A sophisticated, Western-style coffee house, where the TV (usually Eurosport) isn't obtrusive, there are magazines to read and you can get coffee, juices, herbal teas and food. A good place to hang out, with free wi-fi. Daily 7am–3am.

No Big Deal Sharia Sayed al-Bakri, next to Deals bar ☎02 2736 0502, ⓦ nobigdealcafe.com; map p.138. Small, San Francisco-style coffee shop, with home-made cakes and exotic beverages such as Earl Grey tea. Pleasant, but not very Egyptian. Daily 8.30am–1am.

Rigoletto Yamaha Centre, 3 Sharia Taha Hussein ☎02 2735 8684, ⓦ rigolettoicecream.com; map p.138. Espresso, cappuccino, cheesecake and by far the best ice cream in town (£E6 a scoop) – the cinnamon and date flavour is especially good. £E10 minimum charge to eat in. Daily 9am–midnight.

Simonds Coffee Shop 112 26th July St, near Hassan Sabry intersection ☎02 2735 9436; map p.138. Cairo's original French-style coffee shop, with cappuccino, hot chocolate, lemonade, fresh croissants, pastries and *ramequins* (cheese puffs). Daily 7.30am–midnight.

CAIRO 'AHWAS

Cairene men have socialized in hole-in-the-wall coffee houses, or **'ahwas**, ever since the beverage was introduced from Yemen in the early Middle Ages (for a rundown on coffee and tea drinking, see p.37), while there are also a few larger and more sophisticated coffee houses, with high ceilings and tall mirrors, such as *Fishawi's* in Khan al-Khalili and *El Horriya* in Midan Falaki. **All-night** 'ahwas can be found around Midan Ramses and Sharia Qalaa and the Saiyida Zeinab end of Sharia Mohammed Farid and Sharia al-Nasireya. Women can increasingly be seen smoking *sheeshas* in 'ahwas, though generally in more sophisticated, slightly upmarket places rather than old-fashioned hole-in-the-wall ones. In particular, al-Borsa, the area around the stock exchange, is very trendy for 'ahwas, which spread out during the evening into all the surrounding backstreets.

1

DRINKING

Drinking doesn't get a big profile in Cairo, but there's a good range of bars scattered around town. Tourists tend to drink at the bars of **upmarket hotels**, or at pub-style bars, often in Zamalek and Mohandiseen; more upmarket bars often have a minimum charge, which may not be advertised. Alternatively, there are a handful of downtown options, including a couple of fun rooftop bars. For men at least, rough and ready **downmarket bars** can also be a laugh. These spit-and-sawdust drinking dens, euphemistically named "cafeterias", are found in nooks all over Downtown Cairo. Beer is usually served with free nibbles and lots of drunken bonhomie. They're certainly not recommended for women on their own, and even with a male escort you'll be the object of much attention. Some other bars are meeting places for men and prostitutes (the only Egyptian women found there). Most of the establishments we list are places where women shouldn't face too much hassle (exceptions are noted). As throughout Egypt, the sale of alcohol to Muslims is banned during Ramadan and major religious festivals, though available to tourists in some hotels.

DOWNTOWN

Women should be able to get a fairly hassle-free drink in all the bars listed below, except perhaps *El Horryia, Gamayka* and *Bodega Orabi*, though even in *Le Grillon* and *Cafeteria Stella* you may feel happier with a male escort.

★ **Barrel Lounge** 1st floor, Windsor Hotel, 19 Sharia Alfi Bey ☎ 02 2591 5810; map p.71. Some of the furniture is actually made from old wine barrels, and the faded colonial decor and charming olde-worlde ambience almost makes you feel like you've stepped back into the 1930s, when the bar was a popular watering hole for British officers. Women in particular will enjoy the hassle-free

atmosphere, and foreigners can buy alcohol here during Ramadan. Daily 10am–midnight.

Bodega Orabi Opposite 25 Sharia Orabi ☎ 02 2257 4248; map p.71. Basic but friendly bar with a quieter upstairs section overlooking the street. It's small and can sometimes get quite crowded, but is generally more easy-going than other downmarket Cairo bars. Women should be OK here with male company. Daily 11am–4am.

Café Riche 17 Sharia Talaat Harb ☎ 02 2392 9793; map p.70. Once a hangout for artists and intellectuals, this bar-restaurant (not a café, despite the name) has been visited by

---

PATISSERIES, JUICE BARS AND ICE CREAM

Though available at more sophisticated coffee shops, **pastries** are cheaper at patisseries, where traditional Arab sticky sweets such as baklava and burma (see p.36) are sold by the kilo. Many cafés and not a few *kushari* shops and cheap diners also offer puddings such as *mahalabiyya* (blancmange) or rice pudding. For a healthy pick-up before breakfast or lunch, you can't beat Cairo's **juice bars** (usually open 8am–10pm), selling freshly squeezed sugar-cane, orange, guava or other seasonal fruits for £E2.50 to £E4 a glass. Cairenes also love **ice cream,** which comes in all kinds of flavours. The best outlet for ice cream is *Rigoletto in Zamalek* (see p.189).

Al-Rahmany Corner of Khayrat and Mohedayan streets in Saiyida Zeinab; map p.116. Sobia, usually sold in juice shops as a kind of rice milk, is available here in its original form, as a gloopy dessert.

El Abd 25 Sharia Talaat Harb ☎ 02 2392 4407 and 46 Sharia Sherif (at the corner of 26 July) ☎ 02 2393 7770; map p.70. Generally rated the best confectioner in town, this is the place to buy top-notch baklava, burma, konafa, basbousa, nutty crunch (almond, hazelnut or pistachio) and other calorific treats.

El-Sharkia 3 Sharia Alfi Bey ☎ 02 2577 7202; map p.71. The main downtown competitor to El Abd, it isn't quite as renowned, but it has its following, and is usually less crowded.

Farghaly Fruits 45b Midan Dokki, Dokki ☎ 02 3338 7199 (see map, p.139) and 71 Arab League St, Mohandiseen ☎ 02 3338 4375; map p.139. The best juice bar in Cairo, slightly pricier than the others, but

definitely a cut above (they strain their orange and grapefruit juice, for example).

Foontana Sharia Handusa, opposite the north side of Qasr al-Aini Hospital (see map p.126). One of the best places in town to buy rice pudding, topped if you like with basbousa (a confection of semolina, nuts and syrup). It's signed in Arabic only – look for the honey pots in the window).

La Poire 1 Sharia Amerika al-Latina, Garden City ☎ 02 2795 1509; map p.70. Not far from Tahrir Square, this is the original and most central branch of a citywide chain of upmarket patisseries, serving up luscious sticky offerings including home-made baklava (£E77/kilo) and chocolate éclairs (£E8 each).

Mohammed Ali Juices Midan Falaki; map p.71. The best downtown juice bar, unrivalled for its vast selection of drinks, including a wonderful coconut milkshake.

practically every Arab revolutionary of the last century – Saddam Hussein was known to drink here, and the free officers whose coup toppled King Farouk (see p.83) did much of their plotting here. The owner was a pilot during the wars with Israel. Although now largely for tourists, its teak bar still oozes history, but don't bother eating in the mediocre restaurant. Daily 10am–midnight.

Cafeteria Stella Corner of Sharia Talaat Harb and Sharia Hoda Shaarawi, next to Felfela's restaurant; map p.70. Patronized by local barflies, expats and backpackers, this seedy, cramped den often buzzes with life, and the regulars are quite used to tourists popping in for a drink (there's even a ladies' loo). Daily except Fri noon–midnight.

⭐ **El Horryia** Midan Falaki ☎02 2392 0397; map p.71. A large and atmospheric high-ceilinged old-school Cairo café that's hardly changed since the 1930s. Decorated with mirrors and old Stella advertisements, with walls a fine shade of nicotine, it plays host to an eclectic clientele and serves beer as well as tea, coffee and *sheesha*. Chess players meet here in the evening and people gather to watch them play – though drinking isn't allowed round the boards. Daily noon–2am.

Gamayka Sharia al-Bank al-Ahly, off Sharia Sharif; map p.71. Named after the island of Jamaica, this cosy little dive on the edge of the trendy Borsa area is really just an ordinary "cafeteria" bar (women may not feel comfortable here), but it's a little less rough and ready than most, and you can have a *sheesha* with your beer. Daily 24hr.

Happy City Hotel 92C Sharia Mohammed Farid, near Abdeen metro ☎02 2395 9777; map p.71. The rooftop café at this hotel has a view of the Muqattam and tasty complimentary mezze, served when you buy a drink. Daily 6pm–midnight or later.

Le Bistro 8 Sharia Hoda Shaarawi ☎02 2392 7694; map p.71. Pub run by the neighbouring restaurant of the same name (see p.186), with smoochy lighting, red and black decor, soft music and an intimate ambience; a place for a romantic rendezvous. Daily noon–midnight.

Le Grillon 8 Sharia Qasr al-Nil, down a small passage between Qasr al-Nil and Sharia Bustan ☎02 2574 3114; map p.70. A cosy, carpeted bar that's quite large, with lots of space for a quiet chat. It also serves mediocre food and has a smoking garden for *sheesha*. Daily 1pm–2am.

Napoleon Bar Shepheard Hotel ☎02 2792 1000; map p.70. One of the most comfortable bars in town, with soft seating, a refined atmosphere, wood panelling and Napoleonic prints on the walls. As well as drinks, they serve mezze and light meals, and there's live music every night. Foreigners can buy alcohol here during Ramadan. Daily 4pm–2am.

Odeon Palace Hotel 6 Sharia Abdel Hamid Said ☎02 2577 6637; map p.70. The 24hr rooftop bar here is a

popular and very pleasant place for a bit of after-hours drinking, perhaps with a *sheesha*, and draws an eclectic crowd. Minimum charge £E10 7am–9pm, £E15 9pm–7am. Daily 24hr.

ZAMALEK AND MOHANDISEEN

Amici 22 Sharia Taha Hussein, Zamalek (by New President Hotel) ☎0100 661 2596; map p.138. Very trendy upmarket, upstairs bar, with minimalistically dark and stylish decor, where bright young things sip elegantly from a range of well-mixed cocktails at club prices (£E40–45, plus – mentioned only in the small print – 25 percent tax). Daily 6pm–2am.

Bull's Eye 32 Sharia Jeddah, Mohandiseen ☎02 3761 6888, ⓦbullseyepub.com; map p.139. English-style pub featuring, as its name suggests, a dartboard, as well as food and a small dancefloor, and occasional live music. Couples only. Minimum charge £E100. Daily 7pm–2am.

Deals 5 Sharia Sayed al-Bakri, Zamalek ☎02 2736 0502, ⓦdealspub.com; map p.138. This small and rather narrow but homely basement bar, where the tables hug the walls, is one of Cairo's most congenial drinking spots, and one of the few with any kind of atmosphere. It's popular with expats and Egyptians alike, and women can drink here with no fear. There's cold beer (served with popcorn) and decent food, while TVs hang from the walls playing pop videos, though the piped music never matches. There are larger branches in Mohandiseen at 2 Sharia Gol Gamal (☎02 3305 7255) and on the 14th floor of the *Swiss Inn Hotel*, 7 Sharia Higaz; and in Heliopolis at 40 Sharia Baghdad (☎02 2291 0406). Minimum charge Fri & Sat £E150, Sun–Thurs £E125. Daily 3pm–1.30am.

Harry's Pub Marriott Hotel, Zamalek ☎02 2728 3000; map p.138. A favourite with expats, this British-style bar has live music nightly from 10pm, plus karaoke nights and regular screenings of English football. Minimum charge £E200. Daily 6pm–2am.

Piano Bar Marriott Hotel, Zamalek ☎02 2728 3000; map p.138. Sleek bar, more refined than *Harry's* and much frequented by expats, with lots of stately wooden decor in what was the billiard room of Empress Eugénie's palace. Live piano music (from 8pm) enhances the ambience. Daily 6pm–2am.

Pub 28 28 Shagar al-Durr, Zamalek ☎02 2735 9200; map p.138. A smoke-filled bar, very full on a good night, that's also popular as a place to eat, offering a selection of different beers, sangría by the carafe, plus grills, steaks, English-style cold cuts and mezze (among which the *babaghanoug* is highly rated), but it has its regulars, and you may not always get tip-worthy service if you aren't one of them. Daily noon–2am.

1

NIGHTLIFE AND ENTERTAINMENT

Egyptians make a distinction between a **disco**, where you dance to music, and a **nightclub**, where you have dinner and watch a floorshow – if you want to go clubbing, it's a disco, not a nightclub, that you want. For current **listings**, get hold of Saturday's *Egyptian Mail*, the weekly English edition of *Al-Ahram* newspaper, the monthly *Egypt Today*, or the online listings magazines Filbalad at ⓦ filbalad.com and Cairo 360 at ⓦ cairo360.com.

NIGHTSPOTS

Cairo has a fair number of discos but nowhere to rave about. The music is usually last year's hits back home or current Egyptian stuff; light shows are unsophisticated. But dancefloor manners are good, boozy boors are at a minimum and casual dress is acceptable at all but the ritziest places. In addition to the places listed here, one or two bars also have dancefloors, notably *Bull's Eye* (see p. 191).

After Eight 6 Sharia Qasr al-Nil, Downtown ☎0100 339 8000, ⓦ after8cairo.com; map p.70. Sweaty, smoky and quite atmospheric jazz club, with low lights and cocktails. Couples over 25 only; reservation compulsory. £E60 minimum charge (sometimes £E100 at weekends). Sat–Wed 8pm–2am, Thurs & Fri 8pm–3am.

Arabesque 6 Sharia Qasr al-Nil ☎02 2574 8677, ⓦ arabesque-eg.com; map p.70. In the afternoon, this is a restaurant serving Egyptian, French and Levantine cuisine (strong on soups and meat dishes, such as rabbit *molukhiyya* at £E70), but from 9pm onwards it mutates into a disco, with a small dancefloor and DJs playing Arabic and Western hits. There's also a bellydancer (an up-and-coming talent rather than a famous name) from 12.30am on Thurs and Fri nights – or, strictly speaking, Fri & Sat morning. Minimum charge £E150 after 9pm Sat–Wed, £175 Thurs & Fri. Daily noon–2am.

★ **Cairo Jazz Club** 197 26th July St, Mohandiseen ☎02 3345 9939, ⓦ cairojazzclub.com; map p.138. Food, drink and live musicians most nights, but despite the name, jazz only once a week. The lighting is soft, the seating comfortable and the crowd friendly. Happy hour is 7–9pm, when you get two drinks for the price of one. Sat is Middle Eastern music, Sun is usually jazz, but many reckon the best night is Wed, when there's no live band, only a DJ. Couples over 25 only (at least in principle); reservations advisable (lines open 5–10pm). Daily 5pm–3am.

Cancan Fontana Hotel, off Midan Ramses ☎02 2592 2321; map p.85. A very downmarket disco, but fun, playing pop hits for a mix of tourists and Egyptians. Minimum charge £E40. Daily 9pm–2am.

Nirvana (Africana) 41 Pyramids Rd (about halfway along) ☎02 3771 8053; map p.148. Officially renamed *Nirvana* but still universally known as *Africana*, plays African and reggae music, plus some RnB and hip-hop, to a largely sub-Saharan crowd, many of whom seem to be on the game, so it's as much a pick-up joint as a centre for Cairo's African community. It's lively and fun, and the food's good, and the music's great, but don't order spirits here; stick to the beer. £E100 entry including one drink. Daily 11pm–4am (but usually quiet until 1am).

Stiletto Sharia Corniche al-Nil by Midan Galaa, Dokki (opposite Cairo Sheraton Hotel), ☎02 3331 1360; map p.139. Spacious upmarket lounge bar with cocktails, Egyptian and East Asian snacks, and a dancefloor with an eclectic musical mix (Arabic pop, Western pop, house, RnB, even salsa), popular with Cairo's young and rich, but mostly considered a summertime venue. Minimum charge £E150. Thurs–Sat 7pm–2am, Sun 10pm–2am, or later in summer.

LIVE MUSIC AND DANCE

Aside from at *Cairo Jazz Club* and *After Eight* (see above), tourist restaurants and the Opera House, you're unlikely to hear much live Western music. By far the liveliest time of year for Arabic pop music is after the school and university exams (late June–Nov), when El Sawy Culture Wheel (see p.193), *Cairo Jazz Club*, Genaina Theatre (see p.193) and the open-air theatre at the Cairo Opera House (see p.195) are the main venues for everything from Algerian *rai* to Egyptian hip-hop. Concerts are mostly advertised in the Arabic press, although Cairo 360 (ⓦ cairo360.com) usually has relevant listings, and it's especially worth checking their "Cairo Weekend Guide" for a round-up of what's on. Folk music doesn't command a wide following today, but under Nasser (1952–70), troupes of artists were established to preserve Egyptian folk music and dance, and some of these – most famously the Reda Troupe – still perform today, while all of the city's moulids (see pp.196–198) feature religious music in the form of hypnotic Sufi chants. But the really big dance spectacle in Cairo, not to be

---

COUPLES ONLY

Though you might imagine the trend towards a **couples-only policy** is to prevent women from being swamped, locals say that it's to stop discos from becoming gay haunts or pick-up joints for prostitutes. In practice, women can usually get into discos without escorts, but men without women will have more difficulty. Call first to avoid disappointment.

1

GAY LIFE IN CAIRO

There are currently no specific venues for gay men or lesbians in Cairo. In the past, venues such as *Harry's Pub* at the *Marriott Hotel* were popular, but that all changed in 2001 when police raided the *Queen Boat* floating disco, which was popular with both gay and heterosexual couples. Homosexuality as such is not illegal in Egypt, but 52 gay men ("the Cairo 52") were arrested, slung in a cell and charged with offences such as "debauchery" and "contempt of religion", some receiving three-year prison sentences as a result. The religious lobby were delighted, but the gay scene made itself as invisible as possible, and any events that began to attract a gay crowd were quickly closed. After the revolution, things semed to relax for a bit, but the rise to prominence of the Muslim Brotherhood and the Salafists does not bode well. There's been a lesbian scene in Cairo since at least the middle ages, but it's always been more discreet than the gay male scene, and even harder for foreigners to make contacts in.

missed, is the thrice-weekly whirling dervish dance held at the Wikala al-Ghuri.

Balloon Theatre Corniche al-Nil, Aguza ☎ 02 3347 1718; map p.138. This pleasantly old-fashioned theatre by the Nile stages performances of religious and other traditional music. Most importantly, the incredible Reda Egyptian Dance Troupe (founded by Mahmoud Reda in 1959) and the slightly less well-known National Troupe perform traditional dance compositions, with spectacular costumes and excellent musicians.

Darb al-Asfur Darb al-Asfur, Gamaliya; map p.97. The Al-Nil Folk Music Troupe performs for free in the small open space at the western end of this street every Sun at 8pm in summer, 7pm in winter.

El Sawy Culture Wheel Under Zamalek (15th May) Bridge, 26th July St, Zamalek ☎ 02 2736 8881, ⓦ culturewheel.com; map p.138. With a full programme of low-priced folk, jazz and classical concerts, as well as seminars, lectures and movies, the Wheel has fast become one of Cairo's most important cultural centres, and defiantly supported the pro-democracy movement during the 2011 revolution.

Genaina Theatre Al-Azhar Park ☎ 02 2362 5057, ⓦ mawred.org/en/el-genaina-theatre; map p.121. A wonderful open-air venue which hosts not only plays, but also Arabic folk music, the latest Egyptian pop and hip-hop performers, and concerts of Egyptian and foreign classical music (Thurs & Sat at 8.30pm).

Gumhorriya Theatre 12 Sharia al-Gumhorriya ☎ 02 2390 7707; map p.71. As well as plays in Arabic, this downtown theatre often hosts traditional music and dance performances, and some classical concerts, all usually advertised in the weekly English edition of *Al-Ahram*.

★ **MakAn** (Egyptian Centre for Culture and Art) 1 Sharia Saad Zaghloul ☎ 02 2792 0878, ⓦ egyptmusic.org; map p.70. This basement music club hosts performances (Wed at 9pm) of the Zar music of the Sahara, a stirring and deliberately trance-inducing style of tribal music traditionally performed by women to exorcize *jinn*

(malevolent spirits) and heal disease. Also hosts a weekly jam session (Tues at 9pm), involving gypsy, Nubian and Sudanese musicians. £E20 if reserved in advance, or £E30 on the door.

★ **Wikala al-Ghuri** Sharia Sheikh Mohammed; map p.95. Free 90min performances (Mon, Wed & Sat at 8pm) of the famous Mowlawiyya whirling ceremony (see box p.194), or at least, a simulation thereof, are staged at the Wikala al-Ghuri; arrive early to get a good seat, and at least half an hour before the performance in any case. Photos are permitted but not videos. The *wikala* also hosts the International Samaa' Sufi Music Festival every year in Aug, featuring qawwali (trance-inducing Sufi music) from across the Islamic world.

BELLYDANCING

Cairo remains the world's most important bellydancing centre, and every summer (usually late June or early July) hosts the world's premier bellydancing festival, the International Oriental Dance Festival, usually based at the *Mena House Oberoi* hotel. For the latest information on the festival, which features classes and workshops in the daytime and performances in the evenings, plus extra events such as costume shows, check ⓦ raqiahassan.net. There is also a smaller and less prestigious rival festival (ⓦ nilegroup.net), run by the Nile Group four times a year. If you're interested in lessons, Hisham Youssif at the *Berlin Hotel* (see p.180) can arrange coaching with a number of teachers (including some of Cairo's top dancers) at various levels and prices.

VENUES AND PERFORMERS

To see top acts, the place to go is the nightclub of one of the five-star hotels, or a floating restaurant. Of the dancers at these venues, the big names include Randa Kamel, whose sexy moves are very popular with foreigners, though some purists consider them vulgar; she currently performs on the *Nile Maxim* (see p.194). Other top stars are Dina (who performs at the *Haroun al-Rashid*) and Soraya (at the *Empress Show Lounge*). A step down from these are the somewhat sleazy, rip-off nightclubs along

GIVING IT A WHIRL

The **Mowlawiyya** are Arab adherents of a Sufi sect known to Westerners as the whirling dervishes which was founded in Konya, Turkey, during the mid-thirteenth century. Their Turkish name, **Mevlevi**, refers to their original Master, who extolled music and dancing (*samaa*) as a way of shedding earthly ties and abandoning oneself to God's love. The Sufi ideal of attaining union with God has often been regarded by conventional Muslims as theologically suspect, even blasphemous, and only during Mamluke and Ottoman times did whirling dervishes flourish without persecution. They were banned in Turkey by Kemal Atatürk.

While most Egyptian Sufi sects chant and sway as part of their *samaa*, the Mowlawiyya literally whirl themselvs into religious ecstasy. Each element of their whirling dance has symbolic significance. The **music** symbolizes that of the spheres, and the **turning** of the dervishes that of the heavenly bodies. The gesture of extending the right arm towards heaven and the left towards the floor denotes that **grace** is being received from God and distributed to humanity without anything being retained by the dervishes. The camelhair **hats** represent tombstones; the white **skirts** shrouds; and the black **cloaks** (discarded during the *samaa*) the tomb itself.

Pyramids Rd, where the entertainments are varied and sometimes good, but the food is usually poor. For a rather better alternative, the downtown restaurant *Arabesque* (see p.192) hosts up-and-coming dancers and does good food. Cheaper places, with no food to speak of, lurk downtown. These can be fun, but they are extremely sleazy and play dirty tricks (see box p.195) which you need to be aware of if you visit.

FIVE-STAR HOTELS

As well as the places listed below, the nightclubs at the *Mena House Oberoi* and the *Cairo Sheraton* are also good when operating, but were closed at the time of writing.

Empress Show Lounge Cairo Marriott Hotel, Sharia Saray al-Gezira, Zamalek ☏ 02 2728 3000; map p.138. Soraya is curently the star attraction at this top-notch nightclub, where dining is a la carte. Minimum charge £E200. Daily except Mon 10.30pm.

Haroun al-Rashid Semiramis Intercontinental Hotel, Corniche al-Nil ☏ 02 2795 7171; map p.70. The top dancer at this posh (and very expensive) five-star venue is Dina, one of the biggest stars on the bellydancing scene. US$124 including dinner. Tues only at 10.30pm.

FLOATING RESTAURANTS

Nile Maxim Docked in front of the Cairo Marriott Hotel, Sharia Saray al-Gezira, Zamalek ☏ 02 2738 8888, ⊛ maximrestaurants.com; map p.138. Daily dinner cruises at 8pm and 10pm, with a choice of set menus (£E290–395, not including drinks) and an impressive floorshow, including some of Cairo's very best bellydancers, as well as a Sufi-style dervish dance and an Arabic folk band

The Nile Pharaoh & Golden Pharaoh ☏ 02 3570 1000, ⊛ thepharaohs.com.eg; map p.126. A pair of mock-pharaonic barges complete with scarab friezes, picture windows and golden lotus flowers or figures of Horus mounted on the stern and prow. Moored 1km south of the Gama'a Bridge, they cruise for lunch (2.30pm), early dinner (7.30pm) or late dinner (10pm). Cruises cost £E200 and last 2hr; you should check in 30min before sailing. The early dinner cruise is by far the best, featuring music and a bellydancer, the late one has an Arab stand-up comedian and a shorter bellydance show, while lunch cruises have a Middle Eastern band instead.

Scarabee ☏ 02 2794 3444; map p.70. Docked on the Corniche near the Shepheard Hotel, *Scarabee* was Cairo's original floating restaurant, and offers a buffet rather than

BELLYDANCING: A BRIEF HISTORY

The European appetite for exotica in the late nineteenth and early twentieth centuries did much to create the bellydancing art form as it is known today: a sequinned fusion of classical raqs sharqi (oriental dance), stylized harem eroticism and the frank sexuality of the ghawazee (public dancers). During the nineteenth century, many ghawazee moonlighted as prostitutes, so even though most dancers today are dedicated professionals – and the top stars wealthy businesswomen – the association with prostitution has stuck, and the resulting social stigma is deterring young Egyptian women from entering the profession. As a result, most up-and-coming bellydancers today are foreigners. Meanwhile the Islamist parties which rose to dominance after the revolution are staunch critics of bellydancing, and many of their members would like to see it banned – whether they will act on this remains to be seen.

CHEAP TRICKS

Cheap bellydancing joints can be fun to visit, and a lot cheaper than the five-star venues if you are careful, but you need to be aware of how they operate to avoid the scams they pull. Most open their doors at around 10pm, but none really gets going until at least midnight. Most have an entry fee or minimum charge, sometimes both, but will also endeavour to rip you off with **hidden charges and sharp practices**. Napkins, for example, may be placed on your table and then charged on your bill; nibbles may be placed on your table unordered, but they are far from free. You need to be on your toes to keep refusing these extras, as the clubs count on customers getting too drunk to notice, as they do when numbering the drinks on your **bill**, so keep a tally. Venues may also add spurious taxes, or simply refuse to give **change** – even for a £E100 note. **Women** in particular should be aware that the atmosphere at most of these places is generally sleazy, drunken and lecherous. The two we list on p.193 are the best of the bunch, but even in them you need to be wary.

a set menu. It has lunch cruises with a band at 2.30pm, and twice-nightly dinner cruises (7.30pm & 10pm) with an "oriental" floor show, dervish-stye dancer, bellydancer and band. £E250, with promotional rates off-season.

CHEAP VENUES

Palmyra In the passage at 16 26th July St ☎ 0112 428 6660; map p.71. Dancers, singers and other acts. Used to be free from sharp practices (see box above), but has now unfortunately become as bad as the rest. Daily 11pm–4am. Entry £E50 including one beer.

Scheherazade 1 Sharia Alfi Bey; map p.71. The venue itself is a marvellous old vaudeville-style music hall, with a variety of acts, but the usual tricks are played (see box above), and waiters may even try to insist that snacks (lowest price £E20) are compulsory with every beer. Minimum charge £E60. Daily midnight–6am.

CLASSICAL, OPERA AND BALLET

Some classical music performances also take place in the Gumhorriya Theatre (see p.193).

Cairo Opera House Opera House Complex, Gezira ☎ 02 2739 0114, ⓦ cairoopera.org; map p.139. The chief centre for performing arts in the city, its main hall hosts performances by the Cairo Ballet Company (Sept–June) and prestigious foreign acts (anything from kabuki theatre to Broadway musicals). The smaller hall is used by the Cairo Symphony Orchestra (ⓦ cairo-symphony.com), who have weekly concerts, (usually Sat, Sept to mid-June). During July and Aug all events move to the marble-clad open-air theatre; a programme of youth concerts during this period includes everything from Nubian folk-dancing to Egyptian pop. Programme listings appear in *Egypt Today* and the *Al-Ahram* weekly, and are available in more detail from the ticket office. All tickets (£E50–100) should be booked several days in advance (office open daily 10am–3pm & 4–8pm). A jacket and tie are compulsory for men attending events in the main hall.

Manasterly Palace By the Nilometer, Roda Island ☎ 02 2363 1537; map p.127. Hosts some chamber music concerts, which also give you the chance to check out the interior of this mid-nineteenth-century Ottoman rococo palace.

KIDS' ATTRACTIONS

Aquarium Grotto Gabalaya Gardens, Sharia Gabalaya, Zamalek; map p.138. Assorted live and preserved tropical fish amid a labyrinth of passageways that children will love to explore, set in a landscaped garden that was once part of Empress Eugénie's (see p.141) palace grounds. The grottos are original, dating from 1867; the fish tanks were added by British zoologist and conservationist Stanley Flower at the beginning of the twentieth century. They won't impress serious aquarium buffs, but kids should enjoy it, and the attached gardens (same hours and ticket) are a welcome spot of green. Entrance £E1. Daily 10am–4pm.

Cairo Land Sharia Salah Salem, by Fustat Park ☎ 02 2532 4817; map p.116. A small and rather run-down amusement park, but relatively central. There's a mini-rollercoaster and a few other rides, all at low prices (£E3–5). Entrance £E3. Daily: winter 9am–midnight; summer 5pm–1am.

Cairo Puppet Theatre Ezbekiya Gardens, off Midan Ataba ☎ 02 2591 0954; map p.71. A traditional diversion, staging musical puppet versions of Sindbad the Sailor, Ali Baba and other favourites, usually lasting 90min. It's all in Arabic, but there's lots of music and the shows are spectacular enough for the language not to matter too much. Tickets £E10–15. Daily 6.30pm, but arrive for 6pm.

Cairo Zoo Sharia Nahdet Misr, Giza; map p.126. An impressive display of flamingos greets you on entry, and the zoo, formerly part of Khedive Ismail's palace grounds (see p.143) is reasonably humane, as zoos go, with quite large enclosures for most animals, the main exception being the lion house. There's also a hippo pond, which you can walk across, and children will enjoy helping to feed the camels or the elephants. Easily reached from downtown by bus (#8, #115, #124, #900, #998, and minibus #83, from

1

Abdel Mouneem Riyad terminal behind the Egyptian Museum). Avoid Fri and public holidays, when it's packed. £E20, video camera £E30, map £E1. Daily 9am–5pm.

Dreampark Tariq al-Fayoum al-Wahat (Fayoum– Wahat Rd), on the way to 6th October City, 20km southwest of Cairo, beyond the Giza pyramids ☎ 19355, ⓦ dreamparkegypt.com; map p.148. A big (150-acre) modern amusement park with lots of attractions including two rollercoasters (with views of the pyramids from the top), a water chute, dodgems and a little train, plus various fast-food outlets. Expect to pay around £E100 each way by taxi, or take bus #690 from Midan Ramses or a microbus from opposite Giza metro. Entry costs £E60–130, depending on how many rides are included (other rides can be paid for separately). Winter: Sat–Thurs 10am–7pm, Fri 10am–9pm; summer: Sat–Thurs 4pm–midnight, Fri noon–midnight; Ramadan daily 9pm–2am.

Dr Ragab's Pharaonic Village Reached via 3 Sharia Bahr al-Azam, El Moneeb ☎ 02 3572 2533, ⓦ pharaonicvillage .com; map p.127. A kitsch simulation of Ancient Egypt, located on Jacob Island, upriver from Roda. Visitors are taken on a three-hour (or longer) tour, on which you survey the Canal of Mythology (flanked by statues of gods) and see scores of costumed Egyptians performing tasks from their floating "time machines", before being shown around a replica temple and a nobleman's villa. There's also a 3-D cinema, and a dozen

mini-museums, dedicated to Hellenic, Coptic and Islamic civilization, ancient arts, mummification and (a little incongruously) Nasser, Sadat and Napoleon. If you don't take it too seriously, it's a fun place to visit, and quite educational, demonstrating how papyrus is made and how Ancient Egyptians put on their make-up. It's £E15–20 by cab from downtown) or take a bus (#987 from Ahmed Helmi behind Ramses Station, or #107 from Ataba). The nearest metro station is El-Monib, 2km south (a long walk or short cab ride). Entrance £E158–201 depending on the length of the tour. Daily: summer 9am–9pm; winter 9am–5pm;

National Circus Corniche al-Nil, Aguza ☎ 02 3347 0612; map p.138. Old-fashioned circus, with traditional acrobats, clowns, magicians and trapeze artists. Performances (in Arabic, but that won't matter very much) run from 8pm to 11pm daily except Wed (box office open 6–9pm). Tickets £E20–75.

Sindbad Amusement Park Sharia Josip Tito, Heliopolis, near Cairo Airport ☎ 02 2624 4001 or ☎ 02 2624 4002; map p.69. A relatively small but modern fairground whose 21 rides (£E3–5, or £E25 for all of them) include bumper cars, a Ferris wheel and a small rollercoaster, plus play areas for small children. Can get very crowded in summer. To get there, take the Heliopolis metro's Nozha Line from Ramses to the penultimate stop. Entrance £E5. Daily 10am–10pm.

RELIGIOUS FESTIVALS

Cairo's **religious festivals** (moulids) are quite accessible to outsiders, and lots of fun – although the Sufi presence has waned in recent years due to disapproval from religious fundamentalists, particularly Salafists. Many festivals begin with a *zaffa* (parade) of Sufis carrying banners, drums and tambourines, who later perform marathon *zikrs*, chanting and swaying themselves into the trance-like state known as *gazb*. Other traditional entertainers include acrobats, stick dancers and dancing horses, joined nowadays by DJs. The only problem in attending a moulid, aside from the crowds (don't bring valuables, or come alone if you're a woman), is finding out **dates**. Different events are related to the Islamic, Coptic or secular calendars, and sometimes to a particular day or week rather than a certain date, so details below should be double-checked locally.

MUSLIM FESTIVALS

Below is a list of Islamic festivals, ordered according to the Muslim calendar (see p.39).

Ashura (Islamic date 10 Moharram) The anniversary of the martyrdom of Al-Hussein (see p.94) is observed by the city's Sunni Muslims with prayers and charity; the wealthy often feed poor families, serving them personally to demonstrate humility. But aside from *zikrs* (Sufi chanting) outside Hussein's Mosque, there's little to see.

Nezlet al-Hagg (weeks following Eid al-Adha) The return of the pilgrims from Mecca once occasioned great festivities at Bab al-Futuh (see p.101) when they arrived back towards the end of the Islamic month of Safar (the month after Moharram). Nowadays, pilgrims are fêted individually when they return, their homes festooned with bunting and painted with haj scenes, but it's still customary to congregate below the Citadel a week later to render

thanksgiving *zikrs* in the evening.'

Moulid al-Nabi (12 Rabi al-Awwil). The prophet's birthday, celebrated in the evening of the day before – which is known as *Leylat Mubarak* (Blessed Night) – with spectacular processions, fireworks and performances by *munshids* (singers of poetry). Midan al-Hussein, the Rifai Mosque and Ezbekiya Gardens are the best spots to catch the celebrations.

Moulid of al-Hussein This moulid, celebrating Mohammed's grandson Al-Hussein and centred on his mosque (see p.94), gathers pace over a fortnight, culminating in its *leyla kebira* (big night) on the last Wed of the Islamic month of Rabi al-Tani. Hussein's Mosque in Khan al-Khalili is surrounded by dozens of *zikrs* and amplified *munshids*, plus all the usual sideshows.

Moulid of Saiyida Sukayna Held at the Mosque of Saiyida Sukayna on Sharia al-Khalifa (see p.118)

culminating on the second Wed of the Islamic month of Gumad al-Awwil. A smaller affair than that of Sukayna's father, Al-Hussein, and largely confined to celebrants from the local neighbourhood.

Moulid of Saiyida Ruqayya Held at the Mosque of Saiyida Ruqayya at much the same time as the nearby moulid of her niece, Saiyida Sukayna (see above), the *leyla kebira* of Saiyida Ruqayya falling the day after Saiyida Sukayna's.

Moulid of al-Rifai Held at Al-Rifai Mosque (see p.114) on a Thurs and Fri in the middle of the month of Gumad al-Tani, this moulid is attended by Sufis of the Rifai order from all over Egypt. Those carrying black flags belong to the mainstream Rifaiyah; subsects include the Awlad Ilwan (once famous for thrusting nails into their eyes and swallowing hot coals) and the Sa'adiya (snake charmers, who used to allow their sheikh to ride over them on horseback).

Moulid of Saiyida Nafisa Compared with the Moulid of al-Rifai, Sufi dervishes are less evident at this smaller but equally colourful event, held at the Saiyida Nafisa Mosque (see p.118) at variable dates towards the end of the month of Gumad al-Tani, a week or two after the Al-Rifai moulid.

Moulid of Saiyida Zeinab Cairo's wildest moulid, in honour of the city's "patron saint", held at her mosque (see p.117). Attracting up to a million people, the moulid is a high-octane blend of intense devotion and sheer enjoyment, with up to three weeks of celebrations leading to the *yom kebir* ("big day"), on the last Tues of the month of Ragab, and the *leyla kebira* (the subsequent Wed evening).

Moulid of Sheikh al-Dashuti (26 Rajab) A small, local moulid, held at the Mosque of Sheikh al-Dashuti on Sharia Faggala, near the Sakakini Palace (see p.143).

Leylat al-Mirag (27 Ragab). This celebrates a journey

Mohammed made on this night from Mecca to Jerusalem (Koran 17:1); according to legend, he travelled on the back of a winged beast called al-Buraq. The event is commemorated with night-long prayers and *zikrs* in the mosques, and outside the Abdin Palace.

Moulid of Imam al-Shafi'i One of the city's major moulids, held at the Mausoleum of Imam al-Shafi'i in the Southern Cemetery (see p.119). There's a long run-up over the preceding two or three weeks which gathers momentum as it approaches the *yom kebir* (big day), held around the imam's birthday on the Islamic date of 4 Sha'ban, and culminating on the following Wed.

Mid-Sha'ban (15 Sha'ban). This is believed to be the time when Allah determines the fate of every human over the ensuing year. Some people mark it with prayers and fasting, while many visit the Mausoleum of Imam al-Shafi'i (in the aftermath of the moulid just held there) in the hope of gaining *baraka* (the saint's blessing).

Moulid of Sidi Ali al-Bayoumi (early Oct). One of the few Muslim festivals held according to the Western calendar rather than the Islamic one, this is a colourful affair in which a parade of dervishes proceeds from al-Hussein's Mosque to Bab al-Futuh and thence on into the Husseiniya quarter.

COPTIC FESTIVALS

Coptic festivals are primarily religious, with fewer diversions than Muslim ones; the feasts centred around Easter (see ✪ copticchurch.net for dates), Christmas (Jan 7), Epiphany (Jan 19) and the Feast of Annunciation (March 21) have little to offer, unless you're into church services. There's more to enjoy at two festivals in Old Cairo: the **Moulid of Mari Girgis** at the round Church of St George (April 23, St George's Day) and the **Moulid of the Holy Family** at the Church of St Sergius (June 1).

SHOPPING

Cairo is a good place to buy **crafts**, and particularly **clothes** and **textile** products, and is often a good deal cheaper than places like Luxor, Hurghada or Sharm el-Sheikh. Scams and trickery abound, however, and you should never take anyone's word for anything – "let the buyer beware" applies even more here than it does elsewhere in the world. In many places, you'll have to **haggle**, but prices can be very low indeed; on the other hand, the quality of materials and workmanship can be correspondingly low, so always give anything a good once-over before you start bargaining.

SOUVENIRS, ANTIQUES AND COLLECTABLES

Ahmed el Dabba 5 Sikket al-Badestan, Khan al-Khalili ☎02 2590 7823; map p.95. Lots of belle époque, fin-de-siècle items including cigarette boxes, crockery and chandeliers, plus Egyptian and Middle Eastern inlaid chests and furniture, and Persian rugs. Mon–Sat 2–8pm.

Awlad Azouz Salaam 96 Sharia Ahmed Maher, 150m west of Bab Zwayla, Islamic Cairo ☎02 2514 0517; map p.102.. Hole-in-the-wall workshop making and selling

horse equipment, including decorative saddles, reins and horsewhips. Mon–Sat 10am–8pm.

Delta Papyrus Center 3rd floor, 21 Sharia al-Guriya (part of Sharia al-Muizz), Islamic Cairo ☎02 2512 0517; map p.102. If you really want a painted papyrus, the next best thing to Dr Ragab (see p.196) is this shop set up by one of his pupils selling good hand-painted papyruses with pharaonic, Islamic and Orientalist motifs, most copied from tombs and paintings. "Come by yourself, not with a guide or you'll pay more," they quite frankly tell you. Mon–Sat 11am–9pm, Sun 11am–6pm (ring bell).

1

Icon Art Gallery Souk al-Fustat, Old Cairo ☎0122 130 2824; map p.127. Little bric-a-brac shop selling anything from old postcards and photographs to bakelite telephones and brass portraits of Nasser. Worth a browse, though prices are high. Daily 10am–6pm.

Old Shop Sikket al-Badestan, Khan al-Khalili ☎02 2787 0378; map p.95. Large, dusty and very browsable mix of old and new knick-knacks, glassware, furniture, record players and bric-a-brac. Daily 10am–9pm.

Oum el Dounia 1st floor, 3 Sharia Talaat Harb, Downtown ☎02 2393 8273; map p.70. Excellent shop for books on Cairo, Egyptian music CDs, Muski glass (see p.46), Bedouin dresses, bags, purses and all kinds of crafts, especially soft ones. Slightly pricey, but the quality matches. Daily 10am–9pm.

Salon el Ferdaos 33 Sharia Abdel Khaliq Sarwat, Downtown; map p.71. A barber with a counter at the front selling old stamps, coins and banknotes. Mon–Sat 4–9pm.

JEWELLERY

Adly Fam Muski, Khan al-Khalili ☎02 2592 1500; map p.95. Jeweller selling silver figurines, chunky bangles, silver rings and gold cartouches, but you'll need good bargaining skills. Mon–Sat 11am–7pm.

Boutros Trading Sikket Khan al-Khalili ☎02 2590 4153; map p.95. Old family firm selling silver jewellery and other silverware, mostly priced by weight, including rings, bracelets, spoons, plates, bowls and some lovely little pillboxes inlaid with mother-of-pearl and abalone. Mon–Sat 11am–7pm.

Yazejian Opposite the Khan al-Khalili Restaurant, Sikket al-Badestan, Khan al-Khalili ☎02 2591 2321; map p.95. Reliable shop for gold jewellery, including gold cartouche pendants (see below), sold by weight, so expect to pay anything from £E300 to £E2500, depending on how big you want your cartouche. Mon–Sat 2.30–7.30pm.

CLOTHES

Al Trapiche 36 Al-Ghuriya Sharia al-Muizz, Islamic Cairo ☎02 2510 9331; map p.102. The last fez workshop

in Cairo, kept alive by sales to five-star hotels and tourists. Various grades of fez are available, the cheapest going for just £E20. The fez, or *tarboush fassi*, originally from Fez in Morocco, was a mark of Ottoman allegiance, which came to represent the secular, Westernized Egyptian, as opposed to the turbaned traditionalist. Under Nasser it fell from fashion, stigmatized as a badge of the old regime. Waiters and entertainers are the main wearers nowadays, and this is where they get them. Mon–Sat 10am–9pm.

Al-Wikalah 73 Sharia Gawhar al-Qayid, just off Sharia al-Muski, Islamic Cairo ☎02 2589 7443; map p.95. Well-made and good-value bellydancing costumes: a lavishly beaded and sequinned bra and hipband, with a skirt and veil, costs £E800–2000; the more you buy, the lower the price. There's a woman to help fit you, and anything they don't have in stock they can make within a few days. Mon–Sat 11am–9pm.

Amira al-Khattan 27 Sharia Basra, Mohandiseen ☎02 3749 0322; map p.138. Top-notch, bespoke bellydancing costumes. A full costume will set you back US$500–600. Visits by appointment only.

Atlas Silks Sikket al-Badestan, Khan al-Khalili ☎02 2590 6139; map p.95. Made-to-order garments in handwoven fabrics with intricate braidwork; slippers can be made to order too (allow several weeks; keep all receipts). Their cheapest kaftans and *galabiyyas* are dearer than most garments in other shops, but much higher quality. Mon–Sat 10am–8pm.

Auf 116–118 Sharia al-Azhar (on the north side by the pedestrian bridge), Islamic Cairo ☎02 2590 6857; map p.95. Large store stocking a wide assortment of ready-made clothes at reasonable prices, including black dresses with Bedouin-style embroidery, plain white cotton *galabiyyas* and headscarfs, plus cloth by the metre, all at fixed prices. Daily 9am–9pm.

CARPETS, TEXTILES AND FURNISHINGS

APE (Association for the Protection of the Environment) 23 Souk al-Fustat, Old Cairo ☎0122 911 1937, ⓦ ape.org.eg;

ALL THAT GLITTERS

In Islamic Cairo, the **Goldsmiths Bazaar** (Souk al-Sagha) covers Sharia al-Muizz between Sharia al-Muski and Sultan Qalaoun's complex, with scores more shops tucked away on Sikket al-Badestan and Sikket Khan al-Khalili. There are also good silversmiths in the Wikala al-Gawarhergia. Jewellery comes in all kinds of styles, and gold and silver are sold by the gram, with a percentage added on for workmanship. The current ounce **price of gold** is printed in the daily Egyptian Gazette; one troy ounce equals about 31 grams. Barring antiques, all gold work is stamped with Arabic numerals indicating purity: usually 21 carat for Bedouin, Nubian or fellaheen jewellery; 18 carat for Middle Eastern and European-style charms and chains. Sterling silver (80 or 92.5 percent) is likewise stamped, while a gold camel sign in the shop window indicates that the items in the shop are gold-plated brass. **Cartouche pendants** (made from all of these metals) can be inscribed with your name in Ancient Egyptian hieroglyphs; as each syllable has its own symbol, longer names cost more to inscribe.

1

GETTING SNUG WITH A RUG

Pure wool knotted **carpets** and kilims (woven rugs) are an expensive (and bulky) purchase, so serious buyers should read up on the subject before buying one. For cheaper woven rugs and tapestries, the suburban village of **Kerdassa** (see p.160) replicates every style imaginable. The carpet factories around Saqqara – a stopover for many tour groups visiting that ancient site – are all imitators of the famous **Wissa Wassef school** (see p.160). Beware of stitched-together seams and gaps in the weave (hold pieces up against the light) and unfast colours – if any colour wipes off on a damp cloth, the dyes will run when the rug is washed.

map p.127. Run by an NGO working with Cairo's *garbage-pickers*, this shop sells recycled rubbish turned into bags, soft toys, patchwork quilts and other products. Profits go towards education, healthcare and improving life for people in Cairo's poorest social group. Daily 10am–5pm.

AUEED (Association of Upper Egypt for Education and Development) 26 Souk al-Fustat, Old Cairo ☎0122 911 1937, ⊛upperegypt.org; map p.127. Embroidery and woodcarvings by women from Upper Egyptian villages, marketed by an NGO. As in other shops in the Souk al-Fustat, everything is sold at fixed prices. Daily 10am–5pm.

El Assiouty 118 26th July St, Zamalek (entrance in Sharia Aziz Osman) ☎02 2737 1609, ⊛fakhryelassioutycarpets .com; map p.138. Upmarket carpet shop, founded in 1949, whose customers include embassies and diplomats. All the carpets and kilims are Egyptian (though some incorporate Persian designs), and priced by the square metre. Mon–Sat 10am–3pm & 6–9pm.

El Sayd Saleh Ragab Tentmakers' Bazaar (next to Mahmoud al-Kurdi mosque), Sharia al-Muizz, Islamic Cairo; map p.107. Slightly different from the other shops in the Tentmakers' Bazaar, selling bags, pouches and pocketed wall-hangings made out of moulid tent material. No fixed hours, but usually at least noon–5pm daily.

Fair Trade Egypt Apartment 8, 27 Sharia Yehia Ibrahim, Zamalek ☎02 2736 5123 ⊛fairtradeegypt .org; map p.138. Non-profit organization selling crafts made by people from poor communities across Egypt, with a particularly good line in clothes, textiles and kilims. Sat–Thurs 9am–8pm, Fri 10am–6pm.

Fawzi Nouno Tentmakers' Bazaar (north end, west side), Sharia al-Muizz, Islamic Cairo ☎02 2512 7949; map p.107. One of a number of shops in the Tentmakers' Bazaar selling appliqué pillowcases (£E25–75), bedspreads (£E700–1500) and wall hangings (£E200–400), a traditional Cairene craft. Much cheaper is the riotously patterned printed tent fabric used for marquees at moulids (£E6–8/metre). It's worth looking around at what the neighbouring shops have as well, and comparing quality and prices. Mon–Sat 10am–10pm.

GLASS AND CERAMICS

Hassan el Dao'ur 14 Haret al-Birkedar, outside Bab al-Futuh, Islamic Cairo ☎0122 163 0086; map p.97.

Hand-blown Muski glass in navy blue, turquoise, aquamarine, green and purple, at very low prices. The factory is just up the street; they usually allow tourists in (Sat–Thurs 9am–3pm) to watch the glass being blown. To find Haret al-Birkedar, come out of Bab al-Futuh from Sharia al-Muizz, cross the main street (Sharia Galal), and it's about 20m to your right. Daily 9am–10pm.

Saiyid Mageest 8 Sikket Khan al-Khalili ☎02 2592 6258; map p.95. Main outlet for hand-blown Muski glass in the Khan, selling products from factories in the cemetery north of Bab al-Nasr (see p.101). Daily 11am–9pm.

SPICES, HERBS, SOAPS AND PERFUMES

Abd El Rahman Harraz 1 Midan Bab al-Khalq, Islamic Cairo ☎02 2512 8008; map p.71. This venerable herbalist stocks everything from rice and beans to elderflower and pink peppercorns, dates and fresh ginger, dried lizards, frankincense and flowers of sulphur. It's 100m from the Islamic Art Museum as you walk towards Bab Zwayla. Mon–Sat 9am–9pm.

Abdul Latif Mahmoud Harraz 39 Sharia Ahmed Maher, Islamic Cairo; map p.71. The most famous herbalist in Cairo, run by the same family since 1885, this is a dusty, atmospheric place with drawers and jars full of all sorts of herbs, spices, seeds and resins, from *karkaday* and ginseng to gum arabic and frankincense. It stands opposite an Ottoman *sabil*, 200m west of Bab Zwayla (see p.105) in the direction of the Islamic Art Museum. Mon–Sat 10am–8pm.

Karama Perfumes 114 Sharia al-Azhar (corner of Sharia al-Muizz), and also two doors north on Sharia al-Muizz, Islamic Cairo ☎02 2590 2336; map p.95. Most of the other perfume shops in Cairo buy their essential oils here, and then adulterate them with cooking oil before selling them at inflated prices to tourists. It's worth buying your perfume here at source even though they may also sometimes try to overcharge foreigners. Essential oils such as rose or jasmine should cost around 70pt a gram. Mon–Sat 10am–10pm.

Nefertari 15 Sharia al-Marashly, Zamalek ☎02 2735 0480 (see map, p.138) and 27 Souk al-Fustat, Old Cairo ☎0122 210 7736, ⊛nefertaribodycare.com; map p.127. Handmade soaps, organic cotton towels, loofahs, back brushes and massagers, and other bath-time luxuries, all Egyptian made and cruelty-free. Mon–Sat 10am–6pm.

Ragab el Attar 40 & 62 Sharia al-Azhar, east of Midan Ataba ☎ 02 2589 0444, ⊛ ragabelattar.com; map p.71. Two busy branches (one by Midan Ataba, the other by Sharia Bur Said), selling whole and ground spices, incense, joss sticks, and *'amar al-din* (Syrian apricot fruit leather). Mon–Sat 10am–10pm.

BOOKS, MAPS AND NEWSPAPERS

Cairo has plenty of shops selling books in English, many published here by the American University in Cairo (AUC), whose range of Egyptian literature in English, as well as non-fiction books about Cairo and Egypt, is excellent. The best downtown newsstand is on Sharia Mohammed Mahmoud, opposite the AUC entrance, which carries British dailies (usually one day late), the *International Herald Tribune*, *USA Today* and even sometimes the *New York Times*. It also has a pile of secondhand books, but the best place to look for those is the book market in the northeast corner of Ezbekiya Gardens by Midan Ataba (see map, p.71), which has many titles in English.

Al-Ahram 165 Sharia Mohammed Farid, Downtown ☎ 02 2390 4499; map p.71. An outlet for politics textbooks published by *Al-Ahram* newspaper (see p.38) and strategic think-tank; also sells a few maps and has a section of classic English literature downstairs. Daily except Fri 9am–5pm.

Anglo-Egyptian Bookshop 165 Sharia Mohammed Farid, Downtown ☎ 02 2391 4337; map p.71. Academic bookshop, specializing in Arab politics, history and culture, plus some novels, art books and maps. Mon–Sat 9am–8pm.

AUC Bookshop AUC old campus, corner of Sharia Qasr al-Aini and Sharia Sheikh Rihan, Downtown ☎ 02 2797 5929, ⊛ aucpress.com; map p.70. The obvious place to look for AUC publications, with a huge range of stuff on all things Egyptian, plus novels, maps, travel guides and dictionaries. The bookshop entrance may be closed due to revolutionary action, in which case (so long as the bookshop itself is open) access is via the campus's main entrance on Sharia Mohammed Mahmoud (passport needed for entry). There's another branch at 16 Sharia Mohammed Ibn Thakib, Zamalek. Sat–Thurs 10am–6pm, Fri 2–6pm.

Dar al-Salam Publishers 120 Sharia al-Azhar, opposite the Al-Ghuri Palace, Islamic Cairo ☎ 02 2593 2820, ⊛ dar-asalam.com; map p.95. Islamic publisher, frequented by lots of earnest young men in beards and crocheted skullcaps, with some books and pamphlets in English (just next to the door). Among their publications, *Islam and Sex* (£E6.50) is worth perusing. Daily 9am–8pm.

Diwan 159 26th July St, on the corner of Sharia Ishaq Yaakoub, Zamalek ☎ 02 2736 2582, ⊛ diwanegypt .com; map p.138. Bright, modern shop with a wide

selection of books, CDs and DVDs (including a small selection of classic and modern Egyptian films on DVD with subtitles), and a coffee shop. Daily 9am–11.30pm.

Lehnert & Landrock 44 Sharia Sherif, Downtown ☎ 02 2393 7606, ⊛ lehnertandlandrock.net; map p.71. One of the best places to look for maps of Cairo and Egypt, in addition to postcards and greeting cards. They also have a section of prints of old photos of Cairo and Egypt at the back. Daily 10am–7pm.

Romancia 32 Sharia Shagar al-Durr, corner of Sharia Ismail Mohammed, Zamalek ☎ 02 2735 0492; map p.138. For such a poky little shop this place packs an awful lot in – paperback novels (pulp and literary), coffee-table books on Egypt, maps, British newspapers, magazines such as *Time*, *Newsweek* and *The Economist*, and stationery as well. Sat–Thurs 8am–8pm, Fri 9.30am–8pm.

Shorouk 1 Midan Talaat Harb, Downtown ☎ 02 2391 2480; map p.70. Centrally located and very handy for maps, Egyptian novels in translation, books on Egypt and the latest books in English. Daily 9am–11pm.

Zamalek Bookshop 19 Sharia Shagar al-Durr, opposite Pub 28, Zamalek ☎ 02 2736 9197; map p.138. A good place to look for AUC publications, Egyptian novels in English translation, books on Egypt and Cairo in general, plus stationery and British newspapers. Mon–Sat 9am–8pm.

LIQUOR AND SMOKERS' SUPPLIES

Liquor stores are closed during Ramadan (see p.39), though Drinkies still does home deliveries. Refilling stalls all over the city can recharge a lighter for £E1–2, or replace flints for 50pt–£E1.

Babik In the passage by 39 Sharia Talaat Harb, Downtown ☎ 02 2393 5058; map p.71. Wooden tobacco pipes, lighters and numerous brands of cigarette papers and other smokers' requisites. Mon–Sat 9am–9pm.

Drinkies 41 Sharia Talaat Harb, at 26th July St, Downtown ☎ 19330 or ☎ 0800 100 1001, ⊛ alahrambeverages.com; map p.71. Retail outlet for Al Ahram, Egypt's biggest booze company, selling all their brands, including Stella, Sakkara and Heineken, plus wines and spirits. There's another branch at 162a 26th July St (by *Maison Thomas*) in Zamalek (see map, p.138), and they also have a home delivery service (daily 8.30am–2am). Sat–Thurs 10am–midnight, Fri 2pm–midnight.

Nicolakis Corner of Sharia Talaat Harb and Sharia Suq al-Tawfiqiya, Downtown ☎ 02 2576 7419 (see map, p.71). A decent selection of wines, sometimes at slightly better prices than Drinkies; also beer, *zbiba* (Egyptian ouzo) and dodgy lookalike spirits. Daily 7am–10.30pm.

Orphanides 9 26th July St (opposite the High Court), Downtown ☎ 02 2579 9247 and 23 Sharia Bassiouni, Downtown (see map, p.71). Booze store selling beer, wine, *zbiba* and Egyptian brandy, but mostly of interest for

1

the outrageous lookalike brands of spirit it sells (Chefas Rigal, Gorodons, Finelandia Vodka of Egypt and the like), which you definitely shouldn't drink (see p.38). Daily noon–1am.

Souk Bayn al-Qasrayn Bayn al-Qasrayn, on the east side, just south of the Sabil-Kuttab of Abd al-Rahman, Islamic Cairo; map p.95. A covered passage full of shops selling *sheesha* pipes. Prices range from £E25 to £E150, depending on the size and quality; the ones with stainless steel rather than brass fittings are better made and more durable. Neighbouring shops also sell *sheeshas*, but are usually slightly pricier. Mon–Sat 10am–10pm.

MUSICAL INSTRUMENTS AND RECORDINGS

Cairo is a good place to buy traditional musical instruments such as the *kanoon* (dulcimer), oud (lute), *nai* (flute), *rabab* (viol), *mismare baladi* (oboe), tabla (drum), *riq* and *duf* (tambourines; the latter is played by Sufis). There's a whole slew of instrument shops at the top end of Sharia Qalaa (officially renamed Sharia Mohammed Ali, though everyone uses the old name), off Midan Ataba. A good selection of Arabic music on CD is available at Diwan bookshop (see p.201).

Beit al-Oud 164 Sharia Qalaa, off Midan Ataba ⊤0100 686 5192; map p.71. The most renowned and best established of the several oud (lute) makers along this stretch of Sharia Qalaa. An oud here will set you back anywhere from £E150 to over ten times that much, depending on quality and decoration. Daily 11am–11pm.

Gamal al-Sawy Next to Fishawi's, Khan al-Khalili ⊤02 2692 5756; map p.95. Small shop selling bellydancing CDs, DVDs, tapes and videos of the great artistes. Daily 24hr.

Saut al-Musiqa 168 Sharia Qalaa, off Midan Ataba ⊤02 2390 7760; map p.71. The "Sound of Music" (as the name translates) is one of the better musical instrument stores at the top end of Sharia Qalaa, selling drums, ouds and other instruments. Daily 10am–midnight.

Sono Cairo 3 Sharia al-Borsa al-Gadida (an alley between Sharia Talaat Harb and Sharia Qasr al-Nil), Downtown ⊤02 2391 3253; and in the arcade of the Continental-Savoy Hotel on Midan Opera, Downtown ⊤02 2392 1916, Ⓦsonocairo.com; map p.71. Retail outlet for the Sono Cairo label, including quality recordings of Umm Kalthoum, Abdel Wahaab and orchestral music. Also has a good selection of CDs, and DVDs and video CDs of Egyptian and foreign movies (video CDs are much cheaper than DVDs, but don't usually offer subtitles). Daily 10am–10pm.

CONTEMPORARY ART

Espace Karim Francis 1 Sharia al-Sherifein, Downtown ⊤02 2391 6357 Ⓦkarimfrancis.com; map p.71. Not just painting and sculpture, but installations, video art and anything new and fresh. Daily except Fri 1–8pm.

Mashrabia Gallery 1st floor, 8 Sharia Champollion, Downtown ⊤02 2578 4494, Ⓦmashrabiagallery.org; map p.70. Well-established gallery exhibiting works by Egypt's top contemporary artists, especially those working with indigenous styles and materials; also shows work by foreign artists. Daily except Fri 11am–8pm.

Safar Khan Gallery 6 Sharia Brazil, Zamalek ⊤02 2735 3314 Ⓦsafarkhan.com; map p.138. Fine modern art by prominent Egyptian artists, with a permanent collection going back to the 1930s as well as regular exhibitions. Mon–Sat 10am–2pm & 5–9pm.

Townhouse Gallery 10 Sharia Nabrawy, off Sharia Champollion, Downtown ⊤02 2576 8086 Ⓦthetownhousegallery.com; map p.70. Cairo's leading gallery for contemporary art, with regular exhibitions, a stable of good artists and a library of art books. Sat–Wed 10am–2pm & 6–9pm, Fri 6–9pm.

Zamalek Art Gallery 2nd floor, 11 Sharia Brazil, Zamalek ⊤02 2735 1240, Ⓦzamalekartgallery.com; map p.138. One of the best places to see (and buy) work by contemporary Egyptian painters and sculptors. Holds monthly exhibitions, promotes up-and-coming young talent and has a permanent collection of work by pioneering Egyptian artists. Daily except Fri 10.30am–9pm.

DIRECTORY

Banks and exchange There are plenty of ATMs that accept foreign cards, especially around Sharia Talaat Harb, but all over town too. Changing cash or travellers' cheques is usually quick and easy at the 24hr Bank Misr exchange bureaux in the *Ramses Hilton* and the *Shepheard*. Alternatively there are Forex bureaux dotted around town, including a couple on Abdel Khalek Sarwat east of Sharia Talaat Harb, a handful around the junction of Sharia Qasr el-Nil and Sharia Mohammed Farid, and another group on the corner of Sharia el-Gumhoriyya with Midan Opera, which are your best bet for changing currencies such as Libyan dinars, Israeli shekels or Sudanese pounds. Thomas Cook's main office is at 17 Sharia Bassiouni ⊤02 2576 6982 (daily 8am–5pm; full branch list at Ⓦthomascookegypt.com/our_branches.aspx); American Express is at 15 Sharia Qasr al-Nil (daily except Sun–Thurs 9am–4pm; Ramadan 9am–2.30pm). For international transfers, MoneyGram's agents in Cairo include Sphinx Trading at 2 Sharia Sherif and branches of Banque du Caire (for example at 20 Sharia Talaat Harb and 47 Sharia Qasr al-Nil); Western Union's agents are International Business Associates (for example at 1079 Corniche al-Nil in Garden City or downtown at 4

CAIRO'S MARKETS

Although the bazaars deal in more exotic goods, Cairo's markets provide an arresting spectacle, free of the touristy slickness that prevails around Khan al-Khalili. Street markets in central Cairo can be found at Bab al-Luq (on the south side of Midan Falaki; mostly food), Sharia Tawfiqia (off Midan Orabi; fruit, veg and car spares), at the eastern end of Sheikh Rihan (by Sharia Bur Said; food) and the northern end of Sharia Qalaa (phones, electronics, some food) – all do business through the night, accompanied by local coffee houses. With the kilo price displayed on most food stalls, you shouldn't have to bargain unless they try to overcharge. Elsewhere haggling is de rigueur. Canary and budgerigar fanciers may also want to check out Cairo's **bird markets** (10am–2.30pm), which are named after the days on which they're held, including Souk al-Ahad (Sun; Giza Station) and Souk Itnayn w Khamis (Mon & Thurs), in the Abu Rish area of Saiyida Zeinab (see map, p.126). Souk al- Gom'a (see below) also has a bird market in its animal section.

Imam al-Shafi'i Market On and around Sharia Imam al-Shafi'i, Southern Cemetery, Islamic Cairo. Clothes are the mainstay of this street market, which straggles for 1km along the road leading from Al-Basatin to the Imam's mausoleum in the Southern Cemetery area. Market day is Fri, and Fri mornings are by far the busiest time.

Paper Market Sharia al-Geish near Midan Ataba. This daily **market** sells not only all types of paper but also dyed leather, card and other stationery and art materials.

Souk al-Gom'a Southern Cemetery area, south of Islamic Cairo. Once a huge, sprawling flea-market, this market was largely curtailed by the Mubarak regime.

What remains is the pet and livestock market by the Salah Salem overpass, south of the Citadel (see map, p.116), which to a certain extent merges into the Imam al-Shafi'i Market (see above), while half a kilometre to the southeast, junk and furnituire stalls have started to return to the far end of the old Souk al-Gom'a area, although it remains a far smaller affair than before.

Wikalat al-Balah (Souk Bulaq) On and around Sharia Bulaq al-Gadida, Bulaq, behind the Corniche about 200m north of 26th July Street. For secondhand clothes as well as fabrics (from hand-loomed silk to cheap offcuts), tools and much else, you can't beat Bulaq's bustling daily street market.

Sharia Hassan Basha al-Memmary off Sharia Bassiouni) and branches of the Arab African International Bank (for example downtown at 44 Sharia Abdel Khaliq Sarwat, or 54d Sharia al-Gumhorriya at Sharia Alfi Bey).

Cinemas Cheap downtown venues (££10–15), mostly showing a mix of Egyptian and Hollywood films (the latter usually dubbed into Arabic), include Cosmos, 12 Emad al-Din (☎ 02 2574 2177); Diana, 17 Sharia Alfi Bey (☎ 02 2592 4727); and Metro, 35 Sharia Talaat Harb (☎ 02 2393 7566). Plusher venues (££15–25), with a/c and no-smoking, no-chattering rules, include Al-Tahrir, on Sharia Tahrir, Dokki (☎ 02 3335 4726) and the Ramses Hilton cinema in the mall opposite the *Ramses Hilton* hotel (☎ 02 2574 7435). For cinema listings (though not comprehensive), see the weekly English edition of *Al-Ahram*. The Cairo International Film Festival (ⓦ cairofilmfest.org) is held in late autumn.

Courier services EMS, opposite the west side of Ataba post office, in Sharia al-Bedak (daily 24hr) promises worldwide delivery in three to four working days. Private firms (faster but more expensive) include DHL, 38 Abdel Khaliq Sarwat (☎ 02 2393 2145, ⓦ dhlegypt.com), with branches citywide, and UPS, c/o Maadi Express Center, 8 Rd 78, Ma'adi (☎ 02 2981 5099, ⓦ ups.com).

Cultural centres American Research Center in Egypt, 1st floor, 2 Midan Simon Bolivar, Garden City (☎ 02 2794 8239, ⓦ arce.org) has lectures on Egyptian history. The Egyptian

Centre for International Cultural Cooperation (ECIC), 11 Sharia Shagar al-Durr, Zamalek (☎ 02 2736 5419, ⓔ egycenter2008@yahoo.com; daily except Fri 10am–3pm & 5–9pm) organizes exhibitions, recitals and occasional tours. Maulana Azad Centre for Indian Culture (MACIC), by 23 Sharia Talaat Harb (☎ 02 2393 3396; Sun–Thurs 10.30am–5.30pm), has a library (borrowing for members only), and also offers yoga classes. The Netherlands–Flemish Institute, 1 Sharia Mahmoud Azmi, Zamalek (☎ 02 2738 2522, ⓦ institutes.leiden.edu/nvic), has lectures in English about Egypt (Sept–June Thurs 6pm).

Dentists Dr Avedis Djeghalian, 6 Sharia Abdel Hamid Said ☎ 02 2577 7909; Dr Samih Barsoum, 7 26th July St (at Sharia Emad al-Din) ☎ 02 2589 8303.

Doctors Dr Moustafa Chakankiry, *Marriott Hotel* clinic, Zamalek ☎ 02 2739 4625; Dr Samir Kabil, 41 Sharia Talaat Harb (cnr 26th July St) ☎ 02 2392 9846. The US embassy maintains a list of doctors in Cairo, which can usually be found online (currently at ⓦ photos.state.gov/libraries/egypt/19452/pdfs/List_of_Doctors.pdf, for example); the Australian embassy has a shorter list on its web information page at ⓦ egypt.embassy.gov.au/cairo/EgyptInfo.html.

Embassies and consulates Australia, 11th floor, World Trade Centre, 1191 Corniche al-Nil, Bulaq, 200m north of the 26th July Bridge ☎ 02 2575 0444, ⓦ egypt.embassy.gov.au;

1

Canada, 26 Sharia Kamel al-Shenawi, Garden City ☎02 2791 8700, ⌨ canadainternational.gc.ca/egypt-egypte; Ireland, 22 Sharia Hassan Assem, Zamalek ☎02 2735 8264, ⌨ embassyofireland.org.eg; Israel, embassy closed following 2011 attack (see p.142), and still seeking suitable premises at time of writing; Jordan, 6 Sharia Gohini (aka Sharia Bassem al-Kateb), Dokki, two blocks west of the *Sheraton* ☎02 2748 5566, ⌨ jordanembassycairo.gov.jo; Libya, 7 Sharia Saleh al-Ayoub, Zamalek ☎02 2735 1269; New Zealand, 8th floor, North Tower, Nile City Towers, 2005C Corniche al-Nil, Rod al-Farag ☎02 2461 6000, ⌨ nzembassy.com/egypt; South Africa, Building #11, Intersection of Roads 200 & 203, Ma'adi ☎02 2535 3000, ⌨ saembassy-egypt.com; Sudan, 1 Sharia Mohammed Fahmi al-Sayed, Garden City ☎02 2794 9661 (visas issued in 24hr; apply mornings with two passport photos and a letter of recommendation from your embassy, which may charge for issuing it); UK, 7 Sharia Ahmed Ragheb, Garden City ☎02 2791 6000, ⌨ ukinegypt.fco.gov. uk; USA, 5 Sharia Tawfik Diab, Garden City ☎02 2797 3300, ⌨ cairo.usembassy.gov.

Football Cairo's two premier league teams, Ahly and Zamalek, play in season (Sept–May) at the Cairo Stadium in Medinet Nasr (see p.144), the most exciting fixture being the Ahly vs Zamalek derby (buy tickets well in advance).

Golf Cairo and the surrounding region have a number of golf courses. The most central is the eighteen-hole course at the Gezira Sporting Club (☎02 2735 6000; £E50 plus day membership of £E100). The *Mena House Oberoi Hotel* (☎02 3377 3222) has an eighteen-hole course in the shadow of the Giza Pyramids, though this has been closed for renewal (expected to reopen in 2013), and there are a couple more around the ring road out past Heliopolis: the eighteen-hole course at Katameya Heights (☎02 2758 0512 to 17, ⌨ katameyaheights.com), and a 27-hole course at the *JW Marriott Hotel* (☎02 2046 5624). You'll find further information on Cairo's golf courses at ⌨ touregypt.net/golfcourses.htm.

Hammams Hammam el Arbaa, 5 Sharia al-Ansari (aka Sharia al-Hammamat), Bulaq ☎02 2986 0588 (daily: women 9am–5pm; men 6pm–6am). The street is by a juice shop on the left (west) side 600m up Sharia Bulaq al-Gadid (where it forks), which runs north from 26th July St opposite the Abu'l'Ila Mosque.

Hospitals Anglo-American Hospital, 3 Sharia Hadiqet El Zohreya by Cairo Tower, Gezira ☎02 2735 6162, ☎02 2735 6163 or ☎02 2735 6165; Al-Salam International Hospital, on the Corniche in Ma'adi ☎02 2303 0501; Cairo Medical Centre, Sharia al-Ansari, just off Sharia Higaz by Midan Roxi, Heliopolis ☎02 2450 9800. Public ambulances (☎123) will take you for free to whatever hospital is the nearest, or to one of your choice for a small fee.

Internet access Hany, 16 Abdel Khaliq Sarwat (daily 11am–6pm; £E2/hr); Inter Club, in the passage by 12 Sharia Talaat Harb (by *Estoril* restaurant; Sat–Thurs

9am–midnight, Fri 4.30pm–midnight; £E5/hr); Zamalek Center, 25 Sharia Ismail Mohammed, Zamalek (daily 8am–midnight; £E5/hr); Café Paris, Bustan Centre, Sharia Bustan (daily 9am–11pm; £E6/hr).

Language schools Arabic lessons are offered by: International Language Institute (ILI), 4 Sharia Mahmoud Azmi, Sahafayeen (north of Mohandiseen) (☎02 3346 3087, ⌨ arabicegypt.com); Kalimat Language and Cultural Centre, 22 Sharia al-Koroum, behind Mohammed Mustafa Mosque, Mohandiseen (☎02 3761 8136, ⌨ kalimategypt .com), which was set up by former British Council teachers; AUC, 113 Sharia Qasr al-Aini (☎02 2794 2964, ✉ ouc @aucegypt.edu), which is well-respected, though its teaching methods may not be as up-to-date as at Kalimat or the ILI. ILI charges €245 for 40hr of tuition over four weeks in Egyptian Colloquial Arabic, and also offers Modern Standard Arabic, or a combination of both. The *Berlin Hotel* (see p.180) can also organize low-priced, one-to-one tuition.

Passport photos Mitry Colour, 3rd floor, 127 Sharia Ramses, at the corner of Sharia Khalig al-Khouly (Mon–Sat 10am–9pm), charges £E20 for eight photos while you wait, or £E10 for a dozen photos ready the next day. There's an automatic booth on the ground floor of the Mugamma (six photos for £E15 while you wait).

Pharmacies All over town, with some 24hr outlets: Al-Esa'af, 27 26th July St, at the junction with Sharia Ramses (☎02 2574 3369); Atalla, 13 Sharia Sherif, at the junction with Sharia Rushdi (Ramses Station☎ 19955 or ☎02 2575 1052); and Abdallah, 2 Sharia Tahar Hussein, Zamalek (☎02 2738 1988). In cases of emergency, these pharmacies will also deliver medicines.

Photography For prints and CDs from digital cameras, try Kodak, 20 Sharia Adly ☎02 2394 2200. For photographic equipment, try Photo Greenwich, 16 Sharia Adly ☎02 2390 6990. Both of these, and also Mitry Colour (see above), will develop camera film.

Police An alleyway to the left of the Sharia Adly tourist office gives access to an office of the tourist police, though their main office is now at Midan al-Fustat (☎126).

Post offices The central post office is on Midan Ataba (daily except Fri 8am–3pm, Ramadan 9am–2pm), with branches citywide (same hours), including offices on Sharia Tahrir by Midan Falaki, and on Sharia Ramses by the junction with 26th July St. Poste restante is in Sharia al-Bedak, round the corner from the main entrance to Ataba post office, on the west side of the building – enter the last door (Sun–Thurs 8am–2pm; bring your passport). Mail should be addressed to you, with surname in capitals and underlined, at Poste Restante, Post Office Ataba, 11511 Cairo. Letters are held for a month, often filed under the wrong name. Parcels can only be mailed abroad from the Ramses Square post office, round the back (the north side of the building), in an office marked "Foreign Parcels Office" (daily except Fri 8am–3pm). To receive a parcel, go to the main entrance (east side) of the same building, fourth floor.

Swimming pools Best of the hotel pools is at the *Semiramis InterContinental* (£E200), with a much more expensive alternative at the *Cairo Marriott* (£E350 Sun–Wed, £E400 Thurs–Sat). The rooftop pool of the *Fontana Hotel*, off Midan Ramses (summer only, £E25), is OK for dipping but barely big enough for a swim. For more serious swimmers, the Ahli Club (☎02 2735 2202; monthly membership $100), behind the Opera House on Sharia Om Kalthoum, offers an Olympic-size pool and women-only sessions. There's also the Palm Club at Saqqara (see p. 166).

Telephone and fax offices Phone calls can be made, Marhaba Plus cards (see p.58) bought and faxes sent (at per-minute phone rates) or received (for £E1/page), at the following telecom offices: 8 Sharia Adly (☎02 2396 4118); Sharia Alfi Bey by the *Windsor Hotel* (☎02 2589 7635); Sharia Ramses, opposite Sharia Tawfiqia (no fax service at present); 13 Midan Tahrir (☎02 2578 0979), Ataba by the National Theatre (☎02 2578 0979). All are open daily 8am–10pm, and should inform you of your fax's arrival if your name and Cairo phone number are at the top of the page.

Tour operators and travel agents Adventure in Egypt, *Talisman Hotel*, 39 Sharia Talaat Harb ☎0100 106 7673, ⓦadventureinegypt.com; Eastmar Tours, in the passage of

13 Sharia Qasr al-Nil ☎02 2574 5024, ⓦeastmar-travel .com; Samo Tours, 28 Sharia Quday, Shubra ☎0122 313 8446, ⓦsamoegypttours.com. Eastmar also offer Nile cruises (see p.178). Discount flight agents such as Spring Tours (3 Sharia Sayed al-Bakry, Zamalek ☎02 2736 5972, ⓦspringtours.com) may offer discounts and can often find seats when the airline itself swears none exist.

Visa extensions Issued at Mugamma on Tahrir Square (daily except Fri 8am–3pm). For a tourist visa extension, go to windows #13–14 of the immigration section on the first floor (these numbers may change so check at the information desk on the landing), and pick up a form. You need to provide a passport photo plus a photocopy of the pages in your passport bearing your personal details and your Egyptian visa – there are copying and photo facilities on the ground floor, but it's better to get them in advance and avoid the scrum (see "Passport photos" on p.204). Take your form to window #42 to get a stamp (£E11.10), then back to window #13 or #14 where your new visa will be issued. This may be done the same day or next day, or could take longer depending on your nationality and the length of stay requested. A re-entry visa will cost £E51.10 (£E61.10 for two re-entries). Display patience and good humour when dealing with the Mugamma; only stage a tantrum or nervous breakdown as a last resort.

The Nile Valley

FELUCCAS ON THE NILE AT ASWAN

The Nile Valley

Egypt has been called the gift of the Nile, for without the river it could not exist as a fertile, populous country, let alone have sustained a great civilization five thousand years ago. Its character and history have been shaped by the stark contrast between the fecund Nile Valley and its Delta (covered in Chapter 4), and the arid wastes that surround them. To the Ancient Egyptians, this was the homeland or Kemet – the Black Land of dark alluvium, where life and civilization flourished as the benign gods intended – as opposed to the desert that represented death and chaos, ruled by Seth, the bringer of storms and catastrophes.

Kemet's existence depended on an annual miracle of rebirth from aridity, as the Nile rose to spread its life-giving waters and fertilizing silt over the exhausted land during the season of inundation. Once the flood had subsided, the *fellaheen* (peasants) simply planted crops in the mud, waited for an abundant harvest, and then relaxed over summer. While empires rose and fell, this way of life persisted essentially unchanged for over 240 generations, until the Aswan High Dam put an end to the inundation in 1967 – a breathtaking period of continuity considering that Jesus lived only eighty generations ago.

Almost every Nile town is built upon layers of previous settlements – pharaonic, Ptolemaic, Roman and Coptic – whose ancient names, modified and Arabized, have often survived. After a century and a half of excavation by a dozen Western nations – and by the Egyptians since independence – the Valley's ancient **monuments** constitute the greatest open-air museum in the world. Revealed along its banks are several thousand **tombs** (over nine hundred in Luxor's Theban Necropolis alone) and scores of **temples**: so many, in fact, that most visitors feel satiated by just a fraction of this legacy.

TEMPLE OF SETI I, ABYDOS

Highlights

❶ Dahabiyas Cruise the Nile in style aboard a chartered houseboat sailing between Esna and Aswan. **See p.241**

❷ Feluccas A timeless way to view the Nile's scenery and temples, sailing downriver from Aswan to Edfu. **See p.242**

❸ Abydos The carvings in Seti I's mortuary temple are among the greatest produced by pharaonic civilization. **See p.245**

❹ Karnak Temple It took 1300 years to construct this vast cult centre, as large as ten great cathedrals. **See p.278**

❺ Valley of the Kings The most famous of the magnificent burial complexes and mortuary

temples that make up the Theban Necropolis. **See p.292**

❻ Aswan's bazaar This wonderful marketplace sells all kinds of handicrafts, souvenirs and spices. **See p.337**

❼ Nubian music and dance Exuberant and haunting by turns, they're best enjoyed on Sehel or Elephantine Island. **See p.351**

❽ Philae This island sanctuary of the goddess Isis was rescued from Lake Nasser. See **p.355**

❾ Abu Simbel The monumental rock-cut temples of Ramses II and Nefertari are the highlights of Lake Nasser. **See p.366**

HIGHLIGHTS ARE MARKED ON THE MAP ON P.210

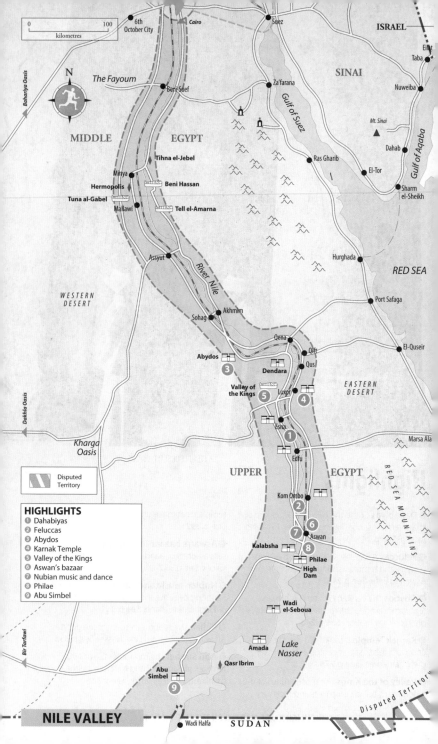

NILE VALLEY

HIGHLIGHTS
1. Dahabiyas
2. Feluccas
3. Abydos
4. Karnak Temple
5. Valley of the Kings
6. Aswan's bazaar
7. Nubian music and dance
8. Philae
9. Abu Simbel

Disputed Territory

N

0   100
kilometres

6th October City
Cairo
Suez
ISRAEL
SINAI
Eilat
Taba
Nuweiba
Za'farana
Gulf of Suez
Mt. Sinai
Dahab
Gulf of Aqaba
The Fayoum
Beni Suef
MIDDLE   EGYPT
Ras Gharib
El-Tor
Sharm el-Sheikh
Tihna el-Jebel
Minya
Hermopolis   Beni Hassan
Tuna al-Gabel
Mallawi   Tell el-Amarna
Bahariya Oasis
Assyut
River Nile
Hurghada
RED SEA
WESTERN DESERT
Akhmim
Sohag
Port Safaga
Dakhla Oasis
Qena
Qift
Abydos
Qus
El-Quseir
Dendara
Valley of the Kings
Luxor
EASTERN DESERT
Esna
Marsa Alam
Kharga Oasis
Edfu
UPPER   EGYPT
Kom Ombo
RED SEA MOUNTAINS
Kalabsha
Aswan
Philae
High Dam
Wadi el-Seboua
Bir Tarfawi
Amada
Lake Nasser
Abu Simbel
Qasr Ibrim
Disputed Territory
Wadi Halfa
SUDAN

To enjoy the Valley, it's best to be selective and mix sightseeing with felucca rides on the river, roaming around bazaars and camel markets, or attending the odd moulid. Most visitors succeed in this by heading straight for **Upper Egypt**, travelling by train or air to **Luxor** or **Aswan**, then making day-trips to the sights within easy range of either base – most notably the cult temple at **Edfu** – in addition to exploring the New Kingdom temples and tombs of **Karnak** and the **Theban Necropolis** from Luxor. Inexpensive **Nile cruises** can be found by shopping around before you leave home; through agents in Cairo, Luxor and Aswan (see pp.239–244); or on boats moored at Aswan, which is also the point of departure for **felucca** cruises to Kom Ombo and Edfu (see pp.242–244). Further north, **Middle Egypt** is chiefly known for its temples at **Abydos** and **Dendara**, but adventurous travellers also visit the tombs of **Beni Hassan** and the ruins of Akhenaten's capital at **Tell el-Amarna**.

Many of the **terms from Egyptology** that fill this chapter may be unfamiliar – for a fuller explanation see the Contexts section on "Ancient Egyptian Temple" (p.676); the various boxes in the text on funerary beliefs and practices under "The Valley of the Kings" (pp.296–297); and the descriptions of gods and goddesses under their respective cult temples (see the main index).

The Nile

The **Nile** is the world's longest river (6695km), originating in the highland lakes of Uganda and Ethiopia, which give rise to the White and Blue Niles. At Khartoum in Sudan these join into a single river which flows northwards via a series of **cataracts** (rocky obstacles and waterfalls) through the Nubian Desert, before forming Egypt's Nile Valley and Delta, through which it travels 1545km to the Mediterranean Sea. The river's northward flow, coupled with a prevailing wind towards the south, made it a natural highway.

As the source of life, the Nile influenced much of ancient Egyptian **society and mythology**. Creation myths of a primal mound emerging from the waters of chaos reflect how villages huddled on mounds till the flood subsided and they could plant their crops. The need for large-scale irrigation works in the Valley and the consequent mobilization of labour consolidated local, regional and ultimately centralized authority – in effect, the state.

Both the Valley and its Delta were divided into **nomes** or provinces, each with a **nomarch** or governor, and one or more **local deities**. As power ebbed and flowed between regions and dynasties, certain of the deities assumed national significance and absorbed the attributes of lesser gods in a perpetual process of religious mergers and takeovers. Thus, for example, Re, the chief god of the Old Kingdom, ended up being assimilated with Amun, the prime divinity of Thebes during the New Kingdom. Yet for all its complexity, Ancient Egyptian religion was essentially practical: its pre-eminent concerns were to perpetuate the beneficent sun and river, maintain the righteous order personified by the goddess Maat, and achieve resurrection in the afterlife.

Abundant crops could normally be taken for granted, as prayers to Hapy the Nile-god were followed by a green wave of humus-rich water around June. However, if the Nile failed to rise for a succession of years there ensued the "years of the hyena when men went hungry". Archeologists reckon that it was **famine** – caused by overworking of the land, as well as lack of the flood waters – that caused the collapse of the Old and Middle Kingdoms, and subsequent anarchy. But each time some new dynasty arose to reunite the land and re-establish the old order. This remarkable conservatism persisted even under foreign rule: the Nubians, Persians, Ptolemies and Romans all continued building temples dedicated to the old gods, and styled themselves as pharaohs.

People of the Nile Valley

Although the Nile Valley and its Delta represents a mere four percent of Egypt's surface area, it is home to 95 percent of the country's population. While Cairo and Alexandria account for about a quarter of this, the bulk of the people still live in small towns and villages and, as in pharaonic times, the **fellaheen** or peasant farmers remain the bedrock of Egyptian society.

Most **villages** consist of flat-roofed mud-brick houses, with chickens, goats, cows and water buffalo roaming the unpaved streets, and elaborate multistorey pigeon coops (the birds are eaten and their droppings used as fertilizer). Children begin work at an early age: girls feed the animals, fetch water and do housework, while by the age of 9 or 10, boys are learning how to farm the land that will one day be theirs.

Rural life might appear the same throughout the Valley, but its character changes as you go further south. The northern reaches of the Valley are unconstrained by the desert hills but fertile land is scarcer; people here have a reputation for being quietly spoken, yet prone to vendettas. By contrast, Egyptians characterize the **Saiyidis** of Upper Egypt as mercurial in character, alternating between hot-blooded passion and a state known as *kismet* – a kind of fatalistic stasis. To non-Saiyidis, they are also the butt of jokes mocking their stubbornness and stupidity. A further ethnic contingent of the southern reaches of the Valley are the black-skinned **Nubians**, whose traditional homeland stretching far into Sudan was submerged by Lake Nasser in the 1960s.

Wildlife of the Nile

The exotic Nile wildlife depicted on ancient tomb reliefs – hippos, crocodiles, elephants and gazelles – is largely a thing of the past, though you might just see a croc on Lake Nasser. However, the Valley has a rich diversity of **birds**. Amid the groves of palms (dates all along the Valley and dom palms south of Assyut), fruit and flame trees, sycamores and eucalyptus, and fields of *besoom* (Egyptian clover) and sugar cane, you can spot hoopoes, turtle- and laughing-doves, bulbuls, bluethroats, redstarts, wheatears and dark-backed stonechats. Purple gallinules, egrets and all kinds of waders are to be seen in the river, while common birds of prey include a range of kestrels, hawks and falcons.

ARRIVAL AND GETTING AROUND   **THE NILE VALLEY**

Setting out from Cairo or the Red Sea Coast, you are faced with a variety of approaches to the Valley, but should bear in mind certain **travel restrictions**. Whereas tourists are unbothered by controls within the security "bubble" of Luxor and Aswan, in **Middle Egypt** the police may insist on escorting visitors, and requiring that they travel by taxi on all excursions. While you have little choice but to comply, and should certainly never get angry, the system is sufficiently inconsistent and fallible enough that you can sometimes persuade the police to cut you some slack.

By plane Planes are the fastest way to travel from one end of the Valley to the other. Depending on demand, there can be from one to a dozen flights a day from Cairo to Luxor, Aswan and Abu Simbel, affording amazing views over the belt of cultivated land surrounded by desert. You can also fly from Aswan to Abu Simbel, and Luxor to Sharm el-Sheikh.

By train Many tourists prefer to take an overnight train directly to Aswan, and then work their way northwards to Luxor (see p.346).

By bus Buses from Cairo's Aboud and Cairo Gateway (Turgoman) terminals to Luxor and Aswan are routed via the Red Sea Coast rather than Middle Egypt. Buses to Beni Suef, Minya, Assyut and Sohag in Middle Egypt do exist, but tourists trying to buy tickets for these may be refused. If you do reach Middle Egypt by train, local cops may tolerate

you using inter-city buses heading south to Luxor. Superjet buses are invariably more comfortable than regular Upper Egypt Bus Co. services.

By service taxi Service taxis are generally out of bounds to tourists throughout the Valley, so we have not detailed routes or prices in this chapter.

By car/motorbike Foreigners can now drive a car or motorbike the length of the Valley, instead of having to detour via the Red Sea highway to travel between Cairo and Luxor. Nonetheless, you should expect scrutiny at checkpoints, if not a police escort at some stage – and beware of farm vehicles on the road. The same goes for **cyclists**.

Tourist coaches and hired taxis may now travel freely in Upper Egypt from 6am to 6pm, except between Aswan and Abu Simbel, where they must join a convoy departing at a set time. In Middle Egypt, a police escort is often mandatory, but rules vary in each governorate and may change at short notice, so it's worth checking with the local tourist office. Coming from Sinai or Hurghada, privately-hired a/c minibuses or cars provide a faster, more comfortable alternative to buses, but must travel in a convoy (three times daily).

TOURS

Tours booked abroad are generally good value, but visitors buying tours in Cairo often pay over the odds for substandard hotels and excursions. Many have complained about touts selling or adapting itineraries from Amigo Tours at huge

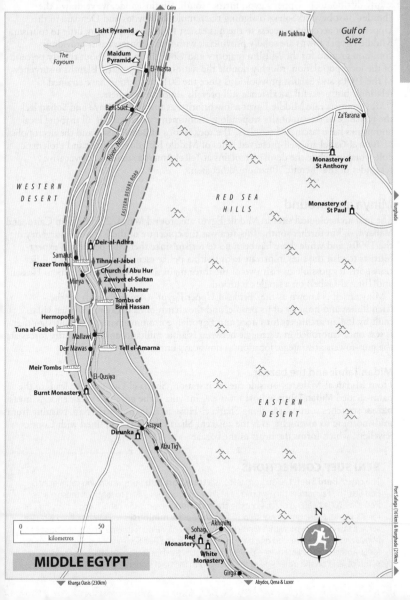

MIDDLE EGYPT

mark-ups (see p.173). If you do want a tour, talk to Samo Tours or Eastmar Tours in Cairo (see p.205) – Eastmar also offers cruises between Luxor and Aswan and on Lake Nasser, and has offices in Luxor and Aswan.

Middle Egypt

It was nineteenth-century archeologists who coined the term **Middle Egypt** for the stretch of river between Cairo and the Qena Bend – a handy label for a region that's subtly distinct from Upper Egypt, further south. (In this guide, we've drawn the "border" just beyond Sohag, assigning the temples of Abydos and Dendara to the Upper Egypt account as access to them is easiest from Luxor.) Owing little to tourism, Middle Egypt's towns are solidly provincial, with social conservatism providing common ground for the Muslim majority and Coptic minority (about twenty percent of the local population, roughly double the national average). The Islamist insurgency of the 1990s and Salafist provocations since the 2011 revolution have strained relations, but peaceful coexistence still prevails almost everywhere.

Most tourists rate Middle Egypt a low priority, as towns like **Minya** and **Sohag** lack the romance of Aswan or the stupendous monuments of Luxor, for all that the local antiquities have fascinated scholars. The rock tombs of **Beni Hassan** and the necropolis of **Tuna al-Gabel** are well-preserved relics of Middle Kingdom artistry and Ptolemaic cult-worship, while the desolate remains at **Tell el-Amarna** stand as an evocative reminder of the "heretic" Pharaoh Akhenaten.

Minya and around

The best archeological sites in Middle Egypt are around **Minya**, 229km from Cairo, and **Mallawi**, 47km further south. This area was the epicentre of the Islamist insurgency of the 1990s, and while there has been no terrorism since then, the police still expect tourists to visit the sites in private taxis (with a police escort) rather than by public transport. It's possible to visit two of the three main sites (Tell el-Amarna, Beni Hassan and Tuna al-Gabel) on a single excursion.

Minya itself is known as the "Bride of Upper Egypt" (Arous al-Sa'id) for the friendliness and honesty of its people, and the charm of its decaying colonial villas, built by Italian architects for Greek and Egyptian cotton magnates. The only sign that it was once embroiled in a struggle between Islamic militants and the security forces are the gun-towers at strategic locations – nowadays unmanned.

Midan Tahrir and the bazaar

From Midan al-Mahatta, outside the train station, Sharia el-Gumhorriya leads to the palm-shaded **Midan Tahrir**, whose most elegant villa is the governor's residence. Minya's **bazaar** stretches southwards along Sharia el-Hussein as far as Midan Sa'a, bustling from mid-morning to midnight, as is the adjacent Sharia Ibn Khasseb, lined with Coptic jewellers, which forms the heart of the bazaar.

BENI SUEF CONNECTIONS

The city of **Beni Suef**, 120km from Cairo, is a **transport hub** from which you can reach the Red Sea, the Fayoum or the Pyramid of Maidum (though it's easier to reach all these places from Cairo). By heading north from the **train station**, crossing the canal bridge, carrying on for 200m and then turning right, you'll find a depot for **minibuses** to El-Wasta, from where a service taxi can get you within range of the Pyramid of Maidum (see p.391). Hourly **buses** to Minya and the Fayoum, and one daily to Za'farana on the Red Sea – running past the turn-off for St Anthony's Monastery (see p.570) – leave from the bus station on Sharia Bur Said, 400m south of (and on the other side of the canal from) the train station.

The Corniche

Minya's Corniche is quiet by comparison, with a riverside park affording views of the striated hills of the Eastern Desert across the Nile. Beyond the white Baroque **Governorate Building,** a stretch of wall beside the Minya Sporting Club displays red and white **murals** glorifying the White Knights, ultra-supporters of Zamalek football club (see p.42), including portraits of members killed during the 2011 Revolution.

The Akhenaten Museum and El-Lamati Mosque

Towards the southern end of the Corniche, you can see the lofty trifurcated pyramid of the unfinished **Akhenaten Museum,** on the east bank of the Nile. Due to open in 2014,

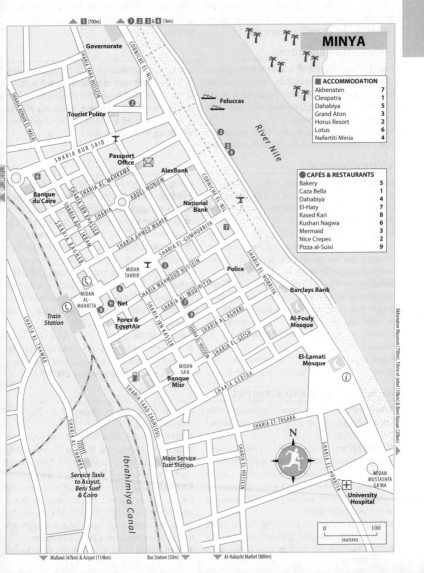

MINYA

■ ACCOMMODATION

Akhenaten	7
Cleopatra	1
Dahabiya	5
Grand Aton	3
Horus Resort	2
Lotus	6
Nefertiti Minia	4

● CAFÉS & RESTAURANTS

Bakery	5
Caza Bella	1
Dahabiya	4
El-Haty	7
Kased Kari	8
Kushari Nagwa	6
Mermaid	3
Nice Crepes	2
Pizza al-Suisi	9

2

the museum will exhibit artefacts from Tell el-Amarna and other sites, but is unlikely to include the iconic bust of Queen Nefertiti held in Berlin (see p.225).

On the west bank of the Nile, the tenth-century **El-Lamati Mosque** is an arrestingly rugged building, with inward-sloping walls topped by crenallations, and a stumpy minaret with a "pencil" finial.

ARRIVAL AND GETTING AROUND

MINYA

Minya is compact enough to walk around, though microbuses (50pt) and taxis (£E5) are widely used by locals.

By train There are roughly seven a/c services daily to Cairo (3hr 30min–5hr), stopping at Beni Suef (2hr) along the way, plus a similar number to Aswan (10hr) via Assyut (2hr), Sohag (4hr), Qena (6hr) and Luxor (7hr).

By bus There are Upper Egypt Bus Co. services to Assyut (4hr) and Cairo (5hr) from the bus station on Sharia Sa'ad Zaghloul, although they're less comfortable than the trains.

INFORMATION AND TOURS

Tourist office Corniche el-Nil, near the El-Lamati Mosque ☎ 086 237 1521 (Sun–Thurs 8.30am–5pm). Contact their helpful English-speaking manager Hussein Farag (☎ 011 1279 9479, ✉ tut_amun2000@yahoo.com) before you arrive to arrange any excursions.

Tours All trips outside town must be by private taxi, accompanied by a policeman. The tourist office offers three

separate eight-hour excursions by taxi (£E150) or limousine (£E200), shared between up to four people: to Beni Hassan (see p.219) and Tell el-Armana (see p.223); to Beni Hassan with the Frazer Tombs, Tihna el-Jebel and Deir al-Adhra (see p.217); or to Tell el-Amarna with Hermopolis, Tuna al-Gabel and Mallawi (see p.221).

ACCOMMODATION

Akhenaten Corniche el-Nil ☎ 086 236 5918, ✉ kingakhenaton@hotmail.com. Centrally located, with friendly staff and en-suite a/c rooms with satellite TV and Nile views. B&B £E232

Cleopatra Sharia Taha Hussein ☎ 086 237 0800, ✉ info@cleopatrahotelmenia.com. A 20min walk from the centre, this high-rise three-star has cosy a/c en-suite rooms and a bar on the seventh floor. B&B £E250

Dahabiya Corniche el-Nil ☎ 010 0199 6829. Minya's most unusual lodgings: a vintage houseboat moored on the Nile. It has two small cabins with fans, TV and heaters in winter, sharing a bathroom – right underneath a restaurant on the top deck, busy till midnight in the summer. B&B £E100

Grand Aton Corniche el-Nil, 1km north of the centre ☎ 086 234 2293. Closed for renovation at the time of

writing, this former *Etap* (still known locally as such) should offer similar amenities to the neighbouring *Horus Resort* (see below) once it reopens, at similar prices.

★ **Horus Resort** Corniche el-Nil, 1km north of the centre ☎ 086 231 6660, ⓦ horusresortmenia.com. Minya's most comfortable option, beside the Nile, has huge a/c en-suite rooms, a pool, kids' entertainments, a restaurant serving alcohol, and wi-fi throughout. B&B $60

Lotus Sharia Bur Said ☎ 086 236 4500. In a quiet-ish part of town, 10min walk from the centre, this faded three-star has a/c rooms with showers and TV, and a top-floor restaurant serving alcohol. B&B £E100

Nefertiti Minia Corniche el-Nil ☎ 086 234 1515, ✉ mgnefertitihotel@yahoo.com. Across the road from the *Grand Aton*, with a fair-sized pool and a large garden, a/c rooms and musty chalets out back. B&B $80

EATING, DRINKING AND ACTIVITIES

Bakery Sharia el-Hussein. A smoke-blackened outlet for freshly baked pitta bread, sweet rolls and sesame-seed pretzels. Daily 24hr.

★ **Caza Bella** Horus Resort ☎ 086 231 6660 ext.1400. Lavishly decorated with red and gold Napoleonic-pharaonic columns, this a/c restaurant offers a bigger menu than other local eateries, and surprisingly low prices. Try a Greek salad (£E8) and veal piccata with mushroom sauce (£E45). Serves alcohol. Daily noon–midnight.

Dahabiya Corniche el-Nil ☎ 010 0199 6829. If it's not too windy, this is a nice place to enjoy a view of the Nile from the boat's top deck or its on-shore garden over a

plate of grilled fish or chicken (£E35–55). Daily 10am–midnight.

El-Haty Sharia el-Hussein. This tiny bazaar eatery wins no prizes for its decor, but their kebabs are perfectly cooked, accompanied by soup, rice, salad, hummous and vegetables – all for only £E27. Daily 10am–midnight.

Kased Kari Midan al-Mahatta. An a/c patisserie selling baklava, *basbousa*, gateaux and ice cream, *Kased Kari* makes a quiet retreat from the heat and hubbub of the square outside the train station, and is popular with families and courting couples. Daily 10am–10pm.

Kushari Nagwa Sharia el-Gumhorriya. An archetypal

kushari outlet, used by locals for takeways. You can sit down and eat your *kushari* at any of the local coffee-houses. Daily 10am–1am.

Mermaid Corniche el-Nil. This floating restaurant does set meals (£E45–75) based around fried fish, kebabs or mixed grills. A bit desolate in the winter months, but busy on summer evenings. Daily noon–midnight.

Nice Crepes Off Sharia Bur Said. Hidden away behind some blocks of flats not far from the Corniche el-Nil, this cheery sit-down café, popular with students, serves sweet and savoury pancakes (mostly under £E20) to eat in or take-away. Daily noon–10pm.

Pizza al-Suisi Sharia el-Hussein. Just along from *El-Haty*, this hole-in-the-wall joint serves freshly baked *fiteer* with savoury or sweet toppings (£E15–25) to either eat at a single table or takeaway. Daily noon–midnight.

DIRECTORY

Banks and exchange AlexBank (Sun–Thurs 9am–2pm) and Barclays (Sun–Thurs 9.30am–2pm), Corniche el-Nil; Banque du Caire (Sun–Thurs 8.30am–2pm), Sharia Sa'ad Zaghloul; Banque Misr (Sun–Thurs 9am–2pm), Midan Sa'a. All these places have ATMs. Forex, Sharia al-Thawra (daily 10am–10pm).

Hospital University Hospital, Midan Mustafa Ga'ma ☎ 086 234 2505.

Internet access Net, in an alley behind Midan al-Mahatta (daily 11am–midnight).

Post office Sharia al-Mahkama (daily except Fri 8.30am–2pm).

Swimming The *Horus Resort* lets non-residents use its pool for £E60.

Telephones Midan al-Mahatta, beside the train station (daily 24hr).

Visa extensions Passport office, Sharia al-Mahkama ☎ 086 236 4193 (daily except Fri 8.30am–2pm). A photo and photocopy of your passport are required.

Around Minya

The main attractions **around Minya** are the rock tombs of **Beni Hassan**, roughly midway between Minya and Mallawi and containing the finest surviving murals from the Middle Kingdom. Nearer to Mallawi on the west bank are the ruins of **Hermopolis** and its partially subterranean necropolis, **Tuna al-Gabel**, while the rock-cut temples of **Tihna el-Jebel** and the Coptic **Monastery of the Virgin** (Deir al-Adhra) lie across the river to the north of Minya, whose bridge provides easy access to the east bank.

TOURS   AROUND MINYA

By private taxi Minya's tourist office can arrange an excursion for up to four people (£E150 by taxi, £E200 by limo) combining Hermopolis, Tuna al-Gabel and Mallawi with Beni Hassan or Tell el-Amarna (see p.216).

The Frazer Tombs
7km northeast of Minya • Daily 8am–5pm • £E15

Across the Nile to the northeast of Minya, farming is constrained by the cliffs of the Eastern Desert, where fallen rocks as big as houses mark the start of a path to the **Frazer Tombs**. Named after their excavator, Gary Frazer, these V and VI Dynasty rock-cut tombs are reached by sunken passageways. The two that are open to visitors once belonged to two dignitaries both named Nika-Ankh. The first contains damaged statues of Nika-Ankh, his wife, their children and grandson, interspersed by hieroglyphs. The effigies in the second tomb are better preserved; note the finely carved pleats on the kilt of Nika-Ankh's statue.

Tihna el-Jebel
15km northeast of Minya • Daily 8am–5pm • Free

Further north, a cleavage in the massif harbours the village of **TIHNA EL-JEBEL** which sits next to the mud-brick **ruins** of the pharaonic town of Dehenet (Forehead), known to the Greeks as Acoris. A long stairway once flanked by altars and statues leads to a craggy massif with two unfinished **rock-cut temples** dedicated to Amun and Suchos (the Greek name for the crocodile-god Sobek). In the penultimate chamber of the first temple are two niches that once held mummified crocodiles: if you carefully circumvent a deep shaft right outside, you can see a remaining croc in a chamber beyond the second temple. Further round the cliff-face, a chapel to the goddess Hathor is carved so high up it seems unbelievable that it was ever used for offerings.

Deir al-Adhra: the Monastery of the Virgin

Gabel et-Teir, 25km northeast of Minya • Daily 8am–8pm • Free

Beyond Tihna el-Jebel the road hugs the base of the cliffs, where men cut limestone boulders into kerb-stones. A flight of 166 steps ascends to the cliff-top village of **GABEL ET-TEIR** (Bird Mountain), nowadays also accessible by road. The mountain is so-named after a legend that all the birds in Egypt gathered there during its monastery's annual feast day.

The **Monastery of the Virgin** (Deir al-Adhra) was once known as the Monastery of the Pulley, after a hoist that was formerly the only means of access before steps were cut into the cliff. A simple nineteenth-century edifice encloses a **rock-hewn church**, reputedly founded in 328 by Helena, mother of the Byzantine emperor Constantine. Its sanctity derives from a tiny **cave** where the Holy Family is believed to have hidden for three days and which now contains an icon of the Virgin credited with miraculous powers. Similar tales surround a baptismal **font** carved into one of the church's Greco-Roman columns.

Usually only visited by local villagers, the church receives nearly two million pilgrims during the week-long **Feast of the Assumption**, forty days after the Coptic Easter. Minibuses run here directly from Minya during the festival.

The Church of Aba Hur

Al-Sawdah, 4km southeast of Minya • Daily 8am–8pm • Free

The east bank road to Beni Hassan runs past the predominantly Coptic village of **AL-SAWADAH** where a sign in English welcomes visitors to the **Church of Aba Hur** (Deir Abu Hor) – you can't miss the modern church that stands in front of a tunnel leading to its subterranean rock-hewn namesake. A blacksmith's son who was born in 310 AD, Aba Hur became a hermit at the age of 20 and took up residence in a disused Ptolemaic temple; his faith under torture converted the Roman governor of Pelusium to Christianity.

Every year on July 6 over one hundred thousand Coptic pilgrims attend the **Moulid of Aba Hur**, camping out in the cemetery beyond Al-Sawadah (see below).

Zawiyet el-Sultan

Zawiyet el-Sultan, 5km southeast of Minya • Daily 7am–sunset • Free

This vast cemetery, called **Zawiyet el-Sultan** (after the next village) or Zawiyet el-Mayyiteen (Corner of the Dead), resembles a field of giant egg-boxes. Thousands of domed mausolea are grouped in confessional enclaves, the Coptic ones topped by a forest of crosses. The Muslim section harbours the tomb of **Hoda Shaarawi** (1879–1947), an early twentieth-century feminist who led demonstrations against British rule and was the first Egyptian woman to publicly remove her veil (in Cairo's Ramses station), inspiring others to do likewise.

Kom al-Ahmar

6km southeast of Minya • Daily 8am–5pm • Free

Beyond Zawiyet el-Sultan the road passes **Kom al-Ahmar** (Red Mound), the site of ancient Hebenu, capital of the Oryx nome, or province. The name Hebenu comes from the Ancient Egyptian word *hbn*, meaning to kill with a knife, and refers to the revenge of the god Horus on his father's murderer, Seth. The site's most interesting feature is a small ruined III Dynasty **pyramid** whose symbolic tomb was never used as such, unlike another tomb dating from the New Kingdom, containing the defaced funerary statue of a local nomarch, Nefer-Skheru.

Beni Hassan

20km southeast of Minya; for details on arranging transport to the site, see "Information and tours" (p.216) • Daily 8am–5pm • £E30 • No photography inside the tombs

The barren cliffs on the east bank to the south of Minya harbour the famous **rock tombs of Beni Hassan**, named after an Arab tribe that once settled hereabouts. The vivid murals in this necropolis shed light on the Middle Kingdom (c.2050–1650 BC), a

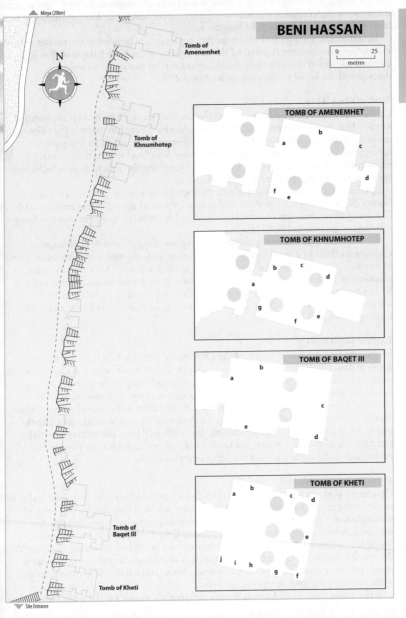

2

period when provincial dignitaries showed their greater independence by having grand burials locally, rather than at Saqqara.

Though most of its 39 tombs are unfinished, the four shown to visitors evince a **stylistic evolution** during the XI–XII Dynasties. Their variously shaped chambers represent a transitional stage between the lateral mastaba tombs of the Old Kingdom and the deep shafts in the Valley of the Kings, gradually acquiring vestibules and sunken corridors to heighten the impact of the funerary effigies at the back. The actual mummies were secreted at the bottom of shafts, accompanied by funerary texts derived from the royal burials of the Old Kingdom.

Pharaonic iconography and contemporary reportage are blended in the **murals**, whose innovative wrestling scenes presaged the battle vistas of the New Kingdom. Though battered and faded in parts, their details reward careful study; the following descriptions are keyed to the tomb plans (see p.219).

Tomb of Kheti (#17)

Of the many chambers hewn into the cliff-side, the first you'll come to is the **Tomb of Kheti**, which retains two of its papyrus-bud columns, painted in places – the colours are quite fresh. As in most tombs of Ancient Egyptian dignitaries, its images are arranged in "registers" (rows) whose height above floor level reflects their spatial relationship. Thus, Nile scenes go below those involving the Valley, above which come desert vistas, the highest ones most distant.

In the murals, hippopotamuses watch the papyrus harvest [a], as desert creatures are hunted [b] above registers of weavers, dancers, artists and *senet* players (*senet* was a bit like draughts or checkers) observed by Kheti and his wife [c], to whom minions bring offerings of gazelles and birds [d].

The rear (east) wall features a compendium of wrestling positions [e], thought to emphasize efforts to defend Egypt against invaders from the east; a now-vanished scene of warriors storming a fortress once explicitly made the point. Don't miss the man standing on his head and in other yoga positions, between the scenes of wine-making [f] and herding cattle [h]. Ploughing [i] is another task overseen by Kheti in his role as nomarch, attended by his dwarf and fan-bearers [g]. Notice Kheti's boats, and bulls locking horns, in the corner [j].

Tomb of Baqet III (#15)

Kheti inherited the governorship of the Oryx nome from his father, buried in the **Tomb of Baqet III**. Its imagery is similar to that in Kheti's tomb, with some scenes better preserved, others not. While the mural of papyrus-gathering in the marshes [a] is quite faded, the desert hunt [b] is rich in details: notice the copulating gazelles near the left-hand corner. Ball players, women spinning and fullers beating cloth appear below. Nearly two hundred wrestling positions are shown on the rear wall [c], with a lovely pair of birds above the funerary niche [d]. The south wall [e] is covered with episodes from the life of this XI Dynasty nomarch. In the second register from the top, his underlings count cattle and beat tax defaulters with sticks.

Tomb of Khnumhotep (#3)

Columned porticos and a niche for statues (which replaced the Old Kingdom *serdab* or secret chamber) are hallmarks of the XII Dynasty tombs, 150m north. The **Tomb of Khnumhotep** is framed by proto-Doric columns and hieroglyphs praising this nomarch, who was also governor of the Eastern Desert. His funeral cortege appears inside the entrance [a]. Servants weigh grain and scribes record its storage in granaries [b], while beneath the desert hunt [c], Semitic Amu tribesmen from Syria in striped tunics pay their respects, their alien costumes, flocks and tribute all minutely detailed – the governor is shown accepting eye paint.

In the niche, images of Khnumhotep's children are visible on the walls but only the plinth of his statue remains. Elsewhere are vivid scenes of Khnumhotep netting birds, hunting with a throwing stick [d] and spearing fish from a punt in the marshes [e]. After the usual offerings [f], he inspects boat-building timber from a litter and then sails to Abydos [g]. Higher and lower registers portray bare-breasted laundrywomen, weavers and other artisans. The hieroglyphic text beneath these scenes has yielded clues about the political relationship between the nomarchs and pharaohs of the XII Dynasty.

Tomb of Amenemhet (#2)

The **Tomb of Amenemhet** belongs to Khnumhotep's predecessor, whose campaign honours are listed beside the door near a text relating the death of Senusret I. Proto-Doric columns uphold a vaulted ceiling painted with checkered reed-mat patterns. A mural [a] of armourers, leatherworkers (at the top) and weavers (below) precedes the customary hunting scene [b], beneath which Amenemhet collects tribute from his estates. Note the scribes berating defaulters on the second register from the bottom. Below the wrestling and siege tableaux, boats escort him towards Abydos [c]. The niche [d] contains mutilated effigies of Amenemhet, his mother and his wife Heptet, who sits at her own table to receive offerings [e]. Fish are netted and spit-roasted above a painted false door flanked by scenes of music making, cattle fording and baking [f].

Hermopolis

Ashmunein, 8km from Mallawi (in theory, you could catch a train or minibus from Minya to Mallawi, then a minibus to Ashmunein for Hermopolis, but the hassle hardly justifies any savings, and you're sure to waste time with the police)

According to one ancient tradition, Creation began on a primordial mound near the city that the Ancient Greeks called Hermopolis Magna, whose pulverized ruins spread beyond the village of **ASHMUNEIN**. Turning right off the main street you'll come to an outdoor **museum** (daily 8am–5pm; free) of antique stone-carvings, fronted by two **giant sandstone baboons** that once sported erect phalluses (hacked off by early Christians) and upheld the ceiling of the Temple of Thoth. Built by Ramses II using masonry from Tell el-Amarna, the temple stood within an enclosure covering 640 square metres, the spiritual heart of the city of the moon-god.

THOTH AND THE HERMOPOLITAN OGDOAD

In Egyptian mythology, **Thoth** was the divine scribe and reckoner of time, the inventor of writing and the patron god of scribes. His cult probably originated in the Delta, but achieved the greatest following in Middle Egypt; later, by association with Khonsu, he acquired the attributes of the moon-god and mastery over science and knowledge. Though usually depicted with a man's body and the head of an ibis (his sacred bird), Thoth also assumed the form of a great white baboon, invariably endowed with an outsize penis. Baboons habitually shriek just before dawn, and the Egyptians believed that a pair of them uttered the first greetings to the sun from the sand dunes at the edge of the world.

Thoth

Thoth's role is rather more complex in relation to the Hermopolitan cosmogony, which ordained that the chaos preceding the world's creation had four characteristics, each identified with a pair of gods and goddesses: primordial water (Nun/Nanuet), infinite space (Heh/Hehet), darkness (Kek/Keket) and invisibility (Amun/Amunet). From this chaos arose the primeval mound and the cosmic egg from which the sun-god hatched and proceeded to organize the world. While stressing the role of this **Hermopolitan Ogdoad** (company of eight), Thoth's devotees credited him with laying the cosmic egg in the guise of the "Great Cackler", so it's difficult to know who got star billing in this creation myth. By the New Kingdom it had generally succumbed to the version espoused at Heliopolis (see p.145), but Thoth's cult continued into Ptolemaic times.

Hermopolis was a cult centre from early Dynastic times, venerated as the site of the primeval mound where the sun-god emerged from a cosmic egg. Like Heliopolis (which made similar claims) its priesthood evolved an elaborate cosmogony, known as the Hermopolitan Ogdoad (see box p.221). Though Ancient Egyptians called the city Khmunu, history remembers it as **Hermopolis Magna**; its Ptolemaic title reflects the Greek association of Thoth with their own god Hermes. However, there's little to see except 24 slender **columns** further south, which were re-erected by archeologists who mistook the ruins for a Greek *agora*. The columns previously supported a fifth-century Coptic basilica, but originally belonged to a Ptolemaic temple.

Tuna al-Gabel

Tuna al-Gabel, 15km from Mallawi • Daily 8am–5pm • £E20

From Ashmunein, a tarmac road continues to the village of **TUNA AL-GABEL**, which takes its name from the ancient necropolis 5km further on into the desert, famous for its extensive catacombs, where thousands of sacred baboons and ibises were buried in ancient times. The name "Tuna" may derive from the Ancient Egyptian *ta-wnt* (the hare) or *ta-hnt* (a place where many ibis birds gather).

Along the way, notice the **boundary stele** on a distant cliff, marking the edge of the agricultural land that was claimed by Tell el-Amarna, across the river.

The necropolis

For millennia, the **necropolis** at Tuna al-Gabel was a cult-centre where pilgrims gave homage to Thoth by paying the priests to embalm ibises – over two million were sacrificed, mostly bred for the chop.

Today, it's awash with sand, wind-rippled drifts casting its angular mausolea into high relief, but obscuring other features. Past the resthouse at the entrance (which sells drinks and has toilets), a path to the right leads to the **catacombs**, which some believe stretch as far as Hermopolis. The accessible portion consists of rough-hewn corridors with blocked-off side passages, where the mummified baboons, which were sacred to Thoth, and ibises were stacked (a few bandages remain). A shrine near the ladder contains a baboon fetish and a pathetic-looking baboon mummy. You can also see the limestone sarcophagus of a high priest of mummification.

Tomb of Petosiris

Further along the main track from the necropolis are several mausolea excavated by Gustav Lefebvre in 1920. The finest is the **Tomb of Petosiris**, High Priest of Thoth (whose coffin is in the Egyptian Museum in Cairo), dating from 350 BC. Its vestibule walls depict traditional activities such as brick-making, sewing and reaping (left), milking, husbandry and wine-making (right) – with all the figures wearing Greek costume. Inside the tomb are colourful scenes from the *Book of Gates* and the *Book of the Dead*. The most vivid scene (on the right-hand wall near the back) shows nine baboons, twelve women and a dozen cobras, each set representing a temporal cycle. Notice the Nubians at the bottom of the opposite wall.

The Well

In the desert off to the right you'll spot some columns from the Temple of Thoth that once dominated the site. More impressive, however, is the ancient **well** that used to supply the necropolis and its sacred aviary with fresh water, drawn up from 70m below the desert by a huge **waterwheel** which still exists, though it no longer works. A spiral staircase gives access to the well-head.

Mallawi

47km from Minya

The town of **MALLAWI** has gone to the dogs ever since Minya supplanted it as the regional capital in the 1960s. Many streets are still unpaved, and hovels are more prevalent than villas. Known to Egyptians as the birthplace of President Sadat's assassin, Khalid al-Islambouli (whose mother remains proud of his deed), it bore the brunt of the state's counter-insurgency campaign in the 1990s.

The police want foreigners to pass through as quickly as possible, but will tolerate a visit to the small **museum** (daily 9am–2pm, Fri 9am–noon; £E10) on Sharia Banque Misr, exhibiting artefacts from Hermopolis and Tuna al-Gabel, and maybe a quick look at the derelict Hindu-Gothic-style **feudal palace** a few blocks away.

2

Tell el-Amarna

12km from Mallawi, 58km from Minya • Daily 8am–5pm • Northern and Southern Tombs £E30; Royal Tomb £E25

TELL EL-AMARNA is the commonly used name for the site where **Pharaoh Akhenaten** and **Queen Nefertiti** founded a city dedicated to a revolutionary idea of God, which later rulers assailed as heretical. During their brief reign, Egyptian art cast off its preoccupation with death and the afterlife to revel in human concerns; bellicose imperialism gave way to pacifistic retrenchment; and the old gods were toppled from their pedestals. The interplay between personalities, beliefs and art anticipates the Renaissance – and for sheer drama their story (see box p.226) beats Shakespeare.

The remains of Akhenaten's city lie on the east bank of the Nile, spread across a desert plain girdled by an arc of cliffs. Away from the palm groves beside the Nile, the site is utterly desolate, a tawny expanse of low mounds and narrow trenches littered with potshards.

Because the city was created from scratch and deserted after Tutankhamun moved the court back to Thebes, its era of glory lasted only twelve years, and many buildings were never completed. Everything of value found during excavations has been removed to museums, leaving only the faintest outlines of the city and the desecrated tombs of Akhenaten and his courtiers to see – yet the site strikes some visitors as a place of mystery whose enchantment grows the more you know about it.One theory is that the site was chosen for its **symbolism**. The arc of cliffs on the eastern horizon has a cleft exactly where the sun rises each morning, having been reborn after a night battling through the underworld (so the Ancient Egyptians believed). By siting his tomb in line with the rising sun, at the epicentre of imaginary rays radiating to boundary stelae (see p.230) which intersected with the city's palaces and temples, Akhenaten identified himself with the deity Aten, and his capital as a divine creation embodying sacred geometery.

The City

Running south from the modern village of El-Till, a tarmac track follows the course of the old **Royal Road** that formed ancient Akhetaten's main axis, known locally as Sikket es-Sultan, the Road of the Sultan. The track passes scores of mounds of sand and debris, partially excavated (and subsequently recovered by sand) since the 1920s, and more recently by the Armana Project, whose website features reconstructions of the city's principal buildings. Many of these were made of **talatat**, small stone blocks whose length was three times their width (hence their Arabic name, "thirds"). These could be quarried faster than the large blocks hitherto used for temples and palaces, enabling Akenaten's architects to build complexes that would have otherwise taken decades.

Great Aten Temple

The **Great Aten Temple** was a brick-walled enclosure 300m deep by 800m wide, bisected by a stone Long Temple with mud-brick pylons. Its northern wall incorporated the Hall of Foreign Tribute where emissaries proffered treasure (as depicted in tombs), while the southern wall was flanked by a field of 720 mud-brick offerings tables.

2

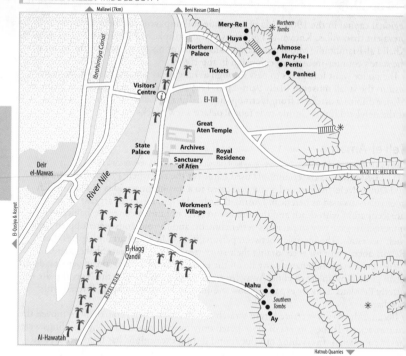

Unlike traditional temples, which got darker as one approached the sanctuary, Aten's was roofless, exposing worshippers to the god's rays during the searing heat of summer – an act of sadism on Akenaten's part, critics maintain. The temple was destroyed after his death on Horemheb's orders; Ramses II quarried its foundations for his temples at Hermopolis, across the Nile. Today, replicas of a complete and a partial lotus-bundle **column** (erected by the Amarna Project) tower incongruously above excavation trenches and foundation walls.

Foreign Office Archives

South of the Great Aten Temple (and hard to distinguish beneath shifting sands) are the remnants of the Foreign Office **Archives**, where the **Amarna Letters** were discovered. Written in the Akkadian script used for diplomatic correspondence with Asiatic states, these clay tablets have revealed much about the period. Over 360 letters have been found, but more were undoubtedly lost, leaving an incomplete puzzle for scholars to piece together and argue over.

Royal Residence

Beyond the Archives come three excavated rectangles that were once the **Royal Residence**. Their private apartments were separated from the stately reception halls that ran through the centre of the huge palace compound. Across the Royal Road stood an even larger **State Palace**, with a dock for the royal barge.

Both palaces were connected by a covered "flyover" spanning the road (part of one pylon remains), into which was set the **Window of Appearances**, whence Nefertiti and Akhenaten showered favoured courtiers with gold collars and other rewards. Its orientation in line with the rising sun ensured that they appeared with the sun directly behind them, bathed in the glow of its rays – an effect frequently depicted in Amarna art (see box p.228).

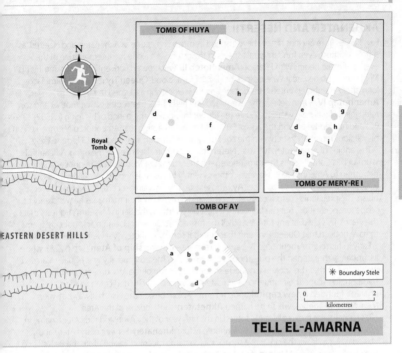

Sanctuary of Aten and beyond

To the south of their residence lay the **Sanctuary of Aten**, probably used for private worship by the royal family, and the home of the High Priest, Panehsi. Beyond spread the city's **residential quarters**: the richest homes beside the road, the poorest hovels backing onto desert.

Also in this quarter was the workshop of the sculptor Tuthmosis, where the famous limestone **bust of Nefertiti** was found in 1912 by Ludwig Borchardt. He deliberately mis-described it as a plaster-cast, so as to take advantage of an agreement that all such finds would be given to Berlin's Ägyptisches Museum. Egypt has long campaigned for its return, and Germany now acknowledges that it has no "moral claim" – but the iconic bust still remains in Berlin.

Northern Palace

The best-preserved outline of an Amarna building is Nefertiti's **Northern Palace** or summer residence, secluded 1500m north of El-Till. Low walls and hollows delineate rooms and courtyards grouped around a garden which once contained a pool that cooled the palace by evaporation. Like all Amarna residences, it was divided into public and private quarters, with north-facing doors to catch the prevailing wind. Rooms were plastered and painted, lit by oil lamps hung from pegs or set in niches, and warmed by braziers over winter. Fitted toilets and bathrooms also featured in the homes of the well-to-do. A magnificent painted floor depicting wildfowl and fish was found here, now in the Egyptian Museum in Cairo. Unlike traditional marsh scenes, Amarna tableaux rarely feature hunting, suggesting that Akhenaten abjured the sport of kings.

The Northern Tombs

Some visitors are content to see just the **Northern Tombs**, 4km from El-Till. Bring a **torch** to spotlight uneven floors and to study the reliefs and paintings (now less clear

2

AKHENATEN AND NEFERTII

Few figures from ancient history have inspired as much conjecture as Akhenaten and Nefertiti, as scholars dispute even fundamental aspects of their story – let alone the interpretation of the events. The tale begins with Pharaoh **Amenhotep III**, who flouted convention by making Tiy, his Nubian concubine, Great Wife, despite her lack of royal blood. **Queen Tiy** remained formidable long after Amenhotep entered his dotage and their eldest son ascended the throne as **Amenhotep IV**. Some believe this event followed his father's death, others that mother and son ruled jointly for twelve years. To square the former theory with the period of his reign (c.1352–1336 BC) and his demise around the age of 30 would mean accepting that Amenhotep IV embarked on his religious reformation between the ages of 9 and 13, though a marriage at 13 is quite likely.

The origins of Amenhotep IV's wife, **Nefertiti**, are obscure. Her name – meaning "A Beautiful Woman Has Come" – suits the romantic legend that she was a Mesopotamian princess originally betrothed to Amenhotep III. However, others identify her as Amenhotep III's child by a secondary wife, or as the daughter of his vizier **Ay**, whose wife, **Tey**, was almost certainly Nefertiti's wet nurse. The pharaonic custom of sister–brother and father–daughter marriages allows plenty of scope for speculation, but the fair-skinned bust of Nefertiti in the Berlin Museum suggests that she wasn't Tiy's child, at any rate. (Amid all the fuss about Cleopatra being black, nobody seems to have noticed that Queen Tiy – and therefore her son, Amenhotep IV – were indubitably so.)

Early in his reign, Amenhotep IV began to espouse the **worship of Aten** (see p.228), whose ascendancy threatened the priesthoods of other cults. The bureaucracy was equally alarmed by his decree that the spoken language should be used in official documents, contrary to all tradition. To escape their influence and realize his vision of a city dedicated to Aten, the pharaoh founded a **new capital** upon an empty plain beside the Nile, halfway between Memphis and Thebes, which he named **Akhetaten**, the "Horizon of the Aten".

It was here that the royal couple settled in the fifth year of their reign and took Aten's name in honour of their faith. He discarded Amenhotep IV for **Akhenaten** (Servant of the Aten) and vowed never to leave the city, while she took a forename meaning "Beautiful are the Beauties of the Aten", styling herself **Nefernefruaten-Nefertiti**. Her status surpassed that of any previous Great Wife, approaching that of Akhenaten himself. Bas-reliefs and stelae show her participating in state festivals, and her own cartouche was coupled with Aten's – an unprecedented association.

There's no sign that their happiness was marred by his decision to take a second wife, **Kiya**, nor of the degenerative condition that supposedly afflicted Akhenaten in later life. However, the great ceremony held at Akhetaten in their twelfth regnal year marked a turning point.

than the copies made by Norman de Garis Davies in the 1900s). Tombs #1 and #2 lack electric lighting and are only shown to visitors who insist. **Photography** is not allowed in any of the tombs.

Tomb of Huya (#1)

As Steward to Queen Tiy and Superintendent of the Royal Harem, **Huya** is shown praying at the entrance, with the text of the *Hymn to Aten* alongside [a]. In the following banqueting scene [b], involving Tiy, the royal couple and two princesses, it may be significant that the dowager queen is merely drinking (which was acceptable by Theban standards of decorum), whereas the Amarna brood tuck in with gusto (an act never hitherto portrayed of royalty). Across the way they imbibe wine, *sans* princesses [c], and then make a royal procession to the Hall of Tribute, where emissaries from Kush and Syria await Akhenaten and Nefertiti [d].

On the rear wall, Akhenaten decorates Huya from the Window of Appearances (notice the sculptor's studio, lower down [e]), who displays his awards [f] on the other side of the portal, the lintel of which portrays three generations of the royal family, including Amenhotep III. Along the east wall, Akhenaten leads Tiy to the temple built for his parents [g]. Huya's mummy was stashed in a burial shaft [h] below the transverse hall, beyond which is a shrine painted with offerings, containing an unfinished statue of Huya [i].

Whether or not this was Akhenaten's true coronation following his father's death, he subsequently launched a **purge against the old cults**. From Kom Ombo in the south to Bubastis in the Delta, temples were closed and statues disfigured, causing public unrest. Although this was quelled by Akhenaten's chief of police, **Mahu**, his foreign minister apparently ignored pleas from foreign vassals menaced by the Hittites and Habiru, and the army was less than zealous in defending Egypt's frontiers. Akhenaten was consequently blamed for squandering the territorial gains of his forefathers.

What happened in the last years of Akhenaten and Nefertiti's reign is subject to various interpretations. The consensus is that Nefertiti and Akhenaten became estranged, and he took as co-regent **Smenkhkare**, a mysterious youth married to their eldest daughter, **Meritaten**. While Nefertiti withdrew to her Northern Palace, Akhenaten and his regent lived together at the other end of the city; the poses struck by them in mural scenes of the period have prompted suggestions of a homosexual relationship. Whatever the truth of this, it's known that Smenkhkare ruled alone for some time after the **death of Akhenaten** (c.1336 BC), before dying himself (see p.298). Nefertiti's fate is less certain, but it's generally believed that she also died around the same time. To date, none of their mummies have been found (or, rather, definitely identified).

The genealogy of Smenkhkare's successor – the boy-king known to posterity as **Tutankhamun** – is obscure. Some hold that his parents were Amenhotep III and his half-sister Sitamun; others favour Ay and Tey, or Akhenaten and Kiya, or even (based on DNA analysis) that he was of Hyksos or Jewish descent. About the only certainty is that he was originally raised to worship Aten, and named Tutankh*aten*.

By renouncing this name for one honouring Amun, he heralded a return to Thebes and the old gods, fronting a **Theban counter-revolution** executed by Vizier Ay and General Horemheb. Some think this was relatively benign while Tut and his successor Ay ruled Egypt, blaming **Horemheb** and Seti I for a later, ruthless extirpation of Atenism.

Seti plundered the abandoned city of Akhetaten for masonry to build new temples, ordered its site cursed by priests to deter reoccupation, and excised the cartouches of every ruler tainted with the "Amarna heresy" from their monuments and the List of Kings. So thorough was this cover-up that Akhenaten and Nefertiti remained unknown to history until the nineteenth century. Since then, they have inspired much scholarly and mystical conjecture, novels such as Naguib Mahfouz's *Akhenaten, Dweller in Truth*, and an opera by Philip Glass.

Tomb of Mery-Re II (#2)

The last resting place of **Mery-Re II**, Overseer of the Two Treasuries, is similar in shape to Huya's tomb, but was constructed late in Akhenaten's reign, since his cartouches have been replaced by Smenkhkare's, and Nefertiti's by Meritaten's. Beyond the entrance (whose adoration scene and *Hymn to Aten* are largely destroyed), the inner walls portray Nefertiti straining a drink for the king, who is seated beneath a sunshade (to the left); and Mery-Re receiving a golden crown, followed by a warm welcome from his household (right). The rear wall bears an unfinished scene of Mery-Re being rewarded by Smenkhkare and Meritaten, drawn in black ink.

Tomb of Ahmose (#3)

This battered tomb is one of the four that visitors usually see. The entrance walls show **Ahmose**, Akhenaten's fan-bearer, praying to Aten, with a now-illegible inscription enjoining the deity to ensure "that there is sand on the shore, that fishes in the stream have scales, and cattle have hair. Let him sojourn here until the swan turns black and the raven white". Inside, you can just discern Ahmose carrying an axe and a fan, his official regalia. On the left-hand wall are bas-reliefs of shield-bearers and pikemen, followed by an outsized horse and chariot outlined in red pigment (presumably intended to represent Akhenaten leading his army into battle, which never happened).

ATEN-WORSHIP AND AMARNA ART

Many herald **Aten-worship** as a breakthrough in human spirituality and cultural evolution: the world's first monotheistic religion. Aten was originally just an aspect of the sun-god (the "Globe" or "Disc" of the midday sun), ranking low in the Theban pantheon until Amenhotep III privately adopted it as a personal deity. Then Akhenaten publicly exalted Aten above other gods, subsuming all their attributes into this newly omnipotent being. Invocations to Maat (representing truth) were retained, but otherwise the whole cast of underworld and celestial deities was jettisoned. Morbid Osirian rites were also replaced by paeans to life in the joyous warmth of Aten's rays (which are usually shown ending in a hand clasping an ankh), as in the famous *Hymn to Aten*.

Similarities between the *Hymn* and *The Song of Solomon* (supposedly written five hundred years later) have encouraged speculation about the influence of Atenism on early Jewish monotheism. Sigmund Freud argued that Moses was an Egyptian nobleman and the biblical Exodus a "pious fiction", while Ahmed Osman advances the theory that Akhenaten's deity derived from tales of the Jewish God related to him by his maternal grandfather Yuya, the Joseph of the Old Testament (see p.626).

Equally intriguing is the artwork of the Amarna period and the questions it raises about Akhenaten. **Amarna art** focused on nature and human life rather than the netherworld and resurrection. Royal portraiture, previously impersonally formalized, was suffused by naturalism (a process which began late in the reign of Amenhotep III). While marshes and wildlife remained a popular subject, these scenes no longer implicitly associated birds and fish with the forces of chaos. The roofless Aten temples made new demands on sculptors and painters, who mixed sunk- and bas-relief carving to highlight features with shifting shadows and illumination.

Most striking is the rendering of **human figures**, especially Akhenaten's, whose attenuated cranium, curvaceous spine and belly, and matronly pelvis and buttocks prompted speculation that the pharaoh may have suffered from Marfan's syndrome – a rare genetic disorder that leads to

feelings of alienation and a slight oddness in physical appearance – or was possibly a hermaphrodite: theories only disproved by DNA testing of royal mummies in 2009. Some argue that the Amarna style reflected Akhenaten's physiognomy, others that such distortions were simply a device that could be eschewed, as in the exquisite bust of Nefertiti. Advocates of the "Akhenaten was sick" theory point out that this was the only time when vomiting was ever represented in Egyptian art; however, Amarna art also uniquely depicted royalty eating, yet nobody asserts that other pharaohs never ate.

Nefertiti and Akhenaten

In the transverse hall are two false doors, a deep vertical shaft, and a defaced, life-size statue of Ahmose in a niche.

Tomb of Mery-Re I (#4)

High Priest **Mery-Re I** (father of Mery-Re II) rated a superior tomb, with a coloured cornice around its entrance [a] and false columns of painted flowers at the rear of the vestibule [b]. Reliefs of Mery-Re and his wife, Tenro, at prayer flank the portal [c] into the main chamber, which retains two of its original papyrus-bud columns. Proceeding clockwise round the room, you see Mery-Re's investiture with a golden collar [d], the royal family leaving the palace [e], and Akhenaten in a chariot (his face and the Aten symbol have been chiselled out, as usual). Scenes of offerings [f] and Aten-worship [g] flank the left side of a doorway into the unfinished rear chamber, which lacks any decoration. More interesting is the eastern wall [h], depicting Akhenaten and the Great Temple (which has helped archeologists visualize the city's appearance). Notice the sensitive relief of blind beggars awaiting alms, low down in the corner [i].

Tombs of Pentu (#5) and Panehsi (#6)

The third tomb in this cluster belongs to **Pentu**, the royal physician. Its papyrus-bundle columns retain traces of paint with chariots visible on the right-hand wall, but there's little else to see. It's better to head 300m south along the cliff path to the isolated tomb of **Panehsi**, overseer of the royal herds and granaries. Unlike most of the others, its decorative facade has remained intact, but the interior has been modified by Copts who used it as a chapel. To the left of the entrance, the royal family prays above their servants. The painted, apse-like recess in the main chamber is probably a Coptic addition – notice the angel's wings.

The Royal Tomb

It's an easy ten-minute drive to the subterranean **Royal Tomb**, in a desolate ravine 5.5km from the plain. A custodian will ride with you to unlock the tomb. Dug into the bed of the wadi, this tomb was the first from the XVIII Dynasty to run directly from a corridor to a burial chamber. Its burial scene and text were virtually obliterated by Amun's priests, and no mummies were ever found there, but in a chamber off the first descending passage, fragmentary bas-reliefs (now clumsily "restored") depict the funerary rites of one of the royal daughters (either Meketaten or Ankesbaten), and a granite sarcophagus bearing Tiy's cartouche was found, suggesting this might have been a family vault. No one knows whether Akhenaten and Nefertiti were interred in the main burial chamber beyond a deep pit (and perhaps dragged out to rot a few years later) or in the Valley of the Kings. Some believe that the mysterious mummy found in tomb KV55 is Akhenaten's (see p.298), or that Nefertiti's has been discovered in tomb KV35 (see p.303).

The Southern Tombs

From El-Hagg Qandil beyond the ancient Workmen's Village, a spur road runs between palm groves to the **Southern Tombs**, scattered over seven low hills in two clusters: #7–15 and #16–25. Amarna notables buried here include Tutu, the foreign minister, and Ramose, Steward of Amenhotep III, but the ones to see are Ay and Mahu.

Tomb of Ay (#25)

Ay's Tomb was never finished, since he built himself a new one at Thebes after the court returned there under Tutankhamun, but such carvings as were executed show the Amarna style at its apogee and the ceiling of its central aisle is painted with a fetching checkerboard pattern.

Both sides of the tomb's vestibule [a] are decorated. On the left, the king and queen, three princesses, Nefertiti's sister Mutnedjmet and her dwarfs lead the court in the worship of Aten. Across the way is a superb relief of Ay and his wife Tey rendering homage and the most complete text of the *Hymn to Aten*; every fold of their skirts and braid in their hair are meticulously depicted. The really intriguing scenes, however, are in the main chamber. On the left side of the entrance wall, Ay and Tey are showered with decorations from the Window of Appearances, acclaimed by fan-bearers, scribes and guards [b]. Palace life is depicted in ink or sunk-relief: a concubine has her hair done, while girls play the harp, dance, cook and sweep. The depth of bowing by courtiers is the most servile ever found in Egyptian art [c]. Along the rear wall are a ruined door-shaped stele [d] and a stairway leading to an unfinished burial shaft.

Ay and Tey are mysterious figures, honoured as "Divine Father and Mother", but never directly identified as being royal. Some reckon Ay was a son of Yuya and Thuya, Akhenaten's maternal grandparents; others that Tey was Nefertiti's wet-nurse, or that both conceived Tutankhamun. Certainly, Ay was vizier to Amenhotep III, Akhenaten and Tutankhamun, and reigned briefly himself (c.1327–23 BC). He was ultimately buried in the Western Valley of the Theban Necropolis (see p.305).

Tomb of Mahu (#9)

Ten minutes' walk away, the **Tomb of Mahu**, Akhenaten's chief of police and frontier security, opens with a rough-cut transverse hall featuring a scene of Mahu standing before the vizier with two intruders, whom he accuses of being "agitated by some foreign power", as minions heat irons in a brazier for their torture (to the left as you enter). Further in are two more chambers at different levels, linked by a winding stairway. Mind your head on the low ceiling.

Boundary stele and quarries

Akhetaten's periphery was defined by **boundary stelae** carved high up on the cliffs, erected over successive years; their inscriptions and family portraits have enabled archeologists to deduce many events during Akhenaten's reign. The most accessible stele is on the clifftop above the Northern Tombs.

Fine alabaster for the temples and public buildings was dragged from the **Hatnub Quarries**, 10km southeast of the city. These had been used since the Old Kingdom, when they were established by the IV Dynasty pharaoh Khufu (as an inscription in Zone P attests). On the way up the wadi are the remains of workmen's huts and pottery from diverse periods. The quarries can only be reached by 4WD.

ARRIVAL AND DEPARTURE   TELL EL-ARMANA

The completion of a river bridge at Deir el-Bersha, near Mallawi, and a road along the east bank from Beni Hassan and Minya, has made Tell el-Amarna far easier to reach than before.

By private taxi Minya's tourist office (see p.216) can arrange a tour for up to four people (£E150 by taxi, £E200 by limousine) combining Tell el-Amarna with Beni Hassan (see p.219), or Hermopolis and Tuna al-Gabel.

By minibus Minibuses run from Minya to Mallawi, and from there to Deir Mawas, where yet another runs to the car-ferry that crosses the Nile to the village of El-Till – as time-consuming as it sounds.

GETTING AROUND

By private taxi Tell el-Amarna is far too large to explore on foot. For those who arrive without a car, there is one at the site that can drive visitors to the Northern Tombs (for £E4/person), the Southern Tombs (£E6/person) or the Royal Tomb (£E50 for up to four people).

TICKETS AND INFORMATION

Tickets Sold at a kiosk midway between El-Till and the Northern Tombs. One ticket covers the Northern and Southern Tombs; a separate one is required for the Royal Tomb.

Visitors' centre A visitors' centre was under construction at the time of writing by the ferry landing stage in El-Till, although nobody knows when it will be finished. The Amarna Project website (@ amarnaproject.com) is the best source of historical information about the site in the meantime.

Assyut and around

ASSYUT (pronounced "As-*yoot*") was an early stronghold of the Islamist insurgency that convulsed Middle Egypt in the 1990s. The city endured nearly a decade of curfews and arrests, leaving it with the mother of bad reputations – so it's hardly surprising that citizens – and the Christian population especially – rejoiced at **apparitions** of the Virgin Mary that occurred (so people swear) in 2000 and 2005 in the form of a light above two churches. Residents remain more ambivalent about the fame of Assyut-born sex bomb **Ruby** – whose pop-videos make Britney Spears look like a nun – and local Mafioso Izzat Hanafi (hanged in 2008, though many believe he was secretly released and now lives in Greece).

A smoggy metropolis of 400,000 people, Assyut has largely erased its own history. Scores of rock tombs west of town are the only sign of pharaonic **Sawty**, a nome capital which the Greeks renamed Lycopolis (Wolf-town) after the local god, Wepwawet, "Opener of the Ways". Represented as a wolf or jackal of the desert, he was an apt symbol for a city which later prospered from slavery, for it was here that survivors of the Forty Days Road (see p.431) emerged from the desert to be traded wholesale. Aside from its atmospheric bazaar, nowadays the only reasons to come are to visit a few sites outside the city, including a pair of fourth-century **monasteries**. As elsewhere in Middle Egypt, it's advisable to contact the tourist office a few days beforehand, to arrange any excursions (see p.232).

2

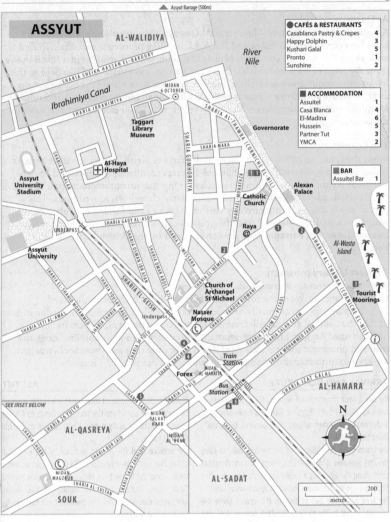

ASSYUT

Assyut Barrage (500m)

AL-WALIDIYA

River Nile

CAFÉS & RESTAURANTS

Casablanca Pastry & Crepes	4
Happy Dolphin	3
Kushari Galal	5
Pronto	1
Sunshine	2

SHARIA SHEIKH HASSAN EL-BAKOUBY

Ibrahimiya Canal

SHARIA IBRAHIMIYA

MIDAN 6 OCTOBER

SHARIA AL-THAWRA (CORNICHE EL-NIL)

Taggart Library Museum

SHARIA MAKA

Governorate

ACCOMMODATION

Assuitel	1
Casa Blanca	4
El-Madina	6
Hussein	5
Partner Tut	3
YMCA	2

SHARIA GUMHORRIYA

Al-Haya Hospital

SHARIA EL-GALAA

Assyut University Stadium

BAR

Assuitel Bar	1

Alexan Palace

SHARIAEL-MOHAFAZA

Catholic Church

Raya @

SHARIA GADY AL-ASDY

UNDERPASS

SHARIA OSMAN IBN AFAN

SHARIA EL-MESSANA

Assyut University

Al-Wasta Island

SHARIA OMAR ABDEL AZIZ

SHARIAEL-NEMEES

Church of Archangel St Michael

SHARIA AL-THAWRA (CORNICHE EL-NIL)

SHARIA FAROUK KIDWANI

SHARIA EL-PETROL

Tourist Moorings

SHARIA EL-GEISH

Underpass

Nasser Mosque

SHARIA TAKSIM EL-PETROL

SHARIA SALAM SALEM

SHARIA EL-SHAHID MOHAMMED

SHARIA TAHRIR FAGER

SHARIA YOUSRY FAGER

SHARIA MASHABA

Train Station

SHARIA MOHAMMED FARID

SHARIA SETI AL-AWAL

SHARIA 26 YULYU

Forex

Bus Station

SHARIA IZAT GALAL

AL-HAMARA

SHARIA 23 YULYU

MIDAN AL-MAHATTA

N

SEE INSET BELOW

SHARIA SARA

MIDAN TALAAT HARB

SHARIA YOUSRY FAGER

SHARIA 26 YULYU

SHARIA SHUKRI

AL-QASREYA

SHARIA BUR SAID

MIDAN AL-BANK

AL-SADAT

MIDAN MAGZOUB

SHARIA SAAD ZAGHLOUL

SHARIA AL-SULTAN

SOUK

0		200

metres

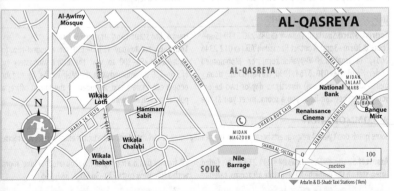

Al-Awimy Mosque

AL-QASREYA

SHARIA 26 YULYU

SHARIA SHUKRI

AL-QASREYA

SHARIA SARA

MIDAN TALAAT HARB

National Bank

MIDAN AL-BANK

Wikala Lotfi

Hammam Sabit

SHARIA BUR SAID

Renaissance Cinema

Banque Misr

N

SHARIA 26 YULYU

SHARIA SAAD ZAGHLOUL

Wikala Chalabi

MIDAN MAGZOUB

SHARIA AL-SULTAN

Wikala Thabat

Nile Barrage

SOUK

0		100

metres

Arba'in & El-Shadr Taxi Stations (1km)

Al-Qasreya

Assyut's old **bazaar** quarter – known as **Al-Qasreya** – is a must-see: a web of shadowy lanes between sharias 26 Yulyu and Bur Said, smelling of incense and offal. To find it, walk along Bur Said till you reach Midan Magzoub, with its remains of a **Nile Barrage** from the reign of Mohammed Ali. Enter the narrow continuation of Bur Said to the left of the mosque and turn right at the first crossroads, to follow the bazaar's main artery – **Sharia al-Qasreya** – past the **Wikala Chalabi** (an old caravanserai) and other Mamluke edifices, emerging on Sharia 26 Yulyu, which you can follow back towards the centre.

The Corniche

From the junction of Sharia 26 Yulyu and Sharia el-Geish, cross the railway tracks via an underpass to stroll along Sharia el-Namees (confusingly signposted "Salah al-Din al-Ayubi" in English), where each evening Assyutis **promenade** past fairy-lit boutiques to a breezy **Corniche** lined with private clubs hosting weddings. This part of town was once inhabited by cotton magnates and foreign consuls, one of whom occupied the **Alexan Palace** (supposedly set for renovation). From here you can see the **Assyut Barrage**, 1km downriver, built by the British between 1898 and 1903.

Taggart Library museum

Midan 6 October • Daily except Fri, Sun & school holidays 8am–2pm • Free

On the northern edge of the town centre next to Midan 6 October, the co-ed Al-Salaam School was originally founded as a boys' college by American missionaries during the colonial era and still retains a somewhat Victorian ambience. Its old-fashioned Taggart Library **museum** displays such curios as mummified dogs and fish, and pharaonic soldiers' dog-tags. If you have time to spare, the school's teachers are keen to introduce their pupils to foreigners, and practice their English.

ARRIVAL AND DEPARTURE ASSYUT

By air Assyut International Airport, 45km southwest of town ☎ 088 231 5481. EgyptAir flies 2–3 times weekly to and from Cairo; other airlines have services to Sharjah, Doha and Jeddah.

By train There are about seven a/c services daily to Cairo (5–7hr), stopping at Mallawi (2hr), Minya (3hr) and Beni Suef (5hr) along the way, plus a similar number calling at Sohag (2hr), Qena (4hr) and Luxor (6hr) en route to Aswan (12hr).

By bus From the bus station in the centre there are services every 2–3hr to Cairo (6–7hr), Sohag (2hr) and

Minya (2–3hr), though all three cities are better reached by train. More useful are the four daily buses to Kharga oasis (4hr); those at 8pm and 10pm run on to Dakhla Oasis (7–8hr).

By service taxi The Arba'in terminal by the El-Mallah canal, 2km from the city centre (£E10 by taxi), serves town along the Valley from Minya to Qena, plus Kharga Oasis (4hr). During Dirunka's Moulid of the Virgin, minibuses run directly to the convent from the nearby El-Shadr taxi terminal.

INFORMATION AND TOURS

Tourist office Sharia al-Thawra ☎ 088 230 5110 (Sun–Thurs 8.30am–3pm). Contact Ramadan Ali (☎ 012 2346 2601, ✉ ramadan.ali48@yahoo.com) or Mohammed Abdel Hamid (☎ 010 6764 1030, ✉ basmalah_doaa_ mohammad@yahoo.com) directly, a day or two before you arrive. They can book you a room, meet you at the

train or bus station and arrange excursions.

Tours Expect to pay £E100–150 for a round-trip to Dirunka, £E250–300 to visit the Burnt Monastery or £E300–350 if combined with the Meir Tombs. Up to four people can share a taxi, arranged by the tourist office; a policeman will ride with you.

ACCOMMODATION

Some hotels don't want foreign guests because of the hassle they entail, so call ahead or ask the tourist office to reserve a room.

Assuitel Sharia el-Thawra ☎ 088 231 2123. This faded three-star on the Corniche has en-suite a/c rooms, satellite

TV, free wi-fi and a rooftop bar. A renovated "deluxe" room with a Nile view costs $20–30 extra. B&B **$65**

Casa Blanca (aka *Dar al-Baydaa*) Sharia Khashaba ☎ 088 233 7662. A few blocks from the train station, this overrated three-star charges way too much for shabby, noisy en-suite a/c rooms, but does at least usually accept foreigners. B&B £E240

El-Madina Sharia Mohammed Farid ☎ 088 237 2507. Near the bus station, so handy for transport but noisy, this dinky two-star has newish a/c en-suite rooms. Some English spoken. £E150

Hussein Sharia Mohammed Farid ☎ 088 234 2532. Next door to *El-Madina*, this older, shabbier hotel is Assyut's cheapest option if the YMCA isn't taking foreigners. No English spoken. £E150

Partner Tut Tourist Moorings ☎ 02 3761 2478. A well-managed hotel-ship beside the Corniche (bookable through *Partner*'s office in Cairo) with a/c en-suite cabins with wi-fi and satellite TV, a restaurant and a swimming pool on deck. B&B $130

YMCA (aka *Nady el-Shaban el-Messihaya*) Sharia el-Namees ☎ 088 232 3218. Contact English-speaking manager Emad Helmy (☎ 012 2293 6396) to arrange to stay. Used by Coptic youth clubs, it has simple rooms with fridges, a large garden and basketball courts out back. £E70

EATING AND DRINKING

Assuitel Bar 6th floor, Assuitel hotel. The only place in town serving alcohol, this shabby rooftop bar has a view of the Nile, Arabic pop videos and cheap beer. Daily 11am–1am.

Casablanca Pastry & Crepes Sharia Khashaba ☎ 088 234 2727. A good spot to eat savoury *fiteer* (Egyptian-style pizzas) or sweet pancakes with various toppings. Daily 11am–10pm.

Happy Dolphin Sharia al-Thawra ☎ 088 229 7575. A floating restaurant, popular with courting couples and wedding parties, serving pizza (£E25–55), mixed grills (£E70) and ice cream. Free wi-fi, and sometimes a DJ. Daily 8am–3am.

Kushari Galal Sharia Sabet. A pit-stop for carbs, selling tasty *kushari* (£E5–8) to eat in or takeaway, although like most such outlets in Middle Egypt, the decor is as basic as it gets. Daily 10am–1am.

★ **Pronto** Sharia el-Namees ☎ 012 0788 8863. Popular with students, this super-clean a/c café serves iced, flavoured and filtered coffee, milkshakes, gateaux and freshly made pizzas (£E25–45). Daily 10.30am–1.30am.

Sunshine Sharia al-Thawra ☎ 088 231 4907. Across the road from the *Happy Dolphin*, this is a bright and cheery place to eat pizza (£E35–55) or mixed grill (£E50–70). Daily 10am–2am.

DIRECTORY

Banks National Bank of Egypt, Midan Talaat Harb (Sun–Thurs 9am–2pm); Banque Misr, Midan al-Bank (Sun–Thurs 9am–2pm). Both have ATMs.

Cinema The small Renaissance Cinema multiplex on Sharia Bur Said (☎ 088 235 3050) screens Western and Bollywood movies, dubbed or subtitled in Arabic.

Hospital Al-Haya, Sharia Mahmoud Rashwan ☎ 088 228 5301.

Internet access Raya, Sharia el-Namees (daily 10am–midnight). There's also free wi-fi for guests at the *Assuitel* hotel and at the *Happy Dolphin* floating restaurant.

Post office Sharia Nahda (Sat–Thurs 8.30am–2pm).

Telephones Sharia el-Geish (daily 24hr).

Tourist police Sharia al-Thawra, above the tourist office ☎ 088 231 7522 (daily 24hr).

Around Assyut

Two **monasteries** in the vicinity of Assyut testify to the roots Christianity put down in this region in the fourth century. Copts believe that these and other sites were actually visited by the **Holy Family** during the four years that Mary, Joseph and the infant Jesus stayed in Egypt to escape King Herod's massacre of the first-born. Although the Bible says little about this period, details of their wanderings were revealed in a dream to Patriarch Theophilus in AD 500, and Copts have made much of this tradition ever since. Indeed, most tourism in the Assyut region involves Copts from other parts of Egypt, making pilgrimages on holy days – although Assyut's tourist office hopes to lure foreigners with the little-visited **Meir Tombs**.

Dirunka: the Convent of the Virgin

12km west of Assyut; to arrange transport to the convent, contact the Assyut tourist office (see p.232) • Daily 8am–5pm (24hr during the Moulid of the Virgin; closed throughout May) • Free

The hilly locality of Dirunka is synonymous with the **Convent of the Virgin** (Deir el-Adhra) that is sited there. Dirunka's caves are believed by Copts to have sheltered the

Holy Family and early Christian hermits. From such troglodyte origins, the present convent has grown into what resembles a fortified campus – cynics might say a refuge for Assyut's Coptic population, should the worst ever occur.

The expansion is justified by the one million pilgrims who attend the **Moulid of the Virgin** (Aug 15–30). This occasions the parading of icons around the spacious cave church where they stand for most of the year. Pilgrims are photographed against a huge portrait of the Virgin, or the verdant plain overlooked by the convent's terrace, below which is a Coptic village where nuns operate a dispensary. About fifty nuns and monks live in the convent.

The Burnt Monastery

Ad-Deir al-Muharraq, 58km northwest of Assyut; to arrange transport to the monastery, contact the Assyut tourist office (see p.232) • Daily except Thurs & Fri 9am–2pm • £E25

Downriver from Assyut, the town of El-Qusiya and its satellite villages have the highest ratio of Christians to Muslims of any region in Egypt. Sporadic anti-Coptic pogroms inspired by local imams have left them fearful, clinging to the spiritual and physical security of the **Burnt Monastery** (Deir el-Muharraq) near the desert's edge, whose **Moulid of the Virgin** (June 21–28) draws hundreds of thousands of pilgrims.

The monastery's tinderbox surroundings explain the name and protective walls; the crenellated inner rampart is still blackened from a conflagration that occurred in the 1990s. Visitors are shown around the thriving modernized establishment, except on fast days. Many of the students at its Theological College will become monks when they turn 25. Within the compound are grouped the Abbot's residence, a fourth-century keep and two ancient churches.

Believers maintain that the **cave sanctuary** of the **Church of the Anointed** (El-Azraq) once hid the Holy Family for six months and ten days, and that the church was the first in the world (consecrated in 60 AD), foretold in the Old Testament as "an altar to the Lord in the midst of the land of Egypt" (Isaiah 19:19–21). It's also said that what is now the altar stone was once used to block the cave's entrance. When an abbot ordered its replacement, the mason's hand was paralysed and a vision of Jesus appeared, intoning "Leave it alone." The icon of the Virgin and Child is said to be painted by St Luke; the apostles in the **Church of St George** come from Ethiopia. Remove your shoes before entering the churches.

The Meir Tombs

62km northwest of Assyut; to arrange transport to the tombs, contact the Assyut tourist office (see p.232) • Daily except Thurs & Fri 9am–2pm • £E25

Named after the village 6km away, the rock-hewn **Meir Tombs** once belonged to the rulers of the fourteenth nome, whose capital Qis or Cusae was the ancestor of El-Qusiya. Nine of its seventeen tombs are open to the public, several of them still vividly coloured.

Tombs #1 and #2 are inscribed with 720 deities, defaced by the Christian hermits that once dwelt there, while in tomb #4 the original grid drawn on the wall to help the artists execute their designs is faintly visible.

Best of all are the splendid desert hunting scene in the tomb of **Senbi-Sa-Ukh-hotep**, and the women's fashions of the XII Dynasty depicted in Chancellor **Ukh-hotep**'s tomb. Model boats from these tombs are exhibited in the Luxor Museum (see p.263).

Sohag and around

Set on a rich agricultural plain bounded by the arid hills of the Eastern and Western deserts, **SOHAG** (pronounced "So*haj*") is a city of 390,000 people with a large Christian community and a small university. Before the troubles of the 1990s, many tourists used Sohag as a base for visiting the nearby **Red and White monasteries** or Abydos Temple, further away (see p.245), having first seen the colossal statue of an Ancient Egyptian princess in the satellite town of **Akhmim**, beyond the east bank district of **Medinet Nasr**.

Though few visitors come nowadays, the authorities hope tourism will eventually pick up with the opening of the **Sohag Museum**, intended to showcase some five thousand artefacts found within the governorate, from the Middle Kingdom until Greco-Roman times. Its inauguration date keeps slipping but is currently forecast for 2014.

Meanwhile, the only other attractions are two local events. The Monday-morning Souk el-Itnayn is a huge **farmers market** that has been held in Sohag since time immemorial. Every week, livestock, fresh produce, farming implements and handwoven baskets are sold in the streets around a cemetery in the southern part of town. A few weeks before the nationwide feast of Eid al-Adha, on the 25th day of the Islamic month of Shawal, people honour the city's patron sheikh with the **Moulid of Al-Aref**, held in and around his mosque, with all-night koranic recitals, Sufi *zikrs* and fairground rides for kids.

Al-Aref Mosque

Sharia el-Mahatta

Sohag's most venerable place of worship is the fourteenth-century **Al-Aref Mosque**, rebuilt in the 1960s. Non-Muslims who express an interest are usually welcome to look inside, although you'll need to put plastic bags over your feet if not wearing socks. Off

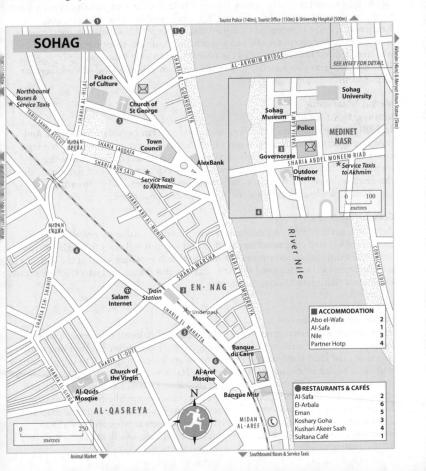

the main prayer hall with its arabesque ceiling is the shrine of Sidi Aref Bellah, a Sufi mystic about whom little is known, though he is credited with great *baraka*. A small cemetery beside the mosque contains the tomb of Murad Bey, the only Mamluke to escape the infamous massacre at Cairo's Citadel (see p.111)

Other mosques and churches

Muslims and Copts worship cheek by jowel in the congested Al-Qasreya quarter, where the Fatimid-style **Al-Quds Mosque** almost backs on to the **Church of the Virgin** in a parallel street. A nearby workshop caters to both faiths, making perfumed floral "pictures" of the Kaaba at Mecca and Christian saints.

The diocese of Sohag is administered from the cathedral **Church of St George**, near Midan Opera. Like the Church of the Virgin, it was built in the twentieth century, but already seems hallowed by time.

Akhmim

On the Nile's east bank, a gaudy statue of a princess marks the municipal boundary between the suburb of Medinet Nasr and the agricultural town of **AKHMIM,** which the sixteenth-century Moorish geographer-historian Leo Africanus reckoned "the oldest city in Egypt". Akhmimis have built on the rubble of their ancestors since Pre-dynastic times. Its name comes from the Coptic "Khmim", recalling a local fertility god, Khente-Min, often represented by a giant **phallus**. Legend has it all the town's men were killed at war except for one lucky youth who had to re-stock the population and was later deified. The Greeks called the town Panopolis, after their own priapic god, Pan. Egyptologists also associate it with the Akhmim Tablet, a kind of worksheet for scribes, defining mathematical units.

Meryut Amun statue

Midan Meryut Amun • Daily 9am–3pm • £E25

In 1981 excavations to build a school uncovered an 11m-high **statue of Meryut Amun**, now displayed in a pit. Since you can see it from street level, it's only worth buying a ticket to examine the statue's finely carved wig and skirt and the cartouches that identify it as Nefertari's eldest daughter, who had to marry her father, Ramses II, after the death of his second wife, Istnofret (as did her half-sister). When found, the limestone figure had rouged lips, but the colour has since faded.

Colossus of Ramses II

Across the street behind Meryut Amun's head, another, smaller pit reveals the plinth and legs of a seated **colossus of Ramses II**. The colossus is reckoned to weigh 700 tons and to be nearly as large as the ones at Abu Simbel; it probably stood at the entrance to a vast temple whose ruins awed the Arab explorer Ibn Batuta, and which is thought to lie beneath Akhmim's Muslim cemetery.

Weaving factory

Midan Meryut Amun • No set hours • Free

The building with green gates to the right of Ramses' colossus is home to a **weaving factory**, one of four built in the 1900s using power-looms from England that nearly wiped out the local hand-weaving industry – a tradition going back to the pharaohs, who were buried in shrouds of Akhmim silk. Hand-weaving was only preserved by a missionary inspired **Women's Cooperative** (Rahabaat) whose tapestries now sell for thousands of dollars. The cooperative's weavers forgo any publicity in order not to irritate their menfolk, who work the power-looms in another section of the factory. The factory, however, may let you see its (male) weavers at work and has a shop downstairs, selling tablecloths, sheets and cuts from bolts of silk or cotton – all in 1950s' patterns.

Monasteries near Sohag

The **Red and White monasteries** southwest of Sohag are both small and dilapidated, yet their near-desolation seems more evocative of the early Christians who sought God in the desert than busier establishments like Dirunka. Only a handful of acolytes tend the chapels, but deeply worn flagstones and a plethora of plastic medallions attest to the hordes of pilgrims who visit them during Shenoudi's moulid in July.

The White Monastery

Ad-Deir al-Abyad, 12km southwest of Sohag; to arrange transport to the monastery, contact the Sohag tourist office (see p.238) • Daily 7am–dusk • Free (but donations appreciated)

Situated at the edge of the cultivated plain, the **White Monastery** (Deir al-Abyad) is named for the colour of its high limestone walls and other masonry, taken from pharaonic or Roman buildings. Supposedly founded by St Helena on her way back from Jerusalem, the monastery once possessed the greatest Coptic library in Egypt (now dispersed among museums worldwide) and was home to over two thousand monks. Today it has only twenty residents, and its courtyard is flanked by ruined cloisters and cells. Despite its fortress-like walls – which are much thicker at the base and topped with a Cavetto cornice in the Ancient Egyptian style – the monastery was often sacked by marauders.

Remove your shoes before entering the **Church of St Shenoudi**, a lofty basilica admitting breezes and birdsong, observed by a stern-faced Christ Pantokrator. Note the monolithic granite pulpit halfway along the northern wall, Roman columns in the apses and pharaonic hieroglyphics on the outer rear wall. The monastery is also known as Deir Anba Shenoudi after its fifth-century founder, who enforced the monastic rule with legendary beatings – on one occasion, fatally. Shenoudi condemned bathing as an upper-class luxury maintained by the sweat of the poor; early monks cleansed themselves by rolling naked in the sand.

It's hard to imagine the monastery packed with pilgrims during **Shenoudi's moulid**, a two-week event attended by over a million people, which reaches its climax on July 14. Among those seeking *baraka* are childless women, who roll down nearby hills in sacks, hoping to obtain divine intervention – a custom dating back centuries, if not millennia.

The Red Monastery

4km northeast of the White Monastery; to arrange transport to the monastery, contact the Sohag tourist office (see p.238) • Daily 7am–dusk • Free (but donations appreciated)

Ad-Deir al-Abyad village straggles beside the road past walled Coptic and Muslim cemeteries, concealing the **Red Monastery** (Deir al-Ahmar) from view. Built of dark red brick, the monastery is attributed to St Bishoi, a penitent armed robber who became Shenoudi's disciple (retaining his club as a reminder); hence its other sobriquet, Deir Anba Bishoi.

The principal **Church of sts Bishoi and Bigol** is remarkable for its sixth- and seventh-century **murals** – covering the walls, pillars and niches – which the American Research Center in Egypt has restored to their original colours. Saints glower from the south apse; peacocks and gazelles graze among the flora and fauna in the eastern apse.

In the courtyard's far corner squats the smaller **Red Church**, whose inner sanctum is barred to women; notice the intricate peg-locks on the doors.

ARRIVAL AND DEPARTURE   **SOHAG**

By air Sohag International Airport, 25km south of town, was created to handle EgyptAir flights to and from Cairo and the Gulf States. None was operating at the time of writing but they might resume in the future.

By train There are about seven a/c services daily to Cairo (6–10hr), stopping at Assyut (2hr), Mallawi (3hr 30min), Minya (4hr) and Beni Suef (5hr) along the way, plus a similar number calling at Qena (2hr) and Luxor (3hr) en route to Aswan (6hr). Only third-class trains stop at Al-Balyana, for Abydos (see p.250).

2

By bus From the bus station south of the centre there are services to Assyut (2hr) and Qena (1hr 30min) every 2–3hr, though both are better reached by train.

By service taxi The terminal near Midan Opera serves Assyut, Minya and other points north. Minibuses to Qena leave from a terminal near the bus station.

GETTING AROUND

By taxi Foreigners must take a private taxi for journeys to Akhmim (roughly £E25/hr), the monasteries and Abydos (see p.245). On the way back from Akhmim, however, you might be able to use local minibuses (£E2). The inconsistency arises because each municipality has its own police command; taxis may have to wait for a change of escort cars at the "border", marked by a statue of a pharaonic princess with a harp.

INFORMATION AND TOURS

Tourist office Medinet Nasr ☏ 093 460 4453 (Sun–Thurs 8.30am–3pm). Contact English-speaking Ahmed Zakaria (☏ 010 1887 9770, ✉ ahmedlion_tower@yahoo.com) a day or two before you arrive to book a hotel room and arrange any excursions by taxi.

Tours Expect to pay £E70–80 for a round-trip by taxi to the Red and White monasteries, or £E100–150 for an excursion to Abydos (see p.245). You will be accompanied by a policeman.

ACCOMMODATION

As in Assyut, hotels may be reluctant to accept foreign guests, so phone ahead to reserve a room.

Abo el-Wafa Midan al-Mahatta ☏ 093 231 9333. Take the lift to reception on the fifth floor of this illuminated high-rise block behind the station, which has small a/c en-suite rooms with TV, and wi-fi throughout. Ask for a room at the back to avoid the noise of trains pulling into the station at all hours. B&B **£E200**

Al-Safa Sharia el-Gumhorriya, 200m north of the Al-Akhmim Bridge ☏ 093 230 7701. The fanciest establishment on the west bank, this well-maintained three-star has a/c en-suite rooms with satellite TV, fridges and balconies facing the river, plus a terrace, restaurant and wi-fi in the lobby. **£E305**

Nile Medinet Nasr ☏ 093 460 6034. Something of a white elephant given how few tourists visit Sohag, this colossal three-star pile on the east bank of the Nile has views from many of its spacious and clean a/c rooms. There's also a pleasant riverside terrace and wi-fi in the lobby. B&B **£E300**

Partner Hotp Corniche Jedid, Medinet Nasr ☏ 010 0992 7323. A sterile hotel-ship moored on the east bank of the Nile, with comfy a/c en-suite cabins, a pool on deck and wi-fi throughout. Sometimes fully booked by Egyptian tour groups, so reserve ahead if you're intent on staying here. B&B **£E130**

EATING

Al-Safa Sharia el-Gumhorriya ☏ 093 230 7701. The breezy Nile terrace is the main attraction of dining here. A meal of kebab or kofta with rice and salad costs about £E80, and they sometimes also serve fish. Daily noon–9pm.

El-Arbala Midan al-Aref ☏ 010 6191 0719. This hole-in-the-wall place near the Al-Aref Mosque does freshly fried fish with rice and salad (£E11), and nothing else. Daily 10am–11pm.

Eman Midan al-Mahatta. Another tiny den with a few tables inside, where you can enjoy freshly baked sweet or savoury *fiteer* (Egyptian pizzas-cum-pancakes). Daily 24hr.

Koshari Goha Off Midan Opera. This busy *kushari* joint has a/c seating upstairs and a takeaway at street-level.

Most locals maintain that its *kushari* is the best in Sohag, but a minority prefer the *Kushari Akeer Saah*. Daily 24hr.

Kushari Akeer Saah Sharia al-Mahatta. Another, smaller *kushari* joint whose name means "Last Hour" (alluding to the fact that it used to be the only 24hr outlet in town), although many of its customers have now defected to *Koshari Goha*, leaving it a bit forlorn. Daily 10am–1am.

Sultana Café Sharia al-Hilal ☏ 093 223 2431. Modelled on *Fishawi*'s in Cairo (see p.189), this friendly retro-arabesque hangout has a shady terrace and a stuccoed a/c interior with a large-screen TV showing pop videos and football. Try their freshly made juices (£E15). Daily 24hr.

NIGHTLIFE

Outdoor Theatre Corniche Jedid, Medinet Nasr. This stone-faced ampitheatre beside the Al-Akhmim bridge-ramp hosts occasional concerts and theatrical performances under the auspices of the Palace of Culture ☏ 093 231 0436.

Palace of Culture Off Midan Opera ☏ 093 231 0436.

The Sohag Folkloric Troupe is noted for its performances of the Taghribat Beni Hilal, a medieval epic relating the Beni Hilal tribe's journey from Arabia to conquer Tunisia. Ask the tourist office to make enquiries if you're interested, as no English is spoken at the Palace of Culture itself.

DIRECTORY

Banks AlexBank (Sun–Thurs 9am–2pm), Banque du Caire (Sun–Thurs 8.30am–2pm) and Banque Misr (Sun–Thurs 9am–2pm) on Sharia el-Gumhorriya all have ATMs.
Hospital Sohag University Hospital, Medinet Nasr ☏ 093 460 9311.

Internet access Dot, in an alley near Midan al-Mahatta (daily 10am–midnight).
Post office Sharia el-Gumhorriya (Sat–Thurs 8.30am–2pm).
Telephone office Sharia el-Gumhorriya (daily 24hr).
Tourist police Medinet Nasr ☏ 093 460 9311 (daily 24hr).

Upper Egypt

2

In antiquity, **Upper Egypt** started at Memphis and ran as far south as Aswan on the border with Nubia. Nowadays, with the designation of Middle Egypt, borders are a bit hazy, though the **Qena Bend** is generally taken as the region's beginning and **Aswan** is still effectively the end of the line.

Within this stretch of the Nile is the world's most intensive concentration of ancient monuments – temples, tombs and palaces constructed from the onset of the Middle Kingdom (c.2050 BC) up until Roman and Byzantine times. The greatest of the buildings are the **cult temples** of **Abydos**, **Dendara**, **Karnak**, **Esna**, **Edfu**, **Kom Ombo**, **Philae** and **Abu Simbel**, each conceived as "homes" for their respective deities and comprising an accretion of centuries of building. Scarcely less impressive are the multitude of tombs in the **Theban Necropolis**, most famously in the **Valley of the Kings**, across the river from **Luxor**, where Tutankhamun's resting place is merely a hole in the ground by comparison with those of such great pharaohs as Seti I and Ramses II.

Monuments aside, Upper Egypt marks a subtle shift of character, with the desert closing in on the river and dom palms growing alongside barrel-roofed houses, designed to reflect the intense heat. One of the greatest pleasures to be had here – indeed one of the highlights of any Egyptian trip – is to absorb the river-scape slowly from the vantage point of a **felucca**. This is easily arranged in Aswan, whence you can sail downriver with no fear of being becalmed; Nile **cruise boats** and **dahabiyas** provide a more luxurious experience. While cruises can be booked at short notice in either city, better deals are usually available in Aswan.

Nile trips

Some people love **Nile cruise boats**, others hate them. On the plus side they offer the chance to travel the river with all the comforts of a four- or five-star hotel. The downside is that you'll visit temples with hundreds of other tourists according to a rigid timetable, amid much noise and air pollution wherever dozens of boats are moored alongside each other – which is hardly surprising when there are over 330 cruisers plying the river between Luxor and Aswan.

For those with money to burn, a **dahabiya** cruise is everything a journey on the Nile should be, recalling a leisurely age of tourism before steamer tours, and as more *dahabiyas* take to the Nile, prices are dropping. At the other end of the scale, **felucca** journeys between Aswan and Luxor are a uniquely Egyptian experience which many travellers rate as the highlight of their visit – though tales of misery aren't uncommon either.

Nile cruise boats

The indubitable advantage of Nile cruises is that they're cheap. **Package tours** from Europe with a return flight and a cruise often cost far less than flights and hotels booked independently. Peak times are Christmas, New Year and Easter, when most (but not all) tour operators raise their prices. In Britain, you can search for deals on ⓦ nilecruisesdirect.com. **Independent travellers** can find bargains in Luxor or Aswan (Cairo is risky unless you deal directly with the company owning the boat). Budget hotels like Luxor's *Oasis* (see p.269) or Aswan's *Nubian Oasis* (see p.349) can book a double cabin in a five-star boat for $60 a night, or $40 a night for a single cabin (except in Dec, when berths may be unavailable), while agencies like Travco and Eastmar offer **deals** on some of the ritzy ships listed below. Alternatively, you can put on smart clothes and go hunting along the Corniche, where boats are moored. The boat manager is likely to quote a lower rate than travel agencies, especially if the boat is

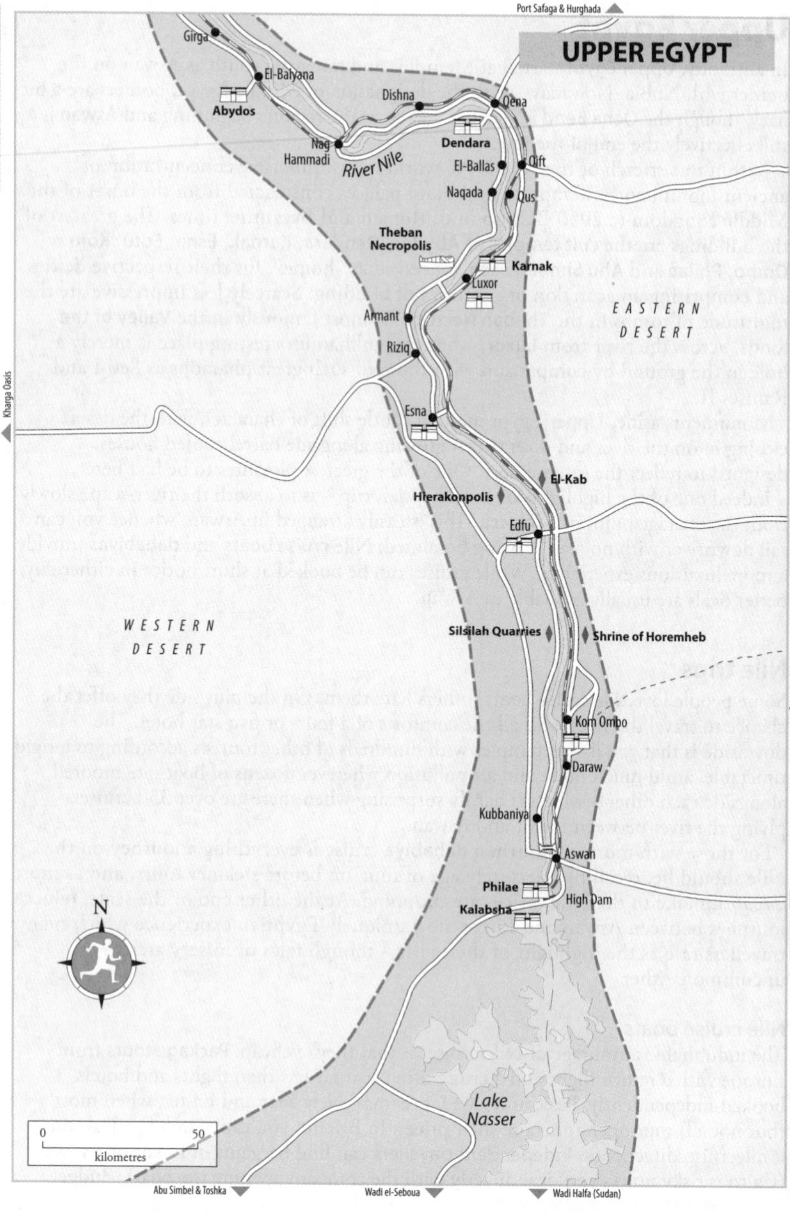

2

Port Safaga & Hurghada

UPPER EGYPT

Girga
El-Balyana
Abydos
Dishna
Qena
Nag Hammadi
River Nile
Dendara
El-Ballas — Qift
Naqada — Qus
Theban Necropolis
Karnak
Luxor
EASTERN DESERT
Armant
Riziq
Esna
El-Kab
Hierakonpolis
Edfu
WESTERN DESERT
Silsilah Quarries — ◆ **Shrine of Horemheb**
Kom Ombo
Daraw
Kubbaniya
Aswan
Philae
Kalabsha
High Dam

Kharga Oasis

N

0 — 50
kilometres

Lake Nasser

Abu Simbel & Toshka — Wadi el-Seboua — Wadi Halfa (Sudan)

near its sailing time and only half full, or you have a bottle of Johnny Walker Black Label to throw into negotiations.

There are two basic **itineraries**: seven nights to Aswan and back starting from Luxor (or vice versa), or a briefer trip commencing at either end, which means two nights' sailing if you start from Luxor or a one-night cruise from Aswan. All these journeys include stopovers at the temples of Edfu and Kom Ombo, and an indeterminate wait to pass through the **locks at Esna**, which makes it unwise to rely on getting back to Luxor or Cairo just in time for a flight home. When the locks are **closed** for a fortnight's maintenance in June and the first half of December, passengers are bussed from Esna to sites up to three hours' distant.

In 2012, Bales (ⓦbalesworldwide.com) and Belle Époque Travel (ⓦdahabiya.com) revived "**full Nile**" cruises between Cairo and Aswan (lasting fifteen days), which had been halted by the Islamist insugency in Middle Egypt during the mid-1990s. At the time of writing, it's too early to say whether these will become a regular fixture or not.

Choosing a boat

You'll be told that all the **boats** rate four or five stars, which the Ministry of Tourism has indeed awarded them, but **standards** vary from bog-average three-star up to the palatial. Even an average vessel will have a/c en-suite cabins, a restaurant, bar, sun deck and swimming pool; superior boats have double beds, large bathrooms, patio doors and balconies. Try to avoid getting a cabin on the lowest deck, where your view of the passing scenery may be restricted by riverbanks.

Though some tourists expect (and pay for) ultraviolet water sterilization, it is basic **hygiene** controls that will determine your health on a Nile cruise. Rather than **tip** your cabin cleaner at the end of the voyage, do so at the beginning as an incentive; cleaners are paid less than £E50 a day.

Other things to consider are the quality of **meals** (included in the price, but ranging from mediocre to sumptuous), the inflated cost of **alcohol** (many people smuggle booze aboard despite prohibition), seating arrangements (independent travellers are obliged to eat at the same table) and **moorings**. Boats in Luxor and Aswan are gradually being moved to new berths far outside town, but those belonging to chains like *Sonesta*, *Sofitel* and *Mövenpick* may continue to dock by their respective hotels.

Boats grossly overcharge for **onshore excursions** in Luxor or Aswan. The management won't mind if you find a cheaper way unless you tell other passengers about it.

Dahabiyas

Egypt's pharaohs loved their pleasure-barges: Cleopatra and Julius Caesar spent nine months sailing round Egypt escorted by four hundred ships. Some of this luxury rubbed off on the houseboats that conveyed Ottoman officials up and downriver, dubbed **dahabiya** (from the Arabic for "gold") after their gilded railings. Despite the advent of Cook's tours in the 1860s, some Europeans still preferred to choose one of the two hundred *dahabiyas* for hire at the Cairo port of Bulaq, but by the 1900s steamers and railways had relegated them to Cairo love nests, which later went to the scrap-yard or were left to rot in the 1960s.

Thirty years later, a few entrepreneurs began refurbishing *dahabiyas* to run exclusive cruises, which proved so successful that replicas are now being built at Esna, Rosetta and Cairo. Though sometimes rented to tour groups, they are often **chartered** for a private cruise by newlyweds, families or friends. Passengers are less constrained by schedules and moorings than on cruise boats, making it feasible to visit sites at quiet times or where larger ships can't moor, so besides the temples at Esna, Edfu and Kom Ombo, you get to explore **El-Kab** and **Silsilah**, which are otherwise difficult to reach (see p.324 & p.329).

A typical *dahabiya* has a spacious salon; wood-panelled cabins ventilated by sliding louvres, with brass fittings and tiled bathrooms; and an upper deck where meals are eaten, whose awning can be rolled back for sunbathing. Besides sightseeing and stopovers there is backgammon, a library of books and CDs, and maybe live music or dancing after supper for entertainment. Meals are lavish, washed down with fruit juices, beer or cocktails. Filtered water and rigorous hygiene mean that sickness is seldom a problem. Unless carefully designed, boats over 38m long can't travel by sails alone and have to use engines (thus technically disqualifying them from being called *dahabiyas*) or be towed by a tug.

Three- to five-day **itineraries** start or end in Esna or Aswan; longer voyages from Luxor to Aswan and back (or vice versa) are also available. If finishing or starting at Esna, transport to or from Luxor is provided. The **price** usually includes transfers, meals and soft drinks, excursions and tickets to the temples en route (but not necessarily in and around Aswan and Luxor) – read the small print carefully.

Feluccas

These single-masted boats have been sailing the Nile since ancient times and offer a unique experience of the river. Sailing so low in the water, the Nile's horizon recedes like an infinity pool, its stillness broken only by passing cruise boats. Evenings often end round a campfire, enlivened by singing and drumming. Most people sleep on mattresses aboard the felucca, but some prefer camping ashore. Each day will be different from the last: stow your phone and take things as they come.

Whether your felucca trip is blissful, tragicomic or unpleasant depends on a host of factors. Nights are chilly in winter and otherwise cool except in summer, when days are scorching. Nile breezes may be cooling, but winds from the desert can suck you dry and the effect of ultraviolet rays is magnified by water.

Itineraries

As the wind nearly always blows south, travelling downstream (towards Luxor) involves constant tacking, unless you simply drift with the sluggish current, but there's no chance of being becalmed, unlike sailing upriver, where the cliffs between Esna, Edfu and Kom Ombo block the wind – which is why almost all journeys start **from Aswan**. Since feluccas are forbidden to sail on the Nile after dark, the distance covered by **itineraries** is reduced and tourists' expectations often exceed reality. Short daylight hours in winter and the low water level between October and May may also cause delays.

Unless the wind is especially strong, a one-day one-night trip usually only gets you to **Kubbaniya** – a few miles beyond the Aswan Bridge – where many boatmen have their family homes, to which you'll be invited for dinner. A two-day two-night trip should take you at least as far as **Darow** if not all the way to **Kom Ombo** (visiting the temple next day), while three days and three nights should include a visit to **Silsilah** and end up somewhere short of **Edfu**. Whatever your final landfall, **onwards travel by minibus** to Luxor – with **stopovers** at Kom Ombo and/or Edfu temples – is usually included in the deal (if not, drivers charge about £E40/person).

Note that it's also possible to hire a felucca for a half-day outing or day-trip, as detailed in the accounts of Luxor and Aswan.

Arranging a felucca trip

Typically, each vessel has an English-speaking Nubian captain and carries six to eight passengers (the largest boats take twelve). Arranging a trip **through a hotel** is easier than doing it yourself, but some places use unreliable captains, or take such large commissions that the disgruntled crew pester passengers for baksheesh. Alternatively, you can **find a captain yourself** after gathering some would-be fellow passengers together. Beware of people claiming to be from this or that family or felucca, who approach you in waterfront restaurants or are recommended by Aswan's tourist office - it's better to contact respected outfits directly

DEIR EL-BAHRI (P.306) >

2

The cost should also cover three **meals** a day: usually simple vegetarian food. It's up to passengers to buy their own bottled **water**, snacks and sweets; crews will purchase **beer** for you if asked. Smoking **dope** is tolerated or encouraged on many, but not all, boats – the Jamaica family (see p.245) has a "no *bango*" rule on its trips. If you're not sure about a crew, **women** will benefit from teaming up with some men for the duration: an all-female group might have problems.

Establish the number of **passengers** before you go and don't be talked into accepting others later on, or food supplies and space will be more limited than you'd expected. It helps if everyone knows what has been negotiated to ensure solidarity in the event of a dispute with the crew. Before departing, you might be asked for a photocopy of your passport for **registration** with the River Police, but many captains don't bother, knowing that the rule is rarely enforced.

Blankets are provided but seldom enough to keep you warm at night during winter, when a sleeping bag is advisable (bring one with you). Ensure that the boat has a canvas awning to protect you from the sun and double as a tent at night; adequate mattresses, a kerosene stove and lamp and a padlocked luggage hold. For those wanting more **comfort**, a few captains have custom-made "deluxe" vessels featuring canvas "cabins" and a fridge, or a shower and a toilet.

Less reputable captains can be careless of **hygiene**, resulting in passengers getting sick. Buy plenty of bottled water, or the crew may dip into the Nile for drinking or cooking purposes. Bring sterilizing tablets to purify the jerry can of Nile water used for washing up, and carbolic soap for handwashing. Also essential are a hat, sunscreen and bug repellent (especially during summer).

NILE TRIPS

CRUISE BOATS

The following cruise boats are a cut above the rest – and costlier.

★ **Misr** ⓦ travelinstyle.com. This Nile steamship was built in 1918 for the British navy and later luxuriantly refitted as King Farouk's private steamer. Its 24 cabins and eight suites accommodate no more than 45 passengers, making it far more intimate than larger cruise ships. A seven-night cruise costs from $3,450/person.

St George ⓦ sonesta.com. The flagship of the *Sonesta* fleet, with a full-service spa and fitness centre, nightly entertainment and over-the-top decor. Seven-night cruises start at $2,240/person, but are considerably cheaper on the *St George*'s less opulent sister ships, the *Star Goddess*, whose cabins are all suites (from $675/person), *Moon Goddess* (from $300), *Nile Goddess* (from $300) and *Sun Goddess* (from $200).

★ **Sudan** ⓦ steam-ship-sudan.com. Commissioned in 1885 for Cook's fleet, this vintage paddle steamer once belonged to King Fouad and was later used as a set in *Death on the Nile*. With only 22 cabins, it has bags of character, which makes up for the lack of a pool. No children under 7. Four- and five-day cruises from €900/1200/person in winter, €600/800 in summer.

Triton Bookable through ⓦ nile-cruise-egypt.com and other tour agencies. Perhaps the ritziest cruise boat on the Nile, with an indoor and outdoor pool, a spa, a gourmet à la carte restaurant, and a steward for each of its twenty staterooms (from $380–510/person/night).

Zahra ⓦ oberoihotels.com. This *Oberoi*-managed boat has all mod cons, with a full-service spa included in the price. Rates for one person sharing a cabin start from €4,340 for a seven-night cruise.

DAHABIYAS

The following are the best of the fifty-odd *dahabiyas* on the Nile.

Africa, **African Queen**, **Candarella**, **Bab el-Nil**, **El Gouna** and **Karim** ⓦ nilesailing.com. Three *dahabiyas* and three *sandales* (Nile cargo sailing boats), designed, built and captained by members of the same family. Their decor is a bit cheesy, but everything else is fine.

Amirat ⓦ sonesta.com. This modern-style boat managed by the Sonesta chain has full-sized bathtubs in its cabin bathrooms, and a jacuzzi on deck. A seven-night cruise costs from $2,236/person.

Assouan, **El-Nil**, **Meröe** and **Melouka** ⓦ nourelnil.com. At 52m, *Meröe* is the largest *dahabiya* on the Nile, with ten spacious cabins and a huge suite. *Melouka*'s six cabins are also on the generous size, while *El-Nil* has room for twenty passengers, and the smaller *Assouan* up to sixteen. Rates start at €1100/person for five nights.

El-Bey (His Lordship), **El-Hanem** (Her Ladyship), **Nesma** (Breeze), **Zahra** (Flower), **Amber** and **Musk** ⓦ dahabiya.com. Run by Belle Époque Travel in Cairo, these 38m-long replica antique vessels each sleep up to twelve passengers in six cabins, panelled in dark wood. None are licensed to serve alcohol, so passengers should bring their own.

★ **Neferu-Ra** ⓦmuseum-tours.com. Built for Omar Pasha in 1910, this 23m-long vessel sleeps up to seven people in three cabins and a suite. The five-day cruise is part of a fifteen-day itinerary including several days in Cairo, which costs $8,250/person. Also available for private charter.

★ **Orient** and **Zekrayaat** (Memories) ⓦnile-dahabiya .com. Run by the owner of *Sofra* restaurant in Luxor (see p.274), these two replica boats are tastefully furnished with antiques. Each has six cabins and a suite; rates are around €175–220/person/day, over three or four nights.

Princess Donia ⓦprincessdonia.com. With its MFI-style decor and TVs in its cabins, this boat bears little resemblance to an antique *dahabiya*, but is nonetheless comfortable. Five- or seven-night cruises from €150/ person a day; also available for private charter.

Royal Cleopatra ⓦbalesworldwide.com. A converted *sandale* with two a/c staterooms (sleeping up to six people). Marketed by Bales Worldwide, mainly to British tourists, a seven-night cruise costs from £2,145/person.

Scheherazade and **Malika Merit** (Queen Merit) ⓦnileboat.com. Two replica vessels with slightly kitsch pharaonic decor, mostly used by French tourists. *Malika Merit* has six cabins and a suite, *Scheherazade* is smaller. Both are used for three- or five-day cruises.

★ **Vivant Denon** ⓦdahabeya.net. Named after the artist on Napoleon's expedition to Egypt, this 30m-long craft built in 1889 for King Fouad would later inspire Agatha Christie to write *Death on the Nile*. It sleeps up to six passengers on cruises from Oct to April, mainly booked by French tourists. Spare cabins available through Audley Travel (ⓦaudleytravel.com).

★ **Zarafa** (Giraffe) and **Dongola** ⓦtravelinstyle .com. These *dahabiyas* were built for Egyptian sultans in the 1830s and owned by 1950s film stars. Their seven-night itinerary includes a private visit to Nefertari's tomb In the Valley of the Queens (see p.318) and costs from $2,400/person on the *Dongola*, $2,800 on the *Zarafa* (which has a/c).

FELUCCAS

The following are some reliable felucca captains and fixers, all based in Aswan.

Ahmed Abd el-Nabi ☏012 2281 3932, ✉ahmedfluck2003@yahoo.com. The *Nile Breeze* can be chartered for £E500/day (plus £E100/person for meals), while the *Five Star* (sleeping up to twelve people in private canvas "cabins", with a fridge to supply cold drinks and fresh food) can be chartered for €600 a day (meals included).

Ahmed Said Gaber (aka "Aco") Nubian Oasis hotel (see p.349) ☏012 2490 8634, ✉AhmedACO72@yahoo.com. A felucca consolidator, charging £E150/person for a one-night trip, £E200 for two nights, £E350 for three nights. Meals and a minibus on to Kom Ombo, Edfu and Luxor included in the price.

Ashraf Mohammed (aka "Captain Bob") ☏010 0387 4053. The veteran skipper of the *Bob Marley*, based in Kubbaniya, invites passengers home for a meal on the first night. His rates vary depending on the length of the trip and the number of people involved. Meals included.

★ **Jamaica family** Near the ferry dock in Siou village on Elephantine Island ☏010 0356 9525 or ☏012 2414 7386. Headed by Captain "JJ", this long-established outfit has eight feluccas, one of them a "deluxe" boat with a shower and toilet, an upper roof deck and *mashrabiya* screens for shade. They charge £E75/person/night, £E150 for the deluxe felucca (meals included).

Abydos

As Muslims endeavour to visit Mecca once in their lifetime and Hindus aspire to die at Varanasi, the Ancient Egyptians devoutly wished to make a pilgrimage to **ABYDOS** (pronounced "Abi-dos"), cult centre of the god Osiris. Those who failed to make it hoped to do so posthumously; relatives brought bodies for burial, or embellished distant tombs with scenes of the journey to Abydos (represented by a boat under sail, travelling upriver). Egyptians averred that the dead "went west", for the entrance to the underworld was believed to lie amid the desert miles beyond Abydos. By bringing other deities into the Osirian fold, Abydos acquired a near monopoly on death cults, which persisted into Ptolemaic times. Its superbly carved **Temple of Seti I** has been a tourist attraction since the 1830s, and many rate its artwork as the finest in Egypt. Its survival owes to the temple being covered by sand for centuries, as suggested by the name of the village where it is located, Al-Araba el-Madfuna (Araba the Buried).

The Temple of Seti I

Al-Araba el-Madfuna • Daily 7am–5pm • £E30

While the temples of Karnak and Deir el-Bahri at Luxor are breathtaking conceptions executed on a colossal scale, it is the exquisite quality of its bas-reliefs that distinguishes

2

THE CULT OF OSIRIS

Originally the corn-god of Busiris in the Delta, **Osiris** attained national significance early in the Old Kingdom when he was coopted into the Heliopolitan Ennead. According to legend, Re (or Geb) divided the world between Osiris and his brother **Seth**, who resented being given all the deserts and murdered Osiris to usurp his domain. Although the god's body was recovered by

Isis, the sister-wife of Osiris, Seth recaptured and dismembered it, burying the pieces at different locations and feeding the corpse to a crocodile. Aided by her sister Nephthys, Isis collected the bits and bandaged them together to create the first mummy, which they briefly resurrected with the help of Thoth and Anubis. By transforming herself into a hawk, Isis managed to conceive a child with Osiris before he returned to the netherworld to rule as lord and judge of the dead. Secretly raised to manhood in the Delta, their child **Horus** later avenged his father and cast Seth back into the wilderness (see p.327).

As the "place of the head" of Osiris (the meaning of its ancient name, Abdjw), Abydos was the setting for two annual **festivals**. The "Great Going Forth" celebrated the search for and discovery of his remains, while the Osiris Festival re-enacted his myth in a series of Mystery Plays. In one scene, the god's barque was "attacked" by minions of Seth and "protected" by **Wepwawet**, the jackal-headed god of Assyut. The total identification of Abydos with **death cults** was completed by its association with **Anubis**, the jackal-headed god of embalming, always present in funerary scenes.

Osiris

Abydos' **Temple of Seti I**. The reliefs are among the finest works of the New Kingdom, harking back to Old Kingdom forms in an artistic revival that mirrored Seti's political efforts to consolidate the XIX Dynasty and recover territories lost under Akhenaten. The official designation of Seti's reign (c.1294–79 BC) was "the era of repeating births" – literally a renaissance.

It was in fact Seti's son, Ramses II (c.1279–13 BC), who completed the reconquest of former colonies and the construction of his father's temple at Abydos. Strictly speaking, the building was neither a cult nor a funerary temple in the ordinary sense, for its chapels contained shrines to a variety of deities concerned with death, resurrection and the netherworld, and one dedicated to Seti himself. Its purpose was essentially political: to identify the king with these cults and with his putative "ancestors", the previous rulers of Egypt, thus conferring legitimacy on the Ramessid Dynasty, whose ancestors had been mere Delta warriors a few generations earlier.

The temple's spell has endured through the ages, as New Age pilgrims follow in the footsteps of Dorothy Eady – known as **Um Seti** (Mother of Seti) – who lived at Abydos for 35 years until she died in 1981, believing herself to be the reincarnation of a temple priestess and lover of Seti I. Her trances and prophetic gifts are related in Jonathan Cott's biography, *The Search for Omm Sety* – available at souvenir stalls here. She is buried in the local cemetery, out near Shunt el-Zibib (see p.249).

The forecourt

The temple's original **pylon** and **forecourt** have almost been levelled but you can still discern the lower portion of a scene depicting Ramses II's dubious victory at Qadesh [a], women with finely plaited tresses [b] and Seti making offerings to Osiris (in a niche, nearby). From the damaged statues currently stored in the upper, second court, your eyes are drawn to the square-columned **facade**, the wall behind pillars covered with scenes of Ramses greeting Osiris, Isis and Horus [c].

The outer Hypostyle Hall

The ponderous sunk-reliefs in the **outer Hypostyle Hall**, completed by Ramses after Seti's death, suggest that he used second-rate artists, having redeployed Seti's top craftsmen on his own edifice. The entrance wall portrays Ramses measuring the temple with the goddess Selket and presenting it to Horus on Seti's behalf, while on the wall to your right Ramses offers a falcon-headed box of papyrus to Isis, Horus and Osiris, and is led to the temple by Horus and Wepwawet (the jackal-headed god of Assyut) to be doused with holy water (represented by the interlinked signs for life and purity) [d]. Guards can point out the

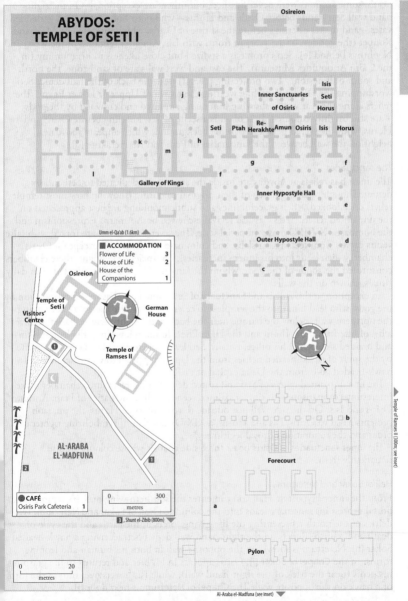

2

"**Abydos helicopter**", a cartouche on a lintel that supposedly shows a helicopter and a submarine. An image first published (1996) in *Alien Encounters* magazine has been proved to have been manipulated, and archeologists dismiss any resemblance to a helicopter as a fluke of erosion (as demonstrated on ⊛members.tripod.com/a_u_r_a/abydos.html).

The inner Hypostyle Hall

The deeper **inner Hypostyle Hall** was the last part of the temple decorated before Seti's death: some sections were never finished, but others are exceptional. On the right-hand wall Seti stands before Osiris and Horus – who pour holy water from garlanded vases – and makes offerings before the shrine of Osiris, who is attended by Maat and Ronpet (the goddess of the year) in front, with Isis, Amentet (goddess of the west) and Nephthys behind [**e**]. Seti's profile is a stylized but close likeness to his mummy (in the Cairo Antiquities Museum). The east and west walls are of sandstone, the north and south of limestone. Two projecting piers [**f**] near the back of the hall depict Seti worshipping the Djed pillar while wearing the crown of Upper or Lower Egypt. The reliefs along the rear wall – showing him being anointed and crowned by the gods – are still brightly coloured. Best of all is a scene of Seti kneeling before Osiris and Horus, with the sacred persea tree in the background, which appears above head height on the wall between the sanctuaries of Ptah and Re-Herakhte [**g**].

The sanctuaries

The finest **bas-reliefs** at Abydos are inside the sanctuaries dedicated to Seti and six deities. Though retaining much of their original colouring (showing how most temple reliefs once looked), their graceful lines and subtle moulding are best appreciated on the unpainted reliefs. Seti's classical revival eschewed both Amarna expressionism and the bombastic XVIII Dynasty imperial style. The seven sanctuaries are roofed with false vaults carved from rectangular slabs, and culminate in false doors (except for Osiris's chamber, which leads into his inner sanctuaries). To Ancient Egyptians, these chambers constituted the abode of the gods, whom the king (or his priests) propitiated with daily rituals, shown on the walls.

An exception to this rule is the **Sanctuary of Seti**, which emphasizes his recognition by the gods, who lead him into the temple and ceremonially unite the Two Lands along the northern wall. Below the barque near the back of the right-hand wall, Seti receives a list of offerings from Thoth and the High Priest Iunmutef, wearing the leopardskin and braided sidelock of his office. Finally, Seti leaves the temple, his palanquin borne by the souls of jackal-headed deities from the Upper Egyptian town of Nekhen and hawk-headed gods from the Delta capital of Pi-Ramses.

The fine unpainted reliefs of Seti and seated deities in Re-Herakhte's chamber make interesting comparison with similar painted scenes in the sanctuaries of Ptah, Amun, Osiris and Isis. On the side wall just outside the Sanctuary of Horus, the pharaoh presents Maat to Osiris, Isis and Horus, a XIX Dynasty motif symbolizing righteous order and the restoration of royal legitimacy.

The **inner sanctuaries of Osiris** boast three side chapels whose colours are still remarkably fresh.

Hall of Sokar and Nefertum

From the inner Hypostyle Hall you can enter the southern wing of Seti's temple. The portal nearest his sanctuary leads into the columned **Hall of Sokar and Nefertum**, two deities of the north representing the life-giving forces of the earth and the cycle of death and rebirth. Reliefs on the right-hand wall depict Seti receiving a hawk-headed Sokar [**h**]; Nefertum is shown on the opposite wall in both his human and leonine forms. In the **Chapel of Sokar** [**i**], Osiris appears in his bier and returns to life grasping his penis (near the back of the right-hand wall), while Isis hovers over him in the form of a hawk on the opposite wall. The **Chapel of Nefertum** is next door [**j**].

The Gallery of Kings

The other portal leads through into the **Gallery of Kings**, so called after the list of Seti's predecessors carved on the right-hand wall – the earliest (Zoser) on the far left of the top row, with Seti at the far end of the bottom register. For political reasons, the Hyksos pharaohs, Hatshepsut, Akhenaten and his heirs have all been omitted, yet the list has proved immensely useful to Egyptologists, naming 34 kings (chiefly from the VI, VII, XII, XVIII and XIX dynasties) in roughly chronological order.

Running off from the gallery are the **Sanctuary of the Boats [k]**, where the deities' barques were kept on platforms; the **Hall of Sacrifices [l]** (closed); and a corridor **[m]** with vivid sunk-reliefs of Seti and Ramses harnessing a bull to present to Wepwawet, and hauling birds in a net. This will bring you out through a rear door to the Osireion, behind the temple.

The rest of the site

The **site of Abydos** covers a huge area, with ruins and mounds scattered across the edge of the desert. Egyptologists from the Penn Museum (ⓦpenn.museum) and the German Archeological Institute (ⓦdainst.org) are excavating several sites, officially off-limits. You can, however, visit two structures near Seti's temple, and Amir Elkarim might be able to arrange trips to others if you're staying at Abydos (see p.250). The longer you stay, the more likely you are to wrangle access to the off-limits areas.

The Osireion

Same opening hours and ticket as the temple of Seti I

When Flinders Petrie excavated here in the 1900s, he uncovered numerous mastabas which he believed to be royal tombs, but which later Egyptologists held to be cenotaphs or Osirian burial places – dummy tombs, built to promote a closer association between the pharaoh's *ka* and Osiris, while his mummy reposed elsewhere. Seti's Cenotaph, known as the **Osireion**, is the only one now visible, albeit half-buried and rendered partly inaccessible by stagnant water. Built of massive blocks, it once enclosed a room containing a mound surrounded by a moat (symbolizing the first land arising from the waters of Chaos at the dawn of Creation), where a pseudo-sarcophagus awaited resurrection. Nearby is a long underground passage that once led to the cenotaph.

Temple of Ramses II

Same opening hours and ticket as the temple of Seti I

Some 300m northwest of the Osireion is a ruined **Temple of Ramses II**, Seti's father, where scenes of the Battle of Qadesh (see p.369) are rendered in exceptional detail on the enclosure walls and pillared courtyard. Ground-penetrating radar has detected a massive structure underneath the sand between Ramses' and Seti's temples that some suspect is another Osireion. Its existence has yet to be announced officially by the Supreme Council of Antiquities, but is an open secret in Egyptological circles.

Shunt el-Zibib

Elsewhere, the Germans have been excavating the Early Dynastic royal cemetery at **Um el-Qa'ab** ("Mother of Pots"), and extensive funerary enclosures at **Shunt el-Zibib** ("Storehouse of Grapes"). Neither site is as spectacular as Seti's temple, but there's an air of impending discovery at Shunt el-Zibib – the Arabic name for the funeral complex of Khasekhemwy, last king of the II Dynasty. It's thought that the pyramids at Saqqara evolved from the enclosure of sunken brick-lined tombs at Abydos, where hieroglyphic writing predating Saqqara's has been found, suggesting the existence of a Pre-dynastic king Hor or Horus who conquered the Delta and united the Two Lands a century before Narmer. Six **Solar Boats** found within Khasekhemwy's enclosure in 1991 may date from the reign of the I Dynasty ruler Aha.

All this raises the possibility that the Early Dynastic burials attributed to Saqqara may have occurred at Abydos instead, and that an intact royal tomb may exist. Since 2004 the Penn Museum team has found evidence that the XII Dynasty **Osirieon of Senusret III** may have really been a royal tomb, looted long ago. A thirty-metre-long shaft was discovered there in 2009.

ARRIVAL AND INFORMATION
ABYDOS

By private taxi/minibus Budget hotels in Luxor arrange excursions to Abydos and Dendara, travelling in a convoy leaving at 8am. Expect to pay £E250–300 for a car seating four, or £E85/person in a minibus. Admission to the temples isn't included in the price. You get to spend an hour at each site. Abydos can also be reached from Sohag by taxi (£E100–150); the local tourist office can arrange an excursion (see p.238).

By train Third-class trains from Luxor (2hr 40min) and

Qena (2hr) stop at the town of El-Balyana, 10km from Abydos. Expect to pay £E50–70 for a taxi to Abydos and back, with an hour's waiting time at the temple.

Visitors' centre Half-built (and abandoned) at the time of writing, this concrete eyesore may eventually feature an exhibition about Abydos. Until then, you can seek information on matters practical or spiritual from Amir Elkarim at the *House of the Companions* or Astet and Horus at the *House of Life*.

ACCOMMODATION, EATING AND DRINKING

Flower of Life Shunt ell-Zibib ☎010 0331 2188, ✉ameer558@yahoo.com. A rustic offshoot of the *House of the Companions* (see below) with mud-brick huts, for communing with nature near the excavations at Shunt el-Zibib. Half board. **£E380**

House of Life Al-Araba el-Madfuna ☎011 4601 6865, ⊕ houseoflife.info. Run by a Dutch woman and her Egyptian partner who call themselves Aset (Isis) and Horus, this "hotel healing centre" has three luxurious flats (each sleeping four people), a restaurant and a pool. Two cheaper

flats (£E200), in a block near the visitors' centre, can also be rented. Full board. **€100**

House of the Companions Al-Araba el-Madfuna ☎010 0331 2188, ✉ameer558@yahoo.com. Another New Age hangout, decorated with murals of Isis and with spacious a/c rooms and self-contained flats. Owner Amir Elkarim also runs the Flower of Life. Half board. **£E380**

Osiris Park Caféteria Al-Araba el-Madfuna. A small, shaded café right outside the temple, which sells tea, cold drinks, packaged snacks and a range of books in English. Daily 7am–10pm.

ACTIVITIES

Ancient Egyptian Healing The *House of Life* runs nine-day courses involving etheric perfumes and oils, meditation

and initiation rituals at sacred sites. Full-board accommodation is included in the cost ($2463).

Dendara

The **Temple of Hathor** at **Dendara** lacks the sublime quality of Seti's edifice at Abydos, but its fabulous astronomical ceiling and nearly intact rooftop sanctuaries offer a unique insight into the solar rituals at other cult sites where they have not survived.

THE GNOSTIC GOSPELS

Driving between Abydos and Dendara you'll pass Nag Hammadi, a town that has given its name to the **Nag Hammadi Codices** found nearby in 1945. Commonly called the **Gnostic Gospels**, they are fourth-century Coptic translations of second-century Greek originals, although the Gospel of Thomas might date from 50–100 AD, and therefore be as early as – or even older than – the gospels of Matthew, Mark, Luke and John. Gnostics (from *gnosis*, Greek for "knowledge") were early mystics who believed that God could only be known through self-understanding and that the world was illusory. Regarding self and the divine as one, they saw Jesus as a spiritual guide rather than the crucified son of God, pointing to his words in the Gospel of Thomas: "If you bring forth what is within you, what you bring forth will save you. If you do not bring forth what is within you, what is within you will destroy you." But the official church thought otherwise and condemned Gnosticism as a heresy; hence the burial of these codices (some of which can be seen today in Cairo's Coptic Museum).

Dendara also shows how Egypt's Greek and Roman rulers identified themselves with the pharaohs and deities of Ancient Egypt by copying their temples, rituals and iconography down to the last hieroglyph – though they did tinker with a few details of reliefs and murals. Goddesses and queens became bustier, and the feet of royalty were shown with all their toes (instead of only the big toe, as the Ancient Egyptians did).

The temple is also pleasing for the completeness of its mud-brick enclosure walls and its rural setting, with rooftop views of lush countryside and the arid hills of the Western Desert. Approaching it by road from Qena, across the Nile, you'll pass fields of onions and clover, donkey carts and camels – an enjoyable ride by *calèche* if you've got time to spare or decide to stay in Qena (see p.255). Most tourists visit Dendara together with the temple at Abydos (see p.250).

The Temple of Hathor

Dendara village, 8km from Qena • Daily 7am–5pm • £E35

Although there have been shrines to Hathor, the goddess of joy, at Dendara since Pre-dynastic times, the existing **Temple of Hathor** is a Greco-Roman creation, built between 125 BC and 60 AD. Since the object of the exercise was to confer legitimacy on Egypt's foreign rulers, it emulates the pharaonic pattern of hypostyle halls and vestibules preceding a darkened sanctuary, with vast mud-brick enclosure walls surrounding the complex.

The facade

The temple **facade** is shaped like a pylon, with six Hathor-headed columns rising from a screen, their headdresses still blue, red and white. Here and inside, Hathor appears in human form rather than her bovine aspect (see below). Because this section was built during the reign of Tiberius, its sunk-reliefs depict Roman emperors making offerings to the gods, namely Tiberius and Claudius before Horus, Hathor and their son Ihy [a], and Tiberius as a sphinx before Hathor and Horus [b] (hard to see). Nineteenth-century engravings show the temple buried in sand almost to the lintel of its portal, which explains why its upper sections bore the brunt of Coptic iconoclasm.

The Hypostyle Hall

Entering the **Hypostyle Hall** with its eighteen Hathor-headed columns you'll be transfixed by its **astronomical ceiling**, now largely restored to its vibrant original colours (mostly blue and white). This is not a sky chart in the modern sense, but a symbolic representation of the heavenly bodies, the hours of the day and night, and the realms of the sun and moon.

Above the central aisle, a row of flying vultures and winged discs separates the left-hand bays representing the southern heavens from those to the right, dedicated to the northern sky. Here, the first row [c] begins with the Eye of Re in its barque, above

---

THE CULT OF HATHOR

Worshipped from the earliest times as a cow goddess, **Hathor** acquired manifold attributes – body of the sky, living soul of trees, goddess of gold and turquoise, music and revelry – but remained essentially nurturing. Her greatest role was that of wet nurse and bedmate for **Horus**, and giver of milk to the living pharaoh. In her human aspect (with bovine ears and horns), the goddess paid an annual visit to Horus at his temple in Edfu. Her barque, escorted by priests and cheered by commoners, proceeded upriver, where Horus sailed out to meet her on his own boat. After much pomp and ritual, the idols were left alone to reconsummate their union while the populace enjoyed a **Festival of Drunkenness**, which led the Greeks to identify Hathor with their own goddess of love and joy, Aphrodite.

Hathor

2

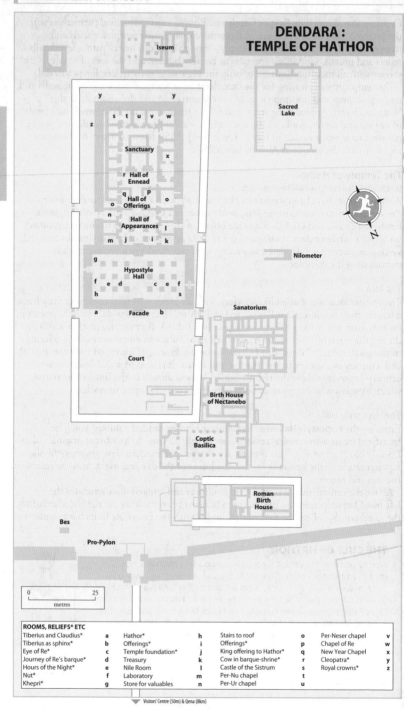

DENDARA : TEMPLE OF HATHOR

Iseum

Sacred Lake

y   y

z   s   t   u   v   w

Sanctuary

x

r   Hall of Ennead

q   p
o   Hall of Offerings   o
n
Hall of Appearances   l

m   j   i   k

g
Hypostyle Hall

f   e   d   c   e   f

h   s

a   Facade   b

Nilometer

Sanatorium

Court

Birth House of Nectanebo

Coptic Basilica

Roman Birth House

Bes

Pro-Pylon

0   25
metres

ROOMS, RELIEFS* ETC

Tiberius and Claudius*	a	Hathor*	h	Stairs to roof	o	Per-Neser chapel	v
Tiberius as sphinx*	b	Offerings*	i	Offerings*	p	Chapel of Re	w
Eye of Re*	c	Temple foundation*	j	King offering to Hathor*	q	New Year Chapel	x
Journey of Re's barque*	d	Treasury	k	Cow in barque-shrine*	r	Cleopatra*	y
Hours of the Night*	e	Nile Room	l	Castle of the Sistrum	s	Royal crowns*	z
Nut*	f	Laboratory	m	Per-Nu chapel	t		
Khepri*	g	Store for valuables	n	Per-Ur chapel	u		

which appear the fourteen days of the waning moon. Beyond the full moon in the centre come the fourteen stages of the waxing moon (each with its own deity), culminating in the full disc worshipped by Thoth, and lastly the moon as Osiris, protected by Isis and Nephthys. Souls in the form of jackals and birds adorn Re's barque as it journeys across the sun's register [d].

Following these are two bands [e] showing the planets, the stars of the twelve hours of the night, and the signs of the zodiac (adopted from Babylonia). The end rows [f] are dominated by Nut, who gives birth to the sun at dawn and swallows it at dusk. On one side, the rising sun Khepri (the scarab beetle) is born [g]; on the other, the sun shines down on Hathor [h].

The Hall of Appearances

The Ptolemaic section of the temple begins with the six-columned **Hall of Appearances**, where Hathor consorted with fellow deities before her voyage to Edfu (see p.251). With a torch, you can examine reliefs on the entrance wall depicting offerings [i], and the foundation of the temple and its presentation to the gods [j]. Notice the "blank" cartouches, which attest to the high turnover of rulers in late Ptolemaic times, when stonemasons were loath to inscribe the names of Ptolemies who might not last for long. Nonetheless, rituals continued at Dendara, where the priests kept holy objects of precious metal in the Treasury [k] and drew water for purification ceremonies from a well reached by the so-called Nile Room [l].

Corresponding chambers across the hall include the laboratory [m], where perfumes and unguents were mixed and stored (notice the reliefs showing recipes, and bearers bringing exotic materials from afar); and another room for storing valuables [n]. A liturgical calendar listing festivals celebrated at the temple appears on the sides of its doorway.

The Hall of Offerings and the Hall of Ennead

Beyond lies the **Hall of Offerings**, the entrance to the temple proper, with twin **stairways** to the roof (see p.254) up which sacrificial animals were led [o]. A list of offerings appears on the rear wall [p], across the way from a relief showing the king offering Hathor her favourite tipple [q].

Next comes the **Hall of the Ennead**, where statues of the gods and kings involved in ceremonies dedicated to Hathor once stood. Her wardrobe was stored in a room to the left, where reliefs show the priests carrying the chests that held the sacred garments. The **Sanctuary** housed Hathor's statue and ceremonial barque, which priests carried to the riverside and placed upon a boat that worshippers towed upriver to Edfu for a conjugal reunion with Horus. Reliefs depict the daily rituals, and the king presenting Maat to Hathor, Horus and Harsomtus (rear wall).

Side chapels

Two corridors with side chapels run alongside (and meet behind) the sanctuary. Above the doorway into the Corridor of Mysteries, Hathor appears as a cow within a wooden kiosk mounted on a barque [r]. Past the chapels of Isis, Sokar and the Sacred Serpent, you'll find the "Castle of the Sistrum" (Hathor's musical instrument), where niches depict her standing on the sky, and the coronation of Ihy as god of music [s]. This is entered via the darkened Per-Nu chapel [t], whence Hathor embarked on her conjugal voyage to Edfu during the New Year festival (which fell on July 19 in ancient times).

The New Year procession began from the Per-Ur chapel [u], where a shaky ladder ascends to a small cache chamber containing reliefs of Hathor, Maat and Isis. In the Per-Neser chapel [v], one of the custodians will lift a hatch and guide you down into a low-ceilinged **crypt** carved with cobras and lotuses. The chapel itself shows Hathor in her terrible aspect as a lioness, for by Ptolemaic times she had assimilated the leonine goddess Sekhmet and the feline goddess Bastet. The temple's most valuable treasures were stored underneath the Chapel of Re [w].

2

The New Year Chapel

If you haven't already stumbled upon it, return to the Hall of the Ennead, bear left through an antechamber and then right, to find the "Pure Place" **[x]** or **New Year Chapel**, whose ceiling is covered by a relief of Nut giving birth to the sun, which shines on Hathor's head. It was here that rituals were performed prior to Hathor's communion with the sun on the temple's roof. Check out the rooftop shrines (see below) before leaving the temple and walking round to the rear wall, where two defaced sunk-reliefs **[y]** of Cleopatra and her son Caesarion feature in a procession of deities. The chubby face is so unlike the beautiful queen of legend that most people prefer to regard this as a stylized image rather than a lifelike **portrait of Cleopatra**. The lion-headed **waterspouts** below the cornice were a Roman innovation.

One last bit of iconography worth noting is the array of royal **crowns** – 22 different kinds appear on the seated kings carved on the third, fourth and fifth registers of the east wall **[z]**.

Rooftop sanctuaries

From either side of the Hall of Offerings, a stairway ascends to the roof of the temple; the scenes on the walls depict the New Year procession, when Hathor's statue was carried up to an open kiosk on the rooftop to await the dawn; touched by the rays of the sun, Hathor's *ba* (soul) was revitalized for the coming year. Besides the sun kiosk there are two suites of rooms dedicated to the death and resurrection of Osiris, behind the facade of the Hypostyle Hall. Although such **rooftop sanctuaries** were a feature of most temples, those at Dendara are uniquely intact.

The one on the left (as you face towards the pylon) is notable for the reliefs in its inner chamber, which show Osiris being mourned by Isis and Nephthys, passing through the gates of the netherworld, and finally bringing himself to erection to impregnate Isis, who appears as a hovering kite.

The other suite contains a plaster cast of the famous **Dendara Zodiac** ceiling filched by Lelorrain in 1820 and now in the Louvre. Upheld by four goddesses, the circular carving features a zodiac which only differs from our own by the substitution of a scarab for the scorpion and the inclusion of the hippo goddess Tweri. The zodiac was introduced to Egypt (and other lands) by the Romans, who copied it from Babylonia. Mind your head on the low doorway.

Best of all is the magnificent **view** of the temple and the countryside from the rooftop. Also notice the **graffiti** left by French troops in 1799, including the names of their commander Desaix and the artist Denon, who sketched frenziedly at Dendara as the Mamlukes drew nearer, melting down bullets for lead when he ran out of pencils.

Outlying buildings

Surrounding the temple are various other structures, now largely ruined. Ptolemaic temples were distinguished by the addition of *mamissi* or Birth Houses, which associated the pharaoh with Horus, the deified king. When the Romans surrounded the temple with an enclosure wall, it split in two the **Birth House of Nectanebo** (XXX Dynasty), compelling them to build a replacement. The **Roman Birth House** has some fine carvings of Hathor suckling Horus on its south wall, and tiny figures of Bes and Tweri on the column capitals and architraves. Between the two *mamissi* lies a ruined, fifth-century **Coptic Basilica**, built with masonry from the adjacent structures; notice the incised Coptic crosses.

As a compassionate goddess, Hathor had a reputation for healing and her temple attracted pilgrimages from the sick. In the **Sanatorium** here patients were prescribed cures during dreams, induced by narcotics. Water for ritual ablutions was drawn from a **Sacred Lake** now drained of liquid and full of palm trees and birds.

Nearby stands a ruined **Iseum** used for the worship of Isis and Osiris, built by Cleopatra's mortal enemy, Octavian, after he became Emperor Augustus.

On your way out of the temple, don't miss the scowling **Bes** – god of dancing girls and licentiousness – carved on a chunk of masonry displayed near the Pro-Pylon.

ARRIVAL AND DEPARTURE DENDARA

By boat Cruises from Luxor on the *Lotus* or *Tiba Star* (Tues, Fri & Sun) involve five hours on the river (with lunch) and an hour at Dendara temple; book through the *Iberotel* hotel (see p.268) or travel agents in Luxor. The cost (£E480) includes lunch and admission to Dendara temple.

By private taxi or minibus Budget hotels in Luxor arrange excursions to Dendara and Abydos, travelling in a convoy leaving at 8am. Expect to pay £E250–300 for a car seating four, or £E85/person in a minibus. Admission to the temples not included in the price. You get to spend an hour at each site.

ACCOMMODATION AND EATING

Accommodation There's nowhere to stay at Dendara (and only one hotel in nearby Qena is willing to take foreigners), but most visitors prefer to stay in Luxor anyway.

Eating Given the limited eating options, it's best to bring a picnic to eat at Dendara. A caféteria (daily 8am–5pm) outside the temple sells overpriced tea, cold drinks and packaged snacks.

Qena

Eight kilometres east of Dendara, **QENA** is a city of two hundred thousand people, whose tidy streets and civic amenities are the legacy of former governor Adel Labib, who wooed back residents embittered by decades of neglect, to prevent any resurgence of sympathy for the militant Islamists who staged Egypt's first terrorist attack on tourists back in 1992. Today, Qena is totally safe to visit and the authorities are even allowing tourists to stay here once again.

Should you be around at the time, Qena's oldest mosque (on the main drag, Sharia Luxor) hosts the **Moulid of Abdel Rahim el-Qenawi**, featuring *zikrs* and dancing horses. The festival kicks off on Sha'ban 14 (the eighth month in the Islamic lunar calender) and finishes the day before the start of Abu el-Haggag's moulid in Luxor (see p.276).

ARRIVAL AND DEPARTURE QENA

By bus Regular services to Cairo, Port Safaga, Hurghada and Suez depart from the bus terminal near Qena's train station.
By train Forty minutes' journey from Luxor, Qena is a stop

for all trains to/from Cairo. A taxi from the station to Dendara should cost about £E40, or £E80 round-trip with an hour's waiting time.

ACCOMMODATION AND EATING

Basma Sharia Nadi el-Bahar, Qena ☎096 533 2779, ✉basmahotel@yahoo.com. The only hotel in Qena currently willing to take foreigners, this plush new three-star right beside the Nile has large, comfortable en-suite rooms overlooking the river, a pool and restaurant. Often

used for conferences and wedding receptions. B&B **£E300**
Prince Sharia el-Gumhorriya. Located beside a major roundabout in the centre of Qena, this humble restaurant serves kofta or grilled chicken with soup and vegetables (£E25–45). Daily 11am–10pm.

Luxor

LUXOR has been a tourist mecca ever since Nile steamers began calling in the nineteenth century to view the remains of **Thebes**, Ancient Egypt's New Kingdom capital, and its associated sites – the concentration of relics in this area is overwhelming. The town itself boasts **Luxor Temple**, a graceful ornament to its waterfront and "downtown", while a mile or so north is **Karnak Temple**, a stupendous complex built over 1300 years. Across the river are the amazing tombs and mortuary temples of the **Theban Necropolis**, and as if this wasn't enough, Luxor also serves as a base for trips to Esna, Edfu, Dendara and Abydos temples, up and down the Nile Valley.

In a town where **tourism** accounts for 85 percent of the economy, it's hardly surprising that you can't move without being importuned to step inside a shop or rent

2

LUXOR (EAST BANK)

Karnak Temple (2km) ◄
Bus Station & Airport ▲

🔷 BARS
Genesis Pub Restaurant	1
Hamees	3
King's Head Pub	4
Murphy's Irish Pub	7
Pub 2000	6
Royal Lounge	5

🔷 NIGHTLIFE
St Katerina	2

Minibus routes (— —)
Tourist bazaars

0 ___ 500 metres

🔷 CAFÉS & RESTAURANTS
Abou Ashraf	6
Abu Hassan el-Shazly	8
Alf Leyl w Leyl	12
Al-Shahaby Lane	3
Amoun	1
A Taste of India	16
Bonduk	10
1896	7
El-Zareem	2
Fortune Cookie/The King and Thai	14
La Mamma	21
Lyaly Zaman	18
Miyako	19
New Oum Kalthoum	5
Nile Terrace Café	3
Nubian National Coffee	4
Oasis Café	17
Puddleduck	15
Quick	11
Shark Restaurant Fish	13
Snobs	20
Sofra	9
Victoria Lounge	7

🔷 SHOPS
Aboudi Bookstore	11
Aboudy Bookshop	5
Al-Ahram Beverages	3
Arkwrights	10
Besheat Store	2
Duty Free Shop	15
Fair Trade Center	4
Gaddis Bookshop	6
Kher Zaman	9
Twinky	7
Winter Akhmeem Gallery	8

🔷 ACCOMMODATION
Boomerang New Peace	14
Egypt Property Sales (agency)	23
El-Luxor	4
Emilio	5
Fontana	17
Happy Land	18
Hilton Luxor Resort & Spa	1
Iberotel	13
Little Garden	15
Luxor Sheraton Resort	27
Mara House	11
Maritim Jolie Ville	26
Morris	20
Nefertiti	7
New Pola	19
Princess	16
Pyramisa Isis	25
Oasis	12
Pavilion Wing	9
Philippe	3
St Joseph	21
Softel Karnak	2
Winter Palace	10
Sonesta St George	22
Steigenberger Nile Palace	24
Susanna	8
Venus	6

ABU JUD

Nile Heritage Centre

SHARIA AL-MATHAR

SHARIA ABDEL HAMID TAHA

Avenue of Sphinxes

SHARIA MAABAD EL-KARNAK

SHARIA AL-GARB

CORNICHE EL-NIL

SHARIA AL-MATHARI

SHARIA TUTANKHAMUN

SHARIA KHALID IBN WALID

Spider Net @
@ Metro Net

Net Café Margareeta @

SHARIA EL-MADINA EL-MINAWRA

River Nile

Luxor Museum

AlexBank 💲

Banque Misr 💲

Protestant Church

SHARIA ST KATERINA

SHARIA ANNIS

SHARIA EL-ZEINI

Institute of Arabic Language

SHARIA YUSSEF HASSAN

Coptic Cathedral

Governorate

BAZAR SAVOY

SHARIA LAHIB IMBACHI

SHARIA AL-MONTAZAH

Catholic Church

Forex

Avenue of Sphinxes

Mosque of Abu

Mummification Museum

Fence

Motorboats & Feluccas

Cruise Boats

Public Ferry

GEZIRA

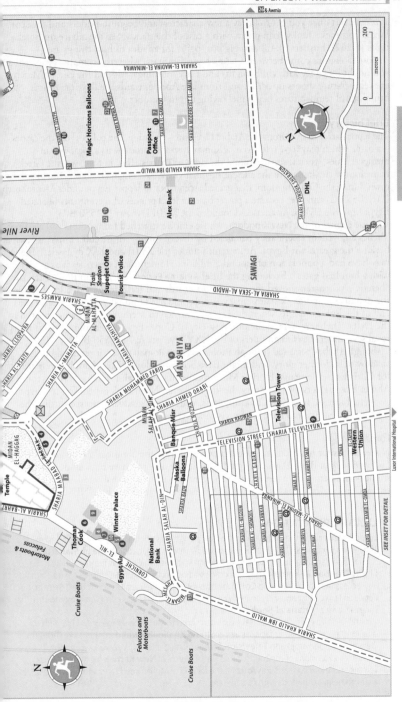

2

26 & Awmia

SHARIA EL-MADINA EL-MINAWRA

Magic Horizons Balloons

Passport Office

SHARIA EL-GAWRA

SHARIA MODERET EL-AMIN

SHARIA KHALID IBN WALID

Alex Bank

River Nile

DHL

SHARIA EL GOMLA SHERATON

Train Station
Superjet Office
Tourist Police

SHARIA RAMSES

MIDAN AL-MAHATTA

SAWAGI

SHARIA AL-SEKA AL-HADID

SHARIA CLEOPATRA

SHARIA AL-SKITA

SHARIA AL-MAHATA

SHARIA MANSHIYA

SHARIA MOHAMMED FARID

MANSHIYA

SHARIA AHMED ORABI

SHARIA AL-DIN

Banque Misr

Television Tower

SHARIA RADWAN

TELEVISION STREET (SHARIA TELEVIZIYUN)

NEFERTITI HOTEL

EL-TAYEB
Western Union

Luxor International Hospital

Temple

MIDAN
EL-HAGGAG

SHARIA MAABD

SHARIA AL-BAHR

Thomas Cook

Winter Palace

Egypt/Air

EL-NIL

National Bank

CORNICHE

MIDAN
NESSIM

Motorboats & Feluccas

Cruise Boats

Feluccas and Motorboats

Cruise Boats

MIDAN SALAH AL-DIN

SHARIA SALAH AL-DIN

Aleska Balloons

SHARIA GADAH

SHARIA AL-SHOMOSL

SHARIA EL-NEGOUM

SHARIA LIBYA AR-LAILA

SHARIA AL-KAWKAB

SHARIA AL-SHUREYA

SHARIA AHMED ESMAT

UMAR ALI

EL-MADINA EL-MINAWRA

SHARIA ABDU HAMID EL-OMRA

SEE INSET FOR DETAIL

SHARIA FARID

SHARIA RADWAN

SENAK

SHARIA KHALID IBN WALID

0   200
metres

N

a *calèche*, but once you get to know a few characters and begin to understand the score Luxor becomes a funky soap opera with a cast of thousands. See the advice on hotel touts (p.267), hustlers (p.43) and gigolos (p.45) for an idea of how things are.

Most foreigners come between October and February, when the **climate** is cooler than you might imagine, with chilly nights and early mornings. Around the end of March the temperature shoots up 10°C, and from late April onwards the daytime heat is brutal, until temperatures begin mellowing out in October.

Brief history

The name Luxor derives from the Arabic El-Uqsur – meaning "the palaces" or "the castles" – a name which may have referred to a Roman *castrum* or the town's appearance in medieval times, when it squatted amid the ruins of **Thebes**. This, in turn, was the Greek name for the city known to the ancient Egyptians as Weset, originally an obscure provincial town during the Old Kingdom, that gained ascendancy in Upper Egypt under Mentuhotep II (c.2055 BC) and later became a power base for local princes who eventually liberated Egypt from the Hyksos invaders and founded the XVIII Dynasty (c.1550 BC).

As the capital of the **New Kingdom**, whose empire stretched from Nubia to Palestine, Thebes enjoyed an ascendancy paralleled by that of **Amun**, whose cult temple at Karnak became the greatest in Egypt. At its zenith under the XVIII and XIX dynasties, Thebes may have had a population of around a million; Homer's *Iliad* describes it as a "city with a hundred gates". Excluding the brief **Amarna Period** (c.1345–36 BC), when the "heretic" Akhenaten moved the capital northwards and forbade the worship of Amun, the dynasty's – and city's – supremacy lasted some five hundred years. Even after the end of the Ramessid line, when the capital returned to Memphis and thence moved to the Delta, Thebes remained the foremost city of Upper Egypt, enjoying a final fling as a royal seat under the **Nubian** rulers of the XXV Dynasty (c.747–656 BC).

Though Thebes persisted through **Ptolemaic** into **Roman** times, it retained but a shadow of its former glory, and might have been abandoned like Memphis were it not for Christian settlements. During Muslim times its only claim to fame was the tomb of Abu el-Haggag, a twelfth-century sheikh. However, Napoleon's expedition to Egypt awakened foreign interest in its **antiquities**, which were gradually cleared during the nineteenth century and have drawn visitors ever since.

Luxor today

Not every visitor has been impressed, however: during the filming of *Death on the Nile*, Hollywood icon Bette Davis remarked that "In my day we'd have built all this at the studio – and better." In a sense she had a point: the temple was half hidden by ramshackle bazaars, and downtown was a mess. But the "solution" approved by UNESCO – whose

---

LUXOR ORIENTATION

Luxor spreads along the east bank of the Nile, its outskirts encroaching on villages and fields. The relatively compact tourist zone is defined by three main roads. **Sharia al-Mahatta** (aka Sharia Sa'ad Zaghloul) runs 500m from the train station towards Luxor Temple, where it meets **Sharia Maabad el-Karnak**, the main drag heading north to Karnak Temple (2.5km). Karnak is also accessible via the riverside **Corniche**, though tourists generally stick to the 1.5km stretch between Luxor Museum and the *Winter Palace* hotel. The "circuit" is completed by a fourth street, known as **Sharia al-Souk** after its bazaar.

In the last two decades Luxor has expanded south towards the village of Awmia, with dozens of hotels and other facilities along **Sharia Khalid Ibn Walid** (running 4km from the *Iberotel* to the *Sheraton*) and **Television Street** (named after its TV tower), which now constitute extensions of the tourist zone. The "suburbs" of **New Karnak** (between Karnak Temple and the *Hilton*) and **Fayrouz** (at the far end of Mohammed Farid and Television streets) are both neighbourhoods with flats for rent.

remit is to preserve the intergity of historic sites – has left the city centre scarred, and citizens embittered. Governor Samir Farag demolished hundreds of homes and shops to create an all-round view of Luxor Temple and expose the Avenue of Sphinxes that once ran out to Karnak. Residents were outraged by the derisory compensation (eighty percent less than allocated by UNESCO), and archeologists appalled by the "excavation" of the sphinxes (using bulldozers, with the damage crudely rectified in concrete). Work has stalled since the Revolution (when Farag was forced to resign), leaving ugly trenches (used as rubbish dumps) rather than the tree-lined promenade originally envisaged.

Luxor Temple

Sharia Maabad el-Karnak • Daily: May–Sept 6am–9pm; Oct–April 6am–8pm • £E50

Luxor Temple stands aloof in the heart of town, ennobling the view from the waterfront and Midan el-Haggag with its grand colonnades and pylons, spotlit at night till 9pm. Though best explored by day – which takes an hour or so – you could come back after dark to imbibe its atmosphere and drama with fewer people around.

Dedicated to the **Theban Triad** of Amun-Min, Mut and Khonsu (see p.279), Luxor Temple was the "Harem of the South" where Amun's consort Mut and their son Khonsu resided. Every spring a flotilla of barques escorted Amun's effigy from Karnak Temple to this site for a conjugal reunion with Mut in an Optet, or fertility festival, noted for its public debauchery, which lasted from two to four weeks.

Brief history

Whereas Karnak is the work of many dynasties, most of Luxor Temple was built by two rulers during a period when New Kingdom art reached its apogee. The temple's founder was **Amenhotep III** (c.1390–52 BC) of the XVIII Dynasty, whose other monuments include the Third Pylon at Karnak and the Colossi of Memnon across the river. Work halted under his son Akhenaten (who erased his father's cartouches and built a sanctuary to Aten alongside the temple), but resumed under Tutankhamun and Horemheb, who decorated its court and colonnade with their own reliefs.

To this, **Ramses II** (c.1279–13 BC) of the XIX Dynasty added a double colonnaded court and a great pylon flanked by obelisks and colossi. Despite additions by later pharaohs and the rebuilding of its sanctuary under Alexander the Great, the temple has a coherence that reproaches Karnak's inchoate giganticism. When the French army first sighted it in 1799, the troops spontaneously presented arms.

The clarity of its **reliefs** is due to the temple having been half-buried by sand and silt, and overlaid by Luxor itself. Nineteenth-century visitors found a "labyrinthine maze of mud structures" nesting within its court. When the French wanted to remove an obelisk, and archeologists to excavate the temple, they had to pay compensation for the demolition of scores of homes.

In recent years, an underground ring-drainage system has been installed to deal with the rising groundwater that had been damaging the temple, and surrounding buildings demolished to reveal more of the Avenue of Sphinxes leading to Karnak and provide an unobstructed view of the temple from all sides.

Approaching the temple

The site is entered by an underground gate beside the coach-park on Sharia Maabad el-Karnak. Behind the ticket office is an **Avenue of Sphinxes** with human faces (a XXX Dynasty addition by Nectanebo I), whose full extent has been recently exposed by excavations. Beyond the **Chapel of Seraphis** dedicated by the Roman emperor Hadrian on his birthday in AD 126, a mound of rubble near the Corniche road shows the level at which the medieval town of Luxor overlaid the ancient city.

The gateway and pylon

The temple **gateway** proper is flanked by massive pylons and enthroned colossi, with a

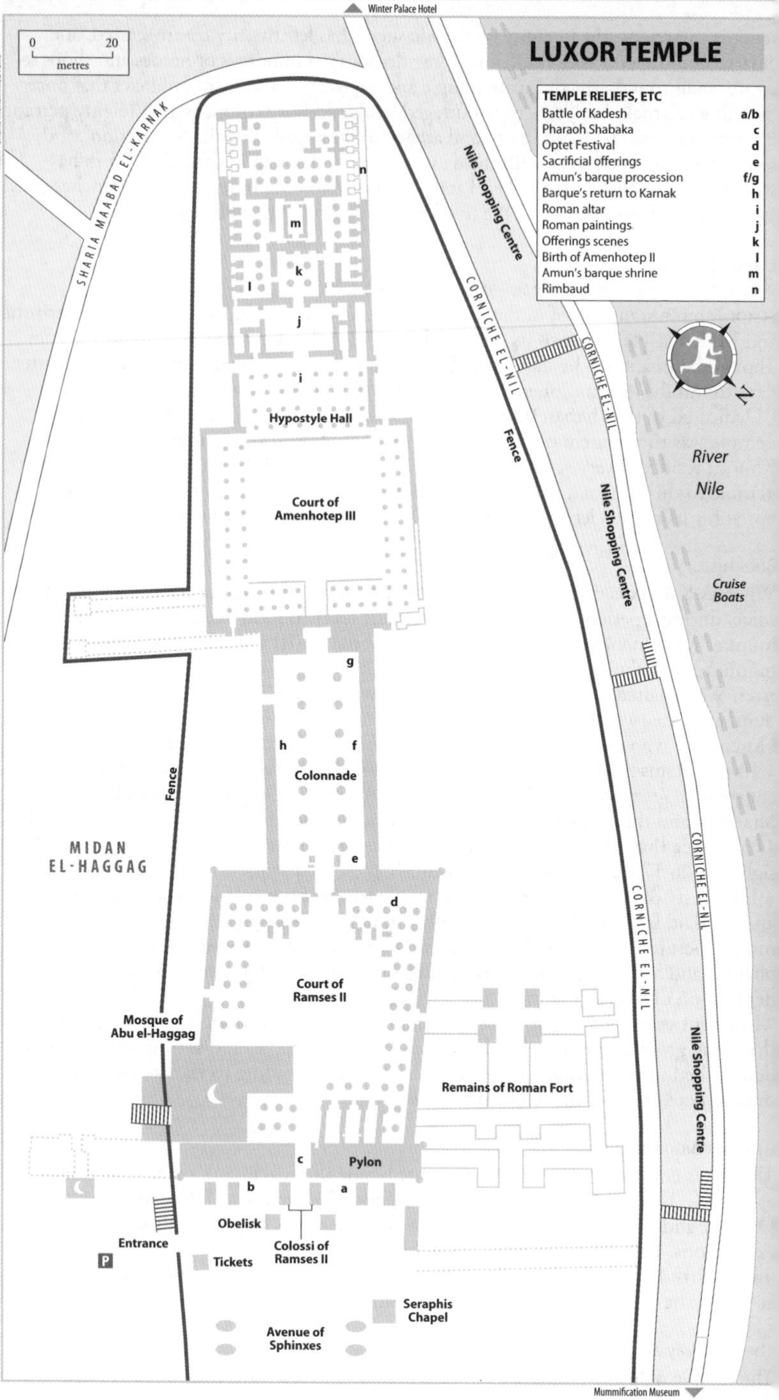

2

Winter Palace Hotel

LUXOR TEMPLE

0   20
metres

TEMPLE RELIEFS, ETC	
Battle of Kadesh	a/b
Pharaoh Shabaka	c
Optet Festival	d
Sacrificial offerings	e
Amun's barque procession	f/g
Barque's return to Karnak	h
Roman altar	i
Roman paintings	j
Offerings scenes	k
Birth of Amenhotep II	l
Amun's barque shrine	m
Rimbaud	n

Sharia Mohammed Farid

SHARIA MAABAD EL-KARNAK

CORNICHE EL-NIL

Nile Shopping Centre

Fence

Nile Shopping Centre

CORNICHE EL-NIL

River
Nile

Cruise
Boats

n

m

k

l

j

i

Hypostyle Hall

**Court of
Amenhotep III**

Fence

g

h   f

Colonnade

MIDAN
EL-HAGGAG

e

d

**Court of
Ramses II**

CORNICHE EL-NIL

Nile Shopping Centre

**Mosque of
Abu el-Haggag**

Remains of Roman Fort

c

b   a

Pylon

Obelisk

Entrance
P

Tickets

**Colossi of
Ramses II**

**Seraphis
Chapel**

**Avenue of
Sphinxes**

Mummification Museum

single **obelisk** soaring 25m high. Carved with reliefs and originally tipped with electrum, this was one of a pair until its mate was removed in 1835, taken to France and re-erected on the Place de la Concorde. The four dog-faced baboons at the base of each obelisk also sported erect phalluses until prudish Frenchmen hacked them off. Behind loom three of the six **colossi of Ramses II** that originally fronted the pylon (four seated, two standing). The enthroned ones have Schwarzenegger physiques and double crowns; reliefs of the Nile-god binding the Two Lands adorn their thrones.

The **pylon** is 65m wide and once stood 24m high; it is notched for flagpoles and carved with scenes of Ramses' supposed victory over the Hittites at Qadesh. You can see Ramses consulting his commanders in the Egyptian camp [a], before charging his foes and battling them until reinforcements arrive [b]. Centuries later, Nubian and Ethiopian kings left their mark: notice the relief of Pharaoh Shabaka running the *heb* race before Amun-Min, high up on the left as you walk through the pylon [c].

Court of Ramses II

Beyond the pylon lies the **Court of Ramses II**, surrounded by a double row of papyrus-bud columns, once roofed over to form arcades. The courtyard is set askew to the temple's main axis, doubtless to incorporate the earlier **barque shrines** of Tuthmosis III, dedicated to Khonsu (to the right as you enter), Amun (centre) and Mut (nearest the river). Incongruously perched atop the opposite colonnade (as best seen from the Corniche), the **Mosque of Abu el-Haggag** is a stocky Fatimid edifice bearing the name of Luxor's patron saint, whose demolition the townsfolk refused to countenance when the temple was excavated. Its interior juxtaposes Islamic motifs with pharaonic hieroglyphs; the prayer niche is hewn from a temple column. Providing it's not prayer-time, non-Muslims might be allowed in – ask at the top of the stairway from Midan el-Haggag.

In the temple itself, you can locate the lower half of a frieze depicting Amun's procession approaching the temple during the Optet festival, when the god was presented with lettuces, symbolizing his fertility [d]. Ramses makes offerings to Mut and Mont (the Theban war god), observed by his queen and seventeen of the hundred or so sons that he sired over ninety years.

Colonnade and Court of Amenhotep III

The portal is flanked by black granite statues of Ramses, their bases decorated with bound prisoners from Nubia and Asia. Beyond lies the older section of the temple, inaugurated by the lofty **Colonnade of Amenhotep III**, with its processional avenue of giant papyrus columns whose calyx capitals still support massive architraves. On the walls are more damaged scenes from the Optet festival, intended to be "read" in an anticlockwise direction. After sacrifices to the boats at Karnak [e], Amun's procession [f] arrives at Luxor Temple [g], returning to Karnak 24 days later [h]. The pharaoh shown here is Tutankhamun, who had the colonnade decorated, but the cartouches honour his successor, Horemheb.

At the end of the colonnade lies the great **Court of Amenhotep III**, surrounded on three sides by colonnades of papyrus-bundle columns with bud capitals. The southern one merges into a **Hypostyle Hall** with 32 papyrus columns, serving as a vestibule to the temple proper. Between the last two columns on the left of its central aisle [i] is a Roman altar dedicated to Emperor Constantine, before his conversion to Christianity.

The inner sanctums

Beyond the hall lies a columned **portico** or antechamber, whose central aisle was flanked by the barque shrines of Mut and Khonsu. Roman legionaries later plastered over the pharaonic reliefs and turned it into a chapel where local Christians were offered a choice of martyrdom or obeisance to the imperial cults. Paintings of Roman emperors are visible near the top of the walls, and around the niche on the south wall [j]; elsewhere the stucco has fallen away to reveal Amenhotep offering sacrifices to

Amun. In the smaller, four-columned **Hall of Offerings**, beyond, reliefs show the pharaoh leading sacrificial cows and presenting incense and sceptres **[k]**.

More interesting reliefs occur in the **Birth Room** of Amenhotep III, whose north wall **[l]** emphasizes his divine paternity, since he was not of direct royal descent. The ravaged lower register shows Thoth leading Amun (disguised as Tuthmosis IV) into the queen's bedchamber, where, the hieroglyphic caption states, "his dew filled her body". Examined from left to right, the middle register depicts Thoth foretelling Amenhotep's birth; Mutemuia's pregnancy and confinement; Isis presenting the child to Amun; and the god cradling his son.

If the Birth Room is inaccessible from the Hall of Offerings you can reach it via the next hall, which Alexander the Great converted into the **Sanctuary of Amun's Barque** by removing four columns and installing a granite shrine **[m]**.

The remaining chambers to the south constituted the private apartments of the gods, but are badly damaged and really only notable for the name Rimbaud, carved high up on the wall near the river **[n]**. The French poet Arthur Rimbaud spent the last sixteen years of his life roaming the Near and Far East; while living in Ethiopia he was feared dead, so Verlaine published his poems (all written by the age of 21), which took Paris by storm and inspired the Decadent movement.

Outside the walls, assorted pharaonic, Roman and Christian **stonework** is stored near the spot where, in 1989, workers uncovered a cache of 26 New Kingdom statues, sixteen of which are on show in the Luxor Museum.

Mummification Museum

Corniche el-Nil • **Museum**: Daily 9am–2pm • £E50 • No photography • **Library**: Daily 9am–1.30pm • Free

Reached by a stairway north of Luxor Temple, the **Mummification Museum** is sunk into the Corniche like a tomb. Its well-presented exhibits lift the lid on Ancient Egyptian mummification techniques and beliefs about death and the afterlife (see pp.296–297). Among the materials and tools is a spoon and spatula, for scraping out the deceased's brain (which was discarded as an unimportant organ). The well-preserved mummy of Maserharti, a XXI Dynasty high priest of Amun, attests to the embalmers' skills, and there are several richly painted coffins. A wooden bed and two linen pillows, found in tomb KV63 in the Valley of the Kings, are recent additions to the museum.

Visitors can consult the museum's Egyptology **library**, which in wintertime may host free **archeological lectures** by such experts as Kent Weeks (studying tomb KV5 in the Valley of the Kings) and Zbigniew Szafranski (of the Polish Mission at Deir el-Bahri).

Luxor Museum

Corniche el-Nil • Daily 9am–2pm • £E80 • No photography

Further north, the **Luxor Museum** displays a superb collection of statues and funerary goods from the Theban Necropolis and temples, dating from the end of the Old Kingdom up until the Late Period. The museum is wheelchair-accessible, and well laid out and labelled in English, making the illustrated guide sold at its bookshop unnecessary.

Cachette Hall

To the right as you enter is a ramp down to the sunken **Cachette Hall**, displaying sixteen of the **royal statues** found beneath Luxor Temple in 1987. It's uncertain whether they were hidden at the start of the Roman occupation or nine hundred years earlier, when Egypt was invaded by the Assyrians. They include an alabaster sphinx of Tutankhamun; Amenhotep III and Horus enthroned, in basalt; a headless cobra poised to strike in the name of the Nubian pharaoh Taharqa; Horemheb kneeling before the god Atum; and a processional effigy of Amenhotep III, its rose quartzite left unpolished to highlight the texture of his kilt, armbands and Combined Crown.

First level

The **first level** opens with a sensitive-faced statue of the adolescent Tutankhamun and a gilded head of the cow deity Mehit-Weret from his tomb in the Valley of the Kings. A colossal **head of Amenhotep III**, found on the west bank in 1957, leads you on to a raised level showcasing more works in stone. Compare the careworn face of Sesostris II and the watchfulness of bureaucrat Yamo-Nedjeh with the serenity of the boy Tut beside the crocodile god Sobek, or the diorite head of Sekhmet from a colossal statue in the Precinct of Mut at Karnak.

2

Thebes Glory

An extension called **Thebes Glory** focuses on the New Kingdom war machine that was honed against Egypt's Hyksos invaders and later unleashed on neighbouring states. Its logistics were so sophisticated that Tuthmosis III was able to move twenty thousand troops 400km in nine days, while Ramses II extended Egypt's strategic reach to 2000km by pioneering the use of oxen (the mainstay of military logistics for the next thousand years).

Tutankhamun's **war chariot**, a relief of Amenhotep II target-shooting and royal **bows** (some recurved and composite) show how the Egyptians mastered the tactics and technology of the Hyksos. A statue of Horemheb and his wife from their unfinished tomb at Memphis, a granite head of Ramses II and a super-sized alabaster Seti I recall the hard men of the XVIII and XIX dynasties.

Best of all, there are two **royal mummies**. That of **Ahmosis I** has a surprisingly delicate physique for the ruler who expelled the Hyksos. His gold-and-electrum axe (found at Dra' Abul Naga on the west bank) and a gold collar with Flies of Valour, from the tomb of Queen Ahhotep (who may have led the Theban army when Ahmosis was a child), are exhibited nearby. The other mummy was returned to Egypt from a museum at Niagara Falls, and might belong to **Ramses I** (see p.305).

Top level

On the museum's **top level** are model boats from the Meir Tombs at Assyut, gilded *shabti* figures from Tut's tomb, and architects' tools from the Workmen's Village at Deir el-Medina. Between two haunting heads of **Akhenaten**, from his Aten temple at Karnak, is a **wall** from the same temple, made of *talatat* (see p.223); the *talatat* were later used as filler for the Ninth Pylon, wherein they were discovered in the 1960s. Reassembled, the painted sunk-reliefs depict Akhenaten's *Sed* festival, with the king and Queen Nefertiti in a litter surrounded by fan-bearers. Their figures have the strange physiognomy associated with Akhenaten's reign (see box, p.228).

A **multimedia display** shows how papyrus was harvested and pressed into sheets for writing and how **scribes** were taught from childhood to read and write hieroglyphics. Trained scribes were managers and bureaucrats, overseeing taxation, irrigation systems and construction projects, whose social status reflected their importance to the state.

Nile Heritage Centre

Sharia Maabad el-Karnak, 1.5km north of Luxor Temple • Daily except Tues 10am–8pm • Exhibition £E10 • Culturama £E80 • Library free

A vanity project from the last years of the Mubarak regime (when it was called the Suzanne Mubarak Library after his wife, and as it's still known to locals), this grandiose edifice has an Egyptology **library** that pointlessly duplicates the one in the Mummification Museum and an **exhibition** of gilded replica Islamic astrolabes and sundials, purely for bling. The centre's intended highlight is **Culturama**, a forty-minute interactive 3D tour of Egypt's ancient civilization, nowadays only screened by prior arrangement (☎012 2907 6243). During the 2011 Revolution the centre narrowly escaped being burnt to the ground. Hardly any tourists ever visit, or even know that it exists.

2

LUXOR BY HOT-AIR BALLOON

Don't miss the experience of drifting over the Theban Necropolis in a **hot-air balloon**, which affords an awesome view of the temples, villages and mountains – you'll probably spend about 40 minutes aloft, depending on the wind. Above the west bank villages, you can hear people in backyards and smell their cooking stoves amidst an eerie silence, broken only by the roar of the balloon's gas-burners.

Booking a balloon-ride through a foreign tour operator will only push up the price. Contact the balloon companies listed below directly to compare quotes. At the time of writing, a ride costs £E250–300 if booked through these companies or budget-hotels such as the *Oasis* and *Happy Land*; local tourist agencies charge £E600. Prices may also reflect the size of the balloon-basket (the largest hold 28 passengers), and your departure "slot". The first flights each day are timed to catch sunrise, but the second series may provide a finer view of the Necropolis in winter time, when mist often lingers over the west bank. The deal should include an early-morning transfer from your hotel to the launch site near Hatshepsut's temple.

Alaska Balloons (off Sharia Salah al-Din ☎095 227 4060).

Hod Hod Soliman Television St ☎095 227 0116, ✉ hodhodoffice@yahoo.co.uk.

Magic Horizon Balloons Sharia Khalid Ibn Walid ☎095 227 4060, ⓦmagichorizon.com.

Sindbad Sharia Abdel Hamid el-Omda ☎010 0330 7708, ⓦsindbadballoons.com.

Sky Cruise ☎095 227 3837, ✉reservations-lxr @skycruise-eg.com.

Viking Air Outside the *Sheraton* hotel ☎012 2569 9393.

ARRIVAL AND DEPARTURE   LUXOR

By air All flights land at Luxor International Airport (☎095 237 4655), 6km southeast of town. Locals pay £E30–40 for a taxi into the centre, but drivers will try to charge more. EgyptAir flies directly to Luxor from Cairo (6–17 flights daily; 1hr) and Sharm el-Sheikh (1–2 weekly; 1hr), with connections from other domestic airports, as well as many foreign capitals. Other airlines' scheduled and charter flights from Europe may only operate in the winter months. Seats on EgyptAir departures should be booked at their office on the Corniche (see p.277) as far ahead as possible to allow for surges in demand. To find seats on charter flights, ask reps at the airport (travellers who overstay the four-week limit on charter return tickets may not get past check-in). Allow 40min to reach the airport.

By train Trains are the best way of reaching Luxor from elsewhere in the Valley, with comfy seating and plenty of leg-room in a/c first- and second-class carriages that allows you to sleep on long journeys (non-a/c second- and third-class should only be considered for shorter rides). Detail of trains from Cairo are covered in chapter 1 (see p.173). Departures from Luxor are subject to similar restrictions. You can only buy tickets for trains #87 (7.15pm), #85 (10.30pm) and #997 (11pm) to Cairo, or #996 (7.30am), #1902 (9.30am) and #980 (6pm) to Aswan – but it's feasible to use other services. Arriving at Luxor's train station on Midan al-Mahatta, tourists are mobbed by hotel touts (some of whom board trains at Qena). As most hotels are less than fifteen minutes' walk away it's fine to strike out towards your preferred option without further ado.

By boat Aside from "full Nile" cruises (see p.241), river journeys to Luxor invariably start from Aswan. Where (or how) you arrive depends on the vessel, and can affect your stay if you're sleeping aboard the boat. Some cruise boats moor by the downtown Corniche within easy walking distance of Luxor Temple and the ferry to the west bank. Moorings further north are less convenient, unless near Karnak Temple, but still better than the New Corniche 6–7km south of town, where you're reliant on taxis to reach the centre (£E30–50), or the west bank via Luxor Bridge. Diesel-fumes are less of a problem here, however. *Dahabiyas* enjoy rustic moorings on the west bank, near Gezi[r]a and the ferry to Luxor. With both sides readily accessible, the only problem is negotiating the gangplank between your *dahabiya* and the shore after dark. Felluccas disembark up to 200km away; passengers travel on to Luxor by minibus (see p.242). Drivers will steer you to whichever hotels pay them a commission, unless you insist on a specific place.

By bus Bus services are run by the Upper Egypt Bus Co. (UEBC) and Superjet (SJ). The main difference between the two companies is that Upper Egypt services terminate at Zanatka Bus Station, 5km outside town near the airport (£E25–30 by taxi into the centre), while Superjet drops passengers at their ticket office (☎095 236 7732) near the train station, in the centre. Upper Egypt Co. also has an office (☎095 237 2118) here, but it only sells tickets for their a/c services; others are handled at the bus station (☎095 232 3218). Upper Egypt services to Cairo, Sharm el-Sheikh, Dahab and Port Said collect passengers outside

2

their train station office 30 minutes before they depart from the bus station. For all other buses to Qena, Port Safaga and Suez you can only buy tickets and board at the bus station. Zanatka is also the terminal for service taxis to (and from) Qena, Edfu and Aswan, but as it's awkward to reach and they only leave when full, there's little point in using service taxis.

Destinations Cairo (2 daily at 6.30pm & 7.30pm; 9hr; UEBC & SJ); Dahab (1 daily at 4.30pm; 16–18hr; UEBC); Hurghada (3 daily at 7.30am, 7.30pm & 8pm; 4–5hr; UEBC & SJ); Sharm el-Sheikh (1 daily at 4.30pm; 15–17hr; UEBC); Port Said (1 daily at 7.30pm; 12hr; UEBC); Port Safaga (3 daily; 4hr; UEBC); Qena (4 daily; 2hr; UEBC); Suez (5 daily; 10hr; UEBC).

By private taxi or minibus a/c private taxis are maginally faster and comfier than buses for travel between Luxor and Hurghada, with the cost shared between passengers (about £E400/£E900 for up to three/six people); these can be arranged through budget hotels or drivers like Tariq Adani (☎ 010 2123 8264). Cars must depart from Luxor in a convoy (8am, 2pm & 6pm). There are no restrictions on travelling directly between Luxor and Aswan via the desert road (roughly £E400). A private taxi is the only way to travel between Luxor and Kharga Oasis (see p.425) by a desert road that enters the Nile Valley near Riziq, 15km south of Luxor (open till 4pm daily). Expect to pay £E500–600 for the two-hour journey; Islam Anwar (☎ 012 2531 9355) quotes £E600 for a ride all the way from Luxor to Dakhla Oasis (or vice versa).

GETTING AROUND

On foot Although the centre is compact enough to explore on foot, many visitors find it offputting to be importuned at every step.

By calèche Fun to ride but a bit pricey for regular use, as drivers charge whatever they can get: £E10 for a brief drive or £E20–30 for an hour's jaunt around the centre seems fair.

By taxi Essential for reaching Luxor's airport (£E30–50), outlying hotels (£E15–20) and cruise-boat moorings (£E30–50), but fairly superfluous around the centre (£E5–10) unless to get back from a disco. It's better to pay what's right at the end rather than haggle over the price at the beginning.

By minbus White-and-blue minibuses are the cheapest way of travelling across town (50pt flat fare). They can be flagged down or drop you off at any point along their routes to several outlying termini; the trick is to know which one relates to your own destination. All **southbound services** run past Luxor Temple, heading either for the International Hospital (mustashfa) or Sharia Medina at the far end of Television St, or past the big hotels on Sharia Khalid Ibn Walid, en route to the village of Awmia. **Northbound minibuses** loop inland via Sharia Manshiya, the train station and Sharia Yussef Hassan, before joining Sharia Maabad el-Karnak near Luxor Temple, running on to Karnak Temple and the Hilton, or turning off near Luxor Museum towards the taxi depot (mogaf) at the end of Sharia al-Mathari. The tactic is to wave down any minibus heading in the right general direction, holler "Awmia", "Karnak" (or whichever other terminus suits you), and hop in if they're going there.

By bicycle Cycling in town isn't advisable due to heavy traffic, but bikes can be useful to reach Karnak Temple (via the Corniche) or for getting around the Theban Necropolis on the west bank (see p.287). Shops on Sharia al-Mahatta and some budget hotels rent them out for £E15 a day. Most bikes are one-speed only and may be defective in some respect, so it's always wise to check the machine and have a short test ride. Some places also rent Motorbikes

INFORMATION

Tourist office Midan al-Mahatta ☎ 095 228 0902 (daily 8am–8pm). Useful for verifying the latest temple opening hours, schedules for Sound and Light shows at Karnak, intercity buses and trains.

Websites Local expat sites feature lots of advice but aren't always up-to-date on prices. Jane Akshar's excellent blog (🖥 luxor-news.blogspot.com) has news of recent developments in Egyptology and local tourism, and there are lively forums on 🖥 luxor4u.com. You can book flats or villas through both these sites.

TOURS

With Karnak Temple and the Theban Necropolis in the immediate vicinity, it'll be a while before you start considering excursions to other sites in the Nile Valley – the **temples of Esna**, **Edfu** and **Kom Ombo** along the way to Aswan, or **Abydos** and **Dendara** to the north of Luxor – any of which makes a feasible day-trip.

BY ROAD

Taxi/minibus excursions Many hotels offer taxi or minibus excursions, the cost split between passengers – the more people, the less each one pays. Edfu and Kom Ombo cost from £E250–300 for one person, down to as little as £E85 each if seven people share a minibus; prices for Dendara and Abydos range from £E250–300 for a solo trip to £E50–85/head for six to ten people (excluding tickets for the temples). Compare quotes from *Happy Land*, the *Oasis*, *Nefertiti* and *Fontana* hotels.

Desert safaris A few local operators offer small-group safaris into the **Western Desert** (see p.374). Ala el-Din at the *Nefertiti hotel* (☎010 0601 6132, ⦿nefertitihotel .com), Hamada El-Khalifa at the *Nile Valley hotel* (☎012 2796 4473, ⦿nile-valley.nl) and Osman Mohammed at the *Eye House* (☎012 2337 1799, ⦿rocktours.dk) stick to the four oases on the "Great Desert Circuit" and seldom venture off-road, while Abou El Naga Gabrail (☎010 0124 0080, ⓔabuelnaga58@yahoo.com) and Azab Safari (☎012 2385 0227, ⓔazab76us@yahoo.com) also offer more ambitious trips to the Great Sand Sea. The cost depends on the number of people and the duration of the tour; meals are included.

BY BOAT

Day cruises to Dendara on the *Lotus Boat or Tiba Star* (Tues & Sun) involve five hours on the river (with lunch) and an hour at the temple: tickets are sold by the *Iberotel* (£E480)

and travel agents (for more), inclusive of admission charges and lunch.

Nile cruises Going for a sail on the river in a felucca is a relaxing way to spend an afternoon, while a sunset cruise is the perfect way to end the day. Haggling with boatmen, expect to pay around £E35/hr for a "local" cruise or £E80 for a trip to Banana Island (see below); slightly more if there are several passengers. The *Steigenberger Nile Palace* runs one-hour cruises with breakfast ($16/person), lunch ($40/person), or cocktails and canapes at sunset ($45). One target for a boat trip is **Banana Island** (Gezira el-Moz), 4km upriver from the centre, a name loosely applied to two banana plantations either side of the river, whose owners charge visitors £E5 each to land. It's enjoyable to wander through the cool, shady groves of mature trees, with their vaulting fronds and pendant flowers; a handful of bananas are included in the price. The round trip takes two to three hours depending on the wind, or half-an-hour each way by motorboat (£E60 return).

ACTIVITIES

Birdwatching on Crocodile Island, site of the *Maritim Jolie Ville*, offers a more peaceful excursion, with sunbirds, glossy ibises, purple herons, pied kingfishers, African rock martins, Sardinian warblers, hooded wheatears and black and whiskered terns amongst the species to be found. The resort's birdwatching guide, Abdou Yussef (☎012 2239 5467), can show you the best spots in his boat.

Horse- and camel-riding Rides in the desert or through the villages on the west bank can be arranged by two

outfits in Gezira: Pharaoh's Stables (☎010 0632 4961) charges £E40 for an hour on a horse or camel, £E90 for three hours' horseriding in the desert; Arabian Horse Stables (☎010 0504 8558) charges £E50 an hour.

Quad-biking The *Oasis*, *Boomerang New Peace* and *Venus* hotels in Luxor can arrange this in the desert on the west bank for £E300/person. The three-hour trip includes pick-up and drop-off at your hotel, a brief camel ride and tea in a Bedouin tent.

ACCOMMODATION

Before choosing a hotel, decide whether you'd rather stay **in Luxor**, or across the river **on the west bank** (which is quieter and hassle-free). The following listings cover both the east and west banks (subdivided into various localities), including the option of **renting an apartment or villa** (see p.272). Officially there are "high" (Nov–April) and "low" (May–Oct) seasons, but in reality prices rise or fall depending on the number of tourists and competition from cruise boats. Many low-budget places employ **hotel touts**, who refer to netting tourists as "fishing" and poach them from rivals by telling outrageous lies. Searching the internet you can get **discounts** of up to fifty percent off the walk-in rates at almost any hotel rated three stars or above. Most low-budget places can be booked through ⦿ hostelworld.com or ⦿ hostelbookers.com, but you're unlikely to save money and might even pay more than if you simply walk in and try haggling.

LUXOR

DOWNTOWN

We've taken downtown to mean anywhere within five minutes' walk of Luxor Temple – an area that includes the main tourist bazaar and the central swathe of the Corniche. The downside of being in the thick of things is that you can hardly step outside without being importuned by a salesman or *calèche* driver, and hotels near the bazaar or main roads can be quite noisy.

El-Luxor Corniche el-Nil, between Luxor Temple and Luxor Museum ☎095 238 0944, ⦿el-luxor-hotel.com; map p.256. Its proximity to the Luxor Museum and its

swimming pool are the main advantages of this refurbished 1970s four-star, still known to locals as the *Etap*. Mainly used by tour groups, the hotel has a restaurant, coffee shop, bar and disco (where a bellydancer performs if there are enough guests). B&B $\underline{\$75}$

Emilio Sharia Yussef Hassan ☎095 237 6666, ⦿emiliotravel.com; map p.256. Sited just off Sharia Maabad el-Karnak, near the Av of Sphinxes leading from Luxor Temple, the *Emilio* is geared to tour groups and can be a bit dismissive of independent travellers. It has comfy a/c rooms with fridges and satellite TV; a rooftop pool, bar and disco, Sun buffet and Saiyidi dance show. B&B $\underline{\$55}$

Iberotel Midan el-Mesaha, 600m south of Luxor Temple ☎095 238 0925, ✉luxor@jaz.travel; map p.257. This former *Novotel* (and still widely known as such) at the southern end of the Corniche has a large atrium and a terrace overlooking the Nile, where their pool is sunk into a pontoon-boat. The a/c en-suite rooms facing the city or Nile ($10–15 extra) are small and bland, and guests must pay for wi-fi, but service is excellent. **$76**

★ **Nefertiti** Sharia Sahaby, off Sharia Maabad el-Karnak ☎095 237 2386, ⊛nefertitihotel.com; map p.256. Beside the tourist bazaar near Luxor Temple, this small boutique hotel is decorated with arabesque murals, tapestries and brass lamps. Guests can dine or smoke a *sheesha* on an awning-shaded rooftop overlooking the temple, or in the outdoor *Al-Sahaby Lane* restaurant (see p.273), in an alley off the bazaar. The hotel has free wi-fi, a buffet breakfast and very helpful staff. Its engaging owner Ala el-Din was on Midan Tahrir during the Revolution and organizes tours to the oases, Cairo, Sinai and Jordan. B&B **£E160**

Philippe Sharia Labaib Habachi, off the Corniche ☎095 237 3604, ⊛philippeluxorhotel.com; map p.256. Conveniently close to the Luxor Museum, the rather faded Philippe has en-suite a/c rooms with fridge and satellite TV; "superior" ones have fancier decor and balconies with a Nile view. Rooftop pool, billiards (£E20/hr), internet (£E20/hr) and massage (£E170/hr). Mainly used by tour groups. B&B **$40**

★ **Susanna** Sharia Maabad el-Karnak ☎095 236 9912, ⊛susannahotelluxor.com; map p.256. Opposite the Avenue of Sphinxes beside Luxor Temple, the super-clean Susanna has a/c rooms with satellite TV and proper bathtubs, an a/c restaurant and a rooftop with a tiny pool, affording great views of the temple. There's a $5/10 premium for street-facing rooms, and those on the top floor (which have the best view). B&B **$40**

Venus Sharia Yussef Hassan ☎095 237 2625 or ☎012 7052 6621, ⊛venus-hotel-luxor.webs.com; map p.256. Legendary hotel now recovering its mojo under energetic new Colombian–Egyptian management, with friendly staff and a funky vibe, free internet, sports TV and a rooftop overlooking the tourist bazaar making up for the noisy location. There are dorm beds, simple a/c rooms (mostly ensuite) plus an apartment sleeping up to five people, and free transfers from the station or airport for pre-booked guests. Balloon rides and excursions also arranged. B&B **£E12**

Winter Palace Corniche el-Nil, 100m from Luxor Temple ☎095 238 0422, ⊛sofitel.com; map p.257. The oldest and grandest of Luxor's hotels, founded in 1887, this Victorian pile has played host to heads of state, Noël Coward and Agatha Christie (parts of *Death on the Nile* were written and filmed here). Rooms in the Palace wing (decorated in colonial style with antique furniture)

overlook the Nile or a vast garden with a heated pool; the adjacent 1970s-retro Pavilion wing only has garden-view rooms, but at lower rates. Besides boasting Luxor's poshest restaurant (see p.272) and bar (see p.275), the *Winter Palace* will also have a health club and arcade modelled on the Mamluke carpet bazaar in Cairo, making it as sumptuous as its sister hotel in Aswan, the *Old Cataract*. Palace wing **€700**; Pavilion wing **€225**

AROUND TELEVISION STREET

Many low-budget hotels cluster around Television St and parallel side streets – mostly no more than fifteen minutes' walk from Luxor Temple or the train station, and accessible by minibus. Despite its littered backstreets, this area is safe, and quieter than downtown.

★ **Boomerang New Peace** Sharia Mohammed Farid ☎095 228 0981, ⊛boomerangluxor.com; map p.257. Managed by an Australian woman and her Nubian husband, *Boomerang* has established itself as a rival to older low-budget hotels. Nicely decorated, tiled and non-smoking throughout, it has free wi-fi, laundry service, internet access (£E5/hr), bike rental (£E15/day), and a rooftop with loungers, a hammock and regular BBQs. All rooms have fans and a/c; some also have private bathrooms, satellite TV and double beds with mosquito nets for £E20–40 more. Felucca cruises, balloon rides, quad-biking, tours and excursions all arranged. Dorm bed **£E25**; rooms **£E90**

★ **Fontana** Sharia Radwan ☎095 238 0663 or ☎010 0733 3238, ⊛fontanaluxorhotel.com; map p.257. A longtime backpackers' favourite on a quiet lane off Television St, owned by the languid Mr Magdy. Clean, well furnished and cheerily decorated, it has informative noticeboards and satellite TV in the lobby, free use of a washing machine and kitchen, and various tours and excursions at negotiable rates. All rooms come with a/c and bathrooms; some have proper bathtubs (but no plugs). B&B **£E50**

★ **Happy Land** Sharia el-Kamrr, off Sharia el-Madina el-Minarwa ☎095 227 1828 or ☎011 1395 7207, ⊛luxorhappyland.com; map p.257. Under the benign management of the ever-helpful Hagg Ibrahim, *Happy Land* is renowned for its cleanliness, honesty and fixed prices. All rooms come with fans, towels and toiletries; a/c, a private bathroom and fridge costs £E15–20 extra. A lavish breakfast is served on the rooftop, which has satellite TV, free wi-fi and a jacuzzi. Mr Ibrahim also offers bike rental, cheap excursions to the Valley temples and the west bank and balloon trips, bus, train and Red Sea ferry tickets. B&B **£E57**

Little Garden Sharia Radwan ☎095 227 9090, ✉littlegardenlxregy@hotmail.com; map p.257. Named after its peaceful palm-garden, this cosy retreat is painted a soothing cream throughout and has a shaded rooftop with sunloungers. All rooms are a/c and ensuite; some are a bit claustrophobic, while others (££200/person) have private terraces with loungers. There's also a library, internet access (££6/hr) and transfers from the train station (free) or airport (€8) for pre-booked guests. B&B **££150**

★ **Oasis** Sharia Mohammed Farid ☏ 010 0380 5882, ⊚ oasishotelluxor.blog126.fc2.com; map p.257. Just off the bazaar in the Manshiya quarter between Television Street and the train station (5mins walk), the *Oasis* is painted a fetching sky blue throughout. Its clean, simple rooms have fans and shared facilities; ££10 extra gets you a/c, a private bathroom and maybe even a double bed. Free tea and cake are served on the sociable rooftop at sunset, and you can order beer and meals. Laundry service and free wi-fi are also available, and genial assistant manager Hassan arranges cheap excursions to the west bank and Valley temples. B&B **££50**

Princess Off Sharia Ahmed Orabi ☏ 095 227 3997, ⊚ princesshotelluxor.com; map p.257. Another backstreet hotel, slightly inferior to the nearby *Fontana*, the *Princess* is decorated with naïve murals of rural life, and has clean en-suite rooms with fans. Manager Hassan Sadek arranges west bank tours (without guide), excursions and balloon rides. B&B **££60**

ALONG SHARIA KHALID IBN WALID

Starting near the southern end of the Corniche and running parallel to the Nile for 4km, Sharia Khalid Ibn Walid is lined with four- and five-star hotels, with restaurants and bars further inland. Even if you stay far from the centre there's never a problem finding a taxi or *calèche*, and public minibuses (to/from Awmia) run until midnight.

Luxor Sheraton Resort 4.2km from Luxor Temple ☏ 095 237 4544, ⊚ sheraton.com/luxor; map p.257. Tranquilly secluded at the far end of Khalid Ibn Walid, the *Sheraton* has good facilities and service. All rooms are a/c and en suite, with LCD TVs. Go for a room in the main building rather than a garden one; costlier "Nile-view" rooms only live up to their billing on the upper floors. Access by free bus from the Luxor Museum seven times daily, or by public minibus as far as Midan el-Salam, five minutes' walk away. B&B **$76**

Maritim Jolie Ville Crocodile Island, 6km from Luxor Temple ☏ 095 227 4855, ⊚ jolieville-hotels.com; map p.257. Locally known to all as the *Mövenpick*, this spacious resort (connected to town by hourly buses to the *Winter Palace* and a motorboat three times daily) is ideal for families, with 320 bungalows in luxuriant grounds, tennis courts, an Italian restaurant (see p.273), a pool and playground. B&B **$75**

Morris Sharia el-Hurriya, 1.7km from Luxor Temple ☏ 095 227 9833, ⊚ info@hotelmorrisluxor.com; map p.257. This high-rise four-star off the main drag has a rooftop pool with Nile views, and large a/c rooms with

fridges, satellite TV and balconies – ask for one with a river view. Serves buffet breakfast (££30), lunch (££50) and dinner (££70). **$60**

New Pola 2.2km from Luxor Temple ☏ 095 236 5081, ⊚ newpolahotel.com; map p.257. A decent mid-range hotel with a/c rooms, a rooftop with a small pool and fabulous Nile views and agreeably kitsch decor throughout. Ask for a room facing the river. B&B **££150**

Pyramisa Isis 3.5km from Luxor Temple ☏ 095 237 0100, ⊚ pyramisaegypt.com; map p.257. This anodyne complex near the end of the street backs onto lush grounds with a big pool and superb views of the river, although its a/c en-suite rooms (either facing the street or Nile) are on the small side. B&B **$85**

St Joseph 2.3km from Luxor Temple ☏ 095 238 1707, ⊚ stjosephhotel@yahoo.com; map p.257. A three-star with a heated rooftop pool and a bar facing the Theban Hills. All rooms are en suite with a/c and free wi-fi; ask for one with a Nile view. They offer aromatherapy and Balinese massage, and can arrange an "Egyptian night" with a snakecharmer and bellydancer, if enough guests are interested. Excellent buffet breakfasts. B&B **££315**

Sonesta St George 2.7km from Luxor Temple ☏ 095 238 2575, ⊚ sonesta.com; map p.257. The fanciest five-star on the street, with oodles of marble, Japanese and Italian restaurants, a heated pool by the Nile and great service. Guests can choose between street- and Nile-view rooms, while the top three floors have deluxe rooms with jacuzzis, large screen TVs and power showers. See their website for best available rates. B&B **$115**

Steigenberger Nile Palace 3.7km from Luxor Temple ☏ 095 236 6999, ⊚ luxor.steigenberger.com; map p.257. Awash with fake marble, this five-star behemoth overlooks a heated pool beside a Nile terrace, and has disabled access to all its street- or river-facing rooms. Amenities include a gym, massage and sauna, plus Italian and Lebanese restaurants. See the website for best available rates. All major cards. B&B **€108**

SAWAGI

If you fancy staying somewhere untouristy and hassle-free, Sawagi, behind the train station, is an artisans' quarter 20 minutes' walk from Luxor Temple. To get there, cross the tracks to the north of the station and follow Sharia Salakhana nearly to the end, before bearing left onto a parallel sidestreet, where you should ask locals for directions to the "Beit Mara".

★ **Mara House** Sharia Salah al-Din al-Ayubi ☏ 010 0757 1855, ⊚ egyptwithmara.com; map p.289. Run by an Irishwoman, Mara, this child-friendly apart-hotel has large a/c en-suite rooms, a restaurant decorated in the khedival style, a bar with wi-fi, a roof-garden overlooking mountains and a library reflecting Mara's passion for Egyptology and spiritual healing. **$100**

2

2

BEYOND KARNAK

If you don't mind being far from Luxor there are two deluxe hotels out past Karnak Temple, both linked to town by free shuttle buses. The *Hilton* is adjacent to a mini tourist-zone of restaurants and bars in New Karnak (accessible by public minibus from Luxor), while the *Sofitel* exists in splendid isolation.

Hilton Luxor Resort & Spa 4km north of Luxor Temple, 1.5km from Karnak Temple ☎ 095 237 4933, ⓦ hiltonluxor.com; map p.289. This opulent five-star resort features a top-class spa and two infinity pools in landscaped grounds beside the Nile. All rooms have balconies with Nile views, soundproof glazing, LCD TVs and DVD players – but no wi-fi (wired access costs $60). Hourly shuttle bus into town. B&B $340

Sofitel Karnak 6km from downtown Luxor, 3km from Karnak ☎ 095 237 8020, ⓦ sofitel.com; map p.289. Secluded amid palms and bougainvilleas, this faux-Moorish hotel has a big heated Nile-side pool, tennis, squash, a sauna and jacuzzi. Advertised abroad as a child-free resort, but not so in reality. All rooms have a private terrace or balcony with garden view, satellite TV and hairdryers. Shuttle bus to the *Winter Palace* in Luxor. B&B $84

WEST BANK

GEZIRA AND RAMLEH

Gezira is only five minutes by motorboat or public ferry from Luxor Temple and on the road to the Theban Necropolis, making it an ideal base from which to explore both sides of the river. With a dozen hotels, plus flats and villas in the riverside Ramleh quarter and a campground further south, visitors are spoilt for choice.

Al-Salam Camp By the Nile 1.6km south of the ferry dock ☎ 010 0682 4067; map p.288. Bookable through Hostelworld, this funky Dahab-style campground exists in a zonked-out world of its own almost cut off by water when the Nile rises. It has circular huts with mosquito-netted sleeping platforms and tiled floors, shared washrooms, a shady yard, rock music and beer. The genial owner, Ahmed, can arrange camel rides. B&B £E60

Amon Gezira ☎ 095 231 0912 or ☎ 010 0639 4585, ⓦ amonhotel.com; map p.288. This quiet backstreet hotel has two blocks flanking a lush garden with a weird silk-cotton tree: the south-facing one has large cool rooms with balconies; the other block, a sun terrace. Most rooms are en suite and a/c, with wi-fi throughout. They also sell beer and wine, and use filtered water for cooking in their restaurant. B&B €20

Cleopatra Gezira ☎ 095 231 4545, ⓦ cleopatrahotelluxor.com; map p.288. At the back of the village, with a view of fields and the Theban Hills, the four-storey *Cleopatra* has large a/c en-suite rooms decorated with arabesques, plus free wi-fi and a rooftop restaurant selling alcohol. B&B $30

El-Fayrouz Gezira ☎ 095 231 2709, ⓦ elfayrouz.com, map p.288. A gorgeous garden shaded by banana and palm trees and a majestic view of the Theban Hills from its rooftop are the main attractions of this four-storey salmon-pink block, named after the Lebanese singer revered throughout the Arab world. The spacious en-suite rooms come with fans (some with a/c); it's worth paying £E25–40 extra for a balcony or rooftop view. Internet access (£E7/hr), meals and alcohol also available. B&B £E150

El-Gezira Gezira ☎ 095 231 0034, ⓦ el-gezira.com; map p.288. Down the first turning off the main street, *El-Gezira* has eleven a/c en-suite rooms with fridges and balconies, an attractive rooftop, a pool table, and a rock-garden with a serpentine watercourse. Guests get free use of the pool and wi-fi at its sister-hotel in Ramleh, *Gezira Gardens* (see below). B&B £E150

El-Mesala Ramleh ☎ 095 231 5004 or ☎ 012 2351 4523, ⓦ hotelelmesala.com; map p.288. A Nile-side newcomer named after the obelisk at Luxor Temple that's visible across the river, this three-storey hotel has large a/c rooms and apartments with bathtubs, satellite TV, free wi-fi, balconies overlooking a pool with sunloungers in the garden and a rooftop restaurant with a view of the temple. B&B: rooms €28; apartments €40

★ **El-Nakhil** Gezira ☎ 095 231 3922 or ☎ 012 2382 1007, ⓦ elnakhil.com; map p.288. Named after the palm trees that shade its garden, this restful enclave of Moorish a/c chalets and suites (some with connecting doors and wheelchair access) has a rooftop with a view of the Theban Hills. Run by a Swiss woman and her Egyptian partner, who serve a buffet lunch if enough guests are staying. B&B €35

★ **Gezira Gardens** Ramleh ☎ 095 231 2505, ⓦ el-gezira.com; map p.288. Under the same Egyptian-German management as *El-Gezira*, this immaculate three-star mini-resort has a/c rooms, and self-catering apartments sleeping up to four (with mosquito nets, private balcony and roof terrace); a swimming pool, bar, two restaurants, billiards, darts, table tennis, wi-fi and satellite TV. Favoured by German tourists. B&B: €35; apartments €60

Kareem Gezira ☎ 010 0184 2083, ⓦ hotelkareemlxr .com; map p.288. Near the Arabian Horse Stables at the back of the village, the *Kareem* ("Merciful") has fake waterfalls and naïve murals in its lobby, slightly uncared for en-suite a/c rooms, free wi-fi and a distant view of Hatshepsut's temple from its rooftop. B&B £E210

★ **Nile Valley** Gezira ☎ 095 231 1477 or ☎ 012 2796 4473, ⓦ nilevalley.nl; map p.288. Located near the ferry dock, with a rooftop restaurant (see p.274) offering a splendid view of Luxor Temple; a big heated pool with a wet-bar out back; en-suite a/c rooms with satellite TV and balconies; and wi-fi throughout. Owned by the ebullient Hamada and his Dutch wife Karin, who also rent apartments, and run tours of the Western Desert (p.267). Serves alcohol. B&B **£E255**

Ramsess Geziva ☎ 095 231 2748, ⍟ ramsesshotel.net; map p.288. Across the way from the *El-Gezira*, this slightly faded hotel built around a yard with fake rock features has garish en-suite rooms with fans, a/c, satellite TV, fridges and balconies, a top-floor restaurant and a rooftop with wi-fi, sunloungers and views of the Theban Hills. B&B **£E140**

Senmut Bed & Breakfast Ramleh ☎ 095 231 3077 or ☎ 012 2736 9159, ⍟ senmut-luxor.com; map p.288. Named after Queen Hatshepsut's courtier (see p.306), the family-friendly *Senmut* has soothing rooms with fans or a/c and bathrooms, a communal living room with a library, satellite TV and internet (£E5/hr); a kitchen for guests' use, service wash and a rooftop overlooking the Nile. B&B **£E180**

Sheherazade ☎ 010 0611 5939, ⍟ hotelsheherazade .com; map p.288. Promising but not really delivering "decadent luxury", this hotel across the road from *El-Fayrouz* has a lofty domed atrium decorated with scenes from the *1001 Nights* and a huge garden, slowly being reduced in size as they build additional wings. All rooms with showers and fans; some have double beds. B&B **£E280**

NEAR THE TEMPLES

Some hotels are within one and fifteen minutes' walk of temples or tombs in the Theban Necropolis, either in villages or on the desert's edge (see map, pp.288–289).

Amenophes Nag Lohlah ☎ 095 206 0078 or ☎ 012 2232 7613, ✉ sayed@hotmail.com; map p.288. Named after the XVIII Dynasty kings whose names are usually rendered as "Amenhotep", this small hotel at the back of the village is only a few minutes' walk from Medinet Habu temple, with clean, pleasantly faded a/c en-suite rooms with TV and balconies – although the view from its rooftop is marred by houses. B&B **£E180**

★ **Beit Sabee Guest House** Nag Lohlah ☎ 011 5400 8230, ⍟ nourelnil.com/beit-sabee-guesthouse.htm; map p.288. A chic mud-brick pile on the far side of Medinet Habu temple, featuring colourful en-suite rooms with a/c or fans, cotton sheets and duvets; ask for one on the upper floor, as downstairs can be dusty. Its location is very quiet but not too remote, so you still feel involved in rural life. Sells beer. B&B **€40**

Habou Nag Lohlah ☎ 095 231 1611 or ☎ 011 4646 5806; map p.288. Immortalized in Richard Critchfield's *Shahhat*, this mud-brick labyrinth of stuffy barrel-vaulted rooms with shared bathrooms is only worth considering for its fabulous view of Medinet Habu temple, directly opposite, since the owners haven't bothered to halt its decline, despite the prime location. B&B **£E120**

★ **Marsam** Gurnat Mura'i ☎ 095 237 2403 or ☎ 010 0342 6471, ✉ marsam@africamail.com; map p.288.

Built for US archeologists and later owned by Sheikh Ali Abdul Rasoul, who helped discover the tomb of Seti I, this rambling mud-brick hotel is a west bank institution, long managed by Czech-born Natasha Baron. Simple rooms with fans (a private shower costs £E25–50 extra) and an Egyptology library surround a restful garden, where meals are served. Fully booked by archeologists in Jan; reservations essential in Dec & Feb. B&B **£E100**

New Memnon Sharia al-Timsalyn, near the Colossi of Memnon ☎ 095 206 0984 or ☎ 010 0471 0033, ⍟ newmemnon.com; map p.288. A recently built walled compound half rented out to the American Research Center in Egypt, with spotless en-suite a/c rooms with TV, fridges and balconies. There's also free wi-fi and a view of the Colossi from its rooftop restaurant. **£E250**

Nour el-Balad 500m beyond Medinet Habu ☎ 095 206 6111 or ☎ 010 0129 5812, ⍟ nourelgournahotel.com; map p.288. The isolated setting on the edge of the desert is the main selling point (or drawback) of "Light of the Country", a mud-brick palace of chic "rustic" rooms equipped with cotton duvets, mosquito nets and fancy bathrooms. The top-floor rooms and rooftop suites are larger and more expensive. B&B **£E200**

Nour el-Qurna Gurnat Mura'i ☎ 095 231 1430 or ☎ 010 0129 5812, ⍟ nourelgournahotel.com; map p.288. The *Nour el-Balad*'s little sister hotel lurks in a palm grove across the road from the Antiquities Inspectorate, offering small, stylish en-suite mud-brick rooms with cotton duvets, mosquito nets and CD players, plus a garden-restaurant and bicycles for rent. B&B **£E200**

Pharaohs Nag Lohlah ☎ 095 231 0702 or ☎ 010 0613 1436, ⍟ hotelpharaohs.com; map p.288. Located beside the road to Medinet Habu, *Pharaohs* has mostly en-suite a/c rooms with free wi-fi, plus a couple of larger ones on the rooftop (costing £E40 more) with a side view of the temple. Beer and meals are served on a shady patio. B&B **£E120**

GURNA TA'RIF AND GABAWY

Off to the east of the Carter House (see p.309), the village of Gurna Ta'rif and the hilltop villa colony of Gabawy harbour three hotels offering peace and seclusion. Gurna Ta'rif can be reached by public transport from Gezira; Gabawy, only by taxi (£E30–40) or bicycle (if you can cope with the steep gradient).

Desert Paradise Lodge Gabawy, 6km from Gezira ☎ 095 231 3036 or ☎ 010 6997 7720, ⍟ desertparadiselodge.com; map p.289. A serenely quiet hilltop lodge that welcomes longstay residents – but not children. Built with a nod to traditional architecture, it has non-smoking flats and mini-suites round a garden with a smallish pool, and domed suites on a rooftop terrace overlooking the Theban Hills. Hosts Ashraf and Farida speak six languages between them and provide a tasty Egyptian breakfast. B&B **€70**

2

Flower of Light Gurna Ta'rif, 5km from Gezira ☎010 6834 3229, ⊚floweroflight.com; map p.289. Set back from the main road with no sign to identify it, this Irish-run hotel doubles as a spiritual retreat, where Antoinette and Donal offer healing workshops, past-life regression, hypnotherapy and tours of sacred sites. It has variously sized en-suite rooms (some a/c with mosquito nets, set around a shady garden with a pool. B&B __££300__

★ **House of Scorpion (Beit al-Aqrab)** Gurna Ta'rif ☎010 0512 8732, on Facebook as "Maison du Scorpion"; map p.289. Don't be put off by the name; this is a lovely, traditional-style mud-brick compound with fruit trees, a Bedouin tent for parties, a library and smoking room, free wi-fi and a well-equipped kitchen for guests. Some rooms have kingsize beds, others grand bathtubs. Owners Tayeb and Christine can arrange music and excursions. The hotel is located right beside the Flower of Light, but entered from around the corner. B&B __££240__

HAGGAR DABA'IYYA

★ **Al-Moudira** Haggar Daba'iyya, 5km from Medinet Habu and 5km from Luxor Bridge ☎012 325 1307, ⊚moudira.com; map p.288. One of the classiest hotels in Egypt, resembling an Ottoman palace, with exquisite courtyards, vast gardens and pool, a Lebanese restaurant, bar and horseriding. Its 54 individually-styled a/c suites are furnished with antiques, mosquito nets, satellite TV and CD players; some have a fountain and a sunken Turkish hammam. The only drawback is that it's miles from anywhere; a taxi from Luxor or to the Necropolis costs around ££70. B&B __€189__

APARTMENTS AND VILLAS

Renting an apartment in Luxor is easy; many regular visitors prefer this to staying at a hotel, for more privacy or to save money. Several hundred foreigners live semi-permanently on the west bank, where there are flats and villas for rent in various localities, some more rural than others.

★ **Flats in Luxor** ☎012 2415 5057 or ☎010 0356 4540, ⊚flatsinluxor.co.uk. Jane and Mahmoud Akshar rent numerous properties, including a family-friendly apartment-complex with a pool and restaurant near Djorf; the Moorish-style *Arabesque House* in El-Tod; and the luxurious *Villa Tahrir* near the desert's edge beyond Medinet Habu temple. They also offer tours, and there's lots of useful information on Jane's "Luxor News" blog (see p.266).

Egypt Property Sales Sharia Radwa Sherifa (see map, p.257) ☎095 238 1723 or ☎010 0614 2722, ⊚egyptpropertysales.com. This agency in Luxor open daily except Fri 10am–9pm) lets and sells properties on both sides of the river: in New Karnak (where a two-bedroom flat costs from ££3000 a month), Gezira (from ££720/££1700/week/month), Ramleh (££690/££2300) and other localities.

Eye House Ramleh ☎012 2337 1799, ⊚eyehouse.dk; map p.288. Owned by a Danish woman and her Egyptian partner, the tranquil *Eye House* (named after the Wadjet Eye of Horus) has apartments with balconies overlooking a garden (sleeping up to four people) and rooftop chalets (sleeping two) with kitchens and views of Luxor Temple and the Theban Hills, both rented on a weekly basis with free wi-fi. __€130/150__/week

Mohammed El-Kady ☎010 0666 9462, ⊚elkady820002000@yahoo.com. Rents several blocks of a/c flats in Ramleh, some sharing a rooftop with fine views, or a garden: a two-bedroom flat costs ££400 a week.

Mousa Ahmed ☎010 0381 7422, on Skype as "Mousaahmed". Rents flats in Djorf, all with a/c and wi-fi and costing ££1500/££4000/week/month for an upstairs flat, ££1200/££3500 for a ground-floor one.

★ **Villa Bahri** Gezira ☎010 0441 3504, ⊚villabahriluxor.co.uk; map p.288. This lovely villa has a two-bedroom garden flat and a large one-bedroom rooftop studio apartment, with arabesque furnishings, wi-fi and a/c. An idyllic west bank retreat, with gorgeous front and back gardens, views of banana plantations and the Theban Hills. Rates vary according to the season. __€140/210__/week

EATING AND DRINKING

Luxor's culinary scene is less diverse than Cairo's, but there's no shortage of places to eat. Upmarket **hotel restaurants** offer various world cuisines and elsewhere you'll mainly find pizzas, kebabs, omelettes and other tourist fodder. Be prepared for the additional service charges and tax (up to 24 percent), though many places don't actually levy them. For self-catering options, see "Shopping" (p.276).

LUXOR (EAST BANK)

★ **1896 Restaurant** ⊚inter Palace hotel, Corniche el-Nil ☎095 238 0422; map p.257. Luxor's grandest dining experience, its classical decor and silver service complementing inventive Mediterranean-French cuisine. Goose liver with nuts and passion-fruit dressing (££203), veal with mushroom sauce (££200) and coconut and caramel fondant with pistachio and kiwi salsa (££83) are

some of the treats on the menu, accompanied by French, Italian or South African wines (££420–1600). An acoustic guitarist entertains guests. Men must wear a jacket and tie (which they'll loan you for the occasion). Daily 7–11pm (sittings at 7pm & 9pm).

Abou Ashraf Sharia al-Mahatta ☎095 237 5936; map p.257. A brightly lit takeaway and sit-down diner just down the road from the train station serving tasty *kushari*

(£E4–8), *shawarma* (£E6), kofta and roast chicken (£E15–20). Pay at the cashiers before eating. Daily 8am–midnight.

Abu Hassan el-Shazly Sharia el-Manshiya; map p.257. Named after Luxor's patron sheikh, this kerbside joint in the spice and hardware souk offers tasty meals of kofta, grilled chicken or stuffed pigeon, salad, rice and dips for about £E50, with a/c seating indoors if you'd rather escape the street life and cats scrounging for leftovers. Daily 9am–1am.

★ **Al-Shahaby Lane** Sharia al-Shahaby, off Sharia Maabad el-Karnak ☎ 095 237 2386; map p.256. With its trellised roof and *mashrabiya* fittings, this airy outdoor restaurant belonging to the *Nefertiti* hotel (see p.268) is a perfect retreat from the tourist bazaar, serving delicious salads (£E15–18), spring rolls (£E10–14), beef *tageen* (£E45), seafood platters (£E70) and camel meat with couscous (£E60). Daily 10am–11pm.

Amoun Bazaar Savoy, off Sharia Maabad el-Karnak ☎ 095 237 0457; map p.256. Although its new setting in a tourist mall is far less funky than its old location beside Luxor Temple, this quiet a/c restaurant still serves hearty Egyptian fare, from soups (£E6–25) and salads (£E8–18) to fish dishes (£E40–120) and kofta with fries (£E40), plus Swiss ice cream. Daily 9am–11pm.

A Taste of India Sharia St Joseph, off Sharia Khalid Ibn Walid ☎ 095 228 0592; map p.257. With its red-and-gold decor and Indian muzak, this British-managed restaurant is the place to satisfy curry cravings, with bhajis (£E22), tandoori chicken (£E55) and other favourites (£E30–80), plus a few European options such as Roquefort steak (£E55) and cottage pie (£E40) plus Egyptian beer, Lebanese wine (£E125) and imported spirits. Daily noon–11pm.

Bonduk Sharia el-Madina el-Minarwa; map p.257. A cheap and cheerful *kushari* diner (portions £E4–8), with tables upstairs. Foreigners staying in hotels off Television St often pop in for a takeaway. You pay at the cashier downstairs. Daily 24hr.

El-Zareem Sharia Yussef Hassan; map p.256. Popular with locals in need of a snack, this busy takeaway (with a few tables upstairs) serves *taamiya*, kofta or shrimp sandwiches, *kushari* and other Egyptian staples, all freshly cooked (£E6–15). Daily 24hr.

Fortune Cookie/The King and Thai Sharia el-Madina el-Minarwa ☎ 012 2701 8638; map p.257. Two nominally separate restaurants currently sharing space (which may occupy separate premises in the future), this a/c British-run establishment celebrates the Hollywood career of the Siberian-born actor Yul Brynner, with still photos and video clips from his films and a menu offering both Thai and Chinese dishes, from pad thai (£E45–65) to duck (£E55) and seafood (£E40–75) recipes. Alcohol served. Daily noon–11pm.

La Mamma Sheraton Luxor Resort & Spa, Sharia Khalid Ibn Walid ☎ 095 227 4544; map p.257. For those with

kids, this Italian restaurant is a good choice, with pizzas (£E58–84) and pasta dishes (£E78–117) just like you'd get at home and space to play outside. Their beef carpaccio (£E65) is fabulous. Only open in the evening at time of writing, but may do lunch in the future. Daily 6–11pm.

Miyako Sonesta St George hotel, Sharia Khalid Ibn Walid ☎ 095 238 2575; map p.257. This posh establishment offers a fairly limited Japanese menu of fresh seafood (£E116–198), sushi appetizers (£E37–64) and beef teriyaki (£E75) – the teriyaki chef whirls his knives at your table and may even invite you to have a go. Smartish dress expected. Alcohol served. Daily 5–11pm.

Nile Terrace Café Winter Palace hotel, Corniche el-Nil ☎ 095 238 0422; map p.257. The hotel's lofty river-facing terrace is an elegant vantage point to watch the sun set over the Theban Hills while consuming a Victorian High Tea (£E72) or quaffing a G&T or a Stella. Smartish dress expected (no shorts). Daily 4–10pm.

Oasis Café Sharia St Joseph, off Sharia Khalid Ibn Walid ☎ 011 1140 0557, ⊛ oasiscafeegypt.com; map p.257. Not to be confused with a similarly named imposter at its previous location near the Luxor Museum, the Oasis Café is a restful a/c retreat decorated with contemporary Egyptian art, with 1940s jazz plus newspapers and the *New Yorker* to read. Try their club sandwiches (£E25–55), Oasis salad (£E30) or specials such as couscous (£E45) or grilled sea bass (£E45). Alcohol served. Daily 10am–10pm.

Puddleduck Sharia el-Madina el-Minarwa ☎ 010 6716 8473, ⊛ puddleduck-restaurant.com; map p.257. Named after the goosey heroine of Beatrix Potter's *Tales of Jemima Puddleduck*, this cosy non-smoking venture run by a British couple might sound twee, but their Jamie Oliver-influenced dishes hit the spot. Try their chicken liver pâté (£E30), Australian lamb shank cooked with wine and mint (£E80) or spinach riccota ravioli (£E60), followed by a vanilla panacotta with strawberry coulis, (£E30). Alcohol served. Daily except Wed 5.30–9.30pm.

Quick Television St ☎ 095 227 2970; map p.257. Aptly named for its speedy service, with a long menu of pizzas, pasta, grills and other high-cholesterol favourites (£E25–60) to take away, have delivered (little English spoken) or eat upstairs, where tables on the balcony provide a respite from the harsh strip-lighting and a vantage point for watching people on the street. Daily 11am–1am.

★ **Shark Restaurant Fish** Sharia el-Madina el-Minarwa ☎ 011 5007 0551; map p.257. A real find, this tiny upstairs seafood diner with marbled tables, in 1920s retro-style, offers imaginatively flavoured recipes and exquisitely presented dishes, like nouvelle cuisine. Diners decide on a main course of fish or seafood (most under £E40); fish soup, salad and rice are included in the price. The quality is amazing – not to be missed – and they even do deliveries. Daily 9am–midnight.

2

Snobs Sharia Radwa Sherifa, off Sharia Khalid Ibn Walid ☎095 227 6156; map p.257. Popular with British expats, this a/c restaurant offers stir-fried chicken with ginger and mango (£E49), apricot sweet-and-sour prawns (£E62), an all-day Sun roast (£E48) and a huge mezze selection for two people (£E250). Daily 11am–midnight.

★ **Sofra** Sharia Mohammed Farid ☎095 235 9752, ⓦsofra.com.eg; map p.257. A *sofra* is a round brass table, which typifies the decor of this romantic restaurant in the backstreets of El-Manshiya, which has a lovely rooftop terrace, a garden with divans for smoking *sheesha* and two khedival-style private dining rooms. Their menu includes all kinds of mezze (£E8–12), flambeed calf's liver (£E20), stuffed duck (£E55), veal stewed with cumin and onions (£E55) and other specialities. Reservations advised in wintertime. Daily 11am–midnight.

WEST BANK

Africa Restaurant Gezira ☎095 231 1488; map p.288. An inviting rooftop with birds nesting in its trellises and a diverting view of Luxor, the *Africa* serves a full Egyptian breakfast (£E20) of *fuul*, *taamiya* and hardboiled eggs; vast combo meals (£E55) of salad, dips, vegetable side dishes and meat or fish main courses; and beer and *sheesha*. Daily 8am–midnight.

African Garden Gezira ☎010 9101 1798; map p.288. Tucked away in a walled yard beside Gezira's taxi station, with colourfully painted vaulted brick arcades shading some of its tables, *African Garden* offers soups, grills, Nubian okra dishes, spag bol and omelettes, at reasonable prices. Daily 8am–9pm.

★ **Al-Moudira** Haggar Daba'iyya ☎012 2392 8322, ⓦmoudira.com; map p.288. This magnificent hotel (see p.272) is the place to go if you want to splurge. Lunch is served by the pool, with a menu of pizzas (£E52), pasta (£E45–58), club sandwiches and wraps (£E40–75). In the evening they serve Mediterranean-Lebanese cuisine (mains £E80–110) in a romantic Moorish courtyard, accompanied by Lebanese wines. Daily noon–3pm & 7–10pm.

Aux 3 ChAcAls 300m from the Colossi of Memnon ☎010 0192 3130; map p.288. "At the Three Jackals" is a friendly French-managed place with a great view of the Theban Hills from its rooftop and a Gallic-Oriental menu including chicken curry (£E45) and shrimp brochette (£E59). Closed June–Aug. Daily except Sun noon–8.30pm.

Happy Habou Nag Lolah ☎010 0002 8165; map p.288. With its spotless toilets and full-on a/c, this is a good place to recuperate after visiting Medinet Habu temple, but gets fewer visitors than the *Maratonga* (see below). Besides serving chicken with lemon sauce (£E55), roast duck (£E65) and fresh juices (£E12–14), they can also arrange parties with a bellydancer if enough people are interested. Daily 24hr.

Maratonga Nag Lolah ☎010 0369 1547, ✉restaurant .maratonga@gmail.com; map p.288. Sited opposite Medinet Habu temple, its restful patio always has a few tables occupied by tourists. They offer two or three different set meals (£E45) each day plus a range of starters, and surreptitiously serve beer and wine (not on the menu). Daily 6am–10pm.

Marsam Gurnat Mura'i ☎095 237 2403 or ☎010 0342 6471; map p.288. This famous hotel (see p.271) serves a hearty set meal of poultry, beef stew or kofta (£E55), plus two different veggie menus (£E25) at lunch. Only vegetarian food is served for dinner, but there's a choice of pizza, pasta, soups and salads. Most ingredients are sourced from local villages. You can eat indoors, or alfresco in a lovely garden. Daily 9am–9pm.

Moon Valley 300m from the Colossi of Memnon ☎012 2796 4850; map p.288. Great-value set meals (£E50) of kofta, *shish tawook*, fish or pepper steak, with soup, rice, salad and a dessert, served on a terrace with views of the Colossi and Hatshepsut's temple, or in an a/c dining room downstairs. Daily 8am–9pm.

Nile Valley Gezira ☎095 231 1477 or ☎012 2796 4473; map p.288. The hotel's rooftop restaurant (accessible by lift) has a fabulous view of Luxor Temple and an extensive menu of Egyptian and European dishes (mostly £E30–55). It's also a nightime hangout for smoking *sheesha*, watching sports TV and drinking beer or wine. If enough tourists are staying, there may be an all-you-can-eat buffet with Saiyidi music and dervish dancing. Daily 8am-midnight or later.

Nour el-Qurna Gurnat Mura'i ☎095 231 1430 or ☎010 0129 5812; map p.288. Phone ahead to place your order at this homely garden restaurant, where chickens peck in the background. A full set meal of whatever they're cooking that day (stuffed vegetables, chicken, duck or pigeon) costs £E25–45. Daily 11am–10pm.

Ramesseum Resthouse Gurna ☎010 0582 4537; map p.288. Generations of Egyptologists and tourists have refreshed themselves at this basic resthouse beside the Ramesseum. Meals (£E60–70) of duck, kofta or grilled chicken with rice and salad are served, but many people come just for a cold beer (£E15) or a bottle of Egyptian wine (£E100). Daily 7am–midnight.

Ramleh Beach Ramleh ☎010 0297 0842; map p.288. An all-night riverside café where you can recline on divans listening to Arabic music with the Theban Hills in the background – the view of the Nile is spoilt by a boatyard. They can rustle up salads (£E8–11), *shawarma* (£E39) or spaghetti bolognese (£E23), but it's probably safer to stick to soft drinks or *sheesha*. Daily 24hr.

Restaurant Mohammed Kom Lolah ☎095 206 0878 or ☎012 2820 4226; map p.288. A peaceful rustic garden with a six hundred-year-old acacia tree where Mohammed and his son Azab serve delicious meals (£E35–50) of grilled chicken, duck or stuffed pigeon (call 2hr ahead to order the pigeon), with fries and salad – and try their marinated goat's cheese too. Beer and wine served. Daily 24hr.

★ **Tout Ankhamon** Gezira ☎ 095 231 0918; map p.288. Hagg Mahmoud used to cook for French archeological missions and his sons continue the tradition, serving gigantic set meals (£E60) of coconut curry or duck with rosemary, accompanied by spicy lentil and vegetable stews, on a rooftop beside the Nile facing Luxor Temple. Daily 8am–9pm.

COFFEE HOUSES

Though traditional coffee shops are exclusively masculine territory, women should feel comfortable in the places listed below (all in Luxor).

Alf Leyl w Leyl Television St; map p.257. With its private booths hung with gilded Arabesque tent-fabric, its fresh juices and big choice of *sheesha* flavours, the "Thousand and One Nights" is popular with Egyptian newlyweds and families. Daily 10am–midnight.

Lyaly Zaman Sharia Radwa Sherifa, off Sharia Khalid Ibn Walid; map p.257. Named "Olden Days" in Arabic, this large, airy tent-covered teahouse has divans for reclining while watching international sports on wide-screen TV. Daily 10am–2am.

New Oum Kalthoum Sharia al-Souk; map p.256. This outdoor coffee shop in the heart of the tourist bazaar does proper espresso, fresh juices and flavoured *sheeshas*. Great for people-watching, and cooled by mist-sprayers. Daily 24hr.

Nubian National Coffee Sharia al-Souk; map p.256. This funky grotto-like tearoom in the heart of the tourist bazaar is the place to meet guys from Aswan and smoke a *sheesha*. Try the coffee spiced with cardamom or fresh juices (£E7). Daily 24hr.

Victoria Lounge Winter Palace hotel, Corniche el-Nil; map p.257. For the princely sum of £E70/person you can enjoy being served cucumber sandwiches, fruit cake and tea, as if the sun had never set on the British Empire. Daily 4–6pm.

BARS

Luxor has a handful of decent bars. On the west bank, drinking mostly takes place in hotels (see p.270) or restaurants (see p.274).

★ **Genesis Pub Restaurant** New Karnak, near the Hilton Luxor Resort & Spa ☎ 095 373 032; map p.289. If a swimming pool with a waterfall isn't tempting enough – and you don't mind a menagerie of ostriches, peacocks, a camel and a horse – this is the best place in Luxor for a fun night out, complete with bubble-blowers and clouds of dry ice, karaoke, HD sports TV, pool (£E20/hr), wi-fi and a bellydancer (Fri). The menu (mains £E55–65) features spicy chicken, pepper steak, a full English breakfast with sausages and bacon, and a Sun roast lunch (reservation required). Daily 9am–4am.

Hamees Sharia Maabad el-Karnak, near Luxor Temple; map p.257. Billed as a restaurant and coffee house but actually a leafy beer garden where British expats gather to whinge over a beer (£E12), or a glass, of Egyptian wine (£E15). Daily 24hr.

King's Head Pub Sharia Khalid Ibn Walid ☎ 095 228 0489; map p.257. Though the king in question is Akhenaten, this place looks and feels like an English pub, offering club sandwiches (£E30) and a Sun lunch of roast beef and Yorkshire pud (£E40), accompanied by cocktails, beer and spirits. Sports TV, free wi-fi, billiards and darts; happy hour 7–8pm & 10–11pm. Daily 10am–2am.

Murphy's Irish Pub Sharia al-Gawazat, off Sharia Khalid Ibn Walid ☎ 012 2494 7562; map p.257. Around the corner from the passport office, *Murphy's* can be livelier than the *King's Head*, with singalongs, Mexican waves, pool matches and sports TV, cheered on by boisterous Brits. They serve steak and chips, wraps and other pub food, and sometimes have karaoke. Daily 1pm–2am.

Pub 2000 Sharia Ali Ibn Abi Talek, off Sharia Khalid Ibn Walid ☎ 012 2332 8563; map p.257. Behind the *Morris* hotel, *Pub 2000* doesn't look much from outside, but its British pub grub is a cut above the average, and owners Asif and Isaac extend a warm welcome. Tues and Thurs are quiz nights. Happy hour 5– 7pm. Daily 11am–2am.

Royal Lounge Winter Palace hotel, Corniche el-Nil ☎ 095 238 0422; map p.257. Furnished with brocade-upholstered armchairs, across the corridor from a lounge-cum-library where you expect Hercule Poirot to gather the suspects in a murder mystery, this staid bar serves cocktails (£E80–120) and Egyptian and French wines by the glass (£E50–60) and bottle (£E150–1250). Daily 3–11pm.

ENTERTAINMENT AND NIGHTLIFE

Luxor's nightlife is a paler shadow of Hurghada's, if only because most tourists are too tired from sightseeing to fancy clubbing. As tourism has plunged since the Revolution, discos have become empty and lifeless, though folklore shows and bellydancing can still be enjoyed at some hotels.

Bellydancing There's a nightly show (8–10pm) in the *Steigenberger Nile Palace*'s bar; the *Sheraton Luxor Resort & Spa* hosts a shorter performance (Fri & Sun 9pm), and there may be one in the *El-Luxor*'s disco (Sun, Tues & Thurs). Other hotels might feature bellydancing as part of a folklore show. Alternatively, you could visit the seedy *St Katerina* club off Sharia Ahmes, where a raucous clientele throws banknotes around. Dancing starts at midnight and runs through till 5am if patrons are still spending. It's best to go with an Egyptian friend to get past the doorman who might claim there's an entry charge, or to argue if they add it to your bill – there isn't one, and you should only pay for drinks.

Folklore shows Otherwise known as "Saiyidi shows" or "Egyptian nights", these feature Saiyidi music, whirling dervishes, stickfighting and sometimes a snakecharmer or

bellydancer. At the time of writing, the only regular show was in the restaurant of the *Sheraton Luxor Resort* & Spa (Mon & Thurs 8pm; free entry, but you must buy drinks), but other hotels such as the *Nefertiti* (£E75) or *St Joseph* (£E95) can arrange shows (with a buffet meal) if enough guests are interested.

SHOPPING

Many souvenir shops that once clustered around Luxor Temple have been moved to the Bazaar Savoy off the Corniche, or the refurbished tourist bazaar on Sharia al-Souk, whose Mamluke-style wooden gateway facing Midan el-Haggag welcomes shoppers. Most shops here are open from 7am to midnight; non-tourist shops elsewhere in town usually close for a siesta (2–5pm). All the following shops are marked on our map of Luxor (see pp.256–257) unless stated otherwise.

BOOKS

Aboudi Bookstore Sharia Maabad el-Karnak, opposite Luxor Temple ☎095 237 2390, ⓦaboudi-bookstore .com; map p.257. This long-established bookshop has recently split into two businesses (see below) run by cousins – hence their slightly different names. Good for Egyptology, politics and sociology, prints and posters. Daily 8am–10.30pm, closed Fri noon–1pm.

Aboudy Bookshop Sharia el-Gawazat, off Sharia Khalid Ibn Walid ☎095 227 3390, ⓔaboudy-lilly@yahoo.com;

map p.257. Has an even larger selection of Egyptology, politics, vintage prints, posters and foreign novels than its near namesake, plus a few shelves of secondhand thrillers. Daily 8am–10pm, Fri 1–10pm.

Gaddis Bookshop Corniche el-Nil, outside the Winter Palace ☎095 238 7042, ⓦgaddis-and-co.co.uk; map p.257. Established in 1907, Gaddis is the finest bookshop in Upper Egypt, stocked with heaps of Egyptology, reproduction and genuine vintage prints and postcards, guidebooks and novels in foreign languages. Daily 10am–9pm.

FESTIVALS IN LUXOR

Visitors coming to Luxor in late January or early February have a good chance of seeing the 22-kilometre **West Bank marathon** (ⓦegyptianmarathon.com), starting and finishing at Deir el-Bahri. In addition, 2012 saw two new festivals that may or not become annual events. The two-day **Luxor African Film Festival** (ⓦluxorafricanfilmfestival.com) in February showcases work from across the continent, with an awards ceremony at the Nile Heritage Centre. Some time in April, DJs and dance crews perform at the **Luxor Spring Festival** (ⓦfacebook.com /Lxr.Spring.Festival/app_20819510258120) an all-night event held at the Royal Valley Golf Club. Transport there and back is included in the cost of tickets (£E65–100).

RELIGIOUS FESTIVALS

Locals have always cared far more about **moulids**, generally held during the two months preceding Ramadan (people can rarely tell you the exact date, but know when one is due). The tumultuous **Moulid of Abu el-Haggag** (pronounced "Hajjaj") pays homage to Luxor's patron sheikh – born in Damascus c.1150 – whose mosque nestles atop Luxor Temple. Giant floats move through the packed streets, some dedicated to trades (the *calèche* drivers' bears a carriage), others in the form of **boats** (often compared to the solar barque processions of pharaonic times; though in Islamic symbolism boats represent the quest for spiritual enlightenment). There are *zikrs* outside Abu el-Haggag's Mosque, **stick fights** (*tahtib*) to the music of drums and *mizmars* (a kind of oboe) and **horse races** (*mirmah*). The festival runs during the first two weeks of Sha'ban, the month before Ramadan. During **Ramadan** itself, townsfolk compensate for its daytime rigours by gathering to hear *zikrs* and musicians on Midan el-Haggag in the evening, where families picnic en masse for three days after the end of Ramadan.

Other moulids during the Islamic month of Rajeb are smaller, local events. **Sheikh Ali Musa of Karnak**'s lasts a week, its *leyla kebira* falling on Rajeb 6. During the moulid you can't miss the music, swings and lights around his tomb, near the entrance to Karnak village. On the other side of town, Awmia village honours its own **Sheikh Ahmed al-Adasi** with a week-long festival, whose curtain raiser is a day of stick fights, horse and **camel races**. Following its *leyla kebira* on Rageb 14, there's a final day of celebrations, when camels and horses are paraded through the streets and villagers throw sweets at each other.

CRAFTS AND CLOTHES

Caravanserai Nag Lolah, west bank ☎ 012 2327 8771, ⓦ caravanserailuxor.com; map p.288. Beside a canal at the back of the village, this charming emporium attached to the owner's house sells pottery, carpets and embroidery from the oases, Muski glass, jewellery, handwoven scarves and colourful ragdolls. Daily 10am–8pm.

Fair Trade Center Sharia Maabad el-Karnak, opposite Luxor Temple ☎ 095 236 0870, ⓔ FTC@EgyptFairtrade .org; map p.257. The local outlet for a Cairo-based NGO marketing the work of nine handicrafts cooperatives, including Hegaza bowls carved from lemon, orange or tamarisk wood; Garagos pottery; embroidery and beadwork from Sinai; recycled paper from Cairo; and cottons, silks and linens from Akhmim (see p.236). Daily 9am–10.30pm.

Nefertari Papyrus Institute Sharia al-Timsalyn, near the Colossi of Memnon ☎ 095 206 0744, ⓦ nefertaripapyrus.com; map p.257. Entirely devoted to papyrus, this shop has a huge selection of designs at fixed prices. Staff can demonstrate how papyrus (grown out back) is turned into sheets, and how to distinguish fakes made from banana leaves from the real thing. Daily 10am–6pm.

Winter Akhmeen Gallery Corniche el-Nil, outside the Winter Palace ☎ 095 238 0422; map p.257. A small shop stuffed with bolts of hand-woven cotton, silk and linen from the women's weaving cooperative in Akhmim (p.236). Besides selling bedcovers, they also make *galabiyyas* and shirts and can copy any other garment to order within 48 hrs. Daily 11am–11pm.

FOOD AND DRINK

Fresh fruit and vegetables are sold at the daily food market on Sharia al-Seka al-Hadid, behind Luxor train station, and on Sharia el-Madina el-Minarwa (Tues & Sun). On the west bank, there's the weekly Souk at-Talaat (Tues) at Gurna Ta'rif, opposite the Temple of Seti I.

Al-Ahram Beverages Sharia Ramses ☎ 095 237 2445; map p.257. Sells the full range of beers, wines and alcopops from Egypt's monopoly alcohol producer, but being run by Christians, it may close for Easter and other Coptic holy days. Daily except Sun 10am–10pm.

Arkwrights Sharia St Joseph ☎ 095 228 2335, ⓦ arkwrights-luxor.com; map p.257. A supermarket aimed at British expats with all kinds of sauces, cereals and other products from home. They also do deliveries and sell freshly made sandwiches and salads to take away. Daily 7am–11pm.

Atta Pastery Baker Gezira, west bank ☎ 010 9738 7350, ⓔ abualata1967@yahoo.com; map p.288. Not what you'd expect to find beside the Arabian Horse Stables: a bakery selling freshly baked focacia with herbs, fruit flans, chocolate eclairs, and cakes for special occasions. Daily 10am–9pm.

Besheat Store Sharia al-Souk; map p.256. Probably the world's only off-licence named after an avatar of the cat-goddess Bastet, this hole-in-the-wall outlet in Luxor's tourist bazaar sells the same products (plus imported beers) as Al-Ahram Beverages. Daily 10am–11pm, closed Sun.

Duty Free Shops Branches at Luxor Airport (irregular hours) and behind the Emilio hotel ☎ 095 237 6331 (daily 10am–2pm & 6–10pm); map p.256. Duty-free alcohol can be purchased within 48hr of arrival in Egypt. You'll need your passport, in which transactions will be noted.

Kher Zaman Television St ☎ 095 228 1496; map p.257. This Cairo supermarket chain has revolutionized local shopping with its huge selection of imported products, European cheeses, fresh meat, salamis, salads and other delicacies. They even do home deliveries. Daily 24hr.

Twinky Sharia el-Manshiya ☎ 095 237 5887; map p.257. Around the corner from the train station, Twinky sells all kinds of Oriental pastries by weight, plus fruit flans and cakes for special occasions. Daily 10am–midnight.

DIRECTORY

American Express Corniche el-Nil, near the *Winter Palace* ☎ 095 237 8333, ⓦ amexfranchise.com (daily except Fri 9am–5pm).

Arabic language courses Institute of Arabic Language, Sharia Yussef Hassan, beside the Emilio hotel (☎ 020 1733 0039, ⓔ luxor@ahlan-egypt.com) runs courses (£E300) over winter and summer.

Banks and exchange Forex bureaux (daily 8am–9pm) on Sharia al-Mahatta and Sharia Maabad el-Karnak offer better rates than Banque Misr and AlexBank on Sharia Labaib Habachi, or the National Bank of Egypt on the Corniche (all with ATMs).

Children's activities Felucca trips (see p.267) are fun for all ages; older children may enjoy horse- or camel-riding

(see p.267) while young ones can ride electric cars on Midan el-Haggag, or carousels at the small amusement park on the corner of Sharia St Joseph and Sharia el-Madina al-Minarwa.

Dentist Dr Fawzi Henri, Sharia al-Mahatta, opposite the post office ☎ 010 0678 0298.

DHL Sharia Founduk Sheraton ☎ 010 6661 8018, ⓦ dhl .com (daily except Fri 9am–5pm).

EgyptAir Outside the *Winter Palace* ☎ 095 238 0580 (daily 8am–8pm); Luxor airport ☎ 095 238 0588.

Golf Royal Valley Golf Club, Sharia Tiba, 8km from Luxor airport, 13km from the centre ☎ 095 928 0098, ⓦ golfluxor .com. A lush eighteen-hole championship course designed by US architect Arthur Davis, with undulating greens, water hazards and a luxurious club house.

Hospitals Luxor International, Television St ☎ 095 238 7194. Hardly up to European standards, but supposedly the best in Upper Egypt.

Internet Many hotels around Television St have free wi-fi for guests; otherwise you'll pay £E5–10/hr in backstreet cyber-cafés, or £E25/hr in a four- or five-star hotel.

Post office Sharia al-Mahatta (Mon–Thurs & Sun 8am–2pm), with a branch in the station (daily 8am–8pm).

Spa treatments Non-residents can enjoy a Turkish bath, sauna or massage (€17–35) at the deluxe Sheraton Luxor Resort & Spa, Hilton Luxor Resort & Spa and Al-Moudira hotels, while the less opulent St Joseph offers aromatheraphy (£E160) and Balinese (£E170) massages.

Swimming Many Luxor hotels let non-residents use their pools for a fee – ranging from the smallish pools at the *New Pola* (£E25), *Susanna* (£E30), *Emilio* (£E30), and *Philippe*

(£E20) hotels, to larger Nile-side pools at the *Iberotel* (£E75) and *Steigenberger Nile Palace* (£E100). On the west bank, try *Gezira Gardens* (£E25), *El-Mesala* (£E20) or the vast pool at *Al-Moudira* (€10).

Thomas Cook Corniche el-Nil, near the *Winter Palace* ☎ 095 237 2402, ✉ tcluxor@thomascook.com.eg (daily 9am–7pm). Money changing, tours and reservations.

Tourist Police Midan al-Mahatta ☎ 095 237 3845 or ☎ 095 237 6620 (daily 24hr). They have a separate Investigations unit for serious problems – both are signposted in English..

Visa extensions Passport office, off Sharia Khalid Ibn Walid ☎ 095 238 0885 (Mon–Thurs & Sat 8am–2pm). A photo and photocopy of your passport required.

Western Union Television Street ☎ 095 227 1187, ⓦ westernunion.com (Sun–Thurs 9am–5pm, Sat 9am–1pm).

Karnak

The temple complex of **Karnak** beats every other pharaonic monument bar the Pyramids of Giza. Built on a leviathan scale to house the gods, it comprises three separate enclosures covering nearly three square kilometres. The grandest is the **Precinct of Amun**, dedicated to the supreme god of the New Kingdom – a structure large enough to accommodate ten great cathedrals and roughly twice the size of the **Precinct of Mut** (Amun's consort), itself twice as large as the **Precinct of Montu** (the Theban war-god since the Middle Kingdom).

Karnak's magnitude and complexity is due to 1300 years of aggrandizement. From its XII Dynasty core, Amun's temple expanded along two axes – west towards the river and south towards the Temple of Mut – while its enclosure wall approached the Temple of Montu. Though Pharaoh Akhenaten abjured Amun, defaced his images and erected an Aten Temple at Karnak, the *status quo ante* was soon restored at the behest of Amun's priesthood.

At the zenith of its supremacy Karnak's wealth was staggering. A list of its assets during the reign of Ramses III includes 65 villages, 433 gardens, 421,662 head of cattle, 2395 square kilometres of fields, 46 building sites, 83 ships and 81,322 workers and slaves. Yet ordinary folk were barred from its precincts and none but the pharaoh or his representative could enter Amun's sanctuary. The whole area was known to the Ancient Egyptians as Ipet-Isut, meaning the most perfect or esteemed of places.

At the time of writing only the Precinct of Amun was accessible, but the Precinct of Mut should open in 2013. Reckon on spending at least two hours at Karnak and be sure to wear a hat and drink lots of water, as there's little shade at the site.

The Temple of Amun

2.5km north of central Luxor • Daily 6am–5pm • Temple £E65, open-air museum £E25

The great **Temple of Amun** seemingly recedes towards infinity in an overwhelming succession of pylons, courts, columned halls, obelisks and colossi, spanning some thirteen centuries of ancient history. Half-buried in silt for as long again, the ruins were

---

Two or three **Sound and Light Shows** are staged nightly at Karnak Temple (schedules posted at the tourist office, or less reliably at ⓦ soundandlight.com.eg). Go for a later show to avoid aural conflict with local muezzins around sunset. Bring mosquito repellent and a torch to light your footsteps during the hour-long odyssey through the temple, whose floodlit forms are more impressive than the show's melodramatic soundtrack. Tickets (£E75) are sold on the spot.

AMUN AND THE THEBAN TRIAD

Originally merely one of the deities in the Hermopolitan Ogdoad (see p.221), **Amun** gained ascendancy at Thebes shortly before the Middle Kingdom, presumably because his cult was adopted by powerful local rulers during the First Intermediate Period. After the expulsion of the Hyksos (c.1567 BC), the rulers of the XVIII Dynasty elevated Amun to a victorious national god, and set about making Karnak his principal cult centre in Egypt.

As the "Unseen One" (whose name in hieroglyphic script was accompanied by a blank space instead of the usual explicatory sign), Amun assimilated other deities into such incarnations as **Amun-Re** (the supreme Creator), **Amun-Min** (the "bull which serves the cows" with a perpetual erection) or ram-headed **Auf-Re** ("Re made Flesh"), who sailed through the underworld revitalizing the souls of the dead, emerging reborn as Khepri. However, Amun most commonly appears as a human wearing ram's horns and the twin-feathered *atef* crown.

His consort, **Mut**, was a local goddess in Pre-dynastic times, who became linked with Nekhbet, the vulture protectress of Upper Egypt. Early in the XVIII Dynasty she was "married" to Amun, assimilated his previous consort Amunet and became Mistress of Heaven. She is customarily depicted wearing a vulture head-dress and *uraeus* and the Combined Crown of the Two Lands.

Amun and Mut's son **Khonsu**, "the Traveller", crossed the night sky as the moon-god, issued prophecies and assisted Thoth, the divine scribe. He was portrayed either with a hawk's head, or as a young boy with the sidelock of youth.

Karnak was the largest of several temples consecrated to this **Theban Triad** of deities.

Amun

Mut

Khonsu

subsequently squatted by *fellaheen* before being cleared by archeologists in the mid-nineteenth century. Ever since then, the temple has been undergoing slow but systematic restoration, epigraphic study and (in some places) excavation.

Since map-boards were installed it's become easier to grasp the temple's convoluted layout; the ruins get denser and more jumbled the further in you go. The temple's **main axis** is perpendicular to the Nile, with a **subsidiary axis** running parallel to the river, the two of them forming a T-shaped whole.

It's worth following the main axis all the way back to the **Festival Hall**, and at least seeing the **Cachette Court** of the subsidiary axis. A break for refreshments by the lake is advisable if your itinerary includes the **open-air museum** or the **Temple of Khonsu**, off the main circuit.

Entering the temple

Walking towards the Precinct of Amun and crossing over a dry moat, you'll pass the remains of an **ancient dock**, from where Amun sailed for Luxor Temple during the Optet festival. Before being loaded aboard a full-size boat, his sacred barque rested in the small **chapel** to the right, which was erected (and graffitied by mercenaries) during the brief XXIX Dynasty. Beyond lies a short **Processional Way** flanked by ram-headed sphinxes (after Amun's sacred animal) enfolding statues of Ramses II, which once joined the main avenue linking the two temples.

2

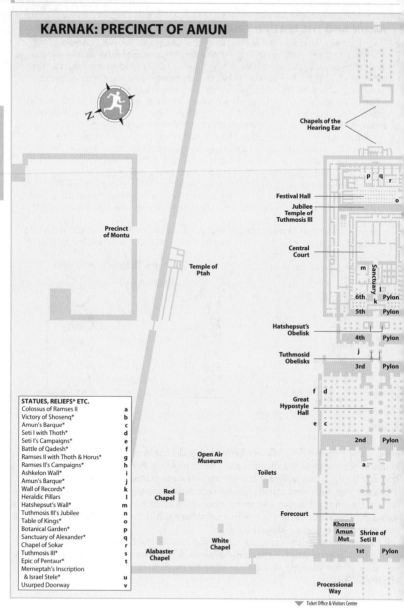

KARNAK: PRECINCT OF AMUN

Chapels of the Hearing Ear

Festival Hall
Jubilee
Temple of
Tuthmosis III

Central Court

Precinct of Montu

Temple of Ptah

Sanctuary

6th Pylon
5th Pylon

Hatshepsut's Obelisk

4th Pylon

Tuthmosid Obelisks

3rd Pylon

Great Hypostyle Hall

2nd Pylon

Open Air Museum

Toilets

Forecourt

Red Chapel

Khonsu Amun Mut Shrine of Seti II

1st Pylon

Alabaster Chapel

White Chapel

Processional Way

Ticket Office & Visitors Centre

STATUES, RELIEFS* ETC.	
Colossus of Ramses II	a
Victory of Shosenq*	b
Amun's Barque*	c
Seti I with Thoth*	d
Seti I's Campaigns*	e
Battle of Qadesh*	f
Ramses II with Thoth & Horus*	g
Ramses II's Campaigns*	h
Ashkelon Wall*	i
Amun's Barque*	j
Wall of Records*	k
Heraldic Pillars	l
Hatshepsut's Wall*	m
Tuthmosis III's Jubilee	n
Table of Kings*	o
Botanical Garden*	p
Sanctuary of Alexander*	q
Chapel of Sokar	r
Tuthmosis III*	s
Epic of Pentaur*	t
Merneptah's Inscription & Israel Stele*	u
Usurped Doorway	v

The First Pylon and Forecourt

At the end of the Processional Way rises the gigantic **First Pylon**, whose yawning gateway exposes a vista of receding portals, dwarfing all who walk between them. The 43-metre-high towers, composed of regular courses of sandstone masonry, are often attributed to the Nubian and Ethiopian kings of the XXV Dynasty, but may have been erected as late as the XXX Dynasty (when Nectanebo I added the enclosure wall).

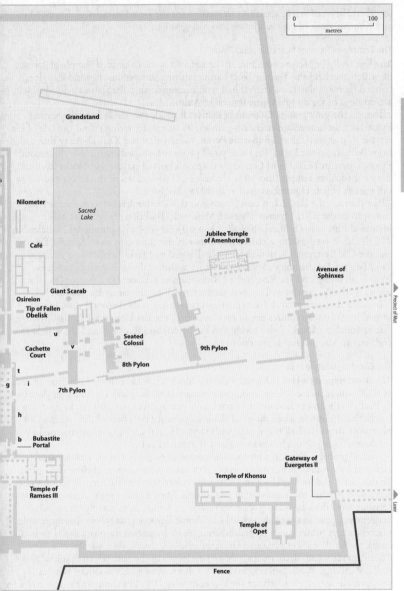

Although the northern tower is unfinished and neither is decorated, their 130-metre width makes this the largest pylon in Egypt.

The **Forecourt** is another late addition, enclosing three earlier structures. In the centre stands a single papyriform pillar from the **Kiosk of Taharqa** (an Ethiopian king of the XXV Dynasty), thought to have been a roofless pavilion where Amun's effigy was placed for its revivifying union with the sun at New Year. Off to the left stands the so-called **Shrine of Seti II**, actually a waystation for the sacred barques of Amun, Mut and Khonsu, built of grey sandstone and rose granite.

The Temple of Ramses III and Second Pylon

The first really impressive structure in the precinct is the columned **Temple of Ramses III**, which also held the Theban Triad barques during processions. Beyond its pylon, flanked by two colossi, is a festival hall with mummiform pillar statues behind which are carvings of the annual Optet festival of Amun-Min.

Though the pink granite **Colossus of Ramses II** beside the vestibule to the Second Pylon [a] is an immediate attention-grabber, it's worth detouring round the side of his temple to pass through the **Bubastite Portal**, named after the XXII Dynasty that hailed from Bubastis in the Delta. En route you'll pass a fish-shaped aperture in the Second Pylon, where in 1820 Henri Crevier uncovered a host of statues and blocks from the demolished Aten Temple (including the colossi of Akhenaten in the Luxor and Cairo museums), which Horemheb used as in-fill for his pylon.

Pass through the Portal and turn left to find the **Shoshenk relief**, commemorating the triumphs of the XXII Dynasty Pharaoh Shoshenk. Traditionally, scholars have identified him as the biblical Shishak (I Kings 14:25–26) who plundered Jerusalem in 925 BC, thus establishing a crucial link between the chronologies of Ancient Egypt and the Old Testament – an orthodoxy challenged by David Rohl's book, *A Test of Time* (see p.625). Although Shoshenk's figure is almost invisible, you can still see Amun, presiding over the slaughter of Rheoboamite prisoners in Palestine [b]. The scenes further along the wall are best seen after visiting the Great Hypostyle Hall.

To reach this, return to the forecourt and pass through the **Second Pylon**, one of several jerry-built structures begun by Horemheb, the last king of the XVIII Dynasty. The cartouches of Seti I (who completed the pylon) and Ramses I and II (Seti's father and son) appear just inside the doorway.

The Great Hypostyle Hall

The **Great Hypostyle Hall** is Karnak's glory, a forest of titanic columns covering an area of 6000 square metres – large enough to contain both St Peter's Cathedral in Rome and St Paul's Cathedral in London. Its grandeur is best appreciated early in the morning or late in the afternoon, when diagonal shadows enhance the effect of the columns. In pharaonic times the hall was roofed with sandstone slabs, its gloom interspersed by sunbeams falling through windows above the central aisle.

The hall probably began as a processional avenue of twelve or fourteen **columns**, each 23m high and 15m round (requiring six people with outstretched arms to encircle their girth). To this, Seti I and Ramses II added 122 smaller columns in two flanking wings, plus walls and a roof. All the columns consist of semi-drums, fitted together without mortar. Their **carvings** show the king making offerings to Theban deities, most notably Amun, who frequently appears in a sexually aroused state. Some Egyptologists believe that the temple priestesses kept Amun happy by masturbating his idol, and that the pharaoh did his bit to ensure the fertility of Egypt by ejaculating into the Nile during the Optet festival.

Similar cult scenes decorate the side and end walls of the hall, which manifest two styles of carving. While Seti adorned the northern wing with bas-reliefs, Ramses II favoured cheaper sunk-reliefs for the southern wing. You can compare the two styles on the Hypostyle Hall's entrance wall, which features nearly symmetrical scenes of Amun's barque procession.

In Seti's **northern wing**, the procession begins on the north wall with a depiction of Amun's barque, initially veiled, then revealed [c]. Thoth inscribes the duration of Seti's reign on the leaves of a sacred persea tree [d] just beyond the doorway. By walking out through this door you'll come upon **Seti I's battle scenes**, whose weathered details are best observed in the early morning or late afternoon. One section [e] relates the capture of Qadesh from the Hittites in Syria (lower rows), and Seti's triumphs over the Libyans (above). Depicted elsewhere **[f]** are his campaigns against the Shasu of southern Palestine and the storming of Pa-Canaan, which the Egyptians "plundered with every evil".

Returning to the Hypostyle Hall, you can find similar reliefs commissioned by Ramses II in the **southern wing**, retaining traces of their original colours. Beyond the barque procession on the inner wall, Ramses is presented to Amun and enthroned between Wadjet and Nekhbet, while Thoth and Horus adjust his crowns **[g]**. On the outer wall are **Ramses II's battle scenes**, starting with the second Battle of Qadesh (c.1300 BC) **[h]**. Though scholars reckon it was probably a draw, Ramses claimed total victory over the Hittites. The text of their **peace treaty** (the earliest such document known) appears on the outer wall of the Cachette Court **[i]**.

This is known as the **Ashkelon Wall** after one of the four battle scenes flanking the treaty; another may depict a fight with the Israelites. Rohl argues that the enemy chariots in this scene contradict established chronology, since the Israelites didn't develop them until King Solomon's reign, but Ramses is conventionally supposed to have been the Pharaoh of the Oppression in the time of Moses, centuries earlier. See Contexts (p.596) for more about Rohl's New Chronology hypothesis.

The Third Pylon

Beyond the XIX Dynasty Hypostyle Hall lies an extensive section of the precinct dating from the XVIII Dynasty. The **Third Pylon** that forms its back wall was originally intended by Amenhotep III to be a monumental gateway to the temple. Like Horemheb forty years later, he demolished earlier structures to serve as core filler for his pylon. Removed by archeologists, these blocks are now displayed – partly reassembled – in the open-air museum. Two huge reliefs of Amun's barque appear on the far wall of the pylon **[j]**.

The narrow court between the Third and Fourth pylons was once enobled by four **Tuthmosid obelisks**. The stone bases near the Third Pylon belonged to a pair erected by Tuthmosis III, chunks of which lie scattered around. Of the pink-granite pair erected by Tuthmosis II, one still stands 23m high, with an estimated weight of 143 tonnes. Once tipped with glittering electrum, the finely carved obelisk was later appropriated by Ramses IV and VI, who added their own cartouches.

The fourth, fifth and sixth pylons

At this stage it's best to carry on through the **Fourth Pylon** rather than get sidetracked into the Cachette Court on the temple's secondary axis. Beyond the pylon are numerous columns which probably formed another hypostyle hall, dominated by the rose-granite **Obelisk of Hatshepsut**, the only woman to rule as pharaoh. To mark her sixteenth regnal year, Hatshepsut had two obelisks quarried in Aswan and erected at Karnak, a task completed in seven months. The standing obelisk is more than 27m high and weighs 320 tons, with a dedicatory inscription running its full height. Its fallen mate has broken into sections, now dispersed around the temple.

The fallen obelisk's carved **tip** can be examined near the Osireion and Sacred Lake. On the way there, you'll pass a granite bas-relief of Amenhotep II target-shooting from a moving chariot, protruding from the **Fifth Pylon**. Built of limestone, this pylon is attributed to Hatshepsut's father, Tuthmosis I.

Though the **Sixth Pylon** has largely disappeared, a portion either side of the granite doorway remains. Its outer face is known as the Wall of Records **[k]** after its list of peoples conquered by Tuthmosis III: Nubians to the right, Asiatics to the left. Beyond the latter is a text extolling the king's victory at Megiddo (Armageddon) in 1479 BC. By organizing tribute from his vanquished foes rather than simply destroying them, Tuthmosis III was arguably the world's first imperialist.

Around the Sanctuary

The section beyond the Sixth Pylon gets increasingly confusing, but a few features are unmistakable. Ahead stand a pair of square-sectioned **heraldic pillars**, their fronts carved with the lotus and papyrus of the Two Lands, their sides showing Amun embracing Tuthmosis III [l]. On the left are two **Colossi of Amun and Amunet**, dedicated by Tutankhamun (whose likeness appears with them) to mark the restoration of orthodoxy after the "heretical" Amarna Period. There's also a seated **statue of Amenhotep II**.

Next comes a granite **Sanctuary** built by Philip Arrhidaeus, the cretinous half-brother of Alexander the Great, on the site of a Tuthmosis-era shrine which similarly held Amun's barque. The interior bas-reliefs show Philip making offerings to Amun in his various aspects, topped by a star-spangled ceiling.

Around to the left of the Sanctuary and further back is a wall inscribed with Tuthmosis III's victories, which he built to hide a wall of reliefs by Queen Hatshepsut, now removed to another room [m]. **Hatshepsut's Wall** has reopened after lengthy restoration, as has the facing portion, where Tuthmosis replaced her image by offerings tables or bouquets, and substituted his father's and grandfather's names for her cartouches (see box, p.306).

Beyond here lies an open space or **Central Court**, thought to mark the site of the original temple of Amun built in the XII Dynasty, whose weathered alabaster foundations poke from the pebbly ground.

The Jubilee Temple of Tuthmosis III

At the rear of the Central Court rises the **Jubilee Temple of Tuthmosis III**, a personal cult shrine in Amun's back yard. As at Saqqara during the Old Kingdom, the Theban kings periodically renewed their temporal and spiritual authority with Bed-sed, or jubilee festivals. The original entrance [n] is flanked by reliefs and broken statues of Tuthmosis in Hed-sed regalia. A left turn brings you into the **Festival Hall**, with its unusual tentpole-style columns, their capitals adorned with blue-and-yellow chevrons. During Christian times the hall was used as a church, hence the haloed saints on some of the pillars.

A chamber off the southwest corner [o] contains an eroded replica of the **Table of Kings** (the original is in the Louvre), depicting Tuthmosis making offerings to previous rulers – Hatshepsut is omitted from the roll call. The so-called **Botanical Garden** is a roofless enclosure containing painted reliefs of plants and animals which Tuthmosis encountered on his campaigns in Syria [p]. Across the way is a roofed chamber decorated by Alexander the Great, who appears before Amun and other deities [q]. The **Chapel of Sokar** constitutes a miniature temple to the Memphite god of darkness [r], juxtaposed against a (now inaccessible) shrine to the sun. A further suite of rooms is dedicated to Tuthmosis [s].

Chapels of the Hearing Ear

Excluded from Amun's Precinct and lacking a direct line to the Theban Triad, the inhabitants of Thebes used intermediary deities to transmit their petitions. These lesser deities rated their own shrines, known as **Chapels of the Hearing Ear** (sometimes actually decorated with carved ears), which straddled the temple's enclosure wall, presenting one face to the outside world. At Karnak, however, they became steadily less approachable and were finally surrounded by the present enclosure wall.

Directly behind the Jubilee Temple is a series of chapels built by Tuthmosis III, centred upon a large alabaster statue of the king and Amun. Further east lie the ruined halls and colonnades of a Temple of the Hearing Ear built by Ramses II. Behind this stands the pedestal of the tallest obelisk known (31m), which Emperor Constantine had shipped to Rome and erected in the Circus Maximus; it was later moved to Lateran Square, hence its name, the **Lateran Obelisk**. As the Ancient Egyptians rarely erected single obelisks, it was probably intended to be accompanied by the Unfinished Obelisk that lies in a quarry outside Aswan, abandoned after the discovery of flaws in the rock.

Around the Sacred Lake

A short walk from Hatshepsut's Obelisk or the Cachette Court brings you to Karnak's **Sacred Lake**, which looks about as holy as a municipal boating pond, with the grandstand for the Sound and Light Show at the far end. The main attraction is a shady (and very pricey) **café** where you can take a break from touring the complex and imagine the scene in ancient times. At sunrise, Amun's priests would take a sacred goose from the fowl-yards which now lie beneath the mound to the south of the lake, and set it free on the waters. As at Hermopolis, the goose or Great Cackler was credited with laying a cosmic egg at the dawn of Creation; but at Karnak the Great Cackler was identified with Amun rather than Thoth.

During the Late Period, Pharaoh Taharqa added a subterranean **Osireion**, linking the resurrection of Osiris with that of the sun. Nearby, a **giant scarab beetle** represents Khepri, the reborn sun at dawn.

The north–south axis

The temple's **north–south axis** is sparser and less variegated than the main section, so if time is limited there's little reason to go beyond the Seventh Pylon. The Gate of Ramses IX, at the southern end of the court between the Third and Fourth pylons, gives access to this wing of the temple, which starts with the Cachette Court.

The **Cachette Court** gets its title from the discovery of a buried hoard of statues early in the twentieth century. Nearly 17,000 bronze statues and votive tablets, and 800 figures in stone, seem to have been cached in a "clearance" of sacred knick-knacks during Ptolemaic times. The finest statues (dating from the Old Kingdom to the Late Period) are now in the Luxor and Cairo museums. The court's northwest corner incorporates a mass of hieroglyphics known as the *Epic of Pentaur* **[t]**, which recaps the battles of Ramses II depicted on the outside of the Great Hypostyle Hall. Diagonally across the court are an eighty-line inscription by Merneptah and a copy of the **Israel Stele [u]** that's in Cairo, which contains among a list of conquests the only known pharaonic reference to Israel: "Israel is crushed, it has no more seed". Rohl argues that the stele has been misread and really relates the achievements of Merneptah's father and grandfather, Ramses II and Seti I.

More proof of the complexities of Egyptology is provided by the **Seventh Pylon**, which was built by Tuthmosis III, but decorated and usurped during the XIX Dynasty, a century or so later, when the cartouches on its door jambs **[v]** were altered to proclaim false ownership. It is fronted by seven statues of Middle Kingdom pharaohs, salvaged from pylon cores. On the far side are the lower portions of two **Colossi of Tuthmosis III**.

The open-air museum

The northern sector of Amun's Precinct contains an **open-air museum**, for which a separate ticket must be bought before entering Karnak. Its prime attractions are two early barque shrines, reassembled from blocks found inside the Third Pylon. From the XII Dynasty comes a lovely **White Chapel**, carved all over with bas-reliefs. While most depict

---

SEKHMET

Sekhmet – "the Powerful" – was the violent counterpart of the Delta goddess Bastet (see p.508). As the daughter of Re, she personified the sun's destructive force, making her a worthy consort for Ptah, the Memphite creator-god. In one myth, Re feared that humanity was plotting against him and unleashed his avenging Eye in the form of Sekhmet, who would have massacred all life had not Re relented and slaked her thirst with red beer, which the drunken goddess mistook for blood.

With the rise of Thebes and Amun's association with Ptah, a corresponding relationship was made between their consorts, Mut and Sekhmet. The New Kingdom pharaohs adopted Sekhmet as a symbol of their indomitable prowess in battle: the statues of the goddess at Karnak bear inscriptions such as "smiter of the Nubians". As "Lady of the Messengers of Death", Sekhmet could send – or prevent – plagues, so her priestesses also served as healers and veterinarians.

Sekhmet

Djed columns, ankhs and other symbols, it's the scenes of Senusret I embracing a priapic Amun-Min that you remember. The plainer **Alabaster Chapel** of Amenhotep I contains more innocuous scenes of the pharaoh making offerings to Amun and his barque.

Along the way you'll pass rows of blocks from Hatshepsut's **Red Chapel**, which archeologists have been unable to reconstruct since each block features a self-contained design rather than a segment of a large relief. This hasn't deterred Egyptologists from trying the same feat with the **Shrine of Tuthmosis III**, with more success. You'll also notice some granite **statues of Sekhmet**, taken from a small **Temple of Ptah** alongside Karnak's enclosure wall, whose ruins aren't much reward for a three-hundred-metre trek across broken ground, though the finest statues of Sekhmet are now in the Luxor Museum.

ARRIVAL AND DEPARTURE   KARNAK

By minibus Public transport (50pt) to Karnak takes a roundabout route past the Gateway of Euergetes II, returning to Luxor along the Corniche el-Nil (where drivers may be loath to pick up tourists, feeling that they ought to take a taxi).
By taxi/calèche After haggling, you should be able to pay £E15 by **taxi** or £E15–20 by **calèche** from Luxor; if you

want your driver for the return trip (£E30 including 2hr waiting time), be sure to remember their licence number.
By bicycle The most direct route (2.5km) from Luxor is along the Corniche el-Nil, which brings you to Karnak's visitors' centre. During summer it's probably better to forgo cycling and conserve your energy for the site.

INFORMATION

Ticket office Around the north side of the visitors' centre. Staff here also sell separate tickets for the Temple of Amun, the open-air museum and the Sound and Light Show (see p.278).
Visitors' centre Behind the Karnak shopping mall facing the Corniche. One of Egypt's better visitors' centres,

featuring photos of Karnak's former ruination, an antique train used to haul masonry during its reconstruction, and scale models of the temple as it looked in ancient times – although it doesn't mention the fact that local residents rioted in protest against the demolition of their homes to create the centre itself. Daily 6am–5pm; admission free.

The Theban Necropolis

Across the Nile from Luxor, the **Theban Necropolis** testifies to the same obsession with death and resurrection that produced the Pyramids. Mindful of how these had failed to protect the mummies of the Old Kingdom pharaohs, later rulers opted for concealment, sinking their tombs in the arid Theban Hills while perpetuating their memory with gigantic mortuary temples on the plain below. The Necropolis straddled the border between the lands of the living and the dead, verdant flood plain giving way to boundless desert, echoing the path of the dead "going west" to meet Osiris as the sun set over the mountains and descended into the underworld.

Though stripped of its treasures over millennia, the Necropolis retains a peerless array of funerary monuments. The grandest of its tombs are in the **Valley of the Kings** and the **Valley of the Queens**, but there's also a wealth of vivid detail in the smaller **Tombs of the Nobles**. Equally amazing are the mortuary temples which enshrined the deceased pharaoh's cult: among these, **Deir el-Bahri** is timelessly magnificent and **Medinet Habu** rivals Karnak for grandeur, while the shattered **Ramesseum** and **Colossi of Memnon** mock the pretensions of their founders. On a humbler level, but still executed with great artistry, are the funerary monuments of the craftsmen who built the royal tombs, and the ruins of their homes at **Deir el-Medina**.

Spread across wadis and hills beyond the edge of the cultivated plain, the Theban Necropolis is too diffuse and complex to take in on a single visit. Even limiting yourself to the Valley of the Kings, Deir el-Bahri and one or other of the major sites, you're likely to feel overwhelmed by the end of the day. Most people favour a series of visits, taking into account the climate and crowds – both major factors in the enjoyment of a trip. In **winter**, mornings are pleasantly hot, afternoons baking but bearable, and most coach tours are scheduled accordingly, making the principal sites crowded between

9am and 2pm. As lots of people come early to beat the crowds, the royal tombs are actually emptiest in the late afternoon. In **summer**, it's simply too hot throughout the afternoon, and you should get here as early as possible.

GETTING TO THE THEBAN NECROPOLIS

There are several ways of crossing **from Luxor** to the west bank. Since the opening of **Luxor Bridge**, 7km south of town at Bogdadi, all coaches, minibuses and taxis from Luxor use this circuitous route, which can take an hour if traffic is heavy. Some operators get round this by sending the vehicle on ahead to meet passengers taken across the Nile by motorboat. Crossing **by boat** remains by far the most pleasant option. You should be able to take bicycles for free on all vessels, but keep safety in mind: overcrowded boats are a recipe for disaster, as was proved in 2001, when 35 passengers drowned after a ferry hit their motorboat in the dark. Stepping across rickety wharfs after dark is a more mundane hazard – watch out for mooring lines and gaps in the planking.

By ferry Public ferries sail frequently during daytime, hourly after 6pm and sporadically after midnight from the landing stage on the Corniche near Luxor Temple signposted "National Ferryboat", to dock near Gezira village on the west bank. Locals pay 25pt for the ride, tourists £E1.

By motorboat/felucca Dozens of motorboats and feluccas inveigle for custom by the water's edge,

charging £E5/boatload (£E10 for more than six passengers) after a brief haggle. Motorboats (called "lunches" in English, *zobak* in Arabic) are the fastest way to cross the river and may land or leave from anywhere along either riverbank, whereas crossing the Nile by felucca is more of a leisurely experience than a quick journey.

GETTING AROUND

Once across the Nile, how you choose to get around will depend on the time of year and what you plan to see, your budget and your sense of adventure. If you intend to visit the Necropolis more than once, try using various modes of transport.

By foot It's quite feasible to explore much of the Necropolis on foot, utilizing public transport to get within walking range. From the taxi depot in Gezira, pick-ups or minibuses (50pt) shuttle passengers to Old Gurna (known to drivers as Gurna Foq), bringing you within fifteen minutes' walk of Medinet Habu, the Valley of the Queens or the Ramesseum. Many run on to Dra' Abu Naga, leaving you closer to the Tombs of the Nobles or Deir el-Bahri.

By taxi Hiring a private taxi is the easiest way of visiting sites according to your own itinerary, but don't pay for unnecessary waiting time. If you're planning to hike over the hills between the Valley of the Kings and Deir el-Bahri (see p.307), arrange for your driver to pick you up later. Taxis are usually hired for 4–6hr, at £E20–30 an hour. Pick-ups (see above) can also be engaged as taxis to whisk up to six passengers from one site to another for £E15 without paying for the driver to hang around while you explore.

By bicycle Assuming that you're fit, the cheapest way to cover the Necropolis is by cycling. Bicycles (*ajila*) can be rented in shops and hotels in Luxor or on the west bank for £E10 a day. Test your bike before hiring; many have no gears, making any uphill stretch against a headwind murder. A day's touring might involve cycling approaching 30km: for example, 3km from the river bank to the main ticket kiosk, 8km from there to the Valley of the Kings (beware of traffic) and 3km from Deir el-Bahri to Medinet Habu. The main drawback is that you can't then walk over

the hills from the Valley of the Kings to Deir el-Bahri. Roads vary from smooth tarmac to stony *pistes*. In winter, you'll feel cool when riding but start sweating once you stop. Cycling during summer is a lot more demanding, so it's imperative to take the gradual uphill stretch to the Valley of the Kings early in the morning, or conserve your energy by getting there by taxi (£E10) with your bike on its roof rack, allowing you to coast back downhill in the afternoon heat. Guard against heatstroke and keep swigging water.

By motorbike Another possibility is to rent a motorbike in Luxor (see p.266) – though this entails crossing the river by the bridge, as motorbikes are too heavy to carry up and down the ferry jetty steps. Be especially careful of children and livestock when riding on the west bank.

By donkey Travelling by donkey offers the thrill of riding up the Theban Hills as mist cloaks the plain, skirting precipices and abandoned tombs before you descend into the Valley of the Kings, and returning via Deir el-Bahri – with fantastic views denied to other travellers. However, it's a physically gruelling five-hour trip, starting at 5am, that's not for anyone with vertigo, nor children. A more laidback donkey option is a village tour of Beirat, using farm trails and backroads, which can be lovely if it's not too hot. You can hire beasts and a guide from Tayeb Khalifa in Gezira (☏012 2743 8266, ✉kingofluxor66@hotmail.com), who charges £E35 for an excursion to the Valley of the Kings and Deir el-Bahri, or the Tombs of the Nobles and the Ramesseum.

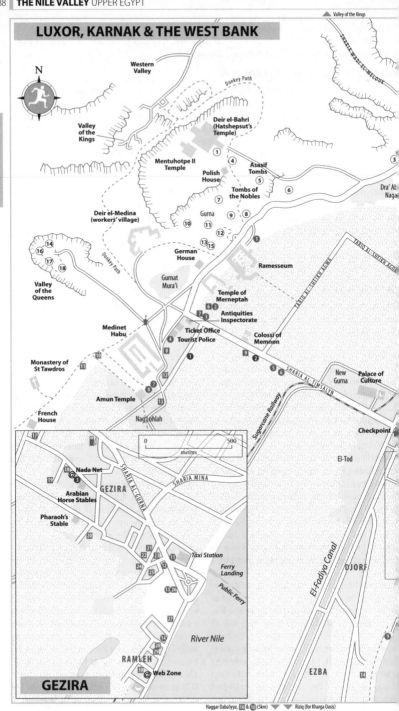

LUXOR, KARNAK & THE WEST BANK

N

Valley of the Kings

Western Valley

Donkey Path

Valley of the Kings

Deir el-Bahri (Hatshepsut's Temple)

Asasif Tombs

Mentuhotpe II Temple

Polish House

Tombs of the Nobles

Dra' Abu' Naga

Deir el-Medina (workers' village)

Gurna

German House

Gurnat Mura'i

Ramesseum

Tarir al-Sheikh Aoui

Valley of the Queens

Donkey Path

Temple of Merneptah

Medinet Habu

Antiquities Inspectorate

Ticket Office
Tourist Police

Colossi of Memnon

New Gurna

Palace of Culture

Monastery of St Tawdros

Amun Temple

French House

Nag' Lohlah

Sharia Al-Timsalyn

Sugarcane Railway

Checkpoint

El-Tod

GEZIRA

Nada Net

Arabian Horse Stables

Pharaoh's Stable

Sharia Al-Gurna

Sharia Mina

0   500
metres

Taxi Station

Ferry Landing

Public Ferry

River Nile

RAMLEH

Web Zone

GEZIRA

El-Fadiya Canal

DJORF

EZBA

Haggar Daba'iyya, 16 & 18 (5km)   Riziq (for Kharga Oasis)

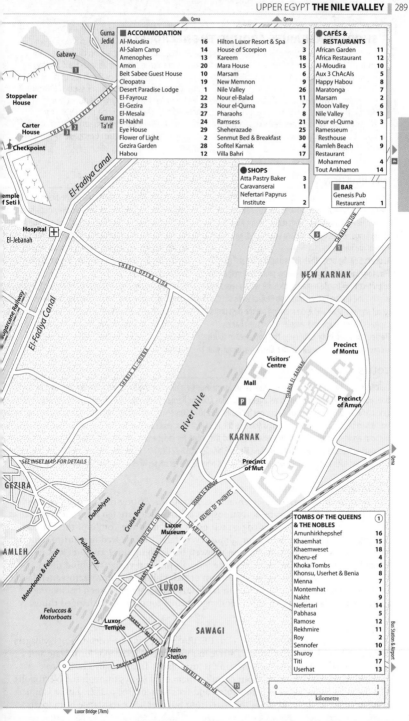

2

■ **ACCOMMODATION**

Al-Moudira	16	Hilton Luxor Resort & Spa	5
Al-Salam Camp	14	House of Scorpion	3
Amenophes	13	Kareem	18
Amon	20	Mara House	15
Beit Sabee Guest House	10	Marsam	6
Cleopatra	19	New Memnon	9
Desert Paradise Lodge	1	Nile Valley	26
El-Fayrouz	22	Nour el-Balad	11
El-Gezira	23	Nour el-Qurna	7
El-Mesala	27	Pharaohs	8
El-Nakhil	24	Ramsess	21
Eye House	29	Sheherazade	25
Flower of Light	2	Senmut Bed & Breakfast	30
Geziza Garden	28	Sofitel Karnak	4
Habou	12	Villa Bahri	17

● **CAFÉS &**
RESTAURANTS

African Garden	11
Africa Restaurant	12
Al-Moudira	10
Aux 3 ChAcAls	5
Happy Habou	8
Maratonga	7
Marsam	2
Moon Valley	6
Nile Valley	13
Nour el-Qurna	3
Ramesseum	
Resthouse	1
Ramleh Beach	9
Restaurant	
Mohammed	4
Tout Ankhamon	14

● **SHOPS**

Atta Pastry Baker	3
Caravanserai	1
Nefertari Papyrus	
Institute	2

■ **BAR**

Genesis Pub	
Restaurant	1

TOMBS OF THE QUEENS ①
& THE NOBLES

Amunhirkhepshef	16
Khaemhat	15
Khaemweset	18
Kheru-ef	4
Khoka Tombs	6
Khonsu, Userhet & Benia	8
Menna	7
Montemhat	1
Nakht	9
Nefertari	14
Pabhasa	5
Ramose	12
Rekhmire	11
Roy	2
Sennofer	10
Shuroy	3
Titi	17
Userhat	13

NEW KARNAK

Precinct
of Montu

Visitors'
Centre

Mall

Precinct
of Amun

KARNAK

Precinct
of Mut

River Nile

El-Fadiya Canal

Gurna
Jedid

Gabawy

**Stoppelaer
House**

**Carter
House**

Gurna
Ta'rif

Checkpoint

emple
f Seti I

Hospital

El-Jebanah

SHARIA OPERA AIDA

Sugarcane Railway

El-Fadiya Canal

SEE INSET MAP FOR DETAILS

GEZIRA

Dahabiyas

Cruise Boats

AMLEH

Motorboats & Feluccas

**Luxor
Museum**

CORNICHE EL-NIL

Public Ferry

Feluccas &
Motorboats

**Luxor
Temple**

LUXOR

SAWAGI

Train
Station

SHARIA AL-MANSHIA

SHARIA AL-MATHAN

AVENUE OF SPHINXES

SHARIA LE-KARNAK

SHARIA AL-QURNA

SHARIA EL-KABBAK

SHARIA HILTON

SHARIA AL-NOSHA

Qena ►

Bus Station & Airport

0		1
	kilometre	

▼ Luxor Bridge (7km)

2

SHORT ITINERARIES AROUND THE NECROPOLIS

For those who like to linger over every carving, the tombs and temples on the west bank could easily fill three or four days. If you're forced to cram the highlights into **half a day**, a minimalist schedule might run: Valley of the Kings (1hr 30min), Deir el-Bahri (20min), the Tombs of the Nobles (30min–1hr), Medinet Habu (30min) and/or the Ramesseum (30min). If you have a **full day**, catch a taxi to the Valley of the Kings before 9am, spend a couple of hours there and then walk over the hills to Deir el-Bahri, arranging to be met there for another ride to Medinet Habu or Deir el-Medina and the Valley of the Queens. Alternatively, you could spend time at the Tombs of the Nobles and the Ramesseum before returning to the landing stage.

INFORMATION

Opening hours The opening hours of the various sites may change with the season and security restrictions, but are generally from 7am to 5pm daily, except for the Valley of the Kings, which opens at 6am year round, and closes at 4pm in the winter.

Tickets See the box, "Theban Necropolis Tickets" (p.291)

Photography Photography is now prohibited in the tombs to protect their fragile murals, which are widely reproduced in print and on the Theban Mapping Project website (W kv5 .com) anyway. Dusk and early morning are the best times to capture the landscape and temples of the west bank.

Police and security Generally, the police leave tourists alone, but the checkpoint at the El-Fadiya Canal won't allow traffic to pass up the road to the Necropolis before 6am – which spoils things for donkey-groups hoping to catch the sunrise, unless they sneak through the fields – and service taxi drivers at Gezira's depot have been told not to take foreigners beyond the west bank security zone, which ends at Haggar Daba'iyya (to the south) and Gurna Ta'rif (to the north).

What to bring Useful things to bring include a torch, plenty of water and small change. If you're planning to cycle or ride a donkey, a hat and double rations of water are vital. A snack, too, is a good idea, as the choice of food and drink is limited, and prices are higher than in Luxor.

TOURS

Guided tours, typically featuring the Colossi of Memnon, the Valleys of the Kings and Queens and Deir el-Bahri, are bookable through any hotel or travel agency. Thomas Cook or Karnak Travel charge €30–40/person (including entrance tickets) for an a/c coach tour, while budget hotels ask £E210–250/person (students £E140–200) to share a minibus or taxi (including tickets and a guide). Even if you like the idea of a tour, don't sign up for the first one offered – at least, not without an idea of what's available elsewhere and the scope for independent travel (see p.287). If you want to hire a personal guide, Mahmoud Abd Allah alias "Mr Sunshine" (T 012 2215 7145, E sunshineluxor@mailcity.com) is a master Egyptologist with forty years' experience who charges only £E200 for his services (excluding transport and tickets).

Gezira and New Gurna

The **west bank villages** are incidental to most tourists visiting the Theban Necropolis, but integral to the landscape and atmosphere. Their fields stretch from the river banks to the temples on the desert's edge; their goats root amid the Tombs of the Nobles. Though land remains paramount, almost every family is involved in tourism, renting out donkeys or making souvenirs on the west bank, commuting to hotel jobs in Luxor or sailing motorboats or feluccas on the Nile. Family and village ties bind them together and help them exploit the stream of rich visitors that flows across their land. Richard Critchfield's *Shahhat* (sold in most Luxor bookshops) gives a fascinating glimpse into their lives two generations ago, before tourism really changed things.

Gezira

Your first village encounter will be with **GEZIRA**, where public ferries disgorge villagers returning from Luxor, and tourists arrive in motorboats. The depot for private and service **taxis** to villages on the west bank is just inland. Traditionally Gezira's role in tourism was to ferry tourists about or guide them on donkeys through the Necropolis, but the village now also has many hotels and flats for rent (see p.272). Luxor Council tried to claim all the land along the waterfront but met fierce resistance from locals

THEBAN NECROPOLIS TICKETS

Confusingly for visitors, **tickets** for the various sites are sold at four separate offices scattered across the Necropolis. To see every site would cost around $120/€80 on tickets at the full rate (roughly half that for students); most people are satisfied to see far less. It's unlikely that you'll use more than six or seven tickets in a day's outing. Tickets are only valid for the day of purchase, with no refunds for unused ones. Last tickets are sold at 4pm.

MAIN TICKET OFFICE (NEAR THE TOURIST POLICE)

Asasif Tombs (Pabasa, Kheru-ef, Ankh-hor)	£E30
Carter House	£E20
Deir el-Medina (any two tombs, excluding Peshedu)	£E30
Khokha Tombs	£E25
Medinet Habu (Temple of Ramses III)	£E30
Ramesseum	£E35
Temple of Merneptah	£E20
Temple of Seti I	£E30
Tomb of Peshedu (Deir el-Medina)	£E15
Tombs of Nakht and Menna (Tombs of the Nobles)	£E25
Tombs of Roy and Shuroy (Dra' Abul Naga)	£E15
Tombs of Userhat and Ramose (Tombs of the Nobles)	£E30

DEIR EL-BAHRI OFFICE

Deir el-Bahri (Hatshepsut's temple)	£E30

VALLEY OF THE KINGS OFFICE

Valley of the Kings (any three tombs except Tutankhamun and Ramses VI)	£E80
Tomb of Tutankhamun	£E100
Tomb of Ramses VI	£E50
Tomb of Ay (Western Valley)	£E25

VALLEY OF THE QUEENS OFFICE

Valley of the Queens (excluding Nefertari's tomb)	£E30

who'd built houses and hotels there, as well as from foreigners who'd bought apartments in the chic new district of **Ramleh**. Many only escaped demolition after the matriarch of the Khalifa family lay down in front of the bulldozers – after which Ramleh was nicknamed "Ramallah" (after the defiant town on the Israeli-occupied West Bank).

El-Tod and New Gurna

Gezira straggles to the **El-Fadiya Canal**, whose murky depths harbour giant **monitor lizards** (warran), which sometimes get sucked into farmers' irrigation pumps, with gory results. Beyond the lackadaisical police checkpoint, **EL-TOD** lies across the main road from **NEW GURNA**, built in the 1940s with government funds to wean villagers away from Old Gurna in the hills. Designed by **Hassan Fathy** (1900–89), an early advocate of appropriate technology through architecture suited to local conditions, the settlement contains two superbly proportioned public buildings – the **mosque** and **Palace of Culture** – made of Fathy's favourite material, mud brick. However, the village failed to attract many Gurnawis, and others moved in instead, to find that Fathy's houses were too small for their extended families, obliging them to add breeze-block extensions.

The Colossi of Memnon

2km from Gezira • Daily 24hr • Free

Looming nearly 18m above fields of clover, the two enthroned **Colossi of Memnon** originally fronted the mortuary temple of Amenhotep III, once the largest complex on the west bank – which later pharaohs plundered for masonry until almost nothing remained but these colossi. Both have lost their faces and crowns, and the northern one was cleaved to the waist by an earthquake in 27 BC. Subsequently, this colossus was heard to "sing" at dawn – a sound probably caused by particles breaking off as the stone expanded, or wind reverberating through the cracks.

Before the colossus ceased "singing" after repairs to the statue in 199 AD, the sound was attributed to the legendary Memnon (whom Achilles killed outside the walls of Troy) greeting his mother, Eos, the Dawn, with a sigh. The Greeks identified the colossi with Memnon in the belief that his father, Tithonus, had been an Egyptian king. Before this, the colossi had been identified with Amenhotep, Steward of Amenhotep III, whom posterity honoured as a demigod long after his royal master was forgotten.

Standing beside the barrier rope you can appreciate what **details** remain on the thrones and legs of the sandstone colossi. On the sides of the nearer one, the Nile-gods of Upper and Lower Egypt bind the heraldic plants of the Two Lands together. The legs of each colossus are flanked by smaller statues of Queen Tiy (right) and the king's mother, Mutemuia (left). They are covered in graffiti, including Roman epigrams, as high as you can reach.

Behind them, the long-lost **Mortuary Temple of Amenhotep III** is being excavated to form a new archeological park and is currently off-limits to the public.

Valley of the Kings

Secluded amid the bone-dry Theban Hills, removed from other parts of the Necropolis, the **Valley of the Kings** (Wadi el-Melouk in Arabic) was intended as the ultimate insurance policy guaranteeing life eternal. These secretive tombs of New Kingdom pharaohs were planned to preserve their mummies and funerary impedimenta for eternity. While most failed the test, their dramatic shafts and phantasmagorical murals are truly amazing, and the descent into the underworld and the fear of robbers who braved the traps is still imaginable in the less crowded, darker tombs.

Surrounded by limestone crags (the loftiest of which was believed to be the abode of Meretseger, snake-goddess of the Necropolis), the valley is a natural suntrap, hot even in winter, the heat permeating the deepest tombs, whose air is musty and humid. The tombs are like portals to another dimension, as alien as the valley itself – which today outwardly resembles a missile base on open-day, with crowds wandering from silo to silo.

The valley is approached by a serpentine road that follows the route of ancient funeral processions, with a tourist bazaar and visitors' centre preceding the ticket office and site entrance (see below). Only ten **tombs** are **open** at any one time (Luxor's tourist office can tell you which); those of Horemheb and Seti I are permanently closed. The signposted tombs are **numbered** in order of their discovery, starting with the tomb of Ramses VII (known in antiquity) – #1 – and ending with the most recent discovery, #64. Egyptologists assign them the prefix KV (short for Kings Valley) to distinguish them from other numbered tombs in the Valley of the Queens.

After you've seen the tombs, you might enjoy **hiking** over the ridge to Deir el-Bahri, for a superb view of Hatshepsut's temple (see box, p.307).

| **INFORMATION** | **VALLEY OF THE KINGS** |

For information on transport to the Valley of the Kings, see "Getting around" (p.287).

Opening hours Daily 6am–5pm

Tickets A single ticket (£E80) is valid for three tombs. Extra tickets can be purchased if you want to see more, while separate tickets are required for the tombs of Tutankhamun (£E100) and Ramses VI (£E50). The first office you come to at the Valley of the Kings sells tickets for the site valid for any three tombs except those of Tutankhamun (£E100), Ramses VI (£E50) and Ay in the Western Valley (£E25), for which separate tickets are sold. Tickets for Ramses VI and Tutankhamun's tombs can also be bought from a kiosk just inside the site's entrance.

Visitors' centre The visitors' centre (daily 6am–5pm; free)

WARDEN WITH KEY AT THE SUN TEMPLE, ABU SIMBEL (P.366) >

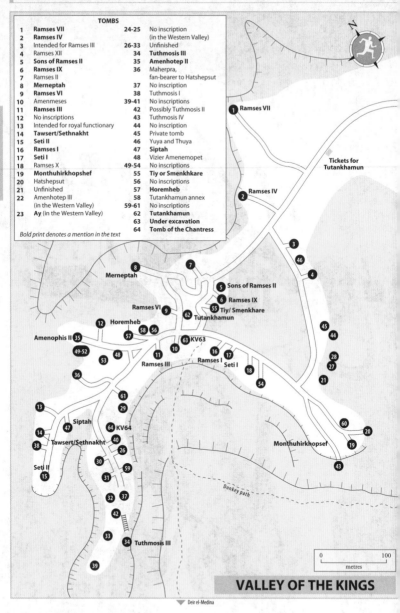

TOMBS

1	**Ramses VII**	24-25	No inscription
2	**Ramses IV**		(in the Western Valley)
3	Intended for Ramses III	26-33	Unfinished
4	Ramses XII	34	**Tuthmosis III**
5	**Sons of Ramses II**	35	**Amenhotep II**
6	**Ramses IX**	36	Maherpra,
7	Ramses II		fan-bearer to Hatshepsut
8	**Merneptah**	37	No inscription
9	**Ramses VI**	38	Tuthmosis I
10	Amenmeses	39-41	No inscriptions
11	**Ramses III**	42	Possibly Tuthmosis II
12	No inscriptions	43	Tuthmosis IV
13	Intended for royal functionary	44	No inscription
14	**Tawsert/Sethnakht**	45	Private tomb
15	Seti II	46	Yuya and Thuya
16	**Ramses I**	47	**Siptah**
17	**Seti I**	48	Vizier Amenemopet
18	Ramses X	49-54	No inscriptions
19	**Monthuhirkhopshef**	55	**Tiy or Smenkhkare**
20	Hatshepsut	56	No inscriptions
21	Unfinished	57	**Horemheb**
22	Amenhotep III	58	Tutankhamun annex
	(in the Western Valley)	59-61	No inscriptions
23	**Ay** (in the Western Valley)	62	**Tutankhamun**
		63	**Under excavation**
		64	**Tomb of the Chantress**

Bold print denotes a mention in the text

VALLEY OF THE KINGS

▼ Deir el-Medina

is located just before the ticket office and features a lovely Japanese-made scale model of the Valley of the Kings crafted from glass to show each tomb's depth and alignment. You can also watch a film of the official opening of Tutankhamun's tomb in 1922, and (if their computers have been replaced) access the Theban Mapping Project's website.

Tuf-tuf An electric road-train, or tuf-tuf (£E4), runs the 400m from the ticket office to the site entrance if you don't fancy walking.

Photography No photography allowed anywhere in the site, and cameras must be deposited before entering – violaters risk having their camera confiscated, and/or a fine.

Websites The comprehensive Theban Mapping Project site (🌐kv5.com) contains plans, images and narrated tours of all the royal tombs, an atlas of the Necropolis and much else, while 🌐kv-63.com features the dig diary of archeologists investigating tomb KV63.

Brief history

Royal burials in the "Place of Truth" (as the Ancient Egyptians called it) date from the early XVIII to the late XX dynasties. The first to be buried here was probably Tuthmosis I (c.1504–1492 BC). Until the time of Ramses I, queens and royal children were entombed here. The tombs were hewn and decorated by skilled craftsmen (known as "Servants at the Place of Truth") who dwelt at nearby Deir el-Medina. Work began early in a pharaoh's reign and never exceeded six years' duration; even so, some tombs were hastily pressed into service, or usurped by later kings.

Broadly speaking, there are two kinds of tombs: the convoluted, split-level ones of early XVIII Dynasty rulers such as Tuthmosis I and Amenhotep II, and the straighter, longer tombs of the XIX and XX dynasties. But there are enough exceptions to make

2

EXCAVATING AND CONSERVING THE VALLEY OF THE KINGS

People have been claiming that there is nothing left to find in the Valley of the Kings almost as long as they have been digging there. Giovanni Belzoni thought so after clearing all the known tombs in 1817; so did Theodore Davis, who scoured over thirty tombs and pits (1902–14). Yet in 1922, Howard Carter's discovery of Tutankhamun's tomb made headlines around the world.

Nothing more was found till 1995, when clues from a papyrus in Turin led Kent Weeks to clear the debris from tomb **KV5** – which Carter had dismissed as looted in antiquity – and uncover the entrance to a mass tomb for the **sons of Ramses II,** reckoned to contain 150 chambers, some huge. While inscriptions suggest that fifty of Ramses' one hundred or so sons were meant to be interred here, the remains of only four adults have been found so far, and the risk of ceilings collapsing has hampered further excavation (see the Theban Mapping Project website, 🌐kv5.com, for news plus images of other royal tombs).

More recently, in 2006, Otto Schaden uncovered an XVIII Dynasty chamber designated **KV63**, containing empty child-coffins and embalmers' gear, while in 2011 Swiss archeologists found an undisturbed burial chamber near the southeastern end of the valley, now designated as **KV64**. Dubbed the "Tomb of the Chantress" after the discovery of a sycamore coffin and resin-impregnated mummy belonging to a temple-chantress called Nehemes-Bastet, it is one of the few non-royal burials in the valley to be definitively identified. Excavations came to a halt during the 2011 Revolution and have yet to resume at the time of writing.

Another, as-yet uncovered, tomb near Tutankhamun's has been located by ground-penetrating radar. Its discoverer, Nicholas Reeves, believes that it might be the final resting place of one or more of the "Amarna women" (Akhenaten's wife Kiya, or his daughters Ankesenamun, Meritaten and Mekataten), but has been denied permission to excavate.

CONSERVATION – AND THE FUTURE OF THE VALLEY

The Valley of the Kings is vulnerable to several hazards. Flash **floods** present a grave danger to the tombs, but clearing the wadis of debris and digging drainage channels risks destroying evidence that might point to undiscovered tombs. The SCA and foreign donors have already spent millions tackling an expanding sub-stratum of grey shale which ruptured several tombs in the 1990s, and installing glass screens and dehumidifiers to reduce the harm caused by **tourism** (the average visitor leaves behind 2.8g of sweat to corrode the murals). The upshot is that some tombs are permanently closed (except for VIPs and a few privileged tour groups), and the rest open according to a rota system. Though frustrating for visitors, this may be the only way to preserve the tombs' fragile artwork for future generations.

As a long-term goal the SCA intends to create life-size **replicas** of all the royal tombs on a site near the Carter House (see p.309). The originals have been laser-scanned to be replicated by digital milling machines, but the Revolution halted their construction before it began. If the project is ever completed, access to the Valley of the Kings will be restricted to a few premium-paying visitors, and ordinary tourists obliged to settle for the replica tombs.

any such generalisations risky; the past twenty years have seen the discovery of tombs consisting of over a hundred rooms, or just a single chamber. Identifying the tombs' owners has often been difficult, thanks to **tomb-robbing** on a massive scale which the weak rulers of the XX Dynasty were unable to prevent. Both the governor and police chief of Thebes were implicated in the disposal of treasure during the XX Dynasty, while many of the robbers were the workmen who had built the tombs, embittered over arrears in pay. In response, the priests reburied many sarcophagi and objects in two **secret caches** that were only discovered in the late nineteenth century (see p.309).

Tomb of Ramses VII (#1)

Set apart near the entrance to the valley, the short tomb of **Ramses VII** lay wide open for millennia, and is now glassed over. Greek and Roman graffiti mar its sunk-reliefs and vivid colours (red, yellow and blue on white), whose freshness is due to restoration. Amid the standard imagery are odd details like the figures entombed in cartouches on the walls of the final corridor, while the hippo-goddess Tweri is prominent in the

---

MUMMIFICATION AND THE UNDERWORLD

The **funerary beliefs** manifest in the Valley of the Kings derive from two myths, concerning Re and Osiris. In that of **Re**, the sun-god descended into the underworld and voyaged through the hours of night, emerging at dawn to sail his barque across the heavens until sunset, when the cycle began anew. **Osiris**, king of the underworld, offered hope of survival in the afterlife through his death and resurrection.

MUMMIFICATION AND BURIAL

To attain the afterlife, it was necessary that the deceased's name (*ren*) and body continued to exist, sustaining the **ka** or cosmic double that was born with every person and inhabited their mummy after death. **Mummification** techniques evolved over millennia, reaching their zenith by the New Kingdom, when embalmers offered three levels of mummification. The deluxe version entailed removing the brain (which was discarded) and the viscera (which were preserved in canopic jars); dehydrating the cadaver in natron salts for about forty days; packing it to reproduce lifelike contours, inserting artificial eyes and painting the face or entire body red (for men) or yellow (for women); then wrapping it in gum-coated linen bandages, and finally cocooning it in mummiform coffins. On the chest of the mummy and its coffin were placed heart scarabs, designed to prevent the deceased's heart from bearing witness against him during the judgement of Osiris.

   Royal burials were elaborate affairs. Escorted by priests, mourners and musicians, the coffin was dragged on a sledge to the Valley of the Kings, where the sarcophagus was already occupied by a *sem* (death) priest, who performed the **Opening of the Mouth** ceremony, touching the lips of the mummy with an adze and reciting spells. As the mummy was lowered into its sarcophagus, priests slashed the forelegs of sacrificial animals, whose limbs were burned as the tomb was sealed. The tomb's contents (intended to satisfy the needs of the pharaoh's *ka* in the afterlife) included food, drink, clothing, furniture, weapons and dozens of *shabti* figures to perform any task that the gods might require. Then the doors were walled up, plastered over and stamped with the royal seal and that of the Necropolis. To thwart robbers, royal tombs featured deadfalls and false burial chambers; however, none of these devices seems to have succeeded in protecting them.

The Journey of Re
From right to left: Sunset; Year; Eternity; Everlasting; Maat (justice); Re; Heka; Sunrise

nocturnal pantheon on the ceiling of the burial chamber, whose sarcophagus is veined with blue imagery. Other Ramessid tombs are finer, however.

Tomb of Ramses IV (#2)

The next tomb, created for **Ramses IV**, is more of a crowd pleaser. Its cheerful colours make amends for the inferior sunk-reliefs and abundant Greek and Coptic **graffiti** (notice the haloed saints on the right near the entrance). The ceiling of the burial chamber is adorned with twin figures of Nut. On the enormous pink-granite **sarcophagus** are magical texts and carvings of Isis and Nephthys to protect the mummy from harm. When these seemed insufficient, priests stashed Ramses in the tomb of Amenhotep II, whence the now empty sarcophagus has been returned. His mummy in Cairo's Egyptian Museum shows him to have been a short, bald man with a long nose. He became pharaoh in his forties after the failure of a conspiracy to usurp the throne from his father, Ramses III (whose "testament" was recorded in the *Great Harris Papyrus*).

THE JOURNEY THROUGH THE UNDERWORLD AND JUDGEMENT OF OSIRIS

Funerary artwork dwelt on the journey through the underworld, whose pictorial representation inverted the normal order, so that each register was topped by sand instead of sky. The **descent** into the underworld (*Duat*) echoed that of a sarcophagus into its tomb, involving ramps, ropes and gateways. Each of the twelve **gates** was personified as a goddess and guarded by ferocious deities. In the darkness between them lay twelve **caverns** inhabited by beings such as the jackal-headed gods who fed on rottenness or the wailing goddesses with bloody axes.

It was Maat's Feather of Truth that was weighed against the deceased's heart (believed to be the seat of intelligence) during the **Judgement of Osiris**. With Anubis operating the scales and Thoth waiting to record the verdict, the deceased had to recite the **negative confession** before a tribunal of 42 **assessor gods**, each attuned to a sin. While the hearts of the guilty were devoured by crocodile-headed Ammut, the righteous were pronounced "true of voice" and led into the presence of Osiris to begin their **resurrection**, which paralleled **Re's passage through the underworld**. Voyaging through the twelve *decans* (hours or "divisions") of the night in his solar barque, Re had to overcome the serpent Apopis and other lesser denizens of **primeval chaos**, which threatened the **righteous order** personified by the goddess **Maat**. Re, helped by Anubis, Isis and Nephthys (often shown as serpents), Aker the earth-god (whose back bore Re's barque) and **Khepri** the scarab beetle, achieves rebirth in the fifth hour, and is fully restored to life by the tenth. Here the two myths part company, for whereas Re emerges from the body of the sky-goddess **Nut** to travel the heavens again, the Osirian journey (that of the righteous deceased) concludes by passing through the reedy **Fields of Yaru** (an Ancient Egyptian metaphor for death, also synonymous with fertility).

Since many of the scenes were supplemented by papyri buried with the mummy, funerary **artwork** is categorized in literary terms. The *Book of the Dead* is the name now given to the compendium of Old and Middle Kingdom Pyramid Texts and Spells, known in the New Kingdom as the *Book of Coming Forth*. Other **texts** associated with the New Kingdom include the *Book of Gates, Book of Caverns, Book of Hours, Book of Day and Night* and *Book of Amduat* (That which is in the Underworld).

The Judgement of Osiris
From left to right: Anubis escorts the deceased and weighs his heart before Ammut and Thoth; then Horus leads him to Osiris, Isis and Nephthys

Tomb of Ramses IX (#6)

The tomb of **Ramses IX** belonged to one of the last rulers (c.1126–08 BC) of the XX Dynasty, towards the end of the New Kingdom. It's indicative of waning majesty that the initial scenes in sunk-relief soon give way to flat paintings, akin to drawings. The walls of its stepped corridor (originally bisected by ramps, for moving the sarcophagus) depict Ramses before the gods and symbolic extracts from the *Book of Caverns*. Notice the solar barques bearing crocodiles, heads and other oddities, on the left-hand wall. The burial chamber is memorable for its *Book of Night* (see p.297). Two sky-goddesses stretch back-to-back across the ceiling, encompassing voids swirling with creatures, stars and heavenly barques. While the king's sarcophagus pit gapes empty, his resurrection is still heralded on the walls by Khepri, the scarab incarnation of the reborn sun at dawn.

Tomb of Tiy or Smenkhkare (#55)

Identifying mummies isn't easy if the tomb was left undecorated and later looted – or the excavation was botched. The tomb designated **KV55** has been a conundrum ever since Theodore Davis failed to record its contents before removing the decrepit mummy in 1907, which he attributed to **Queen Tiy** – the wife of Amenhotep III – due to its pelvic shape and "feminine" position (left arm bound across the chest, right arm alongside the body), and a gilded panel depicting her with Akhenaten.

Later forensic analysis identified the bones as those of a man under 26 with signs of hydrocephalus, which seemingly fitted **Akhenaten**, until another examination in 2000 identified a man no older than his early twenties with a skull similar to Tutankhamun's, which many think was his mysterious predecessor, **Smenkhkare**. DNA analysis has confirmed a familial relationship between the mystery man and Tutankhamun, but the riddle of his identity is still unsolved.

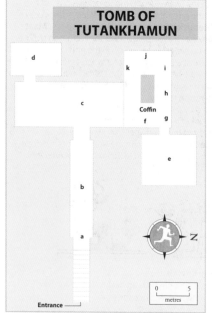

TOMB OF TUTANKHAMUN

d

j

k

i

h

c

Coffin

f

g

e

b

a

N

0 ____ 5
metres

Entrance ____

Tomb of Tutankhamun (#62)

Daily 6am–1pm & 2–5pm • £E100

One of the world's most famous tombs, the tomb of **Tutankhamun** is neither large nor imposing by the standards of the Valley of the Kings, reflecting Tut's short reign, c.1336–27 BC (see p.227) as an XVIII Dynasty boy-pharaoh. Its renown stems from its belated discovery and its amazing hoard of treasures (now mostly in the Egyptian Museum). After archeologist **Howard Carter** had dug in vain for five seasons, his backer, **Lord Carnarvon**, was on the point of giving up when the tomb was found on November 4, 1922. Fears that it had been plundered were dispelled when they broke through the second sealed door – officially on November 26, though in fact Carter and Carnarvon secretly entered the previous night, stole several items and resealed the door. Unpacking everything took nearly ten years, the whole process being recorded in more than 1800 superb photographs by Harry Burton.

THE CURSE OF TUTANKHAMUN

Lord Carnarvon's death in Cairo from an infected mosquito bite in April 1923 focused world attention on a warning by the novelist Marie Corelli, that "dire punishment follows any intruder into the tomb". (At the moment of Carnarvon's death, all the lights in Cairo went out.) The **curse of Tutankhamun** gained popular credence with this and each successive "mysterious" death. The US magnate Jay Gould died of pneumonia resulting from a cold contracted at the tomb; a famous bey was shot by his wife in London after viewing the discovery; a French Egyptologist suffered a fatal fall; Carter's secretary died in unusual circumstances at the Bath Club in London; and his right-hand man Arthur Mace sickened and died before the tomb had been fully cleared. However, of the 22 who had witnessed the opening of Tut's sarcophagus, only two were dead ten years later. Howard Carter died in 1939 at the age of 64, while others closely involved lived into their 80s – not least Dr Derry, who performed the autopsy which suggested that Tut died from a blow to the head, aged about 19. If the most recent explanation for Tut's death is correct, mosquitoes were instrumental in the demise of both the boy-king and Carnarvon (see below).

In 1922, Carter found the door at the bottom of the stairway [a] walled up and sealed with Tut's cartouche and the seal of the Necropolis, but signs of repairs, the detritus in the corridor [b] and another resealed door at the end indicated that robbers had penetrated the antechamber [c] during the XX Dynasty. Most of the funerary objects now in the Egyptian Museum were crammed into the undecorated chambers [c, d (now walled up) and e]. Another wall (now replaced by a barrier) enclosed the burial chamber, which was almost filled by four golden shrines packed one inside another, containing Tut's stone sarcophagus and triple-layer mummiform coffin, of which the innermost, solid **gold coffin** and **Tut's mummy** remain.

In 2005 the mummy was CT-scanned *in situ*, revealing a broken leg that might have given rise to a fatal infection, casting doubt on the theory of a head injury that some had attributed to murder. More recent DNA analysis has revealed that Tut had a hereditary bone disorder and malaria (supported by the discovery of walking sticks and medicines in his tomb), the combination of which may have proved fatal.

The tomb's colourful **murals** run anticlockwise, starting with the funeral procession where nine friends and three officials drag Tut's coffin on a sledge [f]. Next, his successor Ay (see p.229) performs the Opening of the Mouth ceremony [g] and makes sacrifices to the sky-goddess Nut [h]. The deceased king embraces Osiris, followed by his *ka* (in the black wig) [i]. His solar boat and sun-worshipping baboons appear on the left wall [j]. On the hard-to-see entrance wall, Anubis and Isis escort Tutankhamun to receive life from Hathor [k].

Tomb of Ramses VI (#9)

£E50 from the ticket office at the entrance to the Valley of the Kings

One reason why Tut's tomb stayed hidden for so long was that it lay beneath mounds of rubble from the tomb of **Ramses VI** (c.1143–36 BC), which has been a tourist attraction since antiquity, when the Greeks called it the "Tomb of Memnon" (see p.292). The first two corridors have suffered from centuries of graffiti, but worse occurred in 1992, when the ceiling fell down and had to be glued back on in nearly one thousand pieces.

The tomb was begun by Ramses V but usurped and enlarged by his successor, whose offering of a lamp to Horus of the Horizon opens the *Book of Gates* [a], which faces other sunk-reliefs from the *Book of Caverns* [b]. Its astronomical ceiling continues through a series of corridors (note the winged sun-disc over the lintel and Ramses' cartouches on the door jambs [c]). Where the *Book of Gates* reaches the Hall of Osiris [d], a flame-breathing snake and catfish-headed gods infest the *Book of Caverns* [e]. As Re's barque approaches the Seventh Gate, beyond which twelve gods hold a rope

TOMB OF RAMSES VI

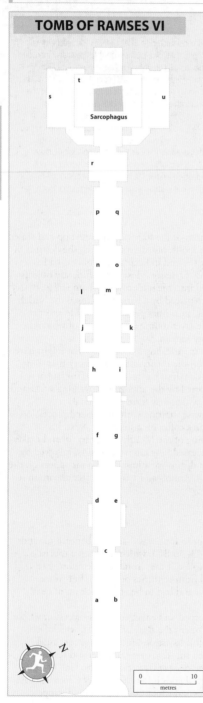

festooned with whips and heads [**f**], the *Book of Caverns* depicts a procession of *ka* figures [**g**]. From here on, the astronomical ceiling features an attenuated sky-goddess and the *Book of Day and Night*.

The eighth and ninth divisions of the *Book of Gates* [**h**] and fifth division of the *Book of Caverns* [**i**] decorate the next chamber, originally a vestibule to the hall beyond, which marked the limits of Ramses V's tomb. This contains the concluding sections of the *Book of Gates* [**j**], the seventh division of the *Book of Caverns* [**k**] and a summary of the world's creation [**l**]. The rear wall also features a scene of Ramses VI making offerings and libations to Osiris. On the pillars, he makes offerings to Khonsu, Amun-Re, Meretseger, Ptah-Sokar, Ptah and Re-Herakhte [**m**].

The descent to the next corridor is guarded by winged serpents representing the goddesses Nekhbet and Neith (left), Meretseger and Selket (right). On the corridor walls appear the introductory [**n**] and middle sections [**o**] of the *Book of Amduat*; on the ceiling, extracts from athe *Books of Re* and the *Book of Day and Night*. Scenes in the next corridor relate the fourth and fifth [**p**] and eighth to eleventh [**q**] chapters of the *Book of Amduat*. The small vestibule beyond contains texts from the *Book of Coming Forth by Day*, including the "negative confession" [**r**]. On the ceiling, Ramses sails the barques of Day and Night across the first register, while Osiris rises from his bier in the second.

Lovely back-to-back versions of the *Book of Day* and *Book of Night* adorn the ceiling of Ramses VI's burial chamber, where his image makes offerings at either end of one wall [**s**]. The rear [**t**] and right-hand walls carry portions of the *Book of Aker*, named after the earth-god of the underworld who fettered the coils of Apopis, safeguarding Re's passage. Incarnated as a ram-headed beetle, the sun-god is drawn across the heavens in his divine barque [**u**].

The king's black granite **sarcophagus** was smashed open by treasure hunters in antiquity, and his mummy left so badly damaged that the priests had to pin the body to a board to provide the remains with a decent burial in another tomb.

Tomb of Merneptah (#8)

Merneptah (c.1213–03 BC), the fourteenth son of Ramses II, didn't become pharaoh until his 50s, having outlived thirteen brothers with prior claims on the throne. On the evidence of his mummy, he was afflicted by arthritis and hardening of the arteries, and underwent dental surgery in old age. Many scholars hold, on the strength of his "Israel Stele" at Karnak and the identification of his father as the Pharaoh of the Oppression, that Merneptah was the Pharaoh of the Exodus, although this is disputed by Rohl (see p.598).

Like other tombs of the XIX Dynasty, his descends in corridors, with a total length of about 80m. In the first corridor, Merneptah is welcomed by Re-Herakhte and Khepri [a], the *Litany of Re* [b] unfolds opposite the sixteen avatars of Osiris [c], Re's barque is pulled through the underworld [d] and Nekhebkau leads his soul towards Anubis [e]. Beyond a pit watched by Thoth and Anubis [f], another corridor decorated with the *Book of Amduat* [g] leads to an antechamber with images of Osiris and Nephthys [h], and Merneptah as Imutef [i].

The next hall is a false burial chamber (a trick that seldom fooled robbers) decorated with hymns to Osiris [j] and scenes from the *Book of Gates*. Notice the binding of the Serpents of Chaos [k], a tug-of-war over a "rope" of human souls [l] and the Osirian avatars above the lintel. The final corridors are largely bare, but for the outer **lid** of Merneptah's sarcophagus – left there by thieves – and the faint image of a monkey [m].

In the real burial chamber, the gods voyage through the night across the ceiling, while murals show the metamorphosis of Khepri into Re, encircled by bird-men requesting the deceased's *ba* (soul) [n], and Khnum piloting a boat with the pharaoh's mummy floating above [o]. There is a carving of the sky-goddess Nut inside Merneptah's massive granite **sarcophagus**.

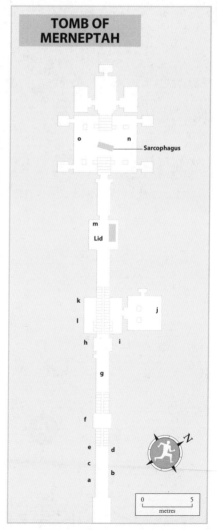

TOMB OF MERNEPTAH

Sarcophagus

Lid

0 — 5 metres

2

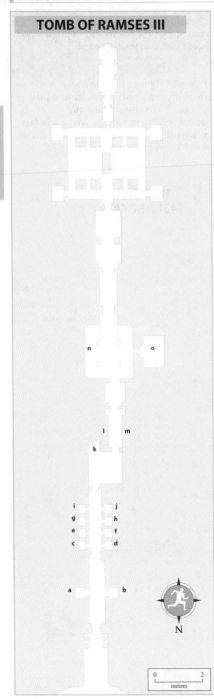

TOMB OF RAMSES III

Tomb of Ramses III (#11)

The grandest of the Ramessid tombs is that of **Ramses III**. His 31-year reign (c.1184–54 BC) marked the heyday of the XX Dynasty, whose power declined under the later Ramessids. Like his temple at Medinet Habu, the tomb harks back to the earlier glories of the New Kingdom. Uniquely for royal tombs, its colourful sunk-reliefs include scenes of everyday life. From another vignette derives its popular name, the Tomb of the Harpists.

Off the entrance corridors lie ten side chambers, originally used to store funerary objects. Within the first pair are fragmentary scenes of butchery, cooking and baking [a] and ships setting sail, those with furled sails bound downriver [b]. Next, Hapy blesses grain-gods and propitiates snake-headed Napret, with her escort of aproned *uraei* [c]. The bull of Meri (right) and the cow of Hesi (left) coexist with armoury scenes [d], while hermaphrodite deities bring offerings [e] to a treasury [f]. Ramses owns cattle and minerals [g], and from his boat inspects peasants working in the Fields of Yaru [h]. In a famous scene, two harpists sing to Shu and Atum, while Harsomtus and Anhor greet the king; the lyrics of the song cover the entrance wall [i]. The twelve forms of Osiris [j] are possibly linked to the twelve divisions of the night.

The dead-end tunnel [k] shows where diggers accidentally broke into a neighbouring tomb, at which point the original builder, Pharaoh Sethnakht, abandoned it and appropriated Tawsert's (see p.303). When construction resumed under Ramses, the tomb's axis was shifted west. The corridor has scenes from the fourth [l] and fifth [m] hours of the *Book of Amduat*. Part of the *Book of Gates* specifies four races of men: Egyptians, Asiatics, Negroes and Libyans (along the bottom) [n]. On the facing wall, the pinioned serpent Apophis is forced to disgorge the heads of his victims, in the fifth chapter of the *Book of Gates*. In the side room [o] are scenes from the *Book of Amduat.* The rest of the tomb has been barred since its ceiling fell down. Ramses III's mummy (in the Egyptian Museum) was the model for Boris Karloff's figure in the 1930s film *The Mummy.*

Tomb of Amenhotep II (#35)

One of the deepest tombs in the valley lies at the head of the wadi beyond Horemheb's tomb. Built for **Amenhotep II** (c.1427–00 BC) midway through the XVIII Dynasty, it has more than ninety steps and gets hotter and stuffier with each level you descend. When the tomb was discovered in 1898, the body of the king was still in its sarcophagus and nine other royal mummies were found stashed in another chamber. The tomb's **defences** included a deep pit (now bridged) and a false burial chamber to distract robbers from the lower levels (which would have been sealed up and disguised).

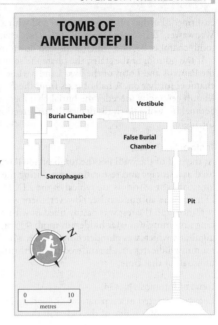

TOMB OF AMENHOTEP II

Vestibule

Burial Chamber

False Burial Chamber

Sarcophagus

Pit

0   10
metres

From a pillared vestibule, steps descend into the huge chamber. On its six square pillars, Amenhotep is embraced and offered ankhs by various gods. Beneath a star-spangled ceiling, the walls are painted pale beige and inscribed with the entire *Book of Amduat,* like a continuous scroll of papyrus. Notice the preliminary pen sketches to the left of the left-hand niche. When found in his quartzite sarcophagus (still *in situ*), the king's mummy had a floral garland around its neck. The second chamber on the right served as a **cache** for the mummies of Tuthmosis IV, Merneptah, Seti II, Ramses V and VI and Queen Tiy, after their original tombs proved insecure.

In 2006 Joann Fletcher rediscovered three mummies that had been catalogued, sealed up and forgotten in 1898. She believes that one might be the mummy of Akhenaten's queen, **Nefertiti**; a theory other Egyptologists dismiss as wishful thinking.

Tomb of Siptah (#47)

Siptah (c.1194–88 BC) was the only son of Seti II, born not of Queen Tawsert but of a Syrian concubine, Sutailja. Since he was only a boy, with an atrophied leg, Tawsert ruled as regent in alliance with an official named Bay (also of Syrian origin). After Siptah came of age, Tawsert married him; some believe that his death six years later was orchestrated by Tawsert and Bay. Siptah's tomb was usurped by a later pharaoh, its contents smashed up in antiquity, and his mummy ended up in the tomb of Amenhotep II. There it was found in 1905, when it was determined that he probably had cerebral palsy or polio as an infant. However, his tomb looks impressive, with a finely dressed Siptah mingling with the gods in the *Litany of Ra* and floating through scenes from the *Book of Amduat.*

Tomb of Tawsert/Sethnakht (#14)

Located en route to Seti II's tomb, this is unusual for having two burial chambers. It originally held the mummy of Seti's wife, Queen **Tawsert**, but was usurped by Pharaoh **Sethnakht** (c.1186–84 BC) after his own tomb (now Ramses III's) ran into difficulties. In the first corridor you find Sethnakht making offerings to Horus and Isis, and Osiris enshrined. Further on, a ram-headed god with a knife is followed by Anubis and Wepwawet. Texts from the *Book of the Dead* cover what was meant to be Tawsert's tomb chamber beyond which steps lead down towards Sethnakht's vault.

At the bottom of the stairs, the pharaoh's soul attains harmony with Maat, cherishing the Papyrus and Lotus of the Two Lands, while Anubis embalms his mummy in a side chamber further on. A hall of texts from the *Book of Caverns* and the Opening of the Mouth ceremony precedes the burial chamber, whose pillars show the gods greeting Sethnakht, while the walls depict the resurrection of Osiris and Re's journey through the night.

Tomb of Seti II (#15)

At the end of the wadi lies the tomb of **Seti II** (c.1200–1194 BC), which Arthur Mace used as a storage and restoration area during the excavation of Tutankhamun's tomb. Its long, straight corridors are typical of the XIX Dynasty, decorated with colourful scenes. Due to Seti's abrupt demise, however, there was only time to carve sunk-reliefs near the entrance, and the rest was hastily filled in with paintings or outline drawings. The king's mummy was later hidden in tomb #35 and replaced by that of an anonymous dignitary, which was plundered by thieves, who left only the sarcophagus lid. His mummy indicates that he suffered from arthritis, but had good teeth, which was unusual for that time.

Tomb of Tuthmosis III (#34)

Likewise secreted in a separate wadi, high up in a cleft, the tomb of **Tuthmosis III** (c.1479–25 BC) is one of the oldest in the valley. Its concealment and (futile) defences make this tomb especially interesting, though some are disappointed by its artwork. Having ascended a wooden stairway to the cleft, you descend through several levels, crossing a pit by footbridge to reach a vestibule. The walls depict 741 deities as stick figures, in imitation of the format used on papyrus texts from the Middle Kingdom onwards, which was favoured for murals early in the New Kingdom. Reduced to their essentials, the ramps and shafts that led into the underworld, and Khepri's role in pulling Re's barque, are clearly visible.

The unusual rounded **burial chamber** is also decorated with outline figures and symbols. Although the yellow background simulates aged papyrus, the texts were only painted after Tuthmosis had been laid to rest; there's a crossed-out mistake on the "instruction" fresco.

Elsewhere you'll notice double images (as at Abu Simbel), believed by some archeologists to have been meant to suggest motion, and others to be the result of overcarving. On one of the pillars, Tuthmosis' mother stands behind him in a barque; the register

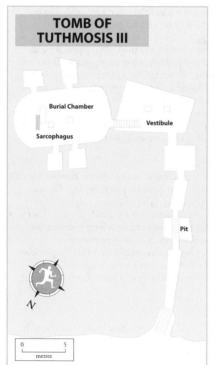

TOMB OF TUTHMOSIS III

Burial Chamber

Sarcophagus

Vestibule

Pit

N

0   5
metres

below shows three wives and a daughter, to the right of which a tree-goddess suckles the young king. By shining a torch inside the quartzite **sarcophagus**, you can admire a lovely carving of Nut, whose arms would have embraced his mummy before priests removed it to a safer hiding place near Deir el-Bahri.

Tomb of Ramses I (#16)

Buried next door to Seti I is his father, **Ramses I**, founder of the XIX Dynasty, who was not of royal blood, but the son of a commander from Avaris. During his one-year reign (c.1295–94 BC), Ramses campaigned in Asia, reopened the turquoise mines of Sinai and married Sitre, the daughter of another soldier from the eastern Delta, siring an heir to continue the dynasty. His tomb has the shortest entrance corridor of any in the valley, leading to a small, finely painted burial chamber, the colours still bright against a blue-grey background. On the left wall are nine black sarcophagi in caverns, above twelve goddesses representing the hours of the night, from the *Book of Gates*. Elsewhere, Ramses appears with Maat, Anubis, Ptah, Osiris and other deities. In 1999, the royal **mummy** was traced to the Niagara Falls Museum, where it had supposedly lain, unidentified, since it was dubiously acquired in 1850. Since being returned to Egypt in 2004, it has been in the Luxor Museum, though the SCA is not convinced that it actually is Ramses.

Tomb of Monthuhirkhopshef (#19)

Sited high up a side-wadi, this seldom-visited tomb casts light on the life of Theban princes – in this case **Monthuhirkhopshef** ("The Arm of Montu is Mighty"), a son of Ramses IX who died in his teens (c.1000 BC). Its corridor is adorned with life-sized reliefs of gods receiving offerings from the prince, who wears the blue-and-gold sidelock of youth, a finely pleated linen skirt and elaborate make-up. Eye make-up was worn by both sexes in Ancient Egypt; it's thought that some of the ingredients helped to prevent eye diseases such as glaucoma.

The Western Valley

2km by dirt road from the Valley of the Kings car park • £E25 (buy a ticket from the Valley of the Kings ticket office before setting off) • The guard with the key to Ay's tomb is in a small house a short way into the valley

The sheer cliffs and eerie silence of the **Western Valley** (Biban el-Gurud) recapture the atmosphere that pervaded the Valley of the Kings before mass tourism and modernization. Though easily reached by taxi, trail-bike or walking (2hr return from the Valley of the Kings car park), the Western Valley sees few visitors and contains only four tombs (two of them royal), of which just one is open.

Halfway up the valley lies a vast tomb (#22) built by **Amenhotep III**, whose son Akhenaten began his own tomb here before moving his capital to Tell el-Armana. Tutankhamun may also have intended to be buried in the Western Valley, but ended up in the Valley of the Kings, leaving an empty tomb to be exploited, farther up the wadi.

This **Tomb of Ay** (#23) is attributed to Tut's successor due to the cartouches in its burial chamber (the only part to be decorated). As vizier, Ay had prepared his own tomb at Tell el-Amarna (p.229), but saw the need to associate himself with earlier kings after becoming pharaoh. Ay's tomb is unique for depicting him hunting fishes, birds and hippopotami in the marshes (typical of nobles' tombs, but not royalty), but is otherwise so similar to Tutankhamun's that it's thought that both were painted by the same artist(s).

Sun Temple of Thoth

Accessible on foot or by donkey (1hr 30min–2hr) via a steep 5km path starting from near the Carter House (see p.309) • No set hours • Free

The images (and mummified remains) of baboons found in Ay's tomb are probably related to a remote **Sun Temple of Thoth** (the god of wisdom to whom baboons were sacred). Perched on a spur 400m above the Western Valley, a mud-brick structure built during the XI Dynasty overlies a stone temple from the Archaic Period – the oldest known one in Upper Egypt. This explains why the Western Valley is sometimes called the Valley of Baboons or Wadi Monkey. The Ancient Egyptians believed it was the abode of the snake-goddess Meretseger ("She who loves Silence"), the guardian of the Necropolis.

2

Deir el-Bahri (Hatshepsut's Temple)

Of all the sites on the west bank, none can match the breathtaking panache of **Deir el-Bahri**. Set amid a vast natural amphitheatre in the Theban Hills, the temple rises in terraces, the shadowed verticals of its colonnades drawing power from the massive crags overhead. Its ramps and courts look modern in their stark simplicity, but in ancient times would have been softened and perfumed by gardens of fragrant trees. The reliefs that cover its colonnades and chapels bespeak of an extraordinary woman, one of the most successful rulers of the XVIII Dynasty (see box below).

Deir el-Bahri (Northern Monastery) is the Arabic name for the **Mortuary Temple of Hatshepsut**, which she herself called **Djeser Djeseru**, the "Splendour of Splendours". Unlike other royal mortuary temples, built on the flood-plain, it was never covered by sand and silt, and has always been the most prominent feature of the Theban Necropolis.

In 1997 Deir el-Bahri tragically made headlines around the world when 58 tourists and four guards were shot or stabbed to death by Islamist terrorists on the temple's Middle Terrace. The day is still remembered on the west bank, especially by the donkey guides who witnessed the **massacre** from the clifftop above.

GETTING AROUND AND INFORMATION   DEIR EL-BAHRI

For information on transport to the Deir el-Bahri, see "Getting to the Theban Necropolis" (p.287).

Opening hours Daily 6am–5pm.
Tickets Tickets (£E30) are sold near the visitors' centre.
Visitors centre The visitors' centre (daily 6am–5pm) is near

the Deir el-Bahri ticket office, beyond the coach park, and features a model of Hatshepsut's temple and the adjacent mortuary temples of Mentuhotpe II and Tuthmosis II.

HATSHEPSUT

Hatshepsut (pronounced "Hat-Cheap-Suit") was not the first woman to rule Egypt – there were female regents during the I, III and VI dynasties – but the length of her reign (c.1473–58 BC) was unprecedented. A daughter of Tuthmosis I, married to his successor Tuthmosis II, Hatshepsut was widowed before she could bear a son. Refusing relegation in favour of a secondary wife who had produced an heir, she made herself co-regent to the young Tuthmosis III and assumed absolute power seven years later.

To legitimize her position, she was depicted in masculine form, wearing a pharaoh's kilt and beard; yet her authority ultimately depended on personal willpower and the devotion of her favourite courtier, **Senenmut**, who rose from humble birth to the stewardship of Amun's estates.

Assisted by Senenmut and her father's architect, Ineni, Hatshepsut commissioned numerous construction projects, from her own mortuary temple to the restoration of the Precinct of Mut at Karnak. Trade flourished during her reign, epitomized by a state-sponsored expedition to the Land of Punt (thought to be modern-day Somalia) which returned with myrrh trees, incense and several Puntites, who became part of her entourage at court.

When **Tuthmosis III** came into his inheritance after her death, he concealed her obelisks at Karnak and later defaced many of her cartouches on monuments, relegating her status to that of regent. This asserted an unbroken chain of succession through the male line, and removed the possibility that her reign might create a precedent. However, Egyptologists deride the notion that Tuthmosis harboured a grudge against his aunt, since he loyally served her as commander of the army, without attempting to use his position to stage a coup against her.

HIKING ACROSS THE HILLS TO DEIR EL-BAHRI

Hiking from the Valley of the Kings over the Theban Hills to Hatshepsut's temple affords a stunning **view** of the Necropolis receding towards the Nile. The fifty-minute hike is easiest in the winter months (over summer, you must start early in the day), and requires a head for heights. Wear a hat and carry plenty of water; walking shoes and sun-cream are also essential. The **trail** starts by the tomb of Seti I (#17), rising steeply for several hundred metres before levelling out and ascending gradually. Donkey-guides and souvenir-vendors will offer assistance, but the route is fairly clear. Where it forks, follow the left-hand track along a flat ridge, before crossing it to behold the Nile Valley. Directly beneath the sheer cliff lies Hatshepsut's temple; to see it, walk right for a bit before peering carefully over the edge. To descend, follow the path alongside a wire fence till you reach a crag where the trail divides. Ignore anyone who tries to lure you down the steepest trail to render "help" for baksheesh – the left-hand path is the one to take, curving around the hillside as it descends to the ticket office for Deir el-Bahri.

The Lower Terrace

In ancient times an avenue of sphinxes probably ran from the Nile to the temple's **Lower Terrace**, which was planted with myrrh trees and cooled by fountains (the stumps of two 3500-year-old trees remain near the final barrier). At the top and bottom of the ramp to the next level were carved pairs of lions (one of each is still visible). Before ascending the ramp, check out its flanking **colonnades**, whose reliefs were defaced by Tuthmosis III, and later by Akhenaten. While Hatshepsut's image remains obliterated, those of Amun were restored after the Theban counter-revolution. Behind the northern colonnade (right of the ramp) can be seen a cow-herd, wildfowl and a papyrus swamp; reliefs in the southern (left) colonnade show the transport by river of two obelisks from Aswan – doubtless the pair that Hatshepsut erected at Karnak.

The **Middle Terrace** once also boasted myrrh trees, acquired from the Land of Punt in an expedition that's depicted along one of the square-pillared colonnades flanking the central ramp to the uppermost level.

The Birth Colonnade

To the right of the ramp is the so-called **Birth Colonnade**, whose faint reliefs assert Hatshepsut's divine parentage. Starting from nearest the ramp, its rear walls show Amun (in the guise of Tuthmosis I) and her mother Queen Ahmosis (seated on a couch), their knees touching. Next, bizarre deities lead the queen into the birth chamber, where the god Khnum fashions Hatshepsut and her *ka* (both represented as boys) on his potter's wheel. Her birth is attended by Bes and the frog deity Heqet; goddesses nurse her, while Thoth records details of her reign. The sensitive expressions and delicate modelling convey a sincerity that transcends mere political expediency.

At the far end of the colonnade, steps lead down into a **Chapel of Anubis** with fluted columns and colourful murals. Tuthmosis III and a falcon-headed sun-god appear over the niche to the right; a yellow-skinned Hathor on the facing wall; offerings by Hatshepsut and Tuthmosis to Anubis on the other walls. As elsewhere, the images of Hatshepsut were defaced in the latter years of Tuthmosis III's reign. Notice the friezes of cobras in the central, barrel-vaulted shrine.

The Punt Colonnade

On the other side of the ramp is the famous **Punt Colonnade**, relating Hatshepsut's journey to that land. Though others had visited Punt to obtain precious myrrh for temple incense, Hatshepsut sought living trees to plant outside her temple. Alas, the faintness of the reliefs (behind a guard-rail) makes it difficult to follow the story as it

2

unfolds (from left to right). The Egyptian flotilla sails from the Red Sea Coast, to be welcomed by the king of Punt and his wife. In exchange for metal axes and other goods, the Egyptians depart with myrrh trees and resin, ebony, ivory and panther skins; baboons play in the ships' rigging. Back home, the spoils are dedicated to Amun and the precious myrrh trees bedded in the temple gardens.

The Punt Colonnade leads into a larger **Chapel of Hathor**, whose face and sistrum (sacred rattle) form the capitals of the square pillars. In the first, roofless, pillared chamber, the goddess appears in her bovine and human forms, and suckles Hatshepsut (whose image has not been defaced here) on the left-hand wall.

The next chamber features delicate reliefs of festival processions (still quite freshly coloured) on the right-hand wall. Peering into the gated sanctuary, you can just about make out another intact Hatshepsut worshipping the divine cow (left), and an alcove (right) containing a **portrait of Senenmut**, which would have been hidden when the doors were open. Apocryphally, it was this humble claim to be recognized within the pharaoh's temple that caused his downfall. After fifteen years of closeness to Hatshepsut and her daughter Neferure (evinced by a statue in the Egyptian Museum, which some regard as proof of paternity), Senenmut abruptly vanished from the records late in her reign.

When archeologists excavated the sanctuary in the early twentieth century they found it stacked with baskets full of wooden phalluses, seemingly used in fertility rituals.

The Upper Terrace

Reached by a ramp with falcon statues at the bottom, the **Upper Terrace** has emerged from decades of research and restoration work by Polish and Egyptian teams. Eight giant statues of Osiris front its portico and a red granite portal into a courtyard flanked by colonnades and sanctuaries. Bodyguards and oarsmen rowing the royal barque are depicted on the inside wall to the left as you enter. On the far wall are eight niches for votive statues, carved with hieroglyphs that rival the delicacy of Seti's reliefs at Abydos.

You can peep into (but not enter) the **Sanctuary of Amun**, dug into the cliff aligned towards Hatshepsut's tomb in the Valley of the Kings on the other side of the mountain. In Ptolemaic times the sanctuary was extended and dedicated to Imhotep and Amenhotep, the quasi-divine counsellors of pharaohs Zoser and Amenhotep III. Beneath it lies another burial chamber for Hatshepsut, presumably favoured over her pro forma tomb in the Valley of the Kings, since it was dug at a later date.

Other temples near Deir el-Bahri

From the heights of Hatshepsut's temple you can gaze southwards over the ruins of two similar edifices beneath the cliffs. The **Mortuary Temple of Tuthmosis III** was long ago destroyed by a landslide, but a painted relief excavated here can be seen in the Luxor Museum.

More remains of the far older **Temple of Mentuhotpe II**, the first pharaoh to choose burial in Thebes (XI Dynasty). Unlike his XVIII Dynasty imitators, Mentuhotpe was actually buried in his mortuary temple; his funerary statue is now exhibited in the Egyptian Museum in Cairo.

How much may still lie undiscovered is suggested by the **Tomb of Montemhat**, mayor of Thebes under Amenhotep II. Presently being excavated, it has a courtyard as big as a tennis court, flanked by giant carvings of heraldic plants, visible 20m beneath the desert's surface – be careful peering over the edge of the pit. You can see a long underground ramp leading to the tomb beside the tuf-tuf terminus of Hatshepsut's temple.

Dra' Abul Naga, the Carter House and the Temple of Seti I

Visible en route to the Valley of the Kings and Deir el-Bahri, **DRA' ABUL NAGA** is a village whose **alabaster workshops** produce the statues and ashtrays sold in tourist shops throughout Egypt. Many of the workshops have garishly painted facades to

---

THE ROYAL CACHE

Whereas Mentuhotpe's remains weren't discovered till modern times, many of the New Kingdom royal tombs were despoiled soon after their burial in the Valley of the Kings. Towards the end of the XXI Dynasty, priests hid forty mummies in a **secret cache** in a hollow to the south above Mentuhotpe's temple, which the villagers of Gurna found in 1875 and quietly sold off for years until rumbled by the authorities, who forced them to reveal the cache's location. Amongst the mummies recovered were Amenhotep I, Tuthmosis II and III, Seti I and Ramses II and III. As the steamer bore them downriver to Cairo, villagers lined the banks, wailing in sorrow or firing rifles in homage – a haunting scene in Shady Abdel Salem's film *The Mummy*, a classic of Egyptian cinema (1975). The royal cache is **not open** to visitors.

---

attract visitors, and if you're curious to see how alabaster is worked, this is the place to look. Otherwise, the village is notable for two tombs in the vicinity.

Tombs of Roy and Shuroy

5km from Gezira • £E15 from the main ticket office (see p.291)

Signposted by the main road beyond Dra' Abul Naga, both these tombs feature remarkably fresh colours. High priest **Roy** from the time of Horemheb has a small rectangular tomb (#255), whose scenes of wailing mourners, sacrificial bulls and funerary offerings are offset by a ceiling checkered with yellow, red, black and white crosses. His near namesake **Shuroy** was a brazier-bearer at Amun's temple during the XIX Dynasty and has a larger T-shaped tomb (#13). Here, the murals are fragmentary or merely sketched in, though there's a fine frieze of dwarfs along the top of the wall to the left inside the transverse hall.

Carter House

Daily 6am–5pm • £E25; tickets sold at the main ticket office (see p.291).

Conspicuously sited on a low ridge overlooking the road to the Valley of the Kings, the **Carter House** is an evocative museum dedicated to the British Egyptologist Howard Carter (1874–1939), who lived here during his five-year search for Tutankamun's tomb (see p.298) and its subsequent excavation.

Simple to modern eyes, the mud-brick house features such Edwardian comforts as a gramophone and a kitchen with a bottled-gas stove; a spare bedroom for Carter's patron Lord Canarvon and his daughters; and a tiny photographer's darkroom used for recording artefacts. You can see Carter's shaving mug, sun-parasols and the magnifying glass with which he pored over excavation plans, seeking clues to the tomb's whereabouts.

A documentary **film** about his discovery of the tomb may be seen if the TV (removed for safety after the Revolution) has been replaced, but the SCA's plan to construct life-size **replicas of the royal tombs** nearby – starting with Tutankhamun's and Seti I's – has been indefinitely put on hold (see p.295).

The **Stoppelaer House**, further uphill, is another former archeological dig-house. German, Polish and French Egyptological missions each have their own houses in the Necropolis, where they live during the winter excavation season.

Temple of Seti I

7.5km from Gezira • Daily 6am–5pm • £E30 from the main ticket office (see p.291)

While nothing remains of the temples of Tuthmosis IV, Tuthmosis II, Ay and Horemheb that once extended towards Medinet Habu, there is a substantial **Temple of Seti I** near Gurna Ta'rif, at the opposite end of the Necropolis. This is the only temple in Egypt where the future Ramses II is depicted as a prince, wearing a tiger-skin tunic and kneeling before his father, Seti – although its reliefs are far inferior to those in Seti's temple at Abydos (see p.245).

2

The Asasif Tombs

6km from Gezira • Daily 6am–5pm • £E30 from the main ticket office (see p.291)

Midway between Deir el-Bahri and the Tombs of the Nobles lies a burial ground known as the **Asasif Tombs**, currently being studied by several archeological teams. While some of its 35 tomb chapels date from the XVIII Dynasty, the majority are from the Late Period (XXV–XXVI Dynasty), when Thebes was ruled by Nubian kings, and then from the Delta.

The most likely to be open is the **Tomb of Pabasa (#279)**, the steward to a Divine Votaress of Amun during the XXVI Dynasty. His tomb reflects the Saïte Dynasty obsession with the Old Kingdom, having a similar design to tombs at Saqqara. Its massive gateway leads into a pillared court with scenes of hunting, fishing and viticulture (note the bee-keeping scene on the central column). A funeral procession and the voyage to Abydos appear in the vestibule.

Also worth noting is the **Tomb of Kheru-ef (#192)**, a steward of Queen Tiy during the Amarna period. His scenes depict a Jubilee Festival, Tiy and Amenhotep III, musicians, dancers and playful animals – as lyrical as those in Ramose's tomb (see p.311).

Gurna

Beyond the Asasif Tombs, the barren, windswept foothills are pockmarked with traces of **GURNA** (often spelt "Qurna" but pronounced with a "G"). For generations this ramshackle village supplied the workforce for archeological digs while quietly **robbing tombs** beneath its own homes. The authorities finally bulldozed the entire village in 2007 under UNESCO's masterplan, compelling its inhabitants to move to the purpose-built settlement of Gurna Jedid.

The wasteland at the crossroads near Gurna Ta'rif is the site for the annual **Moulid of Abu Qusman**, commemorating a local holy man known for his outspokenness (lambasting tourists on the ferry for their immodest attire) and miracles (crossing the Nile on a hankerchief), who died in 1984. The festival is held on the 27th day of the Islamic month of Sha'ban.

Tombs of the Nobles

4–5 km from Gezira • Daily 6am–5pm • Tickets, from the main ticket office (see p.291), cover whichever pairs of tombs are currently accessible, such as Userhat and Ramose (£E30), or Nakht and Menna (£E25), although the exact tombs which are open to visitors is subject to change

The **Tombs of the Nobles** are a study in contrasts to their royal counterparts. Whereas royalty favoured concealed tombs in secluded valleys, Theban nobles and high officials were ostentatiously interred in the limestone foothills overlooking the great funerary temples of their masters. The pharaohs' tombs were sealed and guarded; the nobles' were left open for their descendants to make funerary offerings. Whereas royal tombs are filled with scenes of judgement and resurrection, the nobles' chosen artwork dwells on earthly life and its continuation in the hereafter. Given more freedom of expression, the artists excelled themselves with vivid **paintings** on stucco (the inferior limestone on this side of the hills militates against carved reliefs).

The **tombs' layout** marks a further evolution in funerary architecture since the Middle Kingdom tombs of Beni Hassan. Most are entered via a courtyard, with a transverse hall preceding the burial shrine with its niche containing an effigy of the deceased (or statues of his entire family). Strictly speaking, they are tomb chapels rather than tombs, since the graves themselves lie at the bottom of a shaft (usually inaccessible).

There are four clusters of tombs ranged across an area once occupied by Old Gurna, namely: **Rekhmire and Sennofer**; **Ramose, Userhat and Khaemhat**; **Nakht and Menna**; and **Khonsu, Userhet and Benia**. The first two lie furthest west and back from the road; the next trio downhill towards the Ramesseum; and the last two sets of tombs to the northeast, closer to Deir el-Bahri.

Tomb of Rekhmire (#100)

The richly decorated tomb of **Rekhmire** casts light on statecraft and foreign policy under Tuthmosis III and Amenhotep II, whom Rekhmire served as vizier. The badly damaged murals in its transverse hall show him collecting taxes from Upper [a] and Lower [b] Egypt, and inspecting temple workshops, charioteers and agricultural work [c]. Around the corner from his ancestors [d], grapes are trod in large tubs and the juice is strained and stored in jars [e].

TOMB OF REKHMIRE

Along the rear wall are depicted a desert hunt [f] and a famous scene of Rekhmire receiving tributes from foreign lands [g]. Among the gifts shown are vases from Crete and the Aegean Islands (fourth row); a giraffe, monkeys and elephant tusks from Punt and Nubia (third row); and chariots and horses from Syria (second row).

Growing in height as it recedes towards the false door at the back, the long corridor is decorated with scenes of work and daily life. Slaves store grain in silos [h], whence it was later disbursed as wages to armourers, carpenters, sculptors and other state-employed craftsmen [i]. An idealized banqueting scene with female musicians [j] merges into an afterworld with a lake and trees [k]. Also note Rekhmire's funeral procession and offerings to sustain him in the afterlife [l].

Tomb of Sennofer (#96)

From Rekhmire's tomb, slog 50m uphill to the left to find another colourful tomb, in better condition. Entered by a low, twisting stairway, the tomb of **Sennofer** is known as the "Tomb of Vines" after the grapes and vines painted on the textured ceiling of the antechamber. As mayor of Thebes and overseer of Amun's estates under Amenhotep II, Sennofer had local viticulture among his responsibilities. The walls of the burial shrine depict his funeral procession (left), voyage to Abydos (back, right) and mummified sojourn with Anubis (right). Its square pillars bear images of Hathor, whose eyes follow you around the room. A small tree-goddess appears on the inner side of the rear left-hand pillar.

Tomb of Ramose (#55)

Down a dirt road to the southeast lies the tomb of **Ramose**, who was vizier and governor of Thebes immediately before and after the Amarna revolution. His spacious tomb captures the moment of transition from Amun- to Aten-worship, featuring both classical and Amarna-style reliefs, the latter unfinished since Ramose followed Akhenaten to his new capital. Besides its superb reliefs, the tomb is notable for retaining its courtyard – originally a feature of all these tombs.

Along the entrance wall of its pillared hall are lovely carvings that reflect the mellowing of classicism during the reign of Amenhotep III, Akhenaten's father.

2

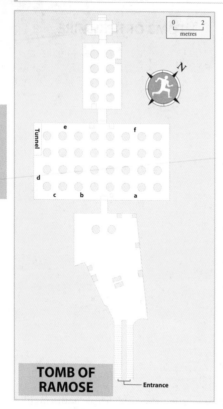

0 — 2
metres

N

Tunnel

e   f

d

c   b   a

TOMB OF RAMOSE

Entrance

Predictable scenes of Ramose and his wife [a], Amenhotep III and Queen Tiy [b] making offerings come alive thanks to the exquisite rendering of the major figures, carried over to their feasting friends and relatives [c]. The sinuous swaying of mourners likewise imparts lyricism to the conventional, painted funerary scene [d], where Ramose, wife and priests worship Osiris.

The onset of Aten-worship and the Amarna style is evident in the reliefs at the back, despite their battered condition. Those on the left [e] were carved before Amenhotep IV changed his name to Akhenaten and espoused Aten-worship, so the pharaoh sits beneath a canopy with Maat, the goddess of truth, receiving flowers from Ramose. (At the far end, note the red grid and black outlined figures by which the artist transferred his design to the wall before relief-cutting took place.) However, the corresponding scene [f] depicts the pharaoh as Akhenaten, standing with Nefertiti at their palace window, bathed in the Aten's rays. Ramose is sketched in below, accepting their gift of a golden chain; his physiognomy is distinctly Amarnan, but rather less exaggerated than the royal couple's (see p.228).

Tomb of Userhat (#56)

Immediately south of Ramose's tomb lies that of **Userhat**, a royal scribe and tutor in the reign of Amenhotep II. Although some of the figures were destroyed by early Christian hermits who occupied the shrine, what remains is freshly coloured, with unusual pink tones. The tomb is also interesting in that it's still illuminated by means of a mirror reflecting sunlight inside, just as it was when the artists decorated the tomb.

Along the entrance wall of the antechamber are scenes of wine-making, harvesting, herding and branding cattle, collecting grain for the royal storehouse [a], and the customary offerings scenes [b]. On the rear wall are reliefs of baking, assaying gold dust and – lower down – a barber trimming customers beneath a tree [c]. The funerary feast scene [d] was extensively damaged by hermits, particularly the female figures. The inner hall contains paintings of Userhat hunting gazelles, hares and jackals from a chariot in the desert [e]; fowling and fishing amid the reeds [f]; and funerary scenes [g]. In a niche at the end is a headless statue of the deceased's wife.

Tomb of Khaemhat (#57)

Next door is the tomb of **Khaemhat**, royal scribe and inspector of granaries under Amenhotep III, which is reached via a forecourt off which two other tombs, now locked, once led. Flanking its doorway outside are battered reliefs of Khaemhat worshipping Re, and the complete set of instruments for the Opening of the Mouth ceremony (right). In the transverse antechamber with its red and black patterned ceiling, the best reliefs are on the left as you enter. Although Renenet the snake-headed harvest-goddess has almost vanished, a scene of grain boats docking at Thebes harbour is still visible nearer the niche containing statues of Khaemhat and Imhotep. In the bottom row to the left of the door into the corridor, Hathor breastfeeds a boy-king, surrounded by sacred cows.

Fishing, fowling and family scenes decorate the right-hand wall of the corridor, leading to a triple-niched chapel containing seated statues of Khaemhat and his family.

Tomb of Nakht (#52)

Northeast of Ramose's tomb lies the burial place of **Nakht**, whose antechamber contains a small museum with drawings of the reliefs (which are covered in glass) and a replica of

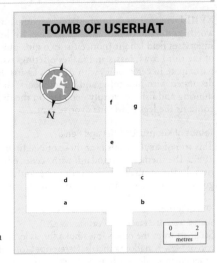

TOMB OF USERHAT

Nakht's funerary statue, which was lost at sea en route to America in 1917. Nakht was the overseer of Amun's vineyards and granaries under Tuthmosis IV, and the royal astronomer, but stargazing does not feature among the activities depicted in his tomb. The only decorated section is the transverse antechamber, whose ceiling is painted to resemble woven mats, with a geometric frieze running above the brilliantly coloured murals.

To one side, Nakht supervises the harvest in a scene replete with vivid details **[a]**. In the bottom register, one farmer fells a tree, while another swigs from a waterskin; of the two women gleaning in the row above, one is missing an arm. Beyond a stele relating

Nakht's life **[b]** is the famous banqueting scene **[c]**, where sinuous dancers and a blind harpist entertain friends of the deceased, who sits beside his wife, Tawi, with a cat scoffing a fish beneath his chair; sadly, their figures have been erased.

The defacement of Nakht's image and Amun's name is usually ascribed to Amarna iconoclasm, but the gouging out of his eyes and throwing sticks in the hunting scene **[d]** suggests a personal animus. Happily, this has not extended to the images in the corner **[e]**, where peasants tread grapes in vats, and birds are caught in clap-nets and hung for curing (below). The plain inner chamber has a false door painted to resemble Aswan granite, and a deep shaft leading to the (inaccessible) burial chamber.

Tomb of Menna (#69)

More scenes of rural life decorate the nearby tomb of **Menna**, an

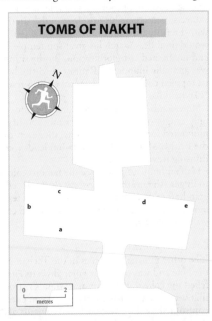

TOMB OF NAKHT

2

XVIII Dynasty inspector of estates. Accompanied by his wife and daughter, Menna worships the sun in the entrance passage. In the left wing of the first chamber, he supervises field labour (notice the two girls pulling each other's hair, near the far end of the third row), feasts and makes offerings with his wife. Across the way they participate in ceremonies with Anubis, Osiris, Re and Hathor. Though chiefly decorated with mourning and burial scenes, the inner chamber also features a spot of hunting and fishing, vividly depicted on the right-hand wall. The niche at the end contains the legs of Menna's votive statue.

Tombs of Khonsu, Userhet and Benia

This trio of small tombs near those of Nakht and Menna was opened to the public in 1992. The themes are standard, with scenes of offerings, hunting, fishing and funerary rites. In the tomb of Userhet (not to be confused with the Userhat in tomb #56), the guard may produce a mummified head for baksheesh.

Khoka Tombs

5km from Gezira • £E25 from the main ticket office (see p.291)

Set apart from the others, the **Khoka** (or, as locals say, "Hookah") tombs were built for a trio of New Kingdom officials. **Neferonpet** (or Kenro) was a treasury scribe; the tomb's inner chamber depicts him assessing deliveries of gold and food, and the work of sculptors and weavers. The golden-yellow, red and blue murals, the brightly patterned ceilings and the votive statues of the deceased and his wives (badly disfigured) are also characteristic of the tomb of **Nefersekheru**, next door. Here, the wives enjoy greater prominence, flanking Nefersekheru pictorially (to the right as you enter) and sculpturally (in niches), and known to posterity as Maatmou, Sekhemui and Nefertari. Their mummies were buried in a shaft off the rear corridor, which leads into the adjacent tomb of Dhutmosi (now inaccessible).

The Ramesseum

4.5km from Gezira • Daily 6am–5pm • £E35 from the main ticket office (see p.291)

The **Ramesseum** or mortuary temple of Ramses II was built to awe the pharaoh's subjects, perpetuate his existence in the afterlife and forever link him to Amun-United-with-Eternity (one of Amun's many avatars). Had it remained intact, the Ramesseum would doubtless match his great sun temple of Abu Simbel for monumental grandeur and unabashed self-glorification. But by siting it beside an earlier temple on land that was annually inundated, Ramses unwittingly ensured the ruination of his monument; its toppled colossi would later mock his presumption, inspiring Shelley's sonnet "Ozymandias".

Nineteenth-century writers knew the ruins as the Memnonium. Their present name only caught on late in the nineteenth century, by which time the Ramesseum had been plundered for statuary – not least the seven-ton head of one of its fallen colossi, now in the British Museum. Its devastation lends romance to the conventional architecture, infusing it with pathos.

Half an hour suffices to see the famous colossi and the best reliefs, but you may care to linger. The nearby *Ramesseum Resthouse* sells cold drinks and hot meals; the owner's grandfather, Sheikh Hussein Abdul, was a teaboy at Carter's excavation in 1922, famously photographed wearing a jewelled collar from Tut's tomb (a copy hangs on the wall inside the resthouse).

Colossi of Ramses II

Like other mortuary temples in the Theban Necropolis, the Ramesseum faces towards the Nile and was originally entered via its **First Pylon**. Wrecked by the earthquake that felled the colossi, the pylon now stands marooned in the scrub beyond a depression that was once the **First Court**. Today, you enter the temple via its **Second Court**, to be confronted by the awesome **fallen colossus of Ramses II**. This seated megalith once

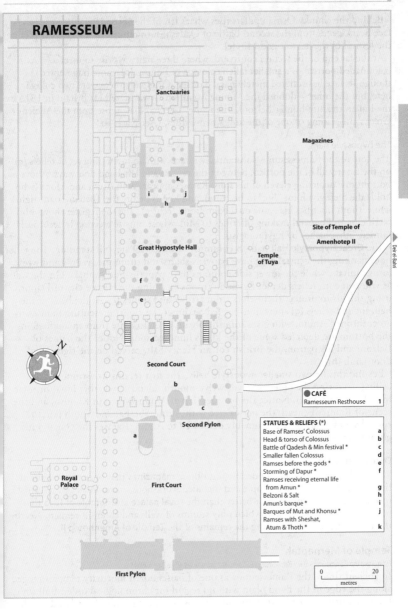

RAMESSEUM

Sanctuaries

Magazines

k

i j

h

g

Great Hypostyle Hall

Site of Temple of

Amenhotep II

Temple of Tuya

Deir el-Bahri

f

e

d

Second Court

b

c

Second Pylon

● **CAFÉ**
Ramesseum Resthouse   1

a

STATUES & RELIEFS (*)

Base of Ramses' Colossus	a
Head & torso of Colossus	b
Battle of Qadesh & Min festival *	c
Smaller fallen Colossus	d
Ramses before the gods *	e
Storming of Dapur *	f
Ramses receiving eternal life from Amun *	g
Belzoni & Salt	h
Amun's barque *	i
Barques of Mut and Khonsu *	j
Ramses with Sheshat, Atum & Thoth *	k

Royal Palace

First Court

First Pylon

0   20
metres

towered over the stairs from the first into the second court [**a**]; over 18m tall and weighing about 1000 tons, it was only surpassed by the Colossi of Memnon thanks to their pedestals. When it toppled some time after the first century AD, its upper half smashed through the Second Pylon into the court, where its head and torso lie today [**b**], measuring 7m across the shoulders; the cartouche on its bicep reads: "Ruler of Rulers". In the lower court are other fragments, notably feet and hands.

Behind the chunky Osirian pillars rises what's left of the **Second Pylon**, whose inner face bears scenes from the second Battle of Qadesh, surmounted by a register depicting the festival of the harvest-god Min [c].

At the far end of the second courtyard, where three stairways rise to meet a colonnaded portico, is a **smaller fallen colossus** of Ramses [d], more fragmented, though its face has suffered merely nasal damage. Originally there were two colossi here, but the other – dubbed the "Young Memnon" – was seized for Britain in 1816 by the Italian treasure-hunter Belzoni. The name "Ozymandias" arose from the Ancient Greeks' misreading of one of the king's many titles, User-Maat-Re.

The hypostyle halls

The core of the Ramesseum is substantially intact, with an interesting set of reliefs [e] on the front wall of the **portico**, between the central and left-hand doorways. Above a bottom row depicting eleven of his sons, Ramses appears with Atum and Mont (who holds the hieroglyph for "life" to his nose), and kneels before the Theban Triad (right) while Thoth inscribes his name on a palm frond (centre). The top register shows him sacrificing to Ptah and making offerings to Min, whose outsize erection is decorously termed "ithyphallic" by Egyptologists.

The **Great Hypostyle Hall** had 48 columns, of which 29 are still standing. The taller ones flanking the central aisle have papyrus shafts and turquoise, yellow and white lotus capitals, while the lower side columns have papyrus-bud capitals. On the wall as you come in, reliefs depict Egyptian troops storming the Hittite city of Dapur, using shields to protect themselves from arrows and stones [f]. At the back of the hall, incised reliefs [g] show lion-headed Sekhmet (far right) presenting Ramses to an enthroned Amun, who gives him the breath of eternal life from an ankh; along the bottom are depicted some of the king's hundred sons. Notice the names of Belzoni and his patron, the British consul Henry Salt, carved on the right-hand door jamb [h].

Beyond this lie two **smaller hypostyle halls**. The first retains its astronomical ceiling, featuring the oldest known twelve-month calendar (whether lunar or solar months is debatable). Notice the barques [i, j] of Amun, Mut and Khonsu, and the scene of Ramses beneath the persea tree with Atum, Sheshat and Thoth [k]. The ruined **sanctuaries** were presumably dedicated to Amun, Ramses the god and his glorious ancestors.

Outlying structures

The whole complex is surrounded by mud-brick **magazines** that once covered about three times the area of the temple and included workshops, storerooms and servants' quarters, that have survived far better than the **royal palace** and **Temple of Tuya** that once adjoined the temple, of which only stumps of walls and columns remain. Nearby, the Italian mission is excavating the remains of the **Temple of Amenhotep II**.

Temple of Merneptah

100m from the Ramesseum • Daily 6am–5pm • £E20 from the main ticket office (see p.291)

In ancient times, the Ramesseum was one of half a dozen mortuary temples ranged along the edge of the flood plain with no regard for chronological order. Built by Ramses' thirteenth or fourteenth son (supposedly the pharaoh of the Exodus), the **Temple of Merneptah** intruded onto the edges of, and reused masonry from, the vast complex of Amenhotep III that once spread to the Colossi of Memnon. The site consists of fragments of the temple, placed in their original positions and supported by modern stonework; its entrance represents the original position of the first pylon.

A **museum** created by the Swiss Institute features plans and finds from the excavation which help you make sense of what little remains. Further in, to the left, stands a copy of the famous **Israel Stele** now in the Egyptian Museum, which was found here by Flinders Petrie in 1896. Visitors can also see a dozen jackal-headed sphinxes originally taken from Amenhotep's III's temple, and other statues pilfered from Deir el-Bahri in a covered storage area that was once the temple's sacred lake.

Deir el-Medina

3.5km from Gezira • Daily 6am–5pm • £E30 from the main ticket office (see p.291) • No photography

Deir el-Medina, the **Workers' Village**, housed the masons, painters and sculptors who created the royal tombs in the Valley of the Kings. Because many were literate and left records on papyrus or *ostraca*, we know such details as who feuded with whom, their sex lives and labour disputes. As state employees, they were supposed to receive fortnightly supplies of foodstuffs and beer, but when these failed to arrive (as often happened during the ramshackle XX Dynasty), the workers downed tools, staged sit-ins at Medinet Habu, or demonstrated in Luxor.

Normally they worked an eight-hour day, sleeping in huts near the tombs during their ten-day shift before returning to their families at Deir el-Medina. In their spare time craftsmen worked for private clients or collaborated on their own tombs, built beneath man-size pyramids. Their own murals appropriated imagery from royal and noble tombs, which was parodied in the famous *Satirical Papyrus*, showing animals judging souls, collecting taxes and playing *senet* (an Ancient Egyptian board game), and humans having sex.

Tombs of Sennedjem (#1) and Ankherha (#359)

The pyramid nearest to the entrance marks the **Tomb of Sennedjem** (or Sennutem), whose vaulted burial chamber is reached by steep flights of steps and two antechambers. Its colourful murals feature ithyphallic baboons (right-end wall), Osiris and the Fields of Yaru, and Anubis ministering to Sennedjem's mummy (facing wall, far left).

The **Tomb of Ankherha** has a similar design: on the left wall of the burial chamber, Ankherha appears with Wepwawet and Khepri; Anubis breathes life into his mummy; his wife adores Horus as a falcon; and his naked daughters make libations.

Tomb of Peshedu (#3)

£E15; requires a separate ticket from the main ticket office (see p.291)

In the **Tomb of Peshedu** one can see the deceased praying beneath the tree of regeneration, below which flow the waters of the Amuntit, the "Hidden Region" where souls were judged. Yellow, black and red are the predominant colours. Peshedu was a stonemason, who may have served as a foreman under Seti I and Ramses II.

Tombs of Iphy (#217) and Iri Nefer (#290)

Unusually for Deir el-Medina, the **Tomb of Iphy**, a sculptor during the reign of Ramses II, eschews ceremonial scenes and deities for tableaux from everyday life. Men fish with a net among lotus plants, as Iphy and his dog draw water from a shaduf (a counter-weighted device introduced to Egypt by its Hyksos invaders).

The nearby **Tomb of Iri Nefer** isn't officially open, but might be viewable for baksheesh. Beautifully decorated with scenes on a yellow background, it features a frieze with baboons and cobras interspersed by a feather, symbol of the goddess Maat.

Ptolemaic temple

Near the village stands a semi-ruined **Ptolemaic temple** dedicated to Maat and Hathor, whose head adorns the pillars between the outer court and *naos*. Each of its three shrines is decorated with scenes from the *Book of the Dead*. Early in the Christian era, the temple and the workers' village were occupied by monks – hence the site's Arabic name of Deir el-Medina (Monastery of the Town).

2

The Valley of the Queens

5km from Gezira • Daily 6am–5pm • £E30 from the Valley of the Queens' ticket office (see p.291)

The **Valley of the Queens** is something of a misnomer, as it also contains the tombs of high officials (interred long before the first queen was buried here during the XIX Dynasty) and royal children. Princes were educated by priests and scribes, taught swimming, riding and shooting by officers, and finally apprenticed to military commands around the age of 12. Less is known about the schooling of princesses, but several queens were evidently well versed in statecraft and architecture.

Originally named the "Place of Beauty", but now known in Arabic as Biban el-Harem (Gates of the Harem), the valley contains nearly eighty tombs, most of which are basically just pits in the ground. Although the finest murals rival those in the Valley of the Kings for artistry, many have been corroded by salt deposits or badly vandalized, and the magnificent **tomb of Nefertari** is so fragile that it is only accessible to VIP groups.

Tomb of Amunhirkhepshef (#55)

After Nefertari's, the best tomb in the valley belongs to **Amunhirkhepshef**, a son of Ramses III who accompanied his father on campaigns and perhaps died in battle at the age of 9. He is shown wearing the royal sidelock of youth, in lustrous murals where Ramses conducts him through funerary rituals, past the Keepers of the Gates, to an unfinished burial chamber containing a granite sarcophagus. A glass case displays a mummified foetus that his mother aborted through grief at Amunhirkhepshef's death, and entombed with her son.

Tomb of Queen Titi (#52)

Sited along the well-trodden route to Amunhirkhepshef's tomb, this cruciform structure was commissioned by **Queen Titi**, wife of one of the Ramessid pharaohs of the XX Dynasty. A winged Maat kneels in the corridor (where Titi appears before Thoth, Ptah and the sons of Horus) and guards the entrance to the burial chamber with Neith (left) and Selket (right).

The burial chamber itself boasts jackal, lion and baboon guardians, plus three side chambers, the finest being the one to the right. Here, Hathor emerges from between the mountains of east and west in her bovine form, while the tree-goddess pours Nile water to rejuvenate Titi, who reposes on a cushion across the room. Sadly, most of these murals are faded or damaged.

Tomb of Prince Khaemweset (#44)

This colourfully painted tomb is reached via a separate path. **Prince Khaemweset** was one of several sons of Ramses III who died in a smallpox epidemic, and the murals in his tomb give precedence to images of Ramses, making offerings in the entrance corridor and worshipping funerary deities in the side chambers. In the second corridor, decorated with the *Book of Gates*, Ramses leads Khaemweset past the fearsome guardians of the Netherworld to the Fields of Yaru, bearing witness for him before Osiris and Horus in the burial chamber. Notice the four sons of Horus on the lotus blossom.

Medinet Habu

3.5km from Gezira • Daily 6am–5pm • £E30 from the main ticket office (see p.291)

Medinet Habu (Habu's Town) is the Arabic name for the gigantic **Mortuary Temple of Ramses III**, a structure second only to Karnak in size and complexity, and better preserved in its entirety. Modelled on the Ramesseum of his illustrious ancestor, Ramses II, this XX Dynasty extravaganza deserves more attention than it usually gets, being the last stop on most tourists' itineraries.

Like Deir el-Bahri and the Ramesseum, the mortuary temple was a focus for the pharaoh's cult, linking him to Amun-United-with-Eternity. The effigies of Amun, Mut and Khonsu paid an annual visit during the Festival of the Valley, while other deities

2

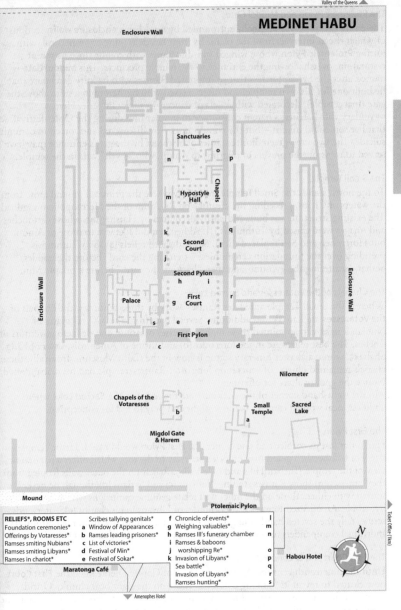

MEDINET HABU

Enclosure Wall

Sanctuaries

o
n p

Chapels

Hypostyle
m Hall

k q
Second
Court l
j

Second Pylon
h i
r
Palace g First
Court
s e f
First Pylon
c d

Enclosure Wall

Enclosure Wall

Nilometer

Chapels of the
Votaresses Small Sacred
b Temple Lake
a
Migdol Gate
& Harem

Mound

Ptolemaic Pylon

Ticket Office (1km)

RELIEFS*, ROOMS ETC			
Foundation ceremonies*	Scribes tallying genitals*	**f** Chronicle of events*	**l**
Offerings by Votaresses*	**a** Window of Appearances	**g** Weighing valuables*	**m**
Ramses smiting Nubians*	**b** Ramses leading prisoners*	**h** Ramses III's funerary chamber	**n**
Ramses smiting Libyans*	**c** List of victories*	**i** Ramses & baboons	
Ramses in chariot*	**d** Festival of Min*	worshipping Re*	**o**
	e Festival of Sokar*	**j** Invasion of Libyans*	**p**
		k Invasion of Libyans*	**q**
Maratonga Café		Sea battle*	**r**
		Invasion of Libyans*	
		Ramses hunting*	**s**

Habou Hotel

N

▼ Amenophes Hotel

permanently resided in its shrines, and Ramses himself often dwelt in the adjacent
palace. Aside from its lack of freestanding colossi, the sandstone temple gives a good
idea of how the Ramesseum must have looked before it collapsed. The complex's
massive enclosure walls sheltered the entire population of Thebes during the Libyan
invasions of the late XX Dynasty and for centuries afterwards protected the Coptic
town of Djeme, built within the great temple.

2

The Ptolemaic Pylon and Migdol Gate

The entire complex was originally surrounded by mud-brick **enclosure walls**, sections of which rise at intervals from the plain. Its front facade is quite asymmetrical, with a jutting **Ptolemaic Pylon** whose winged sun-disc glows with colour since its recent restoration, overshadowing the entrance to the temple precincts. This **Migdol Gate** is named after the Syrian fortress that so impressed Ramses with its lofty gatehouse that he built one for his own temple, and often relaxed with his **harem** in a suite above the gate (inaccessible), decorated with reliefs of dancers in slinky lingerie. Here, a secondary wife hatched a harem conspiracy to murder him during the Optet festival, so that her son could inherit – but the conspirators were discovered and forced to commit suicide. The two grey-green diorite statues of Sekhmet by the gate's entrance may have served to transmit the prayers of pilgrims to Amun, who "dwelt" within the temple.

The Small Temple

To the north stands the **Small Temple**, reputedly where the primeval mound arose from the waters of Chaos, preceding the creator-god Re-Atum of the Hermopolitan Ogdoad. The existing structure was built and partly decorated by Hatshepsut, whose cartouches and images were erased by Tuthmosis III. Akhenaten did likewise to those of Amun, but Horemheb and Seti replaced them. Some defaced reliefs [a] show Tuthmosis presiding over the foundation ceremonies, "stretching the cord" before the goddess Seshat, "scattering the gypsum" and then "hacking the earth" before a priapic Min.

The Chapels of the Votaresses and Sacred Lake

Whereas the Small Temple antedates Ramses' work by three centuries, the **Chapels of the Votaresses** are Late Period additions. Several date from the XXV Dynasty of Nubian kings, who appointed these high priestesses of Amun and de facto governors of Thebes. The best reliefs are in the forecourt [b] and shrine of Amenirdis, sister of King Shabaka, whose alabaster funerary statue is now in the Cairo Museum. Ironically, these chapels remained objects of veneration long after Ramses' temple had been abandoned. Notice the granite altars for offerings.

In the right-hand corner of the enclosure are the remains of a **Sacred Lake** where childless local women came to bathe at night and pray to Isis for conception.

The First Pylon

Had it not lost its cornice and one corner, the **First Pylon** would match Luxor Temple's in size. For baksheesh, a guard may unlock a stairway to the top, which offers a panoramic view of the temple, Theban Hills and Nile Valley. Reliefs on the outer walls (copied from the Ramesseum) show Ramses smiting Nubians [c] and Syrians [d], though he never warred with either. Those on the inner wall relate genuine campaigns with Ramessid hyperbole. An outsized Ramses scatters hordes of Libyans in his chariot [e]. Afterwards, scribes tally the severed hands and genitals of dead foes (third row from the bottom) [f]. Individual commanders may have been rewarded according to their unit's "body count".

The First Court and Second Pylon

Until the nineteenth century, the ruined houses of Coptic Djeme filled the **First Court**, now cleared to reveal its flanking columns. Those on the right bear chunky Osiride statues of the king, attended by knee-high queens. The other side of the court abuts the royal palace (now ruined and entered from outside). In the middle of this wall was a Window of Appearances [g] flanked by sunk-reliefs of prisoners, whence the king rewarded loyal commanders with golden collars.

Yet more scenes of triumph cover the outside of the **Second Pylon**, where Ramses leads three rows of prisoners to Amun and Mut [h] (those in the lowest row are Philistines) and a long inscription lauds his victories in Asia Minor [i]. The vultures on the ceiling of the pylon's gateway are still coloured.

The Second Court

During Coptic times most of the Osirian pillars were removed to make room for a church, and a thick layer of mud was plastered over the reliefs in the **Second Court**. Now uncovered, these depict the annual festivals of Min [j] and Sokar [k], with processions of priests and dancers accompanying the royal palanquin. Elsewhere, the events of Ramses' fifth regnal year are related in a long text lower down the wall [l]. The lotus-bud columns of the rear arcade are coloured blue, red and turquoise.

The Hypostyle Hall and sanctuaries

The now-roofless **Hypostyle Hall**, beyond, once had a raised central aisle like the Great Hall at Karnak, and still has some brightly coloured pillars at the back. To the right lie five **chapels** dedicated to Ramses, his XIX Dynasty namesake, Ptah, Osiris and Sokar. On the opposite side are several (locked) treasure chambers whose reliefs show the weighing of myrrh, gold, lapis lazuli and other valuables bestowed upon the temple [m] – also visible on the outer walls.

Beyond this lie two **smaller halls** with rooms leading off. To the left of the first hall is the funerary chamber of Ramses III [n]; notice the lion-headed deity on the right-hand wall. The other side – open to the sky – featured an altar to Re. On the lintels that once supported the roof [o], Ramses and several baboons worship Re's barque. The central aisle of the next level is flanked by red granite statues of Ramses with Maat or Thoth. At the back are three **sanctuaries** dedicated to the Theban Triad of Mut (left), Amun (centre) and Khonsu (right).

Along the outer walls

Some of the best reliefs at Medinet Habu are on the **outer walls** of the temple, involving a fair slog over broken ground. As most are quite faint, they're best viewed early or late in the day, when shadows reveal details obscured at midday. The famous **battle reliefs of Ramses II** run along the temple's northern wall, starting from the back. Although you'll encounter the last or middle scenes first, we've listed them in chronological order, as Ramses intended them to be seen. The first section [p] depicts the invasion of land-hungry Libyans, early in his reign. In the vanguard of the battle are Ramses, a lion and the standard of Amun. Afterwards, scribes count limbs and genitals to assess each soldier's reward in gold or land. Yet despite this victory, Ramses was soon beleaguered on two fronts, as the Libyans joined with the Sea Peoples (Sardinians, Philistines and Cretans) in a concerted invasion of the Nile Delta. A giant Ramses fires arrows into a melee of grappling ships, in the only Egyptian relief of a sea battle [q]. A third invasion by the Libyans [r] was also thwarted, but their descendants would eventually triumph and rule Egypt as the XXIII and XXIV dynasties.

On the other side of the temple, behind the First Pylon, is a dramatic relief of Ramses hunting antelopes in the desert and impaling wild bulls in a marsh [s], near a ruined **Palace** where he resided during visits. A calendar of festivals appears at the far end of the temple [t], which is surrounded on three sides by mud-brick **storehouses**, eroded into worm-like shapes.

Nag Lohlah

The village of **NAG LOHLAH** beside Medinet Habu will be familiar to readers of Richard Critchfield's *Shahhat* as the birthplace of its eponymous hero and the irascible Hagg Ali, owner of the *Habou Hotel* (which still exists, though Hagg Ali is deceased). Most families have one foot in tourism and the other in farming, so that one finances the other as fortune allows. While Medinet Habu brings customers to their doorsteps, few visitors realise there's also an **Amun Temple** in someone's backyard (no set hours; baksheesh expected). Though small and knocked about, its reliefs retain some of the white background that has faded in other temples.

2

Monastery of St Tawdros

If it's not too hot, the **Monastery of St Tawdros** in the desert beyond Medinet Habu makes an interesting excursion. You can walk here from Medinat Habu in about twenty minutes, or cycle, or, even better, go riding in time for sunset. Be sure to cover your head and bring plenty of water; the unpaved track from Medinet Habu to the French House is easy going, but has no shade at all.

Roughly 200m right off the track into the desert, the monastery is easily identified by its beehive domes. Pharaonic, Greek and Roman masonry is incorporated into the low-vaulted church, whose shrines are dedicated to the Coptic martyrs Tawdros, Elkladius and Foktor. Tawdros (295–306 AD) was a leader in the Roman army before his conversion to Christianity, hence the monastery's alternative name, El Muharrib (The Warrior). The day of his martyrdom (Jan 20) and Easter see crowds of Copts descending on the monastery, but at other times the nuns who live here receive few visitors and seem pleased if anyone rings the bell.

Esna

West bank, 54km from Luxor, 155km from Aswan

Small-town life and ancient stone are boldly juxtaposed at **ESNA**, where a huge pit exposes part of the **Temple of Khnum**, which probably rivals Edfu's Temple of Horus for size. The only part to have been excavated is the Hypostyle Hall, whose somewhat inferior reliefs detract from the forest of columns and lofty astronomical ceiling. The rest lies beneath the surrounding bazaars. The temple is at the southern end of town, 200m inland from the cruise-boat dock, with a covered tourist bazaar leading from one to the other.

Approaching Esna from the north, you'll see two **barrages** that act as bridges over the Nile, with **locks** to allow vessels to pass through, where vendors wait to throw their wares on the ships' decks, hoping that passengers will buy.

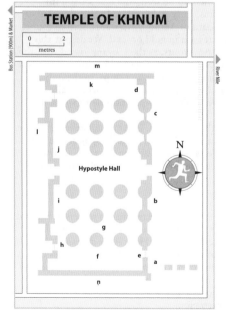

TEMPLE OF KHNUM

0   2
metres

Bus Station (900m) & Market

River Nile

m
k   d
c
l
j
Hypostyle Hall
N
i   b
g
h
f   e   a
n

Temple of Khnum

Sharia el-Shaheed Sa'ad Eid el-Hadry • Daily 8am–5pm •
Tickets sold on the Corniche near the cruise-boat dock • £E50

When Amelia Edwards visited Esna, the **Temple of Khnum** was "buried to the chin in the accumulated rubbish of a score of centuries" and built over with houses. To minimize their destruction, only a portion of the temple was excavated in the 1860s. Now 9m below ground level, the temple resembles a pharaonic Fort Knox, its boxy mass fronted by six columns rising from a screen, the open space above them covered with wire mesh to discourage nesting birds.

The existing temple was a Ptolemaic-Roman replacement for a far older structure dedicated to the ram-headed creator-god of ancient myth (see box p.323). Since what you see is merely the Roman section (dating from the first century AD), the **facade** bears the cartouches of Claudius [a], Titus [b] and Vespasian

KHNUM AND HAPY

In Upper Egypt, **Khnum** was originally the ram-headed creator-god who moulded man on a potter's wheel, and the guardian of the Nile's source (which myth was assigned to the caves just beyond the First Cataract, although the Ancient Egyptians must have known better). Later, however, Khnum was demoted to an underling of Amun-Re and shared his role as river deity with **Hapy**, god of the Nile in flood, who was also believed to dwell in an island cavern near the First Cataract. Shown with a blue-green body and a female breast, wearing a crown of lotus or sedge (the heraldic plants of Upper and Lower Egypt), he should not be confused with Horus's son, Hapi, the ape-headed deity of canopic jars.

Khnum

Hapy

2

[c], and the battered sun-disc above the entrance is flanked by votive inscriptions to these emperors.

Around the **outer walls** of the temple are texts dedicated to Marcus Aurelius [l] and stiffly executed scenes of Titus, Domitian and Trajan smiting Egypt's foes before the gods [m and n]. Several stone blocks from an early Christian church lie in front of the temple.

The Hypostyle Hall

Entering the lofty **Hypostyle Hall**, your eyes are drawn upwards by a forest of columns that bud and flower in variegated capitals. Their shafts are covered with festival texts (now defaced) or hieroglyphs in the form of crocodiles [d] or rams [e]. One is a *Hymn of Creation* that acknowledges Khnum as the creator of all, even foreigners: "All are formed on his potter's wheel, their speech different in every region… but the lord of the wheel is their father too."

The hall's **astronomical ceiling** rivals Dendara's for finesse and complexity, but gloom, soot and distemper render much indiscernible. However, the zodiac register [f] visibly crawls with two-headed snakes, winged dogs and other creatures. Notice the pregnant hippo-goddess Tweri (whom the Greeks called Thoeris), and the scorpion in the next aisle [g]. The registers on the walls below show emperors Septimius Severus, Caracalla and Geta before the gods.

The last Roman ruler mentioned is Decius [h], whose persecution of Christians (249–51) anticipated the "Era of Martyrs" under Diocletian. Further along [i] is the cartouche of Ptolemy VI, whose father began the construction of Esna temple. To the right of the portal, Decius makes offerings to Khnum, including a potter's wheel [j].

The liveliest reliefs are near the foot of the northern wall [k], where Khnum, Horus and Emperor Commodus net fish and malignant spirits. To the left of this tableau stands an ibis-headed Thoth; to the right, Sheshat, goddess of writing.

The rest of town

Directly opposite the temple, the **Emari Minaret** is one of Egypt's oldest minarets, part of a mosque (demolished in the 1960s) founded by vizier Al-Gamali, who built the walls of Fatimid Cairo. About 50m north of the temple stands the **Wikalat al-Gedawi**, a lovely but battered Ottoman caravanserai, where merchants from Sudan, Somalia and Kenya once sold Gum Arabic, ostrich feathers and elephant tusks. On their return journey, caravans were laden with local products such as raw cotton, lentils and medicinal oils.

Lettuce oil (prized as an aphrodisiac since ancient times) is still produced in Esna by pressing seeds at the **Bakour Oil Mill**. This can be found in **Al-Qasreya**, an old covered bazaar south of the temple, where there are several nineteenth-century **houses** with elaborate *mashrabiya* window-screens.

Esna's **Monday market** is held beside the canal beyond Al-Qasreya.

2

Esna rarely features on cruise-boat, felucca or minibus itineraries to Edfu and Kom Ombo, so you'll have get there by private taxi or public transport.

By train An hour's ride from Luxor and 2hr 30min from Aswan; the station is on the east bank of the Nile. Covered pick-ups (*kabouts*) run into town across the river (££1), terminating beside a canal 1.4km north of the temple, which can be reached on foot (20min) or by *calèche* (££10–20).

By service taxi Minibuses from Luxor, Edfu and Aswan drop passengers at a depot near the *kabout* terminus beside the canal (see above).

By private taxi Expect to pay ££250–350 from Luxor or Aswan and back.

EATING

Tourist bazaar The various coffee-houses, *fuul* and *taamiya* stalls in the tourist bazaar (plus others in Al-Qasreya) are as fancy as it gets. They open from mid-morning till late evening.

DIRECTORY

Banks and exchange AlexBank, Corniche, 400m north of the post office (Sun–Thurs 9am–2pm). Exchange kiosk beside the temple ticket office (daily 9am–5pm).

Tourist police Corniche, near the start of the tourist bazaar leading to the temple ☎ 095 240 0686 (daily 8am–8pm).

El-Kab

Eastern Desert Road, 26km from Esna, 15km from Edfu • Daily 8am–4pm • ££30

The east bank Desert Road runs past the little-visited site known as **El-Kab**, where the vast mud-brick walls of the ancient city of Nekheb loom beside the highway. One of the oldest cities in Upper Egypt, it was consecrated to the vulture-goddess Nekhbet. More impressive today for its size than its ruins, El-Kab is chiefly notable for its **necropolis**, just across the highway, where the ticket office is located.

The necropolis

Dug into a ridge on the desert's edge are a dozen small **tombs**, four of them open to visitors. Built for local officials during the early New Kingdom, they have colourful wall-paintings similar to those in the Tombs of the Nobles in the Theban Necropolis, barrel-vaulted ceilings and niches with funerary statues (largely destroyed).

Tomb of Paheri (#3)

The best preserved of the tombs is that of **Paheri**, a mayor of Nekhbet under the XVIII

HIERAKONOPOLIS

On the west bank of the Nile, opposite El-Kab, is another site, although off-limits to visitors. Called Kom al-Ahmar (Red Mound) in Arabic, it is better known to Egyptologists by the name bestowed upon it by the Ancient Greeks: **Hierakonpolis** (City of the Falcon) – itself derived from its Ancient Egyptian name, Nekhen, and its association with a local falcon-god, Nekheny, later amalgamated with Horus.

The city flourished during the late Pre-dynastic and Early dynastic eras (c.4000–2686 BC) and may have been the first administrative capital of the Two Lands, judging by two famous artefacts found here that are now in the Egyptian Museum (see p.75). The **Palette of Narmer** and the **Scorpion Macehead** are the oldest-known symbols of Egyptian kingship, prefiguring the iconography of the dynastic era.

Over a century of research, continuing with the present Hierakonpolis Expedition, has confirmed the site's role in the transition from prehistory to early Egyptian civilization. Among **recent discoveries** are Egypt's oldest mummies (c.3600 BC); an industrial-scale brewery; the first mention of hair-extensions and the use of henna to colour hair; and Egypt's one and only elephant burial. For news of ongoing excavations, visit Whierakonopolis-online.org.

Dynasty, who tutored Tuthmosis I's son, Prince Wadjmose. Its left-hand wall depicts farmers reaping and threshing with oxen, and storing grain; below, Paheri's mummy is conveyed by boat. The other wall shows him sniffing the sacred lotus, and funerary offerings.

Tomb of Setau (#4)

Setau served as high priest of Nekhbet under five rulers of the XIX Dynasty, so offerings to the vulture-goddess, and her sacred barque, feature prominently on his tomb, as does Setau, sniffing the lotus that was the heraldic plant of Upper Egypt, and thus associated with Nekhbet.

Tomb of Aahmes (#4)

The biographical text that covers the right-hand wall of this tomb identifies **Aahmes** as "Captain of Sailors" and cites his feats against the Hyksos during the siege of Avaris (see p.509), for which he was awarded a gold collar and four slaves. Aahmes was the grandfather of Paheri, who is shown making offerings to his illustrious ancestor.

Tomb of Renini (#2)

Renini was mayor of Nekheb during the reign of Amenhotep I, whose duties included supervising harvests, as depicted along with banqueting and offerings scenes, which are crudely carved but brightly coloured. The ceiling is painted with a checker-board pattern to resemble a canopy, and his funerary statue is flanked by protective Wadjet Eyes.

The temples of Thoth and Nekhbet

Clambering through one of the breaches in the ruined city's twelve-metre-thick ramparts, you'll find an expanse of withered grass and mounds of rubble, interspersed by the ruins of two temples that probably originated in Early Dynastic times, in tandem with those of Hierakonopolis, Nekheb's sister-city across the Nile (see box p.324). The existing ruins date from far later, however. The **Temple of Thoth** was begun by Amenhotep II and finished by later rulers of the XVIII Dynasty. During the Late Period, a contiguous **Temple of Nekhbet** was built, using masonry from diverse Middle and New Kingdom structures; its drainage system has been exposed by excavations.

While it's hard to tell one overgrown ruin from another, there are also the remains of a Ptolemaic **Birth-House** and a small **Roman temple**, nearer the river.

ARRIVAL AND DEPARTURE	**EL-KAB**
By dahabiya Passengers can explore El-Kab if their boat moors overnight beside the ruined city.	to a brief stopover at El-Kab.
By private taxi If you've hired a taxi to travel between Luxor and Aswan via the Desert Rd, the driver should agree	**By service taxi** Vehicles taking the Desert Rd between Luxor and Aswan can drop you at El-Kab, but getting a ride back to either city could be problematic.

Edfu

West bank, 115km from Luxor, 105km from Aswan

Roughly midway between Luxor and Aswan, the provincial town of **EDFU** boasts the best-preserved **cult temple** in Egypt, dedicated to the falcon-headed god **Horus** (see box p.327). Though built in the Ptolemaic era, this mammoth edifice respects all the canons of pharaonic architecture, conveying how most temples once looked. In terms of sheer monumental grandeur, it ranks alongside Karnak and Deir el-Bahri as one of the finest sites in the Nile Valley.

2

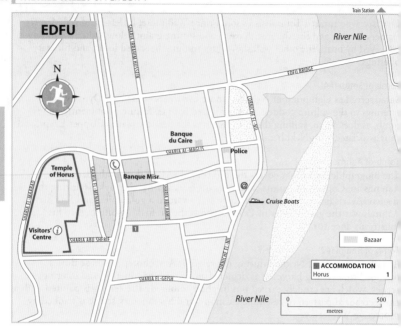

The approach to the temple is designed to distance it from the surrounding town: a sunken high-walled road overlooked by gun-towers, reflecting the paranoia of Mubarak's regime in its final years, which culminates in a car park, tourist bazaar and **Visitors' centre** (no more than an adjunct to the site's toilets). If tourism picks up, there may be a **Sound and Light Show** at the temple in the future (☎097 470 5472 for information). Otherwise you may enjoy Edfu's **bazaar** on Sharia el-Gumhorriya, one block east of the temple, where fruit, vegetable and lingerie stalls mingle in joyous profusion.

Temple of Horus

Sharia el-Mahbad • Daily 7am–6pm • £E50

The **Temple of Horus** lay buried to its lintels until the 1860s, when Auguste Mariette cleared the main building. A splendid drawing by David Roberts shows the courtyard full of sand and peasant houses built atop the Hypostyle Hall. The mammoth task of excavation was nothing compared to the temple's construction, which outlasted six Ptolemies, the final touches being added by the twelfth ruler of that dynasty.

The reliefs and **inscriptions** on the walls include the myth of the struggle between Horus and Seth and an account of the temple's foundation-rituals, known to Egyptologists as the Edfu texts. You can read them *in situ* using Dieter Kurth's annotated text, *Edfu Temple: A Guide by an Ancient Egyptian Priest* (see "Books", p.625).

Birth House and Pylon

Visitors approach the temple as the ancients did, passing through high mud-brick **enclosure walls** and a **Pro-Pylon** (now ruined). Pilgrims seeking a few grains of blessed dust from the temple have left gouge-marks in the stones at head-level.

Off to the left, the colonnaded **Birth House** was a focus for the annual Coronation Festival re-enacting the divine birth of Horus and the reigning pharaoh. Don't miss the reliefs of Horus being suckled by Isis, both as a baby (low down on the rear wall) and as a young man (on the facing columns) [a].

The temple **pylon** was erected by Ptolemy IX before he was ousted from power by his brother Alexander, who was later usurped by another ruler, Neos Dionysos, depicted smiting foes before Horus the Elder [b]. Its gateway is fronted by two giant black-granite **falcons**.

Court of Offerings

Entering the **Court of Offerings**, you can study the festival reliefs on the inner walls of the pylon, which continue around the court along the bottom of the wall. In the *Feast of the Beautiful Meeting*, Horus's barque tows Hathor's to the temple (bottom row), where the deities retire to the sanctuary after suitable rituals [c]. Later they emerge from the temple, embark and drift downstream to the edge of the Edfu nome, where Horus takes his leave [d]. Beneath the western colonnade, Ptolemy IX makes offerings to Horus, Hathor and Ihy [e]; his successor appears before the Edfu Triad across the way [f].

However, most visitors are content to photograph the pair of granite **Horus statues** outside the Hypostyle Hall. One falcon stands higher than a man; the other is missing its lower half.

Hypostyle Hall

The **Hypostyle Hall** of papyrus columns dates from the reign of Ptolemy VII (145–116 BC), known to his contemporaries as "Fatty". With a torch, you can examine two small rooms in the entrance wall: the Chamber of Consecrations, where the king or his priestly stand-in dressed for rituals [g]; and a library of sacred texts adorned with a relief of Sheshat, the goddess of writing [h]. The reliefs showing the foundation of the temple and the deification of Horus [i] have been mutilated by iconoclasts. From here on you encounter the oldest section of the temple, begun by

---

THE CULT OF HORUS

Originally the sky-god of the Nile Valley, whose eyes were the sun and moon, the falcon deity **Horus** was soon assimilated into the Osirian myth as the child of Isis and Osiris (see p.364 & p.246). Raised in the swamps of the Delta by Isis and Hathor, Horus set out to avenge his father's murder by his uncle Seth. During their titanic struggle at Edfu, Horus lost an eye and Seth his testicles. Despite this, Seth almost prevailed until Isis intervened on her son's behalf and Osiris pronounced judgement upon them from the netherworld, exiling Seth back to the wilderness and awarding the throne to Horus. Thus good triumphed over evil and Osiris "lived" through his son.

Horus

All pharaohs claimed to be the incarnation of Horus the "living king" and reaffirmed their divine oneness in an annual **Festival of Coronation**. A live falcon was taken from the sacred aviary, crowned in the central court and then placed in an inner chamber where it "reigned" in the dark for a year as the symbol of the living king. Another event, sometimes called the **Festival of Triumph**, commemorated the Contendings of Seth and Horus in a series of Mystery Plays. At the equally lavish **Feast of the Beautiful Meeting**, his wet nurse and wife Hathor sailed from Dendara aboard the *Lady of the Lake* to be met near Edfu by his own barque, *The First Horus*.

To complicate the cult of Horus still further, he was also associated with the Divine Ennead of Heliopolis and another variant of the Creation myth. The Egyptians, having distinguished the Osirian Horus from the Heliopolitan deity by terming the latter **Horus the Elder**, split him into archetypes such as **Herakhte** (often conjoined with Re), **Hariesis** (stressing his kinship to Isis) and **Haroeris** (see p.332). His priesthood asserted a place for Horus in the Creation myth by crediting him with building the first house amid swamps at the dawn of the world, or even laying the Cosmic Egg whence the sun-god hatched. In rituals associated with the **Myth of the Great Cackler**, they launched a goose onto the sacred lake near Edfu temple, whose egg contained air and the potential for life – crucial elements in the world's creation.

2

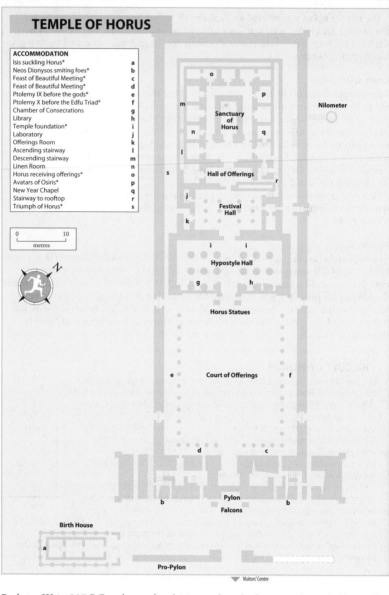

TEMPLE OF HORUS

ACCOMMODATION

Isis suckling Horus*	a
Neos Dionysos smiting foes*	b
Feast of Beautiful Meeting*	c
Feast of Beautiful Meeting*	d
Ptolemy IX before the gods*	e
Ptolemy X before the Edfu Triad*	f
Chamber of Consecrations	g
Library	h
Temple foundation*	i
Laboratory	j
Offerings Room	k
Ascending stairway	l
Descending stairway	m
Linen Room	n
Horus receiving offerings*	o
Avatars of Osiris*	p
New Year Chapel	q
Stairway to rooftop	r
Triumph of Horus*	s

0 ____ 10
metres

Nilometer

Sanctuary
of
Horus

o

p

m

n

q

l

s

Hall of Offerings

r

j

Festival
Hall

k

i   i

Hypostyle Hall

g   h

Horus Statues

e   **Court of Offerings**   f

d   c

b   **Pylon**   b
Falcons

Birth House

a

Pro-Pylon

▼ Visitors' Centre

Ptolemy III in 237 BC and completed 25 years later by his son, who styled himself
Philopator (Father Lover).

Festival Hall

Temple texts rhapsodize about the annual festivals once held here, during which the
Festival Hall was decorated with faïence, strewn with flowers and herbs and perfumed
by myrrh. Incense and unguents were blended according to recipes inscribed on the
walls of the Laboratory **[j]**. Nonperishable offerings were stored in the room next door

[k], while libations, fruit and sacrificial animals were brought in through a passageway connected to the outside world.

Hall of Offerings

The sacred barques of Horus and Hathor appear in glorious detail on either side of the doorway into the **Hall of Offerings**. During the New Year Festival, Horus was carried up the ascending stairway [l] to the rooftop; after being revitalized by the sun-disc, his statue was returned to the sanctuary via the descending stairway [m]. The ritual is depicted on the walls of both stairways, but you'll need a torch, and locked gates may prevent you from going far.

Sanctuary and side chambers

Beyond the Hall of Offerings, the **Sanctuary of Horus** contains a shrine of polished black granite and a replica of his bronze **barque shrine**, where his effigy was kept. There are several chambers worth noting off the corridor surrounding the sanctuary. The Linen Room [n] is flanked by chapels to Min and the Throne of the Gods, while a suite nominally dedicated to Osiris contains colourful scenes of Horus receiving offerings [o] and reliefs of his avatars [p]. Don't miss the **New Year Chapel**, with a dark-blue-coloured relief of the sky-goddess Nut stretched across its ceiling [q]. South of here is another stairway to the rooftop, used for solar rituals [r].

Other sights

Returning to the Festival Hall, you can gain access to an external corridor running between the inner and outer walls, where the priesthood tallied tithes assessed on the basis of readings from the temple's own **Nilometer** (accessible by a passage in the temple's pylon). On the far side of the temple are tableaux from the Triumph of Horus over Seth, depicting Mystery Plays in which Seth was cast as a hippopotamus, lurking beneath his brother's boat in the middle register [s]. At the end of the play, the priests cut up and ate a hippo-shaped cake, to destroy Seth completely.

ARRIVAL AND TOURS
EDFU

Unlike Esna, Edfu is easily reached on excursions arranged by hotels in Aswan or Luxor, and is a mandatory stop for cruise boats and *dahabiyas*.

By cruise boat/dahabiya The tourist dock on the Corniche is roughly 1.2km east of the temple, but a roundabout approach road adds another 500m to the journey, for which taxis charge about £E15, and *calèches* around £E30.
By felucca Travellers coming from Aswan end up at villages south of Esna such as Faris, from which minibuses take them directly to the temple; the ride should be included in the price of any trip.

Tours Edfu is a stopover on all organized trips between Luxor and Aswan. Far more tourists start from Aswan, where you can pay as little as £E85/person travelling by minibus, visiting Kom Ombo en route (excluding entry fees to both).

ACCOMMODATION AND EATING

Besides a simple **restaurant** in the *Horus* hotel, there are *fuul* and *taamiya* stalls around the bazaar, and a few coffee houses near the cruise-boat docks on the Corniche.

Horus Sharia el-Gumhorriya ☎ 097 715 2860. Opposite the Omar Effendi department store off the souk, this hotel is the only one in Edfu worth considering, with en-suite a/c rooms with large beds, clean showers and satellite TV located on the building's kitschly decorated upper floors. B&B **£E260**

Silsilah

42km from Edfu, 85km from Aswan

Between Edfu and Aswan, the Nile is constricted by sheer cliffs on both sides and the bedrock changes from Egyptian limestone to Nubian sandstone. It was here that the

2

Ancient Egyptians quarried sandstone for their sculptures and temples, which was floated downriver on barges, alongside granite from quarries near Aswan. Its ancient name, Khenu (Place of Rowing), suggests that rapids once existed here, as at the First Cataract, or simply the effort required to manoeuvre heavily laden barges on a narrow stretch of river where the cliffs blocked the wind.

The main **quarry** is on the east bank, facing an array of **votive shrines** across the river, spotlit at night for the benefit of passing cruise boats. About the only visitors to either place are New Age tourists to whom Silsilah is marketed as a sacred site, or passengers on *dahabiyas* which moor here to allow a visit to one side of the river – but you can visit either by taxi if you're prepared to pay the price.

The quarry

East bank • Daily 24hr • Free

The quarries at **Gebel al-Silsilah** were principally used during the New Kingdom. It was here the talatat for Akhenaten's temple at Karnak and his new capital at Tell el-Armana were quarried. By eschewing the large blocks of stone favoured by previous rulers in favour of smaller talatat, Akhenaten's chief sculptor Bek was able to supply building-material at a prodigious rate.

Besides Cubist-like spatial excavations from the rock-face, the site features several partially submerged **rampways** to the Nile and the so-called **Stele M**, depicting the quarrying and loading of stone onto barges under the supervision of Ramses II's general, Hapy.

The shrines

West bank • Daily 8am–4pm • £E25

The cliffs on the west bank are riddled with 32 rock-hewn **shrines** (*speos*) dedicated to XVIII and XIX Dynasty pharaohs **Horemheb**, **Seti I**, **Ramses II** and **Merneptah**, where sacrifices were made at the start of the inundation season. The site's southern extremity is marked by a pillar of rock known as the Capstan, after the local belief that there was once a chain (silsilah) strung across the Nile to control shipping. At the northern end, a shrine dedicated to the XXII Dynasty ruler **Shoshenk I** attests to the duration of quarrying at Silsilah, which continued until Roman times.

ARRIVAL AND DEPARTURE   **SILSILAH**

By boat *Dahabiya* passengers can explore Silsilah if their boat moors overnight on one bank or the other. Feluccas on a three-day cruise from Aswan (see p.242) terminate at Faris, 2km from the west bank shrines, but the standard excursion doesn't include a visit to Silsilah.

By private taxi Haggag, of the Luxor west bank *Restaurant Mohammed* (see p.274), can drive up to four people to the quarry and/or shrines for £E300–350.

Kom Ombo

East bank, 170km from Luxor, 45km from Aswan

In ancient times the town of **KOM OMBO** stood at the crossroads of the caravan route from Nubia and trails from the gold mines of the Eastern Desert; under Ptolemy VI (180–145 BC), it became the capital of the Ombos nome and a training depot for African war elephants, which the Ptolemies required to fight the pachyderms of the Seleucid Empire. More recently, many of the Nubians displaced by the creation of Lake Nasser in the 1960s (see p.354) settled around the town.

In 2007 Belgian archeologists discovered what may be Egypt's **oldest rock art**, on boulders in the village of **Qurta**, outside Kom Ombo. Provisionally dated to fifteen thousand years ago (like the famous Lascaux Caves in France), the painted carvings of cattle, gazelles, hippos, fish, and humans with exaggerated buttocks are sure to be off-limits for the foreseeable future, and Kom Ombo remains far better known for its Ptolemaic **Temple of Haroeris and Sobek**. Unlike other temples in the valley, this still stands beside the Nile, making the approach by river one of the highlights of a cruise.

Temple of Haroeris and Sobek

4km south of Kom Ombo • Daily 8am–5pm • £E30

The **Temple of Haroeris and Sobek** stands on a low promontory near a bend in the river whose sandbanks were a basking place for crocodiles in ancient times. This proximity

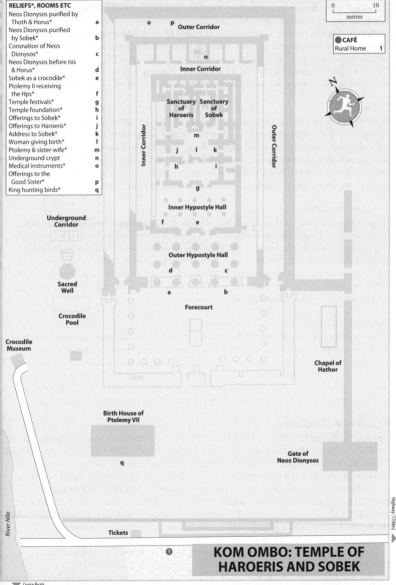

RELIEFS*, ROOMS ETC	
Neos Dionysos purified by Thoth & Horus*	a
Neos Dionysos purified by Sobek*	b
Coronation of Neos Dionysos*	c
Neos Dionysos before Isis & Horus*	d
Sobek as a crocodile*	e
Ptolemy II receiving the Hps*	f
Temple festivals*	g
Temple foundation*	h
Offerings to Sobek*	i
Offerings to Haroeris*	j
Address to Sobek*	k
Woman giving birth*	l
Ptolemy & sister-wife*	m
Underground crypt	n
Medical instruments*	o
Offerings to the Good Sister*	p
King hunting birds*	q

CAFÉ
Rural Home 1

Outer Corridor

Inner Corridor

Sanctuary of Haroeris Sanctuary of Sobek

Inner Corridor   Outer Corridor

Inner Hypostyle Hall

Outer Hypostyle Hall

Underground Corridor

Sacred Well

Crocodile Pool

Crocodile Museum

Forecourt

Chapel of Hathor

Birth House of Ptolemy VII

Gate of Neos Dionysos

Highway (170m)

River Nile

Tickets

KOM OMBO: TEMPLE OF HAROERIS AND SOBEK

Cruise Boats

0   10
metres

2

to the Nile has both preserved and damaged the site, covering the temple with sand which protected it from Coptic iconoclasts, but also washing away its pylon and forecourt. What remains was aptly described by Amelia Edwards as a "magnificent torso"; truncated and roofless yet still imposing.

Its defining characteristic is **bisymmetry**, with twin entrances, sanctuaries and halls nominally divided down the middle. The left side is dedicated to the falcon-headed Haroeris, the "Good Doctor" (a form of Horus the Elder) and his consort Ta-Sent-Nefer, the "Good Sister" (an aspect of Hathor). The crocodile-god Sobek (here identified with the sun as Sobek-Re), his wife (another form of Hathor) and their son Khonsu-Hor are honoured on the right side of the temple.

Approaching the temple, you first sight the **Gate of Neos Dionysos**. Its provenance is obscure, as scholars disagree over the number, order and dates of the various Ptolemies, each of whom adopted a title such as Soter (Saviour), Euergetes (Benefactor) or Philometor (Mother Lover). Some identify Neos Dionysos as Ptolemy XII, others as Ptolemy XIII, but all agree that he fathered the great Cleopatra and was nicknamed "The Bastard".

The facade

With the forecourt (added by Emperor Trajan in 14 AD) reduced to low walls and stumps of pillars, your eyes are drawn to the **facade** of the Hypostyle Hall, whose surviving columns burst in floral capitals beneath a chunk of cavetto cornice bearing a winged sun-disc and twin *uraei* above each portal, their colours still vivid. Bas-reliefs on the outer wall show Neos Dionysos being purified by Thoth and Horus [a], and yet again in the presence of Sobek, whose face has been chiselled away [b].

The Outer Hypostyle Hall

Wandering amid the thicket of columns inside the **Outer Hypostyle Hall**, notice the heraldic lily of Upper Egypt or the papyrus symbol of the Delta carved on their bases. On the inner wall of the facade are splendid carvings of Neos Dionysos's coronation before Haroeris, Sobek, Wadjet and Nekhbet (the goddesses of the north and south) [c], and his appearance before Isis, Horus the Elder and a lion-headed deity [d]. Neos Dionysos makes offerings to the same deities at the back of the hall, whose right side retains part of its roof, decorated with flying vultures.

The Inner Hypostyle Hall

Entering the older, **Inner Hypostyle Hall**, you'll find a relief of Sobek in his reptilian form between the portals [e]. Ptolemy II receives the *hps* (sword of victory) from Haroeris (accompanied by his sister Cleopatra III and his wife Cleopatra IV) in the southwest corner of the hall [f] and makes offerings to gods on the shafts of the pillars, while his elder brother does likewise to Haroeris at the back of the hall, where a list of temple deities and festivals appears all along the wall on the bottom register [g].

Vestibules and sanctuaries

Beyond the Inner Hypostyle Hall lies the first of three, now roofless, **vestibules** (each set slightly higher than the preceding one) decorated by Ptolemy VI. Scenes at the back depict the foundation of the temple, with Sheshat, goddess of writing, measuring its dimensions [h]; and offerings and libations to Sobek [i]. To maintain the temple in a state of purity, these rituals were periodically repeated in the **Hall of Offerings**. The ruined chamber to the right once held vestments and sacred texts, as at Edfu and Dendara. Offerings to Haroeris [j], a description of the temple and an address to Sobek [k] appear on the southern wall, which also features a tiny relief of a woman giving birth, at roughly chest height [l]. Notice the painted vultures on the ceiling, too.

A fine relief between the doors of the sanctuaries [m] shows Ptolemy and his sister-wife being presented with a palm stalk from which hangs a Heb-Sed sign representing the years of his reign. Khonsu does the honours, followed by Haroeris and

Sobek (representing air and water, respectively); Ptolemy himself sports a Macedonian cloak. Because so little remains of the **sanctuaries**, you can glimpse a secret corridor between them, whence the priests would "speak" for the gods; it's accessible via an underground crypt in one of the **shrines** behind the inner corridor [n].

The outer corridor and precincts

In the **outer corridor** between the Ptolemaic temple and its Roman enclosure wall, pilgrims scratched graffiti on the pavements to pass time before their appointment with the Good Doctor, who was represented by a statue behind the central chapel. Ears carved on the walls heard their pleas and the eyes symbolized the health they sought. Though these have been gouged away by supplicant fingers, you can still see reliefs depicting scalpels, suction cups, dental tools and bone saws [o], and Marcus Aurelius offering a pectoral cross to Ta-Sent-Nefer, the Good Sister [o]. Ancient Egyptian medicine is known to have at least eight hundred prescriptions, including one for eye-cataracts, consisting of mashed tortoise brains with honey.

Other rituals centred on a **Sacred Well** with two stairways descending to its depths, which drew water from the Nile to feed a **pool** used for raising sacred crocodiles, accessible by an **underground corridor.**

The Crocodile Museum

South of the Sacred Well, the intriguing **Crocodile Museum** exhibits over twenty **mummified crocodiles**, votive tablets and effigies, found in a cemetery at the nearby village of El-Shabta in the 1970s. The Ancient Egyptians feared and revered crocodiles – associating their stealthy killing skills with the might of the pharaoh – and used crocodile-hide as military body armour. Crocodiles were worshipped at many cult-sites, from Qasr Qaroun in the Fayoum to Kom Ombo, and buried in cemeteries in the vicinity.

Further south stands the ruined **Birth House of Ptolemy VII** – or what's left of it since half the ruins fell into the Nile in the nineteenth century. A customary relief of the king hunting birds appears on its southern wall [q].

ARRIVAL AND DEPARTURE   KOM OMBO

By boat Cruise boats and *dahabiyas* moor near the temple. Feluccas tie up at Kom Ombo town, sending their passengers to the temple by minibus.
By private taxi/minibus Given the temple's distance from town, it's easiest to take an organized excursion from

Aswan (see p.348) or Luxor (see p.266).
By train Kom Ombo train station is 5km from the temple (£E20–30 by taxi). Almost all trains from Luxor (2hr 15min) and Aswan (45min) stop here.

EATING

Rural Home Beside the temple, this pleasant faux-rustic cafeteria serves hot and cold drinks and snacks, and also

puts on henna-painting and other kids' activities if enough tourists materialize. Daily 8am–6pm.

Darow

East bank, 170km from Luxor, 37km from Aswan.

Traditionally, **DAROW** (pronounced "De-*rao*") marks the point where Egypt shades into Nubia, a distinction underlined by its **camel market**, attended by tribesmen from the northern deserts of Sudan, and by a remarkable Nubian house called the **Beit al-Kenzi**. Darow itself is a ramshackle sprawl of mud-brick compounds either side of the highway and railway line.

Camel Market

Held on the eastern outskirts (15min walk from the main intersection) during winter; beyond the vegetable and poultry market over summer – just follow the crowds • Tues 7am–noon year-round and sometimes Sun or Mon (same hours) in winter • Free

For camel-drovers and merchants, Darow's **Camel Market** (Souk el-Gamal) is the main trading stop between the Sudanese town of Dongola and the Birqesh market outside Cairo (see p.172), so business is brisk. Hundreds of camels stand with their forelegs hobbled in the traditional manner, as drovers and buyers drink tea and smoke *sheeshas* beneath awnings. The camels spend two days in quarantine before being sold to *fellaheen* who need a beast of burden, or merchants who plan to sell the camels for a profit at Birqesh. Many are destined to end up on the dinner tables of the poor.

The Souk el-Gamal coincides with a **livestock market** where donkeys, sheep and cows jostle for space with people and trucks. In summer the two markets are often held side by side, with **handicrafts** (as well as saddlery) also sometimes sold at the camel market throughout the winter.

Beit al-Kenzi

Sharia al-Kunuz, beside the Dar Rasoul Mosque (turn right outside the train station, walk along the road and head left) • Daily 8am–noon • £E15

A cooler attraction is the **Beit al-Kenzi** – a fabulous house in the traditional Nubian style, built of mud bricks and dom palms, with beehive domes, inner courtyards and spacious rooms divided by reed-lattice partitions, to allow air to circulate. The house was built in 1912 by the great-grandfather of its present occupant so that his descendants would retain something of the ancestral village that was sacrificed to the first Aswan Dam, and its owner is happy to show visitors around. Call ahead (☏097 273 0970) to check he's at home.

ARRIVAL AND DEPARTURE
DAROW

By train Most trains from Luxor (2hr 30min) and Aswan (25min) stop at Darow, whose station is in the centre of town.

By felucca Feluccas sailing this far downriver from Aswan usually allow passengers a visit ashore if the market is happening that day.

Aswan

Egypt's southernmost city and ancient frontier town has the loveliest setting on the Nile. At **ASWAN** the deserts close in on the river, confining its sparkling blue between amber sand and extrusions of granite bedrock. Lateen-sailed feluccas glide past the ancient ruins and gargantuan rocks of Elephantine Island, palms and tropical shrubs softening the islands and embankments till intense blue skies fade into soft-focus dusks.

Although its own monuments are insignificant compared to Luxor's, Aswan is the base for **excursions** to the **temples of Philae and Kabasha**, near the great dams beyond the First Cataract, and the Sun Temple of Ramses II at **Abu Simbel**, far to the south. It is also the best starting point for excursions to Darow Camel Market, and the temples of Kom Ombo and Edfu, between Aswan and Luxor. Though Kom Ombo and Edfu are easier to reach by road, the classic approach is to travel downriver by felucca, experiencing the Nile's moods and scenery as travellers have for millennia – or on a luxurious cruise (see pp.239–245). Aswan itself is laidback to the point of torpor, with a local **tourism** scene essentially similar to Luxor's but far less dynamic.

Situated near the Tropic of Cancer, Aswan is hot and dry nearly all the time, with average daily temperatures ranging from a delicious 23–30°C in the winter to a searing 38–54°C over summer. In late January and early February, many Egyptians visit Aswan, block-booking seats on trains from Luxor and Cairo. Late autumn and spring are the perfect times to visit, being less crowded than the peak winter period, yet not so enervating as summer (May–Oct), when long siestas, cold showers and air-conditioning are essential, and nocturnal power cuts not only deprive you of cooling and lighting, but mean that food may go bad in fridges overnight.

2

Brief history

Elephantine Island – opposite modern Aswan in the Nile – has been settled since remotest antiquity, and its fortress-town of Yebu became the border post between Egypt and Nubia early in the Old Kingdom. Local governors, entitled Guardians of the Southern Gates, were responsible for border security and trade with Nubia; for quarrying fine red granite; and mining amethysts, quartzite, copper, tin and malachite in the desert hinterland. Military outposts further south could summon help from the Yebu garrison by signal fires and an Egyptian fleet patrolled the river between the First and Second Cataracts.

Besides this, Yebu was an important cult centre, for the Egyptians believed that the Nile welled up from subterranean caverns at the **First Cataract**, just upriver (see p.346). Its local **deities** were Hapy and Satet, god of the Nile flood and goddess of its fertility, though the region's largest temple honoured Khnum, the provincial deity (see p.323).

Classical and Christian Aswan

During settled periods, the vast trade in ivory, slaves, gold, silver, incense, exotic animal skins and feathers spawned a market town on the east bank, but the island remained paramount throughout **classical times**, when it was known by its Greek appellation, **Seyene**. The Alexandrian geographer Eratosthenes (c.276–195 BC) heard of a local well into which the sun's rays fell perpendicularly at midday on the summer solstice, leaving no shadow; from this he deduced that Seyene lay on the Tropic of Cancer, concluded that the world was round and calculated its diameter with nearly modern accuracy – being only 80km out. (Since that time, the Tropic of Cancer has moved further south.)

NUBIA AND THE NUBIANS

Nubia and Egypt have been neighbours since time immemorial. The Egyptians called Nubia Ta-Seti (Land of the Bow), after the weapons for which the Nubians were renowned, while its modern name is thought to derive from *nbw*, the ancient word for gold, which was mined there until Greco-Roman times.

A Nilotic people living between the First and Sixth Cataracts of the Nile (roughly from Aswan to Khartoum) may have been the forerunners of Egypt's civilization. Archeologists have found exquisite figurines predating prehistoric finds in Egypt by three thousand years, and the **world's oldest solar calendar** of standing stones, dating from around 6000 BC, at **Nabta Playa**, 100km from Abu Simbel. Pharaonic and ancient Nubian civilization evolved in similar ways until 3500 BC, when Egypt's unification raised the Old Kingdom to a level from which it could exploit Nubia as a source of **mineral wealth**, exotic goods and **slaves**. The onset of the Middle Kingdom saw the annexation of Lower Nubia – the land between the First and Second Cataracts – while under the New Kingdom, Nubia was ruled by a viceroy entitled the King's Son of **Kush**. It was only at the end of the Third Intermediate Period that Nubia got its own back, as the local rulers of **Napata** took advantage of Egypt's disunity to invade and establish their own **Kushite Dynasty** of pharaohs (747–656 BC), who reigned until the Assyrian invasion of Egypt in 671 BC.

Reconsolidating itself beyond the Fourth Cataract, the Kushite **Kingdom of Meröe** marked the apogee of Nubian civilization, building remarkable **pyramids** and maintaining relations with the Ptolemies, but angering the Romans, who occupied Lower Nubia from 23–272 AD. Before withdrawing, they invited warriors called the **Nobatae** (perhaps Nubia from the Red Sea Hills of Sudan) to fill the vacuum, hastening the decline of Meröe. In the seventh century the Nobatae were converted to Christianity by monks from Aswan's Monastery of St Simeon, and later became the main bulwark against attacks by the Islamic rulers of Egypt during the Fatimid era, until in 1315 the last Christian king was replaced by a Muslim one and most of the population accepted Islam.

Egypt's rulers made little attempt to control Nubia so long as it supplied the ivory and exotica they prized until **Mohammed Ali** visited devastation on Nubia when he sent his son to enslave its male population as cannon fodder for his new army. Resentment smouldered

The potency of the **cult of Isis** at nearby Philae (see p.358) made this one of the last parts of Egypt to be affected by **Christianity**, but once converted it became a stronghold of the faith. From their desert Monastery of St Simeon, monks made forays into Nubia, eventually converting the local Nobatae, who returned the favour by helping them to resist Islamic rule until finally subjugated by Saladin. However, Bedouin raiders persisted through to 1517, when Sultan Selim garrisoned an entire army here, by which time the town's name had changed from Coptic Sawan to its present form, and the population had embraced **Islam**.

2

Colonial and contemporary Aswan

During the nineteenth century Aswan was the base for the conquest of Sudan and the defeat of the Mahadist Uprising (1881–98) by Anglo-Egyptian forces. As British influence grew, it also became the favourite **winter resort** of rich, ailing Europeans, who flocked to Aswan for its dry heat and therapeutic hot sands, luxurious hotels and stunning scenery. Its final transformation into the Aswan of today owes to the building of the **High Dam**, 15km upriver, which flooded Nubia, compelling its inhabitants to settle in new villages built around Kom Ombo and Aswan itself – as related in the city's superb **Nubia Museum**.

The bazaar

Sharia al-Souk (aka Abtal el-Tahrir) running from the train station south to Sharia Abbas Farid • Most shops open Sat–Thurs 10am–2pm & 5–10pm, Fri 10am–noon & 5–10pm.

Aswan's **bazaar** is renowned as the best in Egypt after Cairo's, but – as in Luxor – it's had a kitsch makeover, with Moorish gates at every crossroad and antique

through the reigns of the khedives, drawing in the **British**, who began by supporting khedival forces and ended up underwriting an Anglo-Egyptian government in 1899, when the border between Egypt and Sudan was drawn 40km north of Wadi Halfa and Nubia was divided, yet again.

NUBIAN CULTURE AND CONTEMPORARY SOCIETY

Meanwhile, the **Nubians** remained true to their ancestral homeland and traditional life centred round **villages** of extended families (each with its own compound of domed houses), living by farming the verges of the river, fishing and transporting trade goods. Socially and spiritually, the Nile formed the basis of their existence; villages celebrated births, weddings and circumcision ceremonies with Nile rituals.

This way of life – which had existed pretty much unchanged for five millennia – was shattered by the **Aswan Dams**. The first dam, built in 1902, forced the Nubians to move onto higher, unfertile ground; many menfolk left for Cairo, sending back remittances to keep the villages going. With construction of the High Dam, the Nubians' traditional homeland was entirely submerged, displacing the entire eight hundred thousand-strong community, around half of whom moved north, settling around Aswan and Kom Ombo. Meanwhile the **ancient monuments** of Nubia were moved to higher ground or foreign museums, under a huge project coordinated by UNESCO.

In Egypt, many Nubians took advantage of higher education and business opportunities to make their mark. Others resettled as farmers in villages named after their ancestral homes, maintaining Nubian traditions. Since the 2011 Revolution the desolate shores of Lake Nasser have been reclaimed by settlers (both Nubians from Egypt and other ethnic groups from Sudan), as the state's grip has loosened.

The Nubian **language** is still spoken, but not written; its linguistic ancestor Old Nubian was recorded in a modified Greek alphabet which some scholars maintain has 26 letters, others 30. Among **websites** devoted to Nubian history and culture are ⓦ homestead.com/wysinger/nubians.html (for prehistory and the Meröe pyramids), ⓦ thenubian.net (for cultural commentaries) and ⓦ napata.org (with recordings of spoken Nubian, contemporary and traditional music).

2

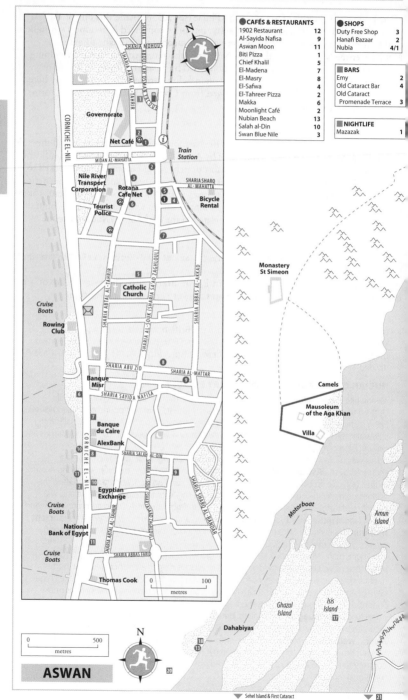

CAFÉS & RESTAURANTS
1902 Restaurant	12
Al-Sayida Nafisa	9
Aswan Moon	11
Biti Pizza	1
Chief Khalil	5
El-Madena	7
El-Masry	8
El-Safwa	4
El-Tahreer Pizza	2
Makka	6
Moonlight Café	2
Nubian Beach	13
Salah al-Din	10
Swan Blue Nile	3

SHOPS
Duty Free Shop	3
Hanafi Bazaar	2
Nubia	4/1

BARS
Emy	2
Old Cataract Bar	4
Old Cataract Promenade Terrace	3

NIGHTLIFE
Mazazak	1

ASWAN

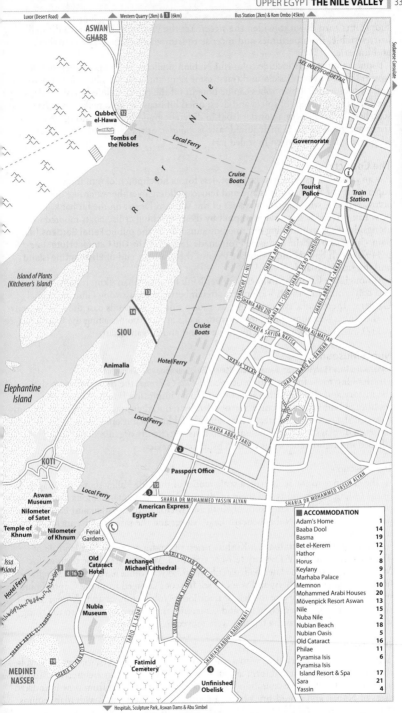

Luxor (Desert Road)

Western Quarry (2km) & **1** (6km)

Bus Station (2km) & Kom Ombo (45km)

Sudanese Consulate

ASWAN GHARB

R i v e r N i l e

Qubbet el-Hawa 12

Tombs of the Nobles

Local Ferry

Cruise Boats

Governorate

Tourist Police

Train Station

Island of Plants (Kitchener's Island)

Island of Plants (Kitchener's Island)

SHARIA ABU ZID

CORNICHE EL-NIL

SHARIA ABTAL EL-TAHRIR

SHARIA EL-SOUK SHARIA SAD ZAGHLOUL

SHARIA ABBAS AL-AKKAD

Cruise Boats

SHARIA SAYIDA NAFISA

SHARIA AL-MATTAR

Elephantine Island

SIOU

Animalia

Hotel Ferry

SHARIA SALAH AL-DIN

SHARIA SHARQ AL-BANDAR

Local Ferry

SHARIA ABBAS FARID

2

KOTI

Local Ferry

Passport Office

Aswan Museum

Nilometer of Satet

Temple of Khnum

Nilometer of Khnum

Ferial Gardens

15
3

SHARIA DR MOHAMMED YASSIN ALYAN

SHARIA DR MOHAMMED YASSIN ALYAN

American Express

EgyptAir

Old Cataract Hotel

Archangel Michael Cathedral

SHARIA SULTAN ABU AL-ALAA

SHARIA AL-GERANA AL-BAHARIYA

4 16 12

Issa Island

3

Hotel Ferry

SHARIA ABTAL EL-TAHRIR

Nubia Museum

TARIQ EL-SADAT

SHARIA ABDUL KADUHANAFI

SHARIA AL-TAHRIR

19

Fatimid Cemetery

4

MEDINET NASSER

Unfinished Obelisk

Hospitals, Sculpture Park, Aswan Dams & Abu Simbel

shopfronts torn down to widen the street. Yet the variety of products and smells is irresistable, from perfumes and incense to fruit and fish, by way of jewellery and lingerie.

Popular **tourist buys** include colourful Nubian skullcaps and long scarves; heavier, woven shawls; woven baskets and trays, some semi-antique and others new. *Galabiyyas* and embroidered Nubian robes can be bought off the peg or tailored to order. Also eye-catching are heaps of spices and dyes; dried hibiscus (used to make *karkaday*), fake so-called "saffron", henna powder (sold in different grades) and peanuts. One product that even locals admit is an acquired taste is *mlouha*, or spicy pickled fish, whose silvery-red flesh stinks even in sealed jars.

The Corniche

Aswan's **Corniche** is the finest in Egypt, less for its hotchpotch of buildings than for the superb vista of Elephantine Island and feluccas gliding over the water like quill pens across papyrus, with the tawny wastes of the Western Desert on the far bank. If the view from riverside restaurants is spoilt by diesel-belching cruise boats moored alongside, it's worth shelling out to enjoy sunset from the public **Ferial Gardens** (daily 9am–5pm; £E5) or the exclusive Promenade Terrace of the **Old Cataract Hotel** (see p.349), which both afford a sublime view of the southern end of **Elephantine Island** and the smaller islands beyond.

Although the Corniche follows the river bank for more than 4km, restaurants, hotels, and banks only line the 1.5-kilometre stretch between the Rowing Club and Ferial Gardens. There traffic swings inland, as a steep side road ascends past the *Old Cataract* to the Nubia Museum. **Public ferries** from docks at three points along the Corniche (see p.347) link downtown with Elephantine Island and Aswan Gharb.

Nubia Museum

Sharia Abtal el-Tahrir • Daily 9am–5pm (Ramadan 9am–3pm) • £E50 • ⓦ numibia.net/nubia/intro.htm

Overlooking town from a hillside above the *Old Cataract*, the **Nubia Museum** showcases the history and culture of this ancient land in an impressive building based on traditional Nubian architecture, surrounded by terraced grounds, which posthumously crowned the career of architect Mahmoud al-Hakim when it opened in 1997. The museum displays some five thousand artefacts, excellently organized and clearly labelled in English; check out their website for a preview.

The collection

At the entrance to the main hall, a **scale model** of the Nile Valley shows the magnitude of the Nilotic civilizations and their architectural achievements. Exhibits lead you from prehistory through the kingdoms of Kush and Meröe into Christian and Islamic eras, until the drowning of Nubia beneath Lake Nasser and the salvage of its ancient monuments.

A striking **quartzite statue** of a Kushite priest of Amun attests to Nubian rule of Thebes during the XXV Dynasty (c.747– 656 BC). While there's little to show for Meröe, tumuli from the later Ballana culture of Lower Nubia have yielded superb **horse armour** and jewellery, and you can see **frescoes** salvaged from the Coptic churches of Nubia. There are life-size models of traditional Nubian houses and photographs of the mud-brick fortresses, churches and cemeteries that were abandoned to the rising waters of Lake Nasser as the temples were moved to higher land.

The grounds

Terraced and boulder-ridden, with a watercourse falling over weirs, the grounds evoke the landscape of Nubia and form an outdoor museum of Nubian architecture. To the south is an artificial cave containing **prehistoric rock art** removed from now inundated areas of Nubia, and a mud-brick **house** furnished as a century ago, with mannequins wearing silver jewellery. Islamic monuments and antiquities, including the **mausoleum** of 77 *wali* (sheikhs), can be found in the opposite direction.

A side-road beside the museum provides a short-cut to the Fatimid Cemetery and the Unfinished Obelisk.

Fatimid Cemetery

Access via Sharia al-Gabana al-Fatemeya, 2.5km from the city centre • Daily 24hr • Free

Covering a dusty slope below the Nubia Museum, Aswan's fenced-off **Fatimid Cemetery** is a sprawl of low mud-brick tombs dating from Tulunid times (ninth century AD) up to the present, ranging from basic enclosures to complex domed cubes. Though not as grand as Cairo's Cities of the Dead (or inhabited by squatters), many have a shape unique to southern Egypt, with protruding "horns" below their domes.

The identities of most of the people buried here have been lost since their marble plaques fell off after a freak nineteenth-century rainstorm and were taken to Cairo without anyone recording their origin, although the tombs of local sheikhs (marked by green flags) are still revered by many Aswanis – but not by Salafists, who abhor such practices as idolatry.

By walking down from the main entrance towards the four-storey building facing the back of the cemetery, you'll emerge on Sharia Dr Abdel Radi Hanafi near the site of the Unfinished Obelisk.

Unfinished Obelisk

Sharia Dr Abdel Radi Hanafi, 3km from the centre (£E30–40 return by taxi; excursions to Abu Simbel often stop here on the way back to Aswan) • Daily 8am–4pm • £E30

The **Northern Quarries** (actually south of town) are the best-known of the many quarrying sites in the hills around Aswan, which supplied the Ancient Egyptians with fine red granite for their temples and colossi. From chisel marks and discarded tools, Egyptologists have been able to deduce quarrying techniques, such as soaking wooden wedges to split fissures, and using quartz sand slurry as an abrasive. A visitors' trail runs through the quarry past some **pictographs** of dolphins and ostriches, painted by ancient quarry workers.

The quarries' fame derives from a gigantic **Unfinished Obelisk**, which was roughly dressed and nearly cut free from the bedrock before being abandoned after a flaw in the stone was discovered. Had it been finished, the obelisk would have weighed 1168 tons and stood nearly 42m high. It's reckoned that this was the intended mate for the so-called Lateran Obelisk in Rome, which originally stood before the temple of Tuthmosis III at Karnak and is still credited as being the largest obelisk in the world.

Elephantine Island

£E1 by public ferry (see p.347) from the docks near Thomas Cook (for Siou) or EgyptAir (for Koti and the Aswan Museum); £E5 by private motor-launch or felucca

Aswan's Elephantine Island takes its name from the huge black **rocks** clustered around its southern end, which resemble a herd of pachyderms bathing in the river. From a felucca you can see cartouches and Pre-dynastic inscriptions carved on the rock faces, which are too sheer to view from the island. Elephantine's spectacular beauty is marred only by the towering *Mövenpick Resort Aswan*, reached by its own private ferry and cut off from the rest of the island by a tall fence. A vast extension is under construction further north.

Siou and Koti

Two **Nubian villages** nestle amid palm groves, their houses painted sky-blue, pink or yellow and often decorated with hajj scenes. Chickens and goats roam shady alleys where elders gossip and women share chores, as their menfolk work in the fields. You can stroll from one village to the other in fifteen minutes, but may be invited into somebody's house.

The northern village, **Siou**, has a small museum, **Animalia** (daily 8am–5pm; £E5, or £E10 with guided tour) in the family home of birdwatching guide Mohammed Sobhi (see p.348). Exhibits include stuffed animals, geological samples and photos of Nubia before it was submerged by Lake Nasser, which he enjoys explaining over tea. Nearer the *Mövenpick* fence, **Baaba Dool** (no set hours; free) is a beautifully painted house whose owner Mustafa (☎010 0497 2608) arranges live music and dancing, henna tattooing by local women (see p.348), and serves tea on a rooftop overlooking the Island of Plants, perfect for birdwatching at sunset.

The other village, **Koti**, has its ferry landing-stage just downhill from the Aswan Museum and the ruins of ancient Yebu (see below).

Aswan Musuem

Daily: May–Sept 7am–5pm; Oct–April 7am–4pm • £E30 (including the Nilometers and ruins)

The small **Aswan Museum** casts light on the island's past, when its southern end was occupied by the town of Yebu or Abu (meaning both "elephant" and "ivory" in the Ancient Egyptian language). Most of the museum's best exhibits have been moved to the Nubia Museum, but a mummified gazelle and jewellery found at the island's Temple of Satet are worth a look, as is the **Annexe**, whose highlights include a life-size granite statue of a seated Tuthmosis III, a colobus monkey embracing a pillar and a pre-nuptial agreement from the reign of Nectanebo II.

The museum was originally the villa of Sir William Willcocks, who designed the first Aswan Dam, and is set amid fragrant subtropical **gardens**.

The Nilometers

In ancient times the Nilometers at Aswan were the first to measure the river's rise, enabling priests to calculate the height of the inundation, crop yields over the next year and the rate of taxation (which peasants paid in kind). There are two on the island, built at the tail end of pharaonic civilization but based on far older practice and used for centuries afterwards.

The easier to find is the **Nilometer of the Satet Temple**, by the riverside; ninety enclosed rock-cut steps lead down to a square shaft with walls graduated in Arabic, Roman and pharaonic numerals, reflecting its usage in ancient times and during the late nineteenth century. To get there from the museum, follow the path southwards for 300m to find a sycamore tree (the pharaonic symbol of the tree-goddess, associated with Nut and Hathor) which shades the structure. Should you approach it by river, notice the rock embankments to the south, which bear **inscriptions** from the reigns of Tuthmosis III, Amenhotep III and the XXVI Dynasty ruler Psammetichus II.

The **Nilometer of the Temple of Khnum** is further inland amid the remains of Yebu. Built in the XXVI Dynasty, it consists of stairs leading down to what was probably a basin for measuring the Nile's maximum level; a scale is etched by the stairs at the northern end.

Ruins of Yebu

The dusty southern end of the island is littered with the **ruins** of the ancient town of Yebu, which covered nearly two square kilometres by Ptolemaic times. You can follow a trail from the Aswan Museum past numbered plaques identifying structures excavated or reconstructed by German and Swiss archeological teams working on Elephantine. The German mission's guidebook, *Elephantine: The Ancient Town* describes its 4400-year history and monuments.

A massive platform and foundation blocks (#6, #12 and #13) mark the site of the **Temple of Khnum**, god of the Aswan nome. The temple was founded in the Old Kingdom but entirely rebuilt during the XXX Dynasty. On its north side are the remains of pillars painted by the Romans, and Greek inscriptions; to the west stands the imposing gateway added by Alexander II, shown here worshipping Khnum.

Immediately to the north lies a Greco-Roman **Necropolis of Sacred Rams** (#11), unearthed in 1906, while further northwest stands the small **Temple of Hekayib**, a VI Dynasty nomarch buried in the Tombs of the Nobles (see below) who was later deified; the stelae and inscriptions found here by Labib Habachi in 1946 revealed much about Aswan during the Middle Kingdom.

Due east is a **Temple of Satet** where excavations continue to produce discoveries. Built by Queen Hatshepsut around 1490 BC, it was the last of more than thirty such temples on this site, dating back four millennia, dedicated to the goddess who incarnated the fertile aspect of the inundation. Beneath the temple archeologists have found a shaft leading 19m into the granite bedrock, where a natural **whirl hole** is thought to have amplified the sounds of the rising water table (the first indication of the life-giving annual flood) and was revered as the "Voice of the Nile". Although the High Dam has since silenced its voice, a half-buried statue near the temple still draws new brides and barren women longing for the gift of fertility.

To the southwest of Khnum's temple, the layered **remains of ancient houses** have yielded Aramaic papyri attesting to a sizeable **Jewish colony** on Elephantine in the sixth century BC. A military order by Darius II permitting the Yebu garrison to observe Passover in 419 BC suggests that they defended the southernmost border of the Persian empire. Although nothing remains of their temple to Yahweh, the Germans used leftover blocks from Kalabsha (see p.360) to reconstruct a **Ptolemaic sanctuary** with decorations added by the Nubian pharaoh Arkamani in the third century BC, at the tip of the island.

Island of Plants (Kitchener's Island)

Best visited as part of a felucca tour (see p.347), otherwise accessible by felucca (£E10–15) from the western shore of Elephantine Island, near Siou • Daily: May–Sept 8am–6pm; Oct–April 8am–5pm • £E15

Almost hidden from sight by Elephantine Island, the verdant **Island of Plants** (or Botanical Garden) is still known to many tourists as "**Kitchener's Island**". Nubians from Elephantine recall how their ancestors were evicted so that the island could be awarded to Sir Horatio Kitchener for his military exploits in Sudan. Here he indulged his passion for exotic flora, importing shrubs and seeds from as far afield as India and Malaysia. Today this island-wide botanical garden is slightly scruffy but still a wonderful place to relax, with birdlife, butterflies and stately palms suffused with the aroma of sandalwood for an hour before sunset.

Tombs of the Nobles

Aswan Gharb, west bank • Public ferry from the Corniche near Midan al-Mahatta (£E1, although they may demand £E5) • Daily 8am–5pm • £E30

Hewn into the cliffside facing Aswan, the **Tombs of the Nobles** recall local governors and other ancient dignitaries, with artwork whose immediacy and concern for everyday life makes a refreshing change from royal art. Situated at different heights – **Old and Middle Kingdom** ones uppermost, **Roman** tombs nearest the river – the tombs are numbered in ascending order from south to north. Taking the path up from the ticket kiosk, you reach the high-numbered ones first.

You can combine a visit to the tombs with the Monastery of Saint Simeon by **walking** 2km across the desert via the domed hilltop Muslim shrine known as **Qubbet el-Hawa** (Tomb of the Wind), from which there's a superb view for miles around. Be sure to wear a hat and carry plenty of water.

Tomb of Sirenput I (#36)

Turn right at the top of the steps and follow the path downhill around the cliffside to find the tomb of **Sirenput I**, overseer of the priests of Khnum and Satet and Guardian of the South during the XII Dynasty. The six pillars of the tomb's vestibule bear portraits and biographical texts. On the left-hand wall Sirenput watches bulls fighting

2

and spears fish from a papyrus raft, accompanied by his sandal-bearer, sons and dog. On the opposite wall he's portrayed with his mutt and bow-carrier, and also sitting above them in a garden with his mother, wife and daughters while being entertained by singers; the lower register shows three men gambling.

Among the badly damaged murals in the **hall** beyond, you can just discern fowlers with a net (on the lower right wall), a hieroglyphic biography (left) and a marsh-hunting scene (centre). Beyond lies a **chapel** with a false door set into the rear niche; the corridor to the left leads to the burial chamber.

Tomb of Pepi-Nakht (#35)

To reach the other tombs, return to the top of the steps and follow the path southwards. Among a cluster of tombs to the left of the steps is a two-roomed structure ascribed to Hekayib (whose cult temple stands on Elephantine), called here by his other name, **Pepi-Nakht**. As overseer of foreign troops during the long reign of Pepi II (VI Dynasty), he led colonial campaigns in Asia and Nubia, which are related on either side of the door of the left-hand room.

Tomb of Harkuf (#34)

Harkhuf was the overseer of foreign troops under Pepi I, Merenre and Pepi II. An eroded biography inside the entrance relates his three trading expeditions into Nubia, including a letter from the eight-year-old Pepi II, urging Harkhuf to bring back safely a "dancing dwarf from the land of spirits" (thought to be a pygmy from Equatorial Africa), whom Pepi desired to see "more than the gifts of Sinai or Punt". The tiny hieroglyphic figure of a pygmy appears several times in the text.

Tomb of Sirenput II (#31)

The largest, best-preserved tomb belongs to **Sirenput II**, who held the same offices as his father Sirenput I under Amenemhat II, during the apogee of the Middle Kingdom. Beyond its vestibule (with an offerings slab between the second and third pillars on the right) lies a corridor with six niches containing Osirian statues of Sirenput, still vividly coloured like his portraits on the four pillars of the chapel, where the artist's grid lines are visible in places. Best of all is the recess at the back, where Sirenput appears with his wife and son (left), attends his seated mother in a garden (right) and receives flowers from his son (centre). Notice the elephant in the upper left corner of this tableau.

Tombs of Mekhu (#25) and Sabni (#26)

At the top of the double **ramps** ascending the hillside (up which sarcophagi were dragged) are the adjacent tombs of a father and son which are interesting for their monumentality – a large vestibule with three rows of rough-hewn pillars, flanked by niches and burial chambers – and for their story. After his father **Mekhu** was killed in Nubia, **Sabni** mounted a punitive expedition that recovered the body. As a sign of respect, Pepi II sent his own embalmers to mummify the corpse; Sabni travelled to Memphis to personally express his thanks with gifts, as related by an inscription at the entrance to his tomb.

Monastery of St Simeon

Accessible on foot (30min) or by camel (£E35–45/hr) from near the Aga Khan's villa, or by walking from the Tombs of the Nobles (see p.343) • Daily 8am–5pm • £E25

Founded in the seventh century and rebuilt in the tenth, the fortress-like **Monastery of St Simeon** (Deir Anba Samaan) was originally dedicated to Anba Hadra, a local saint who encountered a funeral procession the day after his wedding and decided to renounce the world for a hermit's cave before the marriage was consummated. From here, monks made evangelical forays into Nubia, where they converted the Nobatae to Christianity. After the Muslim conquest, the Nobatae used the monastery as a base during their incursions into Egypt, until Saladin had it wrecked in 1173.

One of the custodians will show you around the complex. Its now-roofless **Basilica** bears traces of frescoes of the Apostles, their faces scratched out by Muslim iconoclasts. In a nearby chamber with a font is the place where St Simeon used to stand sleeplessly reading the Bible, with his beard tied to the ceiling so as to deliver a painful tug if he nodded off. The central **keep** has room for three hundred monks sleeping five to a cell; graffiti left by Muslim pilgrims who camped here en route to Mecca can be seen in the last room on the right.

Agha Khan Mausoleum

Accessible by felucca or motorboat as part of a tour (see p.347) or by walking from the Monastery of St Simeon or the Tombs of the Nobles • No admission

The arid west bank is the domain of funerary monuments, ancient and modern. From a walled **villa** with a riverside garden, stairs ascend the hillside to the domed **Mausoleum of the Aga Khan**. Its marble sarcophagus enshrines Aga Khan III, the 48th Imam of the Isma'ili sect of Shi'ite Muslims, who was weighed in jewels for his diamond jubilee in 1945. Drawn to Aswan by its climate and hot sands, which relieved his rheumatism, he fell in love with its beauty, built a villa and spent every winter here till his death in 1957.

Until she was buried beside him in 2000, his widow ensured that a fresh red rose was placed on his sarcophagus every day; legend has it that when none was available in Egypt, a rose was flown in by private plane from Paris on six successive days. The compound has been closed since her death but remains an imposing sight.

Western Quarry

2km from Aswan Gharb by camel with a guide (£E70–100 return; 30min each way) • Daily 24hr • Free

The remote **Western Quarry** in the desert beyond the Tombs of the Nobles is harshly evocative of the effort to supply stone for pharaonic monuments. Huge blocks were prised from the sandstone of Jebel Simaan and dragged on rollers towards the Nile for shipment down-river; the stone for Luxor's Colossi of Memnon may have come from here. An **Unfinished Obelisk** with hieroglyphs extolling Seti I (c.1294–79 BC) was abandoned by the wayside after a flaw in the rock was discovered. This desolate site is seldom visited – beware of snakes.

Sehel Island

4km upriver from Aswan • £E80–150 return by motorboat, £E110–150 by felucca (see p.347) • **Island**: Daily 24hr • Free • **Inscriptions**: Daily 8am–5pm • £E25

On a winter's day there's nothing more relaxing than a cruise to **Sehel Island** by felucca or motorboat, easily arranged in town (see p.347). Bring swimming gear, water and a hat, and come well shod: although the river is cool, the rocks and sand are scorchingly hot. En route, look out for the bougainvillea-festooned villa of pop star Mohammed Mounir, on the east bank of the river.

Landing on Sehel you'll be led by local kids to a Nubian village where **Mohammed Hassan** offers music and meals in his house (☎012 2415 4902) or to the "ruins" (as locals call them) dominating the island. These two hills of jumbled boulders have over 250 **inscriptions** from the Middle Kingdom until Ptolemaic times, mostly recording expeditions beyond the First Cataract or prayers of gratitude for their safe return. Atop the eastern hill, a Ptolemaic **Famine Stele** (#81) backdated to the reign of Zoser relates how he ended a seven-year famine during the III Dynasty by placating Khnum, god of the cataract, with a new temple on Sehel and the return of lands confiscated from his cult centre at Esna, which had provoked Khnum to withhold the inundation.

Sculpture Park

East bank, 6km south of the city centre • £E60 return by taxi • Daily 24hr • Free

Out towards the old Aswan Dam, the arid granite hills overlooking the First Cataract have been quarried since antiquity: an apt setting for Aswan's **Sculpture Park**

2

FEKRA

In Arabic, *fekra* means thought or idea – and the lakeside **Fekra Culture Centre** (ⓦfekraculture.com) near Shallal is brimming with both. Founded by film-maker Ahmed Abdel Mohsen, it's affiliated to Cairo's Townhouse Gallery and Makan club, Zad al-Mostafer in the Fayoum and other art networks abroad, collaborating on projects to share and enrich Nubian culture. Their mud-brick compound of Bedouin tents, chic little rooms and Gaudi-esque toilets open to the sky comes with recording equipment, views of the First Cataract and Philae Temple, birdlife and river bathing. Film-makers, dancers, painters and performers are welcome to apply, but their work must suit the project's theme. The cost of **staying** (with meals) ranges from €100 a night down to nothing, depending on your affluence or poverty. Over summer, rooms or houses might be rented out to tourists if no workshops are scheduled. The back-road that leads here begins near the Sculpture Park.

(El-Mathaf el-Maftouh) of large abstract works by artists attending the international Sculpture Symposium. The park has a superb **view** of the First Cataract (especially at sunset), and may host a **Sound and Light Show** in the future.

Be sure to get a taxi whose driver knows the way from town (about 25min). Take the road for the Aswan Dam but turn off onto an uphill road rather than towards the Shallal docks (for ferries to Philae), continuing until you reach the top; the sculptures are on the right, the still-working **Southern Quarries** to your left. While out here, you could also visit the **Fekra Culture Centre**, 2km away (see map, p.353, and box above).

First Cataract

6km south of the centre (£E60 return by taxi, £E100 by motorboat) • Daily 24hr • Free

Sehel Island, the Sculpture Park and the Aswan Dam all afford wonderful views of the **First Cataract** (Shallal al-Awal), a lush, cliff-bound stretch of river divided into channels by granite outcrops. Before the Aswan Dams, the waters foamed and roiled, making the cataract a fearsome obstacle to upriver travel. In ancient times it was credited as being the source of the Nile (which was believed to flow south into Nubia as well as north through Egypt) and the abode of the deity who controlled the inundation (either Hapy or Khnum, or both in tandem). The foaming waters were thought to well up from a subterranean cavern where the Nile-god dwelt. Offerings continued to be made at Sehel even after the cavern's putative location shifted to Biga Island during the Late Period or Ptolemaic times (see p.355). The Arabic word for cataract, **Shallal**, is the name given to the locality behind the Aswan Dam, which can cause confusion.

ARRIVAL AND DEPARTURE ASWAN

Many tourists travel directly to Aswan from Cairo and begin their exploration of the Nile Valley from here, rather than Luxor. This makes sense, as excursions to the temples at Kom Ombo and Edfu are easier and cheaper, and Aswan is also the starting point for felucca journeys downriver.

By air EgyptAir fly directly to Aswan from Cairo (6–9 daily; 1hr 30min) and Abu Simbel (2–4 daily; 45min), with connections from most other domestic airports and many foreign capitals. Their office is on the Corniche el-Nil ☏097 231 5000; airport ☏097 348 0568 (daily 8am–8pm). Other airlines' scheduled and charter flights from Europe may only operate in the winter. All flights land at Aswan International Airport (☏097 348 0568), 23km south of town; locals pay £E50–60 for a taxi into

the centre, but drivers try to charge foreigners more. EgyptAir departures should be booked at their office on the Corniche. Flying to Abu Simbel not only saves time and avoids an uncomfortable journey but affords a unique view of Lake Nasser and the Sun Temple. Most people opt for a same-day return flight; if you want to stay overnight you have to use the 11am flight. Transfers between the airport and the temple are included in the ticket price.

By train Details of trains from Cairo are given in chapter 1 (see p.174). Travelling to Luxor (3hr), you're supposedly limited to trains #87 (3.45pm), #84 (4pm) and #85 (7.15pm), but can also use regular expresses #981 (5am) and #983 (7am). Arriving at the train station on Midan al-Mahatta you'll be pestered by hotel touts, who are best ignored.

By boat Cruise boats from Luxor either moor by the downtown Corniche el-Nil, or at the New Corniche 3–4km north, where you're reliant on taxis to reach the centre (£E20–30). *Dahabiyas* tie up on the west bank near Ghazal Island, which is pretty remote from everything and requires a motorboat to get anywhere. Feluccas moor all along the Corniche as far south as the *Old Cataract* hotel. A few travellers arrive by the weekly ferry from Wadi Halfa in Sudan at the High Dam (£E20 by taxi to Aswan). Travelling to Sudan, it's best to get a Sudanese visa in Cairo (see p.204), as their local consulate (daily except Fri 9am–4pm; ☎097 232 7231) can't always oblige. The consulate is in a public housing estate north of the train station, with a huge Sudanese flag painted on the wall. Tickets for the ferry to Wadi Halfa are sold by the Nile River Transport Corporation (☎097 230 3348) in the arcade behind the Tourist Police; their High Dam office (☎097 348 0567) may have a better idea of schedules, as the ferry (supposedly leaving Mon afternoon and arriving 24hr later) often breaks down. One-way first- (£E501) and second-class (£E321) fares include meals, but you may wish to bring your own food. Vehicle fares start at £E275 for a motorbike, £E2012 for a car.

By bus and service taxi In theory, Aswan is accessible from several Red Sea resorts, but this can't be taken for granted. About the only reliable departures from Aswan are Superjet (☎097 230 0454) buses to Marsa Alam (4hr), Hurghada (7hr) and Suez (10hr), leaving at 6am, 3.30pm and 5pm (£E35–170), and Upper Egypt Co. buses to Abu Simbel (8am & 5pm; 4hr; £E20). All leave from the Bus Station 3km north of the centre along the Corniche (50pt by minibus; £E10 by taxi), which is also the departure point for service taxis to the same destinations (with similar fares).

GETTING AROUND

Walking or cycling is fine in the centre, but Aswan's islands are only accessible by water, and more distant sites require a taxi.

By bicycle Useful for the Nubia Museum or the Unfinished Obelisk, bikes are rented (£E15/day) on Sharia Sharq al-Mahatta, near the train station.

By minibus Minibuses (50pt–£E1) run the length of the Corniche from the bus station to the Ferial Gardens (where they turn inland), and can be boarded and exited at any point en route.

By taxi Useful if you're laden with luggage, or to reach outlying hotels (£E10), the Nubia Museum, the Unfinished Obelisk, or other distant sites.

By felucca or motorboat Feluccas and motorboats offer the only way to reach certain islands or travel between them. Motorboats are faster (and cheaper), but feluccas (see box below) are best for pleasure cruises.

By ferry Motor-launches acting as public ferries sail from three points along the Corniche: from a dock near EgyptAir to Koti on Elephantine Island (for the Aswan Museum); from near Thomas Cook to Siou, further north on the island; and from the Corniche near Midan al-Mahatta to Aswan Gharb (for the Tombs of the Nobles). In each case the fare is £E1, but boatmen on the ferry to Aswan Gharb may try to charge £E5. Ferries run regularly until 11pm.

On foot Aswan's bazaars and downtown Corniche are compact enough to explore on foot, but it's quite a slog from one end to the other. Stay on the inland side of the Corniche or its central reservation to avoid being hustled by felucca touts.

FELUCCAS AT ASWAN

Feluccas are inseparable from the Aswan experience. It's wonderfully relaxing to drift downstream or tack between rocky islands; yet many visitors end up getting irked by boatmen who fritter away time before demanding baksheesh, or the persistent touts along the Corniche. To avoid disappointment contact reputable captains directly – and beware of imposters using their names. Longer felucca trips downriver towards Luxor are detailed on p.242.

Ahmed Said Gaber at the *Nubian Oasis* hotel can arrange three-hour sailing trips around the islands and west bank trips (£E100/boat) and cruises to Sehel by motorboat for up to three people (£E150/boat).

Jamaica Family The Jamaica Family from Koti on Elephantine – represented by Captain "JJ" (☎010 0356 9525 or ☎012 2414 7386, ☒captainjamaica.com) – has eight feluccas and two motorboats. They ask £E35 an hour to sail around the central islands and west bank, or £E110 for a return trip to Sehel Island (£E80 by motorboat).

INFORMATION

Tourist office Midan al-Mahatta ☎097 231 2811 or ☎010 0576 7594, ✉hak_hus@yahoo.com. Manager Abdel Hakim Hussein can answer most questions, but his felucca recommendations aren't impartial. Daily: May–Sept 8am–3pm & 7–9pm; Oct–April 8am–3pm & 6–8pm; closed Fri noon–3pm.

TOURS

Aswan is a base for **tours** as far south as Abu Simbel (combined with Philae and the Unfinshed Obelisk on the way back on the aptly named "long trip"), or the temples at Kom Ombo and Edfu en route to Luxor (you can stash your luggage on the roof of the minibus, if that's your destination).

Ahmed Said Gaber (ako "Aco") ☎012 2490 8634, ✉AhmedACO72@yahoo.com. Based at the *Nubian Oasis* hotel (see p.349), Ahmed is a reliable consolidator for minibus excursions to Abu Simbel (£E60/person; £E70 including Philae and the Unfinished Obelisk); and Kom Ombo and Edfu with onwards travel to Luxor (£E70). The cost of an excursion by taxi to Philae (£E50) or Kalabsha (£E60) can be shared by up to three people. He also arranges felucca trips (£E150/200/350/person for one/two/three nights) nearly as far downriver as Edfu, and five-star Nile cruises ($30/50/person/night double/single occupancy) to Luxor.

Amr Tours Corniche el-Nil, below the Hathor hotel ☎097 233 0024, ⓦamrtours.net. Minibus excursions to Abu Simbel, Philae and the Unfinshed Obelisk (£E85/person); Kom Ombo and Edfu, with onwards transport to Luxor (£E80/person, or £E300 for a taxi); and Nile cruises to Luxor ($30–50/person/night). Daily 9am–4pm & 7–11pm.

Mohammed Arabi ☎012 2324 0132. Aswan's islands and channels teem with egrets, hoopoes, sunbirds, pied kingfishers, herons and other species. Mohammed Arabi, the "Birdman of Aswan", guides birdwatchers in his motorboat ($30/person), and explains each species' significance in Ancient Egyptian mythology and Nubian culture. Trips start early in the morning.

Mohammed Sobhi ☎010 0545 6420. Mohammed Sobhi of Animalia (see p.342) is another excellent birdwatching guide ($25/person).

ACCOMMODATION

Hotels on the **Corniche** have views of the Nile (if not from the rooms, then from the rooftop) like hotels on Aswan's **islands**, while places in the hilltop suburb of **Medinet Nasser** overlook the First Cataract. The **west bank** provides a laidback alternative to staying in the city, where hotels in the **bazaar** tend to be noisy. As many tourists sleep aboard cruise boats vacancies are plentiful even in winter, and most hotels slash their rates over summer (prices below are for high season). In budget hotels guests are often pressured to sign up for minibus or felucca trips. Such excursions can be an economical way to see the sites, but don't be railroaded into a hasty decision.

ALONG THE CORNICHE

Hathor ☎097 231 4580, ⓦhathorhotel.com. Midway along the Corniche, this aged hotel has en-suite a/c rooms of varying sizes – some facing the Nile, others gloomy – and a rooftop with a small pool, sunloungers and great Nile views. B&B £E110

Horus ☎097 231 3313, ✉arh-2002@yahoo.com. Accessed by lift from a passage, the *Horus* has also seen better days. Their Nile-facing rooms have fans and tiny bathrooms, and the rooftop has fantastic views, but no shade nor any water in its pool. B&B £E100

Marhaba Palace ☎097 233 0102, ⓦmarhaba-aswan .com. This quasi-pharaonic three-star hotel has friendly staff, a pool and health club, fab Nile views from its rooms (with satellite TV and grand bathrooms) and rooftop and a lavish buffet breakfast. B&B $90

Memnon ☎097 230 0483, ⓦmemnonhotel-aswan .com. Similar to the *Hathor* and *Horus*, with a renovated

---

HENNA TATTOOING

Henna has been grown in southern Egypt and Nubia since ancient times and used to dye hair and adorn bodies. Today only a minority of men (usually Salafists) dye their beards red, but many women decorate their hands and feet with intricate designs for weddings. The "tattoos" last for a fortnight or so before fading. Women visitors may be offered tattooing at the Nubian villages on Elephantine, or in Aswan's bazaar. This is women's work – and a great way to spend time with Nubian women – but some local guys see it as an opportunity for lechery, so check who's doing the tattooing. Also beware of black (as opposed to traditional reddish-brown) designs, as these involve the use of a toxic hair dye, PPD, which can cause severe skin damage and allergic reactions.

floor with en-suite a/c rooms (some with bathtubs) and a shadeless rooftop with an empty pool. Reception is on the third floor, reached by a private lift. B&B **£E115**

Nile ✆ 097 231 4222, ⊛ nilehotel-aswan.com. Sited near the end of the Corniche close to EgyptAir, the spacious a/c rooms have Nile views, satellite TV and fridges, and there's also a library of novels and books about Egypt, internet (£E30/day) and helpful staff. B&B **$50**

★ **Old Cataract** ✆ 097 231 6000, ⊛ sofitel.com. Set on a granite outcrop overlooking the river, with a stately garden behind, this magnificent Moorish pile takes you back to the days of Agatha Christie (parts of *Death on the Nile* were filmed here). Following loving refurbishment by the Sofitel chain, its decor and top-class service now make it one of the finest hotels in Egypt. Guests enjoy exclusive use of the pool and terrace, but outsiders can savour a drink on the promenade where King Fouad used to sit, or in the colonial-style bar (see p.351). All rooms come with marble bathrooms, LCD TVs and wi-fi; suites have kingsize beds, butler service and terraces or balconies. **€392**

Philae ✆ 097 231 2090, ⊛ philae-hotel.com. A welcome addition to the Corniche scene, elegantly decorated and sparklingly clean. All rooms are a/c, with bath tubs, wi-fi, LCD TVs, Egyptian cotton duvets and double-glazing to reduce noise. Deluxe rooms have kingsize beds and balconies facing the river, and some suites include kitchens. B&B **$100**

Pyramisa Isis ✆ 097 231 5100, ⊛ pyramisaegypt.com. A mini-resort beside the Nile, whose great location, riverside bar-terrace and swimming pool make it popular with low-budget tour groups. It has comfy a/c chalets in a garden, free wi-fi and an Italian restaurant. B&B **$120**

AROUND THE BAZAAR AND THE TRAIN STATION

Keylany Sharia Keylany ✆ 097 231 7332 or ✆ 010 0107 0275, ⊛ keylanyhotel.com. Owned by deep-sea and Lake Nasser fishing champion Mohammed Keylany, this small hotel is a longtime favourite. Well-run and welcoming, it has a basement jacuzzi and a shaded rooftop with a tiny pool, where pancakes are served for breakfast. Cosy en-suite rooms with fans, a/c, TV, fridges and safes, and there's wi-fi in the lobby and on the rooftop. B&B **$34**

Nuba Nile Off Midan al-Mahatta ✆ 097 231 3353, ⊛ nubanile.com. The best option near the station, family-run and ultra clean, with wi-fi (£E30/day), computer rental (£E10/hr), billiards (£E20/hr), a library and a rooftop with a paddling pool and BBQ parties. Rooms come in all shapes and sizes – ask to see a few before choosing – all have a/c, bath tubs and fridges. B&B **$180**

Nubian Oasis Off Sharia al-Souk ✆ 097 231 2123 or ✆ 012 2490 8634, ✉ nubianoasis_hotel_aswan @hotmail.com. An aged high-rise with erratic hot water, wi-fi and grotty rooms with fans or a/c (bathroom/TV and

fridge £E20/30 extra) that remains popular with backpackers for its low rates, relaxed vibe and engaging manager Ahmed ("Aco"), who arranges minibus excursions, Nile cruises and felucca trips. B&B **£E30**

Yassin Off Sharia al-Souk ✆ 097 231 7109. Heavily touted at the station like the adjacent *Noorhan* (best avoided), the *Yassin* gets mixed reviews. Some complain of being hassled by staff; others praise their helpfulness and rate it a better low-budget option than the *Nubian Oasis* for its cleaner rooms (some en suite) and superior wi-fi coverage. **£E70**

ELEPHANTINE AND ISIS ISLANDS

Baaba Dool Siou, Elephantine Island ✆ 010 0497 2608. About as rustic as you can get within ten minutes' from the Corniche, this traditional mud-brick house in one of the island's Nubian villages has clean, basic rooms (bring a sleeping bag) and shared hot showers. Some have a superb view of the Nile; others are merely fly-ridden. Meals by arrangement. **€10**

Mövenpick Resort Aswan Elephantine Island ✆ 097 230 3455, ⊛ movenpick-hotels.com. Although its ugly tower is long overdue for demolition and they're inexplicably constructing yet more buildings at the far end of the island, the hotel's gardens and views are lovely, and its pool and spa are the best in Aswan. Guests can stay in the main building or in villas in the grounds. The resort is reached by a 24hr ferry from near the *Pyramisa Isis* on the Corniche. B&B **$150**

Pyramisa Isis Island Resort & Spa Isis Island ✆ 097 231 7400, ⊛ pyramisaegypt.com. Built beside a nature reserve containing the only primordial Nilotic vegetation left in Egypt, this swanky resort has villas (with private pools) and chalets in its grounds, and rooms in the main wing. Amenities include a French-managed health club and spa, two pools, minigolf and wi-fi in the lobby. The hotel is reached by a 24hr launch from the docks near EgyptAir. Rooms **€140**; chalets **€130**

MEDINET NASSER

Basma Sharia al-Fanadek ✆ 097 231 0901, ⊛ basmahotel.com. Perched on the hillside above the *Old Cataract*, near the Nubia Museum, this four-star complex has disabled access, a large heated pool and a garden terrace with stunning views of Elephantine, although it's best avoided during the sculpture symposium (see p.352) due to the noise outside. Accessible by hourly free bus from the *Pyramisa Isis* on the Corniche. B&B **$230**

Sara Sharia al-Fanadek, 2km beyond the Nubia Museum ✆ 097 232 7234, ⊛ sarahotel-aswan.com. Built on a clifftop with stunning views over the First Cataract and the Western Desert, the Sara is ideal for chilling out, with a pool, cocktail bar and *sheesha* terrace. All rooms are en suite and a/c with satellite TV; the corner rooms have big balconies, and it's often possible to negotiate discounts. When the splendid isolation palls, there's a free hourly shuttle bus into town. B&B $160

WEST BANK

Adam's Home Nag al-Balida, 7km north of Aswan, 2.5km from the bridge ☎010 0640 4302. A traditional village extended-family home of simple mud-brick rooms round a courtyard, where travellers crossing Africa by motorbike or jeep often stay (sleeping bag required). Owner Yehia (an actor and director) encourages guests to bathe in the Nile and loves sharing his passion for Nubian culture. Though inconvenient for sightseeing in Aswan, it can be reached by taxi from town or a pick-up truck from the Tombs of the Nobles (roughly £E50). **Room £E60**

★ **Bet el-Kerem** Aswan Gharb ☎012 2391 1052, ⓦbetelkerem.com. Five minutes' walk from the Tombs of the Nobles, this charming rustic guesthouse co-owned by a Dutch woman has only nine rooms (all a/c but not all en

suite), so reservations are advised. Its rooftop terrace has Nile views, darts, dominoes and backgammon. Their chef cooks delicious meals, and they organize camel trips, cycle rides and Nubian folklore shows. B&B **€40**

★ **Mohammed Arabi Houses** Near Ghazal Island ☎012 2324 0132. Aswan's top birdwatching guide (see p.348) has invested his savings in four lovely houses with Nubian-style decor, marble floors and fancy bathrooms, built amid a large garden and orchard whose produce is served at dinner on a terrace facing the Nile. It's a wonderful place to relax, but any trip to or from Aswan entails paying for a motorboat. **€100**

Nubian Beach Near Ghazal Island ☎012 2169 9145, ⓦnubianbeachold.com. This folksier Nubian place beside Mohammed Arabi's land offers simple rooms on a B&B or half-board basis, basic three-person tents with the use of a shower, sand saunas (see p.352) and the chance to handle baby crocodiles, although little English is spoken. B&B **€25**; tent **€10**/person

EATING AND DRINKING

Eating out offers the pleasures of fresh fish and Nubian dishes such as okra in spicy tomato sauce in riverside **restaurants**. Most places on the Corniche add 10–25 percent service charge, but hardly anywhere serves **alcohol** or takes cards.

CAFÉS & RESTAURANTS

★ **1902 Restaurant** Old Cataract hotel ☎097 231 6000. With its gourmet cuisine and silver service in a magnificent Moorish hall, 1902 is by far the finest dining in town. Try scallops with asparagus and mango sauce (£E220); mushroom salad with pigeon, Emmental, balsamic and honey sauce (£E180); sauteed beef fillet with foie gras whisky sauce (£E250); and Pavlova with gingery pistachios (£E100). Pearls or tuxedos aren't obligatory but you're expected to dress smartly. Reservations essential. Daily 7–11pm.

Al-Sayida Nafisa Off Sharia Sayida Nafisa. Well known to locals, this humble eatery consists of a yard full of tables with tasty set meals (£E25–35) of chicken, fish or kofta, soup, rice and salad. Daily noon–1am.

Aswan Moon Corniche el-Nil ☎097 231 6108. A spacious floating restaurant hung with colourful tent fabric, although it's become somewhat less popular since it stopped selling alcohol. Food includes fish, chicken, pizzas and pasta dishes (£E25–55), mixed grills (£E45) and salads (£E18) – try the douad basha, meatballs in tomato sauce, baked in an earthenware pot. Daily 8am–midnight.

Biti Pizza Midan al-Mahatta ☎097 230 0948. Tourists are given an English menu of Western-style pizzas (£E38) rather than an Arabic one with more combinations, including flaky fiteer, which they only serve after 2pm. The upstairs dining rooms are a/c, with a view of the square. Daily 10am–1am.

★ **Chief Khalil** Sharia al-Souk ☎097 231 0142. With its friendly Islamist staff, religious TV and kitsch

water-features, this small a/c café is an incongrous place to eat delicious fresh crab or shrimp (£E50), sea bream (£E70), sea bass (£E60) or lobster (£E120), with rice, salad and tahina. Daily 1pm–1am.

El-Madena Sharia al-Souk ☎097 230 5696. A small tiled diner under the same management as Makka (see below); the two are named after the holy cities of Islam. Customers sharing tables tuck into tasty set meals (£E35–55) of liver, chicken or kebab with salad, tahina and vegetable stew. Daily noon–11pm.

El-Masry Sharia Abu Zid ☎097 230 2576. Tucked away on a sidestreet off the bazaar, this quiet family-friendly a/c restaurant (whose name means "The Egyptian") serves kebab and kofta (£E105), grilled pigeon (£E25), fried fish (£E20) and melokheya soup. Daily noon–midnight.

El-Safwa Off Sharia al-Souk. A cheery two-storey diner specializing in kushari that also does "quiches" of macaroni with meat, and has muhalabiyya for dessert, making it ideal for a quick meal under £E10. Daily 24hr.

El-Tahreer Pizza Midan al-Mahatta ☎097 230 7131. Across the square from Biti Pizza, this rival establishment has tables outside and does deliveries. Besides sweet and savoury fiteer (£E20–25) and Western-style pizzas (£E30), they have Egyptian desserts such as muhalabiyya, basboosa and Umm Ali (unusually served cold, though you can ask for it hot). Daily 24hr.

Makka Sharia Abtal al-Tahrir ☎097 230 3232. Slightly fancier than its sister establishment El-Madena, this restaurant is highly rated by locals for its grills, both meat and fish, served with salad, rice, tahina and vegetables.

Prices are similar to *El-Masry* (see above). Daily noon–midnight.

Moonlight Café Midan al-Mahatta ☎ 012 8990 9200. A funky rooftop café above *El-Tahreer Pizza* (entered from Sharia al-Souk), where local online gamers gather to watch TV sports and enjoy fresh juices (£E6–10); try gabana, a Nubian drink made from roasted coffee beans. Free wi-fi. Daily 8am–2am.

Nubian Beach West bank, near Ghazal Island ☎ 012 2169 9145. For £E95/person, you can enjoy a full Nubian meal at this riverside bathing spot (see p.350), with a boat there and back to Aswan. Try their Nubian coffee, spiced with ginger, cardomam and nutmeg. No set hours; by arrangement.

★ **Salah al-Din** Corniche el-Nil ☎ 097 233 2093. Popular with local couples, this terraced restaurant has an a/c dining room and a floating section like the nearby *Aswan Moon*. Try the veal piccata (£E39), fish tageen (£E37) or beef curry (£E35), washed down with a glass of Egyptian wine (£E25) or beer (£E15), or simply enjoy a *sheesha* on the terrace. Like *Emy*, it's a hangout for felucca captains. Daily 9am–midnight.

Swan Blue Nile Corniche el-Nil ☎ 097 231 2131. Next door to the *Marhaba Palace* hotel, its downstairs section does sandwiches (£E2–8), soups (£E4–6) and grills (£E24–36). Upstairs is a palatial lobby and terrace, where diners are entertained by musicians in the tourist season. Daily 24hr.

BARS

Emy Corniche el-Nil ☎ 097 230 4349. A haunt for felucca captains and expats, *Emy* (pronounced "Ee-me") has a double-decker pontoon section with views of Elephantine Island and an enclosed part that's cooler in summer. Most people come to drink chilled beer (£E12) or wine (£E80); the food (dishes £E15–40) is indifferent. Daily 8am–midnight or later.

Old Cataract Bar Old Cataract hotel ☎ 097 231 6000. Wonderfully retro – with arabesque panelling, leather or zebra-patterned armchairs and scarlet-jacketed waiters – you won't find a more elegant (or expensive) place in Aswan to drink cocktails (£E140–170), single-malt whiskies, fine cognacs or French wines. Casual-smart dress required. Daily 10am–2pm.

★ **Old Cataract Promenade Terrace** Old Cataract hotel ☎ 097 231 6000. Aswan's most romantic spot at sundown, with isolated tables along a clifftop promenade facing Elephantine; the one favoured by King Fouad is used for private BBQs. They offer two versions of a Victorian Tea (£E250/350) of sandwiches and pastries, and various cocktails (£E150), whiskies (£E130) and beers (£E35–45). Casual-smart dress required. Daily 10am–10pm.

ENTERTAINMENT AND NIGHTLIFE

After a hard day's sightseeing most tourists opt for an early night, so there's little or no nightlife, at least in the western sense. That's not to say there's nothing happening, but whether you're around when it does rather depends on luck, unless you ask for it to be arranged.

Bellydancing Major hotels may organize shows if enough guests are staying or express an interest. The basement *Mazazak* club (midnight–5am), beside the *Queen Noorhan* hotel two blocks north of the station, is the only regular venue, although it can get rowdy.

Folklore shows The *Mövenpick*, *Basma* and smaller hotels such as *Bet el-Kerem* may stage performances of tahtib (a stickfighting dance) and songs about village life, which can also be arranged at the *Nubian Beach* (see p.350), *Baaba Dool* on Elephantine (see p.349), and Mohammed Hassan's house on Sehel Island (p.345).

Nubian weddings As guests from foreign lands are held to be auspicious, tourists are often invited to attend weddings in the villages around Aswan. Nubian weddings are celebrated on a lavish scale, with musicians costing as much as £E50,000. The bridegroom recoups the expense by inviting hundreds of guests and charging them £E50 each, which makes summer – the wedding season – a costly time for locals, so don't be surprised if you're asked to contribute.

NUBIAN MUSIC

Nubian music ranges from traditional village songs backed by drums and handclapping to urban sounds reflecting the influence of jazz, funk, trance or even classical music. The one thing that all these forms have in common is that they're sung in Nubian. While famous abroad thanks to the late masters Ali Hassan Kuban and Hamza al-Din, in Egypt Nubian music isn't widely popular outside the far south. Nubian CDs and cassettes are sold in Aswan, but contemporary Nubian stars seldom hold public concerts here. As with the jobbing musicians who sometimes play in the Ferial Gardens or the Corniche-side parks at the northern end of town, their main income comes from performing at weddings and other private functions.

Sound and Light Show at Philae Temple Two or three shows nightly; check the schedules at Aswan's tourist office. As at Karnak, the show consists of an hour-long tour through the temple, whose floodlit forms are more impressive than the melodramatic soundtrack. Tickets (£E75) are sold at the dockside just before the first show begins. A four-seater taxi from Aswan and back costs about £E60 (including waiting time), plus the cost of the motorboat ride there and back (see p.360).

SHOPPING

Duty Free Shop Corniche el-Nil ⊕097 231 4939. Sells imported booze (for hard currency; bring your passport for duty free within 48hr of arrival) and Egyptian wine, beer and spirits. Daily 9am–2pm & 6–10pm.

Hanafi Bazaar Corniche el-Nil ⊕097 231 4083. Recognizable by its faux-pharaonic facade, this dusty antique shop owned by the Hanafi brothers is crammed with silk kaftans from all over Africa, amulets, baskets and genuine (not reproduction) Nubian swords. Daily 8am–10pm.

Nubia Sharia al-Souk ⊕097 231 6677. A bookstore chain stocking Egyptology, AUC titles, repro vintage photos, CDs, and foreign novels. There's a second branch at the Unfinished Obelisk (daily 7am–4pm). Daily 9am–midnight.

DIRECTORY

American Express Corniche el-Nil ⊕097 230 6983, ⊛amexfranchise.com (Sun–Thurs 9am–5pm). Exchanges currency and travellers' cheques, holds client mail and organizes tours and travel.

Banks and exchange All the following are on the Corniche and have ATMs. Egyptian Exchange (daily 8am–8pm) offers slightly better rates than Banque Misr (Sun–Thurs 8am–3pm & 5–8pm); Banque du Caire (Sun–Thurs 8.30am–2pm), AlexBank and National Bank of Egypt (Sun–Thurs 9am–2pm).

DHL Corner of the Corniche and Sharia Abbas Farid ⊕097 232 9018, ⊛dhl.com (daily except Fri 10am–2pm & 4–8pm).

Hospitals Ta'mim (Insurance) Hospital, Tariq el-Sadat ⊕09 232 0561; Army Hospital, Tariq el-Sadat ⊕097 231 4709.

Internet Net Café and Rotana Café Net (£E5–10/hr) on Sharia Abtal al-Tahrir (both daily 9am–midnight or later), and at the *Moonlight Café* (see p.351),

Passport Office Police HQ, Corniche el-Nil ⊕097 231 2238 (daily except Sat 8am–2pm & 6–8pm). For visa extensions, use the northern side entrance and head for the second floor; you'll need a photocopy of your passport details and one photo.

Post offices Corniche el-Nil (Sat–Thurs 8am–8pm; Fri 1–5pm); Sharia Abtal el-Tahrir (Sat–Thurs 8am–2pm). Both have EMS.

Spa treatments The *Pyramisa Isis Island* and *Mövenpick Resort Aswan* offer non-residents use of their sauna, steam bath, jacuzzi or whirlpool (€10–35 each). Various massages and scrubs (€17–35) are also available at the *Marhaba Palace* and *Keylany* hotels together with "sugaring", a traditional method of waxing using syrup. Immersion in hot sand has long been used to alleviate arthritis and rheumatism, with "sand saunas" at the *Isis Island* and *Mövenpick* resorts, and the rustic *Nubian Beach* (£E100 including a boat there and back).

Swimming A few hotels let non-residents use their pools. *Pyramisa Isis Island* has both heated and cold pools (£E100 including use of a pool cabin and £E50 worth of drinks) while there's a Nile-side pool at the *Pyramisa* Isis, (£E50 including soft drink) and smaller pools at the *Marhaba Palace* (£E60) and *Nuba Nile* (£E30). Some tourists enjoy bathing in the Nile despite the risk of catching bilharzia (see p.52) near riverbanks and islands that impede the water's fast flow. The safest spot is opposite Seluga Island, upriver from the *Nubian Beach* (see p.350); hire a motorboat (roughly £E50/person; £E30 for lunch). There are other fine locations at the First Cataract and Shallal (see p.346).

Thomas Cook Corniche el-Nil ⊕097 230 6839, ⊛thomascookegypt.com (daily 9am–8pm). Exchanges money, sells travellers' cheques and arranges private tours to Abu Simbel and local sites.

Tourist Police Corniche el-Nil, near Midan al-Mahatta ⊕097 231 4393; also in the train station (both daily 24hr). Pretty ineffectual, but at least they'll write a report for your insurers if anything gets stolen.

FESTIVALS IN ASWAN

Unlike Luxor, Aswan doesn't have any moulids, and the main tourist event is an international **Sculpture Symposium** (mid-Jan to mid-March), when you can see sculptors at work on the terrace of the *Basma Hotel* before their creations are sent to the Sculpture Park (p.345). On **Aswan Day** (Jan 15), the Corniche has traditionally hosted a good-natured parade of civic and military hardware, with fire engines and ambulances following jeep-loads of frogmen and rubber-suited decontamination troops. Now falling only days before the emotive anniversary of the 2011 Revolution, the parade may be cancelled in the future, or at least no longer revolve around Police Headquarters on the Corniche as it formerly did.

The Aswan Dams

The two **Aswan Dams** attest that Egypt's dilemma is more intractable than suggested by one US journalist's pithy diagnosis: "Make more land. Make fewer people. Either solution would alleviate the problem, but neither is easy." Although each dam has brought large areas under cultivation, boosted agricultural productivity and provided hydroelectricity for industry, the gains have been eroded by a population explosion – impelling Egypt to undertake yet more ambitious irrigation projects.

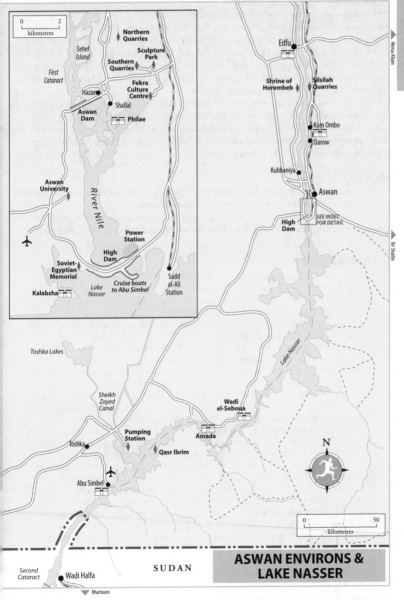

ASWAN ENVIRONS & LAKE NASSER

2

No other nation is reliant on a single man-made structure for its survival; the apocalyptic consequences of the High Dam bursting are envisaged in the novel *Gog – An End Time Mystery* (see p.628). Ever conscious of their significance, Egyptians are inclined to view both dams as tourist attractions, whereas foreigners simply regard them as routes to the temples of Abu Simbel, Philae and Kalabsha. Views from the top of both dams are spectacular, however.

Aswan Dam

7km from Aswan • Daily 7am–5pm • Crossed en route to Abu Simbel • Free

Just upriver from the First Cataract, the British built (1898–1902) the first **Aswan Dam**, later twice elevated to increase its capacity, making it the world's largest dam (50m tall, 2km long, 30m thick at the base and 11m at the top) until the 1920s. Even so it was nearly overtopped in 1946, making a larger dam essential. Since its storage and irrigation functions were taken over by the High Dam, the old dam has generated hydroelectricity for a nearby fertilizer factory.

Driving across the top, notice the 180 **sluice gates** that were once opened during the inundation and then gradually closed as the river level dropped, preserving a semi-natural flood cycle. Philae Temple is visible among the islands to the south, while at the dam's eastern end is a residential suburb for hydro-engineers called **Hazan**, where colonial villas nestle amid verdant gardens.

High Dam

13km from Aswan • Daily 7am–5pm • Crossed on the way back from Abu Simbel • Sightseeing fee of £E20/passenger if vehicles halt for more than a minute • **Visitors' Pavilion**: daily 7am–5pm • Free (but baksheesh expected)

By 1952 it was clear that the Aswan Dam could no longer satisfy Egypt's needs or guarantee security from famine. President Nasser pledged to build a new **High Dam**

LAKE NASSER

As Lake Nasser rose behind the High Dam, flooding ancient Nubia, an international effort ensured that mud-brick fortresses and burial grounds were excavated and photographed, before being abandoned to the rising waters. Half a dozen temples and tombs were salvaged to be reassembled on higher ground or in foreign museums. Since then, however, many temples in Upper Egypt have been affected by damp and salt encrustation, blamed on the rising water table and greater humidity.

Although the human, cultural and environmental costs are still being evaluated, the dam has delivered most of its promised **benefits**. Egypt has been able to convert 3000 square kilometres of cultivated land from the ancient basin system of irrigation to perennial irrigation – doubling or tripling the number of harvests – and to reclaim more than 4200 square kilometres of desert. The dam's turbines have powered a thirty percent expansion of industrial capacity; fishing and tourism on Lake Nasser have developed into profitable industries. Only the **Toshka Project** has turned out to be a failure (see box, p.367).

While the main losers have been the **Nubians**, whose homeland was submerged by the lake, other consequences are still being assessed. Evaporation from the lake has caused clouds and even rainfall over previously arid regions and the water table has risen. Because the dam traps the silt that once renewed Egypt's fields, farmers now rely on chemical fertilizers, and the soil salinity caused by perennial irrigation can only be prevented by extensive drainage projects, which create breeding grounds for mosquitoes and bilharzia-carrying snails. And with no silty deposits to replenish it, the Delta coastline is being eroded by the Mediterranean.

Some fear future **water wars**. When Ethiopia commissioned a study on damming the Abbai River (the source of the Blue Nile), Cairo warned that any reduction of Egypt's quota of Nile water, fixed by treaty at 59 billion cubic metres annually, would be seen as a threat to national security, and that Egypt would, in fact, need a larger share in the future. Egypt and Sudan are boycotting the Nile Basin Initiative by the "upstream" states (Ethiopia, Uganda, Kenya, Rwanda, Tanzania, Burundi and the Democratic Republic of Congo) to renegotiate the treaty.

(Al-Sadd al-Ali) 6km upstream, which would secure Egypt's future, power new industries and bring electricity to every village. When the World Bank reneged on its promised loan under pressure from the US, Nasser nationalized the Suez Canal to generate revenue for the project and turned to the Soviet Union for help. The dam's construction (1960–71) outlasted both his lifetime and the era of Soviet–Egyptian collaboration.

The most visible consequence of the High Dam is **Lake Nasser** (see box p.354), which backs up for 500km, well into Sudan. Over 180m deep in places, with a surface area of 6000 square kilometres, the lake is the world's largest reservoir, and seems more like an inland sea. Since a dam-burst would wash most of Egypt's population into the Mediterranean, its security is paramount. The hills bristle with radar installations and anti-aircraft missiles, and tanks guard strategic locations.

Visiting the High Dam

Most tours simply drive across the top of the dam, so certain features go unnoticed unless you're willing to pay for a closer look. Blink and you'll miss the **Soviet–Egyptian Memorial**, a giant lotus-blossom tower built to symbolize their collaboration and the dam's benefits, as depicted in heroic, Socialist Realist bas-reliefs. A lofty **observation deck**, reached by elevator, allows four people at a time to see how the dam's concrete is crumbling and be stricken by vertigo. Off the road at the far end of the dam is a **visitors' pavilion**, which the curator can unlock. Exhibits include a model of the dam, plans for its construction (in Russian and Arabic) and a photo narrative of the relocation of Abu Simbel.

Some drivers risk stopping midway across the dam to allow passengers a brief look. From this vantage point the dam's height (111m) is masked by the cantilever, but its length (3830m) and width at the top (40m) and base (980m) are impressive. From the southern side of the dam you can gaze across Lake Nasser to Kalabsha Temple. The **view** northwards includes the huge 2100-megawatt **power station** on the east bank and the channels through which water is routed into the Nile, rushing out amid clouds of mist, sometimes crowned by a rainbow. **Philae** lies among the cluster of islands further downriver.

Philae

10km from Aswan • Daily 8am–5pm• £E50

The island of **PHILAE** and its **Temple of Isis** have bewitched visitors since Ptolemaic times, when most of the complex was constructed. The devout and curious were drawn here by a cult that flourished throughout the Roman Empire well into the Christian era. Although the first Europeans to "rediscover" Philae in the eighteenth century could only marvel at it from a distance after their attempts to land were "met with howls, threats and eventually the spears of the natives living in the ruins", subsequent visitors revelled in this mirage from antiquity.

After the building of the first Aswan Dam, rising waters lapped and surged about the temple, submerging it for half the year, when tourists would admire its shadowy presence beneath the translucent water. However, once it became apparent that the new High Dam would submerge Philae forever, UNESCO and the Egyptian authorities organized a massive operation (1972–80) to **relocate** its temples on nearby **Aglika Island**, which was landscaped to match the original site. The new Philae is magnificently set amid volcanic outcrops, like a jewel in the royal blue lake, but no longer faces Biga Island, sacred to Osiris. The Osirian myth and the cult of Isis are the subject of Philae's **Sound and Light Show** (see p.352).

The Temple of Isis

Philae's cult status dates back to the New Kingdom, when Biga Island was identified as one of the burial places of Osiris – and the first piece of land to emerge from the

2

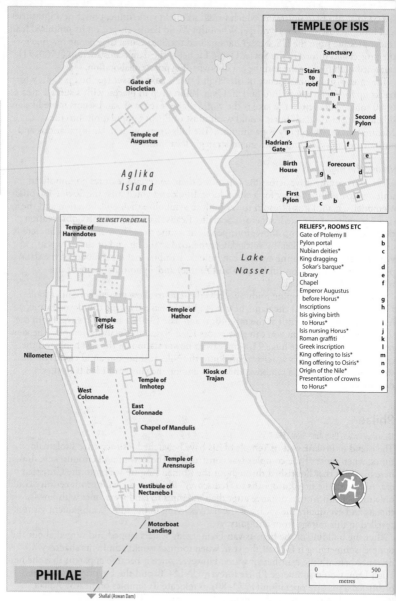

TEMPLE OF ISIS

Sanctuary

Stairs to roof

Second Pylon

Hadrian's Gate

Birth House

Forecourt

First Pylon

Aglika Island

Gate of Diocletian

Temple of Augustus

SEE INSET FOR DETAIL

Temple of Harendotes

Temple of Isis

Lake Nasser

Nilometer

Temple of Hathor

Temple of Imhotep

West Colonnade

East Colonnade

Chapel of Mandulis

Temple of Arensnupis

Vestibule of Nectanebo I

Kiosk of Trajan

Motorboat Landing

PHILAE

▽ Shallal (Aswan Dam)

RELIEFS*, ROOMS ETC	
Gate of Ptolemy II	a
Pylon portal	b
Nubian deities*	c
King dragging Sokar's barque*	d
Library	e
Chapel	f
Emperor Augustus before Horus*	g
Inscriptions	h
Isis giving birth to Horus*	i
Isis nursing Horus*	j
Roman graffiti	k
Greek inscription	l
King offering to Isis*	m
King offering to Osiris*	n
Origin of the Nile*	o
Presentation of crowns to Horus*	p

N

0 — 500
metres

primordial waters of Chaos. Since Biga was forbidden to all but the priesthood, however, public festivities centred upon neighbouring **Philae**, which was known originally as the "Island from the Time of Re".

Excluding a few remains from the Late Period, the existing **Temple of Isis** was constructed over some eight hundred years by Ptolemaic and Roman rulers who sought to identify themselves with the Osirian myth and the cult of Isis. An exquisite fusion of Ancient Egyptian and Greco-Roman architecture, the temple complex harmonizes

FISHING SAFARIS ON LAKE NASSER

Besides antiquities, Lake Nasser is renowned for its **fishing** – for **Nile perch** (the largest caught weighed 176kg, just short of the world record), huge **tilapia**, piranha-like **tigerfish** and eighteen kinds of **giant catfish**. After tilapia (at the bottom of the food chain) spawns in mid-March, perch and catfish thrive in depths of up to 6m till late September, after which big fish are caught in deeper water until February by trolling over submerged promontories or islands, and by shore- or fly-fishing from March to July. The best fishing grounds are in the north of the lake – beyond Amada the fish get eaten by crocodiles. Anglers base themselves on mother ships and fish in twos or threes off smaller boats. Fishing packages include meals, soft drinks and transfers from Aswan in the price; specialist rods can be hired if needed.

African Angler T 097 230 9748 or T 012 749 1892, E enquiries@african-angler.net. Former Kenyan safari guide Tim Bailey organizes one-, six- and thirteen-day fishing trips, marketed in Britain through Tailor Made Holidays.

Lake Nasser Adventure W nilefishing.com. Nubian fisherman Nekrashi (T 012 2350 3825, satellite phone T +88216 333 601 38) and his partner Steven (T 012 2104 0255 or T +88216 333 601 04) have three mother ships on the lake almost all year round. Prices depend on the time of year.

Miskaa T 097 232 8866, W miskaa.com. Another local outfit with eight small boats and mother ships, which does bird- and crocodile-watching safaris as well as fishing trips.

perfectly with its setting, sculpted pillars and pylons gleaming white or mellow gold against Mediterranean-blue water and black Nilotic rock.

Vestibule of Nectanebo

Motorboats land near the southern end of the island. In ancient times, on the original Philae, visitors ascended a double stairway to the **Vestibule of Nectanebo** at the entrance to the temple precincts. Erected by a XXX Dynasty pharaoh in honour of his "Mother Isis", this was the prototype for the graceful kiosks of the Ptolemaic and Roman era. Notice the double capitals on the remaining columns, traditional flower shapes topped with sistrum-Hathor squares that supported the architrave. The screens that once formed the walls are crowned with cavetto cornices and rows of *uraeus* serpents, a motif dating back to Zoser's complex at Saqqara, nearly three thousand years earlier.

The colonnades

Beyond the vestibule stretches an elongated trapezoidal courtyard flanked by colonnades. The **West Colonnade** is the better preserved, with finely carved capitals, each slightly different. The windows in the wall behind once faced Biga, the island of Osiris; the one opposite the first two columns is topped by a relief of Nero offering two eyes to Horus and Isis.

The plainer, unfinished **East Colonnade** abuts a succession of ruined structures. Past the foundations of the **Temple of Arensnupis** (worshipped as the "Good Companion of Isis" in the Late Period) lies a ruined **Chapel of Mandulis**, the Nubian god of Kalabsha. Near the First Pylon, an unfinished **Temple of Imhotep** honours the philosopher-physician who designed Zoser's Step Pyramid and was later deified as a god of healing. Its forecourt walls show Khnum, Satis, Anukis, Isis and Osiris, and Ptolemy IV before Imhotep.

The First Pylon

The lofty **First Pylon** was built by Neos Dionysos (Ptolemy XII), who smites enemies in the approved fashion at either corner, watched by Isis, Horus and Hathor. Set at right angles to the pylon, the Gate of Ptolemy II **[a]** is probably a remnant of an earlier temple. The pylon's main portal **[b]** is still older (dating from the reign of Nectanebo II) and was formerly flanked by two granite obelisks; now only two **stone lions** remain.

Inside the portal are inscriptions by Napoleon's troops, commemorating their victory over the Mamlukes in 1799. The smaller door in the western section of the pylon leads through to the Birth House and was used for rituals; the entrance depicts the personified deities of Nubia and the usual Egyptian pantheon [c]. On the back of the pylon are scenes of priests carrying Isis' barque.

2

The Forecourt

Emerging into the **Forecourt**, most visitors make a beeline for the Birth House or the Second Pylon, overlooking the colonnade to the east. Here, reliefs behind the stylish plant columns show the king performing rituals such as dragging the barque of Sokar [d]. A series of doors lead into six rooms which probably had a service function; one of them, dubbed the Library [e], features Thoth in his ibis and baboon forms, Maat, lion-headed Tefnut and Sheshat, the goddess of writing. At the northern end stands a ruined chapel [f], which the Romans erected in front of a granite outcrop that was smoothed into a stele under Ptolemy IV and related his gift of lands to the temple.

The Second Pylon

Set at an angle to its forerunner, the **Second Pylon** changes the axis of the temple. A large relief on the right tower shows Neos Dionysos placing sacrifices before Horus and Hathor; in a smaller scene above he presents a wreath to Horus and Nephthys, offers incense and anoints an altar before Osiris, Isis and Horus. Similar scenes on the other tower have been defaced by early Christians, who executed the paintings in the upper right-hand corner of the pylon passageway, leading into the temple proper.

The Birth House

The western side of the forecourt is dominated by the colonnaded **Birth House** of Ptolemy IV, which linked his ancestry to Horus and Osiris. Most of the exterior reliefs were added in Roman times, which is why Emperor Augustus shadows Buto, goddess of the north, as she plays a harp before the young, naked Horus and his mother at one end of the central register, behind the Hathor-headed colonnade [g]. Further south and higher up, the Roman reliefs overlie inscriptions in hieroglyphs and demotic characters that partly duplicate those on the Rosetta Stone [h]. Inside, a columned forecourt and

---

THE CULT OF ISIS

Of all the cults of Ancient Egypt, none endured longer or spread further than the worship of the goddess **Isis**. As the consort of Osiris, she civilized the world by instituting marriage and teaching women the domestic arts. As an enchantress, she collected the dismembered fragments of Osiris's body and briefly revived him to conceive a son, Horus, using her magic to help him defeat the evil Seth and restore the divine order. As pharaohs identified themselves with Horus, the living king, so Isis was their divine mother – a role which inevitably associated her with Hathor, the two goddesses being conflated in the Late Period. By this time Isis was the Great Mother of All Gods and Nature, Goddess of Ten Thousand Names, of women, purity and sexuality.

By a process of identification with other goddesses around the Mediterranean, **Isis-worship** eventually spread throughout the Roman empire (the westernmost Iseum or cult temple extant is in Hungary). The nurturing, forgiving, loving Isis was Christianity's chief rival between the third and fifth centuries. Many scholars believe that the cult of the Virgin Mary was Christianity's attempt to wean converts away from Isis; early Coptic art identifies one with the other, Horus with Jesus, and the Christian cross with the pharaonic ankh.

Isis

two vestibules precede the sanctuary, which contains the finest scenes [i]. Although iconoclasts have defaced the goddess suckling the child-pharaoh on the left-hand wall, you can see Isis giving birth to Horus in the marshes at the bottom of the rear wall. Around the back of the sanctuary behind the northern colonnade is a corresponding scene of Isis nursing Horus in the swamp [j].

The Hypostyle Hall

Immediately behind the Second Pylon lies a small open court that was originally separated from the **Hypostyle Hall** by a screen wall, now destroyed. A lovely drawing by David Roberts shows this "Grand Portico" in its rich original colours: the flowering capitals are in shades of green with yellow flowers and blue buds; crimson and golden winged sun-discs are seen flying down the central aisle of the ceiling, which elsewhere bears astronomical reliefs. The unpainted walls and column shafts show the hall's builder, Ptolemy VII Euergetes II, sacrificing to various deities. After the emperor Justinian forbade the celebration of Isis rituals at Philae in 550 AD, Copts used the hall for services and chiselled crosses into the walls. On the left-hand jamb of the portal [k] into the vestibule beyond, a piece of Roman graffiti asserts *B Mure stultus est* ("B Mure is stupid").

The vestibules

As at other temples, the **vestibules** get lower and darker as you approach the sanctuary. By a doorway [l] to the right of the first vestibule, a Greek inscription records the "cleansing" of this pagan structure under Bishop Theodorus, during the reign of Justinian. On the other side of the vestibule is a room giving access to the **stairs** to the roof (see below). The next vestibule has an interesting scene flanking the portal at the back [m], where the king offers a sistrum (left) and wine (right) to Isis and Harpocrates (Child Horus). On the left-hand door jamb, he leaves offerings to Min, a basket to Sekhmet and wine to Osiris, with the sacred bull and seven cows in the background. In the partially ruined transverse vestibule, the king offers necklaces, wine and eye paint to Osiris, Isis, Hathor and Nephthys, outside the sanctuary [n].

The sanctuary

Dimly lit by two apertures in the roof, the **sanctuary** contains a stone pedestal dedicated by Ptolemy III and his wife Berenice, which once supported the goddess's barque. On the left wall, the pharaoh faces Isis, whose wings protectively enfold Osiris. Across the room, an enthroned Isis suckles the infant Horus (above) and stands to suckle a young pharaoh (below, now defaced). The other rooms, used for rites or storage, contain reliefs of goddesses with Nubian features.

Hadrian's Gate

Leaving the temple through the western door of the first vestibule you'll emerge near **Hadrian's Gate**, set into the girdle wall that once encircled Philae Island. Flanking your approach are two walls from a bygone vestibule, decorated with notable reliefs. The right-hand wall [o] depicts the origin of the Nile, whose twin streams are poured forth by Hapy the Nile-god from his cave beneath Biga Island, atop which perches a falcon. To the right of this, Isis, Nephthys and others adore the young falcon as he rises from a marsh.

Above the door in the opposite wall [p], Isis and Nephthys present the dual crowns to Horus, whose name is inscribed on a palm stalk by Sheshat (right) and Thoth (left). Below, Isis watches a crocodile drag the corpse of Osiris to a rocky promontory (presumably Biga). Around the gate itself, Hadrian appears before the gods (above the lintel) and the door jambs bear the fetishes of Abydos (left) and Osiris (right). At the top of the wall, Marcus Aurelius stands before Isis and Osiris; below he offers Isis grapes and flowers.

2

North of the gateway lie the foundations of the **Temple of Harendotes** (an aspect of Horus), built by the emperor Claudius.

Elsewhere on the island

To complete the cast of deities involved in the Osirian myth, a small **Temple of Hathor** was erected to the east of the main complex – really only notable for a relief of musicians, among whom the god Bes plays a harp. More eye-catching and virtually the symbol of Philae is the graceful open-topped **Kiosk of Trajan**, nicknamed the "Pharaoh's Bedstead". Removed from its watery grave by a team of British navy divers, the reconstructed kiosk juxtaposes variegated floral columns with a severely classical superstructure; only two of the screen wall panels bear reliefs.

ARRIVAL AND DEPARTURE   **PHILAE**

By taxi/minibus Organized tours from Aswan (see p.348) are the best way of visiting Philae. A three-hour taxi-tour can cost as little as £E50 (for up to three people). Alternatively, you can visit Philae on the way back from Abu Simbel; a "long tour" (12hr) by minibus (including the High Dam and the Unfinished Obelisk) costs £E70–80/person.

Visitors are dropped at the Shallal dock, 1km from the eastern end of the Aswan Dam, to buy tickets for the temple and board motorboats to the island.
By motorboat A round-trip from Shallal dock for up to eight people should cost around £E50–60; if you spend longer than an hour on the island, baksheesh is expected.

Kalabsha

Lake Nasser, near the High Dam • Daily 8am–5pm • £E35

The hulking **Temple of Kalabsha** broods beside Lake Nasser near the western end of the High Dam, marooned on an island or strung out on a promontory, depending on the water level. Between the site and the dam lies a graveyard of boats and fishy remains, enhancing its mood of desolation. The main temple originally came from Talmis (later known as Kalabsha), 50km to the south of Aswan; in a German-financed operation, it was cut into thirteen thousand blocks and reassembled here in 1970, together with other monuments from Nubia. Strictly speaking, "Kalabsha" refers to the original site rather than the temple itself, which is named after the god Mandulis, and has no historic connection with two smaller monuments in the vicinity, relocated here from other sites in Nubia.

Temple of Mandulis

The **Temple of Mandulis** is a Ptolemaic-Roman version of an earlier XVIII Dynasty edifice dedicated to the Nubian fertility god Marul, whom the Greeks called Mandulis. By Ptolemaic times, Egypt's Nubian empire was a token one, dependent on the goodwill of the powerful kingdom of Napata ruled from Meröe near the Fourth Cataract, about 400km south of Abu Simbel. Having briefly restored old-style imperialism, the Romans abandoned most of Nubia during the reign of Diocletian, falling back on deals with local rulers to safeguard Egypt's southern border. As the linchpin of the last imperial town south of Aswan, the temple bears witness to this patronage and the kingdoms that succeeded the Napatan state, which disintegrated under the onslaught of marauding Blemmye (c.550 AD), a group of nomadic tribes who were perhaps the ancestors of the modern Beja.

Causeway and Pylon

Approaching the sandstone temple from behind, you miss the dramatic effect of the great stone **causeway** from the water's edge, used by pilgrims in the days when Kalabsha was a healing temple, like Edfu and Dendara. For reasons unknown, its chunky **pylon** is skewed at a slight angle to the temple, a blemish rectified by having a trapezoidal **courtyard** whose pillars are set closer together along the shorter, southern side.

Hypostyle Hall

The first batch of reliefs worth a mention occurs on the **facade** of the Hypostyle Hall at the back of the court. While Horus and Thoth anoint the king with holy water in a conventional scene to the left of the portal, the right-hand wall bears a decree excluding swineherds and their pigs from the temple (issued in 249 AD); a large relief of a horseman in Roman dress receiving a wreath from the winged Victory; and a text in poor Greek lauding Siklo, the Christian king of the Nobatae, for repulsing the Blemmye.

The now roofless **Hypostyle Hall** has some interesting reliefs along the rear wall. Left of the portal, a Ptolemaic king offers crowns to Horus and Mandulis, while Amenhotep II (founder of the XVIII Dynasty temple) presents a libation to Mandulis and Min. Across the way, a nameless king slays a foe before Horus, Shu and Tefnet.

Vestibules and Sanctuary

Within the **vestibules** beyond, look out for figures personifying the Egyptian nomes, below a scene of the king offering a field to Isis and Mandulis and wine to Osiris (near the stairs off the outer vestibule); and a rare appearance by the deified sage Imhotep (low down on the left-hand wall of the inner vestibule).

The **Sanctuary** is similar in size to the vestibules and, like them, once had two columns. Along its back wall you can identify (from left to right) the emperor offering lotuses to Isis and the young Horus, and milk to Mandulis and Wadjet; then incense to the former duo and lotuses to the latter. Although the god's cult statue has vanished, Mandulis still appears at either end of the scene covering the temple's **rear wall**: in his royal form, with a pharaonic crown, sceptre and ankh sign (right); and as a god whose ram's-horn crown is surmounted by a solar disc, *uraeus* and ostrich plumes (left).

From the *pronaos*, you may be able to ascend a stairway to the **roof**, which features an abbreviated version of the Osirian shrines found at other complexes. The **view** of Lake Nasser and the High Dam, over the temple courtyards, is amazing. A passageway between the temple and its enclosure wall leads to a well-preserved **Nilometer**.

Kiosk of Qertassi

Re-erected near the lakeside at the same time as Kalabsha Temple, the **Kiosk of Qertassi** resembles a knocked-about copy of the "Pharaoh's Bedstead" at Philae, but actually came from another ancient settlement, 40km south of Aswan. Aside from its fine views of Lake Nasser, this Ptolemaic-Roman edifice is chiefly notable for two surviving Hathor-headed columns, which make the goddess look more feline than bovine. In the forecourt, notice the women pleading for mercy as Ramses seizes their menfolk, and the Nubians paying tribute in the form of gold, ivory, leopard skins, feathers and even an ostrich.

Beit al-Wali

The oldest monumental relic from Nile-inundated Nubia is a temple dug into the hillside behind Kalabsha Temple. Originally hewn under Ramses II, who left his mark throughout Nubia, this cruciform rock-cut structure is known by its Arabic name, **Beit al-Wali** (House of the Holy Man). The weathered reliefs flanking its narrow court depict the pharaoh's victories over Nubians and Ethiopians (left), and Libyans and Asiatics (right). By contrast, scenes in the transverse hall are well preserved and brightly coloured. Here, Ramses makes offerings before Isis, Horus and the Aswan Triad (Hapy, Satet and Khnum), and is suckled by goddesses inside the sanctuary, whose niche contains a mutilated cult statue of three deities.

ARRIVAL AND DEPARTURE   **KALABSHA**

By taxi The only way of getting too Kalabsha is by taxi from Aswan, where the *Nubian Oasis* hotel (p.349) can arrange a trip for up to three people for £E60 (excluding the cost of a motorboat). When the water level is low you can walk across a causeway to Kalabsha; otherwise, take a motorboat from the western side of the High Dam (about £E50 return with an hour's waiting time).

Wadi el-Seboua

100km from the High Dam by cruise boat (see p.364) • Open according to boat schedules • £E45

Cruise boats departing from the High Dam must sail nearly half the length of Lake Nasser before they reach **Wadi el-Seboua**. They usually moor here after dark for passengers to enjoy an awesome floodlit vista of three temples, joined by what appears to be a long processional avenue, which is revealed next morning to be a track across a desert of tan-coloured sand and grey rocks. The landscape is dotted with a few bits of grass and a half-submerged crane that was used to transport the main temple from its original location, 4km away.

Temple of Wadi el-Seboua

Wadi el-Seboua means "Valley of the Lions" in Arabic and refers to the **avenue of sphinxes** leading to the **temple** of that name. The temple was built during the reign of Ramses II by his viceroy of Kush, Setau, using Libyan prisoners of war, who also worked on Abu Simbel. Like Abu Simbel, it was dedicated to Amun-Re, Re-Herakhte and the deified pharaoh, whose role as a conqueror is emphasized by images of Libyan and Asiatic captives carved on the pedestals of the statues of the king that flank its gateway. In the second court, the human-headed sphinxes give way to falcon-headed ones, representing the four forms of Horus.

Beyond the temple **pylon** is an **open court** with columns fronted by Osirian statues of Ramses, notable for their thick legs. Scholars disagree whether this reflected his physique or was merely to make him look stronger, but this feature occurs on all statues of Ramses, whose virility is further attested to by images of his numerous progeny (53 princes and 54 princesses) below the offering scenes on the walls.

The remainder of the temple is cut from rock and once served as a Christian church; its **reliefs** retain much of their scarlet, white and yellow paint due to being covered by plaster for centuries. The best-preserved ones are in the transverse vestibule, including an unusual portrayal of Hathor with a woman's body and a cow's head. You can also see Ramses making offerings to his own sphinx, above and behind the doorway into the sanctuary, where a votive niche contains remnants of the Christian **murals** that once covered the walls, resulting in a surreal tableau of Ramses offering flowers to St Peter.

Temple of Dakka

From Wadi el-Seboua, passengers can walk or ride a camel (£E60) 1.5km across the desert to the hilltop **Temple of Dakka** that once stood 40km north of its present site. Its most striking feature is an elegant freestanding **pylon**, over 12m tall; visitors are sometimes allowed to climb it, which affords a fantastic view of the area. There isn't much carving on the walls but the gateway is crowned by a winged sun-disc, and on its left-hand side is graffiti in Meröitic script thought to have been left by Nubian soldiers retreating from Aswan in 23 AD.

The temple itself was started by **Arkamani**, one of the rulers (218–200 BC) of the Kingdom of Meröe – which at that time controlled Lower Nubia – and was added to by his contemporary, **Ptolemy IV**, and decorated by later Ptolemies. You can see the Hellenistic influence in the composite capitals (combining Greek and Egyptian forms) and scenes in the *pronaos*, where Isis sports big breasts in the Greek style. Also notice the four sacred cobras, carved in the corners of the entrance wall.

On many of the reliefs in the temple the king performing the rituals is simply identified by a generic **cartouche** reading "pharaoh", as the masons didn't know who was in power at the time in Alexandria, or didn't want to inscribe the name of a Ptolemy who wouldn't be on the throne for long. This wasn't the case for Ptolemy IV and his sister-wife Arsinöe, who are shown offering a Maat (truth) figure to Thoth and Wepset on the lintel of the doorway into the vestibule.

The Chapel of Arkamani

At the back of the vestibule, a passageway and stairs lead to the **roof**, which affords a stunning view, while beyond lies the **Chapel of Arkamani** that originally served as the temple's sanctuary. Here, Arkamani makes offerings to the gods beneath a frieze of his cartouche interspersed with falcons and ibises, while on the rear wall is an interesting relief of Thoth as an ape adoring Tefnut, who is shown as a lioness. A baboon worshipping a lion can also be seen in the side-passage leading off the chapel, while another ape consorts with a cow beneath a persea tree low down in the near right-hand corner of the sanctuary, which was built and decorated under the Roman emperors Augustus and Tiberius.

On leaving the temple, walk around the east wall to see a **waterspout** in the shape of a lion's head.

Temple of Maharraqa

A short way downhill back towards the shore stands the small **Temple of Maharraqa**, taken from a site 50km north of its present location, which was the southern frontier of Egypt in Greco-Roman times. Its floral capitals and reliefs were left unfinished – in some places only roughly sketched in reddish-brown paint. The temple's most interesting feature, leading up to the roof, is the **spiral staircase**, the only one known in an Ancient Egyptian building. The temple was probably dedicated to Seraphis.

Amada

125km from the High Dam, 125km from Abu Simbel by Lake Nasser cruise boat (see p.364) • Open according to cruise-boat schedules • £E45

Beyond Wadi el-Seboua, Lake Nasser describes an S-shaped curve past one of the loveliest parts of Nubia, where the rocky desert shoreline is fringed with acacia scrub. Cruise passengers are ferried to **Amada** here by motorboat. Bring a **torch** for examing the reliefs inside the temples.

Temple of Amada

The site is named after the **Temple of Amada**, which is the oldest surviving structure on Lake Nasser and contains some of the finest relief-carving to be seen on any of the Nubian monuments. It was built by the XVIII Dynasty pharaohs Tuthmosis III, Amenhotep II and Tuthmosis IV, and restored and decorated during the XIX Dynasty. Like most of the Nubian temples, it was dedicated to Amun-re and Re-Herakhte, who appear with various pharaohs in the usual offerings scenes.

For archeologists, the site is particulary interesting for its two historic **inscriptions**: the first, carved on a stele on the left side of the entrance, describes the Libyan invasion of Egypt in the fourth year (1232 BC) of Merneptah's reign; while the other, on the back wall of the sanctuary, dates from the second year (1423 BC) of Amenhotep III's reign and relates how he dealt with seven leaders of a revolt in Syria, whose heads and limbs were hung on the gates of Thebes as a warning to other would-be rebels. When Amelia Edwards visited Amada in 1873 she found the temple "half-choked" with sand; judging by the later carvings of **camels** drawn by Bedouin and pilgrims on the cornice of the facade, it was almost completely buried in medieval times. The inner part of the temple consists of a vestibule and sanctuary with a small cult-chamber on either side, whose **reliefs** are as delicate as any produced during the XVIII Dynasty. The ones in the right-hand corner depict the foundation and consecration of the temple; Tuthmosis III and Amenhotep III make offerings to the gods in the other chamber.

Temple of Derr

A few minutes' walk from Amada is the smaller **Temple of Derr**, once located on the east bank of the Nile (the only one in Nubia on that side of the river). With its gateway gone and its pillared forehall reduced to stumps, the temple now confronts visitors with a rugged portico featuring four square pillars and statues of Ramses II only

2

roughed-out up to waist-level. The **interior** of the temple was entirely hewn from rock, with few straight lines or right angles, its sunk-reliefs finished in stucco with painted details. On the side walls of the pillared hall, Re-Herakhte's sacred barque is carried in a procession on the shoulders of priests, as Ramses walks alongside wearing a leopard-skin; the white background and the yellow of the barque are still visible. More colours survive on the walls of the sanctuary, where Ramses burns incense and pours a libation to the barque before annointing Re-Herakhte with his little finger (right). At the back, the four cult-statues that originally represented Ramses, Amun-Re, Re-Herakhte and Ptah were hacked away by Christian iconoclasts.

Tomb of Pennut

Leaving Derr temple, it's worth hurrying on ahead of other tourists to get to the **Tomb of Pennut**, as it's only large enough to hold a few people. Pennut (or Penne) was a high official in Lower Nubia during the reign of Ramses VI, whose tomb was originally dug into a hillside at Aniba, 40km south of its present site. Sunk-reliefs in the rectangular offerings chamber show Pennut and his wife before the gods, mourners at his funeral and Pennut worshipping the cow-goddess Hathor in the Western Mountains.

As you leave the tomb, its custodian delves into a bucket to extract a baby **crocodile**, which he offers to tourists for a photo opportunity. The shallows of Lake Nasser beyond Amada are home to many crocodiles and monitor lizards, but they avoid spots frequented by tourists.

Qasr Ibrim

200km from the High Dam, 50km from Abu Simbel by cruise boat (see below)

Qasr Ibrim – the last stop on the cruise before Abu Simbel – is unique for being the only one of the ancient Nubian sites to remain *in situ*, albeit nowadays on an island rather than the summit of a hill. This continuity has allowed the Egypt Exploration Society to carry out **excavations** every two years since 1961 and establish that Qasr Ibrim was occupied throughout successive periods from the late New Kingdom until the early nineteenth century, when it was inhabited by Bosnian mercenaries of the Ottoman empire, who married into the local Nubian community.

Before the Bosnians' arrival in the sixteenth century, Qasr Ibrim was one of the last redoubts of Christianity in Lower Nubia, as it had previously been the last area to forsake paganism, abandoning the worship of Isis two hundred years after the rest of Egypt. A ruined sandstone **cathedral** dating back to the eighth century overlies a temple of Isis built by the Nubian XXV Dynasty pharaoh Taharka; as many as six temples once existed here. The cathedral's broken vaults rise amid a muddle of dry-stone and cut-masonry walls, riddled with portals, niches and cavities, attesting to the age and complexity of the site.

Due to its fragility and the ongoing excavations, tourists are not allowed to land here, but boats moor so close to the shore that the ruins can easily be seen, or closely examined with **binoculars**.

CRUISES TO WADI EL-SEBOUA, AMADA AND QASR IBRIM

All cruises on Lake Nasser have similar schedules, departing either from the High Dam (lasting four days) or Abu Simbel (three days) to visit the otherwise inaccessible Wadi el-Seboua, Amada and Qasr Ibrim, plus Abu Simbel and Kalabsha temples. Most passengers book abroad, but trips can be arranged in Egypt at short notice, at head offices in Cairo, Luxor's *Happy Land* hotel (see p.268), or tour agencies in Aswan, for around €100/person a night (with buffet meals). Rates are lowest in the summer, highest over Christmas, New Year and Easter.

Eugénie ⓦ eugenie.com.eg. Managed by Belle Époque Travel in Cairo and named after the empress who opened the Suez Canal, this magnificent boat is modelled on a khedival hunting lodge, with a Turkish steam bath, French haute cuisine, cocktails and classical music at Abu Simbel.

DEIR EL-BAHRI FROM THE AIR (P.306)>

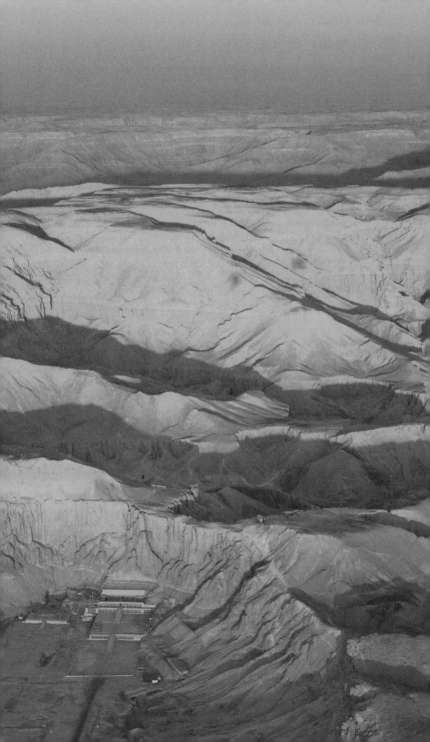

Jaz Omar Khayam and **Tania** ⓦtravco.com. Marketed in Egypt by Travco, the *Jaz Omar Khayam* is comparable to other five-star boats, while the four-star *Tania* is less fancy.

Nubian Sea Its seventy cabins and pool are nothing special, but the buffet meals are superior to all the boats on Lake Nasser except the *Eugénie* and *Qasr Ibrim*. Packages are sold by Audley Travel (ⓦaudleytravel.com) in the US, while cruise-only deals are available from Memphis Tours (ⓦmemphistours.com) in Egypt.

Prince Abbas Operated by the *Mövenpick*, with 55 cabins,

billiards, a mini gym, jacuzzi and a plunge pool on the sundeck. Packages are sold by Audley Travel (see above) in the US, and Longwood Holidays (ⓦlongwoodholidays .co.uk) in Britain, plus cruise-only deals from Memphis Tours (see above) in Egypt.

Qasr Ibrim ⓦkasribrim.com.eg. With its lavish 1930s Art Deco interiors and haute cuisine, this boat is as grand as the *Eugénie*, and is also managed by Belle Époque Travel in Cairo.

Queen Abu Simbel ⓦaggar.4mg.com. Run by Naggar Travel in Cairo, with a sauna, jacuzzi and Turkish bath, billiards and bridge.

Abu Simbel

The great **Sun Temple** of **ABU SIMBEL** ("Father of the Ear of Corn") epitomizes the monumentalism of the New Kingdom during its imperial heyday, when Ramses II (c.1279–13 BC) waged colonial wars from the Beka'a Valley in Lebanon to the Fourth

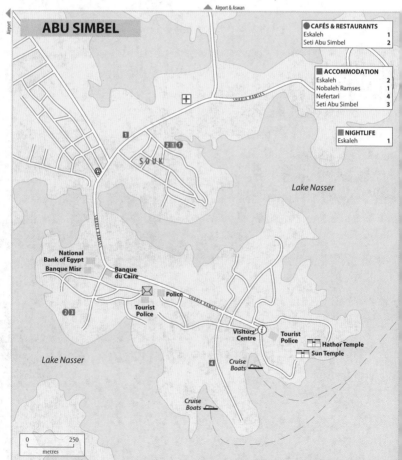

ABU SIMBEL

Airport & Aswan

Airport

● CAFÉS & RESTAURANTS	
Eskaleh	1
Seti Abu Simbel	2

■ ACCOMMODATION	
Eskaleh	2
Nobaleh Ramses	1
Nefertari	4
Seti Abu Simbel	3

■ NIGHTLIFE	
Eskaleh	1

SHARIA RAMSES

S O U K

Lake Nasser

SHARIA RAMSES

National Bank of Egypt

Banque Misr

Banque du Caire

Police

Tourist Police

SHARIA RAMSES

Lake Nasser

Visitors Centre

Tourist Police

Hathor Temple

Sun Temple

Cruise Boats

Cruise Boats

0   250
metres

THE TOSHKA AND EAST OWEINAT IRRIGATION PROJECTS

Inaugurated by President Mubarak in 1997, the **Toshka Project** had the ambitious goals of cultivating 5700 square kilometres of desert northwest of Abu Simbel, and settling six million people there. To irrigate the land, $1 billion was spent on creating the world's largest **pumping station** to extract five billion cubic metres of water from Lake Nasser annually, and digging the **Sheikh Zayed Canal**, named after the president of the United Arab Emirates (a big investor). The main canal (completed in 2002) is 50km long, 30m wide and 6m deep, with four branch canals totaling 159km in length, and a network of roads linking Toshka to another irrigation project at **East Oweinat** in the Western Desert, using aquifer water (see p.435). However, settlers have been disillusioned by the lack of work opportunities and infrastructure, and foreign investors have pulled out since the 2011 Revolution, vindicating critics of both projects, who claimed from the start that they would prove to be white elephants.

2

Cataract. To impress his power and majesty on the Nubians, Ramses had four gigantic statues of himself hewn from the mountainside, whence his unblinking stare confronted travellers as they entered Egypt from Africa.

The temple was precisely oriented so that the sun's rays reached deep into the mountain to illuminate its sanctuary on his birthday and the anniversary of his coronation. The deified pharaoh physically overshadows the sun-god **Re-Herakhte**, to whom the temple is nominally dedicated, just as his queen, **Nefertari**, sidelines **Hathor** in a neighbouring edifice, also hewn into the mountain.

The first European to see Abu Simbel since antiquity was the Swiss explorer Burckhardt, who found the temples almost completely buried by sand drifts in 1813. Although Belzoni later managed to clear an entrance, lack of treasure discouraged further efforts and the site was soon reburied in sand – a process repeated throughout the nineteenth century. Finally cleared, the temple became the scenic highlight of Thomas Cook's Nile cruises.

It was the prospect of losing Abu Simbel to Lake Nasser that impelled UNESCO to organize the **salvage** of Nubian monuments in the 1960s. Behind the temporary protection of a coffer dam, Abu Simbel's brittle sandstone was stabilized by injections of synthetic resin and then hand-sawn into 1041 blocks weighing up to thirty tons apiece. Two years after the first block was cut, Abu Simbel was reassembled 210m behind (and 61m above) its original site, a false mountain being constructed to match the former setting. The whole operation (1964–68) cost $40 million.

The modern **town** of Abu Simbel looks desolate as you roll in past the airport, but once beyond the main intersection it becomes quite picturesque, straggling around rocky headlands replete with beehive-domed houses and crimson oleander bushes. The temples are at the far end of Sharia Ramses, 1km from the town centre.

The Sun Temple

Beside Lake Nasser • Daily 5am–5pm • £E95

Visitors walk around a man-made mountain to be confronted by the great **Sun Temple**, seemingly hewn from the cliffs overlooking Lake Nasser. Its impact is perhaps a little diminished by familiarity (the temple has been depicted on everything from T-shirts to banknotes) and the technicolour contrast between red rockscape and aquamarine water is more startling than the clean-swept facade, which looks less dramatic than the sand-choked Abu Simbel of nineteenth-century engravings. For all

There are two nightly **Sound and Light Shows** (Ⓦsoundandlight.com.eg; £E75) at the temple, starting at 7pm and 8pm from April to October, an hour later from May to September. Images are projected onto the temple facades, with commentary in different languages via headphones.

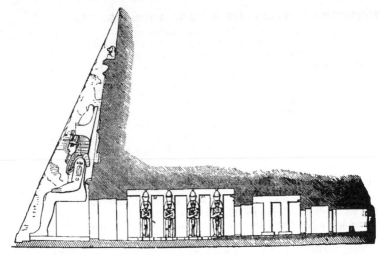

Cross-section of the Sun Temple

the meticulous reconstruction and landscaping, too, it's hard not to sense its artificiality, but gradually the temple's presence asserts itself, and your mind boggles at its audacious conception, the logistics of constructing and moving it, and the unabashed megalomania of its founder.

The colossi and facade

Although Re-Herakhte, Amun-Re and Ptah are also carved on the facade as patron deities, they're clearly secondary to Ramses II, who ruled for 67 years, dying at the age of 96, having sired scores of sons, most of whom predeceased him. The temple facade is dominated by four enthroned **Colossi of Ramses II**, whose twenty-metre height surpasses the Colossi of Memnon at Thebes (though one lost its upper half following an earthquake in 27 BC). Their feet and legs are crudely executed but the torsos and heads are finely carved, and the face of the left-hand figure quite beautiful. Between them stand figures of the royal family, dwarfed by Ramses' knees. To the left of the headless colossus is the pharaoh's mother, Muttuy; Queen Nefertari stands on the right of the colossus, Prince Amunhirkhepshef between its legs. On its right calf, an inscription records that Greek mercenaries participated in the Nubian campaign of the Saïte king Psammetichus II (c.590 BC).

The **facade** is otherwise embellished with a niche-bound statue of **Re-Herakhte**, holding a sceptre and a figure of Maat. This composition is a pictorial play of words on Ramses' prenomen, User-Maat-Re, so the flanking sunk-reliefs of the king presenting the god with images of Maat actually signify Ramses honouring his deified self. Crowning the facade is a corvetto cornice surmounted by baboons worshipping the rising sun. On the sides of the colossal thrones flanking the temple entrance, twin Nile-gods entwine the heraldic papyrus and sedge around the hieroglyph "to unite", with the rows of captives beneath them divided between north and south, Asiatics on the right-hand throne and Nubians on its left-hand counterpart.

The Hypostyle Hall

This schematic division reappears in the lofty rock-cut **Hypostyle Hall**, flanked on either side by four pillars fronted by ten-metre-high statues of Ramses in the Osiris position, carrying the crook and flail (the best is the end figure on the right). Beneath a ceiling painted with flying vultures, the walls crawl with scenes from his campaigns, from Syria to Nubia. On the entrance walls, Ramses slaughters Hittite and Nubian captives before Amun-Re (left) and Re-Herakhte (right), accompanied by eight of his many sons or nine daughters, and his *ka*. But the most dramatic **reliefs** are found on the side walls.

The right-hand wall (all directions assume you're facing the back of the temple) depicts the **Battle of Qadesh** on the River Orontes (1300 BC), starting from the back of the hall. Here you see Ramses' army marching on Qadesh, followed by their encampment, ringed by shields. Acting on disinformation tortured out of enemy spies, Ramses prepares to attack the city and summons his reserve divisions down from the heights. The waiting Hittites ford the river, charge one division and scatter another to surround the king, who single-handedly cuts his way out of the trap. The final scene claims an unqualified Egyptian triumph, even though Ramses failed to take the city. Notwithstanding this, the opposite wall portrays him storming a Syrian fortress in his chariot (note the double arm, which some regard as an attempt at animation), lancing a Libyan and returning with fettered Nubians. Along the rear wall, he presents them to Amun, Mut and himself (left), and the captured Hittites to Re-Herakhte, lion-headed Wert-Hekew and his own deified personage (right).

The eight **lateral chambers** off the hall were probably used to store cult objects and tribute from Nubia, and are decorated with offering scenes. Reliefs in the smaller **pillared hall** show Ramses and Nefertari offering incense before the shrine and barque of Amun-Re (left) and Re-Herakhte (right).

The Sanctuary

Walk through one of the doors at the back, cross the transverse vestibule and head for the central **Sanctuary**. Originally encased in gold, its four (now mutilated) cult statues wait to be touched by the sun's rays at dawn on February 22 and October 22. February 21 was Ramses' birthday and October 21 his coronation date, but the relocation of Abu Simbel has changed the timing of these **solar events** by one day. Perhaps significantly, the figure of Ptah "the Hidden One" (on the far left) is situated so that it alone remains in darkness when the sun illuminates Amun-Re, Re-Herakhte and Ramses the god. Before them is a stone block where the sacred barque once rested.

The Hathor Temple of Queen Nefertari

A little further north of the Sun Temple stands the smaller rock-hewn **Temple of Queen Nefertari**, identified here with the goddess **Hathor**, who was wife to the sun-god during his day's passage and mother to his rebirth at dawn. As with Ramses' temple, the rock-hewn facade imitates a receding pylon (whose corvetto cornice has fallen), its plane accentuated by a series of rising buttresses separating six **colossal statues of Ramses and Nefertari** (over 9m tall), which seem to emerge from the rock. Each is accompanied by two smaller figures of their children, who stand knee-high in the shadows. A frieze of cobras protects the door into the temple, which is simpler in plan than Ramses', having but one columned hall and vestibule, and only two lateral chambers; it runs 24m into the hillside.

The best **reliefs** are in the hall with square, Hathor-headed pillars whose sides show the royal couple mingling with deities. On the entrance wall Nefertari watches Ramses slay Egypt's enemies; on the side walls she participates in rituals as his equal, appearing before Anuket (left) and Hathor (right). In the transverse vestibule beyond, the portal of the sanctuary is flanked by scenes of the royal couple offering wine and flowers to Amun-Re and Horus (left), Re-Herakhte, Khnum, Satet and Anuket (right).

The **Sanctuary** niche contains a ruined cow-statue of Hathor, above which vultures guard Nefertari's cartouches. On the side walls, she offers incense to Mut and Hathor (left), while Ramses worships his own image and that of Nefertari (right).

2

BIRDWATCHING AT ABU SIMBEL

Due to its location on a large body of water surrounded by desert, near the Tropic of Cancer, Abu Simbel sustains both indigenous African and migrant species of birds. Among the rarer species are pink-backed pelicans, yellow-billed storks, long-tailed cormorants, African skimmers and pied wagtails and pink-headed doves. While serious twitchers will haunt the coves with binoculars, casual bird-spotters can see quite a few dazzling birds in the grounds of the visitors' centre or the *Eskaleh* and *Seti Abu Simbel* hotels. The best time for birdwatching is during the **breeding season** in late January/early February.

ARRIVAL AND DEPARTURE
ABU SIMBEL

Abu Simbel lies on the west bank of Lake Nasser, 280km south of Aswan and 40km north of the Sudanese border. Though most tourists make a day-trip from Aswan, some spend the night to enjoy Abu Simbel's laidback ambience and Nubian music at *Eskaleh* (see below).

By air EgyptAir flies to Abu Simbel from Cairo, Luxor and Aswan (2–3 times daily at the time of writing; more if tourism picks up), as well as many foreign capitals. Transfers between the airport and the temple are included in the price.

By minibus/private taxi Excursions from Aswan travel in a convoy leaving at 4am, returning at 10am. This schedule makes sense given the heat of the desert, but means that everyone arrives at once, packing out the temples (the later 11am convoy, returning at 5pm, is for private cars only). You can arrange an excursion by minibus for £E60/person (or hire a taxi for £E450) through the *Nubian Oasis* hotel (see p.349), while a "long trip" including Philae, the High Dam and the Unfinished Obelisk on the way back, costs £E70/person (or £E520 for a taxi). The

Keylany hotel (see p.349) offers similar excursions at fractionally higher rates, while Thomas Cook and other agencies charge considerably more.

By bus/service taxi If you want to escape convoy restrictions, the Upper Egypt Bus Co. runs two services daily from Aswan (8am & 5pm; 4hr), terminating at a roundabout in Abu Simbel that's the pick-up point for the journey back (6am & 1pm). Arrive early to buy a ticket at Aswan's bus station; in Abu Simbel, you pay aboard the bus. If you can't get a seat there's usually a minibus on standby for excess passengers. The fare (£E20) is the same.

By cruise boat The most leisurely – and expensive – way of reaching Abu Simbel, with stopovers at the otherwise inaccessible sites of Wadi el-Seboua, Amada and Qasr Ibrim on Lake Nasser (see pp.362–364).

INFORMATION

There's no tourist office In Abu Simbel and few locals speak English. If you need information on anything, ask Fikry or Yasser at the *Eskaleh* hotel.

Visitors' Centre Beside the ticket office for the temples (daily 5am–5pm; free). A relief model of the Sun and Hathor temples, evocative photos and reams of statistics

(plus film-footage, if the TVs are working) bring home the awesome feat involved in dismantling and reconstructing Abu Simbel.

ACCOMMODATION

Few visitors stay at Abu Simbel, where the choice of hotels is limited and prices are high – but some find the opportunity to savour the temples without other tourists around irresistible.

★ **Eskaleh** Sharia Sa'ad Ibn Abi Wakas ☎012 368 0521, ⊚eskaleh.net. This delightful Nubian-style eco-lodge has a unique vibe conjured up by its musician owner Fikry Kachif. Its name ("Waterwheel") is a tribute to the best-known composition of the Nubian classical musician Hamza el-Din. Entirely built of adobe, *Eskaleh* has en-suite rooms with mosquito nets, a restaurant serving alcohol, a Nubia-related library and wi-fi in the lobby. B&B €120

Nefertari ☎097 340 0508. Sited on a headland overlooking Lake Nasser, only five minutes' walk from the temples, this neglected 1970s holiday village has musty but otherwise comfy a/c chalets, and a wonderful view of the lake from its swimming pool. Call their head office in Cairo (☎02 2683 1677) to get a better deal than their walk-in rates. $123

Nobaleh Ramses Sharia Ramses ☎097 340 1118. A last resort: its domed mud-brick rooms are cool and spacious, but the hotel is practically desolate, with no English spoken or any meals available. **£E300**

Seti Abu Simbel ☏ 097 340 0720 or ☏ 011 1700 0540, ⓦ setifirst.com. On a headland with stunning views of Lake Nasser from its garden and swimming pool, this nominally four-star resort is let down by its faded a/c chalets, lacklustre restaurant and surly staff. **$225**

EATING, DRINKING AND NIGHTLIFE

Eskaleh Sharia Sa'ad Ibn Abi Wakas ☏ 012 368 0521, ⓦ eskaleh.net. Tasty Nubian meals at this delightful eco-lodge (see above), cooked with produce from Fikry's organic garden and served on a breezy terrace with mood-music, beer and wine. A full meal costs about £E90. The kitchen closes at 9pm but you can drink until midnight, with frequent Nubian jam sessions on their gay-friendly rooftop. Breakfast from 8am, lunch from noon, dinner until 9pm.

Seti Abu Simbel ☏ 097 340 0720 or ☏ 011 1700 0540, ⓦ setifirst.com. In theory, this resort (see above) offers a full breakfast ($8), lunch ($26) and dinner ($30) buffet, but this may depend on how full the hotel is – though you can rely on them to sell beer, at least. Daily 9am–10pm.

Souk Sharia Ramses. Two stalls selling *fuul* and *taamiya*, fruit-sellers, grocery shops and several coffee houses (open till midnight), where locals hang out.

DIRECTORY

Banks All the following are on Sharia Ramses and have ATMs. Banque du Caire (Sun–Thurs 8.30am–2pm), Banque Misr (Sun–Thurs 8.30am–2pm), National Bank of Egypt (Sun–Thurs 9am–2pm).

Internet access There's a nameless internet café on Sharia Ramses (daily 11am–10pm), and wi-fi in the lobby at the *Eskaleh* eco-lodge.

Hospital Sharia Ramses ☏ 097 349 9257. Daily 24hr.

Post office Sharia Ramses (Sat–Thurs 8.30am–2pm).

Tourist police Off Sharia Ramses (☏ 097 340 0277; daily 24hr) and at the temple.

The Western Desert Oases

OFF-ROADING THROUGH THE DUNES,
WESTERN DESERT

The Western Desert Oases

For the Ancient Egyptians civilization began and ended with the Nile Valley and the Delta, known as the "Black Land" for the colour of its rich alluvial deposits. Beyond lay the "Red Land" or desert, whose significance was either practical or mystical. East of the Nile it held mineral wealth and routes to the Red Sea Coast; west of the river lay the Kingdom of Osiris, Lord of the Dead – the deceased were said to "go west" to meet him. But once it was realized that human settlements existed out there, Egypt's rulers had to reckon with the Western Desert Oases as sources of exotic commodities and potential staging posts for invaders. Though linked to the civilization of the Nile Valley since antiquity, they have always been different – and remain so.

3

Siwa Oasis, far out near the Libyan border, is the most striking example: its people speak another language and have customs unknown in the rest of Egypt, while its ruined citadels, lush palm groves, limpid pools and golden sand dunes epitomize the allure of the oases. The four "inner" oases of **Bahariya**, **Farafra**, **Dakhla** and **Kharga** lie on the "**Great Desert Circuit**" that travellers can explore starting from Cairo, Assyut or Luxor. Each oasis is different in character due to their diverse landscapes and degree of modernization. The Black and White deserts draw visitors to Bahariya and Farafra, whose village-like "capitals" are trumped by modern towns in Dakhla and Kharga, with Roman temples and fortified villages (qasr) in their hinterlands.

Nearer to Cairo are two quasi-oases: the Fayoum and Wadi Natrun. The **Fayoum** resembles the Nile Valley, with pyramids to prove its importance since the Middle Kingdom, while **Wadi Natrun** is renowned for its Coptic monasteries. Both make good day-trips from Cairo.

The desert

Much of the fascination of this region lies in the desert itself – vast tracts of which were savanna before climate change and overgrazing by Stone Age pastoralists altered it

DUNES AT SIWA

Highlights

❶ Jeep safaris Whether you spend a night in the White Desert, or two weeks in the Great Sand Sea and the Gilf Kebir, you'll never forget the experience. **See p.376**

❷ Birdwatching at Wadi Rayan Senegal coucals, kestrels, kites and herons are among the many species at Wadi Rayan. **See p.389**

❸ The White Desert A surreal landscape of wind-eroded yardangs shaped like falcons, camels, lions and mushrooms, in Farafra Oasis. See **p.409**

❹ The Ghard Abu Muharrik Dune piled upon dune for hundreds of kilometres, beyond the stalactite cave of El-Qaf. **See p.411**

❺ Al-Qasr This fantastic labyrinth of mud-brick dwellings dating back to the tenth century is one of several once-fortified qasr villages in Dakhla Oasis. **See p.418**

❻ Prehistoric rock art *The English Patient* cast a spotlight on the Cave of the Swimmers in the remote Gilf Kebir, and there are many other sites at Jebel Uwaynat. **See p.432**

❼ Siwa Oasis Its citadel, palm groves, rock tombs and salt lakes make Siwa a must for travellers. **See p.441**

❽ Hot springs The best bathing spot is Bir Wahed in the outer dunes of the Great Sand Sea, near Siwa Oasis. **See p.454**

HIGHLIGHTS ARE MARKED ON THE MAP ON P.377

3

DESERT SAFARIS AND TRAVEL PERMITS

The best (and often the only) way to reach many sites, desert safaris are organized by operators in the various oases (see the relevant accounts in the guide for details), Cairo and Europe (see below). **Bahariya Oasis** is the safari-hub of the Western Desert and the best place to arrange one at short notice, particularly to the White Desert. Longer safaris (four to nineteen days) to remoter sites such as the Great Sand Sea or the Gilf Kebir must be booked at least a month ahead and are generally restricted to spring and autumn, due to bureaucracy and the climate. Sadly, some safari outfits fail to respect the **environment**, leaving rubbish behind or even helping foreign collectors to plunder artefacts or minerals. All those we recommend below have good environmental credentials.

TRAVEL PERMITS AND ESCORTS

Several near-fatal incidents in remote areas have prompted tighter controls on travelling in the "deep desert", which the Egyptian Army takes to mean everywhere west of the highway between Bahariya, Farafra, Dakhla and Kharga – namely between Bahariya and Siwa, to Ain Della, the Great Sand Sea or the Gilf Kebir – but not sites east of the highway, such as the White Desert or El-Qaf.

Permits for 24 hours (£E50/person) can only be used to travel by day **between Siwa and Bahariya** (without leaving the road), or to **Ain Della and the Hidden Valley**. Doing either with a safari operator means they'll handle the paperwork, otherwise you'll need to submit a photocopy of your passport and visa (plus your licence and insurance if you're driving) to NGOs in Bahariya (see p.401) or Siwa (p.447), which will process them in 24 hours (except on Fri & Sat).

Only **registered travel agencies** can apply for overnight or multi-day permits for off-road travel between Siwa and Bahariya (£E100/person daily) or to the Gilf Kebir (£E160/person daily). Expect to pay a surcharge if your safari outfit uses a partner agency to apply on its behalf, and allow a month for the application to be processed.

A soldier with a satellite phone accompanies vehicles travelling between Bahariya and Siwa in case of breakdowns. Safaris to the Gilf must have an armed **escort** from the Tourist Safari Police (established so that responsibility no longer lies with the army). Four guards are required for travel below longitude 27° and eight guards below longitude 23°.

TOUR OPERATORS

Ancient World Tours ⓦancient.co.uk. This British firm specializing in archeological travel does a fourteen-day tour of Kharga, Dakhla, Bahariya, the Fayoum, Luxor and Middle Egypt, and an eleven-day tour of Siwa, Bahariya, El-Alamein and Alexandria. Flights from Britain and hotels in Cairo and/or Luxor are included in the price.

Badawiya Expedition ⓦbadawiya.com. Based in Farafra (see p.408) and Dakhla (p.416), although their tours start from Cairo. They arrange camel treks in the White Desert and jeep safaris all over the Western Desert, including such sites as the Cave of the Beasts in the Gilf Kebir and the silica glass area of the Great Sand Sea.

Dabuka Expeditions ⓦdabuka.de. This German company runs safaris in Libya, Sudan, Ethiopia, Tunisia and Jordan as well as Egypt, where they retrace the routes taken by early explorers and run a three-day desert driving course.

Egypt Off-Road ⓦegyptoffroad.com. Peter Gaballa runs expeditions to the Gilf and Sand Sea; off-road safaris from Bahariya to Dakhla via the Ghard Abu Muharrik; and desert driving courses. He speaks English, French, German and Arabic.

Fliegel Jerzerniczky Expeditions ⓦfjexpeditions .com. Travelling in the footsteps of *The English Patient*, this Hungarian company run by András Zboray mounts four or five expeditions a year to the Gilf and Jebel Uwaynat, sometimes venturing into Libya or Sudan. András speaks English and German.

Pan Arab Tours ⓦpanarabtours.com. A Cairo-based agency offering 4WD tours of the oases and tailor-made safaris to the Gilf, Uwaynat, the Sand Sea and the Qattara Depression.

Raid4x4 ⓦraid4x4egypt.com. Rally driver Hisham Nessim (holder of the world record for the fastest crossing of the Sand Sea) runs three different safaris to Uwaynat, a survey of the Gilf and a hunt for the Lost Army of Cambyses (see box, p.410).

Zarzora Expedition ⓦzarzora.com. Former Border Guards colonel Ahmed Mestekawi runs a nineteen-day safari to the Gilf (where he discovered the Cave of the Beasts), and ten-day tours featuring the Al-Baz Crater and silica glass area, or Khufu.

irrevocably. The **Western Desert**, covering 681,000 square kilometres (over two-thirds of Egypt's total area), is part of the North African Sahara belt: its anomalous name was bestowed by British cartographers who viewed it from the perspective of the Nile – and, to complicate matters further, designated its southern reaches and part of Sudan as the "Libyan Desert".

Among its most striking features are the **Qattara Depression** (the lowest point in Africa), the **Ghard Abu Muharrik** (Egypt's longest dune) and the **Great Sand Sea**, which

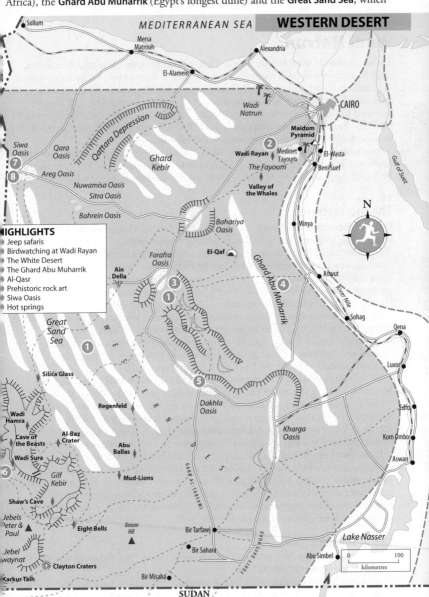

WESTERN DESERT

MEDITERRANEAN SEA

Sollum
Mersa Matrouh
El-Alamein
Alexandria
CAIRO
Wadi Natrun
Maidum Pyramid
El-Wasta
Gulf of Suez
Siwa Oasis 7
Qara Oasis
Qattara Depression
Ghard Kebír
2
Medinet Fayoum
Beni Suef
Wadi Rayan
The Fayoum
Areg Oasis 8
Nuwamisa Oasis
Sitra Oasis
Valley of the Whales
Minya
Bahrein Oasis
Bahariya Oasis
N
El-Qaf
Farafra Oasis
Ain Della
3
1
4
Ghard Abu Muharrik
Assyut
HIGHLIGHTS
▶ Jeep safaris
▶ Birdwatching at Wadi Rayan
▶ The White Desert
▶ The Ghard Abu Muharrik
▶ Al-Qasr
▶ Prehistoric rock art
▶ Siwa Oasis
▶ Hot springs
Sohag
Great Sand Sea
W E S T E R N
1
Qena
Silica Glass
Luxor
Regenfeld
5
Dakhla Oasis
D E S E R T
Edfu
Wadi Hamra
Al-Baz Crater
Kharga Oasis
Kom Ombo
Cave of the Beasts
Abu Ballas
Aswan
Wadi Sura
6
Gilf Kebir
▼ **Mud-Lions**
Shaw's Cave
DARB AL-TARFAWI
Jebels Peter & Paul ▲
Eight Bells
Beacon Hill ▲
Bir Tarfawi
Lake Nasser
FORTY DAYS ROAD
Jebel Uwaynat
Clayton Craters
Bir Sahara
Abu Simbel
0   100
kilometres
Karkur Talh
Bir Misaha
SUDAN

swallowed up an army. Mysterious **craters** and **silica glass** may be due to meteorite strikes, while the **Gilf Kebir** and **Jebel Uwaynat** are rich in prehistoric rock art, made famous by the book and film *The English Patient*.

Cassandra Vivian's *The Western Desert of Egypt: An Explorer's Handbook* is the most comprehensive source of **information** (including GPS waypoints), while Alberto Siliotti's pocket-sized guides to *The Oases* and *Gilf Kebir National Park* contain excellent maps. All are available from bookshops in Cairo and Bahariya.

Wadi Natrun

The quasi-oasis of **Wadi Natrun**, off the Desert Road between Cairo and Alexandria, takes its name – and oasis stature – from deposits of natron salts, the main ingredient in ancient mummifications. Wadi Natrun's most enduring legacy, however, is its **monasteries**, which date back to the dawn of Christian monasticism, and have provided spiritual leadership for Egypt's Copts for the last 1500 years. Their fortified exteriors, necessary in centuries past to resist Bedouin raiders, cloak what are today very forward-looking, purposeful monastic establishments.

Besides the monasteries themselves, Wadi Natrun offers a taste of the beauties of the oases, within easy reach of Cairo. Staying at **Birket al-Hamra** (see p.381) you can enjoy birdwatching, trail-biking or camel-riding around surreally coloured saline lakes.

The monasteries

Christian monasticism was born in Egypt's Eastern Desert, where the first Christian hermits sought to emulate St Anthony, forming simple communities; however, it was at Wadi Natrun that their rules and power were forged, during the persecution of Christians in urban areas under Emperor Diocletian. Several thousand **monks** and hermits were living here by the middle of the fourth century, harbouring bitter grudges against paganism, scores which they settled after Christianity was made the state religion in 330 by sacking the temples and library and murdering scholars in Alexandria (see p.464).

The later Muslim conquest and repeated Bedouin raids encouraged a siege mentality among the monks, who often lapsed into idle dependence on monastic serfs. Nineteenth-century foreign visitors unanimously described them as slothful, dirty, bigoted and ignorant – the antithesis of the monks here today, after decades of monastic revivalism under the late Coptic Pope Sheouda III.

All the **monasteries** have been totally ruined and rebuilt at least once since their foundation during the fourth century; most of what you see dates from the eighth century onwards. Each has a high wall surrounding one or more churches, a central keep, entered via a drawbridge, containing a bakery, storerooms and wells, enabling the monks to withstand siege, and diverse associated chapels. Their low doorways compel visitors to humbly stoop upon entry (don't forget to remove your shoes outside).

Their **churches** – like all Coptic chapels – are divided into three sections. The *haikal* (sanctuary) containing the altar lies behind the iconostasis, an inlaid or curtained screen, which you can peer through with your escort's consent. In front of this is the choir, reserved for Coptic Christians, and then the nave, consisting of two parts. *Catechumens* (those preparing to convert) stand nearest the choir, while sinners (known as "weepers") were formerly relegated to the back.

Deir al-Suryani

9km from Wadi Natrun Resthouse • Sat–Thurs 9am–6pm, Fri 3–6pm; open Sat & Sun only during Lents (opening times can be checked on by calling the Cairo residence on ☎ 02 2592 9658) • Free

The loveliest of the monasteries is **Deir al-Suryani** – a compact maze of honey-coloured buildings. Its tranquillity belies its fractious origins; the monastery was founded by monks who quit St Bishoi's due to a sixth-century dispute over the theological importance of the Virgin. After they returned to the fold it was purchased for a group of Syrian monks, hence its name – the "Monastery of the Syrians". The unscrupulous antiquarian Robert Curzon came searching for ancient manuscripts here in the 1830s and found them lying on the floor "begrimed with dirt". Nowadays, the monastery's antique volumes are lovingly maintained in a modern **library**, including a cache of manuscripts up to fifteen hundred years old. The monastery also boasts the remains of some twelve saints and a lock of hair from Mary Magdalene.

The Church of the Virgin

Deir al-Suryani's principal **Church of the Virgin**, built around 980, contains a *haikal* with stucco ornamentation and the superb ebony **Door of Prophecies**, inlaid with ivory panels depicting the disciples and the seven epochs of the Christian era. Some lovely Byzantine-style **murals** dating back to the church's foundation have been uncovered by restorers. A dark passageway at the back of the church leads to the **cave** where St Bishoi tied his hair to a chain hanging from the ceiling to prevent himself sleeping for four days, until a vision of Christ appeared. The marble basin in the nave is used by the abbot to wash the feet of twelve monks on Maundy Thursday, emulating Christ's act during Passion Week.

Outside, the large **tamarind tree** enclosed by walls is said to have grown from the staff of St Emphram, who, as a monk, thrust it into the earth after his fellows criticized it as a worldly affectation. As Coptic pope, he established cordial relations with the Fatimid caliph in 997.

Deir Anba Bishoi

1km from Deir al-Suryani • Daily: May–Sept 7am–8pm; Oct–April 7am–6pm (opening times can be checked on by calling the Cairo residence on ☎ 02 2591 4488) • Free

Deir Anba Bishoi is the largest of the four monasteries, ringed by several new churches that tower above it, rather spoiling its appearance. Over 150 monks and novices live here and the monastery receives a constant stream of pilgrims that negates any atmosphere of solitude and contemplation.

The legend of **St Bishoi** suggests he was one of the earliest monks at Wadi Natrun. An angel told the saint's mother that he was chosen to do God's work even before his birth in 320; two decades later he moved here to study under St Bemoi alongside John "the Short". Since Bishoi's death in 417 his body has reportedly remained uncorrupted within its casket, which is carried in procession around the **Church of St Bishoi** every

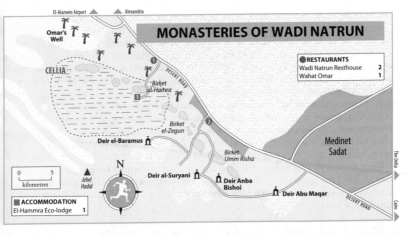

MONASTERIES OF WADI NATRUN

year on July 17. Next to him lies Paul of Tammuh, who was revered for committing suicide seven times. Egypt's beloved Coptic **Pope Shenouda III** was buried here in 2012; several mourners were crushed to death in the hysterical crowd.

St Bishoi's is the oldest of the five churches in the monastery, dating back to the fourth century. The monastery's **keep**, built three to four hundred years later, has chapels at ground level (around the back) and on the second storey, one floor above its drawbridge. There's also a fifth-century **well** where Berber tribesmen washed their swords after massacring the 49 Martyrs of Deir Abu Maqar (see below). The multi-domed building furthest from the entrance is a **Papal Residence**, where Pope Shenouda sometimes pointedly secluded himself to protest at the mistreatment of Copts under the Mubarak regime.

Deir Abu Maqar

6km from Deir Anba Bishoi • Admission only with a letter of introduction from the Coptic Patriarchate in Cairo (next to the Cathedral of St Mark, 222 Sharia Ramses, Abbassiya ☎ 02 282 5374) or Alexandria (in the Cathedral of St Mark, Sharia al-Kineesa al-Kobtiyya ☎ 03 483 5522) • Free

Enclosed by a circular wall ten metres high, **Deir Abu Maqar** requires visitors to pull a bell rope; in times past, two giant millstones stood ready to be rolled across to buttress the door against raiders. Its founder, **St Makarius**, died in 390 "after sixty years of austerities in various deserts", the last twenty of which were spent in a hermit's cell at Wadi Natrun. A rigorous faster, his only indulgence was a raw cabbage leaf for Sunday lunch.

Over the centuries, thirty Coptic patriarchs have come from the monastery; many are buried here, together with the 49 Martyrs killed by Berbers in 444. In 1978, monks discovered what they believed to be the **head of John the Baptist**; however, this is also claimed to be held in Venice, Aleppo and Damascus.

Since its nadir in 1969, when only six monks lived here, the monastery has acquired over a hundred brethren, a modern printing press and a farm employing six hundred workers. The monks have mastered pinpoint irrigation systems and bovine embryo transplant technology in an effort to meet their abbot's goal of feeding a thousand laypersons per monk, by creating orchards and dairy farms.

Deir el-Baramus

10km from the Wadi Natrun Resthouse • Fri–Sun 9am–5pm; closed during Lents (opening times can be checked on by calling the Cairo residence on ☎ 02 2592 2775) • Free

Deir el-Baramus is likewise surrounded by orchards and fields. The monastery was founded by St Makarius in 340, making it the oldest of the four that remain in Wadi Natrun, with eighty monks and novices, one of whom will show you around.

Visitors are greeted outside by a picture of St Moses the Black, a Nubian robber who became a monk under the influence of St Isidore. The monastery's name derives from the Coptic Pe Romios (House of the Romans), referring to Maximus and Domidus, two sons of the Roman Emperor Valentinus who died from excessive fasting; the younger one was only 19 years old. Their bodies are reputedly buried in a crypt below the ninth-century **Church of the Virgin**, whose belfries of unequal height symbolize the brothers' respective ages. Restoration work has revealed layers of medieval **frescoes** in the nave, the oldest (c.1200) as boldly drawn and colourful as comic strips, depicting the Visitation, the Nativity and other biblical scenes. At the western end of the nave is a fourth-century **pillar** with Syriac inscriptions, behind which St Arsanious used to pray with a pebble in his mouth, grudging every word that he spoke (including a statement to that effect).

The monastery's vine-laden courtyard also contains a fortified **keep** built over a well that enabled the monks to withstand seige, two **refectories** and a late-nineteenth-century Byzantine-style **Church of St John the Baptist**, now partly used as a library of theological texts.

Birket al-Hamra

10km off the Desert Road, reach via a spur road turning off at km 112, 100m before the Wahat Omar restaurant (see p.382); a local taxi from the Wadi Natrun Resthouse costs £E7–10 • Daily 24hr • Free

Out beyond Deir el-Baramus are miles of **salt lakes** rimmed by crusts of **natron**, a mixture of sodium carbonate and sodium bicarbonate, which the Ancient Egyptians used for dehydrating bodies and making glass. **Birket al-Hamra** (Red Lake) is magenta-hued and highly saline, with a "miraculous" sweetwater **spring** in the middle – Copts believe that the Virgin Mary quenched her thirst here. You can wade out to the spring (enclosed by an iron well) and taste it for yourself; the mud on the lake-bed is reputedly good for various afflictions.

The local *El Hammra Eco-lodge* (see p.382) can arrange **horseriding**, **camel-trekking** and **birdwatching** (look out for spur-winged plovers, crested larks, jacksnipes and sandpipers). These salt lakes harbour Egypt's last surviving wild **papyrus**, a dwarf subspecies of the plant that once flourished throughout the Nile Valley, but gradually became extinct; the last large papyrus (which could reach 6m) was found in the Delta in the mid-nineteenth century. Today it exists only on plantations, thanks to Dr Rageb, who rediscovered the lost technique of making papyrus paper.

Staff at the eco-lodge can also tell you where to find **petrified mangroves** from the Eocene Epoch, forty million years ago, when the environment resembled how the Florida Everglades are today. Unlike the petrified roots found at the Valley of the Whales (see p.390), these are thick fallen trunks.

ARRIVAL AND DEPARTURE WADI NATRUN

Wadi Natrun Resthouse (known to drivers as "Rest"), at km105 on the Desert Rd, is the jumping off point for exploring the oasis, assuming you don't engage a taxi at the outset in Cairo or Alexandria.

By bus West Delta Co. buses (hourly 5.30am–8.30pm) between Cairo Gateway (see p.175) and Alexandria's Moharrrem Bey Terminal (see p.483) can drop you at the *Resthouse*.

By microbus Midan el-Rameya, near the *Meridien* hotel in Giza, is the terminus for public microbuses to Wadi Natrun, terminating at the *Resthouse*.

By service taxi Service taxis run from Cairo's Aboud terminal (see p.174) to Alexandria; make sure they're travelling via the Desert Rd (not via Damanhur), and that the driver knows you want to be dropped at the *Resthouse*. You'll probably have to pay the full fare to Alexandria.

GETTING AROUND

By private taxi Local taxis (£E30/hr) can be hired at the *Resthouse* to tour the monasteries.

By tuk-tuk Motorcycle-taxis shuttle between the *Resthouse* and Deir Anba Bishoi (£E2–3/passenger), passing Deir al-Suryani en route and enabling you to visit two of the monasteries at little expense.

TOURS

Visiting hours vary from monastery to monastery, as does the extent to which each closes during the Coptic Lents or periods of fasting (June 27 to July 10; Aug 7–21; Nov 25 to Jan 6). On Fri, Sun and public holidays the monasteries are crowded with Coptic pilgrims. Although this isn't the most tranquil time to visit, it might be possible to hitch a ride with one of the busloads of Coptic pilgrims who visit the monasteries on these days – ask around any likely looking bus or minivan (some emblazoned with the name of a parish church or school) outside the *Wadi Natrun Resthouse*, or try hitching by the turn-off to the monasteries.

Organized tours Companies in downtown Cairo run excursions to the monasteries by car or minibus; the cost varies according to the number of people involved, and from agency to agency, so shop around. Holy Family Egypt (⌂ holyfamilyegypt.com), a Dutch–Egyptian agency specializing in Christian tourism, can slot individuals into its group tours by prior arrangement

By private taxi Expect to pay around £E400 for a half-day's excursion from Cairo or Alexandria; be sure the driver knows which monasteries you intend to visit.

3

ACCOMMODATION

The chief reason for staying here is to explore the wildlife of Birket al-Hamra (see p.381), but male visitors interested in experiencing a taste of monastic life have the option of sleeping in a monastery resthouse.

El Hammra Eco-lodge Birket al-Hamra ☎ 045 355 0944, ⊕ elhammraeco-lodge.com. On the western shore of the lake, this charming eco-lodge has comfortable rustic-style bungalows with up to three bedrooms, which can be rented for daytime use (£E100/person with a buffet lunch), or for overnight stays. With a swimming pool, volleyball, trail-bikes, donkeys and camels for rent, you can really make the most of the great outdoors here. Children up to 5 years old stay free and there's a fifty percent discount for under 12s. Half- and full-board deals are also available. B&B **£E300**

Monastery Resthouses With written permission from the Coptic Patriarchate in Cairo or Alexandria (see p.380), men can stay at Deir Anba Bishoi, Deir al-Suryani or Deir al-Baramus (whose lodgings are the least spartan of the three). As other guests are devout pilgrims, you're expected to make at least a token effort to attend prayers, and leave a donation (£E10–20) in return for the tea and bread that's provided.

EATING

Stalls around the *Wadi Natrun Resthouse* sell sandwiches, *fuul* and *taamiya*, but for a proper meal you should head for the *El Hammra Eco-lodge* or *Wahat Omar*.

Wahat Omar Km112, Desert Road. Named after hydrologist Pasha Omar Toussoum, who dug several wells in the area in the 1930s, this well-signposted outdoor restaurant serves Egyptian and Italian dishes (£E30–60) and has a mini-zoo to entertain kids. Daily noon–9pm.

The Fayoum

Likened in Ancient Egypt to a bud on the stem of the Nile, the **Fayoum** depends on river water – not springs or wells, like a true oasis. The water is distributed by a system of canals going back to ancient times, through palm groves and orchards, to flow into the **Lake Qaroun**, the Fayoum depression's main topographical feature since ancient

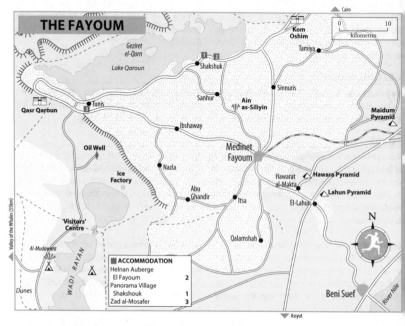

THE FAYOUM

ACCOMMODATION
Helnan Auberge	
El Fayoum	2
Panorama Village	
Shakshouk	1
Zad al-Mosafer	3

times (known as Lake Moeris in the Greco-Roman era). The word "Fayoum" probably derives from Phiom, the Coptic word for "sea", although folklore attributes it to a pharaoh's praise of the Bahr Yussef canal which irrigates the depression: "This is the work of a thousand days" (*alf youm*).

The Fayoum's capital, **Medinet Fayoum**, is far less alluring than the depression's periphery, rich in natural beauty spots, **wildlife** and **antiquities**. West of Lake Qaroun, the artists' colony of **Tunis** makes a relaxed base for exploring **Qasr Qaroun** temple, the wildlife sanctuary of **Wadi Rayan** and the fossilized prehistoric **Valley of the Whales**. Of the Fayoum's **pyramid sites**, the Collapsed Pyramid of **Maidum** marks a step between the first pyramid at Saqqara and subsequent efforts at Dahshur and Giza. **Lahun** and **Hawara** are later, ruined pyramids from the XII Dynasty, which ruled Egypt and ordered the waterworks that transformed the Fayoum from its capital Itj-tway (Seizer of the Two Lands), near **El-Lisht**, where the dynasty's founder built his own pyramid (not covered in this book).

ARRIVAL AND DEPARTURE

Which sites you want to visit may determine how you reach the Fayoum. If you're only interested in the pyramids or the Valley of the Whales, a **day-excursion by taxi** from Cairo makes sense, as getting there by **public transport** is time-consuming, if not impossible. Other sites are theoretically easy to reach from Medinet Fayoum, but the local tourist police may insist you hire a taxi anyway. If you're interested in spending more time in remoter regions, a **jeep safari** could be the best solution (see below). If you're happy to stay in Tunis, the local *Zad al-Mosafer* eco-lodge can arrange a direct transfer from Cairo for a very reasonable rate (see p.388).

TOURS

The Valley of the Whales and Wadi Rayan are also destinations for some safari operators in Bahariya (see box, p.400), in conjunction with the White Desert.

From Tunis Based in Tunis, safari operator Atmen Abood (☎010 0013 3781, ✉atmenabood@yahoo.com) offers day-excursions by jeep from there to the Valley of the Whales (£E400–500 for up to six people). He can also take you to other sites in the Fayoum for a similar day-rate, or on overnight safaris to the Ghard Abu Muharrik, a vast belt of dunes (see p.411), beyond which are the stalactite-cave of El-Qaf (p.411), the famous White Desert (p.409) and the oases of Bahariya (p.394) and Farafra (p.405).

From Cairo Minamar Travel (☎02 2517 3803, ⓦminamar .com) offers an overnight safari from Cairo (from €80), that includes a pick-up from your hotel, a felucca trip on Lake Qaroun, a visit to Wadi al-Rayan and camping at the Valley of the Whales. Their longer trips combine the Fayoum with the White Desert (from €120), El-Qaf (from €260) or Dakhla Oasis (from €290). All prices quoted are per person, for a group of five; fewer travellers are charged more.

Medinet Fayoum

A kind of pocket-size version of Cairo, with the Bahr Yussef in the role of the Nile, **MEDINET FAYOUM** (Fayoum City) makes a grab at the wallets of middle-class Cairenes who come to bask beside Lake Qaroun during summertime. The few foreigners that venture here tend to be whisked through in coaches and remain immured in hotels, so independent travellers draw attention – especially women.

The city and the Fayoum in general are among the most Islamic areas of Egypt, which lived under virtual lockdown during the last decades of the Mubarak regime due to the many militant Islamists who came from or settled here during the 1990s. In the first free elections since the 2011 Revolution, citizens voted solidly for the Muslim Brotherhood or Salafists, but it's too early to say how this will affect **tourism** (which is largely focused beyond the city).

A few hours will suffice to see Medinet Fayoum's atmospheric **souk** and famous **waterwheels.** By coming on a Tuesday you can also catch the local **pottery market,** and there are two colourful **moulids** during the eighth and ninth months of the Islamic calendar (see box, p.386).

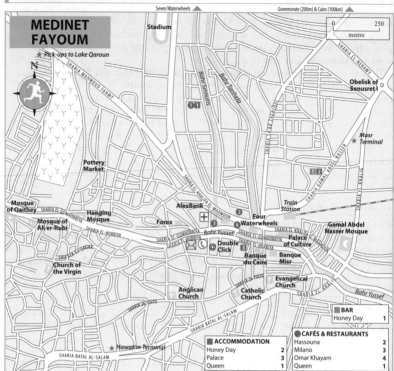

MEDINET
FAYOUM

The Bahr Yussef

Coptic and Muslim folklore ascribes the **Bahr Yussef** (River of Joseph) to its biblical namesake, who's believed to have been the pharaoh's vizier and minister for public works. Originally a natural waterway branching off the Nile near Beni Suef, it was regulated from the XII Dynasty onwards, and now draws water from the Nile at Dairut, nearly 300km further south.

The river (or canal) runs through the heart of the city, spanned by seven bridges. Baskets, pots and other Fayoumi **handicrafts** are sold on the north bank near the Four Waterwheels (see below).

Waterwheels

Four huge wooden **waterwheels** groaning away near the confluence of two canals are a central landmark. The Fayoum has about two hundred such waterwheels, introduced by Ptolemaic engineers in the third century BC. Because Nile water enters the sloping Fayoum depression at its highest point, gravity does half the work of distribution, and the current is strong enough to power the waterwheels for lifting irrigation water. During January the whole system is allowed to dry out for maintenance; the waterwheels have a working life of ten years if properly tarred and maintained.

For a pleasant hour's stroll in the morning or evening, follow the right bank of the Bahr Sinnuris northwards for 3km to reach the **Seven Waterwheels** (not to be confused with the four in the centre). First comes a single wheel near a farm; slightly further on, a quartet revolves against a backdrop of mango trees and palms; the final pair is a little way on, near a bridge.

Souk al-Qantara

Walking westwards beside the Bahr Yussef and crossing the canal, you can follow a street with a wooden roof into the **Souk al-Qantara**, a labyrinth of shops selling copperware and spices, grain and pulses, clothing and other goods. Like Al-Qasreya in Assyut (see p.232), this souk seems little changed since Ottoman times, with not a trace of tourism, let alone the makeovers that have happened to bazaars in Cairo, Luxor or Aswan.

The Christian quarter

Behind the Souk al-Qantara, **Sharia es-Sagha** (Street of Goldsmiths) is crammed with jewellers' shops, mostly owned by Christians. Medinet Fayoum still has a recognisably Christian quarter, reflecting the traditional Islamic division of towns into mahalla based on religion or ethnicity. Ranged along Sharia 26 Yulyu are churches catering to the minor denominations (Anglican, Catholic and Evangelical), which amount to one percent of Egypt's population.

As the largest denomination, the Coptic Orthodox Church has the oldest place of worship, at the heart of the Christian quarter. Built in 1836, the **Church of the Virgin** contains an altar dedicated to the local saint Anba Abram (1829–1912), who was reputedly able to transport himself across distances in a miraculous fashion.

Mosque of Ali er-Rubi

To the west of Souk al-Qantara, the **Mosque of Ali er-Rubi** is dedicated to a local Muslim sheikh whose renown among Fayoumis eclipses even Anba Abram's. His mausoleum, down some steps from the courtyard, is surrounded by an enormous *darih* or carved box-frame, and people muttering supplications. During his moulid, devotees perform *zikrs* and sleep outside the mosque.

Mosque of Qaitbey and around

Facing the Bahr Yussef, the **Mosque of Qaitbey** is the oldest in the Fayoum, built (or restored) by the Mamluke Sultan Qaitbey (see p.120), in honour of his favourite concubine, Asal-Bay. Qaitbey was also responsible for building the humpbacked twin-arched **bridge** nearby, known as the "Bridge of Sighs" because it leads towards the city's Muslim cemetery.

Crossing this, you can head along the riverside to find the **Hanging Mosque**, so called because its north frontage is upheld by five arches, once occupied by workshops. It was built in 1375 by Prince Soliman Ibn Mohammed.

The pottery market

Further north from the Hanging Mosque, backstreets near the Muslim cemetery host a huge Tuesday-morning **pottery market** for red, pink or unglazed pots, casseroles and other traditional products from Nazla. This village in the western Fayoum is notable for its giant pottery-kilns (which cast a smoky pall over the community) and its inexplicable hostility to foreigners (who are strongly advised against visiting).

Palace of Culture and Gamal Abdel Nasser Mosque

East of the train station, the **Palace of Culture** is Medinet Fayoum's modernist landmark, an inverted pyramid housing a cinema, theatre and library. Nearby stands the **Gamal Abdel Nasser Mosque**, one of many that Nasser had built in provincial towns in the 1960s, and which bear his name. The mosque is the site of the "viewing" ceremony (see box, p.386), and its imam leads the procession of floats during the festival.

Obelisk of Senusret I

Entering or leaving town by the Cairo road, you'll pass the thirteen-metre-high red-granite **Obelisk of Senusret I**, the only obelisk in Egypt to have a rounded tip. Senusret was the second king of the XII Dynasty who displayed a special fondness for the Fayoum and was the first ruler to regard it as more than just a hunting ground. The obelisk (actually a stele) was originally sited near the village of Abgig, where the Napoleonic artist Jomard drew it for the Description l'Egypte lying on the ground, broken in two. There it remained until the 1970s, when the antiquities department transported the hundred-ton stone to its present location.

ARRIVAL AND DEPARTURE MEDINET FAYOUM

By train Irregular third-class trains from Ramses and/or Giza station in Cairo take up to four hours to reach Medinet Fayoum. Aside from terminating right in the centre, they offer no advantage over buses or service taxis.

By bus Upper Egypt Bus Co. services (hourly 9.30am–3pm; 2hr) run between Medinet Fayoum's **Masr Terminal**, 1km from downtown, and Cairo's Aboud terminal (see p.174). Buses between Medinet Fayoum and Beni Suef (hourly; 1hr) in the Nile Valley run from the **Hawatim Terminal**

on Sharia Batal al-Salam (£E5–10 by taxi from the centre).

By service taxi Minibuses from Cairo's Midan Orabi, Midan Ramses, Midan Giza and El Moneeb depots run almost nonstop from early morning to late at night to the Masr Terminal. Services from Beni Suef end up at the Hawatim Terminal.

By pick-up Covered pick-ups are the main form of public transport within the Fayoum, departing for Lake Qaroun from a nameless depot on Sharia Mahmoud Fahmy.

INFORMATION

Tourist office In the Governorate Building on Sharia Sa'ad Zaghloul, 2km from the city centre, the city's tourist office (daily 9.30am–3pm; ☎ 084 634 2313) had nothing to offer visitors at the time of writing, although things may improve in the future if the Ministry of Tourism starts paying its local staff – but don't be surprised if doors are locked or the phone isn't answered. A small kiosk beside the four waterwheels (see p.384) might be able to supply some out-of-date brochures.

Tourist police Also in the Governorate Building (☎ 084 630 7298), the tourist police used to keep a close eye on tourists visiting Medinet Fayoum, assigning them a plainclothes minder and only allowing travel within or outside the city by private taxi. Since the Revolution, however, they haven't bothered imposing any restrictions – but whether this will continue is anyone's guess.

ACCOMMODATION

Outside of festivals (see box below) there shouldn't be any difficulty finding a room in town, though none of the hotels is great. You may well prefer to stay out near Lake Qaroun, at Shakshuk or Tunis (see map, p.382), where the ambience is better.

Honey Day 105 Sharia Gamal Abdel Nasser ☎ 084 634 1205 or ☎ 010 0035 7533. Conveniently near Masr bus terminal, this high-rise two-star (whose name is pronounced "honey-die") has decent a/c rooms with TV and fridge, a restaurant and a sleazy bar (if it hasn't been shut down). B&B **£E350**

Palace Sharia Horriya ☎ 084 631 1222. Look out for the sign facing the Bahr Yussef; the entrance is an alleyway,

behind some kiosks. Rooms are clean but musty, with the option of bathrooms and a/c, and the manager speaks English. B&B **£E200**

Queen Sharia Munsha'at Lotfallah ☎ 084 634 6819. Spacious en-suite rooms with satellite TV (a/c costs extra) in a quiet neighbourhood, fifteen minutes' walk from the centre. B&B **£E400**

EATING AND DRINKING

In Egypt the Fayoum is renowned for its tasty vegetables, fruit and poultry (*fayoumi* means "delicious"), but don't expect any fancy restaurants in Medinet Fayoum; there are better options out at Lake Qaroun. Only two places in the oasis serve alcohol.

FAYOUMI FESTIVALS

It's worth visiting Medinet Fayoum simply for its **festivals,** as many local farmers do. Hotels overflow during **Ali er-Rubi's moulid** in the middle of Sha'ban (the eighth month in the Muslim calendar), when the alleys around his mosque are crammed with stalls selling sugar dolls and horsemen, and all kinds of amusements can be tried, while the devout perform *zikrs* in the courtyard. The other big occasion is the "viewing" (*er-ruyeh*) of the new moon that heralds **Ramadan**, celebrated by a parade of carnival floats representing different professions, whose riders bombard spectators with "lucky" prayer leaflets.

Hassouna Sharia Khalifa el-Maamoun ☎ 084 633 3170. One of a few cafés in town that's signposted in English, serving inexpensive *shawarma*, *fuul*, *taamiya* and grilled chicken, to eat in or take away. Daily 9am–11pm.

Honey Day 105 Sharia Gamal Abdel Nasser ☎ 084 634 205. At the time of writing this hotel bar was serving Egyptian beer and spirits and also serving as a hangout for prostitutes, although how long it survives now that local Salafists are in the saddle is anyone's guess. Daily 11am–midnight.

Milano Sharia al-Sadd al-Ali. Not far from the four waterwheels, and identifiable by its green and yellow exterior, *Milano* serves tasty *kushari*, freshly squeezed juice, ice cream or creme caramel. Daily 9am–midnight.

Omar Khayam Sharia al-Sadd al-Ali. Named after the Persian poet (who would surely enjoy its ambience), this vintage teahouse across the road from *Hassouna* has a pleasant shady garden. Their speciality is cold *sahleb*, which comes topped with slices of banana. Daily 24hr.

Queen Sharia Munsha'at Lotfallah ☎ 084 634 6819. The hotel's colourfully decorated restaurant has a longish menu of Egyptian and international dishes – try their shish tawook or *escalope panee*.

DIRECTORY

Banks and exchange The Forex bureau on Sharia er-Ramla has better rates than AlexBank, Banque du Caire or Banque Misr (all with ATMs). Outside of Medinet Fayoum there are no banks or exchange bureaux.

Hospital Arafa Hospital, Sharia el-Gumhorriya (daily 24hr; ☎ 084 636 4747).

Internet access Double-Click, Sharia Khaled Pasha (daily 10am–7pm).

Post office Sharia el-Horriya. Daily except Fri & Sat 8am–7pm.

Telephone office Sharia el-Horriya, beside the post office (daily 24hr).

Lake Qaroun

20km from Medinet Fayoum, 80km from Cairo, accessible by pick-up service taxi (£E1.50) from Medinet Fayoum to the crossroads near the Helnan Auberge El Fayoum, from where other pick-ups run past Shakshuk, towards Tunis and Wadi Rayan.

Short of tankers gliding between the sandbanks of the Suez Canal, Egypt has no weirder juxtaposition of water and desert than **Lake Qaroun** (Birket Qaroun), where colourful fishing boats bob against a backdrop of arid hills. Familiarly known to locals as El-Birka (The Pond), the lake's name may derive from the horn (*qorn*)-shaped peak on an island in the middle, but many Fayoumis believe that it's named after a character in the Koran, who was swallowed up by the earth as a punishment for being "exultant in his riches".

Despite its scrappy beaches of broken shells and saline gunk, the lake has long been a **bathing resort** for wealthy Cairenes, with a year-round "season" (although from Jan to April it's too cold to swim). Shooting wildfowl has been prohibited since it became a nature reserve, but **fishing** is still allowed, at its best between July and September. With

EGYPT'S GARDEN OF EDEN

Drastic fluctuations in Lake Qaroun's water level have occurred throughout history, and its current surface area of 214 square kilometres is a fraction of its size when the Nile first broke into the Fayoum depression, forming a lake 40m above the current level which Ancient Egyptian mythology identified with the waters of chaos and primeval life they called **Nun**. The diversity of wild plant species around the lake, which could be selectively isolated and irrigated, makes the Fayoum a plausible location for Egypt's "Garden of Eden", where Pre-dynastic communities only generations removed from the hunter-pastoralist cultures of the Western Desert learnt the skills of agriculture that would deliver the food surpluses necessary to advance civilization.

Yet if Ancient Egyptian culture was born here, it soon moved on to other locations, only revisiting its roots centuries later. Although the Middle Kingdom emerged at nearby Herakleopolis in the Nile Valley (south of Beni Suef), it wasn't until Amenemhat I (c.1985–55 BC) moved his capital to Lisht that the Fayoum became important. He had canals dug and the channel to the Nile deepened, draining parts for agriculture and submerging a greater area with what the Ancient Greeks and Romans called **Lake Moeris**. The Ptolemies lowered it to reclaim land for their settlements, and by the end of the Roman era the lake had dropped to 36m below sea level, leaving villages and fields high and dry. In modern times, Lake Qaroun has risen again, but still lies well below the level of its ancient predecessors.

binoculars, you can observe the lake's prolific **birdlife** – 88 species, including flamingos, which have a colony on **Geziret el-Qorn** (Horn Island) – from a fisherman's **boat** hired near one of the lakeside hotels (£E30– 50/hr).

The ugly town of **Shakshuk** has nothing to offer visitors, but lends its name to several holiday villages and restaurants. Since 2005 the shore has been embanked against flooding, which almost engulfed the *Helnan Auberge El Fayoum* (once King Farouk's hunting lodge, where Allied and Arab leaders met after World War II to carve up the Middle East) and time-share holiday villages beside the lake.

ACCOMMODATION AND EATING SHAKSHUK

★ **Helnan Auberge El Fayoum** ☏ 084 698 1200, ⓦ helnan.com. Built in 1937 as King Farouk's hunting lodge, this lakeside hotel's Moorish decor is its main selling point – but don't believe its five-star rating. If you can't afford the royal suite, at least check out the banqueting hall or enjoy a cocktail in the *Churchill Lounge*. Only its first-floor rooms can justly claim to have a lake view ($20 extra). Amenities include a swimming pool, bar, billiards and wi-fi in the lobby, while the restaurant (daily noon–11pm) serves tasty grilled calamari (£E105), duck (£E80), club sandwiches (£E30) and alcohol. Sandwiches, cocktails and spirits (£E40) are also

served in the pillared *Churchill Lounge*. B&B $150
Panorama Village Shakshouk ☏ 084 683 1115, ⓔ newpanorama.village@gmail.com. This pleasant lakeside cluster of three-star a/c chalets has a small pool, and free wi-fi throughout. The swish *Dananir* restaurant (daily 10am–midnight; no alcohol) has tables inside and outdoors, an extensive menu of fish, grills and salads, and a singer some nights during the summer holiday season – a nice place to dine if you don't mind the lack of alcohol. Not as grand as the *Helnan Auberge* but good value for money, with half- and full-board deals. B&B £E350

Tunis

45km from Medinet Fayoum, 20km from Shakshuk; pick-up service taxis (£E4) from near the Helnan Auberge El Fayoum run past the village, 200m south of the main road

A bucolic hilltop village turned **artists' colony** where Cairene intellectuals enjoy rusticating, **TUNIS** is well worth a visit in tandem with Wadi Rayan. Its *Zad al-Mosafer* eco-lodge makes an ideal base for exploring Fayoum's beauty spots with **wildlife** guide Ahmed Mansour (☏ 010 0377 9542, ⓔ ahmedmansour05@hotmail.com); **horseriding** (£E50/hr) and **jeep safaris** (see "Tours", p.383) can also be arranged.

In the 1970s Swiss potter Evelyne Porret founded a **pottery school** (☏ 084 682 0405) for local children; former students Abdel Sattar (☏ 084 682 0827) and Rawiaya Abdel Kader Salem (☏ 084 682 0911) now have their own **workshops**, viewable by appointment, like the school itself. Some of their workshops are signposted in English.

At the back of the village, Mohammed Abla's **Fayoum Art Centre** (☏ 012 2338 2810, ⓦ fayoumartcentre.com) runs six-week **courses** (from April), ranging from sculpture to printmaking. Participation is free but there's a daily charge for staying at the eco-lodge. The mud-brick complex also houses an intriguing **Caricature Museum** (no set hours; free), displaying political cartoons about Egypt and the Arab world, from the 1950s until the present.

ACCOMMODATION AND EATING TUNIS

★ **Zad al-Mosafer** ☏ 084 682 0180 or ☏ 010 0639 5590, ⓦ zadalmosaferecolodge.net. Owned by retired Cairo journalist Abdu Gobair, this charming rustic eco-lodge has cosy mud-brick rooms with fans and mosquito nets, plus family rooms sleeping five (£E160) and some en-suite doubles. A small pool, a big play area and a pottery will keep

kids happy, and there are tasty meals cooked from homegrown ingredients – non-residents are welcome to order breakfast (£E25), lunch or dinner (£E45–85), but phone ahead to say you're coming. Horseriding, birdwatching and jeep safaris can also be arranged, as well as transfers from Cairo by car (£E175 for up to five people). £E85

Qasr Qaroun

15km from Tunis, just before the village of Qaroun (accessible by irregular pick-ups from the lakeside road) • Daily 9am–4pm • £E5

According to local legend, the miser Qaroun who was punished by Allah (see p.387)

SOBEK AND CROCODILOPOLIS

The Fayoum's ancient capital, **Crocodilopolis** (later renamed Arsinoë after Ptolemy II's sister-wife), was the centre of the **crocodile cult** supposedly began by Pharaoh Menes, the legendary unifier of Upper and Lower Egypt, whose life was saved by a croc while he was hunting in the Fayoum marshes. The crocodile deity, **Sobek**, was particularly favoured by Middle Kingdom rulers and assumed national prominence after being identified with Re (as Sobek-Re) and Horus. Sobek was variously depicted as a hawk-headed crocodile or in reptilian form with Amun's crown of feathers and ram's horns. At the Sacred Lake of Crocodilopolis, reptiles were fed and worshipped, and even adorned with jewellery, by the priests of Sobek. Today, nothing remains of the ancient city, north of the modern capital.

Sobek

stashed his treasure in **Qasr Qaroun**, which isn't a palace as its Arabic name (pronounced *'asr 'aroun*) suggests, but actually a Ptolemaic **temple** dedicated to the Ancient Egyptian crocodile-god Sobek (see box above).

Outwardly plain but inwardly labyrinthine and riddled with holes dug by treasure-hunters, it needs a torch to explore its warren of chambers, stairs and passageways at different levels. Beware of scorpions, bats, snakes and lizards – the last resemble miniature crocodiles, as befits a temple dedicated to Sobek.

Round about are the **ruins of Dionysias**, a Ptolemaic-Roman town believed to have been abandoned when the lake shrank (it's now 45 minutes' walk away). West of the temple is an even more ruinous **fortress**, constructed during the reign of Emperor Diocletian against the Blemmye (an indication of how far north these Nubian raiders went).

Wadi Rayan

20km from Tunis • By pick-up service taxi from near the Helnan Auberge El Fayoum to a nameless village (ask the driver for Wadi Rayan) beyond Tunis (££4), and then another pick-up to Wadi Rayan (££7) • **Nature Reserve**: daily 24hr • ££19, plus ££5/vehicle

One kilometre beyond Tunis, a well-signposted spur-road turns off the lakeside highway towards **Wadi Rayan**, a separate depression 15km outside the oasis which has become a man-made wildlife haven. The idea of piping excess water from the Fayoum into the wadi was first mooted by the British but only put into practice in 1966, when three lakes and a waterfall were created, vegetation flourished and the area became a major nesting ground for birds.

Wadi Rayan is now a **nature reserve** harbouring the world's sole known population of slender-horned gazelles, eight other species of mammals, thirteen species of resident birds and 26 migrant and vagrant species. The prehistoric fossils of the Valley of the Whales (see p.390) also come under its auspices, supported by several foreign NGOs.

Lakes and waterfalls

Initially cultivated, the valley gets sandier the closer you get to Wadi Rayan's azure lakes, where hordes of visitors descend on Fridays and holidays to sunbathe and play ghettoblasters on the beach. The lake is too saline for swimming, but **boating** (and floating in rubber tyres) is popular, and its tatty lakeside cafés are always busy.

From the main lake a track leads to the **waterfalls** (*shallalat*). The only ones in Egypt, they've appeared in countless videos and films despite being only a few metres high, and are usually busy with families enjoying the novelty of an outdoors power-shower, surrounded by reeds and sand dunes.

Birdwatching, dunes and springs

About 10km beyond the visitors' centre, the road passes a hill known as **Al-Mudawara** which you can hike up for a spectacular **view** of the reed-fringed lake and desert scarp beyond. Soon afterwards is the turn-off for the Valley of the Whales, followed by a signposted turning to a **birdwatching** site by the shore. Besides the ubiquitous cattle egrets, grey herons and little bitterns, there are hard-to-spot wagtails, skylarks, kestrels, kites and Senegal coucals.

Further on, magnificent *seif* **dunes** 30m high run parallel to an inlet fringed by tamarisks, with three sulphur **springs** nearby, before the road crosses a boring stretch of desert to return to the oasis. All of this route can be done in a 2WD car, unlike the route to the Valley of the Whales (see below), separated from Wadi Rayan by the **Garet Gohanimeen** (Mountain of Hell), so-called because the light of the setting sun appears to transform it into an inferno.

INFORMATION AND ACCOMMODATION — WADI RAYAN

Visitors' Centre Near Wadi Rayan car park (daily 11am–3.30pm; free). Closed at the time of writing but set to reopen, it has attractively presented exhibits on the wildlife, geology and prehistory of Wadi Rayan, all captioned in English.

Accommodation Camping (£E40/person) is allowed in specific sites in Wadi Rayan and the Valley of the Whales (contact the reserve's manager, Arafa, for details ☎ 011 1554 4430) but no facilities are provided. The Zad al-Mosafer eco-lodge (see p.388) in Tunis is the nearest hotel.

Valley of the Whales

200km from Cairo, 50km from Wadi Rayan (38km of it by paved road) – a 4WD car is strongly advised as sandstorms can cover the route • Daily sunrise–sunset • £E19, plus £E5/vehicle • Camping is allowed (see above) • A basic café serves hot and cold drinks

Since being declared a World Heritage site in 2005 – and a scandal over Belgian diplomats who pulverized a fossil with their jeep – the **Valley of the Whales** (Wadi al-Hitan) has been patrolled by wardens, and vehicles restricted to marked tracks with walking trails between the fossilized remains. The unique **fossils** consist of amphibious mammals deposited by the swirling waters of the prehistoric Tethys Sea and marine life stranded when it receded forty million years ago. Today they have fallen from (or remain embedded in) hillocks shaped like giant whelks or filigreed slugs, part of the Qasr es-Sagha Formation created by the Tethys Sea, which once extended as far as the Gilf Kebir, now Egypt's most arid region (see p.431).

In 1877, geologist George Schweinfurth found two hundred fossilized skeletons of what he believed was a reptile, which he called "Basilosaurus" (King Lizard), that was later reclassified as a seven-tonne mammal with a slender body 18m long, and small but fully developed hind feet. It's thought that this **Zeuglodon** was a dead-end in the evolution of whales that began when some land mammals migrated into the sea, and that another shark-eating creature, the spear-toothed **Dorudon**, may be the ancestor of modern whales. New skeletons are being discovered all the time – over five hundred have been logged – and there are fossilized **mangrove roots** from a time when the valley resembled the Florida Everglades.

Examples of the fossils in situ are identified in a simple **museum**, due to be upgraded into a visitors' centre like the one at Wadi Rayan.

Kom Oshim (Karanis)

30km from Medinet Fayoum, 70km from Cairo, service taxis in either direction can drop you at "Mathaf Kom Oshim" (the museum by the highway, with the ruins behind it), but getting back is harder, as most passing cars are full • Daily 9am–4pm • £E25

Kom Oshim is the local name for the site of **Karanis**, a Ptolemaic-Roman town founded by Greek mercenaries and their camp followers during the third century BC. With a population of roughly three thousand until the fifth century AD, it was a wealthy farming centre whose sophistication is conveyed by pottery and glassware, terracotta figures used for modelling hairstyles and two "Fayoum portraits" (see p.82) found here by archeologists.

Alas, the site's **museum** has been closed since the Revolution and shows no sign of reopening. Its guardians try to make amends by showing you around the **Beyt Sobek** (House of Sobek), a former archeological dig-house that's been turned into a basic visitors' centre, with a café in the pipeline.

The lowly **ruins** cover a mound guarded by cute wild dogs and bored police, who can point you towards two stone **temples**. A red-stone one, dedicated to two local crocodile gods, was where priests kept a live crocodile in the sanctuary, feeding it on raw meat and honey-cakes. The other (completed by Nero) affords a view of mud-brick ruins and the fertile Fayoum depression further south.

Collapsed Pyramid of Maidum

89km from Cairo, 35km from Medinet Fayoum • From Cairo by taxi take the Assyut Desert Rd for 83km to the Al-Assiouty Resthouse, make a U-turn and drive back past the resthouse to reach the Maidum turn-off; from Cairo by early-morning train to El-Wasta (1hr 30min) and then service taxi to Maidum village (15min), from where it's a 1km walk • Daily 8am–4pm • £E35

The **Collapsed Pyramid of Maidum** is visible from afar, resembling a medieval citadel rising out of the desert in sheer-walled tiers from mounds of debris – a vision almost as dramatic as the act of getting inside used to be, when "visitors had to hang by their hands from the ledge above and drop into the entry guided by a guard" (as *Murray's Handbook* cautioned).

Nowadays you climb an iron stairway on the pyramid's north side, then descend 57m to the bedrock via a steep passageway (high enough to walk comfortably) before ducking through a low portal into the **burial chamber**. Its lofty corbelled ceiling of limestone slabs resembles the chambers in the Bent Pyramid at Dahshur (see p.168), with a cool and slightly humid atmosphere.

Other sights

Around the pyramid are several unfinished mastabas, reduced to mud-brick lumps. It was here that the exquisite "Maidum Geese" frieze and the famous statue of Snofru's son Rahotep and his wife Nofret were found (both are now in the Egyptian Museum). Nearest the pyramid, **Mastaba #17** is exciting to explore, but very dusty and likely to

---

THE RIDDLE OF THE COLLAPSED PYRAMID

Evidently Maidum began as a **step pyramid** (like Zoser's at Saqqara), with four levels, which was then enlarged to an eight-step pyramid, and finally given an outer shell to make it a "true" pyramid. It seems, however, that the design was faulty, distributing stresses outwards rather than inwards, so that its own mass blew the structure apart. When exactly this happened is unknown – and the crux of the riddle of the Collapsed Pyramid.

No inscriptions appeared on the coffin found inside, but New Kingdom graffiti in the nearby mortuary temple led archeologists to attribute the pyramid to the IV Dynasty ruler **Snofru** (see p.170) or to his father **Huni** (c.2637–13 BC). Partisans of Huni argue that Snofru commissioned the Red and Bent pyramids at Dahshur, and would therefore not have needed a third repository for his *ka*.

Most scholars accept Kurt Mendelssohn's theory that the design of the Bent Pyramid at Dahshur was hastily altered because Maidum collapsed during its construction. But critics argue that there is no evidence for the collapse having happened while Dahshur was underway – indeed, Maidum's mortuary temple would not have been built had this happened – and the collapse might have occurred as late as Roman, or even medieval, times.

The nineteenth-century Egyptologist Flinders Petrie calculated that its original height from base to summit was 93.5m (today's ruin is 65m high), with a base-to-height ratio and slope identical to the Great Pyramid at Giza which would have been expressed by the Ancient Egyptian measurement of *seked* (dividing the royal cubit into seven palms and four further digits), specified millennia after the last pyramid was built in the XVII Dynasty *Rhind Mathematical Papyrus*.

rip your clothing as you descend an extremely low and narrow 47-metre-long corridor dug by robbers, and climb a makeshift ladder to the burial chamber. Its sarcophagus is larger than the chamber's entrance, so presumably the mastaba was built around it.

The site ticket also covers admission to a more distant mastaba, a ruined **mortuary temple** and the remains of the **Silah step pyramid** – but frankly they're not worth the effort of walking that far.

Hawara Pyramid

10km from Medinet Fayoum, 12km from Lahun • Service taxis between Medinet Fayoum and Beni Suef can drop you at Hawarat al-Makta, where you cross the Bahr Yussef by a bridge, turn right at the T-junction beyond the village and walk on until the pyramid appears • Daily 8am–4pm • £E30

The royal necropolis of **Hawara** (Great Mansion) may have stood on the shores of Lake Moeris when it was built by the XII Dynasty ruler Amenemhat III (c.1855–1808 BC). Eleven centuries later, it became the finishing point of a one-hundred-kilometre **desert endurance race** instituted by Pharaoh Taharqa (690 BC) to train his troops; the race was revived in 2001 and is now held annually in November (⊕egyptianmarathon.com).

Aside from the race Hawara gets few visitors, as its 54-metre-high **Pyramid of Amenemhat III** has degenerated into a shapeless mound since its limestone casing was removed in antiquity. Unlike most pyramids, its entrance was on the south side: one of many ruses devised to foil tomb-robbers. Alas, due to rising ground water, you can't go inside to examine such ingenious features as the stone portcullises that sealed the corridor or the roof block that was lowered into place once the sarcophagus was in the burial chamber, both operated by ingenious sand-powered mechanisms based on the principle of an hour glass. None of them saved the body of the pharaoh from being looted and burned; his sarcophagus was later stashed alongside that of his daughter, to be found intact with her treasures in 1956.

From its summit (easily reached by climbing the southwest corner) you should be able to see the Lahun Pyramid on the southeastern horizon.

Other sites

Rising ground water has flooded all the excavation pits dug to investigate the site of the fabled **Labyrinth** to the south of the pyramid. Herodotus described it as containing over three thousand chambers hewn from a single rock, but with only column stumps and masses of limestone fragments to show for decades of digging, it's difficult to believe his account of the structure. Most archeologists think that it was Amenemhat III's mortuary temple, although David Rohl argues that it may have been an eternal representation of the bureaucracy and waterworks that Joseph devised to prepare Egypt for the seven years of famine foretold by the pharaoh's dream (Genesis 41:1–4).

During the early excavations at Hawara in the nineteenth century, Flinders Petrie unearthed 146 brilliantly naturalistic **"Fayoum Portraits"** (see p.82) in the Roman cemetery to the north of the pyramid.

El-Lahun and the Lahun Pyramid

5km from El-Lahun on the road between Medinet Fayoum and Beni Suef; service taxis can drop you where the track to the pyramid (800m) leaves the road • Daily 8am–4pm • £E35

West of Hawara, the incoming Nile waters channelled via the Bahr Yussef pass through the village of **EL-LAHUN**, which gets its name from the Ancient Egyptian Le-hone (Mouth of the Lake). Today, the flow of water is regulated by concrete sluices (qantara in Arabic; no photography) not far from a thirteenth-century stone version called the **Qantara of Sultan Qaitbey**, itself modelled on the regulators constructed by Amenemhat III in ancient times. Part of the way to the pyramid follows an earthen **embankment** that was probably part of the barrage that first diverted water into the Fayoum (built by

Amenemhat I), which ends at the desert's edge, where visitors buy a ticket for the site and pick up a police escort to walk the final stretch to the pyramid.

Pyramid of Senusret II

The **Pyramid of Senusret II** was created by Senusret II (c.1880–74 BC), Amenemhat III's grandfather, attesting to the generations of XII Dynasty pharaohs who invested in this site. Built seven or eight centuries after the pyramids at Giza, it employed a new technique devised by his architect Anupy. Its core consists of a limestone knoll on which pillars were based, providing the framework for the mud-brick overlay, which was finally encased in stone. The removal of its casing stones at some point in time left the mud-brick pyramid exposed to the elements, which eroded it into its present mess.

When Petrie entered the pyramid and found Senusret's sarcophagus in 1888 it had been looted long ago, but to the west of the entrance shaft his colleague Guy Brunton discovered the fabulous **jewellery of Princess Sat-hathor**, now divided between the Egyptian Museum and the Metropolitan Museum of Art in New York.

As at Hawara, the pyramid's **entrance** is from the courtyard on the south side, which is why Petrie took so long to find it. This corridor was too narrow to admit the royal sarcophagus, so another shaft was hidden further south, descending for 16m to a **ritual well** whose depths below the water table have never been plumbed. Both lead to an **entrance hall**, from which an ascending corridor takes a ninety-degree turn to reach a gable-roofed **burial chamber** containing a red granite sarcophagus.

Other sites

To the north of the pyramid are eight rock-cut mastabas for Senusret's family, at the far end of which is a shapeless so-called **Queen's Pyramid**, apparently lacking any tomb. In 2009, the SCA discovered dozens of vividly painted coffins in rock-cut tombs dating back as far as the II Dynasty, showing that Lahun was used for burials a thousand years earlier than hitherto reckoned. None are accessible to tourists.

The Great Desert Circuit

The **Great Desert Circuit** extends for around 1400km through four oases, once ruled by pharaohs, Persians, Romans, Mamlukes, Turks and Britons, which have been transformed since the 1970s under the **New Valley** programme (see box below). **Bahariya** and **Farafra** harbour the fantastic Black and White deserts, hot springs and

---

THE NEW VALLEY

The four oases overlie a dead, prehistoric branch of the Nile, tapping a subterranean aquifer estimated to contain fifty thousand cubic kilometres of water. In 1958 Nasser's government unveiled plans to irrigate the desert and relocate landless peasants from the overcrowded Nile Valley and Delta to this **New Valley** (El-Wadi el-Jedid). From this emerged a New Valley governorate charged with running Kharga, Dakhla and Farafra oases, in collaboration with the 6th October City governorate which administers Bahariya Oasis.

Since work began in the 1970s doubts have surfaced about the **aquifer**, which was previously thought to be replenished by underground seepage from Lake Chad and Equatorial Africa but is now believed to be a finite – perhaps rapidly diminishing – resource. The water-table has fallen dramatically in all the oases except Siwa, boreholes must be deeper and the ground water pumped to the surface is hotter. A decade's effort by Mubarak's regime to bring Nile water to Kharga Oasis via the Sheikh Zayed Canal, and exploit the aquifer beneath the desert at East Oweinat, has left several **ghost towns** deserted by settlers disillusioned by the lack of jobs and infrastructure.

palm groves, while in **Dakhla** and **Kharga**, temples and villages attest to historic ties with the Nile Valley and Saharan caravan routes. As well as the inhabited oases there are more remote sites such as the **El-Qaf** stalactite cave and the **Ghard Abu Muharrik** dune, plus uninhabited oases along the road to Siwa.

Visiting the oases

Allow a week to sample all four oases. If you only have a few days, Bahariya and Farafra are the ones to aim for from Cairo; starting from Luxor or Assyut go to Dakhla rather than stopping in Kharga. Each oasis shares the **climate** of Nile Valley towns on the same latitude – Bahariya is like Minya and Kharga like Luxor – although the air is fresher (except during sandstorms). Winters are mild by day and near freezing at night (bring a sleeping bag); in summer temperatures can soar to 50°C at midday and hover in the twenties after dark. Spring and autumn are the best times to visit, with orchards in bloom or being harvested and enough tourists around to make sharing costs easy.

Don't expect any fancy restaurants (though you can look forward to Bedouin parties round a campfire) or be surprised by accommodation and safari operators under the same roof (which can cause problems if you decline their trips). **Tourism** is in the hands of officials and entrepreneurs whose competence and honesty varies. While it pays to shop around, don't let over-suspicion sour things, as you really need local help to get the best from the oases and will have to strike a deal with somebody in the end.

Visitors should respect local values by dressing modestly and observing the conventions on bathing in outdoor **springs** (mostly keyhole-shaped concrete tanks fed by hot water pumped up from below). The ones nearest town are always used by local men; if women bathe there, it is only after dark, never when males are present, and only fully covered by a *galabiyya*. You can avoid these restrictions by bathing in isolated spots, but most **women** cover up anyway. Women on their own should beware of entering palm groves or gardens – regarded here as an invitation to sex.

GETTING AROUND   **THE GREAT DESERT CIRCUIT**

You can embark on the circuit at either end: from Cairo or Assyut by public transport; from Siwa Oasis by jeep; from Luxor by taxi; or even by flying into Kharga Oasis. Details are given under the individual oasis; what follows is an overview.

By plane The Petroleum Service Co. operates twice-weekly flights between Cairo and Kharga Oasis – and maybe also to Dakhla in the future – which afford wonderful views of the desert. Their Cairo ticket office is off Sharia al-Azhar at 45 Afit al-Mahdi ☎ 02 2392 1674 or ☎ 011 1763 1499 (closed Fri).

By bus Daily services linking the four oases to each other, Cairo and/or Assyut, generally suffice, but breakdowns aren't uncommon, so if you have a flight to catch it's safer to use other options.

By minibus or taxi Service minibuses between Siwa Oasis, Mersa Matrouh and Alexandria, or Bahariya and Kharga oases and Cairo, run according to local demand. You can hire a private taxi to travel directly between Luxor and Kharga Oasis.

By jeep Jeeps are the mainstay of safaris to off-road destinations and the only means of travelling directly between Siwa and Bahariya oases. Tourists in their own jeeps may tag along if their driving skills are up to the terrain.

Bahariya Oasis

Bahariya Oasis is the smallest of the four oasis depressions, only 94km long and 42km wide. In the Late Cretaceous era, 94 million years ago, this was a steamy mangrove-swamp inhabited by dinosaurs such as the plant-eating paralititan and the carnivorous carcharodontosaurus (whose bones have been found here). The oasis is known to have been under pharaonic control by the Middle Kingdom, when it exported wine to the Nile Valley, and later thrived as an artery between Egypt and Libya, with Arab armies, merchants and pilgrims passsing through over millennia.

Although it covers 1200 square kilometres, less than one percent is actually cultivated, with date palms, olive and fruit trees, vegetables, rice and corn. Ominously,

AL-QASR, DAKHLA OASIS (P.418)>

3

DUNES

Though gravel plains, limestone pans and scarps account for sixty percent of Egypt's Western Desert, it is the region's **dunes** that captivate the imagination. Lifeless yet restless, they shift and reproduce, burying palm groves, roads and railways in their unstoppable advance. Their shape is determined by prevailing winds, local geology and whatever moisture or vegetation exists. Where sand is relatively scarce and small obstructions are common, windblown particles form **crescent-shaped** *barchan* dunes, which advance horns first, moving over obstacles without altering their height. Baby dunes are formed downwind of the horns, which produces parallel lines of *barchans* with flat corridors between them, advancing up to 20m each year. *Barchans* can grow as high as 95m, extend for 375m, and weigh up to 450 million kilos. However, their mass is nothing compared to **parallel straight dunes**, or *seif* dunes (from the Arabic word for "sword") – some in the Great Sand Sea are 140km long. Formed by a uni-directional wind, they have slipfaces on both sides and a wavy, knife-edged crest along the top. When *seif* dunes fall over an escarpment they reform at the bottom as crescent dunes, which is why *barchans* are the prevailing form in Dakhla and Kharga. Occasionally, they pile one on top of another to create mountainous **whalebacks** or mega-*barchans*. *Seif* and whaleback dunes can combine to form huge **sand seas** or *ergs*. Egypt's Great Sand Sea extends from Siwa Oasis to the Gilf Kebir and far into Libya, where it merges with the Calanscio Sand Sea. When the wind direction alters constantly, it can even form **star-shaped** dunes. These are rare in Egypt, but one has been recorded at Wadi al-Bakht in the Gilf Kebir. Another type of formation is the flat, hard-packed **sand-sheet**, found in the Darb al-Arba'in Desert.

Much of the science of dune formation was discovered by the explorer Ralph Bagnold, whose classic book *The Physics of Blown Sand and Desert Dunes* (1939) later helped NASA to interpret data from its Martian space probes. The book was written with the benefit of five years' experimentation with a home-made wind tunnel and builder's sand; after his desert journeys of the 1920s, Bagnold felt "it was really just exploring in another form".

where ground water was once tapped at a depth of 30m, farmers must now bore 1000m underground; fruit trees have suffered from being irrigated by hotter water, raising fears for Bahariya's future sustainability.

Meanwhile, many people have prospered from **tourism**. Local safari outfits employ hundreds of drivers, cooks and gofers, particularly over Christmas and Easter (when many foreigners living in Cairo come here) and the six-day **Pharaon Rally** in September, when some 150 jeeps and motorbikes race through the oasis, accompanied by TV crews and spectators.

Unlike the three neighbouring oases that comprise the New Valley governorate, Bahariya comes under **6th October City**, one of the high-rise satellite cities built to reduce Cairo's congestion. Plans to build a Museum of the Oases have been stalled for years as the two governorates squabble over whether it should be located in Bahariya or Farafra Oasis.

You'll pass 6th October City en route from Cairo, shortly after the Pyramids of Giza. Thereafter the landscape is flat and featureless, until a grubby halfway **resthouse** followed by a reddish-purple tract of desert whose iron-ore deposits are transported to the Helwan steelworks by a mining-railway.

Bawiti

The oasis "capital" **BAWITI** (pronounced "Ba-weety") has a picturesque nucleus of old houses on a ridge overlooking luxuriant palm groves, but that's not what you see on arrival. Breeze-block dwellings and concrete government buildings line the Cairo–Farafra highway, which doubles as the main street (Sharia Gamal Abdel Nasser/Sharia Masr), busy with trucks, jeeps and donkey-carts. Tourism here is intensely competitive, with touts besieging foreigners the moment they step off the bus.

BAWITI'S ANTIQUITIES TRAIL

All the antiquities in Bawiti – the Golden Mummies in the **Antiquities Inspectorate**; the **tombs of Zad-Amun ef-Ankh and Bannentiu**; the **Temple of Alexander**; and the chapels of **Ain al-Muftillah** – are covered by a single combination **ticket** (£E45) sold at a kiosk 50m downhill from the Antiquities Inspectorate museum, displaying some of the famous "Golden Mummies" (also covered on the same ticket). Ain al-Muftillah and Alexander's Temple are outside town, so you'll need transport to realise the ticket's full value.

Oasis Heritage Museum

2km east of the centre • No set hours • £E10 • 📞 02 3847 3666 or 📞 012 2710 7965, 🌐 camelcamp.com

Bawiti's most visible "sight" is the **Oasis Heritage Museum**, a qasr-like ensemble beside the highway beyond the town limits. Created by Mahmoud Eed, a self-taught sculptor inspired by Badr in Farafra (see p.406), the museum is a work-in-progress. Both artists' figurines portray a way of life that's almost disappeared in the oases, for men at least, whose job it once was to hunt gazelles and weave mats (women's roles haven't changed so much). Besides Mahmoud's terracotta tableaux there's a rather sad **Reptile Collection** of lizards, snakes and hedgehogs, captured in the desert.

Ain Bishmu

Less obvious is Bawiti's **old quarter** of mud-brick homes (reached by following Sharia Safaya and nameless streets northwards), flanked by mastabas where elders sit and gossip. Beyond the domed **Tomb of Sheikh el-Bishmu** you can track down **Ain Bishmu**, a fissure in the bedrock where a spring was hewn in Roman times, gushing hot water (35°C) into a natural basin. Although the ravine is disfigured by a pumping station, there's a wonderful view of the **palm groves** below the ridge, where it's delightful to wander around (especially in spring when the almond orchards are in blossom).

Al-Qasr

The old quarter merges into **Al-Qasr**, built on the site of the former pharaonic capital and continuously inhabited since – though many houses are now abandoned or used as livestock pens. Alleys snake past secretive courtyards and walled gardens, ending in cul-de-sacs or joining up with other lanes. Some houses incorporate stones from a bygone XXVI Dynasty temple, and a Roman triumphal arch which survived until the mid-nineteenth century.

Antiquities Inspectorate

Sharia al-Mathaf • Daily 8am–2pm • Entrance with combination ticket (see box above) £E45

Near Bawiti's hospital, the bunker-like **Antiquities Inspectorate** – locally known as "the museum" (Al-Mathaf) – was built to exhibit **mummies** from a huge cache found

---

VALLEY OF THE GOLDEN MUMMIES

In 1996 a donkey owned by a guard at Alexander's Temple stumbled into a hole in the desert 6km southwest of Bawiti, alerting its master to what turned out to be the largest cache of mummies ever found in Egypt. Surveys revealed that this Greco-Roman era necropolis (no public access) covers ten square kilometres and may contain ten thousand mummies, stacked in family vaults – hundreds have been found so far. Whereas most are simply wrapped in linen, others are in terracotta coffins adorned with human faces, their bodies covered in gilded *cartonage* and their faces with stucco masks. These **Golden Mummies** caught the imagination of the public, and TV networks paid millions of dollars to film the opening of a series of burial chambers. It is widely rumoured that Egypt's former antiquities supremo Dr Zahi Hawass enriched himself with backhanders and by secretly selling the mummies abroad.

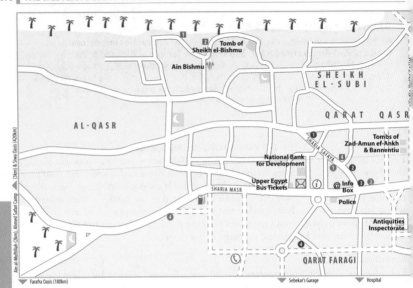

outside Bawiti in 1996 (see box, p.397). Encased in gilded and painted *cartonage* (linen pasteboard), with sculpted stucco masks, the eleven "Golden Mummies" displayed here include a child buried with its parents. The mother's head is inclined towards her husband, and she wears a "chest plate" sculpted with tiny triangular breasts – a funerary fashion in Greco-Roman times, when mummification was often perfunctory. Many of the mummies removed from the earth have since deteriorated – some previously on display are no longer fit to be shown. The museum also has an impish **statue** of Bes, from his shrine at Ain al-Muftillah (see below).

Tombs of Zad-Amun ef-Ankh and Bannentiu

Sharia Yusef Salim • Daily 8.30am–4pm • Entrance with combination ticket (see box, p.397) £E45

From the Antiquities Inspectorate you can walk downhill and cross the main road to reach **Qarat Qasr Salim**, a built-up ridge harbouring two tombs found by Ahmed Fakhry in 1938. Both date from the XXVI Dynasty, when rich local merchants built themselves tombs emulating those of the nobility.

The **Tomb of Zad-Amun ef-Ankh** is sunk in a steep-sided pit. Its votive hall has rounded pillars and is decorated with deities (notice the people bringing gifts, to the left), painted in ochre, brown and black upon a white background. Zad-Amun was wealthy enough to afford his alabaster and limestone sarcophagi to be quarried near Tell el-Amarna and Giza, shipped along the Nile and then dragged 200km overland to Bawiti.

Nearby is the **Tomb of Bannentiu**, his son, at the bottom of a 10m shaft. Mind your head on the steel grating and the low entrance to its votive hall, whose inscriptions acclaim Bannentiu as a priest and a prophet. Here the pillars are square and the murals are in brick red, golden yellow, pale blue and black upon white. Some of the deities have only been sketched in, but there's a fine solar barque at the back, and the embalming process is shown on the right-hand wall.

Ain al-Muftillah

3km northwest of Al-Qasr • Daily 8.30am–pm • Entrance with combination ticket (see box, p.397) £E45

The ancient town once extended to **Ain al-Muftillah**, a spring nowadays on the outskirts of the desert. It's feasible to cycle here but better to go by car, as the route isn't

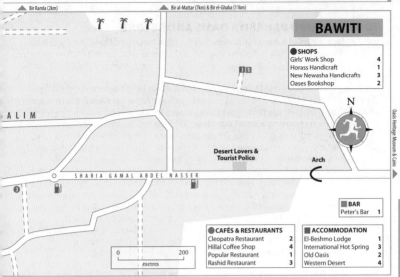

Bir Ramla (2km)

Bir al-Mattar (7km) & Bir el-Ghaba (11km)

BAWITI

SHOPS

Girls' Work Shop	4
Horass Handicraft	1
New Newasha Handicrafts	3
Oases Bookshop	2

Oasis Heritage Museum & Camp

A L I M

Desert Lovers & Tourist Police

Arch

SHARIA GAMAL ABDEL NASSER

0	200
	metres

BAR

Peter's Bar	1

CAFÉS & RESTAURANTS

Cleopatra Restaurant	2
Hillal Coffee Shop	4
Popular Restaurant	1
Rashid Restaurant	3

ACCOMMODATION

El-Beshmo Lodge	1
International Hot Spring	3
Old Oasis	2
Western Desert	4

3

signposted or easy to describe. A little way south of the spring is a wooden-roofed enclosure containing four small **ruined shrines** from the XXVI Dynasty, excavated by Steindorff and Fakhry. Built of friable sandstone streaked with ochre and sienna (which makes them liable to flake and unusually colourful), none conforms to the canons of pharaonic architecture. One was dedicated to Bes, patron deity of musicians, dancers and prostitutes; all that remains of his image is a devilish foot and a tail.

By crossing the rise and a dune beyond, you can enjoy a **panoramic view** of Al-Qasr, Bawiti and the surrounding countryside.

Temple of Alexander

Tibniya, 2km from Ain al-Muftillah • Entrance with combination ticket (see box, p.397) £E45

Ask at the *Ahmed Safari Camp* (see p.401) for directions to the **Temple of Alexander**, 400m away via a sandy track. Built of the same soft stone as the shrines at Ain al-Muftillah, its reliefs have suffered from being sandblasted by the wind for centuries, obliging the SCA to recreate the face and cartouche of Alexander the Great that archeologists recorded in the 1930s. This is (or was) the only temple in Egypt to bear Alexander's figure and cartouche; some believe that he passed through Bahariya en route to Memphis after consulting the Siwan Oracle (see p.452).

ARRIVAL AND DEPARTURE

BAWITI

By bus The Upper Egypt Bus Co. operates four buses daily from Cairo Gateway (see p.175) to Bahariya (5hr; £E35–40), and two from Farafra (see p.407) and Dakhla (see p.414). Buses from Cairo often call at outlying villages before Bawiti – don't get off too early. Arriving in Bawiti, passengers are dropped outside the tourist office, where foreigners are mobbed by touts. Departures are a bit hit-and-miss, as you can only book seats on two buses to Cairo at the ticket kiosk (9am–1pm & 7–11pm) near the post office, from where they leave. Through-services pick up passengers at the *Hillal Coffeeshop* (see p.402) 300m south; tickets are sold aboard the bus.

Departure times change regularly and may involve an hour's margin of error.

By car or minibus Bahariya's *Eden Garden Camp* (see p.402) and *Ahmed Safari Camp* (see p.401) offer direct transfers (4–5hr) from hotels in Cairo to their respective camps (or vice versa) for £E400–450 by car (up to four passengers), £E550 by minibus (up to six people). Transfers are free of the hassles of travelling by bus, but you are expected to stay at least one night at the campground which arranged it. There are also minibuses to Cairo from the *Hillal Coffeeshop* (see above), leaving every few hours depending on demand; if full, passengers pay about £E40 each.

TOURS AROUND BAHARIYA OASIS AND BEYOND

Half-day **local tours** of Bahariya Oasis – visiting the Black Mountain, Bir el-Ghaba and Jebel el-Dist – can be arranged by *El-Beshmo Lodge* (£E300), *Ahmed Safari Camp* (£E400) or freelance drivers (negotiable). The cost can be split between four or five passengers and a 4WD vehicle isn't essential.

Bahariya is a hub for jeep **safaris** throughout the Western Desert, whether to the White Desert in nearby Farafra Oasis, Siwa via the Great Sand Sea, or the Gilf Kebir in the far south. Although this is the best oasis in which to shop around for a deal, price shouldn't be your only benchmark when **choosing a safari operator**. Some are highly experienced but others lack the skills to respond to a sandstorm, a car overturning or a tourist needing to be rushed to hospital after dark – or even carry enough water or fuel to survive getting stranded or lost. The farther off-road into the desert you venture, the more vital their competence becomes.

Outfits attached to hotels or camps using drivers aged over 30 are a safer bet than gung-ho 20-somethings with a borrowed jeep and no back-up – so don't begrudge paying more than the bare minimum charged by novices. Priced on the basis of four passengers, safaris should have a separate supply-jeep for every two or three passenger cars, depending on the terrain and the duration of the trip. Off-road to remote areas requires a **guide** familiar with the terrain from experience, not merely reliant on **GPS** waypoints. Local **drivers** may tell tourists that they have been to the Gilf when really they only know easier terrain closer to home.

The following are highly **reliable** within their stated geographical limits:

Ahmed Safari ☎ 02 3847 1414 or ☎ 012 2492 5563, ✉ ahmed_safari@hotmail.com. Based at their like-named camp (see p.401) outside Bawiti, Ahmed's is prone to rest on its laurals as Bahariya's first safari outfit where others learned their trade, but offers a wide range of safaris, including 4–8 day camel or walking trips in the White Desert (€40/person/day) or the Great Sand Sea (€80/person/day).

★ **Eden Garden Tours** ☎ 02 3847 3727 or ☎ 012 2731 1876, ⊛ edengardentours.com. From *Eden Garden Camp* (see p.402), Talat Mulah organizes off-road jeep safaris throughout the Western Desert, camel treks and walking tours, with faultless logistics and great music (€50/person/day; €120 for the Gilf Kebir).

★ **Yehiya Kandil** ☎ 02 3849 6754 or ☎ 012 321 6790, ⊛ desertshipsafari.com. A guide who can drive you anywhere, from nearby but relatively isolated sites such as El-Qaf (see p.411) to the far Gilf Kebir; also arranges camel trekking (minimum of four people; €60–120/person/day).

★ **Ashraf Lotfi** ☎ 012 2165 3037, ⊛ naturelodge .com. From *Nature Lodge* (see p.401), Ashraf leads camel or walking tours and jeep safaris almost as far as the Gilf for €60/person/day. The food provided on his trips is especially good.

Samy Mansour ☎ 02 3849 7260. From the Bedouin family that owns all the camels in Bahariya Oasis (see p.403), Samy leads camel and walking tours (£E150/person/day). He doesn't speak much English, but Ashraf Lotfi (see above) can broker a deal. If you want to go on an extended walkabout in the desert over summer and learn all about camel-handling, Samy is your man.

Mohammed Senussi (aka "Kosa") ☎ 02 3847 3439 or ☎ 012 224 8570, ✉ aisha_kosa@yahoo.de. Bahariya's best-known guide and driver, his tracking skills have been used by the Egyptian army to chase smugglers, and he often guides others' expeditions to the Gilf.

Western Desert Safari ☎ 02 3847 1600 or ☎ 012 2433 6015, ⊛ westerndeserthotel.com. Samir Abdullah at the *Western Desert* hotel (see p.401) is the only guide who knows the location of the mysterious Sand Volcano (see p.412), visited on a three-day safari together with El-Qaf and the White Desert (£E2500 for up to four people).

White Desert Tours ☎ 02 3847 2322 or ☎ 012 2736 9493, ⊛ whitedeserttours.com. From the *International Hot Spring* hotel (see p.401), owner Peter Wirth guides jeep or all-terrain KMT motorbike safaris all over the Western Desert. Peter speaks English and German, and his artist-photographer wife Miharu speaks Japanese.

By jeep You can avoid the long detour via the Mediterranean coast and Cairo by travelling directly from Siwa Oasis to Bahariya (or vice versa) by jeep across the deep desert (420km; 4–6hr). Local safari outfits charge £E1300–1500 (shared between up to four passengers) plus the cost of a 24-hour permit (see box, p.376) arranged by the NGO Desert Lover (see p.401); arrangements in Siwa (see p.447) and the route (see p.457) are detailed later in this chapter. A military guide and a satellite-phone are mandatory for this journey. Driving yourself, there are no restrictions on travel to the White Desert, but be sure to have enough fuel before leaving Bahariya, as there are no filling stations en route; the nearest is in Qasr al-Farafra.

INFORMATION

Besides the following places, most hotels and safari operators will supply information in the hope of persuading people to go on their tours.

Tourist office Government Building, Sharia Masr ☏ 02 3847 3039 or ☏ 012 2373 6567, ✉ mohamed _kader26@hotmail.com. Manager Mohammed Abdel Kader is helpful, but his safari recommendations aren't impartial. Daily except Fri 8.30am–2pm, Nov–April also 7–8pm.

Desert Lover Sharia Gamal Abdel Nasser, above the tourist police ☏ 02 3847 3439, ⓦ bahariyaoasis-ngo .org. This local NGO handles applications for 24-hour travel permits (see box, p.376), helps train safari drivers, and mounts desert clean-ups. Their office may move to another location in the future. Daily 9am–3pm & 6–9pm.

ACCOMMODATION

Your choice of lodgings may well determine which safari outfit (see box, p.400) you go with – or vice versa – so consider the options well beforehand. Decide if you want the "facilities" of Bawiti close at hand, or desert seclusion, and what kind of scene you prefer in the evening, as locals make music on some campgrounds, while hotels tend to lack nightlife. Most places will send a car into town to collect guests, so by booking ahead and asking to be met, you can escape the mob of touts on arrival (see p.399). A **camp** may have palm-thatch or mud-brick huts with sleeping platforms, or proper en-suite rooms.

BAWITI

El Beshmo Lodge Ain Bishmu ☏ 02 3847 3500, ⓦ beshmolodge.com; map p.398. Located on a ridge overlooking Bawiti's palm groves, its view is the only thing going for this place. The en-suite rooms are none too clean, the tepid spring-fed pool looks uninvitingly murky, and there isn't any garden to speak of. B&B £E150

International Hot Spring 1km west of the centre ☏ 02 3847 2322 or ☏ 012 2321 2179, ⓦ whitedeserttours .com; map p.399. Decorated with prehistoric rock-art motifs from the Gilf Kebir, this comfy German-managed spa hotel has an indoor hot pool, gym, kids' playground, restaurant and bar, plus a striking palm tree growing out of a deep hole in the ground. Under-5s stay free, and there's fifty percent off for under-12s. Rates include half-board. $70

Old Oasis Ain Bishmu ☏ 02 3847 3028 or ☏ 012 2232 2155, ⓦ oldoasissafari.4t.com; map p.398. Sharing the same view as the *El Beshmo Lodge* but far more appealing, it has upper-floor en-suite rooms (a/c £E60 extra) linked by wooden walkways, table tennis, a warm spring-fed pool and a luxuriant garden with a pergola overlooking the palm groves. B&B £E120

Western Desert Sharia Safaya ☏ 02 3847 1600 or ☏ 012 2301 6015, ⓦ westerndeserthotel.com; map p.398. Located amid the tourist bazaar, so sometimes a bit noisy (ask for a room at the back), this well-run hotel has clean en-suite rooms with a/c, satellite TV, wi-fi and a balcony, plus billiards and a rooftop with panoramic views of Bawiti. B&B €35

BETWEEN AGOUZ AND ZABU

Palm Village 5km from Bawiti ☏ 02 3849 6969 or ☏ 012 2468 1024, ✉ palmvalleyhotel@hotmail.com; map p.404. Surrounding a garden with palm trees and rock features, this quiet holiday village has large a/c rooms with bathtubs plus smaller chalets (same price). There's internet

access (but not wi-fi) and billiards in the lobby; fine views of the Black Mountain from the rooftop; horseriding (£E80/hr) and a swimming pool under construction at the time of writing. Rates include half board. €70

TIBNIYA

Ahmed Safari Camp 4km from Bawiti ☏ 02 3847 1414 or ☏ 012 2492 5563, ✉ ahmed_safari@hotmail.com; map p.404. Close to Alexander's Temple (see p.399) but nothing else, Ahmed's mainly caters to overland adventure groups rather than individual travellers. The camp has en-suite rooms with fans or a/c (£E70 more), table tennis, billiards, mulberry orchards and a small menagerie to amuse kids. B&B £E80

TOWARDS BIR AL-MATTAR

Bawitie Oasis Resort 6km from Bawiti, off the Bir al-Mattar road ☏ 010 0772 4942, ⓦ egyptdeserttours .com; map p.404. Owned by a Belgian into spiritual healing and her Egyptian partner, this new-age hotel has cosy en-suite rooms, an impressive circular hall for meditation and healing, a spring for bathing and a Bedouin tent for parties. B&B €55

Qasr el-Bawity (aka "Bawity Palace") 2km from Bawiti, beside the Bir al-Mattar road ☏ 02 3847 1880 or ☏ 012 2258 2586, ⓦ qasrelbawity.com; map p.404. A fantastic cactus garden forms the centrepiece of this stone-built ensemble of en-suite chalets and suites (the top-floor ones with great views), with two tepid indoor plunge-pools and a large cold pool out back. Rates include half board. €80

BIR EL-GHABA

★ **Nature Lodge** 11km northeast of Bawiti ☏ 02 3984 1550 or ☏ 012 2165 3037, ⓦ naturelodge.com; map p.404. With a superb view of Jebel el-Dist and lots of flowers, this lovely camp has stylish huts with mosquito nets, cotton mattresses and towels (but no electricity), plus a library and a kids' playground – and will soon have comfortable chalets too. Their food is exceptionally good. Rates include half board. **££300**

AIN GUFAR

★ **Eden Garden Camp** 10km southeast of Bawiti ☎02 3847 3727 or ☎012 2731 1876, ⓦedengardentours.com; map p.404. Ideal for chilling out or partying, this well-run site in a quiet mini-oasis has a big hot swimming pool fed by a spring, thatched huts (££100) with mosquito nets and electricity, and more expensive a/c en-suite rooms (luxurious chalets are under construction). Guests can help themselves to free hot

drinks in a central pergola upheld by palm trunks, and there is another, enclosed one for parties. Free transport into town, and transfers to or from Cairo (€50 for up to four people) can be arranged. B&B **££150**

EL-HEIZ

Under the Moon Ecolodge 40km southwest of Bawiti ☎012 2423 6580, ⓦhelatravel.com; map p.404. A nice place to relax on the edge of the Black Desert, this rustic eco-lodge has mud-brick rooms (some with mosquito nets), a circular spring-fed pool and extensive gardens, with dunes, fields and farm animals in the vicinity. Rates include half board. **££250**

EATING, DRINKING AND NIGHTLIFE

All hotels and campgrounds serve meals, but two – the *Eden Garden* and *Nature Lodge* – merit a special mention for their food or Bedouin parties (with live music and dancing), arranged on request. The further out of town, the more locals are likely to openly smoke hashish.

Cleopatra Restaurant Sharia Gamal Abdel Nasser. A friendly welcome and tasty *fuul* and *taamiya* for breakfast, or grilled chicken, soup, rice and salad (££20–30) later in the day, await visitors at this family-run place around the corner from the *Popular Restaurant* (see below). Daily 6am–10pm.

★ **Eden Garden Camp** Ain Gufar (see above) ☎02 3847 3727 or ☎012 2731 1876. You needn't be staying at this camp to arrange a fantastic BBQ and pool party (minimum four people), with a lavish meal (££50–70/person; beer, wine and spirits cost extra). The Bedouin drumming and dancing are intoxicating, even without booze or hashish. No set hours.

Hillal Coffeeshop Sharia Masr. This blue-and-white-tiled den tends to overcharge foreigners for soft drinks and hot beverages, but you might still end up spending time on its veranda, which doubles as a bus-stop for through-services. Daily 24hr.

Nature Lodge Bir el-Ghaba (see p.401) ☎02 3984 1550 or ☎012 2165 3037. Phone two hours ahead to order a delicious meal of grilled meats, stews, salads and various trimmings, for ££60–70/person. The views out

here are fabulous. No set hours.

★ **Peter's Bar** International Hot Spring hotel (see p.401) ☎02 3847 2322 or ☎012 2321 2179. The perfect place to spend a few hours, with mellow music and lighting, comfy seating, inexpensive Egyptian beer (££20) and wine (££80 a bottle), imported spirits and vodka, watermelon and lime cocktails. Daily from sunset until the last customer leaves.

Popular Restaurant Sharia Safaya ☎010 0723 8878. Few tourists leave town without visiting Bawiti's oldest eatery, locally known as "Bayoumi's" after its genial owner. It serves *fuul* and *taamiya* for breakfast, soup, chicken or lamb, vegetables, rice and salad (££20–30) for lunch and dinner, and also sells beer (££15) to drink inside or take away. Daily 9am–9.30pm (later for drinking).

Rashid Restaurant Sharia Gamal Abdel Nasser. Often busy with locals whiling away time over soft drinks, tea and *sheeshas*, this café-style place can rustle up a meal of grilled chicken, rice and salad on request, and sells sticky desserts. Daily 7am–1am.

SHOPPING

Girls' Work Shop Qarat Faragi, off Sharia Masr. Sells embroidery, basketware and other handicrafts produced in the oasis by women and girls, for whom it provides a much appreciated source of income. Daily except Fri 10am–1pm.

Horass Handicraft Sharia Safaya. Local handicrafts and souvenirs from other parts of Egypt, including embroidered Bedouin robes and camel-hair socks. If the shop is closed, knock on the door directly across the road. Daily 8am–8pm.

New Newasha Handicrafts Sharia Gamal Abdel Nasser. Sells similar stuff to Horass Handicraft, and rents bicycles (££25/day) a convenient way of exploring local sites around the oasis such as Bir Ramla, Jebel el-Dist and the Black Mountain (see opposite). No set hours.

Oases Bookshop Sharia Safaya. Well-stocked with photo books, posters and maps of the desert, it also has a selection of novels. Daily 10am–10pm.

MEDITATION AND SPIRITUAL HEALING IN BAWITI

Meditation tours are a lucrative sideline for local safari outfits, working with such new-age tour companies as Cosmic Flower (ⓦcosmicflower.nl), Energies of Egypt (ⓦhiddenegypt.com) and The Lightweaver (ⓦthelightweaver.org). At the *Bawitie Oasis Resort* (see p.401), Donny Heuvelmans runs courses in **spiritual healing** based on Ancient Egyptian rituals, and other forms of **natural healing**, while the *International Hot Spring* hotel (see p.401) offers various **massage** treatments (£E200/hr).

DIRECTORY

Banks and exchange National Bank for Development (Mon–Thurs & Sun 9am–2pm) off Sharia Gamal Abdel Nasser exchanges currency, but lacks an ATM. If it's closed, Peter Wirth at the *International Hot Spring* hotel can change money.

Garage Sebekar's garage (daily 24hr) behind Qarat Faragi is where all the safari operators get their Landcruisers fixed, and anyone driving their own jeep should know Sebekar's number (☏012 2275 2644) in case of breakdowns.

Hospital and pharmacies Seek treatment in Cairo rather than at the public hospital off Sharia Gamal Abdel

Nasser (☏02 3847 2390; daily 24hr). Pharmacies on Sharia Masr can deal with minor complaints.

Internet access Info Box, Sharia Safaya (daily 9am–1pm & 2pm–midnight).

Police Sharia Gamal Abdel Nasser (daily 24hr).

Post office Sharia Masr (daily except Fri 8am–2pm).

Telephone office Qarat Faragi, uphill from Sharia Masr (daily 24hr).

Tourist police Sharia Gamal Abdel Nasser, 700m east of the centre ☏02 3847 3900 (daily 24hr).

Northeast of Bawiti

With its palm groves, fields and desert, this scenic area can be explored on a half-day **tour** offered by some hotels and safari outfits (see box, p.400), or by renting a **bicycle** from New Newasha Handicrafts (see p.402). To visit Bir el-Ghaba and Jebel el-Dist involves a round-trip of about 25km.

Hot springs

The nearest spring to Bawiti is **Bir Ramla**, a nice two-kilometre walk past palm and fruit orchards, although the springs are too hot (45°C) for most tourists and quite public. Men can bathe here in shorts; women only at night, in full-length opaque clothing. Similar rules apply to **Bir el-Negba**, 1km further on.

Bir al-Mattar, 5km from Bawiti, is also too hot to bathe in, and there is only a trickle of water at **Bir el-Ghaba** ("Well of the Forest"), 11km from town, yet the locality is worth a visit purely for its scenery, with palm and eucalyptus groves yielding to scrub and tawny mountains in the near distance.

Jebel el-Dist

Jebel el-Dist ("Mountain of the Pot") is more accurately described by guides as "Pyramid Mountain", while the ever-changing play of light across it has inspired another name, "Magic Mountain". Its **dinosaur beds** have been picked bare, but the fields and acacia groves nearer Bir el-Ghaba abound in insects and **birdlife**. You'll also see a herd of **camels** belonging to a Bedouin family (except in July, when the oasis is plagued by camel-ticks and the camels go walkabout in the desert).

Black Mountain

En route to all these sites you'll pass the aptly named **Black Mountain** (Jebel Souda), whose dolomite and basalt mass is crowned by a ruined look-out post used by Captain Williams to monitor Senussi incursions in 1916, for which it is nicknamed the "English Mountain" (Jebel el-Ingleez). Most of the inhabited parts of the oasis are visible from its summit, whose rocks have an oddly sticky texture and smell faintly of biscuits.

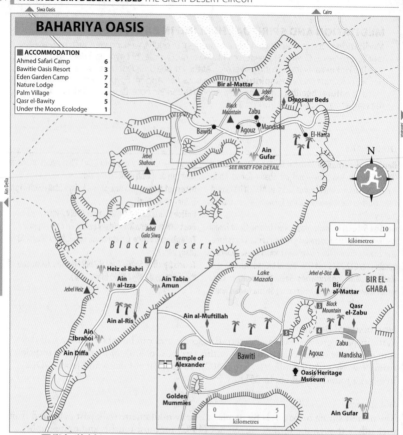

East of Bawiti

Linked by a country back-road which makes them easy to explore by bicycle, the **villages** near Bawiti are unaffected by tourism, and people are friendly and hospitable. **AGOUZ**, only 2km from town, is reputedly inhabited by the descendants of families banished from Siwa Oasis for the loose morals of their womenfolk, but they would rather forget this slur on their ancestors.

Zabu

The back-road to Mandisha passes a field of **dunes** threatening to engulf **ZABU**'s houses and palm groves in sand. Behind the gardens facing the escarpment a track leads into a canebrake harbouring a giant sandstone boulder known as **Qasr el-Zabu**, inscribed by Libyan nomads and other travellers with **petroglyphs**: sun symbols, horses, a charioteer, a woman with her arms akimbo and the name of the explorer Hyde.

South of Bawiti

This part of the oasis is usually visited on jeep safaris to the White Desert. Some drive around the far side of **Jebel Gala Siwa** to see a beautiful **dune** that has formed in the lee of the escarpment – ideal for **sandboarding**. Most stop for lunch at **Heiz el-Bahri**, where tamarisk-mounds and palms surround a cold spring, one of several fertile enclaves in the locality called El-Heiz.

In the desert to the west of the highway, roughly 30km from Bawiti, a white **monument** commemorates Swiss René Michel, a pioneer of tourism to Bahariya, who died here from heatstroke in 1986.

The Black Desert

A hellish landscape of conical and table-top hills with black basalt summits errupting from tawny sand, the **Black Desert** (Sahara Souda) stretches most of the way to Farafra Oasis. Unfairly under-rated compared to the White Desert, this big-sky country eludes efforts to capture its majesty by photography. During winter-time the Black Desert can be seen from the air in a **hot-air balloon** – an unforgetable experience. One-hour flights ($100) with Viking Balloons can be arranged through *Ahmed Safari Camp* (see p.401)

Naqb es-Sillum

The Bahariya and Farafra depressions are separated by a limestone **escarpment** where gigantic drifts of sand flank the road as it traverses the **Naqb es-Sillum** ("Pass of the Stairs"). Two microwave masts relay signals between the oases, and there's a first-aid post with an ambulance by the mast nearest Bahariya. Shortly after the second mast, some safari groups turn off-road towards Agabat and the White Desert (see p.409).

Farafra Oasis

Farafra Oasis is renowned for its **White Desert**, which many tourists visit on safaris from Bahariya rather than from the oasis "capital", **Qasr al-Farafra**, a one-horse town if ever there was. Historically, Farafra was the least populous and most isolated of the four oases. When camels were the only means of travel, the Farafrans had less contact with Bahariya (a journey of four days) than with Dakhla, which was tenuously connected to the Forty Days Road. Fakhry relates how the villagers once lost track of time and could only ascertain the right day for Friday prayers by sending a rider to Dakhla.

Qasr al-Farafra was the only village in the oasis before the New Valley scheme seeded a dozen hamlets across the depression, now inhabited by fifteen thousand settlers from the Assyut region and the Delta.

Qasr has remained a tight-knit community of four extended families and is noted for its piety, apparent during Ramadan, when the mosque overflows with robed imams and sheikhs.

Compared to Bahariya, few people are involved in **tourism** so there's almost no hustling – but little to do at night either. Few tourists stay longer than a night in Qasr, and many simply use it as a pit-stop after camping out in the White Desert and before carrying on to Dakhla Oasis. There are, however, other things to see besides the White Desert, from local **hot springs** to **stalactite caves** far into the desert.

Qasr al-Farafra

The low ground in **QASR AL-FARAFRA** has been colonized by modern infrastructure, which obscures the view of the ancient hilltop village, backing onto palm groves. Even there modernization is apparent, with austerely beautiful old mud-brick houses topped by flowing pediments or crenellations being superseded by breeze-block homes with proper bathrooms. Though Qasr's population has shot up to five thousand in the last twenty years due to better healthcare, its shops and market are still meagre and frugality is the order of the day, despite a few wealthy locals who've built villas on the edge of town.

Come nightfall, there's little to do but hang out in teahouses or maybe wallow in the hot spring at Bir Setta (see p.409), unless you happen to chance upon a **zikr** in somebody's home. These play an important role in the religious and social life of Farafra; foreigners of both sexes are welcome, providing they respect that they are guests at a religious ritual, not spectators at a tourist attraction – which means modest dress and behaviour.

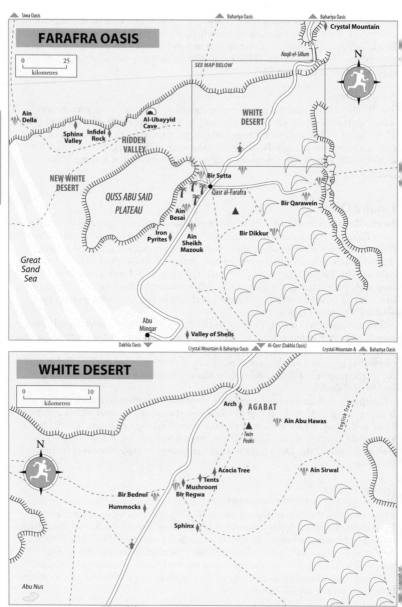

Badr's Museum

Sharia al-Madrassa • Daily 8.30am–sunset • £E10

The creation of Badr Abdel Moghny, a self-taught artist who has exhibited in Europe, **Badr's Museum** resembles a Disneyfied desert mansion, with reliefs of camels and farmers decorating its walls and an antique wooden lock on the door. Its dozen-odd rooms exhibit Badr's rustic sculptures and surreal paintings, stuffed wildlife, weird fossils and pyrites. Here, "Mr Socks" (see p.408) sells handknitted camel-hair mittens, hats and thick woolly socks, for those cold desert nights.

The Fortress

At the highest point in the vicinity, houses merge imperceptibly into the ruined mud-brick **fortress** (*qasr*) that gives the village its name (though the full title isn't used in everyday speech). Until early in the twentieth century, Farafrans would retreat inside whenever marauders came; each family had a designated room, where, during normal times, provisions were stored and guarded by a watchman. Damaged by heavy rainfall, the fortress began to crumble in the 1950s; the less damaged parts are now home to several families.

The palm groves

The extensive **palm groves** behind the village look especially lovely just before sunset. They are divided into walled gardens planted with olive and fruit trees as well as date palms (whose branches are used to fence the land). You can walk the paths freely, but shouldn't enter the gardens uninvited; for single women to do so is regarded as provocative. Likewise, avert your eyes from the **men's bathhouse** on the edge of the village, where youths splash around in a concrete tank fed by a pipe gushing warm water. Foreigners are expected to bathe at other springs, such as Bir Setta (see box, p.409).

QASR AL-FARAFRA

■ ACCOMMODATION	
Badawiya	2
El-Waha	3
Sunrise	1

● CAFÉS & RESTAURANTS	
Badawiya	1
Hussein	4
Mushroom Coffee Shop	2
Samir	3

ARRIVAL AND DEPARTURE

QASR AL-FARAFRA

By bus The Upper Egypt Bus Co. runs buses to Farafra from Cairo Gateway (see p.175) daily at 7am and 8pm (£E40; 9hr). These pass through Bahariya Oasis sometime between 11.30am and noon, and around 11pm, where they can be boarded at the *Hillal Coffeeshop* (see p.402). Arriving in Qasr al-Farafra three hours later, they drop passengers at the *Badawiya* hotel, the petrol station and the souk at the southern end of town. These are the pick-up points for departures to Bahariya and Cairo (around 10am and 10pm),

and buses running on to Dakhla Oasis (around 2.30pm and 2.30am). There may also be an additional daily bus to Cairo operated by the local Express El Wadi company, though this wasn't running at the time of writing. Ask at their ticket office (☎ 012 2288 8215) in the souk if services have resumed.

By minibus There are usually one or two a day between Bahariya and Farafra, charging around £E25/passenger. If you're planning to use one, spread the word so drivers know that you're interested.

3

INFORMATION

Tourist information There isn't a tourist office, so visitors depend on hotels and safari operators for information. The Ali family are the main players: Atif Ali manages the *Badawiya* hotel; Hamdy Ali leads Badawiya Expedition and Sa'ad runs its Cairo office; while their artist cousin Badr has a local museum and gallery (see p.406). The only other people involved in tourism are the family that runs the *El-Waha* and *Sunrise* hotels, with their own safari outfit.

ACCOMMODATION

Your choice of accommodation may determine which safari operator you travel with (or vice versa), as the hotels expect their guests to sign up for safaris, and regard it as bad form for them to go elsewhere.

Badawiya Sharia al-Farafra al-Wahat, 300m north of the petrol station ☎ 092 751 0060 or ☎ 012 8287 9695, ⓦ badawiya.com. Owned by Farafra's leading safari outfit, this large, desert palace-style complex has split-level rooms with fans, raised beds and mosquito nets; spacious a/c suites (€50) with fridges; a big spring-fed pool; and an airy restaurant. B&B €25

El-Waha Off Sharia al-Madrassa ☎ 012 2720 0387, ⓔ wahafarafra@yahoo.com. Located around the corner from Badr's Museum, this small hotel's vine-shaded exterior looks welcoming, but its rooms are pretty basic, with shared bathrooms, and baking hot in summer. Its extremely low prices are the only reason to stay here. €€50

Sunrise Sharia al-Farafra al-Wahat, 600m north of the petrol station ☎ 012 2291 0878, ⓔ wahafarafra @yahoo.com. Built with money earnt from the *El-Waha* hotel, the *Sunrise* has domed brick bungalows with bathrooms, TV and fridges set around a courtyard. Modelled on the *Badawiya* but less stylish and lacking a swimming pool, its rates are lower and its safaris are considerably cheaper too. B&B €180

EATING AND DRINKING

It doesn't take long to sample the culinary delights of Farafra. There are few places to eat, mostly with very limited menus. Nowhere serves alcohol (though non-alcoholic Birell is sometimes available) and any drinking must be done in private to avoid offending local people.

Badawiya Badawiya hotel, Sharia al-Farafra al-Wahat ☎ 092 751 0060. The only proper restaurant in town, with a longish menu of pasta dishes, kofta, kebab and salads prepared from organically grown vegetables. A three-course meal costs £E80–120. Their kitchen closes at 9.30pm but you can order drinks till later. Daily 8.30am–11pm.

Hussein Sharia al-Balad. This basic café with a few tables outside serves *fuul* and *taamiya* for breakfast, and grilled chicken or kebabs with salad, rice and *tahina* (£E45) from noon onwards, with a diminishing choice after 3pm. Daily 8am–8pm.

Mushroom Coffee Shop Sharia al-Madrassa. Named after a rock formation in the White Desert, this laidback café beside Badr's Museum offers omelettes and liver-and-chilli sandwiches up until noon, and hot and cold beverages thereafter. Daily 8am–8pm.

Samir Sharia al-Balad. Genial owner Samir serves home-cooked food in his front parlour, decorated with football banners and happy-puppy-patterned fabric. A meal of grilled chicken or kebabs with rice, salad and stewed vegetables costs £E45. Daily 24hr.

SHOPPING

The antithesis of a shopper's paradise, Farafra has an extremely limited range of goods on sale with only one shop (diagonally opposite the Express El-Wadi ticket office) selling cigarettes.

"Mr Socks" The frontman for a family that earns its living through weaving textiles from camel-hair, Mr Socks harvests the wool and spins it; his uncle makes blankets, his sister sweaters; and he and his mother knit socks and scarves. All are on sale at Badr's Museum and the *Badawiya* hotel.

DIRECTORY

Banks and exchange Banque Misr, Sharia al-Farafra al-Wahat (Sun–Thurs 9am–2pm), doesn't yet have an ATM, but one is planned. It may also be possible to change money at the *Badawiya* hotel.

Hospital Sharia al-Farafra al-Wahat ☎ 092 751 0047 (daily 24hr). Strictly a last resort; if at all possiible, seek treatment in Cairo.

Post office Sharia Bir Setta (daily except Fri 8.30am–2.30pm).

Telephone office Sharia al-Bosta (daily 24hr).

Tourist police Sharia al-Mishtafa Nakhaz (daily 24hr).

White Desert National Park

20km from Qasr al-Farafra, 160km from Bawiti, 570km from Cairo; • Daily 24hr • Officially $5/person and $5/car to enter the park, plus
£E10/person to camp overnight (although these fees may not be levied)

Covering 3010 square kilometres on both sides of the highway, the **White Desert National Park** was established in 2002 to protect this unique landscape from over-exposure to tourism. Heavy fines for littering and the restriction of jeeps to specified tracks forced safari outfits which only cared about making a fast buck to mend their ways. However, after the ticket office was burned down during the 2011 Revolution and park wardens went unpaid, enforcement ceased. At the time of research, safaris were only paying fees to enter or camp in the park if they happened to meet one of the few park wardens on duty.

Crystal Mountain and Agabat

Coming from Bahariya Oasis, you'll enjoy a succession of fantastic views as you enter the Farafra depression, where safaris halt to let passengers admire the **Crystal Mountain** (Jebel al-Izaz), a shiny quartz ridge with a human-high natural arch through the middle, which is why locals call it Hagar al-Makhrum, the "Rock with a Hole".

At this point jeeps can turn off onto a signposted route into the White Desert known as the **English Track** (after the 1920s explorers who first found a way by car), but most traffic continues along the highway, descending the Naqb es-Sillum (see p.405) past the landmark **Twin Peaks**, to the east.

Beyond Twin Peaks lies the spectacularly rugged terrain known as **Agabat** ("Wonders"). Its pale rock "sugarloaves" are a feast for the eyes, but the surrounding soft sand and powdered chalk can easily entrap vehicles – which is why some locals call the locality *Akabat* ("Difficult").

The White Desert

Agabat segues into the famous **White Desert** (Sahara el-Beida) on both sides of the highway. Everywhere you look are chalk *yardangs* (pinnacles) eroded into surreal forms, looming above a dusty pan strewn with shells, crystals and iron pyrites shaped like sea urchins or twigs. The *yardangs* glint pale gold in the midday sun, turn violet and pink around sunset, and resemble icebergs or snowdrifts by moonlight. All originated as deposits of countless sea urchins that thrived in the shallow sea that covered this area during the Cretaceous period, one hundred million years ago. After the sea receded in the mid-Tertiary Era, twenty-odd million years of wind-erosion produced the shapes that amaze visitors today.

BATHING AND FOSSIL-HUNTING IN FARAFRA OASIS

Although most visitors are content to see the White Desert (see above), those with time to spare might consider visiting other beauty spots in the oasis. Farafra has about a hundred wells and natural springs used for irrigation, some of which are also suitable for bathing. **Bir Setta** (Well Six), behind the defunct *AquaSun* hotel 6km northwest of town (£E20–30 by pick-up truck from the petrol station) is a keyhole-shaped tank of sulphurous warm water that stains your clothes brown. Further north, all kinds of birdlife are drawn to the reedy freshwater lake of **Abu Nus** (£E30–40 by pick-up). To the south are **Ain Besai**, a cold pool beside the rock tombs and chapels of a settlement abandoned in Christian times, and **Ain Sheikh Mazouk**, a hot sulphur spring feeding a tank where local men bathe (both are close enough to the highway to be reached by bus, or by pick-up for about £E30).

If you happen to be on a jeep or camel safari to Dakhla Oasis, ask your guide to stop at two sites of geological interest. An area across the highway from Ain Sheikh Mazouk is strewn with hundreds of thousands of **iron pyrites** shaped like flowers, starbursts, twigs or dog turds (their black colour caused by a chemical change from sulphide to oxide), plus fossils of ancient marine creatures such as *Terebratulina* and *Spirobris*. Further south towards Abu Minqar (see p.412) lies the **Valley of Shells** (Wadi el-Khawaka), strewn with prehistoric sea-shells.

Most safaris enter the desert at **Bir Regwa** to follow tracks past such rock formations as the **Mushroom**, the **Tents** and the **Sphinx**. The first two refer to multiple *yardangs*, each a different shape. Another landmark is a large **Acacia Tree** growing from a hillock, whose canopy offers welcome shade. Shrubs and palms dot the landscape where subterranean water nears the surface at **Ain Sirwal** and **Ain Abu Hawas**. Roman **pottery** scattered about suggests that this was once a caravan route between Farafra and Bahariya.

TOURS

THE WHITE DESERT

From Bahariya Although the White Desert is in Farafra Oasis, many tourists visit it with safari outfits from Bahariya (see p.400), whose excursions are competitively priced and come with the scenic bonus of the Black Desert and Naqb es-Sillum en route. Don't choose an outfit simply because they offer the lowest price; this often means they will skimp on food, fuel or water, and lack experience of what to do if a sandstorm blows up – with potentially life-threatening consequences. Cars are restricted to four trails

with designated camping spots. Don't wander far from camp at night – it's easy to get disoriented by the *yardangs*, and several tourists have got lost and nearly died.
From Farafra The *Sunrise* and *El-Waha* hotels charge £E700 for an overnight safari into the White Desert (split between four people), or £E300/person/day for camel treks lasting up to a week, while *Badawiya* quotes from €70/person for jeep or camel safaris. See the accommodation listings (p.408) for contact details.

The Hidden Valley and the New White Desert

50–100km northwest of Qasr al-Farafra • Accessible by safari from Farafra or Bahariya with a 24hr permit (see p.376) • Daily 24hr • Free

Though relatively few safari outfits run trips there – or even know the area from experience rather than mere heresay – the western reaches of the Farafra depression are no less fascinating than the White Desert. The **Hidden Valley** (Wadi al-Ubayyid) behind the Qus Abu Said Plateau looks superficially similar but is more geologically diverse, with volcanic massifs as well as chalk *yardangs*.

The northerly route into the valley passes the well of **Bir Bednui**; a 20-metre-high pinnacle call ed **Al-Qabur** ("The Chisel"); and humped monoliths known as **Hummocks**. In the 1990s, Italian archeologists found the remains of a prehistoric village beside a long-vanished lake, leading to the discovery of the **Al-Ubayyid Cave** 50m up a cliff-face. Its three chambers contain **rock art**, with engravings of gazelles and cattle, and the blown-outlines of human hands. The cave is officially off-limits but some safaris visit it nonetheless.

Further west stands the **Infidel Rock**, an anthropomorphic rock formation that locals believe marks the last known location of the fabled Lost Army of Cambyses (see box,

---

THE LOST ARMY OF CAMBYSES

One of the most famous tales in the *Histories* of Herodotus is that of the Persian conqueror **Cambyses** (525–522 BC), son of Cyrus the Great, who sent an army across the desert to destroy the Siwan Oracle. According to Herodotus, the fifty thousand-strong **army** marched from Thebes (Luxor) for seven days to an "oasis", and thence towards Siwa – which leaves room for doubt as to whether the oasis was Kharga or Farafra. Depending on which you favour, their last watering hole was Ain Amur or Ain Della, beyond which the army ran out of water and perished in the Great Sand Sea after a sandstorm scattered and buried the weakened troops. Some ascribe this disaster to the Persians miscalculating their longitude; others blame their ignorance of the hostile environment. The mystery of where the **Lost Army** disappeared tantalized explorers such as Almássy (see p.437), who claimed to have found the site but never disclosed its location. In 2001, an Egyptian professor announced he had found it after discovering bronze arrowheads and human skeletons north of the Al-Ubayyid Cave, but failed to convince anyone; in 2010, two Italians claimed to have found Persian armour, but were denied permission to excavate. Others theorize that the army numbered far less than fifty thousand soldiers (Persian sources routinely overestimated the size of armies), and was in fact perhaps no larger than five thousand.

p.410). **Sphinx Valley** is a locality where almost every *yardang* calls to mind (and might even have inspired) the famous monument near the Giza Pyramids. The plain beyond is dominated by huge chalk *inselbergs*, or isolated hills, prompting local safari operators to dub this the **New White Desert**.

Ain Della

120km northwest of Qasr al-Farafra • Accessible by safari from Farafra or Bahariya with a 24hr permit (see p.376) • Daily 24hr • Free

Until a decade ago the New White Desert was off-limits due to the proximity of **Ain Della** ("Spring of the Shade"), which has played an epic part in the history of the Western Desert as the last waterhole before the Great Sand Sea. Used by raiders and smugglers since antiquity, explorers in the 1920s and 1930s, and the Long Range Desert Group in World War II, it now has a garrison of Egyptian **Border Guards**. This elite force pursues smugglers using jeeps (rather than camels, as in the days of the Frontier Camel Corps), roaming up to 200km into the Great Sand Sea (see p.440) on four-day patrols. The spring-water is sweet to drink and allows the soldiers the luxury of showers at their barracks in the middle of nowhere.

Off road from Farafra to Dakhla

If you've got time to spare, the off-road journey from Farafra to Dakhla is an amazing two-to-three-day journey that takes you through constantly varying scenery. Safaris starting from Bahariya may travel via the White Desert, or take the easier approach used by outfits in Farafra, via road (62km) to **Bir Qarawein**. This ancient well has now been supplemented by boreholes, allowing watermelons to be grown among dunes that are perfect for **sandboarding**. When the boreholes were first sunk in the late 1990s, enterprising locals grew a far more lucrative crop – marijuana – until their plantations were spotted by chance from an army helicopter.

From Qarawein, jeeps backtrack by road to pick up a track to the sweetwater spring of **Bir Dikkur**, marked by two palms and a camel's skeleton, and into the **dune lanes** advancing in a southeasterly direction. Some have trees protruding from their crests where the dunes have buried whole palm groves on their relentless march towards Dakhla Oasis. Over the next 100km or so, safaris pass through the **Black Valley**, strewn with iron pyrites, and the **Marble Labyrinth**, whose sharp stones are equally hard on cars' tyres. The route ends with a steep **descent** from the plateau to Al-Qasr (see p.418) in Dakhla Oasis.

El-Qaf

210km east of Qasr al-Farafra • Accessible by jeep (6–7hr) from Farafra or Bahariya Oasis, usually on a 3-day safari combined with Bir Qarawein and the White Desert (£E2500–3600 for up to four people) • Daily 24hr • Free

Some safari outfits run trips to **El-Qaf** (also known as Gara or Djara), beyond the limits of Farafra Oasis. Entered via a shallow depression in the desert, this remote **stalactite cave** was known to local Bedouin long before it was "discovered" by Gerhard Rohlfs in 1873, though its whereabouts were subsequently forgotten until it was rediscovered by Carlo Bergmann in 1989. Archeologists have since found stone arrowheads and knives in the cave predating similar tools in the Nile Valley by five hundred years, suggesting that Neolithic technology originated in the desert.

The cave was formed some 100,000 years ago but its limestone formations stopped growing when the rains ceased about 5000 BC. Since then it has filled with sand to a depth of 150m – what's visible today is a fraction of its total size. Some of the pure white stalactites and veil-formations are six metres tall; each one resonates with a different note if gently tapped at its point. Bring lighting, since there's none in the cave.

Ghard Abu Muharrik and the Sand Volcano

230km east of Qasr al-Farafra • Accessible by jeep (7–8hr) from Farafra or Bahariya Oasis, usually on a 3-day safari combined with Bir Qarawein, the White Desert and El-Qaf (£E3600 for up to four people) • Daily 24hr • Free

Safaris to El-Qaf often contiunue 20km further east to see the **Ghard Abu Muharrik**

("Dune with an Engine"). Stretching from Bahariya to Kharga Oasis, this is the **longest whalebacked dune** in the Western Desert, only disqualified from being the longest in Africa by two ridges that trisect the dune into three stretches 100–125km long. It's an awesome sight, dune piled upon dune from horizon to horizon.

Somewhere out in these wastes, Samir from Western Desert Safari in Bahariya (see p.400) has discovered what he calls a **Sand Volcano**, where sand blows up from a subterranean fissure – a phenomenon that has yet to be explained and which can only be seen on his tours, since he jealously guards the secret of its location.

The road to Dakhla

Relatively few vehicles follow the 310-kilometre road between Farafra and Dakhla Oasis. Once you're past Ain Sheikh Mazouk, the desert shifts from white stone to gravel and golden sand until you reach **Abu Minqar** ("Father of the Beak"), an expanse of crops and acacia trees in the wilderness where wells have been sunk and houses built in an effort to attract settlers. It's also the westernmost point on the Great Desert Circuit, and an obligatory tea-stop.

Beyond lie more undulating golden sands, with the escarpment that delineates Dakhla Oasis visible a few kilometres to the left of the highway. Notice the telephone pylons, half-buried by dunes. Entering Dakhla Oasis, you'll pass through Al-Qasr and Mut Talatta before reaching Dakhla's main centre.

Dakhla Oasis

Verdant cultivated areas and a rugged escarpment across the northern horizon make a feast for the eyes in **Dakhla Oasis**. Partitioned by dunes into more or less irrigated, fertile enclaves, the oasis supports 75,000 people living in fourteen settlements strung out along the Farafra and Kharga roads. Although it's the outlying sites that hold the most attraction, the majority of visitors base themselves in or near **Mut**, Dakhla's "capital". Travelling around the oasis, you can see how the Dakhlans have reclaimed land, planted new crops and generally made the best of New Valley developments. Local farmers wear straw sombreros, seldom seen elsewhere in Egypt.

Most **villages** have spread down from their original hilltop maze of medieval houses and covered streets into a roadside straggle of breeze-block houses, schools and other public buildings. Besides Islamic architecture, Dakhla has pharaonic, Roman and Coptic antiquities, dunes, palm groves and hot springs to explore.

Mut

Dakhla's capital, **MUT** (pronounced "moot"), was branded a miserable-looking place by travellers early in the nineteenth century, but has come on apace since the 1950s when the existing town was laid out, complete with wide boulevards. The architect of Mut's low-rise flats is unlikely to have foreseen their balconies being converted into extra rooms or pigeon coops; donkeys chewing hedges in the backstreets add a bucolic touch to the urban landscape.

The main drag, Sharia al-Wadi, runs past an **unfinished tourist village**, designed by Hassan Fathy (see p.291), which later inspired similar domed complexes all over Egypt. As in other oases, locals have embraced modernity and seem keen to forget how previous generations lived.

The old town

Accessible on foot from Sharia al-Ganaim or Midan Gam'a (but best avoided by women on their own) • Daily 24hr • Free

Contrary to the impression conveyed by its modern-day flats, Mut originated as a hilltop *qasr* or **citadel**, divided into quarters separated by gates that were locked at night. Though the summit is in ruins, the mud-brick lanes below are still bustling with life and exciting to explore (beware of lecherous kids and wild dogs). The old town is hidden away behind a ridge, but easy to find. You can enter from the north and exit on to Midan Gam'a, using the Old and New **mosques** as landmarks.

   Midan Gam'a itself used to be the hub of social life but is pretty sleepy nowadays, despite its role as a bus and service taxi terminus.

Mut el-Khorab wildlife

15min walk southwest from Midan Gam'a • Daily 24hr • Free

From Midan Gam'a you can glimpse the remains of **Mut el-Khorab** ("Mut the Ruined"), an ancient city dedicated to the Theban goddess Mut. Mud-brick walls up to three metres high loom over pits left by treasure-hunters, where **Fennec foxes** dwell in burrows, emerging to hunt at dusk. Nearby lies a small field of golden **dunes**, the perfect spot for watching **sunset**. If contacted in advance, Dr Wael Shoudi (📧 wael .elsheikh@yahoo.com) can organize **batwatching**. Dakhla is home to the only species

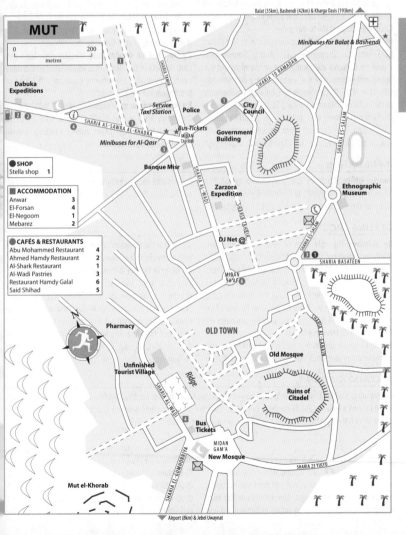

3

of fruit-bat (Rousettus aegyptiacus) found beyond the tropics, of which some 2,500 exist in the oasis. Nocturnal mammals, they feed mainly on dates.

Ethnographic Museum
Sharia es-Salam • Visits by prior arrangement with the tourist office • ££5

Mut's **Ethnographic Museum** is ordered like a family dwelling, with household objects on the walls and a complex wooden lock on the palm-log door. Its seven rooms contain clay figures by the Khargan artist Mabrouk, posed in scenes from village life. Preparing the bride and celebrating the pilgrim's return from Mecca are two scenes that remain part of oasis life today.

ARRIVAL AND DEPARTURE   MUT

By plane Mut's airport is currently closed for renovation, but at some point should become a stopover for twice-weekly flights between Cairo and Kharga Oasis (see p.394). Check with Omar at the tourist office.

By bus The Upper Egypt Bus Co. runs services to Mut (13hr; ££75) from Cairo Gateway (see p.175) daily at 7am and 8pm, routed via Bahariya and Farafra; and an overnight bus via Assyut and Kharga, where a Superjet service also operates (10–11hr; ££80–90). Arriving in Mut, buses drop passengers at Midan Tahrir before terminating at Midan Gam'a, in the southern part of town. Leaving Mut, buses depart for Kharga (3hr) at 6am, 7pm, 8pm and 10pm, continuing on to Assyut (8hr), if not all the way to Cairo (7am & 8pm). Upper Egypt

buses to Farafra (4hr), Bahariya (6hr) and Cairo (13hr) depart at 6am and 5pm. Tickets to Cairo should be purchased the day before; kiosks on Midan Tahrir and beside the *El-Forsan* hotel act as pick-up points for passengers. West-bound buses also pick up passengers at Al-Qasr, near the resthouse.

By minibus or service taxi Irregular departures run from the service taxi depot near Midan Tahrir to the three oases. They charge the same as buses for a full load of passengers, more if half empty.

By private car or minivan Islam (☎ 012 2531 9355) at the *Anwar* hotel quotes ££600–1000 to drive up to six people directly to Luxor, or can arrange a pick-up there to bring tourists to Dakhla Oasis.

INFORMATION

Tourist office Sharia as-Sawra al-Khadra ☎ 092 782 1686 or ☎ 012 2179 6467, ✉ desertlord@hotmail.com. Manager Omar Ahmed is knowledgeable and helpful, and

can organize excursions by taxi all over the oasis (see box, p.415). Daily 8am–2pm, and maybe also 6–9pm.

GETTING AROUND

By minibus The only form of local public transport, minibuses travel out from Mut towards both ends of the oasis. Minibuses to Al-Qasr (££2) and other western villages pick up passengers near the corner of the Al-Qasr road and Midan Tahrir, while vehicles for Balat and Bashendi (££3) leave from two points on Sharia 10 Ramadan. Between 2pm and 3pm you're unlikely to get a ride as all the minibuses are full of schoolkids travelling home.

By taxi Taxis are the priciest option – bargain hard if you want the driver to wait at sites and then return to Mut, or

try Omar at the tourist office (see above), who can fix a taxi with no hassle, or a minibus or 4WD, with driver.

By bicycle Cycling is feasible in winter, depending on your destination and level of fitness. Reaching outlying villages from Mut involves a round trip of at least 60km, but by taking a minibus to Al-Qasr and renting a bike there, you can easily reach several other sites. Bikes can be rented from the *Abu Mohammed Restaurant* (££20/day) in Mut, or the *El-Kasr Resthouse* (££5/day) at Al-Qasr.

ACCOMMODATION

Dakhla offers a wide range of accommodation – less so in Mut itself than out at Mut Talatta springs (see p.417) or further afield in Sheikh Wali (p.420), El-Douhous (p.418), Al-Qasr (p.418), off the road between Rashda and Budkhulu (p.418) or out at Bir el-Gabel (p.418). All except the last two are readily accessible by minibus.

MUT
Anwar Sharia es-Salam ☎ 012 2531 9355; map p.413. Run by the Anwar family, whose son Islam runs excursions around the oasis and will drive tourists as far as Luxor if the price is right. The hotel itself has seen better days, with some of its rooms rather scuffed and

dusty; most have fans or a/c, and a few have private bathrooms. ££90

El-Forsan Sharia al-Wadi ☎ 092 782 1343, ⊕ elforsanhotel.com; map p.413. Overlooking the main drag, the *El-Forsan* has free wi-fi, a hilltop garden and a coffeeshop with views of the old town. Their standard

EXCURSIONS AND SAFARIS AROUND DAKHLA

As some places are hard to reach, and it takes local knowledge of natural beauty spots to get the best from Dakhla, organized **excursions** can be a good idea. Omar at the tourist office can arrange half-day trips either to the east or the west of the oasis (£E150/car) or a full day-trip to both (£E300; £E500 by 4WD), focusing on local antiquities. The *Abu Mohammed Restaurant* and *Anwar* hotel quote £E200 per person for a five-hour trip featuring Al-Qasr, the Magic Spring and dunes at Bir el-Gabal. Nasser at *Elias Camp* charges £E150 per person for an afternoon's **camel trekking**, or £E250 to stay **overnight** in the desert (minimum of three people; meals included).

Ranging further afield, the Bedouin at *El-Douhous Village* offer overnight jeep trips and camel trekking in Farafra's **White Desert**. These cost around £E700 per person per day for a up to six people. Safaris to the remote **Gilf Kebir** (from €130/person daily) are the preserve of the three larger safari operators listed below.

Badawiya Expedition Badawiya Dakhla hotel (see p.416) ☎092 772 7451, ⊕badawiya.com. Based in Farafra, with a branch in Dakhla, Badawiya runs jeep safaris as far afield as Siwa and the Gilf Kebir, plus camel trekking and hiking trips in the White Desert and the Great Sand Sea.

Dabouka Expeditions Sharia as-Sawra al-Khadra ☎092 782 4045, ⊕dabuka.de. A German-based company with a small office in Mut opposite the *Mebarez* hotel offering jeep and camel safaris all over North Africa.

Zarzora Expedition 5 Sharia Tahrir ☎010 0118 8221, ⊕zarzora.com. Another major safari company, offering all kinds of trips and destinations; unlike the others, it actually has its headquarters in Mut, tucked away in a block of flats.

---

rooms have fans and shared bathrooms; en-suite a/c rooms cost £E50 more, but are preferable to the larger, airless bungalows out back (en suite but no a/c; £E100). B&B **£E80**

★ **El-Negoom** Sharia al-Hindaw ☎092 782 0014; map p.413. Located in the backstreets behind the tourist office, *El-Negoom* is quiet, clean and welcoming, with free wi-fi, a large palm garden and a spring-fed swimming pool. Most rooms have a/c, satellite TV and en-suite facilities, although some share a bathroom and fridge with two other rooms. B&B **£E120**

Mebarez Sharia as-Sawra al-Khadra ☎092 782 1524, ✉mebareztouristhotel@hotmail.com; map p.413. This hotel used to be popular with safari groups, and the en-suite a/c rooms are still quite pleasant, although since they got rid of their swimming pool it seems poor value for money compared to *El-Negoom*. B&B **£E150**

MUT TALATTA

Elias Camp 4km from Mut ☎010 0682 6467; map p.417. Hidden away at the end of a track turning right off the side road that leads to the *Mut Inn* (see below), *Elias Camp* comprises a large complex of domed stone chalets, still partly under construction at the time of writing. Its owner, Nasser, runs jeep and camel safaris around the oasis, and offers natural healing (see box, p.416). Rates include full board. **£E400**

Sol y Mar Mut Inn 3km from Mut ☎092 782 1530, ✉mut@solymarpioneers.com; map p.417. Run by the same company as the *Pioneers* hotel in Kharga Oasis, and painted their trademark pink, the *Sol y Mar's* main attractions are its large spring-fed hot pool and the fact that it serves alcohol. Their en-suite chalets are clean and cosy but rather cramped, and the place can get noisy at night when people come to splash around in the pool. Rates include half board. **€70**

SHEIKH WALI

Nasser Hotel & Camp 5km from Mut ☎010 0682 6467; map p.417. Since owner Nasser started building the *Elias Camp* at Mut Talatta (see above), his original hotel has suffered from neglect. A large, lukewarm rooftop pool fed by spring-water only partly makes amends for gloomy, spartan rooms; those with en-suite bathrooms cost £E50 more. **£E50**

EL-DOUHOUS

El-Douhous Village 8km from Mut ☎092 785 0480 or ☎012 8822 3901; map p.417. This hilltop Bedouin "village" keeps on growing as they add extensions, but neglect to maintain the older bits. The two-storey section has en-suite rooms with fans and mosquito nets, which are preferable to the small, dark a/c "chalets" built against the ridge below the dining hall, or the basic reed huts with sleeping platforms. Its Bedouin owner Hagg Abd El Hameed organizes safaris around Dakhla Oasis and the White Desert. B&B: rooms & chalets **£E130**; huts **£E40**

BETWEEN RASHDA AND BUDKHULU

★ **Al Tarfa Desert Sanctuary** 17km from Mut ☎092 910 5007 or ☎010 0100 1109, ⊕altarfa.net; map p.417. Managed by retired desert explorer Wael Abed, this gorgeous deluxe eco-lodge has 32 individually styled a/c suites and rooms set apart for privacy. All suites have their own terrace; a few boast plunge pools. Shared amenities include a sauna, hammam, gym, massage, indoor and outdoor pools. Horse- and camel-rides can be arranged, and rates include a daily guided walk, use of the spa and full board (excluding alcohol). €360

BIR EL-GABAL

Badawiya Dakhla 31km from Mut ☎092 772 7451, ⓦbadawiya.com; map p.417. Built around a bleak hill beside the highway, this latest venture by the Ali family from Farafra (see p.408) has en-suite chalets with a/c, kitchens, sofas and king-size beds, plus shaded terraces and a swimming pool with stunning views of the desert. B&B €56

Bir el-Gabal Camp 37km from Mut ☎012 2106 8227; map p.417. Located out towards the escarpment, this is a small, rustic-style compound of simple rooms with fans sharing bathrooms, with a warm plunge pool nearby. Its

friendly owner, Mohammed Hussein Mohammed, rents bicycles (£E5/day) and hires camels (£E150/day); he is usually to be found at the *El-Kasr Resthouse* (see below), which he also owns. B&B £E120

AL-QASR

El-Kasr Resthouse 32km from Mut ☎092 772 6013 or ☎012 7492 9592; map p.417. Flyblown yet friendly, with triple-bed dorms above a simple 24hr café. The resthouse is favoured by long-stay travellers who like its rock-bottom prices and proximity to Al-Qasr's old town. The owner also rents out bicycles (£E5/day) and can arrange camel trips. B&B £E20/person

Desert Lodge 33km from Mut ☎092 772 7061, ⓦdesertlodge.net; map p.417. Set on a barren hilltop behind old Al-Qasr, this Moorish-style lodge has ravishing desert views, internet, a library and classes in yoga, painting, Arabic and calligraphy – a spa is also planned. All very classy, but its staff could be a lot more welcoming. Rates include half board. €160

EATING AND DRINKING

Nobody ever came to Mut to revel in gastronomy. As in most of the oases, the range of places to eat and dishes on offer are extremely limited, and the word "restaurant" signifies no more than a humble café. You can buy alcohol to takeaway at the Stella Shop (daily 7–10pm) on Sharia es-Salam, around the corner from the Anwar hotel, which sells canned and bottled Stella beer (£E11) behind a dusty window-display that is possibly the world's least-enticing advertisement for any business.

Abu Mohammed Restaurant Sharia as-Sawra al-Khadra ☎010 1267 4553. The English-speaking owner Eid (aka Abu Mohammed) cooks mostly vegetarian dishes, but will prepare grilled chicken or lamb with advance notice. A three-course veggie meal will set you back around £E45, unless you also indulge in beer (£E25) or hook up to his wi-fi (£E15/hr). The leafy front courtyard is a nice place to chill. Daily 8am–9pm (11pm in winter if there are customers).

Ahmed Hamdy Restaurant Sharia as-Sawra al-Khadra ☎092 782 0767. Run by Eid's estranged brother, Ahmed, this place is decidedly meatier, serving juicy grilled chicken or kebabs with all the usual veggie side-dishes at the drop of a hat. Reckon on paying £E60–80 for a full meal. Beer is sometimes sold, but there's no wi-fi. Daily 9am–9pm.

Al-Shark Restaurant Sharia 10 Ramadan. Brightly lit and tiled throughout, *Al-Shark* has yet to be discovered by tourists and its staff only speak Arabic, but by trial and error you could end up with a tasty grilled chicken, kofta or kebab, accompanied by all the usual trimmings. Daily 11am–10pm.

Al-Wadi Pastries Sharia as-Sawra al-Khadra. This hole-in-the-wall joint serves takeaway jam-, apricot- or *sulanta*-filled *fiteer*, or savoury versions if you bring your own cheese, vegetables or meat for cooking on the spot in their oven. Don't expect any frills. Daily 11am–9pm.

Restaurant Hamdy Galal Midan Sa'af. The ebullient Hamdy stokes up his outdoor charcoal grill around noon and serves tasty grilled chicken, kebabs or kofta thereafter, accompanied by soup, salad, rice and vegetable stews, for around £E50. Daily noon–9pm.

NATURAL HEALING AND BATHING IN DAKHLA

As in Bahariya, Mut boasts a niche market in **natural healing** and spiritual tourism. As well as the treatments offered at the three hotels below you could simply head out to Mut Talatta to wallow in the hot pool at *Sol y Mar* (see p.415) for only £E10.

Elias Camp Nasser and his wife at the *Elias Camp* (see p.415) offer massages (£E120/hr), herbal medicine treatments and Islamic prayers and charms for diverse afflictions.

Anwar Staff at the *Anwar* hotel (see p.414) can arrange

bathing at hot springs and a "sand spa" (£E300/person including meals, transport and lodging).

Al Tarfa Desert Sanctuary Guests at the *Al Tarfa Desert Sanctuary* (see p.415) can enjoy Turkish, Finnish, Japanese and Thai spa and massage treatments.

Siad Shihad Off Sharia as-Sawra al-Khadra. Owner Said caters to carnivores with his succulent lamb shish kebabs, served with potatoes in tomato sauce, rice and *tahina*. A few tables outside are as fancy as dining gets in Dakhla Oasis – don't expect any tablecloths. Daily noon–10pm.

Sol y Mar Mut Inn Mut Talatta (see p.415). Just outside town, this is the only place in Dakhla Oasis where you can swim in a large hot pool while quaffing a chilled Stella beer (£E25) or a bottle of Egyptian wine (£E140). The pool can get crowded on Thurs and Fri nights. Daily 24hr.

DIRECTORY

Banks and exchange Banque Misr, Sharia al-Wadi (Sun–Thurs 8.30am–2pm), has an ATM.
Hospital Sharia 10 Ramadan ☎ 092 782 1555 (daily 24hr).
Internet access DJ Net, off Sharia al-Wadi (daily 10am–8pm; £E10/hr). The *Abu Mohammed Restaurant* (see p.416) has wi-fi (£E15/hr).
Police Sharia 10 Ramadan ☎ 092 782 1500 (daily 24hr).

Post office On Midan Gam'a, and also beside the telephone office (both daily except Fri 8am–2pm).
Telephone office Sharia es-Salam (daily 24hr). Menatel card-phones all over town can be used to make international calls.
Tourist police Sharia 10 Ramadan, 400m beyond the hospital ☎ 092 782 1687 (daily 24hr).

North of Mut

Top of the list for most visitors is the medieval settlement of **Al-Qasr**, which is easily reached by minibus. With a bicycle rented from its resthouse, you can go on to explore the **Muzawaka Tombs** and the Roman temple of **Deir al-Hagar**. To also enjoy bathing in local **hot springs**, take one of the excursions offered by local safari outfits or hire a taxi through the tourist office. **Sunset trips by camel** (with the option of sleeping in the desert) are a great way to experience the beauty of the oasis (see box, p.415).

There are two routes to Al-Qasr via different villages. If you can, it's worth following one out and the other one back. Most traffic uses the **main road** (32km), with minibuses stopping at the villages of Rashda and Budkhulu; while along the secondary and longer **loop road** (45km) they call at Qalamoun, Gedida and Mushiya.

Mut Talatta

3km north of Mut • Accessible by minibus from the corner of the Al-Qasr road and Midan Tahrir in Mut

Best visited on the way back, or in the evening, **Mut Talatta** (daily 24hr; £E10) is the nearest of Dakhla's **hot springs**, enclosed by the *Sol y Mar Mut Inn* (see p.415). You don't

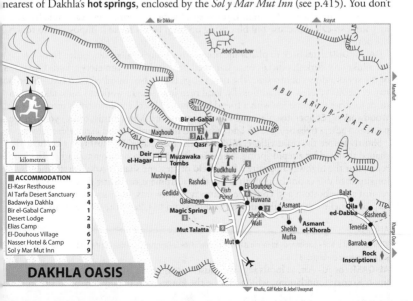

DAKHLA OASIS

ACCOMMODATION
El-Kasr Resthouse	3
Al Tarfa Desert Sanctuary	5
Badawiya Dakhla	4
Bir el-Gabal Camp	1
Desert Lodge	2
Elias Camp	8
El-Douhous Village	6
Nasser Hotel & Camp	7
Sol y Mar Mut Inn	9

have to be a guest to enjoy wallowing in the hotel's large swimming pool of brown, sulphur- and iron-rich water, flowing from a depth of over 1000m, and with chilled beer and wine available, this is a perfect place to relax after a hard day's sightseeing.

The Fish Pond

One kilometre beyond Mut Talatta is the so-called **Fish Pond**, a lake created to serve as a fish farm but which became so polluted with pesticides that it's now merely a drainage lake for irrigation water – but nonetheless great for **birdwatching** (avocet, stilt and coot). Further out, off to the right of the junction where the desert road joins the highway and the loop road begins, you'll glimpse the hilltop *El-Douhous Village* (see p.415), offering jeep and camel safaris.

Budkhulu

If you have a car it's worth detouring east off the main road beyond Rashda to admire the *Al Tarfa Desert Sanctuary* (see p.415), with eucalyptus groves and dunes receding to the escarpment. Back on the highway, olive groves and orchards precede **BUDKHULU**, whose **old quarter** of covered streets and houses with carved lintels harbours a ruined **Ayyubid mosque** with a pepperpot minaret and a palm-frond pulpit. Visible on a hill as you approach is a **Turkish cemetery** with tombs shaped like bathtubs, grave markers in the form of ziggurats and domed shrines: the freshly painted one belongs to a revered local sheikh, Tawfiq Abdel Aziz.

Bir el-Gabal

Shortly before Al-Qasr, the *Badawiya Dakhla* hotel (see p.416) marks the turning off the highway leading to the cluster of houses and bathing tank at **Bir el-Gabal** (6km), set amidst breathtaking scenery on the desert's edge. Here, the *Bir el-Gabal Camp* (see p.416) organizes camel trekking and rents bicycles – making it a feasible base for visiting Al-Qasr.

The loop road: Qalamoun, Gedida and Mushiya

An alternative route to Al-Qasr is via the so-called **loop road**, which links three villages – Qalamoun, Gedida and Mushiya –interspersed by stagnant pools and desert. Just off the road, 1km before Qalamoun, is the **Magic Spring**, a warm, deep waterhole fringed by palms, so-called because bubbles rising up from below make it impossible to touch the bottom.

QALAMOUN dates back to pharaonic times, with many families descended from Mamluke and Turkish officials once stationed here. Its hilltop **cemetery** affords fine views of the surrounding countryside. The next village is only two hundred years old – hence its name, **GEDIDA** ("New"). Traditionally, local men have sought work in Cairo, taking it in turns to share the same job with a friend back home. Local employment is provided by a **Woodworking Cooperative** where (by arrangement with Mut's tourist office) you can see palm and acacia trees being sawn and fashioned into furniture and *mashrabiya* screens.

Shortly before the third village, **MUSHIYA**, the road passes **Bir Mushiya**, a keyhole-shaped tank fed by a tepid spring, where tourists may also be taken to bathe. The loop road joins the highway opposite a **dune field** of crescent-shaped *barchans*, formed by longitudinal dunes on the plateau above the escarpment cascading down the cliff to reform at the bottom and continue their way southwards. Tourists are brought here by jeep or camel to enjoy rolling down the dunes and to take in the view at sunset.

Al-Qasr

32km northwest of Mut • Accessible on any minibus from the corner of the Al-Qasr road and Midan Tahrir in Mut, which may travel by either the main or the loop road

AL-QASR (or Al-'Asr, as locals say) is a must – an amazing Islamic settlement, built upon Roman foundations, which may be the longest continually inhabited site in the oasis and was indubitably Dakhla's medieval capital. Three or four families still live in the mud-brick old town crowning a ridge above palm groves and a salt lake, set back from New Qasr beside the highway. The "border" is marked by handicrafts sellers beside the New Mosque and a **Tour Centre** (daily 8am–5pm) where you can pick up a guide to lead you around and unlock houses and workshops. Pay him at the end: £E15– 20 per group seems fair.

Beyond the twelfth-century **Nasr el-Din Mosque**, whose 21-metre-high minaret has a "pepperpot" finial typical of Ayyubid architecture, you enter a maze of high-walled alleyways and gloomy covered passages. Over thirty **houses** here have acacia-wood lintels whose cursive or Kufic inscriptions name the builders or occupants (the oldest dates from 1518): look out for doorways with Pharaonic stonework and arabesque carvings, archways with *ablaq* brickwork, and a frieze painted in one of the passageways.

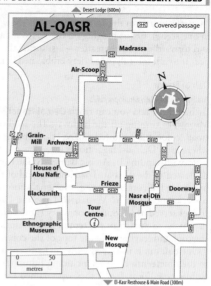

Near the **House of Abu Nafir** – built over a Ptolemaic temple, with hieroglyphics on its door jambs – is a donkey-powered **grain-mill**. Further north, a rooftop *mala'af* or **air-scoop** incorporated into a long T-shaped passage conveys breezes into the labyrinth. Beyond is a tenth-century **madrassa** (school and court) featuring painted *liwans*, niches for legal texts, cells for felons and a beam above the door for whippings. The maze of alleyways also harbours a restored **blacksmith**'s forge.

For more information on these and other facets of the old way of life, check out the **Ethnographic Museum** (daily 10am–5pm; £E10) near the Tour Centre, founded by the anthropologist Aliya Hussein and containing artefacts and photos from all of the oases in the Western Desert.

The best time to **photograph** Al-Qasr is midday, when sunlight falls through skylights to illuminate the maze of shadowy lanes.

If you fancy **staying** here there's the *El-Kasr Resthouse* beside the main road, or the *Desert Lodge* on a hill behind the old town (see p.416 for details). Both serve **meals**.

The Muzawaka Tombs

6km from Al-Qasr • Daily 8am–5pm • £E25

Six kilometres west along the highway from Al-Qasr, a signpost indicates the track to the **Muzawaka Tombs**, a twenty-minute walk or a slow drive through the silent desert, past eerie rock buttes riddled with empty Greco-Roman tombs. Of the three hundred or so recorded by Egyptologist Ahmed Fakhry in 1972, two provoked the word "Muza!" (Decorations!) – hence the name. Both tombs were later closed for many years as restorers strove to reattach their murals to the friable limestone, but are set to be reopened by 2013, while a visitors' centre and caféteria are also planned for the site.

The **Tomb of Petosiris** is vividly painted with Roman-nosed blonds in pharaonic poses, curly-haired angels and a zodiac with a bearded Janus-figure on the ceiling. In the back right-hand corner is a man standing on a turtle holding a snake and a fish aloft – a curious amalgam of Ancient Egyptian and Greco-Roman symbolism. The grapevines symbolize vitality.

Cruder murals in the **Tomb of Sadosiris** show Anubis (weighing the deceased's heart in one scene), Osiris judging on the rear wall, and another Janus – looking back on life and forward into the hereafter – just inside the entrance. Visitors may also be invited to peer into a tomb full of leathery embalmed corpses (baksheesh expected).

Deir al-Hagar

7km from Al-Qasr • Daily 8am–5pm • £E25

By bicycle or taxi you can reach **Deir al-Hagar** via an unmarked road 1km past the Muzawaka turning off the highway. The road runs south past some Roman ruins to a small, colourfully painted village (1km); beyond here a track crosses a ridge, whereupon Deir al-Hagar hoves into view on the right.

Notwithstanding its Arabic name, "Stone Monastery", this was once a Roman temple dedicated to the Theban Triad and the god of the oasis, Seth. The temple's sandstone hypostyle hall, sanctuary and brick enclosure wall were built in the first century AD, under emperors Nero, Vespasian, Titus and Domitian (whose cartouches can be seen). It later served as a Coptic monastery (notice the mural of Christ, the lion and the lamb in a niche to the left of the temple pylon) until a huge dune consumed it, collapsing the roof and leaving only the tops of the columns visible.

One column is inscribed with the names of almost every **explorer** who visited Dakhla in the nineteenth century, including Edmondstone, Drovetti, Cailliaud and the entire Rohlfs expedition. It was they who named Dakhla's only mountain **Jebel Edmondstone**, after the first European to reach the oasis since ancient times; Sir Archibald Edmondstone beat his French rival, Drovetti, by ten days, in 1819, to "discover" it in the name of England.

East of Mut

Villages on the eastern arm of the oasis are more or less accessible from Mut by minibus; most terminate at Balat or Bashendi, but some go as far as Teneida. Heading out of town, you'll see where irrigation canals have enabled wheat, rice and peanuts to be grown on once barren land. **SHEIKH WALI** is on the verge of becoming a suburb of Mut, yet backs onto desert, with olive groves and goat-pens surrounding a Biblical **waterwheel**, while dunes swell in the distance. **ASMANT**, 6km on, has the usual sprawl of modern buildings by the road and a high-walled **old village** on the hill further back, which lends its name to an ancient site 9km further east.

Balat

35km east of Mut • Accessible by any minibus from Sharia 10 Ramadan

After the stretch of desert beyond Asmant, it's delightful to reach **BALAT,** shaded by mature trees, where minibuses drop passengers at a teahouse. Cross the road to explore the old village beyond the TV mast, with its three hundred-year-old **mosque** upheld by

---

ASMANT EL-KHORAB AND THE DAKHLA OASIS PROJECT

Asmant el-Khorab ("Asmant the Ruined"; no public access), 20km east of Mut, is the local name for the **ruins of Kellis**, a Roman and Coptic town inhabited for seven centuries, whose temples and churches mark the shift from pagan Rome to Byzantine Christianity. Excavations have unearthed the remains of aqueducts, farmhouses and tombs, including 34 mummies and wooden codices, casting light on religion and daily life in the third century AD.

Asmant el-Khorab is now the field HQ of the **Dakhla Oasis Project** (DOP), a multi-disciplinary effort to understand the interaction of oasis cultures and their environment, from the Stone Age through until the twenty-first century. Half-a-dozen foreign missions are seeking the holy grail of Egyptology: evidence of links between the Old Kingdom and desert trade routes going back to Neolithic times, which may answer the question: did Ancient Egyptian civilization emerge from the Western Desert?

palm-trunks and a maze of twisting **covered streets** that protect the villagers from sun and sandstorms, and once prevented invaders from entering on horseback. Painted oxblood, salmon, terracotta or pale blue, with carved lintels and wooden peg-locks, its mud-brick **houses** are only slightly less impressive than the ones in Al-Qasr, with many still inhabited.

Qila ed-Dabba and Ain Asil

2–3km from Balat via a track 200m east of the village teahouse; also accessible on foot from Bashendi (2km) • Daily 8am–5pm • £E25

Although the oldest houses in Balat village date only from Mamluke times, this locality was a pharaonic seat of government as long ago as 2500 BC, when the oasis prospered through trade with Kush (ancient Nubia). A few kilometres outside Balat, the ancient necropolis of **Qila ed-Dabba** is home to five mud-brick mastabas (once clad in limestone but long ago reduced to lumps), marking the tombs of VI Dynasty (2345–2181 BC) governors and their families. Like the mastaba-tombs at Saqqara, these consist of mud-brick superstructures used as funerary chapels and built over burial chambers cut deep into the bedrock.

Since the 1980s, the site has been excavated by the Institut Français d'Archéologie Oriental (IFAO), which has a dig-house nearby. Like the Dakhla Oasis Project (see p.420), the IFAO hopes to find evidence of a "missing link" between Egypt's Pre-dynastic civilization and the prehistoric tribes of the desert. Their biggest discovery hereabouts has been the **Tomb of Khenitka**, who governed during the reign of Pepi II (2292–03 BC). Digging 10m down, they found four chambers containing alabaster and terracotta pottery, copper jewellery, statuettes and ostrich eggs (now in the Museum of the New Valley in Kharga Oasis). Faded but elegant reliefs depict Khentika, his wife and son; people ploughing, driving cattle and sailing boats.

The same ticket is also valid for the ruins at **Ain Asil**, 1km northeast of the necropolis, where a fortress and farming community, whose name meant "Our Root is Lasting in the Oasis", existed from the Old Kingdom until Ptolemaic times. From either site, you can see – and walk to – Bashendi (about 2km).

Bashendi

2km off the highway, 40km from Mut • Accessible by minibus • **Tomb of Pasha Hindi**: Daily 8am–5pm • Free •**Tomb of Kitnes**: Daily 8am–5pm • £E25

Minibuses from Mut either terminate at, or pass the turning for, the village of **BASHENDI**, whose name derives from Pasha Hindi, a medieval sheikh who is buried in the local cemetery at the back of the village, where the desert begins. The cemetery dates back to Roman times, and the brick-domed **Tomb of Pasha Hindi** is itself built atop a Roman structure. Empty sarcophagi separate it from the sandstone **Tomb of Kitnes**, whose Ancient Egyptian-style funerary reliefs depict Kitnes meeting the desert-gods Min, Seth and Shu. Its key is held by a villager who can be fetched if you want to look inside. Tombs also form the foundations of many of the village houses, which are painted pale blue or buttercup yellow with floral friezes and hajj scenes, merging into the ground in graceful curves.

Teneida

45km east of Mut • Accessible by minibus from Sharia 10 Ramadan in Mut, or the highway near the turn-off for Bashendi • Daily 24hr • Free

TENEIDA, on the eastern edge of the oasis, is a modern affair centred on a leafy square, whose only "sight" is a **cemetery** with weird tombstones resembling tiny houses. With a car, you can press on to see some **rock inscriptions** off the highway 10km beyond Teneida. The carvings include an ostrich at the base of the sandstone outcrop beside the road, while beyond some fields another rock shaped like a seated camel is covered in prehistoric and Bedouin drawings of giraffes, camels and hunters, as well as the name of Jarvis (British governor of Dakhla and Kharga in the 1930s) and many others. Sadly, recent visitors have covered many of the ancient inscriptions with mindless graffiti.

The road to Kharga Oasis

Beyond the last flourish of greenery, wind-sculpted rocks give way to dun table-tops and gravelly sand, persisting for most of the way from Dakhla to Kharga (193km). Following the Darb el-Ghabari or "Dust Road", the modern road skirts the phosphate-rich Abu Tartur Plateau that separates the two depressions. The appearance of a phosphates factory 45km outside Kharga alerts you for a treat to follow. Golden **dunes** march across the depression, burying lines of telegraph poles and encroaching on the highway. Villagers faced with their advance have been known to add an extra storey to their house, live there while the dune consumes the ground floor and move back downstairs once it has passed on. These dunes are outstretched fingers of the **Ghard Abu Muharrik** (see p.411), of the type known as "whalebacked".

Kharga Oasis

Despite being the nearest of the oases to Luxor and the capital of the New Valley (see box, p.393), **Kharga Oasis** gets far fewer tourists than the others. **El-Kharga**, the "capital" of the oasis, is a 1970s metropolis of eighty thousand people with adequate facilities and a good museum, but otherwise dull, and while the oasis contains many ancient sites, relatively few are accessible without a car, and some can only be reached by jeep.

Submerged by the sea aeons ago, leaving fossils on the high plateau, the Kharga depression is hemmed in by 300-metre-high cliffs, with belts of dunes advancing across the oasis. It's thought that there were no dunes here in Roman times; myth has it that they erected a brass cow on the escarpment, which swallowed up the sand. Many desert trade routes converged on the oasis, notably the **Forty Days Road** (see p.431). Both Roman legionaries and Mamluke troops were stationed here, and deserted Roman forts and villages that claim descent from Mamluke soldiers attest to centuries of firm control by Egypt's rulers, who have used Kharga as a place of exile since antiquity. Under Nasser, Sadat and Mubarak, Islamist militants were incarcearated in the tuberculosis-ridden **Kharga Prison** (visible as one enters the oasis from the north).

Kharga is seen by some as a portent that the New Valley spells ruin for the oases. The influx of *fellaheen* from the Nile Valley has changed agricultural practices; **rice** cultivation has proved more water-intensive than expected, depleting aquifers and turning land saline – leading to strict limits on its production. It's indicative of the mixed antecedents of its citizens that the **name** Kharga may be pronounced "Harga" or "Harjah", depending on who's talking. Both the oasis and its capital are called Kharga; we've used the prefix "El-" to refer to the city.

El-Kharga

As the capital of the New Valley Governorate (comprising Kharga, Dakhla and Farafra oases), **EL-KHARGA** has grown into a sprawl of mid-rise buildings and highways, with the only reminder of its romantic oasis-town origins being the souk and lush palm groves in the "lower" town. The modern town was laid out on higher ground than the original settlement, with banks and government buildings lining the wide **Sharia Gamal Abdel Nasser**, which is too long and monotonous for pleasant walking, despite its ornamental obelisks, arches and shrubs. Public **minibuses** run along its length, en route between the upper and lower parts of town.

Though El-Kharga is no longer encircled by **palm groves**, they still flourish beyond Sharia Bur Said, and dates play an important part in the social calendar. **City Day** (Oct 3) celebrates the beginning of the date harvest with a parade of floats along Sharia Gamal Abdel Nasser, and the marriage season is also timed to coincide with the flowering of the date crop (from July until harvest time).

Museum of the New Valley

Sharia Gamal Abdel Nasser • Daily 8am–5pm • £E30

Housed in an imposing modern building modelled on the Coptic tombs of nearby Bagawat, the **Museum of the New Valley** exhibits artefacts from sites scattered across three oases. The most impressive are Greco-Roman: painted sarcophagi from Maks al-Qibli to the south of Kharga Oasis; death masks from Qasr el-Labeka to the north;

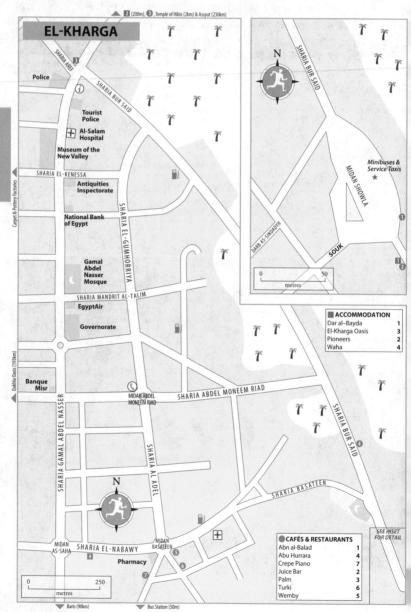

and mummified rams, eagles and ibises from Dakhla Oasis. The Old Kingdom is represented by jewellery, scarabs and headrests from the tombs of the VI Dynasty governors at Qila ed-Dabba, also in Dakhla. Look out for the *ba* birds, representing the soul of the deceased, unearthed at Dush Temple in the far south of Kharga.

The lower town

From **Midan Showla** a busy **souk** runs off into an old quarter of mud-brick houses painted apricot or azure and daubed with the lucky Hand of Fatima. Turn right at the first crossroads and then left to find the **Darb as-Sindadyh**, a dark, serpentine alley roofed with palm trunks which once extended over 4km through a medieval settlement like the qasr in other oases. Most of this has crumbled into ruin, but a short stretch has been restored to remind visitors of what used to exist here.

ARRIVAL AND DEPARTURE   EL-KHARGA

By plane The Petroleum Service Co. (see p.394) operates flights (Tues & Sun; 1hr; about £E500) between Cairo and Kharga, using a small airport 10km from town (£E30 by taxi). Mohsen at the tourist office can book tickets.

By bus The Upper Egypt Bus Co. and Superjet run services (2–3 daily; 7–8hr; £E60) from Cairo Gateway (see p.175), travelling overnight via Assyut in the Nile Valley. Additionally, there are four non-a/c buses to Kharga from Assyut (4hr), some running by day. Arriving in El-Kharga, it makes sense to decide on a hotel and get dropped off at the nearest point, rather than riding on to the bus station off Midan Basateen. Information on departures is hard to obtain there, but Mohsen at the

tourist office (see below) can confirm schedules of buses to Cairo (9pm, 10pm & 11pm) and Dakhla Oasis (2pm & 11pm).

By private car, minibus or service taxi Local drivers charge about £E600 for the two-hour journey from Luxor, via a desert road (275km) that enters the oasis at Baghdad (see p.430), which closes at 4pm. In El-Kharga, drivers on Midan Showla will take people to Cairo by car (£E1000) or minibus (£E1200, shared between up to nine people), and there are service taxis to Dakhla (before 10am or just after 2pm). Alternatively, Mohsen at the tourist office can drive up to three people to Dakhla for £E300, visiting Teneida, Bashendi and Balat (see p.420) en route.

INFORMATION

Tourist office Sharia Gamal Abdel Nasser ☎ 092 792 1206 or ☎ 010 0180 6127, ✉ mohsen_di@yahoo.com. Manager Mohsen Abdel Moneam speaks excellent English and knows everything about Kharga and Dakhla. His tours

(see box below) are one of the few ways of reaching the remoter sites in Kharga, and he can also arrange visits to local carpet and pottery factories. Mon–Thurs & Sun 8.30am–2pm and maybe also 4–10pm.

TOURS

The size of the oasis, the lack of public transport and the remoteness of many sites means that you really need a car (if not a guide) to experience all it has to offer. Taxi drivers on Midan Showla (see above) may agree to take you to Qasr el-Ghweita, Qasr al-Zayan and Dush for £E200–300; otherwise, an organized excursion is the only way to reach these places. As well as the two guides listed below, excursions can also be negotiated with the director of the Antiquities Inspectorate, Dr Mansour (☎ 012 2374 5279).
Dr Mahmoud Youssef ☎ 092 792 0084 or ☎ 010 6330

18237. Alternatively, the director of the New Valley Museum, asks £E1500 a day for a two-day grand tour of all the sites from Ain Um Dabadhib in the north to Dush in the far south – or will guide people with their own 4WD for £E750/day. In both cases, the cost can be shared by up to three passengers.
Mohsen Abdel Moneam c/o the tourist office (see above). Mohsen at the tourist office does day-long tours of Bagawat, Qasr al-Ghweita and Qasr al-Zayan (£E240), and half-day trips to Qasr el-Labeka (£E450) or Ain Um Dabadhib (£E1200).

ACCOMMODATION

There's no problem finding accommodation in El-Kharga, though it's not great value. Staying outside town is only feasible with a car, though both options – the *Hamadalla Sahara City* and *Tabuna Camp* – are within walking distance of ancient temples (see map on p.427).

EL-KHARGA

Dar al-Bayda Off Midan Showla ☎ 092 291 1717; map p.424. Handy for the service taxi station but noisy, this

warren of rooms decorated in lurid colours is the low-budget choice by default. Most rooms have TV and fans, some have baths, and there's wi-fi in the lobby. B&B **£E85**

El-Kharga Oasis Sharia Aref ☎092 792 1206; map p.424. Designed by Soviet architects in the 1960s and nearly always empty, as most of the rooms have gone to pot, while the a/c chalets at the back of its palm garden are plagued by mosquitoes. B&B **£250**

★ **Pioneers** 500m north of the El-Kharga Oasis, on the way out of town ☎092 792 9751, ⓦsolymar.com; map p.424. The only hotel in El-Kharga that can be happily recommended, this pink-painted complex has a/c rooms with satellite TV around a large swimming pool, a lush garden with a coffee shop, a restaurant and a bar. Rates include half board. **€100**

Waha Sharia el-Nabawy ☎092 792 0393; map p.424. Only worth considering if you're broke, or want to stay within walking distance of the bus station, the *Waha* has basic rooms with grungy shared bathrooms; it's worth paying £E6 more for en-suite facilities. **£E24**

QASR EL-GHWEITA

Hamadalla Sahara City 17km from El-Kharga ☎092 762 0240 or ☎010 0255 0742; map p.427. Garishly painted pink and yellow, *Hamadalla Sahara City* makes an incongruous sight beside the highway and a turning leading to Qasr el-Ghweita temple (see p.430). Accommodation is in clusters of domed bungalows with fans and private bathrooms, and there's a restaurant that occasionally sells beer. B&B **£E250**

DUSH

Tabuna Camp 87km from El-Kharga ☎092 910 0688, ⓦdesertinstyle-egypt.com; map p.427. Located within walking distance of the Temple of Dush (see p.430), and offering lodgings in deluxe tents with bathrooms, electricity, dressing rooms and verandas. Camel-trekking and jeep-safaris can be arranged, and there is a telescope for star-gazing. Rates include half board; open Oct–April only. **$200**

EATING AND DRINKING

As in other oases, there isn't a great variety of dishes on offer, and only one place serves alcohol. Grocery shops stock olives, cheese, yogurt and canned food, and there's plenty of fresh fruit and veg in the souks. Almost all shops and stalls close from 2pm to 6pm.

★ **Abn al-Balad** Midan Showla. Its name is the Arabic equivalent of "salt of the earth", alluding to the authenticity of their delicious thin-crust Egyptian pizzas and sweet *fiteer*, which are cooked before your eyes – just a shame they're only open in the evening. Daily 6–10pm.

Abu Hurrara Sharia Bur Said. Many locals rate this the best place in town to eat kofta and kebab (served with all the usual trimmings), and the spartan tiled interior is large enough to allow plenty of leg room. Daily noon–10pm.

Crepe Piano Off Midan Basateen. No English is spoken here, but you can make your request understood by pointing at the pictures of various sweet or savoury pancake options behind the counter. Daily noon–8pm.

Juice Bar Off Midan Showla. A stand-up counter dispensing freshly pressed sugarcane and orange juice, which sometimes also does mango or strawberry juice when they're in season. Daily 10am–2pm & 6–11pm.

Palm Pioneers hotel (see above) ☎092 792 9751. The only restaurant as such in the oasis lays on a buffet supper when tour groups are staying; otherwise you have to discuss with the waiter what you want, according to what's available in the kitchen. Either option costs the equivalent of €10. An adjacent bar sells Egyptian beer (£E30), wine (£E40 a glass) and spirits (£E38–60). Daily 10am–midnight.

Turki Midan Basateen. Of the several simple diners by the fruit and vegetable market in the upper town, *Turki* is the brightest-looking, serving the usual staples of grilled chicken, kebab, soup, rice and salad (meals around £E20). Daily noon–9pm.

Wemby Midan Basateen. Next door to *Turki*, this place looks a bit dingier but is equally popular with locals, serving the same dishes at similar prices. The only significant difference is that *Wemby* doesn't have any signs or menus in English. Daily noon–10pm.

DIRECTORY

Banks and exchange National Bank of Egypt (Sun–Thurs 9am–2pm) and Banque du Caire (Sun–Thurs 8.30am–2pm), on Sharia Gamal Abdel Nasser; the former has an ATM.

EgyptAir Sharia Gamal Abdel Nasser, beside the Governorate ☎092 793 3583 (daily except Fri 9am–5pm). Handles bookings on flights elsewhere in Egypt, but no English is spoken, so any arrangements are best made through the tourist office.

Hospital and pharmacies The private Al-Salam Hospital (☎092 793 3377) on Sharia Gamal Abdel Nasser is preferable to the public hospital on Sharia el-Nabawy

(both 24hr). There's a pharmacy (daily 9am–2pm & 6–10pm) on Midan Basateen, near the latter.

Internet access Cyber cafés come and go on the upper level of the shopping arcade that runs along the north side of Sharia el-Nabawy.

Police Sharia Gamal Abdel Nasser (daily 24hr).

Post office Sharia Abdel Moneem Riad (daily except Fri 8am–2.30pm).

Swimming Non-guests can use the pool at the *Pioneers* hotel for £E50.

Telephone office Sharia Abdel Moneem Riad (daily 24hr).

Tourist police Sharia Gamal Abdel Nasser ☎092 792 1367 (daily 24hr).

Visa extensions Visa extensions are available at the passport office, behind the police station ☎092 792 0096 (daily except Fri 8am–3pm).

North of El-Kharga

Three of the oasis' most evocative monuments lie a few kilometres north of El-Kharga, within walking distance during winter. Here you can see the **Temple of Hibis** juxtaposed against the **Bagawat Necropolis**, one of the oldest Christian cemeteries in Egypt, itself backed by an imposing ruined monastery, **Deir el-Kashef**. Further north and harder to

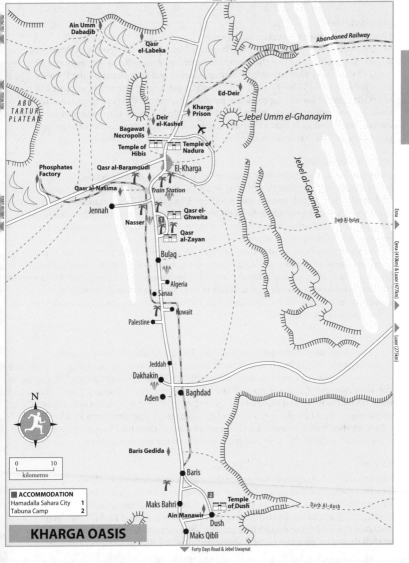

KHARGA OASIS

reach, **Ed-Deir**, **Qasr el-Labeka** and **Ain Um Dabadib** are ancient forts, tunnels and other feats of Roman and Persian engineering.

Temple of Nadura

1km north of town, 500m off the highway • Daily 24hr • Free

Hardly anyone bothers to visit the ruined **Temple of Nadura**, sat atop a 135-metre-high hill in the desert en route to the Bagawat Necropolis. Its eroded sandstone wall and *pronaos* aren't anything special, but the view of the surrounding countryside is great, as suggested by its name, Nadura, meaning "The Lookout". Built during the reign of Antoninus Caesar, Nadura is typical of the Roman temple-forts that once protected the oasis from desert raiders.

Temple of Hibis

2.3km north of town • Not open to visitors, but visible from outside

Sited just off the highway before the Bagawat Necropolis, the **Temple of Hibis** is the largest cult-shrine in any of the oases. Dedicated to Amun-Re, it was begun in the reign of the XXVI Dynasty ruler Psammetichus II and completed by the Persian emperor Darius I (521–486 BC). Fields roundabout cover the site of ancient Hibis, a town that prospered during the same period. The temple was reconstructed after a $20 million conservation fiasco, when it was dismantled to move it to higher ground only for engineers to decide that a drainage system was a better solution to the rising groundwater that was undermining its foundations.

Bagawat Necropolis

2.5km from town • Daily: May–Sept 8am–6pm; Oct–April 8am–5pm • £E30 (ticket also valid for Deir el-Kashef)

Some 200m past the Temple of Hibis you'll see the **Bagawat Necropolis**, consisting of 263 mud-brick chapels spread over a hilltop. Used for Christian burials between the third and sixth centuries (latterly by followers of Bishop Nestorius, who was exiled to Kharga for heresy), the chapels embody diverse forms of mud-brick vaulting or Roman-influenced portals, but are best known for their Coptic murals.

Adam and Eve, Noah's Ark, Abraham and Isaac populate the dome of the fifth-century **Chapel of Peace** near the entrance to the necropolis. Further north, Roman-looking pharaonic troops pursue the Jews, led by Moses, out of Egypt, in the **Chapel of the Exodus**. Flowery motifs and doves of peace can be seen inside **Tomb #25**, one of three adjacent family vaults. The scenes in all these tombs are crudely executed but full of life and vividly coloured.

Deir el-Kashef

3km from town • Daily: May–Sept 8am–6pm; Oct–April 8am–5pm • £E30 (ticket also valid for the Bagawat Necropolis)

From Bagawat's ticket kiosk, a track runs behind the hill past an archeologists' resthouse and rows of rock-cut tombs to reach the dramatic ruins of **Deir el-Kashef** ("Monastery of the Tax Collector"). Named after a Mamluke governor, the five-storey Coptic monastery once housed hermits and travellers in its vaulted cells, and still commands a view of the point where the Darb al-Ghabari from Dakhla crossed the Forty Days Road.

In the valley below you can see the ruins of a small **church** or hermitage, with Greek texts on the walls of the nave and the tiny cells where the monks slept.

Ed-Deir

12km from town • Daily 24hr • Free • Accessible by motorbike with driver, arranged by the tourist office (£E100) •

The best-preserved and most accessible of Kharga's Roman forts is **Ed-Deir**, near the eastern scarp-wall, which once guarded the shortest camel route to the Nile. Built during the reign of the Byzantine emperor Diocletian (244–311 AD), its twelve rounded towers are connected by a gallery, with numerous rooms featuring obscene **graffiti** drawn by generations of Roman, Turkish and British soldiers.

The **abandoned railway** visible in the distance was built by the British in 1906–8, but gradually blocked by advancing dunes. The same fate befell another railway built further south in the 1980s, whose steel tracks were stolen after the 2011 Revolution.

Qasr el-Labeka

40km from town • Daily 24hr • Free • Accessible on a half-day trip organized by the tourist office (££450 for up to three people)

Qasr el-Labeka is the nearest site where you can see the amazing system of **underground aqueducts**, known as *manafis*, that drew on ground water like the *qanats* of ancient Persia (Fakhry suggests that the system originated under Persian rule). Labeka is reached via a spur-road off the highway that turns into a sandy track leading to a tiny oasis, where a farmer has cleared out the *manafi* to irrigate palms and plots. If you don't mind getting your feet wet, the horizontal shaft is narrow but tall enough to venture into. The vertical shafts allowing access from the surface give their name to such aqueducts (*manafi* means "shaft").

You can tell where water lies near the surface from the scrub or palm trees on the plain beyond. Ruined houses and a temple lie half-buried in the sand, with a Roman **fortress** looming from a nearby crag. Its twelve-metre walls enclose sand-choked chambers and the rear gate overlooks a palm grove. If Labeka's Arabic name "Palm-wine Fort" signifies anything, it wasn't the worst posting for a legionary.

Ain Um Dabadib

18km from Qasr el-Labeka • Daily 24hr • Free • Accessible on a full-day trip organized by the tourist office (££1200 for up to three people)

Despite its proximity to Labeka, cars may have to backtrack as far as El-Kharga to find a corridor through the dunes to reach **Ain Um Dabadib.** The largest ancient site in the oasis (covering over 200 square kilometres), it includes a ruined Roman **fortress**, Byzantine **churches** and **tombs**, but is most remarkable for its **underground aqueducts**, the deepest 53m beneath the surface and the longest running for 4.6km. When one of these *manafis* was cleared in the 1900s, water began to flow again. Now choked with sand and inhabited by snakes, scorpions and bats, they are risky to explore.

Ain Amur

48km from the main road • Daily 24hr • Free • Access requires two 4WD vehicles, a guide and a permit, arranged through the tourist office or the Museum of the New Valley (price negotiable)

Further west beyond the limits of the Kharga depression, the isolated **Ain Amur** ("Spring of the Lovely One") is situated 200m up the cliffs of the Abu Tartur Plateau. At 525m above sea level, this is the highest spring in the Western Desert, fed by aquifers in the escarpment rather than deep below the desert floor. Coptic **graffiti** includes the testimony of a traveller "faint from thirst" who stumbled upon Ain Amur late at night, which "saved him". Some believe the spring was the last watering hole of the legendary Lost Army of Cambyses, before it disappeared into the Great Sand Sea (see box, p.410).

South of El-Kharga

Exploring the southern part of the oasis entails flitting between sites off the highway. The temples of **Qasr el-Ghweita** and **Qasr al-Zayn** are both relatively close to town; **Dush** is further out and harder to reach. Dr Mahmoud Youssef (see p.425) can guide visitors to two lesser Roman ruins, amidst the dunes behind Kharga's extravagantly marbled **train station**, moribund since the railway line to Luxor was abandoned to the desert sands in 2008 (its tracks were stolen by looters following the Revolution).

Qasr al-Baramoudi and Qasr al-Nasima

5–7km southwest of El-Kharga • Daily 24hr • Free

Reached by a farming track turning off the highway just before the train station, these two unguarded sites have been looted since the Revolution. **Qasr al-Baramoudi** is a small Roman fort with an oven-shaped pigeon tower which once supplied the garrison with fowl. Such towers have been used in Egypt since antiquity and are still seen in the Nile Valley, but this is exceptional for being Roman and being incorporated into military architecture.

Two kilometres further southwest, **Qasr al-Nasima** is another ruined fort, with an underground shaft which possibly housed an archive of messages transmitted by carrier-pigeons between the forts in the oasis.

Qasr el-Ghweita

16km south of El-Kharga • Daily: May–Sept 8am–6pm; Oct–April 8am–5pm • ££30

Visible from behind *Hamadalla Sahara City*, where a spur-road runs off towards it, **Qasr el-Ghweita** ("Fortress of the Small Garden") is a fortified hilltop temple from the Late Period with a commanding view of the area, which was intensively farmed in ancient times. Its ten-metre-high walls enclose a sandstone temple dedicated to the Theban Triad, built by Darius I on the site of an older shrine. The Hypostyle Hall contains scenes of Hapy the Nile-god holding symbols of the nomes of Upper and Lower Egypt. Inscriptions attest to the quality of the grapes grown hereabouts; wine from Kharga was prized during the New Kingdom, if not earlier.

Qasr al-Zayan

5km from Qasr el-Ghweita • Daily: May–Sept 8am–6pm; Oct–April 8am–5pm • ££30

From Qasr el-Ghweita the spur-road loops south to **Qasr al-Zayan**, a Roman temple that lends its name to a still-thriving village built over the ancient town of Tkhonemyris. This proximity to daily life helps you imagine it as a bustling settlement in antiquity. Dedicated to Amun-Re, the temple is enclosed within a mud-brick fortress, together with living quarters for the garrison, a cistern and a bakery. The plain hereabouts is 18m below sea level, the lowest point in Kharga Oasis.

Bulaq

Returning to the highway, the next settlement, **BULAQ** (meaning "Watch"), consists of a picturesque old village to the west and a larger modern one to the east. Its rustic **hot springs** (open 24hr; free) are visible immediately before you enter town, on the right.

South of Bulaq stretch a string of New Valley settlements founded in the 1980s, named Algeria, Kuwait, Palestine, Baghdad and Aden in a gesture of Arab solidarity.

Baris

Seventy kilometres from El-Kharga, **BARIS** (pronounced "Bar-ees") is named after the French capital, though its foraging goats and unpaved streets make a mockery of a billboard welcoming visitors to "Paris".

Two kilometres before town, you'll pass the abandoned village of **Baris Gedida** (New Baris), begun in the early 1960s by architect Hassan Fathy and based on the principles of traditional oasis architecture, including wind shafts to cool the marketplace. Work was halted by the Six Day War of 1967 and never resumed, so the initial settlers soon drifted away.

More recently, Baris was poised to develop once the **Sheikh Zayed Canal** – drawing water from Lake Nasser – reached Kharga, entering the depression here, but the completion of the final 80km stretch was postponed during the Mubarak era and may never happen now that the Toshka scheme has been discredited (see box, p.367).

Temple of Dush

83km from El-Kharga • Daily: May–Sept 8am–6pm; Oct–April 8am–5pm • ££30 • Accessible by minibus from Midan Showla to Baris (about ££10) and then by private car (about ££30 round-trip), or on an organized excursion (see p.425) •

Reached via a spur-road leaving Baris next to a radio mast, the Roman **Temple of Dush** was built by Emperor Domitian and enlarged by Hadrian and Trajan, who added a monumental gateway. Reputedly once sheathed in gold, the temple is covered in dedications to the last two emperors and the gateway in **graffiti** by Frederic Cailliaud and other nineteenth-century travellers. "Dush" is believed to derive from Kush, the name of the ancient Nubian kingdom.

Abutting the temple to the east is a hilltop **fortress** dating from the Ptolemaic era, now partially buried in the sands, with mud-brick walls up to six metres high, and four or five storeys below ground.

The fortress formerly protected the ancient town of **Kysis**, an agricultural settlement enriched by the Forty Days Road (see box below), that had potters, jewellers and brothels. Since 1976 these sites have been studied by the IFAO (see p.421), which is currently investigating nearby **Ain Manawir**, three deep subterranean aqueducts that once supplied water to Kysis. From October to April visitors will find the IFAO mission in residence near the temple, and also the deluxe *Tabuna Camp*, an idyllic place to stay if you can afford it (see p.426).

Maks Bahri and Maks Qibli

From Dush, it's 32km by road to **MAKS BAHRI** ("Customs North"), a village that once lived off the infamous Forty Days Road, taxing each slave that entered the oasis, selling supplies and pandering to the slavemasters. Caravans going in the other direction were taxed at **MAKS QIBLI** ("Customs South"), where you can see a small mud-brick fort, the **Tabid el-Darawish**, built by the British after the Dervish invasion of 1893. Nowadays, the Forty Days Road has been paved as far south as Bir Tafarwi to link up with the agricultural project at East Oweinat (see box, p.435).

The Gilf Kebir

Egypt's remotest corner is dominated by the **Gilf Kebir** (Great Barrier), a 7,770-square-kilometre plateau that forms an even more formidable obstacle than the Great Sand Sea. Before its discovery by Prince Kemal el-Din in 1926, the Gilf was only known to desert nomads who saw no reason to share their knowledge with outsiders.

What subsequent European explorers found there illuminated Saharan prehistory, later inspiring the book and film *The English Patient*, relating the exploits of explorer

---

THE FORTY DAYS ROAD

Of all the trade routes between North Africa and the tropical south, the **Forty Days Road** (Darb al-Arba'in) was the one most involved in **slavery** – the only business profitable enough to justify the risks and rigours of the thousand-mile journey. The slaves, purchased at the Dongola slave market or kidnapped by the fierce desert tribes, were assembled at **Kobbé**, a town (no longer existing) 60km northwest of El-Fasher, the capital of Sudan's Darfur Province, once an independent kingdom.

After a few days' march from Kobbé, the slaves were unchained from their yokes, for there was no way to escape. With no permanent water source until Bir Natrun, 530km away, they could only survive on the ox skins of water that burdened the camels. While human losses were erased by the sands, the road gained definition from its Bactrian casualties; a 1946 survey of northwestern Sudan noted "a track about one mile wide marked with white camel bones".

Egyptian customs posts taxed caravans arriving in **Kharga Oasis**, the last stage before their ultimate destination, Assyut. As the caravans approached, small boys were hidden in empty water skins to evade tax, but officials would beat them to thwart this ploy. Traffic along the Forty Days Road ended in 1884, after the rise of the Dervish Empire in Sudan closed the border; by the time it reopened, slavery had been prohibited in Egypt. Today, a new form of human trafficking is flourishing in the far southern **Darb al-Arba'in Desert**: smuggling refugees from Darfur, Somalia and Eritrea into Libya, via the remotest region of Egypt (see p.440).

László Almásy and his discovery of the Cave of the Swimmers. This superb example of **prehistoric rock art** is only one of thousands of paintings and petroglyphs in the wadis of the Gilf and **Jebel Uwaynat**, depicting giraffes, ostriches, lions and cattle, and people hunting and swimming – before the decisive shift from savanna to desert occurred at the end of the Holocene wet period, around 5000 BC.

Since then the Gilf Kebir has become one of the **driest places on earth**. Rainfall is less than a millimetre a year, and may fall only every five years, while temperatures range from 0°C to 42°C, with as much as 30°C difference between night and day. With colossal dunes leapfrogging each other to climb the 300-metre-high escarpment, it is (like Chile's Atacama Desert and the dry valleys of Antarctica) one of the places in the world where the environment comes closest to the surface of Mars, and has been intensively studied by NASA.

Yet aeons ago in the late Tertiary age, the Gilf was a watershed draining in all directions; its wadis eroded by water and then by wind and sand over one hundred thousand years. The sheer cliffs on the south and southwest sides are the highest, while the northeasterly ones have been worn down by the Sand Sea. **Dunes** have filled up the valleys and are climbing one on top of the other; white by the Sand Sea, or red around the middle of the Gilf and its southern massif. Despite being so arid, the top of the plateau gets enough rainfall for hardy **flora and fauna** to survive: Barbary sheep, gazelles, foxes, lizards, snakes, birds and butterflies, Roses of Jericho and acacia trees. Visitors may find other surprises, too, like the wreck of a Blenheim bomber discovered on the plateau in 2001 – one of many relics from World War II.

Besides all this, visitors are drawn by the romance of the **explorers** who "discovered" the Gilf – not only Almásy, but Englishmen Ralph Bagnold, Douglas Newbold and Kennedy-Shaw, and Irishman Patrick Clayton. During World War II, they set up the Long Range Desert Group (LRDG) that wreaked havoc behind Italian and German lines, while their former comrade Almásy served on the other side with the Afrika Korps.

In 2007, the Egyptian government established the **Gilf Kebir National Park**, whose 48,533 square kilometres encompass the Gilf, Uwaynat, and the Silica Glass area of the

---

GILF SAFARIS

Jeep-safaris to the Gilf are a major logistical effort involving multiple 4WD vehicles equipped with GPS and satellite phones, authorized by a **permit** and accompanied by an armed escort of **Tourist Safari Police** – all of which add to the basic **cost** of fuel, drivers, food and water. Reckon on paying €120–150 per person per day, once everything has been factored in.

Aside from the cost there's the **bureaucracy**: you must book at least a month if not six months' ahead of the only times when the **temperature** is tolerable (Feb–March & Sept–Nov). Even so, **discomfort** is inevitable: sand gets into every crevice of your body, there's no water to spare for washing and you start to stink – like everybody else. Unless you're willing to rough it and muck in when needed, there's no point in coming at all. But if you do, you're sure to remember it for the rest of your life.

Since the kidnapping of a safari group at Uwaynat in 2008 (a wake-up call for the Egyptian authorities who had previously turned a blind eye to people being trafficked into Libya and failed to anticipate that banditry in Darfur might spill over the border), **security** is now a consideration for anyone travelling this way. Check your own government's travel advice (Germany warns its citizens not to expect to be rescued at the state's expense), and that your **insurance** covers deep-desert journeys and what (if any) back-up exists in case of **emergencies**.

Though the safari operator will supply meals, tents and bedding, you need to **bring** personal essentials such as sun block and skin cream and any luxuries like alcohol or cigarettes (the nearest supply is in Kharga or Dakhla oases). Binoculars are a must, too.

Most safari outfits will take people in their own 4WDs providing they're able to handle the **driving**, which requires experience, skill and nerve. If you have doubts on any of these scores then you should come as a passenger and let the safari team handle all the work.

Sand Sea (see p.440). Protecting this vast area is another matter, especially since the revolutions in Egypt and Libya have weakened authority at every level. Please abide by park regulations (don't disturb or remove anything), and report safari outfits engaged in trafficking artefacts to the Egyptian Environmental Affairs Agency (@eeaa.gov.eg).

Approaching the Gilf

There are two classic approaches to the Gilf. One leads southwest **from Dakhla Oasis** via **Khufu** and **Abu Ballas**, while the other assumes a more easterly starting point **from Kharga Oasis** – or even Aswan or Abu Simbel in the Nile Valley, using the **Darb al-Arba'in** (now paved as far south as Bir Kiseba) to reach **Bir Tarfawi**. It was from there that the first motorized explorers approached Jebel Uwaynat in the mid-1920s, finding the desert easier to cross than they'd expected. Approaching the Gilf **from the Great Sand Sea** to the north is more difficult, but some safaris do it, in which case Regenfeld (see p.441) is a mandatory stopover.

From Dakhla Oasis

This route was known to the Ancient Egyptians, whose Nilotic civilization had links with the desert tribes. Since 2000, German archeologists have excavated 27 way stations en route to the Gilf, part of a pharaonic trade route that may have led as far as Chad and possibly originated in Neolithic times.

Khufu

In 2000, the explorer Carlo Bergmann rediscovered a long-forgotten **site**, 40km southwest of Dakhla, now known as **Khufu** (or "Hofu" to locals). Its name refers to the IV Dynasty pharaoh (better known as Cheops) who is credited with building the Great Pyramid of Giza. His serekh symbol and an inscription attest that Khufu sent an expedition to this desolate spot to obtain mefat (the Ancient Egyptian word for powder). This is thought to refer to pigments for writing and painting, since the Dakhla region is rich in iron oxides, manganese veins and shales, all of which can be used as such. Excavations have found clay seals and pottery bearing the name of his successor, Djedefre, proving that the site was exploited for decades. Alas, much of the evidence has recently been looted.

Abu Ballas

Roughly 200km beyond Khufu, **Abu Ballas** (Father of Pots) is an ancient hillside water cache strategically located between caravan trails and springs. It was named by Prince Kemal el-Din in 1916, who found hundreds of pots big enough to hold about thirty litres of water apiece, some as old as the VI Dynasty, others stashed by Tebu nomads to sustain their raids on Dakhla during Ottoman times. Men from Dakhla eventually found the cache and smashed the pots; archeologists, explorers and tourists have since removed most of the fragments, though a few remain photogenically posed.

In the 1920s, geologist John Ball suggested that the "lost oasis" of Zerzura (see box, p.435) might actually be Abu Ballas, as its name could refer to a *zir* or earthenware water jug, rather than deriving from *zarzur* (the Arabic name for the white-crowned wheatear, a ubiquitous bird), as scholars assumed.

Halfway up the hill's southeast face you can find some **rock art**: a cow suckling its calf, a bearded hunter and his dog chasing an antelope with a bow and arrows, and the profile of a man.

Mud Lions

An hour's drive beyond Abu Ballas is a spectacular field of *yardangs* resembling basking sealions, dubbed the **Mud Lions** (or Red Lions). Formed by a similar process to the chalk *yardangs* of the White Desert (see p.409), but from a different sedimentary

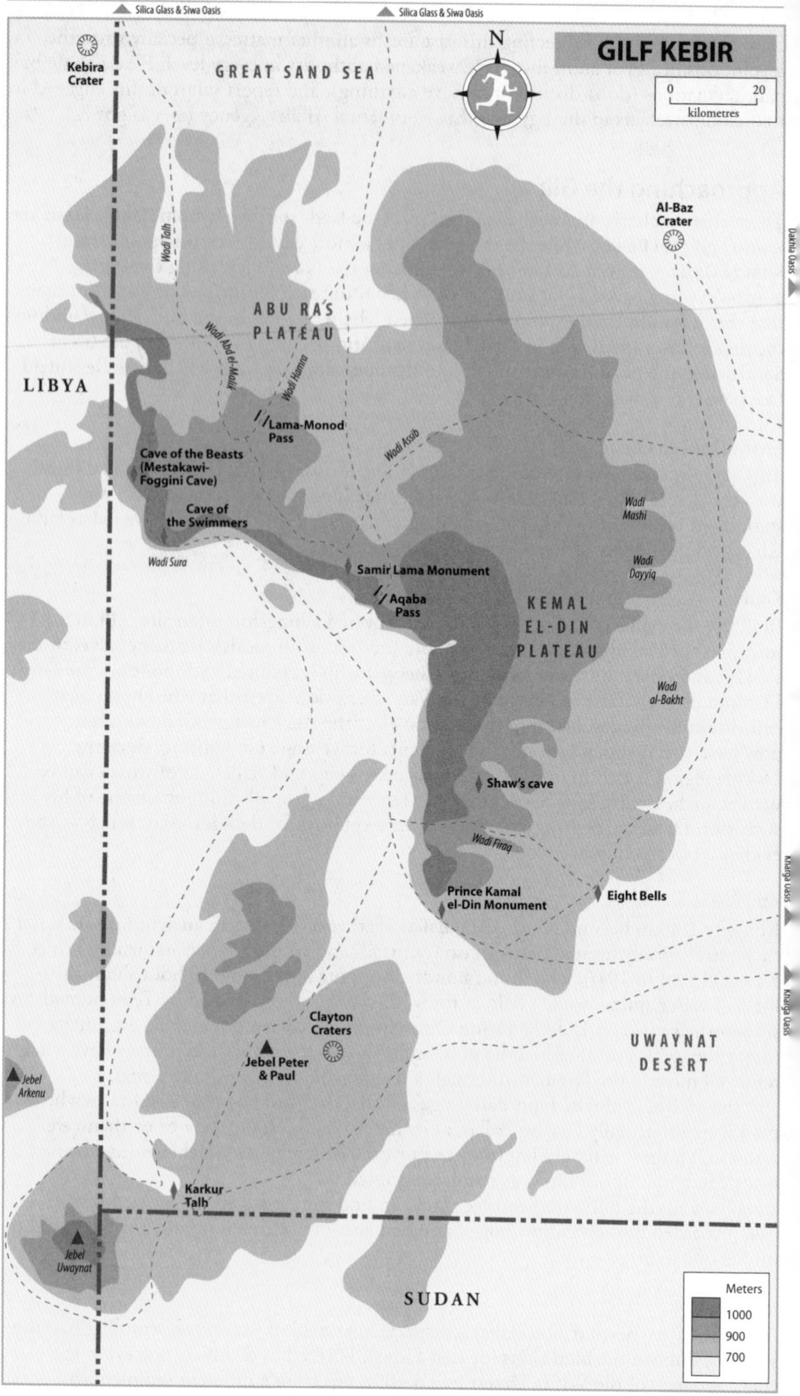

3

Silica Glass & Siwa Oasis   Silica Glass & Siwa Oasis

GILF KEBIR

N

0   20
kilometres

Kebira
Crater

GREAT SAND SEA

Al-Baz
Crater

Wadi Talh

ABU RAS
PLATEAU

Wadi Abd el-Malik

Wadi Mamra

LIBYA

Lama-Monod
Pass

Wadi Asib

Cave of the Beasts
(Mestakawi-
Foggini Cave)

Cave of
the Swimmers

Wadi Mashi

Wadi Dayyiq

Wadi Sura

Samir Lama Monument

Aqaba
Pass

KEMAL
EL-DIN
PLATEAU

Wadi al-Bakht

Shaw's cave

Wadi Firaq

Prince Kamal
el-Din Monument

Eight Bells

Jebel Arkenu

Clayton
Craters

Jebel Peter
& Paul

UWAYNAT
DESERT

Karkur
Talh

Jebel Uwaynat

SUDAN

Meters

1000
900
700

Dakhla Oasis

Kharga Oasis

Kharga Oasis

material, the Mud Lions make an irresistable photo-opportunity. Thereafter, dunes slope imperceptibly to the top of the Gilf, impeding the route to the plateau.

From Kharga Oasis

Depending on how far south you follow the Darb al-Arba'in (see box, p.431) and which roads you use, you may pass the ancient spring of **Bir Tarfawi**, in a depression, surrounded by palms, acacias and tamarisks, which was once filled by two lakes ringed by Neolithic settlements. In 1981, Space Shuttle radar imaging revealed ancient riverbeds that convinced NASA scientist Farouk Al-Baz that vast quantities of fossil water lay beneath the desert.

East Oweinat

Since Al-Baz's hypothesis was confirmed the Egyptian government has sunk wells and established experimental farms collectively named **East Oweinat** (the English spelling differentiates it from Jebel Uwaynat, which is far away, and unrelated to the project). They consist of circular fields irrigated by giant sprinklers, where high-value crops are grown for export to France from an airstrip: a surreal sight, so far into the desert. Beyond here is nothing but wilderness until Kufra Oasis in Libya, 700km away.

The "Zerzura" wadis

The Gilf consists of two massifs – the Abu Ras and Kemal el-Din plateaus – separated by an extrusion of the Great Sand Sea where the **Aqaba Pass** found by Almássy allows drivers to go from the eastern to the western side rather than having to circumvent the Gilf – a short cut that facilitated his search for the "lost oasis" of **Zerzura** (see box below). He was soon convinced that three valleys in the northern plateau (Wadi Abd el-Malik, Wadi Hamra and Wadi Talh) corresponded to Zerzura – but his identification has never been universally accepted and remains debatable. What isn't in doubt is the fantastic rock art that has been discovered in this area, where more will surely be found in the future.

THE SEARCH FOR ZERZURA

First mentioned in 1246 as an abandoned village in the desert beyond the Fayoum, the **"Lost Oasis" of Zerzura** reappeared as a fabulous city in the fifteenth-century Arabic treasure-hunters' *Book of Hidden Pearls*. Its setting was described as three valleys endowed with springs, palm trees, birds and animals, where robbers would find a city "white like a pigeon", with a bird carved on its gate. Inside were riches, and a king and queen asleep in their castle. "Do not approach them, but take the treasure", the book advised.

After the nineteenth-century Egyptologist John Wilkinson learnt of the story, the search for Zerzura obsessed European explorers. As successive desert surveys dashed hopes of finding it anywhere within reach of the known oases, attention turned to the far south, where Jebel Uwaynat and the Gilf Kebir had recently been discovered by Hassanein Bey and Prince Kemal el-Din.

In February 1932 Almássy and Lord Robert Clayton launched the **Zerzura Expedition** (the first to combine cars with light aircraft). Almássy was away visiting Kufra Oasis when Clayton and his observer Penderel flew in their Gypsy Moth biplane over the northern Gilf, sighting "an acacia-dotted wadi". After Almássy's return they made further flights and spotted two such wadis, which they planned to explore by car the following spring. But fate intervened in their plans, for Clayton died of polio on a visit to England, swiftly followed by the expedition's sponsor, Prince Kemal el-Din, leaving Almássy to seek new sponsors and Clayton's widow to continue her husband's quest independently (see box, p.437).

It was a Tebu caravan guide who told Almássy of the existence of a third valley. When asked if he knew of Zerzura, he replied: "Oh, those silly Arab people, they do not know anything, they call these three wadis in the Gilf, Zerzura, but we local people know their real names." Almássy was certain that he had identified the lost oasis at last.

Wadi Abd el-Malik

The longest (120km) of the deep fissures in the Abu Ras Plateau, **Wadi Abd el-Malik** was explored by Almássy and Penderel in 1933 using cars with balloon tyres. They found lots of acacia trees and sites of Tebu encampments, plus a large cave with **drawings** of longhorn cattle, men and a prehistoric dwelling.

Tebu **legend** has it that the valley's name was bestowed by the Senussi of Kufra Oasis, to reward a Bedouin cameleer called Ibrahim Abd el-Malik, who led them to the then-unknown wadi to seize the Tebu's camels. After he returned to Kufra, the valley was soon forgotten again, and only the Tebu remembered its real name – Zerzura. That this refutes what Almássy was told by his Tebu guide exemplifies the contradictions, ambiguities and falsehoods that bedevil all attempts to reconcile the oral folklore of the Western Desert with observable evidence.

Around the wadi

Whether or not this was Zerzura, there's plenty to see in the branches off the main wadi, especially the eastern one where Bagnold found a grotto with **paintings** of bovoids (prehistoric cattle) and **petroglyphs** of giraffes and other wild animals which have since been discovered. The eastern branch of the wadi can be reached from the top of the plateau via the **Lama-Monod Pass**, named after the Saharan explorers who first made the descent by car. **Samir Lama** (1931–2004), "The Master", founded Egypt's first desert-travel agency (1970) and is fittingly remembered by a marble plaque overlooking Wadi Sura, 40km from the pass.

Cave of the Beasts (Mestekawi-Foggini Cave)

In 2002, an expedition exploring a valley to the west of Wadi Abd el-Malik found the largest cave yet known in the Gilf, with a peerless array of prehistoric art. **Paintings** of humans, animals and bizarre headless creatures, **engravings** of cattle and ibexes, and the ghostly blown outlines of three hundred human **hands** give a vivid impression of the far distant past. The cave was initially co-named after the expedition's leader (Ahmed Mestekawi) and sponsor (Massimo Foggini), but French rock-art scholars protested that this contravened academic convention, and it should be called the **Cave of the Beasts**, while German experts preferred the proasic "Wadi Sura 2". Safari operators featuring it on their itineraries may use any of these names.

Wadi Hamra

Wadi Hamra (Red Valley), on the other side of the plateau, is another must-see. Named after its stunning red dunes (the sand is rich in ferrous oxides) offset by black cliffs, the valley resembles a Martian landscape found nowhere else in Egypt. Acacias and spiny bushes provide food for gazelles and Barbary sheep; grasses and herbs appear following freak downpours every ten or twenty years.

Though no paintings have yet been found, the wadi's sandstone rocks abound in **petroglyphs** of giraffes, oryx, ostriches, gazelles and Barbary sheep – the prey that hunter-gatherers killed with dogs, lassos, bows and arrows during the Early Holocene epoch (8000–6000/5000 BC). This rock art is thought to be centuries if not thousands of years older than the images in the Cave of the Swimmers.

Although the valley was first explored by Patrick Clayton in 1933, it was Almássy who discovered that it led up to the Gilf plateau. During the war, he reputedly tried to persuade Rommel to land glider-troops on top of the Gilf and bring them down into Wadi Hamra.

Wadi Sura

Although *The English Patient* locates the Cave of the Swimmers at Jebel Uwaynat, it actually lies in the Gilf's **Wadi Sura** (Picture Valley), where Almássy found it in

LÁSZLÓ ALMÁSSY – THE REAL "ENGLISH PATIENT"

While Michael Ondaatje's novel *The English Patient* and the subsequent Oscar-winning film rescued his name from obscurity, both took liberties with the **truth** to cast "Count Ladislaus de Almasy" as a romantic hero whose love for another man's wife sealed their fates and left him dying of burns in an Italian villa. The real story is rather different – not least because he was, in fact, gay.

Born in 1895, in Hungary, **László Ede Almásy** learned to fly while at boarding school in England. During World War I he was a fighter ace and then an aide to the last Habsburg monarch (who once mistakenly called him "Count" – a title that stuck), serving as his driver during two farcical attempts to regain the throne in 1921. Almássy then became a salesman for the off-road-car manufacturers Steyr, for whom he won many races, and in 1926 took Steyrs into the desert on the first of his numerous Sahara expeditions, about which he wrote several books. The Bedouin called him Abu Ramleh – Father of the Sands.

In 1932 he initiated the **Zerzura Expedition** (see box, p.435), with co-explorers **Lord Robert** and **Lady Dorothy Clayton-East-Clayton** (the fictional Geoffrey and Katherine Clifton), the Irish desert surveyor **Patrick Clayton** (no relation) and Squadron Leader **Godfrey Penderel**. Unlike in fiction, Lord Clayton died of a sudden illness back home, and although his widow returned to the desert to continue searching for Zerzura, she didn't meet Almássy again or share his discovery of the Cave of Swimmers – nor did she perish there in 1939, but rather in a fall from her plane in England six years earlier. Thus the motive for Almássy's collaboration with the Germans in *The English Patient* is pure invention.

As a reserve officer in the Hungarian air force (allied to Nazi Germany), he could hardly refuse being posted to Rommel's **Afrika Korps**, which used his expertise as a spotter and his photos for their official handbook – to the fury of his old companions in Egypt, many of whom were now in the LRDG (see box, p.438). Thanks to the codebreakers of Bletchley Park, the British knew of Almássy's infiltration of two German spies into Egypt, whom he guided through the Gilf to Kharga Oasis in 1941.

He later made amends by visiting Patrick Clayton in an Italian POW camp and getting him moved to a better one. Almássy himself wound up in a Soviet camp where he lost his teeth from scurvy, before a People's Court cleared him of being a Nazi sympathizer after testimony that he had sheltered Jewish neighbours in his flat in Budapest. His **final years** were spent in Africa, where he flew gliders and ran safaris. After catching dysentery in Egypt, he died in a clinic in Salzburg in 1951.

3

1933, with the Frobenius expedition that was searching for rock art at Uwaynat and in the western valleys of the Gilf that had been explored by Patrick Clayton two years earlier. Clayton's son believes that his father found the wadi and its other caves first, but it was Almássy's privilege to discover the Cave of the Swimmers and name the valley.

Shot in Tunisia, the film of *The English Patient* portrays the cave as a deep, convoluted passage, whereas it is really a shallow hollow at the mouth of the wadi, shockingly exposed to the elements (like the Cave of the Archers).

Cave of the Swimmers

The **Cave of the Swimmers** harbours well over a hundred figures in diverse styles. Its famous swimmers are 10cm long and painted in red, with small rounded heads on stalks, tadpole-shaped bodies and spidery arms and legs. Some are diving, implying that a lake once existed here (for which there's geological evidence).

A second group of figures are depicted standing, with clumsy limbs, thick torsos and pea-shaped heads; hands only appear on the larger figures. Most are dark red, with bands of white around their ankles, wrists or waists, similar to the hunters at Karkur Talh (see p.439). Still more intriguing are two yellow figures that seem to be stretching out their arms to welcome a third, smaller, red one, which may be a child and its parents. Cattle, giraffes, ostriches and dogs are also depicted on the walls.

Cave of the Archers

Not far away – beyond a patch of cliff-face where some cretin from London has carved his name – the **Cave of the Archers** contains dark red and white figures of naked men clutching bows, some of them shooting at cattle – whose presence dates these pictures to the Cattle Period (5000–2500 BC) of North African rock art.

Hans Winkler of the 1938 Monod expedition termed the style of the male figures "balanced exaggeration", since they all have wide shoulders and hips, tiny waists and tapering limbs. Feet and hands are rarely shown, and heads often omitted too – unlike the spear-carrying hunters depicted in Karkur Talh at Jebel Uwaynat, which are otherwise similar in style.

Giraffe Cave

On the sandy plain beyond the wadi's entrance, a massive boulder perched upon smaller ones forms the **Giraffe Cave**, found by Clayton in 1931. Inside are giraffes, cattle and dogs, painted in black or white. Anthropologist Roland Keller believes that the giraffe images here prefigure the headless creatures in the Cave of the Beasts (see p.436) as early avatars of the Ancient Egyptian god **Seth**, whose cult accompanied the prehistoric savanna-dwellers as they were forced to move to the Nile Valley by the increasing aridity of their hunting grounds.

The southern massif

The Kemal el-Din Plateau is named after **Prince Kemal el-Din** (1874–1932), who renounced his claim to Egypt's throne so that he could devote himself to exploring the desert using Citroën half-tracks. Besides mapping Uwaynat, he was the first explorer to sight the Gilf (which he named), and a generous patron of other expeditions. The prince is honoured by a simple **monument** near the southern tip of the massif, erected by Almássy.

Prehistoric and wartime relics

The massif's eastern flanks are riven by wadis, some easy to enter, others nearly impassable. **Wadi al-Bakht** (Valley of Luck) is blocked near its far end by a gigantic golden dune which held back an ancient lake ten thousand years ago. Analysis of the dried-out lake bed, or *playa*, has revealed much about climate change over the last twelve thousand years. Archeologists have found the remains of four **prehistoric settlements** where people lived for centuries, hunting ostriches and raising cattle around the lake, until it dried out.

THE LONG RANGE DESERT GROUP (LRDG)

Founded by Ralph Bagnold in June 1940 to reconnoitre Axis forces and engage in "piracy on the high desert", the **Long Range Desert Group**'s motto was "Not by Strength, but Guile." Led by Bagnold and other prewar explorers such as Patrick Clayton, William Kennedy-Shaw and Douglas Newbold, it consisted mainly of New Zealanders, who soon learnt the arts of desert warfare. As with Special Forces ever since, the emphasis was on self-reliance and mobility. Each patrol took all it needed for a cross-desert journey of 1500 miles (which could be doubled by establishing a forward supply dump), in stripped-down Chevy trucks fitted with sand mats and tyre-tracks (doubling as air markers for supply drops) and a sun compass invented by Bagnold. Patrols operated for up to eleven weeks as they spied on convoys or delivered SAS commandos to attack airfields – in ten months, over four hundred planes were destroyed in this way (more than the RAF managed). You can **read** about the LRDG's exploits in Bagnold's *Sand, Wind and War: Memoirs of a Desert Explorer*, Saul Kelly's *The Hunt for Zerzura*, Peter Clayton's *Desert Explorer* (about his father, Patrick), or on the LRDG Preservation Society's website ⓦ lrdg.org.

In **Wadi Dayyiq** (Narrow Valley), a large area is covered by stone-chippings left by prehistoric people shaping knives, blades and arrow-heads from hard rocks. Further north, **Wadi Mashi** (Walking Valley) gets its name because its mountains seemingly vanish and reappear as you approach it, but has yet to yield any finds. Not only prehistory has been preserved. In 1991 a World War II ammunition truck was found in the desert beyond Wadi Dayyiq. After being refuelled it started, and is now in the war museum at El-Alamein (see p.496). There are relics of the **Long Range Desert Group** (see box, p.438) all over the region, from a **Ford lorry** 10km southeast of Kemal el-Din's monument, to hundreds of metal **petrol cans** with the Shell logo, laid out to form route markers. Due to hyper-aridity, these have oxidised with a distinctive black sheen; if removed from the Gilf, they rapidly turn a dull rust-red.

An evocative example of the Long Range Desert Group's exploits is the **airstrip** with a runway marked by concentric rings of petrol cans, near **Eight Bells**, a cluster of hills and depressions in the open desert beyond the massif which is the result of a vast prehistoric drainage system which carried water south into an even larger one that fed a super-lake stretching from Lake Chad to within 600km of the Gilf.

Shaw's Cave

From Eight Bells you can venture into **Wadi Firaq** (Empty Valley), separated from a larger wadi by a col, or promontory. Scramble 100m uphill to find **Shaw's Cave** (also known by its Arabic name, Magaret el-Qantara), an overhanging shelter containing vivid black and white images of cows and more ancient giraffes – the only known **paintings** in the southern Gilf. They were found by Kennedy-Shaw in 1935, who reckoned that they were executed about eight thousand years ago.

Towards Jebel Uwaynat

Before the 2011 revolutions in Egypt and Libya, many Gilf safaris continued south to Jebel Uwaynat (see box below), but whether this will happen in the future is uncertain.

JEBEL UWAYNAT

On a map of North Africa, the ruler-straight borders of Libya, Egypt and Sudan intersect at **Jebel Uwaynat**, the highest, most isolated point in the Libyan Desert. Surrounded by sand-sheets, it rises sheerly to 1898m above the desert floor, just high enough (600m above sea level) to attract a little rainfall, which percolates down to small pools or "springs" at its base, after which Uwaynat is named.

The valleys here (called *karkurs*) are fertile if watered, and sustained communities from prehistoric times until the early 1930s, with **rock art** spanning thousands of years.

In **Karkur Talh** (Acacia Valley), Hassanein Bey found engravings of lions, giraffes, ostriches, gazelles and cows, and Shaw discovered ninety human figures drawn on the roof of a cave. These figures were lither than the hunters in the Cave of the Archers at Wadi Sura but otherwise similar, leading Winkler to conclude that both were the work of the ancient Tebu, who ranged across the Sahara from their mountainous homeland of Tibesti, in Chad (as they still do today).

After the Italians occupied Kufra and placed an outpost at Uwaynat, the possibility that it could be an unguarded back door into Egypt during wartime occurred to both Bagnold and the Italian commander Lorenzini – but not to the HQ staff-wallahs who turned down Bagnold's proposal for car patrols along the frontier. It wasn't until Italy declared war in 1940 that Bagnold was authorized to set up long-range patrols to monitor any activity. In the event, the Italians never tried anything so bold, but Almásy later slipped through from Kufra via Uwaynat and the Gilf, to guide two German spies as far as Kharga Oasis, before returning to Libya.

Since the kidnapping of a safari group at Karkur Talh in 2008, Egyptian **Border Guards** have been stationed there and an **armed resort** of eight Tourist Safari policemen has been mandatory for all expeditions to Uwaynat.

The 150km of hard-packed sand between the Gilf and Uwaynat is a natural highway for **people-traffickers** and other **smugglers** from Sudan and Libya. Although they tend to keep a distance in the event of encountering safari groups, the risk of **banditry** has grown since Gadaffi's overthrow flooded the region with weapons. It's here that safaris appreciate their military escort (who seem pretty superfluous when you're in the Gilf).

Clayton Craters

The route to Uwaynat passes a pair of trachyte peaks known as **Jebel Peter and Paul**, followed by the impressive **Clayton Craters**. Unlike craters north of the Gilf (see below), these twenty geological formations rising 100– 120m from the desert floor (the largest has a diameter of 1.5km) were not caused by meteorite-strikes or volcanic eruptions, but by magma seeping through the Paleozoic sandstone to coalesce into circular dikes.

The Great Sand Sea

Between the Gilf Kebir and Siwa Oasis lies the awesome immensity of dune fields that the explorer Gerhard Rohlfs named the **Great Sand Sea** (Bahr er-Raml in Arabic). Covering 72,000 square kilometres (roughly the size of Ireland), the Sand Sea extends for an average of 650km from north to south and 300km from east to west. Roughly two thirds of this consists of parallel *seif* dunes, sometimes over 100m high and as much as 150km long, separated by flat "corridors" one or two kilometres wide, whose northwest–southeast alignment is determined by the prevailing wind.

While these *seif* dunes are ever-moving, satellite imaging has shown that they sit atop stable whalebacked dunes. Elsewhere in the Sand Sea, *seif* dunes have descended escarpments, they have reformed as crescent-shaped *barchans*. Though shifting sands seem the only "life" in the Sand Sea, a little vegetation exists, lying dormant for years until a brief shower of rain revives it.

This spectacularly alien terrain has long fascinated explorers and scientists; now tourists are venturing in to marvel at its wonders. A **brief excursion** from Siwa Oasis to **Bir Wahed** (see p.454) will let you experience its colossal dunes without spending a fortune, while the following sites can be visited on **deep-desert safaris** (operators are listed under Bahariya, Farafra and Siwa oasis).

Silica Glass area

Among the mysteries of the Sand Sea is an oval-shaped area 80km long and 25km wide, situated north of the 25th parallel, just beyond the Gilf Kebir. Here, the dune-corridors are strewn with pale green translucent **silica glass** – a material scientists believe was created by intense heat (1600–2000°C). Its origin is still debated, but the presence of extraterrestrial elements in the glass points towards a huge meteorite-strike 26 million years ago, or the explosion of a comet high above the desert that fused the sand.

The Egyptian–American scientist Farouk Al-Baz (a pioneer in using satellites to search for water in arid areas) has identified two possible locations for a meteorite's impact. The **Kebira Crater** just across the border in Libya, north of the Gilf Kebir, has a diameter of 30km, but has yet to be proved an impact crater rather than one of volcanic origin. Another possibility is the four-kilometre-wide **Al-Baz Crater** on the other side of the Gilf Kebir, which shows all the signs of an impact crater.

Equally intriguing is the fact that silica glass was known to the Ancient Egyptians, since the **scarab** on Tutankhamun's funerary pectoral cross was carved from this material. Alas, the allure of silica glass has led to wholesale **plundering**; a few years ago, German thieves removed sixteen crates full of the stuff with the help of a safari outfit from Bahariya. With many areas now denuded of glass, please resist the temptation to take a chunk home.

Regenfeld

Another site visited on deep-desert safaris is **Regenfeld** (Rainfield), so named by Rohlfs in 1874. Bent on finding a route from Dakhla to the Libyan oasis of Kufra, Rohlfs had no idea that the Sand Sea extended so far south (though its general existence was known at the time of Herodotus). Eighteen days' march into the dunes, the expedition's camels began dying of thirst, and the party seemed doomed to perish in the Sand Sea.

Then, according to the English version of his adventures, there was torrential rainfall in a spot where barely a drop falls for years, saving their lives and replenishing their water supply. Rohlfs marked the spot with a **cairn** before he left, wondering "Will ever man's foot tread this place again?" However, in the German edition, *Drei Monate in der libyschen Wüste*, he gave no hint of supply problems – attributing his decision to turn north and follow the dune-corridors towards Siwa to sagacity rather than desperation.

Whether or not a miraculous rainfall really saved their lives, Regenfeld became a place of pilgrimage for later explorers, each of whom removed the message left by their predecessor and substituted their own within Rohlfs' cairn. In 1995, Wael Abed discovered a 50km-long swathe of stunted vegetation and plant roots beneath the dunes, which he attributed to a micro-climatic "rain belt" whose cause has yet to be determined. Abed thinks that camels (which can smell rain hundreds of kilometres away) once instinctively followed the belt of vegetation across the Sand Sea, thereby establishing a route used by the Tebu and other desert nomads ever since.

Ammonite Scarp

Heading north from Regenfeld towards Siwa, the Rohlfs expedition encountered one of the few sizable rock outcrops in the Sand Sea, an isolated scarp of fossilized cretaceous rocks from the Mesozoic Era. The expedition's paleontologist Karl von Zittel named it the **Ammonite Scarp** for its profusion of ammonites, an extinct species of mollusc dating back one hundred million years.

Aeons after the waters receded, Palaeolithic hunter-gatherers camped nearby, leaving flint spear-heads, blades and axes to be discovered. When Colonel De Lancey-Forth came this way in the 1920s, he found not only tools but also the ashes of a prehistoric campfire with the shells of baked ostrich eggs, only a few inches beneath the sand.

Siwa Oasis

Isolated by hundreds of kilometres of desert, **Siwa Oasis** remained virtually independent from Egypt until the late nineteenth century, sustaining a unique culture. Yet despite – or because of – its isolation, outsiders have been drawn here since antiquity. The legendary Army of Cambyses was heading this way when it disappeared into a sandstorm; Alexander the Great journeyed here to consult the famous Oracle of Amun; and Arabic tales of Santariyah (as the oasis was known) were common currency into the nineteenth century. In modern times, Siwa has received visits from kings and presidents, anthropologists and generals. Tourism only really began in the mid-1980s but has gathered steam since then.

The oasis offers all you could ask for in the way of desert **beauty spots**: thick palm groves clustered around freshwater springs and salt lakes; rugged massifs and enormous dunes. Equally impressive are the **ruins** of Shali and Aghurmi, labyrinthine mud-built towns that once protected the Siwans from desert raiders. Scattered around the oasis are ruined **temples** that attest to Siwa's fame and prosperity during Greco-Roman times.

Visitors are also fascinated by **Siwan culture** and how it is reacting to outside influences like TV, schooling and tourism. Nowadays, it is mostly only older women who wear the traditional costume, silver jewellery and complex hair-braids; younger wives and unmarried women dress much the same as their counterparts in the Nile Valley. But the Siwans still observe their own festivals and wedding customs; and among themselves they speak **Siwi**, a Berber tongue.

Though things are changing, the Siwans remain sure of their identity and are determined to maintain it. Siwans remain deeply conservative in matters of **dress** and **behaviour**. The tourist office asks visitors to refrain from public displays of affection, and women to keep their arms and legs covered – especially when bathing in pools. Women should also avoid wandering alone in places with few people around, especially palm groves (which is seen here as an invitation to sex). Local people are generally more reserved than Egyptians, and invitations home less common.

The **best time** to come is during spring or autumn, when the Siwans hold festivals and the days are pleasantly warm. In winter, windless days can be nice, but nights – and gales – are chilling. From May onwards, rising temperatures keep people indoors between 11am and 7pm, and the nights are sultry and mosquito-ridden. Even when the **climate** is mild you'll probably feel like taking a midday siesta or a swim.

Brief history

Beyond the fact that it sustained hunter-gatherers in Paleolithic times, little is known about Siwa Oasis before the XXVI Dynasty (664–525 BC), when the reputation of its **Oracle** spread throughout the Mediterranean world. Siwa's population seems to have been at risk from predatory desert tribes, so their first settlement was a fortified acropolis, about which Classical accounts reveal little beyond its name, **Aghurmi**, and its position as a major caravan stop between Cyrenaica and Sudan. The Siwans are related to the Berbers of Algeria, Tunisia and Morocco, and their language is a variant of the Berber tongues, so their society may have originally been matriarchal.

Shali and early Siwan society

According to the **Siwan Manuscript** (a century-old compilation of oral histories whose sole copy is seldom shown to outsiders), repeated Bedouin and Berber raids had reduced Aghurmi's population to a mere two hundred by the twelfth century AD. Around 1203, seven families left Aghurmi to found a new settlement called **Shali**, whose menfolk are still honoured as the "forty ancestors". Later, newcomers from Libya settled in the oasis, giving rise to the enduring distinction between the "Westerners" and the original "Easterners", whose historic feud began after they disagreed over the route of a causeway that both had undertaken to build across the salt lake of Birket Siwa. Nonetheless, both coexisted within a single town built of *kharsif*: a salt-impregnated mud which dries cement-hard, but melts during downpours – fortunately, it rains heavily here only every fifty years or so. Fearful of raiders, Shali's elders forbade families to live outside the walls, so as the population increased Shali could only expand upwards, with passageways regulated to the width of a donkey.

Bachelors aged between 20 and 40 had to sleep in caves outside Shali, guarding the fields – hence their nickname, *zaggalah* (club-bearers). Noted for their love of palm liquor, song and dance, they shocked outsiders with their open **homosexuality**. Gay marriages were forbidden by law in 1928, but continued in secret until the late 1940s. Today, Siwans emphatically assert that homosexuality no longer exists in the oasis – whatever may be said on ⓦgayegypt.com – and resent foreign gays inveigling their youth (who may be ostracized or gaoled as a consequence). Local Salafists believe that gays should be thrown to their death from a high place.

Another feature of Shali was the tradition of violent **feuds** between the Westerners and Easterners, in which all able-bodied males were expected to participate. Originally ritualized, with parallel lines of combatants exchanging blows between sunrise and sunset while their womenfolk threw stones at cowards and shouted encouragement,

feuds became far deadlier with the advent of firearms. Despite this, the Siwans immediately closed ranks against outsiders – Bedouin raiders, khedival taxmen or European explorers. The *Siwan Manuscript* relates how they considered poisoning the springs with mummies in order to thwart the Muslim conquest.

Modern Siwa

Paradoxical as it sounds, Siwa's biggest problem is an excess of water, Smelly, mosquito-infested ponds attest that the **water table** lies only just below the surface, and the water supply is saline or sandy, so residents have to collect water from springs by donkey. Engineers are installing a water-purification plant at Dakhrour, but it will be some years before it's finished.

The road to Mersa Matrouh (completed in 1984) has spurred exports of dates and olives, along with tourism to the oasis, Some five hundred Siwan **women** are now stitching traditional embroidery for an Italian company, earning twice the local wage for an agricultural labourer: the unmarried ones have saved so much money that they can be choosy about taking a husband.

Meanwhile, the Siwans' desire for breeze-block houses with proper bathrooms rather than the traditional dusty mud-brick dwellings has alarmed conservationists. Britain's Prince Charles is among the VIPs backing the **Friends of Siwa Association**, a conservation body set up by **Mounir Nematalla** (see p.454). Many locals regard the Friends of Siwa as a scam to embezzle donations, and resent Nematalla for expropriating part of Shali for his own profit.

In 2002, Italian NGOs helped establish the **Siwa Protected Area** to safeguard some 7,800 square kilometres within and beyond the oasis. The three protected zones harbour mammals (two species of gazelles and four kinds of desert fox), birds (26 species breeding locally, plus seventy migratory) and prehistoric fossils. There are no restrictions on visiting these zones, though a permit (see p.449) is needed for some trips.

Siwa Town

Most visitors rate **SIWA TOWN** and the pools, rocks and ruins around it as the oasis's main attractions. The town has expanded as its population has risen to 25,000 (at least one thousand of them from outside the oasis), and people have moved into modern housing, forsaking traditional mud-brick dwellings – just as their ancestors had previously abandoned the fortified hilltop city of **Shali**, whose ruins overlook the modern town. Wide roads debouch onto a central market area, but the town slips away into a maze of alleyways, and loses itself amid the encircling palms.

Souk and Mosque of Sidi Suleyman

Midan el-Souk is the hub of Siwan life, at its busiest on Fridays, when farmers come in from the villages to sell their produce and buy consumer goods. Plate-glass windows and neon signs have mushroomed in recent years, and noisy tuk-tuks (motorized rickshaws) are displacing carettas (donkey carts) as local transport – all signs of growing prosperity, largely based on tourism and, more recently, smuggling.

For Siwan men, another focal point is the **Mosque of Sidi Suleyman**, built by King Fouad next to the whitewashed **tomb** of Siwa's patron sheikh. According to folklore, the sheikh's miraculous powers were manifest even before he was born, for when his pregnant mother craved fish a pigeon dropped a fully cooked one at her feet. He is also said to have once conjured up a sandstorm to bury an army of Tebu raiders. His devotees perform *zikrs* outside the tomb on Thursday evenings, but no longer hold an annual moulid in his honour (see box, p.448).

Ruins of Shali

The **ruins of Shali**, dramatically floodlit in the evening, are a standing invitation to

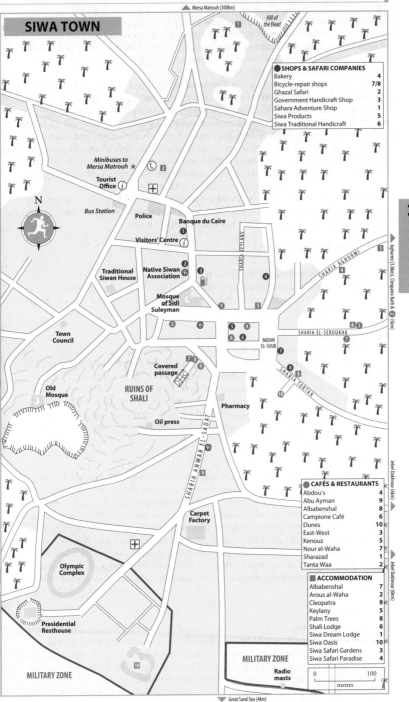

SIWA TOWN

Mersa Matrouh (300km)

Hill of the Dead

Minibuses to Mersa Matrouh ★

Tourist Office

Bus Station

Police

Banque du Caire

Visitors' Centre

Sharia Keylany

Sharia Aghurmi

Aghurmi (3.8km), Cleopatra Bath & (5km)

Traditional Siwan House

Native Siwan Association

Mosque of Sidi Suleyman

Town Council

SHARIA EL-SEBOUKHA

MIDAN EL-SOUK

Old Mosque

RUINS OF SHALI

Covered passage

Pharmacy

SHARIA TOFTAR

Oil press

SHARIA ANWAR EL-SADAT

Carpet Factory

Jebel Dakhrour (4km)

Jebel Dakhrour (6km)

Olympic Complex

Presidential Resthouse

MILITARY ZONE

MILITARY ZONE

Radio masts

0 — 100
metres

Great Sand Sea (4km)

explore. Until the 1890s, this hermetic labyrinth attained a height of over 60m, with many levels of chambers, passages and granaries whose remains cover the entire saddle of rock below Siwa's **Old Mosque**. Built in 1203, its crooked minaret is said to have been the last one in Egypt where the muezzin still shouted out the call to prayer without the benefit of a loudspeaker.

Shali's main entrance is beside the **Albabenshal hotel** (see p.448), seamlessly grafted onto its fortified walls. Many locals are miffed by its owner's expropriation of a listed monument, but not the Friends of Siwa Association (see p.444). From vantage points within Shali you can see the whole modern town, its palm groves, the salt lakes and table-top rocks beyond. Some buildings have recently been bought and restored by foreigners, around 45 of whom live semi-permanently in Siwa. Anglo-Yugoslav **Nada** is currently restoring her house using kharsif and other traditional materials. Should you encounter Nada, you might be invited to see delightfully warped split-level interior (there isn't a straight line in the place), and meet her donkey.

Behind the hill is a donkey-driven **oil-press**, only used in December and January, which dates back centuries. You may also hear a **blacksmith** plying his trade among the abandoned houses used as stables, just outside Shali's walls.

Traditional Siwan House

Mon–Thurs & Sun 9am–2pm • £E5

The **Traditional Siwan House** (Beit Siwi) was set up by a Canadian diplomat's wife who feared that few such kharsif dwellings would survive. The two-storey house is a veritable museum of traditional costumes, jewellery and toys, and a visit can help you to distinguish antiques from replicas in local handicrafts shops.

Hill of the Dead

Jebel al-Mawta, 1km from the centre • Daily 9am–5pm • £E25

By following the Mersa Matrouh road out of town and then bearing right, you'll reach the unmistakable **Hill of the Dead**. Among scores of XXVI Dynasty and Ptolemaic tombs re-used by the Romans, who cut niches (*loculi*) for their own burials, four on the north side of the hill still retain murals or inscriptions. A custodian will unlock them if you buy a ticket, and might let you climb the hill to enjoy the view without paying anything. For baksheesh, he'll also unlock other (unpainted) tombs, to reveal **mummies** found in the necropolis.

Tomb of Si-Amun

Discovered in 1940, when the Siwans dug into the necropolis to escape Italian air raids, the **Tomb of Si-Amun** was promptly vandalized by British soldiers who cut sections from the walls of the corridor – while some murals had already been destroyed in Roman times, when loculi were cut into the walls. Even so, you can still identify Ancient Egyptian gods and the tomb's owner, Si-Amun, thought to have been a wealthy merchant of Greek origin who married an Egyptian and had two sons during the third century BC. He is portrayed in Egyptian dress, with a beard and thick curly hair; one of his sons wears a Grecian-style short cloak. You can also see embalming scenes, the Judgement of Osiris, and an elaborately decorated ceiling in the burial chamber.

Tomb of Mesu-Isis

The **Tomb of Mesu-Isis**, 20m east of the Tomb of Si-Amun, is named after its owner's wife (the only name that could be deciphered). Built around the same time as Si-Amun's tomb, the doorway has a colourful cornice topped by 21 *uraei* and flanked by paintings of Isis and Osiris. An unpainted corridor leads to the burial chamber, where loculi were cut into the side walls in Roman times.

Tomb of the Crocodile

The **Tomb of the Crocodile** reflects Siwa's longstanding ties to the Fayoum, where the crocodile cult once flourished. A yellow-and-red crocodile appears beneath its unknown owner and Amun, to the right of a niche, above which two foxes nibble a stylized fruit tree.

Tomb of Niperpathot

One of the oldest in Siwa, dating from the XXVI Dynasty, the **Tomb of Niperpathot** belonged to a priest of Osiris, identified by lengthy inscriptions in the burial chamber. Its crudely drawn scenes include a depiction of the ceremony called the "dragging of the four calves", originally featured on the walls of temples during the Old Kingdom.

Olympic Stadium and Presidential Resthouse

1km south of the centre at the far end of Sharia Anwar el-Sadat

A vanity project from the Mubarak era, built in support of Egypt's failed bid to host the 2004 Games, Siwa's incongruously pink and empty **Olympic Stadium** lies within an army base to the south of town. With seating for twenty thousand, the stadium could accommodate most of the population of the oasis, but its athletics track and other facilities are only used by a few officers, and guards turn visitors away.

You can, however, glimpse a **Presidential Resthouse** originally built for King Fouad, perched on an outcrop overlooking the road towards Bir Wahed (see p.454). Another gate allows access to the perpetually guestless *Siwa Oasis* hotel, which used to be named after Egypt's former dictator.

3

ARRIVAL AND DEPARTURE   **SIWA OASIS**

Siwa can be approached from two directions only. Almost all traffic uses the road turning off the **Mediterranean coastal highway** near Mersa Matrouh. As the other route – from **Bahariya Oasis** – is only accessible by jeep.

To and from Cairo, Alexandria and Mersa Matrouh
The West and Middle Delta Bus Co. operate daily a/c buses to Siwa. The overnight service (8pm; 9–10hr; ££75) from Cairo Gateway (see p.175) bypasses Alexandria using the El-Alamein Desert Rd, and halts for 30min at Mersa Matrouh bus station, before continuing to Siwa (300km) on the same road taken by buses from Alexandria (10hr; see p.483) and Mersa Matrouh (4–5hr; see p.498). It is also possible to reach Siwa from Mersa Matrouh by minibus (££20/passenger) or private taxi (££300 for up to three people). Leaving Siwa, buy tickets at the bus station near the tourist office the night before to be sure of getting a seat on the morning buses to Mersa Matrouh or Alexandria (7am & 10am). There is also an overnight bus (10pm), and sometimes a 5pm service too. Minibuses from beside the Mosque of Sidi Suleyman run 24hr to Mersa Matrouh, and there are taxi drivers willing to drive to Matrouh (££300), Alex (££600) or even Cairo (££900). All traffic halts briefly at *Bir Nous* (Halfway Well), a grubby resthouse betweeen Siwa and Matrouh selling

tea, soup and soft drinks, and at several military checkpoints en route.

To and from Bahariya Oasis This deep-desert route (420km) has only been tarmacked for 250km and can take anything from four to six hours, depending on how much sand has blown across the road. Travelling in either direction requires a permit (see box, p.449); vehicles usually travel in a convoy, as an army guide with a satellite-phone is mandatory. Anyone planning to drive themselves will need a 4WD with ample fuel and water, and must register their licence number when getting a permit and arranging a guide. Local safari operators in Bahariya (see p.400) and Siwa (see p.449) charge ££1500 for the journey (split between up to four people). In Siwa, you can advertise for fellow travellers at the tourist office or the Native Siwan Association. Always ask whether the quoted price is for a non-stop journey, bypassing all the uninhabited oases off the road, or whether you get to see one or two of them. Some outfits in Siwa offer a ride straight on to the White Desert in Farafra Oasis (see p.409) and camping there, for ££2500–2800 (including meals).

INFORMATION

Native Siwan Association (NSA) Opposite the petrol station, 100m from the centre ☎046 460 2110 or ☎010 0920 2346, ✉siwaegypt.com. On the first floor of a block of flats, this NGO arranges permits for trips to Bir Wahed, Bahariya Oasis and other destinations. They also teach environmental awareness to safari outfits, and

3

SIWAN FESTIVALS

Traditional **Siwan festivals** rooted in Sufism are anathema to the Salafists who have become increasingly powerful in the oasis since the 2011 Revolution. Believing that Muslims should only celebrate Islamic New Year, the Prophet's birthday and the end of Ramadan, they regard other moulids as akin to paganism and have now succeeded in putting an end to the traditional **Moulid at-Tagmigra** (honouring Siwa's patron sheikh, Sidi Suleyman) and **Ashura** celebrations for children, with singing and torchlit processions.

Other Siwans have, however, so far ignored their demands to abolish **Eid el-Siyaha**, when around ten thousand people gather at Jebel Dakhrour to celebrate the date harvest with three days of festivities. Quarrels are resolved, friendships renewed, and everyone partakes of a huge feast after the noon prayer, blessed by a sheikh from Sidi Barrani. Many outsiders come too, and are made welcome – though women should keep a respectful distance from the circles of men performing Sufi *zikrs*. Siyaha occurs during the period of the full moon in October, unless this coincides with Ramadan, in which case it's postponed until November. It's wise to reserve a room well in advance and get there several days early, as buses to the oasis fill up nearer the time.

Another event – far from traditional – is the **Siwan Art Project**, founded by the enterprising Nematalla. Staged every two or three years, the Art Project (featured on ⓦ siwa.com) has previously seen thousands of kites set ablaze on Dakhrour and a "Ship of Siwa" launched on Birket Zeitun. The 2011 event was cancelled due to post-revolutionary insecurity, but it will hopefully take place in 2013.

organize clean-up days in the desert. Daily 9.30am–3pm.

Tourist office Near the bus station, 300m north of the centre ☎ 046 460 1338 or ☎ 010 0546 1992, ✉ mahdi _hweiti@yahoo.com). The tourist office's engaging manager Mahdi Hweiti knows everything about the oasis, can arrange trips to outlying villages and will show you a film about Siwan culture. Should you have any trouble in Siwa, go to Mahdi rather than the police. May–Sept daily 9am–2.30pm & 7–10pm, Fri 11am–1pm; Oct–April daily except Fri 9am–2.30pm & 5–8pm.

Visitors' centre Midway between the NSA and the tourist office ☎ 046 046 0870. An informative two-room exhibition devoted to the fauna, flora and geology of the Siwa Protected Area, sponsored by an Italian NGO. Daily except Fri 9am–3pm.

GETTING AROUND

On foot The best way of exploring Siwa Town, and the only way to visit Shali. If it's not too hot, a walk through the palm groves to Aghurmi (see p.452) or Fatnis (see p.454) can be a pleasure.

By bicycle Many places in the oasis are within cycling range. Bikes can be hired (£E15/day) from bicycle-repair shops on Midan el-Souk; the machines rented out by hotels are generally less reliable.

By caretta Donkey-drawn carts used to be the only form of transport in Siwa, and are still used for ferrying local women around. Usually driven by adolescent boys,

carettas are marginally faster than walking. Aghurmi and Dakhrour are often combined in a round-trip by caretta.

By jeep The only means of reaching Bir Wahed (see p.454), Qara Oasis (see p.456) and other remote sights, with excursions arranged by safari operators and hotels.

By taxi All villages within the oasis can be reached by 2WD. Mahdi at the tourist office (see above) can arrange excursions with a reliable driver.

By tuk-tuk Motorized rickshaws are displacing carettas as local transport.

ACCOMMODATION

Siwa has both budget and upmarket **hotels**, including two lakeside **eco-lodges** 16km from town. While it's worth reserving ahead if you're fussy about where you stay, the only time it's essential to do so is during the Eid el-Siyaha (see box above), when tour groups block-book hotels. People wanting their own space can rent **apartments** sleeping one or two people (£E100/£E800–1000/day/month) through the tourist office. Places out of town are marked on the map of Siwa Oasis on p.453.

SIWA TOWN

Albabenshal Midan el-Souk ☎ 046 460 2399, ⓦ siwa .com. Named the "Door of the Country" in Siwi, this austerely lovely "heritage lodge" occupies several old houses at the base of Shali, built of *kharsif* and salt-slabs

like *Adrère Amellal* (see below) and with wonderful views from its rooftop restaurant. With only eleven rooms, reservations are essential. B&B **£E385**

Arous al-Waha Opposite the tourist office ☎ 046 460 0028. A state-owned hotel, the "Bride of the Oasis" has worn but clean rooms with fans, shower-cabins and fridges. Hardly anyone stays here, but if you don't mind the lack of other guests it's not a bad option. **£E60**

Cleopatra Sharia Anwar el-Sadat ☎046 460 0421. A little way south of the main square, this rather forlorn hotel has simple rooms, some with a toilet, balcony and fan; rooms in the "chalet" block out the back (£E85) also have TV and fridges, but are plagued by mosquitoes. **£E35**

Keylany Midan el-Souk ☎046 460 0415. Initially quite tempting for its central location and rooftop chill-out zone, guests later discover the downside of noise from the bazaar. Some rooms are en suite (£E20 extra), with a/c and balconies (£E50 extra). Their safari trips are worth checking out, even if you don't stay there. **£E50**

Palm Trees Sharia Tortar ☎046 460 1703, ✉M_S_Siwa@yahoo.com. Just off Midan el-Souk, this ultra-laidback, rather grungy hotel is popular for its lovely but mosquito-ridden palm garden and its quiet, central location. Choose between basic rooms with fans (a bathroom costs £E10 extra) and an erratic water supply in the main block, and a/c bungalows (£E75) out the back. **£E55**

Shali Lodge Sharia el-Seboukha ☎046 460 1299, ⊛siwa.com. The prototype for *Albabenshal* and *Adrère Amellal* (and under the same management), this bijou hotel is built of *kharsif* and palm-logs, with rock-walled bathrooms and palm trees growing up through the floor of its rooftop restaurant. B&B **£E385**

Siwa Dream Lodge Near the Hill of the Dead ☎046 460 0272 or ☎010 0099 9255, ⊛siwadreamlodgehotel .com. Existing in splendid isolation a 15min walk from town, with ancient tombs on its doorstep, *Siwa Dream Lodge* has comfortable domed bungalows around a spring-fed pool, and a café with Bedouin-style trimmings. B&B **£E370**

Siwa Oasis Olympic complex ☎046 460 0883, ✉info@ siwaoasishotel.net. Formerly named after Egypt's late dictator, Mubarak, the antiseptic a/c rooms with satellite TV and fridge, chalets with lounges and lavish VIP suites find few takers, despite guests being able to enjoy a jacuzzi, sauna, squash and other sports facilities. Half-board deals available. B&B **£E225**

Siwa Safari Gardens Sharia Aghurmi ☎046 460 2801, ⊛siwagardens.com. Outside town but only 5min walk from the centre, this cosy tourist enclave consists of domed en-suite chalets with wi-fi and a/c in a large shady palm grove with a cold spring-fed pool. Room rates include half board. **£E400**

Siwa Safari Paradise Sharia Aghurmi ☎046 460 1590 or ☎012 2405 8074, ⊛siwaparadise.com. A mini-tourist village comprising a mix of bungalows (with fridges, fans and satellite TV), plus a/c rooms and extra-spacious VIP rooms ($25/50 extra) closer to the hotel's cold spring-fed swimming pool. Wi-fi throughout. All rates include half board. **$55**

PERMITS AND EXCURSIONS FROM SIWA

Though most of Siwa Oasis is freely accessible, you need a **24-hour permit** from Military Intelligence to visit Bir Wahed (see p.454), Shiatta (p.455) and Qara Oasis (p.456), or to travel the road to Bahariya (p.394). In each case there's a fee of £E40 per person, and you must supply a photocopy of your passport details the day before (two days before Fri & Sat). **Applications** can be processed by local safari operators or through the helpful **Native Siwan Association** (see p.447), and any problems can usually be resolved with the help of Mahdi al-Hweiti at the tourist office (see p.448). **Multi-day permits** (for the Qattara Depression or overnight stays in the oases between Siwa and Bahariya) are harder to obtain and need to be submitted through a fully licensed safari operator at least a month in advance.

EXCURSIONS

Jeep safaris are the rule in Siwa, but **camel-trekking** is also possible. Wherever you plan to go, it pays to shop around. Siwa's tourist office can often arrange trips more cheaply than **safari operators** based at hotels, shops or restaurants. Among those worth asking are the *Keylany* and *Palm Trees* hotels; Ali Ashwaraf (☎010 0304 1191) who hangs out at the handicrafts shop next door to *Abdou's*; and Ghazal Safari (☎010 0277 1234, ⊛ghazalsafari.com), near the Native Siwan Association. Camel-trekking is also available (to guests only) at *Adrère Amellal* and the *Taziry Ecolodge*. The Safari Adventure Shop (☎010 0203 0215, ✉elsiway@hotmail.com) near Siwa's bank has a wide range of **equipment** for rent, from sleeping bags to dune-surfing boards and GPS handsets (deposit required).

CAMEL-TREKKING

Sherif Fahmy Based at *Tala Ranch*, Sherif Fahmy charges £E200/person for a 4hr sunset trip into the Sand Sea; £E300 for a half-day trip with lunch; £E350 for an overnight stay in the desert (minimum two people); and £E650/person/day for three-day safaris. On longer trips you can learn how to saddle, mount and feed a camel.

JEBEL DAKHROUR

Al-Zaytuna Resort 3.5km east of town ☎012 2222 4209, ⊛alzaytuna.com. Very peaceful, with a vast garden with mulberry and fig trees, a pool, a playground and views of Dakhrour. The spacious rooms come with duvets and satellite TV (a/c £E20–30 extra) and meals are prepared from organic ingredients. Sand saunas (see p.454) can be arranged. B&B **£E220**

Siwa Shali Resort 5km from town ☎046 921 0064, ⊛siwashaliresort.com. Mainly used by Italian tour groups, this slick *kharsif*-style complex of a/c rooms boasts a 200m-long serpentine pool, a Turkish bath, billiards, a piano and a desert library. B&B **£360**

Tala Ranch 10km from town ☎010 0588 6003, ✉talaranchsiwa@hotmail.com. To get close to the desert, stay at this Bedouin-style residence beside the Sand Sea, which has six stylish *kharsif* chalets smelling enticingly of resin, a Bedouin tent where meals are served and camels to ride in the desert. B&B **£E448**

BIRKET SIWA

Adrère Amellal (aka the *Ecolodge*) 16km from town ☎010 0121 7175 or ☎010 0166 2743, ⊛adrereamellal.net. An amazing mud-brick complex with superb views over the lake, a huge pool and palm garden, and candle-lit rooms encrusted with salt-crystals (see p.454). Amenities include horseriding ($55/hr) and a 24hr bar with imported liquor. Rates include two trips a day into the desert, all meals and unlimited alcohol. **$605**

Taziry Ecolodge 15km from town ☎010 6380 4314, ⊛taziry.com. Around the shore from *Adrère Amellal*, this equally sustainable hotel (whose name means "Moon" in Siwi) is similar in style, though with less greenery around its lakeside pool. Accommodation is in single and double rooms, and chalets ($260) sleeping up to five people; electricity, wi-fi and phone coverage are limited to the reception area. B&B **$145**

EATING AND DRINKING

As oases go, Siwa is good for **eating**, with a couple of places in town whose ambience is chic by desert standards – though nothing compared to *Adrère Amellal or the Taziry Ecolodge* outside town (restricted to guests). Alcohol is only available at *Adrère Amellal*, or in private homes (bought in from Alexandria, or locally distilled from dates), and any **drinking** must be discreet.

SIWA TOWN

★ **Abdou's** Midan el-Souk ☎046 460 1243. The first place in Siwa to serve meals, this shaded outdoor café remains the hub of tourism due to its lengthy menu of breakfasts, pizzas, salads, grills and fresh juices – all at reasonable prices – and its prime location for people-watching. If you want to meet safari guides or find other travellers to share the cost of the journey to Bahariya Oasis, *Abdou's* is where to go. Daily 8.30am–11pm.

Abu Ayman Midan el-Souk. Abu Ayman only cooks one dish: juicy chickens grilled over an old oil-drum, well-seasoned with herbs and served with bread and *tahina* (£E25). His eatery is as basic as it gets in Siwa, but has a loyal following among locals. Daily noon–9pm.

★ **Albabenshal** Midan el-Souk ☎046 460 1499. This moodily lit rooftop restaurant has stunning views of Shali, whose ruins loom above it. The menu is similar to that of its sister-hotel restaurant *Kenouz* (see below), but the cooking is superior and prices slightly higher. Daily 8am–10pm.

Campione Café Midan el-Souk ☎046 460 1719. "Life's too short for bad coffee" is their slogan. You can't fault their Italian espresso (£E8), cappuccino (£E12) or choice of music (Billy Holiday), and it's a good place to watch streetlife from a divan, but their pancakes and pizzas are awful. Daily 7am–1am.

Dunes Sharia Tortar ☎010 0653 0372. One of several simple restaurants amid the palm groves, with a menu covering everything from pancakes to couscous, chicken biryani and grilled pigeon – although nobody minds if you simply linger for an hour or so over a sheesha. Daily noon–10pm.

East-West Midan el-Souk ☎046 460 1212. Named after the historic rival clans of Shali (see p.442), this longstanding competitor to *Abdou's* isn't half as good, with a gloomy interior where the only dishes worth trying are *fuul* or *taamiya*. People mainly come here to sit outside over a tea or juice and watch life go by. Daily 9am–midnight.

Kenouz Shali Lodge, Sharia el-Seboukha ☎046 460 1299. A nice rooftop setting for dinner, offering salads, pizzas and the chef's specialities, chicken with romaniya (brown lentils, olives and corriander; £E55), goose (£E80) and roast goat (£E90) – the last two must be ordered 24hr ahead. Try the date crêpes for dessert. Daily 8am–10pm.

Nour el-Waha Sharia el-Seboukha ☎046 460 0293. The "Light of the Oasis" is another al fresco joint whose menu features all the usual dishes. With plenty of shade, backgammon, dominoes, and occasional live music, you can easily while away time here. Daily noon–10pm.

★ **Sharazad** Midan el-Souk ☎046 460 2014. Named after the story-telling heroine of *A Thousand and One Nights*, this rooftop café is a fine place to relax, with divans, mellow music, wi-fi, sports TV and *sheeshas*. Prices are slightly above average, but everything is delicious – pizzas, spag bol, kofta, savoury pancakes and brownies. Daily 10am–1am.

SIWAN CRAFTS

Traditional crafts still flourish in Siwa, though some designs and materials are new. Authentic **wedding dresses** embellished with antique coins, shells or beads, and black **robes** with orange or red piping, have narrower braiding than the versions made for the tourist market. Women also weave **carpets** and all sorts of **baskets** made from palm-fronds. The largest is the *tghara*, used for storing bread; smaller kinds include the red and green silk-tasselled *nedibash* or platters like the *tarkamt*, used for serving sweets. They also mould **pottery** and fire it at home in bread-ovens, creating robust cooking and storage pots, delicate oil lamps and a kind of baptismal crucible called the *shamadan en sebaa*. Popular buys include the *adjra*, used for washing hands, and *timjamait*, or incense burners.

Unlike the gold-loving Egyptians, Siwans have traditionally preferred **silver jewellery**, which served as bullion for a people mistrustful of banks and paper money. The designs are uniquely Siwan, influenced by Berber rather than Egyptian heritage. Local silversmiths once produced most of it, but in modern times it has largely come from Khan el-Khalili. Broad silver bracelets and oval rings wrought with geometric designs are the most popular items with visitors, while *Al-Salhat*, with its six pendants hung from silver and coral beads, is the easiest type of necklace to identify. You'll also recognize the *tiyalaqan*, a mass of chains tipped with bells, suspended from huge crescents; and the *qasas*, an ornament for the head consisting of silver hoops and bells suspended from matching chunks of bullion.

Margaret May Vale's *Sand and Silver* (sold at the tourist office) is the definitive guide to Siwan handicrafts.

ELSEWHERE

★ **Tanta Waa** Cleopatra's Bath, near Aghurmi ☏ 010 0472 9539. You can't get more chilled than this funky haven with hammocks and *sheeshas*, and a menu featuring salads, meat and pasta dishes – the lasagne alone is worth the journey. It's easy to spend an entire day here, and evening meals or parties can be arranged if you book ahead. Daily 9am–sunset.

SHOPPING

The shops on Midan el-Souk are well supplied with canned goods, sweets, juices and bottled water, while Siwa's market has seasonal vegetables, dates and olives galore, which you can sample before buying.

Bakery Off Midan el-Souk. A hole-in-the-wall outlet for freshly baked pitta bread, while during the Siyaha festival (see box, p.448) and on the Prophet's birthday, they also bake *argheef* (bread sweetened with sugar or dates) and *enkota* (buns flavoured with dates and black pepper). Daily 24hr.

Government Handicraft Shop Near the petrol station. This shop sells Siwan embroidery, jewellery, basketware and pottery at fixed prices, providing a benchmark for haggling at the private shops in the souk. Daily except Fri 9am–4pm.

Siwa Products Midan el-Souk. If you're looking for gastronomic gifts, this is the place to buy locally sourced olive oil, marinated olives and dates (some stuffed with chocolate or almonds). Daily 10am–10pm.

Siwa Traditional Handicraft Midan el-Souk. Of all the private handicrafts shops, this has the widest range of embroidery, jewellery and basketware (some designs made purely for tourists). Daily 10am–8pm.

DIRECTORY

Banks and exchange Banque du Caire (Sat–Thurs 8.30am–2pm, also 5–8pm from Oct–April), reputedly the world's only all-mud-brick bank, has an ATM that usually works. Some hotels may exchange Euros or US dollars.

Hospital Siwa's public hospital on Sharia Anwar el-Sadat (☏ 046 460 0459) lacks such basic equipment as defibrilators, while the Mother and Child clinic facing the tourist office doesn't have any doctors or nurses. If seriously ill, seek treatment in Alexandria or Cairo.

Internet access Desert Net Café (daily 11am–3pm & 7pm–2am), across the landing from the Native Siwan Association; Tiger Shali Net Café (irregular hours), above *Abdou*'s restaurant (accessible by an alleyway to the west).

Pharmacy Sharia Anwar el-Sadat ☏ 046 460 1310 (daily 8am–2pm & 4–11pm). For less than life-threatening complaints, seek help here.

Police In a mud-brick "fort" near the tourist office ☏ 046 460 1008 (daily 24hr).

Tourist police In the same building as the police ☏ 046 460 2047.

Around Siwa Oasis

Although the Siwa depression is some 82km long and up to 28km wide, cultivated areas amount to less than two thousand acres and the total population is only thirty thousand; in some areas both population and cultivation have diminished since salination turned ancient gardens into barren *kharsif*. Nearer town, dense **palm groves** and wiry olive trees are carefully tended in mud- and palm-leaf-walled gardens. Siwa has over three hundred thousand palm trees, each yielding about 90k of dates a year and requiring some 30l of water every day.

Aghurmi

4km east of Siwa Town (follow the road straight on past a crossroads and the modern village to reach the ruins) • Accessible on foot (1hr), by bicycle (20min), or by caretta or tuk-tuk (about £E30 for up to three people for a 2hr circuit including Aghurmi's temples and baths, and Jebel Dakhrour)

From Siwa's Midan el-Souk, you can follow a country road through the palm groves – a pleasant walk if it isn't too hot and you're not intending to venture far beyond **AGHURMI** and the ruins of the ancient Siwans' first fortified settlement. Raised on a hill 12m above the plain and entered by a single gateway, ancient Aghurmi had its own well, rendering it impervious to sieges, and was home to the celebrated Oracle Temple of Amun, whose former petitioners included Alexander the Great. The fortified ruins still afford a superb **view** encompassing the salt lakes of Birket Siwa and Birket Zeitun, Jebel Dakhrour and Siwa Town in the distance, and a great mass of palms.

Oracle Temple

Daily: May–Sept 9am–5pm; Oct–April 9am–4pm • £E25

Fakhry dates Aghurmi's **Oracle Temple** (signposted as the "Alexander Crowning Hall") to the reign of the XXVI Dynasty ruler Amasis the Drunkard (570–526 BC) but reckons it evolved from an older site dedicated to Amun-Re, which others have attributed to the ram-headed Libyan god Ammon. A hilltop **citadel** encloses the temple, along with deep wells that enabled the occupants to withstand seiges.

A Persian army sent to destroy the Oracle was obliterated by the desert (see box, p.410); emissaries from the Athenian statesman Cimon (or Timon, as Shakespeare misspelt it) were told of his death as it happened; and Lysander tried bribery to win the oracle's endorsement of his claim to the Spartan throne. But the most famous petitioner was **Alexander the Great**. Having liberated Egypt from its hated Persian rulers and ordered the foundation of Alexandria (see p.462) he hurried to Siwa in 331 BC. It's thought that he sought confirmation that he was the son of Zeus (who the Greeks identified with Amun), but the oracle's reply – whispered by a priest through an aperture in the wall of the sanctuary – is unrecorded, and Alexander kept it secret unto his death in Asia eight years later.

Temple of Amun

200m from the Oracle Temple • Daily 24hr • Free

In ancient times the Oracle Temple was linked by a ritual causeway to a **Temple of Amun**, which is known locally as "Um Ubayda". Probably founded by Nectanebo II (360–343 BC), who also rebuilt the Temple of Hibis at Kharga Oasis, a bas-reliefed wall and giant blocks of rubble are all that remain of this once-substantial XXX Dynasty creation after it was dynamited by a treasure-hunting local governor in 1897.

Cleopatra Bath

200m from the Temple of Amun • Daily 24hr • Free

From the Temple of Amun follow the path on to reach Ain Juba, known to tourists as the **Cleopatra Bath**. A deep circular pool of gently bubbling spring water, it has no connection with the legendary queen but is a fine place to bathe if you don't mind spectators at the cafés surrounding the pool (there are changing rooms behind *Tanta Waa*) or lots of Siwan men bathing on Friday mornings and at sunset.

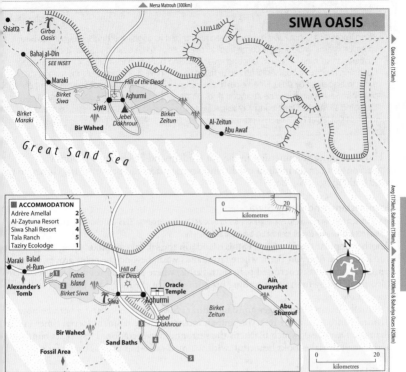

Tamusi Bath

150m back along the trail to the Amun temple, in the palm groves • Daily 24hr • Free

Being fully visible to anyone passing along the trail, Ain Juba has always been shunned by local women in favour of the more secluded **Tamusi Bath** where Siwan brides once ritually bathed and removed their adrim (a silver collar signifying puberty) on the eve of their wedding day. Today, the spring-fed pool is barely less public than the Cleopatra Bath due to the presence of *Ali's Garden,* which serves tea and *sheesha.*

Jebel Dakhrour

5–7km southeast from Siwa Town depending on the route taken • By bicycle (40min), caretta or tuk-tuk (about £E30 for up to three people for a 2hr circuit also including Aghurmi's temples and baths), or on foot from the Cleopatra Bath (15min)

Heading on from the Cleopatra Bath, bear left at the fork and take the first path on the right through clover fields and groves of palms to emerge in the desert near **Jebel Dakhrour.** This rugged massif hosts the annual **Eid el-Siyaha** (see box, p.448) and affords stunning **views.** In contrast to the verdant oasis and the silvery salt lake of Birket Zeitun, the southern horizon presents a desolate vista of crescent dunes and blackened mesas: the edge of the Great Sand Sea.

Visitors can experience a loud **echo** in the basin between the first and second peaks to the right, where Siwans often go to sing. Near the summit of **Jebel Nasra** is a crevice with a vein of red clay that's used to decorate pottery. **Jebel Tunefefan** (Mountain of Pillars) is named for three **caves** with man-made pillars, which were once dwellings and later tombs. Any Siwan in the vicinity can point you towards these two peaks.

> ## SAND SAUNAS
>
> Being immersed in hot sand has long been recognized as good for arthritis, rheumatism and spinal problems, and sufferers come from all over Europe to be treated in Siwa. The treatment is offered from June to September, and involves being buried up to your neck in sand at Jebel Dakhrour. Treatment courses last three to five days, with twenty-minute sessions (two or three daily) interspersed by sips of medicinal tea to induce sweating, and hours of rest in a tent or mud hut. Sand saunas can be arranged through the *Al-Zaytuna Resort* (£E300/person/day including all meals). Don't bring any valuables to the isolated sand-bathing sites, as thefts by locals at Dakhrour have been reported.

Last but not least, immersion in the hot sand around Dakhrour is famously efficaceous for certain medical conditions; several places out here offer the chance to go **sand bathing** (see box above).

Fatnis Island and Birket Siwa

6km southwest from Siwa Town • Accessible on foot (1hr), by bicycle (20min), or by caretta (£E25–30 return for up to three people); take the road out past the town council, then the left-hand road at the first fork

Another popular destination is **Fatnis Island**, on the salt lake of **Birket Siwa**. En route you'll pass the Abu Alif Bath, where farmhands wash; beyond the palm groves, follow a causeway across salt-encrusted pans onto Fatnis, where palms surround a large circular tiled **pool**, fed by fresh water welling up from clefts in the rock 15m below. A stall sells tea and *sheesha*.

Actually, Fatnis is no longer an island. Birket Siwa has receded and a barrage now divides it into a drainage reservoir and an intensely saline remnant (seven times saltier than the Dead Sea), which blackens the surrounding vegetation. Despite its faintly acrid smell the lake looks beautiful, with sculpted table-top massifs on its far shores.

Sidi Jaffar

16km northwest from Siwa Town, via a spur road off the route to Maraki • By taxi (£E30 return) or as an additional stopover on an excursion to Maraki (see p.455)

The largest massif overlooking the lake is called **Sidi Jaffar** by Egyptians but was previously designated by British cartographers as **Jebel Beida** (White Mountain) and is still known to Siwans in their own language as **Adrère Amellal**. Whatever its name, this area deserves a visit just to see the amazing architecture of its two **eco-lodges**.

Adrère Amellal and Taziry eco-lodges

Beside the western shore of Birket Siwa is the extraordinary **Adrère Amellal** eco-lodge (access only with written permission from the *Shali Lodge* in Siwa Town): a vast, fantasy *qasr*-style hotel built entirely of *kharsif*, palm logs and salt slabs (used instead of glass). The brainchild of Cairene entrepreneur and environmental engineer Mounir Nematalla, the eco-lodge is designed to save energy and water and recycle waste products on its organic farm. Being the kind of hotel whose guests arrive by helicopter (or private jet into Siwa's military airport), it can be entirely empty for weeks and then suddenly filled with VIPs, gofers and bodyguards. When not booked out, they don't mind the odd visitor looking around, providing you get written permission first.

The smaller but otherwise similar **Taziry Ecolodge** (see p.450), nearer the Maraki road, doesn't require prior authorisation for a visit.

Bir Wahed

12km southwest of Siwa Town • Jeep excursions for four–five people cost £E140–150/person for a half-day trip ending at sunset or £E165–200 for an overnight stay in a Bedouin tent (meals and blankets provided), plus the cost of permits (see box, p.449)

Perhaps the best excursion Siwa has to offer is **Bir Wahed** (Well One), amid the outer dunes of the Great Sand Sea, which provides an affordable experience of this magnificent landscape, otherwise only available on deep-desert safaris (see p.440).

Two **salt-water ponds** and a freshwater **lake** (where people usually swim on the way back) are followed by a magical **hot pool** the size of a large jacuzzi, irrigating a lush palm garden. The well was dug in the 1960s to find oil, but produced sulphurous water (37°C) instead. To soak up to your chest, puffing a *sheesha*, while the sun sets over the dunes all around, is a fantastic experience. Women may wear bathing costumes without offending any locals. The only downside is that mosquitoes are awful from dusk till dawn.

From here you can pursue a **nature trail** through limestone outcrops strewn with marine **fossils**, and enjoy **sand-surfing** or rolling down the sides of huge knife-edged **dunes** (sand-boards can be rented in town if the safari operator doesn't provide them). Excursions also usually feature some **dune-bashing** (driving over dunes at high speed).

Maraki

25km northwest of Siwa Town • A half-day excursion for two–four people can be arranged by Siwa's tourist office for £E100/person, £E150–200 also including Shiatta

Maraki is the collective name for several **villages** at the western end of the Siwa depression, separated from the main oasis by a rocky desert riddled with over two hundred **tombs** and caves. Although the area was intensively cultivated from Roman times until the fifteenth century, most of the existing buildings are modern breeze-block structures, as the old mud-brick ones were destroyed by a deluge in 1982, which forced residents to shelter in caves at nearby Balad el-Rum.

Balad el-Rum: the "Tomb of Alexander the Great"

In 1991, **Balad el-Rum** (Town of the Romans) made international headlines when Liana and Manos Souvaltzi announced their discovery of the "**Tomb of Alexander the Great**" beneath a ruined **Doric temple**. Egypt's Supreme Council of Antiquities initially endorsed the Souvaltzis' claim, but backed off after the Greeks failed to refute criticism that they'd misread vital inscriptions, revoked their licence and moved all the stones to a depository (not open to the public, though you might be able to look inside for baksheesh).

Girba Oasis and Shiatta

35–55km northwest of Siwa Town • A half-day excursion for two–four people can be arranged by Siwa's tourist office for £E100/person (or £E150–200 including Maraki), or combined with Bir Wahed on a full-day excursion (£E200/person) with safari operators

Beyond the military checkpoint at Bahaj al-Din a track runs off to **Girba Oasis**, which despite its many salt-flats (sabkha) provides grazing for the herds of the Bedouin Al-Shihayat tribe, whose main settlement is at Shiatta, 20km away. During the early twentieth century, both were halts on the Masrab el-Ikhwan (Road of the Brotherhood) from Jaghbub Oasis in Libya, whereby Senussi preachers reached the Western Desert oases (*masrab* is the Siwan word for a camel route, called a *darb* in other oases.)

Since the 2011 revolutions in Egypt and Libya, the thinly guarded international **border** has been crossed with impunity by smugglers armed with AK-47s and RPGs, who have burnt crops to punish local sheikhs for providing information to Egyptian border guards stationed in the vicinity.

Shiatta

Shiatta's beautiful, deep-blue **salt lake** is thought to be the remnant of an ancient, less saline one that stretched as far as Aghurmi. Divers have found **fossils** of fifty-million-year-old crocodiles, an **underground river** (part of the aquifers and waterways beneath the Libyan Desert) and the submerged remains of a Roman or pharaonic **solar boat** that might have been used for ritual voyages to the Oracle Temple (see p.452). Endangered long-horned and Dorcas **gazelles** sometimes graze around its shores. Bring a bottle of fresh water to rinse off the salt after swimming in the lake.

Around Birket Zeitun

East of Siwa Town • Half-day excursions for two–four people can be arranged by Siwa's tourist office (££100/person)

The largest salt lake in the oasis, named after the olive trees that flourished around it in ancient times, **Birket Zeitun** is visible from Jebel Dakhrour, from where a **causeway** crosses acres of mud, attesting to the lake's slow recession. Only the far shore is inhabited, with villages that flourished in Roman times before centuries of slow decline set in.

Ain Qurayshat

The lake's increasing salinity is both the cause and result of depopulation: as fewer irrigation works are maintained, more warm water from the **Ain Qurayshat** spring flows unused into the lake, crystallizing mineral salts as it evaporates. The source is enclosed by an industrial-sized concrete tank where you can bathe – but be careful of underwater ledges.

Abu Shurouf

Better bathing can be found 35km southeast of Siwa Town at **Abu Shrouf**, where there's a large kidney-shaped pool of cool, clear, azure water with bug-eyed fishes, opposite the Hayat mineral water bottling plant. The village beyond is notable for harbouring all the female **donkeys** in the oasis, which are kept and mated here. In Siwan parlance, "Have you been to Abu Shurouf?" is a euphemism for "Have you had sex?"

Al-Zeitun

Further out along the lake, **AL-ZEITUN** was once a model Senussi village tending the richest olive groves in the oasis until it was abandoned after an Italian bombing raid in 1940. Near the far end is a smoke-blackened Ptolemaic kiosk-**temple** where the locals once sheltered from bombs. Hundreds of **Roman tombs** riddle the hills between Al-Zeitun and **Ain Safi**, the last hamlet in the oasis before the Darb Siwa to Bahariya Oasis enters the deep desert (see p.457).

Beyond Siwa Oasis

Beyond the Siwa depression are five smaller oases, visited by relatively few tourists. **Qara**, far away on the edge of the **Qattara Depression**, makes a rewarding day-trip, while travellers bound for Bahariya can see something of **Areg** and **Nuwamisa**, if not the more secluded oases of **Bahrein** or **Sitra**.

Qara Oasis

130 northeast of Siwa Town via the newly upgraded Masrab Kidda (2hr 30min) • A day-trip for up to four people costs ££800–1500, plus permits (see box, p.449)

If you're seriously into desert travel, **Qara Oasis** (often pronounced "Gara" or "Djara") has a compelling fascination. The only inhabited oasis beyond the limits of the Siwa depression, it has been aptly called "Siwa yesterday" due to its isolation. Qarawis still live entirely from their palm groves and vegetable plots, irrigated by seventeen wells. Legend has it that these could only sustain 314 people, so whenever a child was born, an elder would have to leave the oasis.

Until flooding rendered it unsafe in 1982, the Qarawis occupied a Shali-like **fortress** atop "a solitary white mushroom of rock", edged by a "high smooth wall, impregnable to raiders, with one black tunnel for a street", as the explorer Bagnold (see p.396) saw it in the 1920s. Now, most families live in new stone houses on the plain. People trace their ancestry from the Hamudat tribe, a mixture of Bedouin, Berbers and Sudanese (some of them runaway slaves).

Visitors are so rare that the villagers turn out to welcome them and serve a meal in their honour. Qarawis speak Berber among themselves, but Arabic is widely understood.

Qattara Depression

30km from Qara Oasis • Qattara is featured on a few deep-desert safaris; otherwise you might be able to negotiate an excursion from Siwa if the military agrees to grant an overnight permit (see box, p.376)

Beyond Qara the land plummets into the **Qattara Depression**, which is seven times the size of all the Western Desert oases combined and, at its lowest point (141m below sea level), the deepest depression in Africa. The **salt marshes** and **lakes** at the foot of the northern escarpment were regarded as an impenetrable obstacle to Rommel's Panzers during the Battle of El-Alamein.

Planners have long dreamed of piping water 38km from the Mediterranean to the depression, utilizing the fall in height to generate hydroelectricity and run desalination plants and irrigation systems, but all attempts have foundered through lack of capital. There is, however, exploration for **oil** at many points in the desert between Qattara and Mersa Matrouh, with upgraded tracks identified by the logos of oil companies. Local Bedouin are bitter that World War II **minefields** have only been cleared to allow drilling, while their ancestral grazing grounds remain hazardous to enter.

Siwa to Bahariya

Following the ancient Darb Siwa caravan trail, the 420km road (tarmackd for 250km) **from Siwa to Bahariya** takes four to six hours to drive and has six checkpoints which provide assurance that vehicles which break down will be missed, but otherwise there are no sources of water, nor any fuel – and mobile phones are beyond signal range. Safari operators charge £E1500 for up to four people to travel to Bahariya; £E2000 with one or two stopovers en route; or £E2500–2800 to carry on to the White Desert (see p.409) and camp there. Cars must travel in convoy leaving the Carpet Factory at 7am, while travel permits (see box, p.449) and an army guide with a satellite-phone are mandatory

3

Areg Oasis

175km from Siwa

Easily reached on foot from the road, **Areg Oasis** (pronounced "Arej") is surrounded by striated chalk buttes which look like giant brioches that have sat in the oven too long. Regarded as a haunt of bandits by nineteenth-century travellers, its cliffs are riddled with scores of **tombs**. A tablet from Alexandria records that the population of Siwa, Bahrein and other now-deserted oases numbered four hundred thousand in Persian times.

Bahrein Oasis

229km from Siwa

Ten kilometres off the road, **Bahrein Oasis** – named after its two azure salt lakes – is awash with custard-coloured sand, hemmed in by croissant-shaped buttes riddled with Greco-Roman **tombs**. Seductive as they look, the **salt lakes** are surrounded by mushy sand and salt crusts that can trap unwary vehicles, and if safari groups camp here they do so in the palm groves on the far side, away from the mosquitoes and protected from sandstorms.

Nuwamisa and Sitra oases

251km from Siwa to Nuwamisa, 266km to Sitra

Nuwamisa Oasis, roughly 3km off the road from Siwa to Bahariya, looks equally lovely, with a salt lake rimmed by palms and crescent cliffs – but its name, "Oasis of the Mosquitoes", is all too true. Millions of **mosquitoes** swarm as soon as the sun goes down, making camping a nightmare even if you're all zipped up in your tent.

Safari groups prefer to camp in **Sitra Oasis**, 15km away, which isn't so badly infested. Traditionally a watering hole for Bedouin smugglers bringing hashish into Egypt, it is still sometimes used as a fuel-cache by motorized traffickers in various contraband.

For the final 45km of the journey to Bahariya the road skirts the whale-backed **Ghard Kebir** (Great Dunes), voyaging south from the Qattara Depression and destined to arrive in Bahariya in a few hundred years.

Alexandria, the Mediterranean coast and the Delta

BIBLIOTHECA ALEXANDRINA, ALEXANDRIA

Alexandria, the Mediterranean coast and the Delta

Egypt's second city, Alexandria was once a lodestar throughout the ancient world, its lighthouse and library beacons of enlightenment, its rulers synonymous with splendour and depravity. A unique fusion of Hellenistic, Levantine, Egyptian, Jewish and European cultures, its cosmopolitanism took a heavy knock in the Nasser era and has since been diluted further by an influx of provincial Egyptians who deplore its tradition of mixed marriages and cultural curiosity. To those of a nostalgic bent it is the "Capital of Memory", rich in literary and historical associations nurtured by Lawrence Durrell, E.M. Forster and Constantine Cavafy. If Alexandria's monuments are a pale shadow of its ancient glory, its new library and cultural vigour show that the city is still a force to be reckoned with.

For Ancient Egyptians, the **Mediterranean coast** marked the edge of the "Great Green", the measureless sea that formed the limits of the known world. Life and civilization meant the Nile Valley and the Delta – an outlook that still seems to linger in the country's subconscious. For, despite the white beaches, craggy headlands and turquoise sea that stretch for some 500km, much of the Egyptian Med is eerily vacant and underpopulated. Aside from a score of resorts that mainly cater to Egyptians, the only place of note is the World War II battlefield of **El-Alamein**, where the Western Desert campaign was decided.

While the coast's significance has been fleeting and Alexandria is a relative latecomer to the stage of Egyptian history, the Nile **Delta** was one of the Two Lands of Ancient Egypt and remains the archetypal heartland of the nation. Former presidents Sadat and Mubarak relied on grass-roots support from their home province of Menoufiya, yet feared protests by the textile-workers of Mahalla province, the home of Egypt's cotton industry. The Delta is the "real" Egypt, almost untouched by tourism, despite such attractions as the Ottoman mansions of **Rosetta**, the ancient ruins of **Bubastis** and **Avaris**, and colourful moulids at **Tanta** and **Damanhur**.

As for the **weather**, the Mediterranean coast gets hotter and drier the further west you travel, but in winter Alexandria can be cold and windy with torrential downpours and waves crashing over the Corniche, and the Delta experiences showers. The Mediterranean Sea doesn't become warm enough for **swimming** till June, but you can be pretty sure of continuous sunshine from April until November.

DOWNTOWN ALEXANDRIA

Highlights

❶ Bibliotheca Alexandrina The city's library is a stunning example of contemporary architecture, aimed at reviving the legendary Mother Library of antiquity. **See p.475**

❷ Catacombs of Kom es-Shoqafa This eerie subterranean Roman necropolis is full of bizarre carvings, with a dining room for mourners. **See p.476**

❸ Fresh seafood Alexandria is famous for its seafood restaurants, where customers select their meal from a mound of fish and crustaceans. **See p.486**

❹ Coffee houses and patisseries Savour the old-world charm or literary associations of establishments such as Délices. **See p.487**

❺ Diving Explore the remains of Cleopatra's Palace, Napoleonic warships and World War II aircraft in the waters off Alexandria. **See p.482**

❻ El-Alamein The war museum and cemeteries are stark reminders of the decisive battle in 1942. **See p.495**

❼ Rosetta This town has been busy restoring its legacy of Ottoman mansions built in the distinctive Delta style, making it a worthwhile day trip from Alexandria **See p.500**

❽ Moulid of Saiyid Ahmed al-Bedawi Each October, the city of Tanta becomes a seething mass of chanting Sufis, musicians, circus acts and spectators, in the Delta's biggest festival. **See p.503**

HIGHLIGHTS ARE MARKED ON THE MAPS ON PP.492–493 & P.499

Alexandria

ALEXANDRIA (Al-Iskandariya) was Egypt's capital for almost a thousand years before fading into oblivion, only to be reborn in the modern age as a Europeanized metropolis. Since this was built atop the ruins of **ancient Alexandria**, far more antiquities have been lost than found – but each year sees a Greek statue or Roman mosaic unearthed on construction sites or on the seabed, where the ruins of Cleopatra's Palace and the city's ancient lighthouse can be seen by divers.

Another stratum of Alexandria's past is its **colonial heritage**: patisseries, hotels and shops whose names, sepia photographs and other bric-a-brac of a bygone Levantine world give Alexandria a strong whiff of nostalgia. Yet Alexandria is no less febrile than Cairo and has its own dynamic, with a youth culture that made its voice heard during Egypt's 2011 revolution. In Arabic the city is called Al-Iskandariya, after its founder Alexander the Great (who had conquered most of the known world by the age of 33).

For the visitor, the modern city's top three attractions are its iconic **library**, the **Alexandria National Museum** and the **Roman Theatre** (all on the periphery of downtown, fifteen minutes' walk from the central Midan Sa'ad Zaghloul). If you're only here for a day, be sure to allow time to visit the **Catacombs of Kom es-Shogafa**, beyond the city centre. For divers, the sunken ruins and wrecks in the **Eastern Harbour** and **Abu Qir Bay** are ample reason to spend two or three days here, while others will want to savour the city's seafood restaurants, or the jaded ambience and literary mystique of this once-great metropolis.

Brief history

When **Alexander the Great** wrested Egypt from the Persian Empire in 332 BC at the age of 25, he decided against Memphis, the ancient capital, in favour of building a new city linked by sea to his Macedonian homeland. Choosing a site near the fishing village of **Rhakotis**, where two limestone spurs formed a natural harbour, he gave orders to his architect, Deinocrates, before travelling on to Siwa and thence to Asia, where he died eight years later. His corpse was subsequently returned to Egypt, where the priests refused burial at Memphis; its final resting place remains a mystery.

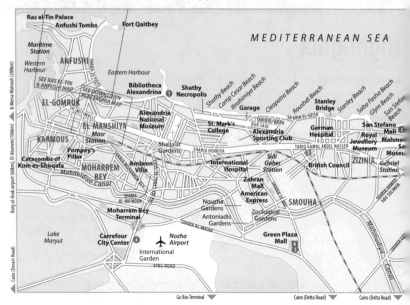

Alexandria under the Ptolemies

Thereafter Alexander's empire was divided amongst his Macedonian generals, one of whom took Egypt and adopted the title Ptolemy I Soter, founding a dynasty (305–30 BC). Avid promoters of Hellenistic culture, the **Ptolemies** made Alexandria an intellectual powerhouse: among its scholars were Euclid, the "father of geometry", and Eratosthenes, who accurately determined the circumference and diameter of the earth. Alexandria's great lighthouse, the **Pharos**, was literally and metaphorically a beacon, rivalled in fame only by the city's library, the **Bibliotheca Alexandrina** – the foremost centre of learning in the ancient world.

While the first three Ptolemies were energetic and enlightened, the later members of the dynasty are remembered as decadent and dissolute – perhaps due to their brother-sister marriages, in emulation of the pharaohs of Ancient Egypt – and relied on Rome to maintain their position. The great **Cleopatra VII** (51–30 BC) came unstuck after her lover, Julius Caesar, was murdered, and his successor in Rome (and her bed), Mark Antony, was defeated by Octavian. The latter hated her and so detested Cleopatra's capital at Alexandria that he banned Roman citizens from entering Egypt on the pretext that its religious orgies were morally corrupting.

Roman rule and Christianity

Whereas local Egyptians and Greeks had previously respected one another's deities and even syncretized them into a common cult (the worship of Serapis), religious conflicts developed under **Roman rule** (30 BC–313 AD). The empire regarded Christianity (supposedly introduced by St Mark in 45 AD) as subversive, and the persecution of Christians from 250 AD onwards reached a bloody apogee under Emperor Diocletian, during whose rule the Copts maintain that 144,000 believers were martyred. (The Coptic Church dates its chronology from 284 AD, the "Era of Martyrs", rather than Christ's birth.)

After the emperor Constantine made **Christianity** the state religion, a new controversy arose over the nature of Christ, the theological subtleties of which essentially masked a political rebellion by Egyptian **Copts** against Byzantine (Greek) authority. In Alexandria, the Coptic patriarch became supreme and his monks waged war against

4

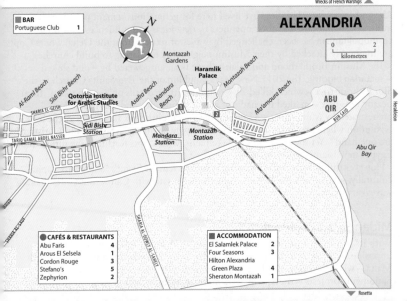

ALEXANDRIA

Wrecks of French Warships

BAR	
Portuguese Club	1

Montazah Gardens

Haramlik Palace

0   2
kilometres

Al-Raml Beach
Sidi Bishr Beach
Asafra Beach
Mandara Beach
Montazah Beach
Ma'amoura Beach

ABU QIR

Heraklion

Qotorba Institute for Arabic Studies

SHARIA EL-GEISH

Sidi Bishr Station

TARIQ GAMAL ABDEL NASSER

Mandara Station

Montazah Station

BUR SAID

Abu Qir Bay

SHARIA AL-SOWLY AL-SAKRY

CAFÉS & RESTAURANTS	
Abu Faris	4
Arous El Selsela	1
Cordon Rouge	3
Stefano's	5
Zephyrion	2

ACCOMMODATION	
El Salamlek Palace	2
Four Seasons	3
Hilton Alexandria	
Green Plaza	4
Sheraton Montazah	1

Rosetta

paganism, sacking the Serapis Temple and library in 391 and later murdering the scientist Hypatia (see box, p.481).

Decline and revival

Local hatred of Byzantium disposed Alexandrians to welcome the **Arab conquest** (641), whose commander, Amr, described the city as containing "4000 palaces, 4000 baths, 400 theatres, 1200 greengrocers and 40,000 Jews". But while the Arabs incorporated elements of Alexandrian learning into their own civilization, they cared little for the city itself. Owing to neglect and the silting up of the waterways that connected it to the Nile, Alexandria inexorably declined over the next millennium, so that when Napoleon's expeditionary force arrived in 1798, they found a mere fishing village with four thousand inhabitants.

The city's **revival** sprang from Mohammed Ali Pasha's desire to make Egypt a commercial and maritime power. The Mahmudiya Canal, finished in 1820, once again linked Alexandria to the Nile, while a harbour, docks and arsenal were created. European merchants erected mansions and warehouses, building outwards from the Place des Consuls (modern-day Midan Tahrir), and the city's population soared to 230,000.

Nationalist resentment of foreign influence fired the **Orabi Revolt** of 1882, in retaliation for which British warships shelled the city. Yet such was Alexandria's commercial importance that it quickly recovered; the next five decades were a Belle Époque that even two world wars only briefly disturbed – notwithstanding the decisive battle of El-Alamein (see p.497), waged only a few hours' drive from Alexandria.

By 1950 the era of European supremacy was nearing its end, as anti-British riots expressed rising **nationalism**. The **revolution** that forced King Farouk to sail into exile in 1952 didn't seriously affect the "foreign" community (many of whom had lived here for generations) until the Anglo-French-Israeli assault on Egypt during the Suez Crisis of 1956, following which Nasser expelled all French and British citizens and nationalized foreign businesses, forcing a hundred thousand non-Egyptians to emigrate. Institutions, street names and businesses were Egyptianized, and the custom of moving the seat of government to Alexandria during the hot summer months was ended.

Alexandria today

Alexandrians whose families have lived here for generations remain proud of their multi-ethnic heritage and their openness to new ideas and influences. But their **cosmopolitanism** has been challenged by waves of settlers from the Delta, where Copts are frequently attacked by their Muslim neighbours for daring to build churches.

The Muslim Brotherhood and Salafists have been empowered by – and stoked – **sectarian bigotry**. The 2011 New Year's **bombing** of the Two Saints Church in the Sidi Bishr district – which killed 21 Copts and inspired calls of "God is Great" from nearby mosques – marked the nadir of sectarian hostility, and was probably orchestrated by Mubarak's secret police. Barely a month later Egypt was swept by a revolution where protesters asserted their unity by chanting "Muslims and Christians are one hand". Yet the sectarian divide remains, with Copts fearful of the future under Egypt's new Islamist government.

However things turn out, Alexandria is sure to remain Egypt's "alternative capital", culturally, socially and politically – sometimes in sync with Cairo, sometimes making waves on its own.

Midan Sa'ad Zaghloul

With its windblown palm trees and tatty lawns, **Midan Sa'ad Zaghloul** is less than imposing. Named after the nationalist leader (see p.87) whose **statue** gazes towards Malta – where he was exiled by the British, returning to a hero's welcome after nationwide protests – the square bears no trace of its ancient glories.

ALEXANDRIA ORIENTATION AND MAPS

Alexandria runs along the Mediterranean for 20km without ever venturing more than 8km inland – a true waterfront city. Its great **Corniche** sweeps around the **Eastern Harbour** and along the coast past a string of city **beaches** to **Montazah** and **Ma'amoura**, burning out before the final beach at **Abu Qir**. In the opposite direction, you need to get past the industrial zone of **Al-Max** to reach the western beaches of **Hannoville** and **El-Agami**. Most foreign tourists frequent the downtown quarter of **El-Manshiya** (see map, p.466), where many restaurants and hotels are within a few blocks either side, or inland, of **Midan Sa'ad Zaghloul**.

The Corniche (and breezes blowing inland) make basic orientation quite simple, but the finer points can still be awkward and even the latest **map** – *Alexandria Key* available for £E25 from local bookshops (see p.490) – doesn't show every backstreet in the centre. A historical map of *Archeological Sites of Alexandria*, published by the Alexandria Preservation Trust, is on sale at bookshops. **Street names** are also problematic, since signs don't always square with the latest official designation or popular usage. In the downtown area, most signs are in English or Arabic, and people may use either when giving directions.

Until the 1870s, visitors could still admire **Cleopatra's Needles**, two lofty obelisks first raised at Heliopolis (see p.145) that were later taken to Alexandria to ennoble the approach to the Caesareum (see below) and finally transplanted on London's Embankment and in New York's Central Park. Their popular name is a misnomer, as they were carved fourteen centuries before Cleopatra's reign and only moved to Alexandria fifteen years after her death.

Today, the square's dominant feature is the pseudo-Moorish **Hotel Cecil**, where British Intelligence hatched the deception plan for the decisive third battle of El-Alamein (see p.497) from a suite on the first floor. The battle marked the turning point in Britain's fortunes in World War II and the end of Nazi Germany's attempts to seize Egypt.

Nearby are three **patisseries** synonymous with social life in colonial times. Nowadays, only *Délices* deserves a visit for its cakes, but the others are worth a peek for their decor or heritage (see box, p.488).

Sharia Nabi Daniel and around

Starting as an alleyway off Midan Sa'ad Zaghloul, **Sharia Nabi Daniel** widens into a busy shopping street leading towards Masr Station, passing a synagogue, a Coptic cathedral and a mosque – each related to different facets of Alexandria's history – on the way. The only trace of what existed here in antiquity however is the street's alignment, which follows the ancient **Street of the Soma**, a wide thoroughfare paved in marble that dazzled the Arabs in 641 even though its finest buildings had already vanished. Before its destruction by feuding Christians in the fourth century, its northern end was crowned by the **Caesareum**, a magnificent temple begun by Cleopatra in memory of Julius Caesar, which her mortal enemy Octavian completed and dedicated to himself.

Eliyahu Ha-Navi Synagogue

Access via Sharia Dr Hassan Fadaly, off Sharia Nabi Daniel • Visits arranged through Ben Youssef Gaon ☎ 012 2700 1031 • Admission free, but a donation of £E10–20 is appreciated

High wrought-iron gates and lethargic police guard the **Eliyahu Ha-Navi Synagogue**, the largest in the Arab world, with seating for seven hundred. Built in 1885 by the philanthropist Baron Jacques de Menasce, the synagogue's Italianate interior features stained-glass windows, giant menorahs, and brass nameplates affixed to the seats of former regular worshippers. Tracing its ancestry back to the city's foundation, Alexandria's Jewish community once numbered seventy thousand – almost all of whom

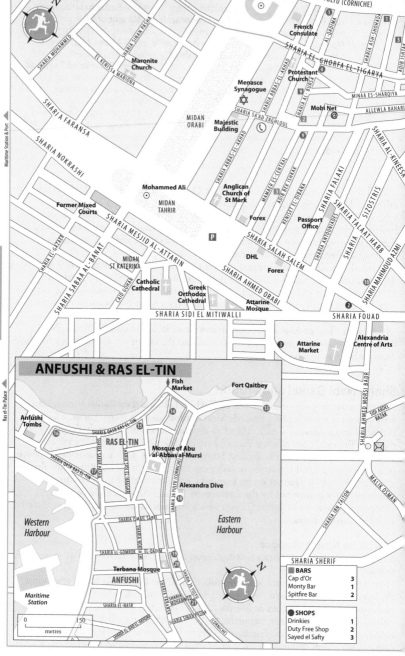

▲ Al-Mursi Mosque (900m) ▲ Fort Qaitbey (1.5km)

DOWNTOWN ALEXANDRIA

N

Unknown Soldier
SHARIA 26 YULYU (CORNICHE)

French Consulate

SHARIA EL GHORFA EL TIGARYA

AL-QADIMA

SHARIA ASH-SHOHADA

ADIB ISHAK

SHARIA MOHAMMED

SHARIA SINAN PASHA

EL KENISSA MARIONA

Maronite Church

Protestant Church

Menasce Synagogue

SHARIA ABBAS-EL-CANAD

SHARIA EL BURSA

MINAA ES-SHARQIYA

Mobi Net
@

ALLEWLA BAHARI

SHARIA FARANSA

MIDAN ORABI

Majestic Building

SHARIA SAAD ZAGHLOUL

SHARIA NOKRASHI

SHARIA ABBAS-EL-AKHID

SHARIA AL-KINEESA

Mohammed Ali
⊙

MIDAN TAHRIR

Anglican Church of St Mark

MAMARL EL-CENTRAL

ADIB BEY ISHAK

KENEDT EL-ZUBANA

SHARIA FALAKI

SHARIA TALAAT HARB

SHARIA SIZOSTRIS

Former Mixed Courts

SHARIA EL-GAZEER

SHARIA MESJID AL-ATTARIN

Forex

Passport Office

SHARIA ANTOUNIABLES

SHARIA

SHARIA MAHMOUD AZMI

SHARIA SABAA AL-BANAT

CATD GOBAN

MIDAN ST KATERINA

Catholic Cathedral

SHARIA SALAH SALEM

DHL

SHARIA AHMED ORABI

Greek Orthodox Cathedral

Forex

Attarine Mosque

SHARIA SIDI EL MITIWALLI

SHARIA FOUAD

Attarine Market

Alexandria Centre of Arts

SHARIA AHMED MOSL BADR

SIDI ABDEL RAZAK

ANFUSHI & RAS EL-TIN

Fish Market

Fort Qaitbey

Anfushi Tombs

SHARIA QASR RAS EL-TIN

RAS EL-TIN

Mosque of Abu al-Abbas al-Mursi

SHARIA QASR RAS EL-TIN

WEST RENIS YUNES

SHARIA SIDI EL-HAGGAG

SHARIA 26 YULYU (CORNICHE)

Alexandra Dive

Western Harbour

SHARIA ISMAIL SABRI

Eastern Harbour

SHERIN NUR AL-DIN

SHARIA AHMED MOSL BADR

MALIK OSMAN

SHARIA IBN FATOM

SHABIA EL-GOMBOR EL-QADIM

Terbana Mosque

ANFUSHI

SHARIA MOHAMMED

SHARIA SINAN PASHA

SHARIA ANFATA

Maritime Station

SHARIA EL-NASR

SHARIA QASR DANT EL-ANDAR

(CORNICHE)

N

0   150
metres

SHARIA SHERIF

■ BARS
Cap d'Or   3
Monty Bar   1
Spitfire Bar   2

● SHOPS
Drinkies   1
Duty Free Shop   2
Sayed el Safty   3

Maritime Station & Fort ◀

Ras el-Tin Palace ◀

4

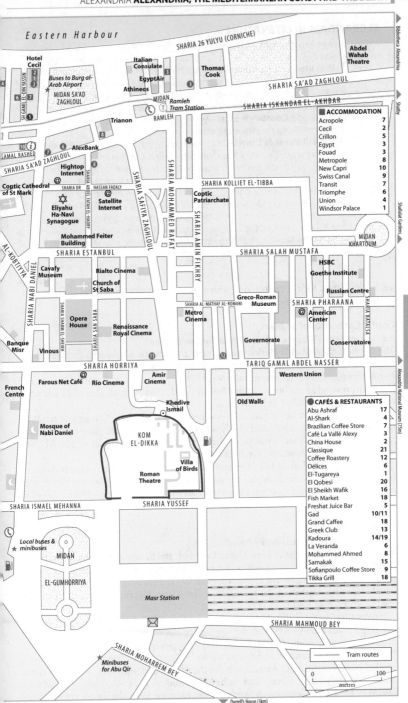

Eastern Harbour

SHARIA 26 YULYU (CORNICHE)

Bibliotheca Alexandrina

Hotel Cecil

Buses to Burg al-Arab Airport

Italian Consulate

EgyptAir

Athineos

MIDAN SA'AD ZAGHLOUL

Thomas Cook

Abdel Wahab Theatre

SHARIA SA'AD ZAGHLOUL

SHARIA ISKANDAR EL-AKHBAR

MIDAN Ramleh Tram Station

RAMLEH

Trianon

Shatby

ACCOMMODATION

Acropole	7
Cecil	2
Crillon	5
Egypt	3
Fouad	3
Metropole	8
New Capri	10
Swiss Canal	9
Transit	7
Triomphe	6
Union	4
Windsor Palace	1

AlexBank

GAMAL RASHED

SHARIA SA'AD ZAGHLOUL

Hightop Internet

HASSAN FADALY

SHARIA DR HASSAN FADALY

SHARIA ABDEL FATAH EL-HADRY

Coptic Cathedral of St Mark

Eliyahu Ha-Navi Synagogue

Satellite Internet

Mohammed Feiter Building

SHARIA MOHAMMED RAFAT

SHARIA SAFIYA ZAGHLOUL

SHARIA KOLLIET EL-TIBBA

Coptic Patriarchate

SHARIA AMIN FIKHRY

MIDAN KHARTOUM

Shallalat Gardens

SHARIA ESTANBUL

SHARIA NABI DANIEL

AL-KOBTIYA

Cavafy Museum

Rialto Cinema

Church of St Saba

SHARIA SALAH MUSTAFA

HSBC

Goethe Institute

Russian Centre

SHARIA AL-MATHAF AL-ROMANI

Greco-Roman Museum

SHARIA PHARAANA

SHARIA BATALSA

American Center

Opera House

SHARIA SHARM EL-SHEIKH

SHARIA SAN SABA

Renaissance Royal Cinema

Metro Cinema

Governorate

Conservatoire

Banque Misr

Vinous

SHARIA HORRIYA

TARIQ GAMAL ABDEL NASSER

Alexandria National Museum (75m)

French Centre

Farous Net Café

Rio Cinema

Amir Cinema

Western Union

Old Walls

CAFÉS & RESTAURANTS

Abu Ashraf	17
Al-Shark	4
Brazilian Coffee Store	7
Café La Vallé Alexy	3
China House	2
Classique	21
Coffee Roastery	12
Délices	6
El-Tugareya	1
El Qobesi	20
El Sheikh Wafik	16
Fish Market	18
Freshat Juice Bar	5
Gad	10/11
Grand Caffee	18
Greek Club	13
Kadoura	14/19
La Veranda	6
Mohammed Ahmed	8
Samakak	15
Sofianpoulo Coffee Store	9
Tikka Grill	18

Mosque of Nabi Daniel

Khedive Ismail

KOM EL-DIKKA

Villa of Birds

Roman Theatre

SHARIA ISMAEL MEHANNA

SHARIA YUSSEF

Local buses & minibuses

MIDAN EL-GUMHORRIYA

Masr Station

SHARIA MAHMOUD BEY

SHARIA MOHARREM BEY

Minibuses for Abu Qir

Tram routes

0   100
metres

Durrell's House (3km)

ALEXANDRIA IN LITERATURE

With relatively few monuments to show for its ancient lineage, Alexandria's past is found in its faded coffee houses, minutiae such as old nameplates, the reminiscences of aged Arabs and Greeks, and in its **literary dimension**. The English novelist **E.M. Forster** (author of *A Room with a View* and *A Passage to India*) wrote the first guidebook to Alexandria (where he had his first sexual relationship, with an Egyptian tram-conductor, while serving as a nurse during World War I), but reckoned that the best thing he did was to publicize the work of the Alexandrian Greek poet **Constantine Cavafy** – odes to nostalgia, excess, loss and futility.

Cavafy was the model for the character Balthazar in *The Alexandria Quartet*, written by a deracinated Briton, **Lawrence Durrell** (1912–90). This verbose tetralogy of novels, relating the same events from the perspective of four characters living out the Ancient Greek myths in Alexandria before, during and after World War II, was widely acclaimed in the 1960s for its "relativity In space and time", but is little read today. Durrell based the character of Justine on his Alexandrian Jewish lover Eve Cohen, a survivor of childhood incest. The plot twist that once shocked readers seemed far more sinister after their daughter Sappho hanged herself in 1985, leaving letters hinting at incest with Durrell, blighting his posthumous reputation.

Durrell had little time for Egyptians and his novels are not well regarded in Egypt, where people prefer the late Nobel laureate **Naguib Mahfouz**'s *Miramar* as an evocation of post-colonial Alexandria from an Egyptian standpoint.

left in the 1950s. Of the twenty-odd Jews who remain today, Ben Youssef Gaon – in his fifties – is the youngest.

Coptic Cathedral of St Mark

Access via Sharia al-Kineesa al-Kobtiyya, off Sharia Nabi Daniel • Daily 8am–8pm • Free

The **Coptic Cathedral of St Mark** is named after the Apostle Mark, who brought Christianity to Alexandria and was martyred by local pagans in 67 AD. Dragged by horses through the streets, his remains were held by a local church until 828, when the Venetians smuggled the body out of Muslim-ruled Alexandria in a barrel of salt pork, to rebury it at the Basilica di San Marco.

A novel reinterpretation of this story was proposed by Andrew Chugg (see p.624), namely that Alexander the Great's body was secretly buried in the guise of St Mark's relics after Emperor Theodosius prohibited the worship of Alexander in 391 AD, and was later smuggled abroad by Venetians unaware of its true origin.

The existing cathedral – built of reinforced concrete in the 1950s – pays stylistic homage to Byzantine basilicas and the ancient churches of Wadi Natrun. Its western entrance incorporates six marble pillars from an earlier cathedral, itself the successor to a church founded by St Mark himself.

Cavafy Museum

4 Sharia Sharm el-Sheikh • Daily except Mon 10am–5pm • £E15

Wandering off Nabi Daniel onto Sharia Estanbul, the flamboyant **Mohammed Feiter Building**, emblazoned with majolica coronets, can help you locate a narrow lane across the road, called Sharia Sharm el-Sheikh. Near its far end, a sign in Greek identifies the **Cavafy Museum**, recreating the second-floor flat where Alexandria's greatest poet spent the last 25 years of his life.

Constantine Cavafy (1863–1933) was born into a wealthy family that fell on hard times, obliging him to become a clerk at the Ministry of Public Works. His poems are odes to nostalgia, excess, loss and futility. Living in genteel poverty above a bordello near the Greek Orthodox Church of St Saba, he wrote: "Where could I live better? Below, the brothel caters for the flesh. And there is the church which forgives sin. And there is the hospital where we die." Cavafy died, as he had predicted, in St Saba's hospice, and was buried in the Greek Cemetery at Shatby, where his grave bears the simple epitaph, *Poet*.

Visitors can see his brass bed, icons, books and death mask, and the modest desk where he wrote *The Barbarians*, *Ithaca* and his elegiac *The City*. The museum's custodian relates how "Cavafis" (as he is known) had nine brothers, loved candlelight and died of throat cancer from drinking – but draws a veil over his homosexuality ("He never married").

Church of St Saba
Sharia San Saba • Daily 8am–8pm • Free

Visible from the Cavafy Museum, but only accessible from a parallel street, is the Greek Orthodox **Church of St Saba**, built over an ancient temple of Apollo. The seventeenth-century church contains a marble columnar tablet on which St Catherine (see p.566) is said to have been beheaded, and sanctified relics of Patriarch Petros VII, who was killed in a helicopter crash on Mount Athos in 2004.

The Opera House
Accessible from Sharia San Saba or Sharia Horriya

From the Church of St Saba, Sharia San Saba runs southwards past Alexandria's **Opera House**, originally the Theatre Mohammed Ali and now better known as the **Sayed Darwish Theatre**. A splendid Beaux Arts edifice, it fuses elements of the Odéon Théâtre in Paris and the Vienna Opera House. Classical musicians from Cairo and around the world often perform here (see p.489).

Sharia Horriya

The junction of Sharia Nabi Daniel and **Sharia Horriya** is another landmark in the geography of ancient Alexandria, marking the approximate site of its central crossroads, where the Street of the Soma met the city's east–west axis, the **Canopic Way**, leading from the Gate of the Sun where visitors entered the city. The fabled Soma and Mouseion (see box, p.470) are thought to have stood here in antiquity. Mindful of this, **Lawrence Durrell** (see p.468) located many of his fictional characters nearby; he himself lived with Eve Cohen (the model for Justine) in a flat at 40 Sharia Fouad.

The nearby **Banque Masr** on Sharia Talaat Harb occupies a copy of the Palazzo Farnese in Rome, built for an Italian bank by the Jewish fascist Guiseppe Loria (who also designed the *Hotel Cecil*); its lavish Moorish-Gothic interior is worth seeing.

Mosque of Nabi Daniel
Sharia Nabi Daniel • Daily 6am–8pm • Free

The **Mosque of Nabi Daniel** that lends its name to the street would hardly merit a glance were it not for legends that **Alexander the Great's tomb** lies beneath its crypt. In 1850, a local dragoman (guide), Ambrose Schilfizzi, claimed to have seen a body in a crystal coffin at the end of a subterranean passage. A more creditable report, by the engineer Mahmoud Bey Falaki, describes a network of passages of finely cut masonry. However, later excavations revealed no trace of the Soma and further digging has been vetoed by the religious authorities.

Kom el-Dikka
Sharia Yussef • Daily 9am–4.30pm (Ramadan until 3pm) • Site £E20; Villa of Birds £E15

In 1959, Polish archeologists searching for Alexander's tomb beneath the Turkish fort and slums on **Kom el-Dikka** ("Mound of Rubble") found a stratum of Roman remains that they're still excavating today. During Ptolemaic times this was the Park of Pan, a hilly pleasure garden with a limestone summit carved into the shape of a pine cone (of which nothing remains).

The site's most striking feature is a well-preserved **Roman Theatre** with marble seating for seven to eight hundred, cruder galleries for the plebs and a forecourt with two patches of mosaic flooring. Along the northern side of the theatre's portico are thirteen

THE MOUSEION AND THE SOMA

Chroniclers have left tantalizing descriptions of two edifices that once overlooked the crossroads of the ancient city. Our word "museum" derives from the **Mouseion** (Shrine of the Muses), a complex incorporating lecture halls, laboratories, observatories and the legendary Mother Library (see p.476), founded by Ptolemy I (323–282 BC), the first dynasty to rule Alexandria in antiquity. Across the way stood the **Soma** (literally, "dead body"), a temple where Alexander the Great was entombed alongside several Ptolemies. Alexander reposed in a gold sarcophagus until Ptolemy IX melted it down to mint coins during a crisis, but his body remained on view long after the dynasty had fallen. The victorious Octavian paid his respects to Alexandria's founder but disdained his heirs, stating, "I wished to see a king, I did not wish to see corpses." According to one chronicler, Octavian accidentally broke Alexander's nose while bending to kiss the dead conqueror.

What happened to **Alexander's body** later remains a mystery. Folklore has it that his tomb lies beneath the Mosque of Nabi Daniel, but most scholars now believe that the Romans reburied him outside the Royal Quarter, in what is now Shatby, where the Christian cemeteries are today (see p.478). Another theory is that it reposes in Venice's Basilica di San Marco (see p.468).

auditoria that might have been part of Alexandria's ancient **university**, with an annual enrolment of five thousand students. **Opera** concerts are staged in the Roman Theatre over summer; see Alex Agenda for details.

The Villa of Birds

It's worth buying a separate ticket to view the **Villa of Birds**. Built during the reign of Hadrian (117–138 AD), this dwelling burnt down the following century, but some of its wonderful mosaic floors have survived. The largest depicts peacocks, parrots, quail, pigeons and other birds. Others feature a panther, and stylised flower designs.

En route to the villa you'll pass a laboratory for cleaning antiques, with masonry dredged from the sea bed laid outside. Archeologists are currently unearthing a **Temple of Bastet** discovered in 2010 on the northern edge of Kom el-Dikka (off-limits).

Sharia Safiya Zaghloul

Exiting Kom el-Dikka and turning northwards round the corner of the site, you'll come to a **statue of Khedive Ismail** that once stood by the Corniche. It was removed in 1956 when Ismail became reviled by nationalists as a dupe of colonialism, and has only now been granted a permanent home here.

From the statue, cross over Sharia Horriya and head north along **Sharia Safiya Zaghloul**. In Cavafy's day this was called the Rue Missala and known for its billiard halls and rent boys; today it is named after the wife of the nationalist leader and noted for its shops and cinemas.

The Quartier Grec

The turning just beyond the Metro Cinema leads to the heart of what was once the **Quartier Grec**, or Greek Quarter, one of five urban zones allotted to different ethnic groups by Mohammed Ali that became as rich and cosmopolitan as Alexandria itself. Many of its villas now house foreign **cultural centres** (see p.490), including the American Center, previously owned by the philanthropist and Zionist Georges Menasce.

The quarter's most famous building is the **Greco-Roman Museum**, whose Classical facade is visible at the far end of Sharia al-Mathaf ar-Romani. Formerly home to Egypt's best collection of classical antiquities, it is currently closed indefinitely pending the construction of a second floor.

Alexandria National Museum

110 Tariq Gamal Abdel Nasser • Daily 9am–4.30pm • £E35 • ⓦ alexmuseum.org.eg

Occupying an Italianate mansion once owned by a wood merchant, the **Alexandria National Museum** displays some of the amazing archeological finds made in and around the city since the 1990s. Artfully lit and with informative English labelling, the museum also has an impressive art and history bookshop.

The ground floor

The ground floor affords pride of place to Hellenistic artefacts from **Herakleion** and **Canopus** (see p.481–482). A diorite sphinx, a priest of Isis carrying a Canopic jar and a statue of the goddess share the spotlight with a granite stele of Nectanebo II that once stood at the mouth of the Canopic branch (see p.481) of the Nile. From **ancient Alexandria** come an effigy of Emperor Caracalla in pharaonic headgear, a **mosaic** of Medusa found beneath a cinema and the **head of Briniky**, the wife of Ptolemy II. The latest exhibit is a marble statue of a naked warrior, presumed to represent **Alexander the Great**, which was found beneath the Shallalat Gardens in 2009.

The upper floor

Upstairs, mother-of-pearl-inlaid doors and *mashrabiyas* precede **Coptic** stelae and friezes carved with lions, sheep or grapevines, followed by icons, priestly garments and accoutrements. The **Islamic** artefacts include sashes and capes of Persian or Turkish origin, gold coins minted under the Fatimid and Byzantine empires and Mamluke and Ottoman weaponry. A final room entitled "Alexandria in the Twenty-First Century" juxtaposes photos of colonial street scenes and a satellite view of the city with tableware, jewellery and medals from King Farouk's collection. Look out for the life-size silver fish with a flexible body.

4

Sharia Sa'ad Zaghloul

The old heart of "European" Alexandria lies less than 500m west of Midan Sa'ad Zaghloul, a short walk along **Sharia Sa'ad Zaghloul**, which starts as a busy shopping street aglow with neon, and ends as a shadowy alley. Along the way you can see traces of the past in Art Deco frontages and faded plaques bearing Greek, French or Armenian names, and stop at atmospheric coffee houses or bars for refreshment (see pp.486–488).

At the far end you'll find the **Majestic Building** where the British novelist E.M. Forster (author of *A Room with a View* and *A Passage to India*) stayed when it was a hotel, during World War I. Across the road stands the derelict **Menasce Synagogue**, a relic of the area's social complexion a century ago, like the German **Protestant Church** on Sharia el-Akkad el-Boustra.

Midan Orabi and Midan Tahrir

Emerging from Sharia Sa'ad Zaghloul onto **Midan Orabi** you'll see a Neoclassical **Monument of the Unknown Soldier** facing the seafront, where a naval guard of honour is changed every hour on the hour. The square is named after the leader of the 1882 Orabi Revolt, Egypt's first attempt to cast off European colonial rule, punished by a naval bombardment of the city.

Midan Tahrir

Midan Orabi forms a T-shape with an even larger square, whose equestrian **statue of Mohammed Ali** rears outside the former **Mixed Courts**, where foreigners were once tried under their own jurisprudence rather than Egyptian law. After the 1952 revolution it was named **Midan Tahrir** (Liberation Square), where, on the revolution's fourth anniversary, Nasser delivered a speech climaxing in the announcement that Egypt had taken possession of the Suez Canal. More recently, it was the site of million-strong demonstrations against the Mubarak regime during Egypt's 2011 revolution.

Sharia Salah Salem

Running off the eastern end of Midan Tahrir is the erstwhile Bond Street (as the British conceived it) of Alexandria, now called **Sharia Salah Salem** and less chic than in colonial times, but still the place to find antiques and jewellery.

THE PHAROS

Alexandria's lighthouse, the **Pharos**, was one of the Seven Wonders of the ancient world. Transcending its practical role as a navigational aid and early-warning system, it became synonymous with the city itself: a combination of aesthetic beauty and technological audacity, exceeding 125m (perhaps even 150m) in height, including the statue of Zeus at its summit.

Possibly conceived by Alexander himself, the Pharos took twelve years to build under the direction of an Asiatic Greek, Sostratus, and was completed in 283 BC. Its square base contained three hundred rooms which, according to legend, once housed the seventy rabbis who translated the Hebrew scriptures into Greek, and perhaps also machinery for hauling fuel up to the lantern in the cylindrical third storey, whose light is thought to have been visible 56km away. Some chroniclers also mention a "mirror" that enabled the lighthouse keepers to observe ships far out at sea.

Around 700 AD the lantern collapsed, or was demolished by a treasure-hunting caliph; the base survived unscathed and Ibn Tulun restored the second level, until an earthquake in 1303 reduced the whole structure to rubble, which is now strewn over the seabed beyond Fort Qaitbey.

Divers have located over 2500 stone objects **underwater** at depths of 6–8m, including the head of a colossus of Ptolemy as pharaoh, and the base of an obelisk inscribed to Seti I, both of which have been brought to the surface. In addition, there are several **monoliths**, weighing 50–70 ton apiece and embedded in the rock by the impact of their fall, which can only have belonged to the lighthouse.

Five hundred metres offshore **wrecks** of Greek and Roman trading vessels laden with amphorae of wine and fish sauce have been found, along with over fifty **anchors** of all eras – more pieces in the mosaic picture of ancient Alexandria that's emerging from surveys of the Eastern Harbour.

Divers may explore these and other sites for themselves (see box, p.482).

Further along on the left, the building at **2 Sharia Mahmoud Azmi** is associated with Lawrence Durrell (who worked at a propaganda bureau here in 1942) and the **Al-Fayeds** (of Harrods fame), who founded their first trading company here (its sign remains) and went on to become international business moguls – a far cry from their impoverished childhood in Anfushi.

Sharia Mesjid al-Attarin

The parallel **Sharia Mesjid al-Attarin** is named after the fourteenth-century **Attarine Mosque** that stands on the site of the fourth-century Church of St Athanasius, from which Napoleon's forces removed a seven-ton sarcophagus, thought to be Alexander's but later attributed to the XXX Dynasty pharaoh Nectanebo I. The neighbouring **Greek Orthodox** and **Catholic cathedrals** are the heart of their respective communities, while the lane running between Sidi el Mitiwalli and Ahmed Morsi Badr streets harbours the **Attarine antique market**, an intriguing place to browse.

Northwest of Midan Tahrir

Northwest of Midan Tahrir, grandiose edifices give way to **souks** spreading off **Sharia Nokrashi** – heaving with fruit and vegetable stalls, butchers and hardware stores – and **Sharia Faransa** (French), devoted to clothes and dressmaking materials. Before the 1952 revolution, Nokrashi was notorious for its child bordellos. In *The Alexandria Quartet*, Justine sought her kidnapped daughter here, the diplomat Mountolive was mauled by child prostitutes and Scobie (modelled on "Bimbashi" McPherson, the paedophile head of the prewar British secret police) killed his neighbours with moonshine whisky.

Anfushi

Tram #15 from Midan Ramleh runs one block inland from the Corniche, past or within walking distance of all the Anfushi and Ras el-Tin sights

Although the **Eastern Harbour** is no longer the busy port of ancient times, its graceful curve is definitely appealing. As it sweeps around towards Fort Qaitbey, bureaucratic monoliths give way to stately palms and weathered colonial mansions, likened by author Michael Palin to "Cannes with acne". Walking at least some of the way along the Corniche is highly recommended, but you may wish to use minibuses or trams for longer distances.

In ancient times, a seven-league dike – the **Heptastadion** – connected Alexandria to a towering lighthouse on an island – the Pharos (see box, p.472). Allowed to silt up after the Arab conquest, the causeway gradually turned into a peninsula that the newcomers built over, creating the **Anfushi** quarter (or El-Anfushi). Its Ottoman mosques, ramshackle *mashrabiya*'d houses and bustling streetlife makes Anfushi ripe for exploration.

Terbana and Abu al-Abbas al-Mursi mosques

Sharia Faransa • Daily 6am–8pm • Free

The seventeenth-century **Terbana Mosque** incorporates a public drinking fountain and numerous antique columns; a huge pair with Corinthian capitals supports the minaret. Further north, the **Mosque of Abu al-Abbas al-Mursi** honours the patron saint of local fishermen and sailors, a thirteenth-century Andalucian sheikh. The existing mosque was built in 1938 by an Italian architect, but its keel-arched panels, elaborately carved domes and cornices look as old as the sixteenth-century original.

Fort Qaitbey
Sharia Qasr Qaitbey · Daily 9am–4pm · £E25

One tram stop after Al-Mursi's mosque, take a short walk past a fishing port and **shipbuilding** yard full of brightly painted wooden boats to reach a narrow promontory culminating in **Fort Qaitbey.** Built in the 1480s by the Mamluke Sultan Qaitbey (see p.120), and later beefed up by Mohammed Ali, this Toytown citadel is an Alexandrian landmark, its limestone ramparts buffeted by wind-borne spray, its flag forever rippling.

The fort's keep contains a small museum of maritime artefacts, but the real justification for the admission fee is its sweeping **view** of the city, with fishing boats bobbing on the Mediterranean and the futuristic library glinting across the Eastern Harbour. In addition, notice several huge **red-granite pillars** incorporated in the fort's outer walls, which are thought to have come from the Pharos that once stood here (see box, p.472).

Ras el-Tin
Tram #15 runs past the fish market and the Anfushi Tombs, near Ras el-Tin Palace garden

The **Ras el-Tin** (Cape of Figs) quarter covers a headland flanking the Western Harbour, whose Mediterranean shoreline hosts Alexandria's fabulous **fish market**, where freshly netted fish and crustaceans are haggled over by merchants and housewives waving scaling-knives and shopping bags. Come early to catch the market in full swing; it begins winding down after 10am. Later in the day, you can enjoy a meal at one of the **fish restaurants** on Sharia Safar Pasha, further inland.

Ras el-Tin Palace
Sharia Qasr Ras el-Tin · Garden: Daily 24hr · Free

The headland is distinguished by the **Ras el-Tin Palace** overlooking the Western Harbour, whose audience hall was sited so that Mohammed Ali could watch his new fleet at anchor while reclining on his divan. On July 26, 1952 it witnessed **King Farouk's abdication** following the Free Officers' coup in Cairo three days earlier. Farouk departed on the royal yacht to a 21-gun salute, accompanied by an English nursemaid, three Albanian bodyguards, a dog trainer and 244 trunks, to spend the rest of his life in exile.

Although the palace is off-limits, its formal **garden** is open to the public.

The Anfushi Tombs
Sharia Qasr Ras el-Tin · Daily 9am–5pm · £E20

Near the entrance to the garden of Ras el-Tin Palace you'll find the rock-cut **Anfushi Tombs**, uncovered in 1901 – thought to be part of a subterranean necropolis extending as far as Ras el-Tin Palace. Sited in pairs around a staircase, the four tombs are painted to simulate costly alabaster or marble and belonged to third-century BC Greek Alexandrians who adopted Ancient Egyptian funerary practices. The right-hand set has pictures of Egyptian gods, warships and feluccas; a Greek workman has also immortalized his mate's virtues in graffiti.

The submerged Royal Quarters
On the other side of the Eastern Harbour, some 4km from Anfushi, a narrow promontory juts from the shore near the library. Its Arabic name, **Silsilah**, refers to an iron chain fastened here in medieval and ancient times, which could be strung across the harbour to prevent ships from entering or leaving.

Nowadays occupied by the navy and out of bounds, Silsilah's interest lies in the **underwater** discoveries made since 1996 by Franck Goddio and his team, whose survey of the seabed five metres down has revealed extensive submerged ruins from the **ancient Royal Quarters** of Alexandria, including granite columns, votive statues, sphinxes, pavements, ceramics and a pier (see ⓦunderwaterdiscovery.org). Goddio was quick to claim that they had found the site of **Cleopatra's palace** on the island of Antirrhodos (where she met her death), which had been plunged into the sea by an earthquake and a tsunami in 365 AD – an assertion questioned by archeologists until he found inscriptions verifying his claim. Ever since, the Supreme Council of Antiquities (SCA) has dreamt of creating the world's first underwater museum – with Plexiglas tunnels that would allow visitors to stroll below the surface – but so far nobody has figured out how to prevent algae from obscuring the view from the tunnels.

Meanwhile you can investigate the ruins by **diving**, with visibility at its best (from 7–20m) from April to June and October to December. Contact Alexandria Dive (see p.482) for all arrangements. Besides seven or eight sphinxes (one 5m long), a giant obelisk and numerous columns, divers can see the wreck of a British **Beaufort bomber** that narrowly missed crashing into the *Hotel Cecil* in 1942; the pilot's flight mask is fused into the rock.

The Bibliotheca Alexandrina

Inland from Silsilah, the city's futuristic **Bibliotheca Alexandrina** resembles a giant discus embedded in the ground, representing a second sun rising beside the Mediterranean. Pictograms, hieroglyphs and letters from every alphabet are carved on its exterior, evoking the diversity of knowledge embodied in the ancient library and the aspirations of the new one. Seventeen years in the building at a cost of $355 million, the library was controversial even before its inauguration in 2002 (when an exhibition of books from every nation featured the *Protocols of the Elders of Zion* as Israel's entry), but no one doubts its impact on the city's cultural scene or its must-see status with tourists.

In and around the library

On the inland side facing Sharia Bur Said, a **colossus of Ptolemy II** dredged from the Eastern Harbour watches over ticket kiosks and a cloakroom (where all bags must be checked in). Inside, maps, engravings and photos in the **Impressions of Alexandria** exhibit show how the city has evolved since antiquity and its ruination by the British in 1882. A fine **Antiquities Museum** in the basement displays a giant head of Serapis, a black basalt Isis salvaged from Herakleion and two mosaic floors unearthed during the building of the library, one depicting a dog beside a brass cup, the other a gladiator locked in combat. Ancient scrolls and tomes can be seen in the dimly lit **Manuscripts Museum** on the entrance level. Or simply wander at will through the vast **reading area** – a stunning cascade of levels upheld by stainless-steel pillars suggestive of the columns in pharaonic temples.

The library's stunning design (by a Norwegian–Austrian team) is matched by the diversity of events at the **Arts Centre** in the block opposite the entrance – see the website for what's on. The entire area is a wi-fi zone, where Alexandrians gather with their laptops and smartphones. There's also the **Planetarium**, a Death Star-like spheroid on the plaza facing the sea, screening IMAX science movies (£E25) for children.

INFORMATION **BIBLIOTHECA ALEXANDRINA**

Opening hours Sat–Thurs 11am–7pm, Fri 3–7pm
Tickets Choose between a basic library ticket (£E10; no children under 6) or a combination ticket (£E45; no student discount) which also covers the Antiquities and Manuscripts museums inside. Alternatively, individual tickets for these (£E20 each) are sold on the spot.

Tours Free tours in English leave every 45min from just inside the entrance.
Website ⓦ bibalex.org
Photography Photography is permitted in the reading room if you buy a permit (£E20), but not in the museums or exhibitions.

ANCIENT ALEXANDRIA'S LIBRARY

Founded shortly after the city itself, on the advice of Ptolemy I's counsellor Demetrius of Phalerum, in antiquity Alexandria's library stood beside the Mouseion (see p.470) in the heart of the city. Dedicated to "the writings of all nations", the library welcomed scholars and philosophers and supported research and debates. By law, all ships docking at Alexandria were obliged to allow any scrolls on board to be copied, if they were of interest. By the mid-first century BC it held 532,800 manuscripts (all catalogued by the Head Librarian, Callimachus), and later spawned a subsidiary attached to the **Temple of Serapis**. The two were known as the "**Mother**" and "**Daughter**" libraries and together contained perhaps 700,000 scrolls (equivalent to about 100,000 printed books today).

As many as 40,000 (or even 400,000) scrolls were burned during Julius Caesar's assault on the city in 48 BC, when he supported Cleopatra against her brother Ptolemy XIII; as compensation, Mark Antony gave her the entire contents of the Pergamum Library in Anatolia (200,000 scrolls). But it was Christian mobs that destroyed this vast storehouse of "pagan" knowledge, torching the Mother Library in 293 and the Daughter Library in 391, though medieval Europe later mythologized its destruction as proof of Arab barbarism. An apocryphal tale had the Muslim leader Amr pronouncing: "If these writings of the Greeks agree with the Koran they are useless, and need not be preserved; if they disagree, they are pernicious, and ought to be destroyed."

Pompey's Pillar

Sharia Amoud el-Sawary • Daily 9am–4.30pm, Ramadan 9am–3pm • £E20 • £E20 by taxi from the centre

The poor **Karmous quarter** in the southwest of the city contains two ancient monuments, best seen together. Though the two are sufficiently close to each other that strolling between them is feasible, it's easier to catch a taxi from the centre than to walk here from Midan el-Gumhorriya (about 30min). Note that taxi drivers know Pompey's Pillar by its Arabic name, Amoud al-Sawary.

Pompey's Pillar is easy to spot: an elegant column hewn from red Aswan granite, towering 30m above a ridge beside a cemetery. Named by nineteenth-century Europeans after the Roman consul Pompey – who was treacherously murdered while seeking asylum in Egypt in 48 BC – the pillar was actually erected in 291 AD to bear a statue of Emperor Diocletian, who threatened to massacre Alexandria's populace "until their blood reached his horse's knees", but desisted when his steed slipped and bloodied itself prematurely.

The pillar stands on the site of the **Temple of Serapis**, a deity invented by the Ptolemies to link their Greek god Dionysus with the Ancient Egyptian cult of the Apis bulls at Saqqara (see p.165). The temple later housed Cleopatra's "Daughter Library" of 42,800 texts, which outlived the Mother Library by almost a century, only to be destroyed by Christian mobs in 391 AD. All that remain are three subterranean **galleries** where the sacred bulls were interred, several **sphinxes** (originally from Heliopolis) and Egypt's most northerly **Nilometer**. Given what used to exist here, it's hard not to be disappointed.

Catacombs of Kom es-Shoqafa

Sharia el-Shenity Abu Mandour • Daily 9am–4.30pm (Ramadan 9am–3pm) • £E35 • No photography • £E20 by taxi from the centre or 10min walk from Pompey's Pillar (turn right around the corner after leaving Pompey's Pillar and follow the road on for five minutes; the entrance to the catacombs is on the left 150m beyond a small square)

The **Catacombs of Kom es-Shoqafa**'s prosaic Arabic name, "Mound of Shards", hardly does justice to their wonderful amalgam of spookiness and kitsch. The catacombs were discovered in 1900 when a donkey disappeared through the ground. Hewn 35m into solid rock, with the deepest of its chambers about 20m below street level, this is the largest known Roman burial structure in Egypt, and one of the last major constructions to pay tribute to the Ancient Egyptian religion, albeit in a distorted

form. For more information, buy Jean-Yves Empereur's excellently illustrated *A Short Guide to the Catacombs of Kom es-Shoqafa*, available at the site.

Reached via a spiral **stairway** beside the shaft down which bodies were lowered on ropes, the catacombs probably began as a family crypt in the second century AD, growing into a labyrinth as extra chambers were dug to accommodate more than three hundred bodies over the three centuries that it remained in use. Today, the lowest level has been partially submerged by the rising water-table.

Off the bottom of the staircase is a niched **Rotunda** with a central well, plummeting to the flooded depths. As originally constructed, this led only to the principal tomb (straight ahead; see below), and a **Triclinium**, or banqueting hall (to your left), where relatives toasted the dead from stone couches; the first archeologists to enter it found wine jars and tableware.

Close by, tomb-robbers had already dug through into an older, separate crypt, featuring a lofty chamber riddled with *loculi* (family burial niches) which were sealed with plaster slabs once full. European scholars named it the **Hall of Caracalla** after the Roman emperor who massacred Alexandrian youths at a festival in 215 AD. A **mural** beside the hole between the two sections depicts the mummification of Osiris and the kidnapping of Persephone by Hades, illustrating how Ancient Egyptian and Greek funerary myths coexisted in Alexandria.

The most dramatic relic of the time when "the old faiths began to merge and melt" (in E.M. Forster's words) is the **Principal Tomb,** one level beneath the Rotunda. Its vestibule is guarded by reliefs of bearded serpents with Medusa-headed shields and muscle-bound statues of the Egyptian gods Sobek and Anubis wearing Roman armour.

Bab Sharq

Bordering El-Manshiya, the affluent **Bab Sharq** district can be easily approached from the Quartier Grec (see p.470) or en route to the Corniche beaches (see p.479). Its nexus is **Midan Khartoum**, an L-shaped park whose Ptolemaic **column** (erected to celebrate Britain's recapture of Khartoum in 1898) is a local landmark at the junction of Sharia Horriya and the Sharia Canal El Suez.

Shallalat Gardens

Midan Khartoum • Daily 24hr • Free

Flanking Midan Khartoum, the hilly **Shallalat Gardens** are ablaze with scarlet flame trees in summer. Their nineteenth-century designer utilized remnants of the Arab city walls and a canal to create rockeries and ornamental ponds. Here, E.M. Forster had his first date with Mohammed el-Adl, a tram conductor whom he met at Ramleh in the winter of 1916–17. The racial, class and sexual barriers that their relationship challenged underlie the finale of *A Passage to India*, which Forster was struggling with when he learned of Mohammed's death in 1922. Near the northwest corner of the Gardens is the **Ibn el-Nabih Cistern** (dawn–dusk; free), its three levels upheld by antique columns from older structures.

The Bab Sharq cemeteries

Beyond Sharia Canal El Suez lies a sprawling necropolis of **cemeteries** consecrated to diverse faiths, full of lavish mausolea and sculptures. Though most date from the nineteenth or twentieth centuries, burials have occurred here since ancient times. An **alabaster antechamber** (off-limits) near Sharia Anubis (the road that bisects the necropolis) is believed by some to be part of a tumulus that might once have contained Alexander the Great's tomb.

Smouha

The **Smouha** district in the southern suburbs is a magnet for wealthy Alexandrians,

---

THE AMBRON VILLA

Aficionados of **Lawrence Durrell** may wish to track down his last Alexandrian residence, in the suburb of Moharrem Bey, to the east of the Karmous quarter. Once home to Alexandria's mercantile elite, Moharrem Bey's mansions have become slums since the 1950s, but you can still see the **Ambron Villa** where Durrell and his muse Eve Cohen rented the top floor in 1943–44; *Prospero's Cell* and *The Dark Labyrinth* were written in the corner tower. Though it's now a listed building, the villa has been allowed to decay and developers have built flats in the garden where the painter Gilda Ambron shared a studio with their neighbour, Clea Badaro, who inspired the character Cleo in *The Alexandria Quartet*. As the villa can't be entered, only hardcore fans will find it worth the expense of a taxi (£E20). Get someone to write the address (19 Sharia al-Ma'amoun) in Arabic to show to the driver.

---

thanks to the **Zahran and Smouha Malls**, 300–400m from Sidi Gaber Station, and the **Green Plaza Mall** and **Carrefour City Center** (run by the French chain Carrefour), out near Lake Maryut. The district is named after the Baghdad-born Jewish architect Joseph Smouha, whose Smouha City (as it was originally called) was the local equivalent of Cairo's Heliopolis, a modern suburb for the upper-middle classes. Though all the "foreigners" were dispossessed by Nasser, their legacies – and names – survive in present-day Alexandria.

The Antoniadis, Zoological and Nouzha Gardens

Embellished with Classical statuary, the **Antoniadis Gardens** (daily 9am–4pm; £E10) were once the private grounds of a wealthy Greek family and now host opera concerts over the summer. Nearby are the **Zoological Gardens** (same hours; £E5) and **Nouzha Gardens** (same hours; £E5), laid out under Khedive Ismail. In ancient times, this was a residential suburb inhabited by the likes of Callimachus (310–240 BC), the Head Librarian of the Bibliotheca Alexandrina.

4

East along the coast

Alexandria's beaches are an overworked asset. Hardly a square metre of sand goes unclaimed during high season, when millions of Egyptians descend on the city. Before June the beaches furthest out are relatively uncrowded, except on Fridays, Saturdays and public holidays. Aside from the paying beaches at Montazah (see p.481) and Ma'amoura, baladi modesty prevails, with women sunbathing or wading into the sea fully clothed – no wonder foreigners prefer beach holidays at European-style resorts on the Red Sea. Many visitors also travel further out to **Abu Qir** for its seafood (though you can eat just as well closer in to Alexandria) or go **diving** shipwrecks or sunken ruins. There are also various attractions on land including the **Royal Jewellery Museum** in Glym (if it's reopened), the **Mahmoud Said Museum** in San Stefano and the extensive grounds of the **Montazah** palace, further along the coast.

Shatby

Beyond the library the district known as **Shatby** is overshadowed by **St Mark's College**, a massive, red-brick, neo-Baroque edifice whose dome is visible from afar. Founded to educate the city's Christian elite, it now forms part of Alexandria University.

On the far side of Sharia Bur Said is the grandly named **Shatby Necropolis** (daily 9am–4pm, Ramadan 9am–3pm; £E20), a small pit exposing some rock-cut ossuaries and sarcophagi from the third century BC. The adjacent **Camp Cesar** looks no grander for its association with Julius Caesar (who camped here during the battle that left Cleopatra at his mercy), while neighbouring **Ibrahimiya** was the birthplace of Hitler's deputy Führer, Rudolf Hess.

Bacos to Stanley Bay

Shortly before Cleopatra beach, tram #2 turns further inland, passing through the **Bacos** quarter where Gamal Abdel Nasser was born on January 15, 1918. Tram #1 runs closer to **Cleopatra** beach, which has no connection with the lady herself, although the nearby **Roushdi** district was the site of Nikopolis, which Octavian founded because he hated living in Alexandria. Today, Roushdi is the centre of the city's expat life, but a vestige of its origins remains in the form of the **Mustafa Kamel Necropolis** (daily 9am–4pm; £E20). Its four tombs, discovered in 1933, date from the second century BC; two are upheld by Doric columns and one contains a mural of a horseman. To get here, catch tram #2 from Ramleh to Roushdi tram station and walk towards the Corniche along Sharia al-Mo'asker al-Romani.

Travelling along the Corniche, you'll cross the **Stanley Bridge**, whose supporting towers mimic the Turko-Florentine architecture at Montazah. From the bridge, which takes only eastbound traffic, you can see **Stanley Bay**'s tiers of concrete sun terraces and bathing cabins, built by the British in the 1920s.

Royal Jewellery Museum

27 Sharia Ahmed Yehia • Daily 9am–2pm & 5–7pm (when it reopens) • £E35 • Tram #2 from Midan Ramleh to the El-Fenoun el-Gamilia or Qasr el-Safa stop

Three blocks inland from Glym Beach, the **Royal Jewellery Museum** has been closed since the 2011 revolution to safeguard its treasures from looters – ask at the tourist office to see if it has reopened. The museum is housed in a mansion built for Mohammed Ali's granddaughter, Princess Fatima el-Zaharaa and her husband, that's as splendidly vulgar as the treasures on display. Among the highlights are Mohammed Ali's diamond-inlaid snuffbox, King Farouk's gold chess set, a platinum crown with 2159 diamonds and his diamond-studded gardening tools. The gallery downstairs is lined with stained-glass cameos of courtly love in eighteenth-century France, while images of Provençal farmers, milkmaids and food decorate the service corridors. Upstairs are the wildest his 'n' hers bathrooms: hers with tiled murals of nymphs bathing in a waterfall; his with scenes of Côte d'Azur fishermen.

Mahmoud Said Museum

Sharia Mahmoud Said Pasha • Daily except Mon 10am–6pm • £E10 • Tram #1 or #2 from Midan Ramleh to Gianaclis (the stop after the Jewellery Museum)

The **Mahmoud Said Museum** – in an Italianate villa that once belonged to its namesake – showcases the work of three Egyptians who pioneered the European art of easel-painting from the 1920s onwards. Together, they forged a "national" tradition of figurative painting where none had existed under Islam, inspired by the Fayoum Portraits of the Greco-Roman era.

A judge who painted as a hobby, **Mahmoud Said** (1897–1964) was the first Egyptian artist to receive a state prize, yet he disliked official commissions such as the wall-sized *Inaugural Ceremony of the Suez Canal* that greets visitors to the museum, preferring to paint pensive, sensual women or landscapes of Alexandria and Lebanon.

Upstairs, six rooms are devoted to the brothers Seif (1906–79) and Adham (1908–59) Wanly, who founded the first Egyptian artists' studio in 1942. **Seif** was an Expressionist who depicted such bourgeois delights as casinos, nightclubs and horse-racing, while **Adham** was into Cubism, abstraction and Socialist Realism, producing such polemical works as *Hunger* and *Palestine*.

Montazah

16km east of the centre; entry from Sharia Malak Hefni • Daily 24hr • £E6 • Minibus #11, #260, #729 & #766 via the Corniche, or #729 & #768 from Masr Station; £E35 by taxi

The Corniche ends at **Montazah**, a former royal retreat that's now the city's pleasure ground. Created by Khedive Abbas Hilmy (1892–1914) as a summer refuge from the

HYPATIA OF ALEXANDRIA

After Cleopatra, the most famous woman of Egypt's Greco-Roman era was **Hypatia of Alexandria** (c.350–415 AD). Her mathematician father Theon (the last head of the Daughter Library) had Hypatia educated in Athens and Italy, where she imbibed the philosophy of Aristotle, Plato and Plotinus, which she taught after returning home. Besides developing Neo-Platonist philosophy, she wrote (or co-authored with Theon) many mathematical treatises; reputedly charted celestial bodies (quite likely); and invented the hydrometer for measuring the specific gravity of liquids (almost certainly untrue).

As the personification of a Hellenistic tradition of enquiry – and an influential learned woman – Hypatia was hated by early Christians as a pagan sorceress. Her atrocious murder was instigated during Lent by a monk called Peter the Reader; a Christian mob stripped her naked, dragged her to the Caesareum and flayed her alive using oyster shells or ceramic tiles. Historians dispute the culpability of Bishop Cyril (later made a Coptic saint) in her murder, but few doubt that it marked the end of Alexandria's glory as a centre of enlightenment.

In modern times she has been acclaimed as a feminist icon, portrayed in novels such as Brian Trent's *Remembering Hypatia* and the 2009 Hollywood film *Agora*. Science has also honoured her, bestowing her name on an asteroid belt, a lunar crater and a species of moth.

heat of Cairo, it was embellished by his successors, who cherished Montazah's privacy, surrounded by high walls and the sea.

Today, Alexandrians flock here to enjoy the lush gardens and flamboyant Turko-Florentine architecture. Avenues of palms and flowerbeds converge on the Disneyesque **Haramlik Palace**, whose tower is modelled on one at the Palazzo Vecchio in Florence. Commissioned by King Fouad, the palace served as a Red Cross hospital during World War I – E.M. Forster worked here as a nurse. Restored by Sadat as a presidential residence and guesthouse, it remains off-limits to the public. Further inland, the **El Salamlek Palace**, built in the form of an Alpine chalet for the Austrian mistress of Khedive Abbas, is now the *El Salamlek Palace* hotel (see p.485).

Venezia Beach

The largest of Montazah's rocky bays is rimmed by **Venezia Beach** (£E15 admission, including use of a beach chair and umbrella), where the dress standards for women are fairly liberal. A promontory ending in an ornate "Turkish" **Belvedere** and a **lighthouse** encloses the bay, providing a sheltered spot for windsurfing and snorkelling in summer. The lighthouse is thought to occupy the site of the temple of Taposiris Parva, whose last high priestess was Hypatia of Alexandria (see box above).

Ancient Canopus

Further east along the coast, beyond the paying beach and villas of Ma'amoura, naval bases occupy the site of ancient **Canopus** (no access). This once-great Delta city flourished when a branch of the Nile reached the sea by the nearby "Canopic Mouth". Myth has it that Canopus was founded by a Greek navigator returning from the Trojan Wars, whom the locals later worshipped in the form of a jar with a human head – hence the term **Canopic jars,** bestowed on similar receptacles used to preserve mummies' viscera.

Although **diving** offshore is rarely permitted by the navy, you can see life-size statues of Ptolemaic rulers and some of the thousands of bronze pots and incense burners found on the sea bed in 2004 in the Alexandria National Museum (see p.471) and the Antiquities Museum (p.475).

Abu Qir

21km from the centre • Minibus #260 or #766 via the Corniche, or #729 or #768 from Masr Station; £E40 by taxi

The seaside suburb of **Abu Qir** (pronounced Abu Ear) is popular with Alexandrians for its al fresco **seafood restaurants** (see p.487), but its tatty beach is less alluring to

DIVING IN ALEXANDRIA

Blocks from the Pharos litter the sea bed near Fort Qaitbey, with Roman trading vessels lying 500m offshore (see box, p.472), while the ruins of Cleopatra's Palace can be dived near Silsilah (see p.474). Both these sites are only 5–8m underwater, so even uncertified divers may be accepted if they can pass a try-out. Diving in **Abu Qir Bay** requires more open-water experience, whether you're exploring Napoleonic wrecks or the ruins of ancient Herakleion (see below). Still more experience is required on three-day **wreck-diving safaris** along the coast as far west as Mersa Matrouh that explore sunken German U-boats and Allied cargo ships. For all these excursions you must supply your passport details up to four days ahead. Images of ancient ruins and wrecks around Alexandria can be seen on ⓦcealex.org under "Excavations".

Alexandra Dive Sharia 26 Yulyu, Eastern Harbour ⓘ012 2906 5477, ⓦalexandra-dive.com. Reputable operator offering one-day boat excursions (££60 including lunch and permit; equipment ££20 extra) to four different sites, with two dives at each location. They also do PADI courses, from Open-Water (££280) up to Divemaster.

foreigners than the waters of **Abu Qir Bay,** whose submerged shipwrecks and ancient ruins are fantastic for **diving**. This must be arranged several days beforehand (see box above) and entails choosing between two different dive sites: Napoleonic wrecks or the ruins of ancient Herakleion (unless you dive both on consecutive days).

The wrecks

The **wrecks** of the warships **L'Orient**, **Sèrieuse** and **Artèmise** were first discovered in the 1960s by an Egyptian diver at a depth of 9–11m, 8km offshore, but their location was forgotten until 1983, when they were relocated by a Frenchman whose own records were lost when he died two years later. Not until 1998–99 did Franck Goddio's team re-locate and excavate the wrecks. Much of *L'Orient*'s timber framing has survived, though its top deck has collapsed onto the lower ones, posing snag hazards for divers. Anchors, cannons and other hardware can still be seen.

All three ships belonged to the French fleet that was sunk by England's Admiral Nelson in the so-called **Battle of the Nile** (1–3 Aug, 1798) that scuppered Napoleon's dream of an eastern empire. Though the two fleets were evenly matched, Admiral Bruey had his ships cabled together in shallow water when Nelson's fleet charged them amidships, inflicting carnage at close quarters. The French lost eleven ships and seventeen thousand men, the English two ships and 218 sailors.

Underwater ruins of Herakleion

Two years after excavating *L'Orient*, Goddio's team found the **ruins of Herakleion** 6.5km offshore. This ancient port fell into the sea some 1300 years earlier due to coastal erosion, earthquakes, and/or a tsunami, being buried by sediment 23–30m underwater. Its identity was only confirmed by a granite stele inscribed with the city's Ancient Egyptian name, Toins, and part of the Temple of Hercules seen by Herodotus in the fifth century BC (who dismissed the legend that Hercules once blocked the Nile to prevent a flood).

Marine archeologists have examined the remnants of vast buildings, harbours and a dozen ships, salvaging several statues and stele from the sea bed – but thousands of artefacts remain half-buried in silt or covered in seaweed, for divers to discover.

ARRIVAL AND DEPARTURE   ALEXANDRA

Most tourists reach Alexandria from Cairo, either by **train** (the easiest way, arriving in the downtown area), **bus** (the next best option, ending up on the outskirts), **service taxi** (less comfortable) or **plane** (no time-saver, taking the airport journeys and check-in into account). Buses and service taxis offer two routes, travelling either by the verdant **Desert Road** past the turn-off for Wadi Natrun (whose monasteries are covered in Chapter 3), or via the congested **Delta Road** (or Agricultural Road), which is much slower, though the distance is roughly similar (about 225km).

BY AIR

EgyptAir flies directly to Alexandria (2–4 daily; 45min) from Cairo airport's terminal 3, with connecting flights (4–5 weekly) from Luxor, Aswan, Sharm el-Sheikh and Hurghada. At the time of writing, no foreign airlines flew to Alexandria, but Emirates, British Airways, Lufthansa, Air France and Olympic may do so in the future.

AIRPORTS

Borg al-Arab All flights currently land at Borg al-Arab airport (☏ 03 459 1483), 40km from the city centre (see map, p.493). Bus #555 (£E20) runs directly to the *Hotel Cecil* (see p.485) in the centre; buses to the airport depart three hours before scheduled flights (tickets are sold at a kiosk facing the *Cecil*). A taxi costs around £E140–175.

Nozha airport The smaller Nozha airport (☏ 03 425 0527) is only 6km from the centre (see map, p.462), but is closed for an upgrade at present. When it reopens, EgyptAir and other carriers might use it instead of Burg al-Arab, in which case a taxi should cost around £E75.

Al-Alamein airport Previously, some charter flights used Al-Alamein airport, 130km west of Alexandria (see map, p.493), for package holidays. A taxi from here to the city costs about £E275.

AIRLINES

Air France 6 Sharia Horriya ☏ 03 486 8547.

British Airways Burg al-Arab airport ☏ 03 459 2834.

EgyptAir 19 Midan Ramleh ☏ 03 486 5937.

BY TRAIN

There are nineteen daily a/c services to Alexandria from Cairo's Ramses Station (platforms 1–4), all requiring seat reservations. Seven are nonstop, and four halt only at Tanta in the Delta, with a journey time of 2hr 30min. The others stop at five to eight stations en route (2hr 45min–3hr 30min total journey time). There are also some forty non-a/c trains, with third- and sometimes second-class carriages only; these cost a fraction of the price of a/c services, stop everywhere, and can take four hours or more to reach Alex. All trains terminate at Alexandria's Masr Station (Mahattat Masr), about 1km south of downtown Midan Sa'ad Zaghloul (see map, p.467), which you can reach by walking up Sharia Nabi Daniel (10–15min). Some trains also stop at Sidi Gaber and/or Ma'amoura stations, in the eastern part of the city.

BY BUS

To and from Cairo Three companies run services from Cairo to Alexandria (£E25–30): Superjet, the West and Middle Delta Bus Co. and Go Bus. Superjet buses are the comfiest, with a/c, toilets and hostesses serving (pricey) tea and snacks. West and Middle Delta buses are similar, but without hostess service. Both run hourly (7am–6pm;

3hr) with less frequent services up until 11pm, all departing from Cairo's Aboud Terminal (see p.174). Superjet buses can also be boarded near the *Ramses Hilton* in downtown Cairo, where there's a ticket office. Returning to Cairo, both West Delta and Superjet have frequent services, some running on to the airport. The third company, Go Bus, run just two services daily, departing at 11am and 3pm from their ticket office near the *Ramses Hilton* in downtown Cairo. The convenience of boarding there is outweighed by hassle at the other end, as they only allow you to alight near the Carrefour City Center mall (see map, p.462), before speeding off to a remote depot on the Ring Road (£E30 by taxi to the centre if you're lucky).

To and from the rest of Egypt Many places featured in the rest of this chapter can be reached from Alexandria by bus, making day-trips to Rosetta and Tanta in the Delta easy; despite being nearer, El-Alamein and the Monastery of St Menas are awkward, while the Monasteries of Wadi Natrun (see p.378) require a taxi at least part of the way. Buy a ticket beforehand at the bus company offices listed below. West Delta buses run directly to Siwa Oasis (10hr); alternatively, you could stay overnight at Mersa Matrouh and carry on to Siwa next day. Many buses to El-Alamein and Mersa Matrouh continue to Sollum (£E35), though if you're travelling to Libya it's easier to take an international bus from Cairo to Tripoli (see p.175).

Destinations El-Alamein (West Delta hourly; Superjet services at 7.15am during summer; 1hr); Hurghada (Superjet 9pm; West Delta 9am & 6.30pm; 9–10hr); Ismailiya (West Delta 7am & 2.30pm; 5hr); Mersa Matrouh (West Delta hourly; Superjet services at 7.15am during summer; 4hr); Port Said (West Delta 6 daily; Superjet 3 daily; 4hr); Rosetta (West Delta: 7am, 8am & 3.30pm; 1hr); Sharm el-Sheikh (West Delta 9pm; Superjet 10pm; 8–10hr); Siwa Oasis (West Delta 8.30am, 11am and 10pm; 10hr); Tanta (West Delta hourly 6am–6pm; 1hr 30min); Zagazig (West Delta 8am, 9am & 2pm; 2hr).

GETTING INTO TOWN

Superjet and West Delta buses from all over Egypt arrive at the vast **Moharrem Bey Terminal** on the southern outskirts of Alexandria (see map, p.462). Often called the New Terminal (El-Mogaf Geddid), it's 20min by taxi (£E15–20) from the centre; don't be alarmed if the driver takes a roundabout route to avoid traffic jams.

BUS COMPANY OFFICES

West Delta Corner of Midan Sa'ad Zaghloul and Sharia el-Ghorfa el-Tigarya, downtown (☏ 03 480 9685), near Sidi Gaber Station beside a fountain opposite the station (☏ 03 420 6701) and at Moharrem Bey Terminal (☏ 03 363 3993).

Superjet Moharrem Bey Terminal (☏ 03 363 3551) and opposite Sidi Gaber Station (☏ 03 543 5222).

BY SERVICE TAXI

Minibuses and cars from Cairo do the run in about three hours, departing from outside Ramses Station and the Aboud Terminal, and Midan el-Rameya at the start of the Alexandria Desert Rd, their drivers yelling Iskandariya! Iskandariya! Service taxis are more cramped than buses and won't leave until nearly full, but you don't need to bother about tickets, and they sometimes make faster time. Most end up at the Moharrem Bey Terminal, but a few terminate at Masr Station or the seaside suburb of El-Agami – be sure to ask at the start of your journey. Moharrem Bey is also the point of departure for service taxis to the Delta and Canal cities; fares are approximately the same as buses to the same destinations (see above).

BY BOAT

Cruise boats While scheduled ferries from Greece, Cyprus or Syria are a distant memory, some cruise boats still feature a stopover at Alexandria on their Mediterranean itineraries. These invariably dock at the Maritime Station in the Western Harbour, access to which is restricted, so that taxis can only be hailed (or drop off passengers) outside the perimeter.

GETTING AROUND

On foot Downtown is compact enough to walk around, and a stroll along the Corniche is recommended, at least as far as the Library (15min), if not all the way out to Fort Qaitbey (35–50min). However, you really need transport to reach other outlying areas.

By tram Trams run from 5.30am to 1am, with fares of 50pt or 75pt. Destinations and route numbers are in Arabic only, but you can get an idea from the vehicle's livery where it's heading: trams between Midan Ramleh and Ras el-Tin (to the west) are painted yellow with a red or blue trim; trams between Midan Ramleh and points east are painted blue and white. On trams with three carriages, the middle one is reserved for women. Over summer, a 1936-vintage wooden tram (£E2) runs from Ramleh out to Zizinia (between Glym and Stanley).

By bus or minibus Buses (£E1.50–2) are grossly overcrowded, with passengers boarding on the run – except for the red double-decker buses (£E3) that infrequently run between downtown and Montazah. Minibuses (£E1.50–2) offer seating-only rides on many of the same routes – most usefully the #11, running along the Corniche all the way from Ras el-Tin to Montazah, via Midan Sa'ad Zaghloul and the Library.

By taxi Black-and-yellow taxis seldom use meters and will charge whatever they can get away with (especially to Masr Station or other departure points). You should pay about £E10 for a ride across downtown (say, to Shatby Beach), and £E35 for a trip all the way east to Montazah. There are also rarely seen City Taxis (silver-grey Toyota Corollas) with meters which can be booked on freephone ☎ 0800 999 9999.

By car With driving in the city so crazy, renting a car makes sense to visit El-Alamein, west of Alexandria (see pp.495–497). For self-drive rental, Avis in the *Hotel Cecil* (☎ 03 485 7400; daily 8am–8pm) charges $56/day for a Chevrolet Aveo, including 100km of mileage. For hiring a car with an English-speaking **driver**, you're better off going to Thomas Cook (see p.492).

By calèche Horse-drawn carriages solicit passengers with cries of *calèche, calèche* outside Masr Station and along the Corniche. You'll have to negotiate a price – reckon on about £E60 an hour.

INFORMATION AND TOURS

Tourist office The main office is off the southwest corner of Midan Sa'ad Zaghloul (Sun–Thurs 8.30am–6pm; Ramadan 9am–4.30pm; ☎ 03 485 1556), staffed with helpful English-speakers who can supply a city map and *Alex Agenda* (see below). There are other, less efficient branches at Masr Station (Sun–Thurs 8.30am–6pm; ☎ 03 392 5985), the Maritime Station (irregular hours; no phone) and Nozha airport (☎ 03 420 2021).

Listings For latest listings information, see two free monthly publications: the booklet *Alex Agenda* (available from hotels and the tourist office – they're also on Facebook), and *Alex Times* magazine (from Al-Ahram newspaper stands and the Fish Market restaurant).

Websites None of the tourist-oriented Alexandria sites is up-to-date, but the city's ancient and modern history is well covered on ⊕ houseofptolemy.org.

Tours Zahraa Adel Awad (☎ 010 0272 4324, ✉ egypt_tourguide@hotmail.com) leads informative walking tours ($40–60/4hr, depending on the size of the group). Her Roots Tour – aimed at people with ancestral ties to the city – can be tailored to personal wishes, such as finding the house where their grandparents once lived. Other tours are devoted to Durrell, Cavafy and E.M. Forster, or Italianate or Art Deco architecture. She also does taxi tours of Alexandria and Rosetta.

ACCOMMODATION

A sea view is a big plus, and hotels charge a premium even for side-seaview rooms. One drawback that only later becomes apparent is **tram noise** – basically, you either learn to live with it or move further inland. **Reservations** are essential in high season (June–Sept). If you don't mind being out of the centre, there are **upmarket hotels** at San Stefano, Montazah and near Alexandria's southern edge. Look for discount rates online.

DOWNTOWN

Acropole 4th floor, 27 Sharia Gamil el-Din Yassin ☎03 480 5980, ✉acropole_hotel@hotmail.com; map p.467. Very central, but within earshot of trams, this shabby 1940s *pension* has side-seaview rooms with washbasins, grungy shared bathrooms and free wi-fi. The *Transit hotel* (see below) across the landing is better, but more expensive. B&B **£E150**

Cecil 16 Midan Sa'ad Zaghloul ☎03 487 7173, ⊛sofitel .com; map p.467. An Alexandrian institution: dead central, and with wonderful views of the Eastern Harbour. Durrell, Churchill, Noel Coward and Josephine Baker head the list of former guests, but modernization and *Sofitel* management have dispelled its once decadent ambience. Regular rooms are plush with a/c but nothing special (sea view costs $74 extra) and there's a bar, nightclub and rooftop Oriental restaurant. B&B **$186**

Crillon 5 Sharia Adib Ishtak ☎03 480 0330; map p.466. A time-warped prewar *pension* on the Corniche, with a lobby full of stuffed birds and faded Art Deco rooms with seaview balconies and clean shared bathrooms on the third floor, plus pokier en-suite rooms upstairs. Guests can have an Egyptian or continental-style breakfast served on their balcony. Half board is obligatory in high season. B&B **£E142**

Egypt 3rd floor, 1 Sharia Degla ☎03 481 4483, ⊛egypthotel.7p.com; map p.467. Occupying part of a century-old Italianate apartment block on a side-street between Ramleh and the Corniche, this three-star hotel has a/c en-suite rooms with TV and fridges, seaview suites sleeping up to four people, and free wi-fi in its columned lobby. It's worth paying a little extra for a seaview room. B&B **$55**

Fouad 2nd floor, 1 Sharia Degla ☎03 487 0684, ✉messi_pop23@yahoo.com; map p.467. One floor below the *Egypt*, its lobby and rooms are less elegant, but come with TV, fans and fridges; some also have bathrooms, and seaview balconies. Their suites (£E500), sleeping up to five people, are a good deal for groups. Free wi-fi. B&B **£E250**

★ **Metropole** 52 Sharia Sa'ad Zaghloul ☎03 486 1467, ⊛paradiseinnegypt.com; map p.467. Situated just off Ramleh with most rooms facing Midan Sa'ad Zaghloul or the sea, this renovated 1900s four-star has bags of character, a gloriously over-the-top lobby, a/c rooms and palatial fittings; side- or full seaview costs $20/40 extra. Suites are furnished with antiques, king-size beds and jacuzzis, and there's free wi-fi throughout, plus a 24hr business centre. B&B **$179**; suite **$259**

New Capri 5th floor, 23 Sharia Minaa es-Sharqiya ☎03 480 9310; map p.467. This 1930s *pension* creates a favourable impression with its Arabesque decorative touches, free wi-fi, library and buffet breakfast, but its rooms (some with private bathrooms, balconies and sea views) are pretty shabby. B&B **£E132**

★ **Swiss Canal** 14 Sharia al-Bursa al-Qadima ☎03 480 8373; map p.466. Named after the Suez Canal (according its Egyptian pronunciation), this invitingly bright, old-fashioned hotel, up the road from the *Spitfire Bar* (see p.488), has an Art Deco pharaonic foyer and spacious en-suite rooms with soft beds, fridge, TV, fans or a/c (£E13 extra), painted salmon pink throughout. No breakfast. **£E90**

★ **Transit** 4th floor, 27 Sharia Gamil el-Din Yassin ☎03 485 1198 or ☎012 2648 4117, ⊛hotel-alexandria .net; map p.488. A welcome newcomer on the scene, whose super clean a/c rooms have cotton duvets, satellite TV and shower-toilet cabins; some have views of Midan Sa'ad Zaghloul and the sea. There's also free wi-fi, kitchen, internet access (£E5/hr) and laundry service, and pick-ups from Burg al-Arab airport (£E150) and excursions to El-Alamein and the Monastery of St Menas can be arranged. B&B **Dbl $30**

Triomphe 5th floor, 26 Sharia Gamil el-Din Yassin ☎03 480 7585; map p.467. Pleasantly kitsch, with lots of plants in the lobby, this place remains popular with long-stay guests, although its high-ceilinged rooms have seen better days. Double rooms have side-sea views; ensuite costs £E30 extra. Free wi-fi but no breakfast. **£E120**

Union 5th floor, 164 Sharia 26 July ☎03 480 7312, ✉unionhotelalex@gmail.com; map p.467. Not as well run as it used to be, but still popular for its pleasant en-suite rooms (with TV, a/c and sea- or side-views), and its lounge overlooking the Eastern Harbour, where they sell beer. B&B **£E113**

Windsor Palace 17 Sharia ash-Shohada ☎03 480 8256, ⊛paradiseinnegypt.com; map p.466. Run by the same chain as the *Metropole*, this refurbished Edwardian hotel charms with its wrought-iron elevators, rich green and gold decor and high-ceilinged rooms – it's worth paying $20 more for a view of the Eastern Harbour. Free wi-fi. B&B **$139**

OUTSIDE THE CENTRE

El Salamlek Palace Montazah Gardens ☎03 547 7999, ⊛sangiovanni.com; map p.463. Built by Khedive Abbas for his mistress, this bijou hunting lodge in the grounds of the royal palace (30–40min by taxi from the city centre) has six rooms and fourteen suites (from $635) furnished with antiques, a swanky restaurant, a private beach and a casino (open to non-residents with passports). B&B **$127**

★ **Four Seasons** 399 Sharia el-Geish, San Stefano ☎03 581 8000, ⊛fourseasons.com/alexandria; map p.462. Setting new standards for luxury in Alex, this marbled five-star behemoth (20min by taxi from the centre) has balconies, CD players, LCD screens and deep tubs in all its rooms. Facilities include a wellness spa, private beach and marina, and an infinity pool overlooking the Med, plus sushi and Italian restaurants. **$330**

4

Hilton Alexandria Green Plaza 14 May Bridge, Smouha (20min by taxi from the centre) ☎ 03 420 9120, ⊚ hilton.com; map p.462. With its five-star amenities and the Green Plaza Mall on its doorstep, who cares if you're beside a motorway on the city's edge. B&B **$140**

Sheraton Montazah Sharia el-Geish, Montazah ☎ 03 548 0550, ⊚ sheratonmontazah.com; map p.463. Situated on a busy junction overlooking the Montazah Gardens, its sea views are the main attraction of this five-star tower, whose facilities include a sauna and an outdoor pool. B&B **$115**

EATING AND DRINKING

Alexandria can't match Cairo for culinary variety, but it beats the capital when it comes to **seafood restaurants,** where fish and crustaceans are laid out for diners to select their own, priced per kilo, ranging from grey mullet (£E50) and sea bream (£E85) up to lobster (£E280) and super jumbo shrimps (from £E320). When these pall you can always fall back on Egyptian favourites like *shawarmas*, pizzas, *fuul* and falafel. **Coffee houses**, too, are an Alex speciality, and there are some good **bars** if you know where to look.

CAFÉS AND RESTAURANTS

The following establishments more or less cover Alexandria's culinary and budgetary spectrum. Unless stated otherwise, credit cards aren't accepted and alcohol isn't served.

DOWNTOWN

Al-Shark Sharia al-Bursa al-Qadima ☎ 03 577 4999; map p.466. Fronted by a veritable jungle of plants, this brightly lit café (whose name means The East) serves kebabs by the kilo and traditional Egyptian dishes such as mutton *fatta* (£E35), rice with gizzards and baked macaroni, to eat indoors or take away. Daily 10am–10pm.

★ **China House** 6th floor, Hotel Cecil, Midan Sa'ad Zaghloul ☎ 03 487 7173; map p.467. Enjoy a wonderful rooftop view of the Eastern Harbour, while eating dishes prepared by Chinese, Thai and Indian chefs. Try the wonton soup (£E18) or chicken satay (£E32), followed by a Thai seafood salad (£E38) or chilli shrimps (£E66), washed down with cold beer. Minimum charge £E25/person. Daily 5–11.30pm.

Gad Sharia Horriya and Sharia Mahmoud Azmi; map p.467. Two branches of the popular Egyptian fast-food chain, selling delicious takeaway kebabs, kofta, *shawarma*, *fuul* and shrimp sandwiches, all freshly prepared and costing under £E10. Daily 24hr.

★ **La Veranda** 46 Sharia Sa'ad Zaghloul ☎ 03 486 1432; map p.467. A mellow a/c bistro in the long hall of *Délices* patisserie (see opposite) offering great onion soup, baked fish, steak with Roquefort sauce and French-style chicken curry served with a flourish, together with beer, reasonably priced Egyptian wine and real Greek ouzo. Daily 11am–11pm.

Mohammed Ahmed 17 Sharia Abdel Fatah el-Hadry ☎ 03 483 3576; map p.467. One of the cheapest places for a takeaway or a meal on the run, serving tasty *fuul*, falafel and other vegetarian dishes (all under £E5). Try the *fuul iskandarani*: fava beans topped with tomatoes, onions, *tahina* and chilli powder. Daily 6am–1am.

ANFUSHI AND RAS EL-TIN

Abu Ashraf 28 Sharia Safar Pasha ☎ 03 481 6597; map p.466. Accessible by tram #15, this street is full of fish and kebab restaurants, tempting passers-by with their outdoor grills. *Abu Ashraf* is devoted to seafood, which is always excellent. Try the seabass stuffed with garlic and herbs or the creamy shrimp *kishk* (casserole). Daily 24hr.

Fish Market Sharia 26 Yulyu ☎ 03 480 5119; map p.466. Sited above the *Tikka Grill*, this posh a/c seafood restaurant has a wonderful view of the Eastern Harbour. The mandatory salad platter (£E15/person) is a meal in itself; if you don't fancy choosing your own seafood from the display on ice, the menu includes squid tageen (£E35). Daily noon–2am (1am in winter).

Grand Caffee Sharia 26 Yulyu ☎ 03 480 5119; map p.466. Under the same management as the nearby *Fish Market* and *Tikka Grill*, but far less formal, with leatherette armchairs outside and a/c tables indoors. The menu features pizzas (£E22–34), Caesar salad (£E28), ice cream, milkshakes and flavoured *sheeshas*. Minimum charge £E20/person. Daily 8am–1am.

★ **Greek Club** Sharia Qasr Qaitbey ☎ 03 480 2690; map p.466. With its spacious rooms and a terrace that catches the breeze from the harbour, this is a great place to eat fish (grilled with olive oil, lemon and oregano; baked with tomato; or rubbed with salt and spices and charred, Egyptian style), moussaka or mezze, or simply enjoy a glass of beer or wine at sunset. Daily noon–11pm.

Kadoura 33 Sharia Bairam el-Tonsi ☎ 03 480 0405 and 147 Sharia 26 Yulyu ☎ 03 480 0967; map p.466. An Alexandrian institution, *Kadoura* (pronounced Adoura) is devoted to seafood; all orders come with salad, rice and dips. Meals are served at tables in the street at the scruffy old *Kadoura* in Anfushi; the new branch on the Corniche has a/c and indoor seating. Daily noon–midnight.

Samakmak 42 Sharia Qasr Ras el-Tin ☎ 03 481 1560; map p.466. Owned by retired Alexandrian bellydancer Zizi Salem and popular with actors and other celebrities, this upscale fish place is renowned for its crab *tageen*, crayfish, and spaghetti with clams. All their seafood is extremely fresh and comes with various dips and salads. In the summer you can eat outdoors in a large tent. Serves alcohol. Daily noon–midnight.

Tikka Grill Sharia 26 Yulyu ☎ 03 480 5114; map p.466. More Levantine than Indian – its menu ranges from veal piccata (£E55) to marinated spicy chicken (£E39) – but nonetheless recommended for its delicious *puris* (spelt boury on the menu) and grilled meats. Daily 1pm–1am.

FURTHER OUT

Abu Faris International Garden, Suez Canal Bridge ☎ 03 382 5333; map p.462. This popular Syrian restaurant has a full menu of grills, seafood and salads, but many people come simply for the spicy lamb and chicken *shawarmas*, served in roasted flatbread. It's located about 1km before the Carrefour City Center mall, on the other side of the road, beside Alexandria's International Garden. Only accessible by taxi (£E25), but they do home deliveries. Daily noon–11pm.

★ **Arous El Selsela** Shatby beach; map p.462. A stone's throw from the library, this is the only place in the centre where you can dine al fresco beneath palm-frond umbrellas with the waves breaking under your nose. Generous-sized steaks (£E40), calamari (£E45) and pizzas (£E21–39) make it excellent value, and they don't mind if you simply want to chill out over a fresh juice or a flavoured *sheesha*. Look for the flight of steps near the white monument shaped like three ship's masts. Daily 24hr.

Cordon Rouge Green Plaza Mall, 14 May Bridge, Smouha ☎ 03 420 8666; map p.462. A slick Mediterranean-style restaurant-cum-bar, popular with well-heeled locals, and with a menu featuring pasta, salads, grills and cocktails. On Thurs nights, a guest DJ keeps dancers happy with hip-hop, techno or RnB music. Daily noon–2am.

Stefano's Four Seasons hotel, 399 Sharia el-Geish ☎ 03 581 8000; map p.462. This stylish restaurant specializes in southern Italian cuisine, including seafood, risotto and fresh pasta dishes, from an open kitchen, with a princely Italian wine list. Reckon on paying £E300 a head, without alcohol. Formal/smart casual dress required. Daily 7pm–1am.

Zephyrion Abu Qir beach ☎ 03 562 1319; map p.463. Fronted by a cactus garden, *Zephyrion* (Greek for sea breeze) is the most identifiable of Abu Qir's seafood spots (others are simply tables on the beach), with a summer veranda and ample seating indoors. They don't serve alcohol but you can bring your own bottle and they'll uncork it. Daily noon–midnight.

COFFEE HOUSES, PATISSERIES AND JUICE BARS

Although most of Alexandria's prewar coffee houses and patisseries have fared badly (see box, p.488), a new breed of youth-friendly places has emerged, and some of the old-style *'ahwas* are still going strong. As a general rule, the many coffee houses along the Corniche that cater to the summer tourist trade are nothing special.

DOWNTOWN

Brazilian Coffee Store 44 Sharia Sa'ad Zaghloul ☎ 03 486 5059; map p.467. The aroma of freshly roasted coffee draws you in from the street, to find an antique roasting and grinding machine beneath a giant glass map of Brazil. There's seating in the modernized section upstairs, favoured by women and courting couples; downstairs, men smoke standing over their cappucinos. Besides coffee, they sell croissants and pastries; pay at the cash-desk before collecting your order. Daily 7.30am–10pm.

Café La Vallé Alexy Midan Ramleh; map p.467. If you're looking for a place to meet English-speaking Alexandrians, this female-friendly coffee house and juice bar fits the bill, with free wi-fi, flavoured *sheeshas* and MTV. Daily 24hr.

Coffee Roastery 48 Sharia Fouad ☎ 03 483 4363; map p.467. Popular with hip Alexandrian youth for its preppy ambience, free wi-fi and loud MTV. The Illy coffee, milkshakes and fresh-fruit smoothies are great, while the chicken Alfredo is the best bet if you're tempted to eat. Daily 7.30am–1am.

★ **Délices** 46 Sharia Sa'ad Zaghloul ☎ 03 486 1432; map p.467. Run by the Moustakas family since 1922, *Délices* catered for King Farouk's coronation and was recently voted the best patisserie in Egypt. From their cake shop, a long hall running through to Midan Sa'ad Zaghloul contains three seating areas with different retro decors; the middle section houses a Mediterranean restaurant, *La Veranda* (see opposite). Daily 7am–11pm.

El-Tugareya Sharia 26 Yulyu; map p.466. Nearly a century old, this sprawling multi-roomed *'ahwa* is an informal hub of commerce and trade where deals are sealed with a handshake, and also a lively youth hangout. The section facing Sharia el-Ghorfa el-Tigraya is devoted to business, backgammon and gossip; the Corniche side is frequented by women, students, film-makers and writers. Daily 9am–late.

Freshat Juice Bar 18 Sharia Amin Fikhry, off Midan Ramleh; map p.467. The best place to quench your thirst downtown, offering 26 different juices, made with or without sugar, as you wish. Daily: summer 7am–1am; winter 9am–midnight.

Sofianopoulo Coffee Store 18 Sharia Sa'ad Zaghloul ☎ 03 484 5469; map p.466. A vintage coffee merchants furnished with silver bean-grinders and wooden allegorical statues. Croissants are sold in the morning in the sit-down annexe next door, decorated with kitsch mosaics. Daily 8am–midnight.

ANFUSHI AND RAS EL-TIN

Classique 60 Sharia 26 Yulyu; map p.466. This super clean a/c patisserie has a sumptuous array of European

4

VINTAGE COFFEE HOUSES AND PASTISSERIES

Before the 1952 revolution, Alexandria's coffee houses, patisseries and tearooms were the hub of bourgeois society, where artists, writers and socialites philosophized and pursued affairs, like Durrell's characters in *The Alexandria Quartet*. Since then some have closed, while others depend on a dwindling clientele of elderly Egyptian gentlemen or tourists. Only a few can be recommended for their food or ambience (see p.487), but others deserve a look (or at least a mention) for their period decor or literary mystique, constituting a kind of **heritage trail**.

Two of the most famous are on Midan Sa'ad Zaghloul. *Délices*, dating from 1922, has retained its elegant long hall and teak bar, its French name belying the fact that it was founded by Alexandrian Greeks, like the nearby **Trianon**, built on the site of Cleopatra's Needles. The *Trianon* was used for filming the British war movie *Ice Cold in Alex* (1959), whose characters stranded in the desert dream of quaffing Stella beer if they ever get out alive. Before the war, it was frequented by the poet Cavafy (see p.468), who worked upstairs as a clerk for the First Circle of Irrigation.

Across Midan Ramleh from the *Trianon* stands **Athineos**, a Greek cultural landmark whose classical friezes and fixtures seem unchanged since its 1940s heyday (rather like their cakes). In the other direction along Sharia Sa'ad Zaghloul, both the **Brazilian Coffee Store** and the **Sofianpoulo Coffee Store** grind and roast beans using 1920s machinery, and are still going strong.

En route between them, notice the name **Baudrot** in flowing 1930s typography, which reminds locals of a rendezvous for lovers that closed a few years ago. **Pastroudis** on Sharia Horriya (which shut in the 1990s) was another haunt of Durrell's, as was **Vinous** on the corner of Sharia Nabi Daniel, which seems unlikely to survive much longer, as its Art Deco fittings are riddled by termites.

---

gateaux and Middle Eastern pastries, and is non-smoking throughout. Daily 10am–11pm.

El Qobesi 51 Sharia 26 Yulyu ☎ 03 486 7860; map p.466. Serving wonderful freshly squeezed juices (£E7–10) – ranging from mango to apple and peach –in chilled glasses. No sign in English, but you can't miss the fruit stacked outside, or the fairy-lit palm trees after dark. Daily 24hr.

El Sheikh Wafik Sharia Qasr Ras el-Tin; map p.466. If you fancy a dessert after trying Anfushi's seafood or kebab restaurants, this corner café serves delicious *couscousy* (couscous with grated coconut, raisins, nuts and sugar, drenched in hot milk) and ice cream. Daily 9am–4am.

DRINKING

Although Alex is the centre of Egypt's wine and spirits industry (the vineyards are at Gianaclis, near Lake Maryut), bars have a low profile nowadays due to the rising tide of Islamic fundamentalism. If you just want a carry-out, Drinkies (see p.490) is right in the centre, and there's also a duty-free shop selling imported liquor (see p.490).

★ **Cap d'Or** (aka *Sheikh Ali*) 4 Sharia Adib Bek Ishtak, off Sharia Sa'ad Zaghloul ☎ 03 487 5177; map p.466. A real slice of old Alex, furnished with Art Nouveau mouldings and model ships, where bohemians and expats rub shoulders over grilled sardines and bottles of whisky or tequila. It has a friendly atmosphere, and is popular with the gay community after midnight, when there may be live oud (lute) music. A seafood and salad meal with a beer costs about £E90. Daily 24hr.

Monty Bar 1st floor, Hotel Cecil, Midan Sa'ad Zaghloul ☎ 03 487 7173; map p.467. Named after General Montgomery (Monty), who is said to have plotted the Battle of El-Alamein here (despite being a teetotaller), its overstuffed chairs, silk drapery and dark panelling create a soporific atmosphere, enlivened by a singer of chansons (10pm–midnight). Test the barman's knowledge of cocktails (£E50) by ordering a Monty – a martini mixed at a ratio of 15:1, so-called because he supposedly refused to go into battle unless his advantage over the enemy was similarly high. They also sell beer (£E25) and non-alcoholic yogurt fizzes (£E20). Daily 5.30pm–2am.

Portuguese Club (aka *Centro de Portugal* or *Nady Portugali*) 42 Sharia Abd el-Qader Ragab, Roushdi ☎ 03 542 7599; map p.463. A country club-cum-singles' bar frequented by expats, with pool and darts competitions and party nights. It's located 3km from the centre, off Tariq Gamal Abdel Nasser; catch tram #2 to the Egyptian-American Center and walk two blocks inland to find the first side street off Sharia Kafr Abdou – which is the name to give if you take a taxi (£E20). Drinks are purchased by a system of pre-paid credits. Their menu includes pasta, seafood and peppered steak. Daily 3pm–1am.

Spitfire Bar 7 Sharia al-Bursa al-Qadima ☎ 03 480 6503; map p.466. A block from Cap d'Or, this easily overlooked den dating back to the 1900s is plastered with stickers from oil companies, warships and overland travel groups (the kind of foreigners that frequent the place). Playing 70s rock music and TV sports, it's fun for groups, but rather a downer on your own. Mon–Sat noon–1am.

NIGHTLIFE AND ENTERTAINMENT

Thursday and Friday are the big nights out in Alex, but there's usually something happening throughout the week at one venue or another – see *Alex Agenda* for details. Regular clubbing is restricted to the *Cordon Rouge* and *Portuguese Club*; other clubs, in four- and five-star hotels, only come alive over summer, and restrict entry to mixed-sex couples. Otherwise, look out for flyers promoting one-off appearances by guest DJs on the rooftop of the Rio Cinema on Sharia Horriya (see map, p.467). Besides the places listed below, it's worth checking out what's on at cinemas (see p.490) or foreign cultural centres (see p.490), while over summer, operas are also staged at the Roman Theatre (see p.469), in the Antoniadis Gardens (see p.479), and sometimes at other sites such as Fort Qaitbey.

Alexandria Centre of Arts (aka Freedom Centre of Creativity) 1 Sharia Horriya ☎03 495 9155, ⓦaca.org.eg (in Arabic only); map p.466. Housed in a whitewashed villa, this centre hosts art exhibitions, poetry readings, contemporary Arabic drama and music. Upstairs is an artists' studio, a library and a cinema where they screen foreign movies (Mon 6pm). Sat–Thurs 9am–9pm.

Bibliotheca Alexandrina Arts Centre Corniche ☎03 483 9999, ⓦbibalex.org; map p.462. The library's arts and conference centres host performances of both European and Arabic classical and contemporary music, modern dance and drama (tickets £E20–60), and also show foreign and Egyptian films (free).

Cecil Nightclub 1st floor, Hotel Cecil, Midan Sa'ad Zaghloul ☎03 487 7173; map p.462. About the only place downtown where you can see bellydancers performing three nights of the week all year-round. Minimum charge £E75/person. Thurs, Sat & Sun 12.30–5am.

Cordon Rouge Cordon Rouge restaurant, Green Plaza Mall; map p.462. The only dance spot that's active all year-round, other than the *Portuguese Club* (see p.488), the *Cordon Rouge* sets its mirror-ball spinning every Thurs night, as local DJs like Shioni (hip-hop and RnB) crank up

the volume.

Conservatoire de Musique d'Alexandrie 90 Sharia Horriya ☎03 487 5086; map p.467. This music college hosts concerts of European and Arabic classical music, vocal and piano recitals and classes.

Garage (aka Jesuit Cultural Centre) 298 Sharia Bur Said, Sidi Gaber ☎03 542 3553; map p.462. Alexandria's most avant-garde venue, occupying a former garage and hosting Arab hip-hop bands and protest singers, contemporary drama and performance art. Besides screening art-house movies (Sat), the Jesuit centre runs workshops for local film-makers and supports other projects. Most events are free.

Opera House (aka Sayed Darwish Theatre) 22 Sharia Horriya ☎03 480 0138, ⓦcairoopera.org/sayed _darwish.aspx; map p.467. This splendid one-thousand-seat auditorium hosts performances by the symphony, opera and ballet companies of the Cairo Opera House, visiting orchestras and the Alexandria Opera Ensemble for Music and Arab Singing.

Portugali Disco *Portuguese Club*, Roushdi; map p.463. Tues is disco night, but their upstairs dancefloor can be quiet as a morgue unless the clientele is in the mood or everyone turns up for a monthly themed party-night.

FESTIVALS

Summer is the busiest time in Alex's cultural calendar with all sorts of events at the city's leading arts centres, plus some other venues that throw open their doors to visiting artists. Should you happen to be here over **New Year**, beware the blizzard of crockery that Alexandrians throw out of their windows at midnight – a local ritual derived from the Greek custom of smashing plates at funerals or weddings.

Summer Dance (Aug). The Rida Troupe (Ballet Rida) or the National Troupe (El-Fir'a el-Qawmiyya) perform folk dances at the outdoor Abdel Wahab Theatre (☎03 486 3637), east of Midan Ramleh, and a circus sets up at St Mark's College in Shatby (☎03 592 2709 for performance times).

International Film Festival ☎03 578 0042, ⓔalexfilmfest@gmail.com (Sept). Formerly cherished as a rare opportunity to watch foreign movies in an uncensored state; now a litmus test of cultural politics under Egypt's Islamist government. The Convention Hall en route to the library is the main venue, but every cinema in town (see p.490) screens a few.

International Yachting Regatta (Sept). Various competitive events at sea beyond the Eastern Harbour, whose participants are likely to be found afterwards

celebrating their victories or drowning their sorrows at the *Greek Club* (see p.486).

Alexandria Biennial (Oct in odd-numbered years). An exhibition of art from Mediterranean countries that allowed Mubarak's cultural supremo, Farouk Hosny, to wax lyrical about creativity – it may face the axe under an Islamist government that views most forms of modern art as anathema.

International Marathon (Oct). Prior to the 2011 revolution, Alex's marathon was held along the Corniche between Ras el-Tin and Montazah. Details of future races will appear on ⓦegyptianmarathon.com, if it ever resumes.

Ramadan The Muslim holy month is punctuated with five consecutive moulids honouring revered local sheikhs, starting with *zikrs* outside the Mosque of Al-Mursi in Anfushi (see p.473). The day after its "big night" the action shifts to Sidi Gaber's mosque, then Sidi Bishr's; these are followed by the moulids of Sidi Kamal and Sidi Mohammed al-Rahhal. These moulids have long been a part of popular culture but are despised by fundamentalist Salafists, whose growing power in Alexandria may curtail them in the future.

SHOPPING

Downtown Sharia Sa'ad Zaghloul and Sharia Nabi Daniel are usually thronged with families window-shopping for clothes, shoes and toys, while antique shops on Sharia Salah Salem and Sharia Masguid al-Attarine are fun for visitors to explore. Shopping malls are wildly popular with locals as places to mingle with the opposite sex, entertain children or eat out, in a stylishly modern air-conditioned environment.

Carrefour City Center KM6, start of the Cairo Desert Rd ☎ 03 397 0017, ⊛ carrefour.com.eg; map p.462. Run by the French chain Carrefour, this hypermarket sells everything from gorgonzola cheese to plasma TVs. Its fast-food outlets and entertainments are supplemented by those in the International Garden, across the road. A taxi from the centre costs about £E20. Daily 9am–1am, Thurs & Fri till 2am.

Drinkies Corner of Sharia Gamil el-Din Yassin and Sharia el-Ghorfa el-Tigarya ☎ 19330; map p.467. Downtown liquor-store stocking the full range of Egyptian-made beers (£E7–11), wines (£E41–89), spirits (£E20–140) and alcopops (£E10–14); they will deliver orders over £E100. Daily 11am–1am.

Duty-free Shop 31 Sharia Salah Salem ☎ 03 482 9919; map p.467. A limited selection of imported spirits, wine and beer, purchasable with US dollars, sterling, euros or Visa cards only. Daily 11am–10pm (Ramadan 11am–2pm & 8–10pm).

San Stefano Mall 388 Sharia el-Geish, behind the Four Seasons hotel ☎ 03 582 3589; map p.462. Alexandria's ritziest mall has four levels of shops, a food court, a kids' zone with a ten-screen cinema, and a 24hr supermarket. May–Sept: daily 11am–1am. Oct–April: daily 11am–11pm, Fri–Sun till midnight;

Sayed el Safty 63 Sharia Mesjid al-Attarin ☎ 03 392 2972; map p.466. A few blocks from the Attarine market, this wonderful shop is crammed with antique and reproduction furniture, china, statues, backgammon sets and knick-knacks. Mon–Sat 10am–10pm.

DIRECTORY

American Express El-Saladya Building, Sharia 14 Mai (see map, p.462) ☎ 03 420 1050. Based in a travel agent out in Smouha, it's a nuisance to reach. Daily except Fri & Sat 9am–5pm.

Arabic courses Qortoba Institute for Arabic Studies, corner of Sharia Mohammed Nabeel Hamdy and Sharia Khalid Ibn Walid, Miami (see map, p.463) ☎ 03 556 2959 or ☎ 010 0584 3483, ⊛ qortoba.net. Offers one-on-one tuition for €4/hr and can arrange student accommodation (from €100/month) or flat rental (from €170/month) nearby, to avoid you having to slog across town for lessons.

Banks and exchange AlexBank, 59 Sharia Sa'ad Zaghloul; Banque Misr, 1 Sharia Talaat Harb; HSBC, 47 Sharia Sultan Hussein; National Bank of Egypt, *Cecil* hotel. All of these places have ATMs, although Forex bureaux on Midan Ramleh and Sharia Salah Salem offer better rates of exchange. All are open Sun–Thurs 9am–2pm.

Bookshops Diwan, Bibliotheca Alexandrina forecourt, shop #4 ☎ 012 2600 0169, ⊛ diwanegypt.com. An excellent shop with a wide range of books on Egypt, foreign-language novels and Egyptian music CDs. Daily 10am–10pm.

Cinemas Downtown venues include the three-screen Royal Renaissance (☎ 03 485 5725) near the Opera House, and the 3D Amir cinema (☎ 03 391 7972) on the corner of Sharia Horrya and Sharia Safiya Zaghloul. Suburban multiplexes include the Green Plaza Mall Cineplex (☎ 03 420 9155) in Smouha, and the Renaissance in Carrefour City Center (☎ 03 397 5897) and in the San Stefano mall (☎ 03 490 0056).

Consulates Ireland, 55 Sharia Sultan Hussein ☎ 03 485 2672 (Mon–Thurs & Sun 8am–1pm); UK, 3 Sharia Mena, Roushdi ☎ 03 546 7001 (Mon–Thurs & Sun 8am–1pm); USA, 3 Sharia Phara'ana ☎ 02 486 1009 (Mon–Thurs & Sun 9am–3pm). Australia, New Zealand and Canada have no consular representation; for other consulates, ask at the tourist office.

Cultural centres American Center, 3 Sharia Phara'ana ☎ 03 486 1009, ✉ aca@internetalex.com (Mon–Thurs & Sun 10am–4pm); British Council, 11 Sharia Mahmoud El-Ela, Roushdi ☎ 03 545 6512, ⊛ britishcouncil.org.eg (daily except Fri 11am–7pm); French Centre, 30 Sharia Nabi Daniel ☎ 03 392 5580, ⊛ cfcc/eg.org (daily except Fri & Sat 9am–noon & 5–7.30pm); Goethe Institute, 10 Sharia al-Batalssa ☎ 03 484 1037, ⊛ goethe.de/Alexandria (Mon–Thurs 9am–1pm, Sun 9am–2pm); Russian Centre, 5 Sharia Batalsa ☎ 03 486 5645 (Mon–Thurs & Sun 10am–1pm & 5–8pm).

Dentist Royal Dental Care, 457 Tariq Gamal Abdel Nasser, Mandara ☎ 03 550 6865.

DHL 9 Sharia Salah Salem, El-Manshiya ☎ 03 487 3603 (daily except Fri 9am–5pm).

MOSAIC, BIBLIOTHECA ALEXANDRINA, ALEXANDRIA (P.475) >

Hospitals German (Al-Almani) Hospital, 56 Sharia Abdel Salaam Aref, Glym ☎ 03 584 1806; tram #2 to the Saba Pasha stop (see map, p.462). International Hospital, 20 Sharia Beha al-Din, Smouha (see map, p.462) ☎ 03 420 7243. Both are well equipped, with English-speaking doctors.

International calls There are Menatel booths all over town. The 24hr exchange on Midan Ramleh has direct-dial phones and sells phonecards; the exchanges on Midan el-Gumhorriya and Sharia Sa'ad Zaghloul (both daily 8am–11pm) work on the pre-booking system.

Internet access Cyber cafés come and go, but try Farous Net Café, Sharia Horriya (daily 10am–midnight); Hightop Internet, 71 Sharia Nabi Daniel (daily 10am–11pm); Mobi Net, Sharia Allewla Bahari Gamal Rashed (daily 9.30am–2am); or Satellite Internet, Sharia Dr Hassan Fadaly (Mon–Sat 11am–11pm), downtown. Most charge £E3–4/hr.

Passport Office 25 Sharia Talaat Harb (see map, p.466) ☎ 03 484 7873 (Mon–Thurs 8.30am–2pm, Fri 10am–2pm, Sat & Sun 9–11am). Visa extensions (from window #6 on the first floor) require one photo and a copy of the relevant pages of your passport; there's a photo studio and copier across the street. No applications accepted after noon.

Pharmacies Khalil, Sharia el-Ghorfa el-Tigarya, off Midan Sa'ad Zaghloul ☎ 03 480 6710 (Mon–Sat 9am–10pm, Sun 10am–10pm). There are many other pharmacies on Midan Ramleh, Sharia Safiya Zaghloul and Sharia Nabi Daniel.

Photography Kodak Express, 36 Sharia Safiya Zaghloul ☎ 03 486 4072 (daily 10am–11pm). Sells memory cards for digital cameras, and prints photos.

Post offices Midan Ramleh (daily 8am–3pm), Sharia el-Ghorfa el-Tigarya (same hours) and Masr Station (daily 8am–5pm). Express Mail Service is open till 2pm at all the main post offices.

Thomas Cook 15 Midan Sa'ad Zaghloul (see map, p.467) ☎ 03 487 5118, ⓦ thomascook.com.eg (daily 8am–5pm). Currency exchange, travellers' cheques and tourist excursions.

Tourist police Above the tourist office (☎ 03 485 0507), in the Maritime Station (no phone), at the Roman Theatre (☎ 03 390 2904), Fort Qaitbey (☎ 03 480 9144) and Montazah Gardens (☎ 03 547 5025). All except the last are open 24hr.

Western Union 73 Sharia Horriya, inside the Arab African International Bank (see map, p.467) ☎ 03 492 0900 (daily except Fri 9am –5pm).

The Mediterranean coast

Egypt's 500km-long **Mediterranean coast** (known as Al-Sahel) has beautiful beaches and sparkling sea all the way to Libya. However, many stretches are still mined from World War II or off-limits due to military bases, while all the most accessible sites have been colonized by holiday villages catering mainly to Egyptians, whose beach culture is

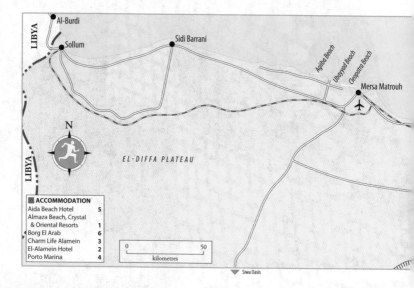

ACCOMMODATION

Aida Beach Hotel	5
Almaza Beach, Crystal & Oriental Resorts	1
Borg El Arab	6
Charm Life Alamein	3
El-Alamein Hotel	2
Porto Marina	4

0   50
kilometres

▼ Siwa Oasis

so different from Westerners' that most foreigners prefer the Sinai and Red Sea resorts.

Travelling between Alexandria and the World War II battlefield of **El-Alamein** you'll pass a slew of **resorts** reserved for elite sections of Egyptian society such as the army and diplomatic corps, and others open to anyone who can afford to stay, though for independent travellers they're simply blights on the landscape which make the colonial-era beach resort of **El-Agami** (20km from downtown Alexandria and now a commuter suburb) seem historic by comparison. With the ancient lighthouse at Abu Sir and the ruins of Taposiris Magna off-limits, the only accessible "sight" is the Coptic **Monastery of St Menas**, off the highway between Alexandria and El-Alamein.

ACCOMMODATION ALONG THE MEDITERRANEAN COAST

Heading along the coast you'll pass a string of holiday **resorts**, many only functioning over summer, when rich Egyptians move in. The **beach scene** is staid by Western standards; bikinis, cocktails and discos are only found at a handful of resorts also taking European package tourists, and while a sandy white beach can be taken for granted, a hotel's four- or five-star rating may not signify much in other ways. After the 2011 revolution, many charter flights were cancelled and domestic tourism also fell sharply. A lot of resorts shut down for a year, or cut back on services, catering and maintenance. In Egypt, local travel agents offer their own (half- or full-board) deals for resorts on the Mediterranean coast. Simple accommodation is also available in Mersa Matrouh (see p.498).

ALEX TO EL-ALAMEIN

Aida Beach Hotel El-Alamein Highway, kilometre 77 ☎ 046 410 2802, ✆ aidagroup.com. This four-star resort has a large pool and a beach; tennis, squash, billiards and a children's playground. All rooms have wi-fi and balconies with sea views, but the overall dÈcor is rather cheesy. B&B $75

Borg El Arab El-Alamein Highway, kilometre 52 ☎ 03 374 0730. A former *Hilton* now owned by the Iberotel chain, this four-star has a huge beach and pool, and an animation team to entertain children, but its rooms have seen better days. B&B $88

Porto Marina El-Alamein Highway, kilometre 105 ☎ 046 445 2711, ✆ golfportomarina.com. Popular with wealthy Cairenes, this Venetian-themed five-star resort boasts canals, lagoons, gondolas, and a golf course, with many rooms overlooking a lagoon or the sea. All meals are buffet-style. Open in summer only. B&B $285

EL-ALAMEIN TO MERSA MATROUH

Almaza Bay 37km before Mersa Matrouh. This mega-development has a splendid beach shared by three five-star hotels: *Almaza Beach* (☎ 046 436 0000, ✉ almaza@jaz .travel); the chandeliered *Crystal* (☎ 046 436 0020, ✉ crystal@

4

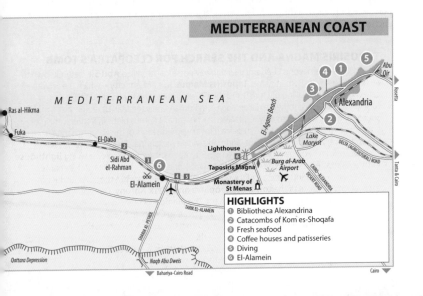

MEDITERRANEAN COAST

MEDITERRANEAN SEA

Ras al-Hikma
Fuka
El-Daba
Sidi Abd el-Rahman
El-Alamein

Lighthouse
Taposiris Magna
Monastery of St Menas
Burg al-Arab Airport

El-Agami Beach
Lake Maryut
Alexandria
Rosetta
Abu Qir

TARIK EL-ALAMEIN
SHARA EL-PETROL
Qattara Depression
Naqb Abu Dweis
Bahariya–Cairo Road

CAIRO–ALEXANDRIA DESERT ROAD
DELTA (AGRICULTURAL) ROAD
Tanta & Cairo
Cairo

HIGHLIGHTS
1. Bibliotheca Alexandrina
2. Catacombs of Kom es-Shoqafa
3. Fresh seafood
4. Coffee houses and patisseries
5. Diving
6. El-Alamein

jaz.travel); and the Moroccan-themed *Oriental* (☎046 436 0030, ✉oriental@jaz.travel), whose rooms cost roughly four times as much as the other two. Shared amenities include a dive centre, jet-skiing, sauna, jacuzzi; buffet-style, Italian and Lebanese restaurants, bars and discos. B&B $\overline{200-1000}$

Charm Life Alamein (aka *Ghazala Regency*) Ghazala Bay, kilometre 140 ☎02 266 8902, ⊚charmlifehotels .com. Only 19km from El-Alamein airport, this five-star resort has a superb beach, a heated indoor pool, dive centre, spa and child-oriented entertainments, all geared to French and Italian tourists. B&B $\overline{250}$

El Alamein Hotel Sidi Abdel Rahman, 10km beyond El-Alamein ☎046 468 0140, ✉alameinreservation @emaar.ae. An ugly three-star hotel with a large serpentine pool and a lovely beach. B&B $\overline{70}$

Monastery of St Menas (Abu Mina)

Ezbet Mohammed Farid, 75km from downtown Alexandria, 65km from El-Alamein, 15km off the coastal highway • Daily 9am–sunset • Admission free but donation appreciated • ⊚stmina-monastery.org.

If you're curious about the early history of Christianity in Egypt or the Coptic faith today, it's worth visiting the **Monastery of St Menas** (aka Abu Mina or Deir Mari Mina). Egypt's most important Coptic pilgrimage site after the monasteries of Wadi Natrun and the Red Sea Hills, it can be visited as a side-trip by car en route to El-Alamein, or a separate excursion by minibus.

While its belfry towers are visible from far away, high walls enclose the concrete buildings of the modern monastery, erected in 1959. Its **cathedral** is adorned with Italian marble, black and rose Aswan granite, and stained glass. Busloads of pilgrims arrive daily, particularly on November 11, **St Menas's Day**, when the cathedral overflows. In addition to Menas, the crypt houses the body of Pope Kyrillos VI (1959–71), whom Copts regard as a saint, writing petitions on his marble grave.

St Menas (285–c.309) was born near Memphis to Christian parents who had almost given up hope of children and regarded his birth as a miracle. Due to his father's position as a Roman official, Menas was fast-tracked as a legionary but quit after three years' service to become a hermit. A vision of being crowned by angels for martyrdom inspired his declaration of faith under torture; his corpse was burned for three days but remained intact, to be returned to Alexandria by his sister.

When the Era of Martyrdom ended, Coptic pope Athanasius had a vision that Menas's body should be loaded on a camel set to roam in the desert – it was buried at the spot where the camel refused to go any further. Miraculous events at the site persuaded others to exhume Menas in 350 and build a church over his grave, later enclosed within a huge basilica.

TAPOSIRIS MAGNA AND THE SEARCH FOR CLEOPATRA'S TOMB

Thirty kilometres beyond El-Agami the highway passes a site called **Abu Sir**, better known to archeologists by its Roman name, **Taposiris Magna**. This ancient **city** – which the Egyptians called Per Usiri ("Dwelling of Osiris") and the Greeks Busiris – had one port on the Mediterranean and another on Lake Maryut. In Roman times the Maryut region was a major source of grain, shipped to Italy to placate the potentially riotous plebs in Rome. A chain of lighthouses from Alexandria to Cyrenaica (Libya) warned sailors of the abrupt change from sea to sand along a coastline devoid of landmarks. While Alexandria's Pharos (see p.472) has disappeared, archeologists have gleaned clues to its shape from the sole surviving **lighthouse** in the chain, at Abu Sir – which most believe was a one-tenth scale replica of the Pharos.

Today, both the lighthouse and Taposiris Magna are off-limits while the SCA conducts excavations in search of the **tomb of Cleopatra and Mark Antony**. The Dominican scholar Kathleen Martinez believes it lies beneath the city's Temple of Osiris, having found the mummies of ten nobles just outside, and coins bearing Cleopatra's face and an alabaster mask with a cleft chin similar to portraits of Antony within the temple precincts. Her belief is also founded on the historian Plutarch's assertion that Octavian allowed the couple to be buried together after their respective suicides in 30 BC. If Martinez is right and finds their mummies, it will be the greatest discovery since Tutankhamun's tomb.

A wealthy **pilgrim city** grew up as camel trains spread his fame (Menas is depicted between two camels), and "holy" water from local springs was exported throughout Christendom. Sacked during the Muslim conquest and abandoned after its springs dried up in the twelfth century, the city's extensive **ruins** were placed on UNESCO's Endangered World Heritage list in 2001, due to the rising water-table rendering its structures unstable.

ARRIVAL AND DEPARTURE	**MONASTERY OF ST MENAS**
By minibus Irregularly scheduled, privately operated minibuses run from Alexandria's Moharrem Bey Terminal (see p.483) to the Bunga Sukar stop, right outside the monastery. On the feast of St Menas and other holy days, pilgrims travel there by hired minibuses directly from churches in Alexandria; ask at the Cathedral of St Mark ☎ 03 483 5522 (see p.468) for details.	**By hired car or taxi** Thomas Cook in Alexandria (see p.492) quotes £E270 for a four-hour excursion to the monastery, or about £E500 with El-Alamein, while the *Transit Hotel* (see p.485) will do both for £E400. You probably won't save money by negotiating a taxi, and driving yourself isn't advised due to the confusing signage en route between Alexandria and the monastery.

El-Alamein

Before Alamein we never had a victory. After Alamein we never had a defeat.

Winston Churchill, The Hinge of Fate

The utterly misnamed "city" of **EL-ALAMEIN** squats on a dusty plain 106km west of Alexandria, situated along a spur road that turns inland from the highway. Anyone driving past could blink and see nothing except construction debris until they pass the Italian war memorial 9km down the highway. Still, El-Alamein ("Two Worlds" or "Two Flags") is an apt name for a place that witnessed the turning point of the North African campaign, determining the fate of Egypt and Britain's empire. When the Afrika Korps came within 111km of Alexandria on July 1, 1942, control of Egypt, Middle Eastern oil and the Canal route to India seemed about to be wrested from the Allied powers by Germany and Italy. Instead, at El-Alamein, the Allied Eighth Army held, and then drove the Axis forces back, to ultimate defeat in Tunisia. Some eleven thousand soldiers were killed and seventy thousand wounded at El-Alamein alone; total casualties for the North African campaign (Sept 1940–March 1943) exceeded one hundred thousand.

Travellers who wish to pay their respects to the dead or have an interest in military history should find the **memorials** and **war museum** worth the effort of getting there. While you can be sure of finding the **cemeteries** open, it's worth phoning ahead to check about the museum (☎046 410 0021), as it closes now and again for some reason or another.

The Allied memorials and cemetery

Beyond the checkpoint where Sharia al-Petrol turns off towards the Qattara Depression, look out for signs by the highway, indicating Allied war memorials. The first is the **Greek Memorial**, resembling a classical temple, approached by an avenue of oleanders, followed 600m later by the **South African Memorial**, whose inscription ("South Africans outspanned and fought here during their trek from Italian Somaliland to Germany 1939–1945") evokes the Boer Voortrekkers.

Another kilometre west is the entrance to the **El-Alamein War Cemetery** (daily 9am–4pm; free), 400m off the highway. Secluded on the reverse slope of a hill, it is a tranquil site for the graves of 7367 Allied soldiers (815 of them nameless, only "known unto God"), with memorial cloisters listing the names of 11,945 others whose bodies were never found. Though over half were Britons, the dead include Australians, New Zealanders, Indians, Malays, Melanesians, Africans, Canadians, French, Greeks and Poles. If you want to find a particular headstone, the Commonwealth War Graves Commission (☎cwgc.org) in London can tell you exactly where to look.

4

Walking down to the cemetery, you'll pass the **Australian Memorial**, honouring the 9th Australian Division that stormed Point 29 and Thompson's Post during the penultimate phase of the Third Battle. At the start of the Third Battle the area now occupied by the cemetery was a staging area for Allied forces; the front line was about 12km west, running 65km inland from where the Italian Memorial stands today to the edge of the Qattara Depression, which formed an impassable obstacle to tanks.

The War Museum

600m west of the Australian Memorial, along a secondary road • Daily 9am–5pm • £E20, photography £E10 • (using public transport, ask to be dropped on the highway near a Sherman tank, follow the turn-off uphill to a T-junction and bear left to reach the museum)

Allied troops reached their staging areas by what is now a minor road, running further inland from today's highway, past El-Alamein's **War Museum** (locally known as Al-Mathaf). An illuminated map showing each phase of the battle, and an Italian documentary, provide an overview of the conflict, while uniforms, photos and models convey the harsh conditions in the field. Notice the section on Almássy, of *The English Patient* (see p.437) and his role in guiding two German spies through the desert.

Outside are armoured vehicles, cannons and trucks, including a lorry belonging to the Long Range Desert Group (see p.483) found in the desert in 1991. There's also a restored **Command Bunker** that was used by Monty during the battle, which you'll have to ask a guide to unlock.

The Axis memorials

Roughly 2km west, look out for an **Italian plaque** on the south side of the highway, marking the furthest point of the Axis advance, which asserts: *Mancò la Fortuna, Non il Valore* ("Lacking Fortune, Not Valour"), *1.7.1942, Alessandria 111km*. The Allies denigrated the Italians as cowardly buffoons whose officers enjoyed field-brothels at the front, but many of their units fought bravely and endured the same hardships as the other combatants.

Three kilometres on you'll spot the **German Memorial** atop **Tell el-Issa**, a ridge overlooking the sea north of the highway. A squat octagonal structure modelled on the Castel del Monte in Apulia, its courtyard lies over a mass grave of 4280 soldiers, whose names are recorded on plaques beside stone sarcophagi, representing their home provinces. The memorial's custodian can open a gate leading to the **German Memorial Beach**, 1km away – one of the nicest, most deserted beaches on the coast.

The **Italian Memorial**, 5km west, is also visible from the highway. A white marble tower at the end of an oleander-lined avenue, it has a small museum and a chapel dedicated to the 42,800 Italian soldiers, sailors and airmen who died during the campaign. Only 4,800 bodies were recovered, due to the efforts of Colonel Paolo Dominioni, who spent ten years and his entire fortune scouring the desert and building the memorial. The surrounding area is still mined, so don't stray off the paths.

The battlefield

The **battlefield** itself is generally far too dangerous to explore, due to the **minefields** laid by both sides. A staggering sixteen million landmines are estimated to remain in the Western Desert, which still kill and maim local Bedouin to this day (only tracts of land where companies are drilling for oil have been de-mined). Britain, Germany and Italy have always rejected Egyptian and Libyan demands that they fund mine-clearance programmes – the current excuse is that Egypt hasn't signed up to the Ottawa Convention banning the manufacture of mines.

A few local Bedouin with 4WDs are prepared to take people to strategic strongpoints such as **Kidney Ridge** (which the 51st Highland Division was disconcerted to find was actually a depression, leaving them exposed to enemy fire) via known routes through the minefields. To enter this area requires permission from the

THE BATTLE OF EL-ALAMEIN

Rather than the single, decisive clash of arms that many people imagine, the Battle of El-Alamein consisted of three savage bouts of mechanized warfare separated by relative lulls over a period of five months (July–Nov) in 1942. In the **First Battle** of El-Alamein, the German **Afrika Korps**' advance was stymied by lack of fuel and munitions and stiff Allied resistance organized by General Auchinleck. Once resupplied, however, Field Marshal Erwin **Rommel** was able to press the advantage with 88-millimetre cannons that outranged the Allies' guns, as well as faster, better-armoured tanks, used with an élan that earned him the title "the Desert Fox".

In August, General Bernard **Montgomery** ("Monty") took over the Allied **Eighth Army**, vowing that it would retreat no further. He negated his army's weaknesses by siting its tanks "hull down" in pits with only their gun turrets above ground, protecting them until the Panzers came within range. Aware that the Allies were being resupplied, Rommel attacked the Alam Halfa Ridge in the **Second Battle** of El-Alamein (Aug 31 to Sept 6). Repulsed with heavy losses and desperately short of fuel, the Afrika Korps withdrew behind a field of five hundred thousand landmines. Monty patiently reorganized his forces, resisting pressure from his superiors to attack until he had amassed one thousand tanks. A stage illusionist, Jasper Maskelyne, concealed them in the desert and constructed fake tank parks as part of an elaborate deception plan to mislead Rommel as to where and when the Eighth Army's main offensive would occur.

Shortly after nightfall on October 23, Monty launched the **Third Battle** of El-Alamein with a barrage of 744 guns that was heard in Alexandria. Having cracked the Nazi Enigma code, the Allies knew that Rommel was convalescing in Italy; when the Eighth Army punched a corridor through the minefields of the central front, the Germans were taken unawares. Rommel managed to return two days later, but was obliged to concentrate his mobile units further north, stranding four Italian divisions in the south. The Allies had established a commanding position at Kidney Ridge, from where Monty launched the decisive strike on November 2, leaving Rommel with only 35 operational tanks by the end of the day. On November 5 the Eighth Army broke out and surged westwards; the Afrika Korps fought rearguard actions back through Libya until its inevitable surrender in Tunisia six months later.

4

Egyptian army, without which visitors have no right to assistance in the event of an accident, and can be fined if caught by a patrol.

ARRIVAL AND DEPARTURE

EL-ALAMEIN

By bus and minibus From Alexandria's Moharrem Bey Terminal (see p.483), hourly West Delta buses and minibuses bound for Mersa Matrouh (£E20–35) can drop you at any point along the highway from the Greek to the Italian memorials – but knowing where to ask the driver to stop can be difficult, and travelling from one site to another this way is extremely time-consuming. Returning to Alex, most minibuses terminate at the satellite-city of Amriya,

from which it's at least £E20 by taxi to Alexandria – so public transport is a bad option if you want to visit more than one sight at El-Alamein, let alone the Monastery of St Menas (see p.494).

By car or taxi Thomas Cook in Alexandria (see p.492) quotes about £E350 for a four-hour excursion to El-Alamein, like the *Transit Hotel* (see p.485). You probably won't save money by negotiating for a taxi on your own.

Mersa Matrouh

The Mediterranean governorate capital, **MERSA MATROUH**, is also a summer resort, but its beach scene is ultra-conservative and the few Westerners that come here do so off-season, en route between Alex and Siwa (see p.441). A ramshackle metropolis that once attracted Libyan tourists to whom it seemed enticingly louche, Matrouh resembles a Borat joke, with every woman veiled and gloved so as not to arouse male lust, and Salafist preachers condemning the evils of *kuffar* from loudspeakers (not only on Fri).

Despite the vast **Ubayyad Beach** and a beautiful cove at **Agiiba Beach**, 14km and 24km west respectively, Matrouh is the last place where you could relax wearing a bikini or sipping a cocktail – unless of course you go to the *Almaza Bay Resort* (see p.493), 37km east.

ARRIVAL AND DEPARTURE

By bus or minibus Hourly West Delta buses and irregular minibuses from Alexandria's Moharrem Bey Terminal take 4hr to cover the 290km to Matrouh. The bus terminal is beside the highway, 3km from the centre (£E15 by taxi or £E1.50 by local pickup). From here, a/c buses (7.30am, 1.30pm & 4pm; 4–5hr) and minibuses run to Siwa Oasis, or you can hire a taxi seating up to three people for £E300.

MERSA MATROUH

By air From June to Sept, EgyptAir flies to and from Cairo (1hr) on alternate days, using Mersa Matrouh international airport (£E30 from the centre by taxi). The local EgyptAir office (☏ 046 493 6573; daily except Fri 8am–5pm) is on Sharia al-Matar, opposite the National Bank of Egypt.

INFORMATION

Tourist office Behind the Governorate building on Sharia al-Iskandariya ☏ 046 493 1841. Drop in to check bus schedules and pick up a free map of town from the helpful staff. Daily 8.30am–5pm, June–Sept till 7pm.

ACCOMMODATION AND EATING

Booking accommodation is essential over summer, when hotels hike their rates (prices below are for off-season).

Riviera Palace Sharia al-Iskandariya ☏ 046 493 3045. Near the Corniche end of Matrouh's main drag, this three-star hotel has large a/c en-suite rooms with fridges and fake stuffed tigers in the foyer, although it gets block-booked by Cairenes over summer. B&B $\underline{\$73}$

Rommel House Sharia al-Galaa ☏ 046 493 2485. Four blocks east of Sharia al-Iskandariya, this simple hotel has en-suite rooms with fans, balconies and TV, and doesn't charge vastly more over summer. B&B $\underline{\underline{£E120}}$

EATING

Besides the following places, there are *fuul* and *taamiya* stalls and 24-hour coffee houses around the fruit and vegetable market on Sharia Omar Mukhtar, one block west of Sharia al-Iskandariya.

Abdu Kofta Sharia Tahrir ☏ 012 2314 4989. Three blocks east of the main drag, this popular place serves kofta and grilled meat by the kilo, with salad and mezze. Daily 11am–10pm.

Abu Aby Pizza Sharia al-Iskandariya. Across the road and a little way north of the *Riviera Palace* hotel, Abu Aby does not-quite-western-style pizzas, to eat upstairs or takeaway. Daily 11am–midnight.

Hammo al-Temsah Fish Sharia Tahrir. Next door to *Abdu Kofta*, this tiled diner specializes in fish rolled in a salty mixture that forms a charred crust when grilled, leaving the inside moist and tender. Daily noon–10pm.

DIRECTORY

Banks and exchange Banque Misr on Sharia al-Galaa (Sun–Thurs 9am–2.30pm & 6.30–8pm) has an ATM; National Bank of Egypt, Sharia al-Matar (Sun–Thurs 9am–2pm & 6–9pm).

Hospital Military Hospital, Sharia ash-Shaati ☏ 046 493 5286 (daily 24hr).

Internet access Crazy Net, Sharia ash-Shaati (daily 24hr).

Tourist police Sharia Omar Mukhtar, behind the tourist office ☏ 046 493 5575 (daily 24hr).

The Delta

The Nile **Delta** is Egypt's most fertile and (barring Cairo) its most heavily populated region – nearly half the people in Egypt live here, and despite the lack of ancient sites, a scoot around the Delta on service taxis and third-class trains gives a feel for today's Egypt in a way that visits to tombs and temples do not. Although several pharaonic dynasties arose and ruled from this region – Lower Egypt – little of their capitals remain beyond mounds of debris known as *tell* or *kom*. The pharaohs themselves plundered older sites of sculptures and masonry, and with a yearly rainfall of nearly 20cm (the highest in Egypt) and an annual inundation by the Nile that coated the land in silt, mud-brick structures were soon eroded or swept away. More recently, farmers have furthered the cycle of destruction by digging the mounds for a nitrate-enriched soil called *sebakh*, used for fertilizer; several sites catalogued by nineteenth-century

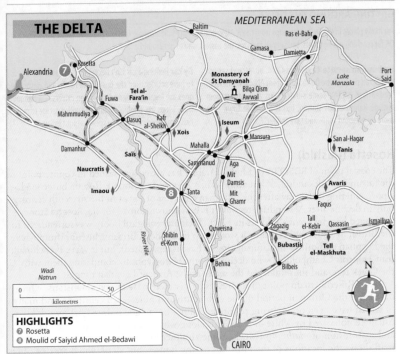

THE DELTA

HIGHLIGHTS
- ❼ Rosetta
- ❽ Moulid of Saiyid Ahmed el-Bedawi

4

archeologists have now all but vanished. On those that remain, there's good information at ⓦegyptsites.wordpress.com/category/delta.

Rosetta is a charming little town, with a special architecture of its own, but the main cities of the Delta, including **Mahalla**, **Tanta** and **Damietta**, are of interest not so much for any sights or attractions, but because they do not have any, and thus represent a chance to see the ordinary, workaday "real" Egypt which usually escapes most tourists. The Delta also abounds in **moulids** (popular festivals), the largest of which draw crowds of over a million. Companies of *mawladiya* (moulid people) run stalls and rides, Sufi *tariqas* perform their *zikrs*, people camp outdoors, and music blares into the small hours. Smaller, rural moulids tend to be heavier on the practical devotion, with people bringing their children or livestock for blessing, or the sick to be cured.

The Delta's other main attraction is its flat, intensely green **landscape**, riven by waterways where feluccas glide past mud-brick villages and wallowing buffalo. The northern **lakes** are a wintering ground for **birdlife** – in ancient times, wealthy Egyptians enjoyed going fowling in the reeds, using throwing sticks and hunting cats; their modern-day counterparts employ shotguns. The Delta is also still a habitat for wildcats and pygmy white-toothed shrews, but boars have been driven out, and the last hippopotamus was shot in 1815.

More sombrely for the ecology, the Delta is one of the world regions most vulnerable to the effects of **global warming**. Oceanographers predict that a one-metre rise in the sea level would swamp Alexandria and submerge the Delta as far inland as Damanhur, destroying six percent of Egypt's cultivable land and displacing 3.3 million people. The freshwater Delta lagoons, which provide much of the nation's fish, would also be ruined. A more immediate threat is **erosion** by the Mediterranean. Now that the Delta is no longer renewed by silt from the Nile, its coastline is being worn away.

GETTING AROUND THE DELTA

For many places in the Delta, day-trips from Cairo, Alexandria or Port Said are more feasible than overnight stays. Trains are OK for reaching major towns, but service taxis are the easiest way to get around.

By bus and service taxi From Cairo, buses and service taxis to all parts of the Delta leave from Aboud terminal in Shubra (see p.174); some service taxis also depart from outside Ramses train station, but these leave town by a more roundabout route and take longer.

By car Renting a car isn't necessarily a good idea: it's easy to have accidents on the busy Delta roads, and unsurfaced ones are legally off-limits to foreign drivers – a hangover from 1960s spy-phobia. Should the police decide to make a fuss, you could conceivably spend a night in jail.

Rosetta (Rashid)

The coastal town of **ROSETTA** (Rashid in Arabic) has waxed and waned in counterpoint to the fortunes of Alexandria, 65km away. When Alex was moribund, Rosetta burgeoned as a port, entering its heyday after the Ottoman conquest of Egypt in the sixteenth century, only to decline after Alexandria's revival. It is best known abroad for the **Rosetta Stone**, discovered here by French soldiers in 1799. Their archeological booty was surrendered to the British in 1801, which is how it wound up in London's British Museum (from where the Egyptian authorities are campaigning to have it repatriated), but it was a Frenchman, Jean-François Champollion, who deciphered the hieroglyphs by comparing them with the Greek text, and thus unlocked the secret of the Ancient Egyptian tongue.

Today, Rosetta's main point of interest is its distinctive **Delta-style mansions**, which date from the Ottoman period of the eighteenth and nineteenth centuries, and many of which have been or are being restored. Hallmarks include pointed brickwork, usually emphasized by white or red paint, along with inset beams and carved lintels, and a profusion of *mashrabiya*-work. Some incorporate ancient columns. Our map shows the locations of the most interesting houses, not all of which are described individually in the text, but which make a good basis for exploring the town.

Around mid-November, the chain of festivals that started in Tanta the previous month (see p.503) should reach Rosetta. Don't despair if you come a few weeks earlier,

ROSETTA

since similar **moulids** occur at Fuwa, Mahmudiya and Dasuq, further inland. Salted fish (*fisikh*) and hummus are the traditional snacks at these events.

Sharia Azouz Sama and around

The places of interest start opposite the service taxi station, on **Sharia Azouz Sama**, home to some fine Delta-style houses, all dating from the eighteenth century. **Kohiya House** stands next to the fine **Al-Araby Mosque**. Two doors further on stand the trio of **Ramadan House, Maharem House** and **Al-Gamal House**, with **Abouhoum House** just across the street.

Sharia Azouz Sama continues down to the Corniche, which runs along the river. One block north of Azouz Sama, shortly before you reach the Corniche, you'll find the **Damaksi Mosque**, built in 1714, a curious mosque, located one storey above street level. Next to it is **Al-Baqrawali House**, a Delta-style mansion built in 1808.

VIEWING ROSETTA'S MANSIONS

Though the restored mansions look great from the outside, most are not currently open to the public. To find out what's open, go to **Al-Amasyali House** (see below), where they'll sell you a ticket for that house and the neighbouring **Abu Shahim Mill**. In the past, the same ticket also covered entry to the **Hammam Azouz** bathhouse (see below) and one other mansion, but none of those were open at the time of writing. Alternatively, **caretakers** at certain restored mansions may allow you in to have a look.

Sharia Sheikh Qanadili

Further examples of Rosetta's Delta-style architecture lie on, or just off, **Sharia Sheikh Qanadili**, which runs north (parallel to the river), one block east of Al-Gamal House. Heading north along it from Azouz Sama, you pass **Thabet House**, one of the oldest of the Delta-style houses, built in 1709. On Haret al-Haj Youssef (the next left heading north from Thabet House), **Al-Manadili House** is now sadly derelict, its upper storeys having collapsed relatively recently, but its portico survives, supported by two ancient columns that are evidently of pharaonic or Greco-Roman origin.

Two blocks north, back on Sharia Sheikh Qanadili, the street opens out into a square. On its south side is **Al-Amasyali House** (daily 9am–4pm; £E16), whose upstairs reception room is ennobled by a superb wooden ceiling and mother-of-pearl-inlaid *mashrabiyas*. The house is open to the public (see box above), as is the **Abu Shahim Mill** next door (same hours; included in Al-Amasyali ticket), with its huge wooden grinders and delicately pointed keyhole arches. The mill was built around 1808 for the Turkish Agha, Ali al-Topgi, who bequeathed them both to his servant Al-Amasyali.

Ali al-Mahaldi Mosque

In a busy market street, a couple of blocks east and one block north of Abu Shahim Mill, the 1722 **Ali al-Mahaldi Mosque** is held up by an amazing miscellany of pilfered columns, some Greco-Roman, others looking suspiciously like the columns used to hold up the pulpits of Coptic churches. The mosque is under restoration and currently closed to the public, although if the door is open you can see the columns from outside.

Rashid Museum

Midan al-Hurriya • Daily 9am–4pm • £E25

On Midan al-Hurriya, the town's main square, the eighteenth-century **Kili House** contains the small **Rashid Museum**. Exhibits include some old swords, guns and documents, but the main attraction is the restored upstairs rooms, giving a feeling of what the house must have been like in its heyday. Also included in the ticket is the pleasant garden opposite, decorated with a few unlabelled cannons and columns.

Hamman Azouz

A couple of hundred metres south of Sharia Azouz Sama, three blocks off the Corniche, is the nineteenth-century **Hammam Azouz**, a fine example of a traditional bathhouse with a lovingly restored interior decorated with marble floors and fountains. It's not in use today, however, and was closed at the time of writing, but has been open to the public in the past: ask for latest information at Abu Shahim Mill (see above)

Zaghloul Mosque

One block south and one block west of Hamman Azouz, the 1545 **Zaghloul Mosque** (Gama'a Zaghloul) is Rosetta's oldest and largest mosque, bigger than Al-Azhar in Cairo – although it's currently under restoration and closed to the public. The mosque's roof is covered with over fifty domes, and as in other local mosques, the three hundred columns holding it up are a motley miscellany, taken from older

4

buildings of assorted historical periods. In 1807, the minaret gave out the rallying cry for the townspeople to (successfully) fight off an invading British force hoping to occupy the town against Napoleon.

Fort Qaitbey

7km north of town • Daily 9am–4pm (Ramadan 9am–3pm) • £E15 • Take a service taxi from the Corniche just north of Midan al-Hurriya (50pt), a green-and-white taxi (£E5) or a boat (around £E100 for the round trip, depending on your bargaining skills)

Built in 1479 to guard the mouth of the Nile and protect Egypt's spice trade against predatory maritime powers, **Fort Qaitbey** (Borg Qaitbey in Arabic) was reinforced in 1799 by Napoleon's troops. It was during these reinforcements that a sharp-eyed French officer by the name of Pierre-Francois Bouchard noticed the Rosetta Stone, which must have been among masonry recycled for the fort's construction.

The fort was originally modelled on Fort Qaitbey in Alexandria (see p.474), but was built in honey-coloured local stone. The brickwork is Napoleonic rather than Mamluke, and the fort itself isn't tremendously exciting in itself, but it's a pleasant few hours' excursion, and you can climb the ramparts to enjoy the view downriver towards the sea (the coast having shifted a few kilometres since the fort was built), and upstream, past the brick factories which occupy the river bank between here and Rosetta.

Mosque of Abu Mandur

3km south of Rosetta

For an alternative river trip (or a long walk up the Corniche), head for the tranquil, eighteenth-century **Mosque of Abu Mandur**, 3km south of Rosetta, which contains the tomb of a local saint and is thought to stand on the site of Bolbitine, an ancient Egyptian port which fell into disuse after the construction of Alexandria. You can hire a boat to reach the mosque along the Corniche (for example, at the dock 200m south of *El Nile Hotel*; expect to pay £E50–70 for the round trip).

ARRIVAL AND DEPARTURE   **ROSETTA**

By service taxi The service taxi station is at the western end of Sharia Azouz Sama, with **taxis to** Alexandria's Midan al-Gumhorriya (1hr) and to Damanhur (1hr 15min). To get here from Cairo, change at Damanhur (2hr); if you get to Damanhur by train, you'll then need to take a cab (£E2) to the bus and servees station for your onward connection.

By train The station is 500m north of town along Sharia Sheikh Qanadili. There is only one direct train a day to Alexandria's Masr station (1hr 30min), but eight to Ma'amoura (1hr), with connections to Alexandria. There are no train services between Rosetta and Dasuq, Damanhur, Tanta or Cairo.

ACCOMMODATION AND EATING

The restaurant of the *Rasheed International* offers the best **eating** in town. For cheap eats, your best bet is the slew of places opposite the service taxi stand. A local product that you'll often find on sale in the street or along the Corniche is fresh **palm heart**, which is very cheap here and well worth trying.

El Nile Hotel On the Corniche, 300m south of Midan al-Hurriya ☏ 045 292 2382. Not for the picky, and really only for serious budgeteers, this little place is very basic, with rather hard mattresses and shared bathrooms, but some rooms have balconies overlooking the river, and most have river views. Even so, it isn't worth the saving over the *Rasheed International* except if you're alone, single rooms being exactly half the price of doubles. **£E100**

Hotel Rasheed International On the south side of the park, south of Midan al-Hurriya ☏ 045 293 4399, ✉ rasheedhotel@yahoo.com. Rosetta's best hotel is great value, with neat a/c en-suite rooms, some giving views over Midan al-Hurriya or (from the top storeys) the river. B&B **£E130**

Damanhur and around

Most of the land between Alex and Tanta is given over to **cotton**, Egypt's major cash crop, whose intensive cultivation began under Mohammed Ali. Hardly surprising, then, that local towns are heavily into textiles, particularly the Beheira governorate capital, **DAMANHUR**, once Tmn-Hor, the City of Horus.

Damanhur is rather drab, but blossoms during its festival, **Moulid of Sheikh Abu Rish**, held in late October and early November, when turbaned Sufis perform *zikrs* and *munshids* to enthusiastic crowds. This occurs a week after Dasuq's moulid (see below); with venues so close together, the *mawladiya* (moulid people) can easily move on to the next event: barbers, circumcisers and all.

Egypt's only **Jewish moulid**, held over two days in January, is a very different scene. The shrine of **Abu Khatzeira** ("Father of the Mat"), a nineteenth-century mystic, has often been suspended in recent years; when the moulid is held, it is cordoned off by security police who rigorously exclude non-Jewish Egyptians, fearing a terrorist attack or violent anti-Israel protests. Within the cordon a few thousand visitors, mostly from Israel, bring sick relatives or bottled water to be blessed, and "bid" for the key to Abu Khatzeira's shrine; the money raised supports its upkeep.

Tell al-Fara'in (Buto)

Ibtu village (5km north off the Dasuq–Kafr al-Sheikh road), 30km northeast of Damanhur, 12km northeast of Dasuq

On the edge of marshes north of the village of Ibtu lies the large *tel* known as **Tell al-Fara'in** ("Mound of the Pharaohs"). This was the site of **Buto**, which is the Greek name for a dual city known to the Ancient Egyptians as Pr-Wadjet. **Wadjet**, the cobra-goddess of Lower Egypt, was worshipped in one half of the city, known as Dep. The other half, Pe, was dedicated to Djbut, the heron-god, later supplanted by Horus. The site has a *kom* at each end, with a Temple of Wadjet in the middle, but nothing of great significance to an untrained eye. For more on Tell al-Fara'in, check the Deutsches Archäologisches Institut website at ⓦdainst.org/en/project/buto, or go to ⓦegyptsites .wordpress.com//category/delta and click on "Tell el-Fara'in".

ARRIVAL AND DEPARTURE
DAMANHUR

Damanhur is the main transport hub for the Western Delta, with regular **trains** to Cairo and Tanta, or to Alex, plus **service taxis** to all those places and to Rosetta or Dasuq (change there for Kafr al-Sheikh) from its new bus and *servees* station (£E2 by cab from the train station).

Tanta and around

A bustling industrial city (Egypt's fifth-largest), **TANTA** marks the end of the cotton harvest in October with Egypt's largest festival, the **Moulid of Saiyid Ahmed al-Bedawi**, when its population jumps from 430,000 to nearly three million as visitors pour in from the Delta villages, other parts of Egypt and the Arab world. The moulid honours the founder of one of Egypt's largest Sufi brotherhoods. Born in Fez in Morocco in 1199, **Saiyid Ahmed al-Bedawi** was sent to Tanta in 1234 by the Iraqi Rifaiyah order, and later established his own *tariqa* (brotherhood), the Ahmediya. Streets and squares fill with tents and stalls for the moulid, thousands camp out amidst heaps of blankets and cooking pots among the music and chanting, vendors and devotees, Sufi *zikrs*,

---

TWO MOULIDS: DASUQ AND FUWA

A week or so after Tanta's festival (see above), and a week before Damanhur's (see above) the agricultural town of **Dasuq** (the "q" usually pronounced as a glottal stop) holds the **Moulid of Ibrahim al-Dasuqi** (starting Oct 10), drawing almost as many people. **Al-Dasuqi** (1246–88) was the only native-born Egyptian to found a major Sufi order, the Burhamiya, whose chosen colour is green: the other brotherhoods originated abroad, or were started here by foreigners. Buses and service taxis run to Dasuq from Damanhur, as do service taxis from Kafr al-Sheikh and Rosetta. Service taxis from Dasuq will take you to **Fuwa**, 13km northwest, which has its own local saint's festival every year in late October or early November.

even a circus with tigers and a levitation act. Events focus on the triple-domed, Ottoman-style **mosque** (some 300m northeast of the railway station) wherein Bedawi and a lesser sheikh, Abd al-Al, are buried. The climax to the eight-day festival occurs on a Friday, when the Ahmediya – whose banners and turbans are red – parade with drums behind their mounted sheikh. If you attend the moulid, it is best to leave your valuables somewhere safe: pickpocketing is rife and people quite often suffer injuries from crushing or fist-fights in the dense crowds.

Tanta is known for its roasted chickpeas (hummus in Arabic, though it does not necessarily mean that they are mashed with garlic and tahini). They can be bought at any of the multitude of sweet shops surrounding the mosque.

Saïs

30km northwest of Tanta, 20km south of Dasuq

Nothing but a few pits and blocks of masonry remains of the once great city of **SAÏS**, beside the Rosetta branch of the Nile on the northern edge of the modern village of **Sa al-Hagar**, just west of the Tanta–Dasuq road. Founded at the dawn of Egyptian history, it was always associated with the goddess of war and hunting, **Neith**, identified by the Greeks with their goddess Athena. The city became Egypt's capital during the **Saïte Period**, under the XXVI dynasty (664–525 BC). For more information about the site, go to ⓦ egyptsites.wordpress.com/category/delta and click on "Sa el-Hagar (Sais)".

ARRIVAL AND INFORMATION

TANTA

4

Regular trains, buses and service taxis from Alex and Cairo run from early morning till nigh on midnight. All the bus depots are connected with each other and with the train station by regular service taxi microbuses (50pt) or by taxi (££2–3).

By train From the handsome railway station in the city centre, there are 12 a/c services a day to Cairo and Alexandria, including eight which stop at Benha and Damanhur, plus innumerable slow ones to all of those destinations, as well as five to Mansura (1hr 15min), three to Damietta (2hr 35min) and twelve to Zagazig (1hr 25min–2hr).

By bus Regular buses to Cairo's Aboud terminal (every 30min 6am–10pm; 1hr 30min) leave from Gomla bus station, 2km northwest of the city centre, where you will also find buses to Damanhur and Alexandria (hourly 7am–7pm), Port Said (3 daily) and Suez (3 daily). Buses to

Mahalla leave every 15min from Mura Shaha station.
By service taxi Service taxis to Cairo (1hr 15min), Damanhur (1hr) and Alex (2hr 15min) run from Gomla (same location as the bus station). For Mahalla (30min), Sammanud (40min), Mansura (1hr), Ismailiya (2hr) and Zagazig (1hr) they run from Mura Shaha, and for Kafr al-Sheikh (1hr) they leave from a place called Staad, between Mura Shaha and the city centre.
Banks On Midan al-Gomhurriya, opposite the street leading to the Green House, the Ahli United Bank changes money and has an ATM.

ACCOMMODATION

It's easy to come to Tanta on a day-trip, but if you want to stay here during the moulid, you'll need to book a room as far in advance as possible.

Green House Hotel Sharia al-Borsa, off Midan al-Gomhurriya, about 600m northeast of the station ⓣ 040 333 0761/2, ⓕ 040 333 0320. The carpets here (green, naturally) are a little bit worn around the edges, but the hotel is homely and very friendly, and the staff can organize most things for you on request. B&B **££350**

New Arafa Hotel Southern end of Midan al-Mahata, near the station ⓣ 040 340 5040, ⓦ newarafahotel .com. This well-appointed if rather impersonal city-centre hotel could not be more conveniently located. Its rooms are a good size and equipped with a/c, TV and a minibar, and there's even a rooftop swimming pool. B&B **££420**

Mahalla al-Kubra and around

Located 24km northeast of Tanta, **MAHALLA** (Al-Mahalla al-Kubra, to give it its full title) is Egypt's fourth largest city and a big textile centre. Egypt's cotton industry is one of the few in the country with relatively strong unionization, and the failure of

THE MOULID OF ST GEORGE

The **Coptic Moulid of St George** (Aug 2–28), held around the Church of Mar Girgis in the village of **Mit Damsis**, is notable primarily for its **exorcisms**. Copts attribute demonic possession to improper baptism or deliberate curses, and specially trained priests bully and coax the *afrit* ("demon") to leave through its victim's fingers or toes rather than via the eyes, which is believed to cause blindness. Both Copts and Muslims attend the moulid, usually harmoniously, although in 2009 it had to close a day early due to sectarian clashes between Christian and Muslim youths. The Muslims apparently objected to this Christian moulid being allowed while, using the swine flu scare of that year as a pretext (see p.125), a similar Muslim event earlier in the year had been banned. The ban was, ironically, a sop to the Islamic fundamentalist lobby.

Mit Damsis village is near the Damietta branch of the Nile on the Mit Ghamr–Aga road between Zagazig and Mansoura. Because the moulid is well attended there's a fair chance of lifts along the seven-kilometre track that turns west off the main road, 15km south of Aga. Mit Damsis rarely appears on maps; don't confuse it with Damas, which does.

wages to keep up with inflation was highlighted by an April 2008 textile workers' strike, supported by opposition activists nationwide. This led to riots when the government banned all protests and attempted to quell them by force. Police used live ammunition against the demonstrators and killed at least three people including a schoolboy. Forty-nine protestors were charged with offences arising from the riots, and many were tortured by police before getting sentences of three to five years in prison.

4

Sammanud

Just six kilometres east of Mahalla, the riverside town – almost a suburb, these days – of **SAMMANUD** is where the Holy Family are believed to have stayed during their sojourn in Egypt. In pharaonic times this was **Djebnetjer**, capital of the Twelfth Nome, but all that survives of ancient Djebnetjer today is a large mound and a scattering of red and black granite blocks just west of Sammanud's taxi depot, near the hospital at the western end of town. This marks the site of the Temple of Onuris-Shu, rebuilt to grace the city under Nectanebo II (360–343 BC), the last XXX Dynasty pharaoh, and the last ruler of Egypt until Nasser who wasn't either foreign or of foreign origin.

Djedu (Busiris)

Another ancient city, **Djedu** (usually referred to by its Greek name, **Busiris**), occupied a bluff overlooking the river 5km south of Sammanud, near the modern-day village of Abu Sir Bana. A major cult centre of the underworld god Osiris, its temple was an important pilgrimage site in Old Kingdom times, but all that remains of it today are part of a XXVI Dynasty basalt statue and fragments of a monumental gateway.

ARRIVAL AND DEPARTURE · MAHALLA AL-KUBRA

Service taxis to Mansura (30min), Damietta (2hr 30min) and Alexandria (3hr), along with frequent local buses to Tanta, leave from a depot near the train station (400m up Sharia Talaat Harb from the *Omar Khayyam* hotel).

Intercity buses, and service taxis for Tanta (30min) and Cairo (1hr 45min), leave from Midan al-Shur, nearly 1km south of the *Omar Khayyam* on 23rd July St, by a clock in the form of the Eiffel Tower.

ACCOMMODATION

Omar Khayyam Midan Setta w'Ashreen Yulyu (23rd July Square), 300m north of the train station along 23rd July St, aka Sharia al-Bahr ☏040 223 4866, ⊛omarelkhayamnew.com. Mahalla's top hotel, this good-value two-star is clean and well-kept, with a choice of smaller rooms with shared bathrooms or larger en-suite rooms with a/c. B&B **£E140**

Mansura

MANSURA was founded as the camp of Sultan al-Kamil's army during the 1218–21 siege of Damietta, in which Al-Kamil – Saladin's nephew and the fifth Ayyubid sultan – successfully managed to see off the Crusaders. Unfortunately, its name ("The Victorious") was a premature boast, since the Crusaders reoccupied Damietta in 1247. Weakened by cancer and tuberculosis, al-Kamil's son, Sultan al-Salih, was unable to dislodge them, and died here in 1249. His death was concealed by his widow, Shagar al-Durr, who issued orders in Al-Salih's name, buying time until his heir could return from Iraq. Encouraged by the Mamlukes' withdrawal, France's Louis IX (later canonized as Saint Louis) led a sortie against the enemy camp, slaying their general in his bath. But with victory in sight, the Crusaders were struck by food poisoning after eating fish deliberately fed on corpses by the townspeople of Damietta, just before a devastating counterattack launched by Baybars (see p.144). Louis was captured and ransomed for Damietta's return, and later died in Tunisia while engaged on yet another ill-fated crusade.

Aside from the **house** where Louis was imprisoned (now the Mansura National Museum), the town is mostly modern, with tree-lined avenues, a university and a central mosque on Sharia al-Guesh whose twin minarets, visible from afar, make it a very handy landmark. For outsiders, the town's most interesting feature is its delicious buffalo-milk **ice cream**, which can be sampled at the sweet shops on Sharia al-Habasy, a couple of blocks west of Sharia Bur Said.

Mansura National Museum

Sharia Bur Said, 50m south of the Corniche next to a large mosque • Daily except Mon 8am–6pm (although closed for renovation at the time of writing) • £E3

The medieval house where Louis IX was imprisoned, Beit Ibn Luqman, is now the **Mansura National Museum**. As well as the room where Louis was held prisoner, the museum has a hall of artworks portraying the events and characters of the defence of Mansura, most notably a wonderful tableau by Abdel Aziz Darwish in which a tired crusader knight is about to have his head hewn off by an Egyptian soldier, while one to his left holds aloft a severed head, and one to his right is busy throttling a Crusader with his bare hands. There are also some swords and pieces of armour from the battle.

ARRIVAL AND DEPARTURE

By train The train station is on Midan al-Mahata (Station Square), slap-bang in the middle of town, 200m south of the Corniche.

Destinations Cairo (6 daily; 3hr 20min–4hr 30min); Damietta (5 daily; 1hr 30min); Mahalla (8 daily; 35–55min); Tanta (5 daily; 1hr–1hr 10min); Zagazig (10 daily; 1hr 20min–2hr).

By service taxi Most service taxis leave from Utubis al-Gadid station (the new bus station, although almost no buses serve it), 2km southeast of the centre (1.5km south from the Corniche on Sharia al-Guesh, then 500m east from

the Ramses statue). Destinations include Cairo (2hr 30min), Damietta (2hr) and Zagazig (2hr). For Tanta (1hr), Alexandria (3hr 30min), Mahalla al-Kubra (30min) and Kufr al-Sheikh (1hr 30min), service taxis run from Talkha station across the river (50pt by microbus from across the bridge opposite the end of Sharia Bur Said).

By bus The bus station is on Sharia al-Guesh, 500m east of the train station (along Sharia Gamal al-Din al-Afghani).

Destinations Cairo (every 30min; 3hr 30min); Sharm el-Sheikh (6 daily; 7hr); Suez (6 daily; 3hr 30min); Zagazig (7 daily; 2hr).

ACCOMMDOATION

Marshal el-Gezirah Sharia al-Mashaya al-Sofeya, 2km west of the town centre along the Corniche ☎ 050 221 3000. Mansura's top hotel, dating from 1923, with a very grandiose lobby all done out in marble. It's slightly less grand when you get upstairs, but it still has large a/c rooms, with balconies overlooking the river. B&B **£E400**

★ **Marshal Hotel** Opposite the station on Midan al-Mahata ☎ 050 233 3920. A two-star hotel run by the

same firm as the *Marshal el-Gezirah*, slightly more modest, but a lot friendlier and more conveniently located, and excellent value, with a/c carpeted rooms – ask for a big one, as they all cost the same – and a café and pastry shop downstairs. Coming here by taxi, ask for Midan al-Mahata – if you ask for the funduq *Marshal* they'll take you to the *Marshal el-Gezirah*. B&B **£E168**

Damietta (Dumyat)

Sited near the mouth of the eastern branch of the Nile, the port city of **DAMIETTA** became prosperous in medieval times through its trade in coffee, linen, dates and oil. However, it was always wide open to seaborne invasions and was seized by the Crusaders in 1167–68 and 1218–21, on the latter occasion accompanied by St Francis of Assisi – who ignorantly imagined that the Sultan al-Kamil knew nothing of Christianity, although he numbered Copts amongst his advisors. In 1247, the townspeople managed to get rid of the Crusaders by selling them fish fed on rotting corpses (see p.506). With the opening of the Suez Canal, Damietta had to reorient its trade towards Port Said, some 70km east; nowadays it's a thriving port city known as a centre for the manufacture of furniture, which is the local cottage industry. The centre of town is marked by a sharp bend in the river, with the main Corniche on its eastern side.

Lake Manzala

Damietta offers the chance to see the "real Egypt", far from any major tourist sights, and most foreigners who stay here simply use it as a base for **birdwatching** on **Lake Manzala**, 7km southeast of town. The lake is Egypt's most important wetland habitat, although pollution and encroachment by farmland and fish farms are nowadays severely threatening the lake's continued existence. The lake's average depth is 1.3m, and only the northern part is navigable, in flat-bottomed boats; you'll need to find a boatman to punt you through the reeds. Winter is the best time to see herons (*balashon* to locals), spoonbills (*midwas*), pelicans (*begga*) and flamingos (*basharus*).

ARRIVAL AND DEPARTURE   DAMIETTA

By train Damietta's train station is on the west side of the river, 200m north of the bend in the river, although rail services are slow and infrequent.

Destinations Cairo (1 daily; 3hr 30min); Mansura (5 daily; 1hr 30min); Tanta (4 daily; 2hr 30min); Zagazig (1 daily; 1hr 50min).

By bus and service taxi The bus station is at the junction of Sharia Bab al-Haras and Sharia al-Gala', 800m east of the Corniche (a 10min walk, or 50pt by *servees*). Service taxi stands are strung out along Sharia Bab al-Haras south from the bus station. Hourly buses (6am–5pm) and regular service taxis run to Mansura (2hr) and Cairo (4hr), with service taxis (but only two daily buses) to Port Said (45min), and four daily buses to Alexandria (3hr).

ACCOMMODATION AND EATING

⭐ **El Manshy** 5 Sharia al-Nokrashy (just off Sharia al-Gala', 150m from the Corniche) ☎ 057 233 3400. Less well equipped than the *Soliman Inn* but friendly and homely in a lived-in kind of way, with cosy if smallish rooms, tiny balconies, blue carpets and salmon-pink walls. It also has a decent restaurant. B&B **£E140**

Soliman Inn (aka *Seleman Inn*) 5 Sharia al-Gala', 100m off the Corniche (entrance on Sharia Souk al-Khodar) ☎ 057 237 6050. Three-star hotel with a/c, TV and fridge in every room, but it's pot luck whether you'll find anyone at the reception desk. B&B **£E248**

Zagazig

The charmingly named **ZAGAZIG** (usually pronounced "Za'a'zi") was founded in 1830, and is actually a grimy industrial town. **Ahmed Orabi** (1839–1911), leader of the 1882 revolt against British rule, was born here, and has a statue outside the station. Zagazig is the source of most of the **papyruses** sold in tourist shops throughout Egypt, which are manufactured in sweatshops and sold to dealers for as little as £E3–4 apiece. From a tourist's standpoint, its attractions are the **Moulid of Abu Khalil**, held outside the main mosque during the month of Shawwal (currently July or Aug), and the paltry ruins of **Bubastis**.

Bubastis (Tel Basta)

Sharia al-Shohada (1.5km southeast of the town centre) • Daily 8am–4pm • £E20 • Take your passport and expect a grilling on entry from the guards, who are not used to foreign visitors, and may follow you around the site • To reach the site from Midan Orabi (the square in front of Zagazig station), cross the railway via the underpass on the left-hand side of the station and continue straight ahead (southeast) along Sharia Mustafa Kamel for just over 1km to the end of the street, either on foot, or by microbus from the beginning of Farouq (50pt), or by taxi (£E3); the site is about 200m to your right on the left-hand side of Sharia al-Shohada

There's little to see of **Bubastis** (Bubasta in Arabic) beyond the few displayed artefacts, but archeologists have found Old and New Kingdom cemeteries and vaulted catacombs full of feline mummies, and the city was known to the Ancient Egyptians as Pr-Bastet ("House of Bastet"), after the cat-goddess daughter of the sun god Re, who was honoured with licentious festivals. Fifth-century BC Greek historian Herodotus said that its seven hundred thousand revellers consumed more wine than "during the whole of the rest of the year", and described how the city lay on raised ground encircling a canal-girt temple, "the most pleasing to look at" in all of Egypt. Begun by the VI Dynasty pyramid-builders, Bubastis reached its apogee after its rulers established the XXII Dynasty in 945 BC, though the capital at this time was probably still Tanis (see p.509).

ARRIVAL AND DEPARTURE
ZAGAZIG

By train The railway station is slap-bang in the middle of town, and could be said to mark its centre. Destinations Cairo (11 daily; 1hr 40min–2hr 30min); Ismailiya (7 daily; 1hr 20min); Mansura (10 daily; 1hr 20min–2hr); Port Said (7 daily; 2hr 40min).

By bus The main bus station is west of the train station on the south side of the tracks (from the square in front of the train station, cross the tracks via the pedestrian underpass, then turn left, alongside the railway, and it's 250m ahead on the right). Buses for Tanta, Mansura and Faqus leave from the Mansura bus station, 2km northwest of the centre on Sharia Abdel Aziz Ali and served by microbus (50pt) from outside the train station.

Destinations Alexandria (3 daily; 3hr 30min); Cairo (every 30min until 6pm; 1hr 30min); Ismailiya (every 30min until 6pm; 2hr); Mansura (7 daily; 2hr); Port Said (2 daily; 4hr); Suez (4 daily; 4hr).

By service taxi There is a regular service from just by the railway station to Cairo's Aboud terminal (1hr 15min). Service taxis for Ismailiya (1hr 30min) and Port Said (3hr) leave from the Ismailiya *servees* station, 5km east of the town centre on Sharia al-Sadat, while those for Tanta (1hr), Mansura (2hr) and Faqus (40min) leave from the Mansura bus station (see p.506). Both the Ismailiya and Mansura stations are served by microbus (50pt) from outside the train station.

ACCOMMODATION

Marina 58 Sharia Gamal Abdel Nasser, near al-Fatr Mosque ☎ 055 231 3934. Two-star hotel overlooking the local side-branch of the river. The rooms are a little bit scuffed, but quite large, with a/c and balcony, and there's a restaurant downstairs. B&B **£E246**

Opera Midan Orabi (entrance down a side alley off the square in front of the train station; sign in Arabic only) ☎ 055 230 3718. Cheap and very simple, with hard beds, sparse bedding and shared bathroom facilities, but you do get a fridge and TV in your room, a ceiling fan and a little balcony. If that still isn't enough, a brand new hotel, the *Rotaj*, is about to open next door. **£E60**

Tanis, Avaris and the "Land of Goshen"

According to the Bible (Genesis 47:27), the ancient Israelites lived in a land called **Goshen** and (Exodus 1:11) toiled as slaves there, building "treasure cities" called Pithom and Raamses, before Moses led them out of Egypt to the Promised Land. Victorian archeologists strove to uncover these biblical locations, some shrewdly plugging the biblical connection to raise money for digs. Pithom may have been **Tell al-Maskhuta**, an enormous *kom* off the road between Zagazig and Ismailiya, while Raamses has usually been identified as **Pi-Ramses**, the royal city of the XIX Dynasty pharaoh Ramses II – which is why his successor, Merneptah, regularly gets fingered as the pharaoh of the Exodus.

In the 1930s, French archeologist Pierre Montet discovered the *kom* at **Tanis** and suggested that this was Pi-Ramses, but work by Austrian archeologist Manfred Bietak in the 1960s showed that in fact Pi-Ramses centred on the modern-day village of **Qantir**, and extended to the nearby site of **Avaris**.

DATING TANIS

Originally identified by archeologists with Avaris, the capital of the Hyksos, or the much later city of Pi-Ramses, Tanis is now thought to have come into existence long afterwards, during the Third Intermediate Period (1070–664 BC). Confusingly for scholars, the founders of Tanis plundered masonry from cities all over the Delta (some predating the Hyksos, who had earlier usurped it). In 1939, Pierre Montet discovered the **tombs of Psusennes II and Osorkon II**, containing the "Treasure of Tanis", which is now in the Cairo Museum. Perplexingly, it was soon noted that the tomb of the XXI Dynasty ruler Psusennes seems to have been built after that of Osorkon, who is supposed to have lived well over a century later, during the XXII Dynasty. In his book *A Test of Time* (see p.596), British Egyptologist David Rohl argues that the two dynasties were actually contemporary, and that by assuming that they were sequential, archeologists have overestimated the duration of the Third Intermediate Period by at least 140 years – thus distorting the whole chronology of Ancient Egypt. Rohl uses his "new chronology" to try to match archeological evidence with events described in the Bible, but it should be said that most Egyptologists do not take his arguments seriously.

Avaris

Avaris had previously been the capital of the **Hyksos** (XV Dynasty), whose name derives from *hekau-khasut* ("princes of foreign lands"). The Hyksos rulers had Semitic names, but in 1991, **Minoan-style frescoes** were unearthed at a Hyksos-era palace on the western edge of the site, evincing strong links with the Minoan civilization of Crete, though most still believe that the Hyksos originated in Palestine or Syria. Avaris existed long before the Hyksos invasion, however, and before finding the frescoes, Bietak's team excavated what had been a hilly residential quarter, uncovering grave goods which suggested that the bulk of the population originated from Palestine and Syria. This lay above a stratum of evidence for an older, more sophisticated community of non-Egyptians, where 65 percent of the burials were of children below the age of two. David Rohl (see p.596) argues that this represents the **Israelites** during their sojourn in Egypt and the culling of their male newborn by the "pharaoh who did not know Joseph" (Exodus 1:8), and that the Exodus occurred during the XIII Dynasty rather than the New Kingdom, as biblical scholars believe.

The main archeological site at Avaris is **Tell al-Daba**, 7km north of Faqus, but it is not open to tourists, though there are plans afoot for an archeological museum near the site. For information on Tell al-Daba, see ⓦegyptsites.wordpress.com/category/delta; the official website of the Austrian excavation team at ⓦauaris.at includes a map of the area

Tanis

The Delta's largest archeological site is a huge *kom* near the village of **San al-Hagar**, 167km northeast of Zagazig and best known by its Greek name, **TANIS**, though it was called Zoan in the Bible (Numbers 13:22; Isaiah 19:11 and 13, and 30:4; Ezekiel 30:14), and known to the Ancient Egyptians as Djanet. In *Raiders of the Lost Ark*, it is here that Indiana Jones uncovers the Ark of the Covenant.

The **site** looks as if the huge Ramessid **Temple of Amun** was shattered by a giant's hammer, scattering chunks of masonry and fragments of statues everywhere. The ruins aren't all that impressive in themselves and few tourists come here, so you'll have the site pretty much to yourself.

ARRIVAL AND DEPARTURE	SAN AL-HAGAR

San al-Hagar is most easily reached from Faqus, 37km to the south, which is connected by service taxi to Ismailiya, Cairo and Zagazig, by bus from Zagazig and Cairo's Aboud terminal (hourly 9.15am–7pm; 2hr). From Faqus, you can catch a local bus or service taxi to San al-Hagar, or hire a private taxi for the round trip.

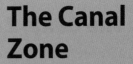

The Canal Zone

THE SUEZ CANAL

5

The Canal Zone

Once feted as a triumph of nineteenth-century engineering and regarded as the linchpin of Britain's empire, the Suez Canal nowadays seems as the author Joseph Conrad described it: "a dismal but profitable ditch", connecting the Red Sea and the Mediterranean. Except around the harbour mouths or where ships are glimpsed between sandbanks, it's a pretty dull waterway relieved only by the interesting cities of Port Said and Ismailiya.

Foreigners generally unfairly overlook both Port Said and Ismailiya, prejudging them on the basis of **Suez**, a neglected and untidy city but a vital transport nexus between Cairo, the Sinai and the Red Sea Coast. The Canal scarcely impinges on the leafy, villa-lined streets of **Ismailiya**, once the residence of the Suez Canal Company's European staff and now a popular honeymoon destination for Egyptians. By contrast, with its evocative waterfront, beaches and duty-free shopping, **Port Said** feels like Alexandria minus its cultural baggage – and a place that's somehow more authentic as a maritime city.

Brief history

The **first attempts** to connect the Red Sea and the Mediterranean are usually attributed to Necho II (610–595 BC). However, it was Persian emperor **Darius**, around 500 BC, who completed the region's first canal, linking the Red Sea and the Great Bitter Lake, from where an older waterway connected with Bubastis on the Nile and from there on to the Mediterranean. Refined by the Ptolemies and Trajan, these waterways were restored by **Amr,** following the Muslim conquest, and used for shipping corn to Arabia until the eighth century, when they were deliberately abandoned to starve out rebels in Medina.

The idea of a direct Red Sea-Mediterranean canal was first mooted – then vetoed – by Napoleon's engineers, who miscalculated a difference of ten metres between the two sea levels. The later discovery of this error encouraged junior French consul **Ferdinand de Lesseps** to present his own plan to Said Pasha, who approved it despite British objections.

Work began in 1859 and continued throughout the reign of Said's successor, Ismail, who went bankrupt attempting to finance his £19 million sterling investment. In 1875, he was forced to sell his shares to Britain – swooping before France could make an offer – for £4 million sterling. When the Canal opened in 1888, its vast profits went abroad with the **Suez Canal Company**, while two world wars transformed the **Canal Zone** into the world's largest military base.

Post World War II

In the wake of World War II, guerrilla attacks in the Zone led to the British assault on Ismailiya's police barracks, sparking Cairo's "Black Saturday" (see p.89). After the 1952 Revolution, Egypt demanded the British army's withdrawal and a greater share of the Canal's revenue, and when the West refused to make loans to finance the Aswan High Dam, Nasser announced the Canal's **nationalization** (July 26, 1956). Britain and France agreed to use Israel's advance into Sinai that October as a pretext

WALKING BY THE CANAL, PORT SAID

Highlights

❶ Ship-watching on the Suez Canal
International ferries and supertankers are among the many giant ships that ply the 163km-long Suez Canal, which remains an important trade link between the Red Sea and the Mediterranean. **See p.517**

❷ Ismailiya This European-style garden city was constructed for the foreign employees of the Suez Canal Company, and some of Ismailiya's leafy boulevards lined with colonial villas still look much as they did in the 1930s. **See p.518**

❸ Limbo Festival Not what you might assume, this fascinating festival is held annually in Ismailiya a week after Easter and involves locals burning dolls symbolizing pet hates – footballers and politicians are popular targets. **See p.521**

❹ Colonial architecture Port Said's crumbling but atmospheric nineteenth-century townhouses highlight the city's blend of French, British and Italian influences – some of the timber-porched buildings even have a touch of New Orleans about them. **See p.521**

HIGHLIGHTS ARE MARKED ON THE MAP ON P.514

5

for "safeguarding" the Canal by bombarding and invading its cities. But by standing firm and appealing to outraged world opinion, Nasser emerged victorious from the **Suez Crisis**.

The **1967 War** with Israel, and the subsequent "War of Attrition", led to the closure of the Canal until 1969. The Egyptians then stormed the Israeli-fortified Bar-Lev Line along the Canal's east bank during the 1973 **10th Ramadan/Yom Kippur War**. Although

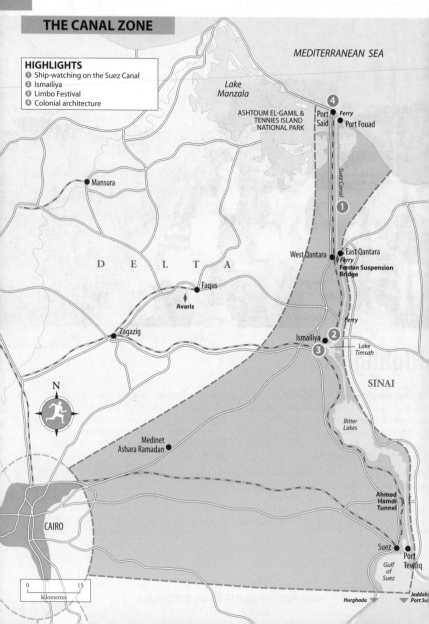

THE CANAL ZONE

HIGHLIGHTS
1. Ship-watching on the Suez Canal
2. Ismailiya
3. Limbo Festival
4. Colonial architecture

MEDITERRANEAN SEA

Lake Manzala

ASHTOUM EL-GAMIL & TENNIES ISLAND NATIONAL PARK

Port Said — *Ferry* — Port Fouad ④

Suez Canal ①

Mansura

West Qantara — East Qantara — *Ferry* — **Ferdan Suspension Bridge**

D E L T A

Faqus

Avaris

Zagazig

Ferry

Ismailiya ② — *Lake Timsah* ③

SINAI

Bitter Lakes

Medinet Ashara Ramadan

N

Ahmed Hamdi Tunnel

CAIRO

Suez — Port Tewfiq

Gulf of Suez

Jeddah Port Su...

Hurghada

0 15
kilometres

SUEZ CANAL FACTS AND FIGURES

The 163km long Suez Canal, the world's third longest, generally handles up to fifty ships a day (though its full capacity is 75) with an average transit time of fifteen hours. During its closure in the early 1970s, supertankers were built to travel around Africa – and proved too large to pass through Suez once it reopened. The Canal was subsequently widened in places, but is still not wide enough for continuous two-way traffic. In 2008–2009, the canal earned a record $5.11 billion, but the subsequent fall in global trade means this may not be matched for some time to come. For more information, visit ⓦ suezcanal.gov.eg.

the Canal was reopened in 1975, both sides remained dug in on opposite banks until 1982, when Israel withdrew from Sinai.

The cities of the Canal Zone played an important role in the **uprisings** that led to the overthrow of President Mubarak in early 2011, notably Suez, where anti-regime protests were a catalyst for demonstrations throughout the country. In February 2012, 74 people were killed at a riot at a football match in Port Said. Many believe the violence was politically motivated, and rumours that the police had failed to intervene sparked days of clashes across Egypt in which a further sixteen people died.

Suez

Unlike Port Said and Ismailiya, **SUEZ** (Es-Suweis in Arabic) has a history long predating the Canal, going back to Ptolemaic Klysma. As Arabic Qulzum, the port prospered from the spice trade and pilgrimages to Mecca throughout medieval times, remaining a walled city until the eighteenth century. The Canal brought modernization and revenues, later augmented by the discovery of oil in the Gulf of Suez, though the city was later devastated during the wars with Israel. Today most of Suez's 490,000 inhabitants live in prefabricated estates or the patched-up remnants of older quarters, while noxious petrochemical refineries, cement and fertiliser plants ring the outskirts. The city is mainly used by travellers as an interchange between Cairo, the Sinai Peninsula and Hurghada. There is a distinct lack of things to do in Suez, and although local people are friendly, modest dress is advised.

Sharia al-Geish

The main street, **Sharia al-Geish**, is a two-kilometre-long swath where cruising minibuses drop and collect passengers along the way to Port Tewfiq. Dusty palms and decrepit colonial-era buildings (including several churches) are followed by a strip of hotels, restaurants and currency exchanges. The **Convent of the Good Chapel Sisters** is an imposing colonial-style building given to the international sisterhood in 1872 by the Suez Canal Company after one of its directors recovered from a mystery illness while in their care. A decline in their numbers led the nuns to give their chapel to the Coptic church, but they still run a primary school and a dispensary for the poor.

Sharia Sa'ad Zaghloul and around

The backstreets to the south of Sharia al-Geish harbour cheap cafés, while **Sharia Sa'ad Zaghloul** runs southwest past consulates and an amusement park towards the police headquarters. North of Sharia al-Geish, a tawdry souk overflows along **Sharia Haleem**, presaging a quarter of workshops, crumbling century-old apartments with wooden balconies and modern government-built low-rises. There's another, and better, **bazaar** a short walk away to the northwest in the Arba'in area.

5

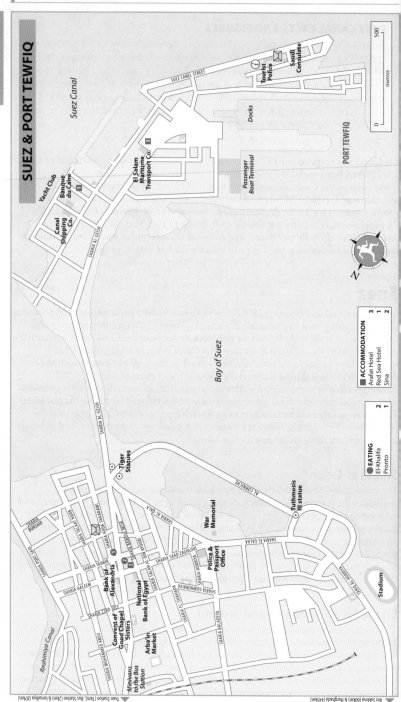

SUEZ & PORT TEWFIQ

Suez Canal

Yacht Club

Canal Shipping Co.

Banque du Caire **1**

SHARIA AL-GEISH

El Salam Maritime Transport Co. **3**

SUEZ CANAL STREET

Tourist Police ⓘ

Saudi Consulate ✉

Docks

Passenger Boat Terminal

PORT TEWFIQ

N

0   500
metres

Bay of Suez

SHARIA AL-GEISH

Tiger Statues

Tuthmosis III statue

AL CORNICHE

War Memorial

Police & Passport Office

SHARIA EL GALAA

SHARIA AL-QALA

SHARIA SAAD ZAGHLOUL

SHARIA SALAH EL-DIN NOUBI

SHARIA L CHAMDA

SHARIA GUMHORRIYA

SHARIA EL-CHAMDA

SHARIA SALAH AL-TINA NOUBI

SHARIA WORRIYA

SHARIA BRAIMIYA

Bank of Alexandria ⓘ

National Bank of Egypt ⓘ

Convent of Good Chapel Sisters

Arba'in Market

SHARIA TAHRIR

SHARIA HALEEM

SHARIA OREZ KHEIR

SHARIA TALAKA KIBIR

SHARIA HUDA SHAARANI

SHARIA PORT SAID

SHARIA MOHAMMED ABDU

SHARIA BURSAID

Ibrahimiya Canal

2

Stadium

TARIK EL-GEISH

◄ Train Station (1km); Bus Station (2km) & Ismailiya (87km)
◄ Minivans to the Bus Station

Ain Sukhna (60km) & Hurghada (445km) ▼

■ ACCOMMODATION	
Arafat Hotel	3
Red Sea Hotel	1
Sina	2

● EATING	
El-Khalifa	2
Pronto	1

CROSSING THE CANAL

Heading from the Canal Zone to the southern part of the Sinai you'll cross the Canal via either the **Ahmed Hamdi Tunnel** (12km north of Suez) or the **car ferry** (7km north of Ismailiya), which runs almost non-stop during the day. Destinations in the northern Sinai, which is very unsettled at the moment (see p.567), are served by the passenger ferry at **Qantara** (Arabic for "bridge"), 44km from Ismailiya and 80km from Port Said, and the nearby 4.1km **Ferdan Suspension Bridge**.

A couple of kilometres to the south is the **Ferdan Railway Bridge**, built on the site of an old track constructed to transport army troops to Gaza during World War I, but dismantled by the Israelis in 1968. The world's largest retractable bridge, with a span of 340m, it was devised in the late 1990s, when a rail network running the Orient Express was planned, linking Egypt to Turkey and Europe via Palestine, Israel and Lebanon. This has since been put on hold, but you can still see the bridge – which sits alongside the Canal when not in use – in operation daily (9–11am & 9pm–1am) to allow trains and cars to cross the Canal.

Al Corniche and the port

An imposing statue of the pharaoh Tuthmosis III stands at the western end of **Al Corniche** street, which overlooks the Bay of Suez; meanwhile, on either side of the road at the eastern entrance, you'll see statues of two tigers growling and crouching as if ready to pounce. Signifying strength, they were built to guide ships through the canal. Similar tiger statues, destroyed by the Israelis in the 1967 war, originally stood on either side of the Canal's entrance.

The premier Suez activity is, of course, to take a trip to the port area to look at the enormous freighters and supertankers on the Canal. Don't be tempted to take photographs, however; it's illegal, and there are security officers stationed in the area. In the spring, migratory **birds of prey** (including Griffon vultures and eagles) make an arresting sight.

ARRIVAL AND DEPARTURE   SUEZ

By train The train station is 1.5km west of the city centre's Arba'in Market. There are trains to Cairo (7 daily; 3–4hr), but they are significantly slower and less comfortable than buses or service taxis.

By bus Buses arrive at and depart from the Arba'in Terminal (☎062 322 0753) on the Cairo road on the outskirts of the city, a 5–10min taxi (£E10–20) or microbus ride into the centre of Suez. If you're travelling from Hurghada (hourly; 6–7hr) and want to head on to the Sinai the same day, you should aim to arrive in Suez by noon/1pm to be sure of getting an onward connection; the

same advice applies travelling in the opposite direction. Most buses to the Sinai start their journey in Cairo.
Destinations Alexandria (4–5 daily; 6hr); Aswan (2–3 daily; 10–12hr); Cairo (every 30min; 1hr 30min–2hr); Dahab (1 daily at 11am; 7–8hr); Ismailiya (every 30min–1hr; 1hr–1hr 30min); ; Luxor (5 daily; 8–10hr); Port Said (5 daily; 2hr 30min–3hr); Sharm el-Sheikh (5–6 daily; 6–7hr).

By service taxi Service taxis arrive at and depart from the Arba'in Terminal; they serve a similar set of destinations as the buses, though fares vary wildly depending on demand.

INFORMATION

Tourist office The tourist office (officially Mon–Wed & Sun 8am–8pm, though it doesn't always keep to these times; ☎062 333 1141) and the tourist police (daily 24hr;

☎062 333 3543) are on the edge of Port Tewfiq (Bur Tewfiq in Arabic) on Suez Canal St; reachable by minibus along Sharia al-Geish.

ACCOMMODATION

Outside the hajj season, finding a room in Suez is straightforward, but hotel standards are low and rates rather high.

Arafat Hotel Off Sharia al-Geish, Port Tewfiq ☎062 333 8355. The only budget option in the port area, *Arafat* has small and clean – if tatty – rooms with balconies and fans; some also have bathrooms. The manager can provide information about passenger ships heading elsewhere in

the Middle East. £E40
Red Sea Hotel 13 Sharia Riad, Port Tewfiq ☎062 319 0190. One of the smarter hotels in Suez, though still nothing to write home about. The dated, slightly cramped rooms come with baths, phones, balconies and TVs, while

5

the hotel's *Mermaid Restaurant* has good views of the canal. Rates include breakfast. **£E350**
Sina 21 Sharia Banque Misr ☏ 062 333 4181. If money is tight, the centrally-located *Sina* has inexpensive rooms with fans and either shared or private bathrooms. It's a bit shabby, with lots of peeling paint, but just about okay for a night. The nearby *Star*, at no.17, is very similar. **£E40**

EATING AND DRINKING

Decent eating out options are pretty limited in Suez: in addition to the places listed below, you can also get snacks and fresh juices from shops in the streets behind El-Khalifa.

El-Khalifa 320 Sharia al-Geish ☏ 064 333 7303. Your best bet for seafood is the bustling El-Khalifa: there's no menu; just wait for the proprietor to bring out a platter of fish and simply point to what looks best. They often have *umm el-khaloul*, a popular local shellfish, though in hot weather avoid it if it looks as though it might have been left standing around. Mains from £E30. Daily noon–9/10pm.
Pronto Sharia al-Geish. Fast-food canteen in the centre of town, popular with local teenagers and dishing up a variety of inexpensive (from around £E20) burgers, pizzas and sandwiches to eat in or take away. Daily noon–10pm.

DIRECTORY

Banks and exchange You can change money at the Bank of Alexandria on Sharia al-Geish, the National Bank of Egypt on Sharia Sa'ad Zaghloul or the Banque du Caire in Port Tewfiq. There are numerous ATMs on Sharia al-Geish.
Post office There are post offices in Port Tewfiq and on Sharia Hoda Sharawi, in the centre of the city (both daily except Fri 8am–3pm)

Visa extensions Visa extensions can be made at the passport office (daily except Fri 8am–2pm) inside the police headquarters on Sharia Horriya; arrive early with your passport and photo, pen, something to read and a sense of humour.

Ismailiya

ISMAILIYA is popular with Egyptian tourists and honeymooners, who come to enjoy the beaches along Lake Timsah. While many might think that the place came into being with the building of the Suez Canal in 1862, historical research dates human settlement in the region to biblical times – the area is mentioned in the Bible itself. Today the city has a schizoid character, defined by the rail line that cuts across it. South of the tracks lies the European-style **garden city** built for foreign employees of the Suez Canal Company, which extends to the verdant banks of the Sweetwater Canal. Following careful restoration, its leafy boulevards and placid streets, lined with colonial villas, look almost as they must have done in the 1930s, with bilingual street signs nourishing the illusion that the British Empire has just popped indoors for a quick cocktail. North of the train tracks is another world of hastily constructed flats grafted onto long-standing slums, and a quarter financed by the Gulf Emirates that provides a *cordon sanitaire* for the wealthy suburb of **Nemrah Setta** (Number Six).

THE MUSLIM BROTHERHOOD

Ismailiya was the birthplace of the **Muslim Brotherhood** (see p.614) and its founder Hassan al-Banna, who mounted a series of attacks against the British and an economic boycott in the Canal Zone. The British suspected that the Islamist group was being aided by elements in the Egyptian police, and on January 25, 1952, tried to disarm Ismailiya's main barracks. Fifty officers were subsequently killed, sparking rioting in Cairo the following day, which became known as "Black Saturday". The Brotherhood was subsequently banned in 1954 but continued to operate and expand underground, putting up independent candidates for election. After the 2011 Egyptian revolution, the organization was legalized and its influence has continued to grow, with its candidate, Mohammed Morsi, triumphing in the June 2012 presidential elections.

House of Ferdinand de Lesseps

Mohammed Ali Quay, near the junction with Sharia Ahmed Orabi

The large, vaguely Swiss-looking building on Mohammed Ali Quay is the **house of Ferdinand de Lesseps**, who lived here during the construction of the Suez Canal and whose carriage stands outside, encased in glass. Unfortunately, it now serves as a private hotel for guests of the Suez Canal Authority and so isn't open to the public, although lone visitors might chance a peek inside if the rear gate is open.

Ismailiya Museum

Off Mohammed Ali Quay • Mon–Thurs, Sat & Sun 9am–4pm, Fri (and daily during Ramadan) 9.30am–noon & 1.15–4pm • £E15

A small sphinx stands guard outside the tiny **Ismailiya Museum**, which has four

ISMAILIYA

Port Said (80km)

CIRCULAR ROAD

Suez Canal
University

Bus Station &
Service Taxis

AL ESHREEN

AL ESHREEN

RIDA

Approx 2 km

■ **ACCOMMODATION**
Crocodile Inn	2
Mercure Forsan Island	3
New Palace	1
Youth Hostel	4

● **EATING & DRINKING**
George's	2
King Edward	1

AL-TOGARI

Approx 1 km

★ Service Taxis

Train
Station

SHARIA AL-HORRIYA   MIDAN
ORABI   SHARIA AL-HORRIYA

National
Bank of Egypt   @   SHARIA TAHRIR

SHARIA TAHRIR   Bank of   Metro
Alexandria   Mosque   Supermarket

St. Mark   HSBC ATM
Coptic Cathedral   SA'AD ZAGHLOUL

SHARIA SAAD   ZAGHLOUL   MIDAN   SHARIA   MIDAN
GUMHORRIYA   SHARIA M. KAMIL

Passport
Office   SHARIA AL-GEISH

SHARIA AL-GEISH   Ismailiya
Museum
Police   Garden
of Steles

MOHAMMED ALI QUAY   De   SHARIA SALAH SALEM
Lesseps
House   Sweetwater Canal
Mallaha
Park

SHARIA AL-MONTANISHAT

0   Central area only   250
metres

Customs   Suez
Canal
Authority

Lake Timsah

◢ 4 & Beach

5

thousand Greco-Roman and pharaonic artefacts, plus a section devoted to the waterways of Ramses and Darius. Highlights include a fourth-century mosaic depicting Phaedra, Dionysos, Eros and Hercules, and a beautiful collection of tiny glass vases for "preserving tears". Other sections cover the Canal in modern history, the Battle of Ismailiya and the "Crossing" of October 1973. With permission from the museum, you can also see some plaques and obelisks from Ramses II's time in the **Garden of Steles** just to the west.

Mallaha Park and the Sweetwater Canal

Off Mohammed Ali Quay

If you fancy a stroll head to **Mallaha Park**, just south of the Ismailiya Museum, which has around five hundred acres of exotic shrubs and trees. The nearby **Sweetwater Canal** was dug to provide fresh water for labourers building the Suez Canal. Previously, supplies had to be brought across the desert by camels, or shipped across Lake Manzala to Port Said.

Lake Timsah

Taxi (around £E10) from the city centre, or a 1km walk along Sharia Talatini.

Notwithstanding its name, which translates as "Crocodile Lake", **Lake Timsah** has a nice **beach**. You can dine outside near picturesque fishing boats, or pay a small fee to use the manicured lawns and beaches of the private resorts and clubs, though many of these places close outside high season. Wealthier citizens patronize the *Mercure Forsan Island* (see below), which has waterskiing, windsurfing and tennis.

ARRIVAL AND DEPARTURE   ISMAILIYA

By train The train station is the junction of Midan Orabi and Sharia al-Horriya. There are trains to Cairo (6 daily; 3–5hr), but they're slower and less comfortable than buses and service taxis.

By bus All buses arrive at and depart from the bus station on the ring road outside Ismailiya, opposite the massive Suez Canal University building, a 5–10min taxi (£E5–10) or

minibus ride into the town centre.

Destinations Cairo (every 30min; 2hr); Port Said (hourly; 1hr 30min–2hr); Suez (every 30min–1hr; 1hr–1hr 30min).

By service taxi Service taxis also leave from the bus station, serving the same destinations as buses, although they're generally somewhat quicker.

ACCOMMODATION

While most of Ismailiya's accommodation has seen better days, the majority of places are safe, reasonably clean and fairly inexpensive, and only really get busy during festivals and the summer (May–Sept). Rates for all include breakfast.

Crocodile Inn 172 Sharia Sa'ad Zaghloul ☎ 064 391 2555. This centrally located hotel (also known as the *Timsah Hotel*) is a reliable and economical choice, with spacious en-suite rooms, all with a/c, TV, bathtubs and small balconies (though no views). **£E200**

Mercure Forsan Island 2km east of town ☎ 064 391 6316, ⓦ mercure.com. This leafy resort, set in fifty acres of grounds, is the best in town, with minimalist en-suite rooms and villas with TVs, a/c and minibars. There's also a swimming pool and a private beach on the lake. Good online discounts available. **$85**

New Palace Midan Orabi ☎ 064 391 6327. This wonderfully pretentious nineteenth-century pile has a pink exterior and good-value rooms with TV, a/c and private bathrooms. Popular with honeymooners and often full, so try to book in advance. **£E100**

Youth Hostel Sharia Imhara Siyahi, 1km from the centre ☎ 064 392 2850, ⓦ hihostels.com. Overlooking Lake Timsah, this Hostelling International-affiliated youth hostel has its own beach on the lake, a café-restaurant, and reasonable double, triple and dorm rooms, all en suite. Dorm **£E17**; rooms **£E70**

EATING AND DRINKING

Ismailiya's dining options are adequate, if nothing special, though there is one gem, *George's*. When the weather's fine, locals head to the fishing port on Lake Timsah to dine alfresco; it's worth the cost of a taxi (£E5–10) out along Sharia Talatini

FESTIVALS IN ISMAILIYA

Around Easter time, Ismailiya is a good place to witness the spring festival of **Sham al-Nessim**, when families picnic in the park between the Sweetwater Canal and Lake Timsah, vehicles are decorated with flowers and little girls compete for the coveted title of "Miss Strawberry". Even better is the "**Doll-Burning**" or **Limbo Festival**, held a week later. Its curious title refers to a hated nineteenth-century local governor – Limbo Bey – effigies of whom were torched by the citizenry. Ever since then, it has been customary to burn dolls resembling your pet hate: footballers are popular targets whenever Ismailiya's club does poorly. The dolls are burned on the streets after dark.

to eat fish straight from the lake, or try the local speciality, *umm al-khaloul* (see p.518). Otherwise, there are several decent restaurants clustered together in the centre. In addition to *George's* and *King Edward*, the *Mercure Forsan Island*'s bar is a good place for an alcoholic drink.

★ **George's** Sharia Sultan Hussein ☎ 064 391 8327. This Greek place dates back to 1950 and has an illicit, speakeasy-feel with dim lighting, white-shirted waiters and tasty steak, offal and seafood (mains around £E50–60): try the meatballs in tomato sauce. Daily noon–late.

King Edward Sharia Tahrir ☎ 064 332 5451. This a/c restaurant-bar is a popular haunt of expat engineers and other passing foreigners. The menu features a mix of continental dishes and Egyptian staples, plus cold beer. Mains around £E40–60. Daily noon–late.

DIRECTORY

Banks and exchange You can change money at the Bank of Alexandria or the National Bank of Egypt – both are just off Midan Orabi. There's an HSBC ATM outside Metro Supermarket on Sharia Sultan Hussein.

Internet access Anosh Net, just off Sharia Tahrir.
Post office The post office (daily except Fri 9am–4pm) is just off Midan Orabi.

Port Said

Founded at the start of the Canal excavations, **PORT SAID** (*Bur Said* in Arabic) was by the late nineteenth century an important port where all the major maritime powers had consulates. It was long synonymous with smuggling and vice, and the French adventurer Henry de Monfreid was amused by the Arab cafés where "native policemen as well as coolies" smoked hashish in back rooms, supplied by primly respectable Greeks. Nowadays, this bustling city of around 540,000 remains an important harbour and fuelling station for ships passing through the Suez Canal. A faintly raffish atmosphere lingers and its timber-porched houses have something of the feel of New Orleans' French Quarter.

Before the downturn in tourism caused by the global financial crisis and the Egyptian revolution, Port Said had been attempting to lure tourists away from Alexandria by promising better shops and less crowded beaches. These days, however, aside from day-trippers from the cruise liners, foreign tourists seldom visit the city.

Colonial Port Said

On the southern side of the city centre, the area around **Ahmed Shawki** and **Al-Guesh** streets, close to the Arsenal Basin, are good places to see some of Port Said's dusty nineteenth-century European-style colonial houses, which although dilapidated remain wonderfully evocative. Sadly, with new constructions springing up constantly, these buildings may not be there much longer.

Sharia al-Gumhorriya and the bazaar

The city centre's principal thoroughfare, **Sharia al-Gumhorriya** reflects Port Said's metamorphosis from salty entrepôt to slick commercial centre, with plate-glass facades

5

PORT SAID

De Lesseps Plinth

Al Salam Mosque

Shopping Centre

US Consulate

Yacht Basin

PORT FOUAD

Tourist Port

Suez Canal

Beach

SHARIA TARH AL-BAHR

SHARIA PALESTINE

SHARIA TRIESTINE

Thomas-Cook

Egypt Air

AL GUISH ST.

@

Misr Travel

AL CORNICHE

Ferial Gardens

Tourist Police & Post Office

BAZAAR

SHARIA ORABI

SHARIA FAIDI AL-BAHR

Customs

Former Italian Consulate

SHARIA SALAH SALEM

SHARIA NAGI ST.

PEDESTRIAN PROMENADE

Governor's Building

Suez Canal Authority

Beach

Military Museum

SHARIA 23RD JULY

SHARIA SAFIA ZAGHLOUL

SHARIA SAAD ZAGHLOUL

Arsenal Basin

AHMED SHAWKI STREET

SHARIA MUSTAFA KAMEL

Train Station

Sherif Basin

AL NASR ST

AL SHOHAD ST.

Service Taxis ★

NABIL MANSOUR ST.

IBN EL KASSEM ST.

RAMZES ST.

EL BOSTA ST.

FARHI AL-MASRI ST.

AL DORA ST.

HAMDY ST.

EL GONI ST.

SHARIA ORABI

AL MINA ST.

AL CORNICHE

Stadium

SHARIA SAAD ZAGHLOUL

MOHAMED AL SAYED SARRAN ST.

AL MINA ST.

NEHRU ST.

NEHRU SUEZ ST.

ASFAR ST.

AL-SALAM ST.

EL TABAKH ST.

GAMAL GAMEL ST.

0   300
metres

■ ACCOMMODATION

Hotel de la Poste	3
New Continental	4
Nora's Beach Hotel	1
Resta	2

● EATING & DRINKING

Abou Essam	1
Cecil Bar	5
Gianola	4
Maxim	2
Pizza Pino	3

▲ Asthoum Al-Gamil & Tennis Island National Park

▲ Bus Station (1.5km)

superseding early 20th-century balconies as the street progresses north from the Arsenal Basin to Sharia 23rd July. The adjacent **bazaar** ranges from humble stalls on Salah al Din Street to smart boutiques on Sharia en-Nahda and at the junction between Sharia al-Gumhorriya and Sharia 23rd July. There's another fine selection of old colonial buildings just east of Sharia al-Gumhorriya on **Memphis Street** – particularly the glorious old Woolworths store.

The Corniche

Bounding the northern side of the centre is Port Said's shell-strewn **beach** (loungers, parasols and windbreakers available to rent), backed by the city's long **Corniche**, from where you can watch dozens of vessels at anchor in the Mediterranean waiting to go through the Canal. At the eastern end of the Corniche is a massive sandstone plinth that bore a huge **statue of de Lesseps**, before it was torn down following the 1952 Revolution.

The Military Museum and around

Sharia 23rd July • Daily 9am–3pm (in theory, although only erratically open on Fri) • £E5

West of the centre (and south of the Corniche), Port Said's **Military Museum** provides a strong sense of the Suez Canal's embattled history. The 1956 Anglo–French–Israeli invasion is commemorated by lurid paintings and dioramas, while another room is dedicated to exhibits from the 10th Ramadam/Yom Kippur War.

Around 450m east of the Military Museum along Sharia 23rd July is the **former Italian consulate**, once grand, now abandoned, which has an interesting World War I memorial dedicated to 22 Italian soldiers on its eastern wall. An inscription (in Italian) reads: "Empowered by civic pride, they all rushed to the call from the homeland and sacrificed their lives for Italy's glory. 1915–18."

Port Fouad

Connected by ferry (every 10–15min) to a dock just east of Port Said's bazaar at the end of Sharia Saad Zaghloul

Founded as a suburb for Canal bureaucrats in 1927, **PORT FOUAD** is quieter than its sister city across the water. Residents describe their daily commutes to Port Said as journeying between Asia and Africa; the battered ferry responsible offers an enjoyable ride, though it reeks of everything but intercontinental status. The suburb's decrepit but stylish **1930s architecture** can be appreciated by making a tour of its Art Deco flats, colonial villas and well-tended gardens.

Ashtoum al-Gamil and Tennies Island National Park

7km west of Port Said, just off the coastal Damietta Road • No fixed opening times • Free

The **Ashtoum al-Gamil and Tennies Island National Park** has been a small nature reserve since 1988. Covering roughly thirty square kilometres of inlets connecting the Mediterranean with Lake Manzala, it's a prime spot for birdwatching, particularly if you can find a boatman to take you through the reeds. Its dunes and lagoons are home to residents and winter migrants including flamingos, pelicans, kingfishers, plovers, spoonbills and ducks. There are no fees or permits to visit the area, and if you're driving, you can just pull off the road.

ARRIVAL AND DEPARTURE   **PORT SAID**

By train There are trains to Cairo (5 daily; 4hr), but travelling by bus or service taxi is a much better bet.
By bus The bus station is about 3km from downtown, just off the main road from Ismailiya; a taxi into the

city centre costs around £E5–10. Heading to Cairo, the most comfortable services are run by Superjet (☎ 066 321 1779).

Destinations Alexandria (2 daily; 4hr); Cairo (every 30min;

5

3hr); Ismailiya (hourly; 1hr 30min–2hr); Suez (5 daily; 2hr 30min–3hr).

By service taxi Service taxis to Suez, Ismailiya, Cairo and other destinations arrive and depart from a stand on Sharia Mustafa Kamel, near the train station.

INFORMATION

Tourist office The tourist office on Sharia Filastin (daily except Fri 10am–5pm; ☎ 066 323 5289) has a useful free town map. There's also a tourist information booth at the train station (daily except Fri 10am–2pm; ☎ 066 322 3909).

ACCOMMODATION

Standards are pretty low at Port Said's hotels. Rates for all include breakfast, unless stated otherwise.

★ **Hotel de la Poste** 46 Sharia al-Gumhorriya ☎ 066 322 9655. Port Said's most atmospheric hotel is a 1940s-style place offering high-ceilinged rooms with fans and either private or shared bathrooms; TVs, fridges and breakfast cost extra. It's professionally run, very good value and popular, so book ahead. There's also a restaurant, bar and patisserie. **£E90**

New Continental 30 Sharia al-Gumhorriya ☎ 066 322 1355. A very welcoming family-run hotel that does the basics well: the en-suite rooms are clean and compact and come with a/c, TVs, fridges and tiny private balconies. Breakfast costs extra. **£E140**

Nora's Beach Hotel Al-Corniche ☎ 066 332 9834. This huge beachside complex has two hundred apartments and suites – all a bit frayed around the edges – with a/c, private bathroom, TVs, minibars, and balconies or terraces. Popular with Egyptian families, *Nora's* has three pools, a gym and a disco. **£E600**

Resta Sharia Sultan Hussein, off Sharia Filastin ☎ 066 332 5511, ⓦ restahotels.com. Way overpriced and in need of a revamp, the *Resta* is nevertheless the most comfortable option in Port Said. It has a good location overlooking the canal entrance and the fishing harbour, variable en suites with a/c and TVs, a pool and a decent restaurant. **$170**

EATING AND DRINKING

There are several good places to eat in Port Said: fresh seafood is readily available, and most restaurants have tables outside, allowing you to take in the bustling street life. Sharia al-Gumhorriya has plenty of patisseries and coffee houses to pass the time in, and there's the odd atmospheric bar.

Abou Essam Al-Corniche, near the mosque ☎ 066 323 2776. A good place to sample local fish and seafood without paying over the odds (a full meal costs around £E40–60), and there's a fine selection of mezze too. Daily 1–10.30pm.

Cecil Bar Sharia al-Gumhorriya, diagonally across from the *New Continental* hotel. This atmospheric spit-and-sawdust bar is one of the few places in Port Said to serve alcohol and as such draws an eclectic array of characters. It is located below the scruffy *Reana House* restaurant (Chinese and Korean food), and hidden away behind tinted windows. Open daily 5/6pm–late.

Gianola Sharia al-Gumhorriya, near the *New Continental* hotel ☎ 066 324 0001. This stylish, long-running a/c coffee shop is ideal for breakfast, a sandwich – you can even get one with smoked salmon – or a hot drink. Sandwiches and snacks cost about £E20–40. Daily 9am–10/11pm.

Maxim In the shopping centre on the corner of Sharia al-Gumhorriya and Al-Corniche ☎ 065 323 4335. With panoramic canal views and live music most evenings, this restaurant is a good place for seafood or steak, pasta and chicken options. Mains around £E30–70. Daily noon–11pm/midnight.

Pizza Pino On the corner of Sharia al-Gumhorriya and 23rd July sharia. A busy Italian restaurant with an a/c dining area, quick service and sport and music videos on the TV. Chefs work nonstop in the open kitchen to produce a wide range of fairly authentic pizzas, pastas, grills and seafood dishes (mains £E30–40), plus tempting ice creams. Daily noon–10/11pm.

DIRECTORY

Banks and exchange Most of the banks along Sharia al-Gumhorriya have ATMs. Thomas Cook is also on Sharia al-Gumhorriya (daily 8am–5pm; ☎ 066 322 7559, ⓦ thomascookegypt.com), and there are numerous private exchanges on Sharia en-Nahda.

Hospitals The best-equipped hospital is Al-Soliman, near the sports stadium (☎ 066 333 1533).

Internet access Try the Xpress cyber café, next to Ferial Gardens.

Post office The main branch (daily except Fri 9am–2pm) is on Sharia al-Gumhorriya, near the southeast corner of Ferial Gardens.

Tourist police On the first floor of the main post office building (☎ 066 322 8570).

Travel agents Misr Travel, near the tourist office on Sharia Filastin (☎ 066 322 6610, ⓦ misrtravel.net).

Visa extensions The passport office is in the governor's building on Sharia 23rd July (Thurs & Sat 8am–2pm).

Sinai

VIEW FROM MOUNT SINAI

Sinai

The Sinai peninsula has been the gateway between Africa and Asia since time immemorial, and a battleground for millennia. Prized for its strategic position and mineral wealth, Sinai is also revered by disparate cultures as the site of God's revelation to Moses, the wanderings of Exodus and the flight of the Holy Family. As Burton Bernstein wrote, "It has been touched, in one way or another, by most of Western and Near Eastern history, both actual and mythic," being the supposed route by which the Israelites reached the Promised Land and Islam entered North Africa, then a theatre for Crusader–Muslim and Arab–Israeli conflicts, and finally transformed into an internationally monitored demilitarized zone.

Though mostly wilderness, Sinai is both dramatic and beautiful. The interior of southern Sinai is an arid moonscape of jagged ranges harbouring **Mount Sinai** and **St Catherine's Monastery** – pilgrims climb from the site of the Burning Bush to the summit where God delivered the Ten Commandments. Further north, the vast **Wilderness of the Wanderings** resembles a Jackson Pollock canvas streaked with colour. The Sinai is also home to a remarkably high number of plants and wildlife; over sixty percent of Egypt's plant life thrives in this area, and 33 species are unique to it, including the world's smallest butterfly, the Sinai Baton Blue. Hyenas, ibex and the rabbit-like hyrax also inhabit the region. Venture into this "desert" on a jeep or **camel safari** and you will also find remote springs and lush oases, providing insights into **Bedouin culture**.

Above all, the south has the lure of exquisite coral reefs and tropical fish in the **Gulf of Aqaba**, one of the finest **diving** and **snorkelling** grounds in the world. The beach resorts at **Sharm el-Sheikh** (which includes **Na'ama Bay**), **Dahab** and **Nuweiba** cater to every taste and budget. From Sharm el-Sheikh you can make expeditions to Egypt's deepest reefs and most diverse aquatic life at **Ras Mohammed**, a mini-peninsula at the southern tip of Sinai, and the **Tiran Strait**, scattered with the wrecks of ships that have floundered on the reefs of this narrow passageway connecting the Red Sea to the Gulf of Aqaba. Northwest of here, the **Gulf of Suez** pales by comparison with its eastern counterpart, with no reefs and few sites to interest the general visitor – although it's great for windsurfers and kiteboarders.

The differences between Sinai and mainland Egypt can induce **culture shock**. For those accustomed to the rest of the country, Sinai will seem amazingly uncrowded,

Highlights

❶ Reefs and wrecks The Sinai has an excellent range of dive sites, including the Thistlegorm, a British ship sunk by German bombers in 1941. **See p.535**

❷ Ras Mohammed Egypt's first national park, at the southern tip of the Sinai peninsula, offers some world-class diving. **See p.538**

❸ Na'ama Bay Egypt's premier resort, whose buzzing bars and clubs teem with hedonists every night. **See p.540**

❹ Dahab Chill out in Dahab, renowned for its diving, laidback beach cafés and backpacker vibe. **See p.548**

❺ Desert safaris Explore the dramatic interior of the Sinai on a camel, horse or jeep safari with a Bedouin guide. **See p.559**

❻ St Catherine's Monastery Built by the Byzantine Empress Helena to commemorate the site of the burning bush at the foot of Mount Sinai. **See p.562**

❼ Mount Sinai Climb the mountain where Moses received the Ten Commandments and see dawn break over the Sinai desert. **See p.563**

HIGHLIGHTS ARE MARKED ON THE MAP ON P.530

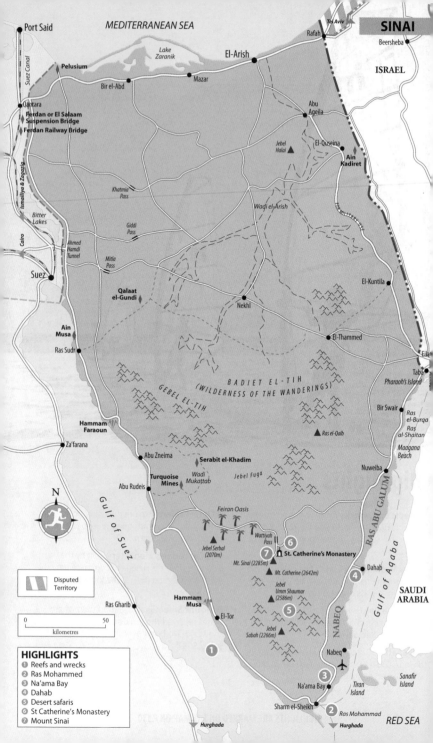

laidback and hassle-free – especially for women. Even the customary salutation is different: "*kif halak?*" ("How is your health/situation?") instead of "*izzayak?*".

Brief history

Fifty million years ago the Arabian Plate began shearing away from the African landmass, tearing the Sinai peninsula from the mainland while the Red Sea inundated the gap. Bronze Age Semites from Mesopotamia were the first to exploit Sinai's lodes of copper ore and turquoise, foreshadowing the peninsula's colonization by the III Dynasty pharaohs, who enslaved its Semitic population. **Pharaonic rule** continued until the invasion of the Hyksos "Shepherd Kings", whose occupation of northern Egypt lasted well over a century, till Ahmosis I finally destroyed their last bastion in Gaza. This was subsequently the route by which Tuthmosis III and Ramses II invaded Palestine and Syria.

The Exodus

Enshrined in the Old Testament and by centuries of tradition, the **Exodus of the Israelites** is a historical conundrum, as no archeological evidence of their journey through Sinai has been found – though excavations at Avaris in the Delta (see p.509) suggest this was the "City of Bondage" from which they fled. Though this is generally agreed to have happened c.1447 BC, scholarly opinion is divided as to the identity of "pharaoh", with most fingering Tuthmosis III or another ruler of the XVIII Dynasty, while David Rohl argues that it was actually the XIII Dynasty king Dudimose (according to his New Chronology see p.598).

VISITING SINAI

Approaches to the Sinai **from Israel and Jordan** are covered in Basics (see p.28). Serious divers and trekkers should acquire the 1:250,000 *Sinai Map of Attractions*, an English-language tourist map sold at most resorts.

VISAS

You can visit part of the peninsula on a free **Sinai-only visa** (see p.50), valid for two weeks and covering south Sinai only. If you wish to visit Ras Mohammed, other parts of Sinai's interior or mainland Egypt, you'll need a **regular visa**, which can be obtained upon arrival at Sharm el-Sheikh airport.

SINAI'S CLIMATE

Sinai's **climate** is extreme. On the coast, daytime temperatures can reach 50°C (120°F) during summer, while nights are sultry or temperate depending on the prevailing wind. In the mountains, which receive occasional snowfall over the winter and the odd rainstorm during spring, nights are cooler – if not chilly or freezing. Outside of winter, you should wear a hat, use high-factor sunscreen and drink four to six litres of water a day (more if you're trekking) to avoid sunburn and heatstroke. During summer, the heat is likely to make you spend less time on the beach and more time in the water, and to forgo trekking or camel riding entirely.

SECURITY

Although the overwhelming majority of tourists visit Sinai without incident, it is important to be aware of the security situation. Between 2004 and 2006 a series of **bomb attacks** struck Sharm el-Sheikh, Dahab and Taba, and the risk of further terrorist attacks in the future remains real. It is important to keep up to date with the latest security situation (see p.540).

Armed Bedouin groups – who often clash with the police – kidnapped several groups of tourists in early 2012 on the roads between Nuweiba, Dahab and St Catherine's Monastery, although all the tourists were released unharmed within hours. There have also been cases of **roadblocks and robberies** on these highways, as well as on the Suez–Sharm el-Sheikh road, which is currently unsafe to travel at night – SUVs are particularly at risk.

The situation in **northern Sinai** (see p.567) is volatile and often violent, and travellers are currently advised to avoid the region.

Scholars have compared Biblical descriptions with physical features and tried to reconcile myths with realities. The "**Red Sea**" is a mistranslation of the Hebrew *yam-suf*, or **Sea of Reeds**, which fits the salt lakes and marshes to the north of Suez, known today as the Bitter Lakes. From there, the Israelites proceeded to **Ain Musa** and followed **Wadi Feiran** inland towards **Mount Sinai**, although an alternative theory has them trekking across northern Sinai and receiving the Ten Commandments at **Jebel Halal**. Either way, the subsequent forty years in the wilderness are only explicable in terms of a lengthy stay at "Kadesh Barnea", identified as the oasis of **Ain Kedirat**, where there are extensive ruins.

6

Christianity and Islam

Over the next millennium or so, Sinai was invaded by Assyrians, Hittites and Babylonians, recaptured by Egypt, and conquered in turn by the Persians, Greeks and Romans. Whether or not the **Holy Family** had previously crossed Sinai to escape Herod's massacre, the region had begun to attract hermits even before Emperor Constantine legalized **Christianity**. In 639–40 the **Arabs** swept into Sinai, fired with the zeal of **Islam**. Northern Sinai eventually became a pawn in the **Crusades**, the area between Aqaba and Rafah belonging to the Frankish Kingdom until its collapse at Acre. After the Crusades, the victorious Mamlukes reopened Sinai's trade routes but the peninsula remained Egypt's Achilles heel, as the Ottoman Turks and Mohammed Ali demonstrated with their conquests of 1517 and 1831.

Twentieth-century Sinai

Sinai's strategic importance increased with the completion of the **Suez Canal**, and in 1892 Britain compelled Turkey to cede it as a buffer zone. Backed by Germany, the Turks retook it in 1914. Anglo-Egyptian forces only dislodged them after a prolonged campaign.

During World War II Sinai saw little fighting, but the **creation of Israel** brought it back into the front line. In 1948 the Israelis repulsed Arab attacks from all sides and took the **Gaza Strip** and **El-Arish** before an armistice was signed, only withdrawing under British pressure. Nasser brought together British and Israeli interests by closing the Gulf of Aqaba to Israeli shipping and nationalizing the Suez Canal. Israel's advance into Sinai in October 1956 was the agreed pretext for Anglo-French intervention in the **Suez Crisis**; the three states, though militarily successful, were compelled to quit by international opposition, and UN peacekeeping forces established a buffer zone in Gaza and guaranteed free passage through the Gulf of Aqaba.

However, when Egypt ordered the UN to leave and resumed its blockade in 1967, Israel launched a pre-emptive strike and captured the entire peninsula, which it retained after the **Six Day War**. In the **October War of 1973**, Egypt broke into Sinai but then suffered a devastating counterattack across the Suez Canal.

The Camp David Accords and after

US-sponsored peace negotiations culminated in President Sadat's historic visit to Jerusalem, the **Camp David Accords** and a peace treaty signed in 1979. Under its terms Israel evacuated all settlements founded during the occupation of Sinai and the territory reverted to Egypt. The phased transition was completed in 1982, except for the disputed enclave of Taba, finally resolved in 1989. The Multinational Force and Observers (MFO) based at Na'ama Bay monitors Sinai's demilitarized zones.

Tourism, introduced to Sinai by the Israelis, initially suffered from the handover, as the Camp David Accords forbade any development for five years. Since 1988, however, its recovery has shifted into overdrive. While the areas of Ras Mohammed, Abu Galum and Nabeq are protected as nature reserves, the entire coastline north of Nuweiba, and from Sharm el-Sheikh to Nabeq, is highly developed, with new resorts springing up all the time and innumerable charter flights from Europe into Sharm el-Sheikh airport.

The mercurial nature of Middle Eastern politics, however, means tourism along the Sinai coast is a fickle business. Unrest in the West Bank and Gaza has greatly slowed tourist traffic from Israel, while the 2004 **terrorist attacks** in Taba, with more attacks in Sharm el-Sheikh and Dahab in 2005 and 2006 respectively, have worsened the situation further. While tourists have flocked back to Sharm el-Sheikh and Dahab, the coast around Nuweiba and Taba is very quiet. The global recession and the unrest caused by the ongoing Egyptian revolution are unlikely to improve matters.

The gulf coasts

Sinai rises and tapers as the peninsula runs towards its southern apex, red rock meeting golden sand and deep blue water along two gulf coasts. Even the **Gulf of Suez**, as E.M. Forster noted, looks enticing from offshore – "an exquisite corridor of tinted mountains and radiant water" – though it's nowadays transformed after dark into a vision of Hades by the flaming plumes of oil rigs.

For most travellers, however, Suez is merely an interlude before the **Gulf of Aqaba**, whose amazing coral reefs and tropical fish have given rise to a number of popular resorts. The beach scene here is the best in Egypt, and trips into the **interior** are easy to arrange. Even from the beach, the view of the mountains of Sinai and Saudi Arabia is magnificent.

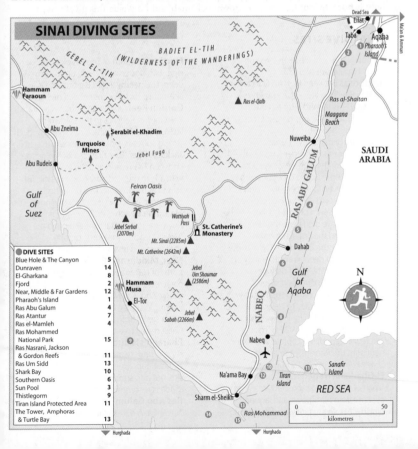

SINAI DIVING SITES

● DIVE SITES	
Blue Hole & The Canyon	5
Dunraven	14
El-Gharkana	8
Fjord	2
Near, Middle & Far Gardens	12
Pharaoh's Island	1
Ras Abu Galum	4
Ras Atantur	7
Ras el-Mamleh	4
Ras Mohammed National Park	15
Ras Nasrani, Jackson & Gordon Reefs	11
Ras Um Sidd	13
Shark Bay	10
Southern Oasis	6
Sun Pool	3
Thistlegorm	9
Tiran Island Protected Area	11
The Tower, Amphoras & Turtle Bay	13

Diving and snorkelling

Much of the diving in Sinai is easy to access and relatively sheltered from harsh winds and currents, making it a popular destination for those who have little or no experience. It's an inexpensive place to learn open-water diving and gain a PADI, BSAC or CMAS certificate, entitling you to dive anywhere in the world.

Prices and packages

Prices for diving courses tend to be lower (often significantly so) in Dahab and Nuweiba than Sharm el-Sheikh; the best deals for all destinations are generally to be had online. Boat trips to dive sites usually include equipment, though lunch is often extra (about £E50–60).

Dive packages can be a good deal, costing around €200–260 for ten dives. Liveaboards can work out cheaper than staying in a hotel and buying a dive package separately, averaging around €100 per person per day, including full board. Where equipment rental isn't covered, count on an extra €25–30 per day. During quiet periods, bookings can be arranged at short notice, but to be sure of what you're getting it's best to book in advance.

Dives and courses

The type of diving and the degree of experience required at each dive site are mainly determined by underwater topography and currents. Around Sharm el-Sheikh the chief activity is **boat diving**. Up the coast towards Dahab and Nuweiba this gives way to

---

SINAI DIVE SITES

The following sites are all marked on the Sinai dive sites map (p.533).

Amphoras Between Ras Um Sidd and Na'ama Bay. This site – also known as "Mercury" – is named after a Turkish galleon laden with amphoras of mercury that lies on the reef.

Blue Hole 8km north of Dahab. The challenge of this 107m-deep hole in the reef is to swim through a passage 60m down and come up the other side: this is highly risky even for expert divers and a number of people – including dive-masters and instructors with prior experience of the Blue Hole – have died here. You can safely snorkel around the rim of the hole.

Canyon Near the Blue Hole. This narrow reef crack, 50m deep, is another famous site, and one that should only be attempted by experienced divers.

Dunraven The *Dunraven* steamship was en route from Bombay to Newcastle when it steered onto a reef in fine weather in 1873, capsized and sank 25m. Though its 25 crew escaped, the captain was found negligent (he fatuously remarked, "Twenty-five is my lucky number!").

El-Gharkana Nabeq This luxuriant reef – part of the Nabeq protected area – lies offshore from mangroves and lagoons which are home to rare waterfowl and flora.

Fjord 10km south of Taba. A picturesque cleft with underwater reefs, up to 16m deep. The nearby "Fjord Banana" site is an alternative for less experienced divers.

Gordon Reef Off the coast of Ras Nasrani. The Gordon Reef lies in the shipwreck-littered Tiran Strait, which has sharks and strong currents. Not for beginners.

Jackson Reef Near Tiran Island. A large reef between Tiran Island and the mainland, with a 70m drop-off, sharks and pelagic fish, as well as the shipwreck *Lara*. Strong currents make it dangerous for beginners.

Maagana Beach 5–10km north of Nuweiba. The reef falls sheer around the "Devil's Head" to the north, getting shallower and less impressive further south.

Near, Middle and Far Gardens 1–5km north of Na'ama Bay. A series of lovely coral reefs, good for easy diving and snorkelling. The Near Gardens are within walking distance of Na'ama. In 2010 there was a series of shark attacks in the Middle Garden area (see box, p.540).

Pharaoh's Island Near Taba. There's superb underwater scenery, easy access by boat and a spectacular wall dive at this site, but also strong currents; a diving guide is recommended.

Ras Abu Galum 50km south of Nuweiba. A 400-square-kilometre

shore diving, where you wade or swim out to the reefs. **Liveaboards** (also called safari boats) allow you to spend days or weeks at sea, cruising the dive sites and shipwrecks of the north Red Sea around Ras Mohammed and the Tiran Strait (or the more southerly reefs beyond Hurghada). They also give access to less-visited sites out of "peak hours", and the chance to make up to five dives a day.

Choosing a dive centre

When **choosing a dive centre**, stick to operators that have been around longest and have proper links with organizations like PADI. The Chamber of Diving and Watersports (ⓦcdws.travel) has a list of all legal dive centres in the Sinai, as well as those that have been blacklisted. When visiting a centre, ask to see a card proving the instructor is qualified to teach the relevant course (PADI, BSAC, or whatever), and isn't merely a dive-master. Many dive centres offer courses not only in English but also in various other European languages. Finally, a number of Sinai dive centres charge an optional €1 per day levy on all divers to pay for the upkeep of the local hyperbaric chamber (see p.542).

Snorkelling

Snorkelling is also great fun and much cheaper than diving. Equipment can be rented at most of Sinai's dive centres (€5–10/day), but if you're planning to snorkel a lot, it's cheaper to bring your own gear from home. Note that coral reefs and spiny urchins can rip unprotected feet to shreds; in all events you should only walk in designated

protected area with a deep virgin reef wall and a range of sea life.

Ras Atantur Between Dahab and Nabeq. Colourful, abundant reef, with a shipwreck – the *Maria Schroeder* – 10km further south. Access by 4WD.

Ras el-Mamleh 20km south of Nuweiba. A slab of virgin reef wall on the northern edge of the Ras Abu Galum protected area. Access by 4WD or boat.

Ras Mohammed National Park 25km southwest of Sharm el-Sheikh. Wonderful corals, mangrove lagoons, anemone gardens and crevice pools, with shark reefs offshore. It's also the site of the *Yolanda* shipwreck (see below).

Ras Nasrani Near Tiran Island. Sheer reef wall riddled with shark caves; the "Light" and the "Point" are notable spots. Large turtles are a common sight on the reef slope. Beware of sharks and strong currents. Not for inexperienced divers.

Ras Um Sidd Sharm el-Sheikh. Within walking distance of Sharm el-Sheikh at the north point of the harbour, this site features exquisite fan corals and fish.

Shark Bay 10km north of Na'ama Bay. Colourful reef just off the beach of a small resort. Good for novices and experienced divers alike, and snorkellers.

Southern Oasis 7km south of Dahab. A gently sloping reef, the Southern Oasis

offers easy diving and snorkelling.

Sun Pool 10–15km south of Taba. A gorgeous diving beach along a shallow reef extending as far north as the Fjord.

Thistlegorm Near El-Tor in the Gulf of Suez. This British ship, sunk by German bombers in 1941, was laden with rifles, uniforms, trucks and jeeps – and also packed full of ammunition, which exploded, ripping the ship apart and killing most of the crew. Tubeworms grow out of the bathtub in the captain's cabin and you can still see many of the armoured vehicles the ship was carrying. Discovered by Jacques Cousteau, it's a popular dive from Sharm el-Sheikh.

Tiran Island Protected area East of Na'ama Bay. An archipelago with over twenty dive sites, all amazing, although sharks and strong currents means the sites are only for experienced divers unless explicitly stated otherwise.

The Tower South of Na'ama Bay. A sheer reef pillar dropping 60m, with easy access from the beach and mild currents. Good for novice divers.

Turtle Bay Between Ras Um Sidd and Amphoras. This shallow bay has turtles and is good for beginners.

Yolanda Off Ras Mohammed. This Cypriot freighter struck a reef during a storm in 1981; its cargo includes a BMW and scores of porcelain lavatories.

6

"corridors" to protect the corals – if the water is too shallow to allow you to float above them. However cool the water may feel, the sun's rays can still burn exposed flesh, so always wear a T-shirt and use waterproof sunscreen.

Between Suez and Sharm el-Sheikh

There's little point stopping during the 338km journey between **Suez** and **Sharm el-Sheikh,** unless you are an avid windsurfer or kiteboarder. Such attractions as exist along (or off) the route are otherwise awkward to reach, so most travellers pass them by. Although the resort of **Ras Sudr** is essentially an oil town, its proximity to Cairo (130km) means it is becoming popular with Cairenes as a weekend getaway, while it also attracts windsurfers from further afield year-round. Further south, and inland, the pharaonic ruins at **Serabit el-Khadim** also draw visitors. Beyond **El-Tor**, the area's administrative capital, there's little of interest until you reach **Ras Mohammed**.

Ras Sudr

Famed for the variety of seashells washed up on its beach, the flyblown town of **RAS SUDR** (or Ras Sidr) is marred by a reeking oil refinery that doesn't seem to bother the middle-class Cairenes who frequent its holiday resorts. This part of the coast is so windy it is often overlooked by travellers who seek the calmer reef-fringed shores of Sharm el-Sheikh, although the year-round cross-shore gusts make it a haven for **kiteboarders** and **windsurfers** – for equipment and tuition try the *Moon Beach Resort* (see below).

ACCOMMODATION   **RAS SUDR**

Moon Beach Retreat 40km south of Ras Sudr ☎069 340 1501, ⓦmoonbeachretreat.com. Although it is a taxi ride away from Ras Sudr, this is just about the best place to stay in the area, with simple rooms in a/c stone chalets, private beach, pool, restaurant and bars. There's a good windsurfing school – conditions are ideal for beginners – plus yoga and massage. Half-board **€100**

Hammam Faraoun

Fifty-five kilometres south of Ras Sudr, a turn-off leads to **HAMMAM FARAOUN** ("Pharaoh's Bath"), several near-boiling **hot springs** which Arab folklore attributes to the pharaoh's struggles to extricate himself from the waves that engulfed his army as he chased the Israelites. Local Bedouin use the springs for curing rheumatism, and it's possible to take a dip in the waters. A cave in the hill beside the shore leads into "the sauna", a warren of chambers awash with hot water, but it's more comfortable to bathe where the springs flow into the sea.

Serabit el-Khadim

Built upon a 755-metre-high summit reached by a tortuous path, the rock-hewn temple known as **Serabit el-Khadim** is Sinai's only pharaonic temple, surrounded by some of the region's grandest scenery. Erected during the XII Dynasty, when turquoise mining in the area was at its peak, it is an enduring symbol of pharaonic power.

PROTECTING THE REEFS

Egypt's coral reefs are fragile organisms, vulnerable even to wave motion and excessive sunlight, as well as accidental damage from tourists. Dive boats that come too close and divers who break or disturb corals have resulted in many sites near Sharm el-Sheikh being "over-dived", while other reefs have been damaged or destroyed by tourism-related work. For divers and snorkellers alike, the fundamental rule is to look but not touch. In marine parks such as Ras Mohammed, it's also forbidden to feed the fish or remove anything from the sea. And don't buy aquatic souvenirs – their export is illegal. Even shells from the beach may be confiscated when you leave Egypt, with a hefty fine given in return.

Though Bedouin still glean some turquoise by low-tech methods, the amount that remains isn't worth the cost of industrial extraction.

Wadi Mukattab and Wadi Maraghah

Serabit el-Khadim is becoming a popular stop on jeep safaris from points south, approached via a track leading off the road from St Catherine's into **Wadi Mukattab** – the Valley of Inscriptions. There are dozens of hieroglyphic texts carved into the

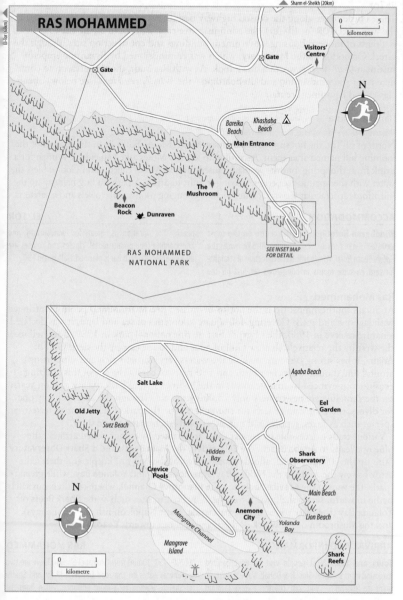

rocks, alongside Proto-Sinaitic inscriptions that continue into **Wadi Maraghah**, where ancient mine workings and stelae were damaged when the turquoise mines were revived by the British (before going bust in 1901). Most travel agencies in Sharm el-Sheikh and many in Dahab can organize day- and overnight trips here, while Desert Divers (see p.551) run a four-day tour (€220) taking in Serabit el-Khadim, Wadi Mukattab and St Catherine's (see p.562).

El-Tor

There's little to see along the coastal highway besides a scattering of holiday resorts all the way to **EL-TOR** (or El-Tur), the administrative capital of south Sinai. The town itself is a mass of modern housing, government buildings and construction sites, though the Greek Orthodox **Raithu Monastery**, which was commissioned by Byzantine emperor Justinian (527–65), is worth a quick look. As with Ras Sudr, the main reason to come here is for the **windsurfing** and **kiteboarding** – the *Windhaven Hotel* (see below) offers classes and equipment rental.

Hammam Musa
4km north of El-Tor • No fixed hours, but open most days • £E25

North of El-Tor, the **hot springs** of **Hammam Musa** (Moses' Bath) lie in the shadow of the looming hill named after them. According to legend, Moses asked an elderly woman for a drink from the spring, but the woman refused him, so Moses called upon God to bless the water with therapeutic properties, making it unfit to drink. A path leading halfway up the hill affords spectacular views; facilities include changing rooms with towels and a cafeteria.

ACCOMMODATION   **EL-TOR**

Windhaven Hotel North of the centre on the coast ☎ 069 377 4343, ⓦ oceansource.net. Also known as the *Habibi Beach Hotel*, *Windhaven* has a collection of straightforward en-suite rooms in bungalows set just off the beach. The location is great for windsurfing and kiteboarding (equipment rental, classes and courses are all available). A beach bar is planned. Half-board €90

Ras Mohammed

At Sinai's southernmost tip is the not-to-be-missed **RAS MOHAMMED** peninsula, fringed with lagoons and reefs. Covering 480 square kilometres of sea and land, it was declared a nature reserve in 1983, then Egypt's first marine **national park** in 1989. Bordered to the west by the relatively shallow Gulf of Suez and to the east by the deep Gulf of Aqaba, it has strong currents, making the waters very nutrient-rich and supporting around one thousand species of fish and 150 types of coral. The age of this amazing ecosystem is evinced by marine fossils in the bedrock dating back twenty million years; on the shoreline are newcomers only 75,000 years old. Though the area is chiefly one for **divers**, there are calmer reefs for **snorkellers** too. The park is also home to terrestrial species such as foxes, reptiles and migratory birds such as the white stork.

Various trails – accessible by regular car – are marked by colour-coded arrows. The blue one leads to **Aqaba Beach**, the **Eel Garden**, the **Main Beach** and a **Shark Observatory** 50m up the cliffside, which affords distant views of the odd fin. Purple and then red arrows show the route to the **Hidden Bay**, **Anemone City** and **Yolanda Bay**, while green marks the way to the **Crevice Pools** and the **Mangrove Channel**, where children can safely bathe in warm, sandy shallows. Divers head by boat to sites such as the **Shark Reefs** off Yolanda Bay (the place to see sharks, barracuda, giant Napoleon fish and manta rays), and **the Mushroom** or the **wreck** of the *Dunraven*, out towards **Beacon Rock**.

ARRIVAL AND INFORMATION   **RAS MOHAMMED**

Tours and taxis Most people visit on an organized excursion from Sharm el-Sheikh or Dahab, but – if you only want to snorkel – you can charter a taxi (around £E200–250; 30min) from Sharm el-Sheikh. There are two perimeter gates on the road between El-Tor and Sharm el-Sheikh, leading to a main entrance, 20km from the nearest reefs. You need a full Egyptian visa – not a Sinai-only one – to visit Ras Mohammed.

Opening hours Daily sunrise–sunset

Entrance charge €5

Visitor centre The visitor centre (daily except Fri 10am–sunset) has a library, shop, restaurant and free telescopes (which can also be found at the Shark Observatory and at Suez Beach).

Camping You can camp (around ₤E30/person per night) at a site near Khashaba Beach; enquire at the main entrance and brings supplies with you from Sharm.

Sharm el-Sheikh and Na'ama Bay

Although technically one destination, **Sharm el-Sheikh** comprises several different areas – and constant development means more are added each year. Sharm el-Sheikh is often referred to simply as **Sharm**: if you're outside the resort that term refers to the whole resort, including Na'ama Bay, while once you're within the resort itself, the name "Sharm" refers only to the downtown area of **Sharm el-Maya**, home to a market, port and marina. Glitzy **Na'ama Bay**, 7km up the coast, is where the bulk of the best hotels, restaurants and nightlife venues are based.

Sharm el-Sheikh and Sharm el-Maya

A hunk of sterile buildings on a plateau commanding docks and other installations, **SHARM EL-SHEIKH** was developed by the Israelis after they captured the town in the 1967 war. Their main purpose was to thwart Egypt's blockade of the Tiran Strait and to control overland communications between the Aqaba and Suez coasts. Tourism was an afterthought – though an important one, helping to finance the Israeli occupation and settlements, which Egypt inherited between 1979 and 1982.

Since then, Sharm's infrastructure has expanded in fits and starts, without much enhancing its appeal. Despite some plush hotels it basically remains a dormitory town for workers servicing neighbouring Na'ama Bay – while the port area of **Sharm el-Maya** retains a local ambience reminiscent of Suez or Cairo which can come as a shock to tourists leaving their resorts for the first time. Whereas beachwear is de rigueur in Na'ama, tourists

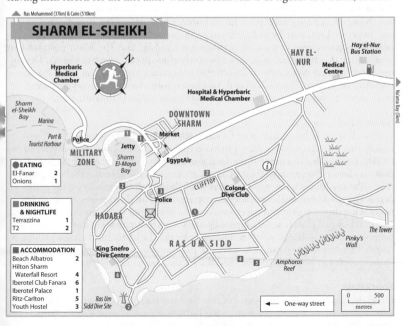

SECURITY AND SAFETY IN SHARM AND NA'AMA BAY

Sharm and Na'ama Bay tragically hit the headlines on July 24, 2005, when a series of coordinated bomb attacks struck the resort, killing around eighty people and injuring more than two hundred. **Security measures** have been heightened since, but travellers should always be vigilant. In December 2010 there was a series of **shark attacks** close to the shoreline in Sharm: a German tourist was killed in the Middle Garden reef and four other people badly injured. Shark attacks of any kind are very unusual in the Red Sea, but it is advisable to check local updates.

---

in Sharm el-Maya should **dress** modestly off the beach to avoid unwelcome attention.

The only foreigners here tend to be divers and a few backpackers who take advantage of its cheapish accommodation and commute into Na'ama Bay. Sharm has a **beach**, but its small bay doesn't match Na'ama's, although the Sharm el-Maya area does have some good restaurants and souvenir shops. The new **Sharm el-Sheikh National Museum** (due to open in 2013–14) will feature around seven thousand exhibits tracing the country's history from pharaonic times to the present day.

Ras Um Sidd

Southeast of Sharm el-Maya bay, a string of hotels and villas has sprouted along the stretch of coast known as **Ras Um Sidd**. The swankiest resorts are perched close to the coast, while cheaper hotels fill up the land behind, although in general it's a pretty bleak area, with poor beaches, and guests have to rely on shuttle buses to get them to the better amenities of Na'ama Bay. The main attraction is the nearby **Ras Um Sidd dive site**. The area is basically all coral reef, without any natural sandy beaches – what sand there is has been imported by the hotels to create their own beaches, inevitably increasing the debris many divers now encounter underwater in this area.

The Tower

From Ras Um Sidd, a paved road lined with holiday resorts and hotels runs to **The Tower**, a fine diving beach colonized by the big *New Tower Club* hotel. The real lure, however, is a huge **coral pillar** just offshore, which drops 60m into the depths. It's easy to get to The Tower by taxi from either Sharm or Na'ama, but it is no longer possible to access most of the reefs between Ras Um Sidd and The Tower from land, as hotels along this stretch of coast now effectively block public access to the sea. Diving these reefs by boat, you come to (in order of appearance after Ras Um Sidd) Fiasco, Paradise, Turtle Bay, Pinky's Wall and Amphoras. **Turtle Bay** has sun-dappled water that's lovely to swim in, even if there are fewer green turtles than you'd hope.

Na'ama Bay

With its fine sandy beach and smart facilities, **NA'AMA BAY** has transformed itself so rapidly that even the residents have trouble keeping up. Now a glitzy, over-developed tourist centre with a vast array of fast-food joints, international restaurants, bars and clubs, it's far from an authentic Egyptian experience, and the general feel of the place is much like any Mediterranean package resort. Nightlife and sunbathing are the main draws, though diving and snorkelling are popular too, with dive centres, hotels and malls being the only points of reference along the beachfront strip. The **beach** is divided into hotel-owned plots that are supposedly open to anyone providing they don't use the parasols or chairs – though scruffier-looking types may be hassled and topless bathing is illegal. There are also two public beaches (£E10), though they are no more than narrow strips squeezed in beside the *Novotel* and the *Hilton Fayrouz Resort* beaches.

Shark Bay

Hotel development continues past Na'ama Bay, and resorts – some up to a square kilometre in size – line the coast up to **Ras Nasrani** and even beyond to the borders of

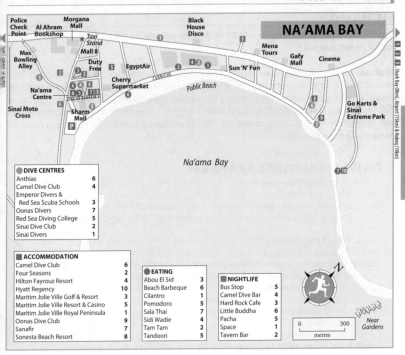

NA'AMA BAY

DIVE CENTRES	
Anthias	6
Camel Dive Club	4
Emperor Divers &	
Red Sea Scuba Schools	3
Oonas Divers	7
Red Sea Diving College	5
Sinai Dive Club	2
Sinai Divers	1

ACCOMMODATION	
Camel Dive Club	6
Four Seasons	3
Hilton Fayrouz Resort	4
Hyatt Regency	10
Maritim Jolie Ville Golf & Resort	3
Maritim Jolie Ville Resort & Casino	5
Maritim Jolie Ville Royal Peninsula	1
Oonas Dive Club	9
Sanafir	7
Sonesta Beach Resort	8

EATING	
Abou El Sid	3
Beach Barbeque	6
Cilantro	1
Pomodoro	5
Sala Thai	7
Sidi Wadie	4
Tam Tam	2
Tandoori	5

NIGHTLIFE	
Bus Stop	5
Camel Dive Bar	4
Hard Rock Cafe	6
Little Buddha	5
Pacha	5
Space	1
Tavern Bar	2

the **Nabeq** protected area. The once-beautiful and isolated retreat of **SHARK BAY**, 8km north of Na'ama, has now been overwhelmed by numerous large holiday resorts, although it still boasts a fine beach, and views of Tiran Island, and continues to attract many visitors, including scores of day-trippers from Na'ama. Despite the bay's forbidding name (Beit el-Irsh, "House of the Shark" in Arabic), the sharks have been scared away by divers, leaving a benign array of tropical fish and coral gardens just offshore, with deeper reefs and bigger fish further out. There's an £E10 charge to use the beach.

ARRIVAL AND DEPARTURE

SHARM EL-SHEIKH AND NA'AMA BAY

By plane Sharm el-Sheikh airport, 10km north of Na'ama Bay, has regular flights to Cairo, Hurghada and elsewhere in Egypt, as well as a host of international services (many of them charter flights). Visas are easy to pick up at the airport (ignore the tourist agency touts who try to do it for you for an inflated fee); if you're travelling beyond the Sinai coast, make sure you get a full visa rather than a Sinai-only one (see p.50). The airport has ATMs and a moneychanger. Independent travellers will need to get a taxi into Na'ama Bay or Sharm (around £E70, though you'll have to haggle).

By bus All buses leave from the Hay el-Nur bus station (📞 069 366 0666) around 2km from both Sharm (to the south) and Na'ama (to the northeast); a taxi to either costs around £E50. If you're heading to Cairo, the four daily Superjet buses make fewer stops and tend to be quicker

than the much more frequent East Delta services; you'll need to buy your ticket in advance in person at the bus station to be sure of getting a seat. Bus timetables are notoriously subject to change, so ask around to check the latest information.

Destinations: Alexandria (1 daily; 8–10hr); Cairo (22–24 daily; 7–8hr); Dahab (10 daily; 1hr 30min); Ismailiya (about 20 daily; 7–8hr); Luxor (2 daily; 12–14hr); Nuweiba (3 daily; 2hr–2hr 30min); Suez (3 daily; 6–7hr); Taba (1 daily; around 4hr 30min).

By boat The useful catamaran service between Sharm el-Sheikh and Hurghada was suspended at the time of writing, but may restart in the future.

By taxi Taxis are the easiest way to travel between Na'ama Bay/Sharm and Shark Bay (around £E30–50).

6

GETTING AROUND

Since the 2005 terrorist attack, Na'ama Bay's tourist area has been pedestrianized and vehicles are no longer permitted south of the main coast road.

Minibuses Frequent minibuses carry local workers between Sharm el-Maya and Na'ama (generally ££1–2/person). You can flag them down at any point along the main road, but bear in mind you won't be sharing space with cosmopolitan Egyptian holidaymakers, so it's advisable to be modestly dressed

Taxis Taxis are easy to find in downtown Sharm, on Peace Road and at the stand in Na'ama Bay. Drivers are used to tourists paying inflated prices, so you'll generally have to haggle hard to avoid being ripped off; the journey between Na'ama Bay and downtown Sharm or Hadaba should cost about ££30-40.

DIVING IN SHARM AND NA'AMA BAY

The fabulous array of **dive spots** around Sharm and Na'ama is the chief attraction of both resorts, offering endless scope for boat and shore diving. Divers are not allowed to explore the reefs near Na'ama and Sharm el-Sheikh independently; all diving must be done with a guide, which in practical terms means sticking with trips run by the dive operators listed below.

A plethora of **dive centres** offer an extensive range of courses, trips and equipment rental. All the centres listed here are open daily (mostly 8.30am–6pm). Dive boats leave around 9am from the **Sharm el-Maya marina**, and most centres will collect you from your hotel and drop you off again. Trips to the **Gordon** and **Jackson reefs** in the Tiran Strait (see p.534) or **Ras Mohammed** (p.538) cost €55–65; a one-day **Thistlegorm** trip (see p.535) €90–120. Space permitting, **snorkellers** can join any boat for about €25. Some of the centres offer **liveaboards** too. Before signing up for any courses, ask where you'll be doing your training: the water in Sharm el-Maya is less pleasant than in Na'ama Bay thanks to the former's proximity to the marina. All Sharm and Na'ama dive centres are members of the **South Sinai Association for Diving and Marine Activities** (☎069 366 0418, ⓦsouthsinai.org), which regulates and promotes the diving industry in the region and organizes regular clean-ups of the sea.

In case of **diving emergencies**, contact Dr Adel Taher at the Hyperbaric Medical Centre near the marina (☎069 366 0922 or ☎0122 212 4292). There is also a 24-hour emergency hotline (☎012 333 1325) and a second decompression facility at the International Hospital in Hay el-Nur (☎069 366 8094). Dive schools charge an optional €6/££48 per diver for three weeks' cover allowing emergency use of the chambers. For more information, visit ⓦdeco-international.com.

DIVE CENTRES

Anthias *Sonesta Beach Resort* ☎0100 117 5500, ⓦanthiasdivers.com. Austrian-run outfit that delivers proven service and varied diving options, including liveaboards.
Camel Dive *Club Camel Dive Club Hotel* ☎069 360 0700, ⓦcameldive.com. Good facilities and lots of daily trips. Popular with UK travellers.
Colona Dive *Club Amar Sina*, Hadaba ☎069 366 3670, ⓦcolona.com. Courses, trips and liveaboards.
Emperor Divers & Red Sea Scuba Schools *Bay View Hotel* ☎0122 350 2433, ⓦemperordivers.com. Well-run operation offering liveaboards and the usual range of courses and trips.
King Snefro *Club el Faraana Reef* ☎069 366 1202, ⓦkingsnefro.com.

Liveaboard operator with around twenty years' experience.
Oonas Divers *Oonas Dive Club* ☎069 360 0581, ⓦoonasdivers.com. Five-star PADI dive centre.
Red Sea Diving College Sultana Building, Na'ama beach ☎069 360 0145, ⓦredseacollege.com. Fine facilities and tuition, plus liveaboards.
Sinai Dive Club *Hilton Fayrouz Resort* ☎069 360 0136, ⓦdive-club.com. Courses, day-trips and liveaboards.
Sinai Divers *Ghazala Hotel* ☎069 360 0697, ⓦsinaidivers.com. Efficient, experienced setup offering liveaboards.
Tornado Marine Fleet ⓦtornadomarinefleet.com. Six luxurious liveaboards. Online bookings only.

SNORKELLING AND WATERSPORTS IN SHARM AND NA'AMA BAY

Unless you join a dive boat (see p.542), visiting the local reefs involves some walking. The best reefs – known as **coral gardens** – run for several miles **north of Na'ama Bay**. They don't get many divers but are ideal for **snorkelling**, although they are regularly visited by glass-bottom boats, so take care while you're in the water. Several agencies – including Sun 'n Fun, on the Corniche near the *Hilton Fayrouz Resort* in Na'ama Bay (069 360 1623) – run snorkelling trips to the mangrove forests of **Nabeq** (see p.548) or boat trips to reefs at **Ras Mohammed**, **Ras Nasrani** and **Shark Bay**.

There's also a wide variety of **watersports** on offer, including sailing, windsurfing, waterskiing, parasailing, jetskiing, banana boats, tube rides and pedalos. **Glass-bottom boat** trips are run by Sun 'n Fun (see above), with trips (every 2hr; $10/£E60) leaving throughout the day from the beachfront near their office. **Submarine trips** are advertised too, but there have been serious acccidents with similar vessels in Hurghada (see box, p.577).

6

Car, moped and bike rental Cars can be rented from Avis in Na'ama Bay's Morgana Mall (0122 789 4063, avisegypt.com). It is illegal for unaccompanied foreigners to go off-road, as there are still many unexploded landmines in Sinai. Mopeds are available from Red Sea Star Sports Centre ($60–70/day negotiable; 012 407 7216), near the *Tam Tam* restaurant in Na'ama; bicycles are also available for rent (around £E30/hr).

INFORMATION

Tourist office The isolated and not particularly helpful tourist office (daily except Fri 9am–3pm; 069 366 4721) is a couple of kilometres northeast of Hadaba.

ACCOMMODATION

Most visitors visit on package tours. Mid-range and top-end hotels are plentiful but generally not as luxurious as their star rating would imply (knocking off one star normally gives a more accurate picture). The rates below are for bed and breakfast, unless stated otherwise. There's a surge of European package tourists over spring, autumn and Christmas, and Egyptian holiday periods (Dec 22–Feb 2, March 1–May 3 and July 19–Oct 31) can also be busy; try to book in advance during these times – online and package deals are often cheaper.

SHARM EL-SHEIKH

The accommodation in Sharm el-Sheikh is generally a bit cheaper than in Na'ama Bay, though you're generally a taxi ride away from the action.

Beach Albatros Sharm el-Maya 069 366 3923, pickalbatros.com. All-inclusive mid-range resort on the cliff above Sharm el-Maya with good views from the pool and the best beach in this part of town (reached via lift, or a very long staircase) which was created by filling in – and killing – a stretch at the back of the reef. €90

Hilton Sharm Waterfall Resort Ras Um Sidd 069 366 3232, hilton.com. Fine beachside hotel with a complex of seven pools, a small beach (linked to the resort by cable car), several good restaurants and very competitive prices – although the room decor could do with freshening up. $80

Iberotel Club Fanara Ras Um Sidd, next to the lighthouse 069 366 3966, iberotel.com. A well-designed all-inclusive on one of the few good beaches (especially for snorkellers) in the area. Rooms have a/c, TVs and terraces, and many are geared towards families. Great service. €70

Iberotel Palace Sharm el-Maya 069 366 1111, iberotel.com. Decent hotel with clean and comfortable rooms, a large section of beach, pool, several restaurants and bars, and a range of sports facilities. Excellent service. €60

Ritz-Carlton Ras Um Sidd 069 366 1919, ritzcarlton.com. This huge resort has stylish and very comfortable rooms, a beach with direct access to a reef (good for snorkelling and diving; bad for swimming), two pools with a "river" and waterfall, and Italian, Middle Eastern and Japanese restaurants. $120

Youth Hostel Clifftop 069 366 0317, hihostels.com. Either noisily full of young Egyptians or bleakly empty, this hostel offers the cheapest digs around. The dorms and private rooms are pretty cramped, although bathrooms are generally fairly clean. Dorms £E70; rooms £E150

NA'AMA BAY

Luxurious resorts featuring acres of marble floors and lush landscaped gardens are the norm in Na'ama Bay. Make sure you're not shunted into one of the hotel "extensions", which generally have a lower standard of accommodation and are a highway crossing away from the sea.

Camel Dive Club King of Bahrain St 069 360 0700, cameldive.com. Attached to one of Na'ama's best diving centres is this well-designed hotel filled with trellis-style walls

6

and climbing plants. Its a/c en suites have TVs and kettles, and are arranged around the pool. The central location, however, means noise can be a problem. **€80**

★ **Four Seasons** Northeast of Na'ama Bay ☎ 069 360 3555, ⓦ fourseasons.com. This tranquil hotel is just about the best in town, with stunning Arabian-style architecture, large and airy en suites with attractive lattice-work decor, smart service, a spa, four pools and fine restaurants. Well worth a splurge. **$290**

Hilton Fayrouz Resort On the beach ☎ 069 360 0136, ⓦ hilton.com. This excellent resort has spotless and spacious – but slightly dated – a/c chalets set in pretty landscaped gardens with one of the largest beaches in Na'ama Bay. Service is on point, and there are good options for eating and drinking. **$110**

Hyatt Regency Just north of Na'ama Bay ☎ 069 360 1234, ⓦ sharmelsheikh.regency.hyatt.com. Overlooking one of Na'ama's premier diving sites, the Gardens, this expensively bedecked resort has opulent, extremely comfortable, though somewhat generic en suites. While the beach isn't great, guests can take advantage of the beautiful landscaped grounds, pool and top notch Thai restaurant (see p.546). **$160**

Maritim Jolie Ville Golf & Resort 7km north of Na'ama Bay ☎ 069 360 3200, ⓦ jolieville-hotels.com. Away from the scrum of Na'ama Bay, this relaxing resort offers elegant, fully equipped en suites and no less than twelve restaurants and bars. As well as an award-winning eighteen-hole golf course, there's a tennis academy, the best swimming pool in the area and a small beach. Free shuttle buses run to Na'ama Bay. **$220**

Maritim Jolie Ville Resort & Casino Centre of Na'ama Bay ☎ 069 360 0100, ⓦ jolieville-hotels.com. This well-run hotel is so big that it uses golf carts to shuttle occupants from one end of its immaculate grounds to the other. The tasteful rooms have king-sized beds and flatscreen TVs, and there's also a popular beach bar and a casino. **$160**

Maritim Jolie Ville Royal Peninsula 6.5km north of Na'ama Bay ☎ 069 360 4200, ⓦ jolieville-hotels.com. Close to the Jolie Ville Golf & Resort, the *Royal Peninsula* has clusters of very spacious en-suite rooms surrounded by bird- and flower-filled gardens. There's an excellent pool, gym and spa, several good restaurants (including a Thai and an Italian) and bars, and free shuttle buses to Na'ama Bay and the hotel's private beach. **$85**

★ **Oonas Dive Club** At the northern end of the bay ☎ 069 360 0581, ⓦ oonasdiveclub.com. Popular and good-value mid-range hotel, aimed at divers (you can score a good deal on accommodation if you also book a diving package). Neat and tidy en-suite rooms come with a/c, TV, kettles and balconies. There's a small book exchange, and guests can use the beach and pool at the nearby *Sonesta*. **€60**

Sanafir King of Bahrain St ☎ 069 360 0197, ⓦ sanafirhotel.com. One of Na'ama's first hotels, with a much-imitated white-domed compound of (adequate) a/c rooms. If you plan to party all night, this place – home to both the *Bus Stop* bar and *Pacha* club (see p.546) – is a good option; if you're after peace and quiet, however, head elsewhere. **$70**

Sonesta Beach Resort At the northern end of Na'ama beach ☎ 069 360 0725, ⓦ sonesta.com. Beautifully designed resort with over five hundred rooms that manages to make you feel it's the only hotel on the beach. Each chalet is designed in traditional Arabian style, with whitewashed archways, domed roofs and spacious interiors; facilities include tennis courts, two restaurants, seven swimming pools, spa and casino. **$105**

SHARK BAY

★ **Sharks Bay Umbi Diving Village** Central Shark Bay ☎ 069 360 0942, ⓦ sharksbay.com. This economical lodge has a mix of wooden cabins on its private beach and slightly more expensive domed "Bedouin Village" rooms on the cliffside; all have a/c, private bathrooms and fridges; the latter also have TVs, phones and balconies or terraces. There's also a restaurant, bar and dive centre, and staff can organize inland safaris. **€35**

EATING   SHARM EL-SHEIKH AND NA'AMA BAY

Sharm and Na'ama Bay offer an extensive range of restaurants, with Italian, Japanese, Indian, Chinese, Thai, Moroccan and Lebanese – as well as Egyptian – among the cuisines on offer. Standards are generally pretty high, though inexpensive options are thin on the ground. Tap water is not drinkable here (or indeed anywhere else in the Sinai).

SHARM EL-SHEIKH

The Sharm el-Maya area is a good spot for cheap eats (particularly fish and seafood), while Il Mercato shopping complex on the clifftop has a range of smarter and chain restaurants and coffee shops. *Terrazzina* (see p.546) is also worth checking out.

El-Fanar Ras Um Sidd Lighthouse ☎ 069 366 2218, ⓦ elfanarsharm.com. The stunningly located and very romantic *El-Fanar* ("lighthouse" in Arabic) serves up quality Italian food (mains £E50–160) and has a vast sea view taking in Ras Mohammed. It's also great for an evening drink, and turns into a nightclub on Wed. Daily noon–late.

Onions Il Mercato shopping complex. This modern, a/c restaurant is a good option for a snack or light meal, with a menu featuring good-value sandwiches (including a "super Viagra" seafood-filled one, if you need perking up), pizzas, pastas and burgers (£E20–50). Daily 10am–11pm.

6

NA'AMA BAY

Prices tend to be higher along the Corniche (the beach promenade) where every hotel offers at least one beachside restaurant, and on the inland King of Bahrain Street. Both stretches are busy, with back-to-back bars and restaurant tables spilling out on to the street (several also have cooling water-vapour machines, but the water used is not the cleanest).

Abou El Sid Hard Rock Café ☏ 069 360 3910. As authentically Egyptian as you'll get in Na'ama, with an appealing rooftop dining area, carved wooden bar and innumerable lanterns. There are interesting specialities like pigeon stuffed with rice, spicy sausages, rabbit with *molukhiyya* (Jew's mallow), and "Circassian chicken" served with a walnut sauce. Mains £E42–85. Daily 12.30–midnight.

Beach Barbecue On the Corniche. Canopied restaurant on the beach serving chargrilled steaks and seafood (and sometimes combinations of the two, such as the sirloin and shrimp); the pizzas, however, are better elsewhere. Go for the mango cheesecake for dessert. Mains £E59–139. Daily noon–4pm & 6.30–10.30pm.

Cilantro On the Corniche, near the Hilton Fayrouz Resort ☏ 069 360 3506, ⓦ cilantro-café.com. Pleasant, palm tree-shaded branch of the Egyptian coffee shop chain, with a range of hot and iced coffees (£E14–30) and all manner of sandwiches, salads, cakes and ice creams. Daily 9am–10.30pm.

Pomodoro Camel Dive Club ☏ 069 360 0700. Reliable restaurant serving pretty authentic thin-crust pizzas (£E46–78), plus snacks like potato wedges and nachos, sandwiches and burgers, and a few pasta dishes, though prices are a bit on the high side. Daily 12.30–11.30pm.

★ **Sala Thai** Hyatt Regency ☏ 069 360 1234. Refined, romantic and suitably expensive Thai restaurant (complete with Thai chef) that's excellent for a special occasion or if you just fancy a splurge. Expect to pay around £E200–250/person for a good meal. Daily 6–11.30pm.

Sidi Top floor, Na'ama Centre ☏ 0128 802 1418, ⓦ sidiwadie.com. Classy Moroccan joint with tagines, couscous, spicy *harira* soup, and an interesting seafood pastilla (mains from £E70). Next door, sister restaurant *Fairuz* serves up good Lebanese food. Daily 12.30–10.30pm.

Tam Tam On the Corniche, in front of Hotel Ghazala ☏ 069 360 0155. Tasty Egyptian and Lebanese food – including hot and cold mezze, grilled meat and seafood, delectable sweets like Umm Ali (see p.36) and a breezy roof terrace with low tables, rugs and cushions. There's also an Egyptian floor show with music and dance several nights a week. Mains £E60–150. Daily 12.30–midnight/1am.

Tandoori Camel Dive Club ☏ 069 360 0700. Some of the area's best Indian food (mains £E40-80) is served here, including plenty of veggie options such as *paneer jalfrezi* and *tarka dhal*, as well as – of course – tandoori meat dishes. Daily 6.30–11.30pm.

SHARK BAY

Soho Square Near White Knights beach, between the Savoy and Sierra hotels ☏ 0100 160 9544, ⓦ soho-sharm.com. This flashy development is home to several good restaurants, cafés and bars (including an ice bar), as well as a nightclub, bowling alley, children's play area, ice rink and several shops. Daily 10am–late.

DRINKING AND NIGHTLIFE

Alcoholic drinks are widely available in Sharm and Na'ama – perhaps more so than anywhere else in Egypt – although generally at European prices.

SHARM EL-SHEIKH

There are a couple of decent bars here, but most of the action is a taxi ride away in Na'ama Bay. El-Fanar (see above) is also worth checking out.

Terrazzina Sharm el-Maya beach ☏ 0100 500 6621, ⓦ terrazzina.com. This restaurant-bar-club – which has various offshoots in and around Sharm – is the liveliest joint outside of Na'ama Bay, offering beach parties, full-moon events and a revolving roster of DJs. Good seafood too. Daily mid-afternoon–3/4am.

T2 Clifftop ☏ 0122 117 1855, ⓦ thetavernbar.com. An offshoot of the Tavern Bar (see below) in Na'ama Bay, this British-style pub has a welcoming atmosphere, sport on the TV, regular live bands, and BBQs on the terrace; check the website to see what's on. Daily 10am–3/4am.

NA'AMA BAY

The Corniche is lined with open-air bars attached to the resorts, while King of Bahrain Street has several drinking spots too; many places also offer *sheesha*. Most hotels offer Egyptian **floor shows**; the best, however, is at the *Tam Tam* restaurant (see above). There's a good club scene, plus several **casinos** including ones at the *Maritim Jolie Ville Resort & Casino* and the *Sonesta* hotels; take your passport.

Bus Stop Sanafir hotel ☏ 0128 277 9880. Popular place (beer around £E20–25) and warm-up spot for those heading on to neighbouring *Pacha*, with live-sport screenings, plenty of games consoles to play on and a daily happy hour (8–9pm). Mon–Fri 4pm–1am, Sat & Sun 2pm–1am.

Camel Dive Bar Camel Dive Club ☏ 069 360 0700, ⓦ cameldive.com/about/camel-bar. A favourite starting

TOURS AND ACTIVITIES AROUND SHARM

All the hotels, most dive centres and travel agencies such as Sun 'n Fun (see p.543) can arrange **tours** by jeep, camel, motorcycle or quad bike. Some of the most popular day excursions include snorkelling visits to **Nabeq**; jeep trips to the **Coloured Canyon** followed by snorkelling at Nuweiba/Dahab; overnight trips to **St Catherine's Monastery** and **Mount Sinai**; and sunset visits to **Wadi Mandar**. Several companies also offer excursions to **Serabit el-Khadim** and **Hammam Faraoun** (p.536), and longer desert trips (though these are generally cheaper from Dahab or Nuweiba). Most day-trips cost around $40–70; beware of very cheap deals, as these are likely to involve travelling by bus.

Horseriding in the desert can be arranged at the *Sofitel hotel's* equestrian centre (☎069 360 0081) or through Sun 'n Fun; the latter also offer quad bike tours and operate the Sinai Moto Cross **quad bike** circuit (€25 for 30min) in Na'ama, while there's **go-karting** at the state-of-the-art Ghibli Raceway (☎069 360 3939, ⋓ghibliraceway.com; €16 for 10min), just off the Airport Road, near the entrance to the *Hyatt Regency*.

6

point for an evening out, this friendly place has a chilled roof terrace shaded by an awning and a livelier bar downstairs (happy hour 5–8pm). It's a good place to swap dive stories, watch sports on TV or listen to a DJ. Beer from ££20, cocktails from ££45. Mon–Fri 3.30pm–3/4am, Sat & Sun 1pm–3/4am.

Hard Rock Café Just off the main strip ☎069 360 2664, ⋓hardrock.com. An unmissable giant guitar marks the entrance to this unfeasibly popular international chain which serves as a restaurant during the day (sandwiches, burgers and snacks from around ££40), a bar during the evening and a club after midnight. Daily noon–3/4am.

Little Buddha Just off King of Bahrain St ☎069 360 1030, ⋓littlebuddha-sharm.com. This slick lounge has low seats and equally low lighting, burning incense and a cutting-edge sound system. The enormous circular bar and dancefloor surround a downstairs dining area where quality Asian fusion food is served (mains ££62–110), while a giant Buddha presides over the two storeys. Daily 1pm–3.30am.

Pacha Sanafir hotel ☎069 360 0197, ⋓pachasharm .com. Sharm outpost (entry around ££75) of the legendary club chain, open 365 days a year, with top DJs and weekly Ministry of Sound, HedKandi and House Nation nights, as well as a swimming pool and the inevitable VIP room. It also puts on regular events at *Echo Temple*, a desert venue accommodating up to eight thousand people, and on the Pacha Boat. Daily 11pm–4am.

Space Just off Peace Rd next to the Panorama Naama Heights hotel, ☎0111 012 2020, ⋓spacesharm .com. Offshoot of the famous Ibiza club with a great sound system graced by local and international DJs. Entry around ££75. The main nights are Mon, Wed & Fri (11pm–4am), though there are often events on other nights too; check the website for details.

Tavern Bar In a small mall behind the Na'ama Centre ☎0122 765 2800, ⋓thetavernbar.com. One of the main hangouts for British expats and tourists, with a pub-style atmosphere, cold beer (around ££20), pub grub such as Sun roasts and full English breakfasts, live sport on TV, karaoke and DJs. Daily 10am–3/4am.

DIRECTORY

Banks and exchange Most hotels in Sharm and Na'ama have their own mini banks and/or ATMs. The National Bank of Egypt has branches in the *Maritim Jolie Ville Resort & Casino* and *Hilton Fayrouz Resort*. You can get cash advances on Visa and MasterCard at Banque Misr (daily except Fri 9am–1.30pm & 5–8pm) in the Sharm Mall. For changing cash, Swiss Exchange in the Morgana Mall (daily 9am–midnight) may offer slightly better rates than the banks.

Books and newspapers Vendors pushing carts along the beachfront in Na'ama sell international magazines and newspapers. Many hotels have book exchanges, and some souvenir shops sell books. The Al Ahram Bookshop, just off the main road in Na'ama, has a small range of English language books (mainly Naguib Mahfouz and Agatha Christie titles).

Hospitals and pharmacies The Sharm International Hospital (☎069 366 0894; there's a good pharmacy next door too) and the Sharm Medical Centre (☎069 366 1744) are both in Hay el-Nur. Other pharmacies include Towa in the Sharm Mall (☎069 360 0779), which offers free delivery. In Na'ama, the *Jolie Ville Resort & Casino* is home to the Mount Sinai Clinic (☎069 360 0100). For diving emergencies, see p.542.

Internet access Most hotels offer internet and wi-fi access (the latter is provided by many restaurants and bars too, usually for free). Cyber cafés are also common, though charges are much higher than the rest of Egypt, at around ££30/hour.

Police The police (☎069 366 0415) and tourist police (☎069 366 0311), both open 24 hours, share a building near the arcade and beyond the mosque in Hadaba.

Post office The post office (daily except Fri 8am–3pm) is in Hadaba, though most of the bigger hotels have shops that sell stamps and can post items for you.

Shopping A number of malls and and recreated "souks" compete to attract tourists, but there's little here you can't find in Cairo or Luxor at lower prices.

Travel agents Thomas Cook, in Na'ama's Gafy Mall (daily 9am–2pm & 6–8pm; ☎ 069 360 1809), offers the usual range of travel services, plus Visa cash advances. Mena Tours at the *Marriott* (☎ 069 360 0190, ⓦ menatours .com.eg) can book flights and – if the service starts up again – Hurghada catamaran tickets.

6 The Tiran Strait

The headland of Ras Nasrani beyond Shark Bay marks the beginning of the **Tiran Strait**, where the waters of the Gulf of Suez flow into the deeper Gulf of Aqaba, swirling around the small islands and reefs of the **Tiran archipelago**. This was declared a protected area in 1992 and is now a popular spot for **divers** although there are no facilities (or admission charges); the only access is by boat from Sharm el-Maya or Shark Bay. The straits are not a destination for novice divers, however, as the sea can be extremely rough and chilling (bring high-calorie drinks and snacks to boost your energy). Sharks, manta rays, barracuda and Napoleon fish are typical of the deepwater sites around the **islands of Tiran** and **Sanafir**, though there are also shallow reefs like the Small Lagoon and Hushasha. The multitude of **shipwrecks** in the Gulf is due to treacherous reefs and currents, insurance fraud and Egypt's blockade of the strait in the 1960s. The **Jackson Reef** has a spectacular seventy-metre drop-off and the wreck of the *Lara* to investigate, while the **Gordon Reef** boasts the hulk of the *Lucila*. Two notable sites at **Ras Nasrani** are the **Light**, with a forty-metre drop-off and pelagic fish; and the **Point**, with a dazzling array of reef fish.

Nabeq

Beyond the mouth of the Gulf of Aqaba, a ninety-kilometre section of coast stretching north to Dahab has been designated as another protected area, named after the small oasis and Bedouin village of **NABEQ** (or Nabq). Most visitors come here on half-day trips from Sharm el-Sheikh or Dahab to explore Nabeq's **mangrove forests** – the most northerly in the world, and home to ibex, hyrax, foxes and other wildlife. There are also some pristine **reefs** offshore – quieter than those at Tiran or Ras Mohammed given that few dive boats come here from Na'ama.

INFORMATION   NABEQ

Entrance charge Admission to the Nabeq protected area costs €5; the only facilities are a cafeteria and a small

visitors' centre (daily 8am–5pm).

ACCOMMODATION

A small collection of resorts around Nabeq village offer easy access to the protected area, although transport connections are limited to hotel shuttle buses, and the beaches can be poor.

Radisson Blu 17km north of Na'ama Bay ☎ 069 371 0315, ⓦ radissonblu.com. One of the best beachfront hotels in Nabeq, this top-end resort has smart though

characterless rooms, most with sea views. There's the requisite private beach, several good restaurants, three pools and a dive centre and spa. **$88**

Dahab

Jagged mountains ranged inland accompany the road 95km northwards from Na'ama Bay, providing a magnificent backdrop for **Dahab**'s tawny beaches, from which its name – Arabic for "gold" – derives. For travellers, Dahab divides into two main parts: a cluster of resorts set around the **lagoon**, close to Dahab City, and the settlement of **Asilah** (or Asalah), 2.5km up the coast, where younger and independent travellers hang out in a kind of "Goa by the Red Sea" – though as Asilah gets smarter, the distinction between the two areas is blurring.

Like Sharm and Taba before, Dahab's relaxed ambience was shattered when three **bombs** went off in Asilah at 7.30pm on April 24, 2006, destroying several restaurants, shops and a supermarket, killing 23 people and injuring 60. Today there is a noticeable **security presence**, and whether you are on public or private transport, you'll probably be asked to show your **passport** at checkpoints on leaving or entering Dahab.

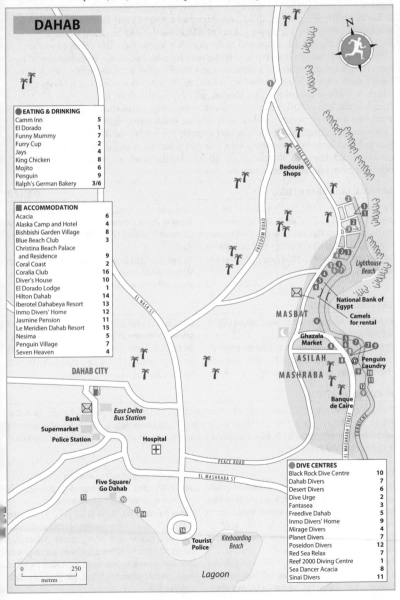

DAHAB

● EATING & DRINKING

Camm Inn	5
El Dorado	1
Funny Mummy	7
Furry Cup	2
Jays	4
King Chicken	8
Mojito	6
Penguin	9
Ralph's German Bakery	3/6

■ ACCOMMODATION

Acacia	6
Alaska Camp and Hotel	4
Bishbishi Garden Village	8
Blue Beach Club	3
Christina Beach Palace and Residence	9
Coral Coast	2
Coralia Club	16
Diver's House	10
El Dorado Lodge	1
Hilton Dahab	14
Iberotel Dahabeya Resort	13
Inmo Divers' Home	12
Jasmine Pension	11
Le Meridien Dahab Resort	15
Nesima	5
Penguin Village	7
Seven Heaven	4

DAHAB CITY

Bedouin Shops

Lighthouse Beach

National Bank of Egypt

MASBAT

Camels for rental

Ghazala Market

ASILAH

MASHRABA

@ Penguin Laundry

Banque de Caire

East Delta Bus Station

Bank

Supermarket

Police Station

Hospital

Five Square/ Go Dahab

Tourist Police Kiteboarding Beach

Lagoon

FREEDOM ROAD

PEACE ROAD

EL MASR ST

EL MASHRABA ST

PEACE ROAD

EL MASHRABA ST

EL MASHRABA STREET

CORNICHE

0   250
metres

● DIVE CENTRES

Black Rock Dive Centre	10
Dahab Divers	7
Desert Divers	6
Dive Urge	2
Fantasea	3
Freedive Dahab	5
Inmo Divers' Home	9
Mirage Divers	4
Planet Divers	7
Poseidon Divers	12
Red Sea Relax	7
Reef 2000 Diving Centre	1
Sea Dancer Acacia	8
Sinai Divers	11

6

6

Dahab City and the lagoon

Don't be discouraged by **DAHAB CITY**'s unappealing sprawl of municipal housing and government offices – the only time you're likely to come here is when you arrive or depart from the bus station. To the south of Dahab City is the far more attractive **lagoon** area, home to numerous holiday resorts and boasting a great stretch of sandy beach, while the lagoon itself is a great place to windsurf or kiteboard (see p.554).

Asilah

With its breathtaking views, quiet ambience and string of great beachside restaurants and hotels, the gentrified hippie colony of **ASILAH** is the Red Sea coast's best backpacker hangout. Its reputation as *the* place for hippie travellers emerged in the 1960s, when Israeli troops started coming here for a bit of R&R. Nowadays, buildings stretch back behind scores of restaurants and hotels, while a section of the beach has been paved to create a pedestrianized corniche. There are two main areas: **Mashraba**, which is south of the bridge, and **Masbat**, which is north of the bridge.

Such is the lure of Asilah that visitors often stay longer than they'd expected, getting stuck in a daily routine of café life, or if they are more active, diving and snorkelling. Given Asilah's reputation, it's important to stress the hedonistic limits: women can generally sunbathe without any hassle, but **going topless** is illegal, and there are periodic crackdowns on **drugs**. Finally, stick to bottled water to avoid the risk of **hepatitis** from contaminated cisterns.

ARRIVAL AND DEPARTURE
DAHAB

By bus Most independent travellers arrive at the bus station (☎069 364 1808) in Dahab City. The community-run Bedouin Bus (☎0101 668 4274, ⓦbedouinbus.com) runs buses to St Catherine's leaving from outside Marine Garden Camp, near Ralph's German Bakery, at 5pm on Tues and Fri; buy tickets on board.

Destinations Cairo (5 daily; 7–8hr); Nuweiba (3 daily; 1hr); Sharm el-Sheikh (at least 10 daily; 1hr–1hr 30min); St Catherine's Monastery (2 weekly; 2hr); Taba (1 daily; 2hr 30min).

By taxi Hotels and diving companies can arrange taxis to Sharm el-Sheikh (around £E280) and St Catherine's (around £E400-450 return with waiting time).

GETTING AROUND

By bike Most dive centres hire out bikes (around £E10/hr or £E40/day).
By taxi Taxis and pick-ups meet buses at the bus station; the journey to either Asilah or the Dahab Bay resorts should cost £E10–15, though you'll have to haggle; a taxi between

Dahab Bay and Asilah costs roughly the same. In Asilah, you'll generally be dropped off by the parking lot near the bridge.
On foot Asilah's central streets are pedestrianized, and it's easy to get around on foot. It takes around 30min to walk from here to Dahab Bay.

ACCOMMODATION

There's an excellent range of accommodation, whatever your budget. The bigger resorts are dotted around Dahab Bay, and are good choices if you just want to lounge on the beach. The backpacker lodges, B&Bs and smaller (generally independently owned) hotels are in more characterful Asilah, which is also where you'll find the best selection of restaurants, bars and shops.

THE LAGOON
The holiday resorts here are self-contained, with private beaches (non-guests can use them for around £E50–100) and access to a coral reef on the headland, though there's nothing else in the immediate vicinity; online deals can make them very good value. The rates below are for bed and breakfast unless stated otherwise.
Coralia Club Dahab Bay ☎069 364 0301, ⓦaccorhotels .com. At the eastern end of the resort strip, monopolizing a windswept bay enclosed by a sandbar – a fabulous spot to

learn how to windsurf – the *Coralia* has some of Dahab's most stylish rooms, as well a range of sports facilities, an organic farm and the area's biggest beach. €55
Hilton Dahab By the lagoon ☎069 364 0310, ⓦhilton .com. Set in an attractive complex of articifical lagoons, manicured gardens and white, domed Nubian-style chalets. Rooms are a little old-fashioned, but come with their own hammocks, and there's a pleasant stretch of beach, several restaurants and bars, and plenty of aquatic activities. $70

DIVING AND SNORKELLING IN DAHAB

Shore diving is the norm in Dahab. The nicest reefs are to the north of the lagoon; the reefs at Asilah are meagre, except for the area around the lighthouse, and much of the seabed is covered in rubbish. Experienced divers should look out for occasional free "trash dives", organized to clear the rubbish, mostly plastic bags blown into the sea, which sea turtles can mistake for jellyfish and choke on.

Most divers head 8km up the coast where you can find the Eel Garden, Canyon and Blue Hole dive sites, trips to which are arranged by most dive centres. The **Canyon** is a dark, narrow fissure that you reach from the shore by swimming along the reef and then diving to the edge of a coral wall. It can be frightening for inexperienced divers, as it sinks to a depth of 50m, but there's plenty to see at the top of the reef. Further north lies the notorious **Blue Hole**, which has claimed several lives (usually experienced divers who dive too deep for too long). This spectacular shaft in the reef plunges to 80m; the challenge involves descending 60m and swimming through a transverse passage to come up the other side. Divers who ascend too fast risk getting "bent"; inexperienced divers should not attempt this dive under any circumstances. Fortunately, the Hole can be enjoyed in safety by staying closer to the surface and working your way round to a dip in the reef known as the Bridge, which swarms with colourful fish and can even be viewed using snorkelling gear.

The main destination for day-long **dive safaris** is the Ras Abu Galum protected area, a 30km stretch of coast with three diving beaches, accessible by jeep or camel (see p.554). **Naqb Shahin** is the closest to Dahab of the three, and has fantastic coral and gold fish, but the sea is very turbulent, so many divers prefer **Ras Abu Galum** or **Ras el-Mamleh**, further north. All three sites have deep virgin reefs with a rich variety of corals and fish.

PRICES

While renting equipment is generally costlier than in Sharm el-Sheikh, **diving courses** are normally cheaper. Competition means cut-price deals, especially when business is quiet, but you should keep a sense of perspective – the rockbottom outlets are unlikely to be rigorous about your safety. The more established centres charge around €35 for an introductory shore dive; around €90–110 for a one-day dive in Ras Abu Galum; around €120–150 for a diving trip to Ras Mohamed; around €125–170 for a diving trip to the *Thistlegorm*; and around €200–250 for a PADI Open Water course.

FREE DIVING AND SNORKELLING

Expert training in **free diving** – which is done on a single deep breath, without the aid of scuba gear – is available from Lotta Ericson of Freedive Dahab (☏0100 545 9916, ⊕freedivedahab.com), who offers a two-day beginner course (€170), as well as more advanced courses lasting up to four days. Most participants find they can hold their breath for up to four minutes after the longer course, enabling them to dive to 15m or deeper. As for **snorkelling**, for a more ambitious jaunt than just wading out from the shore, arrange an excursion to the Blue Hole (€10–15 for a half-day), which can be done through a number of operators, including Desert Divers.

DIVE CENTRES

Black Rock Dive Centre *Ganet Sinai Hotel* ☏0106 143 9420, ⊕blackrockdivecentre.com.
Dahab Divers Lighthouse Beach ☏069 364 0381, ⊕dahabdivers.com.
Desert Divers Masbat ☏069 364 0500, ⊕desert-divers.com.
Dive Urge Masbat ☏069 364 0957, ⊕www.dive-urge.com.
Fantasea *Coral Coast Hotel* ☏069 364 1373, ⊕fantaseadiving.net.
INMO Mashraba ☏069 364 0370, ⊕inmodivers.de.

Mirage Divers *Mirage Village* ☏069 364 0341, ⊕miragedivers.com.
Planet Divers *Planet Oasis Hotel*, near Lighthouse Beach ☏069 364 1090, ⊕planetdivers.com.
Poseidon Divers *Le Meridien* ☏069 364 0091, ⊕poseidondivers.com.
Red Sea Relax Masbat ☏069 364 1309, ⊕red-sea-relax.com.
Sea Dancer Acacia *Acacia* hotel ☏069 364 0404, ⊕seadanceracacia.com.
Sinai Divers *Hilton Dahab* ☏069 364 0100, ⊕sinaidivers.com.

6

Iberotel Dahabeya Resort By the lagoon ☎069 364 1264, ⊛iberotel.net. The architecture of the *Iberotel* has a Mediteranean feel, and the hotel is popular with package tourists and families. There are 144 functional mid-range rooms (only eighteen have sea views), pools, windsurfing and dive centres, and a kids' club. Half-board **€68**

★ **Le Meridien Dahab Resort** West of the lagoon ☎069 364 0425, ⊛lemeridiendahab.com. The pick of the resorts, in a secluded position west of the lagoon, with chic and spacious rooms, beautiful pools, a good beach, windsurfing and dive centres, and excellent service. Look out for the Omar Khayyam poems dotted around the resort. **$90**

ASILAH

Asilah's accommodation ranges from simple, budget guesthouses and campgrounds to swish hotels; standards are generally high across the board. Bear in mind that anything on the main strip in Masbat is likely to suffer from noise unless set well back from the main drag. Rates include breakfast unless stated otherwise.

Acacia Mashraba ☎069 364 0401, ⊛acaciadahab .com. Justifiably popular, beautifully designed hotel whose swish en-suite rooms have a cool, minimalist feel; all have TVs, fridges and a/c, though you'll have to pay a bit extra to secure a private terrace. There's also a pool, good restaurant and a cocktail lounge with regular live music. **$66**

★ **Alaska Camp and Hotel** Masbat ☎069 364 1004, ⊛dahabescape.com. Extremely welcoming low-cost hotel with a relaxed vibe, a Bedouin tent-style communal area and simple but super-clean en-suite rooms; there are also more expensive (but still very good value) options with a/c and private balconies. Breakfast costs extra. **£E100**

Bishbishi Garden Village Mashraba ☎069 364 0727, ⊛bishbishi.com. Operated by the indefatigable Jimmy, this bustling backpacker hangout is a great place to meet other travellers. It has a good range of rooms – from very basic options with shared bathrooms to a/c en suites – while bike and snorkel rental, luggage storage and laundry services are all available. Breakfast costs extra. **€5**

★ **Blue Beach Club** 200m north of Lighthouse Beach ☎069 364 0411, ⊛bluebeachclub.com. Professionally run hotel with attractive budget, standard and superior rooms; all are fine options, particularly the superior rooms, which have partial sea views, kettle, safe and flatscreen TV. There's a small pool, beach area, dive centre, restaurant, the *Furry Cup* bar (see p.553), and numerous activities, including yoga, massage, Arabic language-classes and horseriding. **€40**

★ **Christina Beach Palace and Residence** Mashraba ☎069 364 0390, ⊛christinahotels.com. A range of tasteful en-suite rooms in whitewashed blocks with domed ceilings. Choose between the more sophisticated rooms on the Corniche and comfortable but

much less expensive "backpacker" rooms on the main road. There's a good pool, but you pay extra for a/c. Excellent service. Backpacker rooms **$27**; Corniche rooms **$60**

Coral Coast 300m north of Lighthouse Beach ☎069 364 1195, ⊛fantasearedsea.com. Away from the bustle of Masbat, this sizeable hotel has a good selection of a/c rooms – all have balconies or terraces, but you have to pay more for ones with a kettle, fridge and sea views. There's a small pool and a branch of Fantasea Divers. **€38**

Diver's House South of Mashraba ☎069 364 0451, ⊛divers-house.com. Rambling hotel with a variety of quirky rooms: the cabin-like room with huge domed ceiling or the a/c en suite with sea views are the ones to go for. Those at the back are best avoided. Breakfast costs extra. **$25**

El Dorado Lodge 350m north of Lighthouse Beach ☎069 364 1027, ⊛eldoradodahab.com. In a peaceful location, this Italian-run hotel has immaculate wooden a/c cabins, free from clutter; the more expensive ones have private bathrooms. Also has its own dive centre and an excellent restaurant (see p.553). Shared bathroom **€30**; en suite **€50**

Inmo Divers Home Mashraba ☎069 364 0370, ⊛inmodivers.de. Run by a German–Egyptian couple, Inmo has simple rooms with shared bathrooms aimed at backpackers as well as more comfortable a/c en suites with balconies and sea views. There are attractive bamboo walkways and communal areas, pool, playground and dive centre. Shared bathroom **€20**; en suite **€30**

Jasmine Pension On the Corniche ☎069 364 0852, ⊛jasminepension.com. A small budget hotel right on the Corniche with an economical café and a handful of tidy en-suite rooms: all are a/c but only the pricier ones (an extra £E50) have balconies and sea views **£E200**

Nesima Mashraba ☎069 364 0320, ⊛nesima-resort .com. Arguably the most beautiful hotel in Asilah – if somewhat overpriced – with white domes, a curvaceous pool and flower-filled pathways. The standard rooms, though attractively furnished, are a little on the small side, though the most expensive options are very appealing. There's also a small massage centre. **€63**

Penguin Village Mashraba ☎069 364 1047, ⊛penguindahab.com. Popular backpackers' haunt offering dorms, simple rooms with fan and shared or private bathrooms, and a few smarter a/c en suites with sea view. Also arranges lots of activities, trips and inexpensive ways to pass the time. Breakfast costs extra. Dorms **€4**; fan rooms **€8**; a/c rooms **€14**

Seven Heaven Masbat ☎069 364 0080, ⊛7heavenhotel.com. Economical option in a central location between the bridge and Lighthouse Beach, drawing a regular stream of travellers, especially divers. The basic rooms are pretty worn, but clean and acceptable for a night or two. **$8**

EATING

There are scores of **restaurants** in Asilah: house, trance and chill-out music fills the air, and floor cushions and posters reflect the mix of Bedouin and hippie influences – you can sit around for hours without being required to eat, although not all places have alcohol licences. Outside the resorts, there are no really good restaurants (or bars) in the lagoon area.

Camm Inn Masbat. The cane furniture and overgrown plants give this place the feel of a safari lodge, and its global menu demonstrates a touch more imagination than most, with the Malaysian dishes particular highlights. Mains £E35–90. Daily 9am–11pm/midnight.

★ **El Dorado** El Dorado Lodge ☎ 069 364 1027. The best of Dahab's Italian restaurants, offering home-made pasta, thin-crust pizzas and delectable desserts such as panna cotta, *affogato* and tiramisu. The location, right on the beach, is tranquil, and service couldn't be friendlier. Mains £E45–100. Daily except Tues noon–10pm.

Funny Mummy Corniche ☎ 0100 046 6177. A travellers' favourite, with an attractive roof terrace festooned with twinkly lights, and a downstairs area strewn with cushions and low tables; you'll generally find several kittens to play with too. There's a wide-ranging food and drinks menu (the Egyptian-style dishes tend to be the best options), plus *sheesha* pipes. Mains £E24–90. Daily 9am–11pm/midnight.

Jays Masbat ☎ 0100 188 8907. *Jays* is popular both for its menu – which includes Italian dishes, soups, salads, sandwiches, steaks and seafood, plus desserts such as banoffee pie – and its "no hassle policy", which means you won't be bothered by touts every time you walk by. There's often live music in the evening. Mains £E30–130. Daily 9am–11pm/midnight

King Chicken Mashraba. A modest eatery that's always busy with both locals and frugal travellers. You can get a chicken quarter, rice, salad, soup, bread and hummus for just £E17.50, as well as kebabs and koftas for not much more. Daily noon–10.30pm.

Penguin Corniche. Next door to *Funny Mummy*, the very similar – and equally popular – *Penguin* has a laidback vibe, tasty food and great milkshakes and smoothies (£E18–20), plus *sheeshas* (£E6). Daily 9am–11pm/midnight.

Ralph's German Bakery Mashraba ☎ 069 364 1998. All manner of strudels, cakes, pastries, croissants, sandwiches and proper Lavazza coffee are on offer at this café. There's another branch next to the Ghazala supermarket close to the bridge. Cakes £E8–25. Daily 7am–9pm.

DRINKING AND NIGHTLIFE

Many of the restaurants in Asilah double as bars, often putting on live music, though nightlife is a lot more sedate than in Sharm el-Sheikh or Hurghada.

Furry Cup Blue Beach Club. This open-walled wooden construction, perched right on the seafront, is a particularly good spot for a sundowner, with imported alcohol and a daily happy hour (6–8pm). A beer costs around £E20. Daily noon–midnight.

Mojito Masbat. As its name suggests, Mojito is a good place for a cocktail (around £E40) and has a friendly atmosphere, drawing both locals and travellers with its regular live music and DJ events, dance classes, film nights and *sheesha* pipes. Daily noon–midnight/1am.

DIRECTORY

Arabic classes *Blue Beach Club* has a language school offering both introductory classes (£E60/45min) and week-long courses. Classes are also available from *Inmo Divers Home*.

Banks Asilah has several ATMs, including one by Desert Divers in Masbat and another close to the big Ghazala Market. Near *Christina Beach Palace* is the Banque du Caire, which also has an ATM. Several of the resorts around the lagoon have their own ATMs and mini bank branches, including the Hilton.

Festivals If you visit in April, make sure you check out the Bedouin (ⓦ bedouinfestival.com) and Dahab (ⓦ dahabfestival.info) festivals, which have a range of cultural activities and events.

Hospital Dahab's hospital (☎ 069 364 5208) is in Dahab City, southeast of the bus station.

Internet Most hotels and restaurants in Asilah provide free wi-fi (the lagoon resorts tend to charge). There are also several cyber cafés in Asilah, including Penguin Internet Café, outside Penguin VIllage, and Aladin Internet Café, Masbat (both daily 8am–10/11pm; £E8/hr).

Laundry Most hotels provide inexpensive laundry services (generally around £E3–5/item); alternatively, try Penguin Laundry, near Penguin Village.

Massage, yoga and dance Several places – including *Blue Beach Club* and *Nesima* – offer massage (from around £E200/hr). *Blue Beach Club* also offers reiki courses (from £E1200), Egyptian- and bellydancing classes (£E120/hr) and drop-in yoga sessions (£E60–70). Desert Divers also offer yoga classes, as well as overnight yoga and chi gong sessions in the desert (from €120).

6

WATERSPORTS AND ACTIVITIES AROUND DAHAB

The wind blows for an average of around 270 days a year in Dahab, making it a haven for **windsurfers** and **kiteboarders**. Five Square/Go Dahab (☎0122 756 8358, ⊕go-dahab.ru), based at the *Panda Resort* by the lagoon, run beginners windsurfing classes (€40/1hr or €145/3 days) and kiteboarding (€90/2hr), and rents out equipment (from €10/day). The *Hilton*, *Iberotel* and *Le Meridien* hotels also have windsurfing/kiteboarding centres.

RIDING, ROCK-CLIMBING AND DESERT SAFARIS

If you fancy **riding** on the beach, local boys rent out horses or camels (around £E50/hr); they tend to hang out by the restaurants in Masbat. Alternatively, *Blue Beach Club* offers more organized horse rides down the beach (£E100/hr), as well as lessons (£E150/hr); you can also do overnight trips into the desert and the mountains.

A more exciting option is to sign up for trips into the rugged **interior**, which can be organized at most hotels, travel agencies and dive centres. Trips (see p.556) can involve trekking, camel rides and quad biking, cost around €40–50 per day, and range in length from a single day to around two weeks. Desert Divers also offer a range of **rock-climbing** courses and day-trips for both beginners (from €65) and those with previous experience.

Newspapers, magazines and books You can buy foreign newspapers and magazines from the vendor who travels around central Asilah during the day. Aladin Internet café has a sizeable collection of secondhand books for sale or exchange.

Post office There's a post office in Dahab City, but many shops in Asilah sell stamps and will send items for you.

Supermarkets The best-stocked supermarket is Ghazala Market in Asilah (daily 8am–late).

Tourist police There's a tourist police booth opposite the *Coralia Club* resort.

Ras Abu Galum

The coast between Dahab and Nuweiba is hidden from view as the road veers inland, but this remote area, the **Ras Abu Galum** Protectorate, harbours some of Sinai's richest wildlife. Access is limited to a coastal track (walking or camel only) from Dahab or an unpaved road (4WD required) that branches off from the main road 20km short of Nuweiba. There are a couple of modest shops and restaurants, but it's wise to bring food and water if you plan on staying awhile. It is possible to walk from Dahab (Ras Abu Galum is approximately two hours from the Blue Hole) or you can rent a 4WD pick-up truck (around £E40–50). Some of the tour operators stop here on the way to the Blue Hole, but for more in-depth exploration, the eco-tourism outfit Centre for Sinai (☎0100 666 0835, ⊕centre4sinai.com.eg) can introduce you to a Bedouin guide who organizes trips by jeep or camel.

Nuweiba and Tarabeen

Beautiful but desolate, **NUWEIBA** is another resort on the Gulf of Aqaba, consisting of a **port** with nearby tourist complexes, followed 4km up the coast by **Nuweiba "City"**, an administrative and commercial centre grafted on to a former Israeli *moshav* (cooperative village). During the late 1970s, thousands of Israeli and Western backpackers flocked here to party and sleep on the beach, but today tourism is at a virtual standstill. The beach is beautiful, but – with the exception of a few patches of privately owned sand – covered with rubbish. For most travellers, Nuweiba now serves primarily as a stepping stone for onward travel by bus to **Eilat** in Israel or by boat to **Aqaba** in Jordan.

Around 500m north of Nuweiba City is the neighbouring Bedouin settlement of **TARABEEN**, named after a local Bedouin tribe and attracting younger travellers.

ARRIVAL AND CITY TRANSPORT

NUWEIBA AND TARABEEN

By bus Nuweiba's main bus station is at the port, though the Taba bus also stops on the highway close to Nuweiba City. There are buses to Dahab and Taba, but no direct buses to Sharm el-Sheikh. The community-run Bedouin Bus (☎0101 668 4274, ⓦbedouinbus.com) runs to St Catherine's (2hr) on Wed and Sun, departing from the bus stop near the hospital at 2pm and also picking up passengers opposite the main bus station at 2.30pm. Buy tickets on board.

Destinations Dahab (2 daily; 1hr); St Catherine's (2 weekly; 2hr); Taba (3 daily; 1hr 30min).

By taxi Taxis charge £E15–30 from the port to Tarabeen, and about £E10–20 from Nuweiba City to Tarabeen. You can walk from Nuweiba City to Tarabeen in twenty minutes along the beach; it takes slightly longer by road.

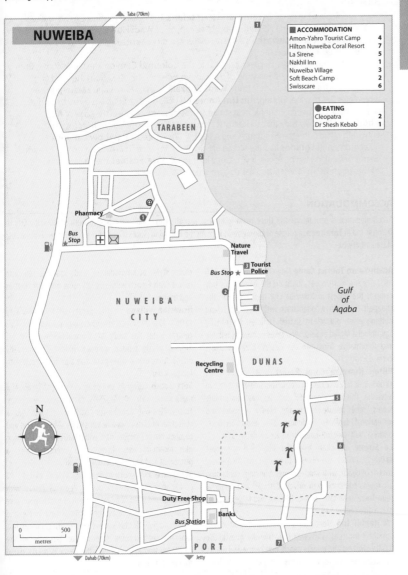

NUWEIBA

▲ Taba (70km)

ACCOMMODATION
Amon-Yahro Tourist Camp	4
Hilton Nuweiba Coral Resort	7
La Sirene	5
Nakhil Inn	1
Nuweiba Village	3
Soft Beach Camp	2
Swisscare	6

EATING
Cleopatra	2
Dr Shesh Kebab	1

TARABEEN

Pharmacy

Bus Stop

Nature Travel

Bus Stop

Tourist Police

Gulf of Aqaba

NUWEIBA CITY

DUNAS

Recycling Centre

N

Duty Free Shop

Banks

Bus Station

PORT

0   500
metres

▼ Dahab (70km)   ▼ Jetty

6

6

DIVING, SNORKELLING AND SAFARIS IN NUWEIBA

Diving in Nuweiba is mostly from the shore thanks to a lack of jetties and safe anchorages. There are several shallow **reefs** offshore, the best of which is the **Stone House**, beyond the southern promontory. Though fine for **snorkelling**, they're not so great for **diving** unless you're a novice, so the divers that come here usually travel to Ras Abu Galum (p.554) or sites north of Nuweiba (see p.557). These trips can be arranged by any of Nuweiba's **dive centres**, including Emperor Divers at *Hilton Nuweiba Coral Resort* (☎ 069 352 0320, ☷ emperordivers .com) and Scuba Divers at *La Sirene* (☎ 069 350 0705, ☷ scuba-divers.de).

SAFARIS

There are also a wide range of **camel and** jeep **safaris**. The nearest destinations are the oasis of **Ain el-Furtaga** and the colourful sandstone canyon of **Wadi Huweiyit**. Slightly further north lies **Moyat el-Wishwashi**, a large rainwater catchment cistern hidden in a canyon between imposing boulders.

One of the most popular jeep excursions is to the **Coloured Canyon**; the name comes from the vivid striations on the steep walls of the canyon, which is sheltered from the wind and eerily silent. Other destinations include **Wadi Ghazala**, with its dunes and acacia groves where gazelles may be spotted; **Ain Um Ahmed**, whose deep torrent, fed by snow on the highest peaks of the Sinai, shrinks to a stream as the seasons advance; the oasis of **Ain Khudra**, supposedly the Biblical Hazeroth, where Miriam was stricken with leprosy for criticizing Moses; and the beautiful – and relatively untouristed – **Rainbow Canyon**.

Recommended **guides** include Morad el Said at *Amon-Yahro Tourist Camp*, an English- and German-speaking Egyptologist. If you fancy learning to **ride a camel**, the *Habiba* camp, next to the *Amon-Yahro Tourist Camp* has its own school (☷ sinai4you.com/crs).

ACCOMMODATION

Accommodation is concentrated in three main locations: near the **port**; along the beach south of Nuweiba City in **Dunas**; and in **Tarabeen**, a couple of kilometres north. All the following places include breakfast in their rates unless stated otherwise.

Amon-Yahro Tourist Camp Nuweiba City ☎ 069 350 0555, ☷ amonyahro.net. Right on the beach, this tidy camp is the closest in Nuweiba City to Dunas, and the cheapest too, with wooden huts with mattresses (and nothing else), plus clean shared facilities. It's run by Egyptologist Morad el Said, who takes visitors on reliable and informative trips into the desert. Breakfast costs extra. **E£100**

Hilton Nuweiba Coral Resort East of the port ☎ 069 352 0320, ☷ hilton.com. The smartest hotel in Nuweiba, this large, peaceful complex has comfortable rooms, pool, private beach and plenty of sport and recreational facilities (including dive and waterports centres). Half- and full-board deals are available. **$70**

La Sirene Between Nuweiba City and the port ☎ 069 350 0701, ☷ nuweiba-lasirene.com. On a lovely stretch of beach, with sand-coloured buildings containing a/c rooms equipped with private bath, TV and colourful rugs. There's also table tennis, billiards and table football, plus a dive centre. **€48**

★ **Nakhil Inn** North Tarabeen ☎ 069 350 0879, ☷ nakhil-inn.com. This well-run, friendly guesthouse has its own reef and private beach, dive centre and plenty of activities on offer. Choose between split-level chalet-style accommodation and spacious en-suite rooms with French windows; all come with a/c, kettles and fridges. **$45**

Nuweiba Village In the centre of Nuweiba City ☎ 069 350 0401, ☷ nuweibavillageresort.com. This central hotel has snug a/c bungalows with TV set around neatly tended gardens, plus a (sporadically open) disco, dive centre, pool, and a private beach with laidback bar. **$55**

Soft Beach Camp At the southern end of Tarabeen's main street ☎ 0100 364 7586, ☷ softbeachcamp.com. This chilled-out German-run backpacker place has a collection of classic Sinai beach shacks – basic wood and bamboo huts of varying sizes with mattresses on the floor, plus mosquito nets. There's also internet access, a restaurant and a book exchange. **E£100**

Swisscare 3km south of Nuweiba Village ☎ 069 352 0640, ☷ swisscare-hotels.com. Peaceful resort with whitewashed villas, a private stretch of beach, pool, dive centre, restaurants, massage facilities and horse and camel riding. All the suite-style rooms come with a separate seating area (balcony or terrace), private bathroom and a/c, although the decor is pretty dated throughout. **$50**

EATING, DRINKING AND NIGHTLIFE

Tarabeen has a couple of budget restaurants, while the shops in Nuweiba City are good for self-caterers. Nightlife boils down to an occasional disco in the *Nuweiba Village* hotel, or playing guitars, drums or backgammon and getting stoned in Tarabeen. If you want a beer, try the bars in the smarter hotels.

Cleopatra Nuweiba City, 220m south of Nuweiba Village. Decked out with a mix of Ancient Egyptian and maritime kitsch, this restaurant serves good seafood, pizzas, pastas, mezze and chicken dishes (mains around £E30). Open daily for lunch and dinner.

Dr Shesh Kebab Nuweiba City's bazaar. A long-standing budget traveller favourite serving falafel, baba ganoush, pizza, spaghetti, seafood and excellent kebabs (mains £E10–40). The gracious Dr Shesh Kebab, as the owner styles himself, is usually around in the evenings, when he's happy to talk to tourists and offer travel advice. Open daily for lunch and dinner.

DIRECTORY

Banks There are mini banks and ATMs at the *Nuweiba Village* and *Hilton* hotels, and in the port area.

Doctor There is a doctor on call at *Nuweiba Village* hotel. Nuweiba Hospital is poorly equipped, so head for Sharm el-Sheikh if you're seriously ill (see p.547).

Internet Almostakbal (£E5/hr), on the main street in Nuweiba City.

Police The tourist police (☎069 350 0231) can be found just outside the *Nuweiba Village* hotel.

Post office In the centre, two blocks east of the bus stop (daily except Fri 9am–2pm).

Travel agent Nature Travel (☎069 350 0391, ⓦnaturetravelegypt.com), near Nuweiba Village, runs a range of trips throughout the Sinai (including to the Coloured Canyon and St Catherine's Monastery) and to Petra, and can also book catamaran tickets to Jordan (see below).

Between Nuweiba and Taba

The 70km of coastline between **Nuweiba** and the **Taba** border crossing into Israel was for a long while relatively untouched, scattered with just a few appealing low-key resorts. During the 1990s these were joined by plenty of new resorts and the massive Taba Heights tourist development. However, since September 11, 2001 many of these hotels have been virtually empty due to the dearth of Israeli visitors, with some closing down completely. Visitor numbers took a further knock after bombings in 2004 in Taba (see p.558) and at Ras al-Shaitan. As a result, independent travellers who venture this way will get long stretches of beautiful beach more or less to themselves.

Maagana Beach and around

North of Nuweiba, the first notable spot is **MAAGANA BEACH**, whose southern end – called **Lami Beach** – begins 8km from Tarabeen. Though its reefs are quite shallow and unimpressive, the beach itself is nice and has striking rock formations. Two kilometres further on lies the picturesque headland of **RAS AL-SHAITAN**, where the **reef** drops off sharply to the north, making it ideal for shore diving and snorkelling. A few kilometres beyond Ras al-Shaitan lies the headland of **RAS EL-BURQA**, home to the best resort in the area, *Basata* (see p.558). Next up is the Bedouin settlement of **BIR SWAIR**, which has a good stretch of beach.

> ## VISITING JORDAN
>
> A catamaran departs daily from Nuweiba's port (☎069 352 0427) at 6am to Aqaba in Jordan (around 1hr 30min; $85 one-way, $125 return); in the opposite direction, it leaves Aqaba at 7pm/7.30pm. Tickets are available from Meenagate (☎0112 059 5506, ⓦmeenagate.com); book by phone or email at least 24 hours in advance and arrive at the port an hour before departure. Late departures are not uncommon and bad weather can cause extensive delays. One-month **Jordanian visas** are currently free for most nationalities arriving via Aqaba. Day-trips (around $250) to Petra can be arranged through Nature Travel (see above); a more comprehensive two-night visit costs about $450 (£E2700).

By bus Buses travelling between Nuweiba and Taba can drop you off at – or near – any of the resorts mentioned below.

Banks and shopping There are no banks outside of Nuweiba and Taba, and few places to buy food.

ACCOMMODATION

★ **Basata** Ras el-Burqa ☎069 350 0480, �🌐basata .com. Egypt's most eco-friendly resort has its own organic gardens, desalination plant, and recycling programme. Alcohol, TV and loud music are banned, and the ambience is family-oriented with a New Age ethos. There are camping spots, simple huts and more comfortable chalets. You'll either feel at home with *Basata's* New Agers or find them unbearably cliquey. Camping €12/person; rooms €40

Bawaki Around 10km north of Ras al-Shaitan ☎069 350 0470, �🌐bawaki.com. This domed holiday resort is a reasonable mid-range choice, with a selection of modest whitewashed a/c bungalows (including some larger options suitable for families or groups), restaurant, bar, pool and private beach. Rates are all-inclusive. $555

Ras Satan Ras al-Shaitan ☎0100 525 9109, �🌐ras-satan.com. This sleepy shoestring camp has basic wooden huts with mattresses and colourful rugs, and a restaurant serving decent local and international dishes; regular music workshops are also held here. Note that on top of the room rate each guest is required to buy at least two meals a day at the camp's restaurant. £E80

Taba and the border

Hugging the Gulf of Aqaba's northernmost reaches lies the much-disputed territory of **TABA**. Following its withdrawal from the Sinai, Israel claimed Taba lay outside the jurisdiction of the Camp David Accords, and demanded $60 million compensation for its return to Egypt. It took ten years of bitter negotiations until international arbitration finally returned the town to Egypt in 1989. After a period of relative calm, Taba's peace was shattered on October 7, 2004 when a massive car bomb tore away a side of the *Hilton Taba Resort*, killing 32 people.

Taba is now a town in two parts: the unassuming border settlement of **Taba** itself – little more than a handful of hotels, cafés, shops and a bus terminal – and, around 18km south, the huge **Taba Heights** development (🌐tabaheights.com). Dubbed the "Red Sea Riviera", this complex features several top-end resorts plus a casino, restaurants, bars, shops and a medical centre. It's all pretty characterless, however, and unless you're en route to Israel or just want to lie by the hotel pool or on the beach (there's a particularly good one 3km north of Taba Heights), there's not much to do.

Pharoah's Island

Seven kilometres south of Taba you'll see **PHAROAH'S ISLAND** (Gezirat Faraoun; known to Israelis as "Coral Island"), its barren rocks crowned by the renovated ruins of a

---

CROSSING THE ISRAELI BORDER

The **border with Israel** is open 24 hours except during Yom Kippur and Eid el-Adha. Avoid crossing after mid-morning on a Friday or any time on Saturday, however, as most public transport and businesses in Israel shut down over *shabbat*. The whole process can be very quick, unless you get caught behind a large group. For details of entering Egypt at Taba, and entry and departure taxes, see Basics (p.28). If you're **arriving from Israel**, don't listen to any taxi drivers who say you need to take a taxi to reach Taba bus station – it's less than five minutes' walk.

Israel issues free three-month **visas** to EU, US, Australian and New Zealand citizens. However, if you plan on travelling to Syria or other Arab countries that do not recognize Israel, ask immigration on both sides of the border to leave your passport unstamped. Travellers must walk across the no-man's land between the Egyptian and Israeli checkpoints; from the Israeli checkpoint you need to catch a shared taxi or #15 bus for the 10km trip into Eilat. If you need to **change money**, the exchange rate on the Egyptian side, at Bank Misr, which also has an ATM, is better than the Israeli bank where you pay your exit tax.

crusader fort built in 1115 to levy taxes on Arab merchants while ostensibly protecting pilgrims travelling between Jerusalem and St Catherine's Monastery. The fort was subsequently captured by Saladin but abandoned by the Arabs in 1183. It is only 250m offshore, so can be admired from the mainland; alternatively, boat trips can be organized via the the nearby *Salah al-Deen* hotel. The main reason to come here, however, is to **dive or snorkel** in the maze of reefs off the northeastern tip of the island. As the currents are strong and the reefs labyrinthine, it's best to take a guide.

ARRIVAL AND DEPARTURE ┄┄┄┄┄┄┄┄┄┄┄┄┄┄┄┄┄┄┄┄┄┄┄┄┄┄┄┄┄┄┄┄┄┄┄┄┄┄┄ TABA

By bus The East Delta bus terminal (☎ 069 353 0205) is a few hundred metres before the Israeli border. There are services to Nuweiba (3 daily; 1hr), one of which usually continues to Dahab (around 3hr).

ACCOMMODATION

TABA

Hilton Taba Resort & Nelson Village Taba ☎ 069 353 0140, ⊛ hilton.com. Offering the smart service and range of amenities you'd expect from a *Hilton*, with very comfortable rooms (though the cheapest lack sea views), several good restaurants and bars, a decent-sized pool, private beach (and reef, which is great for snorkelling), dive centre and casino. $100

Tobya Boutique Hotel 1km south of Taba ☎ 069 353 0275, ⊛ tobyaboutiquehotel.com. *Tobya* has a bit more character than many of the somewhat bland international chains in the area, with a stylish Egyptian-Nubian architectural feel. There's a decent restaurant, a pool, a small private beach and the obligatory casino. $80

TABA HEIGHTS

El Wekala Golf Resort ☎ 069 360 1212, ⊛ threecorners.com. Not as smart, but also a bit cheaper, than its Taba Heights neighbours, *El Wekala* overlooks an eighteen hole golf course, a five-minute bus ride from the beach. Rooms are comfortable, though nothing special, and there are three pools and a spa. Popular with families. €55

Hyatt Regency ☎ 069 358 0234, ⊛ taba.regency .hyatt.com. Huge five-star in faux-Nubian style with artificial lagoons and landscaped gardens. As well as swish rooms, the resort has a private beach, several good pools, four restaurants, four bars, health club and tennis courts. $140

The interior

The **interior of the Sinai** is a baking wilderness of jagged rocks, drifting sand and wind-scoured gravel pans, awesome in its desolation. Yet life flourishes around its isolated springs and water-holes, or whenever rain falls, renewing the vegetation across vast tracts of semi-desert. Hinterland settlements bestride medieval pilgrimage routes, which the Turks transformed from camel tracks into dirt roads, and the Egyptians and Israelis then improved and fought over. Both sides also built and bombed the airstrips which international peacekeepers now use to monitor the Sinai's demilitarized zones.

The only readily accessible parts of the interior are **St Catherine's Monastery**, **Mount Sinai** and **Feiran Oasis**, although some other, smaller oases can be reached by jeep or camel from the coast or St Catherine's (see below). That said, most buses from Cairo to Nuweiba traverse the **Wilderness of the Wanderings** via **Nekhl** and the **Mitla Pass**, allowing you to see something of the peninsula's interior. Because of the unexploded ordnance lying around, **driving yourself** is officially restricted outside the St Catherine's and Feiran Oasis areas.

Inland safaris and treks

Inland safaris range from half-day excursions to two-week treks. Travelling by **jeep** is obviously faster and makes few or no physical demands, but tends to distance you from the landscape, unlike travel by **camel** (see p.565), which feels totally in keeping with the terrain.

For those with more time and stamina, the most rewarding option is **trekking**. Treks can be arranged at the village of St Catherine's (where you can also obtain maps for one-day walks in the area) or at certain points along the roads into the interior, and also with many of the Bedouin who run trips from the coastal resorts. The list of destinations below should give an idea of what's on offer.

Practicalities depend on your destination and mode of travel. Day excursions from the coast can be made on a Sinai-only visa, but to travel for any longer or to explore the High Mountain Region beyond the immediate vicinity of St Catherine's

6

SAFARI DESTINATIONS IN SINAI

The following are all shown on the map on p.561.

Ain el-Furtaga 16km from Nuweiba by road. A palm-filled oasis at the crossroads of trails to the Coloured Canyon, Wadi Ghazala and Ain Khudra Oasis.

Ain Khudra Oasis One of Sinai's loveliest oases, reached by hiking from the St Catherine's road, with help from local Bedouin guides, or from the south by 4WD.

Ain Kid Oasis A red-walled canyon 14km off the road between Sharm el-Sheikh and Dahab (reached via Wadi Kid). A spring appears here in rainy years, while the oasis has a freshwater well.

Ain Umm Ahmed Another beautiful oasis, accessible by 4WD or camel from Bir es-Sawa and a possible base for climbing expeditions to Ras el-Qalb (see below).

Arched Canyon Sinuous gorge accessible only on foot; drop-off and pick-up by 4WD from Ain el-Furtaga or Bir es-Sawa.

Bir es-Sawa Small oasis with a spring issuing from a cave, beside the El-Thammed road.

Blue Valley 12km from St Catherine's. A canyon painted blue by a Belgian artist in 1978.

Coloured Canyon 17km north of Ain el-Furtaga. Two rainbow-hued canyons, great for walking or rock-climbing (no water). One of the most popular day-trips from Nuweiba and Dahab.

El-Haduda The biggest sand dune in the eastern Sinai, reached from Sheikh Hamid (see below).

Feiran Oasis Over twelve thousand palm trees, monastic remains and access to Jebel Serbal. The wadi in which the oasis is situated may have been the route taken by the Israelites to reach Mount Sinai.

Forest of Pillars A unique natural phenomenon of petrified tree stumps on the cliffs of Jebel el-Tih, 15km northeast of Serabit el-Khadim. Access by 4WD or camel only; guide essential.

Jebel Sabah A 2266m peak in the southern Sinai, from which Saudi Arabia and mainland Egypt are visible on clear days. For experienced hikers only, with abundant food and water. Permit required.

Jebel Serbal Near Feiran Oasis, this is one of the loveliest mountains in Sinai, with ruined chapels lining the trail to the summit (2070m). No climbing skills needed, but guide and permit required.

Jebel Um Shaumar Sinai's second-highest peak, whose summit (2586m) affords a view of the entire southern horn of the peninsula. Experienced climbers only. Permit required.

Nuwamis Prehistoric site with 5550-year-old graves and inscriptions 6km from Ain Khudra. Reached on foot (2hr 30min) from Sheikh Hamid, by appointment only.

Ras el-Qalb Isolated mountain (999m) associated in Bedouin folklore with the monster Ula. For climbers only; no water. Permit required.

Serabit el-Khadim Hilltop temple overlooking the Gulf of Suez, with ancient turquoise mines and inscriptions in the surrounding valleys; it's covered on p.536. Access by 4WD, then on foot.

Sheikh Hamid Bedouin settlement on the road to St Catherine's, 7km from the Dahab–Nuweiba road. This is the starting point for walking or camel treks to Ain Khudra, Nuwamis, El-Haduda and remoter destinations (up to two weeks).

Wadi Ghazala Links Ain el-Furtaga and Ain Khudra Oasis (see above). Acacia groves, dunes and gazelles.

Wadi Huweiyit North of Nuweiba. Colourful canyon with typical desert flora; easy hiking.

Wadi Mandar 40km north of Sharm el-Sheikh. Bedouin camel races held here on January 1.

Wadi Naseb Runs down from Mount Catherine towards Dahab. The verdant upper reaches of the wadi are inhabited by Bedouin. 4WD essential.

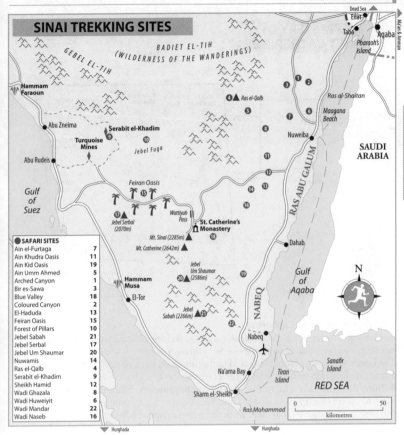

SINAI TREKKING SITES

BADIET EL-TIH
(WILDERNESS OF THE WANDERINGS)

GEBEL EL-TIH

Dead Sea
Eilat
Taba
Pharaoh's Island
Aqaba

Hammam Faraoun

Ras el-Qalb

Ras al-Shaitan

Maagana Beach

Abu Zneima

Serabit el-Khadim

Turquoise Mines

Jebel Fuga

Nuweiba

SAUDI ARABIA

Abu Rudeis

Gulf of Suez

Feiran Oasis

RAS ABU GALUM

Jebel Serbal (2070m)

Wattiyah Pass

St. Catherine's Monastery

Mt. Sinai (2285m)

Mt. Catherine (2642m)

Dahab

Hammam Musa

Jebel Um Shaumar (2586m)

Gulf of Aqaba

El-Tor

Jebel Sabah (2266m)

NABEQ

Nabeq

N

Nabeq

Sanafir Island

Na'ama Bay

Tiran Island

RED SEA

Sharm el-Sheikh

Ras Mohammad

0   50
kilometres

SAFARI SITES

Ain el-Furtaga	7
Ain Khudra Oasis	11
Ain Kid Oasis	19
Ain Umm Ahmed	5
Arched Canyon	1
Bir es-Sawa	3
Blue Valley	18
Coloured Canyon	2
El-Haduda	13
Feiran Oasis	15
Forest of Pillars	10
Jebel Sabah	21
Jebel Serbal	17
Jebel Um Shaumar	20
Nuwamis	14
Ras el-Qalb	4
Serabit el-Khadim	9
Sheikh Hamid	12
Wadi Ghazala	8
Wadi Huweiyit	6
Wadi Mandar	22
Wadi Naseb	16

Hurghada   Hurghada

Monastery and Mount Sinai you must have a full Egyptian visa. To climb mountains you must also have a **permit** from the police, which can be obtained by your Bedouin guide. It's illegal – and highly risky because of unexploded ordnance and the likelihood of getting lost – to go trekking without a guide. To help you select destinations and plot routes, buy the 1:250,000 *Sinai Map of Attractions*. Other things to **bring** are listed in the "High Mountain Region and Feiran Oasis" section (p.565).

St Catherine's Monastery and Mount Sinai

Venerated by Christians, Jews and Muslims as the site of God's revelation of the Ten Commandments, **Mount Sinai** overlooks the valley where Moses is said to have heard the Lord speaking from a burning bush.

The bush is now enshrined in **St Catherine's Monastery**, nestling in a valley at the foot of the Mount, surrounded by high walls and lush gardens. As tourists have followed pilgrims in ever greater numbers, the sacred mount has witnessed unseemly quarrels between Bedouin over the shrinking amount of sleeping space for the climbers at the peak, and the monastery itself shows signs of strain. Yet for most travellers it remains a compelling visit, while other seldom visited peaks offer equally magnificent views if you're prepared to make the effort to reach them.

6

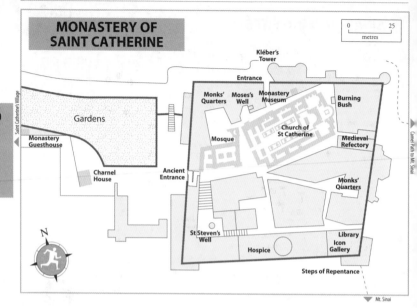

The Monastery of St Catherine

Mon–Thurs & Sat 9–11.45am, Fri 10.45–11.45am; officially closed Sun and Greek Orthodox holidays, but will sometimes open briefly on these days, in order to accommodate tourist demands. • Free (but modest dress required)

The Greek Orthodox **Monastery of St Catherine** dates back to 337 AD, when the Byzantine **Empress Helena** ordered the construction of a chapel around the putative **Burning Bush**, already a focus for hermits and pilgrimages. Since then, the monastery has had cycles of expansion and decline, on occasion being totally deserted. Most of the monks today have come here from the monasteries of Mount Athos in Greece.

Kléber's Tower and the walls

Entrance is through a small gate in the northern wall near **Kléber's Tower** (named after the Napoleonic general who ordered its reconstruction) rather than the main west-facing portal, which has a funnel that was used for pouring boiling oil onto attackers. Built of granite, 10–15m high and 2–3m thick, St Catherine's **walls** are essentially unchanged since Stephanos Ailisios designed them in the sixth century.

Moses' Well and the Burning Bush

As you emerge from the passage, a right turn takes you past **Moses' Well**, where the then fugitive from Egypt met Zipporah, one of Jethro's seven daughters, whom he married at the age of 40. Walking the other way and around the corner, you'll see a thorny evergreen bush outgrowing an enclosure. This is the transplanted descendant of the **Burning Bush** whence God spoke to Moses: "Come now therefore, and I will send thee unto Pharaoh, that thou mayest bring forth my people the children of Israel out of Egypt" (Exodus 3:10). Sceptics may be swayed by the fact that it's the only bush of its kind in the entire peninsula and that all attempts to grow cuttings from it elsewhere have failed. The bush was moved to its present site when Helena's chapel was built over its roots, behind the apse of St Catherine's church.

Nearby is the **Monastery Museum** (£E50), which has Byzantine icons, crosses and chalices, reams of aged manuscripts, fragments of the world's oldest bible and other pieces from the library (see below). Exhibits are labelled in English and Arabic.

St Catherine's Church

A granite basilica, **St Catherine's Church** was erected by Justinian between 542 and 551; the walls and pillars and the cedarwood doors between the narthex and nave are all original. Its twelve pillars – representing the months of the year and hung with icons of the saints venerated during each one – have ornately carved capitals, loaded with symbolism.

At the far end, behind the iconostasis is the **Chapel of the Burning Bush**, only viewable by special dispensation. The narthex displays a selection of the monastery's vast collection of **icons**, running the gamut of Byzantine styles and techniques, from encaustic wax to tempera. The church's **bell** is rung 33 times to rouse the monks before dawn.

The rest of the monastery

Other parts of the monastery are usually closed to lay people. Among them are an eleventh-century **mosque**, added to placate Muslim rulers; a **library** of over three thousand manuscripts and five thousand books; and a **refectory** with Gothic arches and Byzantine murals. You can usually enter the **charnel house**, however, which is heaped with monks' skeletons; the cemetery itself is small, so corpses have to be disinterred after a year and moved into the ossuary. The cadaver in vestments is Stephanos, a sixth-century guardian of one of the routes to the Mount.

Mount Sinai

While some archeologists question whether **Mount Sinai** really was the Biblical mountain where Moses received the Ten Commandments, it's hard not to agree with the nineteenth-century American explorer John Lloyd Stephens that "among all the stupendous works of Nature, not a place can be selected more fitting for the exhibition of Almighty power". Its loftiest peak, a craggy, sheer-faced massif of grey and red granite "like a vengeful dagger that was dipped in blood many ages ago", rises 2285m above sea level. Strictly speaking, it's only this that the Bedouin call Jebel Musa ("Mount Moses"), though the name is commonly applied to the whole massif. Some Biblical scholars reckon that Moses proclaimed the Commandments from Ras Safsafa, at the opposite end of the ridge, which overlooks a wide valley where the Israelites could have camped.

Many people ascend by the camel path and descend by the Steps of Repentance (see below). You could start your ascent around 5pm (earlier during winter) to avoid the worst of the heat and arrive in time to watch the spellbinding sunset and then sleep overnight at the summit. With a torch, you could also climb the camel path (but not the steps) by night, though not during winter.

The camel path

You'll have to hire a Bedouin guide (£E125) to **climb the mountain**; don't let them hurry you – do it at your own pace. The longer but easier route is via the switchback **camel path**, starting 50m behind the monastery. It's possible to rent a camel for most of

---

THE BEDOUIN OF SINAI

The Bedouin community in St Catherine's – and throughout the Sinai – is severely marginalized to the extent that the Egyptian authorities do not even collate official statistics on them. Few Bedouin work in the region's hotels, restaurants and travel agencies, and **guiding** is generally the only legal form of employment available – little surprise that some Bedouin become involved in illegal activities (see p.567). A few NGOs are working to improve the situation, including the **Community Foundation for South Sinai** (ⓦ southsinaifoundation.org), which is based in St Catherine's and supports sustainable development, education, employment, health and conservation projects.

6

the ascent (around £E110), but it's really worth the effort of walking (2–3hr). You can stock up on water at the shops outside the monastery before setting off, and there are refreshment stalls along the way. Prices rise the higher you go, but restocking on the mountain saves you carrying extra weight right at the start. Bedouin entrepreneurs at the peak rent out blankets and mattresses for the night (£E10–20).

Steps of Repentance

Beyond the cleft below the summit, the path is joined by the second route up the mountain, known as the Sikket Saiyidna Musa ("Path of Our Lord Moses") or **Steps of Repentance**. Hewn by a penitent monk, the 3750 steps make a quicker but much steeper ascent from the monastery (1hr 30min), which is hell on the leg muscles; some of the steps are a metre high. Two buildings top the summit, a mosque and a Greek Orthodox church, both usually locked. Next to the mosque is the cave where God sheltered Moses: "I will put thee in a cleft of the rock, and will cover thee with my hand while I pass over" (Exodus 33:22). A little lower down the slope, a bunch of semi-permanent structures have sprung up, offering weary travellers a place to sleep.

Around 300m below the summit you enter a depression known as the Plain of Cypresses or **Elijah's Hollow**, where pilgrims pray and sing; a five hundred year-old cypress tree stands here. This is also where Elijah is believed to have heard God's voice (I Kings 19:9–18) and hid from Jezebel, being fed by ravens. One of the two chapels is dedicated to him, the other to his successor, Elisha.

ARRIVAL AND DEPARTURE   ST CATHERINE'S MONASTERY

All vehicles stop about 10km before the monastery at a petrol station/police checkpoint/ticket office for the St Catherine protectorate, where foreigners must purchase a **ticket** ($3) to enter the area. Most tourist facilities are in **St Catherine's village**, 3km from the monastery. **Shared taxis** (around £E5) shuttle regularly between the village and the monastery, though you could also walk (a pretty hot and dusty 40–50min).

By bus A daily public bus travels to (6am) and from (11am) Cairo via Suez; the journey takes around seven hours. The community-run Bedouin Bus (☎0101 668 4274, ⍟bedouinbus.com) has services to (11am) and from (5pm) Dahab every Tues and Fri, as well as to (8am) and from (2pm) Nuweiba every Wed and Sun. Both journeys take around two hours. Buses depart from the centre of town, opposite the mosque. Buy tickets on board.

By taxi A taxi from Dahab or Nuweiba should cost around £E350–450 for the return journey (including waiting time); from Sharm el-Sheikh, it's roughly double the price.

INFORMATION AND TOURS

Tours You can visit St Catherine's on an organized tour from Sharm el-Sheikh, Dahab, Nuweiba, Cairo, Hurghada or Eilat. Many trips include a moonlit ascent of Mount Sinai; you sleep at the peak and return to the monastery in the morning after sunrise. Bear in mind that night-time temperatures are around 10°C during summer and near zero over winter (when frosts and snow are common); a sleeping bag is essential (blankets are normally available to rent at the summit too). There is often little room at the top and it can be very uncomfortable; if the summit is too busy, you may have to sleep further down at Elijah's Hollow (see above).

Walking Maps of short walks in the area can be purchased from the St Catherine Protectorate visitor centre at the end of the road before the monastery. If you're planning to do any trekking in the High Mountain Region, visit the *Bedouin Camp El-Milga* (see 565), where you'll find Sheikh Mousa (☎069 347 0457, ⍟sheikhmousa.com), the chief of the Bedouin guides who lead expeditions. For more details, see "The High Mountain Region and Feiran Oasis" section (p.565).

ACCOMMODATION AND EATING

There's a decent range of budget and mid-range **hotels** in the village, as well as an atmospheric option next to the monastery itself. Most people eat at their lodgings, though there are a few simple **restaurants** in the centre of the village, as well as a snack bar outside the monastery.

Al-Karm Ecolodge Around 35km northeast of St Catherine's, near the settlement of Sheikh Awad in Wadi Gharba ☎0100 132 4693, ⍟awayaway-sinai .net. A Bedouin-owned and operated camp with just a handful of rooms in a wonderfully remote location (4WD is needed to get here; phone for more detailed directions) with hikes and cultural trips on offer. It's run along environmentally friendly lines, with composting toilets and solar-powered showers, but no electricity. **££200**

Bedouin Camp El-Milga In the El-Milga area of the village, beyond the main square and around 150m northwest of the petrol station ☏ 069 347 0457, ⓦ sheikhmousa.com. Run by the chief of the local Bedouin guides, this friendly lodge has a range of accommodation options from camping spots to en-suite rooms. There also are plenty of hikes and activities on offer, plus free wi-fi, a laundry service and a restaurant. Camping **££15**; dorms **££25**; rooms **££85**

Catherine Plaza Just outside the village ☏ 069 347 0288, ⓦ catherineplaza.com. Large mid-range hotel offering reasonable though pretty dated rooms with bath tub, a/c, phone and TV. There's also an inviting pool, restaurant, bar and billiards table. Half-board rates only. **££450**

Desert Fox Camp 800m from the village, near the main intersection ☏ 069 347 0344 or ☏ 010 9473 2417,

ⓦ desertfoxcamp.com. This backpacker hangout is the cheapest place in the area, with basic stone cabins. If money is really tight, you can camp in the pleasant grounds (tents provided, or bring your own). There's a communal kitchen, simple restaurant and sometimes live music in the evenings. Ten percent of all online bookings go to the Community Foundation for South Sinai (see p.563). Camping **££15**; rooms **££50**

Safary Moonland Camp and Hotel 500m from the village behind Catherine Plaza ☏ 018 658 4550, ⓔ mnland2002@yahoo.com. The dorms and private rooms here are popular with backpackers and overlanders, and it's the only budget place hereabouts where you can sleep on a bed rather than a mattress on the floor. Dorms **££25**; rooms **££100**

★ **St Catherine's Monastery Guesthouse** Just outside the monastery walls ☏ 069 347 0353. Sheltered by the towering red cliffs of Mount Sinai, this guesthouse has a dramatic setting unmatched in the Sinai. The en-suite twin-bedded rooms are small and basic, simple meals (breakfast and dinner) are included and the views are glorious. Half-board **££400**

DIRECTORY

Banks and exchange There's a bank (but no ATM) in the arcade in the centre of the village.

Tourist police A small tourist police booth is located in the village centre, on the opposite side of the road to the bank.

Shops Fansina (☏ 069 347 0155, ⓦ fansina.net; daily 9.30am-3pm), an EU-supported shop, sells handicrafts produced by local Bedouin women, including lovely purses, bags and cushion covers.

The High Mountain Region and Feiran Oasis

The area around St Catherine's is sometimes termed the **High Mountain Region**, as it contains numerous peaks over 2000m. Snow frequently covers the ground in winter and flash floods can occur year round. The scenery is fantastic, with phalanxes of serrated peaks looming above wadis full of tumbled boulders and wiry fruit trees. This harsh but beguiling land is the stamping ground of the Jebeliya and Aulad Said tribes, some of whom act as guides for **treks** on foot or by camel; the terrain is generally too rough for vehicles, even 4WDs. Foreigners are legally forbidden to embark on such expeditions without a Bedouin guide.

Trekking is possible in winter if you are prepared to put up with chilly nights and possible snow flurries; in the summer it's just a case of being fit enough to stand up to the heat. The main **starting point for treks** is the El-Milga area of St Catherine's (see above), where Sheikh Mousa will organize everything. An all-inclusive trek, including guide, food and transport, costs around £E300–350 per day. You'll need comfortable hiking boots, warm clothes, a sleeping bag, sunglasses, sunscreen, lip salve, bug repellent, toilet paper and water purification tablets (unless you're willing to drink from springs). A good map of south Sinai (see p.561) and a compass are also useful.

Mount Catherine

Egypt's highest peak, **Mount Catherine** (Jebel Katerina; 2642m), is roughly 6km south of Mount Sinai and can be reached on foot in five to six hours. The path starts behind St Catherine's village, running up Wadi el-Leja on Mount Sinai's western flank, past the deserted Convent of the Forty and a Bedouin hamlet. Shortly afterwards the trail forks, the lower path winding off up a rubble-strewn canyon, Shagg Musa, which it eventually quits to ascend Mount Catherine – a straightforward but exhausting climb. On the summit are a chapel with water, two rooms for pilgrims to stay overnight, a meteorological station and **panoramic views**.

According to tradition, priests found **St Catherine's remains** here during the ninth or tenth century. Believers maintain she was born in 294 AD in Alexandria of a noble family, converted to Christianity and subsequently lambasted Emperor Maxentius for idolatry, confounding fifty philosophers who tried to shake her faith. Following an attempt to break her on a spiked wheel (hence Catherine wheels), which shattered at her touch, Maxentius had her beheaded; her remains were transported to Sinai by angels.

The Blue Valley

If climbing Mount Catherine seems too ambitious, consider visiting the **Blue Valley**, 5km southeast of the intersection of the roads to St Catherine's, Nuweiba and Feiran Oasis. This can be done as a day-trip from Dahab or in half a day from St Catherine's Village by hiring a jeep and a guide. The canyon's name derives from a Belgian who in 1978 painted its rocks a deep blue in emulation of the Bulgarian artist Christo, who hung drapes across the Grand Canyon.

Feiran Oasis

It's thought the ancient Israelites reached Mount Sinai by the same route that buses coming from the west use today, via Wadi Feiran and Wadi el-Sheikh. Travelling this road in the other direction, you might glimpse the **Tomb of Nabi Salah** near the **Watiyyah Pass**, where Bedouin converge for an annual **moulid** on the Prophet Mohammed's birthday. Beyond the pass lies El-Tafra, a small and dismal oasis village.

Roughly 60km from St Catherine's the road passes a huge walled garden marking the start of **FEIRAN OASIS**. A twisting, granite-walled valley of palms and tamarisks, the

---

LONGER TREKS AROUND ST CATHERINE'S

The two **four-day treks** outlined here give an idea of local trekking opportunities; other possibilities are mentioned under the "Feiran Oasis" section (see above).

ST CATHERINE'S TO AL GALT AL AZRAQ

The first trek, starts off in El-Milga and begins by taking the path through the **Abu Giffa Pass** down into Wadi Tubug, passing walled gardens en route to **Wadi Shagg**, where you'll find Byzantine ruins and huge boulders. The next day you follow the trail through **Wadi Gibal** and climb one of two hills offering magnificent views, before descending to **Farash Rummana** camping spot. On the third day you strike north through a canyon to the water-holes of **Galt al-Azraq**, pushing on to camp at Farsh Um Sila or Farsh Tuweita. The final day begins with an easy hike down towards Wadi Tinya, before climbing **Jebel Abbas Pasha** (2383m), named after the paranoid ruler who built a palace there (now in ruins). You then follow a path down through the Zuweitun and Tubug valleys, back to Abu Giffa and El-Milga. If you want a more detailed account of the trek, track down a copy of Francis Gilbert and Samy Zabat's *A Walk in Sinai: St Catherine's to Al Galt Al Azraq*.

ST CATHERINE'S TO FARSH ABU TUWEITA

The second trek starts at **Abu Sila** village, 3km from El-Milga, where there are some rock inscriptions. You'll probably camp out near Bustan el-Birka's sweetwater spring. Day two involves descending into **Wadi Nugra**, below Jebel el-Banat, where you can bathe in pools fed by a twenty-metre-high waterfall. You then press through Wadi Gharba to the tomb of **Sheikh Awad**, where the Aulad Gundi tribe holds an annual feast in his honour. Having spent the night here, you have a choice of three routes to **Farsh Abu Tuweita**, the final night's camping spot. On the fourth day you follow the same route as the final leg of the first hike.

NORTHERN SINAI

While jagged mountains dominate the gulf coasts and interior of the peninsula, **northern Sinai** is awash with pale sand dunes. Security concerns (see p.531), however, mean that travellers are currently advised to avoid all but essential travel to the area north of the Suez–Taba road. The smuggling tunnels around the divided and tense **Rafah** border crossing are the main source of goods for the Gaza Strip, while **El-Arish** and the surrounding area are other notable flashpoints, with repeated clashes between security forces and Islamic militants, attacks on gas pipelines to Jordan and Israel and, in 2011, the rape of a British woman, allegedly by an Egyptian army officer.

In addition, every year thousands of **refugees** – mainly from Eritrea, Ethiopia and Sudan – attempt to cross the Sinai to Israel, but few make it. A CNN report at the end of 2011 revealed widespread enslavement of refugees by Bedouin people-smugglers, rape, extortion, blackmail, and even evidence of organ-harvesting.

oasis belongs to the tribes of the Tawarah, who have houses and wells here. Feiran was the earliest Christian stronghold in the Sinai, with its own bishop and **convent**, ruined during the seventh century but now rebuilt. Further back in time, this was reputedly the Rephidim of the Amalakites, who denied its wells to the thirsty Israelites, causing them to curse Moses until he smote the Rock of Horeb with his staff, making water gush forth. Refreshed, they joined battle with the Amalakites the next day, inspired by the sight of Moses standing on a hilltop, believed to have been the conical one the Bedouin call **Jebel el-Tannuh**, with ruined chapels lining the track to its summit (1hr). Other **hiking** possibilities in the area include **Jebel el-Banat** (1510m), further north, and the highly challenging ascent of **Jebel Serbal** (2070m), south of the oasis.

A **guide** can be arranged through Sheikh Mousa (see p.565). Feiran Oasis lacks any accommodation, but you could probably **camp** in the palm groves with local consent.

The Wilderness of the Wanderings

Separating the granite peaks of south Sinai from the sandy wastes of the north is a huge tableland of gravel plains and fissured limestone, riven by wadis: the **Wilderness of the Wanderings** (Badiet el-Tih), through which the children of Israel are said to have passed. Life exists in this desert thanks to sporadic rainfall between mid-October and mid-April, which refills the cisterns that irrigate groves of palms and tamarisks. During Byzantine times, these cisterns sustained dozens of villages along the Sinai–Negev border; nowadays, the largest irrigated gardens are in Wadi Feiran and Wadi el-Arish.

Crossing the Wilderness via Nekhl and the Mitla Pass

The shortest route between Nuweiba and Cairo (470km; 6–7hr) crosses the Wilderness via Nekhl and the Mitla Pass. The heat-hazed plateau is stupefyingly monotonous but contains several historic locations (which you can visit by hiring a taxi for the day or getting a travel agency in Sharm or Dahab to organize a trip for you). The road from Nuweiba heads north to El-Thammed before cutting west across Wadi el-Arish. **NEKHL**, at the heart of the peninsula, has a **derelict castle** built by Sultan al-Ghuri in 1516. South of one of the wadi's many tributaries lies **Qalaat el-Gundi**, a **ruined fort** built by Saladin; it can also be reached by a track from Ras Sudr on the Gulf of Suez. To the west, the road descends through the 480-metre-high **Mitla Pass**, one of three cleavages in the central plateau. The outcome of three Arab-Israeli conflicts was arguably determined here in some of the bloodiest **tank battles** in history.

The Red Sea Coast

SWIMMING WITH SPINNER DOLPHINS, RED SEA

The Red Sea Coast

An entrepôt since ancient times, the RED SEA COAST, stretching 1250km from Suez to the Sudanese border, was once a microcosm of half the world, as Muslim pilgrims from as far away as Central Asia sailed to Arabia from its ports. Though piracy and slavery ceased towards the end of the nineteenth century, smuggling still drew adventurers and explorers long after the Suez Canal had sapped the vitality of the Red Sea ports. Decades later, the coastline assumed new significance with the discovery of oil and its vulnerability to Israeli commando raids. The latter led to large areas being mined, which is one reason why tourism didn't arrive until the 1980s – although it has boomed since then, fuelled by the region's good-value resorts and superlative dive sites.

7

Along **the coast**, turquoise waves lap rocky headlands and windswept beaches, while inland the Nile Valley is divided from the coast by the arid hills and mountains of the **Eastern Desert**, home to the Red Sea monasteries. Cairenes appreciate the beaches at Ain Sukhna, south of Suez, but the region's real lure are the fabulous island reefs near the brash resort of **Hurghada** and the less touristy settlements of **Port Safaga**, **El-Quseir** and **Marsa Alam** to the south.

South from Suez to Ain Sukhna

The coastal route south from Suez is of little interest, passing numerous oil and natural-gas refineries, while in the distance you can also see the **Jebel Ataqa**, the northernmost range in the Eastern Desert and an old Bedouin smuggling route.

Around 55km south of Suez is the town of **AIN SUKHNA**, whose beaches are popular with Egyptians but attract few foreigners. The town's name derives from the **hot springs** (35°C) originating in the Jebel Ataqa. Light patches offshore indicate **coral reefs**, while barbed-wire fences delineate areas sown with landmines (mainly beneath the cliffs). The quality of resorts here is generally low, and it's better to head on to El Gouna or Hurghada rather than stopping off here.

The Red Sea monasteries

Secreted amid the arid Red Sea Hills, Egypt's two oldest **monasteries** – dedicated to St Paul and St Anthony – trace their origins back to the infancy of Christian monasticism, observing rituals that have scarcely changed over sixteen centuries. You don't have to be religious to appreciate their tranquil atmosphere and imposing setting, however, and there's also scope for **birdwatching** in the vicinity.

Highlights

❶ Monasteries Deep in the desert, St Paul's and St Anthony's are the oldest monasteries in Egypt and still draw thousands of Copts from across Egypt each year. **See p.570**

❷ Diving Hurghada is a great place to arrange an inexpensive PADI Open Water course, a half- or full-day diving trip to one of the many nearby reefs, or an extended stay on a liveaboard. **See p.580**

❸ Hurghada nightlife This resort is renowned for its lively bar and club scene, with many of the best venues to be found in the Hurghada Marina. **See p.584**

❹ Red Sea Mountains Experience the wadis and Bedouin culture of the Red Sea Mountains on a camel or jeep safari. **See p.585**

❺ Marsa Alam The camps and resorts dotted along the coast north and south of Marsa Alam provide access to some of the best and least-visited dive sites in Egypt. **See p.591**

HIGHLIGHTS ARE MARKED ON THE MAP ON P.572

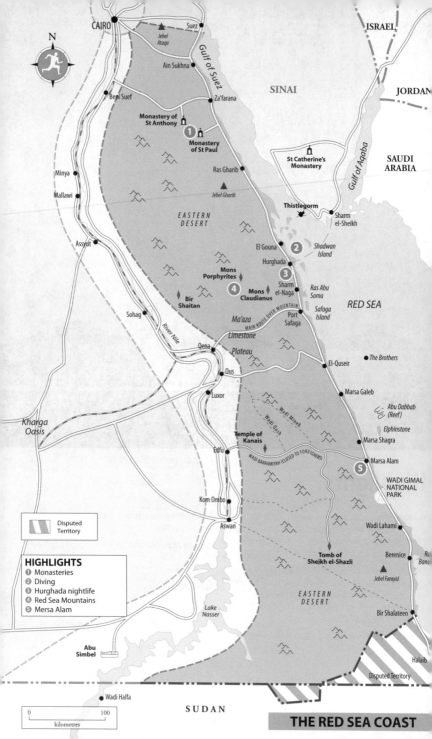

THE RED SEA COAST

N

CAIRO
Suez
ISRAEL

Jebel
Ataqa

Gulf of Suez

Ain Sukhna

Beni Suef

Za'farana

SINAI

JORDAN

Monastery of
St Anthony

①

Monastery
of St Paul

St Catherine's
Monastery

SAUDI
ARABIA

Ras Gharib

Gulf of Aqaba

Minya

Jebel Gharib

Mallawi

E A S T E R N
D E S E R T

Thistlegorm

Sharm
el-Sheikh

Assyut

El Gouna

②

*Shadwan
Island*

Hurghada

③

*Ras Abu
Soma*

Mons Porphyrites

④

Sharm
el-Naga

RED SEA

Bir
Shaitan

Mons
Claudianus

*Safaga
Island*

Sohag

Ma'aza

MAIN ROUTE OVER MOUNTAIN

Port
Safaga

River Nile

Limestone

Qena

Plateau

El-Quseir

● *The Brothers*

Qus

Luxor

Marsa Galeb

*Abu Dabbab
(Reef)*

*Kharga
Oasis*

Elphinstone

Wadi Mineh

Temple of
Kanais

Wadi Qash

Marsa Shagra

Edfu

WADI BARRAMIYAH (CLOSED TO FOREIGNERS)

Marsa Alam

⑤

WADI GIMAL
NATIONAL
PARK

Kom Ombo

Aswan

Wadi Lahami

Tomb of
Sheikh el-Shazli

Berenice

*Ra
Banc*

**Disputed
Territory**

Jebel Farayid

HIGHLIGHTS
① Monasteries
② Diving
③ Hurghada nightlife
④ Red Sea Mountains
⑤ Mersa Alam

*Lake
Nasser*

E A S T E R N
D E S E R T

Bir Shalateen

Halaib

Disputed Territory

Abu
Simbel

● Wadi Halfa

S U D A N

0 ———— 100
kilometres

Be aware that large areas of the coastline and many wadis in the region are still **mined**: any area with barbed-wire fencing (however rusty) is suspect, and you should never wander off public beaches or into the desert without a guide.

The Monastery of St Anthony

Around 30km south of Ain Sukhna, the fly-bitten town of **ZA'FARANA** is the nearest settlement to the Red Sea monasteries. West from here, a wide valley cleaves the Galala Plateau and sets the road on course for the Nile, 168km away. Called **Wadi Arraba**, its name derives from the carts that once delivered provisions to the monastery, though legend attributes it to the pharaoh's chariots that pursued the Israelites towards the Red Sea.

Travelling for 33km along this road brings you to a turn-off to the south, from where a dramatic ridge of cliffs known as Mount Qalah can be seen in the distance, with the **Monastery of St Anthony** situated beneath. The monastery was founded shortly after Anthony's death in 356, although a sojourn by St John the Short is all that's recorded of its early **history**. An influx of refugee monks from the monasteries at Wadi Natrun (see p.378) occurred during the sixth century, followed by a wave of Melkite monks in the seventh. Subsequently pillaged by Bedouin and razed to the ground, the monastery was restored during the twelfth century by Coptic monks, from whose ranks several Ethiopian bishops were elected. After a murderous revolt by the monastery servants, it was reoccupied by Coptic, Syrian and Ethiopian monks.

The permanent **brethren** who now live at the monastery are university graduates and ex-professionals – not unlike the kind of people drawn to monasticism in the fourth century AD. A typical day at the monastery begins at 4am, with two hours of prayer and hymns followed by communion and Mass, all before breakfast.

Inside the monastery

The monastery is effectively a self-contained village complete with lanes of two-storey dwellings, churches, mills and gardens of vines, olives and palms, surrounded by lofty walls with an interior catwalk – although most of the buildings themselves are recent compared to the monastery's foundation. An English-speaking monk will give you a partial tour of the monastery, though some areas are off-limits. Highlights include the **keep**, a soot-blackened **bakery** and a **library** of over 1700 manuscripts.

The oldest of the five **churches** is dedicated to the monastery's namesake, who may be buried underneath it. Don't miss the **wall paintings**, some of which date from the seventh century and have been restored to their former glory. During Lent (when the gates are locked and deliveries are winched over the walls) monks celebrate the liturgy in the twelve-domed **Church of St Luke**, dating from 1776. A small **museum** details the monastery's history; next door is a well-stocked bookshop. The community remains dependent on water from the monastery's **spring**, where Arab legend has it that Miriam, sister of Moses, bathed during the Exodus.

St Anthony's Cave

Early morning or late afternoon is the best time to go up to **St Anthony's Cave** (*maghara*), 2km from – and 276m above – the monastery (bring water). After passing a sculpture of St Anthony carved into the mountain rock, you'll face 1200 steps (a 45min walk) up to the cave, but the stunning views from 680m above the Red Sea reward your effort. Technicolour wadis and massifs spill down into the azure gulf, with Sinai's mountains rising beyond. The cave where Anthony spent his last 25 years contains medieval graffiti and modern *tilbas*, scraps of paper bearing supplications inscribed with "Remember, Lord, your servant", which pilgrims stick into cracks in the rock. **Birdlife** – hoopoes, desert larks, ravens, blue rock thrushes and pied wagtails – is surprisingly abundant, and you might glimpse some shy **gazelles**.

The Monastery of St Paul

The **Monastery of St Paul** has always been overshadowed by St Anthony's. Its titular founder (not to be confused with the apostle Paul) was only 16 and an orphan when he fled Alexandria to escape Emperor Decius' persecutions, making him the earliest known hermit. Shortly before his death in 348, Paul was visited by Anthony. Paul begged him to bring the robe of Pope Athanasius, for Paul to be buried in. Anthony departed to fetch this, but on the way back had a vision of Paul's soul being carried up to heaven by angels, and arrived to find him dead. While Anthony was wondering what to do, two lions appeared and dug a grave for the body, so Anthony shrouded it in the robe and took Paul's tunic of palm leaves as a gift for the pope, who subsequently wore it at Christmas, Epiphany and Easter.

The monastery (called Deir Amba Bula or Deir Mari Bolus) was a form of posthumous homage by Paul's followers: its turreted walls are built around the cave where he lived for decades. To a large extent, its fortunes have followed those of its more prestigious neighbour. In 1484 all its monks were slain by Bedouin, who occupied St Paul's for eighty years. Rebuilt by Patriarch Gabriel VII, it was again destroyed near the end of the sixteenth century.

Inside the monastery complex

The **monastery complex** is much smaller than St Anthony's and a little more primitive looking. It boasts four churches, but the **Church of St Paul** is its spiritual centre, a cave-church housing the remains of the saint. The church walls are painted with murals generally thought inferior to those of St Anthony's, though they have been well preserved. A monk will show you round the chapels and identify their icons: notice the angel of the furnace with Shadrach, Meshach and Abednego, and the ostrich eggs hung from the ceiling – a symbol of the Resurrection. The southern sanctuary of the larger **Church of St Michael** contains a gilded icon of the head of John the Baptist on a dish. When Bedouin raided the monastery, its monks retreated into the five-storey **keep**, supplied with spring water by a hidden canal. Nowadays this is not enough to sustain the monks and their guests, so water is brought in from outside.

ARRIVAL AND DEPARTURE	**THE RED SEA MONASTERIES**

The **Monastery of St Anthony** is around 45km west of Za'farana , while the **Monastery of St Paul** is about 35km southeast across the desert from St Anthony's (and around 40km southwest of Za'farana by road). The cheapest way to see the monasteries is to use public transport combined with walking (or hitching, though this carries inherent risks and shouldn't be attempted alone): carry ample water, and don't attempt to walk during the hottest months of the year (roughly June to Sep). It's possible to hike during the cooler months between the two monasteries along a demanding trail across the top of the plateau, although it's strongly recommended you hire a guide, which is easier to do at St Paul's than at St Anthony's.

By bus Any bus from Cairo or Suez to Hurghada can drop you at the turn-off for St Paul's (26km south of Za'farana), recognizable by its plastic-roofed bus shelter. The monastery is 13km uphill from here.

By service taxi Service taxis running between Beni Suef (see p.214) and Za'farana pass within striking distance of St Anthony's. Get off at the signposted turn-off 33km west of Za'farana, from where it's 15km uphill to the monastery.

By taxi Chartering a taxi for the return trip to the monasteries costs around £E1000 from Hurghada or Cairo or about £E700 from Suez, depending on your negotiating skills.

Tours Travel agencies in Hurghada can organize a trip to the monasteries. Alternatively, if you're happy to travel with devout believers you can join a pilgrimage tour arranged by the Coptic Patriarchate in Cairo (22 Sharia Ramses, Abbassiya; ☎ 02 2396 0025) or the YMCA (72 Sharia al-Gumhorriya, downtown; ☎ 02 2591 7360).

ACCOMMODATION AND EATING

There are dormitories at both monasteries if you want to stay, but you'll need prior written permission from the residence office (☎02 2590 0218) at St Mark's Church in Heliopolis, Cairo. Both monasteries also have cafeterias, although it's worth bringing some food and drink with you as the menus are quite limited. Smoking and drinking alcohol are forbidden at both monasteries.

INFORMATION

Opening times Both monasteries are open daily 4am–4.45pm except during Christmas and Lent, when they are closed to visitors.

Entrance Free at both monasteries.

El Gouna

Around 22km north of Hurghada lies the vast tourist resort of **EL GOUNA** (ⓦelgouna .com), popular with the Egyptian jet set and Western package tourists. Built on a series of islands linked by purpose-built bridges and canals, El Gouna covers 37 square kilometres and packs in a lot, including an eighteen-hole golf course, casino, two shopping centres, (the main one with an open-air cinema), cafés, restaurants, bars, nightclubs, banks, travel agencies and a post office, plus a museum, aquarium, winery, a cheese factory and an international airport. Most hotels have **dive centres** attached – for a list of nearby dive sites, see the Hurghada account (p.581) – and watersports, horseriding, go-karting, tennis, squash and microlight flights are also available. El Gouna's state-of-the-art private **hospital** (emergencies ☎065 354 0011, ⓦelgounahospital.com.eg) has a decompression chamber (☎0122 218 7550).

ARRIVAL AND DEPARTURE EL GOUNA

By plane Charter flights serve El Gouna's small airport, but most tourists fly into Hurghada (see p.578).

By bus The El Gouna Transport Company (☎065 354 1561) runs regular buses to Cairo (12–14 daily; 6hr) and Hurghada (12–14 daily; 30min) from its ticket office on the central plaza; it's worth booking tickets in advance.

By taxi A taxi to or from Hurghada costs around £E60–80, though you'll have to bargain hard.

ACCOMMODATION, EATING AND DRINKING

There are more than a dozen three- to five-star **hotels** in El Gouna, plus numerous private villas. Among the profusion of **eating**, **drinking** and **dancing** venues are poolside snackbars, karaoke joints, discos, Bedouin tents, formal restaurants and *sheesha* cafés. Holidaymakers on full-board packages can use the "dine around" system to patronize other hotels.

Mövenpick Resort & Spa El Gouna ☎065 354 4501, ⓦmoevenpick-hotels.com. Swish a/c rooms with balconies or patios overlooking the sea, lagoon or gardens. There are four pools, a good dive centre (ⓦemperordivers .com), kiteboarding and windsurfing facilities, a 3km stretch of beach, plus spa, massage and aromatherapy centre. B&B $185

★ **Sheraton Miramar** El Gouna ☎065 354 5606, ⓦstarwoodhotels.com. Built across nine islands, the *Sheraton* is probably the pick of the hotels in El Gouna. The sparkling rooms (each accessed via a small bridge) have terraces, sea views and all the modcons you'd expect, and there are two main pools, three more for children and a dive centre. B&B €120

Three Corners Ocean View El Gouna ☎065 358 0350, ⓦthreecorners.com. Not as smart as some of its neighbours, but also a fair bit cheaper, *Ocean View* has airy, if rather plain en-suite rooms, a couple of great pools, a health centre, and a range of reasonably priced bars and restaurants. Rates are all-inclusive. €88

Hurghada and around

Over the last 25 years **HURGHADA (Ghardaka)** has been transformed from a fishing village into a booming town of around 180,000 people. This phenomenal growth is almost entirely due to **tourism**, though it's worth taking Hurghada's claims to be a seaside resort with a handful of salt: its public beaches are distant or uninviting, while the best marine life is far offshore. The town itself is pretty charmless: a sprawl of

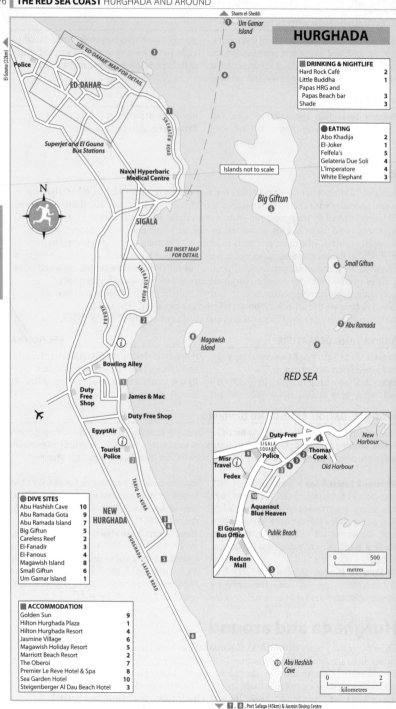

HURGHADA

Sharm el-Sheikh

Um Gamar Island

El Gouna (22km)

Police

ED-DAHAR

SEE ED-DAHAR MAP FOR DETAIL

SHERATON ROAD

Superjet and El Gouna Bus Stations

Naval Hyperbaric Medical Centre

SIGALA

SEE INSET MAP FOR DETAIL

N

7

SHERATON ROAD

HADABA

Islands not to scale

Big Giftun

Small Giftun

Abu Ramada

Magawish Island

RED SEA

Bowling Alley

Duty Free Shop

James & Mac

Duty Free Shop

EgyptAir

Tourist Police

TARIQ AL-KUBA

NEW HURGHADA

HURGHADA - SAFAGA ROAD

DRINKING & NIGHTLIFE
Hard Rock Café	2
Little Buddha	1
Papas HRG and Papas Beach bar	3
Shade	3

EATING
Abo Khadija	2
El-Joker	1
Felfela's	5
Gelateria Due Soli	4
L'Imperatore	4
White Elephant	3

DIVE SITES
Abu Hashish Cave	10
Abu Ramada Gota	9
Abu Ramada Island	7
Big Giftun	5
Careless Reef	2
El-Fanadir	3
El-Fanous	4
Magawish Island	8
Small Giftun	6
Um Gamar Island	1

ACCOMMODATION
Golden Sun	9
Hilton Hurghada Plaza	1
Hilton Hurghada Resort	4
Jasmine Village	6
Magawish Holiday Resort	5
Marriott Beach Resort	2
The Oberoi	7
Premier Le Reve Hotel & Spa	8
Sea Garden Hotel	10
Steigenberger Al Dau Beach Hotel	3

Duty Free

SIGALA SQUARE

Police

Misr Travel

Fedex

Thomas Cook

New Harbour

Old Harbour

Aquanaut Blue Heaven

El Gouna Bus Office

Public Beach

Redcon Mall

0   500
metres

0   2
kilometres

Abu Hashish Cave

7 , 8 , Port Safaga (45km) & Jasmin Diving Centre

utilitarian structures, garish hotels, gaudy shops and patches of waste ground. If you're not into diving – a score of coral islands and reefs are within a few hours' reach by boat, and many other amazing sites can be visited on liveaboards – or lazing on the beach at one of the resorts, you'll quickly find the place lacks appeal. Hurghada is extremely popular with Eastern Europeans and especially Russians, hundreds of thousands of whom visit each year; while their custom is welcome, cultural differences sometimes cause tension with locals.

There's a good **public beach** in Sigala (see below), but to **sunbathe** without unwanted attention in Hurghada you'll have to go for the private beaches. Most of the bigger hotels and resorts in Ed-Dahar and New Hurghada allow non-residents to use their beaches and pools for a fee (generally around £E30–70).

Ed-Dahar

Hurghada stretches for nearly 40km, and is divided into three main zones. The town proper – **Ed-Dahar** – is separated from the coast by a rock massif known as Jebel el-Afish. Its amorphous downtown embraces a touristy bazaar and a strip of restaurants, shops and hotels on **Hospital Street**. The main thoroughfare is **Tariq el-Nasr**, whose busiest stretch lies between the bus station and the old telephone exchange. The coastal **Corniche** is often referred to as the "Sheraton road", in reference to a now-closed hotel.

The Red Sea Aquarium

Daily 9am–10pm • £E15

If you want a glimpse of the Red Sea's wonders without getting wet, the tiny **Red Sea Aquarium** on the Corniche is worth checking out (though the tanks appear seriously undersized) with a collection including reef sharks, turtles, angelfish, puffer fish and groupers, as well as some truly fierce-looking moray eels.

Sigala and New Hurghada

From Ed-Dahar, two main roads run south to **Sigala**, which contains the modern **port** and the smart **Hurghada Marina**, home to some of Hurghada's best restaurants, bars and clubs, and a mass of hotels and resorts. The **public beach** here (daily 8am–sunset; £E5) has been transformed from a wasteland where no foreign tourist would be seen dead to a tidy shore with sunshades and small refreshment kiosks – although sunbathing female tourists may still attract a fair bit of attention.

Beyond Sigala is nothing but desert and an endless array of **resorts** and building sites dignified with the name of **New Hurghada**.

WATERSPORTS AND BOAT TRIPS IN HURGHADA

Powerful gusts make Hurghada a great place for **windsurfing** and **kiteboarding**. Several resorts have lagoons and rent out boards (around €55/day) and kites (around €85/day), and some places offer instruction: Happy Surf (**☎**0122 240 9888, **✆**happy-surf.de) at the *Hilton Hurghada Plaza* organizes windsurfing classes; Pro Center at *Jasmine Village* (**☎**0100 667 2811, **✆**tommy-friedl.de) and Colona Watersports at *Magawish Village* (**☎**0100 344 1810, **✆**colonawatersports.com) offer kiteboarding lessons.

With a couple of days' notice, Prince Safaris (**☎**012 248 4015, **✆**prince-diving.com), on Dr Sayed Koryem Street, can arrange **deep-sea fishing** day-trips for around €100 per boat including equipment. An international fishing competition is held off Hurghada's shores every February.

Most of the hotels and travel agencies can get you tickets for **glass-bottomed boat trips** (around £E50/hr). **Submarine trips** are also advertised but are not recommended as there were a couple of serious accidents in early 2012 in which several tourists died.

7

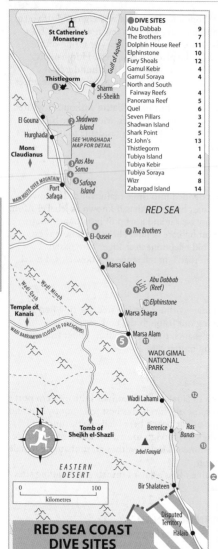

DIVE SITES	
Abu Dabbab	9
The Brothers	7
Dolphin House Reef	11
Elphinstone	10
Fury Shoals	12
Gamul Kebir	4
Gamul Soraya	4
North and South	
Fairway Reefs	4
Panorama Reef	5
Quel	6
Seven Pillars	3
Shadwan Island	2
Shark Point	5
St John's	13
Thistlegorm	1
Tubiya Island	4
Tubiya Kebir	4
Tubiya Soraya	4
Wizr	8
Zabargad Island	14

RED SEA COAST DIVE SITES

Diving

It was **diving** that really put Hurghada on the map. There are more coral islands here than reefs, including about ten islands within day-trip range and many more that can be visited on extended dive safaris or liveaboards. Sharks, giant moray eels and manta rays can also be found in deeper waters. More detailed information on Red Sea dive sites around Hurghada and elsewhere can be found in Guy Buckles's *Dive Sites of the Red Sea*.

Hurghada welcomes hordes of tourists each week, and has more than a thousand tour boats. To help combat the environmental impact of this, the **Underwater National Parks of the Red Sea and Protected Islands** enforces a daily "environmental tax" (€3) for all divers and snorkellers, the proceeds of which are ploughed back into environmental projects. This is in addition to the standard per-person charge of €3 per day to dive the Giftun Islands and the nearby reefs and €5 per day for sites further south, such as Brothers and Zabargad. The problem is also being tackled by **HEPCA** (Hurghada Environmental Protection and Conservation Association; ⓦhepca.com), which is trying to raise ecological awareness. Tourists can help by using dive centres which belong to HEPCA and display a certificate from the **Egyptian Underwater Sports Federation**.

There are **decompression chambers** in El Gouna (see p.575) and the Mubarak Naval Hyperbaric & Emergency Medical Centre (ⓣ065 354 9150 or ⓣ354 4195) in Ed-Dahar, about 500m northwest of the police station.

ARRIVAL AND DEPARTURE

BY PLANE

The airport (ⓣ065 344 3974) is 15km south of Ed-Dahar. There are daily EgyptAir flights to Cairo, regular flights to Sharm el-Sheikh and occasional flights to Luxor, as well as international connections. If you've arrived on one of the latter without a visa, you can get one from the row of bank tellers on the left before you pass through immigration; ignore the tourist agency touts who try to do it for you for an

inflated fee. A taxi to Ed-Dahar, Sigala or one of the holiday resorts should cost around £E40–50, though you'll have to haggle hard.

BY BUS

Bus timetables are notoriously subject to change, so it's advisable to ask around to find out the latest information. Superjet and (to a lesser extent) El Gouna Transport

Company buses tend to be quicker and more comfortable than those from the main bus station.

Main bus station The main bus station (☏ 065 354 7582) is on the southern edge of downtown Ed-Dahar. It's worth buying tickets for Cairo, Luxor and Aswan in advance.

Destinations Aswan (2 daily; 7hr); Cairo (10–12 daily; 6–7hr); El-Quseir (3–4 daily; 3hr); Luxor via Qena (6–7 daily; 5hr); Marsa Alam (3–4 daily; 5hr); Safaga (hourly; 1hr); Suez (12 daily; 6–7hr).

Superjet The Superjet terminal (☏ 065 355 6188) is about 1km south of Ed-Dahar along Tariq el-Nasr. Superjet has 3–4 daily services to Cairo, some of which generally continues to Alexandria (9hr), as well as a morning bus to Luxor (usually 7am; 5–6hr); buy tickets for all destinations in advance.

El Gouna Transport Company The El Gouna Transport Company terminal (☏ 065 354 1561) is next to the Superjet one and has 12–14 buses daily to Cairo via El Gouna.

BY SERVICE TAXI

Service taxis arrive at the **taxi station** on Tariq el-Nasr, near the Police Station. A fair price for seven people to hire a taxi to Luxor is around £E200/person; ignore anyone who says there's a "convoy charge" for foreigners. Groups can also consider taking a taxi all the way to Sharm el-Sheikh (upwards of £E1000) – which avoids the tedious interlude at Suez (see p.517).

Destinations Cairo (6–7hr); El-Quseir (around 2hr); Marsa Alam (3–4hr); Safaga (45min); Suez (around 5hr).

By boat The useful catamaran service between Hurghada and Sharm el-Sheikh was suspended at the time of research, but may well restart in the future.

GETTING AROUND

While **walking** is fine for getting around Ed-Dahar, transport is needed to reach Sigala or anywhere further south.

By private minibus Private minibuses run up and down the coast along the Corniche 24 hours a day, as well as along Tariq el-Nasr to the airport and beyond. They can be flagged down at any point on their route, and cost a few Egyptian pounds.

By bicycle Some tourists scoot around on rented bicycles, which are fine in town if you can handle the traffic, but are not up to trips down the coastal highway, which is often buffeted by strong crosswinds. Lots of places around

Ed-Dahar's bazaar rent bikes for £E5–10/hr.

By taxi Depending on your negotiating skills, taxis should cost around £E25–40 for journeys between Ed-Dahar and Sigala, and around £E50–70 between Ed-Dahar and the New Hurghada holiday resorts.

Car rental Avis, opposite *Aqua Village Hotel* in Sigala (☏ 065 344 4146, ⊛ avisegypt.com), has a good range of cars (including 4WDs).

INFORMATION

Travel agencies, hotels, dive centres and individual fixers are all ready to help – however, the information (especially regarding dive centres) you're given by any of these should be taken with a hefty pinch of salt as everyone earns a commission on whatever you can be induced to spend.

Tourist office Hurghada's helpful tourist information centre (daily 9am–8pm; ☏ 065 346 3221) is somewhat let down by a lack of useful leaflets; it's near EgyptAir in New Hurghada. There's a second branch (daily 4–11pm;

DANGERS OF THE DEEP

Common sense and conservation-mindedness should keep you from touching any underwater flora or fauna, particularly coral, which can be extremely sharp and is easily damaged. It's also important to avoid aggravating any potentially dangerous creatures such as **moray eels**, which may bite when threatened, or **stingrays**, which can deliver a painful dose of venom. Contact with **jellyfish**, meanwhile, can cause a mild skin irritation. Very few Red Sea species behave aggressively towards people, though there have been some well-publicised **shark** attacks (see p.534 and 540). **Poisonous creatures** to look out for include the spiny, bottom-dwelling scorpion fish, and the nocturnal lionfish, with its elaborate array of strikingly marked fins. The lethal stonefish, camouflaged as a gnarled rock, is harder to spot but fortunately rare.

Arguably the biggest dangers to divers, however, are their own actions and those of their diving company. In 2008, for example, two Danish tourists and one Egyptian went missing, presumed drowned, on a private diving trip just off the coast of Marsa Shagra, just north of Marsa Alam – a pertinent reminder of the importance of following full diving safety procedures. Then, in June 2009, a French tourist on a boat trip near Marsa Alam mistook a shark for a large fish, jumped into the water to have a closer look, and was attacked and killed by it.

⊙ 065 346 3221) around 2km north, near the *La Perla Hotel*. **Websites** The Red Sea Pages (ⓦ redseapages.com) and Hurghada Tourism (ⓦ hurghada-tourism.com) websites both have local information.

ACCOMMODATION

There are well over a hundred **hotels** in Hurghada, with many more being built. With a few honourable exceptions, standards are not that high – a good guide would be to subtract one star from whatever rating a hotel claims to have. As tour groups come year round, there's no real "off" season; **peak times** are Christmas, Easter and August–September. Budget hotels tend to be most in demand during the winter. Arriving at the bus station, you'll be mobbed by **touts**, offering free transport to their establishment. If you're set on locating a hotel on your own, bear in mind that few streets have names or house numbers. If you're coming for the diving, **package deals** organized through a dive centre tend to be the cheapest options. Hotels catering to **independent travellers** get a commission for each guest they sign up for a diving course, so if you book one with your hotel when you get there, you may be able to negotiate a discount on the price of a room.

ED-DAHAR

Most **budget places** cluster around the bazaar or the strip of cafés and shops between Sharia Abdel Aziz Mustafa and the Corniche, while **mid-range hotels** are sited off the main road near the Esh-Shahid Mosque. **El Arosa** Just off the Corniche ⊙ 065 354 8434,

---

DIVE CENTRES AND SITES AT HURGHADA

Your life may depend on **choosing the right diving centre**; always check that the instructor is qualified, with valid ID and insurance, not merely photocopies. Many are freelancers who change jobs frequently, so even the best centres sometimes get bad instructors. As a rule of thumb, it's safer to dive with the large outfits attached to the resorts than with backstreet operators taking clients sent by budget hotels (whose recommendations can't be trusted). Of Hurghada's hundred or so dive centres, most are run by Europeans and tend to have higher standards than the locally managed outfits. The ones listed below are affiliated to HEPCA and are thus subject to monitoring.

The dive centres that are members of the **Diving Emergency Centre Organization** (DECO; ⊙ 0122 218 7550, ⓦ deco-international.com) encourage clients to pay around €6 for three weeks' cover, which includes free use of the decompression chambers in Hurghada, El Gouna or Marsa Alam, doctor's fees, as well as equipment and medicines used in treatment, though not hospitalization or any transport for the injured person.

Most **dive sites** (see below) within day-trip range are to the east and northeast of Hurghada. Inexperienced divers should be wary of the northerly reefs, where the currents are strongest. While many liveaboards go as far north as Ras Mohammed, sites to the south are regarded as more prestigious. All of the following are within day-trip range unless stated otherwise.

PRICES

Never hand over cash to someone on the street who promises to arrange a trip; book through a dive centre. A four- or five-day PADI Open Water course costs around €350, while an Advanced Open Water course will set you back about €250. Scuba **equipment** is included in the price of courses, but otherwise costs around €25 extra per day. The average rate for a day's **boat diving** is €50–60; most trips include two dives and lunch. For longer trips, several centres including Colona (see opposite) can arrange **liveaboards** and diving packages (mostly lasting for a week) that go south to sites near Safaga, Marsa Alam, Wadi Gimal and Wadi Lahami, or even as far as the Zabargad Islands, about 100km southeast of Berenice. Expect to pay at least €90 per person per day.

SNORKELLING

If you don't fancy diving, there are also opportunities for snorkelling, the gear for which can be rented for €5–6 a day from most dive centres. The small reefs offshore from the *Shedwan Hotel* complex in Ed-Dahar and the *Jasmine Village* in Hurghada have been subject to noticeable damage though they do offer snorkellers a glimpse of the fish and corals that are more common further out to sea. Most dive centres offer **snorkelling trips** (around €25–40/day) and can recommend good locations at the Giftun Islands or elsewhere where you may also spot dolphins. An especially good deal is offered by Prince Safaris (see p.577), run by friendly Bedouin brothers, who can arrange snorkelling trips to the Giftun Islands for about €25.

✉ elarosahotel@yahoo.com. Reasonable though fairly small en-suite rooms with a/c and TV. Guests can use the beach at the pricier *Geisum Village* across the road, a far better option than taking a dip in the rather grotty in-house pool. Breakfast included. **££180**

Hilton Hurghada Plaza South end of the Corniche ☏ 065 354 9745, 🌐 hilton.com. Massive but isolated five-star perched on an arid hill between Ed-Dahar and Sigala. Rooms are suitably smart and come with good sea views, service is attentive and the food is of a high standard. Breakfast included. **$135**

Four Seasons Dr Sayed Koryem Street ☏ 065 354 5456, ✉ fourseasonshurghada@hotmail.com. Not to be confused with the luxury international chain of the same name, this friendly budget hotel is slightly shambolic, but acceptable at the price. Rooms come with

old a/c units, TVs and private bathrooms (many of which could do with modernization). Breakfast included. **££100**

Sea View Corniche ☏ 065 354 5959, 🌐 seaviewhotel .com.eg. A bit away from the action, *Sea View* has clean a/c rooms with white and green decor, prints of Ancient Egypt and TVs; most also have small balconies overlooking the sea across the busy Corniche. Residents can use the beach at the nearby *Sea Horse Hotel*. Breakfast included. **$30**

Three Corners Beach Resort Corniche ☏ 065 354 7816, 🌐 threecorners.com. A slight step-up in class from its sister *Empire Hotel*, this competitively priced hotel has its own beach, pool and manicured gardens. The comfortable en-suite rooms have TVs and a/c; more expensive ones also have sea views. The food is okay, though nothing to write home about. Rates include full board. **€50**

7

DIVE CENTRES

Aquanaut Blue Heaven *Regina Resort*, Sigala ☏ 065 344 0892, 🌐 aquanaut.net.

Aquarius Diving Club *Marriott Beach Resort*, New Hurghada ☏ 065 344 6950, 🌐 aquariusredsea.com.

Colona *Magawish Holiday Resort*, New Hurghada ☏ 065 346 4631, 🌐 colona.com.

Easy Divers *Three Corners Beach Resort*, Ed-Dahar ☏ 0122 230 5202, 🌐 easydivers-redsea.com.

Emperor Divers *Hilton Hurghada Plaza*, just outside Ed-Dahar ☏ 0122 737 2125, 🌐 emperordivers.com.

James & Mac Giftun *Azul Resort*, New Hurghada ☏ 0122 311 8923, 🌐 james-mac.com.

Jasmin Diving Center *Grand Seas Resort*, New Hurghada ☏ 065 346 0334, 🌐 jasmin-diving.com.

Subex Just off the Corniche, downtown Ed-Dahar ☏ 065 354 7593, 🌐 subex.org.

DIVE SITES

Abu Hashish Cave An underwater cave in a reef that was once used by dope smugglers to hide their wares.

Abu Ramada Island South of Giftun Island, this island is surrounded by a coral reef covered in psychedelic-hued soft corals; a good place for drift diving.

Abu Ramada Gota Also known as the "Aquarium", this spot has amazing standing ergs and 1500-year-old stony corals, with a profusion of bannerfish, sweetlips and spotted groupers.

Brothers Around 70km northeast of El-Quseir, these two islands – Little Brother and Big Brother – are home to two shipwrecks and several types of sharks, including hammerheads. Popular liveaboard destination.

Careless Reef North of Giftun Island, and only accessible in mild weather conditions, this popular reef has two coral towers and is home to an extended community of moray eels.

Dolphin House Reef A horseshoe-shaped reef 15km south of Marsa Alam, widely used by dolphins as a nursery for their young. HEPCA has installed buoys to

prevent boats from entering. See p.578.

El-Fanadir Located to the north of Sigala, this is one of the best dive sites in the area, with a beautiful reef slope and large table corals.

El-Fanous These coral gardens, located just off Big Giftun Island, are good for both diving and snorkelling.

Giftun Islands Most of the reefs on the Big and Small Giftun Islands have been ruined by years of dive boats dropping their anchors onto the coral, and are now mostly visited by snorkellers. Two notable spots for both snorkellers and divers are the Small Giftun Drift (fine reef wall and lovely fan corals), and the Stone Beach on the northeast side of Big Giftun.

Shadwan Island Halfway to Sharm el-Sheikh (so out of day-trip range), with sheer walls and deep trenches attracting reef and oceanic sharks.

Thistlegorm This wreck (see p.535) is cheaper and slightly easier to reach from Sharm el-Sheikh.

Um Gamar Island Sheer walls and caves, brilliant for drift diving. You can swim through a cave filled with thousands of silvery glassfish.

7

Three Corners Empire Hotel Hospital St ☏ 065 354 7186, ⓦ threecorners.com. Dominating the skyline, this large, dated hotel is an economical choice. The a/c rooms are spacious and clean, though rather stark; all have a/c, TVs and balconies overlooking the pool. Guests can use the beach at the *Three Corners Beach Resort*. Breakfast included. **€20**

SIGALA

Despite being close to a decent range of places to eat and drink, it's hard to see why anyone would want to stay in Sigala, since there are better budget and mid-range options in Ed-Dahar and ritzier resorts in New Hurghada.

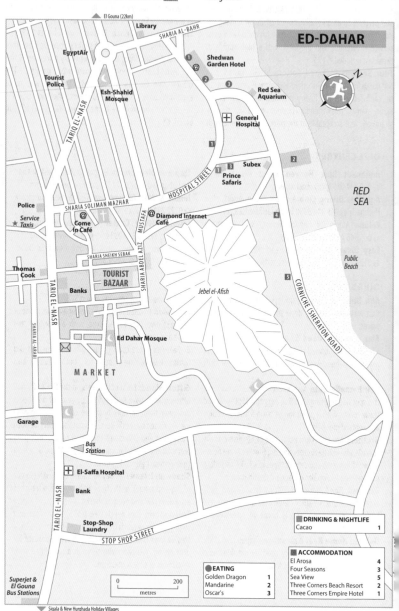

El Gouna (22km)

ED-DAHAR

Library
SHARIA AL-BAHR
EgyptAir
Shedwan Garden Hotel
Tourist Police
Esh-Shahid Mosque
Red Sea Aquarium
General Hospital
TARIQ EL-NASR
Subex
Prince Safaris
HOSPITAL STREET
Police
Service Taxis
SHARIA SOLIMAN MAZHAR
Come In Café
Diamond Internet Café
MUSTAFA
SHARIA SHEIKH SEBAK
RED SEA
Thomas Cook
TOURIST BAZAAR
SHARIA ABDEL AZIZ
Banks
Public Beach
TARIQ EL-NASR
SHARIA AL-ARABI
Jebel el-Afish
Ed Dahar Mosque
CORNICHE (SHERATON ROAD)
MARKET
Garage
Bus Station
El-Saffa Hospital
Bank
TARIQ EL-NASR
Stop-Shop Laundry
STOP SHOP STREET
Superjet & El Gouna Bus Stations
Sigala & New Hurghada Holiday Villages

DRINKING & NIGHTLIFE
Cacao 1

ACCOMMODATION
El Arosa 4
Four Seasons 3
Sea View 5
Three Corners Beach Resort 2
Three Corners Empire Hotel 1

EATING
Golden Dragon 1
Mandarine 2
Oscar's 3

0   200
metres

Golden Sun Just off Sheraton Rd ☎ 065 344 4403, ✉ goldenkhalid@hotmail.com. With friendly staff, a small garden out front, fake papyrus prints on the walls, an internet café and functional a/c rooms, *Golden Sun* does the best with what it has. **££100**

Sea Garden Hotel Off Sheraton Rd ☎ 065 344 7495, ⓦ seagarden.com.eg. The clean but plain rooms could do with a touch-up, but all have a/c, private bathrooms and wi-fi. There's a nice garden and pool, and it's close to the attractions of Hurghada Marina. Breakfast included. **$90**

NEW HURGHADA

The fully-contained **resorts** of New Hurghada are a good option if you want to spend a few days lazing on the beach or by the pool. All have a/c and private beaches. The smartest options are located at the southern end of the strip, in the Sahl Hasheesh area. All are located on the coast road; the distances stated below are measured from Ed-Dahar's bus station. Although rough prices are given below, rates for the resorts fluctuate and good deals can often be found online.

Hilton Hurghada Resort 17km ☎ 065 346 5036, ⓦ hilton.com. With a full range of facilities and the same five-star rating as its sister *Plaza* hotel (see p.581), the *Hilton Hurghada Resort* is a reliable, if unspectacular hotel. Highlights include friendly service, three pools and a modern health and fitness centre. Breakfast included. **$135**

Jasmine Village 21km ☎ 065 346 0475, ⓦ jasminevillage.com. The highlight of this simple family-friendly resort is its great little beach with a reef and windsurfing lagoon. There are also tennis and squash courts, mini golf and a small zoo and aviary, as well as straightforward rooms with TVs and fridges. All inclusive **$90**

Magawish Holiday Resort 19km ☎ 065 346 2621, ⓦ magawish.com. A former *Club Med*, *Magawish Holiday Resort* offers simple mid-range rooms, as well as a big beach and decent sports facilities, especially for windsurfing and kiteboarding, plus a children's playground. All inclusive **$100**

Marriott Beach Resort 11km ☎ 065 344 6950, ⓦ marriott.com. Although the rooms could do with a revamp, the Marriott remains a solid choice and often offers good last-minute deals. There's a large pool, small sandy beach, marina and fitness centre, as well as several restaurants and bars. Breakfast included. **$100**

★ **The Oberoi** 28km ☎ 065 344 0777, ⓦ oberoihotels .com. Located in the Sahl Hasheesh area and run by the luxury Indian chain, the award-winning *Oberoi* is the most opulent resort in the region. Attractive domed buildings house stylish rooms with sunken bath tubs overlooking private gardens; the most expensive options have their own pools. There are several excellent restaurants (including one serving Indian cuisine), great pools, spa, fitness centre and acres of lush grounds. Breakfast included. **€450**

Premier Le Reve Hotel & Spa 28km ☎ 02 2267 8560, ⓦ tropicanagroupegypt.com. In the Sahl Hasheesh area, this exclusive hotel gets consistently good reports from travellers: there are spacious en-suite rooms (most with sea views), four pools, a spa complex, numerous restaurants and bars, and several free daily shuttle buses into Sigala. All inclusive **€200**

Steigenberger Al Dau Beach Hotel 16km ☎ 065 346 5400, ⓦ steigenbergeraldaubeach.com. Large, very good-value resort with its own nine-hole (par three) golf course, comfortable rooms, pools, excellent spa and decent restaurants and bars; make sure, however, that you're not shunted into the - far less impressive - annex over the road. Breakfast included. **€67**

EATING

All the resort hotels have restaurants, often with **live music** in the evening, while some of the best restaurants (and bars, clubs and boutiques) are at the Hurghada Marina in Sigala. Alternatively, for an inexpensive meal, check out the many (often nameless) kebab, fish and pizza restaurants in Ed-Dahar and Sigala. Almost everywhere adds around ten per cent in **service taxes** to the bill – some resorts bump things up by more than twenty percent. Few restaurants have fixed opening times; most open and close depending on how many customers (or potential customers) are around. Also note that it's not advisable to drink the tap water in Hurhgada.

ED-DAHAR

Golden Dragon Hospital Street ☎ 065 355 5051. Kitsch, faux oriental decor – expect snarling dragons, red lanterns and pagoda-style roofs – but a genuine Chinese chef and great food (mains £E50–90): the salt and pepper squid is a particular highlight. Daily 1–11pm/midnight.

Mandarine Hospital Street ☎ 065 354 7007. Located close to the *Shedwan Garden Hotel*, this reliable Lebanese restaurant has a range of mixed grills, *shawarmas* and kebabs from around £E50. The house speciality is grilled pigeon with

tomato and onion. Daily 1–11pm/midnight.

Oscar's Corniche. If you can block out the road noise, this restaurant is a decent choice, with a menu featuring a range of dishes; opt for the Egyptian options – notably the kebabs – rather than the pseudo-European ones. Mains £E30–70. Daily 7am–midnight.

SIGALA

Abo Khadija East of Sigala Square. If you want an inexpensive lunch or dinner and a bit of local colour, head

7

to this tiny eatery, where you can get a hearty meal of soup, rice, salad, beans and grilled meat for around £E10–20. Daily 10am–9pm.

El-Joker Near the police station in Sigala Square ☎ 065 344 3146. This glass-walled restaurant claims to be the best seafood restaurant in town, a boast it almost lives up to. Generous portions are served at very good prices (mains from £E20) – try the calamari soup. Daily 11pm–1am.

Felfela's Sheraton Rd, south of Redcon Mall ☎ 065 344 2410. This spacious branch of the Cairo chain serves decent Egyptian food at reasonable prices (mains around £E30–60), and has a great view of the harbour. It's good for vegetarians too. Daily 8.30am–midnight.

Gelateria Due Soli Hurghada Marina ☎ 0100 138 3147. This tiny café and ice cream parlour is attached to the

L'Imperatore and is a good stop-off during the day or after dinner. It has around twenty different flavours of home-made ice cream (from £E9/scoop), plus waffles, smoothies and Illy coffee. Daily 11am–midnight.

L'Imperatore Hurghada Marina ☎ 0100 482 4903. One of the better Italian restaurants in Hurghada, with good thin-crust pizzas, a range of pasta and seafood options, friendly service and – of course – red-and-white-checked table cloths. Mains £E40–120. Daily 9am–midnight/1am.

White Elephant Hurghada Marina ☎ 0100 102 5117. This popular Thai restaurant serves tasty and nicely presented Thai food (mains £E35–110): highlights include the red and yellow curries, pad thai, *tom yam gung* and the house speciality, blue shell crab. Daily 1pm–midnight.

DRINKING AND NIGHTLIFE

A lot of **drinking** goes on in clubs, restaurants and hotels, though there aren't that many independent bars; some of the best ones are to be found at Hurghada Marina. Most restaurants don't sell alcohol during Ramadan or before 1pm on Fridays, but the holiday resorts are exempt from these restrictions. Hurghada has some of the liveliest **nightlife** in mainland Egypt, but the music is mostly mainstream. Posh places baulk at shorts or trainers; smart-casual **dress** is universally acceptable. Most charge an entry fee (generally upwards of £E25), and men on their own or in groups may not be allowed in. Many of the bigger resorts put on bellydancing shows in the evenings; any hotel or travel agency can book tickets.

ED-DAHAR

Cacao Dr Sayed Koryem St. Busy bar with regular drinks promotions, live music and plenty of wooden seats to perch on, plus burgers, pizzas and snacks if you need something to soak up the alcohol. There's also regular live music (Mon & Thurs nights) and a daily happy hour (3–6pm). Daily 24hr.

NEW HURGHADA

Hard Rock Café Across from the El-Smaka Hotel, New Hurghada ☎ 065 346 5170, ⓦ hardrock.com. Popular branch of the international chain, decorated with the usual rock memorabilia. There's a spacious outdoor area, a pricey menu featuring burgers, nachos and sandwiches (from £E40), frequent live music and DJs after midnight. Daily noon–3am.

★ **Little Buddha** Sindbad Beach Resort, New Hurghada ☎ 065 345 0120, ⓦ littlebuddha-hurghada .com. An offshoot of the *Buddha Bar* in Paris, *Little Buddha* has a good atmosphere, slick decor, subdued

lighting, tasty Southeast Asian fusion food and sushi (upwards of £E50) and potent cocktails. It turns into a DJ bar later on. Daily 4pm–4am.

SIGALA

Papas HRG and Papas Beach Bar Hurghada Marina ☎ 0106 883 1436, ⓦ papasbar.com. This buzzing bar-restaurant is a Hurghada institution and very popular with foreigners, offering a wide range of events – including pool competitions, live music and karaoke nights – and is a good spot to watch sport on the big screen. Decent food is available too (mains £E39-85). Later on, the crowd heads to the attached *Papas Beach Bar* nightclub. Daily 9am–3/4am.

Shade Hurghada Marina ☎ 0100 344 1813, ⓦ theshadebar.com. Next door to *Papas HRG*, *Shade* has a similarly buzzing atmosphere, though is somewhat less frenetic. There are scores of large bean bags to recline on whilst listening to some excellent live music and DJs and sipping a well-made cocktail (around £E55). Good food, too. Daily 1pm–2am.

DIRECTORY

Banks There are innumerable ATMs spread throughout Hurghada, including inside many of the bigger hotels. The National Bank of Egypt (Sat–Thurs 8.30am–2pm & 6–9pm) on Tariq el-Nasr in Ed-Dahar changes travellers' cheques.

Hospitals The best hospitals in the area are the El-Salam Hospital (☎ 065 354 8787, ⓦ elsalamhospital.com) on the

Corniche between the *Hilton* and the port, and the hospital in El Gouna (see p.575). Hotels and resorts have doctors on call.

Internet cafés Most hotels and many restaurants and bars offer (often free) wi-fi. There are also plenty of cybercafés (usually charging around £E5/hr), including dozens in Sigala, notably around *McDonald's*. In Ed-Dahar, try Come In Café on Sharia Soliman Mazhar or Diamond Internet Café on Hospital St.

Laundry Many hotels have in-house laundries (£E5–25/item). Alternatively try Stop-Shop off Tariq el-Nasr, 300m south of the bus station in Ed-Dahar.

Pharmacies There are several pharmacies on Sharia Abdel Aziz Mustafa and Tariq el-Nasr in Ed-Dahar, and outside the hospitals.

Post office On Tariq el-Nasr, 200m north of the bus station (daily except Fri 8.30am–2.30pm).

Tourist police The tourist police are next to the tourist office in New Hurghada (daily 24hr; ☏ 065 344 7773). To contact the police in Ed-Dahar, call ☏ 065 354 3365.

Tours Most hotels and scores of travel agencies – including Misr Travel in Sigala (☏ 065 344 2131, ⓦ misrtravel.org) – offer excursions to Luxor, Karnak, Sinai, Cairo and the Red Sea monasteries.

Travel agent Thomas Cook is in Sigala at 8 Sheraton Rd (daily 9am–2pm & 6–9pm; ☏ 065 344 3338) and in Ed-Dahar at 2 Tariq el-Nasr (same hours; ☏ 065 354 1807).

Inland from Hurghada: the Red Sea Mountains

Inland from Hurghada, the barren plains erupt into the **Red Sea Mountains**, which follow the coast southwards towards Ethiopia. This geologically primitive range of granite, porphyry and breccia contains Egypt's highest mountains outside Sinai. They are home to a few thousand Bedouin, who are perfectly at ease in the wilderness – unlike isolated groups of miners and soldiers, who feel almost as exiled as the slaves who quarried here in ancient times.

Jebel Abu Dukhaan and around

Twenty kilometres north of Hurghada, a track quits the highway and climbs inland towards **Jebel Abu Dukhaan**, the 1161-metre-high "Mountain of Smoke". Anciently known as Mons Porphyrites, this was the Roman Empire's main source of fine red porphyry, used for columns and ornamentation. Blocks were dragged 150km to the Nile, or by a shorter route to the coast, from where they were shipped to far-flung sites such as Baalbek in Lebanon or Constantinople. Round about the extensive quarries lies a ruined town of rough-hewn buildings with two large cisterns and an unfinished Ionic temple.

Under the emperors Trajan and Hadrian, the pale, black-flecked granite quarried at **Mons Claudianus**, 50km from Mons Porphyrites, was used to construct the Pantheon and Trajan's Forum in Rome. Around the quarries, beneath Jebel Fatira and Jebel Abu Hamr, you'll find numerous abandoned columns.

Jebel Gattaar and Jebel Shaayib el-Banat

Between Jebel Abu Dukhaan and Mons Claudianus rise the highest mountains in the Eastern Desert: Jebel Gattaar and Jebel Shaayib el-Banat. **Jebel Gattaar** (1963m) is esteemed by the Bedouin for its permanent springs and comparatively abundant vegetation. Further south, **Jebel Shaayib el-Banat** (at 2187m the highest in mainland Egypt) rises to a summit that the geographer and mountaineer George Murray likened to a "monstrous webbed hand of seven smoothed fingers".

TOURS   **THE RED SEA MOUNTAINS**

The Red Sea Mountains are best visited through travel operators on day excursions from Hurghada. Many companies offer half-day camel or jeep safaris ending at sunset, including a barbecue and Bedouin entertainments for around €35; try Prince Safaris in Ed-Dahar (see p.577). Red Sea Desert Adventures (see p.592) in Marsa Alam offer similar tours, as well as longer trips lasting several days taking in Mons Porphyrites and Mons Claudianus (around €100/day) and desert stargazing excursions.

South of Hurghada

Down the coast from Hurghada, the stream of holiday resorts becomes less dense until three belated spurts of development on the outskirts of **Port Safaga** (58km), **El-Quseir** (a further 85km) and **Marsa Alam** (a further 132km). Little more than an

ECO-TOURISM OR GREENWASHING?

The Red Sea Coast's booming tourism industry has prospered at serious cost to the **environment**. Rampant development, over-fishing, pollution, the degradation of coral reefs and increased pressure on water supplies are just a few of the problems. As the Hurghada Protection and Conservation Association (see p.578) warns: "Environmental deterioration is no longer a threat but a reality. Each day in the Red Sea we are witness to the depletion of the very resource base that attracts so many visitors here in the first place." In recent years numerous "**eco-lodges**" have sprung up in the region. While some – such as those run by Red Sea Diving Safari (see p.592 & 000) – have genuine green credentials, many others are simply indulging in greenwashing. Similarly not all the dive centres and travel agencies are as conservation-minded as their promotional literature might suggest. The key thing for eco-minded travellers to do is to ask lots of questions – How is waste disposed of? What is recycled? How is power usage minimized? How does the local community benefit? What conservation efforts are being made? – before deciding who to stay and dive with.

7

overgrown, grubby port, Safaga has few charms, though it is within boat range of some stunning offshore reefs, while El-Quseir retains a sleepy quality unlike anywhere else on the Red Sea. The region around Marsa Alam is home to several isolated diving camps and resorts, as well as the **Port Ghalib** tourist development, of which construction is ongoing.

Further south, communications become tenuous and bureaucratic obstacles loom as you head towards the Sudanese border. From **Bir Shalateen**, you need military permission to proceed further south, or into the mountains. The principal attraction of the far south is its reefs, which can be reached on dive boats operating out of Hurghada, Safaga, El-Quseir and Marsa Alam.

Sharm el-Naga and around

The highway south of Hurghada initially runs several kilometres inland before regaining the coast. About 40km after Hurghada and 18km before Safaga, a signpost indicates the turn-off for the wide bay of **SHARM EL-NAGA**, home of the *Sharm El-Naga Resort & Diving Centre* (☎0100 123 4540; see below). The main attraction here is the **beach diving** and **snorkelling**, and day-trippers from overcrowded Hurghada often come here to use the beach.

The luxury development of **Soma Bay**, a couple of kilometres to the south (ⓦsomabay .com), boasts a Gary Player-designed eighteen-hole golf course and a spa and thalassotherapy centre. Further south, just before Safaga, is the similar **Makadi Bay** complex.

ARRIVAL AND DEPARTURE   SHARM EL-NAGA AND AROUND

By bus Buses between Hurghada and Safaga pass by the resorts listed below, but almost all guests book package tours which include transfers.

ACCOMMODATION

Iberotel Makadi Beach Makadi Bay ☎065 359 0000, ⓦiberotel.de/en. The best hotel in Makadi Bay, the *Iberotel* offers friendly service, an extensive array of activities (from dance classes to watersports), a pool, a dive centre and comfortable en-suite rooms with sea, pool or garden views. All inclusive €146

Sharm El-Naga Resort & Diving Centre Sharm El-Naga ☎0100 111 2942, ⓦsharmelnaga.com. Although it's a bit cut off, this resort is a good option if you just want to lounge on the beach, dive or snorkel and comes with simple, sparsely furnished en-suite chalets, a big pool, bar and restaurant. All inclusive $80

Sheraton Soma Bay Soma Bay ☎065 354 5845, ⓦsheraton-somabay.com. Vast, top-notch resort with six classes of rooms, numerous restaurants and bars, a nightclub, elaborate mosaic-patterned pool, private beach and a wide range of activities (which makes it popular with families). B&B €85

TROPICAL SEA LIFE, HURGHADA (P.578)>

Port Safaga

PORT SAFAGA (Bur Safaga in Arabic) amounts to very little. Coming in from the north, you pass a slip road curving off to a series of holiday resorts on a headland, catering mainly to divers. The town, whose economy is driven by the nearby phosphate mines, begins 3km later and consists of a single windswept avenue running straight on past concrete boxes with bold signs proclaiming their function, until the bus station and a final mosque, 4km south. Silos and cranes identify the port, which runs alongside (but remains out of bounds) for most of this distance. Safaga's only attractions are the **reefs** to the north, and there's not much reason to hang around otherwise.

ARRIVAL AND GETTING AROUND   PORT SAFAGA

By bus The bus station is in the southern part of town, not far from the port.
Destinations Cairo (6–7 daily; 7–8hr); El-Quseir (3–4 daily; 2hr); Hurghada (hourly; 1hr); Luxor (6–7 daily; 4hr); Marsa Alam (3–4 daily; 4hr); Qena (6–7 daily; 3hr).
By service taxi Service taxis leave from the depot 500m

south of the port entrance and run in between buses to Hurghada and Qena for similar rates, though it can take a long time to muster enough passengers for El-Quseir.
By minibus Numerous minibuses run around Safaga and can be used to reach the resorts to the north of the town.

ACCOMMODATION

In Safaga itself, accommodation includes several pricey **hotels** near the beach and a few mid-range options on the Corniche. If you're diving, you'll probably be staying at one of the cluster of holiday resorts, all of which are around 3–5km north of town.

Lotus Bay Resort & Gardens Around 3km north of town ☎ 065 326 0003, ⊛ lotusbay.com. Peaceful resort with neat and tidy rooms in a collection of whitewashed villas spread across a nice garden. There's also a gym, spa, tennis and squash courts, a big pool and dive and windsurfing centres. B&B $70
Menaville Resort Around 5km north of town ☎ 065 326 0064, ⊛ menaville-resort.com. The climbing plants that cover the whitewashed buildings give a Mediterranean feel to this resort, which also boasts a large pool, gardens and clean and simple rooms. It's also home to a spa and

"climatotherapy centre", which offers treatment for psoriasis and rheumatism, capitalizing on Safaga's supposedly propitious natural enivronment – including high UV levels in the sunshine and some radioactivity in the sands. B&B $70
Nemo On the Corniche ☎ 065 325 6777, ⊛ nemodive .com. This Belgian and Dutch-owned hotel is firmly geared towards divers, with a range of economical accommodation-and-diving packages. Staff are friendly, rooms are clean, there's a children's play area and the hotel's private beach has its own reef. B&B €38

DIVING AND SNORKELLING IN SAFAGA

Boats and instructors at the main **dive centres** tend to be committed to groups, though they will take on independent travellers if they have space: expect to pay around €300 for a PADI Open Water course or around €50 for two boat dives. As in Hurghada, an **environmental fee** of €3 a day is levied on all divers and snorkellers. The main diving grounds lie 6–8km offshore from the holiday resorts between Safaga Island and the Ras Abu Soma headland to the north. **Tubiya Island** is ringed with corals just off its beach, while dive boats drop their clients directly over the sunken **North and South Fairway Reefs** or the twin pairs of sites known as **Tubiya Kebir**, **Tubiya Soraya**, **Gamul Soraya** and **Gamul Kebir**. Other sites include the **Seven Pillars** off Ras Abu Soma, and the **Panorama Reef** and **Shark Point**, 10km east of Safaga Island. Most of them are notable for their coral pillars and strong currents. Note that among the big fish prevalent in these waters are aggressive **hammerhead sharks**.

DIVE CENTRES

Barakuda Diving *Lotus Bay* ☎ 065 325 3911, ⊛ barakuda-diving.com.
Ducks Diving *Safaga Palace* ☎ 0100 138 6091, ⊛ ducks-diving.com.

Orca *Hotel Orca Village* ☎ 065 326 0111, ⊛ orca-diveclubs.com.
Shams Safaga Resort Dive Centre *Shams Safaga Resort* ☎ 065 326 0044, ⊛ shamshotels.com.

Safaga Palace Resort Around 5km north of town ☎ 065 326 0100, ⓦ safagapalaceresort.com. Large, long-standing resort with an outsized curvy pool at its centre, several restaurants and bars (including a British-style pub), dive, kiteboarding and windsurfing centres and a health club and spa. Rooms are comfortable and many have sea views, though the decor is drab. B&B **£E500**

EATING

All the hotels and resorts have their own restaurants, but there are also a few inexpensive places to eat in town.

Ali Baba 2km north of the town centre. Popular restaurant offering tasty, good-value Egyptian/Middle Eastern cuisine, including mezze, fresh fish and seafood, and grilled meats. As ever, the Western-style dishes are more hit and miss. Mains from £E30. Daily noon–10pm.

DIRECTORY

Banks and exchange There are several banks and ATMs, including the National Bank of Egypt in the town centre and Banque du Caire in an arcade near the *Safaga Palace Resort*.

Hospital On the main street, Sharia el-Gumhorriya, in the centre of town.
Police station On the main street, 500m south of the hospital.

El-Quseir

EL-QUSEIR, 85km from Safaga, is another phosphates extraction centre, though with fewer inhabitants and more appeal. In pharaonic times, boats sailed from here to the "Land of Punt" (thought to be Yemen or Somalia), as depicted in reliefs within Hatshepsut's temple at Deir el-Bahri. The Romans knew it as Leukos Limen ("White Harbour"), while under Arab rule El-Quseir was the largest Red Sea port until the tenth century, remaining a major transit point for pilgrims until the 1840s, when Flaubert caught its last flickers of exoticism.

Today, El-Quseir is a sleepy place, mostly unaffected by tourism, despite the resorts on its outskirts. Life moves pretty slowly, except on Fridays, when Ma'aza and Ababda Bedouin flock in for the weekly **market**. The best **dive sites** nearby are the Brothers, east of El-Quseir, and the Elphinstone and Abu Dabbab reefs, down towards Marsa Alam, although the Quei and Wizr reefs are closer. All the resorts have their own **dive centres** although they may not allow outside divers to join their trips; it's best to book a dive package deal from the outset.

The fortress

Daily 9am–5pm • £E10

Smack in the town centre, just past the main traffic roundabout, sits El-Quseir's most impressive landmark, the sixteenth-century crumbling **walled fortress**, which now houses a museum. Designed to protect trade routes used by the Ottomans, the fortress declined after trade was diverted around the Cape of Good Hope. Napoleon's army raised the French flag here in 1799, only to attract the attention of British warships sailing off the coast. The French survived a brief assault, but abandoned the fort two years later. Its most recent occupant was the Egyptian army, stationed here until 1975. The cistern, watchtower (climb up for excellent views) and rooms built into the walls of the fortress each contain small exhibits on the history and traditions of the Red Sea coast.

The rest of the town

In addition to the fortress, El-Quseir has a few other sights that are worth a quick look, including a small **harbour** where you can see local boat-builders at work, and a beachside **promenade**, good for a stroll. A few blocks back from the waterfront, past a number of shuttered and balconied houses, are the thirteenth-century **Faran Mosque** and an imposing former **quarantine hospital** dating back to the nineteenth century.

ARRIVAL AND DEPARTURE

EL-QUSEIR

By bus The bus station is about 3km north of the fortress; you can take a taxi (around £E10–20) or a minibus to the town centre.

Destinations Cairo (5 daily; 10–11hr); Hurghada (5 daily; 3hr); Marsa Alam (4 daily; 2hr); Safaga (5 daily; 2hr); Suez (1 daily; 9–10hr).

By service taxi Service taxis to Cairo, Hurghada, Safaga and Marsa Alam depart when full from a stand next to the bus station.

ACCOMMODATION

Hotel Al Quseir Hotel Sharia Port Said in the town centre ⓣ065 333 2301, ⓦalquseirhotel.com. Occupying a refurbished 1920s home with charming rooms, this atmospheric hotel is a welcome break for mid-range travellers tired of boxy concrete bungalows – although rates may seem a bit steep considering the facilities. None of the rooms is en suite, but the more expensive ones have a/c and sea views. B&B **£E138**

7

★ **Mövenpick Resort El Quseir** 7km north of town ⓣ065 333 2100, ⓦmoevenpick-hotels.com. This Nubian-style resort is one of the few in this part of Egypt that has managed to blend with the local environment and culture, offering classy rooms and every facility imaginable, including a dive centre and spa. B&B **$115**

Radisson Blu 3km north of town ⓣ065 335 0260, ⓦradissonblu.com. Running a close second to the Mövenpick, this beautifully designed hotel has swish rooms (all with private balcony or terrace) in pinkish domed buildings, a trio of pools, a dive centre, private beach and lagoon and a spa featuring Balinese and Ayurvedic treatments. B&B **$80**

Rocky Valley Diver's Camp 10km north of town ⓣ065 326 0055, ⓦrockyvalleydiverscamp.com. Located close to several great reefs, *Rocky Valley* has a mix of bungalows and Bedouin-style tents, plus a restaurant and diving facilities. The camp is often booked up by tour groups, so independent travellers should call or email in advance. Also offers all-inclusive packages including diving and pick-ups. B&B **€100**

EATING AND DRINKING

There is only a handful of places to eat in the town, and if you want an alcoholic drink you'll have to head to one of the resorts.

Marianne Sharia Port Said, in the town centre ⓣ0100 946 8198. This inexpensive joint, located in the atmospheric older part of town, is a good place to sample some local seafood (mains from around £E30), with the calamari dishes a particular highlight. Daily noon–9/10pm.

ROCK ART

The **rock art** of the Eastern Desert is one of Egypt's best-kept secrets. Spread over 24,000 square kilometres of desert east of Luxor and Edfu, the sites vary from a single boulder to cliff walls dotted with pictures of people and animals, flotillas of boats and herds of giraffes, ostriches and elephants. They are difficult to reach, however, and it's easy to get lost – at least one group has died in the area – so it's vital to go with a guide. There are three main places of interest: two are partially accessible by 2WD, using the roads between El-Quseir and Qift or Marsa Alam and Edfu, but all of the wadis between them require 4WD.

Created before the unification of Egypt (c.3100 BC), the rock art sheds light on the origins of Egyptian civilization. The oldest human figures are gods or chieftains in ostrich-feather headdresses, brandishing maces – intriguingly similar to the "Conquering Hero" motif in pre- and Early Dynastic art at Hierakonopolis in the Nile Valley. They often appear standing in boats, and are frequently surrounded by ostriches, elephants or cattle. Both Hans Winkler, who did seminal research in the 1930s, and David Rohl, who made recent studies, believe the oldest boats represent "Eastern Invaders" from Mesopotamia, who reached Egypt by the Red Sea and conquered the indigenous people of the Nile Valley, kickstarting Egyptian civilization.

Permits are required for visiting these sites: both Red Sea Desert Adventures (see p.592) and Ancient World Tours (UK ⓣ020 7917 9494, ⓦancient.co.uk) can obtain them and organize excursions.

DIRECTORY

Banks and exchange The National Bank of Egypt is on Sharia el-Gumhorriya, 150m north of the roundabout, but it doesn't have an ATM.

Between El-Quseir and Marsa Alam

The coastal road south of El-Quseir runs through some of the most amazing landscapes in Egypt, with a shimmering turquoise sea, long empty stretches of beach and huge expanses of desert disappearing into the distance. The 132km stretch to Marsa Alam is sprinkled with holiday resorts, but although this part of the Red Sea Coast is growing in popularity with holiday-makers and divers, its tourist infrastructure is far from developed.

Next to Marsa Alam's international airport, 50km north of the town, is **Port Ghalib** (ⓦportghalib.com), a Kuwaiti-funded development similar in style – though not yet in scale – to El Gouna (see p.575). Construction work is ongoing, but when it is completed it will stretch along 18km of coast, with shops, a golf course, apartments, hotels, a promenade and a three-hundred-berth yacht marina. Several resorts are already open.

7

ACCOMMODATION   BETWEEN EL-QUSEIR AND MARSA ALAM

★ **InterContinental The Palace Port Ghalib Resort** Port Ghalib ☎065 336 0000, ⓦintercontinental .com. This impressive hotel is currently the best in Port Ghalib, with stylish rooms, attentive service and modern facilities including spa and gym, a large pool and a saltwater "lagoon", as well as a private beach. B&B €70

Oasis 25km north of Marsa Alam ☎0100 505 2855, ⓦoasis-marsaalam.com. The peaceful German-run *Oasis* is a good option for divers, offering clean Bedouin-style chalets (#23 has a bath with a sea view), a large pool, massage and beauty treatments, and a range of excursions, as well as a branch of Sinai Divers (see p.592). Half board €56

★ **Shagra Village** 20km north of Marsa Alam ☎065 338 0021, ⓦmarsa-shagra.org. The northernmost of three camps run by Red Sea Diving Safari, *Shagra Village* is an eco-friendly beachside dive centre that aims to minimize the impact of diving and tourism, with comfortable tents, huts and en-suite chalets. Underwater weddings – with the bride and groom in full scuba gear – are available. Full board: tents €40; huts €45; chalets €55

Marsa Alam

The town of **MARSA ALAM** itself is undistinguished, consisting of a large army base, some government buildings and apartment blocks constructed for the expected influx of hotel staff to the area, grafted onto a fishing port where liveaboards now moor. The area around the town, however, has become a diving hub, and there are some excellent **dive sites** within striking distance. The best places to stay are outside Marsa Alam to the north (see above) and the south (see p.593).

ARRIVAL AND INFORMATION   MARSA ALAM

By plane Some 50km north of the town Marsa Alam's airport (ⓦmarsa-alam-airport.com) has regular flights to Cairo and destinations in Europe and the Middle East. There's no public transport from the airport so you'll need to arrange a pick-up with your hotel or resort.

By bus The bus stand is on the edge of town, 800m west of the traffic circle.

Destinations Bir Shalateen (generally 1 daily, though the service isn't too reliable; 4hr); El-Quseir (3–4 daily; 2hr); Hurghada (3–4 daily; 5hr); Safaga (3–4 daily; 4hr).

By service taxi Service taxis depart from a stand on the northern edge of the town, serving most of the same destinations as the buses, but usually a bit quicker.

Banks Several of the bigger resorts in the area, including the *Kahramana Hotel*, 25km north of town, have mini bank branches and ATMs.

South of Marsa Alam

For keen divers who have made it this far, there are several camps and hotels to the south of town offering the opportunity to explore the most remote **dive sites** in the

7

El-Quseir, Airport & Port Ghalib

MARSA ALAM

2

Marsa Shagra

3

Hyperbaric Medical Centre

N

RED SEA

Marsa Alam

Bus Station/ Service Taxis

1

```
0          10
    kilometres
```

● **DIVE SITE**
Dolphin House Reef   1

■ **ACCOMMODATION**
InterContinental The Palace Port Ghalib Resort	1
Lahami Bay	7
Marsa Nakari Village	4
Oasis	2
Shagra Village	3
Shams Alam	5
Wadi Lahami Village	6

5 , 6 , 7 , Wadi Gimal National Park, Wadi Lahami ▼ & Berenice

4

southern Red Sea – and to experience an eerily empty and barren region of mountains, ocean and reef far removed from the commercialized northern Red Sea coast.

One of the most popular of these dive sites is the **Dolphin House Reef** (also known as Samadai Reef), a crescent-shaped protected area set up in 2001 to protect the area's spinner dolphins. Tourist numbers to the reef have been capped at two hundred per day – previously there were up to 2,500 – and it's now a great spot for snorkelling as well as diving. Other notable dive sites include **Elphinstone**, a 300-metre-long reef ideal for drift diving; **Abu Dabab**, a series of sheltered reefs; **Fury Shoals**, a set of reefs rich in marine life; and **St John's**, a site with caves, black coral and – if you're lucky – sharks.

Wadi Gimal National Park

The closest park entrance to Marsa Alam is 50km south of town, close to the Shams Alam Beach Resort • Daily sunrise–sunset • £E20

A unique protected area covering 6000 square kilometres of land and 4000 square kilometres of sea, **Wadi Gimal National Park** is home to an interesting mix of archeological sites and wildlife. The area once lay on an important trading route, and there are several pharaonic and Roman ruins to explore, including the village of Geli and an old emerald mine. Wild gazelle can also be seen, while in spring and the autumn you may be able to spot migrant birds such as osprey, falcons, white-eyed gulls and the occasional flamingo. Red Sea Desert Adventures (ⓦredseadesertadventures.com) and the *Shams Alam Beach Resort* (see p.593) can organize dives, excursions and overnight camping in the park.

DIVING AND DESERT SAFARIS AROUND MARSA ALAM

There are some excellent diving opportunities in and around Marsa Alam. Two good **operators** are Sinai Divers (ⓣ0100 505 2855, ⓦsinaidivers.com) at the *Oasis* resort, and Red Sea Diving Safari (ⓣ0122 399 3860, ⓦredsea-divingsafari.org) at *Shagra Village*. *Shagra Village* is also home to Egypt's most southerly decompression chamber, the Hyperbaric Medical Centre (ⓣ0122 165 3806); divers are encouraged to take out cover in case they have to use it (around €6 for three weeks).

If you want to **explore the interior**, Red Sea Diving Safari also offers a range of trips, including birdwatching in Wadi Gimal National Park (see above) and stargazing excursions in the desert.

Lahami Bay 138km south of Marsa Alam ☎02 2753 7100, ⓦlahamibay.com. The southernmost resort on the Red Sea coast, the top-end *Lahimi Bay* features Mediterranean and Far Eastern touches, stylish rooms decorated with local artwork, several restaurants, cafés and bars, plus tennis courts, sauna, fitness centre and windsurfing facilities. Its dive area is a further 50km south at the port of Ras Banata, whose island reefs are home to one of the few undisturbed breeding grounds for sea turtles in the region. All inclusive €185

Marsa Nakari Village 40km south of Marsa Alam ☎065 338 0021, ⓦmarsa-nakari.org. Run by Red Sea Diving Safari, this camp faces a sheltered bay and offers accommodation in tents, huts and chalets; the first two share bathrooms, the latter are en suite. As well as diving, kayaking, massages and desert safaris are all available. Full

board: tent €40; hut €45; chalet €55

Shams Alam 50km south of Marsa Alam ☎0122 244 4931, ⓦshamshotels.com. This large resort is ideal for anyone who wants to explore the neighbouring Wadi Gimal National Park. As well as comfortable (though slightly overpriced) rooms surrounding the pool, there's also a dive centre, health club and plenty of activities on offer. All inclusive $140

Wadi Lahami Village 135km south of Marsa Alam, near the village of Hamata ☎065 338 0021, ⓦwadi-lahami.org. Also run by Red Sea Diving Safari, *Wadi Lahimi* caters for experienced divers, with a mix of accommodation in tents and en-suite chalets, offering diving courses and trips, free diving, kiteboarding and birdwatching in the nearby mangroves. Full board: tents €40; chalets €55

7

The far south

As the coast road heads southwards to the Sudanese border, the seemingly endless coastline is almost completely empty except for the occasional mangrove, grazing camel or cluster of tanks left by the military. Some 145km south of Marsa Alam is the town of **BERENICE**, named after Ptolemy II's wife, on whose suggestion a trading port was established here in 275 BC. Abandoned during the fifth century AD, the site was excavated in 1818 by Belzoni, who found a Temple of Semiramis.

Nowadays, Berenice amounts to a few characterless buildings clustered together in a windswept bay. Its hinterland, however, has several would-be attractions. For climbers, there is the challenge of Egypt's "most aggressive peaks", **Jebel Farayid** and the **Berenice Bodkin** – one of the largest rock spires in the whole of North Africa and the Middle East. Here, too, are the ruins of the Ancient **Emerald Mines of Wadi Sakait**, which were worked from pharaonic through to Roman and Islamic times, before being abandoned. Nearby is a small Ptolemaic rock temple, dedicated to Isis and Serapis.
Red Sea Desert Adventures (see opposite) can organize trips from Marsa Alam taking in Berenice and Wadi Sakait.

Off the coast 100km southeast of Berenice is **Zabargad Island**, whose deep reefs teeming with fish and corals are a favourite destination for liveaboards.

South to the Sudanese border

For geopolitical reasons, the area south of the town of Bir Shalateen has long been off-limits. During the early 1980s, the US military staged war games here. More recently, it has been a bone of contention between Egypt and Sudan, whose common border was arbitrarily set by the British in 1899. After independence, both countries agreed this was unfair on the Bishari nomads whose tribal grounds straddled the border, so a slice of Egyptian territory was placed under Sudanese administration – this worked fine until Sudan granted a Canadian oil company offshore exploration rights, and Egypt responded by sending in troops to reassert its sovereignty. Since 1992, the region from **Bir Shalateen** down to **Halaib** has been under military rule.

At present, tourists are allowed to travel at least as far as **Bir Shalateen**, which has a daily camel market; Red Sea Desert Adventures (see opposite) runs interesting trips here.

WALL PAINTING, TOMB OF SETI I, VALLEY OF THE KINGS

Contexts

History

The present borders of Egypt are almost identical to those in pharaonic times, territories such as Sinai and Nubia being essentially marginal to the heartland of the Nile Valley and its Delta, where Egyptian civilization emerged some five thousand years ago. The historical continuity is staggering: the pharaonic era alone lasted thirty centuries before being appropriated by Greek and Roman emperors.

Egypt's significance in the ancient world was paramount, and the country has never been far from the front line of world history. Although neither Christianity nor Islam was born in Egypt, both are stamped with its influence. In modern times, when the Arab world sought to rid itself of European masters, Egypt was at the forefront of the anti-colonial struggle, while its peace treaty with Israel altered the geopolitics of the Middle East. Today, Egypt is once again in the news, having elected an Islamist president, with far-reaching implications for the region.

Prehistoric and Pre-dynastic Egypt

Stone tools from the gravel beds of Upper Egypt and the Gilf Kebir in the Western Desert attest to the presence of **hunter-gathering hominids** over 250,000 years ago, when the Sahara was a lush savanna that supported zebras, elephants and other game. Between around 70,000 and 24,000 BC, there were fluctuating wet and dry periods, when lakes rose or shrank and grasslands expanded or receded, and tribes are assumed to have moved backwards and forwards between the Nile and the oases. While most still lived by hunting and fishing, herding cattle emerged even before cereal cultivation, sheep and goat herding filtered through from the Near East (c.7000 BC).

During the **Neolithic** era, Middle Egypt and the Delta had **settled communities** that cultivated wheat and flax, herded flocks and wove linen. Although some reverted to nomadism after the rains of the Neolithic era checked the process of desertification, others remained to develop into agricultural societies. Between 6600 and 4700 BC, human occupation of the Western Desert reached its peak, giving rise to the **rock art** in the Cave of the Swimmers and other sites at the Gilf Kebir and Jebel Uwaynat.

The impetus for development came from southern Egypt. At **Nabta Playa**, 100km west of Abu Simbel, archeologists have identified the world's **oldest calendar** of standing stones and sculpted monoliths – dating from around 6000 BC – that attests to a Neolithic culture with a knowledge of astronomy and the resources and organization to create such a site. And then there are the mysterious **boats** drawn in the Eastern Desert perhaps a thousand years later, which some believe represent "Eastern Invaders" who conquered the indigenous people of the Nile Valley.

Evidence of later agricultural societies is less impressive. The **Naqada I** period, from about 4000 BC onwards, was characterized by larger settlements and a distinctive style of pottery. Clay and ivory figurines show Naqada menfolk sporting beards and

c.250,000 BC	c.25,000 BC	c.6000 BC	c.5000 BC
Hunter-gathering hominids roam the vast savannas to the west of the Nile Valley.	Late Paleolithic era. Onset of desertification until rains of Neolithic era.	Middle Neolithic era. Intensive occupation of the Western Desert by hunter-gatherers.	Pastoralism becomes widespread in the Eastern and Western deserts, while Badarian culture takes root in the Nile Valley.

penis shields, like their Libyan neighbours. More extraordinary are the narrow-necked vases carved from basalt, which can't be reproduced by twenty-first-century technology. **Naqada II** graves (containing copper tools, glazed beads and lapis lazuli from Asia) evolved from simple pits into painted tombs lined with mats and wood and, later still, brick.

The development of extensive **irrigation** systems (c.3300 BC) boosted productivity and promoted links between communities in Upper and Lower Egypt, giving rise to two loose **confederations**. As power coalesced around Naqada in the south and Behdet in the Delta, each confederation became identified with a chief deity and a symbol of statehood: Seth and the White Crown with **Upper Egypt**, Horus and the Red Crown with the **Delta**.

Later, each acquired a new capital (Hierakonpolis and Buto, respectively) and strove for domination; the eventual triumph of the southern kingdom resulting in the **unification of the Two Lands** (c.3100 BC) under the quasi-mythical ruler **Menes** (aka Narmer). Some identify him as pharaoh Aha, whose tomb is the earliest found at Saqqara, but if the Greek name "Menes" is derived from the Egyptian *mena* (Establisher), it may not refer to any actual individual.

The Archaic Period and Old Kingdom

The **Early Dynastic** or **Archaic Period** was the formative epoch of Egyptian civilization. Its beginnings are a mix of history and myth, relating to the foundation – supposedly by Menes – of the city of **Memphis**, located at the junction between Upper and Lower Egypt: the first imperial city on earth. From Memphis, the third and fifth kings of the **I Dynasty** (c.3100–2890 BC) attempted to bring Sinai under Egyptian control. Writing, painting and architecture became increasingly sophisticated, while royal tombs at Saqqara and Abydos developed into complex mastabas. At this time, royal burials were accompanied by the deceased's servants – a practice that later dynasties abandoned.

Also indicative of future trends was the dissolution of the unified kingdom as

---

ALTERNATIVE CHRONOLOGIES

Egyptology is riddled with uncertainties, not least in its chronology of dynasties and kingdoms (not an Egyptian concept, but a modern invention enabling scholars to get a handle on three thousand years of history). In *A Test of Time*, **David Rohl** argues that only one of the "Four Pillars" of synchronicity between Ancient Egyptian and Biblical history is impeccable, and that evidence calls for the Third Intermediate Period to be shortened by 300 years, with knock-on effects on earlier times. Rohl's **New Chronology** puts the Exodus in the XIII rather than the XIX Dynasty, and makes Akhenaten a contemporary of David and Saul. In the 1990s, disputes over the age of the Sphinx provided support for the theory advanced by **Anthony West** in *Serpent in the Sky*, that the Egyptian temples embody the legacy of a far older, greater civilization. In this book we've stuck to **orthodox chronologies**, about which even mainstream Egyptologists differ and acknowledge margins of error. These are up to a hundred years in the period around 3000 BC, seventy-five years around 2000 BC, and between ten and fifteen years around 1000 BC. From 500 BC onwards, dates are fairly precise until the Ptolemaic era, when the chronology gets hazy, only firming up again in Roman times.

---

c.4000 BC	c.3100 BC	c.2686–2613 BC	c.2613–2494 BC
Naqada I culture in Upper Egypt.	Unification of the Two Lands (Upper and Lower Egypt) by Menes. Foundation of Memphis.	III Dynasty: Zoser; Sekhemkhet; Huni. Building of the first pyramids at Saqqara and Maidum.	IV Dynasty: Snofru; Cheops; Chephren; Mycerinus. Bent Pyramid at Dahshur; Pyramids of Giza.

centralized authority waned. Although briefly restored by Raneb, regional disputes persisted throughout the **II Dynasty** (c.2890–2686 BC), inspiring the mythological **contendings of Seth and Horus**. Rivalry between the regions and their respective deities appears to have been resolved under Khasekhemwy, the last king of the dynasty – paving the way for an era of assurance.

During the **III Dynasty** (c.2686–2613 BC), technological advances and developments in culture raised Egypt to an unprecedented level of civilization. The dynasty's foremost ruler was **Zoser** (or Djoser), whose architect, **Imhotep**, built the first **Step Pyramid** at Saqqara in the 27th century BC. Its conception and construction was a landmark, and later generations deified Imhotep as the ultimate sage. The III Dynasty also sent expeditions into Sinai, to seek gold and copper and subjugate the local Bedouin.

Scholars differ over whether the III Dynasty belongs to the Archaic Period or the succeeding **Old Kingdom**, when pyramid-building and expansionism were likewise pursued during the **IV Dynasty** (c.2613–2494 BC), whose first king, **Snofru** (aka Sneferu), raised two pyramids at Dahshur and raided Nubia and Libya. His successors, **Cheops** (Khufu), **Chephren** (Khafre) and **Mycerinus** (Menkaure), erected the **Pyramids of Giza**, expanded trade relations with the Near East and developed mining in Nubia. Though Snofru's line expired with the death of **Shepseskaf**, his widow Queen **Khentkawes** is believed to have married a high priest to produce an heir.

During the **VI Dynasty** (c.2345–2181 BC), nobles were buried in their own **nomes** (provinces) rather than at Saqqara, and these nomarchs became increasingly powerful, until the situation reached the point of no return under **Pepi II** (aka Neferkare), whose death heralded the **end of the Old Kingdom**.

The Middle Kingdom

There followed a century of internal strife, known to Egyptologists as the **First Intermediate Period**. The Greek historian Manetho records seventy rulers during the brief VII Dynasty; no one knows the number during the VIII Dynasty. When famine struck, weak principalities allied themselves with **Herakleopolis**, the capital of the Twentieth Nome, whose ruler, **Achthoes**, gained control of Middle Egypt and founded the **IX Dynasty** in 2160 BC. While this controlled the north, Upper Egypt was contested by the rulers of Edfu and Luxor (known to history as **Thebes**), until the Theban ruler Inyotef Sehertowy triumphed, founding the **XI Dynasty**.

The struggle between north and south was finally resolved by **Nebhepetre Mentuhotpe II**, who reunited the Two Lands in 2055 BC, establishing the **Middle Kingdom**. During his fifty-year reign, mines and trade routes reopened; incursions into Libya, Nubia and Sinai resumed; and arts and crafts flourished again. His successors sent expeditions to the Land of Punt (present-day Somalia), one of them commanded by **Amenemhat I**, who returned the capital to Memphis, annexed northern Nubia, furthered trade with Palestine and Syria, and founded the **XII Dynasty** (c.1991–1786 BC).

Under **Senusert I** (aka Sesostris I) the administrative capital was transferred to the **Fayoum**, where massive waterworks were undertaken. Amenemhat II curbed the power of the nomarchs, while Senusert III may have abolished the office completely. These kings also built **the last pyramids**, at Lahun, El-Lisht and Hawara, where the final

c.2494–2345 BC	**c. 2345–2181 BC**	**c.2181–2025 BC**	**c.2160–2130 BC**
V Dynasty: Userkaf; Sahure; Neferefre; Nyuserre; Unas.	VI Dynasty: Teti; Pepi I; Pepi II. More pyramids at Saqqara.	VII and VIII dynasties: period of anarchy and fragmentation of power.	IX and X dynasties: Achthoes. Capital at Herakleopolis, near Beni Suef.

pyramid was erected by Amenemhat III.

According to Rohl's New Chronology, it was **Amenemhat III** who took **Joseph** as his vizier and let the **Israelites** settle in the Delta. Graves at Avaris suggest a large Semitic population stricken by calamities, akin to the Biblical account of the events leading up to the Exodus, which Rohl assigns to the reign of the XIII Dynasty pharaoh **Dudimose**. These attributions are utterly at variance with orthodox chronology, which places the Exodus during the New Kingdom, over two hundred years later.

Yet there's no doubt that the late XII Dynasty was a **troubled time**, with floods bringing poor harvests and famine in their wake. The faces of the statues of pharaohs of this era are uniquely stern and careworn. Whether or not Egypt was also smitten by plagues and disrupted by an exodus from the Delta, it was obviously in poor shape to resist an invasion.

The Hyksos invasion

Under the XIII Dynasty Egypt slid towards an era of disorder termed the **Second Intermediate Period**. For the first time, Lower Egypt fell into the hands of "rulers of foreign lands" or *heka kaswt* – later rendered by the historian Manetho as **Hyksos**. Manetho relates that "invaders of obscure race" appeared in the reign of Dudimose, but many archeologists believe that they gradually filtered into the Delta and only took over later. They had weapons and technology which gave them an edge over the Egyptians: chariots, bronze armour, helmets and swords, and recurved bows that outranged the Egyptian ones. Although Egyptian chronicles describe their rule as anarchic, the *Rhind Mathematical Papyrus* suggests that the Hyksos fostered aspects of native culture, and their introduction of the *shaduf* (counterweighted draw-well) irrigation device proved of lasting benefit to Egyptian agriculture.

Ruling Lower Egypt from the Delta city of **Avaris**, the Hyksos tolerated a separate XIV or Xois Dynasty in the western Delta until about 1650 BC, and pursued peaceful trade with Thebes until the **Theban XVII Dynasty** ruler Sekenenre Tao II resumed war with Lower Egypt. His son **Khamose** was within striking distance of Avaris when he died, whereupon his brother, **Ahmosis I**, finally expelled the Hyksos from Egypt (c.1550 BC), ushering in a new era.

The New Kingdom

The **XVIII Dynasty** (c.1550–1295 BC) founded by Ahmosis I inaugurated the **New Kingdom**, a period of stability, wealth and expansion, whose rulers include some of the most famous names in Egyptian history. Their formidable war machine subdued **Nubia** (yielding gold, ivory, ebony, gems and slaves) and established colonies or local satrapies in Syria and Palestine. An influx of immigrants into Egypt introduced new customs, ideas and technology.

The effects are evident at **Thebes**, capital of the New Kingdom, where a spate of temples and tombs symbolize the pre-eminence of the god Amun and the power of the pharaohs. While **Tuthmosis I** (c.1504–1492 BC) built the first tomb in the Valley of the Kings, his daughter **Hatshepsut** raised the great mortuary temple of Deir el-Bahri, ruling as pharaoh (c.1473–58 BC) despite her stepson's claim on the throne.

Having belatedly assumed power, **Tuthmosis III** embarked on conquests beyond the

2133–1991 BC	c.2055–1985 BC	c.1985–1795 BC	c.1750–1650 BC
XI Dynasty (Thebes only): Inyotef Sehertowy.	XI Dynasty (all Egypt): Nebhepetre Mentuhotpe II reunites Two Lands (c.2055 BC).	XII Dynasty: Amenemhat I; Senusert I and II; Amenemhat III. Pyramids at Lahun, Lisht and Hawara.	XIII Dynasty (1795–1650 BC) and XIV Dynasty (c.1750–1650BC).

Fourth Cataract in Nubia and across the Euphrates to the borders of the Hittite Empire. Many biblical scholars believe that Tuthmosis III was the pharaoh of the Exodus (though other XVIII rulers have also been fingered).

His successor **Amenhotep II** (c.1427–1400 BC) penetrated deeper into Nubia, and **Tuthmosis IV** (c.1400–1390 BC) strengthened the empire by marrying a princess of Mitanni, a state bordering the Hittites.

The zenith of Egyptian power coincided with the reign of **Amenhotep III** (c.1390–52 BC), who devoted himself to the construction of great edifices such as Luxor Temple. During the same period, a hitherto minor aspect of the sun-god was increasingly venerated in royal circles: the **cult of Aten**, which the pharaoh's son would subsequently enshrine above all others. By changing his name from Amenhotep IV to **Akhenaten** and founding a new capital at Tell el-Amarna, he underlined his commitment to a new monotheistic religion that challenged the age-old priesthood and bureaucracy (see p.226).

This **Amarna Revolution** barely outlasted Akhenaten's reign (c.1352–36 BC) and that of his successor, **Smenkhkare**, for the boy king **Tutankhamun** (c.1336–27 BC) was easily persuaded to abjure Aten's cult and return the capital to Thebes, heralding a **Theban counter-revolution** that continued under **Ay** and **Horemheb**. Though Horemheb (c.1323–1295 BC) effectively restored the *status quo ante*, his lack of royal blood and, more importantly, an heir, brought the XVIII Dynasty to a close.

The Ramessid dynasties

The **XIX Dynasty** (c.1295–1186 BC) began with the brief reign of Horemheb's vizier, **Ramses I** (c.1295–1294 BC), whose family was to produce several warrior-kings who would recapture territories lost under Akhenaten. **Seti I** (c.1294–79 BC) reasserted pharaonic authority in Nubia, Palestine and the Near East, and began a magnificent temple at Abydos. His son **Ramses II** (c.1279–13 BC) completed the temple and the reconquest of Asia Minor, commemorating his dubious victory at Qadesh with numerous reliefs, but later concluding a treaty with the Hittites. At home, Ramses usurped temples and statues built by others, and raised his own monumental edifices – notably the Ramesseum at Thebes and the sun temples at Abu Simbel.

His son **Merneptah** (c.1213–03 BC) faced invasions by the "Sea Peoples" from the north and Libyans from the west, but eventually defeated them in the Delta. He is also popularly believed to be the pharaoh of the **Exodus**, though most scholars reckon that this occurred under the XVIII Dynasty. The XIX Dynasty expired with **Seti II** (c.1194 BC), to be followed by some years without a ruling dynasty.

The **XX Dynasty** (c.1186–1069 BC), begun by Sethnakhte, was the last of the New Kingdom. His successor **Ramses III** (c.1184–53 BC) repulsed three great invasions by the Libyans and Sea Peoples, and built the vast temple-cum-pleasure palace of **Medinet Habu**. Under the eight kings who followed (all called Ramses), Egypt lost the remains of its Asiatic empire, and thieves plundered the royal necropolis. **Ramses XI** (c.1099–69 BC) withdrew to his palace in the Delta, delegating control of Upper Egypt to **Herihor**, high priest of Amun, and Lower Egypt to Vizier **Smendes**.

The Late Period

Their successors consolidated this division, ruling their respective halves of Egypt from

c.1650–1550 BC	c.1650–1550 BC	c. 1550–1295 BC
XV and XVI (Hyksos) dynasties: Khyam; Apophis I and II. Capital at Avaris in the Delta.	XVII Dynasty (Thebes): Khamose wars against the Hyksos.	XVIII Dynasty: Two Lands reunited. Ahmosis; Amenhotep I; Tuthmosis I and II; Hatshepsut; Tuthmosis III; Amenhotep II and III; Akhenaten; Smenkhkare; Tutankhamun; Ay; Horemheb.

Thebes and **Tanis**, with the Theban priest-kings acknowledging the Tanite pharaohs' superiority; scholars designate both ruling houses as the **XXI Dynasty** (c.1069–945 BC). Towards the end of this era, **Shoshenk I** founded the **XXII Dynasty** (c.945–715 BC) of **Libyan** extraction, which ruled Egypt from **Bubastis** in the Delta until a rival line seized power in Upper Egypt, precipitating civil war between the Bubastite monarchs and the Theban **XXIII Dynasty** (c.818–720 BC), which was further complicated by a brief **XXIV Dynasty** (c.727–715 BC) of **Ethiopian** kings.

The lifespan of these four dynasties – termed the **Third Intermediate Period** (TIP) – is one of the murkiest eras of Egyptian history, yet crucial to Rohl's New Chronology hypothesis, as the accepted dates for the New Kingdom hinge on the length of the TIP. Rohl contends that the XXI and XXII dynasties overlapped for generations, and that the duration of the TIP should therefore be reduced accordingly – with knock-on effects down the line.

Egypt's prolonged instability was brought to an end by the intervention of neighbouring Nubia. The Nubian king **Piankhi** (c.747–716 BC) advanced as far north as Memphis, while his brother **Shabaka** (c.716–702 BC) went on to conquer the Delta and reunite the Two Lands. The **XXV Dynasty of Nubian kings** (c.747–656 BC) was marked by a revival of artistic and cultural life. The dynasty's later, **Ethiopian**, rulers had to contend with the **Assyrians**, who were thrown back from the gates of **Thebes** in 671 BC and eventually sacked the city in 664 BC.

After the Assyrians withdrew from Egypt to defend their homeland from the Babylonians, the vacuum was filled by **Psammetichus I**, the fourth ruler of the **XXVI Dynasty** (664–525 BC). Known as the Saïte Dynasty after its capital at **Saïs** in the Delta, this was the last great age of pharaonic civilization – termed the **Late Period** – harking back to the glories of the Old Kingdom in art and architecture, but also adopting new technologies and allowing colonies of Greek merchants at Naucratis and Jewish mercenaries at Elephantine.

Necho II (c.610–595 BC) defeated Josiah, King of Judah, at Megiddo, and is credited with starting to build a canal to link the Nile with the Red Sea. Though **Psammetichus II** (c.595–589 BC) enjoyed several victories, his successor was overthrown following defeat in Libya, the throne passing to **Amasis** "the Drunkard", who relied on Greek allies to stave off the Persian Empire.

The **Persian invasion** of 525 BC began a new era of rule by foreigners that essentially lasted until Nasser overthrew Egypt's monarchy in 1952. The Persian emperors **Cambyses** and **Darius I** completed Necho's canal, founded a new city near Memphis, called **Babylon-in-Egypt** (today's Old Cairo), and built and restored temples to enhance their legitimacy, yet **rebellions** attested to Egyptian hatred of this foreign **XXVII Dynasty**. After this was ousted the native **XXX Dynasty** faced repeated Persian assaults, which **Nectanebo I** repulsed with Greek help, but resulted in a crushing defeat for **Nectanebo II** in 343 BC. Egypt remained under Persian control until 332 BC, when their entire empire succumbed to **Alexander the Great**.

The Ptolemies, Roman rule and Christianity

During his brief stay in Egypt, Alexander offered sacrifices to the gods of Memphis and visited Amun's temple at Siwa; reorganized the country's administration, installing

c. 1295–1186 BC	c. 1186–1069 BC	c.1069–945 BC	c.945–715 BC
XIX Dynasty: Ramses I; Seti I; Ramses II; Merneptah; Seti II.	XX Dynasty: Sethnakhte; Ramses III (and eight other minor Ramses).	XXI Dynasty: authority divided between Tanis and Thebes. Smendes; Herihor; Psusennes I and II. Capital at Tanis.	XXII Dynasty: Shoshenk; Osorkon.

himself as pharaoh; and founded the coastal city of **Alexandria**; he then went off to conquer what remained of the known world. Upon his death in 323 BC, Alexander's Macedonian generals divided the empire, Ptolemy becoming ruler of Egypt and establishing the **Ptolemaic Dynasty** in 332.

Under Ptolemy I, **Greek** became the official language, and Hellenistic ideas had a profound effect on Egyptian art, religion and technology. Although Greek deities were also introduced, the Ptolemies cultivated the Egyptian gods and ruled much like Egyptian pharaohs, erecting great cult temples such as Edfu and Kom Ombo. They also opened new ports, established the great Library of Alexandria and had Hebrew scriptures translated into Greek by rabbis.

All this did nothing to check growing **Roman intervention** in Egyptian affairs. In 54 BC **Julius Caesar** took Alexandria by force, only to be seduced by **Cleopatra VII**, the last of the Ptolemies, who bore a son by him – Caesarion – and after Caesar's death formed a similar alliance with **Mark Antony**. However, their joint fleets suffered disaster against **Octavian** at the Battle of Actium, and both committed suicide rather than face captivity. Octavian had Caesarion murdered and reduced Egypt to the status of a province of the Roman Empire (30 BC).

Like the Ptolemies, the **Roman emperors** adopted many of the Egyptian cults, building such monuments as Trajan's kiosk at Philae and temples at Dendara and Esna. Their main interest in the new colony was as a grain supplier to Rome. In terms of culture, language and administration, **Hellenistic influence** barely diminished and Alexandria continued to thrive as an important centre of Greek and Hebrew learning.

Although the **Holy Family's flight to Egypt** from Palestine cannot be proven, Egypt's Jewish colonies would have been a natural place of refuge, and many sites remain associated with the episode. According to Coptic tradition, **Christianity** was brought to Egypt by **St Mark**, who arrived in the time of Nero. Mark converted many to the new underground faith, founding the Patriarchate of Alexandria in 61 AD.

Politically, the most significant ruler was **Trajan** (98–117), who reopened Necho's Red Sea Canal. Trade flourished, but the *fellaheen* were growing increasingly discontented with heavy taxation and forced recruitment into the Roman army.

The Copts

First-century Egypt was fertile ground for the spread of **Christianity**. The old gods had lost credibility over the millennia of political manipulations and disasters, while the population – Egyptians and Jews alike – was becoming increasingly anti-Roman and nationalistic in its outlook. The core of Christianity, too, had a resonance in ancient traditions, with its emphasis on resurrection, divine judgement and the cult of the great mother.

As Egypt's Christians – who became known as **Copts** – grew more assertive, there was conflict with the Roman authorities. **Persecutions** began in 202, reaching their height under Emperor **Diocletian** (284–305), when thousands of Coptic Christians were massacred. Copts date their calendar from the massacres in 284.

The legalization of Christianity and its adoption as the imperial religion by Emperor **Constantine** in 313 did little to help the Copts. The Roman rulers, in their new capital at **Byzantium**, embraced an orthodox faith that differed fundamentally from that of their Egyptian co-religionists. Attempts at reconciliation at the **Council of**

c.818–715 BC	c.747–656 BC	c.664–525 BC	525–404 BC
XXIII and XXIV dynasties (the latter contemporary with the XXV Dynasty in Upper Egypt).	XXV (Nubian) Dynasty: Piankhi; Shabaka; Taharqa; Tanutamun.	XXVI (Saïte) Dynasty: Psammetichus I; Necho II; Psammetichus II; Apries; Amasis.	XXVII (Persian) Dynasty: Persian invasion. Cambyses; Darius I; Xerxes; Artaxerxes I. Foundation of Babylon-in-Egypt (Cairo).

Nicaea (325) failed, and the split had become irrevocable by the time it was formalized at the **Council of Chalcedon** (451), following which the Copts established their own completely separate Patriarchate at Alexandria.

The same period also saw the emergence of **monasticism**, which took root in the Egyptian deserts. The monasteries of St Catherine in the Sinai, those of Wadi Natrun and Sohag, and St Anthony's and St Paul's in the Red Sea Mountains, all originated in these years.

The Caliphal era

Egypt remained under **Byzantine rule** until the **advance of Islam** in the seventh century. The Muslim armies, led by the Prophet Mohammed's successor, Abu Bakr, defeated the Byzantine army in 636. General Amr Ibn al-As then advanced on the fortress town of Babylon-in-Egypt, which soon surrendered, followed by the capital, Alexandria, in 642.

Amr built his own capital, **Fustat**, north of Babylon-in-Egypt, in what is today Old Cairo. However, Egypt was merely a province in the vast Islamic **Caliphate** that was governed from Damascus and Baghdad; as in Roman times, Egypt was regarded as a bread basket for the empire. Inside Egypt, **Arabization and Islamicization** were hastened by the discriminatory poll-tax (*jiziya*) levied on Copts and Jews by Caliph Omar. Much depended on the character of the caliphs and clannish power struggles, whose impact was felt throughout the empire. In 750, the ruling **Umayyad** dynasty was defeated by the armies of Abu al-Abbas (a descendant of Abu Bakr), and an **Abbassid** caliphate came to power in Baghdad, administering Egypt, along with its other territories, for the next two centuries.

The Tulunids and Ikhshidids

In 868, **Ahmed Ibn Tulun**, sent to administer Egypt on behalf of Caliph al-Mu'tazz, declared the territory independent and founded a dynasty that ruled Egypt for 37 years. Like previous rulers, he built a new capital city, **Al-Qitai**, whose vast mosque still remains. But the **Tulunid dynasty** proved ephemeral; all his heirs were assassinated, and by 905 Abbassid rule was reimposed.

Egypt remained under the direct control of Baghdad until 935, when Mohammed Ibn Tughj was granted the title Ikhshid (ruler or king) by the caliph. Like the Tulunids, the **Ikhshidid dynasty** functioned virtually independently, until a combination of famine, drought and instability opened the way for an invasion of the **Shia Fatimids** from Tunisia in 969, whose armies swept on to conquer Syria. Now it was Egypt's turn to host the imperial capital.

The Fatimid caliphs

The early **Fatimid caliphs** ruled half the Muslim world, with Egypt forming the central portion of an empire that included North Africa, Sicily, Syria and western Arabia. **Gohar**, commander of the caliphal forces, built the city of **Al-Qahira** (the Triumphant) as a new capital in 969, its walls containing opulent palaces and the great mosque-university of Al-Azhar. From there, **Caliph al-Muizz** ruled an empire with a vast multi-racial army including Europeans, Berbers, Sudanese and Turks.

Whereas Al-Muizz and his successor were efficient, tolerant rulers under whom Egypt

404–380 BC	380–343 BC	343–322 BC	332–30 BC
XXVIII and XXIX dynastie.	XXX Dynasty: Nectanebo I and II.	Second period of Persian occupation.	Alexander the Great conquers Egypt and founds Alexandria. His successors, the Ptolemies, make the city an intellectual beacon for the Mediterranean world.

flourished, the third caliph – **Al-Hakim** (996–1021) – was a capricious despot, whose destruction of the Church of the Holy Sepulchre in Jerusalem later provided a pretext for the First Crusade. By the long reign of his grandson, **Al-Mostansir** (1035–94), decay had set in. Though able governors restored order and prosperity for a further century, the Fatimid Empire felt increasingly vulnerable after the loss of Syria to the Seljuk Turks, and confronted by new forces in Europe.

The **Crusades** (after 1097) obliged the Fatimids to fight for their possession of the Holy Land, and defend Egypt itself after 1167. Outraged by the feebleness of the Fatimids and fraternization between Muslims and Crusaders in Palestine, the Seljuk Sultan, Nur al-Din, sent an expedition to repel the Europeans. His nephew, Salah al-Din al-Ayyubi – known to Europe as **Saladin** – took possession of Alexandria and routed the Crusaders.

The Ayyubid sultans

On the death of the last Fatimid caliph in 1171, Saladin became ruler of Egypt. To this day he remains an Arab hero, renowned for his modesty, generosity and wisdom. Having no pretensions to religious leadership, he took the secular title of Al-Sultan ("The Power") rather than that of caliph. Of his 24-year reign, he spent only eight years in Cairo, the rest being spent at war against the Crusaders. By 1183, Syria had been won back and in 1187 Jerusalem was recaptured.

In Cairo, he built a fortress – today's Citadel – and expanded the Fatimid walls to enclose the city. To propagate Sunni orthodoxy, he introduced the Seljuk institution of the **madrassa** or teaching mosque, thus turning Cairo into a great centre of learning.

Following his death in 1193, the Sultanate's eastern territories fragmented, but Egypt remained united under the **Ayyubids**. His nephew, **Al-Kamil** (1218–38), repulsed the Fifth Crusade, and the last of the dynasty, **Ayyub** (1240–49), built up a formidable army of Qipchak slaves from the Black Sea region.

When Ayyub died without leaving an heir, his widow **Shagar al-Durr** took power, ruling openly as sultana until the Abbassid caliphs insisted that she take a husband, quoting the Prophet Mohammed's words: "Woe to the nations ruled by women." Having wed she had him murdered by a henchman, **Baybars the Crossbowman**, who clawed his way to power after she was killed in 1250.

The Mamlukes

Baybars was a commander (emir) among the **Mamlukes**, the foreign slave-troops on whom the later Ayyubids depended. Originally drawn from Central Asia and later from all over the Near East and the Balkans, they became a self-perpetuating caste whose emirs ruled Egypt for the next three centuries, each sultan intriguing his way through the ranks to assume the throne by *coup d'état* or assassination. Frequent changes of ruler were preferred, since contenders had to spread around bribes.

The Turkic **Bahri** ("River") **Mamlukes** (so-called after their garrison by the Nile) gave rise to the first Mamluke dynasty, founded by **Qalaoun**, who poisoned Baybars' heirs in 1279. He sponsored many buildings in Cairo, established relations with potentates around the Indian Ocean and concluded treaties with European sovereigns. **Mohammed al-Nasir** (1294–1340) was another great builder and power-broker, who concluded treaties with the Mongols after defeating them in Syria – but his heirs

30 BC	45 AD	249–305	313
Octavian (Augustus) annexes Egypt to the Roman Empire after the death of Cleopatra VII, the last of the Ptolemies.	St Mark brings Christianity to Egypt.	Persecution of Coptic Christians under Decius and Diocletian.	Edict of Milan legalizes Christianity. Foundation of monasteries of Wadi Natrun, St Anthony, St Paul and St Catherine.

struggled to hold the throne amidst perpetual intrigues by Mamluke factions.

In 1382 the sultanate was seized by **Barquq**, of the Circassian **Burgi** ("Tower") **Mamlukes** garrisoned below the Citadel. To finance his campaigns against the **Mongols** in Syria, he imposed taxes that beggared the economy. Hardships were exacerbated by famine and plague during his son's reign, and it was only under Sultan **Barsbey** (1422–37) that Egypt regained some of its power, establishing friendly relations with the Ottoman Turks and expanding trade in the Indian Ocean.

Though Egypt enjoyed peace and prosperity during the long reign of **Qaitbey** (1468–95), his lavish building programme was unsustainable by his successors. Egypt's spice-trade monopoly was dealt a crippling blow by the discovery of the Cape route to the Indies, depriving the 46th (and penultimate) sultan, **Qansuh al-Ghuri** (1501–16), of revenue, just as the **Ottoman Turks** attacked Mamluke domains in Syria. Following Al-Ghuri's death in battle at Aleppo, his successor **Tumanbey** was crushed by the Ottoman onslaught and executed in Cairo in 1517.

Ottoman and French occupation

Even after the Turkish conquest, the Mamlukes remained powerful figures in the administration of what was now a province of the **Ottoman Empire**. Government was provided by a series of **pashas**, officials trained in Istanbul. The Mamluke army continued to grow with the import of Caucasian slaves; by the end of the sixteenth century its senior **beys** were infamous for their intrigues, arbitrary taxes and profligate ways. Egypt's **decline** was accelerated by a plague epidemic in 1719, which left the country depopulated and its capital crumbling away amidst mounds of rubbish, as the French traveller Volney described in 1784.

At the end of the century, Egypt became a pawn in the struggle between France and Britain. **Napoleon** saw it as a means to disrupt British commerce and rule in India. In 1798, his fleet landed at Alexandria, where he issued a proclamation that began with the Islamic *bismillah* ("In the name of God"), promising to liberate Egypt from the "riffraff of slaves", and that he respected Islam more than the Mamlukes did.

Although Napoleon routed the Mamlukes and occupied Cairo, he left his fleet exposed at Abu Qir Bay, where it was destroyed by the British under Nelson. With his grand vision in tatters, Napoleon returned secretly to France, leaving the army behind. After General Menou proclaimed Egypt a **French protectorate** the British invaded Alexandria, combining with Ottoman forces to take Cairo, forcing the French to surrender. Under the Capitulation Agreement, the archeological treasures gathered by Napoleon's savants were surrendered to Britain – which is why the **Rosetta Stone** ended up in the British Museum rather than the Louvre.

While Europeans marvelled at the wonders of Ancient Egypt, Egyptians were left awed by the defeat of the "invincible" Mamlukes and such wonders of Western technology as printing presses and hot-air balloons (which the French introduced to Cairo). While Ottoman rule had been restored, things would not be the same.

Mohammed Ali and his heirs

Among the Turkish officers left in charge was **Mohammed Ali** of the Albanian Corps,

395	451	640–642	661–750
Partition of Roman Empire into East and West; Egypt falls under Eastern, Byzantine, sphere.	Council of Chalcedon leads to expulsion of Copts from Orthodox Church.	Arab conquest of Egypt; introduction of Islam. Foundation of Fustat (Cairo).	Egypt forms part of Umayyad Caliphate, ruled from the dynasty's capital at Damascus.

whose dynasty was to change Egypt more radically than any ruler since Saladin, and is thus regarded as the founder of modern Egypt. Having been confirmed as **pasha** in 1805, he proceeded to decapitate the Mamluke leadership (see p.108), confiscated private land and set about modernizing Egypt with European expertise, building railways, factories and canals. His son Ibrahim led a murderous campaign to subjugate northern **Sudan**, of which the only positive result was the introduction of a special kind of **cotton** – henceforth Egypt's major cash crop.

When Mohammed Ali died insane in 1849, his successor **Abbas** (1848–54) closed the country's factories and secular schools and opened Egypt to free trade, thus retarding industrialization. **Said Pasha** (1854–63) granted a concession to a French engineer, Ferdinand de Lesseps, to build the **Suez Canal** (see p.512) – a project completed in 1869, by which time **Khedive Ismail** (1863–79) was in power. He transformed Cairo, spending lavishly on modernization, but exorbitant interest rates had to be paid on European loans. To stave off bankruptcy, he sold his Suez Canal shares to the British government in 1875.

Ismail was deposed by his son **Tewfiq** (1879–92), whose own fiscal power was limited by the French and British, to the disgust of patriotic Egyptians. A group of army officers forced him to appoint their leader, **Ahmed Orabi**, as Minister of War. France and Britain responded by sending in the gunboats, shelling Alexandria and landing an army which routed Orabi's forces at Tell el-Kebir and restored Tewfiq as a puppet ruler under British control.

British occupation and Egyptian nationalism

Britain's stated intention was to set Egyptian affairs in order and then withdraw, but its interests dictated a more permanent involvement. From 1883 to 1907, Egypt was controlled by the British Consul-General, Sir Evelyn Baring, later **Lord Cromer**, who coined the term **Veiled Protectorate** to describe the relationship between the two countries. Egyptian resentment at this usurpation of authority found expression under **Abbas II**, who came to power in 1892, and in a nationalist movement led by the lawyer **Mustafa Kamel**. Egypt was effectively a colony, with Britain supplying all the country's manufactured goods, and encouraging Egyptian dependence on cotton exports.

When Turkey entered **World War I** on the side of Germany in 1916, Egypt was still nominally a province of the Ottoman Empire, so to safeguard its strategic interests Britain declared Egypt a protectorate and tightened its grip. By 1917, **Fouad**, the sixth son of Ismail, was khedive of Egypt, with Reginald Wingate its High Commissioner. The **nationalist movement** flourished under wartime conditions; in 1918 its leader, **Sa'ad Zaghloul**, presented Wingate with a demand for autonomy, which was rejected. The request to send a delegation (*wafd*) to London led to Zaghloul's arrest and deportation to Malta (rescinded after nationwide riots). In 1922 Britain abolished the protectorate and recognized Egypt as an independent state but kept control of the judiciary, communications, defence and the Canal, while Fouad assumed the title of king.

The next twenty years saw a struggle for power between the king, the British and the nationalist **Wafd Party**. Fouad's son, **King Farouk**, succeeded him in 1935 and signed a twenty-year **Anglo-Egyptian treaty**, which ended British occupation but empowered their forces to remain in the Canal Zone. In 1937, Egypt joined the League of Nations,

750–935	935–969	969–1171
Abbassids depose Umayyads and form new dynasty, ruling from Baghdad. In 870 Egypt's governor, Ibn Tulun, declares independence, founding a dynasty which rules until 905.	Ikhshidid dynasty takes power in Egypt.	Shi'ite Fatimid dynasty conquers Egypt and seizes the Islamic Caliphate, which it rules from Cairo.

but the outbreak of World War II halted its move to complete independence.

World War II and postwar manoeuvrings

World War II saw Rommel's **Afrika Korps** coming within 111km of Alexandria, though they were repulsed by the **Eighth Army** under General Montgomery at the **Battle of El-Alamein** in October 1942. Thereafter the tide of war turned in the Western Desert campaign and the Allies continued to advance across North Africa, through Libya and Tunisia.

During the war, the Wafd leadership kept dissent muted on the tacit understanding that full independence would be granted after the war, when they demanded the evacuation of British troops and unification with Sudan (contrary to Britain's plans for its self-government). Popular resentment was expressed in riots and strikes, supported by the **Muslim Brotherhood (see p.518)**, which led to clashes with British troops in the Canal Zone.

Following the declaration of the state of **Israel** in May 1948, Egypt joined Iraq, Syria and Jordan in a military invasion. The defeat of the Arab forces was followed by a UN-brokered treaty that left the **Gaza Strip** under Egyptian administration. Many of the Egyptian officers who fought in this war were disgusted by the incompetence and corruption of their superiors: these veterans formed the core of a revolutionary conspiracy known as the **Free Officers**.

The 1952 Revolution

Following Egypt's first **elections** in ten years, the Wafd won a majority and formed a government with Nahas Pasha as prime minister. In 1952, Nahas was dismissed by King Farouk after abrogating the Anglo-Egyptian treaty, and the Egyptian army was sent out onto the streets to quell protests. On July 23, the Free Officers staged a bloodless **coup**, forcing **Farouk's abdication** three days later. Their nominal leader, General Naguib, became head of the armed forces and prime minister, but real power lay in the hands of the nine officers of the **Revolutionary Command Council** (RCC), foremost among who was Colonel **Gamal Abdel Nasser**.

The constitution was revoked, political parties dissolved, the monarchy abolished and Egypt declared a **republic** (July 26, 1953). Meanwhile, a struggle for power raged behind the scenes, as Naguib attempted to step beyond his figurehead status and moderate the RCC's radicalism. After being implicated in an attempt on Nasser's life in 1954, Naguib was placed under house arrest; Nasser became acting head of state and in June 1956 was confirmed as president.

The Nasser era

President Nasser dominated Egypt and the Arab world until his death in 1970, his ideology of **Arab nationalism** and socialism making him supremely popular with the masses from Iraq to Morocco. Under his leadership, Egypt was at the forefront of **anti-colonialism**, supporting liberation struggles in Algeria and sub-Saharan Africa, and co-founding the Non-Aligned Movement.

In 1954 he reached agreement for the withdrawal of British troops from the Canal Zone, though the Canal's management and profits were to remain in foreign hands.

1171–1250	1250–1382	1382–1517	1517
Saladin founds Ayyubid dynasty and liberates land conquered by the Crusaders. Intrigues of Shagar al-Durr open the way to Mamluke takeover.	Bahri Mamlukes: Qalaoun, Khalil and Mohammed al-Nasir.	Burgi Mamlukes: Barquq, Farag, Barsbey, Qaitbey and Qansuh al-Ghuri.	Selim the Grim conquers Egypt. For the next three centuries the country is ruled as an Ottoman province from Istanbul.

Meanwhile he was seeking credits from the World Bank to finance construction of the Aswan High Dam, and weapons to rearm Egyptian forces. When the Soviet Union offered to supply arms, the United States vetoed loans for the dam, leaving Nasser with no alternative but to **nationalize the Canal** to secure revenue, in July 1956.

This was regarded by Britain and France as a threat to their vital interests. Both concluded a secret agreement with Israel, whose **invasion of Sinai** in October 1956 was to provide the pretext for their own intervention to "safeguard" the Canal. Following bombardments and British paratroop landings in Port Said, the United States stepped in, threatening to destabilize Britain's economy unless its forces withdrew. The canal reopened under full Egyptian control and Nasser emerged from the **Suez Crisis** as a champion of Arab nationalism.

On a wave of **pan-Arab** sentiment, Egypt and Syria united to form the **United Arab Republic** in 1958, an unworkable arrangement that foundered within three years. Egypt moved closer to the Soviet Union, accepting technical and military assistance on a massive scale, to build the Aswan High Dam and counter an increasingly well-armed Israel by staging *Fedayeen* raids from Gaza.

When Israel threatened to invade Syria in 1967, Nasser sent Egyptian forces into Sinai and blockaded the Tiran Straits, cutting shipping to the Israeli port of Eilat. Israel responded with a pre-emptive strike, destroying Egypt's air force on the ground and seizing Sinai, Gaza, the West Bank and the Golan Heights. The **Six Day War** was a shattering defeat for the Arabs and Nasser in particular, who proffered his resignation, only resuming the presidency after mass demonstrations of support on the streets. The conflict had no formal resolution, subsiding into a **War of Attrition** which dragged on for the next two years, with Israeli forces shelling the Canal cities from Sinai while Egypt rearmed and struggled to host millions of refugees.

Amid the drama of Suez and wars with Israel, it's easy to overlook the **social achievements** of the Nasser era. One of the RCC's first acts was to break up the old feudal estates, transferring **land** to the *fellaheen*. As a result of the **Aswan High Dam**, the amount under cultivation increased by fifteen percent (surpassing population growth for the first time) and the dam's turbines powered a huge **industrial base**, created virtually from scratch. There was similar progress in **education and health care**; average life expectancy rose from 43 to 52 years. The downside was a Soviet-style system where all political parties were merged into the **Arab Socialist Union** (ASU), and censorship, torture and internment were widespread. Nevertheless, **Nasser's death** – from a heart attack – in 1970 came as a profound shock to the whole Arab world. His funeral procession in Cairo was the largest Egypt has ever seen.

Egypt under Sadat

Nasser's deputy, **Anwar Sadat**, was confirmed as president by the ASU hierarchy to reform a country demoralized by defeat, stagnation and austerity. His "**corrective revolution**" reversed decades of centralized economic control, while the mass-expulsion of Soviet advisors masked secret planning with Syria and Jordan to launch a new campaign against Israel. On October 6, 1973, Egyptian forces crossed the Canal, storming the "invincible" Bar-Lev Line to enter Israeli-held Sinai. This **October War** (aka 10th Ramadan/Yom Kippur War) ultimately turned against the Arabs, but enhanced

1798–1802	1805	1854–63	1863–79
French occupation of Egypt. Discovery of the Rosetta Stone.	Mohammed Ali seizes power and begins a programme of ruthless modernization.	Reign of Said Pasha. Suez Canal begun.	Reign of Khedive Ismail. Completion of Suez Canal.

their bargaining position and dealt a blow to Israeli self-confidence; Egypt also regained a strip of territory to the east of the Canal, enabling Sadat to claim victory.

After the war, an amnesty was granted to political prisoners, censorship was lifted and some political parties, including the Muslim Brotherhood, were allowed. Equally important was Sadat's *infitah* or "**open door**" policy, to encourage private and foreign investment and reduce the role of the state in the economy. Helped by Gulf Arab investments – a reward for the October War – and stimulated by the reconstruction of the Canal cities, the economy boomed. However, while the number of millionaires rose from five hundred to seventeen thousand and an affluent middle class developed, the condition of the urban poor and *fellaheen* worsened. Some five million families subsisted on less than $30 a month, and one and a half million Egyptians migrated to work in the Gulf States.

In 1977, when the International Monetary Fund insisted on the removal of subsidies on basic foodstuffs, there were nationwide **food riots**. Needing an injection of Western capital and convinced that Israel's acquisition of nuclear weapons made an Arab victory impossible, Sadat became the first Arab leader to visit Jerusalem, signing the **Camp David Agreement** (1978), whereby Egypt recognized Israel's right to exist and Israel agreed to withdraw from Sinai. Outraged, the Arab League severed links with Egypt and moved its headquarters from Cairo to Tunis.

At home, Sadat had encouraged the rise of Islamic groups to counter leftist influences, but as the Muslim Brotherhood grew stronger and protested against the Camp David Accord he ordered wholesale arrests – resulting in **Sadat's assassination** by Islamic militants in October 1981.

Mubarak's Egypt

Sadat's successor, **Hosni Mubarak**, was the third president to emerge from the armed forces, ruling through an authoritarian system essentially unchanged since Nasser's time. Under the **emergency laws** passed after Sadat's murder, demonstrations and strikes were crushed by riot police; **torture** by the security forces was rife; and **elections** were shamelessly rigged.

Having been "re-elected" president four times already, Mubarak was obliged to open the election to other candidates when he ran for a fifth term in 2005. His opponent **Ayman Nour** was jailed on charges of forging signatures as MP of a new liberal party, Al-Ghad (Tomorrow), while meetings of the reformist alliance **Kifaya** (Enough) were broken up by thugs (*baltagiyya*) paid by the state.

As the octogenarian Mubarak schemed to ensure that his son **Gamal** would inherit the presidency, Egyptians seethed. They saw government ministers become billionaires through the privatization of state assets and generals enjoying sumptuous country clubs and villas, while ordinary people faced soaring food prices, unemployment and a future without hope. With almost one third of Egypt's population aged under 25, a generational tidal wave was set to emerge from the depths of despair.

The 2011 Revolution

The overthrow of the Tunisian dictator Ben Ali early in 2011 inspired Arabs across North Africa and the Gulf to revolt. In Egypt, activists called for a "**Day of Rage**" on

1879–92	1935–52	1952–53	1956
Reign of Khedive Tewfiq. British crush the Orabi Revolt (1882–83). Tewfiq reinstated as a puppet ruler.	Reign of King Farouk; during World War II Egypt stays under British control.	Farouk overthrown by Free Officers. Egypt declared a republic.	Nasser becomes President; Suez Crisis. Major industrialization programme.

January 25, using Facebook, Twitter and SMS to mobilize protestors on Cairo's main square, Midan Tahrir (see box, p.72).

As happened in Tunisia, protestors chanting *Slimiyya*! (Peacefully) were tear-gassed and beaten. On the second night, crowds trying to march on the National Assembly and Interior Ministry were fired on by snipers. But each day saw people returning to Tahrir to defy the regime, with hundreds of thousands pouring onto the square after Friday prayers. Mosques became first-aid posts and well-wishers sent water, food and blankets. (State TV claimed that foreign agents were supplying Kentucky Fried Chicken and drugs to the protestors.)

As the battered riot police withdrew from central Cairo, its suburbs were hit by a wave of looting blamed on convicts escaped (or released) from prisons in the Delta, or the infamous *baltagiyya*. This was seen as a ploy to scare protestors into returning home, but only encouraged the formation of vigilante groups in every neighbourhood and an even greater contempt for the regime.

When **army** tanks appeared on Tahrir many feared a Tiananmen Square-like bloodbath, but others hailed the soldiers as a shield against the *baltagiyya*, who had staged repeated attacks and even charged into the square on horses and camels. When the army High Command announced that the protest was "legitimate", even larger crowds came onto the streets in cities across the country.

With Egypt at a standstill and the economy losing $30 million a day, the stalemate couldn't continue for long. As protestors began a "million man march" from Tahrir to the Presidential Palace on February 11, Mubarak was secretly boarding a jet bound for his villa in Sinai. At 6pm, **Mubarak's resignation** was announced by his vice president and spy-master, causing nationwide celebrations.

In the euphoria, most people welcomed the news that authority was now vested in a **Supreme Council of the Armed Forces** (SCAF) headed by Field Marshal Tantawi, which pledged to oversee Egypt's transition to democracy.

Egypt since the revolution

SCAF's first acts complied with popular demands for the dissolution of **parliament** and the suspension of the **constitution** (both tainted by Mubarak's regime). Free elections and a constituent assembly would follow within six months, SCAF pledged. Besides mourning ceremonies for revolutionary martyrs, Tahrir now saw protests by striking state employees, ignoring SCAF's exhortations that citizens should cease protesting and return to work.

Protestors' raids on secret police headquarters found evidence of vote-rigging, mass surveillance and torture, intensifying demands that Mubarak and his cronies should face justice. On the night of March 9, soldiers forcibly cleared Tahrir and sealed it off. Arrested women activists were subjected to forced "virginity tests", and Egypt's caretaker cabinet decreed that protestors would be gaoled or fined $100,000.

It was a foretaste of what lay ahead, as suspicions of SCAF grew and the popular unity manifest during the revolution fragmented. In May, hardline **Salafists** (see p.615) burned down three churches in the Cairo suburb of Imbaba, followed by attacks on other churches outside the capital. Throughout July hundreds of thousands demonstrated in Cairo, Alexandria and Suez, demanding immediate reforms and prosecutions of former officials of the Mubarak regime. A march on the Defence

1967	1970	1973	1977–78
Six Day War with Israel; massive damage to Canal cities.	Nasser dies and is succeeded as president by Sadat. Aswan High Dam completed.	October War with Israel.	Sadat's trip to Jerusalem leads to Camp David Agreement.

Ministry was attacked by *baltagiyya*, and in August, soldiers once again tore down protestors' tents on Tahrir.

In early October, Copts protesting outside the State TV building were crushed by armoured personel carriers, leaving 28 dead and 212 injured. As the **Maspero massacre** was happening, state TV urged "noble patriots" to rally against "violent Copts" and "foreign infiltrators". Late November saw six days of fighting in several cities, leaving nearly forty dead and over two thousand injured, but calls for a boycott of **parliamentary elections** were ignored by the electorate. The result was a triumph for Egypt's **Islamists**, with the Muslim Brotherhood's Freedom and Justice Party (FJP) winning forty percent of seats and the Salafist Al-Nour party twenty percent.

Liberal fears that Islamists would also win the presidency led some to demand the postponement of the next round of elections, but most Egyptians wanted the issue resolved. Soaring unemployment, crime and insecurity had made life even harder for the forty percent living below the poverty line.

The 2012 presidential elections

The first round of voting (May 23–24) confounded pundits who had predicted a narrow lead for the "stability candidate" Amr Moussa, or the moderate Islamist Dr Abul Fatouh. Instead, the Muslim Brotherhood's candidate **Mohammed Morsi** came first with 26 percent, slightly ahead of **Ahmed Shafiq**, Mubarak's last prime minister – ensuring that the second round would be a contest between two extremes of the political spectrum.

Mohammed Morsi was a last-minute replacement for the Brotherhood's original candidate (disqualified by SCAF), mocked by detractors as the "spare tyre". His rival, Shafiq, was a *fuloul*, or remnant, of the old regime, who pledged to curb the Brotherhood. Liberals faced a choice between two evils that seemed a travesty of their hopes for democracy, so many abstained from voting – unlike Egypt's Copts, who rallied behind the *fuloul* Shafiq as their only hope of averting a Brotherhood victory.

The political landscape shifted week by week, with the lifting of the emergency laws; the sentencing of Mubarak and his Interior Minister to life imprisonment; and a Constitutional Court ruling invalidating the 2011 elections which enabled SCAF to dissolve parliament overnight. Just before the second round of voting began on June 16, SCAF promulgated an interim constitution, reserving itself sweeping powers and restricting those of the president and parliament, to ensure that the armed forces kept their privileges no matter who was elected.

While both sides claimed victory and accused the other of fraud, it soon became clear that the FJP's candidate had won a slim majority (51.7 percent, on a reduced turn-out of fifty percent), and Shafiq promptly fled Egypt to avoid prosecution for corruption. On June 25, Mohammed Morsi was declared Egypt's first freely elected **president**, to rejoicing by supporters massed on Tahrir Square.

While he vowed to be a president "for all Egyptians", and a spokesman hinted that a Christian or a woman might be chosen as vice president, Morsi's victory speech on Tahrir included an uncompromising reiteration of the Brotherhood's credo: "The Koran is our constitution, the Prophet is our leader, Jihad is our path and death in the name of Allah is our goal. "

Morsi's first act was to defy SCAF's decree dissolving parliament by ordering MPs to

1981	1996	1997	2001
Assassination of Sadat. Presidency assumed by Mubarak.	Valley of the Mummies, Egypt's largest cache of mummies, is discovered in Bahariya Oasis.	Fifty-eight foreigners killed by Islamist terrorists at Hatshepsut's Temple, near Luxor. Toshka Project inaugurated.	Discovery of the underwater city of Herakleion in Abu Qir Bay on the Mediterranean coast.

reconvene. A month later, Jihadists in Sinai killed sixteen Egyptian soldiers, stole their armoured cars and launched an attack on Israel. Morsi seized the opportunity to **consolidate his power** by retiring Marshal Tantawi and other SCAF figures, and promoting pro-Brotherhood generals. The media, too, was reined in, using laws from the Mubarak era and new ones promulgated by parliament.

Christians and liberals now fear that the FJP and Salafists are intent on creating a hardline sharia state. Israeli and Western governments are alarmed by the remilitarization of Sinai, and the prospect that Egypt may revoke the Camp David Accords. Meanwhile, long-standing problems are getting worse. Only three percent of Egypt's land is usable for agriculture, while the **population** rises by a million every nine months (at the time of writing, it stands at 85 million). Egypt must import half the food it needs, and without $2 billion a year in **US aid** the economy would collapse. A creeping **environmental crisis** in the Delta – where land is being lost to rising sea-levels and soil-salinization – and the risk of a new epidemic of bird flu – add to the uncertainty surrounding Egypt's future.

2002	2011	2012
Inauguration of the Bibliotheca Alexandrina, and the completion of the main branch of the Sheikh Zayid Canal at Toshka.	Mubarak overthrown by a popular revolution which sees Cairo's Tahrir Square become the epicentre of Egyptian politics.	An Islamist becomes Egypt's first freely elected civilian president since the overthrow of Egypt's monarchy sixty years earlier.

Islam

Islam was born on the Arabian Peninsula, beyond the periphery of Greco-Roman civilization. Its founder, **Mohammed**, was a merchant from the city of Mecca, in what is now Saudi Arabia. At the age of 40 (c.609 AD), he began to have visions of an angel commanding him to recite divine revelations. As "God's Messenger", he proclaimed the oneness of **Allah** (God), the evil of idolatry in a city worshipping several deities (of whom Allah was one) and the need for submission (*islam*) to Allah's will. Forced to flee Mecca with his followers in 622 (the *hijra* that marks the beginning of the Muslim calendar), he spent eight years uniting the Bedouin tribes of Medina to finally conquer Mecca, dying two years later.

Mohammed's recitations – he was illiterate – were later transcribed into the Islam's holy book, the **Koran** (or "recitation"), which asserted that Allah was the same God worshipped by Jews and Christians, but that the message of Abraham (Ibrahim), Moses (Musa) and Jesus (Issa) had been distorted and was only truly expressed by Mohammed, the "Seal of the Prophets".

The Pillars of Faith

Muslims (believers) face five essential requirements, the so-called "**Pillars of Faith**": prayer five times daily, the pilgrimage (*Hajj*) to Mecca, the Ramadan fast, giving alms (*zakat*) and – most fundamental of all – the belief that "there is no God but Allah and Mohammed is His Prophet". Ritual prayers are the most visible of these obligations, punctuating the Islamic day (which begins at sunset) at dawn, noon, mid-afternoon, sunset and after dark. Prayers can be performed anywhere, but preferably in a mosque.

In the past, a muezzin (prayer crier) would climb his minaret each time and summon the faithful. Nowadays, the call is most likely pre-recorded; even so, this most distinctive of Islamic sounds has a beauty all of its own. The message is simplicity itself: "God is most great (*Allahu Akbar*). I testify that there is no God but Allah. I testify that Mohammed is His Prophet. Come to prayer, come to security. God is great." Another phrase is added in the morning: "Prayer is better than sleep."

Prayers are preceded by ritual ablutions. Facing Mecca (the direction indicated in a mosque by the *mihrab* or niche), worshippers recite the *Fatihah*, the first chapter of the Koran, and then repeat the same words twice in the prostrate position, with interjections of *Allahu Akbar*. A highly ritualized procedure whose obeisance symbolizes Muslims' submission to God, the sight of thousands of people going through the same motions simultaneously in a mosque is a powerful one. On Islam's holy day, Friday, all believers are expected to attend prayers led by local imams, who also deliver a *khutba*, or sermon.

Ramadan is the name of the ninth month in the lunar Islamic calendar, the month in which the Koran was first revealed to Mohammed. For the whole of the month, believers must obey a rigorous fast (the custom was originally modelled on Jewish and Christian practice), forsaking all forms of consumption between sunrise and sundown; this includes food, drink and any form of sexual contact. Only certain categories of people are exempted: travellers, children, pregnant women and warriors engaged in *jihad* (see p.613). Given the climates in which many Muslims live, the fast is a formidable undertaking, but in practice it becomes a time of intense celebration.

The pilgrimage, or **Hajj**, to Mecca is an annual event, with millions flocking to Mohammed's birthplace from all over the world. Here they go through several days of rituals, the central one being a sevenfold circumambulation of the sacred Kaaba shrine. Islam requires that all believers go on a Hajj as often as is practically possible, but for the poor it may well be a once-in-a-lifetime occasion, and is sometimes replaced by a series of visits to lesser, local shrines – in Egypt, for instance, to the mosques of Saiyida Zeinab or El-Hussein in Cairo.

Development in Egypt

Mohammed's successors – the four Rightly Guided Caliphs – spread Islam far beyond Arabia in a great **jihad** (holy war); within a century of the Prophet's death they had forged an Islamic Empire extending from the Atlantic Ocean to Central Asia. Egypt fell readily in 640, its Byzantine rulers hated by a native population who acquiesced to, or welcomed, the Muslim conquest after its leader, Amr, promised to respect Egypt's Christians and Jews as "people of the book".

In accordance with Koranic precepts codified by Caliph Omar, they had to pay a poll-tax (*jizia*) and submit to restrictions affirming their inferior status, in return for which their lives and property were protected. Even these weren't guaranteed under Caliph Al-Hakim, who destroyed many churches and synagogues during his reign. Despite such powerful incentives to convert to Islam, it was not until the eleventh century that Cairo attained a **Muslim majority**, and not until the thirteenth century for Egypt as a whole.

The original Arab dynasties of Egypt subscribed to **Sunni Islam** – the more "orthodox" branch of the religion, dominant then, as now, in most parts of the Arab world. However, the Fatimid dynasty, which took control of Egypt in 969, signalled a shift to **Shi'ite Islam**, which was to continue (among the rulers, at least) until late in the twelfth century. Under the Ayyubid dynasty that followed, Egypt reverted, permanently as it turned out, to Sunni adherence, with orthodoxy propagated through the new institution of the **madrassa** – a theological college attached to a mosque.

The Grand Sheikh of Cairo's **Mosque of Al-Azhar** is the ultimate theological authority for most Sunnis outside the Gulf Arab states, issuing *fatwas* (opinions) on a wide range of questions submitted by believers, from family matters to financial affairs – in person, by post or email.

Sheikhs and Sufis

Alongside this formal religious establishment, Egypt also developed a **popular religious culture**, manifested in the veneration of sheikhs and the formation of Sufi brotherhoods – both of which remain important today. **Sheikhs** are basically local holy men: people who developed reputations for sanctity and learning.

Although the Koran prohibits monasticism and isolation from the community, Islam soon developed religious orders dedicated to asceticism and a mystical experience of God. Collectively known as the **Sufis** (possibly derived from *safa*, the Arabic word for "purity", or *suf*, referring to the woollen cloaks worn by early Muslim ascetics); these groups generally coalesced around a charismatic teacher, from whom they derived their name. The largest of these brotherhoods (*tariqas*) in Egypt are the **Rifai**, the **Ahmediya** and the **Shadhiliyya** – who can be seen at moulids ("saint's day" festivals) parading with their distinctive banners.

Decline and revival

While Europe was in the Dark Ages, the Islamic world, straddling the Near East, India and the Mediterranean, developed and disseminated **knowledge** from Classical civilizations and Asia in fields from chemistry to cartography. The medical treatises of Ibn Sina (known in Europe as Avicenna) and the piped water and sewage systems of Fustat are just two Egyptian examples. Yet despite this contribution to the European Renaissance and the lucrative trade in spices and other luxuries, relations between Islam and Christendom were more antagonistic than amicable. The Crusades, and Saracen and Ottoman attacks on Europe, had an enduring impact on both sides.

As Europe moved towards the Age of Enlightenment, the Islamic world grew more introverted and hostile to innovation, and by the end of the eighteenth century Europe was poised to take advantage. Napoleon's expedition to Egypt in 1798 marked the beginning of a century in which virtually every Islamic country came under the control of a **European power**. While Islam couldn't be held solely responsible, its centrality and the reality of European technological superiority posed a question that provoked a **crisis in religious self-confidence**: Why had Islam's former power now passed to infidel foreigners?

The Islamist response

Responses to this question veered between two extremes. There were those who felt that Islam should try to incorporate some of the West's secularism and materialism; on the other side, there were movements holding that Islam should turn its back on the West, purify itself of all corrupt additions and thus rediscover its former power.

The earliest exponent of the latter view was the **Muslim Brotherhood** (Il-Ikhwan il-Muslimeen, or Ikhwan for short), founded in Ismailiya by **Hassan el-Banna** in 1928. The Brotherhood preached a moral renewal of Islam, established a network of schools and training centres, and later set up clandestine paramilitary groups. Aimed as much against corrupt feudal institutions as against Western imperialism, the Brotherhood spread throughout Egypt and spawned offshoots across the Middle East. Its terrorist activities prompted a violent state response, being banned by King Farouk, whose bodyguards assassinated El-Banna in 1949.

His mantle was assumed by **Sayyid Qutb**, whose conversion to radical Islam followed two years in the USA, where he was appalled by American women, the "animal-like" mixing of the sexes and jazz music. Jailed for ten years after an abortive attempt by two Brothers to assassinate Nasser, Qutb wrote a manifesto, *Milestones* (smuggled out of prison), asserting that Muslim states had reverted to Jahiliyya (the pagan era before Islam) by failing to apply Sharia law. On the day of Qutb's execution in 1966, a 15-year-old follower vowed to continue his work by forging an Islamist vanguard: **Ayman al-Zawahiri**, the future founder of Jihad Islami and Al-Qaida's deputy leader.

In Egypt, the Brotherhood remained underground until the Sadat era, when the government regarded it as a useful counterweight to the Left. Its tacit cooperation with the state led to the emergence of more radical groups; the most effective was **Al-Jihad**, which assassinated Sadat and attempted to launch a revolution in Assyut in 1981.

Under Mubarak, the mainstream Islamist opposition was allowed to establish clinics and schools for the poor, **Gamaat Islamiya** (Islamic Societies) captured the professional unions and thousands of Egyptians put their savings into Islamic investment houses. When these went bankrupt amid accusations of fraud the Islamic movement's credibility was badly dented, but its prompt distribution of aid after the 1991 Cairo earthquake redeemed its reputation amongst the urban poor.

The following year **Islamic militants** launched an insurgency in Middle Egypt, killing tourists, policemen and Copts. Gamaat Islamiya (not to be confused with the aforementioned Islamic Societies, despite their overlapping membership and ideology) and the smaller Jihad Islami (Islamic Jihad) claimed divine sanction for attacks on the "Pharaonic regime", "infidel" tourists and Christians who refused to pay *jizia* (extortion money, justified as an Islamic "poll tax" on infidels).

While the insurgency was crushed following the 1997 Luxor massacre and the ceasefire declared by imprisoned leaders of Gamaat Islamiya, the authorities later deferred to the Islamist agenda by jailing three hundred Egyptians for converting to Christianity, and turning a blind eye to rapes and other violence directed against the Copts, from Alexandria to Middle Egypt.

Meanwhile the exiled leaders of Jihad Islami, Ayman al-Zawahiri and Mohammed Atef, joined **Osama Bin Laden** in Afghanistan, merging with Al-Qaida to form the World Islamic Front Against Jews and Crusaders. Their assault on the World Trade

Center on 9/11 was a devastating reprise of an earlier attack in 1993 inspired by the Egyptian sheikh Omar Abdel Rahman (now serving a life sentence in the US).

The **Arab Spring** of 2011 was initially heralded as proof that democracy, not violent Islamism, was the future, rendering Al-Qaida irrelevant. But popular revolutions in Tunisia, Libya and Egypt have empowered Islamists of all stripes far more than secular liberals, to the latter's dismay.

The Muslim Brotherhood's march to power through the ballot box has been mirrored by the **Salafists** (from *salaf*, meaning "ancestor" or "predecessor"), who follow the example of the earliest Muslims, rejecting all forms of innovation and speculative theology in favour of a literal application of the Koran and *ahadith* (sayings and deeds attributed to the Prophet). Their hostility to the cult of sheikhs has resulted in the vandalism of Muslim shrines in Libya and Tunisia, while Egyptian Salafists have burnt down churches and spoken of re-imposing the *jizia* on non-Muslims.

Ancient Egyptian Temples

Two types of temple were built in Egypt from the earliest times. **Mortuary temples** were devoted to the worship of a dead king, whereas **cult temples** were dedicated to the principal god or goddess of a region, whose effigy was honoured with daily rituals and periodically taken to visit its divine spouse in another temple. Most temples embody centuries of work by successive kings, some of whom added major sections while others merely decorated a wall or carved their name on another pharaoh's statue, usurping it for their own glory.

Layout

The general form and layout of temples hardly changed over millennia. Most temples were surrounded by high mud-brick **enclosure walls** (still intact at Karnak, Medinet Habu and Dendara) which defined the holy precincts. Generally inaccessible to commoners, these contained priestly residences, storehouses and a **Sacred Lake** for ritual ablutions. In Greco-Roman times there was also a **Birth House** or mamissi containing scenes asserting the king's divine ancestry, while at certain "healing" temples – notably Dendara and Karnak – ordinary folk could submit prayers to **Chapels of the Hearing Ear** by the outer rear wall.

Entering the temple proper meant passing through massive stone **pylons**, whose facades bore giant reliefs of the pharaoh making offerings to the gods and smiting Egypt's foes (depicted begging for mercy or with their amputated hands and genitals being tallied by royal scribes). Some temples also had **obelisks** with tips sheathed in gold or electrum (an alloy of gold and silver), guardian **colossi** representing a pharaoh or a diety, and open **courts** flanked with colonnades of Osiride pillars.

Another pylon marked the transition to the **Hypostyle Hall**, whose forest of columns was meant to resemble a papyrus thicket. Beyond lay a series of **vestibules**, climaxing in a **sanctuary** where the deity's idol and a gilded boat-shaped shrine, or barque, reposed.

Some temples had a **rooftop shrine** for an annual ritual celebrating the resurrection of Osiris, whose idol was carried to the roof to be touched by the sun at dawn. The best preserved shrine is at Dendara, which depicts Isis restoring Osiris to life by copulating with his mummy.

It has been argued that the **configuration** of certain temples is based on "sacred geometry". Luxor Temple supposedly embodies the proportions of the human figure, and the entire site of Tell el-Amarna may have been aligned to the sun's rays emanating from a cleft in the cliffs on its western horizon.

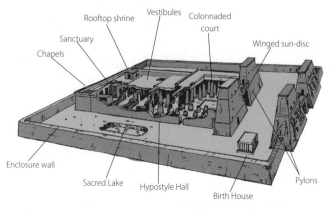

Rooftop shrine · Vestibules · Colonnaded court · Sanctuary · Chapels · Winged sun-disc · Enclosure wall · Sacred Lake · Hypostyle Hall · Birth House · Pylons

Decoration

As in Ancient Greece and Rome, Egyptian temples were whitewashed and painted all over, looking far gaudier than today, when a bit of remaining **colour** makes an exciting change from monochrome masonry. Virtually every wall is covered in **reliefs**, either carved proud (bas-reliefs, the most delicate and time-consuming method), recessed into the surface (sunk-reliefs) or simply incised (the quickest form to execute) in rows called "registers".

Pillars and columns were both structurally essential and boldly decorative. Square-sectioned **pillars** were faced with a statue of the pharaoh as a god (usually Osiris, hence the term Osiride pillars) or crowned with the head of the goddess Hathor (occasionally with a cow's face, but more often with cow's ears). **Columns** derived from plant forms, with different permutations of shafts and capitals. Palm columns had a plain shaft and leafy capital, papyrus columns chevron markings and an open (flowering) or closed bud capital, with a shaft sometimes resembling a bundle of stems.

Some Ptolemaic temples feature **astronomical ceilings** combining Ancient Egyptian and Babylonian cosmology, with the sky-goddess Nut swallowing and giving birth to the sun, planets and stars juxtaposed with bulls, scorpions and other zodiac symbols. The finest example is in the Hypostyle Hall at Dendara.

Imagery and cartouches

Much of the imagery of Ancient Egypt referred to the union of the **Two Lands** – the Nile Valley (Upper Egypt) and its Delta (Lower Egypt) – represented by the vulture-goddess **Nekhbet** and the cobra-goddess **Wadjet**. They were often combined on the lintels of doorways as a **winged sun-disc**; represented by their **heraldic plants**, the sedge and the lotus, bound together by the Nile-god Hapy; or by the ribbed **Djed pillar**, symbolizing unity and stability.

Hapy binding the two lands

The union of the Two Lands was also symbolized by royal crowns. At state rituals, the pharaoh customarily wore first the **White Crown** of the Delta and then the **Red Crown** of the Valley, although by the time of the New Kingdom (c.1570 BC) these were often subsumed into the **Combined Crown**. Pharaonic crowns also featured the **uraeus** or fire-spitting cobra, an incarnation of Wadjet believed to be the guardians of kings.

Winged sun-disc

Additional symbols of royal authority included the **crook** (or staff) and the **flail** (or scourge), which are often shown crossed over the chest – in the so-called Osiride position – on pharaonic statues. A ubiquitous motif was the **ankh**, symbolizing breath or life, which pharaohs are often depicted receiving from the gods in tombs or funerary texts.

The archetypal symbol of kingship was the **cartouche**, an oval formed by a loop of rope, enclosing the hieroglyphs of the pharaoh's nomen and prenomen. The **prenomen** (usually compounded with the name of Re, the sun-god) was one of four names adopted on accession to the throne, while the **nomen** roughly corresponded to a family name, and is the name by which pharaohs are known to posterity (eg Ramses or Seti).

At Early Dynastic temples and remote quarries, the ruler's name was represented by a **serekh**, a lozenge-shaped cartouche combining the pharaoh's "Horus name" with the image of a falcon.

White crown

Red crown

Combined crown

Uraeus

Djed pillar

Crook

Flail

Ankh

Music

Egypt's traditions in music, as with other cultural spheres, date back to pharaonic times, though the primary influences are Arab and Islamic. Cairo is the centre of the Arab recording industry – a dominance partly acquired thanks to the decline of its rivals in Lebanon, Libya and Kuwait, but one which is now being challenged by studios and labels in Saudi Arabia and the Emirates. Still, Egypt's vast and youthful population makes it the most important market for Arab music; what follows is the briefest of introductions to the various major genres.

Ancient Egyptian music

Nobody is sure what **Ancient Egyptian music** sounded like, but enough is known about the instruments for musicologists to have tried to recreate the hymns and songs that accompanied rituals and court life in ancient times. Flutes and clarinet-type instruments go back to the Old Kingdom (if not Pre-dynastic times), as do harps, trumpets, cymbals and castanets. By the Middle Kingdom, harps were accompanied by the *sistrum* (a kind of rattle associated with the goddess Hathor), tambourines, clappers and a type of guitar. The lute and lyre were probably introduced by the Hyksos, while other instruments came into Egypt as a result of the various foreign invasions after the fall of the New Kingdom.

Religious music

Although the call to prayer and the recitation of the Koran are not regarded in Egypt as music, they are certainly listened to for pleasure. The *tajwid*, or musically elaborate style of Koranic recitation, reached its apogee in Egypt; virtuosity is maintained by rigorously testing reciters before they are awarded the title of *moqri*. Among the masters of this genre are **Sheikh Mohammed Mahmoud al-Tablawi**, **Sheikh Abdelbasset Abdessamad** and **Mohammed Rifaat**.

Performers may be **munshids** – professionals who move from one festival to another – or simply the **muezzin** or **imam** of the local mosque. In everyday life, all muezzins have their individual styles of phrasing, and the Mubarak government's proposal to replace diverse voices with a single nationwide **azan** was fiercely resisted. Recitals at **moulids** are often more participation than performance, with lines of Sufi devotees chanting and swaying to the accompaniment of a drum. These recitals, known as **zikrs**, can last for days. **Sufi music** gained a wider following in Egypt in the late 1990s thanks to **Yassin al-Tuhami**, who revitalized a once-forgotten moulid in the Muqattam Hills that now draws *fellaheen*, Cairene and foreign Sufi enthusiasts alike.

Coptic liturgical music is quite different in spirit and only to be heard at church services. Some maintain that it is descended from Ancient Egyptian temple chants, as the Coptic language has many similarities with Ancient Egyptian and cymbals are played during the liturgy (distinguishing Coptic from Orthodox ritual music, which is purely choral). Much Coptic music on the web actually hails from churches in the US rather than Egypt (see links on ⓦcopticchurch.org and ⓦcoptic.org), but CDs of local Coptic choirs are sold at churches and monasteries in Egypt.

Another form – which many would deny is religious at all – is **zar** music, performed at rituals that are often likened to exorcisms, though their aim is not to expel a spirit from its host but to harmonize relations between them. *Zars* are usually private events reserved for women but occasionally occur at public moulids.

Classical Arabic music

The antecedents of **classical Arabic music** can be traced back to the **Bedouin** war bards of the Arabian Peninsula, whose metre matched that of a camel's stride, but also to the refined **court music** of the great caliphal cities of Baghdad and Damascus, and Ottoman Constantinople, which nurtured instrumental and compositional skills for generations.

During the twentieth century the form was characterized by oriental scales, orchestras and male choirs, bravura rhetoric and soloists filled with yearning. **Sayyid Darwish** was its father, blending Western instruments and harmony with Arab musical forms and Egyptian folklore, but its greatest exponent was **Umm Kalthoum**, whose fifty-year career spanned the advent of gramophones, radio and long-distance broadcasting, making her the most popular singer in the Arab world. In Egypt she was a national institution, accorded a weekly concert on radio and, later, TV; her funeral in 1975 drew the largest crowd since that of President Nasser (who timed his speeches around her broadcasts).

Almost as revered was **Mohammed Abdel Wahab**, a nightclub singer who composed the music for Egypt's national anthem, "Biladi, Biladi". His career was linked to the birth of the Egyptian film industry in the 1930s, which also saw the rise of Lebanese-born **Farid al-Atrache** and his sister **Asmahan** (killed in a car crash in 1944). Another superstar was the actor/singer **Abdel Halim Hafez**, the "Nightingale of the Nile", whose film recordings are still loved though he died in 1977. Wahab survived all of the above, but lay low for nearly twenty years before releasing his last song shortly before his death in 1991. His protégée, **Warda al-Jaza'iriya**, was a true Mediterranean – French, Algerian, Lebanese and Egyptian by birth, heritage and residency – and at the forefront of Arab music for decades until her death in 2012.

Regional/ethnic music

The different types of folk or popular music you'll come across vary greatly with the region and environment: Cairo, the Nile Valley, the Delta and the desert all have their own characteristic sounds, rhythms and instruments.

Saiyidi

The music of Upper Egypt – known, like its people, as **Saiyidi** – has a characteristic rhythm to which horses are trained to dance, based upon two instruments: the *nahrasan*, a two-sided drum hung over the chest and beaten with sticks; and the *mismar saiyidi*, a kind of wooden trumpet. **Omar Gharzawi** is known for his rebuttals of the stereotyped image of stupid, hot-headed Saiyidis; **Sayed Rekaby El-Genena** revels in poetic rapping competitions (a tradition in his home village); while **Rabia el-Bakaria**'s music and lyrics are likened by admirers to Egyptian reggae. On a more official standing is *Raïs* ("Boss") **Met'al Gnawi**, who has represented Egypt at music festivals abroad, with a band promoted as **Les Musiciens du Nil**. At home he is best known for his hit "Ya Farula!" ("My Strawberry"), full of fruity sexual allusions.

Fellahi

The northern counterpart to Saiyidi music, found in the Delta, is known as **fellahi** (peasant) music. It is generally softer, with a fondness for the *matsoum* (4/4) rhythm, and use of instruments like the *rababa*, a two-stringed viol, and the *mismar*, a kind of oboe.

Sawaheeli

Found along the Mediterranean coast and in the Canal Zone, **Sawaheeli** music is characterized by the use of a harp-like stringed instrument, the *simsimiya*. Another form, specific to Alexandria, also features the accordion, the result of the city's Greek and Turkish influences. The most famous Sawaheeli singers are **Aid el-Gannirni** from Suez and **Abdou el-Iskanrani** from Alex, while Port Said is home to Zakaria Ibrahim's band **El Tanbura**.

Bedouin

There are two kinds of **Bedouin** music in Egypt: one found in the Western Desert, the other in the Eastern Desert and Sinai. Both have songs recounting old tales to a strong rhythmic accompaniment featuring handclapping and frame drums called *duf* or *darabukka*, depending on their size. This polyrhythmic sound has been a major influence on *shababi* music (see p.621), but **Awad al-Malki** aside, Bedouin artists have yet to achieve widespread popularity in Egypt or the international success of Nubian musicians.

Nubian

Nubian music found a global audience in the 1990s, when **Ali Hassan Kuban** hit the world-music charts with "From Nubia to Cairo" and "Walk Like a Nubian". Born in 1933, he sang on boats as a child, played at weddings and founded a succession of bands that introduced brass sections, electric guitars and soul vocals to Nubian music, releasing his last album shortly before his death in 2001. Kuban, the female vocalist **Tété Alhinho** and other Nubian musicians cut several CDs under the name **Salamat** for the Piranha label (💿piranha.de).

Drummer **Mahmoud Fadl** began his career as a limbo dancer at weddings and has produced four albums of his own plus *Umm Kalthoum 7000*, a Nubian homage to the Arab diva featuring the singer **Salma Abu Greisha**, who also appears on Fadl's *The Drummers of the Nile Go South*, with drummers **Gaafar Hargal** and **Hamdi Matoul**. Until his death in 2006, another international star was **Hamza al-Din**, whose compositions for the oud (lute) and tar (single-skinned frame drum) were influenced by his Sufi beliefs and conservatory training. His haunting *Escalay* ("The Waterwheel") was a lament to his birthplace, drowned by Lake Nasser; he also wrote pieces for ballet companies and the Kronos Quartet.

Pop music

In Cairo and other cities, rural traditions have mixed with more elite styles and adapted to reflect urban preoccupations. By the mid-1980s two main types of music had developed: **shaabi** and **shababi**. Nowadays, some would say that the distinction between them is moot, and artists such as Hakim can rightfully claim to have a foot in each camp, while pop idol Amr Diab has spearheaded attempts to stake a claim on the world market. For news and clips of stars, visit **websites** 💿mazika.com, 💿albawaba .com and 💿sotwesoora.com, or Internet **radio stations** like Al Madina FM (💿almadinafm.com).

Shaabi

Shaabi (People) music was born in the working-class quarters of Cairo, and blends the traditional form of the *mawal* (plaintive vocal improvisations) with a driving beat; the lyrics are often raunchy, satirical or provocative. It was rarely broadcast via the media but was popular at weddings and parties throughout working-class Cairo and at nightclubs along Pyramids Road, and was played on battered cassettes in taxis, buses and cafés across Egypt.

The original *shaabi* singer was **Ahmed Adaweyah**, who, from 1971 on, introduced the idea of street language, to which later imitators added elements of rap and disco, in the manner of Algerian *raï* music. **Sha'ban Abdel Rahim** was a laundry ironer until a television appearance catapulted him to stardom. His earthy persona infuriated Egypt's cultural arbiters, but eventually he was embraced by the government and recorded "The Word of Truth", a paean to Mubarak crediting him with making running water and mobile phones available to the masses. Rival *shaabi* superstar **Hakim** tried to reach an international crossover audience with a remix of his hits by Transglobal Underground, following the example of Amr Diab (see p.621).

Shababi

Shababi or "youthful" music – also known as **Al-Jeel** (The Generation) music – followed hot on the heels of *shaabi* in the 1980s. It took disco elements like drum tracks and synthesized backing and mixed them with Nubian and Bedouin rhythms – the latter introduced by Libyan musicians who had fled to Cairo after Gaddafi's cultural crackdown, notably **Hamid el-Shaeri**, whose 1988 back-room recording of "*Lolaiki*" sung by **Ali Hamaida** launched the genre. Some call *shababi* "Mediterranean Music", acknowledging the crosscurrents of influences within the Arab world and its European diaspora – while others simply see it as classic Arabic pop.

Whatever the name, it's big business – though piracy means that most artists receive little from sales of tapes and CDs, earning their money from appearances at weddings and concerts instead. That said, Egypt's foremost pop idol, **Amr Diab**, broke into the international market with the song "Nour el Ain" and had another international hit with "Akhtar Wahed". But his career in Egypt might not recover from his craven response to the revolution, when Diab fled aboard his private jet – unlike rival *shababi* star **Mohammed Mounir,** whose plaintive songs of city life and pan-Arab yearning took on a political edge when he sang on Tahrir Square.

Shababi has a galaxy of female stars that compete on satellite channels across the Arab world. Many are foreigners – the Moroccan **Samira Saeed** or the Lebanese **Elissa**, **Nancy Ajram** and **Haifa Wahbe** – who are based in Cairo or at least sing in the Egyptian dialect, but the most controversial singer is homegrown. Born in the Islamist stronghold of Assyut, **Ruby** set Egyptian eyes agog with the sexuality of her videos and the assertiveness of her lyrics. By contrast, **Shireen Abdel Wahab** is seen as respectable, performing at official functions and benefit concerts. Other popular artists include the musician and actor **Mustafa Amar** and the lutist and singer **Ehab Tawfik**.

Protest music

The Arab Spring produced a blizzard of **protest music** across North Africa and the Middle East, which provided the soundtrack to Egypt's 2011 Revolution – performed live on Tahrir Square by local artists, or via the internet from abroad.

Ramey Essam is Egypt's best known protest singer, for his "Taty, Taty" ("Leave, Leave"), a mash-up of inventive slogans on Tahrir, where he stayed in the tent village and played almost every hour throughout the revolution on one of the square's many stages. *Shababi* star Mohammed Mounir voiced his support with "Ezzay?" ("How Come?") and recorded the rousing "Sout al-Horeya" ("Voice of Freedom") with Essam and Cairo rockers **Cairokee.**

Electronic music was a "safe" subversive genre that flourished below the state's radar in the last years of Mubarak's regime, personified by the multi-talented **Ahmed Basiony**, who died of injuries sustained on the second day of the revolution. People on Tahrir were also entertained by amateur musicians' improvised responses to voices from the crowd. Most of this music has yet to be released on CD, but can be found on the internet.

Discography

Although CDs and internet-streaming are increasingly popular in Egypt, cassettes remain the people's medium of choice, being robust, cheap and easy to copy. Recordings of traditional music are issued by the Centre for Culture and Art (Ⓦegyptmusic.org). In Europe or North America you can find a more limited range of vintage albums – mostly Umm Kalthoum and the like – with a few more contemporary releases on labels such as Mondo Melodia, Piranha or Axiom.

ANCIENT EGYPTIAN MUSIC

Michael Atherton *Ankh: The Sound of Ancient Egypt* (Celestial Harmonies). Haunting suites developed from songs or poems.

RELIGIOUS MUSIC

Mohammed Rifaat and Sheikh Abdelbasset Addessamad *Le Saint Coran* (Clube du Disque Arabe). Two masters of Koranic recitation featured on a series of French CDs.

Al-Hamidiyah Brotherhood *Saint Egypt: La Châdhiliya* – *Sufi Chants from Cairo* (Institut de Monde Arabe). An offshoot of the Shadhiliyya Sufi order.

Umm Sameh, Umm Hassan and Nour el-Sabah Mazaher. Three *zar* priestesses on CD and video, available in Cairo from the Egyptian Center for Culture and Art.

CLASSICAL ARABIC MUSIC

Abdel Halim Hafez *Abdel Halim Hafez – Twentieth Anniversary Memorial Edition* (EMI Arabia). This double CD includes some of his 1930s film-score songs and experimental arrangements from the 1960s.

Farid al-Atrache *Les Années '30* (Clube Du Disque Arabe). Remastered songs from the 1930s, when Farid was at his hottest.

★ **Mohammed Abdel Wahab** *Treasures* (EMI Arabia).

A double-CD featuring works from his later period including "The Last Blessing", an amazing forty-minute recital.

★ **Umm Kalthoum** *Al-Awia fil Gharam; Al-Atlaal; Enta Omri* (Sono Cairo). Three of her greatest live recordings, available on CD or DVD.

Warda *Warda* (EMI Hemisphere). A CD compilation of her work, including the hit "Barwanness Beek".

SAIYIDI MUSIC

★ **Les Musiciens du Nil** *Charcoal Gypsies* (Real World). Met'al Gnawi's ensemble fuses African and Middle Eastern percussion with traditional Saiyidi sounds, to irresistible effect.

Sayed Rekaby el-Genena *Jaafra*. Poetic rapping, oud and *duf* music from his home village, available on CD from the Egyptian Center for Culture and Art.

NUBIAN MUSIC

★ **Ali Hassan Kuban** *From Nubia to Cairo; Walk Like a Nubian;* and *Real Nubian* (Piranha). An infectious mix of wedding songs, brass bands and African percussion.

★ **Hamza ad-Din** *Escalay* (Nonesuch). Classical oud music inspired by Nubian sounds and Sufism.

★ **Mahmoud Fadl** *The Drummers of the Nile Go South;*

The Drummers of the Nile in Town (Piranha). The Nubian master-percussionist whips up a storm with Saiyidi musicians and the Hasaballah brass band.

★ **Salamat Mambo** *El Soudani – Nubian Al Jeel Music from Cairo and Ezzayakoum* (Piranha). Stonking percussion and frenzied sax and trumpet riffs.

SAWAHEELI

El Tanbura *The Simsimyya of Port Said* (Institut du Monde Arabe); *Friends of Bamboute* (Proper). Their debut album features Sufi and traditional songs; their twentieth-anniversary release adds dance music and trancelike chanting.

SHAABI

★ **Ahmed Adaweyah** *Al-Tareek; Adaweat*. Two soulful albums featuring the father of *shaabi* at his best; both are widely available in Egypt.

Hakim *Lela* (EMI Arabia). Sizzling *shaabi* with guest appearances by Stevie Wonder and the late James Brown.

SHABABI

★ **Amr Diab** *Akhtar Wahed; Kemmel Kalamak* (Rotana). The first is an excellent introduction to Diab's singing, while the second marks his debut as a composer.

Mohammed Mounir *Ahmar Shafayef* (Mondo Melodia).

Plaintive songs of life and the city, with a political edge.

Ruby *Fein Habibi* (MSM Egypt). This 2004 album set a new benchmark for the daringness of its lyrics and video clips; her 2007 *Meshit Wara Ehsasy* is tamer.

PROTEST MUSIC

At the time of writing, the following music is only available online.

Ahmed Basiony *Copia*. Killed during the Revolution, Basiony's (and others') electronic compositions can be heard on Mohammed Refat's 100 Radio Station (Ⓦ 100radiostation.com).

Arabian Knightz *Rebel* (YouTube). A remix of Lauryn Hill's "I find It Hard to Say" by Cairo's best known rap group.

★ **Cairokee** *Ya el-Medan* (YouTube). A wistful ballad to the spirit of Tahrir, with guest-vocalist Aida el-Ayouby accompanying herself on the oud.

Mohammed Mounir *Ezzay?* (YouTube). Unlike other pop stars, Mounir supported the Revolution from the outset, likening his bittersweet love for Egypt to an abusive relationship.

Ramy Essam Taty *Taty* (YouTube and Ⓦ facebook.com/RamyEssamOfficial). Dedicated to Mubarak, "Leave, leave" was first sung on Tahrir.

Books

Most of the books listed below are in print; those that are out of print (o/p) should be easy to track down in secondhand bookstores. Books that are only published in Egypt are generally most easily available in Cairo.

Books aside, there are a few **periodicals** which are worth seeking out if you're seriously into Egyptology. The *Journal of Egyptian Archeology*, published annually by the Egyptian Exploration Society (EES, ⓦees.ac.uk) is the world's leading Egyptology forum: all new theories and discoveries get printed here first. The EES also publishes the magazine *Egyptian Archeology*, illustrated and with a popular slant. Or you can subscribe to *Ancient Egypt* magazine (ⓦancientegyptmagazine.com), featuring easy-to-read articles by academics, plus details of lectures, conferences and events held by Egyptology societies in Britain.

Travel

GENERAL

Amelia Edwards *A Thousand Miles up the Nile*. Verbose, patronizing classic from the 1870s. All books on Egypt have their Amelia quotes – the *Rough Guide to Egypt* included.

Gustave Flaubert *Flaubert in Egypt*. A romp through the brothels, baths and "native quarters" of Egypt, by the future author of Madame Bovary.

Amitav Ghosh *In An Antique Land*. Wry tales of life in a Delta village during the early 1990s, interspersed with snippets of less absorbing historical research.

E.W. Lane *Manners and Customs of the Modern Egyptians*. Facsimile edition of this encyclopedic study of life in Mohammed Ali's Cairo, first published in 1836. Highly browsable.

Christopher Pick (ed) *Egypt: A Traveller's Anthology*. By a mixed bag of observers from the eighteenth and nineteenth centuries, including Disraeli, Mark Twain, Vita Sackville-West, Flaubert, E.M. Forster and Freya Stark.

Paul William Roberts *River in the Desert*. Chiefly interesting for its eyewitness account of a *zar* (exorcism) and a chapter on the Kushmaan Bedouin of the Eastern Desert.

★ **Anthony Sattin** *The Pharaoh's Shadow*. Fascinating discourse on the "survival" of Ancient Egyptian religious beliefs and practices in modern-day Egypt.

CAIRO

★ *Mamluk Art: The Splendour and Magic of the Sultans*. A guide to Mamluke architecture in Cairo, Alexandria and Rosetta, with concise essays by various scholars illustrated with colour photos, plans and walking routes.

★ **Maria Golia** *Cairo: City of Sand*. Focuses on the domestic life, housing and nitty-gritty of contemporary Cairo, including its satellite cities, ring road and other prestige projects.

Richard Parker *Islamic Monuments of Cairo: A Practical Guide*. A detailed handbook to the monuments and history of seventh- to nineteenth-century Cairo, illustrated with black and white photos.

★ **Max Rodenbeck** *Cairo: The City Victorious*. This superb history of Cairo includes the best anecdotes from earlier histories and follows events up until 1999.

ALEXANDRIA

Andrew Chugg *The Lost Tomb of Alexander the Great*. Chugg's theory, expounded in *The Lost Tomb*, that Alexander's body is buried in Venice under the guise of St Mark, caused a stir in 2004.

★ **Jean-Yves Empereur** *Alexandria Revealed; Alexandria Rediscovered*. As director of the Centre d'Etudes Alexandrines, responsible for excavating the Pharos, the Catacombs and lesser-known sites, Empereur has unearthed a mass of evidence about the ancient city. In *Alexandria Rediscovered* he writes about the problems of working in a city whose buried past is all too fragile. Both books are very readable and profusely illustrated.

E.M. Forster *Alexandria: A History and a Guide*. This 2004 Abinger Edition is replete with erudite notations to Forster's 1922 guidebook, and includes his collection of essays on Alexandrian life, Pharos and Pharillon.

★ **Michael Haag** *Alexandria: City of Memory*. An evocative and beautifully written account of the city as experienced by Forster, Cavafy and Durrell, illustrated with many rare photographs from the 1920s, 1930s and 1940s.

THE DESERT

★ **Wael Abed** *The Other Egypt: Travels in No Man's Land (Zarzora Expedition)*. A tour d'horizon of the natural wonders of the Western Desert, illustrated with eighty colour photos, plus rare black-and-white photos from the 1920s and 1930s.

Ahmed Fakhry *The Oases of Egypt*. Volume I, covering Siwa, is fascinating and has been republished in paperback; Volume II, on Bahariya and Farafra, is heavier going and remains out of print, but can be found in Cairo bookshops.

★ **Saul Kelly** *The Hunt for Zerzura: The Lost Oasis and the Desert War*. A detailed account of the real drama that inspired *The English Patient*.

★ **Alberto Siloitti** *The Oases; The Fayoum; Gilf Kebir National Park*. An excellent series of pocket guides to the Western Desert, profusely illustrated in colour.

★ **Margaret Mary Vale** *Sand and Silver*. The most comprehensive study yet of Siwan jewellery, costumes and customs, by an Englishwoman who has been visiting the oasis since 1984.

★ **Cassandra Vivian** *The Western Desert of Egypt: An Explorer's Handbook*. This exhaustive, recently updated guidebook covers all the oases and off-the-beaten-track sites, with maps and GPS waypoints. Fits the dashboard of a 4WD, but too heavy for a rucksack. Sold in Cairo and Bahariya Oasis.

Ancient history

GENERAL

★ **Mark Collier & Bill Manley** *How to Read Egyptian Hieroglyphics: A Step-By-Step Guide To Teach Yourself*. A bestseller, thanks to its clarity and the exciting sense of knowledge that it confers.

★ **George Hart** *British Museum Pocket Dictionary of Egyptian Gods and Goddesses; Routledge Dictionary of Egyptian Gods and Goddesses*. Two highly useful guides to the deities and myths of Ancient Egypt, illustrated with line drawings. The former is easier to carry when visiting temples in Egypt.

Colin J. Humphreys *The Miracles of Exodus: A Scientist's Discovery of the Extraordinary Natural Causes of the Biblical Stories*. With a title like that, who could resist a look? Some of the explanations therein seem quite plausible, others less so.

Dieter Kurth *The Temple of Edfu: A Guide by an Ancient Egyptian Priest*. A complete translation of the hieroglyphic inscriptions on the enclosure wall of Edfu Temple, describing the rituals and daily life within its walls.

Dimitri Meeks & Christine Favard-Meeks *Daily Life of the Egyptian Gods*. Scholarly study of the rituals and beliefs surrounding the gods; a TV spin-off focused on the more salacious bits.

★ **David Rohl** *A Test of Time: The Bible – From Myth to History; Legend: The Genesis of Civilisation*. The former is a stimulating argument for revising the chronology of Ancient Egyptian and Biblical history; the latter advances an unusual theory of Egypt's Pre-dynastic era. Both are closely argued and worth reading even if you're sceptical (as most Egyptologists are).

Ian Shaw *The Oxford History of Ancient Egypt*. An excellent survey taking in theories and discoveries up until 2003, with many fine illustrations and site plans.

★ **Ian Shaw and Paul Nicholson** *British Museum Dictionary of Ancient Egypt*. Richly illustrated, paperback-sized dictionary, especially good for site plans and assessments of fairly recent discoveries.

Joyce Tyldesley *Hatshepsut: The Female Pharaoh; Nefertiti: Egypt's Sun Queen; Ramses: Egypt's Greatest Pharaoh*. Readable and illuminating biographies of some of the most famous rulers of the New Kingdom.

Jean Vercoutter *The Search for Ancient Egypt*. Pocket-size account of Egypt's "discovery" by foreigners, packed with drawings, photos and engravings.

★ **Kent Weeks** *The Lost Tomb; The Treasures of Luxor and the Valley of the Kings; Atlas of the Valley of the Kings*. The first describes Weeks' discovery and excavation of the mass tomb of the sons of Ramses II; the second is an illustrated guide to treasures from Luxor and its necropolis; and the third is the first volume of an ongoing magnum opus, showcased on the Theban Mapping Project's website, ⓦ kv5.com.

John Anthony West *Serpent in the Sky: High Wisdom of Ancient Egypt; The Traveler's Key to Ancient Egypt: A Guide to the Sacred Places of Ancient Egypt*. New Age interpretations of Ancient Egyptian culture. *Serpent* is quite heavy going and marred by rants, but *Traveler's Key* is a lively on-site guide that points out inconsistencies in orthodox Egyptology and presents alternative theories.

PYRAMIDOLOGY

Guillemette Andreu *Egypt in the Age of the Pyramids*. Nicely illustrated study of the pyramids' evolution in the context of Ancient Egyptian life and culture, by a French Egyptologist.

Robert Bauval *The Orion Mystery*. Postulates that the Giza Pyramids corresponded to the three stars in Orion's

Belt as it was in 10,500 BC.

I.E.S. Edwards *The Pyramids of Egypt*. Lavishly illustrated, closely argued survey of all the major pyramids, overdue for an update since it was last revised in 1991.

Graham Hancock *Fingerprints of the Gods; The Message of the Sphinx; The Mars Mystery; Heaven's Mirror*. Asserts that the pyramids, Angkor Wat temple and the statues of Easter Island were all created by a lost civilization propagated by extraterrestrials.

Peter Hodges *How the Pyramids were Built*. As a professional stonemason, Hodges has practical experience, rather than academic qualifications, on his side. An easy read and quite persuasive.

THE AMARNA PERIOD/TUTANKHAMUN

Cyril Aldred *Akhenaten, King of Egypt*. A conventional account of the Amarna period by a British Egyptologist.

★ **Michael Haag** *The Rough Guide to Tutankhamun*. A pocket-sized guide, covering not just the life of its subject but also the history of the Valley of the Kings and the lives of Howard Carter and Lord Carnarvon. Illustrated throughout with both archive and modern photographs.

Dominic Montserrat *Akhenaten: History, Fantasy and Ancient Egypt*. An interesting study of how Akhenaten's image has evolved and resonated in popular culture since he was "discovered" in the nineteenth century.

Ahmed Osman *Moses and Akhenaten; Stranger in the Valley of the Kings*. These two books argue that Akhenaten was actually Moses, and his grandfather Yuya the Biblical Joseph, in a substantial rewrite of the Exodus story.

Julia Samson *Nefertiti and Cleopatra*. Fascinating account of Egypt's most famous queens, by an expert on Amarna civilization. Samson concludes that Smenkhkare, Akhenaten's mysterious successor, was actually Nefertiti; her coverage of Cleopatra is rather less controversial.

PTOLEMAIC, ROMAN AND COPTIC EGYPT

Christian Cannuyer *Coptic Egypt – The Christians of the Nile*. A pocket-sized, easy-to-read study of Coptic history and culture, fully illustrated throughout.

Dominic Montserrat *Sex and Society in Graeco-Roman Egypt*. In-depth study of sexual mores and practices in a famously licentious era.

Győző Vörös *Taposiris Magna: Port of Isis*. A richly illustrated look at the ancient port city whose lighthouse is commonly thought to be a scaled-down copy of the Pharos at Alexandria, though Vörös argues it was actually a prototype.

MEDIEVAL AND MODERN HISTORY

Said K. Aburish *Nasser: The Last Arab*. A new look at an old hero, who embodied the aspirations and contradictions of Arab nationalism. As the author of books on Saddam Hussein, Arafat and the House of Saud, Aburish mourns the lack of a new Nasser to inspire the Arabs today.

Alaa Al-Aswany *On the State of Egypt: What Caused the Revolution*. A collection of articles by the bestselling novelist (see p.627), dating from 2005 onwards, that stops short of the Revolution but clarifies its genesis.

★ **Stephen Bradley** *Inside Egypt: The Land of the Pharaohs on the Brink of a Revolution*. First published in 2008, this prescient book examines the darkest corners of Mubarak's Egypt.

★ **Stephen Bungay** *Alamein*. Concise, highly readable and enlightening on the interplay between strategy, tactics, logistics and intelligence during the Western Desert campaign.

Steven Cook *The Struggle for Egypt: From Nasser to Tahrir Square*. An accessible overview of Egyptian history since the 1950s and the dilemmas facing the country in the twenty-first century.

★ **Wael Ghonim** *Revolution 2.0*. Google's Middle East marketing director, Ghonim set up the "We are all Khaled Saeed" Facebook page that mobilized the first protest on Tahrir Square that led to the Revolution. This is a personal account of his experiences, including eleven days in a state security prison.

Amin Maalouf *The Crusades through Arab Eyes*. A Lebanese Copt, Maalouf has used the writings of contemporary Arab chroniclers to retrace two centuries of Middle Eastern history and concludes that present-day relations between the Arab world and the West are still marked by the battle that ended seven centuries ago.

Ayman Mohyeldin & Mia Gröndahl *Tahrir Square: The Heart of the Egyptian Revolution*. Stunning photos from Tahrir by a Swedish photo-journalist based in Cairo, with a forward by Al Jazeera's Egypt correspondent.

Adhaf Soueif *Cairo: My City, Our Revolution*. A heartfelt, beautifully written account of Soueif's involvement in the Revolution, by the author of *The Map of Love* and other novels (see p.627).

SOCIOLOGY AND FEMINISM

★ **Galal Amin** *Whatever Happened to the Egyptians?; Whatever Else Happened to the Egyptians?* Two insightful, wryly readable accounts of social changes from the 1950s to the present. Subjects covered range from car ownership

and Westernization in the first book through to TV, fashions and weddings in the second.

★ **Nayra Atiya (ed)** *Khul-Khaal: Five Egyptian Women Tell Their Stories*. Gripping biographical accounts by women from diverse backgrounds revealing much about Egyptian life a generation ago that still holds true today. Widely sold in Egypt.

★ **R. Critchfield** *Shahhat: An Egyptian*. A wonderful book based on several years' resident research with the Nile Valley *fellaheen*, across the river from Luxor. Moving, amusing and shocking, by turn. Widely sold in Egypt.

Nawal el-Saadawi *The Hidden Face of Eve*. Egypt's best-known woman writer, this is her major polemic, covering a wide range of topics – female circumcision, prostitution, divorce and sexual relationships. Her website (⊛ nawalsaadawi.net) embraces literature, sociology and politics; see also the "Egyptian fiction" section (below).

Islam

A.J. Arberry (trans.) *The Koran* (Oxford University Press). The best English-language version of Islam's holy book, whose revelations and prose style form the basis of the Muslim faith and Arab literature.

★ **Karen Armstrong** *Muhammed: A Prophet for Our Times; Islam: A Short History*. Two widely acclaimed books by a religious scholar and former nun, sympathetic to Islam and its Prophet.

Titus Burckhardt *Art of Islam: Language and Meaning* (o/p). Superbly illustrated, intellectually penetrating overview of Islamic art and architecture.

★ **Robert Spencer** *The Truth about Muhammed: Founder of the World's Most Intolerant Religion*. A forensic indictment of the Prophet's life and legacy, to be read as an antidote to Armstrong's biography (or vice versa), but not taken to Egypt.

Wildlife

Bertel Bruun *Common Birds of Egypt*. A slim illustrated guide you can slip into your pocket.

★ **Guy Buckles** *Dive Guide: The Red Sea*. An illustrated guide to over 125 diving and snorkelling sites from Sinai to Eritrea, with notes on access, visibility and diving

conditions, as well as the species that you'll see.

David Cottridge & Richard Porter *A Photographic Guide to Birds of Egypt and the Middle East*. This ornithology guide is better illustrated than Brunn's, but heavier to carry around.

Egyptian fiction and poetry

★ **Alaa Al-Aswany** *The Yacoubian Building; Chicago*. Al-Aswany's first novel was a controversial bestseller in the Arab world, portraying the tenants of a Cairo apartment block as a microcosm of Egyptian society. His second, *Chicago*, set among Egyptian émigrés abroad, is equally perceptive about Egyptians, but its American characters verge on caricature.

★ **Salwa Bakr** *The Golden Chariot; The Wiles of Men and Other Stories*. A novel set in a women's prison near Cairo; the inmates' tales highlight different facets of women's oppression in Mubarak's Egypt. Touching and disturbing.

C.P. Cavafy *The Collected Poems of C.P. Cavafy: A New Translation*. Elegiac evocations of the Alexandrian myth by the city's most famous poet, in a new translation by Aliki Barnstone.

Waguih Ghali *Beer in the Snooker Club*. A wryly bittersweet novel about drunken Anglophile Cairene wasters trying to square their youthful idealism with the realities of the Nasser era.

★ **Gamal al-Ghitani** *The Zafarani Files; Zayni Barakat; Pyramid Texts*. The *Zafarani Files* is a dark satire about paranoia and credulity, while *Zayni Barakat* is a convoluted drama set in the last years of Mamluke rule. His latest novel, *Pyramid Texts*, is a series of Sufistic parables about the human condition, inspired by the Sphinx and the Giza Pyramids.

Yusuf Idris *The Cheapest Nights; Rings of Burnished Brass* (o/p). Two superb collections by Egypt's finest writer of short stories, who died in 1991. Uncompromisingly direct, yet ironic.

★ **Naguib Mahfouz** *Palace Walk; Palace of Desires; Sugar Street; Miramar*. The late Nobel laureate's novels have a nineteenth-century feel, reminiscent of Balzac or Victor Hugo. His "*Cairo Trilogy*", comprising the first three books listed here, is a tri-generational saga set during the British occupation, while *Miramar* looks back on the 1952 Revolution from the twilight of the Nasser era. Favoured themes include the discrepancy between ideology and human problems, and hypocrisy and injustice.

★ **Nawal el-Saadawi** *Woman at Point Zero; The Fall of the Imam; God Dies by the Nile*; and others. Saadawi's novels are informed by her work as a doctor and psychiatrist in Cairo, and by her feminist and socialist beliefs, on subjects that are virtually taboo in Egypt. *Point Zero*, her best, is a powerful and moving story of a woman condemned to death for killing a pimp. You will find very few of her books on sale in Egypt, though *The Fall of the Imam* is the only one officially banned. See also the "Sociology" section (above).

Ahdaf Soueif *Aisha; In the Eye of the Sun; The Map of Love; I Think of You*. Born in Cairo, Souief was educated in Egypt and England. Her semi-autobiographical novels are acclaimed for their sensibility: *In the Eye of the Sun* explores love and destiny in the Middle East during the 1960s and 1970s; *The Map of Love* (shortlisted for the Booker Prize) and *I Think of You* focus on sexual politics.

★ **Bahaa Taher** *Aunt Safiyya and the Monastery*. Beautifully crafted novella set in a village in Upper Egypt, where a blood feud is challenged by a Muslim farmer and a Coptic monk.

Foreign fiction

Will Adams *The Alexander Cipher; The Exodus Quest*. A pair of pacey thrillers featuring Egyptologist Daniel Knox on the trail of the long-lost tombs of Alexander the Great and Akhenaten.

Michael Asher *The Eye of Ra; Firebird*. Two gung-ho thrillers with a supernatural edge, involving outlaw desert tribes and the lost oasis of Zerzura.

Noel Barber *A Woman of Cairo*. Ill-starred love and destiny amongst the Brits and westernized Egyptians of King Farouk's Cairo; from that perspective, a good insight into those times.

Agatha Christie *Death Comes at the End; Death on the Nile*. The latter is a classic piece of skullduggery solved by Poirot aboard a Nile cruiser. *Death Comes at the End* is a lamer effort, set around Luxor.

★ **Len Deighton** *City of Gold*. Hard-boiled thriller set in 1941, when vital information was being leaked to Rommel. Its period detail is excellent.

Paul Doherty *The Mask of Ra*. A pharaonic whodunnit set at the time of Hatshepsut's accession.

Lawrence Durrell *The Alexandria Quartet*. Endless sexual and metaphysical ramblings (see p.468), occasionally relieved by a dollop of colonial Alex atmosphere or a profound psychological insight.

Ken Follet *The Key to Rebecca*. Fast-paced thriller based on the true story of a German spy who operated in Cairo during 1942, with a walk-on role for Sadat.

Robert Irwin *The Arabian Nightmare*. Paranoid fantasy set in the Cairo of Sultan Qaitbey, where a Christian spy contracts the affliction of the title. As his madness deepens, reality and illusion spiral inwards like an opium-drugged walk through a medina of the mind.

T.S. Learner *Sphinx*. The discovery of an ancient underwater artefact off the coast of Alexandria opens a pandora's box of murderous intrigue, with potentially world-shaking consequences.

★ **Michael Ondaatje** *The English Patient*. The novel takes liberties with the truth when portraying Almássy and his co-explorers (see p.457) but its brilliance is undeniable, and its equal focus on Kip and Dorothy make it more multi-layered than the film.

Michael Pearce *The Mamur Zapt and the Donkey-vous; The Mamur Zapt and the Girl in the Nile; The Mamur Zapt and the Men Behind; The Mamur Zapt and the Return of the Carpet; The Mamur Zapt and the Spoils of Egypt*. A series of yarns set in khedival Egypt, featuring the chief of Cairo's secret police.

Dan Richardson *Gog – an End Time Mystery*. Set in a flood-ravaged Egypt after the destruction of the High Dam, this near-future thriller (written by one of the authors of this guide) has some memorable Egyptian characters and plot twists, played out amid the ruins of Cairo, a Pre-dynastic tomb on the Giza Plateau and other locations.

Wilbur Smith *River God; The Seventh Scroll; Warlock*. A blockbuster trilogy that crams the Hyksos invasion and liberation of Ancient Egypt into two volumes, interspersed by the search for the lost tomb of pharaoh Mamose in modern times.

★ **Paul Sussman** *The Last Secret of the Temple; The Lost Army of Cambyses; The Hidden Oasis; Labyrinth of Osiris*. Four intelligent thrillers featuring police inspector Yusuf Khalifa, embroiled in ancient mysteries and present-day turmoil across the Middle East.

Glossary

Ablaq Striped. An effect achieved by painting, or laying courses of different coloured masonry; usually white with red or buff. A Bahri Mamluke innovation, possibly derived from the Roman technique of *opus mixtum* – an alternation of stone and brickwork.

Ain (Ayn, Ein) Spring.

Ba The Ancient Egyptian equivalent of the soul or personality, often represented by a human-headed bird; also used to describe the physical manifestation of certain gods.

Bab Gate or door, as in the medieval city walls.

Bahr River, sea, canal.

Baksheesh Alms or tips.

Baladi National, local, rural or countrified; from balad, meaning country or land.

Baltagiyya A rent-a-mob of ex-convicts, drug addicts and thieves, used by Mubarak's state security apparatus to disrupt protests and intimidate opposition activists.

Baraka Blessing.

Beit (Beyt) House. Segregated public and private quarters, the *malqaf*, *maq'ad* and *mashrabiya* are typical features of old Cairene mansions.

Bey (Bay) Lord or noble; an Ottoman title, now a respectful form of address to anyone in authority.

Bir (Beer) Well.

Birka (Birqa, Birket) Lake.

Burg (Borg) Tower.

Calèche Horse-drawn carriage.

Caliph Successor to the Prophet Mohammed and spiritual and political leader of the Muslim empire. A struggle over this office caused the Sunni–Shia schism of 656 AD.

Canopic jar Sealed receptacle used in funerary rituals to preserve the viscera of the deceased after embalming. The stomach, intestines, liver and lungs each had a patron deity, sculpted on the jar's lid.

Cloisonné A multi-step enamelling process used to produce jewellery, vases and other decorative objects.

Corniche Seafront or riverfront promenade.

Dahabiya Nile houseboat.

Darb Path or way; can apply to alleyways, thoroughfares or desert caravan routes.

Deir Monastery or convent.

Djed pillar Ancient Egyptian symbol of stability, in the shape of a pillar with three or four horizontal flanges, possibly derived from a pole around which grain was tied.

Electrum An alloy of gold and silver, used by the Ancient Egyptians to sheath the tips of obelisks.

Emir Commander, prince.

Feddan A traditional measure of land equivalent to 4200 square metres.

Fellaheen (sing. fellah) Peasant farmers who work their own land or as sharecroppers or hired labourers for wealthier farmers.

Felucca Nile sailing boat.

Finial Ornamental crown of a dome or minaret, often topped by an Islamic crescent.

Galabiyya Loose flowing robe worn by men.

Gezira Island.

Ghard (Ghird) Extended belt of sand dunes.

Hajj (Hadj) Pilgrimage to Mecca.

Hagg/Hagga One who has made the pilgrimage to Mecca.

Haikal Sanctuary of a Coptic church.

Hammam Turkish bathhouse.

Haramlik Literally the "forbidden" area, ie women's or private apartments in a house or palace.

Heb-Sed An Ancient Egyptian festival symbolizing the renewal of the king's physical and magical powers, celebrated in the thirtieth year of his reign and every three years thereafter.

Islamist(s) Groups aiming to replace secular with Sharia law and re-align Egypt's foreign policy – some by peaceful means, others violently.

Ithyphallic Decorous term for a god with an erection; Min, Amun and Osiris were often depicted thus by the Ancient Egyptians.

Jebel (Gebel, Gabal, etc) Hill or mountain

Jedid/Jedida (Gadid/Gadia) "New" in Arabic; the ending depends on whether the subject of the adjective is masculine or feminine. In Upper Egypt, the first syllable is pronounced as a soft je; in Lower Egypt, as a hard ga sound.

Ka Ancient Egyptians believed that an individual's life-force served as the "double" of his or her physical being and required sustenance after their death, through offerings to the deceased's *ka* statue, sometimes secluded in a *serdab*.

Khan Place where goods were made, stored and sold, which also provided accommodation for travellers and merchants, like a *wikala*.

Khanqah (or zawia) A "monastery" or hostel for Sufis or dervishes.

Khedive Viceroy.

Kom Mound of rubble and earth covering an ancient settlement.

Kufic The earliest style of Arabic script; Foliate kufic was a more elaborate form, superseded by Naskhi script.

Kuttab Koranic school, usually for boys or orphans.

Leyla kebira "Big night": the climactic night of a popular religious festival.

Liwan An arcade or vaulted space off a courtyard in mosques and madrassas; originally, the term meant a sitting room opening onto a covered court.

Maabad (Mabad) Temple (Arabic).

Madrassa Literally a "place of study" but generally used to designate theological schools. Each madrassa propagates a particular school of Islamic jurisprudence.

Malqaf Wind scoop for directing cool breezes into houses; in Egypt, they always face north, towards the prevailing wind.

Mamissi Birth House. A pseudo-Coptic term coined to describe a structure attached to temples from the Late Period to Roman times, where rituals celebrating the birth of Horus and the reigning king were performed.

Mashrabiya An alcove in lattice windows where jars of water can be cooled by the wind; by extension, the projecting balcony and screened window itself, which enabled women to watch street-life or the *salamlik* without being observed.

Masr (Misr, Musr) Popular name for Egypt, and Cairo, dating back to antiquity.

Mastaba Mud-brick benches outside buildings; Egyptologists use the word to describe the flat-roofed, multi-roomed tombs of the Old Kingdom, found at Saqqara and other sites.

Merlons Indentations and raised portions along a parapet. Fatimid merlons were angular; Mamluke ones crested, trilobed (like a fleur-de-lis) or in fancier leaf patterns.

Midan An open space or square; in Tulunid Cairo most were originally polo grounds.

Mihrab Niche indicating the direction of Mecca, to which all Muslims pray.

Minaret Tower from which the call to prayer is given; derived from minara, the Arabic word for "beacon" or "lighthouse".

Minbar Pulpit from which an address to the Friday congregation is given. Often superbly inlaid or carved in variegated marble or wood.

Mosque A simple enclosure facing Mecca; in its original form, the mosque acquired minarets, *riwaqs*, madrassas and mausolea as it was developed by successive dynasties.

Moulid Popular festival marking an event in the Koran or the birthday of a Muslim saint. The term also applies to the name-days of Coptic saints.

Muezzin A prayer-crier (who nowadays is more likely to broadcast by loudspeaker than to climb up and shout from the minaret).

Muqarnas Stalactites, pendants or honeycomb ornamentation of portals, domes or squinches.

Naos The core and sanctuary of a Coptic or Byzantine church, where the liturgy is performed.

Naskhi Form of Arabic script with joined-up letters, introduced by the Ayyubids.

Nomarch A Greek title, used to describe a provincial governor in Ancient Egypt.

Nome A Greek term, used to describe a province of Ancient Egypt.

Nomen The name that a pharaoh was given at birth, which equates more or less with a family name, eg Tuthmosis in the XVIII Dynasty or Ramses in the XIX Dynasty.

Ostracon (pl. ostraca) A Greek term used by archeologists to describe potsherds or flakes of limestone bearing texts and drawings, often consisting of personal jottings, letters or scribal exercises.

Pasha (Pacha) Ruler – a lord or prince. Nowadays, a respectful term of address for anyone in authority, pronounced "basha".

Prenomen The "throne name" assumed by a pharaoh at his coronation. When inscribed in a cartouche it is usually preceded by the symbols for Upper and Lower Egypt, and followed by the suffix Re.

Pronaos Vestibule of a Greek or Roman temple, enclosed by side walls and a row of columns in front.

Pylon A broad, majestic gateway that formed the entrance to temples from the XVIII Dynasty onwards, or a series of gateways within large complexes such as Karnak.

Qadim/Qadima (masc./fem.) "Old", as in Masr al-Qadima, or Old Cairo.

Qalaa Fortress, citadel.

Qasr Palace, fortress, mansion. Also used to describe semi-fortified villages in the oases, such as Qasr al-Farafra.

Qibla The direction in which Muslims pray, indicated in mosques by the wall where the *mihrab* is located.

Qubba Dome, and by extension any domed tomb or shrine.

Ras Cape, headland, peak.

Repoussé A technique in which malleable metal is ornamented by hammering from the reverse side to form a raised design on the front, which is often combined with the opposite technique of chasing (hammering from the front) to form a finished piece.

Riwaq Arcaded aisle around a mosque's *sahn*, originally used as residential quarters for theological students; ordinary folk may also take naps here.

Sabil Public fountain or water cistern. During the nineteenth century it was often combined with a Koranic school to make a *sabil-kuttab*.

Sahn Central courtyard of a mosque, frequently surrounded by *riwaqs* or *liwans*.

Salafist(s) Islamist movement advocating a strictly literal application of the Koran and *ahadith*, that is hostile to the veneration of dead sheikhs, and any form of religious innovation.

Salamlik The "greeting" area of a house; ie the public and men's apartments.

Sanctuary The *liwan* incorporating the *qibla* wall in a mosque, or the shrine of a deity in an Ancient Egyptian temple.

Senussis An Islamist movement, strong in the Libyan Desert between 1830 and 1930, which resisted British and Italian colonialism in Egypt and Libya.

Serdab The Arabic word for a cellar beneath a mosque. Also used by Egyptologists to describe the room in mastaba tombs where statues of the deceased's *ka* were placed, often with eye-holes or a slit in the wall enabling the *ka* to leave the chamber, and offerings to be made to the statue from the tomb's chapel.

Shabti (ushabti) Ancient funerary figurines, whose purpose was to spare their owner from having to perform menial tasks in the after-life.

Sharia Street (literally "way"). With the Arabic feminine ending added (the resulting word is sometimes transliterated Shariah), it refers to laws based on Koranic precepts.

Sharm Bay.

Squinch An arch spanning the right angle formed by two walls, so as to support a dome.

Sufis Islamic mystics who seek to attain union with Allah through trance-inducing *zikrs* and dances. Whirling Dervishes belong to one of the Sufi sects.

Supreme Council for Antiquities (SCA) The state organization responsible for Egypt's ancient monuments, formerly called the Egyptian Antiquities Organization.

Supreme Council of the Armed Forces (SCAF) Military junta that assumed power after Mubarak's overthrow, on behalf of Egypt's "deep state".

Tariqa A Sufi order or dervish brotherhood.

Tell Another word for *kom*.

Thuluth Script whose vertical strokes are three times larger than its horizontal ones; Thuluth literally means "third".

Tuf-tuf A form of transport in some tourist areas, consisting of an engine pulling open-sided carriages, but running along roads; similar to a Noddy train.

Uraeus (pl. uraei) The rearing cobra symbol of the Delta goddess Wadjet, worn as part of the royal crown and often identified with the destructive "Eye of Re".

Wadi Valley or watercourse (usually dry).

Wahah Oasis.

Wikala Bonded warehouse with rooms for merchants upstairs. Here they bought trading licences from the *muhtasib* and haggled over sales in the courtyard. *Okel* is another term for a *wikala*.

Yardang Freestanding, wind-eroded rock formations, typical of the White Desert.

Zikr Marathon session of chanting and swaying, intended to induce communion with Allah.

Zawia See *khanqah*.

Small print and index

A ROUGH GUIDE TO ROUGH GUIDES

Published in 1982, the first Rough Guide – to Greece – was a student scheme that became a publishing phenomenon. Mark Ellingham, a recent graduate in English from Bristol University, had been travelling in Greece the previous summer and couldn't find the right guidebook. With a small group of friends he wrote his own guide, combining a highly contemporary, journalistic style with a thoroughly practical approach to travellers' needs.

The immediate success of the book spawned a series that rapidly covered dozens of destinations. And, in addition to impecunious backpackers, Rough Guides soon acquired a much broader readership that relished the guides' wit and inquisitiveness as much as their enthusiastic, critical approach and value-for-money ethos.

These days, Rough Guides include recommendations from budget to luxury and cover more than 200 destinations around the globe, as well as producing an ever-growing range of eBooks and apps.

Visit **roughguides.com** to see our latest publications.

Rough Guide credits

Editor: Gavin Thomas
Layout: Ankur Guha
Cartography: Deshpal Dabas
Picture editor: Lisa Jacobs
Proofreader: Anita Sach
Managing editor: Keith Drew
Assistant editor: Jalpreen Kaur Chhatwal
Production: Charlotte Cade
Cover design: Nicole Newman, Ankur Guha
Editorial assistant: Olivia Rawes

Senior pre-press designer: Dan May
Design director: Scott Stickland
Travel publisher: Joanna Kirby
Digital travel publisher: Peter Buckley
Reference director: Andrew Lockett
Operations coordinator: Becky Doyle
Publishing director (Travel): Clare Currie
Commercial manager: Gino Magnotta
Managing director: John Duhigg

Publishing information

This ninth edition published February 2013 by
Rough Guides Ltd,
80 Strand, London WC2R 0RL
11, Community Centre, Panchsheel Park,
New Delhi 110017, India
Distributed by the Penguin Group
Penguin Books Ltd,
80 Strand, London WC2R 0RL
Penguin Group (USA)
375 Hudson Street, NY 10014, USA
Penguin Group (Australia)
250 Camberwell Road, Camberwell,
Victoria 3124, Australia
Penguin Group (NZ)
67 Apollo Drive, Mairangi Bay, Auckland 1310,
New Zealand
Penguin Group (South Africa)
Block D, Rosebank Office Park, 181 Jan Smuts Avenue,
Parktown North, Gauteng, South Africa 2193
Rough Guides is represented in Canada by Tourmaline
Editions Inc. 662 King Street West, Suite 304, Toronto,
Ontario M5V 1M7
Printed in Singapore by Toppan Security Printing Pte. Ltd.

Help us update

We've gone to a lot of effort to ensure that the ninth
edition of **The Rough Guide to Egypt** is accurate and up-
to-date. However, things change – places get "discovered",
opening hours are notoriously fickle, restaurants and
rooms raise prices or lower standards. If you feel we've got
it wrong or left something out, we'd like to know, and if
you can remember the address, the price, the hours, the
phone number, so much the better.

Please send your comments with the subject line
"**Rough Guide Egypt Update**" to ❸ mail@uk.roughguides
.com. We'll credit all contributions and send a copy of the
next edition (or any other Rough Guide if you prefer) for
the very best emails.

Find more travel information, connect with fellow
travellers and book your trip on ⓦ roughguides.com

Readers' letters

Thanks to all the readers who have taken the time to write in with comments and suggestions (and apologies if we've
inadvertently omitted or misspelt anyone's name):

Thanks to all the readers who have taken the time to write
in with comments and suggestions (and apologies if we've
inadvertently omitted or misspelt anyone's name): Ahmed

Abed; Wael Abed; Omar Ahmed; Zahraa Adel Awad; S.D.
Baylis; Jan Bennell; John Houston; Mahdi Hweiti; Marlene
LeGates; Paul Sussman; Wendy Tyson; Chris Wood.

ABOUT THE AUTHOR

Before joining Rough Guides, **Dan Richardson** worked as a sailor on the Red Sea and lived in Peru. Since then, he has authored or co-authored guides to Moscow, St Petersburg, Hungary, Budapest, Romania, Bulgaria and Egypt, lectured at the Foreign Office and been a volunteer aid worker in Albania. He is also the author of *Gog – an End Time Mystery*, an apocalyptic whodunit set in near-future Egypt, and has been a special-effects actor since 2010.

Acknowledgements

Dan Richardson Thanks to Saber in Cairo; Hussein Farag in Minya; Ramadan Ali and Mohammed Abdel Hamid in Assyut; Ahmed Zakaria in Sohag; Abdel Hagg Ibrahim, Hamada and Karin El-Khalifa, Aladin Al-Sahaby and Hassan in Luxor; Mahmoud Yussef and Mohsen Abdel Monaem in Kharga Oasis; Talat Mulah and Peter Wirth in Bahariya Oasis; Mahdi Hweiti in Siwa Oasis; and Zahra Adel Awad and all the staff of the tourist office in Alexandria. In London, thanks to Gavin Thomas for his incisive editing and forbearance of missed deadlines.

Daniel Jacobs Big thanks to Hisham Youssef (*Berlin Hotel*), Salah Mohammed (SAMO Tours), Hamdi Shora, Caroline Evanoff, Abdul Al Sharawy and Mohamed Saied.

Shafik Meghji Thanks to all the locals and travellers who helped out along the way. A special *shokran* must go to Dan Richardson and Daniel Jacobs for their advice and support; Gavin Thomas for his excellent editing skills; Pru and David at On The Go Tours; Rosie Hegarty; Andy Turner; Jessica Jacobs; Tanis Newman; Hany George; Jean, Nizar and Nina Meghji; and Sioned Jones, for all her love and support.

Photo credits

All photos © Rough Guides except the following:
(Key: t-top; c-centre; b-bottom; l-left; r-right)

p.1 Getty Images: Pyramids of Giza
p.2 Getty Images: Red Sea boat
p.4 Olivier Goujon/SuperStock: Valley of the Kings
p.5 Getty Images: Feluccas
p.9 Getty Images: Street hawker (t); Green turtle (b)
p.11 Getty Images: Bahariya
p.13 Getty Images: Little egrets (t); Temple of Queen Nefertari (b)
p.14 Getty Images: Mount Sinai
p.15 Getty Images: Islamic Cairo (t); Prisma/SuperStock: Diving and snorkelling (c); Robert Harding Picture Library/SuperStock: Valley of the Kings (b)
p.16 Toño Labra/age fotostock/SuperStock: Catacombs of Kom es-Shoqafa (t); Getty Images: Mezze (c); age fotostock/SuperStock: Feluccas (b)
p.17 Getty Images: Alexandria (t); Pyramids of Dahshur (b); bbbar/Fotolia.com: White Desert (c)
p.18 Getty Images: Balloon rides (t); davemhuntphoto/Fotolia.com: Aswan (cl); Eddie Gerald/Dorling Kindersley: Karkaday (cr); George Nazmi Bebawi/Fotolia.com: Abu Simbel (b)
p.19 Eddie Gerald: Jewellery (t); age fotostock/SuperStock: Egyptian Museum (c); Radius/SuperStock: Dahab (b)
p.20 Sinidex/Fotolia.com: Karnak temple (t); Travelshots/SuperStock: Bellydancing (b)
p.21 Getty Images: The Pyramids and Sphinx at Giza (t); age fotostock/SuperStock: Abydos (cl); Eddie Gerald: St Catherine's Monastery (cr); Alamy: Dahabiya cruises (b)
p.22 Aleš Nowák/Fotolia.com: Jeep safari (t); Getty Images: Fresh juice (bl); Med-Man/Fotolia.com: Street food (br)
p.23 age fotostock/SuperStock: Ras Mohammed (t); Elena Moiseeva/Fotolia.com: Siwa Oasis (b)
p.24 Galyna Andrushko/Fotolia.com: The White Desert
p.26 Getty Images: Donkey cart
p.62 Getty Images: Reading in mosque
p.65 Getty Images: Islamic Cairo
p.91 Roger d'Olivere Mapp/Rough Guides: Egyptian Museum (t); Getty Images: Man holding prayer beads (b)
p.123 Getty Images: Bedouin at the Giza Pyramids
p.147 Getty Images: Cairo bazaar (t); Roger d'Olivere Mapp/Rough Guides: Mosque of Ibn Tulun (b)

p.181 Alamy: Revolutionary graffiti
p.197 AWL: Islamic Cairo (t); age fotostock/SuperStock: Tutankhamun, Egyptian Museum (b)
p.206 James May/Purestock/SuperStock: Feluccas at Aswan
p.209 Getty Images: Abydos temple
p.243 Getty Images: Deir el-Bahri
p.265 Getty Images: Deir el-Bahri (t); Eddie Gerald: Karnak Temple (b)
p.293 Getty Images: Temple warden, Abu Simbel
p.335 Getty Images: Nubian hats (tl); Luxor Temple (tr); Feluccas, Aswan (b)
p.365 Getty Images: Deir el-Bahri
p.372 Getty Images: Off-roading, Western Desert
p.375 Getty Images: Dunes at Siwa
p.395 AWL: Al-Qasr
p.423 Max Alexander/Dorling Kindersley: Dakhla Oasis (t); Ritterbach/Huber/4Corners: The White Desert
p.443 Hemis.fr/SuperStock: Farmers, Dakhla Oasis
p.458 Roger d'Olivere Mapp/Rough Guides: Bibliotheca Alexandrina
p.461 Getty Images: Downtown Alexandria
p.477 Getty Images: Boats in harbour, Alexandria (t); Fish market, Alexandria (b)
p.491 Getty Images: Bibliotheca Alexandrina
p.510 Getty Images: Suez Canal
p.513 Getty Images: Port Said
p.526 Eddie Gerald: Mount Sinai
p.529 Denis Rybin/Fotolia.com: Windsurfers, Dahab
p.545 Minden Pictures/SuperStock: Camels in Sinai (t); Getty Images: Diving, Ras Mohammed (b)
p.568 Getty Images: Dolphins, Red Sea
p.571 Getty Images: Hurghada
p.587 Manfred Bortoli/SIME/4Corners: Sea life, Hurghada
p.594 Alistair Duncan/Dorling Kindersley: Tomb of Seti I

Front cover Mask of Tutankhamun © Guido Alberto Rossi/Tips/Axiom
Back cover Aswan © Peter Phipp/Alamy (top); Karnak Temple © Jan Wlodarczyk/Alamy (left); Camel at sunset © JLImages/Alamy (right)

Index

Maps are marked in grey

Map symbols

The symbols below are used on maps throughout the book

✉	Post office	✈	Airport	⊞	Temple	▢	Building
ⓘ	Information point	★	Transport stop		Tomb	⊡	Church
⊞	Hospital	☂	Oasis/palm grove	⚲	Monastery/convent	▢	Mosque
P	Parking	☈	Spring	✡	Synagogue	⬭	Stadium
🅖	Garage/fuel station	☇	Waterfall	⛰	Mountain range	⊞	Christian cemetery
ℂ	Telephone	☈	Viewpoint	▲	Mountain peak	⊻	Muslim cemetery
◆	Point of interest	🗼	Lighthouse	◥	Mountain pass	⬚	Park/national park
@	Internet access	♟	Checkpoint	⌒	Cave	⬚	Beach/dunes
⊤	Fountain	⚔	Battlefield	ﺑﺳﻣﷲ Reef		⬓	Delta
⊙	Statue	△	Pyramid	✺	Crater	⬚	Saltpan
⚓	Swimming Pool	☠	Shipwreck	⊔⊔⊔	Cliff face/escarpment		

Listings key

- ■ Accommodation
- ● Restaurant/café
- ■ Bar/pub/club
- ● Shop
- ● Diving site
- ● Safari site

MAKE THE MOST OF YOUR CITY BREAK

NEW YORK CITY · HONG KONG & MACAU · BERLIN · MARRAKESH · ROME

FREE PULL OUT MAP WITH EVERY SIGHT AND LISTING FROM THE GUIDE

ESSENTIAL ITINERARIES AND RELIABLE RECOMMENDATIONS

ROUGH GUIDES

SO NOW WE'VE TOLD YOU
HOW TO MAKE THE MOST
OF YOUR TIME, WE WANT
YOU TO STAY SAFE AND
COVERED WITH OUR
FAVOURITE TRAVEL INSURER

WorldNomads.com
keep travelling safely

GET AN ONLINE QUOTE
roughguides.com/insurance

RECOMMENDED BY
ROUGH GUIDES

MAKE THE MOST OF YOUR TIME ON EARTH[TM]